THE COMPLETE GUIDE TO

# GARAGES

Includes:

- Building a New Garage
- Repairing & Replacing Doors & Windows
- Improving Storage
- Maintaining Floors
- Upgrading Electrical Service
- Complete Garage Plans

Creative Publishing international

MINNEAPOLIS, MINNESOTA
www.creativepub.com

Creative Publishing international


400 First Avenue North, Suite 300
Minneapolis, Minnesota 55401
1-800-328-0590
www.creativepub.com


Printed in the United States of America

10 9 8 7 6 5 4 3 2 1

Library of Congress Cataloging-in-Publication Data

The complete guide to garages : includes building a new garage, improving storage, maintaining floors, upgrading electrical service, repairing & replacing doors & windows.
p. cm.
"Black & Decker."
Includes index.
Summary: "Includes wide selection of garage projects, from simple organization to planning and building an all-new garage"--Provided by publisher.
ISBN-13: 978-1-58923-457-4 (soft cover)
ISBN-10: 1-58923-457-X (soft cover)
1. Garages--Design and construction--Amateurs' manuals,
2. Garages--Maintenance and repair--Amateurs' manuals,
I. Black & Decker Corporation (Towson, Md.) II. Title.

TH4960.C66 2009
690'.898--dc22

2009020709

*President/CEO:* Ken Fund
*VP for Sales & Marketing:* Kevin Hamric

**Home Improvement Group**

*Publisher:* Bryan Trandem
*Managing Editor:* Tracy Stanley
*Senior Editor:* Mark Johanson
*Editor:* Jennifer Gehlhar

*Creative Director:* Michele Lanci-Altomare
*Senior Design Managers:* Jon Simpson, Brad Springer
*Design Manager:* James Kegley

*Lead Photographer:* Joel Schnell
*Set Builder:* Bryan McLain
*Photo Coordinator:* Cesar Fernandez Rodriguez
*Shop Help:* Charlie Boldt

*Production Managers:* Laura Hokkanen, Linda Halls
*Project Editor/Contributing Writer:* Chris Marshall
*Page Layout Artist:* Heather Parlato

*The Complete Guide to Garages*
*Created by:* The Editors of Creative Publishing international, Inc., in cooperation with Black & Decker.


## NOTICE TO READERS

For safety, use caution, care, and good judgment when following the procedures described in this book. The publisher and Black & Decker cannot assume responsibility for any damage to property or injury to persons as a result of misuse of the information provided.

The techniques shown in this book are general techniques for various applications. In some instances, additional techniques not shown in this book may be required. Always follow manufacturers' instructions included with products, since deviating from the directions may void warranties. The projects in this book vary widely as to skill levels required: some may not be appropriate for all do-it-yourselfers, and some may require professional help.

Consult your local building department for information on building permits, codes, and other laws as they apply to your project.

# Contents

## The Complete Guide to Garages

**Introduction** .5

**Gallery of Garages** .7

**Building a New Garage** .23

Making Plans 24
Overview: Building a Garage 26
Building the Foundation 28
Framing & Raising Walls 34
Installing Roof Framing 44
Sheathing Walls 52
Installing Fascia & Soffits 56
Building the Roof 60
Installing Windows & Service Doors 68
Installing Overhead Garage Doors 76
Installing Siding & Trim 82

**Garage Plans** .91

Single Detached Garage 92
Additional Garage Plans 98
Compact Garage 102
Gambrel Garage 116
Carport 132
Garage Workshop 142

**Garage Improvements** .151

Storage & Workspace Improvements 152
Electrical & Lighting Improvements 178
Floor Improvements 206
Installing Roll-out Floor Covering 214
Installing Interlocking Floor Tiles 216

**Garage Maintenance** .221

Renewing a Garage Floor 222
Tuning Up Garage Doors 226
Garage Door Openers 232

**Resources/Credits** .235

**Metric Conversion Charts** .236

**Index** .237

# Introduction

First and foremost, a garage is a sheltered building where you can park your vehicles safely. But it can be much more than that, and it often is. A garage may also serve as an organized and climate-controlled workspace to pursue hobbies or as a utility shed for storing gardening and snow-removal equipment. It may be a workshop, a walk-in sports locker, or an overflow storage area. How can one room do it all? Truth be told, having a versatile, hard-working, well-organized garage is a very tall order—but with practical projects and the right approach it can definitely be done. You can have the garage you've always wanted, and this book will help you achieve it.

In *The Complete Guide to Garages*, we'll start from scratch and build from there. The "Gallery of Garages" section (pages 7 to 21) introduces you to a wide range of garage styles and spotlights the many and various ways we use them. It's a chance to let your imagination go and an opportunity to dream big. But if your garage space or budget requires you to keep things manageable, even one or two ideas from these gallery photos could open up a new storage idea or workspace possibility that you can adapt to your own space.

If your home does not have a garage or if your current model is basically a tear-down, this is one of the few books on the market that will teach you how to build a garage yourself. The first major section of the book, "Building a New Garage," walks you step by step through the process of constructing a detached, single-car garage. You'll learn how to frame and erect walls and build a rafter-style roof. We'll show you how to sheathe the structure, trim and shingle the roof like the pros do, and then install siding, windows, and doors.

Next, you'll find a complete set of measured plans for the garage seen in the first chapter, along with plans and how-to photos for two additional garages, a carport, and a garage workshop conversion. Or, use these three detailed garage projects to help acquaint yourself with the skills you'll need in order to build whatever garage you choose.

The second half of this book focuses on garage improvements to help you transform an existing garage. In "Garage Improvements," you can finish those bare stud walls and ceiling and then outfit them with pegboard, shelving, wall tracks, and cabinets to maximize every available inch of storage space. To bring lights to your many projects, turn to the "Electrical & Lighting Improvements" section for help. We'll show you how to insulate, run new outlets, hang a shop light, install a skylight, and add a heater—improvements that pay dividends in the long run. Maybe your dull, damp garage floor could use a facelift. The final section offers several painting and floor-covering options that will give you stunning results in less than a weekend's time.

Now is the perfect time to begin planning your new garage or tackling that first improvement project. Doing it yourself—and doing it right—is easier than you think. Let us show you how.

# Gallery of Garages

It's remarkable what your garage can become when you approach it creatively and set the bar high. The gallery that follows will take you on a tour of several residential garages. As you're about to see, there's simply no reason why that covered parking spot at the head of your driveway can't evolve into the perfect entertainment room, mechanic's space, woodworking shop, or art studio you dream about. Sure, some of these examples might stretch the limits of budgets and practicality for everyday folks, but they testify to the fact that homeowners everywhere love their garages. Keep in mind that many of these homeowners would call their garage a perpetual "work in progress." Transforming a garage into an attractive, functional and even exciting part of your home doesn't happen overnight. It takes place slowly, one project at a time. But, it will never happen without that first good improvement project and the determination to get the job done.

So, enjoy this behind-the-scenes glimpse into truly inspirational garage spaces. We hope you catch the fever; then step out into your own garage and start dreaming.

**With the right architecture,** a garage can be far more than a spot to park cars. Here, the area above this garage provides another living space and elegantly ties the garage and home together.

**Even a small detached garage** can give you the room you need to explore that restoration project or other latent hobby. If you're up to the challenge, consider building the garage yourself.

**A skylight** is an effective way to bring natural light into your garage without creating the security concerns that arise when a window is installed.

**Sometimes organized clutter still looks cluttered.** The beauty of garage cabinetry is that it hides what you would ordinarily see. You effectively get a "less is more" feeling without actually losing any storage capability.

**Racking and shelf systems** offer the ultimate in garage storage organization. Creating a dedicated spot for everything is the best way to prevent creeping clutter from taking over your garage space.

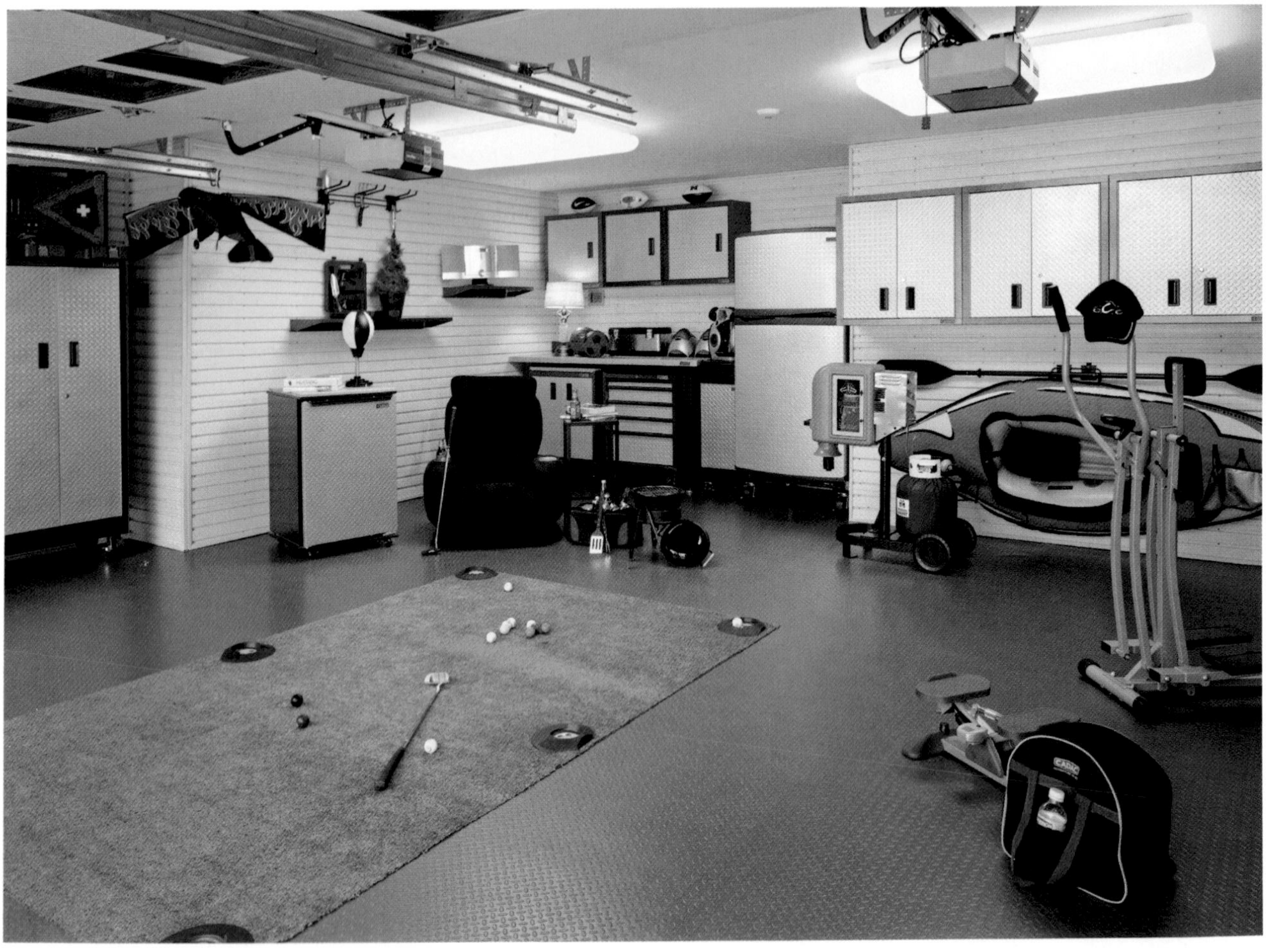

**If a workout or relaxation space** is what you need, your garage can adapt to that purpose. No matter what your family's recreational pursuits may be, a garage can become that perfect work station with the right wall-hanging and storage systems.

**Installing a durable floor covering** adds years to your garage floor's life, as well as giving it a finished look.

**No matter how modest your budget** may be, even a few garage organizers will help you take back wasted space in your garage so you can put it to more productive use.

**Garage windows** don't have to be plain. An architecturally interesting window can be installed just about anywhere to fend off the monotony of the utility window.

**Think carefully about how to organize** your shelving layout. Integrate shelves around windows, the workbench, and areas for hanging items to make the best use of available wall space.

**Give your garage a professional, industrial look** by outfitting it with metal-clad cabinets and wall-hanging systems. You can buy these cabinets with polished chrome or brushed-finish surfaces, depending on the look you want.

super
Ugly

**Want the "show" face of your garage** to make a dramatic statement? Replace your ordinary sectional garage doors with custom frame-and-panel wood doors. There are a wide variety of wood types, styles, and window arrangements from which to choose.

**It's a trophy garage space** that's equipped for even your most prized possession.

**Freestanding base cabinets** and track-mounted wall units are combined with a removable slatted wall "backsplash" to form a work center that is sturdy, efficient, and portable.

**Heavy-duty wall brackets,** wire bins, and shelving can transform an empty garage wall into an organized storage spot for all your favorite sports equipment.

**A single corner of your garage** can offer serious storage potential when it's outfitted with the right set of cabinets.

**A little natural lighting** goes a long way toward making your garage more inviting and functional. Here, a service door with divided glass really serves as an entrypoint and a window.

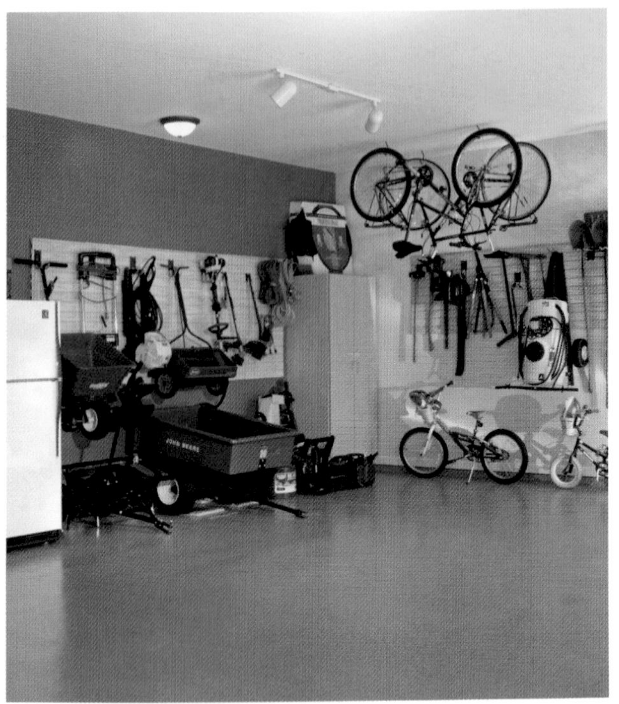

**A wall-track system**, heavy-duty hooks, or even a ceiling hoist can get those seldom-used items up and out of the way.

**Epoxy-based garage floor paint** comes in several attractive colors. You can even add granules to the paint to improve traction or enhance its appearance. Floor paint is applied much like wall paint, but be sure to check the moisture content of the concrete first, and clean the slab thoroughly.

**White cabinets** not only make your garage workspace look neat and clean, but they'll also help make the most of the room's available lighting.

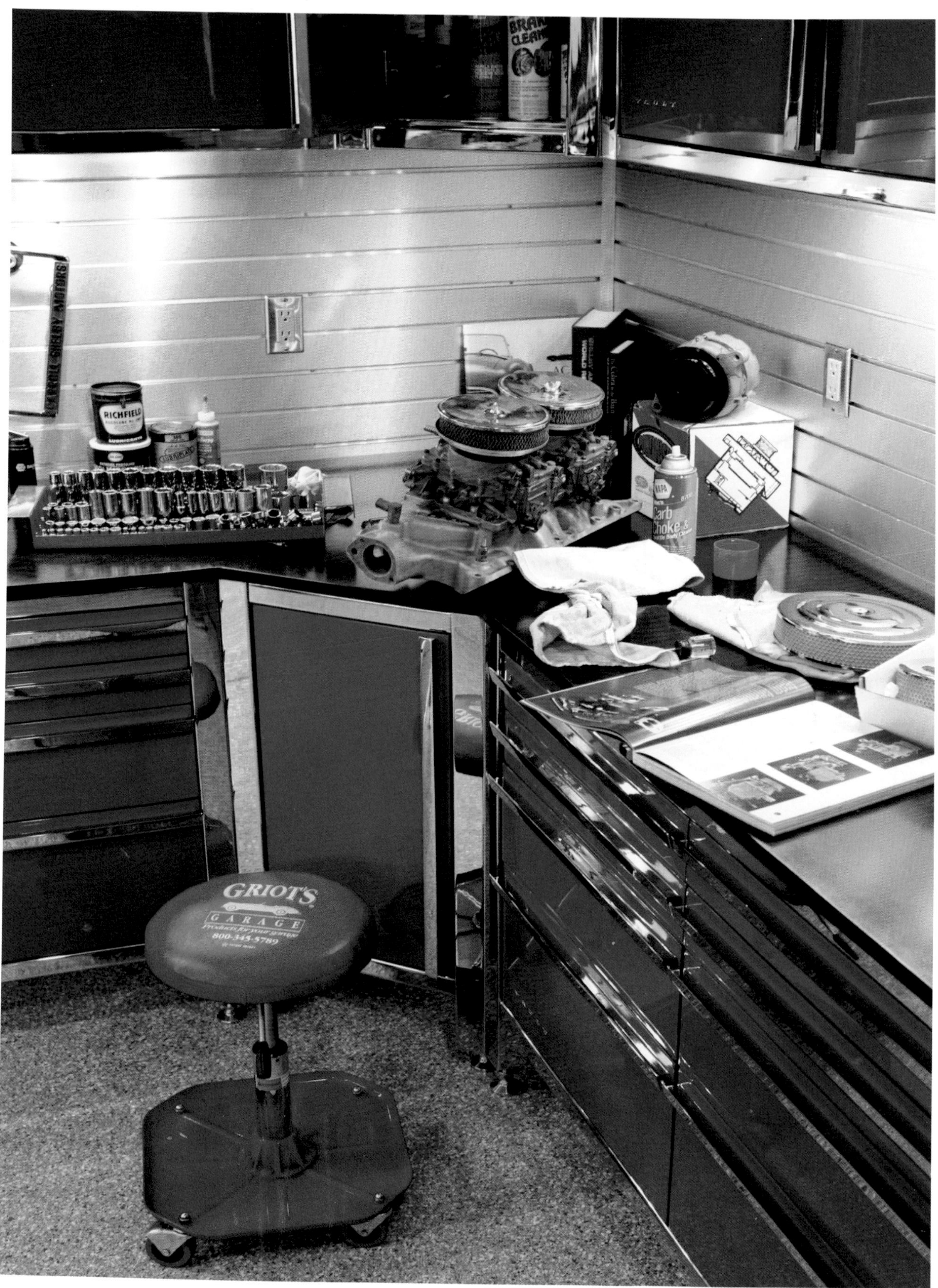


**Color choices, modular configurations,** and specialized features continue to expand every year. Here, corner cabinets and a wall truck system combine for effective storage.

**The first step** to organizing a garage effectively is to identify what you really need to keep and store. Reduce unnecessary clutter, then come up with a plan that makes efficient use of the available space.

**Heavy-duty shelf standards** and brackets provide an effective system for storing bulky or seldom-used items.

**Painting the floor** is a low-cost way to add years to your garage base. It's easy, and paints are available in many colors.

**Safety and organization** are directly related when it comes to garage planning. Having dedicated cabinets (preferably lockable) for storing poisonous and flammable products greatly decreases the chances that an accident will occur.

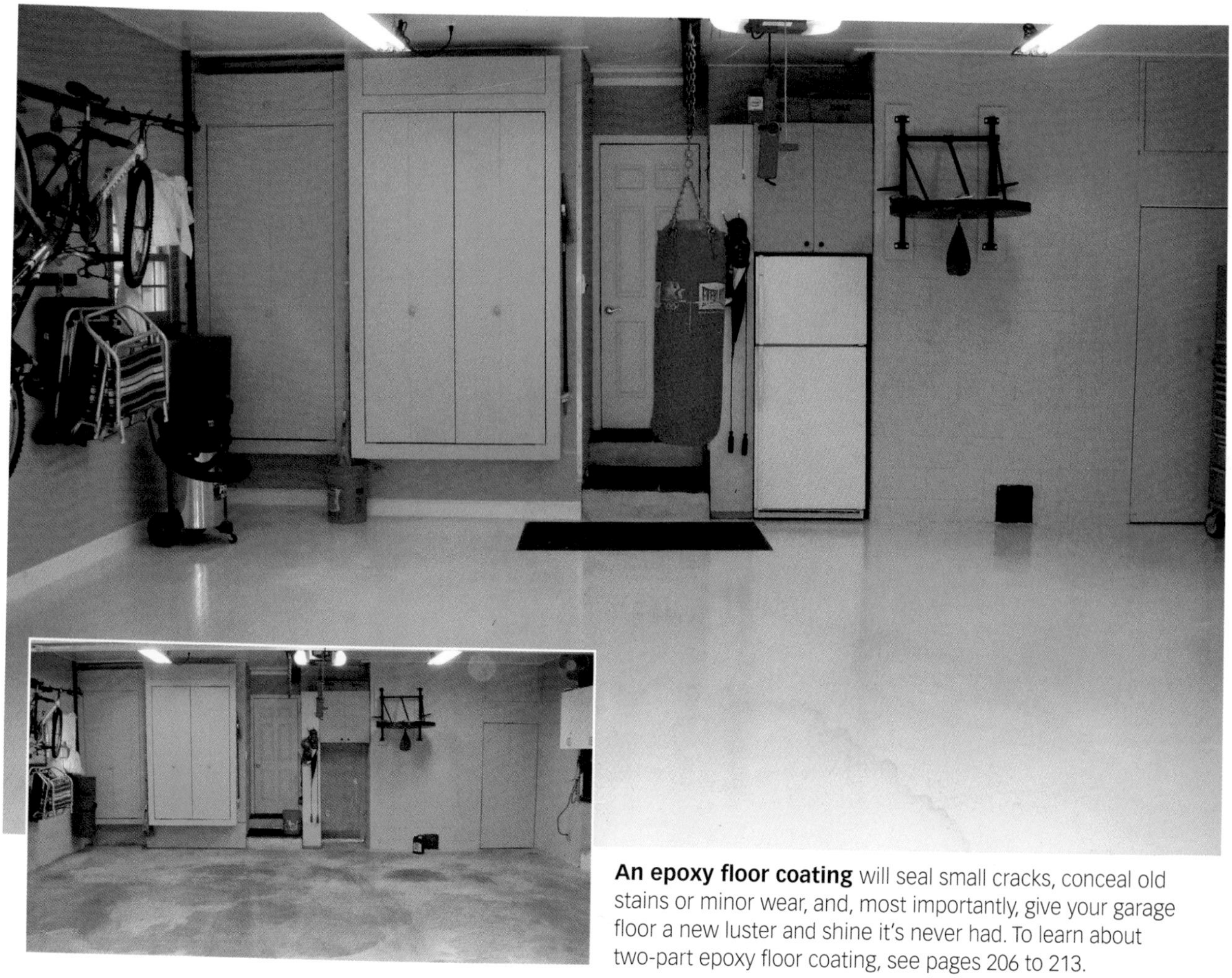

**An epoxy floor coating** will seal small cracks, conceal old stains or minor wear, and, most importantly, give your garage floor a new luster and shine it's never had. To learn about two-part epoxy floor coating, see pages 206 to 213.

**Recessed can lights** and a translucent door will make your garage seem more welcoming at night. Accessory lighting also improves your home's security.

**By installing some texturized flooring,** adding a few matching cabinets, and choosing two or three colors to paint the walls (and even the floor), you've suddenly given the room a whole new dimension.

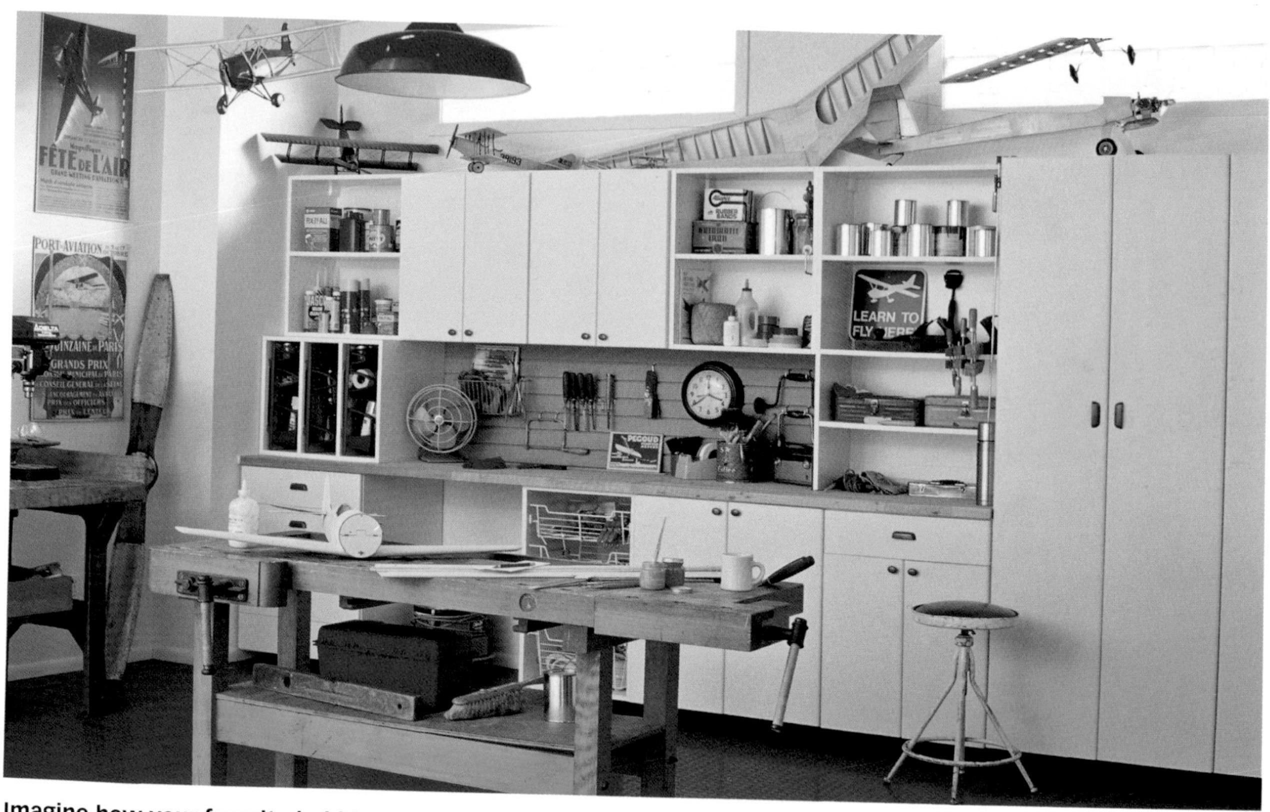


**Imagine how your favorite hobbies** could grow if you just had a dedicated place to pursue them.

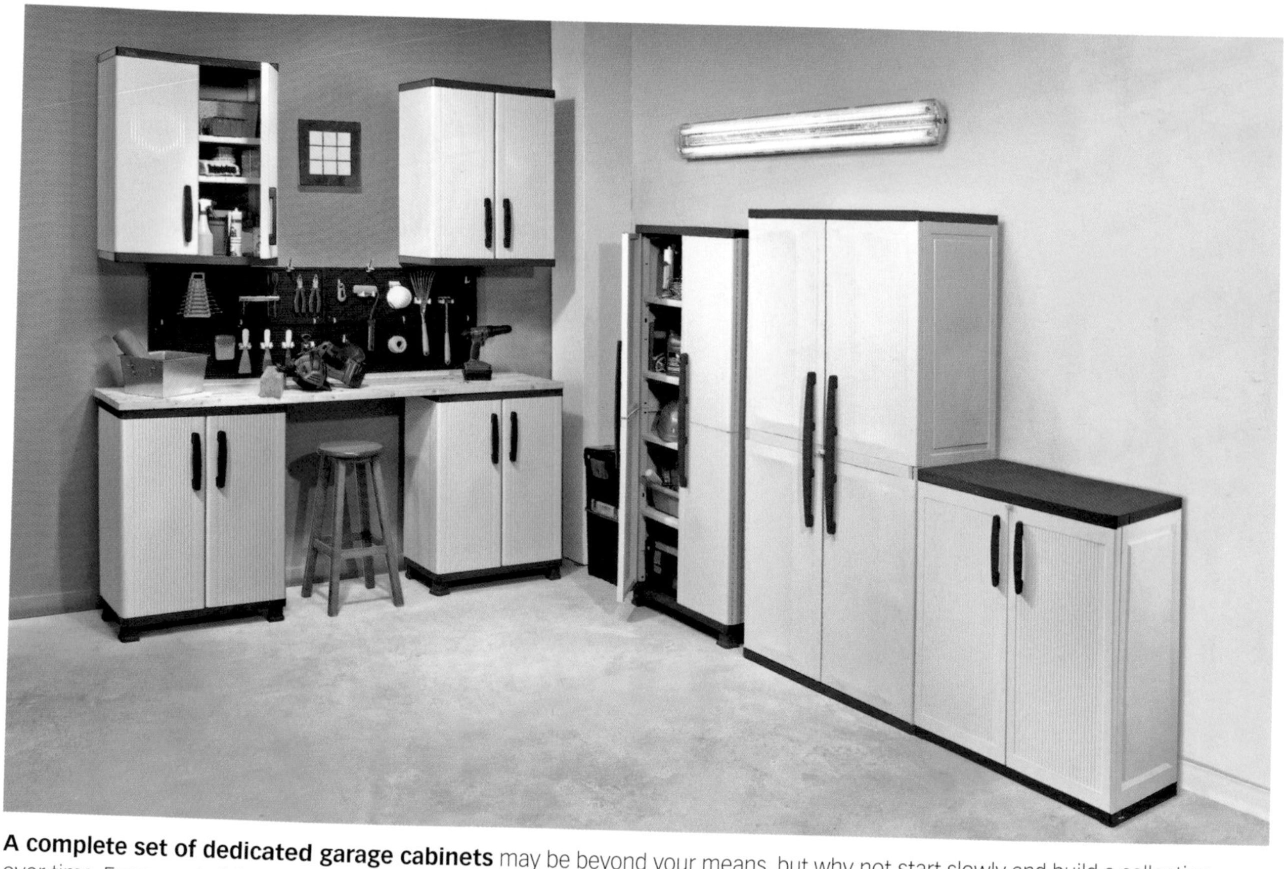

**A complete set of dedicated garage cabinets** may be beyond your means, but why not start slowly and build a collection over time. Even one tall floor cabinet can provide lots of space for lawn and garden chemicals, sports equipment, extra paint or automotive supplies. Add more cabinets when you can, and before you know it, you'll have the most organized garage on the block!

MOTORCYCLE
RACES
PEORIA FAIR GROUNDS
SUNDAY MAY 28

# Building a New Garage

Here you have the opportunity to follow along as we build a detached single-car garage from scratch. As you'll see in the plans on pages 94 to 101, the overall design is straightforward, so this structure will blend well with most home styles. There is still plenty of room to add your own special touches with the siding, roofing, doors, and windows you select. Even if you choose not to build this exact garage design, you can use the project to learn construction methods and techniques that can be adapted to whatever garage you decide to build.

Building a new garage can be an incredibly gratifying experience for an experienced do-it-yourselfer. You have the opportunity to practice a variety of skills, from pouring a foundation to framing and erecting walls and rafters to hanging soffits and fascia. If you've never dared to install siding or shingle a roof, this garage project provides a manageable way to explore those skills so you can bolster your confidence for bigger projects. We'll even show you how to install windows, a service door, and a sectional garage door so you can truly take on every aspect of this job.

**In this chapter:**

- Making Plans
- Overview: Building a Garage
- Building the Foundation
- Framing & Raising Walls
- Installing Roof Framing
- Sheathing Walls
- Installing Fascia & Soffits
- Building the Roof
- Installing Windows & Service Doors
- Installing Overhead Garage Doors
- Installing Siding & Trim

# Making Plans

To successfully build your own garage you must have a complete set of construction drawings. At a minimum that will include a site drawing that shows your garage in situ relative to your house, including property boundaries and municipal sidewalks; elevation drawings from the front, back, and both sides; and a plan view drawing. You will need these along with a cost estimate for your building permit applications. Additional drawings, such as detail drawings of rafters or trusses and finishing details, and materials and cutting lists are also helpful. Finally, draft a plan with hard dates to create an overall project schedule. Be sure to flag any points where you'll need deliveries (such as ready-mix concrete for the slab) or a helper or two. It is important to be realistic when making plans.

Some of the projects in this book include complete construction drawings in the style of architectural blueprints (see Garage Plans, pages 91 to 101). If you're not familiar with reading plans, don't worry; they're easy to use once you know how to look at the different views. Flipping back and forth between the plan drawings and the project's step-by-step photos will help you visualize the actual structure.

**A complete plan** for building your garage starts with detailed construction drawings. Based on your drawings, break the project into smaller tasks and try to estimate how long each phase will take and whether you will need to enlist help.

**BUILDING SECTION**

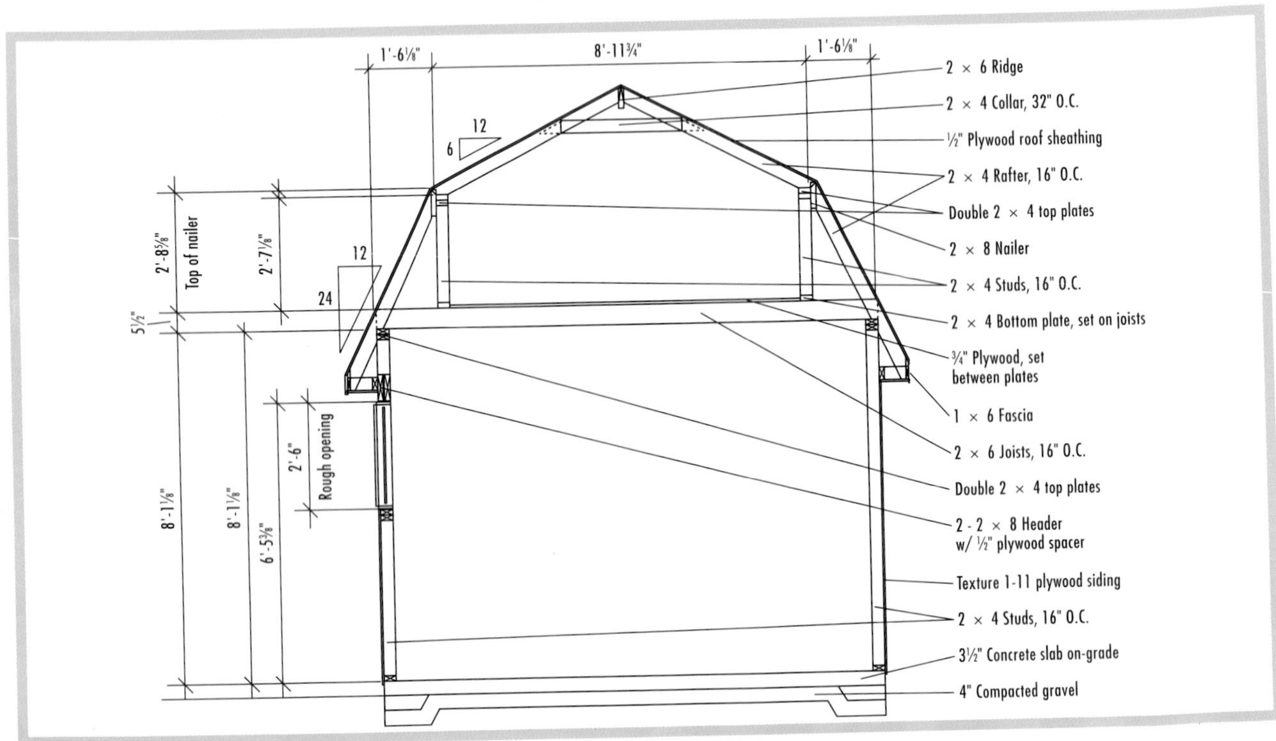


**A building section** is the most comprehensive drawing, giving you a side view of the structure sliced in half down the middle. It shows both the framing and finish elements.

FRONT FRAMING ELEVATION

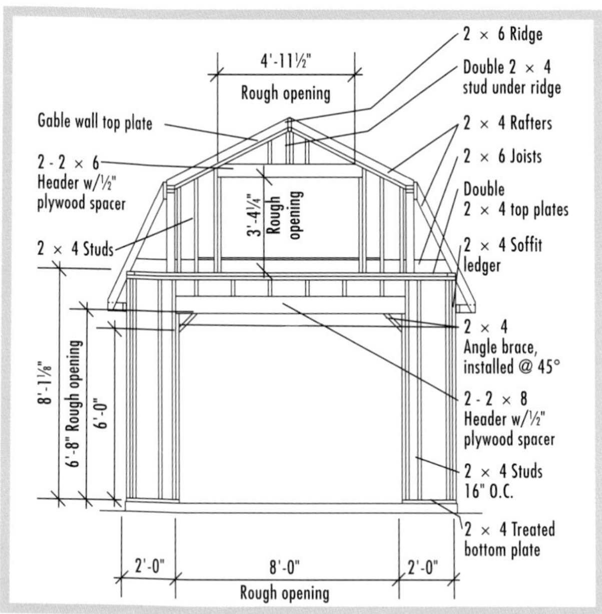


**Elevations** give you a direct, exterior view of the building from all sides. Drawings may include elevations for both the framing and the exterior finishes.

SILL DETAIL

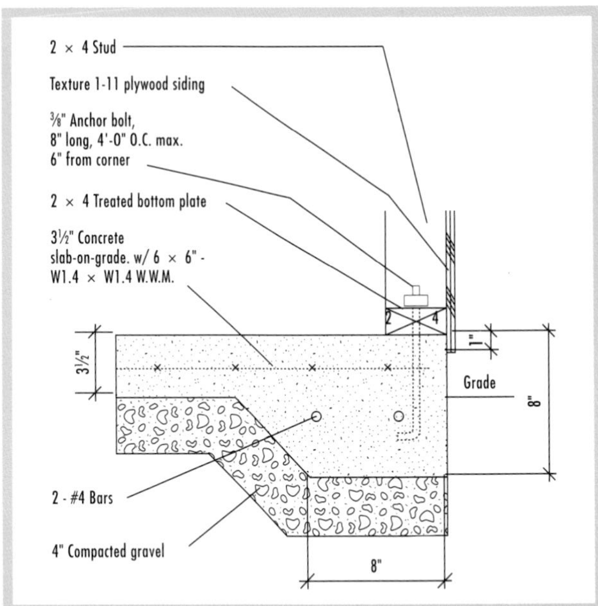


**Detail drawings and templates** show close-ups of specific areas or parts of the structure. They typically show a side or overhead view.

FLOOR PLAN

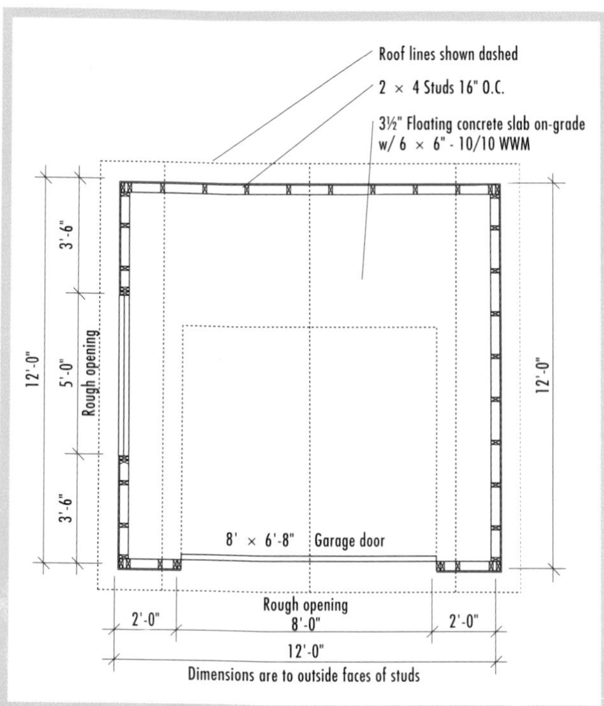


**Plan views** are an overhead perspective, as if looking straight down from above the structure. Floor plans show the layout of the walls or upright supports with the top half of the structure sliced off. There are also foundation plans, roof framing plans, and other plan views.

## Planning Considerations ▸

In most cases, deciding where to locate a detached garage is pretty obvious. But here are some points to keep in mind as you evaluate possible locations:

- **Soil and drainage:** To ensure that your foundation will last (whatever type it is), locate your garage on solid soil in an area that won't collect water.
- **Utility lines:** Contact local utility providers to find out where the water, gas, septic, and electrical lines run through your property. Often, local ordinances and utility companies require lines to be marked before digging.
- **Building permits:** Obtain permits, if your local jurisdiction requires them.
- **Setback requirements:** Most zoning laws dictate that all buildings, fences, etc., in a yard must be set back a specific distance from the property line. This setback may range from 6" to 3 ft. or more.
- **Neighbors:** Out of respect—and to prevent complaints that could later interfere with the building process—talk to your neighbors about your project.

# Overview: Building a Garage

**Building the Foundation** (pages 28 to 33)

**Framing & Erecting Walls** (pages 34 to 43)

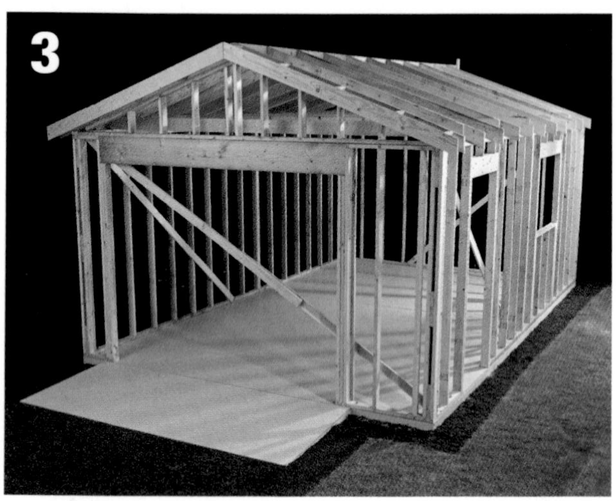


**Installing Roof Framing** (pages 44 to 51)

**Sheathing Walls** (pages 52 to 55)

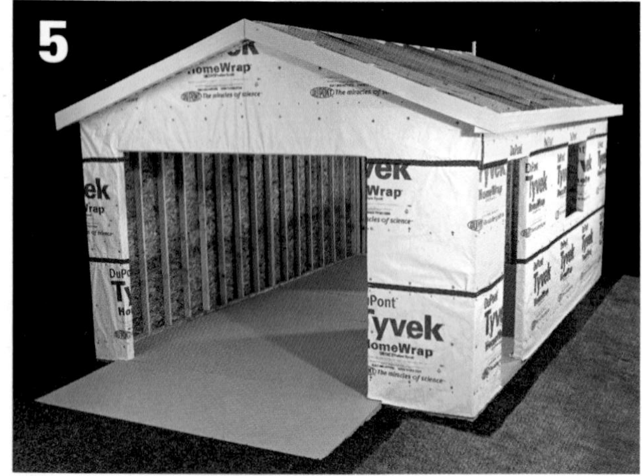


**Installing Fascia & Soffit** (pages 56 to 59)

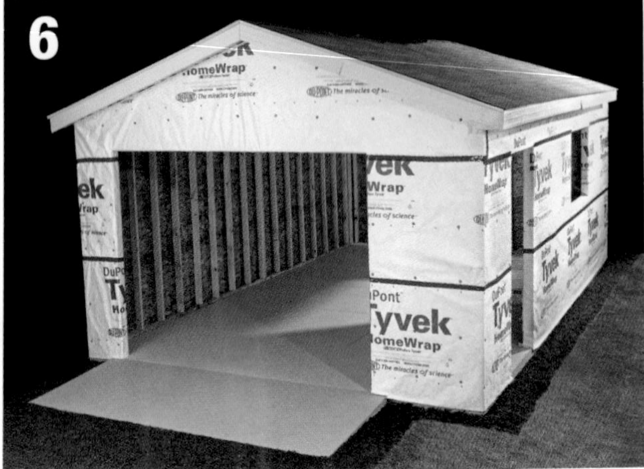


**Building the Roof** (pages 60 to 67)

**Installing Windows & Service Doors** (pages 68 to 75).
**Installing Overhead Garage Doors** (pages 76 to 81)

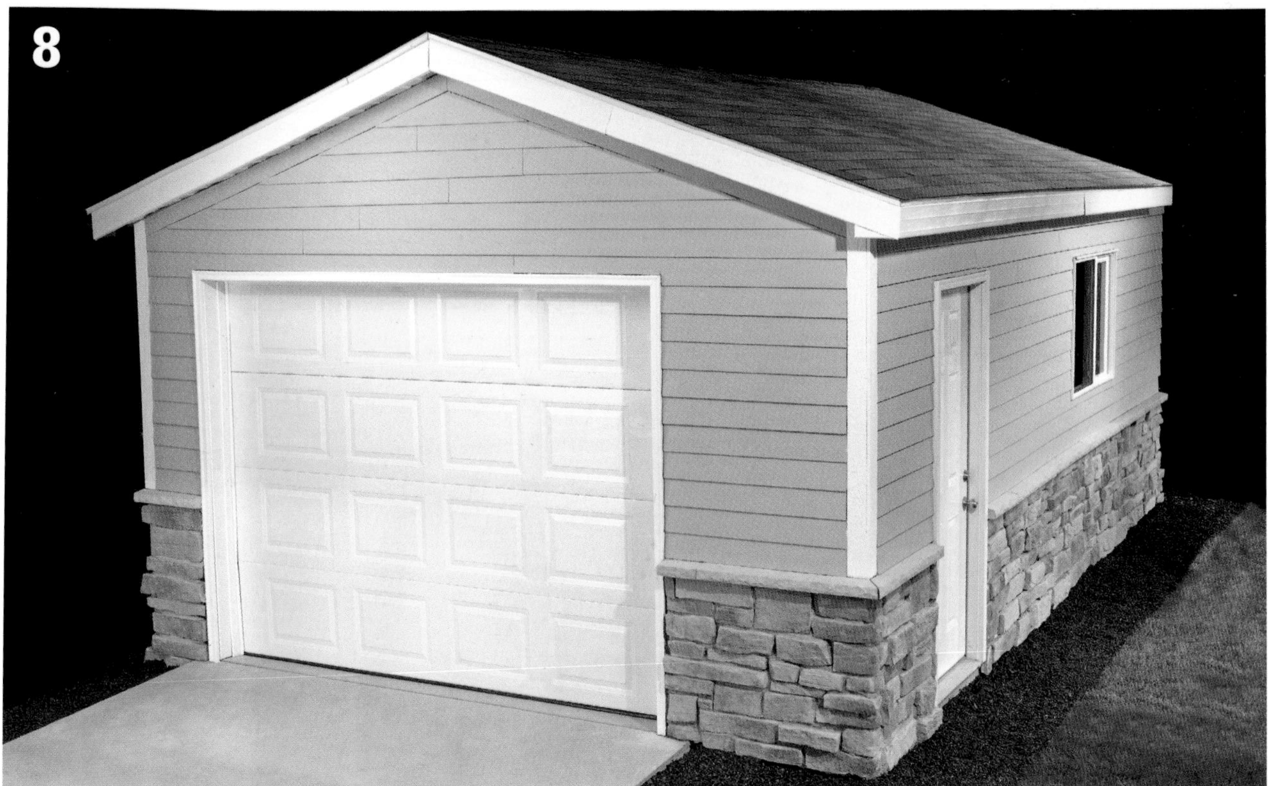


**Installing Siding & Trim** (pages 82 to 89)

# Building the Foundation

**A concrete slab** with an adjoining concrete apron and driveway is the most common garage foundation setup.

The slab foundation commonly used for garages is called a slab-on-grade foundation. This combines a 3½- to 4"-thick floor slab with an 8- to 12"-thick perimeter footing that provides extra support for the walls of the building. The whole foundation can be poured at one time using a simple wood form.

Because they sit above ground, slab-on-grade foundations are susceptible to frost heave; in cold-weather climates they are suitable only for detached buildings. Specific design requirements also vary by locality, so check with the local building department regarding the depth of the slab, the metal reinforcement required, the type and amount of gravel required for the subbase, and whether a plastic or other type of moisture barrier is needed under the slab.

The slab shown in this project has a 3½"-thick interior with an 8"-wide × 8"-deep footing along the perimeter. The top of the slab sits 4" above ground level (grade). There is a 4"-thick layer of compacted gravel underneath the slab and the concrete is reinforced internally with a layer of 6 × 6" 10/10 welded wire mesh (WWM). In some areas, you may be required to add rebar in the foundation perimeter. Check the local code. After the concrete is poured and finished, 8"-long J-bolts are set into the slab along the edges. These are used later to anchor the wall framing to the slab.

A slab for a garage requires a lot of concrete. Considering the amount involved, you'll probably want to order ready-mix concrete delivered by truck to the site (most companies have a one-yard minimum). Order air-entrained concrete, which will hold up best, and tell the mixing company that you're using it for an exterior slab.

## Tools & Materials ▸

- Work gloves & eye protection
- Stakes & boards
- Mason's lines
- Plumb bob
- Shovel
- Long level
- Tape measure
- Drill
- Wheelbarrow
- Bull float
- Wood or magnesium concrete float
- Concrete groover tool
- Concrete edging tool
- Paint roller
- Compactable gravel
- 2 × 8 lumber
- 3" deck screws
- Metal mending plates
- Re-wire mesh
- Concrete
- J-bolts
- Concrete cure & seal

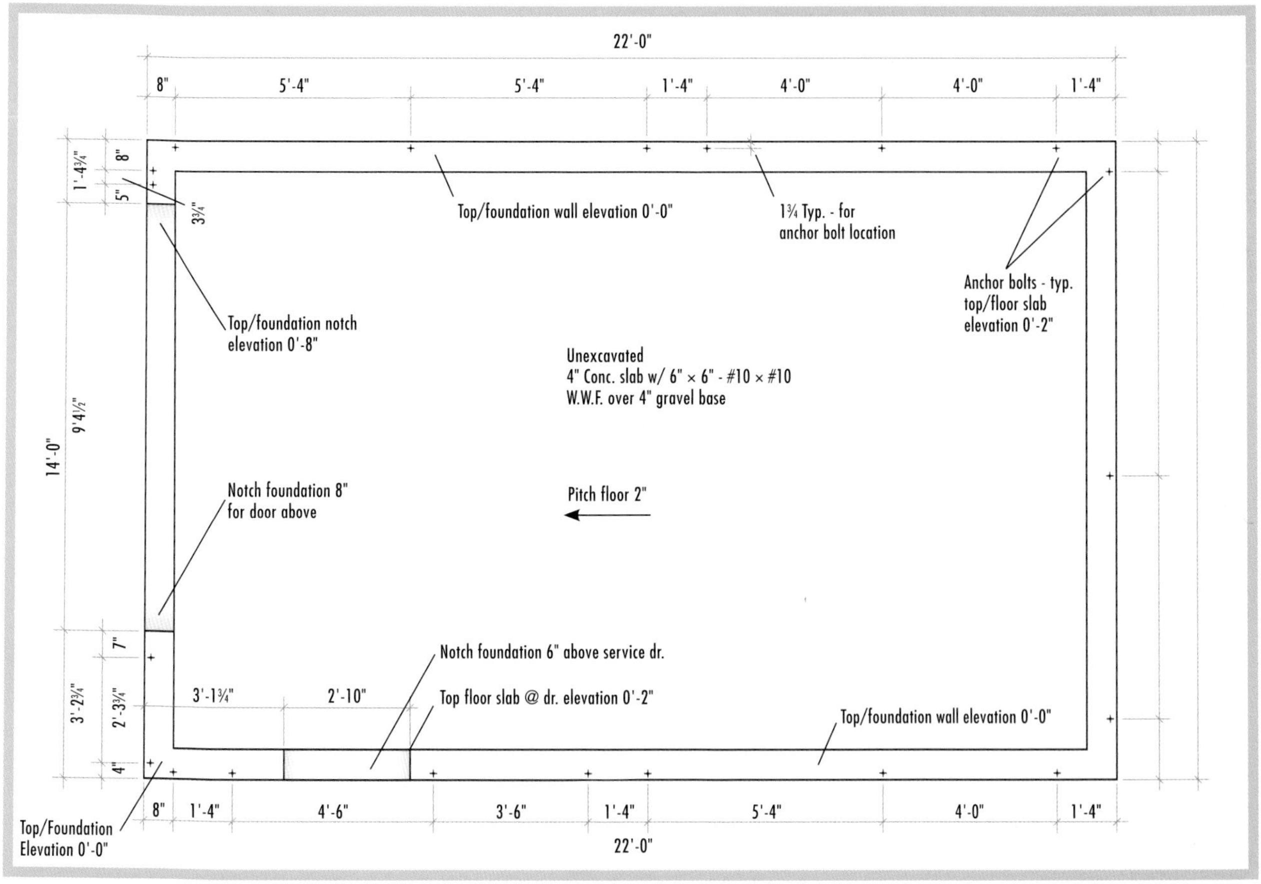

22'-0"
8"
5'-4"
5'-4"
1'-4"
4'-0"
4'-0"
1'-4"
Top/foundation wall elevation 0'-0"
1¾ Typ. - for anchor bolt location
Anchor bolts - typ. top/floor slab elevation 0'-2"
Top/foundation notch elevation 0'-8"
Unexcavated
4" Conc. slab w/ 6" × 6" - #10 × #10 W.W.F. over 4" gravel base
Notch foundation 8" for door above
Pitch floor 2"
Notch foundation 6" above service dr.
Top floor slab @ dr. elevation 0'-2"
Top/foundation wall elevation 0'-0"
3'-1¾"
2'-10"
Top/Foundation Elevation 0'-0"
8"
1'-4"
4'-6"
3'-6"
1'-4"
5'-4"
4'-0"
1'-4"
22'-0"
14'-0"
9'4½"
1'-4¾"
8"
5"
3¾"
7"
3'-2¾"
2'-3¾"
4"


**A plan view** of the slab should include J-bolt locations, door locations, and footing sizes. Also indicate the overall dimensions and the direction and height of the floor pitch.

2½ proj.
6"
6" × 6" - #10 × #10 W.W.F.
To extend 6" below local frost line
8"
16"


Temporary form stakes
2½ proj.
4"
18"
Min. 12"
6" × 6" - #10 × #10 W.W.F.
2 - #4 rods
Remove form boards after concrete sets.


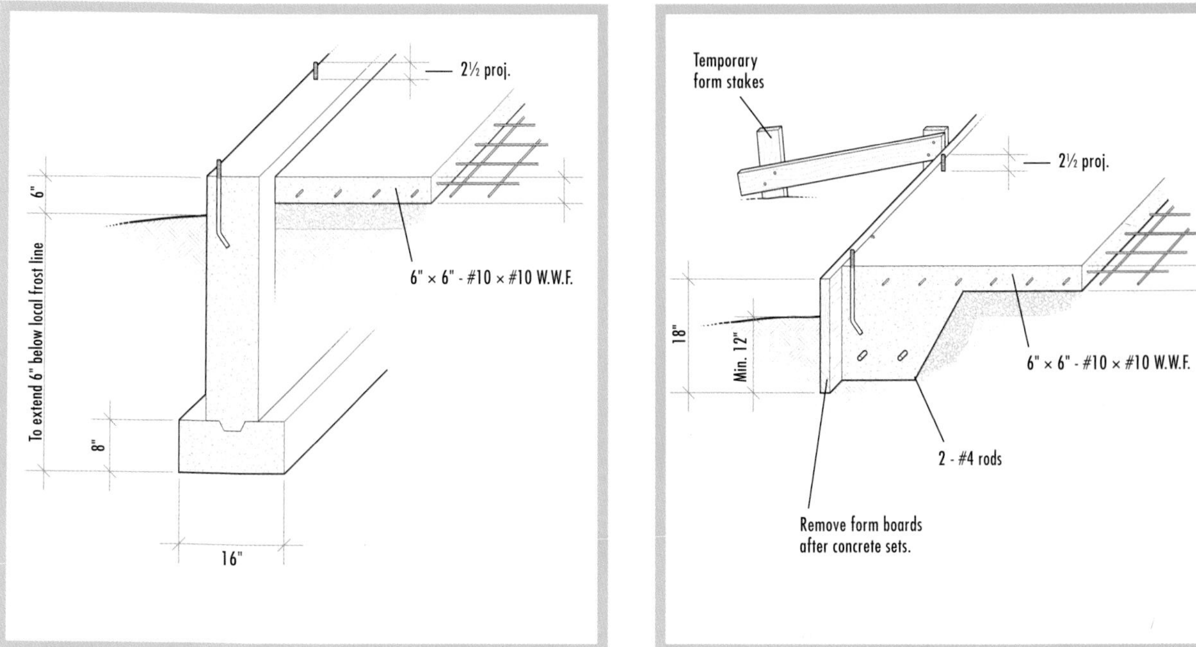

**The garage slab** cannot simply float on the ground. It requires footings around the perimeter. For detached garages, an 8 × 16" footing will comply with most local codes. For attached garages, the footings must extend past the frostline. In both cases, an ample layer of drainage rock is required to help minimize movement from freezing and thawing.

# How to Pour a Concrete Slab

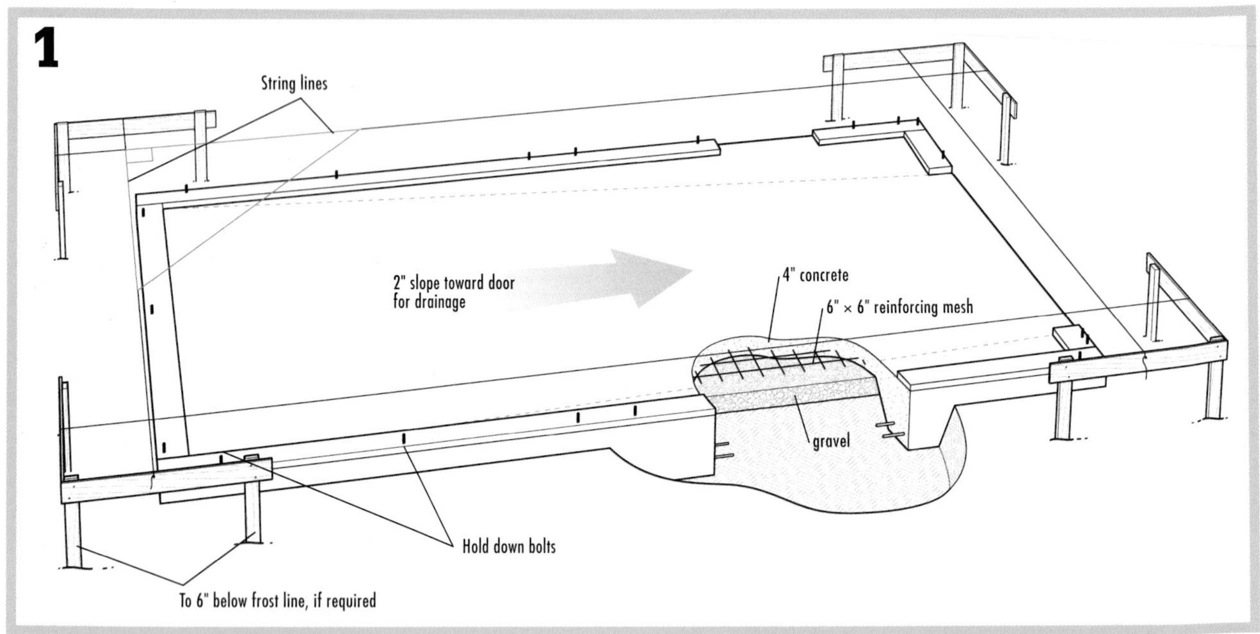


**Begin to lay out the excavation** with pairs of batterboards installed at each corner of the garage slab site. Position them about 2 ft. outside the perimeter of the slab area so you'll have plenty of room to work. Run level mason's lines between the batterboards to establish the final size of the slab. Drop a plumb bob down from the intersections of the strings, and drive a stake at each corner.

**Excavate the area** about 2 ft. wider and longer than the staked size of the slab. The poured slab should slope 2" total from the back wall to the overhead door wall to facilitate drainage. Remove 3 to 4" of soil from the excavation area, and dig a deeper trench around the perimeter for the footing. The outside of the footing should line up with the mason's lines. Slope the soil to create a transition between the excavated interior and the footing. Check your local building codes to determine the correct footing size and depth for your climate and soil conditions.

**Fill the excavation area** with 4" of compactable gravel, letting it spill down into the 12"-deep footings that frame the perimeter. Tamp the gravel level and smooth it with a rented plate compactor. The gravel surface should maintain the 2" total back-to-front slope. Depending on your soil conditions, some concrete contractors recommend laying 6-mil polyethylene sheeting over the compacted base to form a moisture barrier. *Tip: Install electrical conduit underneath the slab if you will be providing underground electrical service.*

**Build a form** for pouring the slab using 2 × 8 lumber or strips of exterior-rated plywood. The inside dimensions of the form should match the final slab size. If necessary on long runs, join the lumber end-to-end, reinforcing the butt joints with metal mending plates screwed to the outside surfaces. Fasten the form pieces together at the corners with 3" deck screws. Position the form so it aligns with the mason's lines. The form should also follow the 2" total back-to-front slope.

**Drive wood stakes** along the outsides of the form at 4-ft. intervals. Place two stakes at each corner. Set the tops of the stakes flush with the top edges of the form (or slightly below the tops). As you drive the stakes, periodically check the form for level and measure from corner to corner to ensure that it's square. Measure down from the mason's lines to position the form 4" above grade. Attach the stakes to the form with deck screws to hold the form in place.

**Add re-wire reinforcement** according to the requirements in your area. Here, rows of 6 × 6 10/10 wire mesh are set onto spacers (chunks of brick) in the pour area. Overlap the sheets of mesh by 6", and stop the rows about 2" in from the insides of the form. Fasten the mesh together with wire tie. *Option: Reinforce the footings by laying out two rows of #4 rebar 2" above the bottom of the trench by wire-tying it to shorter pieces of rebar driven into the gravel. Space the rows about 4" apart. You'll need to dig out the gravel to accomplish this.*

## Estimating Concrete ▸

Calculate the amount of concrete needed for a slab of the design shown on this page using this formula:

Width × Length × Depth, in feet (of main slab)
Multiply by 1.5 (for footing edge and spillage)
Divide by 27 (to convert to cubic yards).

Example—for a 12 x 12-ft. x 3½" slab:
12 × 12 × 3½" = 42
42 × 1.5 = 63
63 ÷ 27 = 2¹¹⁄₁₆ approx. (2.33 cubic yards)

**Concrete Coverage**

| Volume | Slab Thickness | Surface Area |
|---|---|---|
| 1 cu. yd. | 2" | 160 sq. ft. |
| 1 cu. yd. | 3" | 110 sq. ft. |
| 1 cu. yd. | 4" | 80 sq. ft |
| 1 cu. yd. | 5" | 65 sq. ft. |
| 1 cu. yd. | 6" | 55 sq. ft. |
| 1 cu. yd. | 8" | 40 sq. ft. |

(continued)

**Pour the concrete.** Have ready-mix concrete delivered to your job site and place it into the forms with wheelbarrows and shovels (make sure to have plenty of help for this job). Fill a form with concrete, starting at one end. Use a shovel to settle the concrete around the reinforcement and to remove air pockets. Fill the form to the top. *Note: In most municipalities you must have the forms and subbase inspected before the concrete is poured.*

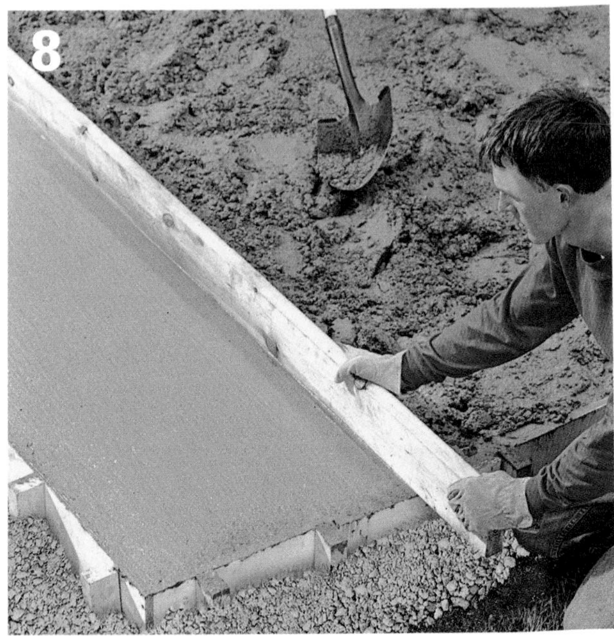

**Strike off the concrete** once a section of a form is filled. The best way to do this is to have two helpers strike off (screed) the wet concrete with a long 2 × 6 or 2 × 8 that spans the width of the form. Drag the screed board back and forth along the top of the form in a sawing motion to level and smooth the concrete. Fill any voids ahead of the screed board with shovelfuls of concrete.

**Smooth the surface** further with a bull float as soon as you're finished screeding, working across the width of the slab. Floating forces aggregate down and draws sand and water to the surface to begin the smoothing process.

**Push J-bolts** down into the concrete, wiggling them slightly to eliminate air pockets. Twist the bottom hooked ends so they face into the slab. Position the J-bolts 1¾" from the edges of the slab, aligned with your layout marks. Leave 2½" of bolt thread exposed, and make sure the J-bolts are plumb. Smooth the surrounding concrete with a wooden or magnesium concrete float.

## Bleed Water ▸

Timing is key to an attractive concrete finish. When concrete is poured, the heavy materials gradually sink, leaving a thin layer of water—known as bleed water—on the surface. Let bleed water dry before proceeding with other steps. Follow these rules:

- Settle and screed the concrete and add control joints immediately after pouring and before bleed water appears.
- Let bleed water dry before floating or edging. Concrete should be hard enough that foot pressure leaves no more than a ¼"-deep impression.
- Do not overfloat the concrete; it may cause bleed water to reappear. Stop floating if a sheen appears, and resume when it is gone.

**Optional:** Cut control joints using a groover (left photo) if your local codes require them (dividing slabs into 10 × 10-ft. sections is standard). Lay a long 2 × 12 to span the slab and line up one edge so it's centered on the slab's length. Use a 2 × 4 (or the 2 × 12) as a guide for cutting across the slab with a groover tool. Then, round the edges of the slab next to the forms using an edging tool (right photo). *Note: Instead of grooving, you may cut control joints in the dried concrete using a concrete saw.*

**Use a magnesium or wood hand-held float** to refine the slab's finished surface as soon as the bleed water evaporates (see Bleed Water, left). Work the float back and forth, starting from the middle of the slab and moving outward to the edges. Use large scraps of 2"-thick rigid foam insulation as kneeling pads while you work.

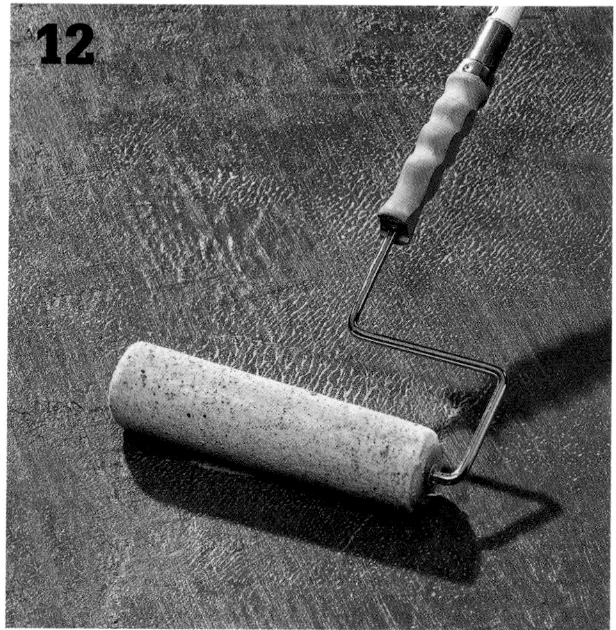


**Apply a coat of cure and seal** product (See Resources, page 235) to the surface once it dries so you do not have to water the concrete surface during the curing stage. After a couple of days, strip off the forms. Wait at least one more day before you begin building on the slab.

# Framing & Raising Walls

Framing and erecting walls should prove to be one of the more enjoyable aspects of your new garage project. You'll be able to assemble the entire skeleton of the building fairly rapidly, especially if you work with a helper or two and use a pneumatic nail gun for fastening and a power miter saw for cutting. Assembling walls isn't a complicated process. In fact, if you set aside a full day for the job, you'll probably have all the walls assembled and standing on the slab before sundown—maybe even sooner.

We'll use fundamental stick-framing techniques and 2 × 4s to assemble the walls of this garage. In terms of the tools you need, be sure to have a circular saw or power miter saw on hand with a quality (carbide-tipped) crosscutting or combination blade installed. You also need a framing square, speed square, or combination square; a long level, a 25- or 50-foot tape measure, string line, and a framing hammer or pneumatic framing nailer.

As you lay out each wall section, carefully inspect the studs and top and bottom plates to make sure they're straight and free of large splits, knots, or other defects. Separate your lesser-quality lumber for use as wall braces or shorter pieces of blocking. If you end up with a lot of bad studs, call your supplier and request a better supply.

## Tools & Materials ▸

- Work gloves & eye protection
- Combination square
- Drill & spade bit
- Miter saw
- Marker
- Speed square
- Tape measure
- Hammer (or pneumatic nailer)
- Caulk gun
- Mason's line
- Reciprocating saw
- Stakes
- Pressure-treated 2× lumber for sole plates
- 2× pine lumber (2 × 4, 2 × 8, 2 × 12)
- Galvanized common nails (8d, 10d, 16d)
- 1 × 4 bracing
- Deck screws
- Galvanized washers & nuts for J-bolts
- ½" plywood
- Construction adhesive

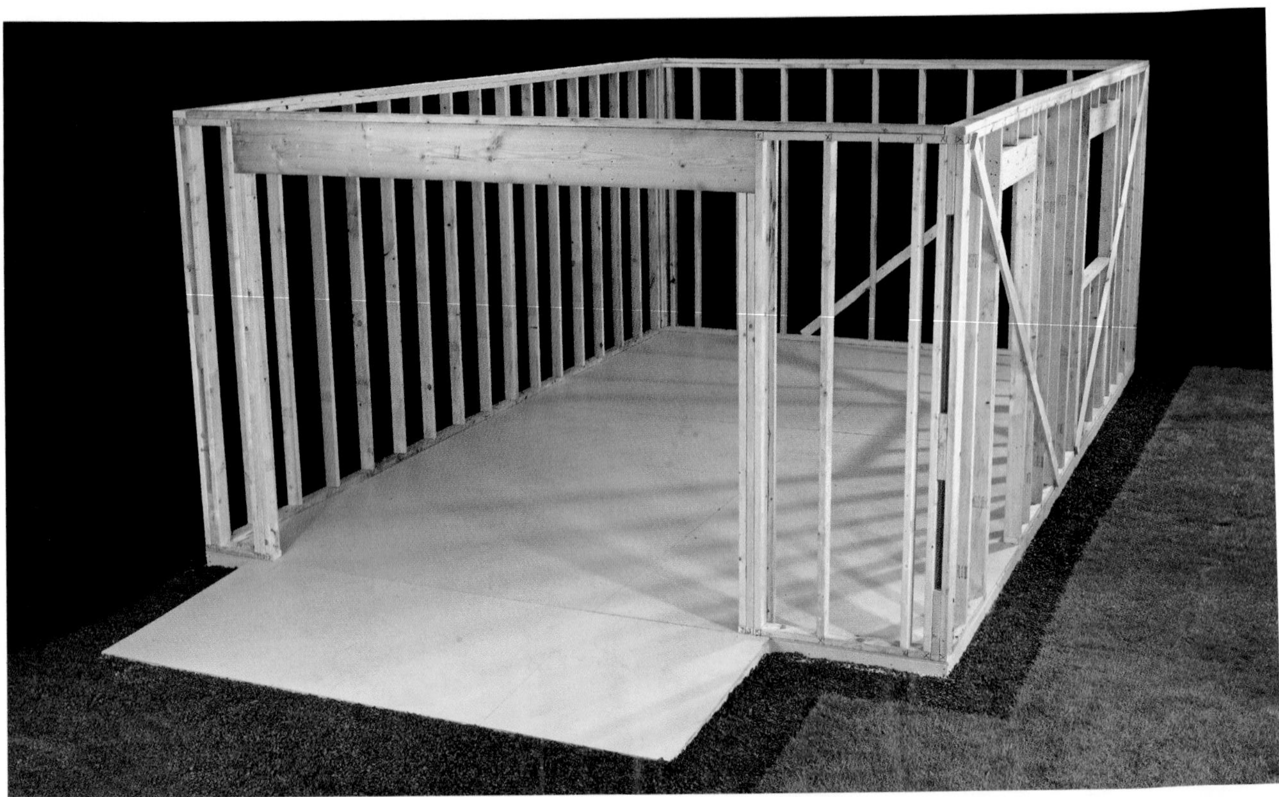

**Raising the garage walls** is an exciting time in your project, as the structure begins to emerge rapidly with relatively little effort.

## Tips for Framing ▸

**The best hand-nailing technique** for joining framing members depends on whether you assemble the framed wall and then raise it, or you add boards one at a time in their final position. If you're assembling the wall on the floor or ground, end-nail the studs to the plates whenever you can (left sample). End-nailed joints, usually made with 10d common nails, are strong and fast to make. To double up wall studs or headers, facenail the parts (right sample) with 8d common nails. Facenailing is also used for attaching jack studs to king studs. To fasten a vertical stud to a top or sole plate that is already in place, toenailing (middle sample) is your best option.

**A pneumatic framing nailer** makes fast work of frame carpentry. Typical collated strips have nails with diameters roughly equivalent to an 8d nail and varying in length between 2⅜" and 2½". Framing nailers can be relatively expensive but are also available for rent at larger rental centers.

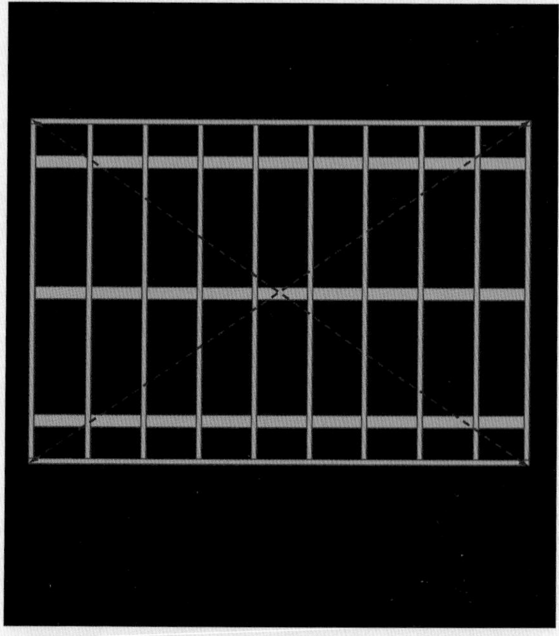

**Measure the diagonal distances** once you have assembled each wall. The distances between opposite corners will be equal when the walls are square.

# How to Frame a Garage

**Prepare the sole plates.** Select straight pressure-treated lumber for the wall sole plates and cut them to length. Position the bottom plates on the slab and up against the J-bolts. Follow your plans to determine which walls run to the edges of the slab (called through walls) and which butt into the other walls (called butt walls). Use a combination square and pencil to extend a line across the bottom plate at each J-bolt location.

**Drill guide holes for J-bolts.** Make a tick mark on the J-bolt layout marks 1¾" in from the outside edge of the bottom wall plates to determine where to drill the J-bolt through-holes. Drill through the bottom plate at each hole location with a ⅝" or ¾" spade bit to allow some room for adjusting the plate on the slab. Slip a backer board beneath the workpiece before finishing the hole.

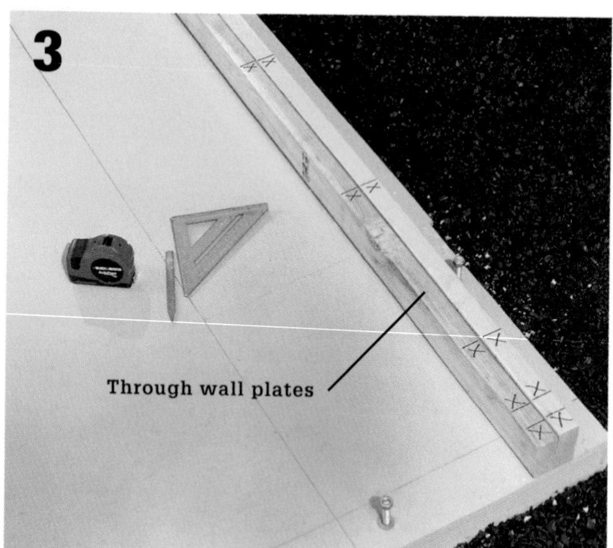


**Make plates for the through walls:** Cut a cap plate for the first wall so its length matches the sole plate. Stand both plates on edge and line up the ends. If the first wall is a through wall, make marks at 1½" and 3" to indicate the end stud and extra corner stud. Mark the next stud at 15¼" according to your stud layout. Step off the remaining studs at 16" on center. Mark double studs at the opposite end of the wall. Draw Xs to the side of each of these marks to designate on which side of the marks the studs should go. Extend these stud layout marks across both edges of the cap and sole plates.

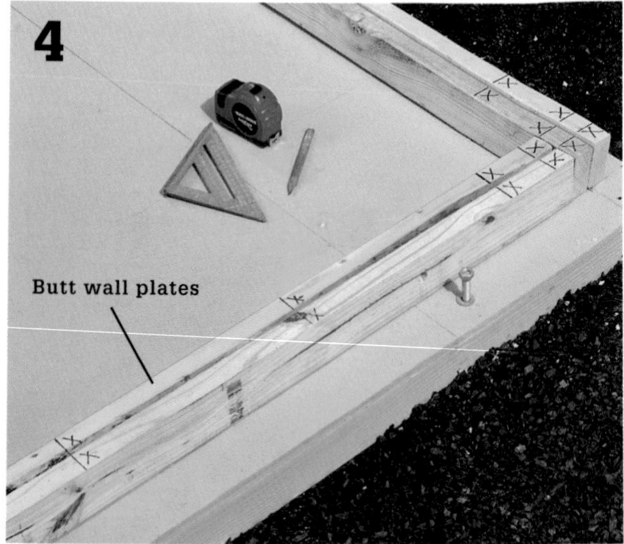


**Make plates for butt walls:** For laying out the stud spacing on butt walls, the end studs will be aligned with the ends of the top and bottom plates. Mark the second stud 15¼" from the plate ends, and step off the rest of the studs at 16" on center. Extend the lines across both wall plates and draw Xs to the right of your stud marks.

**Cut wall studs to length.** Select the number of studs you'll need to build the first wall, and sight down their edges to make sure they're straight. Inspect for deep end checks or loose knots (a check is a lengthwise separation of the wood; an end check is one occurring on an end of a piece). Set defective studs aside for use as blocking. For the single garage shown here, cut the studs to 7 ft., 8⅝" (92⅝").

**Assemble the back wall.** Position the marked wall plates about 8 ft. apart with the stud markings facing up. Lay out the studs between the plates, and start by nailing the bottom plate to the wall studs with pairs of 16d galvanized common nails or pneumatic framing nails. Make sure the edges of the studs and plates are flush and the studs line up with their layout marks on the plate. Drive two nails through the plate into the stud ends to secure them. Nail the top plate to the studs the same way.

**Add end blocking for through wall.** Cut three 12" lengths of 2 × 4s to serve as blocking between the end and second studs on through walls. Space the blocking evenly top to bottom along the inside face of the end studs. Nail the blocking in place.

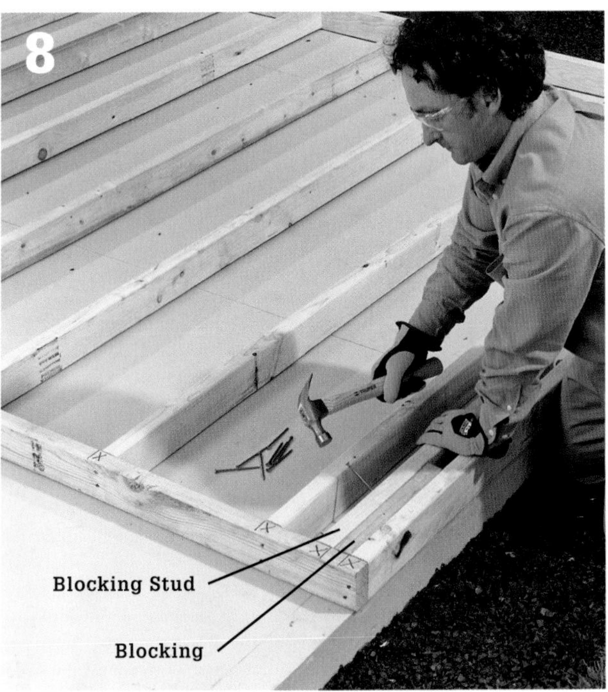


**Nail blocking stud in place.** Butt the second stud against the blocking, and nail the top and bottom plates to it. Drive more nails through the second stud and into the blocking.

(continued)

**Square up the wall.** Check the wall for squareness by measuring from corner to corner and comparing the diagonals (see page 35). If the measurements are not equal, push the longer-dimension corners inward as needed until the diagonals are the same.

**Install temporary bracing.** Once the wall is square, install a temporary 1 × 4 brace across the wall plates and studs to stabilize the wall and keep it square. Use deck screws or 8d nails to tack the brace diagonally across the wall, driving two fasteners into the top and bottom plates and one nail into every other stud. Leave these braces in place until the walls are ready to be sheathed.

**Set up the back wall.** Before standing the first wall up, nail a temporary brace to each end stud to hold the wall in position after it is raised. Drive one 16d nail through the brace and into the end stud about 7 ft. up from the bottom plate to act as a pivot. Tip the wall up and onto the J-bolts with the aid of a helper. Swing the end braces out into the yard, and attach them to stakes in the ground. Check the wall for plumb with a long level held against the studs before fixing the braces to the stakes. Erect any adjoining walls that do not have window or door openings.

**Anchor the wall plates.** Use a hammer to tap the bottom plate into final position on the slab, and attach it to the J-bolts with galvanized washers and nuts.

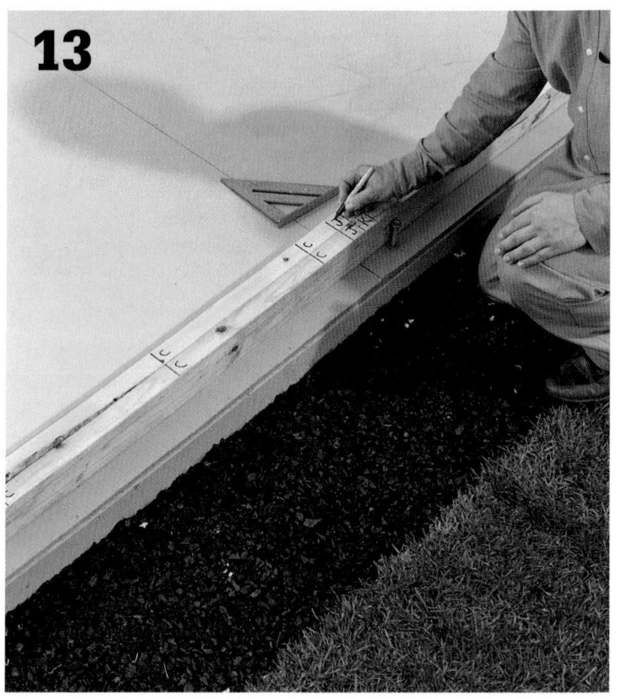


**Mark window and door openings.** For walls with windows or a service door, mark the positions of king and jack studs when you are laying out the top and bottom plates. Identify these studs with a K or J instead of an X to keep them clear. Mark the cripple studs with a C as well.

(continued)

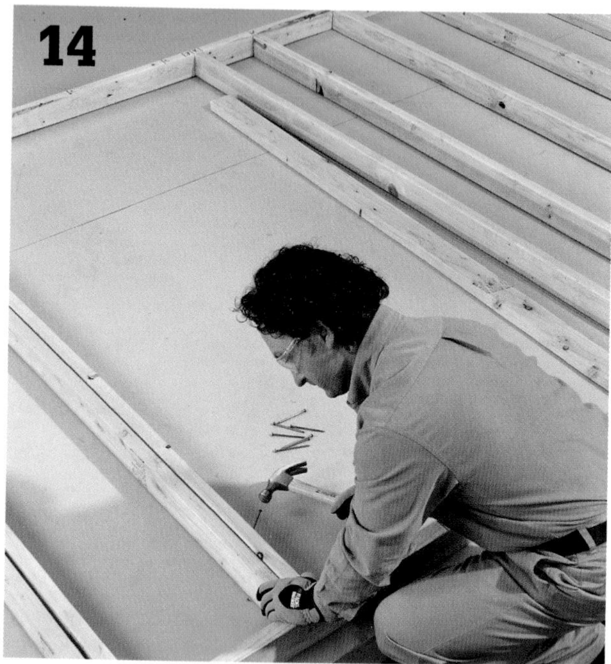

**Frame window and door openings.** Measure and cut the jack studs to length following your garage plans. For either window or door jack studs, make the jack stud length equal to the height of the rough opening minus 1½" for the bottom plate (door framing) or 3" for a double rough sill (window framing). Facenail the jack studs to the king studs with 10d common nails spaced every 12".

**Make the headers.** The header seen here is assembled from doubled-up 2 × 8 lumber sandwiched around a piece of ½" plywood sized to match. Fasten the header pieces together with wavy beads of construction adhesive and 16d nails spaced every 12". Make sure the ends and edges are aligned. Drive the nails at a slight angle to keep them from protruding, and nail from both sides of the header.

**Install the headers.** Set the headers in position on top of the jack studs and drive 16d nails through the king studs and into the ends of the header to fasten it in place. Use six nails (three per end) for 2 × 8 headers.

**Install cripple studs above.** First, cut the cripple studs to fit between the header and the wall's top plate, and then toenail them in place with three 8d nails on each end. Drive two nails through one face and one nail through the center of the opposite face.

**Install cripple studs below.** When framing for a window, measure down from the bottom edge of the header to position the rough sill and establish the rough opening dimensions. Cut two rough sill pieces to length from 2 × 4s and facenail them together with 10d nails. Toenail the sill to the jack studs with 16d nails. Cut and nail cripple studs between the rough sill and the wall's bottom plate to complete the window framing.

**Join wall sections.** For long walls, your garage plans may require you to build the wall in two sections and nail these together before erecting the wall. Facenail the wall sections with pairs of 8d nails spaced every 12" along the adjacent end-wall studs.

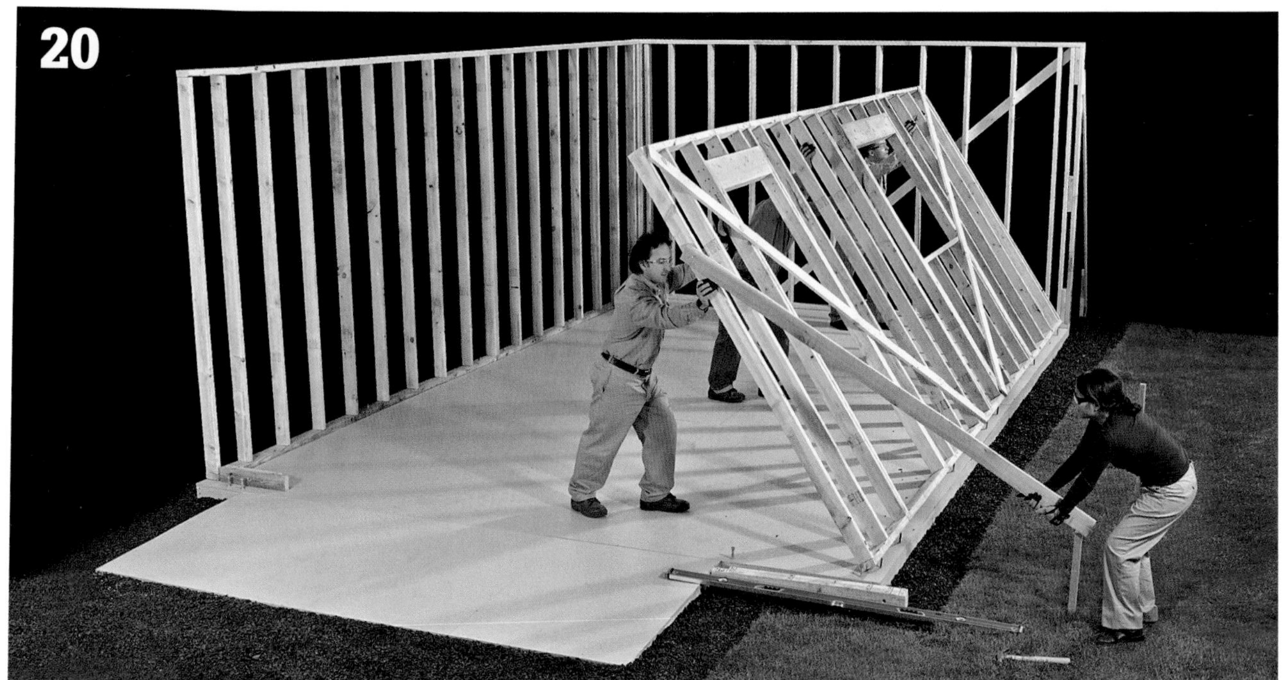


**Raise window/door wall.** You'll need three or four helpers to tilt the heavy wall up and into position on the slab. Adjust the wall as needed so it butts against the short wall and lines up properly on the slab. Check the wall for plumb along several studs, and attach a temporary staked brace to the unsupported end. Install washers and nuts on the J-bolts to fasten the wall to the slab.

(continued)

**Nail walls together.** Drive 16d nails through the end stud of the butted wall into the end studs and blocking of the through wall. Space these nails every 12" along the length of the walls. Prior to nailing the second long wall, you can remove the temporary brace and stake that hold the back wall in position.

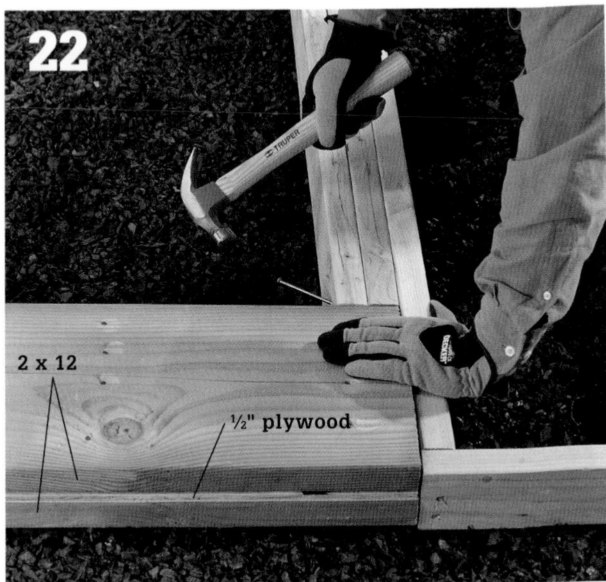


**Assemble the garage door wall.** Follow the instructions in your garage plans to assemble the front wall and the sectional garage door rough framing. Sectional garage doors typically have a doubled-up 2 × 12 header sandwiching a piece of ½"-thick plywood. Build the header just as you would a window or service door header. The header will be supported by double jack studs. This wall may or may not have a continuous top wall plate and cripple studs above the header, depending on the height of your garage walls.

**Position the front wall.** Remove temporary braces and stakes supporting the front and side walls, then tip the front wall up and into position against the side walls. Line up the ends of the side walls with the front wall, and nail the walls together through the end studs with 16d nails. Install washers and nuts on the front wall J-bolts.

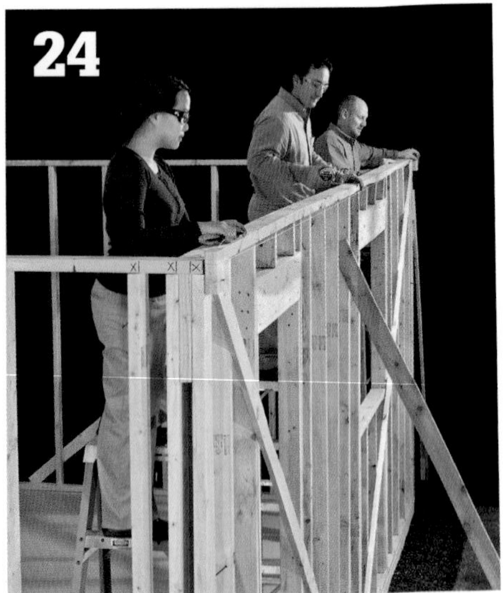


**Test walls for flatness.** Check the long walls for bowing by tacking a scrap block of 2 × 4 at the top outside corner of each wall. Drive another nail partially into these blocks, and then string a mason's line between the nails. Pull the line taut, and measure the distance between the string and the wall's top plate. The distance should be 1½" all along the wall.

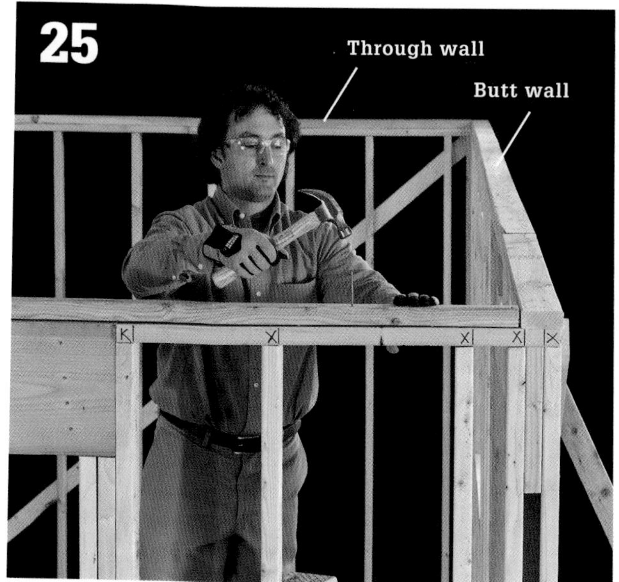


**Lock the walls together.** Cut top plates to length from 2 × 4s to make tie plates. Make the through-wall tie plates 7" shorter than the through-wall top plate 3½" on each side. Cut the tie plates for butted walls 7" longer than the butt-wall top plate. This way, the double top plates on butted walls will overlap the through-wall top plates, locking the walls together. Facenail all four tie plates to the wall top plates with 10d nails. Drive two nails in the overlapped corners, then single nails every 16" along the plates.

**Cut out the threshold.** Cut away the bottom plate from the rough opening of the service door with a reciprocating saw with the blade installed upside down. Make these cuts flush with the edge of the jack studs so the door jamb will fit properly in the opening.

**Frame the overhead door opening.** *Note: If you have already purchased your sectional garage door, check the door opening requirements in the installation manual and compare them to these instructions before proceeding with this step.* Facenail a 2 × 6 around each side and the top to frame the sectional garage door rough opening on the inside face of the front wall. These boards form blocking for installing the garage door and garage door opener later. Position the blocking flush with the faces of the jack studs and the bottom edge of the door header. Fasten the blocking with 10d nails. Wait until you are preparing to install the door to install trimboards and stop molding.

# Installing Roof Framing

This garage has a simple gable-style roof consisting of only two roof planes with flat gable end walls. For that reason, we'll frame the roof using rafters as the principal structural members. Rafters extend from the wall top plates and meet at a ridgeboard at the roof's peak. They're a traditional form of roof construction on both simple and complex roof designs, and rafters are also a more economical option than custom-built trusses. If you're unfamiliar with roof framing, constructing this rafter roof will be an excellent opportunity to learn some important basic skills.

Building the roof frame is a departure from wall framing because you can't nail whole sections of the roof together at once and set them in place. Instead, you'll cut all the rafters to size and shape to match the slope of the roof, and then install them in pairs "stick built" style. For a garage this small, 2 × 6s spaced 24" on center are sufficiently strong to serve as rafter boards, unless your area is beset with extreme snow loads. Since the garage's roof ridge runs from front to back, rafters are installed perpendicular to the length of the building. A third important component of rafter framing—horizontal collar or rafter ties—span the width of the structure and can function as ceiling joists. Collar ties help keep the walls from spreading apart by locking several pairs of rafters together into triangulated frames, similar to a roof truss.

## Tools & Materials ▸

- Work gloves & eye protection
- Carpenter's pencil
- Speed square
- Tape measure
- Miter saw
- Framing square
- Ladders
- Jigsaw
- Circular saw
- Hammer (or pneumatic nailer)
- Long level
- 2 × 6 lumber
- 2 × 4 lumber
- Rafter ties
- Galvanized common nails (10d, 16d)
- 2 × 4 braces
- Collar ties

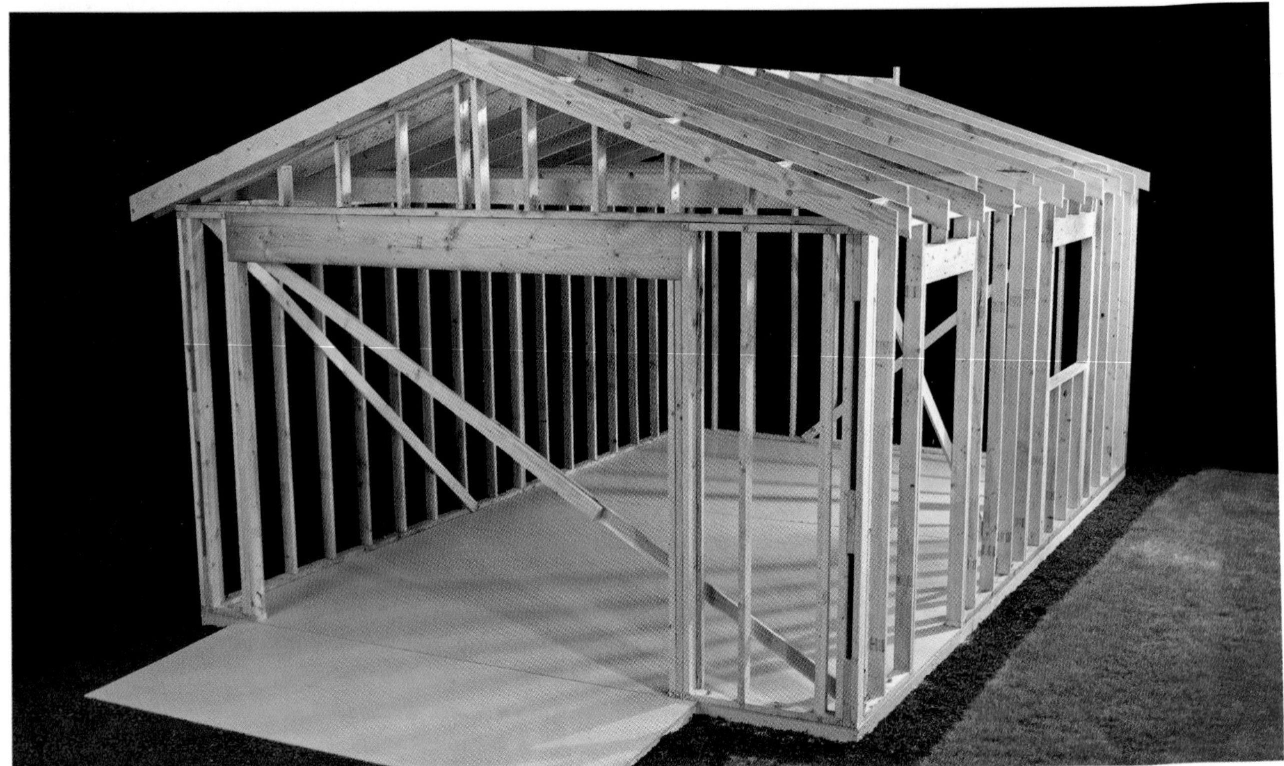

**A system of rafters,** ridgeboard, and collar ties creates the framework for this garage's simple gable-style roof. Rafters are a traditional, sturdy, and economical option for this project, but custom-built trusses are another viable option here.

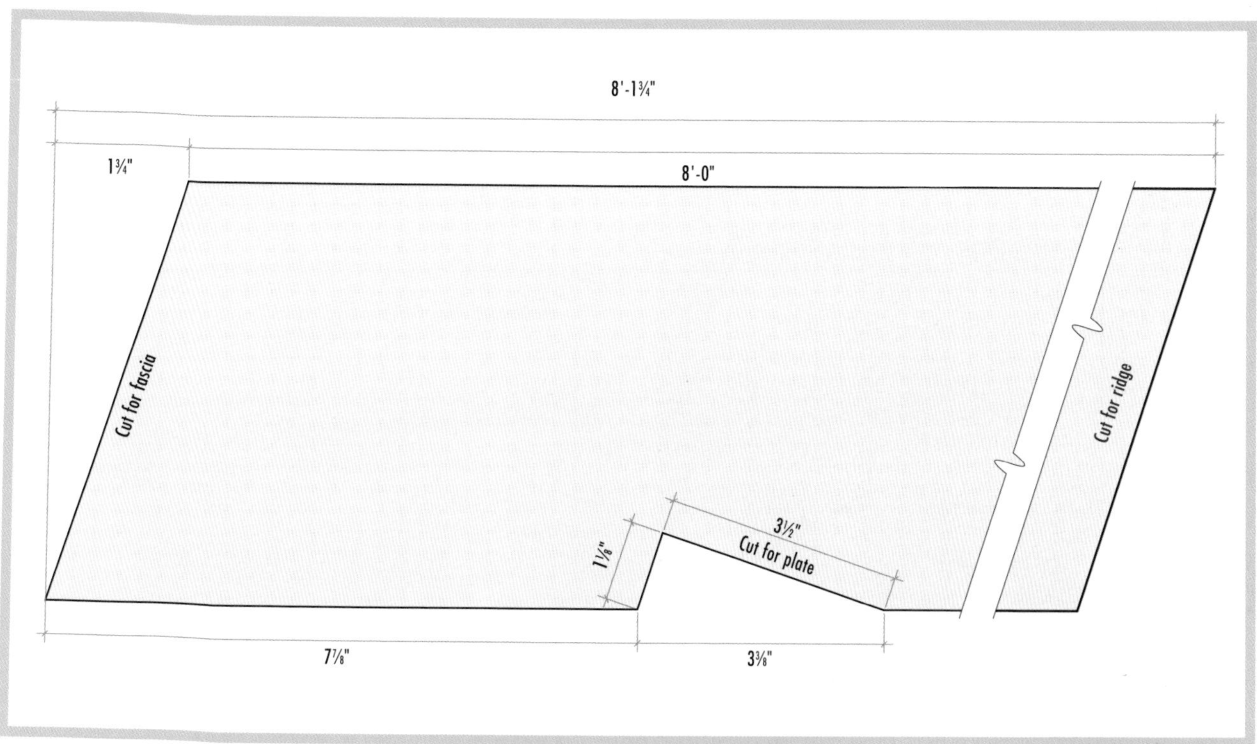


**This template** may be used as a guide for laying out the birdsmouth cuts on the rafter ends for the garage project seen here.

## Using a Speed Square ▸

A speed square is a handy tool for marking angled cuts using the degree of the cut or the roof slope. Set the square flange against the board edge and align the pivot point with the top of the cut. Pivot the square until the board edge is aligned with the desired degree marking or the rise of the roof slope, indicated in the row of common numbers. Mark along the right-angle edge of the square.

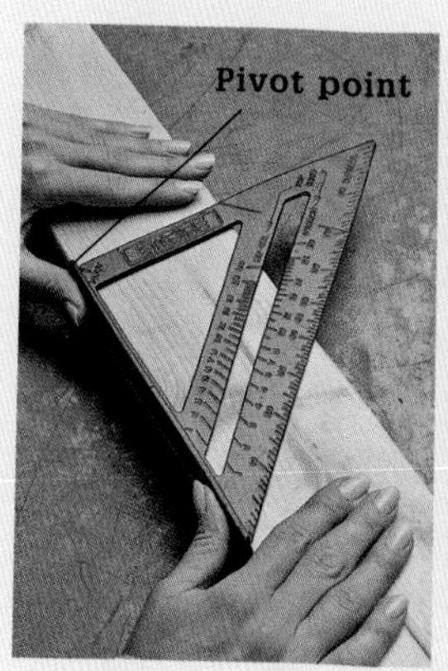


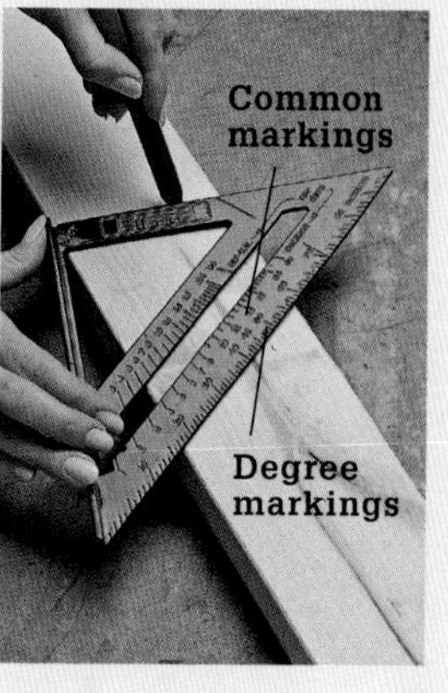


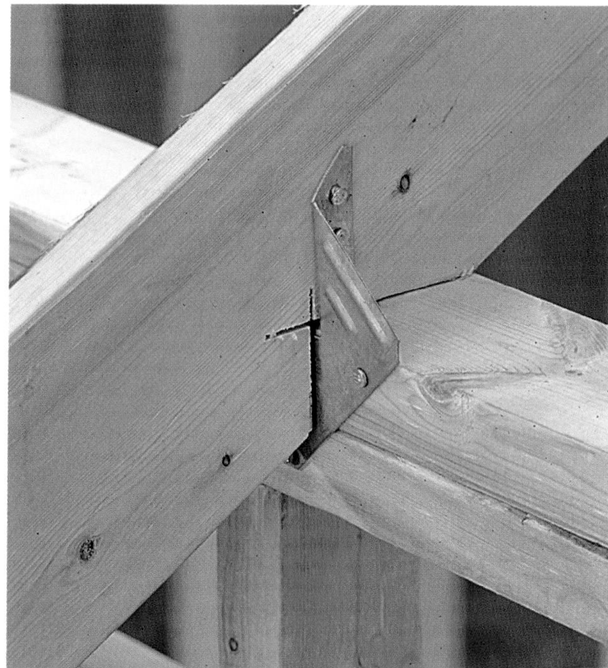

**Metal rafter ties** add strength to the connection between the rafter and the top plate of your garage walls. They also help with alignment and minimize any splintering of the rafter caused by toenailing. In some areas of the country where hurricanes and tornadoes are common, metal rafter ties are required by local codes.

## How to Install Roof Framing

**Make a pair of pattern rafters.** Choose two straight 2 × 6s to create a full-size pattern rafter for each leg of a rafter pair. Mark a cutting line on one end of each pattern with the correct angle formed with the ridgeboard. Refer to your garage plans to determine the correct roof pitch (which determines the cutting angle). Then, measure from the top of the ridge angle along the rafter to determine its overall length and draw a second reference line for the plumb cut at the eave end. Make the plumb cuts with a power miter saw (best choice) or a circular saw. Lay out and cut the birdsmouths on the pattern rafters, using a speed square (page 45). Use a framing square to create the level and plumb lines that form the birdsmouth cuts. The birdsmouth will enable the roof rafters to rest on the wall double top plates at the correct roof pitch. Use the pattern rafters as templates for marking the rest of the rafters.

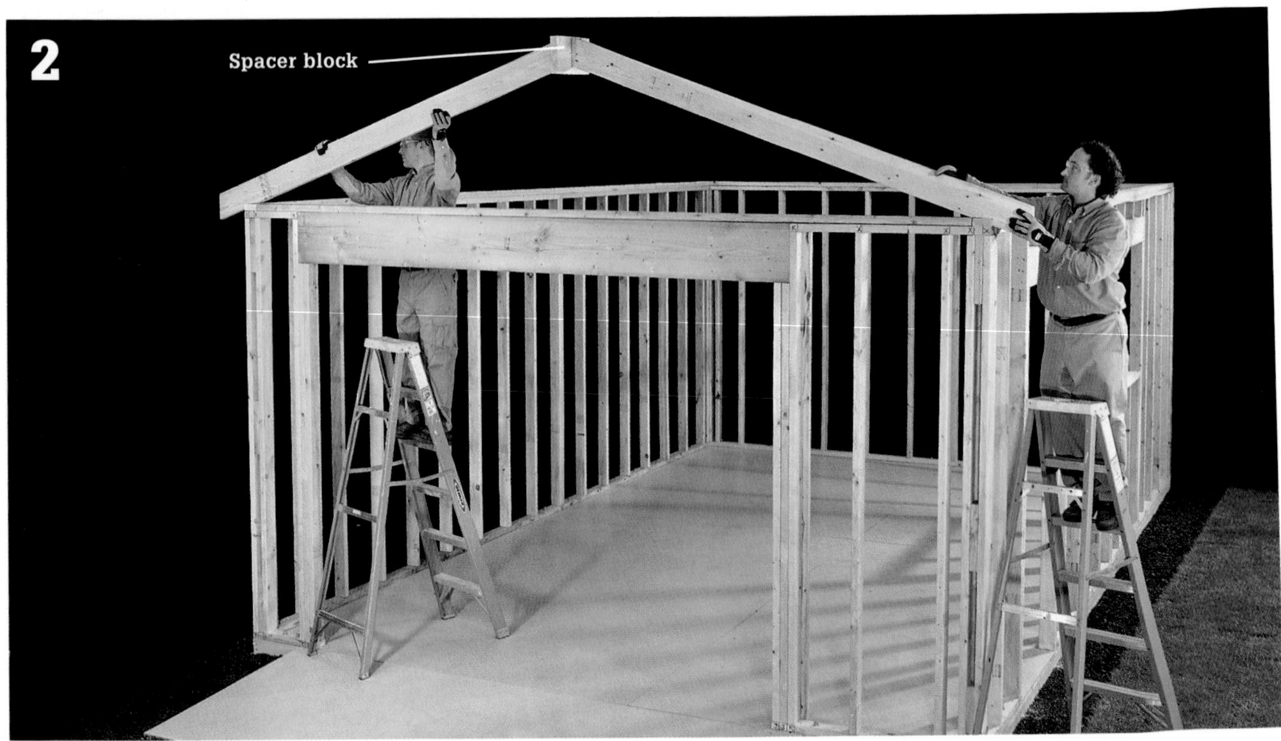


**Check the fit.** Set your pattern rafters in position on top of the side walls with a 2 × 8 spacer block tacked between them to represent the ridgeboard. You'll know you have a good fit if the top angled ridge cuts meet the ridgeboard flush and the birdsmouth cuts sit flush on the wall plates. Have a helper position and check the fit of these parts. Adjust the angles, if necessary, to improve the fit of the parts.

**Cut all the rafters.** Use the pattern rafter to trace the plumb cuts and birdsmouth onto the workpieces for all of the rafters. Set the cutting angle on your power miter saw to match the plumb cut and cut each rafter at the cutting lines. Then, finish the rafters by cutting the birdsmouths with a jigsaw, or circular saw and handsaw.

**Plot the rafter locations.** Mark the location of each rafter on the doubled top plates. The rafters begin at the ends of the walls, and the intermediate rafters should line up over the wall studs that are spaced 16" on center. Use a speed square to extend a rafter layout line up from each wall stud layout line to the top plate. Mark an X next to the line to indicate which side of the line the rafter should go. Mark the position of all the rafters.

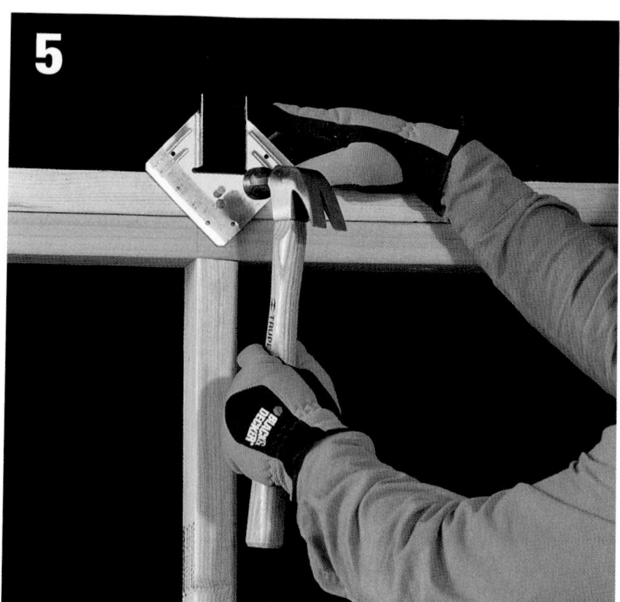

**Install rafter ties.** If building codes in your area require it, or if you simply want a stronger structure, nail metal rafter connector plates (often called rafter ties) to the wall top plates before installing the rafters.

**Mark the ridgeboard.** Select a straight, flat 2 × 8 for the ridgeboard. It should be several feet longer than the roof length. Lay the board face-down over the tops of the end walls and flush against a side wall. Adjust the ridgeboard so it overhangs the end walls evenly. Use a square to transfer the rafter layout lines and X marks from the wall double top plate to the ridgeboard. Then, flip the ridgeboard over and mark the rafter locations on the opposite face.

(continued)

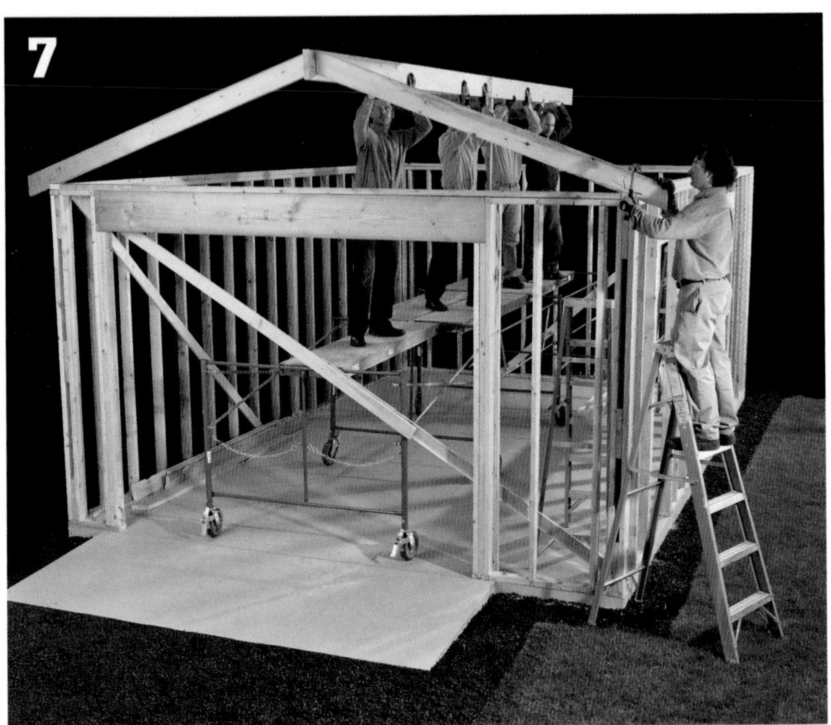


**Install the ridgeboard.** To make it easier to begin the rafter installation, nail the first two end rafters to the ridgeboard before lifting them into place on the walls. Facenail the ridgeboard to one end rafter through the top plumb cut with three 16d nails. Make sure the rafter is properly lined up with the ridgeboard layout line. Toenail the opposite rafter to the ridgeboard. Then, with several helpers lift the end rafters and ridgeboard into position on the wall plates. Have a helper hold up the opposite end of the ridgeboard while you toenail the end rafters to the wall plates.

**Install a temporary brace.** Toenail a temporary 2 × 4 brace vertically to the opposite end wall. Choose a brace longer than the roof will be high. Rest the ridgeboard against the brace and adjust it until it is level. Use 10d nails to nail the ridgeboard temporarily to the brace to hold it in position.

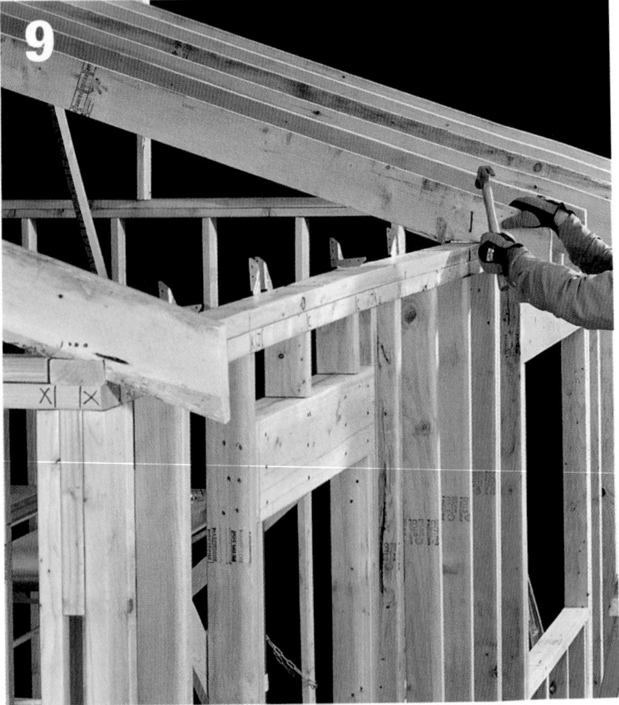


**Install the rest of the rafters.** With the ridgeboard braced and leveled, fit and install the rest of the rafters, fastening them with 16d nails. Toenail the rafters to the metal rafter ties at birdsmouths, and either facenail or toenail the rafters to the ridgeboard, depending on which rafter you are installing for each pair. Check the ridgeboard periodically for level as you work. When you reach the opposite end of the roof, remove the temporary ridge brace and install the end rafters.

**Install collar ties.** Follow your garage plans to lay out and cut collar ties to size. Collar ties prevent the garage walls from spreading apart under roof loads. Angle-cut the top ends of each collar tie if necessary to match the roof slope. Install the collar ties by facenailing them to the rafters with three 10d nails at each end.

**Install gable top plates.** On the gable ends of the roof, you'll need to install additional studs under the rafters to provide nailing surfaces for wall sheathing. Start by cutting a pair of 2 × 4 gable wall top plates that will extend from the sides of the ridgeboard down to the wall double top plates.

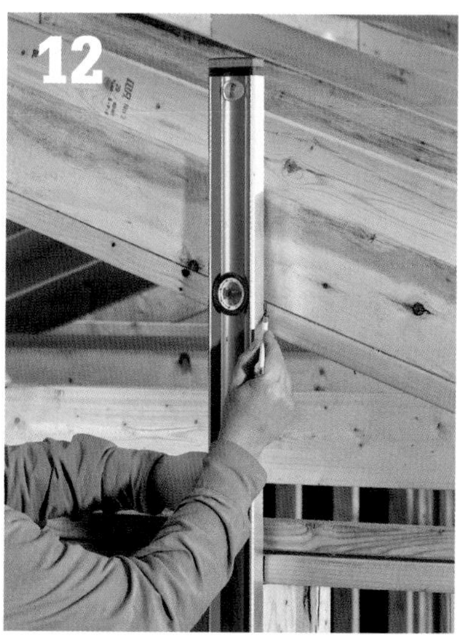


**Lay out and install gable studs.** These should be positioned by holding a long level against the wall studs and transferring layout lines to the edges of the gable top plates. Plan for a gable stud to line up over each wall stud. Cut the gable studs to fit and toenail them to the gable and wall top plates.

**Install lookouts.** Follow your plans to lay out the locations of the lookout blocking that will form gable overhangs on the roof. Cut the blocking to size, and facenail through the end rafters to install it to the outside faces of the end rafters. Make sure the top edges of the blocking and rafters are flush before driving the nails. Also mark the gable overhang length on each end of the ridgeboard, and cut it to final length with a circular saw or handsaw.

**Complete the overhang.** Lay out and cut the gable overhang rafters to size and shape using your pattern rafter as a template. *Note: Gable end rafters do not have birdsmouths. Nail these rafters to the lookout blocking and ridgeboard to complete the roof framing.*

## Option: Roof Trusses ▸

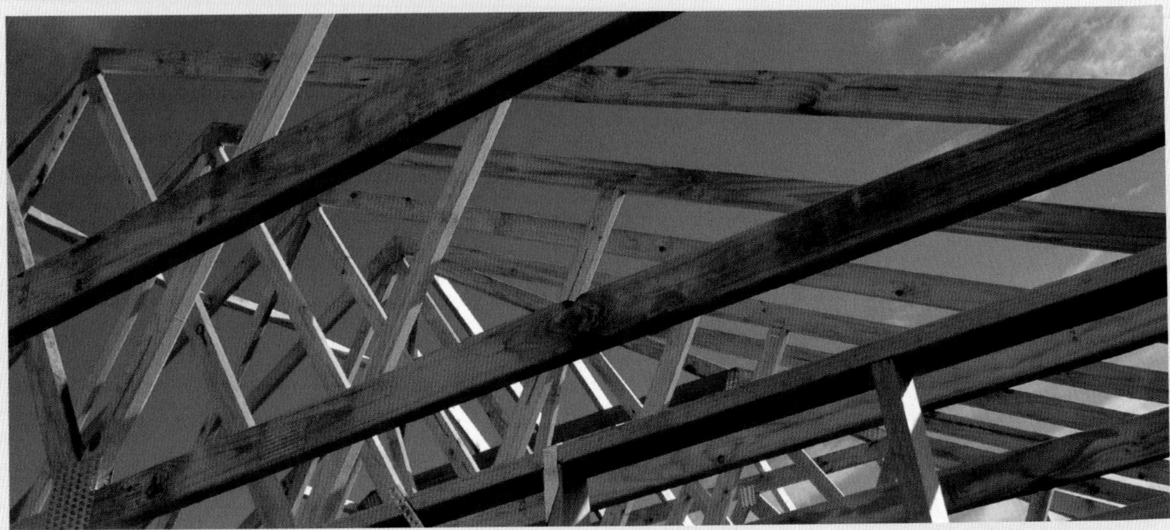

**Custom-made roof trusses** save time and practically guarantee that your roof will be square and strong. They add considerably to the project cost, however, and must be ordered well in advance.

Trusses are engineered roof support members that can be used instead of hand-cut rafters to support your roof. You can build them yourself or you can order them premade to match your building size and preferred roof pitch. A truss has a triangular shape with two matching top chords that meet a horizontal bottom chord. Diagonal crossbracing, called webs, are fitted between the top chords and the bottom chord. Typically, the joints between chords and web members are reinforced with metal or plywood gusset plates.

Trusses are designed so the ends of the bottom chord rest on the top plates of the side walls. Consequently, you don't have to cut tricky birdsmouths or rafter angles—you simply fasten the bottom chord by toenailing or using metal hangers. The relative ease that can be installed may make up for the higher costs compared to rafters. But unless your garage is very small, you will likely need to rent a crane, forklift, or other mechanical assistant to raise the trusses into position.

Most professional garage contractors employ trusses because they go up quickly and don't require complicated cutting. There are limitations, however. If you are purchasing the truss premade, you can pretty well wager that the quality of the lumber won't be as high as the dimensional lumber you'd use to make rafters. The presence of the bottom chord will cut into your open space in a garage, potentially limiting the storage options. But if you are planning to install a ceiling in your garage, the chords can be put to work as ceiling joists.

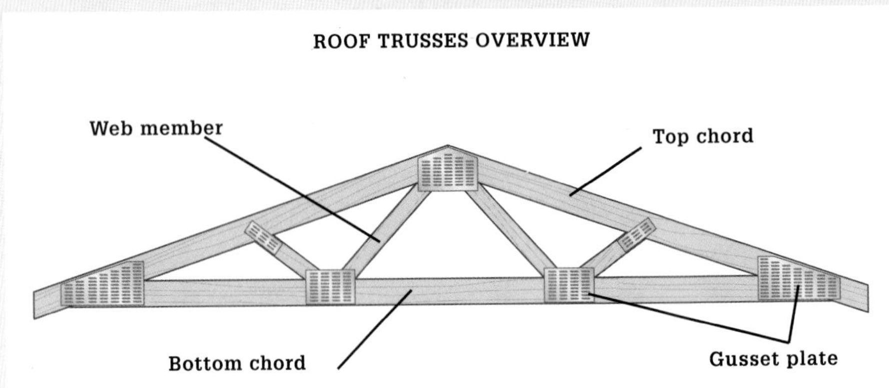


**A manufactured truss** consists of two top chords and a lower chord with web members installed between chords for strength. The joints are usually reinforced with metal or plywood gussets. Unlike rafter roofs, a truss roof does not have a ridgepole.

# Working with Trusses

**Use long 2 × 4 braces** clamped to the end wall to temporarily clamp or tack the end truss in position. If the truss is sized correctly there should be no need to adjust it side to side, but you'll need to make sure it is flush with the end wall and plumb before you nail it into place.

**Secure the trusses** to the walls with metal truss ties or rafter ties. These are required in high-wind areas but are a good idea anywhere because they strengthen the roof and help in alignment.

**Toenail trusses** to wall plates with 16d nails. Typically, the two end trusses are installed first and then a mason's line is stretched between the tails of the top chords to use as an alignment reference. A temporary brace with truss spacing marked to match the wall plates is installed as you go to stabilize the trusses and create the correct spacing. Remove the brace before installing the roof decking.

## Dos & Don'ts for Working with Trusses ▸

- DO set trusses on blocking for their protection when storing.
- DO have plenty of help when it's time to raise the trusses.
- DO NOT cut trusses for any reason.
- DO NOT exceed the span spacing for which the truss is rated.
- DO provide your truss dealer with an accurate plan drawing of your garage.
- DO NOT walk on trusses if they are being stored lying flat.
- DO NOT install trusses in high winds.
- DO use temporary braces to ensure that trusses stay plumb during installation.

# Sheathing Walls

Once the garage walls are framed and erected, all exterior wall surfaces, including the angled areas up the gable walls, should be covered with a layer of oriented strand board (OSB) or CDX plywood sheathing. Wall sheathing serves two basic purposes: it strengthens the wall framing by locking the studs to a stiff outer "skin," and it provides a uniform backing for nailing the siding and trim in place. The minimum sheathing thickness for 16" O.C. stud walls is ⅜", and ½" material is even better.

Provided you've framed your garage walls correctly, you should be able to install sheathing in full 4 × 8 sheets because the stud spacing will enable the sheets to be nailed along the edges and ends evenly. You can hang sheathing horizontally or vertically, but generally the horizontal approach makes large sheets easier to manage. Install a bottom coarse of sheathing first all around the building so you can use the top edge as a handy ledger for resting and nailing off the top course. To speed the process along, sheathe right over service door and window openings, and then cut these openings again once all the sheathing is in place.

Even exterior-rated sheathing isn't immune to the effects of wind-driven rain, especially around nail holes. It's good practice to cover sheathing with 15-pound building paper or housewrap. Install it horizontally, working from the bottom of the walls up and overlapping the seams by at least 2". If you use housewrap, be sure to tape all seams with housewrap tape recommended for the brand of wrap you are using. Housewrap will begin to degrade from sunlight in just a few weeks, so be sure to get your permanent siding on promptly.

## Tools & Materials ▸

- Work gloves & eye protection
- Chalk line
- Tape measure
- Marker
- Hammer (or pneumatic nailer)
- Drill & bits
- Reciprocating saw
- Cap nails
- Utility knife
- OSB sheathing
- Common nails (6d)
- Housewrap
- Housewrap tape

**Wall sheathing** stiffens building wall framing and creates a uniform backing for siding and trim. A layer of building paper or housewrap seals the sheathing from moisture infiltration.

## How to Install Wall Sheathing

**Snap a layout line.** Use a chalk line to create a level line 47" up the walls, measured from the bottom of the bottom plate. Snap a line the full length of each wall. At this height, the bottom course of sheathing will cover the bottom wall plate and overlap the foundation by 1", minimizing water infiltration. Several inches of slab should still be visible after the sheathing is installed. Sheathing should not contact the soil.

**Install the first sheet.** Position the first full sheet of OSB sheathing in one corner so the top edge lines up with the chalk line. One end of the sheet should align with the edge of the framed wall and the other should fall midway across a stud. Attach the sheathing with 6d common nails. Space the nails every 6" around the perimeter and every 12" at the intermediate studs. Before nailing, snap chalk lines across the sheet to show the centerlines of every wall stud. Install all first-course panels. *Note: Go ahead and sheath over door and window openings. You can cut out the sheathing later.*

**Install the second course.** Begin this course with a half sheet of OSB to establish a staggered pattern. Snap chalk lines across this sheet, too, to show nailing locations of studs. If necessary, trim the second-course panels so the tops are flush with the top edges of the wall-cap plate. Maintain a gap of ⅛" between the first and second course panels to allow for expansion and contraction (6d nails can be used as spacers between panels).

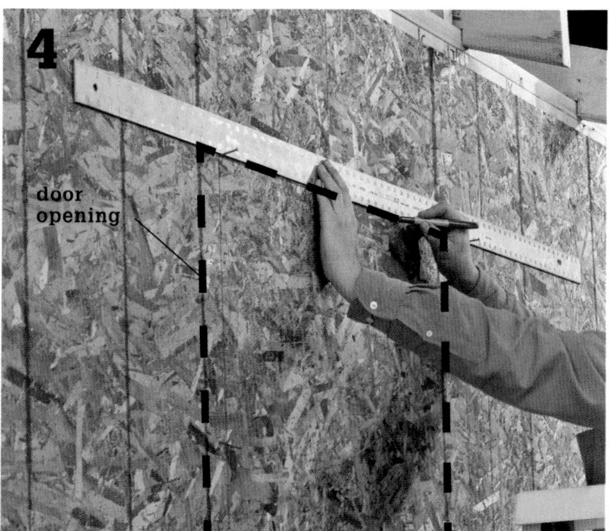


**Mark the door and window openings.** Drill through the sheathing at all corners of the door and window openings (you can drive nails if you prefer), and then connect the holes (or nails) with straight cutting lines.

(continued)

**Cut out the door and window openings,** using a reciprocating saw. Cut carefully so the sheathing does not extend into the opening.

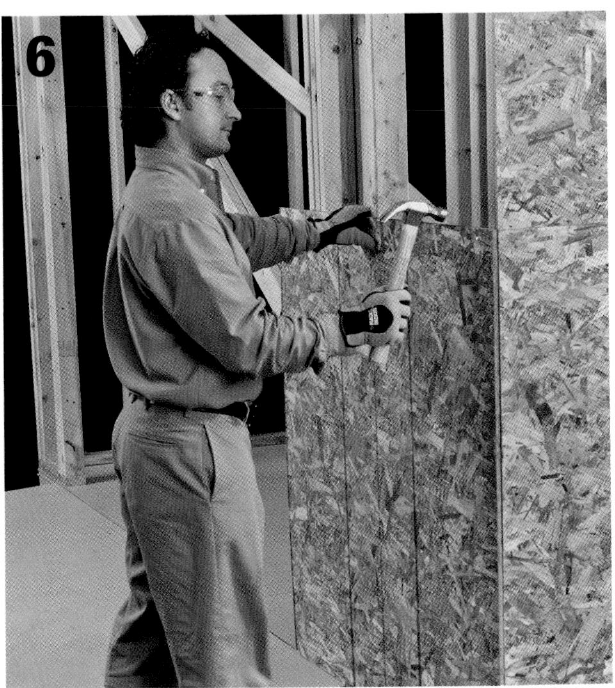


**Sheath the next wall frame.** The panels for the adjoining wall should overlap the ends of the panels on the first wall without extending beyond them. Complete installing full panels on all four walls.

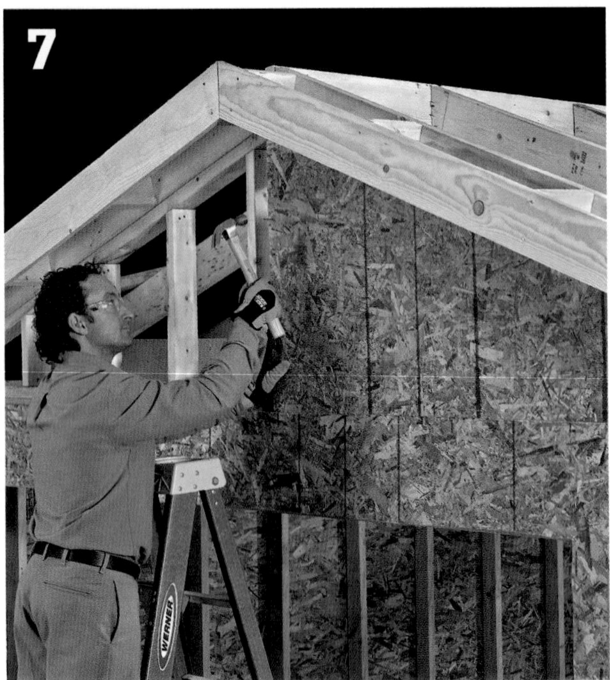


**Install sheathing in gable areas.** After the first courses are installed on the walls with roof gables, lay out and cut second-course panels that follow the eave line. Mark stud locations and attach these gable sheathing panels with 6d nails, maintaining ⅛" gaps between panels.

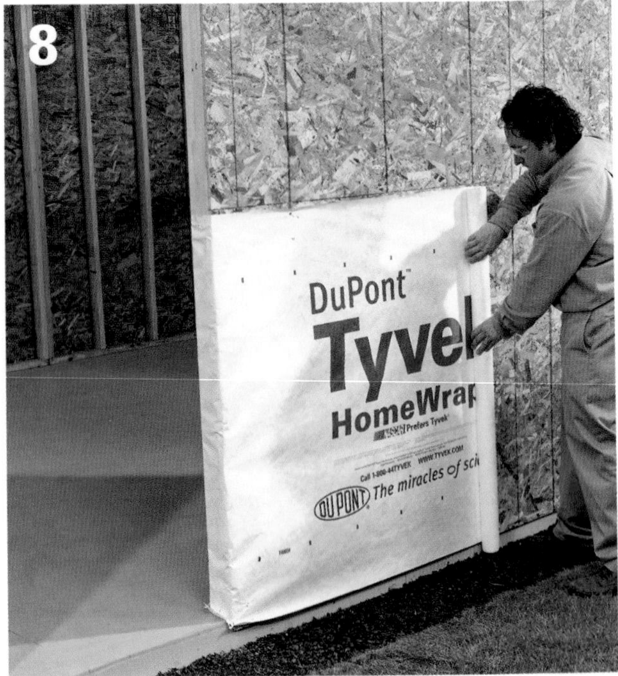


**Begin installing housewrap.** Begin at the bottom courses if the product you're using is not wide enough to cover a wall in one piece. *Note: Housewrap is a one-way permeable fabric that helps keep moisture from entering the structure from the exterior. Installing it makes sense only if you are planning to add finished interior walls in the garage.*

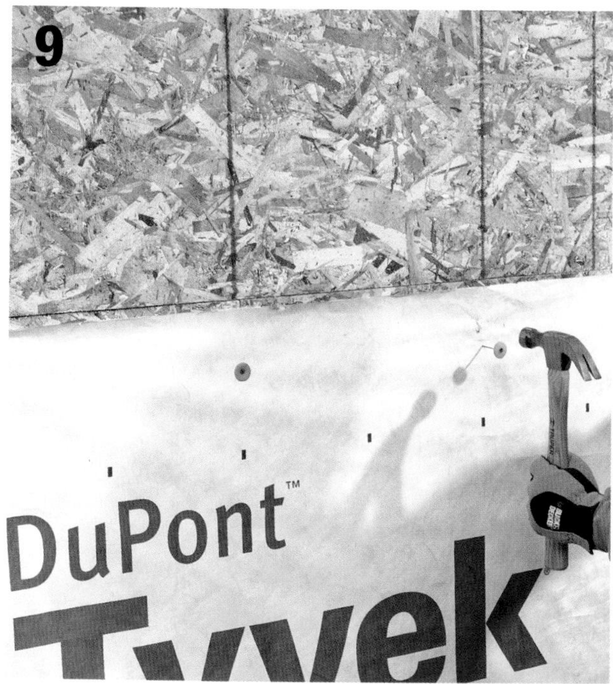


**Attach the housewrap with housewrap nails.** Drive at least three housewrap nails spaced evenly along each wall stud.

**Finish installing the housewrap.** All seams should overlap by at least 6 to 12", with horizontal seams overlapping from above.

**Cut out windows and doors.** Make a long X cut in the housewrap, connecting corners diagonally at window and door openings. Use a utility knife to make the cut. Staple down the extra housewrap in the window rough opening so it wraps around the jack studs, header, and rough sill.

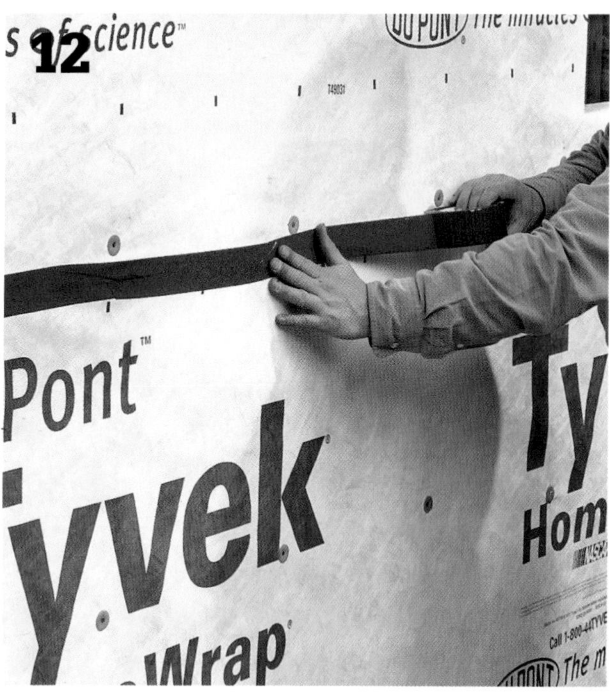


**Tape the seams.** To seal the housewrap, apply housewrap tape along all horizontal and vertical seams. *Note: Housewrap is not rated for long-term exposure to the sun, so do not wait more than a few weeks after installing it before siding the garage.*

# Installing Fascia & Soffits

Fascia and soffits form transitions from your garage's roof to the wall siding. Fascia consists of 1× pine or cedar boards, sometimes called subfascia, that cover the ends of the rafters at the roof eaves to keep weather and animal pests out. It also serves as an attachment surface for gutters. The faces of the gable end rafters are also covered with fascia boards to continue the roof trim pattern all around the building. Generally, fascia boards are installed before the roof sheathing to ensure that the roof sheathing will overlap them once it's in place. You can paint your garage fascia to protect it, or cover it with manufactured aluminum fascia that matches the soffit color.

A soffit extends from the fascia to the wall. It encloses the bays between the rafters or trusses and provides an important means of ventilation beneath the roof deck. Sometimes a soffit is made of exterior plywood with vents cut into it, but the soffit we show here is ventilated aluminum strips, available in a range of colors to match aluminum or vinyl siding. Install your garage soffit before hanging the siding so you can nail it directly to the wall sheathing.

## Tools & Materials ▸

- Work gloves & eye protection
- Miter saw
- Hammer (or pneumatic nailer)
- Speed square
- Chalk line
- Circular saw
- Aviation snips
- Caulk gun
- 1 × 8 lumber
- Common nails (16d)
- Galvanized casing nails (8d)
- 2 × 2 lumber (if needed)
- 2 × 6 scrap lumber
- Vented aluminum soffit panels with mounting strips
- Rolled aluminum flashing with color-matched nails
- Fascia covers
- Color-matched caulk

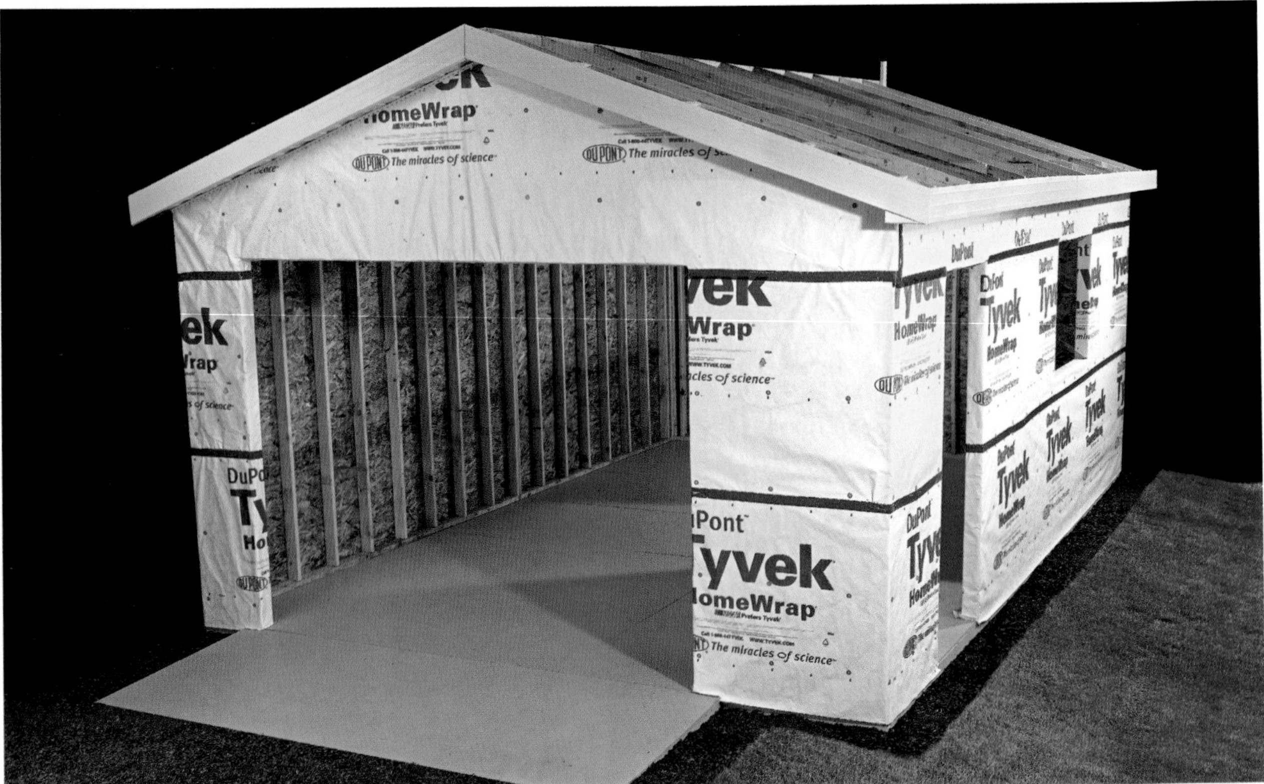


**Fascia and soffits** enclose roof rafters to keep weather and pests out while providing a means of roof ventilation and a graceful transition from the roof to the walls.

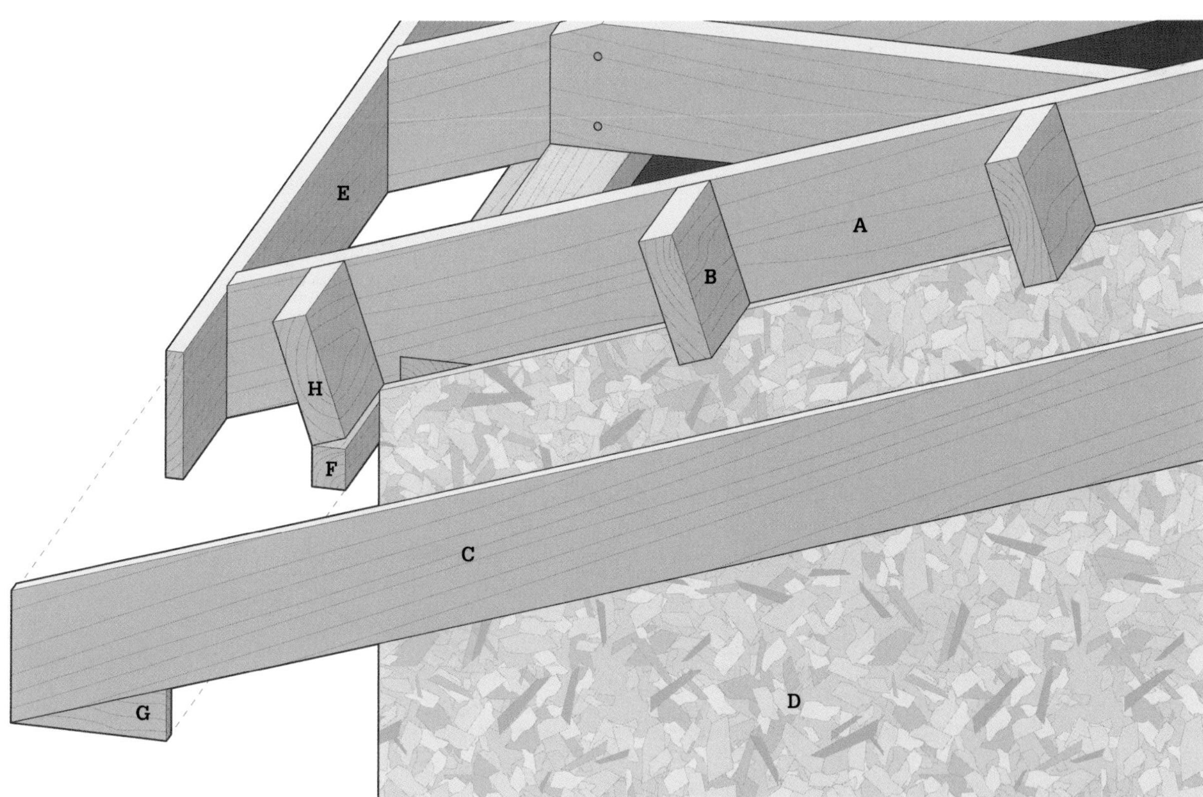


**Components of the cornice system built here include:** (A) End rafters, (B) 2× lookout blocking, (C) Gable overhang rafters, (D) Wall sheathing, (E) 1 × 8 subfascia (eaves), (F) 2× soffit blocking-eaves (continuous strip along wall), (G) 2× gable rafter blocking, (H) 2× cornice blocking.

**Install the subfascia.** Cut pieces of 1 × 8 to make subfascia strips that fit into the fascia area. Attach them to the rafter tails with 8d galvanized casing nails. The ends of the subfascia should be flush with the faces of the gable overhang rafters. Use a speed square held against the top edges of the rafters to adjust the subfascia up or down until the square meets it halfway through its thickness. This will allow the roof sheathing to overhang the rafter tails for proper drainage. Once the subfascia is properly adjusted, drive three nails per rafter tail to secure it.

**Make vertical joints.** If your subfascia or fascia boards are not long enough to cover a wall in one piece, use overlapping scarf joints to join the ends. Miter cut the ends of the scarf joint parts so they overlap and fall over a rafter tail. Drive three 8d nails through both joint parts to secure them to the rafter.

(continued)

**Option:** If you will be installing wood soffit panels, install 2 × 2 soffit blocking. (The garage seen here will be equipped with metal soffits that do not need backer blocking.) The blocking should be positioned so the bottom edge is flush with the soffit groove or backer in the fascia. Cut the soffit blocking so it extends beyond the ends of the walls to create a nailing surface for any filler pieces that will be installed with the cornice. Nail the soffit blocking to the wall studs with 10d nails, one nail per stud.

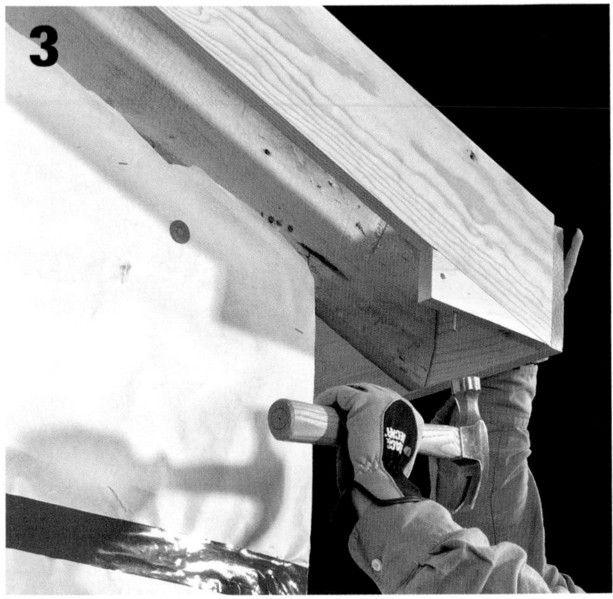


**Add cornice filler pieces.** Measure and cut triangular blocking to fit underneath the gable end rafter tails. Lay out the blocking so it forms a plumb bottom to the rafter tails. Toenail this blocking to the rafters. If soffit blocking is present, screw or nail the cornice blocking to the end of the soffit blocking. Lay out, cut, and nail 1× subfascia boards to cover the gable rafters and the ends of the ridgeboard. Miter cut the ends of the subfascia where they meet at the roof ridge.

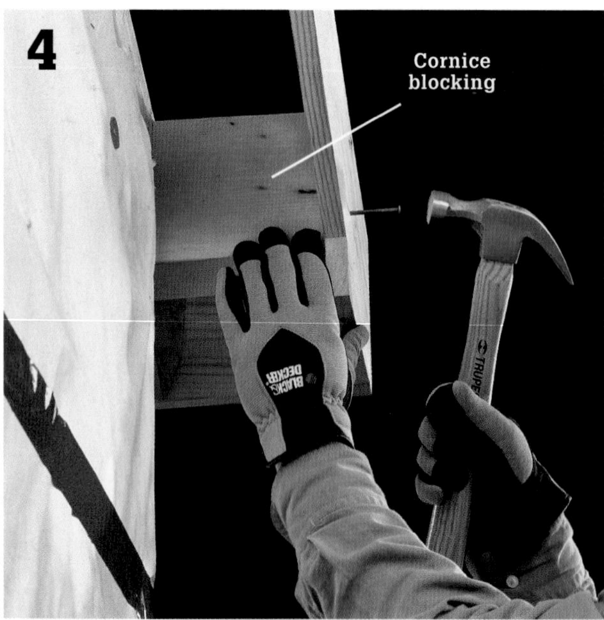


**Install cornice blocking.** Cut and fit short lengths of 2 × 6 scrap between the gable and end rafters and the wall to box in the cornice. Drive 16d nails through the subfascia and end rafters to attach the blocking.

**Enclose the eaves.** Cut strips of vented aluminum soffit to enclose the eaves of the roof. Hang mounting strips for the soffit panels on the garage walls (if you did not install backer boards—see Option, above). Attach the free edges of the soffit to the bottom of the subfascia with siding nails. The soffit panels should stop flush with the subfascia.

**Install soffit in the gables.** Lay out and snap chalk lines on the gable walls for installing soffit hanger strips, and then mount the hanger strips (or the blocking). Cut, fit, and nail the soffit panel strips to the subfascia and soffit blocking to close up the rake ends of the roof.

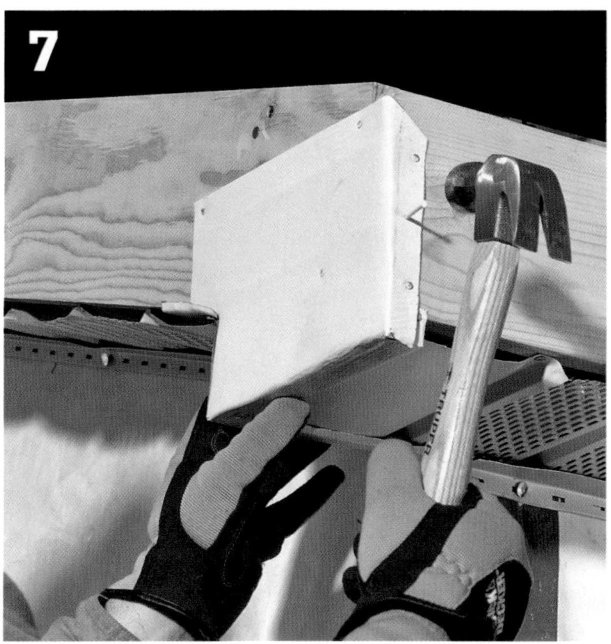


**Enclose the cornices.** Cut and bend pieces of rolled aluminum flashing to fit over the roof cornices and cover the blocking. Nail this flashing to the cornices with color-matched siding nails. Wrap this flashing around the eave subfascia boards by 1 to 2" so you can install metal fascia to overlap it.

**Install fascia covers.** Measure the width of the subfascia boards, and cut fascia covers to fit. Fit the fascia in place over the subfascia boards so the bottom lip overlaps the soffits. Nail through the lip every 16" into the subfascia with color-matched siding nails. Fasten the top of the fascia within ½" of the cut edge so the nail heads will be covered by drip edge molding later. At the cornice, bend the last piece of fascia cover at a right angle to turn the corner (make relief cuts with aviation snips first).

**Finish installing fascia covers.** Install the fascia covers on the gable ends, stopping just short of the cornices. At the cornices, bend a piece of fascia cover to turn the corner, and trim the end so it will make a straight vertical seam. Caulk the seam with caulk tinted to match your fascia cover color.

# Building the Roof

Now that your garage fascia and soffits are installed, it's time to sheathe the roof deck, install roofing, and add a ridge vent (optional). The purpose of roof sheathing is obvious: it reinforces the rafters to help stiffen the roof, and it provides a flat, continuous surface for attaching the roofing. As with wall sheathing, you can use either oriented strand board (OSB) or CDX plywood for roof sheathing, but make sure it's at least ½" thick to carry the combined weight of the roofing material and snow loads (if applicable). If you accurately placed your rafters at the roof framing stage, the sheathing should install quickly, with minimal waste, and all seams should fall at the rafter locations. Stagger the joints from one row of sheathing to the next.

After constructing the roof deck, install a layer of 15# or 30# roofing felt (also called building paper). Roofing felt protects the sheathing and serves as an important second line of defense against leaks beneath the roofing. Roll out and nail the felt horizontally, starting at the eaves and overlapping the felt as you work your way up to the peak. Once the felt is in place, you can install a metal drip edge around the roof perimeter and then proceed with the roof covering. We used asphalt shingles for this project, but feel free to use roofing material to match your home's roof—cedar shingles, metal roofing, or even clay tiles are other good options.

Finally, you can provide excellent ventilation by topping off your garage roof with a continuous ridge vent. A ridge vent combined with vented soffits allows convection to draw cool air in through the eave or gable vents and exhaust hot air out at the roof peak.

## Tools & Materials ▸

- Work gloves & eye protection
- Tape measure
- Hammer (or pneumatic nailer)
- Circular saw
- Aviation snips
- Stapler
- Utility knife
- Chalk line
- Roofing hammer
- Framing square
- ½" CDX or OSB sheathing panels
- Box nails (8d)
- Metal drip edge
- Roofing nails
- Building paper (15# or 30#)
- Shingles
- Continuous ridge vent (optional)

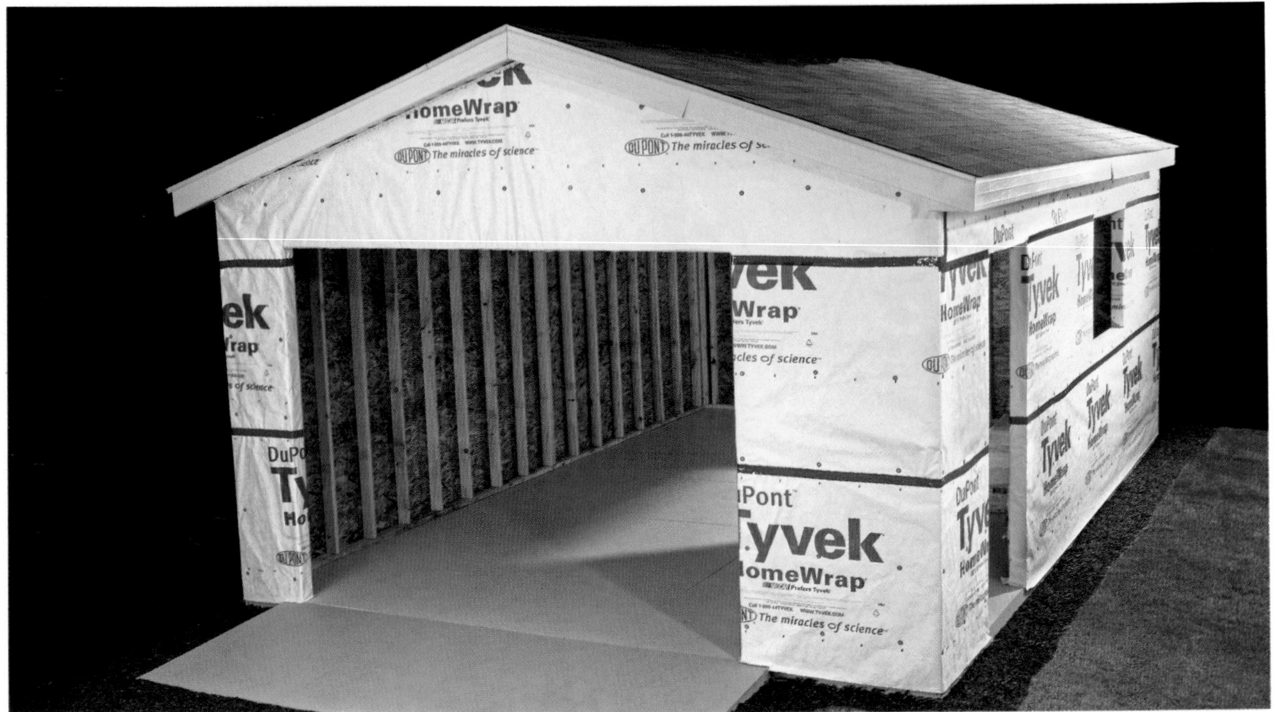


**A top-notch garage roof includes** roof deck sheathing, drip edge, roofing felt, shingles, and a continuous ridge vent. When properly installed, your garage roof should last as long as your house roof.

## Asphalt Shingles ▸

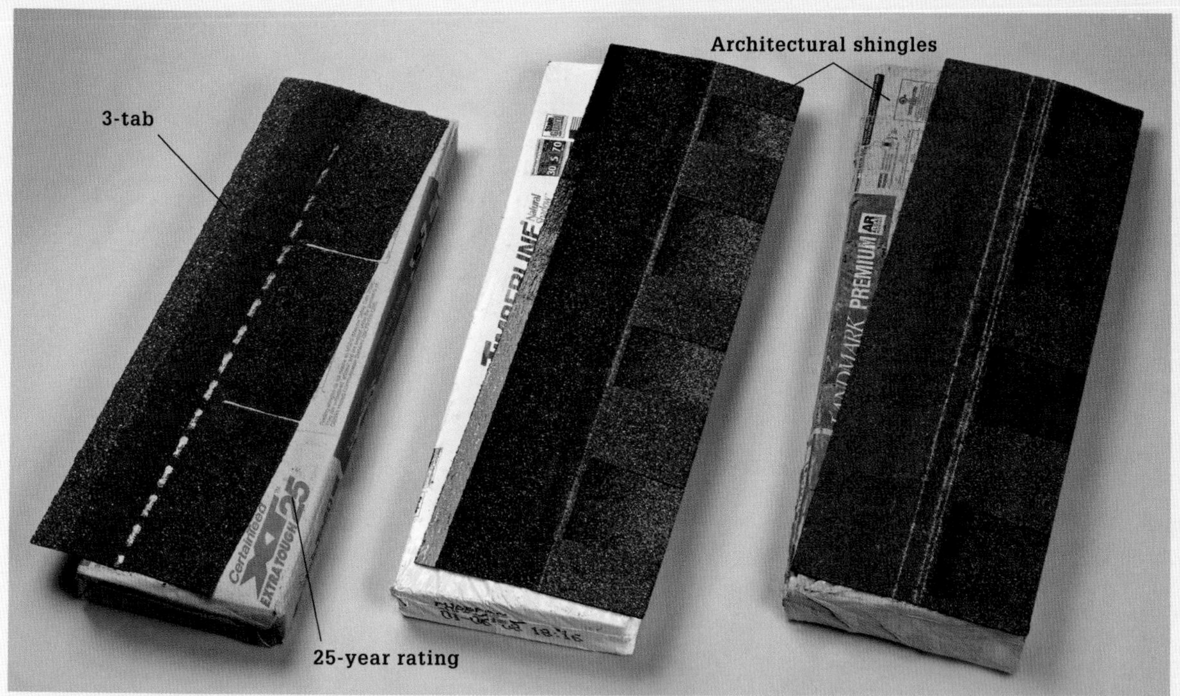

Asphalt shingles are usually rated by life span, with 20-, 25-, and 40-year ratings the most common (although some now claim to be 50-year shingles). Functionally, these ratings should be used for comparison purposes only. In fact, the average life span of an asphalt shingle roof in the United States is 8 to 10 years.

The term multitab shingle refers to any asphalt shingle manufactured with stamped cutouts to mimic the shapes of slate tile or wood shakes. Multitab cutouts are made and installed in single thickness 3-ft. strips, so these tabbed reveals show up. The ubiquitous term for them is three-tab, but two- and four-tab styles are also available. Generally, the tabs are spaced evenly along each sheet of shingle to provide a uniform appearance and a stepped, brick-laid pattern on the roof. However, some manufacturers also offer styles with shaped corners or randomly spaced tabs trimmed to different heights for a more unique look.

## How to Prepare the Roof Deck

**Install the first course of roof decking.** Start sheathing the roof at one of the lower corners with ½" CDX plywood or oriented strand board (OSB) that's rated for sheathing. Where possible, use a full 8-ft.-long sheet or a half sheet with the seam still falling midway across a rafter or truss. Align the sheet so it overlaps the gable subfascia and touches the eave subfascia. Fasten the sheet to the rafters with 8d box nails spaced every 6" along the edges and 12" along the intermediate rafters. Lay out and install the rest of the sheathing to complete the first row, spacing the sheets ⅛" apart to allow for expansion.

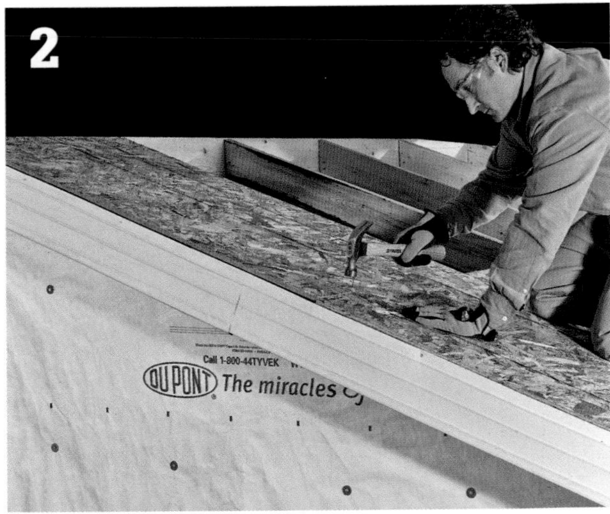


**Install the second row of decking.** Start with a half sheet (approximately) to stagger the vertical gaps between rows. Make sure the end of the half sheet falls midway along a rafter. Continue to sheathe the roof up to the ridge, but stop nailing within 6" of the ridge. This area will be cut away to install a continuous ridge vent later. Add decking to the other side of the roof up to the ridge.

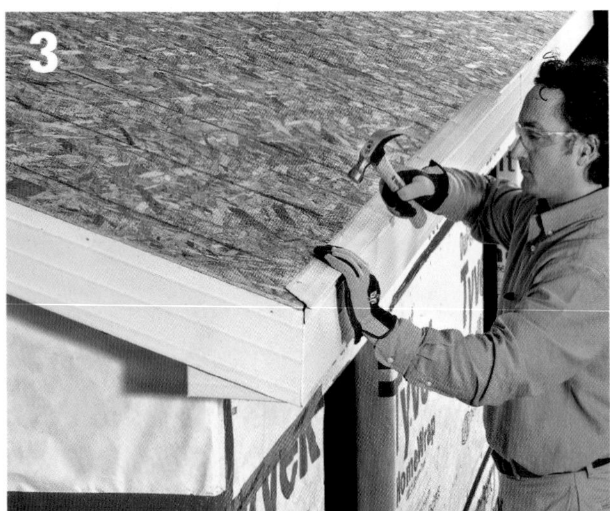


**Install drip edge on eaves.** Cut a 45° miter at the end of a piece of drip edge flashing and position it along one eave edge of the roof. The mitered end should be positioned to form a miter joint with the drip edge that will be installed on the rake edge after the building paper is laid. Attach the drip edge with roofing nails driven every 12". Install drip edge up to the ridge, overlapping any butt joints by 2". Flash both eave edges.

**Begin installing building paper.** Snap a chalk line across the roof sheathing 35⅝" up from the roof edge. At this location, the first row of building paper will overhang the drip edge by ⅜". Roll out 15# or 30# building paper along the eaves with the top edge aligned with the chalk line. Staple it to the sheathing every 12" along the edges and one staple per sq. ft. in the field area. Trim the gable ends of the paper flush with the edges of the sheathing. If you live in a cold climate and plan to heat your garage, install self-adhesive ice-guard membrane for the first two courses.

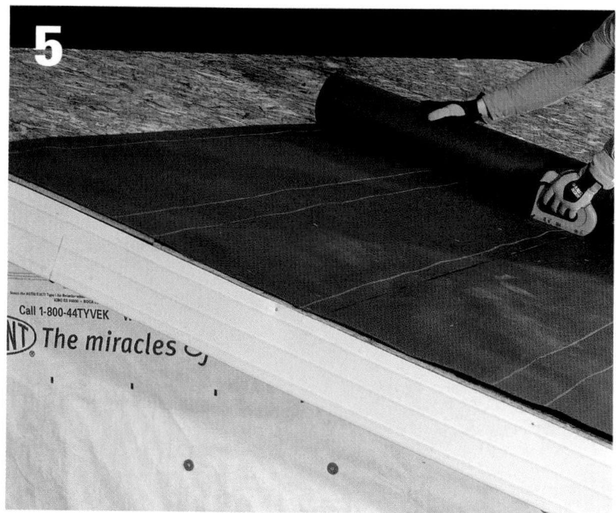


**Install the second underlayment course.** Snap another chalk line across the first row of underlayment, 32" up from the eaves. Roll out the second row of building paper with the bottom edge following the chalk line to create a 4" overlap. Staple it in place. Cover the entire roof up to the ridge with underlayment, overlapping each row by 4".

**Install drip edge on rakes.** Cut a 45° miter at the end of the first piece of drip edge, and install it along the rake edge of the roof, covering the underlayment. Fit the mitered end over the eave's drip edge, overlapping the pieces by 2". The gable drip edge should be on top. Nail the drip edge all the way to the peak, and then repeat for the other three rake edges.

## How to Install Shingles

**Mark starting lines.** Snap a chalk line for the starter course on each roof deck. The lines should be created all the way across the roof deck, 11½" up from the eave edge (½" less than the height of the shingle) to mark the top edge of the starter course of shingles for each roof deck. This will result in a ½" shingle overhang for standard 12" three-tab shingles.

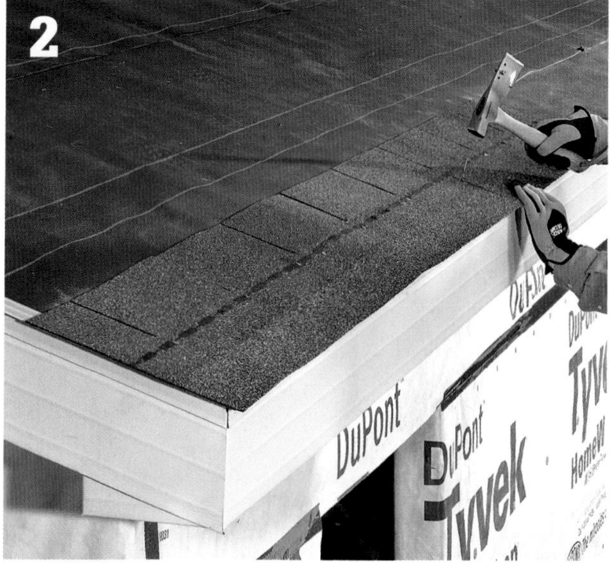


**Install the starter course.** Trim off one half of an end tab on a shingle. Position the shingle upside down so the tabs are aligned with the chalk line and the half tab is flush against the rake edge of the roof. Drive roofing nails near each end, 1" down from each slot between the tabs. Continue the row with full shingles nailed upside down to complete the starter course. Trim the last shingle flush with the opposite rake edge.

(continued)

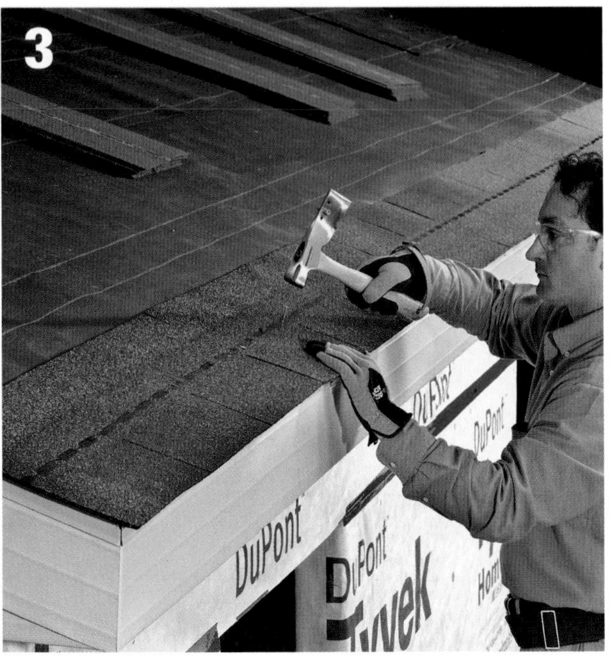


**Install the first full course.** Apply the first full course of shingles over the starter course with the tabs pointing down. Start from the same corner you began the starter course. Place the first shingle so it overhangs the rake edge by 3/8" and the eaves by 1/2". The top edge of the first course should align with the top of the starter course.

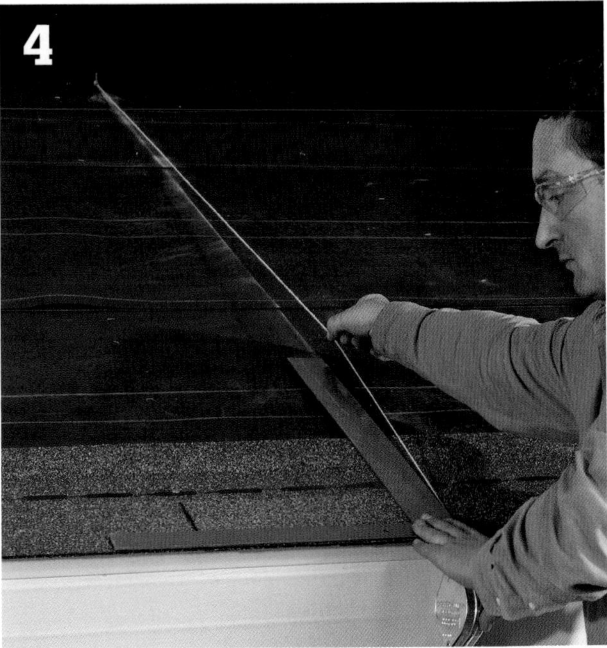


**Create a vertical reference line.** Snap a chalk line from the eave's edge to the ridge to create a vertical line to align the shingles. Choose a spot close to the center of the roof, located so the chalk line passes through a slot or a shingle edge on the first full shingle course. Use a framing square to establish a line perpendicular to the eave's edge.

## Working on Roofs ▸

When working on the roof and staging heavy bundles of shingles, it's a good idea to share the job with a helper. Set up ladders carefully, stay well clear of overhead power lines, and work cautiously near the eaves and rake ends of the roof to prevent accidents. Get off the roof if you are tired, overheated, or if impending bad weather threatens your safety.

**Set shingle pattern.** If you are installing standard three-tab shingles, use the vertical reference line to establish a shingle pattern with slots that are offset by 6" in succeeding courses. Tack down a shingle 6" to one side of the vertical line and 5" above the bottom edge of the first-course shingles to start the second row. Tack down a shingle for the third course 12" from the vertical line. Begin at the vertical line for the fourth course. Repeat.

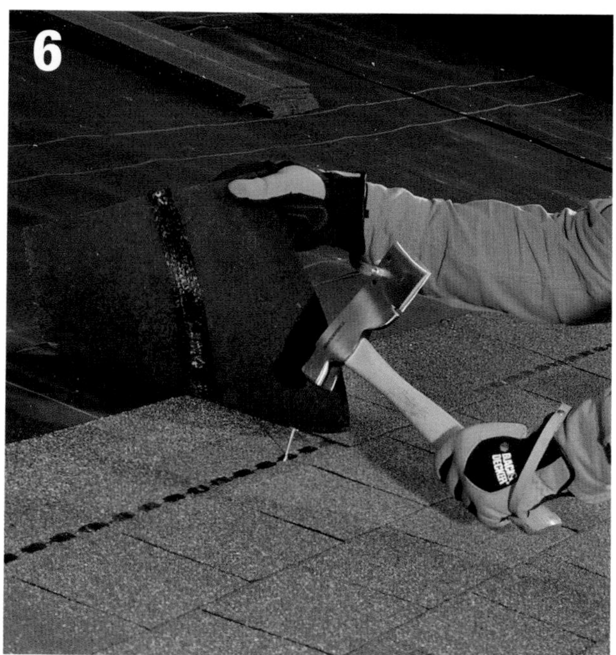


**Fill in shingles.** Add shingles in the second through fifth courses, working upward from the second course and maintaining consistent reveals. Insert lower-course shingles under any upper-course shingles left partially nailed, and then nail them down.

**Test shingle alignment regularly.** After each three-course cycle, measure from the bottom edge of the top row of shingles to the closest layout line on the building paper, and take several of these measurements along the course. If the row is slightly out of alignment, make incremental adjustments over the next few courses to correct it—don't try and get it back all in one course.

## Cutting Ridge Caps ▸

**Cut three 12"-sq. cap shingles** from each three-tab shingle. With the back surface facing up, cut the shingles at the tab lines. Trim the top corners of each square with an angled cut, starting just below the seal strip to avoid overlaps in the reveal area.

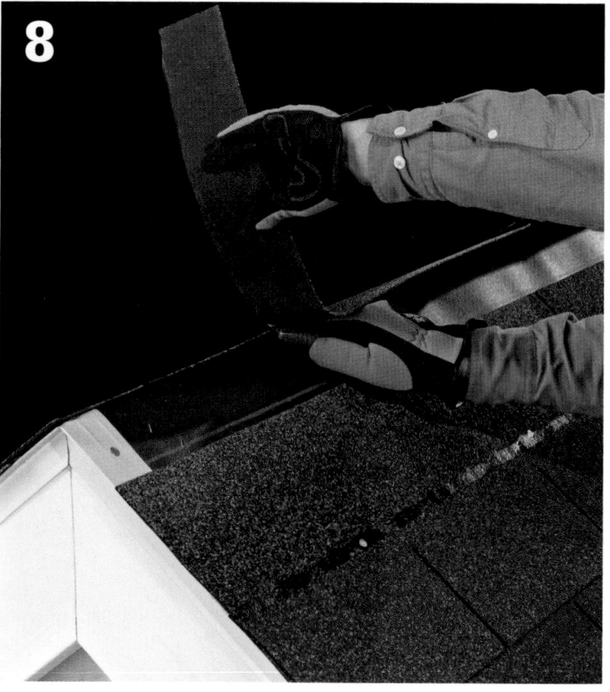


**Shingle up to the ridge.** At the ridge, shingle up the first side of the roof until the top of the uppermost reveal area is within 5" of the ridge (for standard three-tabs). Trim the shingles along the peak. Shingle the other side of the roof up to the peak. If you plan to install a continuous ridge vent, skip to page 66.

(continued)

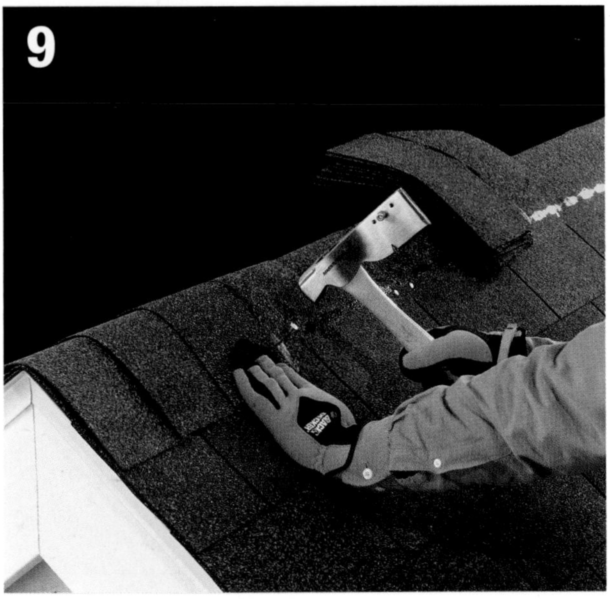


**Install ridge cap shingles.** Start by installing one shingle at one end so equal amounts hang down on each side of the ridge. Measure this distance and snap straight chalk lines to the other end of the roof, extending the lines formed by the edges of the shingles. Nail in the tapered area of each shingle so the next shingle will cover the nail head. Complete the installation of the ridge shingles.

**Trim shingles.** Mark and trim the shingles at the rake edges of the roof. Snap a chalk line down the roof to trim neatly and accurately. Use old aviation snips to cut the shingles. You may use a utility knife with backer board instead. Let the shingles extend ⅜" beyond the rake drip edge to form an overhang.

## How to Install a Continuous Ridge Vent

**Mark cutting lines.** Measure from the ridge down each roof the distance recommended by the ridge vent manufacturer. Mark straight cutting lines at this distance on each deck, snapping a pair of chalk lines.

**Cut out roof sections.** Using a circular saw equipped with an old blade, cut through the shingles and sheathing along the cutting lines. Be careful not to cut into the rafters. Stop both cuts 6 to 12" from the gable ends. Make two crosscuts up and over the ridge to join the long cuts on the ends. Remove the shingles and sheathing from the continuous ridge vent area. Drive additional roofing nails through the shingles and sheathing along the cut edges to secure the roof to the rafters.

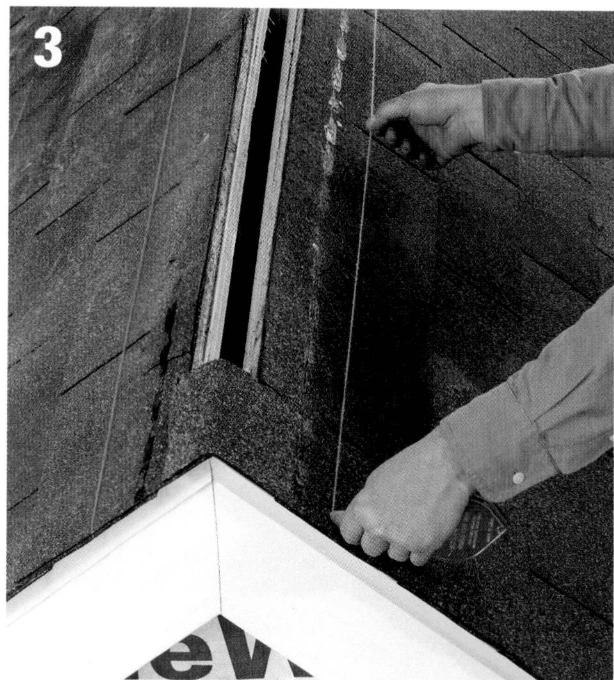

**Mark installation reference lines.** Test-fit the continuous ridge at one end, measuring down from the ridge half the width of the ridge vent, and marking that distance on both ends of the roof. Join the marks with two more chalk lines to establish the position for the edges of the continuous ridge vent.

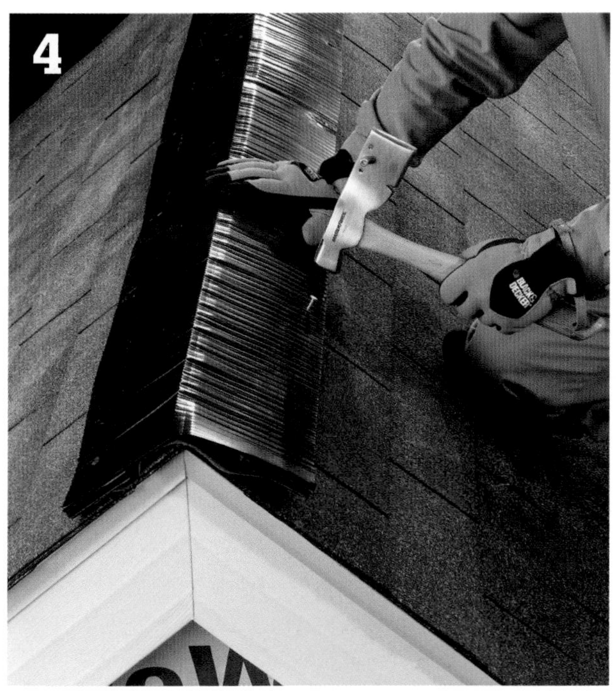

**Attach the ridge vent.** Center the ridge vent over the opening, aligning the end with the rake edge of the roof. The edges of the vent should be even with the chalk lines. Drive long (1½") roofing nails through the vent and into the roof where indicated by the manufacturer.

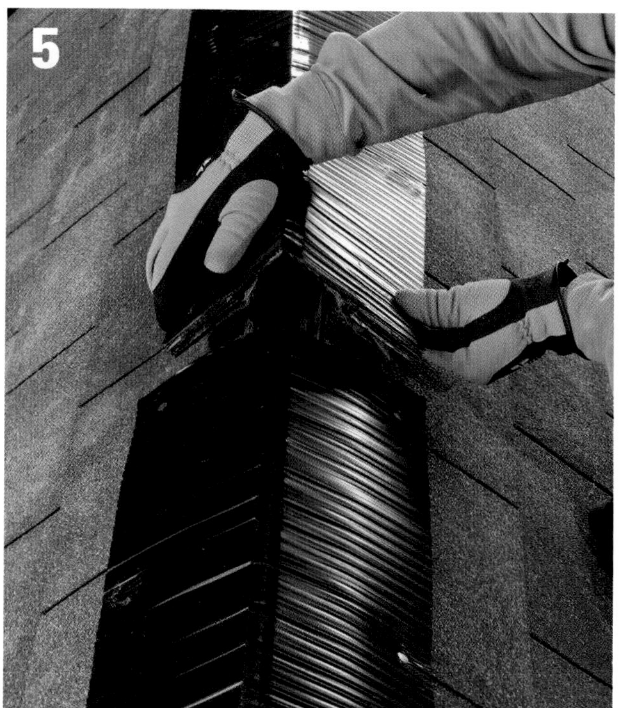

**Add sections.** Butt new pieces of continuous ridge vent against the pieces you have installed and nail the ends. Install the vent along the full length of the roof, including the end areas with shingles still intact.

**Add ridge cap shingles** (see page 66, step 9). Cover the ridge vent with ridge cap shingles, nailing them with two 1½" roofing nails per cap. Overlap the shingles as you would on a normal ridge. Trim the end ridge cap shingle flush with the other rake-edge shingles.

# Installing Windows & Service Doors

Most garages, like the detached garage featured here, have a service door for added safety and accessibility. A window also makes sense for a garage, bringing improved ventilation and a pleasant source of ambient light. This section will show you how to install both features. If you already have experience hanging doors and windows, you'll find the process for installing them in a garage is no different from installing them in a home. However, it's a good idea to review these pages to refamiliarize yourself with the techniques you should follow to do the job correctly.

Installing doors and windows are similar operations. First, you'll need to seal the rough openings in the walls with self-adhesive flashing tape to prevent moisture infiltration. Tape should be applied from the bottom of the doorway or the windowsill first, working up to the header and overlapping the tape to shed water. Once you've inserted the window or door in its opening, you'll need to shim it, adjusting for level and plumb, before nailing the jamb framework and brick mold in place.

When you have the option, hang the service door and window before proceeding with the siding (which we'll cover in the next section). That way, you'll be able to fit the siding up tight against the brickmold for a professional finish.

## Tools & Materials ▸

Work gloves & eye protection
Utility knife
Caulk gun
Level
Hammer
Screwdriver
9" self-adhesive flashing tape
Silicone caulk
Window
2" Roofing nails
Shims
Casing nails (6d)
Drip cap
Expanding foam insulation
Service door
Lockset

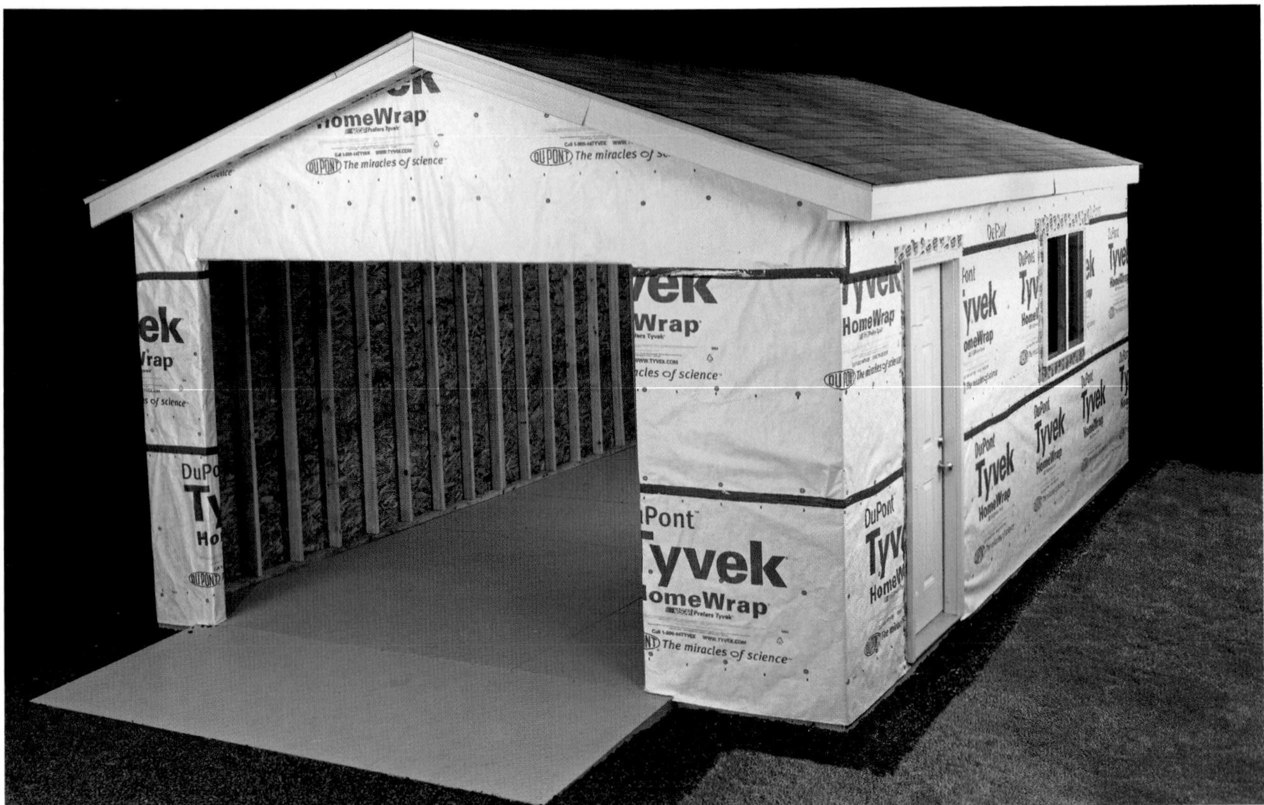


**A sturdy service door** and lockset will give your new garage added accessibility without compromising security. Installing one is a fairly simple project. A vinyl- or aluminum-clad garage window will bring a breath of fresh air and improve your task lighting when working in the garage.

## Tips for Sizing & Framing ▸

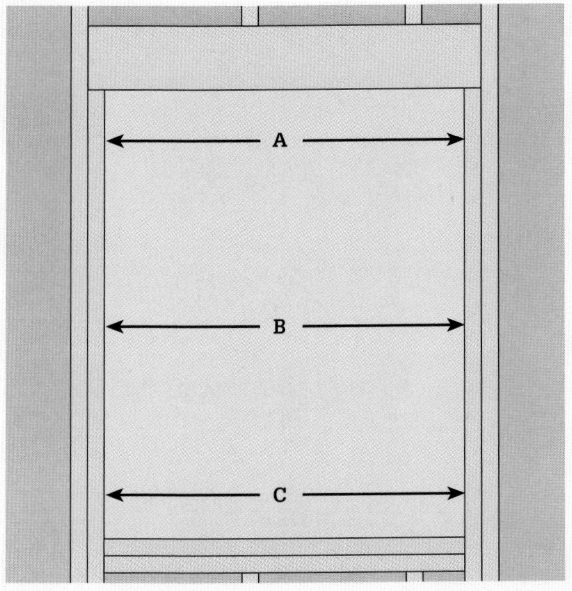


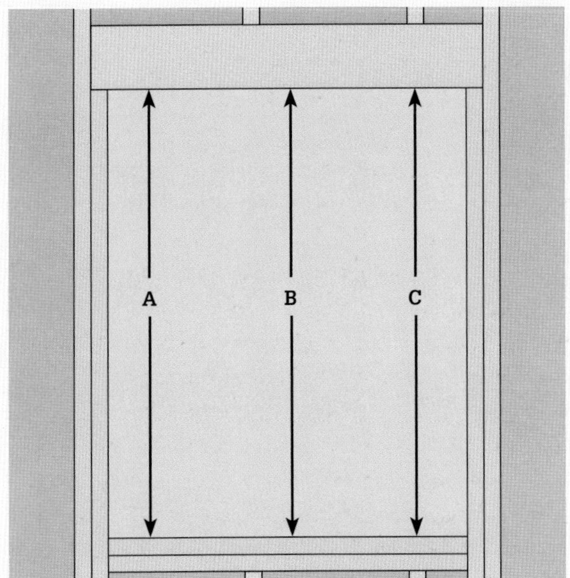


**Determine the exact size of your new window** or door by measuring the opening carefully. For the width (left photo), measure between the jack studs in three places: near the top, at the middle, and near the bottom of the opening. Use the same procedure for the height (right photo), measuring from the header to the sill near the left edge, at the middle, and near the right edge of the opening. Use the smallest measurement of each dimension for ordering the unit.

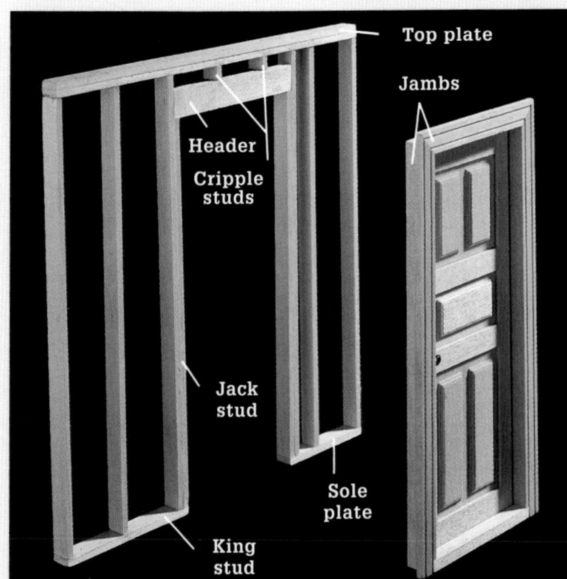


**Door opening:** The structural load above the door is carried by cripple studs that rest on a header. The ends of the header are supported by jack studs (also known as trimmer studs) and king studs that transfer the load to the sole plate and the foundation of the house. The rough opening for a door should be 1" wider and ½" taller than the dimensions of the door unit, including the jambs. This extra space lets you adjust the door unit during installation.

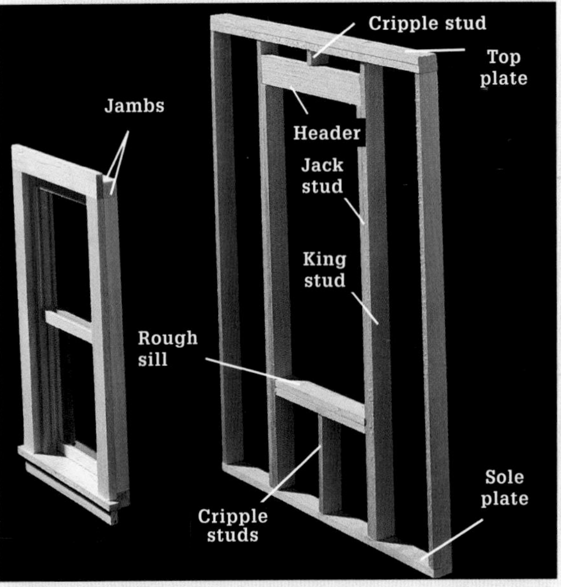


**Window opening:** The structural load above the window is carried by a cripple stud resting on a header. The ends of the header are supported by jack studs and king studs that transfer the load to the sole plate and the foundation of the house. The rough sill, which helps anchor the window unit but carries no structural weight, is supported by cripple studs. To provide room for adjustments during installation, the rough opening for a window should be 1" wider and ½" taller than the window unit, including the jambs.

# How to Install a Garage Window

**Flash the rough sill.** Apply 9"-wide self-adhesive flashing tape to the rough sill to prevent moisture infiltration below the window. Install the flashing tape so it wraps completely over the sill and extends 10 to 12" up the jack studs. Fold the rest of the tape over the housewrap to create a 3" overlap. Peel off the backing and press the tape firmly in place. Install tape on the side jambs butting up to the header, and then flash the header.

**Option:** You can save a step (and some material) by installing the flashing on the sides and top after the window is installed, as seen in this skylight installation. The disadvantage to doing it this way instead of flashing the entire opening and then flashing over the window nailing flanges after installation (see step 8) is that the inside faces of the rough frame will not be sealed against moisture.

**Caulk the opening.** Apply a ½"-wide bead of caulk around the outside edges of the jack studs and header to seal the window flange in the opening. Leave the rough sill uncaulked to allow any water that may penetrate the flashing to drain out.

**Position the window.** Set the window unit into the rough opening, and center it side to side. Check the sill for level.

**Tack the top corners.** Drive a roofing nail through each top corner hole of the top window flange to tack it in place. Do not drive the rest of the nails into the top flange yet.

**Plumb the window.** Have a helper hold the window in place from outside while you work inside the garage. Check the window jamb for square by measuring from corner to corner. If the measurements are the same, the jamb is square. Insert shims between the side jambs and rough opening near the top corners to hold the jambs in position. Use additional shims as needed to bring the jamb into square. Recheck the diagonals after shimming.

**Nail the flange.** Drive 2" roofing nails through the flange nailing holes and into the rough sill to secure it. Handnail this flange, being careful not to damage the flange or window cladding.

**Nail the jambs.** Drive 6d (2") casing nails through the jambs and top corner shims to lock them in place. Add more shims to the centers and bottom corners of the jamb, and test the window action by opening and closing it. If it operates without binding, nail through the rest of the shims.

(continued)

**Flash the side flanges.** Seal the side flanges with flashing tape, starting 4 to 6" below the sill flashing and ending 4 to 6" above the top flange. Press the tape firmly in place.

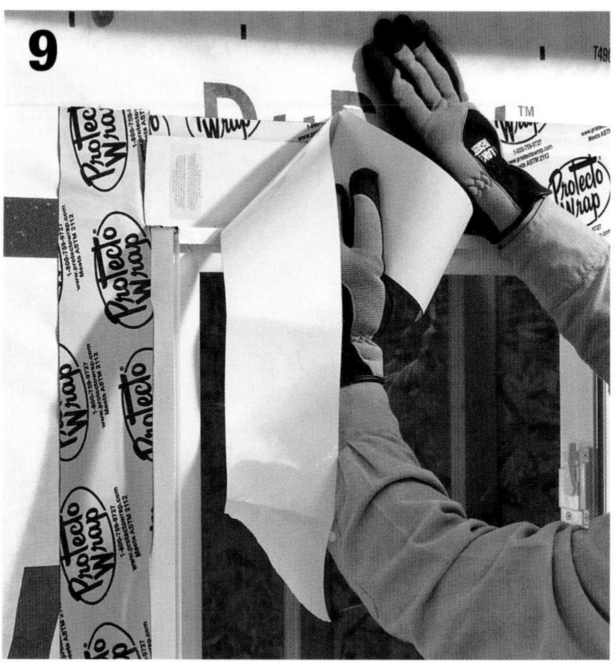


**Install the drip cap.** Cut a piece of metal drip edge to fit over the top window jamb. This is particularly important if your new window has an unclad wooden jamb with preinstalled brickmold. Set the drip edge in place on the top jamb, and secure the flange with a strip of wide flashing tape. Do not nail it. Have the tape overlap the side flashing tape by 6". *Note: If you plan to trim the window with wood brickmold or other moldings, install the drip edge above that trim instead.*

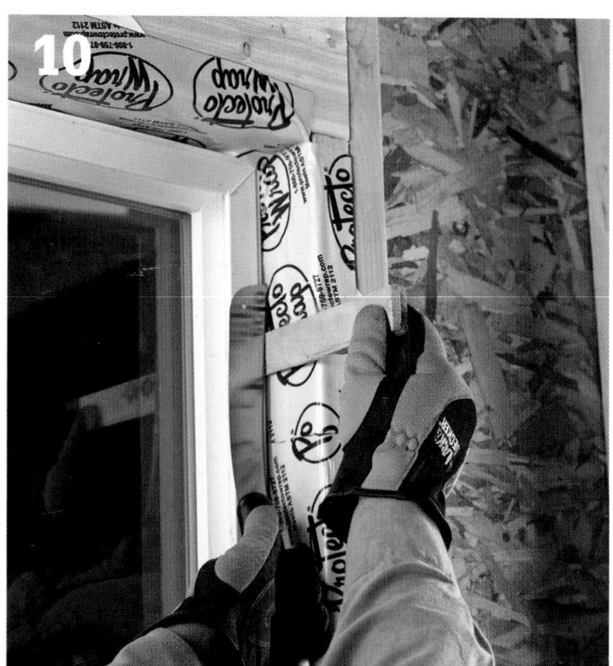


**Finish the installation.** Cut the shim ends so they are flush with the inside of the wall using a utility knife or handsaw.

**Spray expanding foam** insulation around the perimeter of the window on the interior side if you will be insulating and heating or cooling your garage.

## Service Door Buyer's Tips ▸

- If you plan to use your new garage as a workshop, buy the widest service door that will suit your building. That way, you won't have to open your sectional garage door every time you want to pull out the lawnmower or trash cans.
- Although primed wood service doors are less expensive than aluminum- or vinyl-clad doors, they're generally not a better value in the long run. Normal wear and tear and the effects of the elements will mean you'll need to keep up with regular scraping and painting in order to keep your wooden door in good condition. A clad door, on the other hand, requires little or no maintenance over the life of the door.
- Another option for many of today's quality service doors is to purchase a jamb made of composite materials instead of wood. A composite jamb will not wick water up when it rains, and it's impervious to rot and insects.

## How to Install a Service Door

**Flash the opening sides.** Apply two strips of 9"-wide self-adhesive flashing tape to cover the jack studs in the door's rough opening. Cut a slit in the tape and extend the outer ear 4 to 6" past the bottom edge of the header. Fold the tape over the housewrap to create a 3" overlap. Peel off the backing and press the tape firmly in place.

**Flash the header.** Cover the header with a third piece of self-adhesive flashing tape, extending the ends of the tape 6" beyond the side flashing. Fold the extra tape over the housewrap to form a 3" overlap.

**Seal the opening.** Apply a ½"-wide bead of caulk up the outside edges of the jack stud area and around the header to seal the brickmold casing.

(continued)

**Position the door in the opening.** Set the bottoms of the side jambs inside the rough opening, and tip the door into place. Adjust the door so it's centered in the opening.

**Adjust the door.** Orient pairs of shims so the thick and thin ends are reversed, forming a rectangular block. Insert the shims into the gap between the rough framing and the hinge-side jamb. Spread the shims closer together or farther apart to adjust the total thickness until they are pressure-fitted into the gap. Space the shims every 12" along the jamb, and locate two pairs near the hinges. Check the hinge jamb for plumb and to make sure the shims do not cause it to bow. Drive pairs of 6d casing nails through the jambs at the shim locations.

**Shim the latch side.** Insert pairs of shims every 12" in the gap between the latch-side jamb and the rough framing. With the door closed, adjust the shims in or out until there's a consistent ⅛" gap between the door and the jamb. Then drive pairs of 6d casing nails through the jamb and shims to secure them.

**Attach the brickmold.** Drive 2½" galvanized casing nails through the brickmold to fasten it to the jack studs and header. Space the nails every 12". Trim off the shims so they are flush with the inside wall using a utility knife or handsaw.

## How to Install a Lockset

**Insert the lock bolts** for the lockset (and deadbolt, if installing one) into their respective holes in the door. These days, new exterior doors are almost always predrilled for locksets and deadbolts. Screw the bolt plates into the premortised openings.

**Fasten the lock mechanisms** by tightening the screws that draw the two halves together. Do not overtighten.

## Door Security

**Add metal door reinforcers** to strengthen the area around the lockset or deadbolt. These strengthen the door and make it more resistant to kick-ins.

**Add a heavy-duty latch guard** to reinforce the door jamb around the strike plate. For added protection, choose a guard with a flange to resist pry-bar insertion. Attach the guard with 3" screws that will penetrate through the jamb and into the wall studs.

# Installing Overhead Garage Doors

Your sectional garage door will bear the brunt of everything Mother Nature and an active household throws at it—seasonal temperature swings, moisture, blistering sunlight, and the occasional misfired half-court jump shot. If that isn't enough, the average sectional garage door cycles up and down at least four times per day, which totals up to around 1,300 or more uses every year. For all of these reasons, it pays to install a high-quality door on your new garage so you can enjoy a long service life from it.

These days, you don't have to settle for a drab, flat-panel door. Door manufacturers provide many options for cladding colors, panel texture and layout, exterior hardware, and window styles. Today's state-of-the-art garage doors also benefit from improved material construction, more sophisticated safety features, and enhanced energy efficiency. When you order your new door, double-check your garage's rough opening and minimum ceiling height to be sure the new door will fit the space properly.

Installing a sectional garage door is easier than you might think, and manufacturers make the process quite accessible for average do-it-yourselfers. With a helper or two, you should have little difficulty installing a new garage door in a single day. The job is really no more complex than other window and door replacements if you work carefully and exercise good judgment. Garage door kits come with all the necessary hardware and detailed step-by-step instructions. Since garage door styles vary, the installation process for your new door may differ from the photo sequence you see here, so always defer to the manufacturer's instructions. This will ensure the door is installed correctly and the manufacturer will honor the product warranty.

## Tools & Materials ▸

- Work gloves & eye protection
- Tape measure
- Long level
- Drill with nut drivers
- Stepladder
- Ratchet wrench with sockets
- Adjustable wrench
- Hammer
- Sectional garage door with tracks & mounting brackets
- 16d nails
- Doorstop molding

**The sectional garage door** you choose for your garage will go a long way toward defining the building's appearance and giving you trouble-free performance day in and day out.

**Measure for the door.** Measure the width of the header, the headroom clearance to the rafter collar ties (or bottom truss chords), and the inside opening of the doorway. Check these measurements against the minimum requirements outlined in the instruction manual that comes with your sectional garage door.

**Assemble door tracks.** Working on the floor, lay out and assemble the vertical tracks, jamb brackets, and flag angle hardware. Install the door bottom seal and the roller and hinge hardware on the bottom door section.

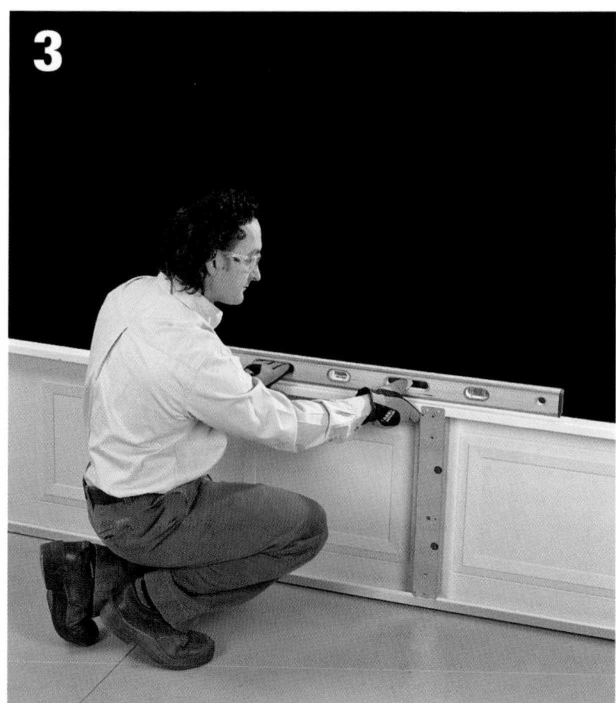


**Install the first section.** Set the bottom door section into position against the side jambs, and adjust it left or right until the side jambs overlap it evenly. Check the top of the door section for level. Place shims beneath the door to level it, if necessary. Have a helper hold the door section in place against the jambs until it is secured in the tracks.

**Attach the tracks.** Slip a vertical track over the door section rollers and against the side jamb. Adjust it for plumb, then fasten the jamb brackets to the side jamb blocking with lag screws. Carefully measure, mark, and install the other vertical track as well.

(continued)

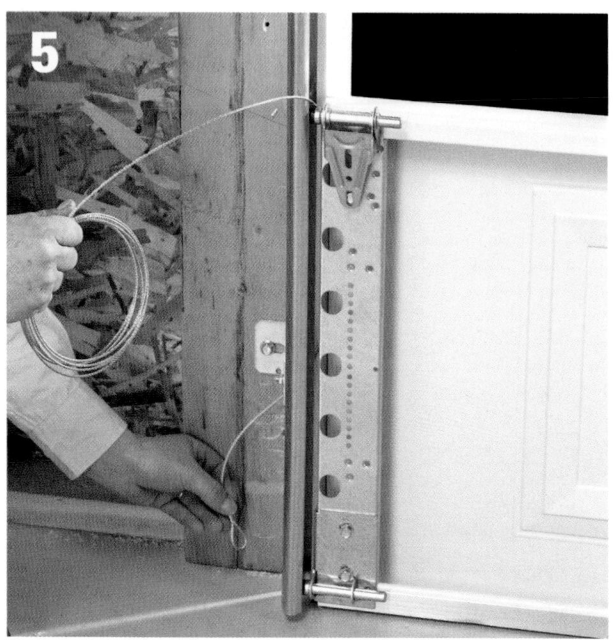


**Attach the lift cables.** Depending on your door design, you may need to attach lift cables to the bottom door section at this time. Follow the instructions that come with your door to connect these cables correctly.

**Install the door hinges.** Fasten the end and intermediate hinges to the bottom door section, and then install roller brackets and hinges on the other door sections. Attach hinges to the top edges of each door section only. This way you'll be able to stack one section on top of the next during assembly.

**Add next sections.** Slip the next door section into place in the door tracks and on top of the first section. Connect the bottom hinges (already attached to the first section) to the second door section. Repeat the process until you have stacked and installed all but the top door section.

**Option:** The top door section may require additional bracing, special top roller brackets, and a bracket for securing a garage door opener. Install these parts now following the door manufacturer's instructions.

**Install the top section.** Set the top door section in place and fasten it to the hinges on the section below it. Support the door section temporarily with a few 16d nails driven into the door header blocking and bent down at an angle.

**Complete track installation.** Fasten the horizontal door tracks to the flag angle brackets on top of the vertical track sections. Temporarily suspend the back ends of the tracks with rope so they are level.

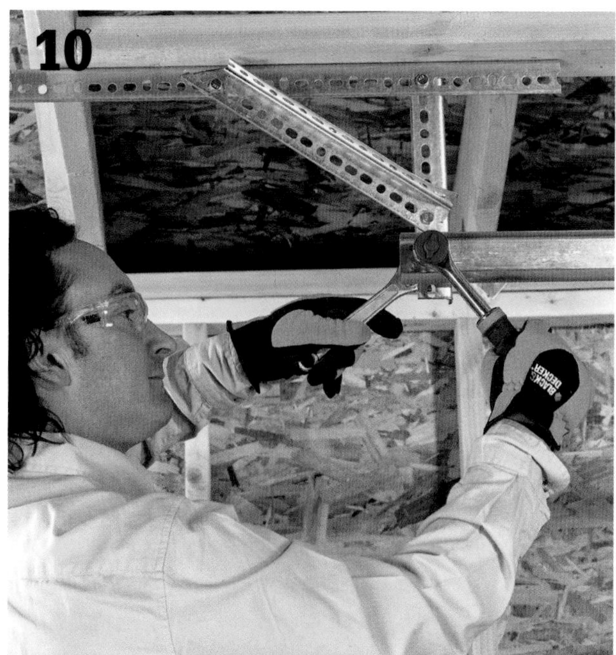


**Install rear hanger brackets.** This step will vary among door opener brands. Check your door instruction manual for the correct location of rear hanger brackets that will hold the horizontal door tracks in position. Measure, cut, and fasten sections of perforated angle iron together with bolts, washers, and nuts to form two Y-shaped door track brackets. Fasten the brackets to the collar tie or bottom truss chord with lag screws and washers following the door manufacturer's recommendations.

**Attach the extension springs.** The door opener here features a pair of smaller springs that run parallel to the horizontal door tracks, not parallel to the door header as larger torsion springs are installed. The springs are attached to cables that attach to the rear door hanger brackets.

(continued)

**Test to make sure the door tracks properly.** Raise it about halfway first. You'll need at least one helper here. Slide a sturdy support underneath the door bottom to hold the door and then inspect to make sure the rollers are tracking and the tracks are parallel.

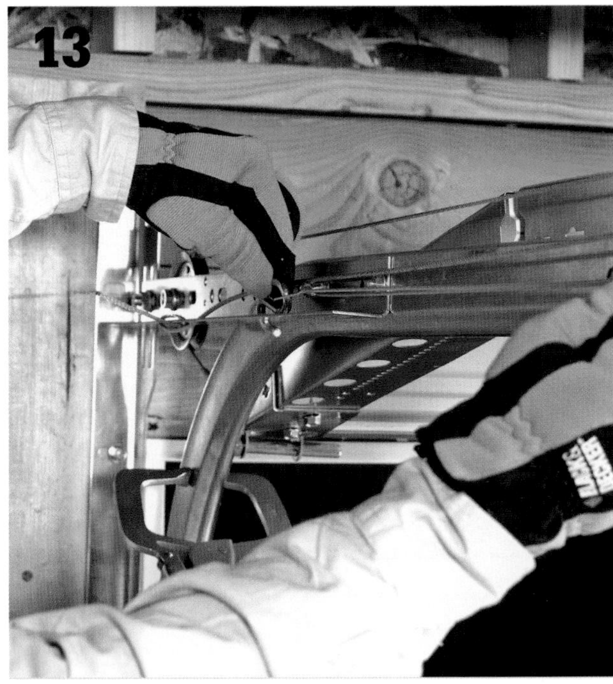


**Attach the spring cables.** The door should be fully raised and held in place with C-clamps tightened onto the tracks to prevent it from slipping down. The tension in the springs should be relieved. The cables in this case are tied off onto a 3-hole clip that is then hooked onto the horizontal angle bracket near the front of the tracks.

**Attach the doorstop molding.** Measure, cut, and nail sections of doorstop molding to the door jambs on the outside of the door to seal out weather. A rolled vinyl doorstop may come with your door kit. If not, use strips of 1 × 2 treated wood or cedar for this purpose.

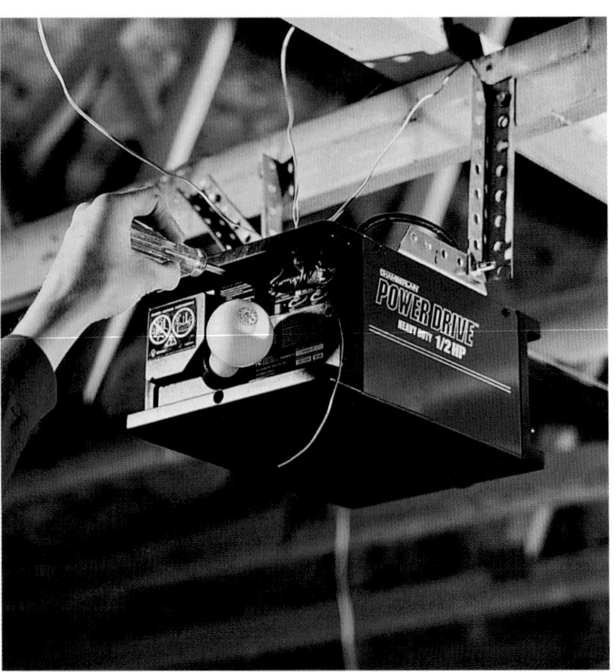


**Option:** Install a garage door opener. See pages 232 to 234.

## Garage Door Opener Safety Tips ▸

Whether you're adding an opener to a new or an old garage door, these tips will help make it a safe part of your home. (Also see pages 226 to 231 for information on repairing garage doors.)

- Before beginning the installation, be sure the garage door manually opens and closes properly.
- If you have a one-piece door, with or without a track, read all additional manufacturer's installation information.
- The gap between the bottom of the garage door and the floor must not exceed 1/4". If it does, the safety reversal system may not work properly.
- If the garage has a finished ceiling, attach a sturdy metal bracket to the structural supports before installing the opener. This bracket and hardware are not usually provided with the garage door opener kit.
- Install the wall-mounted garage door control within sight of the garage door, out of reach of children (at a minimum height of 5 ft.), and away from all moving parts of the door.
- Never use an extension cord or two-wire adapter to power the opener. Do not change the opener plug in any way to make it fit an outlet. Be sure the opener is grounded.
- When an obstruction breaks the light beam while the door is closing, most door models stop and reverse to full open position, and the opener lights flash 10 times. If no bulbs are installed, you will hear 10 clicks.
- To avoid any damage to vehicles entering or leaving the garage, be sure the door provides adequate clearance when fully open.
- Garage doors may include tempered glass, laminate glass, or clear-plastic panels—all safe window options.

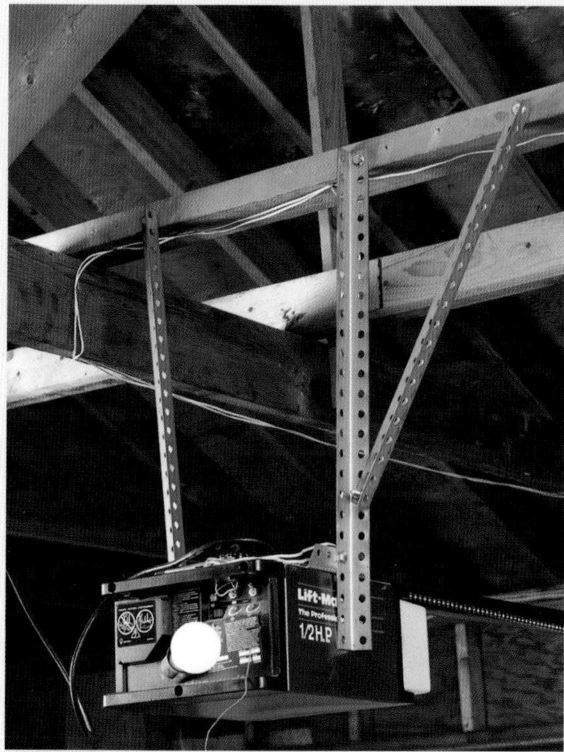


**Make sure your garage door opener** is securely supported to trusses or ceiling framing with sturdy metal hanging brackets.

**Use the emergency release handle** to disengage the trolley only when the garage door is closed. Never use the handle to pull the door open or closed.

# Installing Siding & Trim

Siding will protect your new garage from the elements, of course, but it also serves as a way to visually tie the garage to your home. Ideally, you should choose the same siding for the garage as you have on your house, but if you decide to go with a different material it should mimic the same pattern, such as horizontal laps, overlapping shakes, or vertical boards and battens. These days, material options for garage siding are more varied than ever. You might choose wood, vinyl, aluminum, fiber-cement lap siding, cedar or vinyl shakes, faux brick and stone, or stucco. Or, depending on your home's siding scheme, it might be a combination of two different siding materials that complement one another.

Each type of siding will typically have its own unique installation process, and each application requires the correct underlayment, fasteners, and nailing or bonding method. The installation process can even vary among manufacturers for the same product type.

For the garage project shown here, we install a combination of fiber-cement lap siding and cast veneer stone.

## Tools & Materials ▸

Work gloves & eye protection

**For stone veneer:**

Aviation snips
Hammer
Trowel
Mixing trough
Stiff-bristle brush
Angle grinder with diamond blade
Mason's hammer
Trowel
Grout bag
Jointing tool
Expanded metal lath
Building paper
Type N mortar
Masonry sand
Veneer stone
Sill blocks
2 × 2" zinc-coated L-brackets
Metal flashing

**For Fiber-cement siding:**

Work gloves & eye protection
Hammer
Tape measure
Bevel gauge
Circular saw
Paint brush
Chalk line
Drill with bits
Cementboard shears
Caulk gun
Jigsaw with masonry blades
Fiber cement corner boards
Casing nails (6d)
Fiber cement frieze boards
Primer paint
Fiber cement siding
Dust respirator
Silicone caulk
Paint

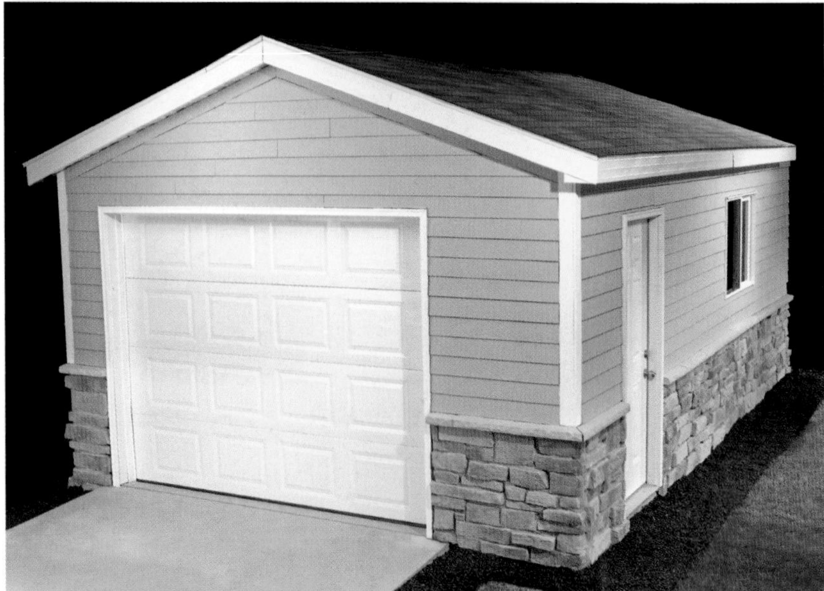

**A combination of faux stone** and lap siding, with accenting corner trim, transforms what could otherwise be an ordinary garage into a structure that adds real curb appeal to your home.

# Garage Siding Types

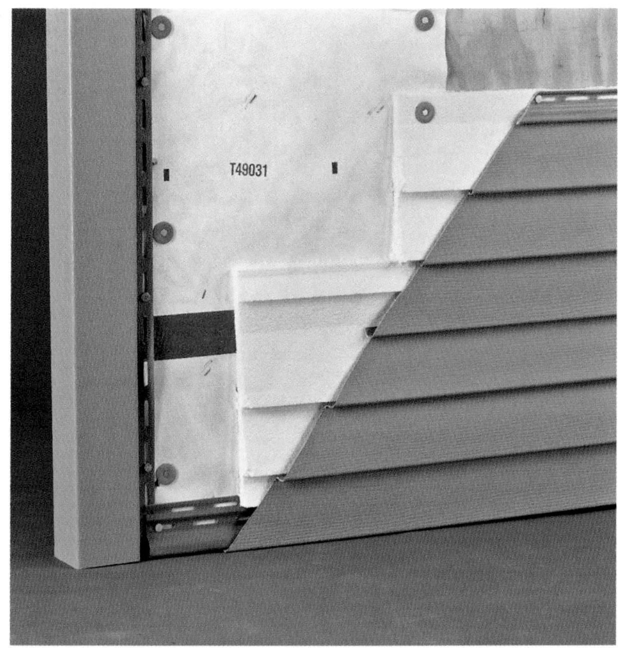


**Vinyl lap siding** is inexpensive, relatively easy to install, and low maintenance. Some styles can be paired with custom profiled foam insulation boards. Matching corner trim boards are sold, but you can also make your own wood trim boards and paint them.

**Wood lap siding** comes in wide or narrow strips and is normally beveled. Exterior-rated wood that can be clear coated is common (usually cedar or redwood). Other wood types are used, too, but these are usually sold preprimed and are suitable for painting only.

**Fiber-cement lap siding** is a relative newcomer but its use is spreading quickly. It is very durable but requires some special tools for cutting and installation.

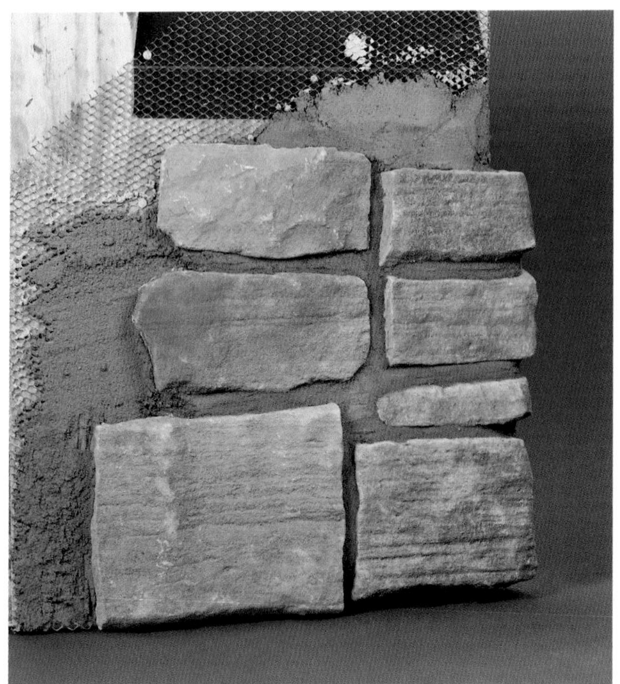

**Specialty siding products** like these cast veneer stones are often used as accents on partial walls (see the photo on previous page). They can also be used to side one wall of a structure. For the most part, their effectiveness (and your budget) would be diminished if they were used to cover the entire structure.

**Cast veneer stones** are thin synthetic masonry units that are applied to building walls to imitate the appearance of natural stone veneer. They come in random shapes, sizes, and colors, but they are scaled to fit together neatly without looking unnaturally uniform. Outside corner stones and a sill block (used for capping half-wall installations) are also shown here.

## How to Install Cast Veneer Stone

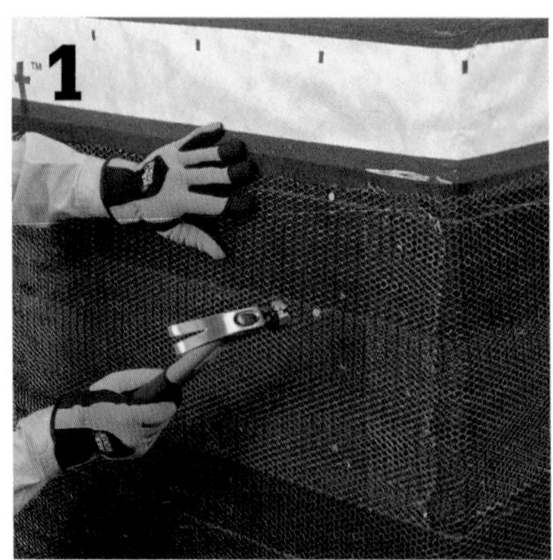

**Prepare the wall.** Veneer stones can be applied to a full wall or as an accent on the lower portion of a wall. A top height of 36 to 42" looks good. A layer of expanded metal lath (stucco lath) is attached over a substrate of building paper.

**Apply a scratch coat.** The wall in the installation area should be covered with a ½- to ¾"-thick layer of mortar. Mix one part Type N mortar to two parts masonry sand and enough water to make the consistency workable. Apply with a trowel, let the mortar dry for 30 minutes. Brush the surface with a stiff-bristle brush.

**Test layouts.** Uncrate large groups of stones and dry-lay them on the ground to find units that blend well together in shape as well as in color. This will save an enormous amount of time as you install the stones.

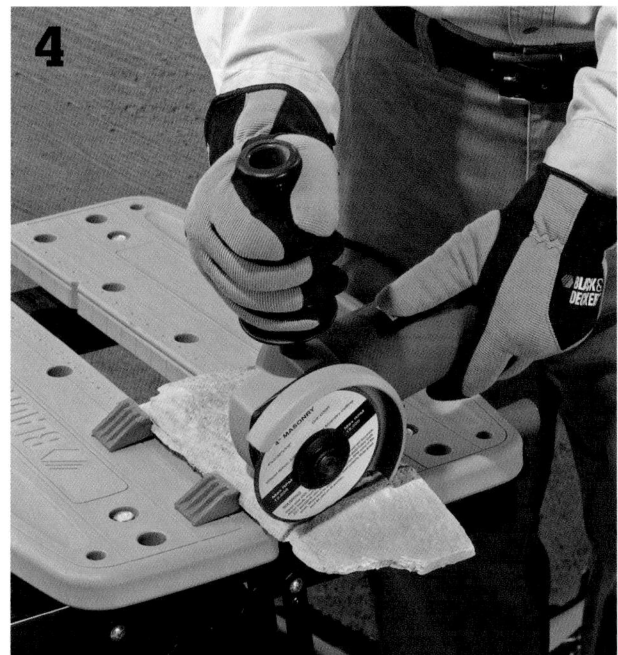


**Cut veneer stones,** if necessary, by scoring with an angle grinder and diamond blade along a cutting line. Rap the waste side of the cut near the scored line with a mason's hammer or a maul. The stone should fracture along the line. Try to keep the cut edge out of view as much as you can.

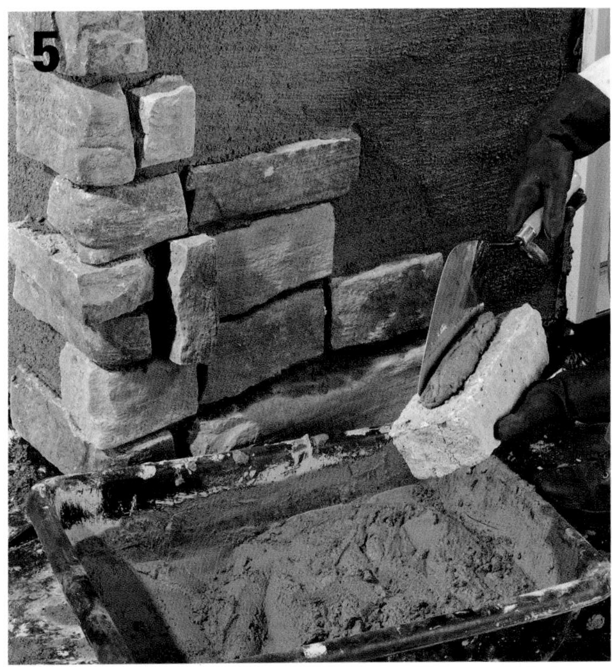


**Apply the stones.** Mix mortar in the same ratios as in step 2, but instead of applying it to the wall, apply it to the backs of the stones with a trowel. A ½"-thick layer is about right. Press the mortared stones against the wall in their position. Hold them for a few second so they adhere.

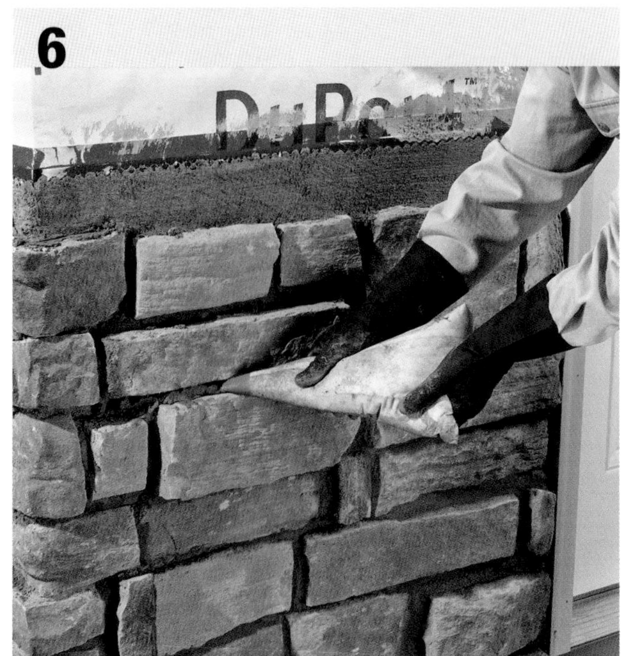


**Fill the gaps** between stones with mortar once all of the stones are installed and the mortar has had time to dry. Fill a grout bag (sold at concrete supply stores) with mortar mixture and squeeze it into the gaps. Once the mortar sets up, strike it smooth with a jointing tool.

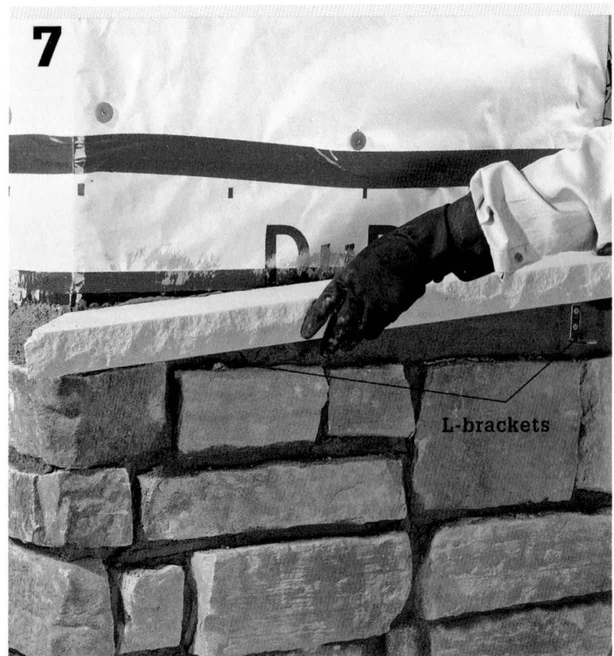


**Install sill blocks.** These are heavier and wider than the veneer block so they require some reinforcement. Attach three 2 × 2" zinc-coated L-brackets to the wall for each piece of sill block. Butter the backs of the sill blocks with mortar and press them in place, resting on the L-brackets. Install metal flashing first for extra protection against water penetration.

## Tools for Working with Fiber-cement Siding ▸

The garage shown here will be covered with durable and rot-resistant fiber-cement lap siding. The best tool for cutting it is electric cementboard shears (available at rental centers) that make straight cuts without raising harmful silica dust. You can also cut fiber-cement with a circular saw and fiber-cement blade or with a jigsaw, but both will create more dust than shears create. Bore holes with a drill and twist bits or hole saws. To install fiber-cement siding, drill pilot holes and hand nail with siding nails; or use a pneumatic coil nailer with special fiber-cement siding nails. Wear a quality dust respirator when cutting or drilling fiber cement.

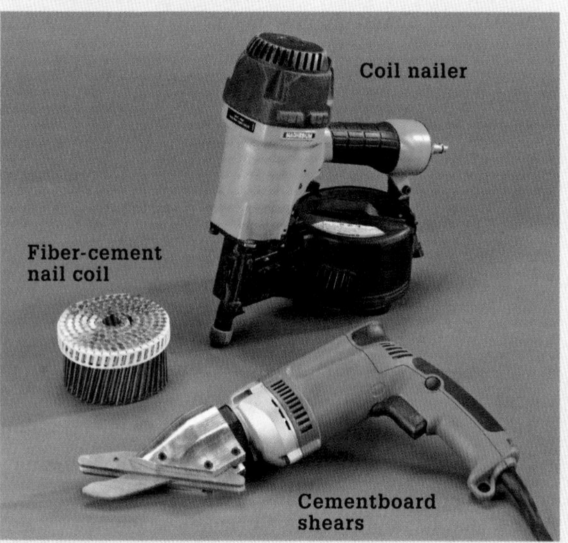


## How to Install Fiber-cement Lap Siding

**Install corner boards.** Nail one board flush with the wall corner and even with the bottom of the wall sheathing using 6d galvanized casing nails. Keep nails 1" from each end and ¾" from the edges. Drive two nails every 16". Overlap a second trim board on the adjacent side, aligning the edge with the face of the first board, and nail in place.

**Trim windows and doors.** Measure and cut brickmold or other trim to fit around the windows and doors. The trim joints can either be butted or mitered, depending on your preference. For miter joints, cut corners at 45° and nail with 2½" galvanized casing nails. Drive pairs of nails every 16".

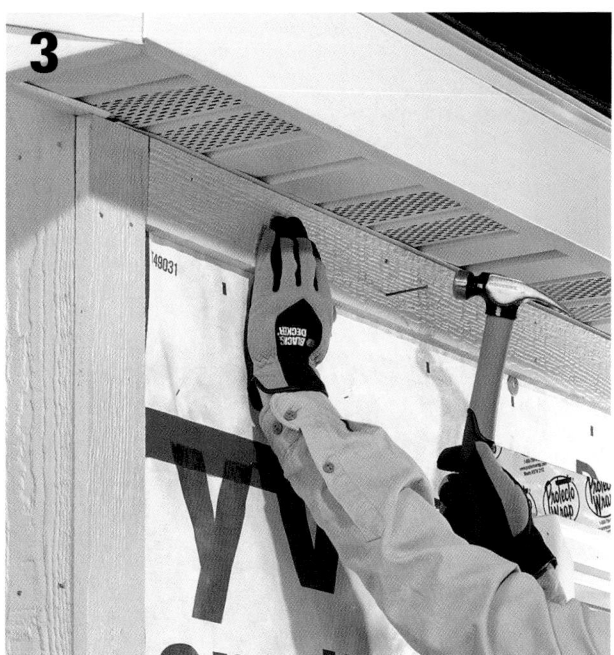


**Install frieze boards.** Cut the frieze boards to match the width of the corner boards. Butt them against the corner trim, and nail them to the wall studs directly under the soffits on the eaves with 6d galvanized casing nails.

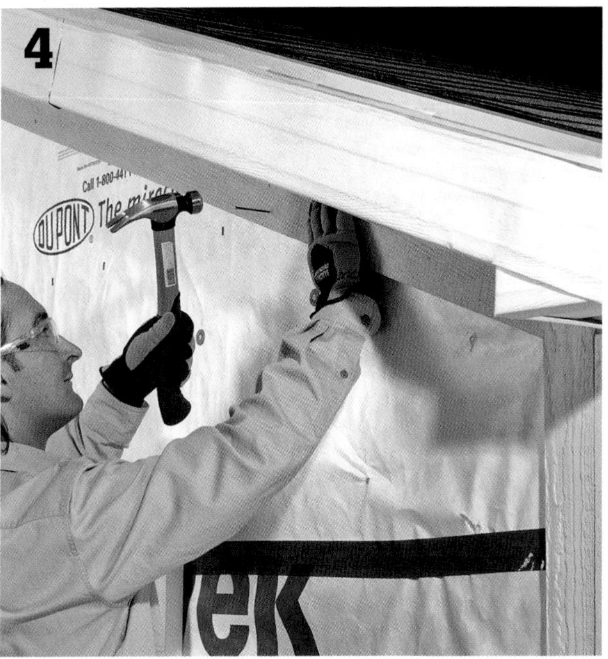


**Install gable frieze boards.** Use a bevel gauge to transfer the gable angle to the frieze boards, and miter cut the ends to match. Install the gable frieze boards so they meet neatly in a miter joint at the roof peak. Nail them to the gable wall plates and studs with pairs of 2" 6d galvanized casing nails every 16".

**Install starter strips.** Install strips of lath (or narrow pieces of siding) along the bottom of the walls, flush with the bottom edges of the wall sheathing. The lath will tip the first row of siding out to match the overlap projection of the other rows. Attach the lath to the wall studs with 6d galvanized casing nails. Snap vertical chalk lines to mark wall stud locations.

**Install first board.** Cut the first siding board so it ends halfway over a stud when the other end is placed ⅛" from a corner trim board. Prime the cut end before installing it. Align the siding with the bottom edge of the lath, keeping a ⅛" gap between the siding and the corner board. Nail the panel at each stud location 1" from the top edge with siding nails. Keep nails at least ½" in from the panel ends to prevent splitting.

(continued)

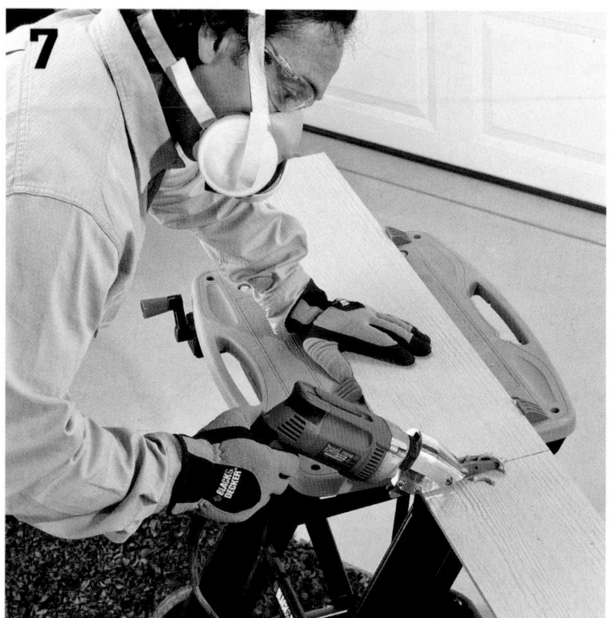


**Install second board.** Mark and cut the second piece of siding to length. Wear a dust respirator when cutting the siding, especially if you use a circular saw instead of electric cementboard shears.

**Install the next board.** Set the second siding board in place over the lath, spaced to create a gap of ⅛" where it would butt against the first board. Nail the siding board to the wall at stud locations. Install more siding boards to complete the first row. Snap level chalk lines across the wall to mark layout lines for the remaining rows of siding. Set this pattern so each row of siding will overlap the row below it by 1¼".

**Install next rows.** As you install each row of siding, stagger the joints between the end boards to offset the seams by at least one wall stud.

**Work around windows and doors.** Slide a piece of siding against the horizontal trim, and mark the board ⅛" from the outside edges of the trim. Use these marks to draw perpendicular lines on the board, and make a mark on the lines to represent the correct overlap. Connect these marks with a long line, and make the cutout with a jigsaw equipped with a masonry blade. Fit and nail the notched panel around the opening.

**Install top row.** Unless you get lucky or have planned very carefully, the top row of siding boards will likely require rip-cutting to make sure that your reveals and setbacks are maintained. With a circular saw and a straightedge guide, trim off the top of the boards so the cut tops butt up against the frieze. Nail the cut boards in place.

**Transfer gable angles.** Use a bevel gauge to determine the roof angle on the gable ends of the roof. Transfer the angle to the siding panels that butt against the gable frieze boards, and cut them to fit.

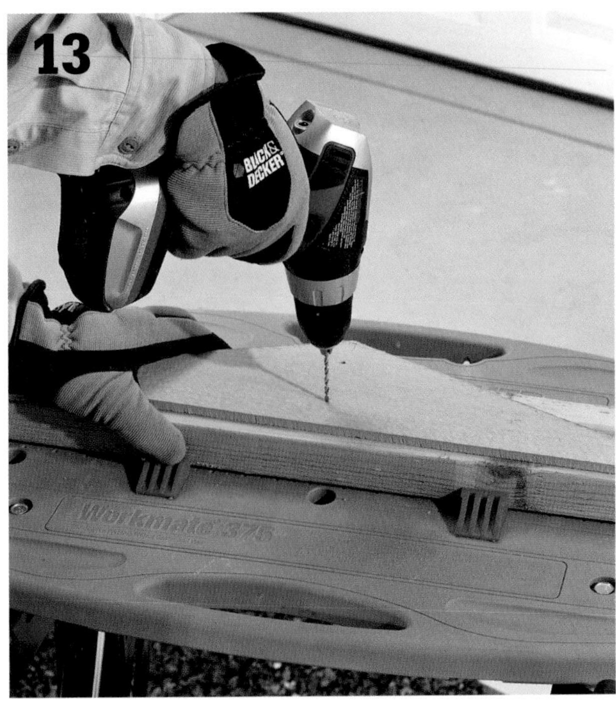


**Fill in under gables.** Drill pilot holes though the angled corners of gable siding pieces to keep them from splitting. Drive the nails through the holes to install the boards.

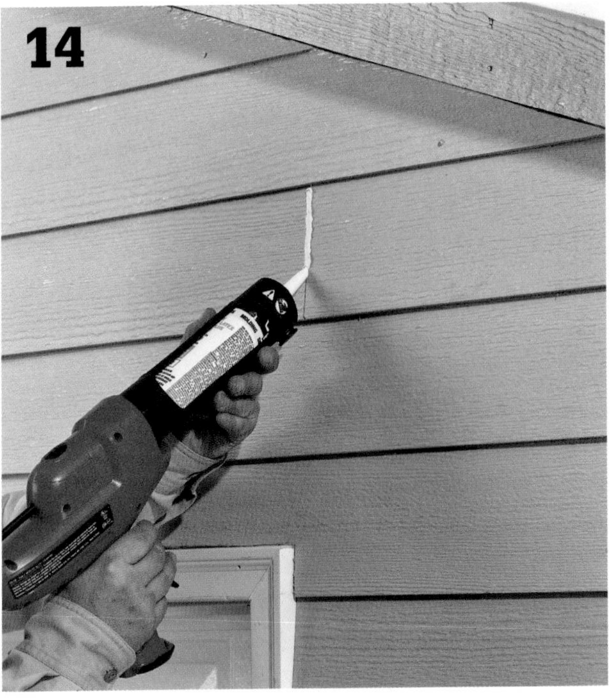


**Caulk gaps.** Fill all gaps between boards and between boards and trim with flexible, paintable caulk. Paint the siding and trim as desired.

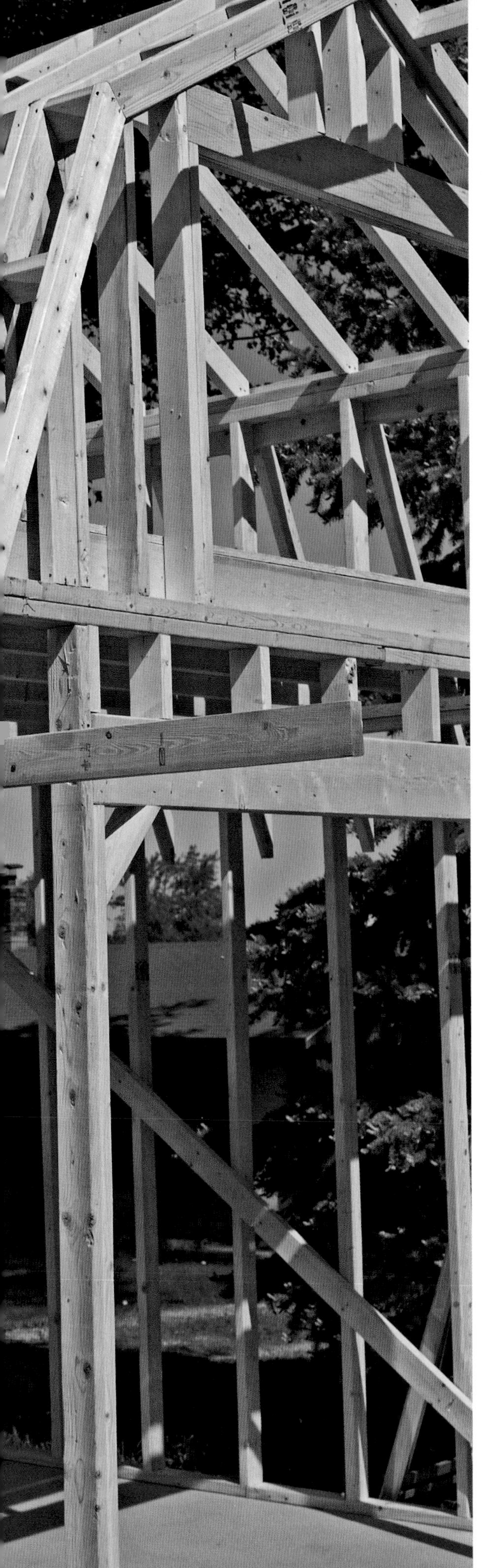

# Garage Plans

A garage is a major structure, so building one should not be done without a complete set of plan drawings. In fact, you will need an accurate set of plans just to get the building permit for your garage. You'll also need a detailed materials list for ordering supplies and making a plan. Most of the plans featured in this book were created and sold as complete plan packages by a building plan publisher (see Resources, page 235). You'll find many vendors who sell these products online, through mail order businesses, or at bookstores and building centers.

You may also hire a local architectural firm to help you design the structure and draft plans. Or, if you are an inveterate do-it-yourselfer, you can design the garage and draw up the plans yourself. This is a bit chancy if you don't have a lot of experience, but there are computer-assisted design programs that can help. Or, many home centers provide software-based design and estimating assistance if you purchase your materials through them.

**In this chapter:**


- Single Detached Garage
- Additional Garage Plans
- Compact Garage
- Gambrel Garage
- Carport
- Garage Workshop

# Single Detached Garage

Building a detached garage is quite possibly the most complex DIY job you ever undertake. But if you have a good working plan and approach the job realistically with measured confidence, you can do it. The one-stall detached garage featured here (see Resources, page 235) is about as simple a design as you'll find. The only really tricky part is cutting the rafter ends and making the cornices. You can simplify these tasks, however, by replacing the rafters with a truss system (see pages 50 to 51).

The plan drawings that follow on the next five pages deal primarily with the structure of the building. Finished details such as trim and siding are left somewhat open, since it is likely that you'll choose appearances and products that match your own house. The one built here features fiber-cement siding on top, with the bottom section of each wall sided with cast veneer stone. As shown, this garage is 14 feet wide and 22 feet from front to back. If you choose to alter any of the dimensions for your project, do so with great care and make certain to update all of your part dimensions.

On the four pages following the plan drawings for this garage, you'll find a few additional garage plans that may fit your needs a little more closely or inspire you to create your own design or modified design.

**This efficient garage** is built from the ground up using common building materials available at any building center. This plan was the basis for the Building a New Garage chapter featured on the previous pages. The materials lists and plan drawings are included in the following five pages of this chapter.

# Materials & Cutting List ▸

## Material List

| Description | Quantity/Size | Board Ft. |
|---|---|---|
| Wall plate treated | 1 pc. / 2 × 4 × 14' | 9 |
| Wall plate treated | 5 pcs. / 2 × 4 × 12' | 40 |
| Precut wall studs | 58 pcs. / 2 × 4 × 8' | 309 |
| Wall plates | 3 pcs. / 2 × 4 × 14' | 28 |
| Wall plates | 6 pcs. / 2 × 4 × 12' | 48 |
| Wall plates | 3 pcs. / 2 × 4 × 10' | 20 |
| Header over garage door | 2 pcs. / 2 × 12 × 10' | 40 |
| Header blocking | 2 pcs. / 2 × 4 × 10' | 13 |
| Header over sash & door | 2 pcs. / 2 × 8 × 10' | 27 |
| Cripple studs | 6 pcs. / 2 × 4 × 8 | 32 |
| Garage door hardware surround | 1 pc. / 2 × 4 × 10' | 7 |
| Garage door hardware surround | 2 pcs. / 2 × 4 × 8' | 11 |
| Corner brace | 6 pcs. / 1 × 4 × 12' | 24 |
| Rafter tie | 5 pcs. / 2 × 6 × 14' | 70 |
| Rafters & gable blocking | 12 pcs. / 2 × 6 × 18' | 216 |
| Ridgeboard | 2 pcs. / 2 × 8 × 12' | 32 |
| Gable studs | 3 pcs. / 2 × 4 × 12' | 24 |
| Gable nailer | 4 pcs. / 2 × 4 × 8' | 21 |
| Soffit nailer | 4 pcs. / 2 × 2 × 12' | 16 |
| Horizontal hardboard siding 10½ exp. | 617 sq. ft. / 7⁄16" × 12" | 617 sq. ft. |
| Metal corners for siding | 40 pcs. | |
| Rake fascia | 2 pcs. / 1 × 8 × 18' | 12 |
| Rake soffit | 2 pcs. / 1 × 6 × 18' | 18 |
| Rake shingle mold | 36 L.F. | |
| Fascia & soffit | 8 pcs. / 1 × 8 × 12' | 64 |
| Aluminum foil kraft paper | 1 roll / 36" wide | |
| C-D Ext. plywood roof sheathing | 13 pcs. / 4' × 8' × ½" | 416 sq. ft. |
| Roofing felt | 1 roll / 15# | |
| Asphalt shingles | 4⅓ sq. / 235# | |
| Sliding window unit | 1 ea. / 4 × 3' | |
| Exterior caulk | 2 tubes / 101 | |

| Description | Quantity/Size | Board Ft. |
|---|---|---|
| Garage service door 5 panel | 1 ea. / 2'8" × 6'8" | |
| Sectional up & over garage door | 1 ea. / 9 × 7' | |
| Door jambs | 42 L.F. / 1 × 4' | |
| Brickmold casing | 42 L.F. | |
| Shingle mold stop | 42 L.F. | |
| Concrete slab foundation & floor | 8 cu. yd. | |
| Concrete figures | | |
| Wire mesh | 308 sq. ft. / 6 × 6 × #10 | |
| Reinforcing bars | 144 L.F. / ½" dia. | |
| Exterior paint | 3 gal. | |

### Nails

| | |
|---|---|
| 16d common nails coated | 20 lb. |
| 10d common nails coated | 2 lb. |
| 8d common nails coated | 2 lb. |
| 6d common nails coated | 5 lb. |
| 8d galvanized siding nails | 5 lb. |
| 1¼" galvanized roofing nails | 15 lb. |
| 8d casing nails | 2 lb. |
| Anchor bolts w/ nuts & washers | 20 ea. / ½" dia. × 12" |
| Key in knob cylinder lockset | 1 ea. |
| Door butts | 1 pr. / 3½ × 3½" |

### Optional

| | |
|---|---|
| Ext. plywood sheathing (corner bracing) | 8 pcs. / 4' × 8' × ½" |
| Insulating sheathing | 12 pcs. / 4' × 8' × ½" |
| Galvanized nails | 10 lb. / 1½" |

### Optional for Alternate Formed Foundation

| | |
|---|---|
| Concrete for footing | 3 cu. yd. |
| Concrete for walls | 6 cu. yd. |
| Concrete for floor | 4 cu. yd. |

*These plans have been prepared to meet professional building standards. However, due to varying construction codes and local building practices, these drawings may not be suitable for use in all locations. Results may vary according to quality of material purchased and the skill of the builder.*

## Foundation Plan

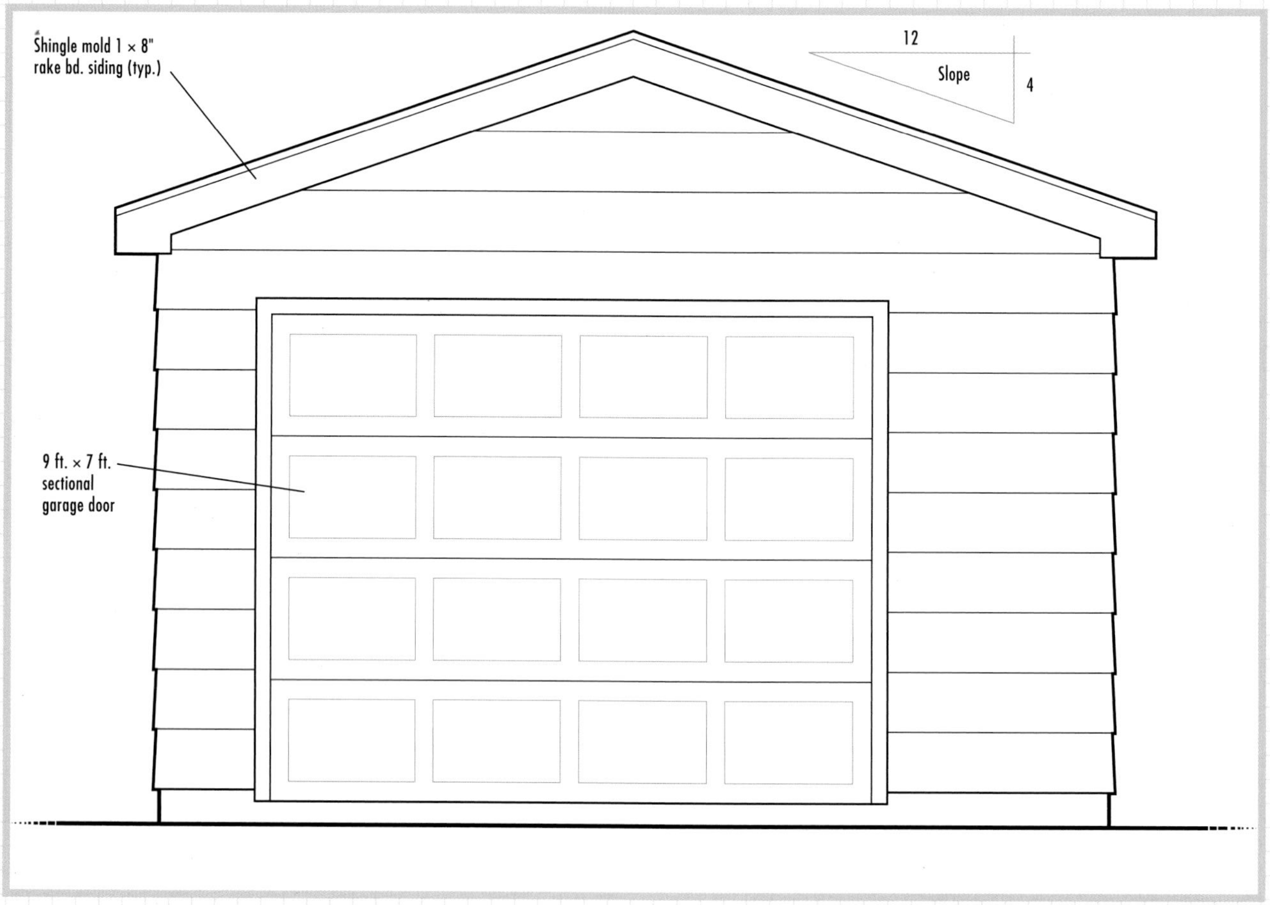

Shingle mold 1 × 8"
rake bd. siding (typ.)
12
Slope
4
9 ft. × 7 ft.
sectional
garage door

## Elevations

Self-seal asphalt shingles
1" × 8" fascia
1" × 8" lap
siding (typ.)
7½"
6"
Rear
Right side
Left side

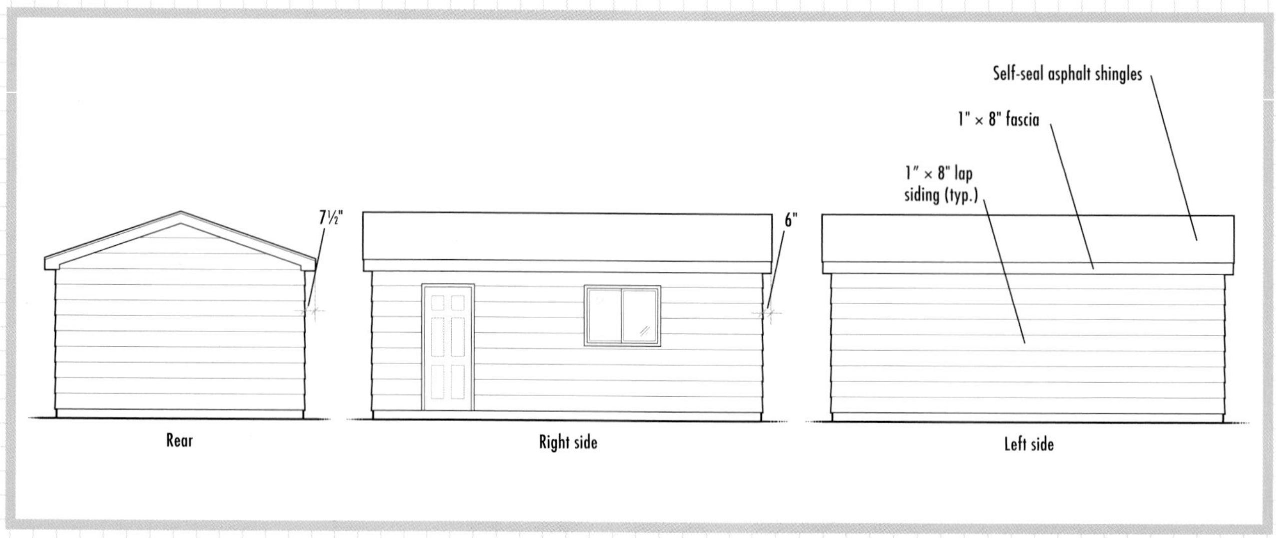

# Wall Framing Plan

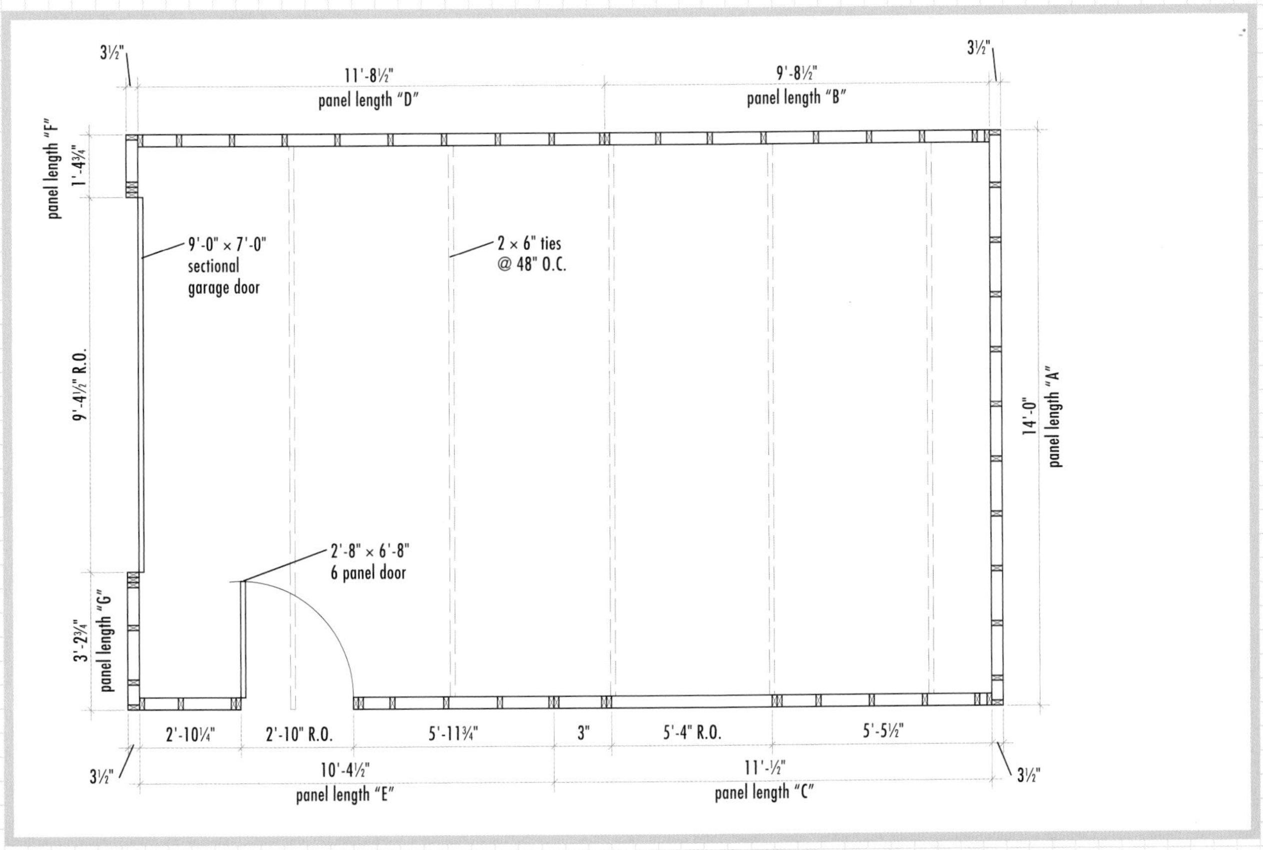

3½"
11'-8½"
panel length "D"
9'-8½"
panel length "B"
3½"
panel length "F"
1'-4¾"
9'-0" × 7'-0"
sectional
garage door
2 × 6" ties
@ 48" O.C.
9'-4½" R.O.
14'-0"
panel length "A"
2'-8" × 6'-8"
6 panel door
3'-2¾"
panel length "G"
2'-10¼"
2'-10" R.O.
5'-11¾"
3"
5'-4" R.O.
5'-5½"
3½"
10'-4½"
panel length "E"
11'-½"
panel length "C"
3½"

## Overhead Door Jamb Detail

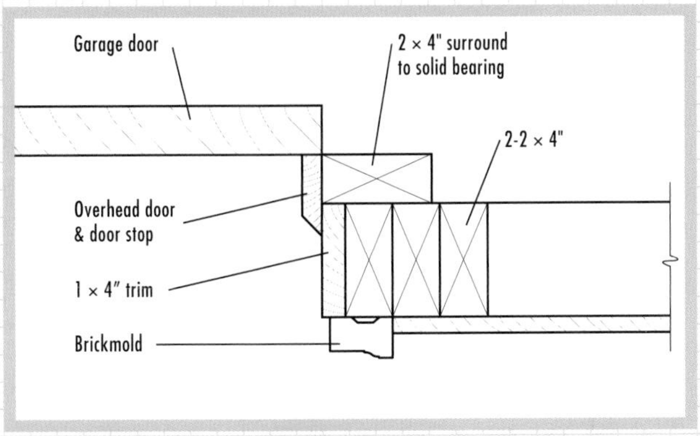

Garage door
2 × 4" surround
to solid bearing
2-2 × 4"
Overhead door
& door stop
1 × 4" trim
Brickmold

## Typical Corner Detail

2 × 4" stud
Note: If interior finish is used,
add 2" × 4" stud & blocking
at each corner.

## Service Door Jamb Detail

⅜ × ⅝ 6-panel door
¼" shim space
2-2 × 4"
Door stop
1 × 4" trim
Brickmold
Siding

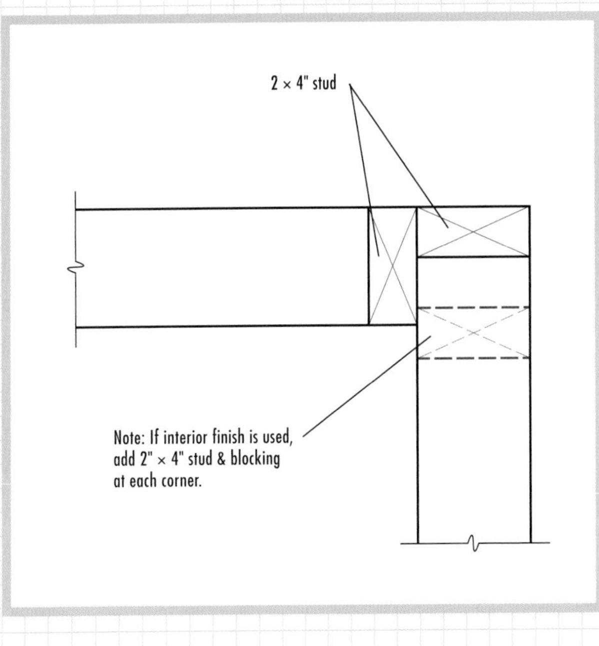

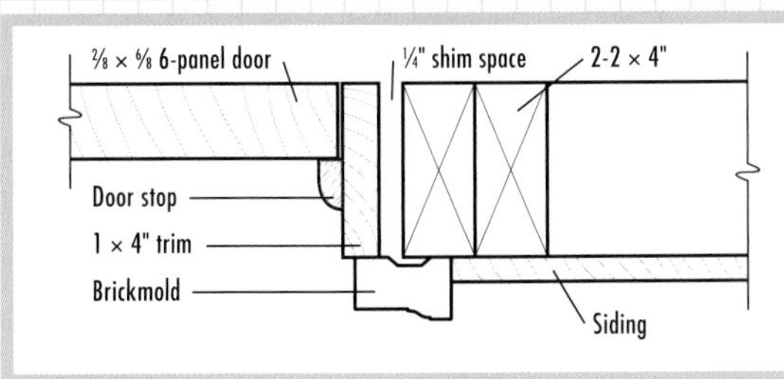

# Foundation Plan

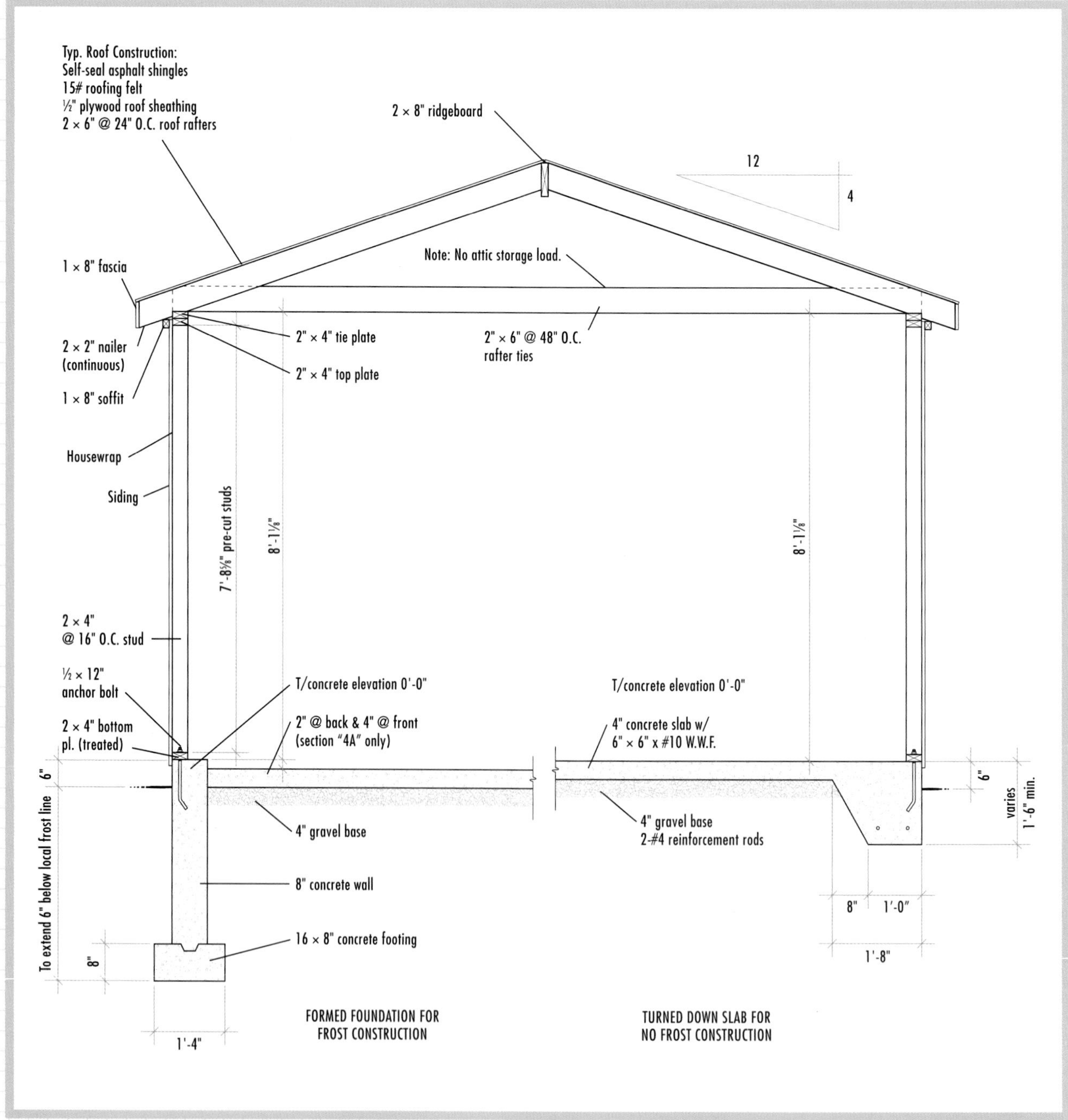

## Side Wall Framing Plan

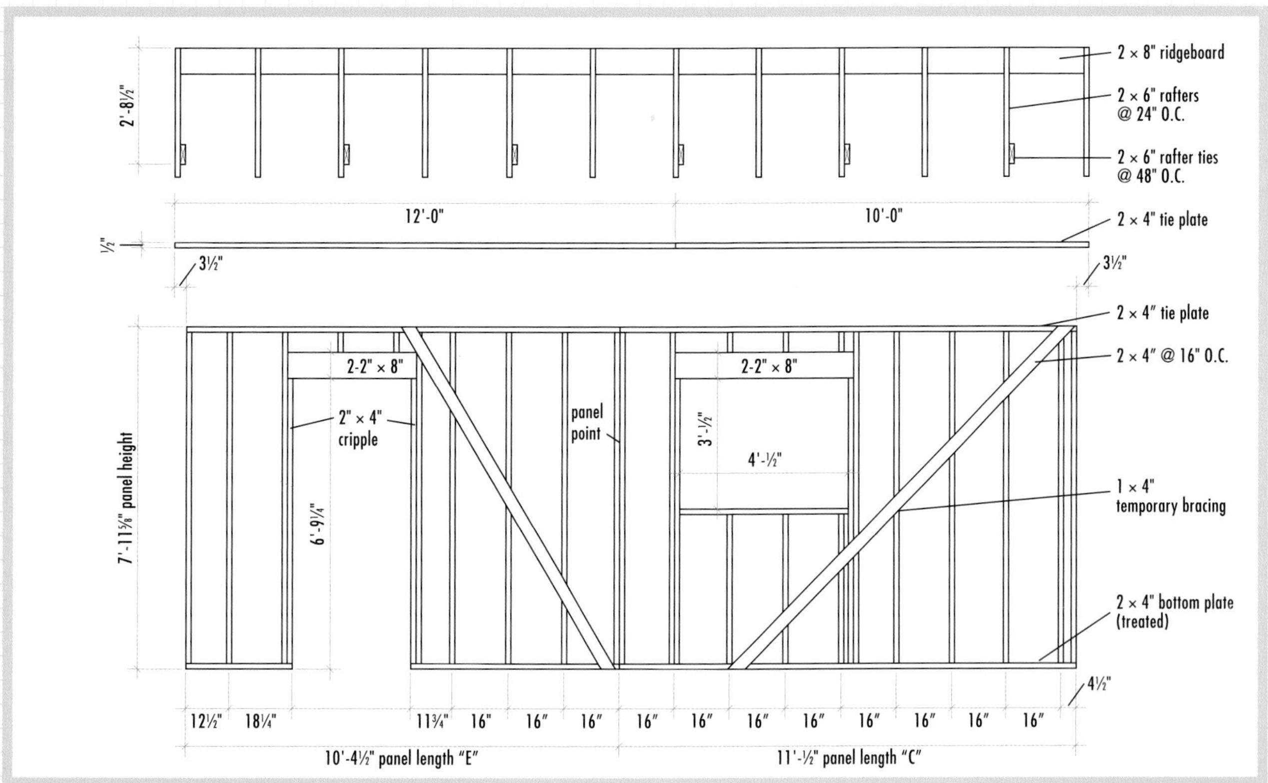

2 × 8" ridgeboard
2 × 6" rafters @ 24" O.C.
2 × 6" rafter ties @ 48" O.C.
2'-8½"
12'-0"
10'-0"
2 × 4" tie plate
½"
3½"
3½"
2 × 4" tie plate
2 × 4" @ 16" O.C.
2-2" × 8"
2-2" × 8"
2" × 4" cripple
panel point
3'-½"
4'-½"
1 × 4" temporary bracing
7'-11⅝" panel height
6'-9¼"
2 × 4" bottom plate (treated)
4½"
12½" 18¼" 11¾" 16" 16" 16" 16" 16" 16" 16" 16" 16" 16" 16"
10'-4½" panel length "E"
11'-½" panel length "C"

## Front Framing Plan

2 × 8" ridgeboard
2 × 4" siding nailer
2 × 6" gable end rafter
2 × 4" gable end studs
2'-8½"
7½" 20" 16" 16" 16" 16" 16" 16" 16" 16" 20" 7½"
½"
2 × 4" tie plate
3½"
3½"
13'-5"
2 × 4" top plate
2 - 2" × 12" headers
2 × 4" studs @ 16" O.C.
11¼"
2 × 4s as required
2 × 4" cripples each side
7'-11⅝" panel height
7'-⅜"
2 × 4" bottom plate (treated)
3"
3"
1'-1¼" 16 8"
1'-3¼"
9'-7½" header length
3'-1¼"

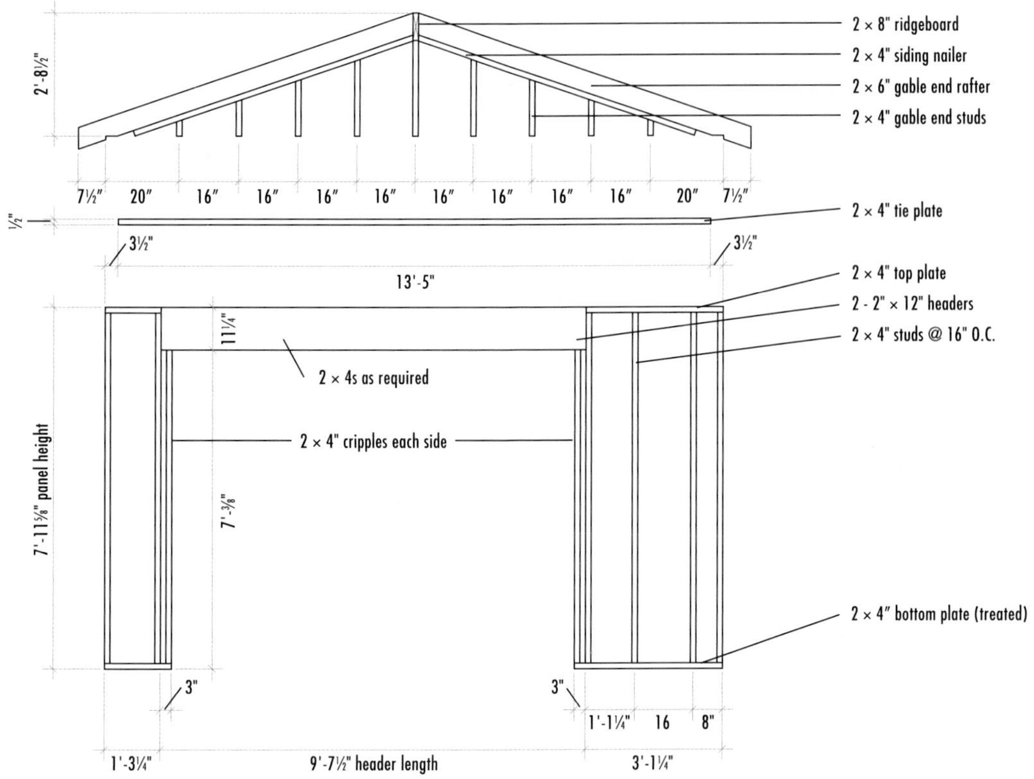

# Additional Garage Plans

## Garage with Covered Porch

- Size: 24 × 22 ft.
- Building height: 13 ft.
- Roof pitch: 5/12
- Ceiling height: 8 ft.
- Overhead door: 9 × 7 ft.
- Roomy garage has space for storage
- Distinctive covered porch provides perfect area for entertaining

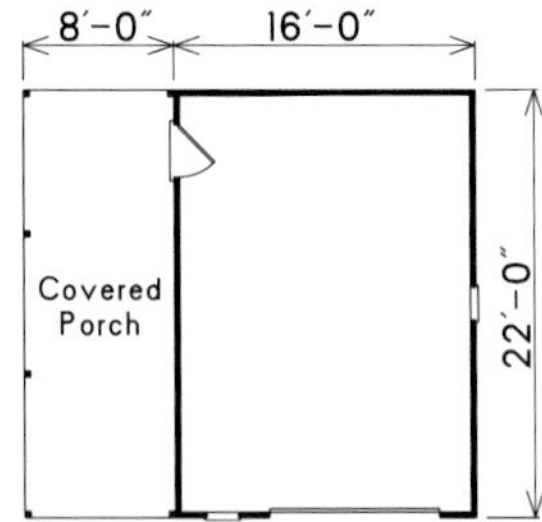


**Design #002D-6010**

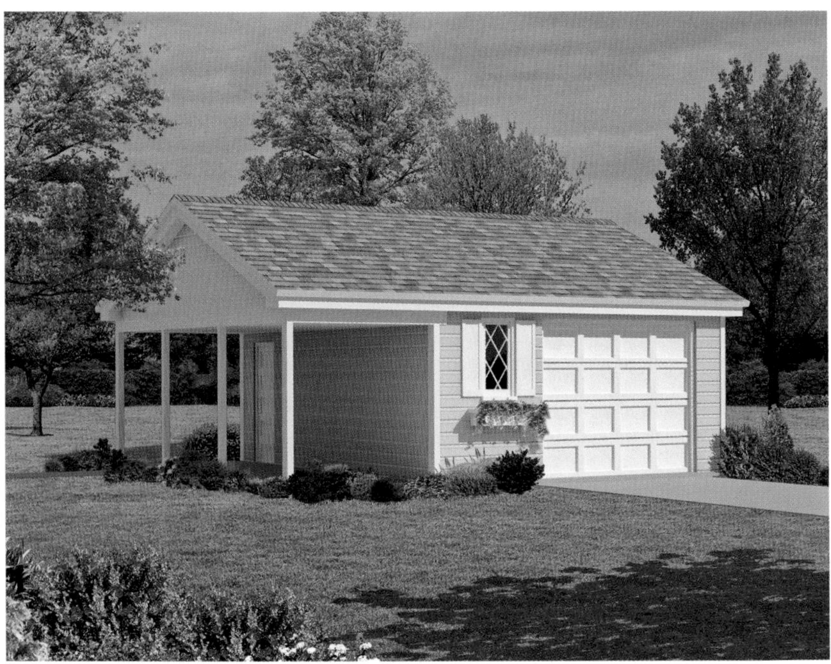

## Three-Car Detached Garage

- Size: 32 × 22 ft.
- Building height: 12 ft., 2"
- Roof pitch: 4/12
- Ceiling height: 8 ft.
- Overhead doors: 9 × 7 ft., 16 × 7 ft.
- Side entry for easy access
- Perfect style with many types of homes

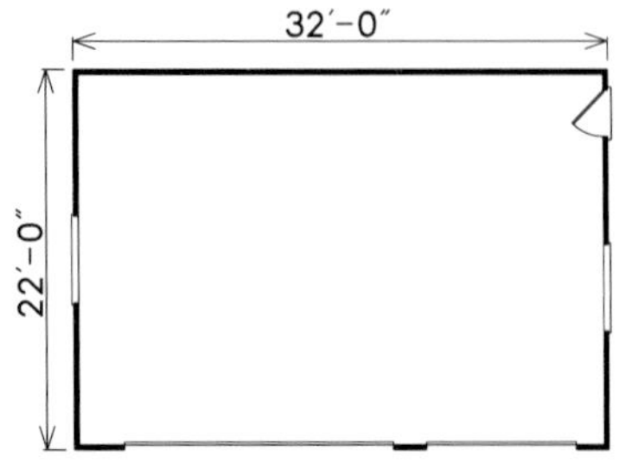


**Design #002D-6011**

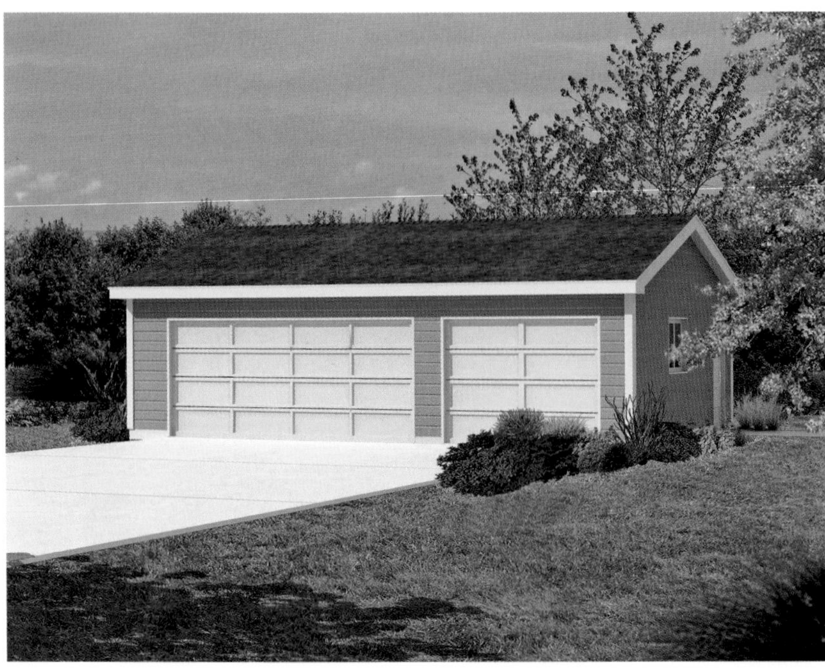

*Visit www.projectplans.com to order and view garage plans.*

## Two-Car Detached Garage

- Size: 24 × 22 ft.
- Building height: 14 ft.
- Roof pitch: 6/12
- Ceiling height: 8 ft.
- Overhead door: 16 × 7 ft.
- Design with wonderful versatility

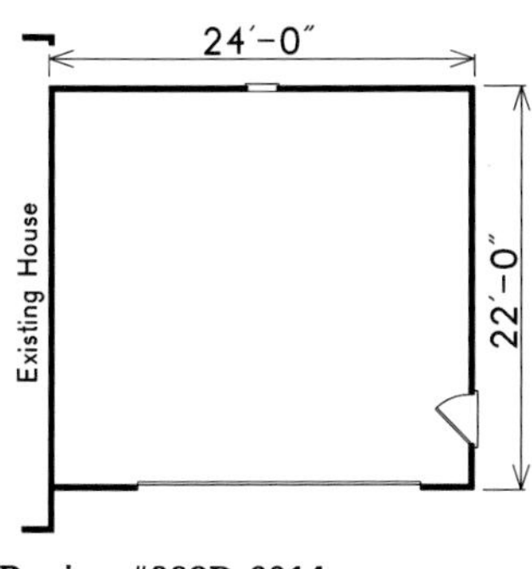


**Design #002D-6014**

## Victorian Garage

- Size: 24 × 24 ft.
- Building height: 16 ft., 7"
- Roof pitch: 8/12
- Ceiling height: 8 ft.
- Overhead doors: (2) 9 × 7 ft.
- Accented with Victorian details
- Functional side entry

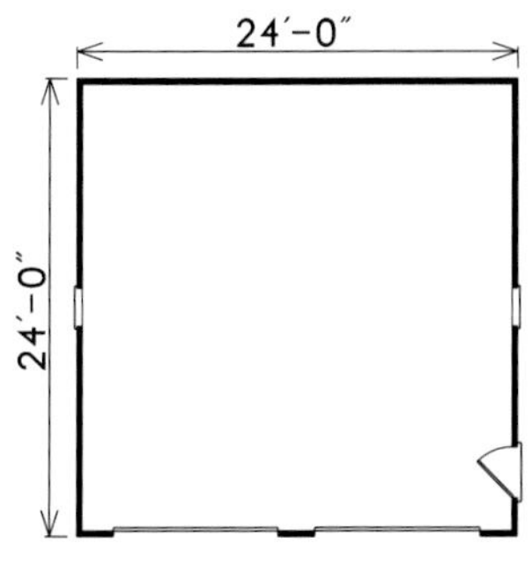


**Design #002D-6018**

*Visit www.projectplans.com to order and view garage plans.*

## Reverse Gable Garage

- Size: 24 × 22 ft.
- Building height: 14 ft., 8"
- Roof pitch: 5/12, 8.5/12
- Ceiling height: 8 ft.
- Overhead doors: (2) 9 × 7 ft.
- Roof overhang above garage doors adds custom look
- Handy side door

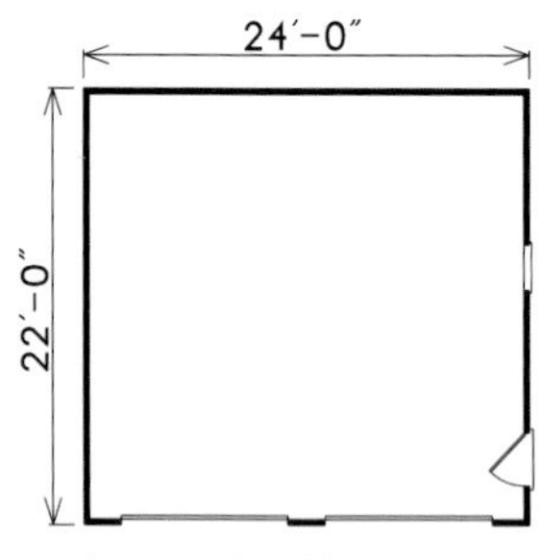


**Design #002D-6040**

## Three-Car Garage/Workshop

- Size: 24 × 36 ft.
- Building height: 14 ft., 6"
- Roof pitch: 4/12
- Ceiling height: 10 ft.
- Overhead doors: (2) 9 × 8 ft.
- Oversized for storage
- Ideal size for workshop or maintenance building

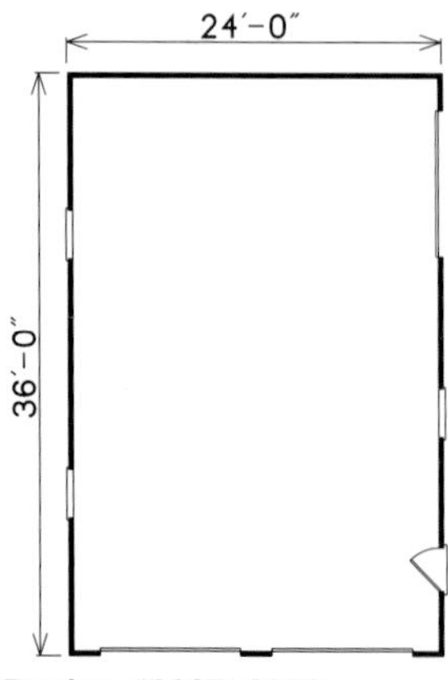


**Design #002D-6042**

*Visit www.projectplans.com to order and view garage plans.*

## Three-stall Garage

- Size: 40 × 24 ft.
- Building height: 15 ft., 6"
- Roof pitch: 6/12
- Ceiling height: 9 ft.
- Overhead doors: (3) 9 × 7 ft.
- Oversized with plenty of room for storage
- Side door for easy access

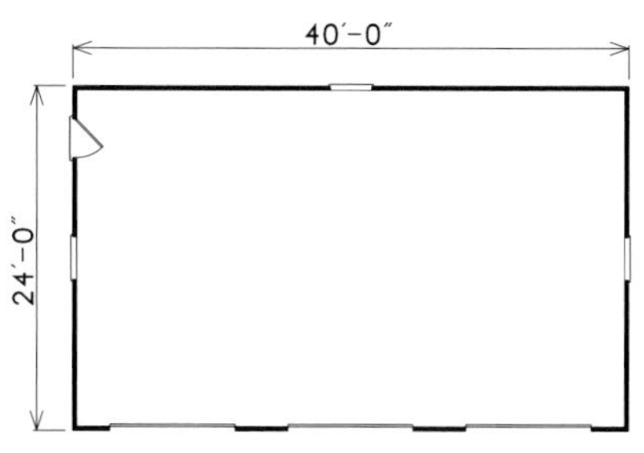


**Design #002D-6046**

## Garage with Loft

- Size: 22 x 25 ft. 4"
- Building height: 20 ft., 6"
- Roof pitch: 7/12 (main), 3/12 (roof dormer)
- Ceiling height: 8 ft.
- Overhead door: 18 × 7 ft.
- Slab foundation

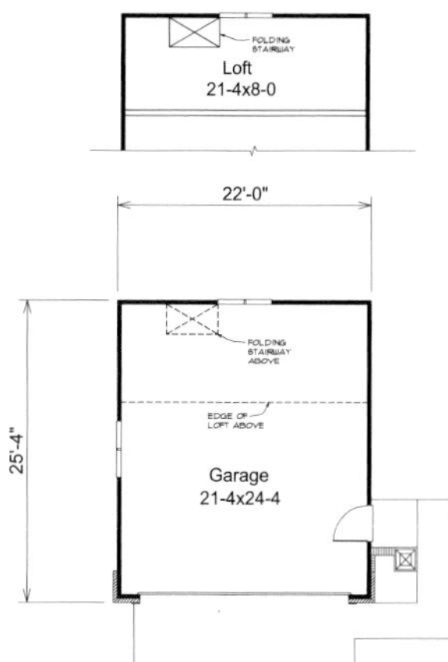


**Design #002D-6008**

*Visit www.projectplans.com to order and view garage plans.*

# Compact Garage

The compact garage is named for its exceptional versatility and ample storage space. This classic gabled outbuilding has a footprint that measures 12 × 16 feet and it includes several useful features. For starters, its 8-foot-wide overhead garage door provides easy access for large equipment, supplies, projects, or even a small automobile. The foundation and shed floor is a poured concrete slab, so it's ideal for heavy items like lawn tractors and stationary tools.

To the right of the garage door is a box bay window. This special architectural detail gives the building's façade a surprising houselike quality while filling the interior with natural light. And the bay's 33"-deep × 60"-wide sill platform is the perfect place for herb pots or an indoor flower box. The adjacent wall includes a second large window and a standard service door, making this end of the garage a pleasant, convenient space for all kinds of work or leisure.

Above the main space of the compact garage is a fully framed attic built with 2 × 6 joists for supporting plenty of stored goods. The steep pitch of the roof allows for over 3 feet of headroom under the peak. Access to the attic is provided by a drop-down staircase that folds up and out of the way, leaving the workspace clear below.

The garage door, service door, staircase, and both windows of the garage are prebuilt factory units that you install following the manufacturer's instructions. Be sure to order all of the units before starting construction. This makes it easy to adjust the framed openings, if necessary, to match the precise sizing of each unit. Also consult your local building department to learn about design requirements for the concrete foundation. You may need to extend and/or reinforce the perimeter portion of the slab, or include a footing that extends below the frost line. An extended apron (as seen in the Gambrel Garage, page 116) is very useful if you intend to house vehicles in the garage.

## Cutting List ▸

| Description | Quantity/Size | Material |
|---|---|---|
| **Foundation** | | |
| Drainage material | 2.75 cu. yd. | Compactible gravel |
| Concrete slab | Field measure | 3,000 psi concrete |
| Mesh | 200 sq. ft. | 6 × 6", W1.4 × W1.4 welded wire mesh |
| Reinforcing bar | As required by local code | As required by local code |
| **Wall Framing** | | |
| Bottom plates | 1 @ 16', 2 @ 12' 1 @ 10' | 2 × 4 pressure treated |
| Top plates | 2 @ 14', 4 @ 12' 4 @ 10' | 2 × 4 |
| Standard wall studs | 51 @ 8'* *may use 92 5/8" precut studs | 2 × 4 |
| Diagonal bracing | 5 @ 12' | 1 × 4 (std. lumber) |
| Jack studs | 5 @ 14' | 2 × 4 |
| Gable end studs | 5 @ 8' | 2 × 4 |
| Header, overhead door | 2 @ 10' | 2 × 12 |
| Header, windows | 2 @ 10' | 2 × 12 |
| Header, service door | 1 @ 8' | 2 × 12 |
| Header & stud spacers | | See Sheathing, right |
| **Box Bay Framing** | | |
| Half-wall bottom plate | 1 @ 8' | 2 × 4 pressure-treated |
| Half-wall top plate & studs | 3 @ 8' | 2 × 4 |
| Joists | 3 @ 8' | 2 × 6 |
| Window frame | 4 @ 12' | 2 × 4 |
| Sill platform & top | 1 sheet @ 4 × 8' | 1/2" plywood |
| Rafter blocking | 1 @ 8' | 2 × 8 |
| **Roof Framing** | | |
| Rafters (& lookouts, blocking) | 36 @ 10' | 2 × 6 |
| Ridgeboard | 1 @ 18' | 2 × 8 |
| **Attic** | | |
| Floor joists | 16 @ 12' | 2 × 6 |
| Floor decking | 6 sheets @ 4 × 8' | 1/2" plywood |
| Staircase | 1 unit for 22 × 48" rough opening | Disappearing attic stair unit |
| **Exterior Finishes** | | |
| Eave fascia | 2 @ 18' | 2 × 8 cedar |
| Gable fascia | 4 @ 10' | 1 × 8 cedar |

| Description | Quantity/Size | Material |
|---|---|---|
| Drip edge & gable trim | 160 lin. ft. | 1 × 2 cedar |
| Siding | 15 sheets @ 4 × 8' | 5/8" T 1-11 plywood siding w/ vertical grooves 8" on center (or similar) |
| Siding flashing | 30 lin. ft. | Metal Z-flashing |
| Overhead door jambs | 1 @ 10', 2 @ 8' | 1 × 6 cedar |
| Overhead door stops | 3 @ 8' | Cedar door stop |
| Overhead door surround | 1 @ 10', 2 @ 8' | 2 × 6 |
| Corner trim | 8 @ 8' | 1 × 4 cedar |
| Door & window trim | 4 @ 8', 5 @ 10' | 1 × 4 cedar |
| Box bay bottom trim | 1 @ 8' | 1 × 10 cedar |
| **Roofing** | | |
| Sheathing (& header, stud spacers) | 14 sheets @ 4 × 8' | 1/2" exterior-grade plywood roof sheathing |
| 15# building paper | 2 rolls | |
| Shingles | 4 2/3 squares | Asphalt shingles—250# per sq. min. |
| Roof flashing | 10'6" | |
| **Doors & Windows** | | |
| Overhead garage door w/hardware | 1 @ 9/0 × 7/0 | |
| Service door | 1 unit for 38 × 72 7/8" rough opening | Prehung exterior door unit |
| Window | 2 units for 57 × 41 3/8" | Casement mullion window unit—complete |
| **Fasteners & Hardware** | | |
| J-bolts w/nuts & washers | 14 | 1/2"-dia. × 12" |
| 16d galvanized common nails | 3 lb. | |
| 16d common nails | 15 lb. | |
| 10d common nails | 2 1/2 lb. | |
| 8d box nails | 16 lb. | |
| 8d common nails | 5 lbs. | |
| 8d galvanized siding nails | 10 lb. | |
| 1" galvanized roofing nails | 10 lb. | |
| 8d galvanized casing nails | 3 lb. | |
| Entry door lockset | 1 | |

## Foundation Plan

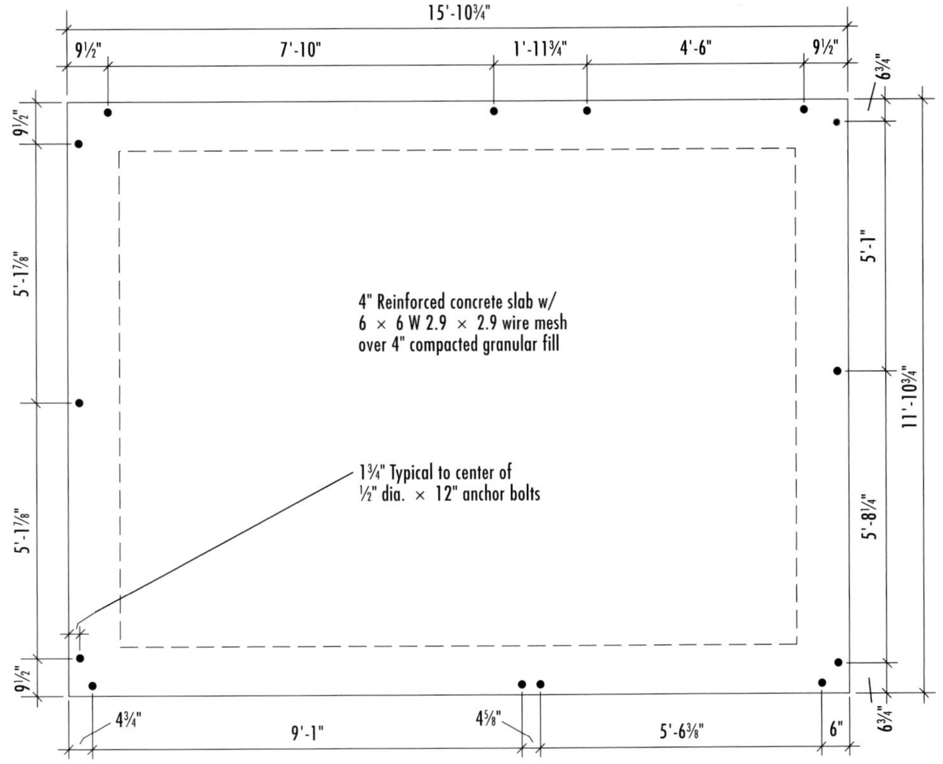

15'-10¾"
9½"
7'-10"
1'-11¾"
4'-6"
9½"
6¾"
9½"
5'-1⅞"
5'-1⅞"
9½"
5'-1"
11'-10¾"
5'-8¼"
6¾"
4" Reinforced concrete slab w/
6 × 6 W 2.9 × 2.9 wire mesh
over 4" compacted granular fill
1¾" Typical to center of
½" dia. × 12" anchor bolts
4¾"
9'-1"
4⅝"
5'-6⅜"
6"


## Foundation Detail

1¾" Typical to center of
½" dia. × 12" anchor bolts
Grade
6"
4" Reinforced concrete slab
w/6 × 6 W 2.9 × 2.9
wire mesh over 4" compacted
gravel
3"
2 - #4 Bars
1'-0"
To extend below
local frost line
(12" min.
w/no frost line)


## Building Section

2 × 8 Ridgeboard
½" Plywood flooring
12
8
Disappearing
stairway
12'-4½"
to slab
3'-2⅛"
6"
8'-1⅛"
11'-9¼"
1'-6"
1 × 6
Trim board
4'-9"
T1-11
Siding
7'-8⅝"
2 × 4 Top plate
½" Plywood door
1'-0"
½" Plywood shelf
1'-3½"
2 × 4
Wall stud
2 × 2
Shelf supports
4"
2"
T1-11 Siding
3"
2 × 4 Wall stud
11'-10¾"
2 × 4 Bottom plate
1'-0"
4" gravel bed, compacted

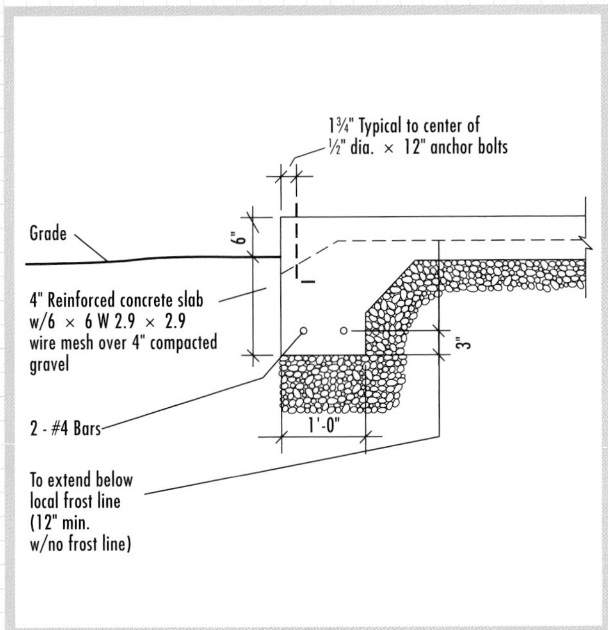

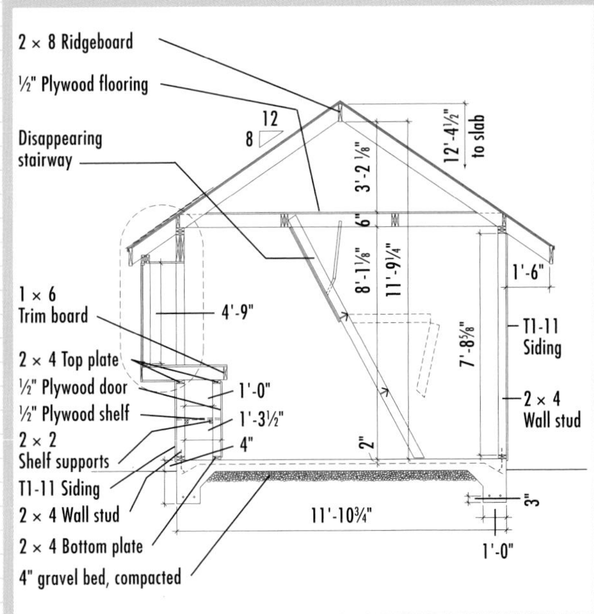

## Front Elevation

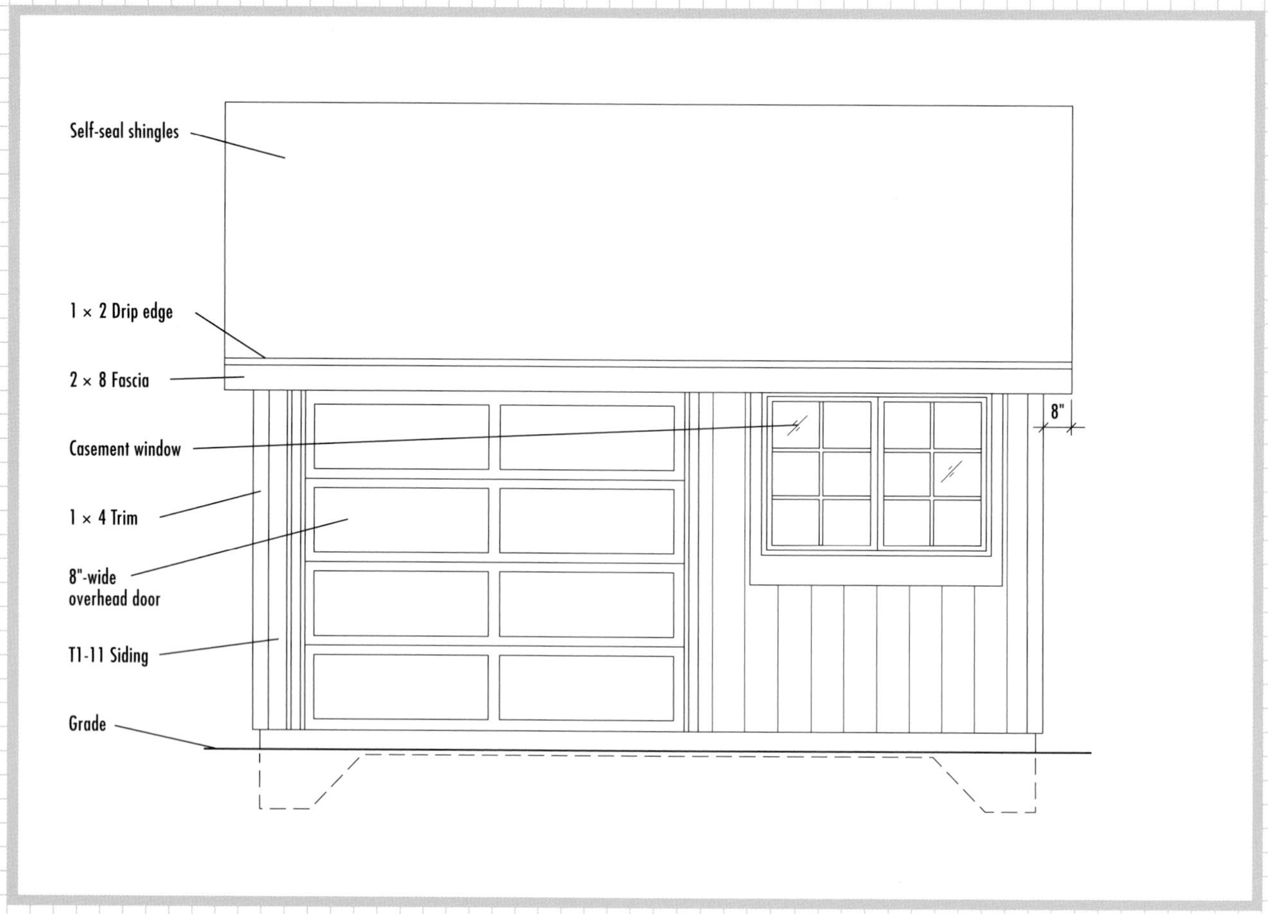

Self-seal shingles
1 × 2 Drip edge
2 × 8 Fascia
Casement window
1 × 4 Trim
8"-wide overhead door
T1-11 Siding
Grade
8"


## Right Side Elevation

12
8
1 × 2 Drip edge
1 × 8 Fascia
1 × 2 Trim
Z-flashing
1'-6"
Casement window
1 × 4 Trim
T1-11 Siding
Grade
Concrete slab


## Rear Elevation

Self-seal shingles
8"
1 × 4 Trim
Grade
Concrete slab
T1-11 Siding w/ grooves, 8" O.C.

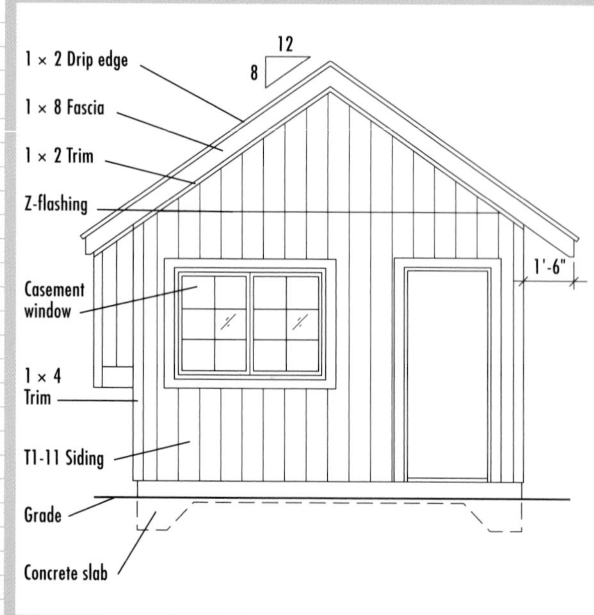

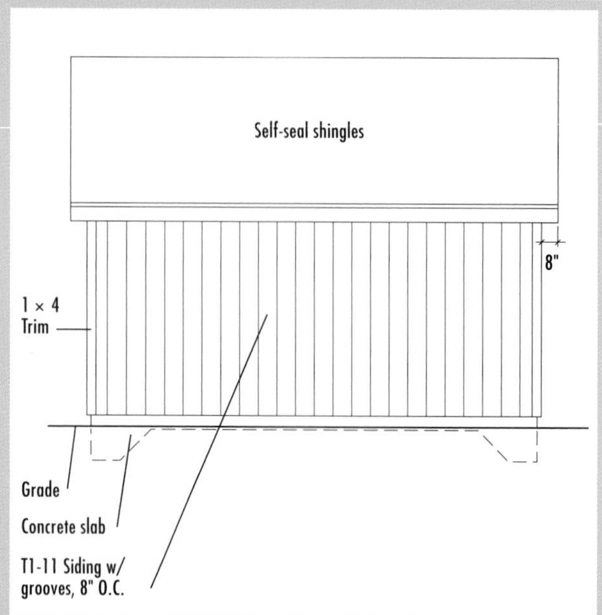

## Wall Framing Plan

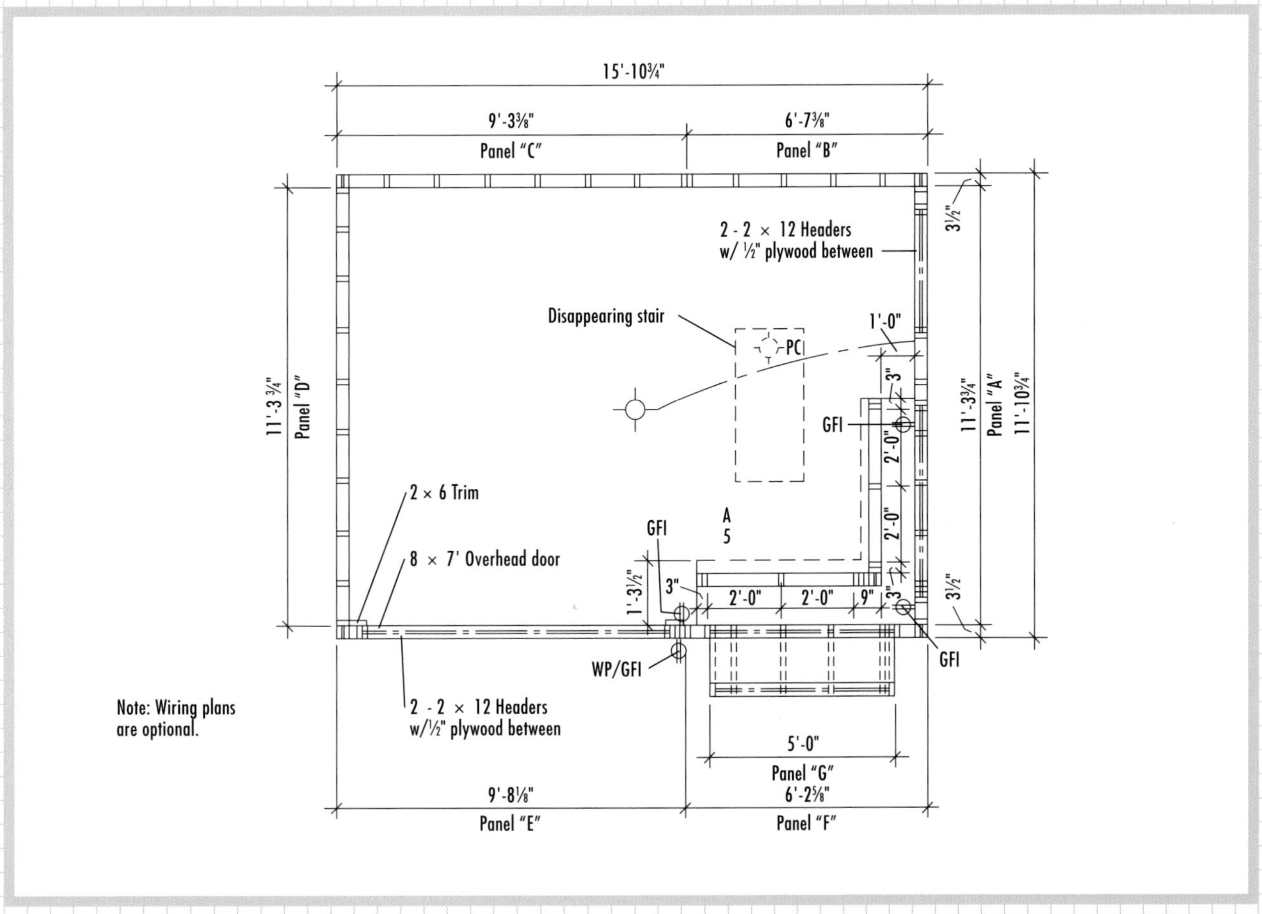

15'-10¾"
9'-3⅜"
Panel "C"
6'-7⅜"
Panel "B"
3½"
2 - 2 × 12 Headers
w/ ½" plywood between
Disappearing stair
PC
1'-0"
3"
11'-3¾"
Panel "D"
GFI
2'-0"
2'-0"
11'-3¾"
Panel "A"
11'-10¾"
2 × 6 Trim
GFI
A
5
8 × 7' Overhead door
1'-3½"
3"
2'-0"
2'-0"
9"
3"
3½"
GFI
WP/GFI
Note: Wiring plans
are optional.
2 - 2 × 12 Headers
w/½" plywood between
5'-0"
Panel "G"
6'-2⅝"
9'-8⅛"
Panel "E"
Panel "F"

## Back Side Framing

15⅝"
15⅝"
8"
16" 16" 16" 16" 16" 16" 16" 16" 16" 16"
8"
2'-0"
2'-0"
2 × 8
Ridgeboard
2 × 6 Rafters
2 × 6 Attic
floor joists
@ 16" O.C.
9'-0⅝"
6'-3⅛"
2 × 4
Tie plate
3½"
3½"
2 × 4 Top plate
1 × 4
Diagonal bracing
Blocking between
corner studs
45°
2 × 4 Wall studs
3½"
16" 16" 16" 16" 16" 16" 16" 16" 16" 16"
3½"
6'-7⅜"
9'-3⅜"
Panel "B"
Panel "C"
11⅞"
11⅞"
2 × 4
Bottom plate

## Left Side Framing

12
8
2 × 8 Ridgeboard
2 × 4 Gable studs
2 × 6 Rafters
15⅝" 16" 16" 16" 8" 8" 16" 16" 16" 15⅝"
2 × 4 Tie plate
11'-10¾"
3½"
3½"
2 × 4
Top plate
1 × 4
Diagonal
bracing
2 × 4
Wall studs
2 × 4
Bottom plate
45°
11⅝" 16" 16" 16" 16" 16" 16" 16" 11⅝"
11'-3¾"
Panel "D"

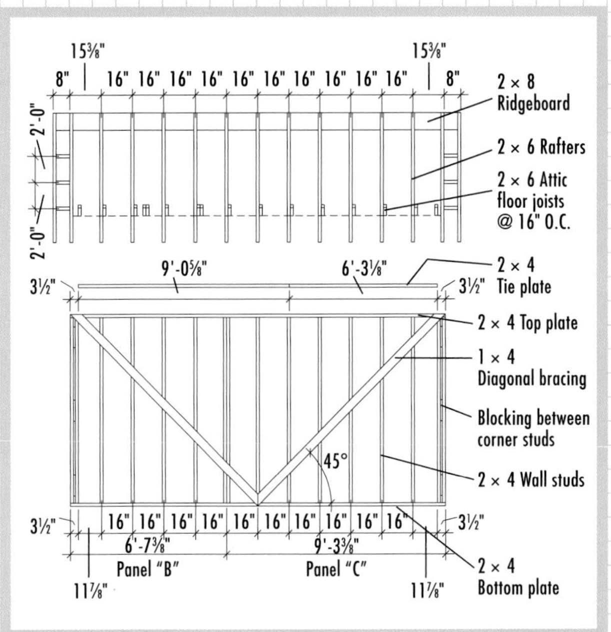

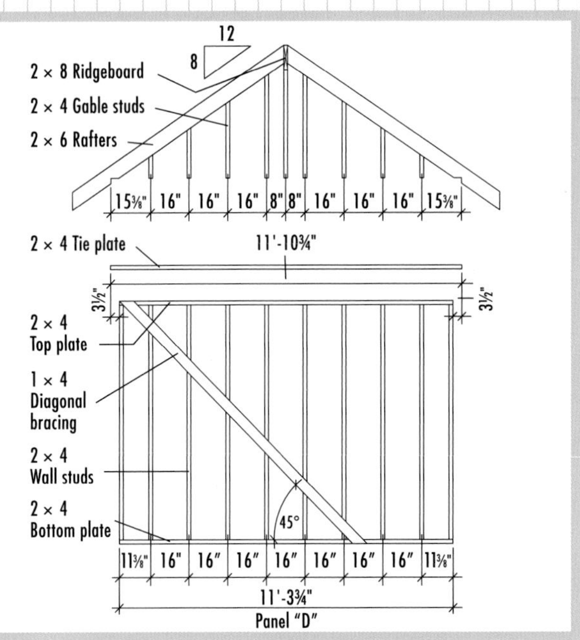

## Front Side Framing

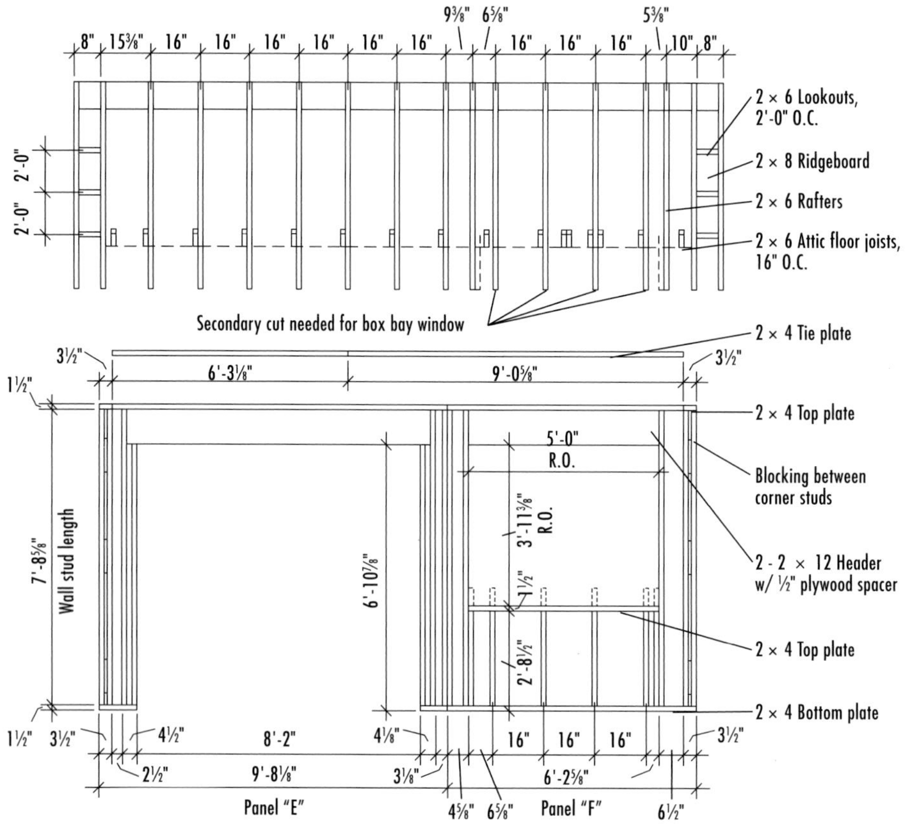

## Attic Floor Joist Framing

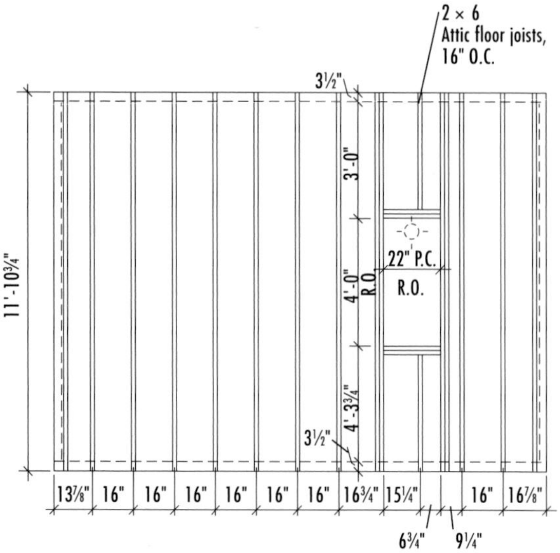

## Box Bay Window Framing

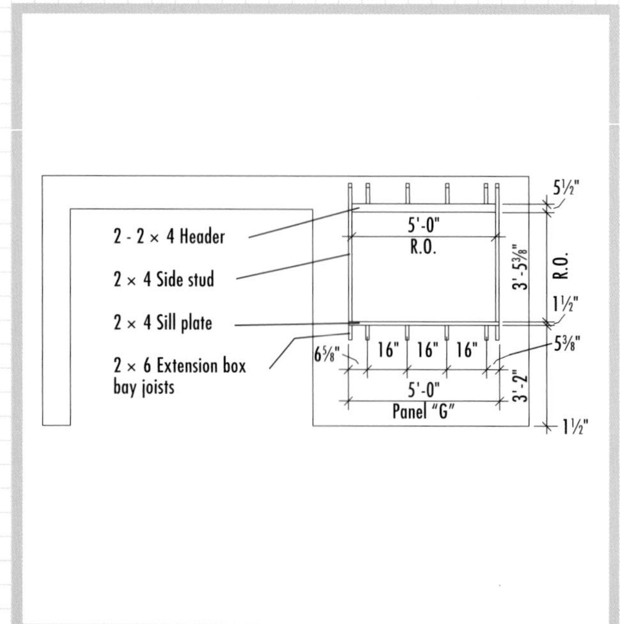

# Overhead Door Header Detail

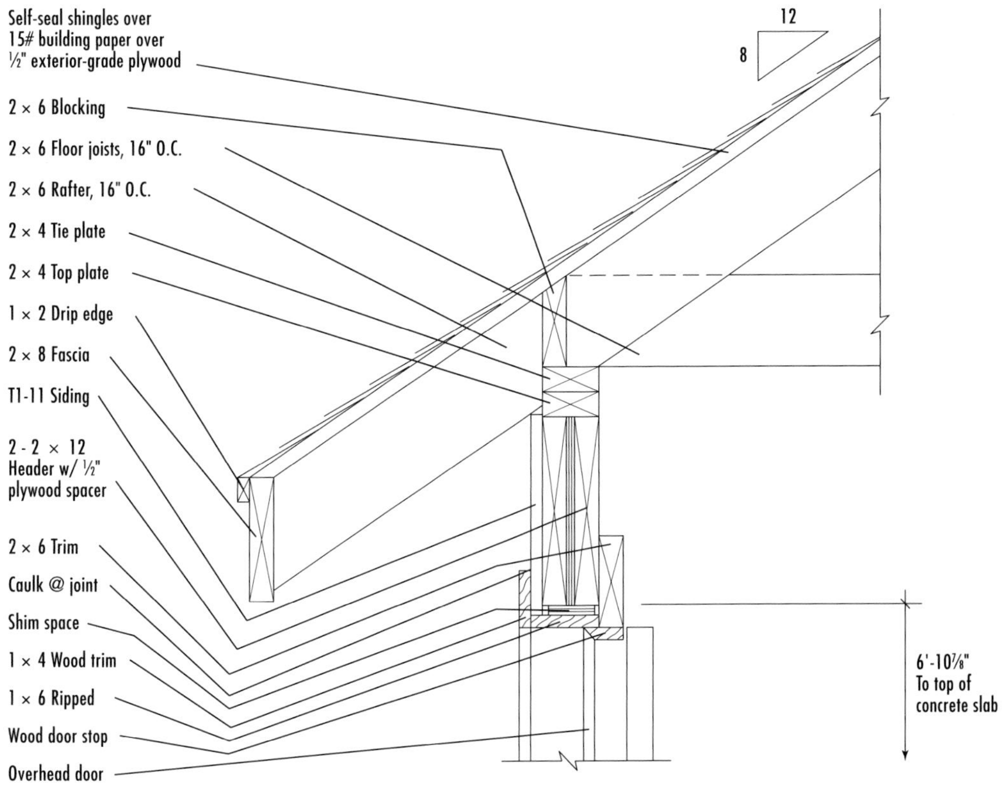

Self-seal shingles over
15# building paper over
½" exterior-grade plywood
2 × 6 Blocking
2 × 6 Floor joists, 16" O.C.
2 × 6 Rafter, 16" O.C.
2 × 4 Tie plate
2 × 4 Top plate
1 × 2 Drip edge
2 × 8 Fascia
T1-11 Siding
2 - 2 × 12 Header w/ ½" plywood spacer
2 × 6 Trim
Caulk @ joint
Shim space
1 × 4 Wood trim
1 × 6 Ripped
Wood door stop
Overhead door
12
8
6'-10⅞" To top of concrete slab

# Overhead Door Jamb Detail

2 × 6 Surround
Overhead door
Wood door stop
Shim space
2 × 4 Wall stud
1 × 6 Ripped
1 × 4 Wood trim
Caulk @ joint

# Service Door Header/Jamb Detail

2 × 4 Tie plate
2 × 4 Top plate
2 - 2 × 12 Header w/ ½" plywood spacer
T1-11 Siding
Caulk @ joint
Shim space
1 × 4 Wood trim
1 × 6 Ripped
Wood stop
2 × 4 Wall stud
Shim space
Service door
Wood door stop
1 × 6 Ripped
1 × 4 Wood trim
T1-11 Siding
Caulk @ joint

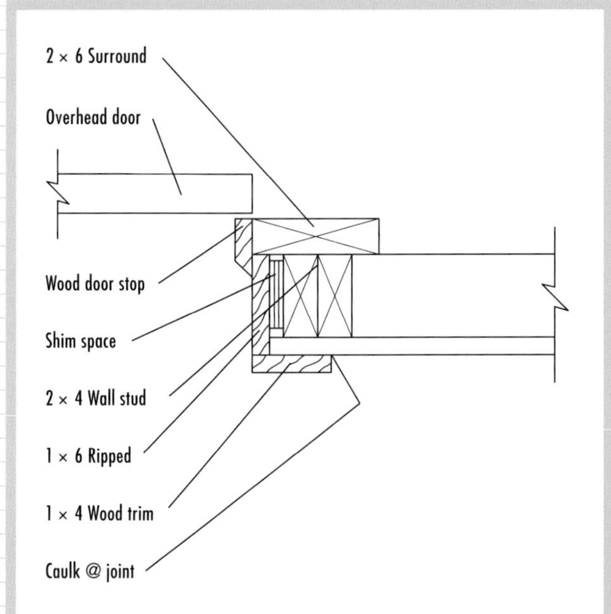

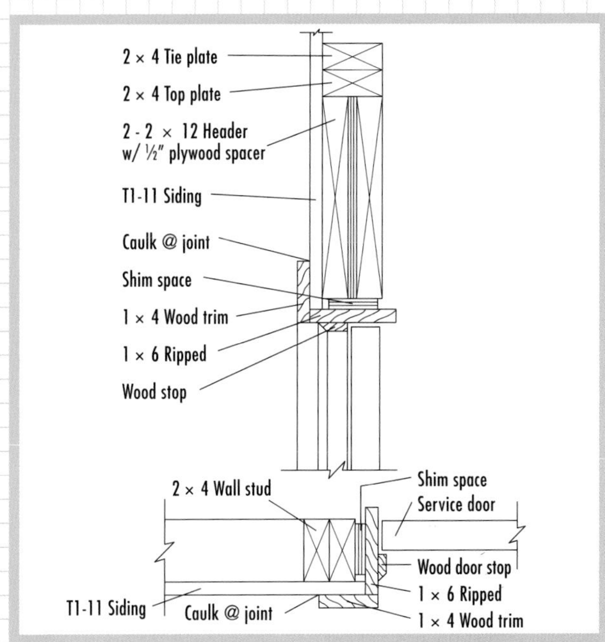

## Rafter Template

9'-2⅛"
3⅝"
8'-10½"
5½"
1"
1½"
2⅜"
3½"
2 × 6 Rafter
3⅝"
1³⁄₁₆"
1'-9⅝"
4¼"
6'-8⅝"
3⅝"
Secondary cut for rafters over box bay window only
3"
¹⁵⁄₁₆"
1¼"

## Corner Detail

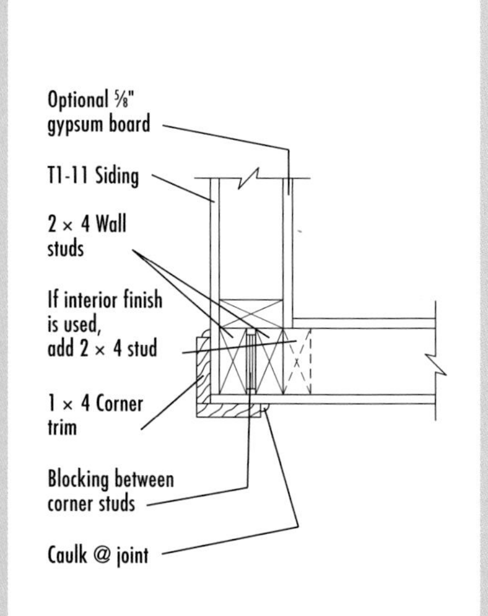


## Box Bay Window Detail

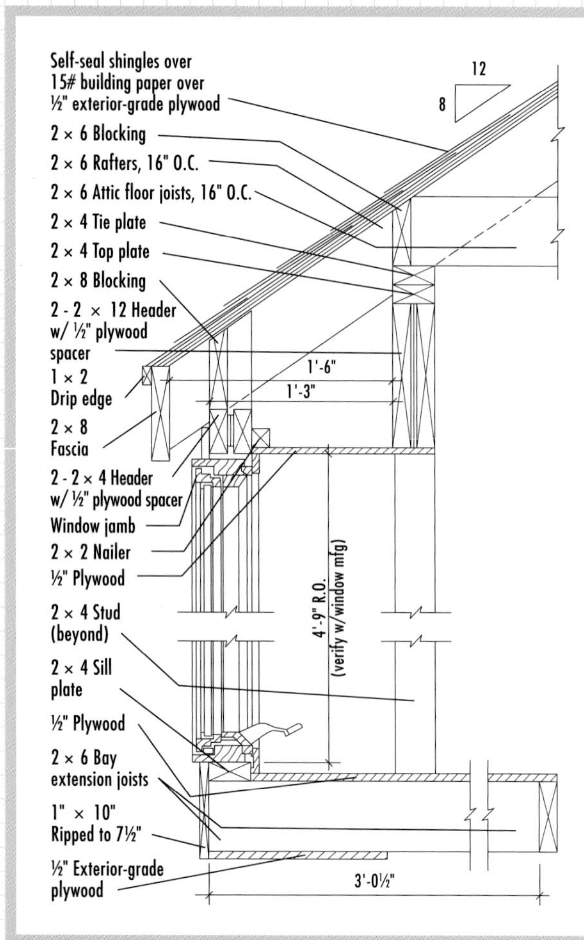


## Isometric

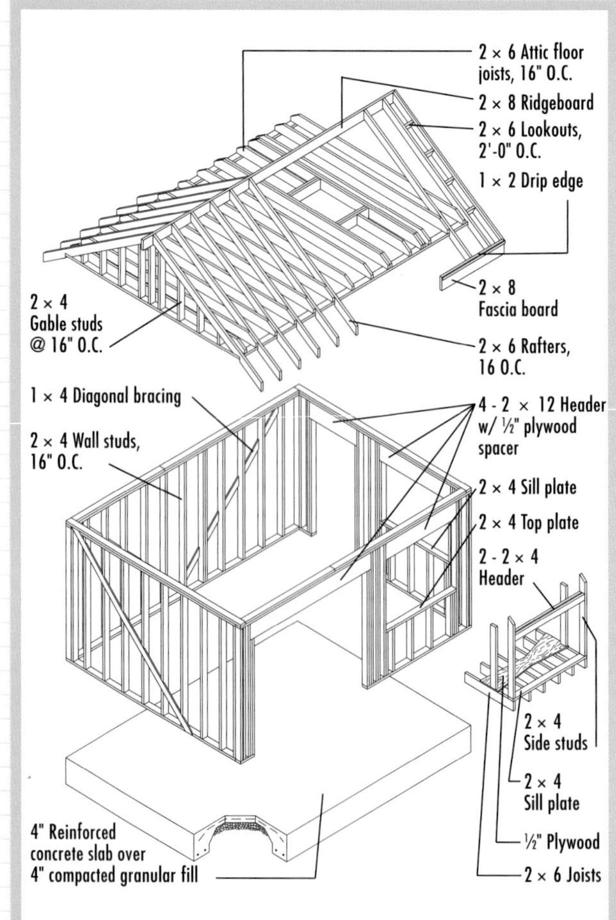

# How to Build the Compact Garage

**Build the concrete foundation** using the specifications shown in the Foundation Detail (page 105) and following the basic procedure on pages 28 to 33. The slab should measure 190¾" × 142¾". Set the 14 J-bolts into the concrete as shown in the Foundation Plan (page 105). *Note: All slab specifications must comply with local building codes.*

**Snap chalk lines** for the bottom plates so they will be flush with the outside edges of the foundation. You can frame the walls in four continuous panels or break them up into panels A through F, as shown in the Wall Framing Plan (page 107). We completely assembled and squared all four walls before raising and anchoring them.

**Frame the back wall(s)** following the Back Side Framing (page 107). Use pressure-treated lumber for the bottom plate, and nail it to the studs with galvanized 16d common nails. All of the standard studs are 92⅝" long. Square the wall, then add 1 × 4 let-in bracing.

**Raise the back wall** and anchor it to the foundation J-bolts with washers and nuts. Brace the wall upright. Frame and raise the remaining walls one at a time, then tie all of the walls together with double top plates. Cover the outside of the walls with T1-11 siding.

(continued)

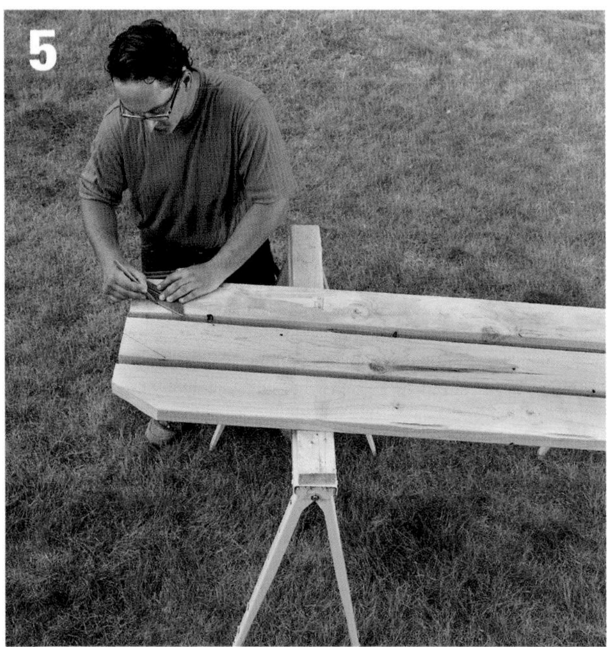


**Cut fifteen 2 × 6 attic floor joists** at 142¾". Cut the top corner at both ends of each joist: Mark 1⅞" along the top edge and 15⁄16" down the end; connect the marks, then cut along the line. Clipping the corner prevents the joist from extending above the rafters.

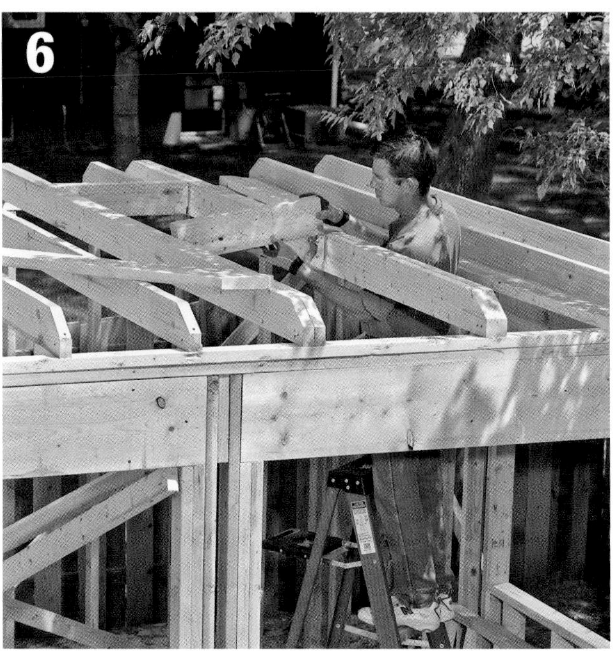


**Mark the joist layout** onto the wall plates following the Attic Floor Joist Framing (page 108). Leave 3½" between the outsides of the end walls and the outer joists. Toenail the joists to the plates with three 8d common nails at each end. Frame the rough opening for the staircase with doubled side joists and doubled headers; fasten doubled members together with pairs of 10d nails every 16". Install the drop-down staircase unit following the manufacturer's instructions.

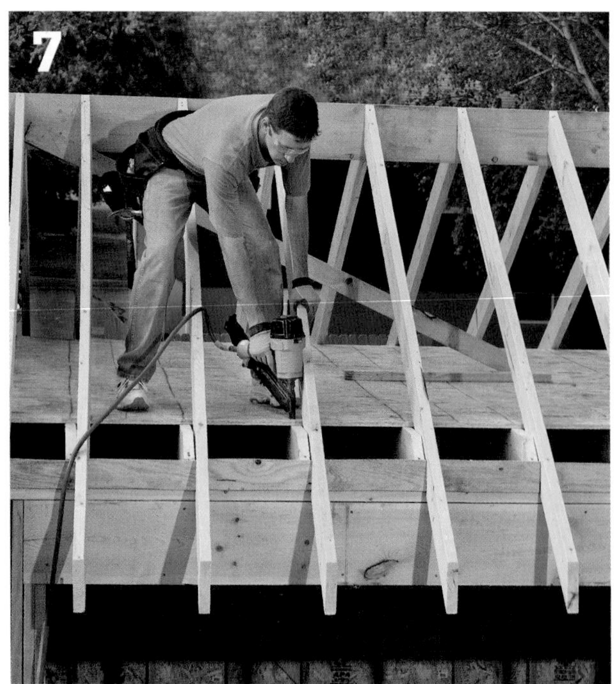


**Cover the attic floor** with ½" plywood, fastening it to the joists with 8d nails.

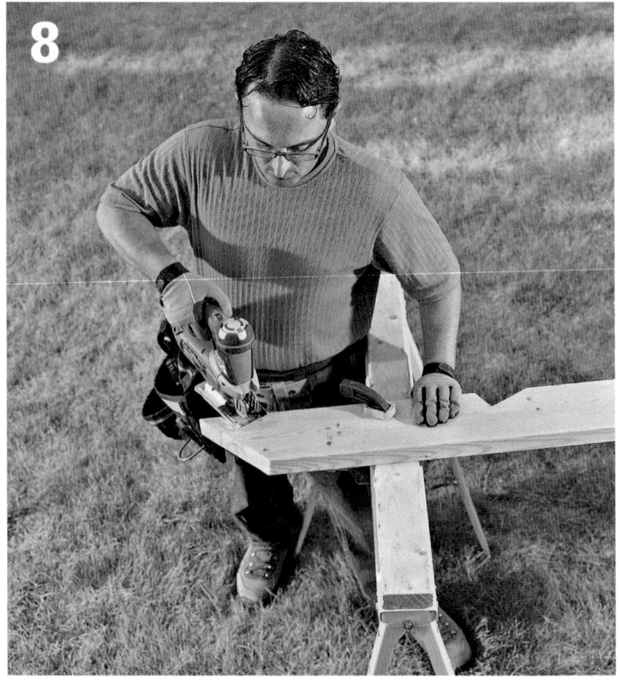


**Use the Rafter Template** (page 110) to mark and cut two pattern rafters. Test-fit the rafters and adjust the cuts as needed. Cut all (24) standard rafters. Cut four special rafters with an extra birdsmouths cut for the box bay. Cut four gable overhang rafters—these have no birdsmouths cuts.

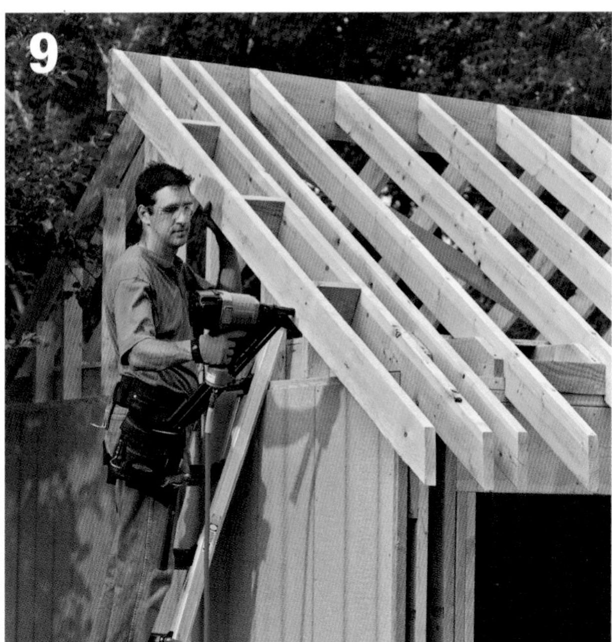


**Cut the 2 × 8 ridgeboard** at 206¾". Mark the rafter layout on the ridge and wall plates as shown in the Front Side Framing (page 108) and Back Side Framing (page 107). Frame the roof following the steps on pages 46 to 51. Install 6½"-long lookouts 24" on center, then attach the overhang rafters. Fasten the attic joists to the rafters with three 10d nails at each end.

**Mark the stud layout** for the gable end walls onto the end wall plates following the Side Framing (page 107). Transfer the layout to the rafters, using a level. Cut each of the 2 × 4 studs to fit, mitering the top ends at 33.5°. Install the studs flush with the end walls.

**Construct the 2 × 4 half wall** for the interior apron beneath the box bay. Cut two plates at 60" (pressure-treated lumber for bottom plate); cut five studs at 32½". Fasten one stud at each end, and space the remaining studs evenly in between. Mark a layout line 12" from the inside of the shed's front wall (see the Building Section page 105). Anchor the half wall to the slab using masonry screws or a powder-actuated nailer.

**Cut six 2 × 6 joists** at 36½". Toenail the joists to the inner and outer half walls following the layout in the Box Bay Window Framing (page 108); the joists should extend 15" past the outer shed wall. Add a 60"-long 2 × 4 sill plate at the ends of the joists. Cut two 2 × 4 side studs to extend from the sill plate to the top edges of the rafters (angle top ends at 33.5°), and install them. Install a built-up 2 × 4 header between the side studs 41⅜" above the sill plate.

(continued)

**Install a 2 × 2 nailer** ½" up from the bottom of the 2 × 4 bay header. Cover the top and bottom of the bay with ½" plywood as shown in the Box Bay Window Detail on page 110. Cut a 2 × 4 stud to fit between the plywood panels at each end of the 2 × 4 shed wall header. Fasten these to the studs supporting the studs and the header.

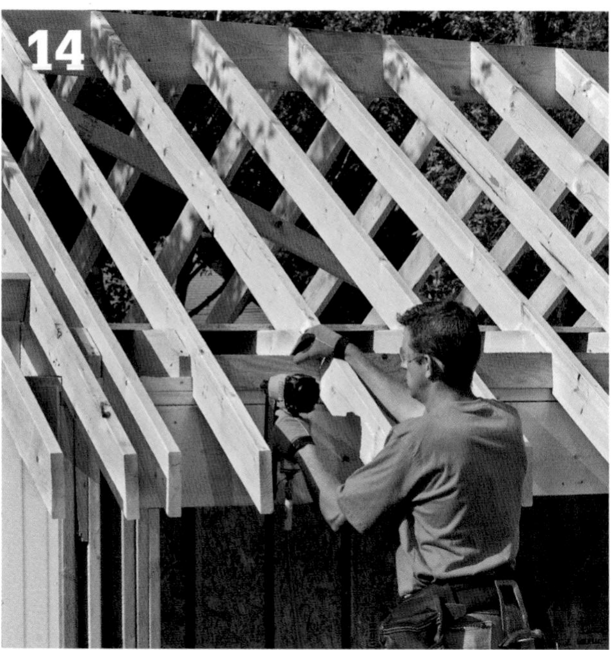


**Bevel the side edge** of the 2 × 6 blocking stock at 33.5°. Cut individual blocks to fit between the rafters and attic joists, and install them to seal off the rafter bays. See the Overhead Door Header (page 109). The blocks should be flush with the tops of the rafters. Custom-cut 2 × 8 blocking to enclose the rafter bays above the box bay header. See the Box Bay Window Detail on page 110.

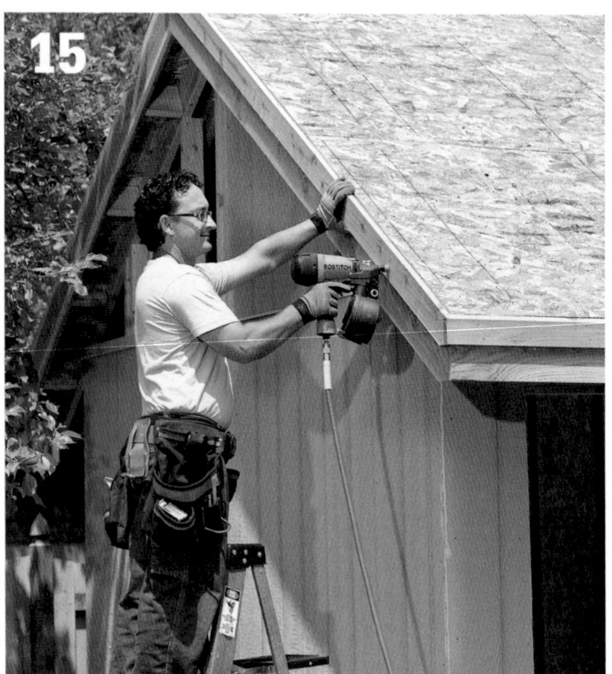


**Add 2 × 8 fascia to the ends of the rafters** along each eave so the top outer edge is flush with the top of the roof sheathing. Cover the gable overhang rafters with 1 × 8 fascia. Add 1 × 2 trim to serve as a drip edge along the eaves and gable ends so it will be flush with the top of the roof sheathing.

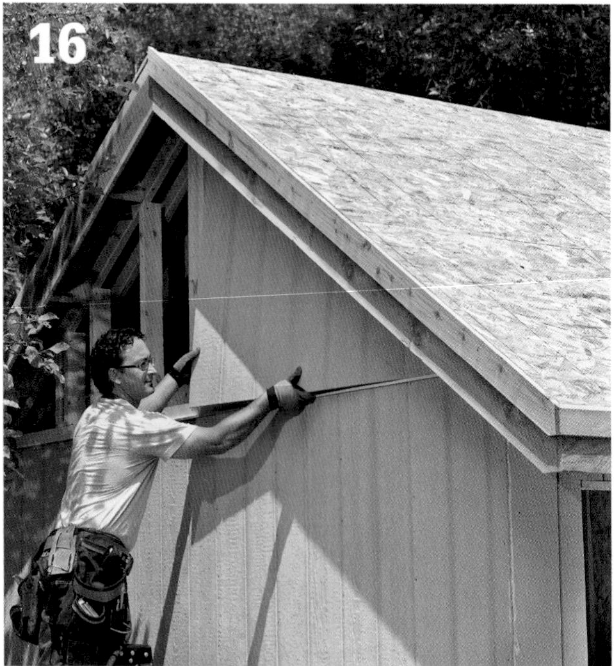


**Add Z-flashing above the first row** of siding, then cut and fit T1-11 siding for the gable ends. Cover the horizontal seam with 1 × 4 trim snugged up against the flashing.

**To complete the trim details,** add 1 × 2 along the gable ends and sides of the box bay. Use 1 × 4 on all vertical corners and around the windows, service door, and overhead door. Rip down 1 × 10s for horizontal trim along the bottom of the box bay. Also cover underneath the bay joists with ½" exterior-grade plywood.

**Rip cut 1 × 6 boards** to 4⅛" wide for the overhead door jambs. Install the jambs using the door manufacturer's dimensions for the opening. Shim behind the jambs if necessary. Make sure the jambs are flush with the inside of the wall framing and extend ⅝" beyond the outside of the framing. Install the 2 × 6 trim as shown in the Overhead Door Header and Overhead Door Jamb on page 109.

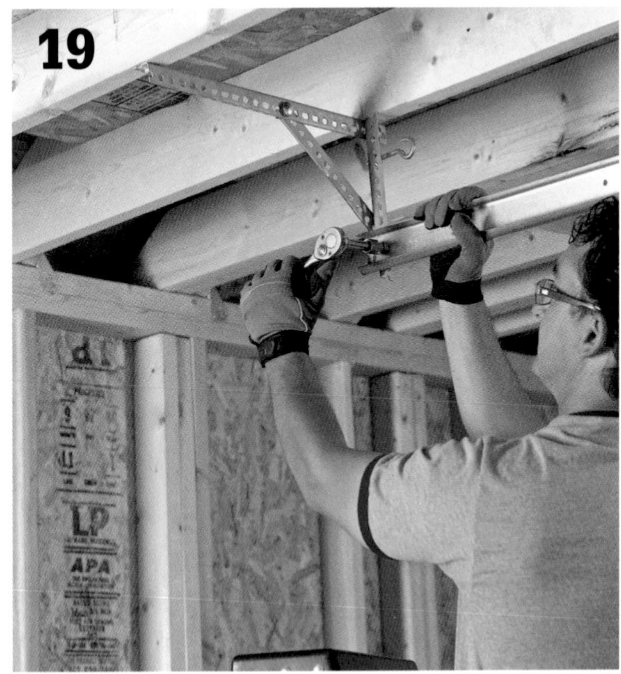


**Install the two windows and the service door** following the manufacturers' instructions. Position the jambs of the units so they will be flush with the siding, if applicable. Install the overhead door, then add stop molding along the top and side jambs. See the Service Door Header/Jamb Detail on page 109.

**Install ½" plywood roof sheathing** starting at the bottom ends of the rafters. Add building paper and asphalt shingles following the steps on pages 62 to 67.

# Gambrel Garage

Following classic barn designs, this 12 × 12-foot garage has several features that also make it a workshop. The garage's 144-square-foot floor is a poured concrete slab with a thickened edge that allows it to serve as the building's foundation. Designed for economy and durability, the floor can easily support heavy machinery, woodworking tools, and recreational vehicles.

The garage's sectional overhead door makes for quick access to equipment and supplies and provides plenty of air and natural light for working inside. The door opening is sized for an 8-foot-wide × 7-foot-tall door, but you can buy any size or style of door you like—just make your door selection before you start framing the garage.

Another important design feature of this building is its gambrel roof, which maximizes the usable interior space (see next page). Beneath the roof is a sizeable storage attic with 315 cubic feet of space and its own double doors above the garage door. *Note: We added a patio section to the front of this garage. This optional slab will appear throughout the how-to photos.*

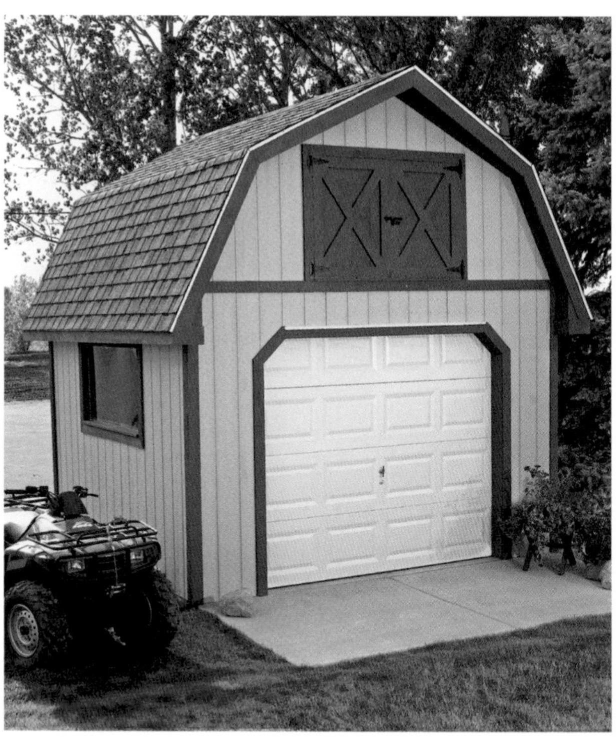

## The Gambrel Roof ▸

The gambrel roof is the defining feature of two structures in American architecture: the barn and the Dutch Colonial house. Adopted from earlier English buildings, the gambrel style became popular in America during the early seventeenth century and was used on homes and farm buildings throughout the Atlantic region. Today, the gambrel roof remains a favorite detail for designers of sheds, garages, and carriage houses.

The basic gambrel shape has two flat planes on each side, with the lower plane sloped much more steeply than the upper. More elaborate versions incorporate a flared eave known as a Dutch kick, that was often extended to shelter the front and rear façades of the building. Barns typically feature an extended peak at the front, sheltering the doors of the hayloft. The main advantage of the gambrel roof is the increased space underneath the roof, providing additional headroom for upper floors in homes or extra storage space in outbuildings.

## Cutting List ▸

| Description | Quantity/Size | Material |
|---|---|---|
| **Foundation** | | |
| Drainage material | 1.75 cu. yd. | Compactible gravel |
| Concrete slab | 2.5 cu. yd. | 3,000 psi concrete |
| Mesh | 144 sq. ft. | 6 × 6", W1.4 × W1.4 welded wire mesh |
| **Wall Framing** | | |
| Bottom plates | 4 @ 12' | 2 × 4 pressure treated |
| Top plates | 8 @ 12' | 2 × 4 |
| Studs | 47 @ 92⅝" | 2 × 4 |
| Headers | 2 @ 10', 2 @ 6' | 2 × 8 |
| Header spacers | 1 @ 9', 1 @ 6' | ½" plywood—7" wide |
| Angle braces | 1 @ 4' | 2 × 4 |
| **Gable Wall Framing** | | |
| Plates | 2 @ 10' | 2 × 4 |
| Studs | 7 @ 10' | 2 × 4 |
| Header | 2 @ 6' | 2 × 6 |
| Header spacer | 1 @ 5' | ½" plywood—5" wide |
| **Attic Floor** | | |
| Joists | 10 @ 12' | 2 × 6 |
| Floor sheathing | 3 sheets @ 4 × 8' | ¾" tongue & groove exterior-grade plywood |
| **Kneewall Framing** | | |
| Bottom plates | 2 @ 12' | 2 × 4 |
| Top plates | 4 @ 12' | 2 × 4 |
| Studs | 8 @ 10' | 2 × 4 |
| Nailers | 2 @ 14' | 2 × 8 |
| **Roof Framing** | | |
| Rafters | 28 @ 10' | 2 × 4 |
| Metal anchors—rafters | 20, with nails | Simpson H2.5 |
| Collar ties | 2 @ 6' | 2 × 4 |
| Ridgeboard | 1 @ 14' | 2 × 6 |
| Lookouts | 1 @ 10' | 2 × 4 |
| Soffit ledgers | 2 @ 14' | 2 × 4 |
| Soffit blocking | 6 @ 8' | 2 × 4 |
| **Exterior Finishes** | | |
| Plywood siding | 14 sheets @ 4 × 8' | ⅝" Texture 1-11 plywood, grooves 8" O. C. |
| Z-flashing—siding | 2 pieces @ 12' | Galvanized 18-gauge |
| Horizontal wall trim | 2 @ 12' | 1 × 4 cedar |
| Corner trim | 8 @ 8' | 1 × 4 cedar |
| Fascia | 6 @ 10', 2 @ 8' | 1 × 6 cedar |
| Subfascia | 4 @ 8' | 1 × 4 pine |
| Plywood soffit | 1 sheet @ 10' | ⅜" cedar or fir plywood |
| Soffit vents | 4 @ 4 × 12" | Louver w/ bug screen |
| Z-flashing—garage door | 1 @ 10' | Galvanized 18-gauge |

| Description | Quantity/Size | Material |
|---|---|---|
| **Roofing** | | |
| Roof sheathing | 12 sheets @ 4 × 8' | ½" plywood |
| Shingles | 3 squares | 250# per square (min.) |
| 15# building paper | 300 sq. ft. | |
| Metal drip edge | 2 @ 14', 2 @ 12' | Galvanized metal |
| Roof vents (optional) | 2 units | |
| **Window** | | |
| Frame | 3 @ 6' | ¾ × 4" (actual) S4S cedar |
| Stops | 4 @ 8' | 1 × 2 S4S cedar |
| Glazing tape | 30 lin. ft. | |
| Glass | 1 piece—field measure | ¼" clear, tempered |
| Exterior trim | 3 @ 6' | 1 × 4 S4S cedar |
| Interior trim (optional) | 3 @ 6' | 1 × 2 S4S cedar |
| **Door** | | |
| Frame | 3 @ 8' | 1 × 6 S4S cedar |
| Door sill | 1 @ 6' | 1 × 6 S4S cedar |
| Stops | 1 @ 8', 1 @ 6' | 1 × 2 S4S cedar |
| Panel material | 4 @ 8' | 1 × 8 T&G V-joint S4S cedar |
| Door X-brace/panel trim | 4 @ 6', 2 @ 8' | 1 × 4 S4S cedar |
| Exterior trim | 1 @ 8', 1 @ 6' | 1 × 4 S4S cedar |
| Interior trim (optional) | 1 @ 8', 1 @ 6' | 1 × 2 S4S cedar |
| Strap hinges | 4 | |
| **Garage Door** | | |
| Frame | 3 @ 8' | 1 × 8 S4S cedar |
| Door | 1 @ 8' × 6' - 8" | Sectional flush door w/2" track |
| Rails | 2 @ 8' | 2 × 6 |
| Trim | 3 @ 8' | 1 × 4 S4S cedar |
| **Fasteners** | | |
| Anchor bolts | 16 | ⅜" × 8", with washers & nuts, galvanized |
| 16d galvanized common nails | 2 lb. | |
| 16d common nails | 17 lb. | |
| 10d common nails | 2 lb. | |
| 10d galvanized casing nails | 1 lb. | |
| 8d common nails | 3 lb. | |
| 8d galvanized finish nails | 6 lb. | |
| 8d box nails | 6 lb. | |
| 6d galvanized finish nails | 20 nails | |
| 3d galvanized box nails | ½ lb. | |
| ⅞" galvanized roofing nails | 2½ lb. | |
| 2½" deck screws | 24 screws | |
| 1¼" wood screws | 48 screws | |
| Construction adhesive | 2 tubes | |
| Silicone-latex caulk | 2 tubes | |

# Building Section

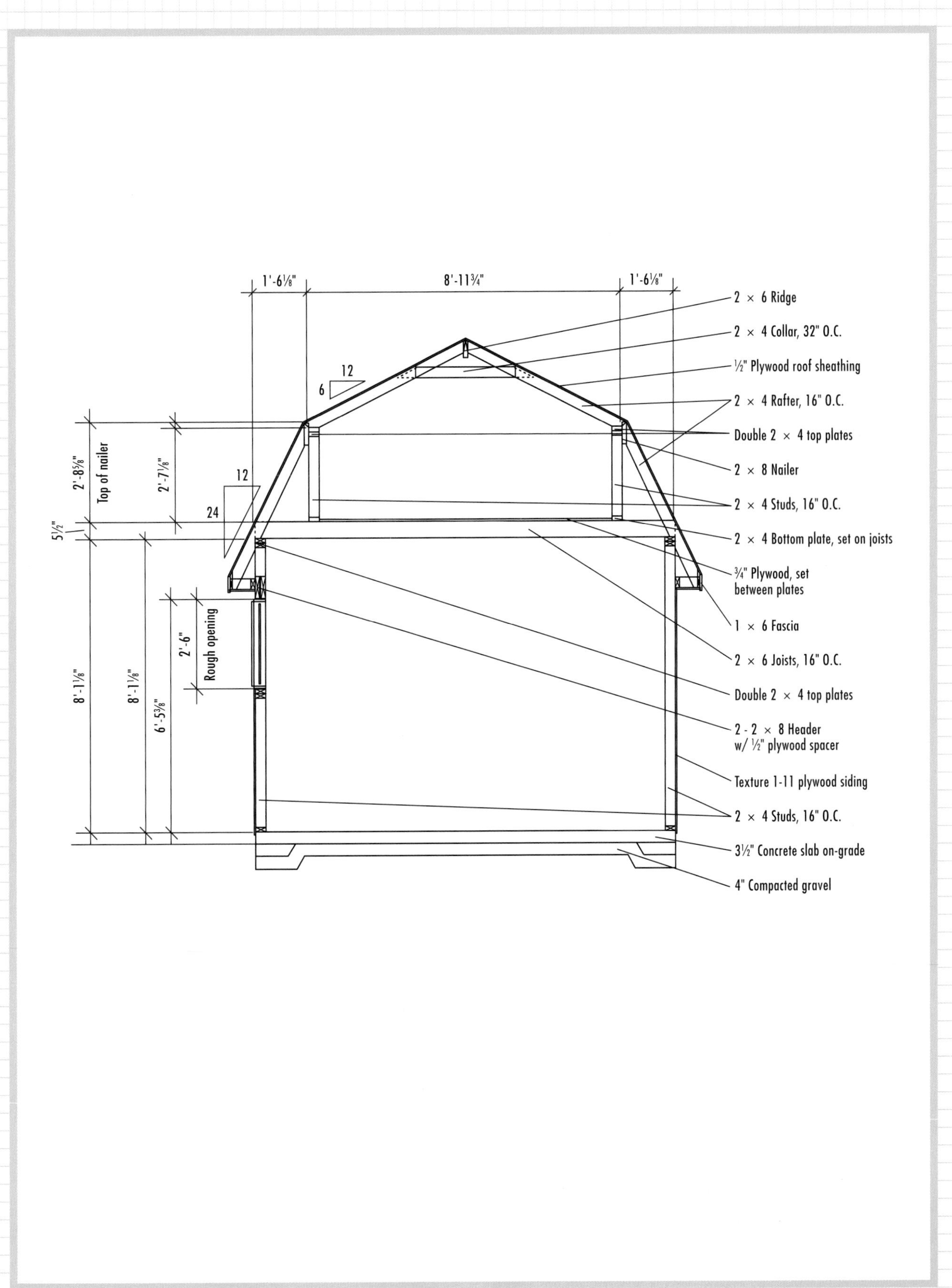

1'-6⅛"
8'-11¾"
1'-6⅛"
12
6
12
24
2'-8⅝"
Top of nailer
2'-7⅛"
5½"
2'-6"
Rough opening
8'-1⅛"
8'-1⅛"
6'-5⅜"
2 × 6 Ridge
2 × 4 Collar, 32" O.C.
½" Plywood roof sheathing
2 × 4 Rafter, 16" O.C.
Double 2 × 4 top plates
2 × 8 Nailer
2 × 4 Studs, 16" O.C.
2 × 4 Bottom plate, set on joists
¾" Plywood, set between plates
1 × 6 Fascia
2 × 6 Joists, 16" O.C.
Double 2 × 4 top plates
2 - 2 × 8 Header w/ ½" plywood spacer
Texture 1-11 plywood siding
2 × 4 Studs, 16" O.C.
3½" Concrete slab on-grade
4" Compacted gravel

## Floor Plan

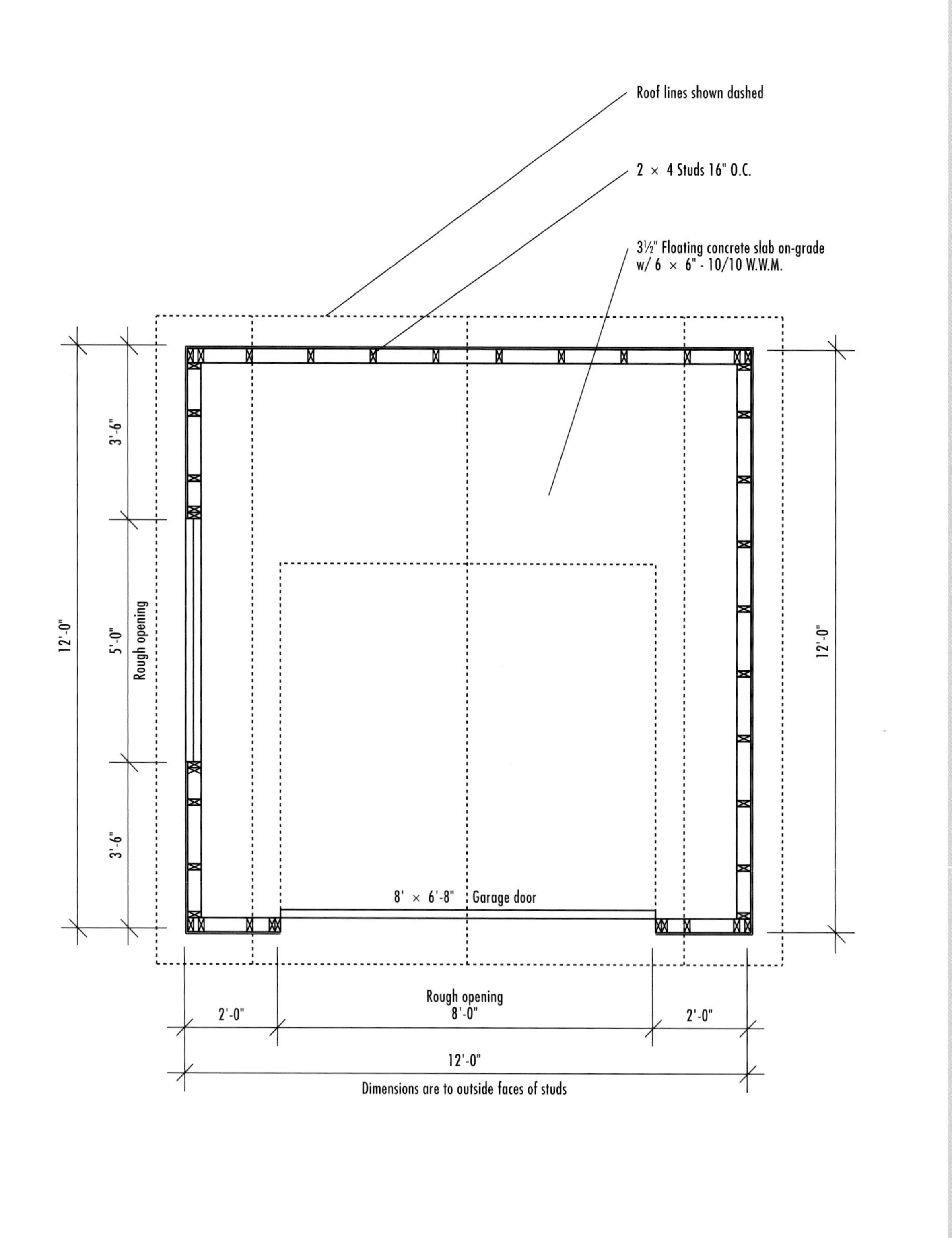

Roof lines shown dashed
2 × 4 Studs 16" O.C.
3½" Floating concrete slab on-grade w/ 6 × 6" - 10/10 W.W.M.
12'-0"
3'-6"
5'-0"
Rough opening
3'-6"
12'-0"
8' × 6'-8" Garage door
2'-0"
Rough opening 8'-0"
2'-0"
12'-0"
Dimensions are to outside faces of studs

## Rafter Templates

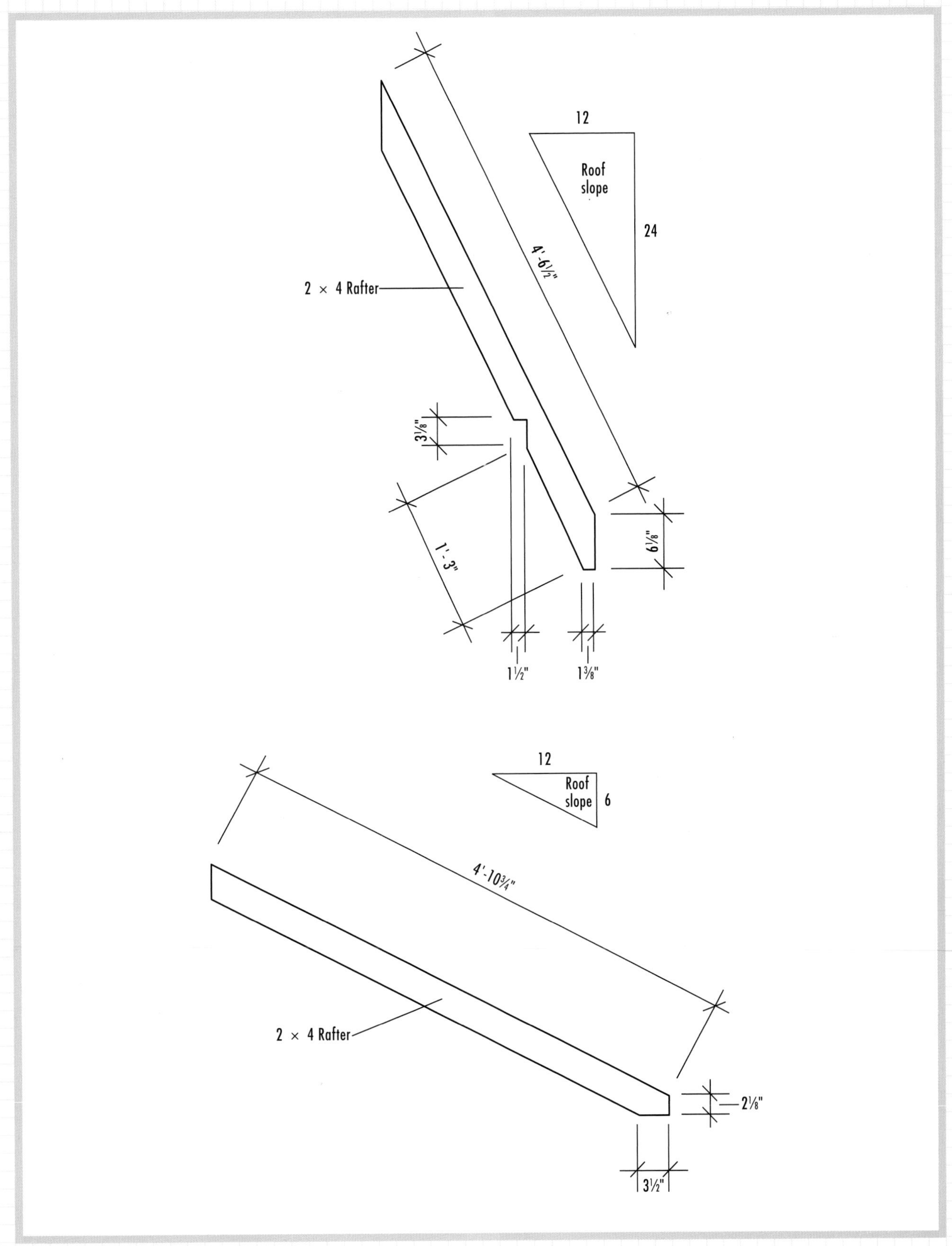

## Front Elevation

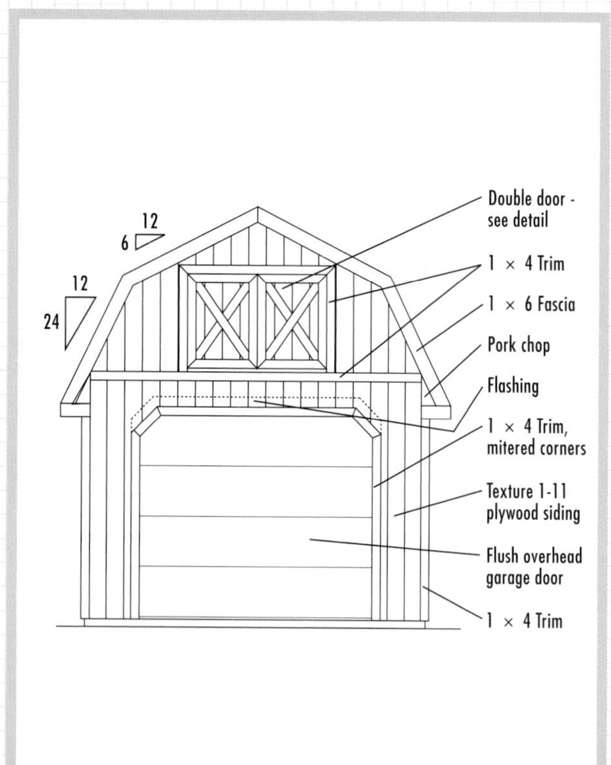


## Left Side Elevation

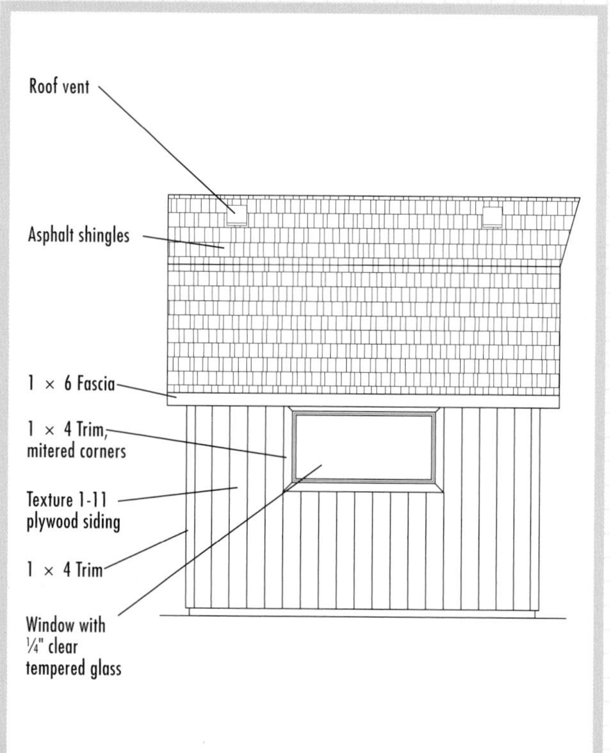


## Rear Elevation

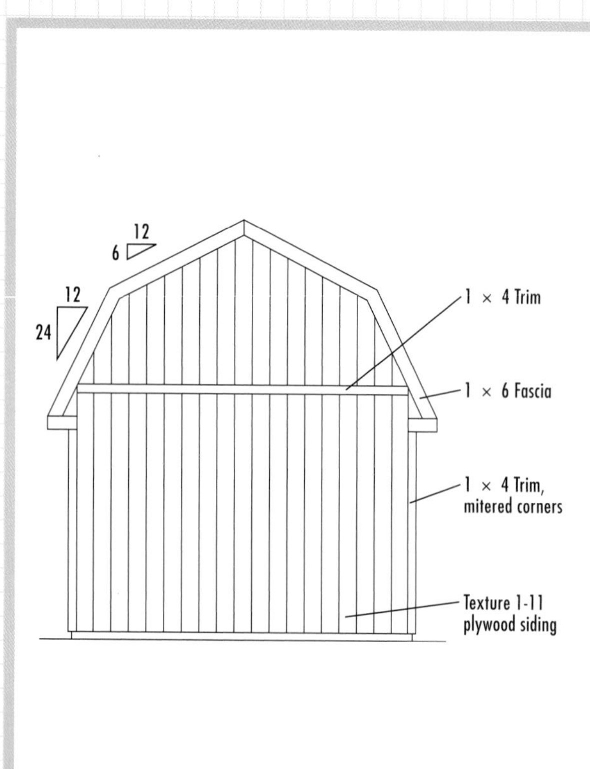


## Right Side Elevation

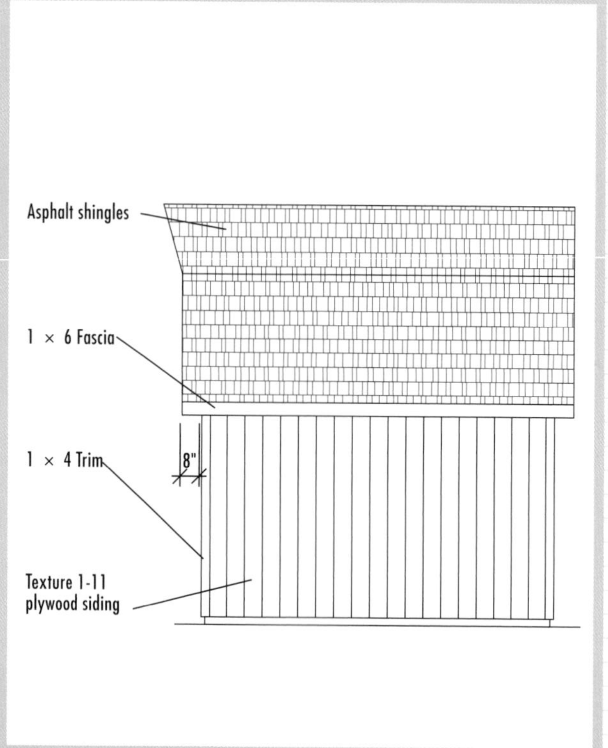

## Gable Overhang Detail

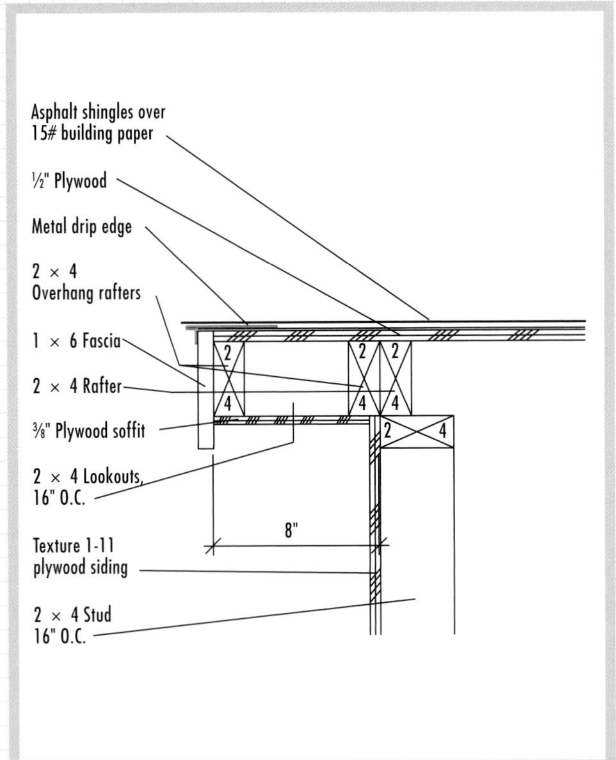


## Gable Overhang Rafter Details

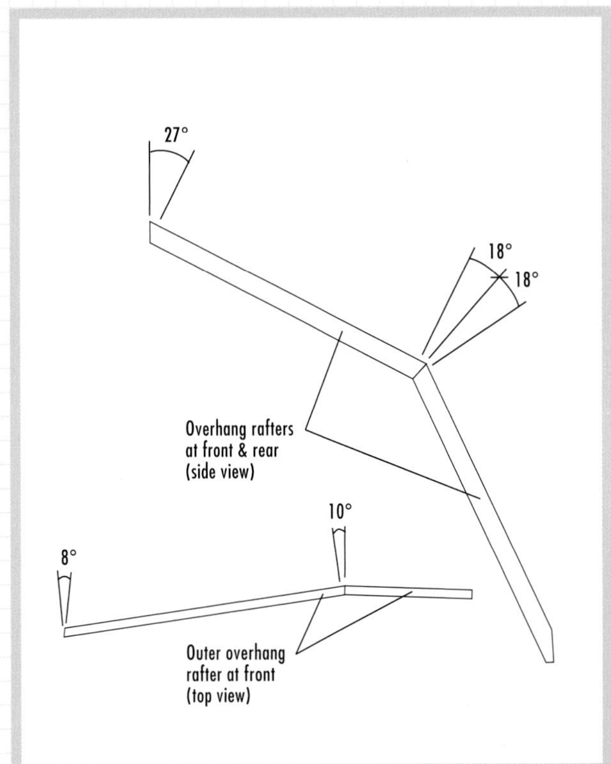


## Eave Detail

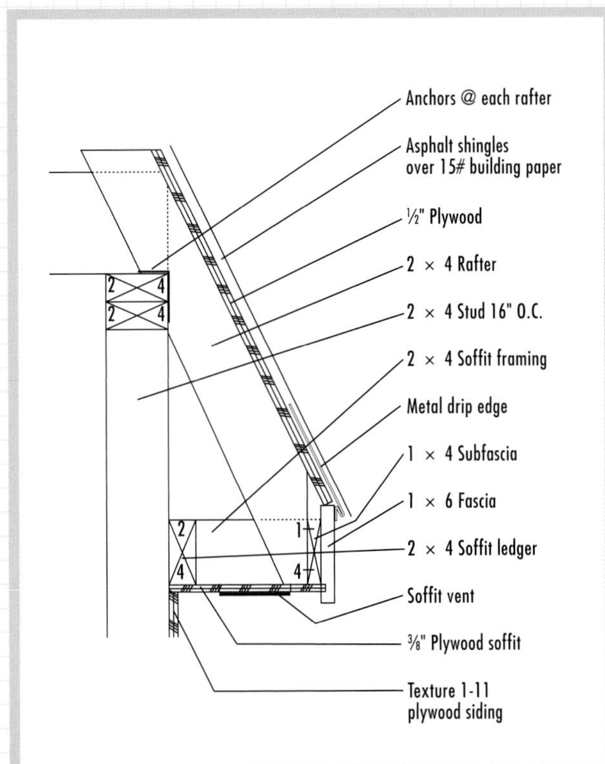


## Sill Detail

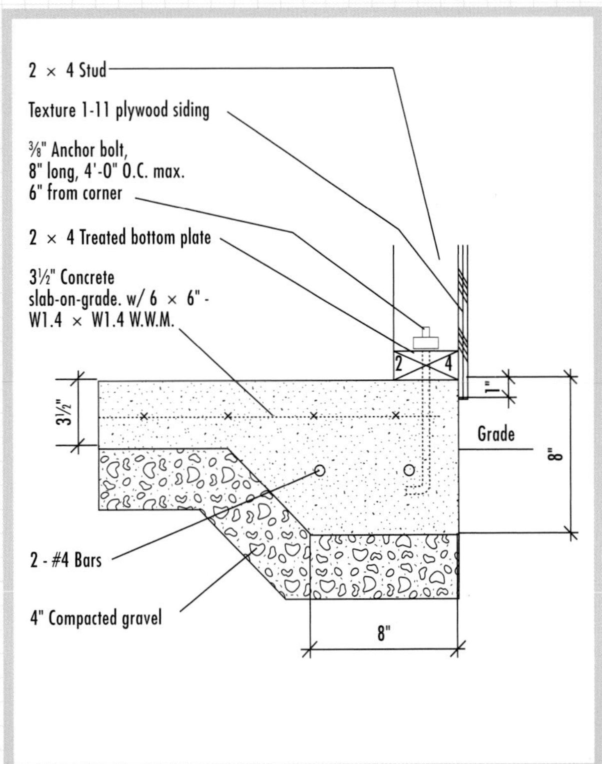

## Attic Door Elevation

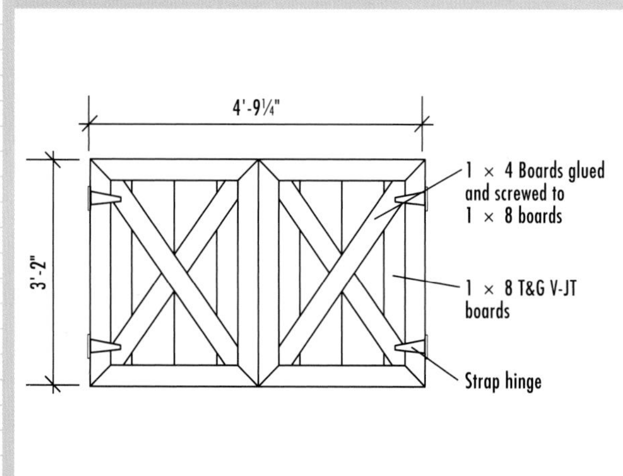


## Attic Door Jamb Detail

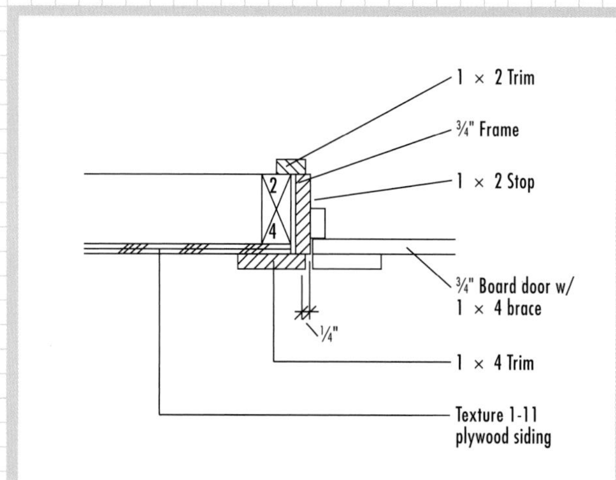


## Garage Door Trim Detail

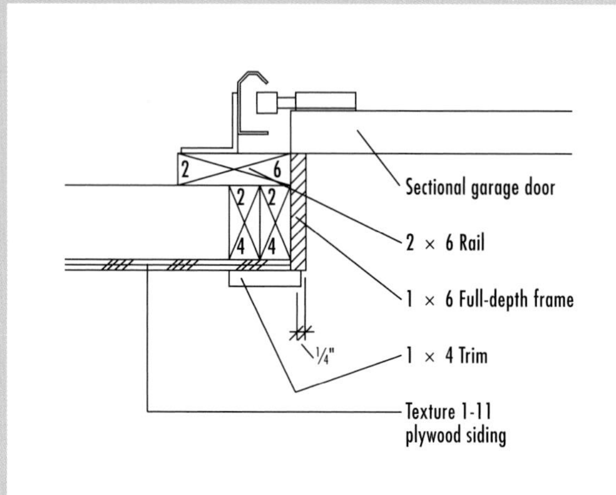


## Attic Door Sill Detail

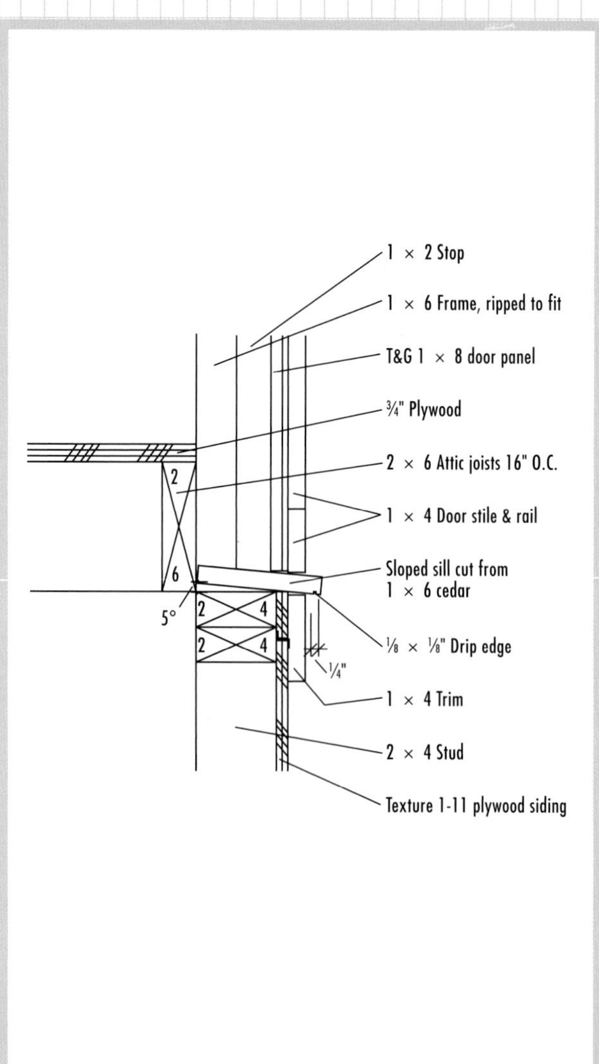


## Window Jamb Detail

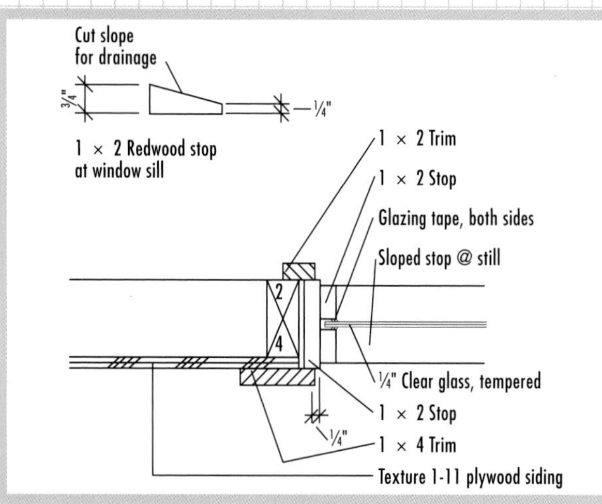

## Front Framing Elevation

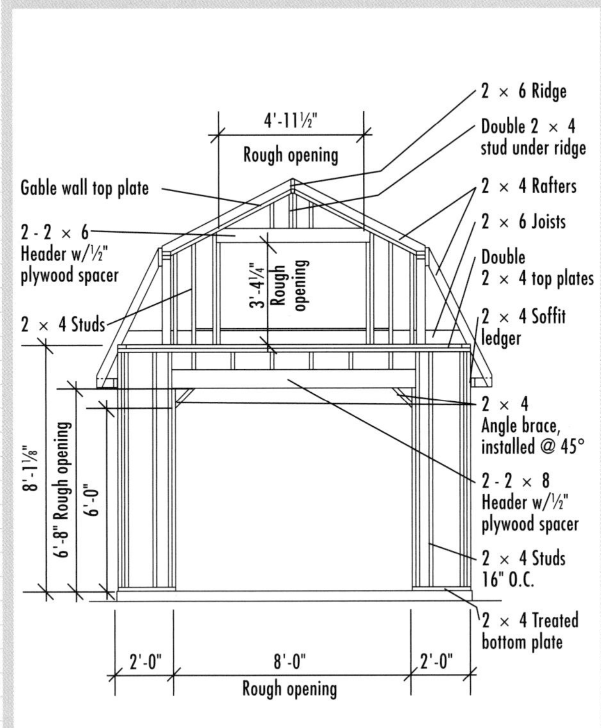


## Left Side Framing Elevation

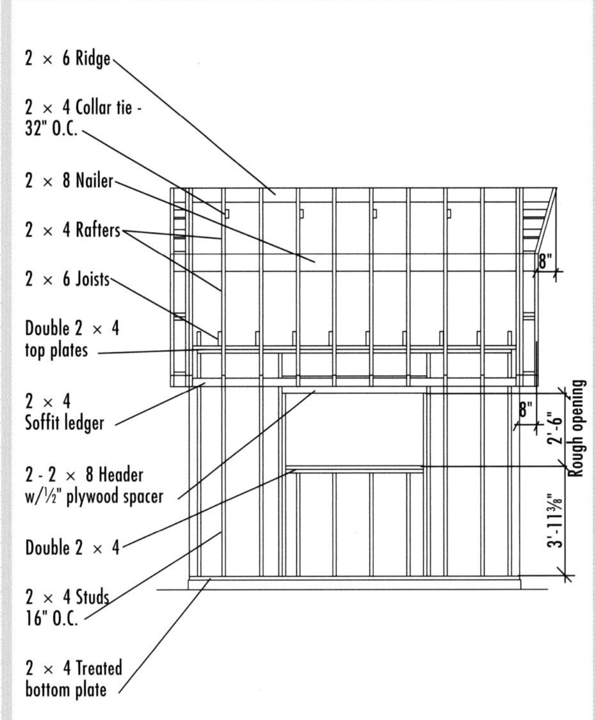


## Rear Framing Elevation

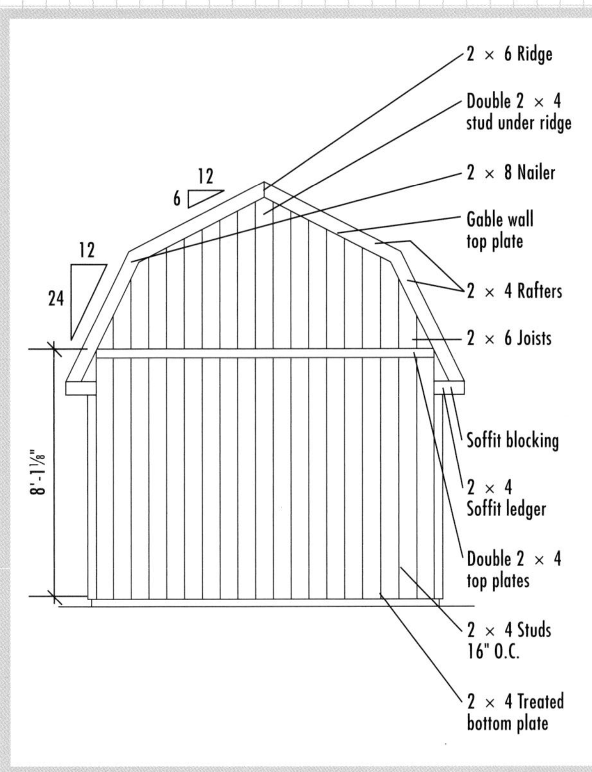


## Right Side Framing Elevation

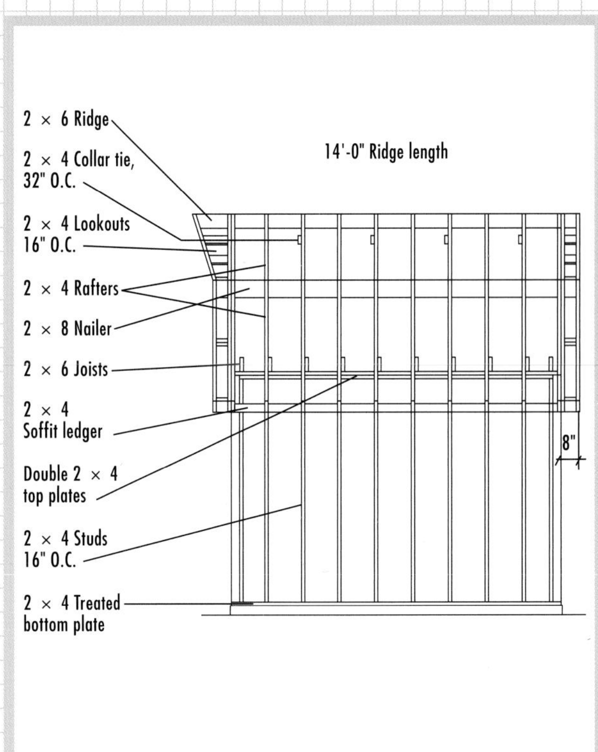

## How to Build the Gambrel Garage

**Build the slab foundation** at 144" × 144". Set J-bolts into the concrete 1¾" from the outer edges and extending 2½" from the surface. Set a bolt 6" from each corner and every 48" in between (except in the door opening). Let the slab cure for at least three days before you begin construction.

**Snap chalk lines on the slab** for the wall plates. Cut two bottom plates and two top plates at 137" for the sidewalls. Cut two bottom and two top plates at 144" for the front and rear walls. Use pressure-treated lumber for all bottom plates. Cut 38 studs at 92⅝", plus 2 jack studs for the garage door at 78½" and 2 window studs at 75⅞". *Note: Add the optional slab now, as desired.*

**Construct the built-up 2 × 8 headers** at 99" (garage door) and 63" (window). Frame, install, and brace the walls with double top plates one at a time following the Floor Plan (page 120) and Elevation drawings (page 122). Use galvanized nails to attach the studs to the sole plates. Anchor the walls to the J-bolts in the slab with galvanized washers and nuts.

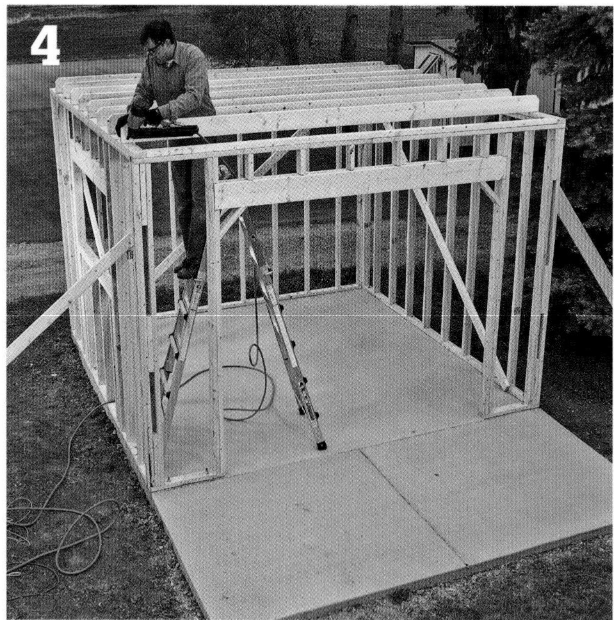

**Build the attic floor.** Cut ten 2 × 6 joists to 144" long, then clip each top corner with a 1½"-long, 45° cut. Install the joists as shown in the Framing Elevations drawings (page 125), leaving a 3½" space at the front and rear walls for the gable wall studs. Fasten the joists with three 8d nails at each end.

**Frame the attic knee walls.** Cut four top plates at 144" and two bottom plates at 137". Cut 20 studs at 26⅝" and 4 end studs at 33⅝". Lay out the plates so the studs fall over the attic joists. Frame the walls and install them 18⅛" from the ends of the joists, then add temporary bracing. *Option: You can begin building the roof frame by cutting two 2 × 8 nailers to 144" long. Fasten the nailers to the knee walls so their top edges are 32⅝" above the attic joists.*

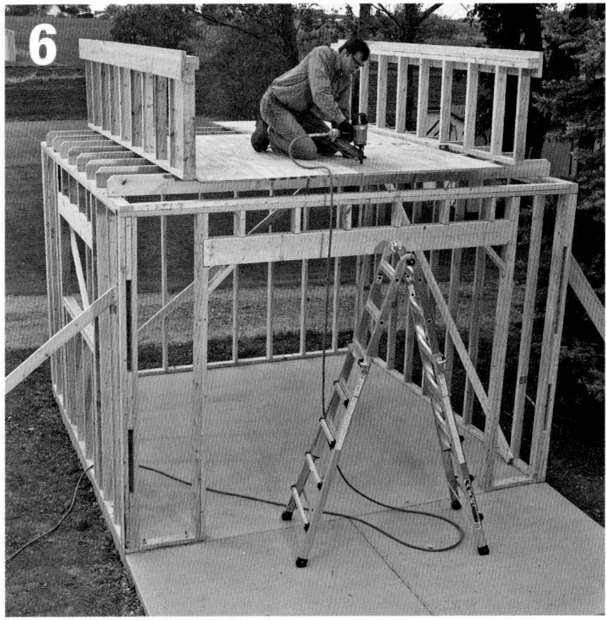


**Cover the attic floor between the knee walls** with ½" plywood. Run the sheets perpendicular to the joists, and stop them flush with the outer joists. Fasten the flooring with 8d ring-shank nails every 6" along the edges and every 12" in the field of the sheets.

**Mark the rafter layouts** onto the top and outside faces of the 2 × 8 nailers; see the Framing Elevations drawings (page 125).

**Cut the 2 × 6 ridgeboard** at 168", mitering the front end at 16°. Mark the rafter layout onto the ridge. The outer common rafters should be 16" from the front end and 8" from the rear end of the ridge.

(continued)

**Use the Rafter Templates** (page 121) to mark and cut two upper pattern rafters and one lower pattern rafter. Test-fit the rafters and make any needed adjustments. Use the patterns to mark and cut the remaining common rafters (20 total of each type). For the gable overhangs, cut an additional eight lower and six upper rafters following the Gable Overhang Rafter Details (page 123).

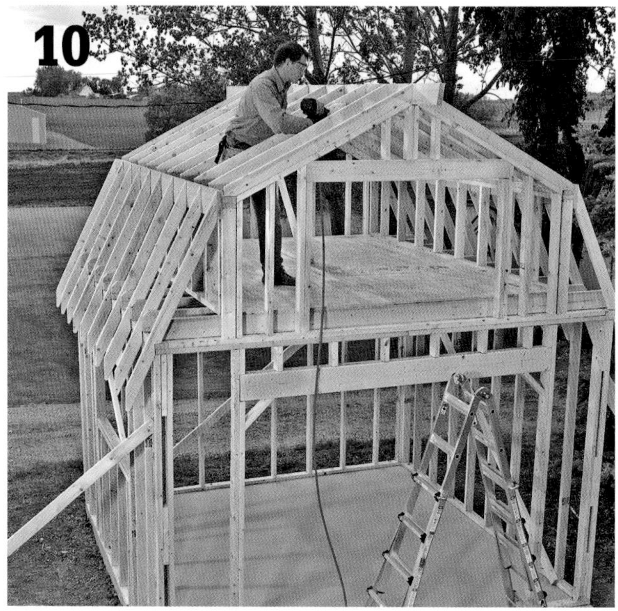


**Install the common rafters.** Then reinforce the joints at the knee walls with framing connectors. Also nail the attic joists to the sides of the floor rafters. Cut four 2 × 4 collar ties at 34", mitering the ends at 26.5°. Fasten them between pairs of upper rafters, as shown in the Building Section (page 119) and Framing Elevations drawing (page 125).

**Snap a chalk line across the sidewall studs,** level with the ends of the rafters. Cut two 2 × 4 soffit ledgers at 160" and fasten them to the studs on top of the chalk lines with their ends overhanging the walls by 8". Cut twenty-four 2 × 4 blocks to fit between the ledger and rafter ends, as shown in the Eave Detail (page 123). Install the blocks.

**Frame the gable overhangs.** Cut twelve 2 × 4 lookouts at 5" and nail them to the inner overhang rafters as shown in the Left and Right Side Framing Elevations (page 122). Install the inner overhang rafters over the common rafters using 10d nails. Cut the two front (angled) overhang rafters; see the Gable Overhang Rafter Details (page 123). Install those rafters; then add two custom-cut lookouts for each rafter.

**To complete the gable walls,** cut top plates to fit between the ridge and the attic knee walls. Install the plates flush with the outer common rafters. Mark the stud layout onto the walls and gable top plate. See the Front and Rear Framing Elevations (page 125). Cut the gable studs to fit and install them. Construct the built-up 2 × 6 attic door header at 62½"; then clip the top corners to match the roof slope. Install the header with jack studs cut at 40¼".

**Install siding on the walls,** holding it 1" below the top of the concrete slab. Add Z-flashing along the top edges, and then continue the siding up to the rafters. Below the attic door opening, stop the siding about ¼" below the top wall plate. As shown in the Attic Door Sill Detail (page 124). Don't nail the siding to the garage door header until the flashing is installed.

**Mill a ⅜"-wide × ¼"-deep groove** into the 1 × 6 boards for the horizontal fascia along the eaves and gable ends (about 36 lin. ft.); see the Eave Detail (page 123). Use a router or table saw with a dado-head blade to mill the groove, and make the groove ⅞" above the bottom edge of the fascia.

**Install the 1 × 4 subfascia along the eaves,** keeping the bottom edge flush with the ends of the rafters and the ends flush with the outsides of the outermost rafters. Add the milled fascia at the eaves, aligning the top of the groove with the bottom of the subfascia. Cut fascia to wrap around the overhangs at the gable ends but don't install them until step 17.

(continued)

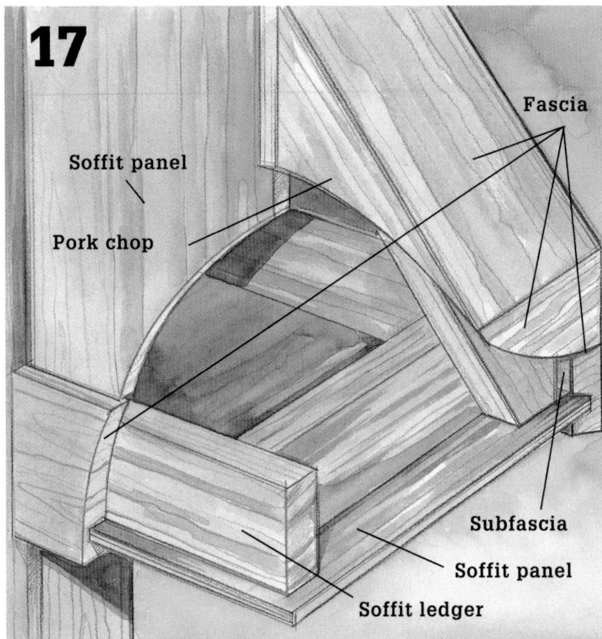


**Add fascia at the gable ends,** holding it up ½" to be flush with the roof sheathing. Cut soffit panels to fit between the fascia and walls, and fasten them with 3d galvanized nails. Install the end and return fascia pieces at the gable overhangs. Enclose each overhang at the corners with a triangular piece of grooved fascia (called a pork chop) and a piece of soffit material. Install the soffit vents as shown in the Eave Detail (page 123).

**Sheath the roof** starting at one of the lower corners. Add metal drip edge along the eaves, followed by building paper; then add drip edge along the gable ends over the paper. Install the asphalt shingles (see pages 63 to 66). Plan the courses so the roof transition occurs midshingle, not between courses; the overlapping shingles will relax over time. If desired, add roof vents (pages 66 to 67).

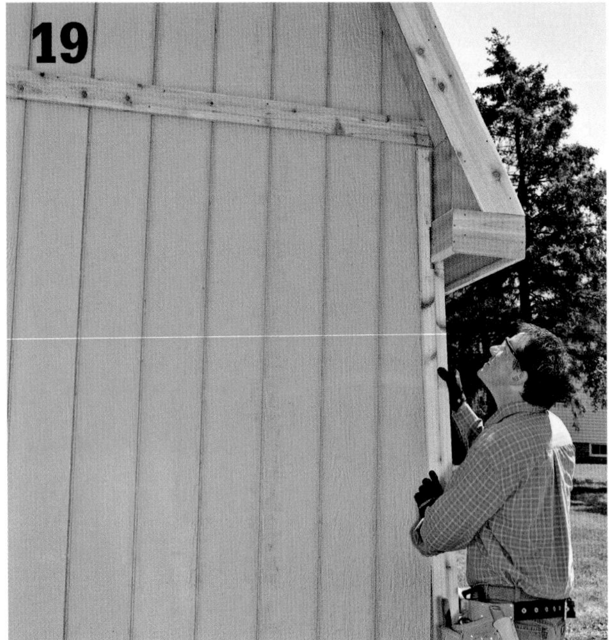


**Cover the Z-flashing at the rear wall** with horizontal 1 × 4 trim. Finish the four wall corners with overlapping vertical 1 × 4 trim. Install the 2 × 6 rails that will support the garage door tracks following the door manufacturer's instructions to determine the sizing and placement; see the Garage Door Trim Detail (page 124).

**For the garage door frame,** rip 1 × 8 trim boards to width so they cover the front wall siding and 2 × 6 rails, as shown in the Garage Door Trim Detail (page 124). Install the trim, mitering the pieces at 22.5°. Install the 1 × 4 trim around the outside of the opening, adding flashing along the top. See the Front Elevation (page 122).

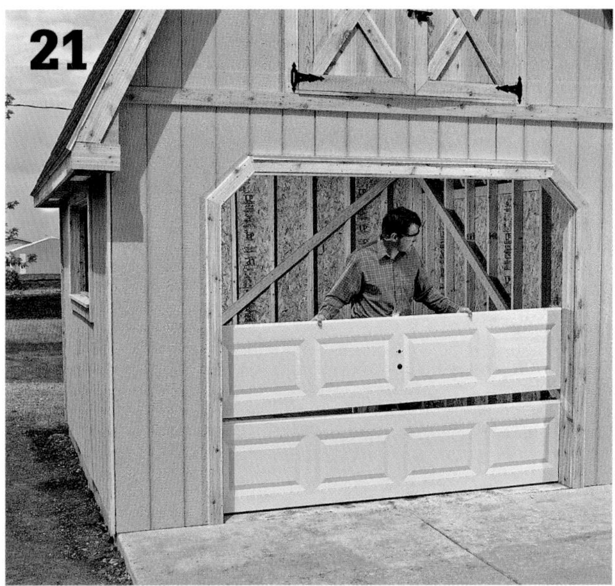


**Install the garage door in the door opening** following the manufacturer's directions.

**Build the window frame,** which should be ½" narrower and shorter than the rough opening. Install the frame using shims and 10d galvanized casing nails, as shown in the Window Jamb Detail (page 124). Cut eight 1 × 2 stop pieces to fit the frame. Bevel the outer sill stop for drainage. Order glass to fit or cut your own plastic panel. Install the glazing and stops using glazing tape for a watertight seal. Add the window trim.

**For the attic door frame,** rip 1 × 6s to match the depth of the opening and cut the head jamb and side jambs. Cut the sill from full-width 1 × 6 stock; then cut a kerf for a drip edge (see the Attic Door Sill Detail, page 124). Fasten the head jamb to the side jambs and install the sill at a 5° slope between the side jambs. Install the door frame using shims and 10d casing nails. Add shims or cedar shingles along the length of the sill to provide support underneath. The front edge of the frame should be flush with the face of the siding. Add 1 × 2 stops at the frame sides and top ¾" from the front edges.

**Build the attic doors** as shown in the Attic Door Elevation (page 124), using glue and 1¼" screws. Each door measures 28⅝" × 38", including the panel braces. Cut the 1 × 8 panel boards about ⅛" short along the bottom to compensate for the sloping sill. Install the door with two hinges each. Add 1 × 4 horizontal trim on the front wall up against the doorsill; then trim around both sides of the door frame. Prime and paint as desired.

# Carport

A carport provides a low-cost alternative to a garage, protecting your vehicle from direct rain, snow, and sunlight. Because it is not an enclosed structure, a carport is not held to the same building restrictions as a garage. This carport plan provides a 10 × 16-foot coverage area that is large enough to accommodate most full-size vehicles. To help ease the building process, premanufactured trusses are used. When ordering trusses, specify the roof pitch, distance being spanned, and the amount of overhang of the rafter tails. Also, place your order a few weeks in advance of your project start date. Many home centers and lumber yards carry in-stock trusses in standard dimensions and roof pitches, such as a 10-foot span with a 6-in-12 pitch—the dimensions used in this project.

This project also features metal roofing panels, an attractive and easy-to-install roofing material that does not require a roof deck. The trusses are tied together with 2 × 4 purlins, which also provide nailers for the metal roof panels. The panels are fastened with self-tapping metal roofing screws with rubber washers to prevent water leakage. Because of the scale of this project, recruit the help of at least one other person.

**A carport** is faster, easier, and cheaper to build than a full garage, but the storage and security benefits these structures offer are more limited.

## Materials & Cutting List ▸

| Description | Quantity/Size | Material |
|---|---|---|
| **Foundation** | | |
| Batterboards/braces | 10 @ 8'-0" | 2 × 4 |
| Drainage material | 1⅔ cu. ft. | Compactible gravel |
| Concrete tube forms | 6 @ 14"-dia. | |
| Concrete | field measure | 3,000 psi concrete |
| **Beam Framing** | | |
| Posts (6) | 6 @ 12' | 6 × 6 rough-sawn cedar |
| Side beams (4) | 4 @ 16' | 2 × 8 pressure treated |
| End beams (2) | 2 @ 12' | 2 × 8 pressure treated |
| Lateral beams (4) | 4 @ 10' | 2 × 8 pressure treated |
| Diagonal supports (8) | 4 @ 8' | 4 × 4 cedar |
| **Roof Framing** | | |
| Gable braces (8) | 4 @ 10', 2 @ 8' | 2 × 4 |
| Trusses, 2 end and 11 common (13) | 13 @ 10' span | 2 × 4 with 6-in-12 pitch |
| Purlins (10) | 20 @ 8' | 2 × 4 |
| Metal hurricane ties | 22, with nails | Simpson H-1 |
| Metal hurricane ties | 4, with nails | Simpson H-2.5 |
| **Roofing** | | |
| Metal roofing panels | 8 @ 4' × 8' | with ridge cap and sealer strip |
| Gable Finishes | | |
| Gable-end purlin blocking (16) | 3 @ 8' | 2 × 2 |
| Blocking (8) | 5 @10' | 1 × 6 |
| Gable sheathing (4) | 2 @ 4 × 8' | ¾" CDX plywood |
| Gable end fascia (4) | 4 @ 8' | 1 × 6 cedar |
| Side fascia (2) | 4 @ 10' | 1 × 8 cedar |
| **Siding** | | |
| Siding (14) | 14 @ 8' | cedar siding with 6" reveal |

| Description | Quantity/Size | Material |
|---|---|---|
| **Fasteners** | | |
| 1½" deck screws | | |
| 2½" deck screws | | |
| 6d galvanized common nails | | |
| 8d galvanized common nails | | |
| 8d joist hanger nails | | |
| 10d galvanized common nails | | |
| ⅜" x 4" galvanized lag screws | 48, with washers | |
| ⅜" x 5" galvanized lag screws | 12, with washers | |
| 10d ringshank nails | | |
| 6d galvanized casing nails | | |
| 6d siding nails | | |
| 1" self-tapping metal roofing screws with rubber washers (as specified by metal roofing manufacturer) | | |
| 2½" self-tapping metal roofing screws with rubber washers (as specified by metal roofing manufacturer) | | |

## Front Elevation

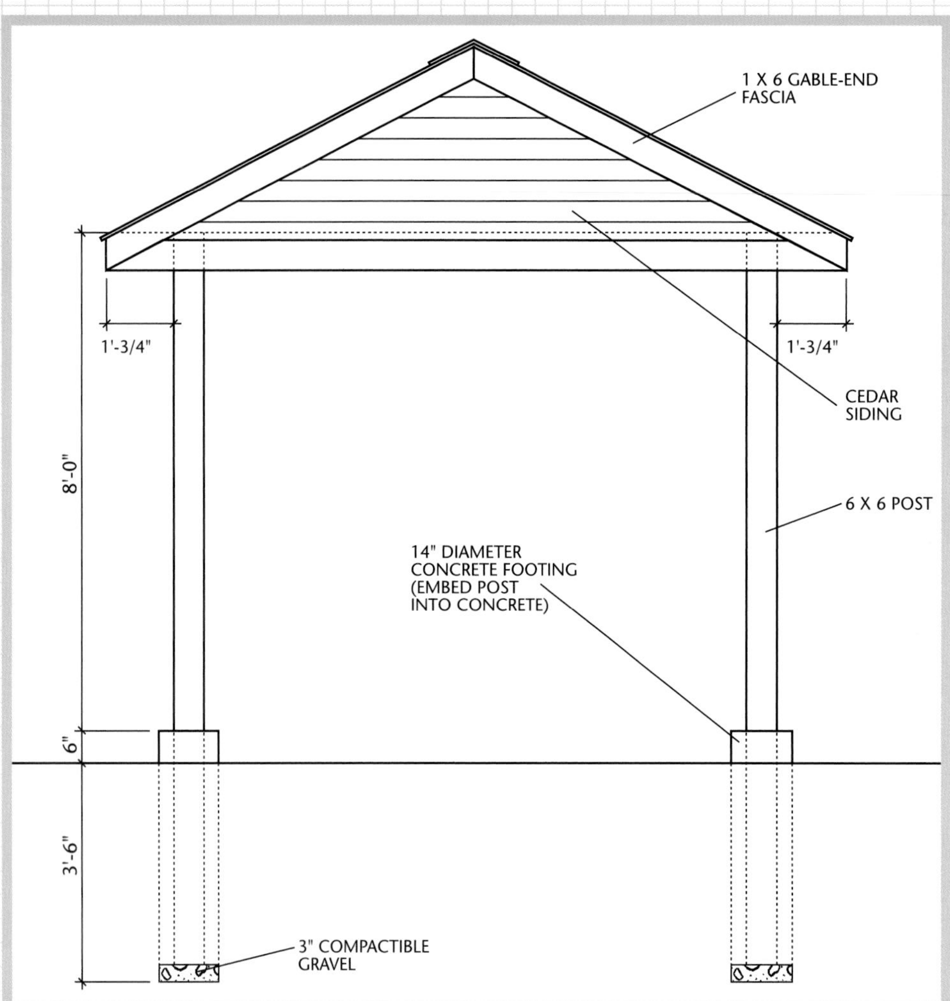


## Side Elevation

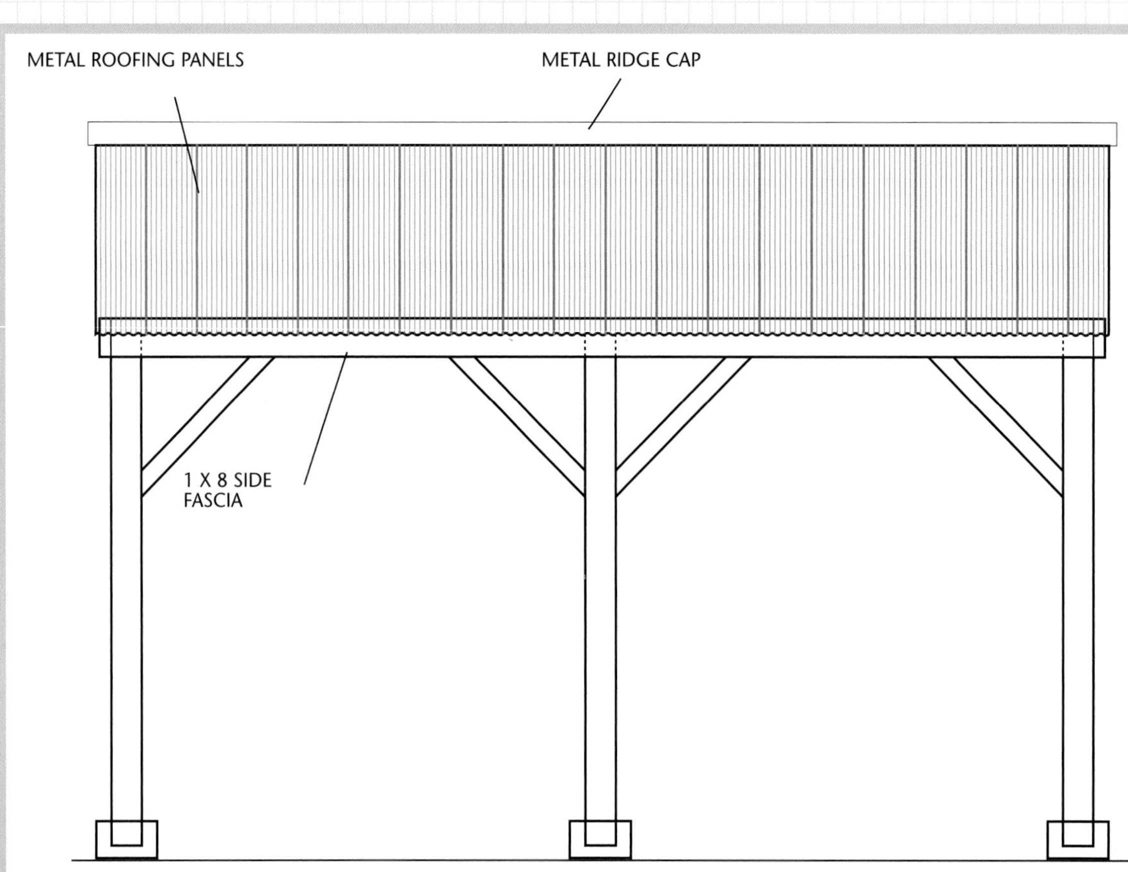

## Front Section

PREMANUFACTURED 2 X 4 TRUSS
12
6
1'-6"
1'-6"
1'-6"
1'-6"
6-1/4"
PURLINS
2 X 8 DOUBLE
SIDE BEAM
9'-6"
12'-0"
2 X 8 END BEAM

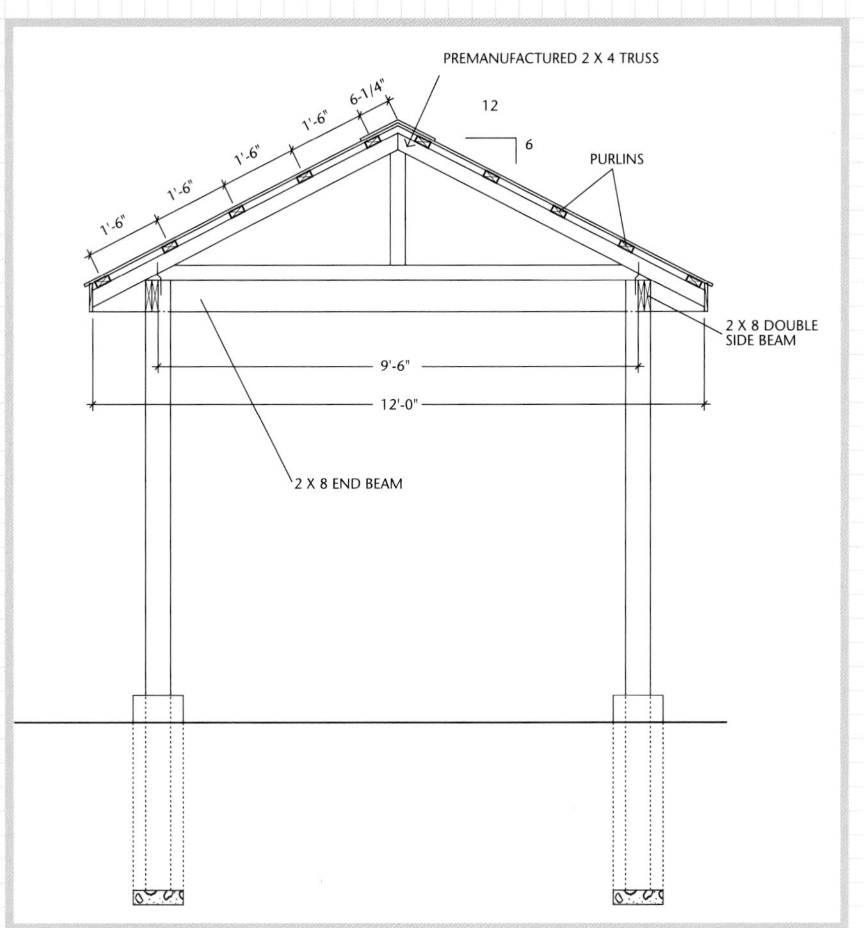

## Side Section

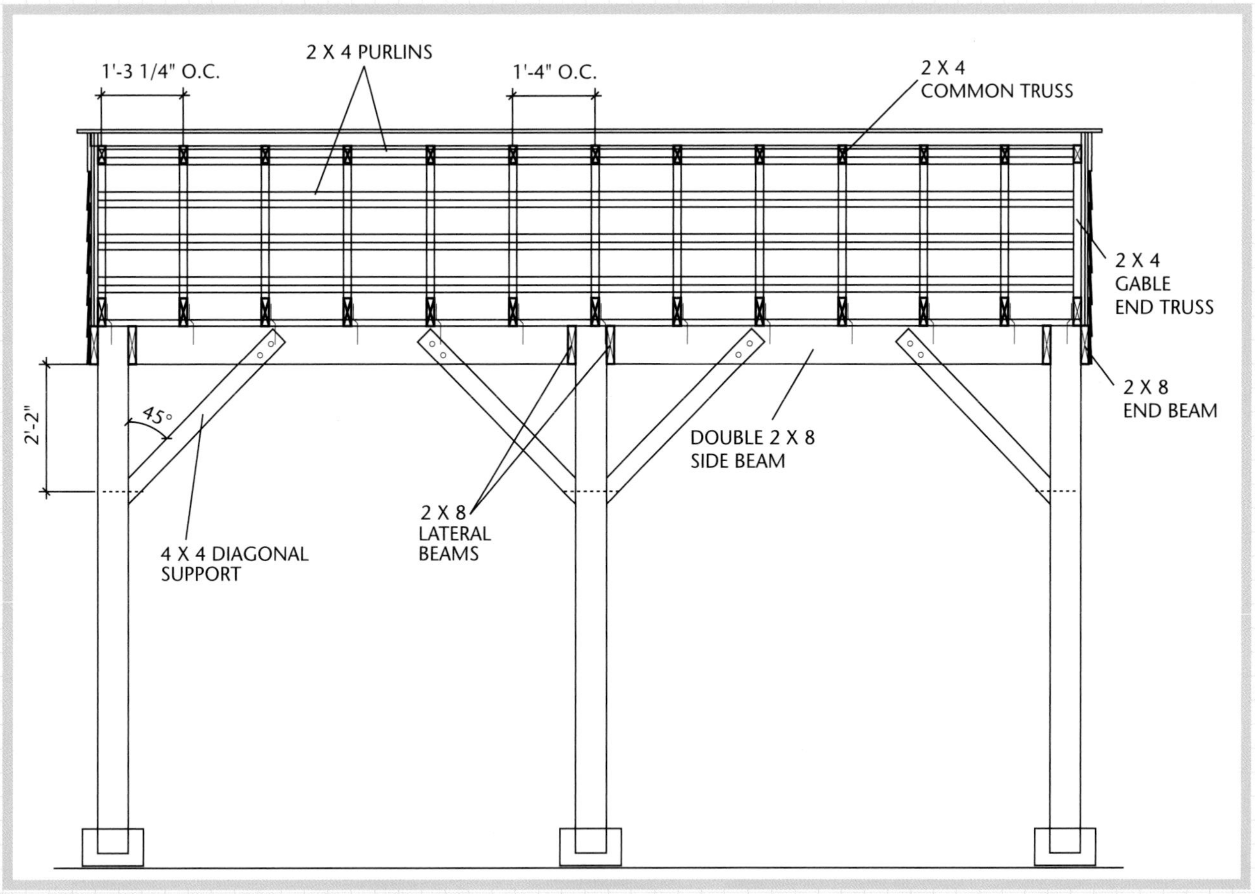

2 X 4 PURLINS
1'-3 1/4" O.C.
1'-4" O.C.
2 X 4
COMMON TRUSS
2 X 4
GABLE
END TRUSS
2 X 8
END BEAM
2'-2"
45°
DOUBLE 2 X 8
SIDE BEAM
2 X 8
LATERAL
BEAMS
4 X 4 DIAGONAL
SUPPORT

## Beam Framing Plan

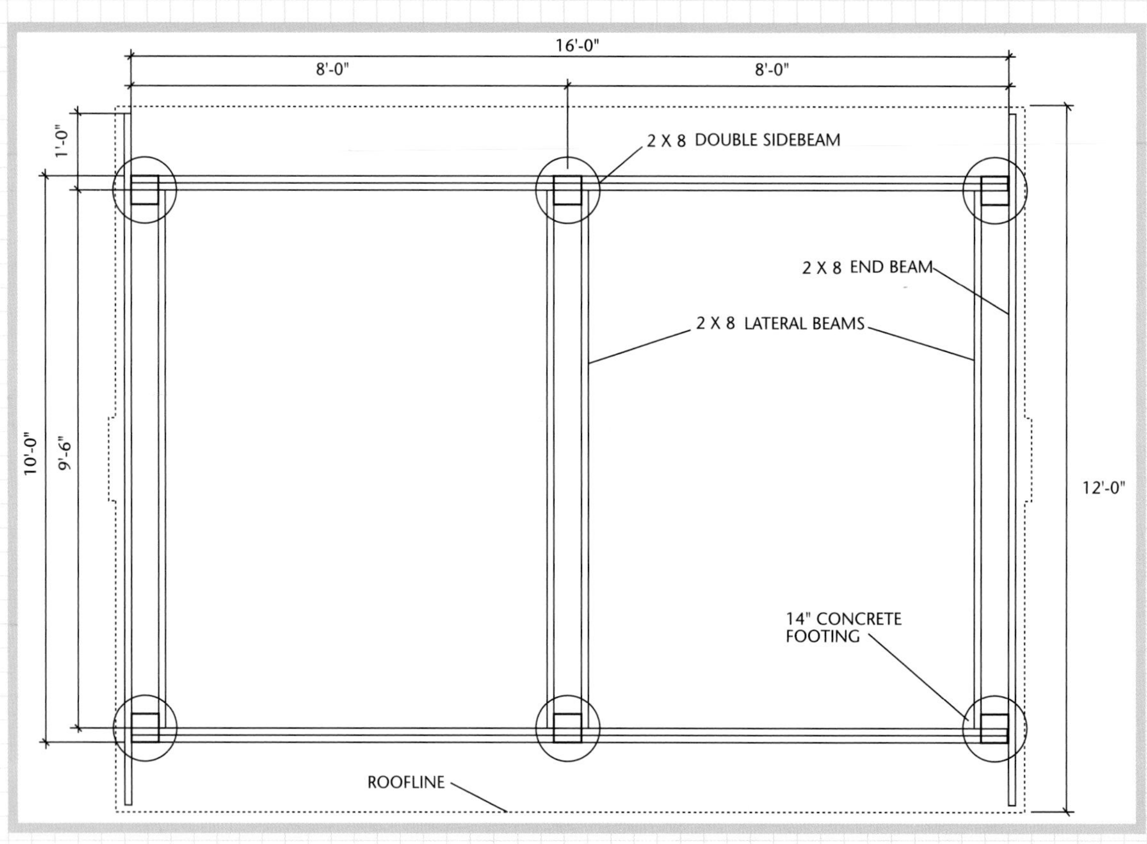


## Diagonal Support Detail

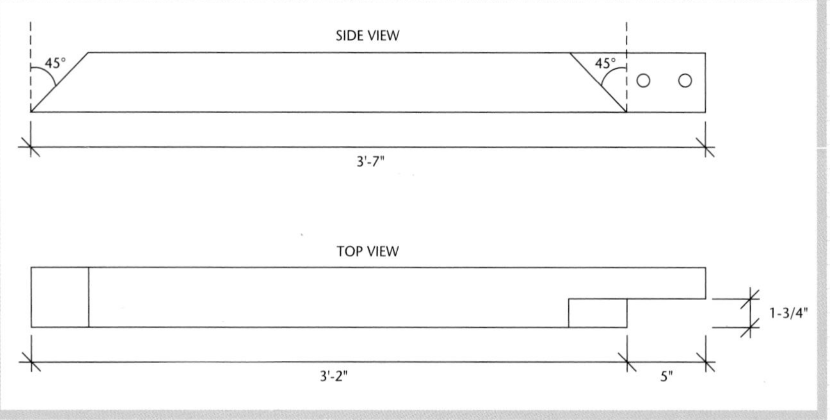


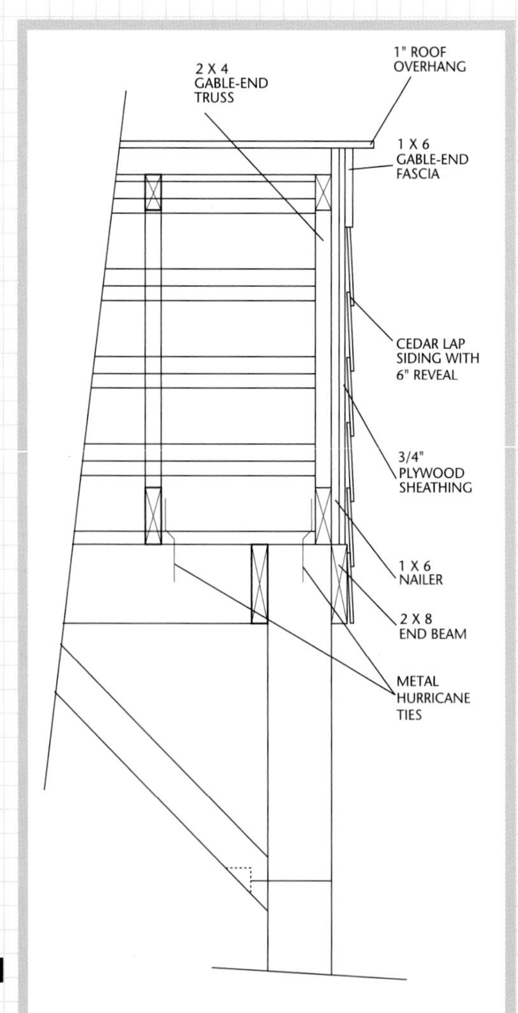

## Gable End Detail

# How to Build a Carport

**Lay out the rough location** of the carport with stakes and string, creating an area 10 feet wide and 16 feet long. Install ten 2 × 4 batterboard sets with crosspieces about 2" below the tops of the stakes. Run level mason's strings between the batterboards at planned post locations. Measure and mark the exact post locations on the layout strings according to your plan, and then drive wooden stakes to mark their locations on the ground.

**Dig post footing holes** for 14"-dia. footings at least 6" deeper than your local frost line. Use a power auger or clamshell digger. Make sure the holes are centered on the stakes. Many local building codes require bell-shaped flares at the footing bases. Pour 2 to 3" of compactable gravel into each footing hole. Set a concrete tube form into each hole, then insert a 6 × 6 post that's slightly longer than the final post height. Brace and plumb the posts, check alignment, and then fill footing holes with concrete.

**Trim the post tops.** Mark the finished height onto one post and draw a cutting line. Transfer the cutting line to all other posts using a mason's string and line level or a laser level as a reference. Trim the posts to height. Scribe a 3"-wide × 7¼"-deep notch on the outside face of each post, and then cut the notches with a circular saw.

**Install the side beams.** Cut four 2 × 8s at 192" using a circular saw. Then clamp the boards together in pairs and facenail with 10d common nails to make the side beams. Lift the beams into the notches and clamp into position so the ends of the beams are flush with the edges of the posts. Fasten each beam with two ⅜ x 5" galvanized lag screws and washers.

(continued)

**Install end beams.** Cut two 2 × 8 end beams at 144" using a circular saw. Then lift and position the end beams against the ends of the posts with the top edges flush with the post tops. The beams should extend 12" past each post on each end. Securely clamp the beams in position and fasten with two ⅜ × 4" lag screws with washers per joint.

**Install lateral beams.** Cut four 2 × 8 lateral beams to size and lift each beam into position between the side beams. Make sure the top edges of the beams are flush with the top of the posts and clamp in place. Drill a pair of ½"-deep counterbore holes using a 1" spade bit, then drill 3½"-deep, ¼" pilot holes at each location. Fasten the lateral beams with ⅜ x 4" lag screws with washers.

**Install corbels.** Cut eight 4 × 4 diagonal supports (corbels) to size, beveling one end and notching the other. At each post, measure down from the side beam and mark at 26". Position the beveled end of the support against the post aligned with the mark, and the notched-out end against the bottom edge of the inner member of the side beam. Clamp the support to the side beam and attach with ⅜ × 4" lag screws with washers.

**Install the first truss.** Place a gable truss on the ends of the side beams. Extend a pair of long 2 × 4s to the ground and clamp them to the truss so the truss is held in place in vertical position. Align each truss with the reference marks on the side beams, and then measure the overhang of each rafter tail to ensure proper placement. Use wood shims at the braces to keep the truss plumb, if necessary. Toenail the truss in place using 10d galvanized common nails. Install the truss at the other end of the carport. *Tip: Tack a chalk line to the rafter tails at each carport end so it spans the length. Draw the lines taut and use them as references for installing the common rafters.*

**Install common trusses.** Lift each truss up so its ends rest on the side beams—it's easier to do this if the truss is upside down (with the peak facing downward). When you are ready to install it, flip the truss right-side up and position it on the beams. Trusses do not always need to follow conventional rafter spacing (16 or 24" O.C.). Here, the carport design has the trusses spaced 27¼" apart O.C. Toenail the trusses to the beams with 10d nails. Install the trusses in order, tacking a 1 × 4 brace to the top chord to maintain the correct spacing and alignment. If you will be installing purlins for a panel roof, install one now in lieu of a brace.

**Install the purlins.** Metal and fiberglass roof panels don't require a deck, but they normally need to have evenly spaced sets of wood strips beneath them for reinforcement. Called purlins, these strips are mounted perpendicular to the trusses or rafters. Often, they are used to secure a profiled filler strip that fits underneath the roofing panel to support the profiled shape and create a seal. Snap chalk lines for alignment, and then install the purlins.

(continued)

**Close off the gable ends.** Install 1 × 6 blocking to fur out the chords and struts of the gable-end trusses. Measure the triangular shape of the gable-end wall from the top edge of the end beam to the top edge of the blocking. Divide the area into two equal-size triangular areas, and cut ¾" plywood sheathing to fit. Attach the sheathing with 1½" deck screws.

**Cut 1 × 6 fascia boards**—two for each gable end—long enough to extend from the peak to several inches past the ends of the rafter tails. Use a rafter square to mark the peak ends of the boards for the roof pitch, and then cut the angles. Fasten the gable-end fascia boards to the gable sheathing using 6d galvanized casing nails. Cut 1 × 8s to size for the side fascia boards and fasten with 6d galvanized casing nails driven into the ends of the rafter tails. Make sure the top edge of the fascia boards do not protrude above the top of the last row of purlins. Trim the ends of the gable-end fascia flush with the side fascia using a handsaw.

**Install roofing panels.** Lay the first metal roofing panel across the purlins and position it so the finished edge of the panel extends approximately 1" beyond the gable-end fascia, and 1" past the side fascia. Drive 1" metal roofing screws with rubber washers through the roof panel into the purlins (these are sometimes called pole barn screws). Space the fasteners according to the manufacturer's directions. Install all panels, overlapping each preceding panel according to the manufacturer's directions. Work from one gable end to the other. Install the final panel so the finished edge overhangs the gable-end fascia by 1".

## Ridge Caps ▸

A cutaway view of the ridge cap shows how the cap fits over the sealer strip. The caulk and the rubber sealer strip form a barrier to water and pests.

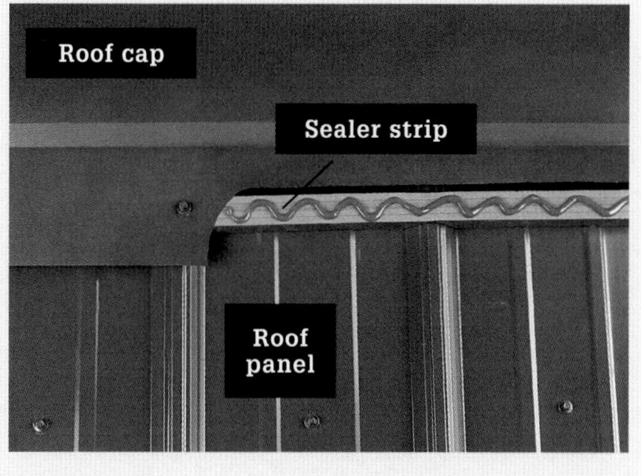


**Install the ridge cap (left).** To seal the roof ridge, a metal cap piece that matches the roof panels is screwed over the open seam. Mark the location for the rubber sealer strip on the starter purlin 6¼" from the peak of the roof. Run a bead of caulk along the reference line, and then install sealer strips on both sides of the peak. Apply a caulk bead to the tops of the sealer strips, and then center the preformed metal ridge cap over the peak so it overhangs the finished edges of the gable-end roof panels by 1". At each ridge of the metal roof panels, drive 2½" metal roofing screws with rubber washers through the ridge cap and sealer strip.

**Install siding.** Choose a style and color of siding that matches or blends with your house siding and install it in the gable area. Here, cedar lap siding is being installed. Use a framing square or rafter square to mark cutting lines on the ends of each piece to match the roof pitch. Install a 2"-wide starter strip at the bottom, and then work your way up toward the gable peak. Maintain a consistent reveal, and nail the siding in areas that will be covered by the next course. Stain or seal any exposed cedar, such as the gable ends, side fascia, and posts.

# Garage Workshop

There is no better spot for your dream workshop than in the garage. Because things you do in a workshop tend to produce noise and mess, a garage workshop has the advantage of isolation from the rest of the household. Whether your interests tend toward woodworking, metalworking, small engine repair, or just plain tinkering away with the ballgame on the radio, you'll spend plenty of quality time in your garage workshop.

In more temperate climates, garages often make better shops than basements. Ventilating the shop is as easy as opening the garage door or rolling machinery outside for doing dusty work. Garages usually have high finished ceilings or open trusses, so you can maneuver larger building materials and make taller projects without overhead restrictions. Having a shop on ground level also saves your back from straining when you need to move machinery, supplies, and projects in and out of the workshop.

If you'd rather not dedicate your entire garage to a workshop, you can still keep one or more stalls available for parking a car, bicycles, or a lawn tractor by simply mounting your tools and workbench on wheels. Wheels make it possible for one person to easily move even the largest machinery.

One problem with most garages is they don't have enough electrical outlets. Those that are present are often fed with an inadequate electrical supply. Many garages, even on new homes, are wired with a single circuit. Some garages on older homes have no electricity at all, especially if they are detached from the house. When a garage serves only as parking and storage space, a single electric circuit is sufficient for servicing a garage door opener, an overhead light, and maybe a few light-duty outlets. But once your garage becomes a workshop, you're going to need more electricity to power tools with larger motors, such as table saws and planers.

**Creative use of space** in and around your garage lets you build a workshop that meets your needs without making your garage unusable for other functions.

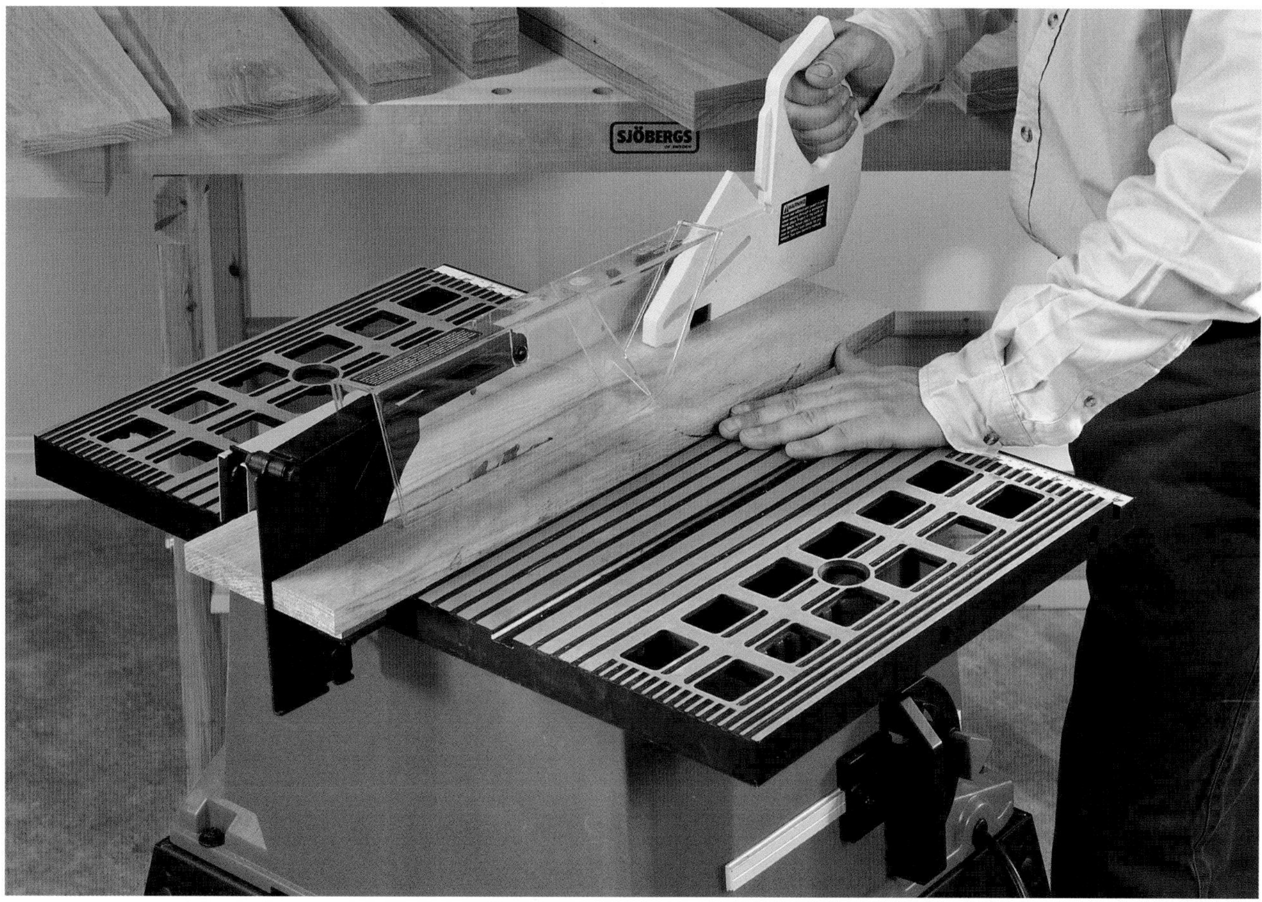


**Bench-top power tools** can be used on your workbench or you can build rolling bases to make them easy to transport from place to place. Either way, they offer excellent flexibility and efficiency.

With ample cross-ventilation, a garage shop is pleasant to work in during spring and fall months, especially if you work in the cool of the day. Winters and summers are a different story, depending on where you live. Garage walls are often uninsulated, so your workshop can become nearly intolerable to work in on bitterly cold days or during hot, humid summers. Uninsulated spaces will be difficult to heat or cool efficiently. Wood glues and finishes won't cure properly below 55°F, so you'll have to move gluing and finishing tasks indoors or save them until spring.

A couple of heating options can make winter shop time more tolerable and even pleasant. Standard "milk house" style electric heaters designed for heating a room simply won't generate enough heat to warm an entire garage. Kerosene or propane-fueled heaters, especially those with built-in blowers, will do the job more efficiently. A higher output, 240-volt heater will also work. Either choice is safe to use in a garage, provided you open a window or door or raise your garage door a few inches to exhaust carbon monoxide. You'll also need to turn off the heater when routing or sawing for long periods of time so the heater flame doesn't ignite the dust.

Cooling a garage shop during the summer can be equally challenging. Cross-ventilation will help draw breezes through the shop, especially if you use a fan to help move the air.

Unfinished garage walls make it easy to store supplies, lumber, and tools. Mount shelving, workbenches, lumber racks, and pegboard directly to the wall studs. You can even store lumber and other odds and ends overhead if the roof trusses are accessible.

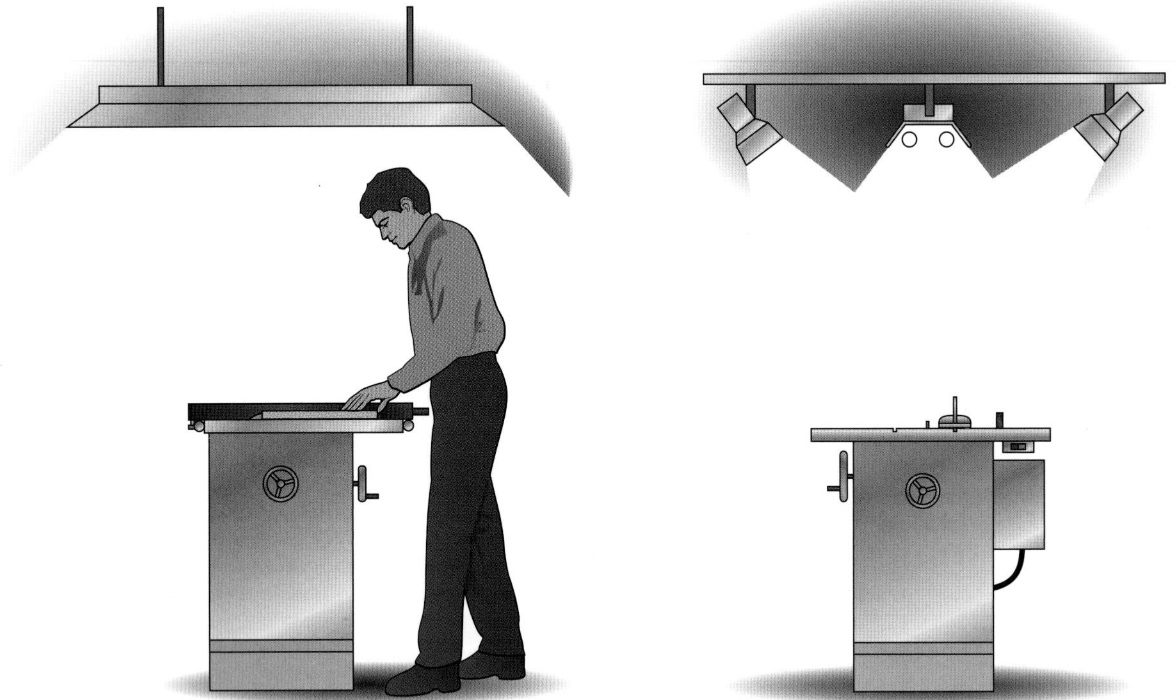

**A combination of light sources** should include natural light, general overhead lighting—preferably from a fluorescent tube fixture (see pages 192 to 193)—and directed task lighting provided by a trouble light or other lamp fitted with a compact fluorescent or LED bulb.

## Preparing the Garage

Getting your garage workshop up and running is one thing, but refining it to suit your specific working style will take years. Most DIYers enjoy the process of creating and recreating a workshop as their tools amass and their skills improve. For our purposes, we'll discuss the basics of turning a space into a workshop. Of course you'll need to adapt this general advice to fit your context, budget, and personal preferences. Depending on your space limitations and expectations, the job may be as easy as clearing out some clutter and putting up a workbench.

It's probably impossible to have too much light in a workshop. Try to have enough light so you won't be forced to work in the shadows. In addition to natural light from windows and skylights, workshops should be lit with a combination of overhead and task lighting. Overhead lights illuminate the general workspace, while task lighting directs focused light on the workbench and other machines where you need it most.

Ordinary ceiling-mounted incandescent light bulbs provide a reasonable amount of light in the immediate area under the fixture, but the light drops off quickly as you move away, creating shadows. If you're adding new fixtures, plan for one single-lamp fixture to illuminate about 16 square feet of floor space. Your garage shop should be equipped with fixtures that have protective covers over the lamps.

Make the most of natural light if your workspace has windows. Sunlight produces wonderful workshop lighting. A few windows, a skylight, or simply opening garage and service doors can largely replace artificial lighting during the daytime. Natural light makes even small shops more pleasant to work in while providing some radiant heat. Install skylights so they face north or east if you live in a hot climate. You'll get the benefit of indirect sunlight brightening your space without all the extra heat. For cooler climates, position skylights southward to capture more direct sunlight.

## Fluorescent Lights ▸

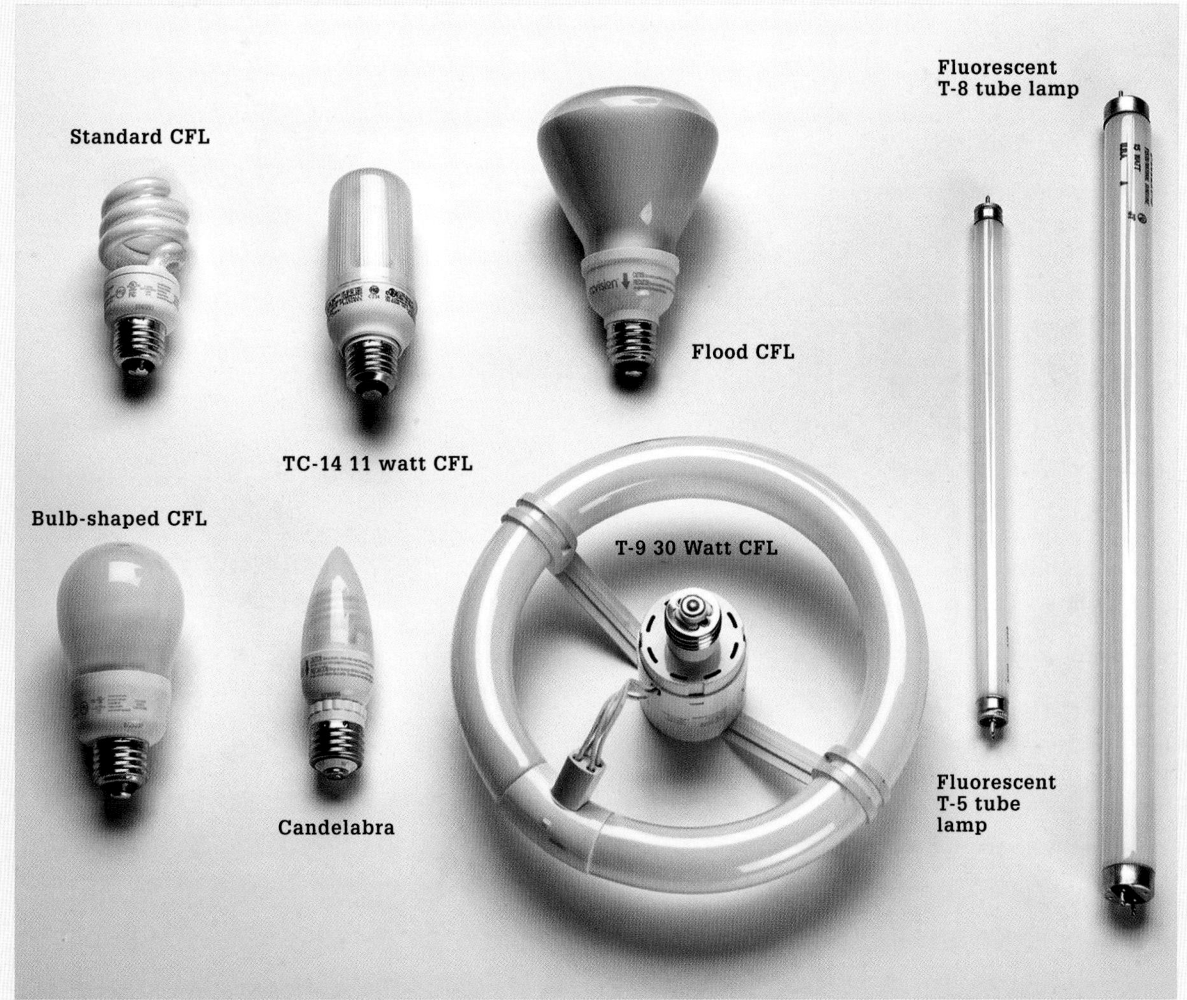


**Compact fluorescent lamps** are better than incandescents because they provide the same light output with only a third of the wattage. Depending on the type, CLFs can be used with standard incandescent fixtures, fluorescent fixtures, and those with dimmer switches.

Fluorescent lights are well suited for your garage because they provide diffuse, even light. They are inexpensive to buy, and they operate on a fraction of the energy used by incandescent light bulbs, yet they produce about five times as much light and last about ten times as long. Fluorescent fixtures and bulbs come in a rapidly expanding range of sizes, shapes, and qualities. On the low end, you can buy 4-foot "shop lights" for less than $10 each. However, these budget-priced fixtures have low-quality ballasts that often make an annoying buzzing sound when the lights are on. In colder temperatures, the ballasts warm up slowly and make the bulbs flicker or light dimly. For about two or three times the price of economy fixtures, you can buy better quality 4-foot lights with "industrial" ballasts that start quickly in cold weather. The ballasts operate quietly and outlive their cheaper cousins.

For larger workspaces, consider installing 8-foot fluorescent lighting (see pages 192 to 193). Each fixture will cost $50 to $100 on average, which is usually still more economical than buying two premium 4-foot lights. Long fluorescent fixtures are made for commercial applications, so you'll be assured of good-quality ballasts designed for cold-weather use. Long fixtures also make for easier installation. You'll only need to hang and wire half as many lights.

## Lighting & Electrical

Along with ample lighting, you'll need sufficient electricity in your shop. At a minimum, workshops require two circuits. One 15-amp circuit should be dedicated to shop lighting. Otherwise, you could be left in the dark if you trip a circuit breaker while using a machine. The other circuit supplies power for electrical outlets. Read the labels on your tools to identify how many amps they draw at peak loads, then use a circuit rated 20 to 30 percent over this number. For smaller corded power tools, a 15-amp circuit is usually sufficient. Full-size table saws, planers, jointers, and dust collectors should draw power from a 20-amp circuit. Large tools that produce 2 hp or more are generally wired for 220-volt operation, which requires at least a 30-amp circuit. If you don't have room to add two or more new circuits for the shop, a licensed electrician can install a smaller panel of additional circuit breakers, called a subpanel (pages 188 to 191). Subpanels are also useful when your shop is located in the garage far from the main service panel. Having a subpanel in the shop allows you to switch circuits on and off conveniently without having to walk all the way to the main panel.

*Caution: Adding new circuits to the main service panel may exceed its amperage capacity, even if there are slots available for more circuits. An electrician can determine whether adding more circuits or a subpanel will be safe for your current main panel. See pages 178 to 191.*

You'll likely need to use extension cords to deliver power where it's needed or move machines around

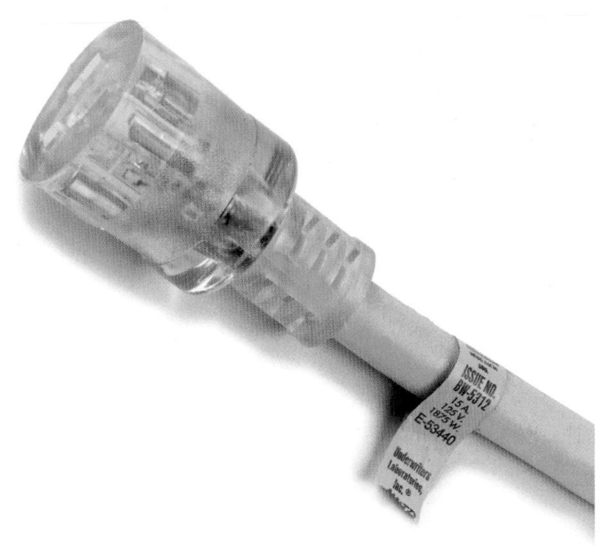


**Use heavy-gauge extension cords** in the shortest usable lengths to power your tools. This cord will be adequate for tools drawing 15 amps or less, provided it's not overly long.

the shop in order to plug them in. Extension cords can be used safely to power most tools, provided the cord's amperage rating is greater than the tool's peak amperage draw. In other words, if the tool draws 12 amps under maximum load, use an extension cord rated for 15 or more amps. Keep the length of the extension cords as short as possible without causing tripping hazards. Long extension cords can starve tools of optimal amperage to operate properly.

## Air Quality & Ventilation

Sawdust and fumes from stains, varnishes, and other finishing supplies can compromise the air quality in your shop. Contaminated air isn't just unpleasant to breathe, it's unhealthy. Use portable fans to move the air through windows and doors when you are sanding, sawing, or routing. Place the fan in a window or doorway opposite another open window or door to create a cross breeze. When your woodworking tool arsenal grows large enough to include those really dusty tools, especially table saws, stationary sanders, and planers, invest in a dust collector to capture dust, wood chips, and other debris right at the source.

## Workbenches

Woodworking supply catalogs and home centers sell workbenches, but you can probably build a bench of equal or better quality yourself for less than what you'll pay for a ready-made bench. Project books often include plans for workbenches, and woodworking magazines publish workbench stories nearly every year.

Benches fall into three broad categories: traditional cabinetmaker's benches, utility workbenches, and metalworking benches. Traditional benches are those with thick hardwood tops and sturdy wooden leg bases. They're freestanding, so you can position them wherever you need to and work around all four sides.

Bench dimensions are typically 2 feet wide and 4 to 6 feet long. The top work surface tends to be a laminated blank of hard maple, beech, or other hardwood. The extra thickness helps absorb vibrations produced by heavy pounding, and the added weight keeps the bench stationary. Bench tops are often outfitted with a series of holes along one long edge or at the end. Wood or metal pegs, called bench dogs, fit into these holes and work in conjunction with a vise on the bench to hold long boards or large workpieces. If you buy a traditional bench, expect to pay more than $500 for a good one.

Utility workbenches are easy to build and a good value for woodworking and general home-improvement tasks. These benches may resemble cabinetmaker styles with a heavy top and a skeletal base, or they can be as simple as a sheet of plywood on top of a closed cabinet or two. A utility workbench can be freestanding, or you can fasten it to wall studs. Your bench will be more useful with a vise, but you can often forego the vise and use C-clamps or other short clamps to secure your work to the bench top. Or buy a clamp-on bench vise.

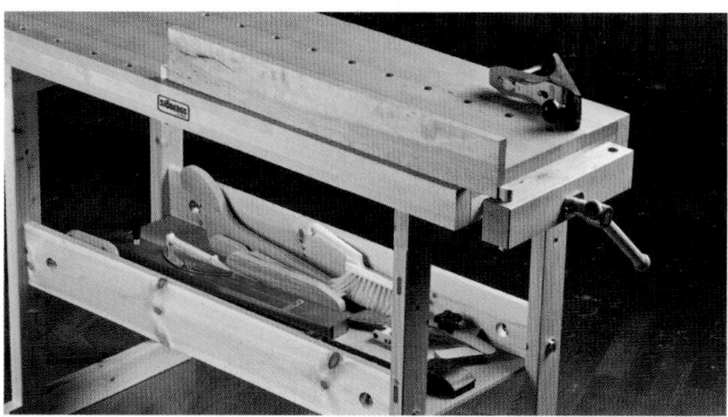

**Woodworking bench**

**Utility bench**

**Metalworking bench**

## Shop Layout

Arranging tools, materials, and fixtures in your shop will depend on the shape of the space you have; where doors, windows, and outlets are located; and the size and mobility of the machinery you own. Your vehicle parking and general storage needs will impact the shop too, of course. The following two pages include four sample floor plans. Here are some general guidelines to start with when laying out your shop:

- Locate shelves or racks for storing lumber or sheet goods close to entry doors and stairwells.
- Table saws require at least 4 to 8 feet of clear space on all sides so there's room to work without hitting walls or other obstructions. Place the saw near the center of the shop.
- Keep your thickness planer and jointer near the table saw so you can move easily from jointer to planer to table saw for sizing and surfacing stock efficiently.
- Arrange other machines and shop fixtures where they are convenient for you.
- Have a bin near the miter saw for collecting short scraps. Place your stationary sanding station near a window to draw out the airborne dust.
- Router tables and band saws can be stored anywhere, provided they are on wheels.
- A drill press should stand against a wall where it's less likely to tip over.
- Keep measuring and marking tools, hand tools, containers of fasteners, and glue close to the workbench.

# Sample Garage Workshop Floor Plans

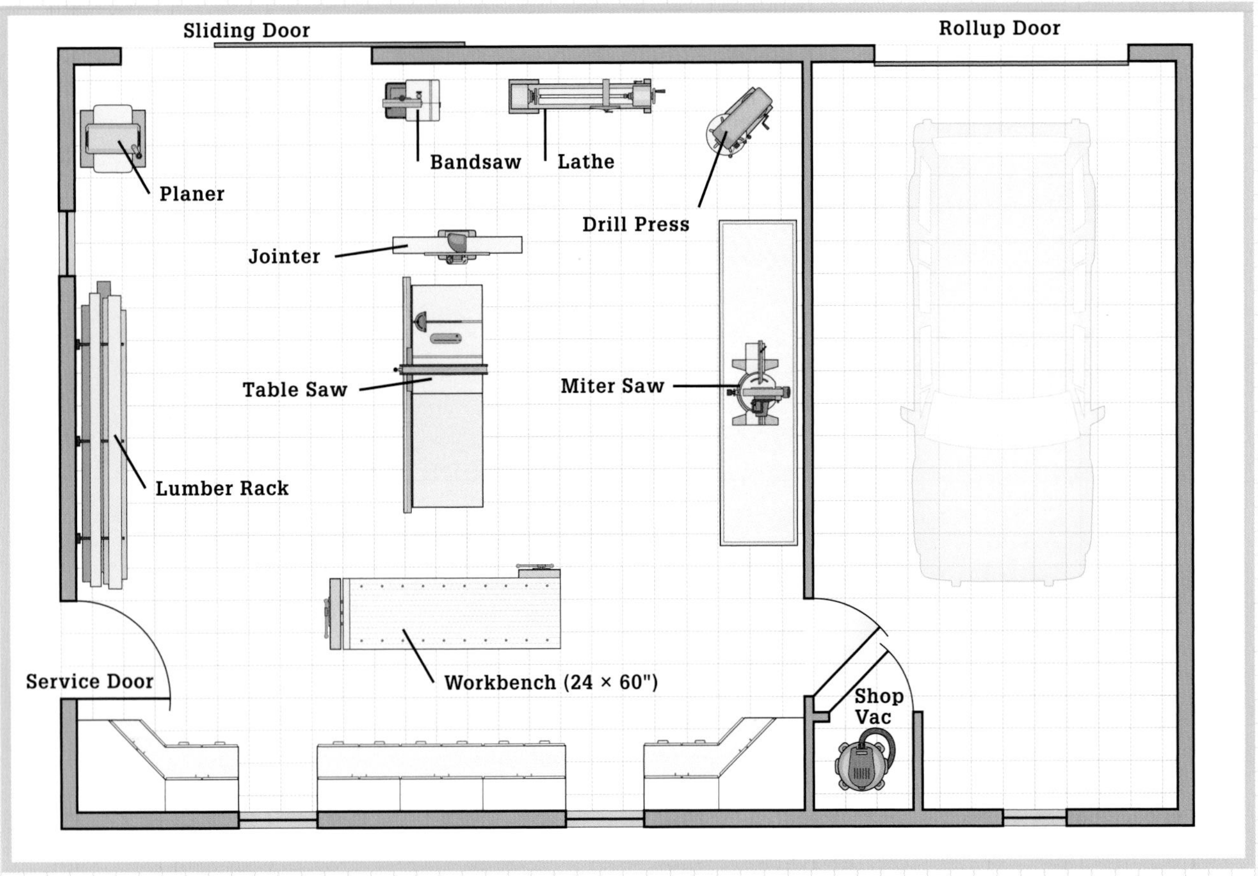

Sliding Door
Rollup Door
Bandsaw
Lathe
Planer
Drill Press
Jointer
Table Saw
Miter Saw
Lumber Rack
Service Door
Workbench (24 × 60")
Shop Vac


Air Compressor
Workbench (30 × 80")
Bandsaw
Rolling tool chest
Planer
Router Table
Jointer
Drill Press
Sanding Station
Outfeed Table (storage cabinet under)
Rollup Door

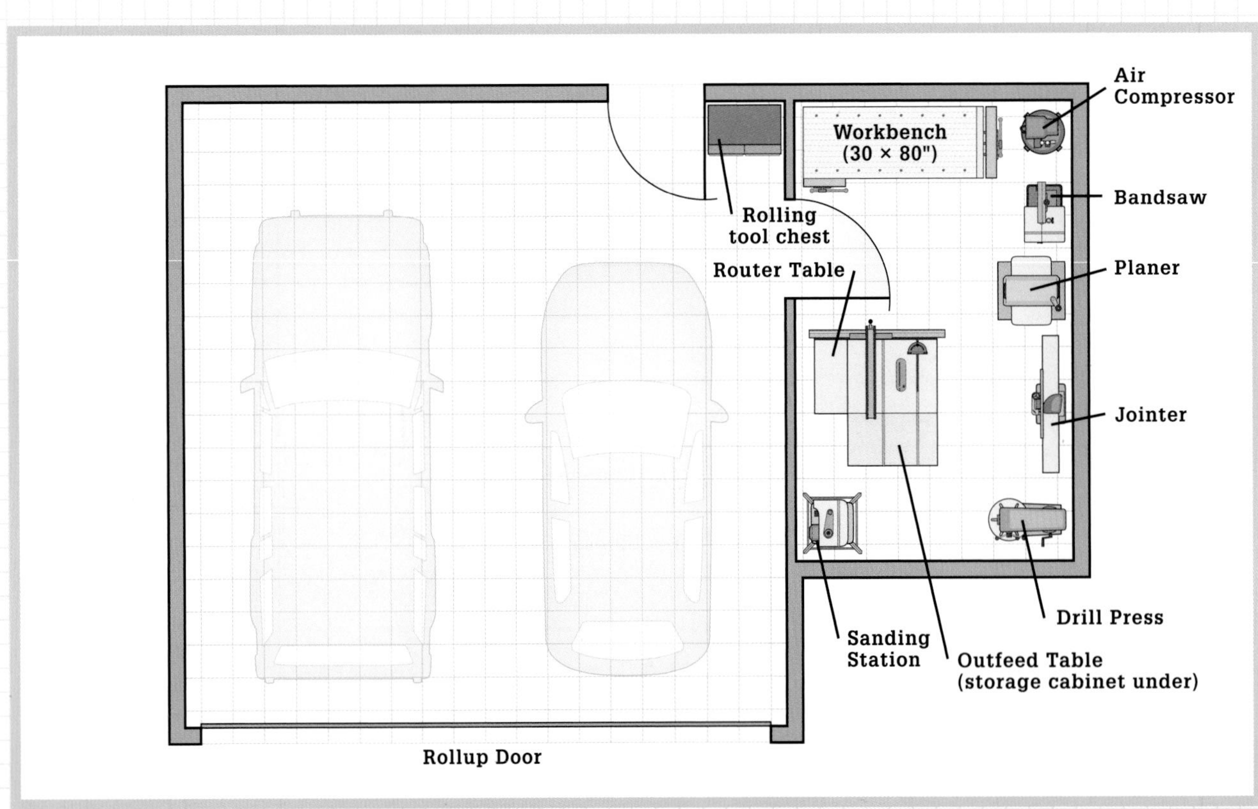

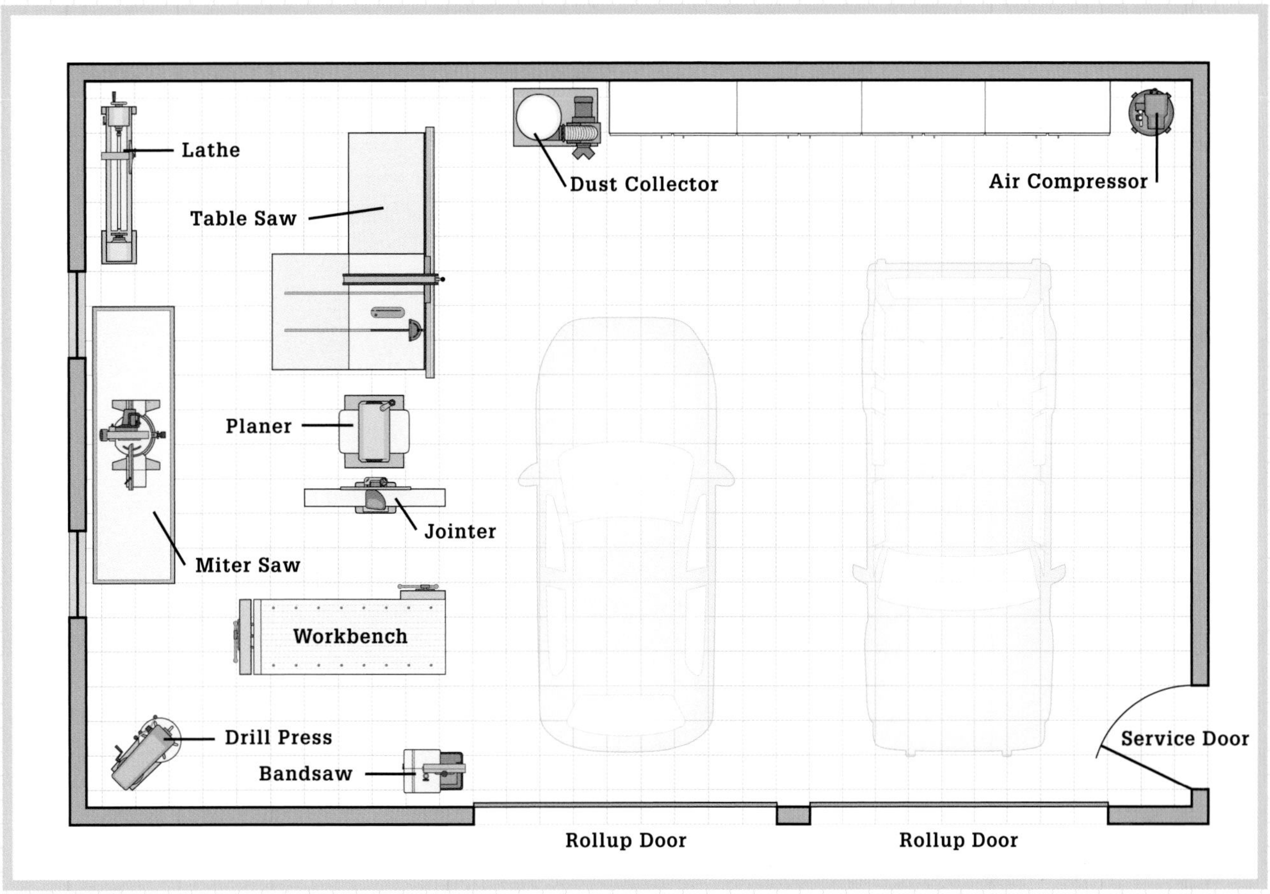

Lathe
Dust Collector
Air Compressor
Table Saw
Planer
Jointer
Miter Saw
Workbench
Drill Press
Bandsaw
Service Door
Rollup Door
Rollup Door

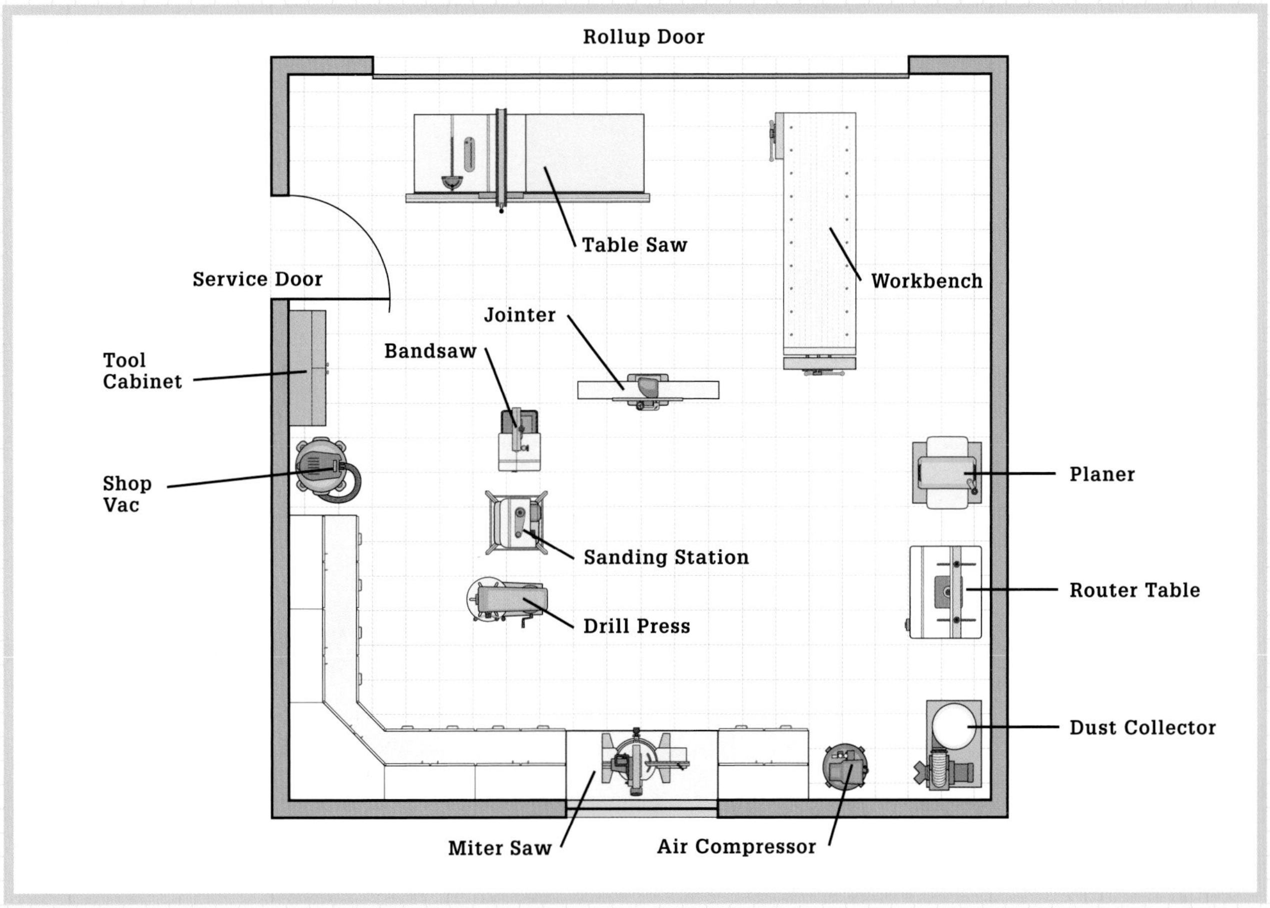

Rollup Door
Table Saw
Service Door
Workbench
Jointer
Bandsaw
Tool Cabinet
Shop Vac
Planer
Sanding Station
Router Table
Drill Press
Dust Collector
Miter Saw
Air Compressor

DALE JR
8

# Garage Improvements

Whether you use your garage primarily for parking and storage or you dream of converting it into a customized space for pursuing woodworking, auto restoration, or other hobbies, you'll only be able to use the space effectively if some basic organizational and infrastructure needs are met. This "Garage Improvements" chapter is filled with practical solutions to help you turn your garage into the space you've always wanted it to be. The first several projects focus on wall and ceiling storage options, and each could easily be completed in a weekend or less. The next six projects address electrical and lighting improvements. If you have moderate wiring skills already, you'll be able to handle each of these projects safely without hiring an electrician to do the work. The last few projects provide practical alternatives for either sprucing up your existing cement slab floor or installing a durable new covering over it.

In its present state your garage may be a dank and unusable cave, or it may simply be plain and uninspired. But once you set your mind to accomplishing even one of these projects, you'll start the ball rolling toward a much better workspace and storage area. It's not impossible, and the benefits will far outweigh the initial effort.

## In this chapter:


- Storage & Workspace Improvements
- Electrical & Lighting Improvements
- Floor Improvements
- Installing Roll-out Floor Covering
- Installing Interlocking Floor Tiles

# Storage & Workspace Improvements

Garages tend to be catch-all spaces for anything and everything that doesn't quite fit in the house. Old boxes of mementos or bags of sporting equipment, collections of stuff intended for that next yard sale, a dorm room's contents home for summer, the broken-down lawn mower that never quite made it to the curb . . . the possibilities are virtually endless. We simply have stuff to spare, and once the basement or attic reaches its fill, the garage is the next logical spot for overflow. All that's really required to manage your mess is a bit of planning and organization. Even if you are among those rare folks who can keep the disorder down to a dull roar naturally, making storage and workspace improvements to your garage can help you free up space to use in other ways, such as pursuing a garage-based hobby.

Whatever your garage demands are, the first step in organizing it is evaluating exactly what you need to store. Do you have tools and equipment that should be hung up or can they lay flat? Maybe those boxes in the corner are light enough to store on a shelf or even place on a rack that hangs from the ceiling. Cans, odd-shaped containers, small power tools, and the like will stow well in cabinets, while the really small stuff might fit best in a series of drawers. Does your inventory of necessary chemicals and compounds include hazardous or flammable material with special storage needs? Take stock of your stuff, reducing or recycling what you really don't need, then you'll be ready to come up with a garage storage plan that works.

This section offers storage solutions for anything and everything in your garage. Most of these projects are relatively inexpensive, and you may even have the materials needed already. Generally, no single storage solution will do the whole job. So try to compartmentalize areas of your garage for certain kinds of storage, and keep your options open for how best to use the wall, floor, and ceiling space. Two or three different options could provide the ideal system for your garage.

**Your garage can be the picture of neatness** and function with the right combination of storage systems. No matter what you need to organize your space, there's a project or product option that can help get the job done.

## Insulating Your Garage Walls ▸

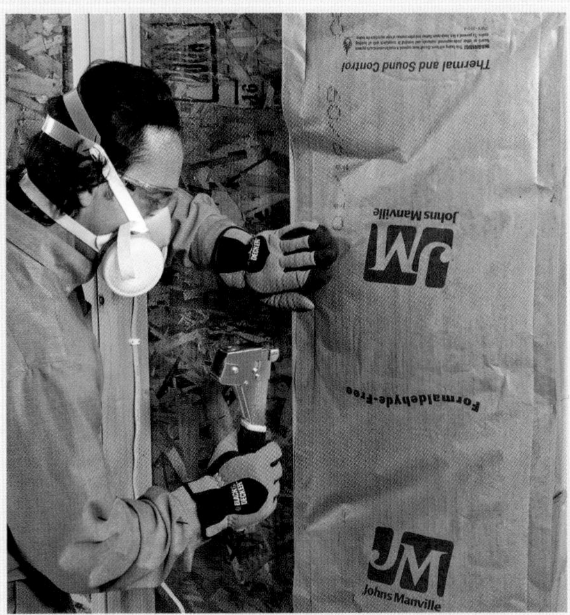


**Use faced fiberglass insulation** batts to insulate your garage walls. Staple the backing tabs to the wall studs, driving a staple every 8 to 10". The tabs should be perfectly flat against the studs to block air movement. Do not compress the insulation.

**Work around obstacles** in the wall cavities. For wiring cables and conduit, split the batts by separating them into two layers. Tuck the unfaced layer behind the cable or conduit and then install the faced layer over both.

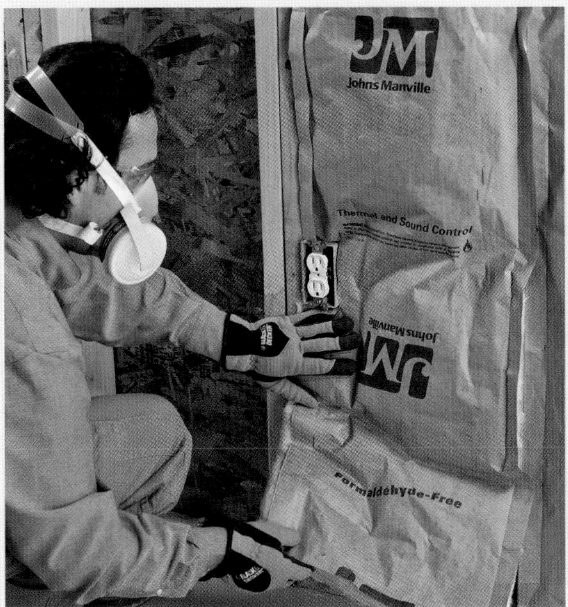


**Fit the batts** around electrical boxes by cutting the insulation with scissors, not by stuffing it. Tuck a small piece of the insulation behind the box if there's room.

**Cut around windows and doors.** Lay a batt on a piece of scrap plywood with the facing down. Set a wide straightedge, such as a metal rule, across the batt at the cutting point. Press down on the straightedge to compress the insulation and then slice through with a sharp utility knife. Be sure to wear gloves and face protection (such as a respirator).

# Finishing Interior Walls

**Finishing your garage walls** with drywall or other panel products improves the appearance of your garage and also can serve practical functions such as forming a fire block or concealing wiring or plumbing.

Whether or not to install finished interior walls on your garage is mostly a matter of preference. The only time wall surfaces are required is when your garage shares a wall with your house (an attached garage) or if one of the walls in your detached garage runs parallel to the house and is constructed within 3 feet of the house. In both cases only the shared or closest walls need to be finished to block the spreading of fire. Typically, a wall covering of ½"-thick (minimum) drywall with taped seams is required. Some circumstances may demand that you install fire-rated, Type X drywall or a double layer of drywall. The seams between drywall panels on fire-blocking walls must be finished with tape embedded in joint compound or with adhesive-backed fire-blocking tape.

If the area above the garage is occupied by a habitable room, the garage walls should be covered with ½" drywall to provide rigidity and structure, and the ceiling should be finished with ⅝"-thick Type X drywall. Ceiling seams should be covered with tape and compound. Fastener heads do not need to be covered with compound except for visual reasons.

If your goal is to create a garage with walls that are finished to interior standards or serve to prevent fire spreading, then drywall is an excellent wall covering. Although the price and availability of diverse building materials fluctuates rather dramatically, drywall is typically one of the more economical choices. But because drywall is relatively susceptible to damage from impact (for example, from tools or bicycles) and doesn't withstand exposure to moisture well, many homeowners choose other wall coverings for their garage. Exterior siding panels are thick enough to hold fasteners and withstand moisture well but are relatively costly, and most have a rougher texture that some find bothersome on interior spaces. Interior paneling has only minimal structural value and some styles are fairly inexpensive, but it may be more visually pleasing to you.

Plywood and oriented strand board (OSB) are popular products for garage walls. Thicker panels (½ to ¾" thick) give excellent rigidity to the walls and are suitable for holding some fasteners. They can be left unfinished, clear-coated for protection with polyurethane finish (or comparable), or you may choose to paint them. A lighter colored wall paint in semigloss or gloss is a good choice. Sheet goods that have a pleasing color or woodgrain may be finished with either a clear coating or a protective deck/siding stain. Lauan plywood underlayment, for example, has a natural mahogany color that can be pleasing when treated with a reddish exterior stain or clear coat. It is also inexpensive but it is thin (¼" on average) and can only support very light-duty fasteners with little load, such as a stickpin holding a wall calendar.

## Finishing Garage Walls ▸

**Fire-rated drywall** (Type X) is often required on walls that separate the garage and house, but more often it is installed on garage ceilings when a habitable space is located above the garage.

**Tape the seams** in fire-rated walls. If you are installing fire-rated drywall that won't be painted, you can save time and effort by using self-adhesive firewall tape (see Resources, page 235).

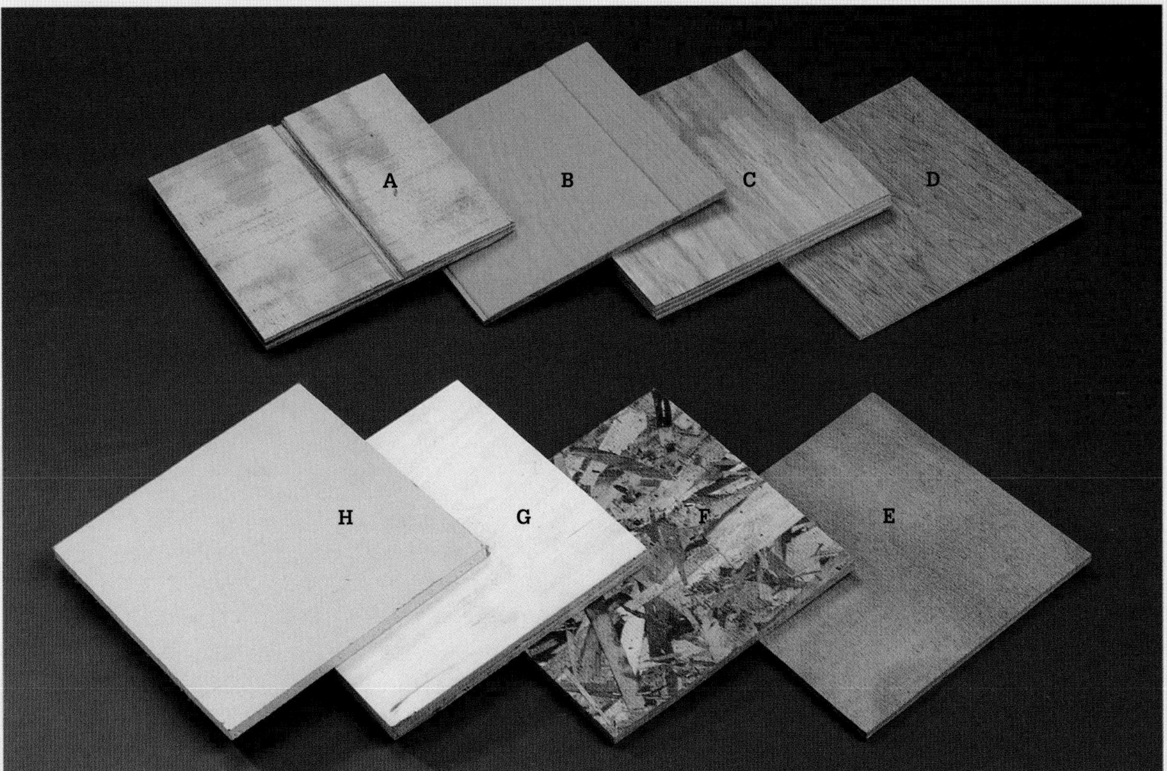


**Sheet goods** that may be used for interior garage walls include: (A) Siding panels (T1-11 shown); (B) fiber-cement siding panels; (C) ¾" interior grade plywood; (D) ¼"-thick underlayment (lauan shown); (E) cedar siding panels; (F) oriented strand board; (G) hardwood plywood (birch shown); (H) drywall (½" shown).

# How to Hang Drywall in a Garage

**Begin installing drywall panels** in a corner. You can install the panels vertically or horizontally, depending on the wall height and how much cutting is involved. Garage walls are seldom a standard 8 ft., as are interior walls. If you are finishing a ceiling with drywall, cover the ceiling first so you can press the tops of the wall panels up against the ceiling panels. This helps support the ends of the ceiling panels. Drive coarse 1¼" drywall screws every 16".

**Cut drywall pieces to fit** around doors and windows. Take special care if you are covering a firewall since any gaps will need to be filled with joint compound and taped over. Make straight cuts that run full width or length by scoring through the face paper with a utility knife and then snapping along the scored line. Finish the cut by slicing through the paper of the back face.

**Mark and make cutouts** for electrical and utility boxes. Use a drywall saw, key hole saw, or spiral-cutting saw to make the cutouts. Make sure the edges of the front boxes are flush with the face of the drywall (move the boxes, if necessary). Finish installing all panels.

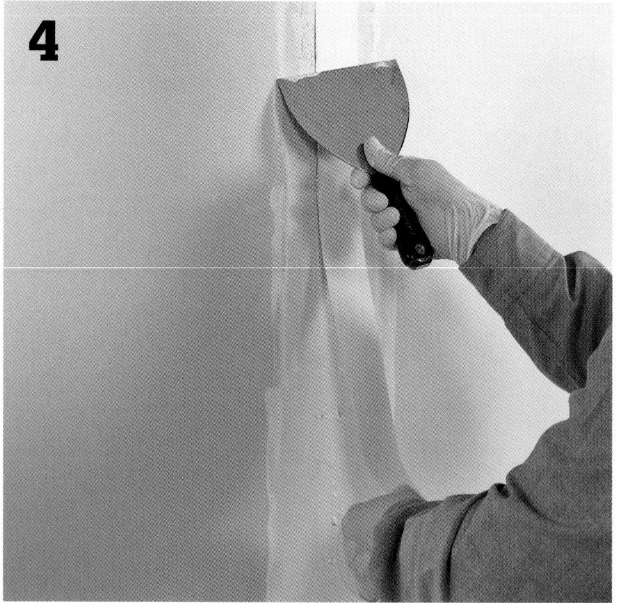

**Cover seams** between drywall panels with joint compound; use drywall tape on walls that serve as firewalls. Cover tape with two layers of feathered-out joint compound, and then cover all fastener heads if you will be painting the walls. Give the panels a coat of drywall primer before painting.

# How to Finish Walls with Sheathing

**Begin installing full panels** of sheathing at one corner. Apply a bead of construction adhesive to the faces of the wall studs before installing each panel. For best holding power, use drywall screws or deck screws instead of finish nails or pneumatic nails. Drive the screws so the heads are countersunk just below the wood surface.

**Make cutouts** for boxes with a jigsaw. Cut panels to fit using a circular saw for straight cuts and the jigsaw for any other interior cuts. Install all wall panels, making sure the seams fall at wall stud locations. Leave gaps of ⅛ to ¼" between panels.

**Use screen retainer strips** or T-molding to cover the seams between sheathing panels if you will be painting the walls. Attach the strips with panel adhesive and brad nails. Sand back any splinters around fastener heads, and then cover the heads with joint compound or wood putty.

**Paint the sheathing** with a semigloss or gloss paint that's easy to clean and will reflect light well. Use a paint roller or a high-volume low-pressure sprayer to apply the paint. Apply two or three thin coats.

# Hanging Pegboard

Pegboard, also called perforated hardboard or perfboard, is one of the simplest and least expensive storage solutions for hanging tools and other lightweight objects. When mounted to the wall and outfitted with metal hooks, pegboard provides a convenient way to keep items from getting lost in the back of a drawer or the bottom of a tool chest. Pegboard also makes it easy to change the arrangement or collection of your wall-hung items, because you can reposition the metal hooks any way you like without measuring, drilling holes, or hammering nails into the wall. In fact, pegboard has served as a low-cost storage option for so long that there are a multitude of different hooks and brackets you can buy to accommodate nearly anything you want to hang. Any home center will carry both the pegboard and the hooks.

You need to install pegboard correctly to get the most value from it. If your garage walls have exposed studs, you can simply screw pegboard to the studs. The empty bays between the studs will provide the necessary clearance for inserting the hooks. On a finished wall, however, you'll need to install a framework of furring strips behind the pegboard to create the necessary clearance and provide some added stiffness. It's also a good idea to build a frame around your pegboard to give the project a neat, finished appearance.

If your garage tends to be damp, seal both faces of the pegboard with several coats of varnish or primer and exterior paint; otherwise it will absorb moisture and swell up or even delaminate.

## Tools & Materials ▸

| | |
|---|---|
| Eye protection | Stud finder |
| Marker | Level |
| Tape measure | Drill |
| Circular saw | Pegboard panels |
| Straightedge | 1 × 2 lumber |
| Miter saw | 1" drywall screws |
| Caulk gun | Panel adhesive |
| Paint roller | Paint or varnish |

**Pegboard systems** are classic storage solutions for garages and other utility areas. Outfitted with a variety of hangers, they offer flexibility and convenience when used to store hand tools and other small shop items.

## Pegboard & Hanger Hardware Styles ▸

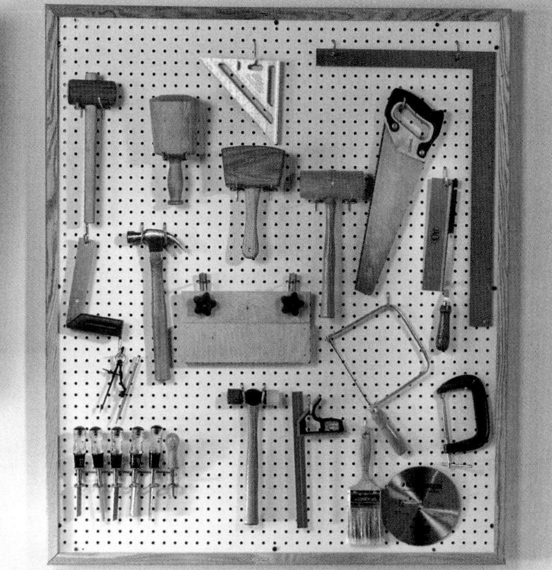

**Hanger hardware** comes in many shapes and sizes, from the basic J for hanging a single tool to double-prong hangers for hammers and even shelf standards. You can buy assorted hangers in kits or stock up on the type you're likely to use the most.

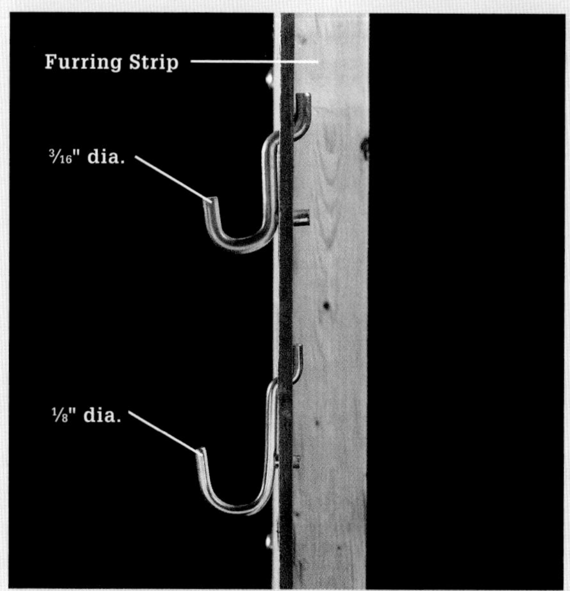


**Two common thicknesses** for pegboard hangers are 1/8"-dia. and 3/16"-dia., both of which fit into standard pegboard hole configurations. The thicker the hanger, the more it can handle. Both types rely on the mechanical connection with the pegboard and can fail if the holes in the board become elongated. The pegboard must have furring strips on the back side to create a recess for the hangers.

**Pegboard** is a single-purpose sheetgood material. It is used to create a wall surface with storage function (occasionally it may be used as a cabinet back where ventilation is desired). Although it comes in 1/8"-thick panels, avoid them in favor of 1/4"-thick material. Most larger home centers carry it unfinished and in pre-finished white. Woodgrain and other decorative panels can be found, and you can also buy metal pegboard panels. The standard size holes are 1/4"-dia. and spaced in a 1"-on-center grid.

## How to Install a Pegboard Storage System

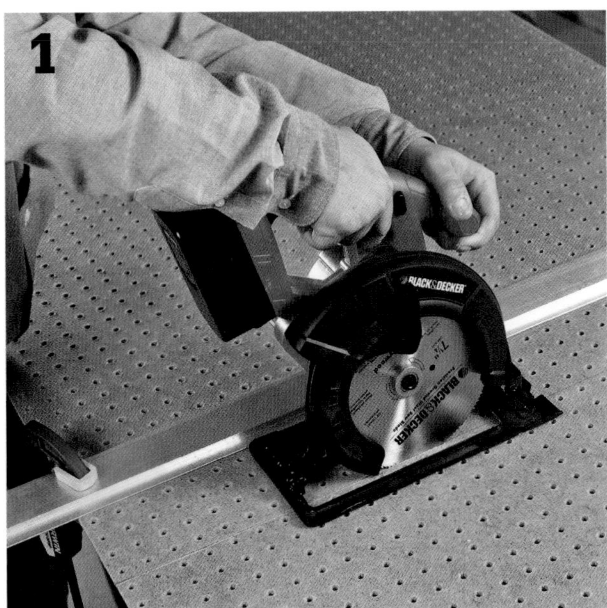

**Cut your pegboard panel to size** if you are not installing a full sheet (most building centers sell 2 × 4-ft. and 4 × 4-ft. panels in addition to the standard 4 × 8 ft.) If you are cutting with a circular saw, orient the panel face-up to prevent tearout on the higher-grade face. If cutting with a jigsaw, the good face of the panel should be down. If possible, plan your cuts so there is an even amount of distance from the holes to all edges.

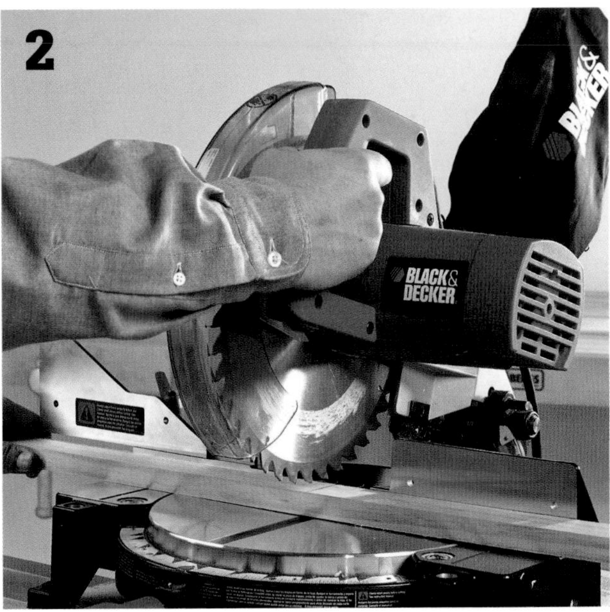

**Cut 1 × 2 furring strips** to make a frame that is attached to the back side of the pegboard panel. The outside edges of the furring strips should be flush with the edges of the pegboard. Because they will be visible, cut the frame parts so the two side edge strips run the full height of the panel (36" here). Cut a couple of filler strips to fill in between the top and bottom rails.

**Attach the furring strips** to the back of the panel using 1" drywall screws and panel adhesive. Drive the screws through countersunk pilot holes in the panel face. Do not drive screws through the predrilled pegboard holes. Use intermediate furring strips to fill in between the top and bottom. These may be fastened with panel adhesive alone.

**Option:** Make a frame from picture frame molding and wrap it around the pegboard to conceal the edge grain and the furring strips. If you can't find picture frame molding with the correct dimensions, mill your own molding by cutting a 3/8"-wide by 1"-deep rabbet into one face of 1 × 2 stock.

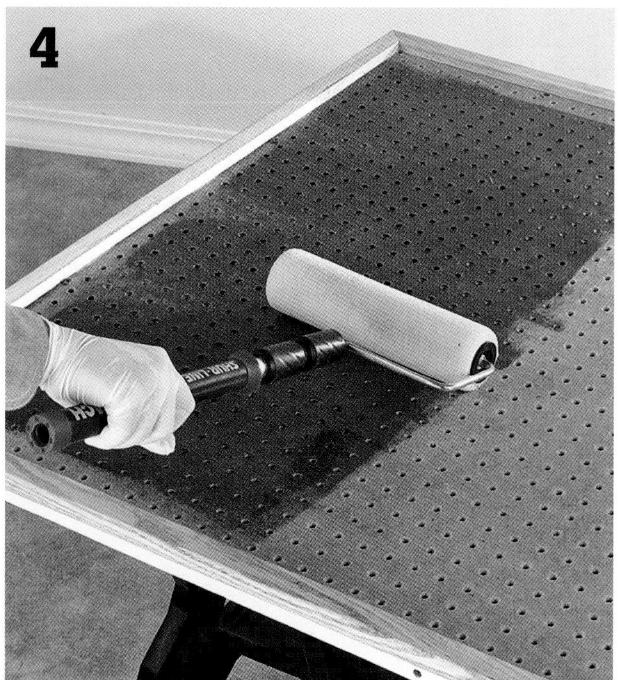

**Paint or topcoat the pegboard.** You can leave the pegboard unfinished, if you prefer, but a coat of paint or varnish protects the composite material from nicks and dings and hardens it around the hole openings so the holes are less likely to become elongated. A paint roller and short-nap sleeve make quick work of the job.

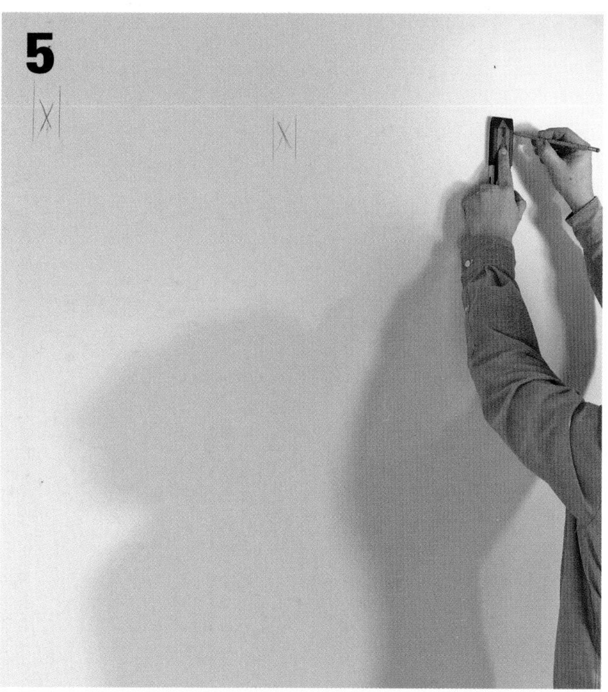

**Locate and mark wall studs** if your garage wall has a wall covering. Make sure the marks extend above and below the pegboard location so you can see them once the pegboard is positioned on the wall.

**Tack the pegboard** and frame to the wall in the desired location. Drive one 2½" screw partway through the top frame at the center of the pegboard. Place a long level on the top of the pegboard and adjust it to level using the screw as a pivot point.

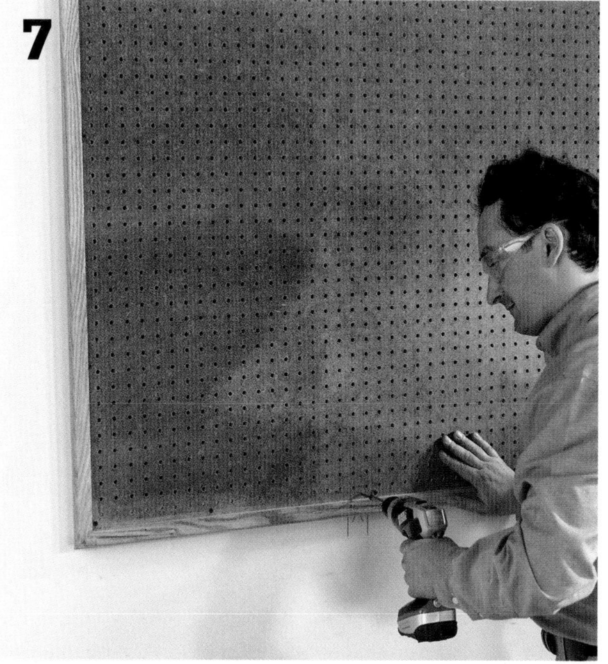

**Drive a drywall screw** through the top and bottom frame rails at each wall stud location. Drill countersunk pilot holes first. Double-check for level after driving the first screw. Insert hangers as desired.

# Installing Adjustable Shelving Systems

Some garage stuff is simply stored best on shelving, particularly if it's too large to fit into a cabinet but still relatively lightweight. Empty planters, gas cans, boxed supplies, and half-full cans of paint are ideal candidates for a sturdy shelving system. You could go to the effort and build your garage shelving from scratch, but going that route will require you to come up with a means of supporting shelf boards on the wall. It's doable, of course, but you'll have to make the standards and brackets yourself. Plus, most shop-made shelving is fixed in place, so you can't reposition the shelves easily if your storable items change.

A more convenient option is to buy metal shelf standards that fasten to the wall studs and shelf brackets that clip into a series of slots on the standards. Home centers carry these adjustable shelving systems in several colors and they come with shelf brackets in a range of lengths to suit various shelf widths. For garage applications, it's a good idea to buy heavy-duty standards and brackets. The components are made of thicker-gauge metal than regular-duty hardware, and the shelf brackets have two mounting lugs instead of one to reinforce the attachment points.

When you install your shelving, locate the top of the standards just high enough so you can reach the top shelf from the floor. If you plan to load your shelving with fairly heavy items, mount a standard to every wall stud in the shelf area. Use strong screws recommended by the manufacturer and fasten them to wall studs only—never to paneling, trim boards, or wallboard alone. Be sure to use sturdy shelf boards and firmly tap the brackets into mounting slots before loading up the shelves.

## Tools & Materials ▸

| | |
|---|---|
| Eye protection & work gloves | Straightedge |
| Level | Stud finder |
| Drill | Rubber mallet |
| Tape measure | Shelf standards with brackets |
| Circular saw | ¾" plywood |

**Sturdy, adjustable shelves** are easy to install and offer a convenient place to safely store those larger, lightweight items off the floor.

## How to Install Bracket Shelves

**Install the first standard** at one end of the installation area. The standards seen here (70" long) are centered on wall studs with the tops level. Align the top of the standard with the top level line and drive one screw through a mounting hole. Hold a level against the side of the standard and adjust it until it is plumb. Drive screws through the remaining mounting holes.

**Install the remaining standards.** For fail-proof results, install the two end standards first, and then establish a level line between them so you can butt the intermediate standards against the line. Use a level against each standard to make sure it is plumb. *Note: If you need to cut the standards for length, align all cut ends of the standards in the same locations (either at the top or bottom).*

**Prepare your shelf stock.** For excellent results, rip cut quality ¾" plywood to width (usually 11½") with a circular saw and a straightedge. Avoid particleboard or MDF shelving as it is prone to sagging and will degrade quickly if exposed to moisture. Most premilled shelving (usually coated with vinyl or melamine) is made from particleboard and is a bit too light-duty for garage storage.

**Install shelf support brackets** in the standards using light blows from a rubber mallet to make sure they're fully seated. Set the shelving onto the standards, adjusting as desired.

# Installing Slatted Shelving Systems

Have you ever marveled at those floor-to-ceiling, slatted-track wall storage systems used for product display in many retail stores? You might not think of that approach as a viable option for your garage, but slatted wall systems are definitely available to consumers—and they're easy to install. The slatted panels are made of PVC or composite material in 4 or 8" pieces and in a variety of colors. Panels are packaged in cartons that cover between 30 to 40 square feet of wall space. The panel color is blended through the material, so slatted wall systems never need painting. Panels are washable and waterproof, making them perfect for a damp garage. Best of all, slatted wall systems can be outfitted with a variety of hooks, brackets, baskets, shelving, and even cabinetry to store just about anything. Aside from the hanging accessories, manufacturers also offer color-matched screw plugs, trim pieces for surrounding outlets, switch plates, and baseboard and moldings for accommodating room corners.

Installing a slatted wall system is a straightforward project. The installation methods do vary quite a bit, depending mostly on whether you select standard or heavy-duty products. Whatever the method, you need to locate and mark the wall studs in the project area and snap a plumb chalk line to establish the height of the bottom row of slatted panels. Depending on the system you choose, you can attach the panels by driving screws through them and into the wall studs or by attaching clips to the wall first and hanging the panels on the clips. Panels can be attached end-to-end with interlocking dowels and then hung as longer pieces. Then, each subsequent row clips to the row below it for an unbroken, seamless look. Slatted wall panels can be cut, drilled, and sanded with ordinary tools, so there's no special bits or blades to buy.

## Tools & Materials ▸

- Tape measure
- Chalk line
- Level
- Circular saw
- Drill
- Wood glue
- Slatted wall panels
- Wall clips and connective dowels
- Screws

**A slatted wall system** combines easy installation, durability, and a range of hanging accessories to form an integrated solution for most any garage storage need. It can be customized for differing load demands, it's fairly easy to install, and it has a more finished appearance with greater durability than pegboard.

# How to Install Slatted Walls

**Lay out vertical and horizontal reference** lines if you are installing the slatted wall system on a finished wall. The bottom reference line should be 16" above the floor in most installations. Also mark all wall stud locations. For bare stud wall applications, establish horizontal reference lines that are parallel to the floor.

**Attach installation accessories** to the wall if you'll be using them. Here, special hangers are attached at stud locations so the wall slat panels in this heavy-duty system can be positioned accurately. For maximum holding power you will also need to drive screws through the mounting slots in each panel.

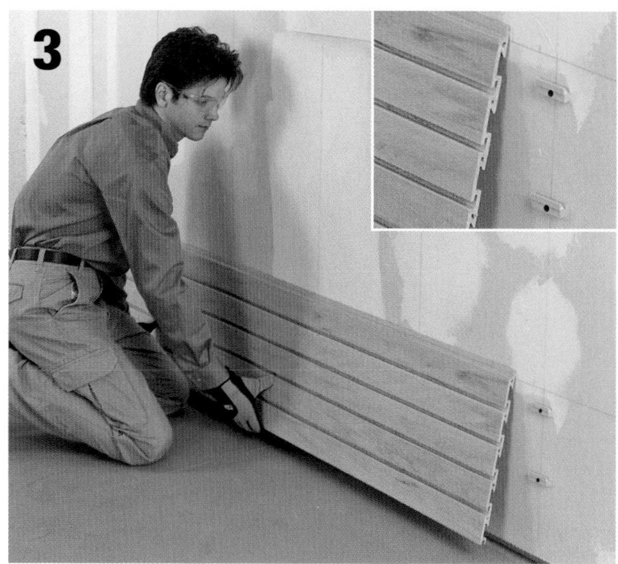

**Begin installing slatted panels,** starting at the bottom. Make sure the panel is oriented correctly, with the dovetailed side of the slot facing up so it can slip over the angled edge of the installation accessory (inset photo).

**Prepare butted joints** between panels. In this system, dowel holes are drilled by enlarging predrilled pilot holes in the panel ends where the panels meet. Barbed dowels are inserted into the dowel holes and glued in place to reinforce the joint. If you do not intend the slatted wall to be permanent, do not use glue. The dowel reinforcement is unnecessary if the butt joint between panels falls at a wall stud location.

(continued)

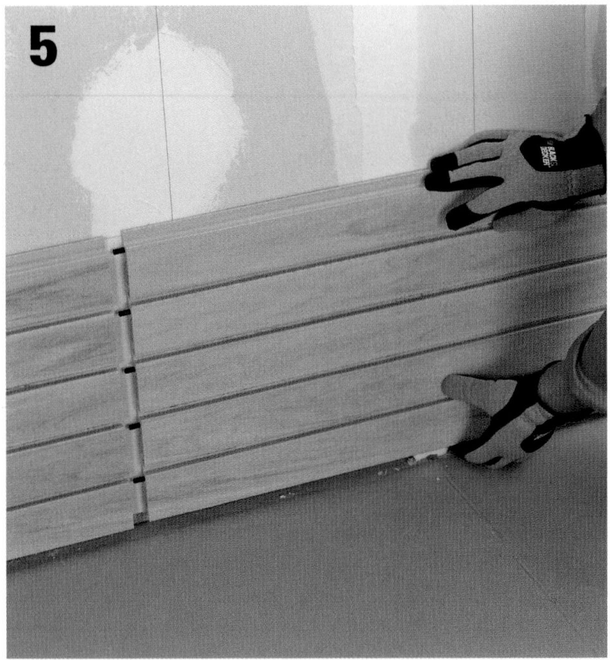

**Make butted joints** at panel ends by sliding doweled panels together. If the ends do not fit together easily, try rapping the free end of the second panels with a wood block to seat it against the first panel.

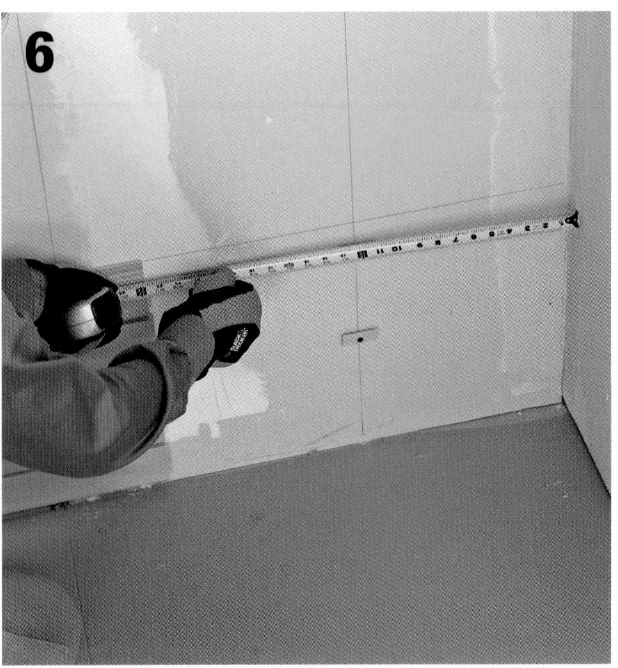

**Measure to find the required length** of the last panel in the first row of panels (if you are doing a full-wall installation). Subtract ⅛" from the distance to allow for expansion of the PVC plastic or composite panels.

**Cut the end panel** to length using a circular saw with a straightedge cutting guide. Orient the panel with the good side facing down to minimize tearout from the saw blade. Any general-purpose blade with carbide-tipped teeth will work. *Tip: Set the workpiece on a backer of scrap plywood and set your saw cutting depth so it is slightly deeper than the panel thickness but not deep enough to cut through the backer.*

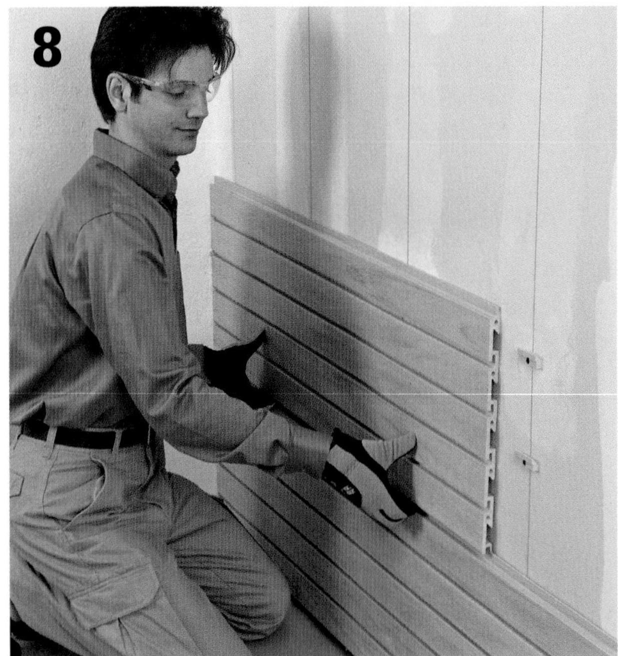

**Install the second course** of panels above the first course. Start with a half-length panel to create a staggered running-bond pattern (seams are not aligned between courses).

**Measure for any cutouts** in the panel, such as windows, receptacles, or switches. To find the edges of the cutout, hold the panel directly below the obstruction with the end aligned flush against the panel it will fit against.

**Make cutouts** for obstructions by following the cutting line with a jigsaw or handsaw. If you are making long, straight cuts, you will get a truer cut with a circular saw and straightedge guide, and then complete the cut at the corners with a jigsaw.

**Install the top row.** Most panels are sized so that they will fit onto an 8-ft. wall without cutting to width. But if you need to cut the panels to width, use a circular saw and straightedge cutting guide or a table saw for the job. Make sure to cut from the same side of all cut panels. Install hangers and brackets as desired.

## Making Corners ▸

If your slatted wall plan calls for making a corner with the material, the easiest way to treat the panels is to butt one panel against another at inside corners or to miter cut the mating panel ends at outside corners. Most slatted wall system manufacturers also sell corner trim that may be installed on outside corners for a neater appearance.

# Utility Shelves

You can build adjustable utility shelves in a single afternoon using 2 × 4s and plain ¾" plywood. Perfect for use in a garage, utility shelves can be modified by adding side panels and a face frame to create a finished look.

The quick-and-easy shelf project shown on the following pages creates two columns of shelves with a total width of 68". You can enlarge the project easily by adding more 2 × 4 risers and plywood shelves. Do not increase the individual shelf widths to more than 36". The sole plates for the utility shelves are installed perpendicular to the wall to improve access to the space under the bottom shelves.

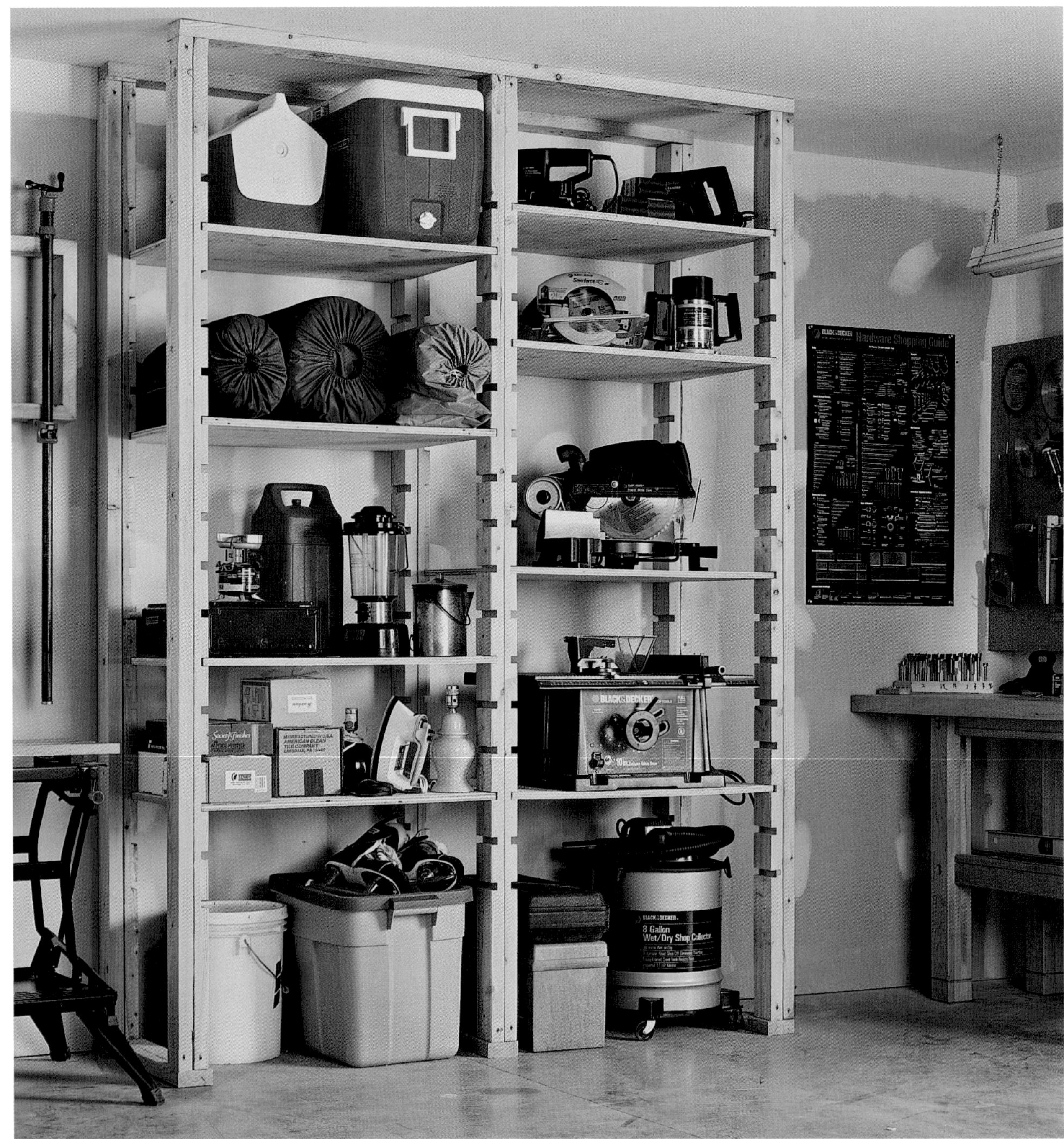


**Utility shelves** built with ordinary 2 x 4s and plywood are an easy, inexpensive way to create flexible storage in a garage.

## Tools & Materials & Cutting List ▸

**Tools**

Tape measure
Level
Framing square
Drill/driver
Plumb bob
Powder-actuated nailer
Clamps
Router
Circular saw
Grease pencil
Straightedge guide

**Materials**

(15) 2 × 4 × 8 pine
(2) ¾ × 4 × 8 plywood
Wood glue
Shims
Drywall or deck screws (2½", 3")
Finishing materials
Shelf supports

**Cutting List**

| Part | No. | Desc. | Size | Material |
|---|---|---|---|---|
| A | 2 | Top plates | 68" | 2 × 4s |
| B | 3 | Sole plates | 24" | 2 × 4s |
| C | 8 | Shelf risers | 93" | 2 × 4s |
| D | 4 | End risers | 93" | 2 × 4s |
| E | 12 | Shelves | 30¾ × 24" | ¾" plywood |

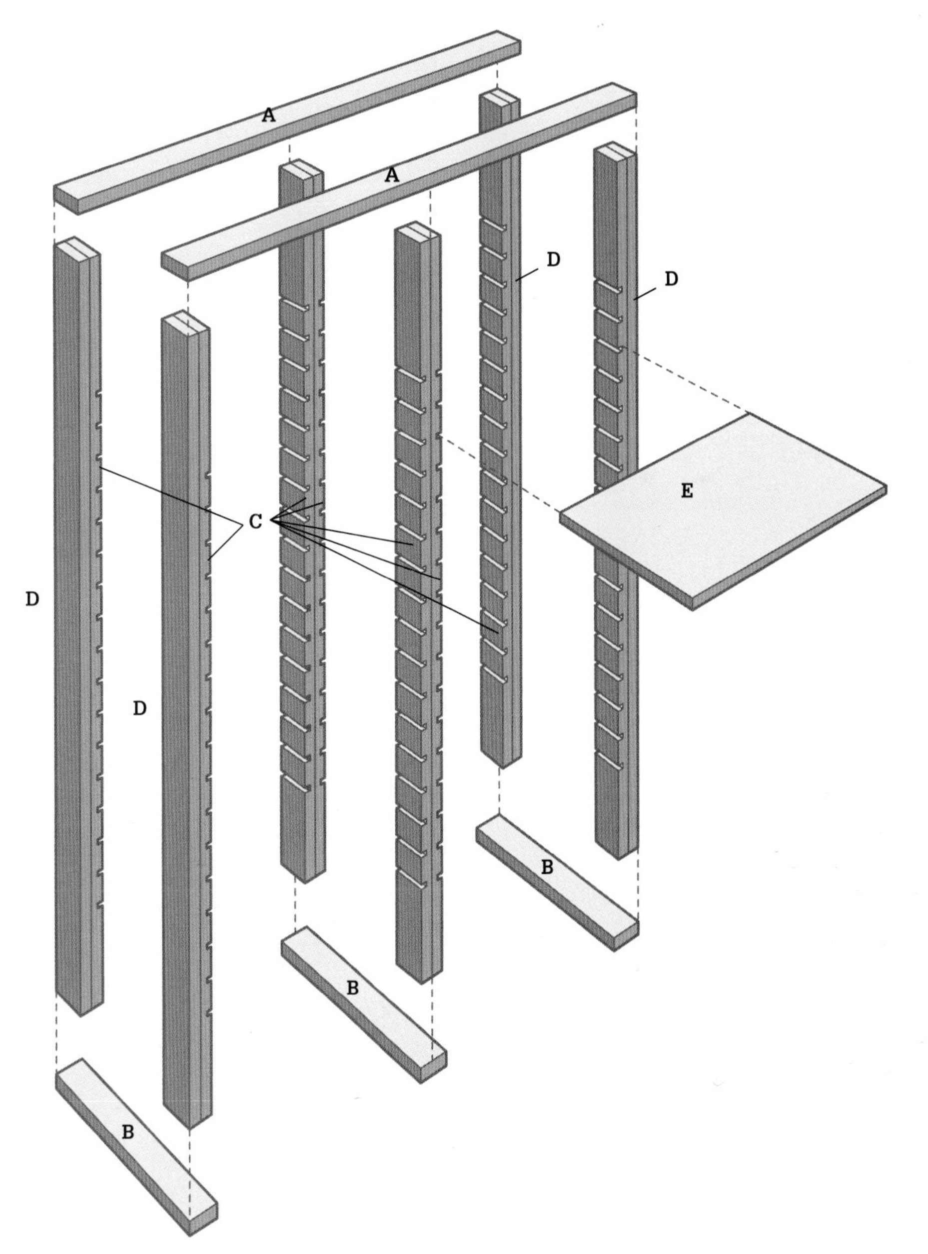

## How to Install Utility Walls

**Mark the location of top plates** on the ceiling. One plate should be flush against the wall, and the other should be parallel to the first plate, with the front edge 24" from the wall. Cut 2 × 4 top plates to full length of utility shelves, then attach to ceiling joists or blocking using 3" screws.

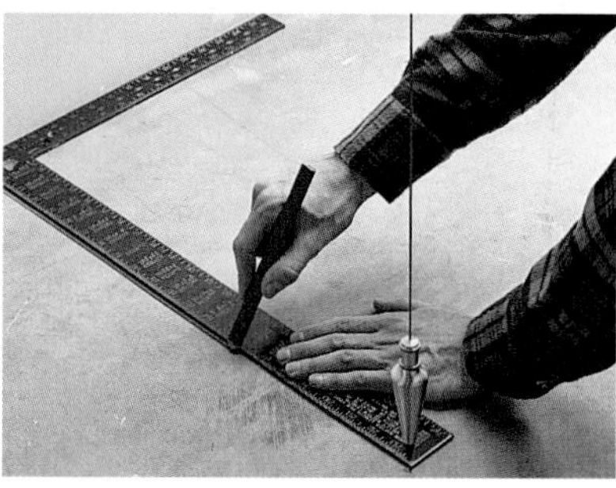

**Mark points directly beneath** the outside corners of the top plates to find the outer sole plate locations using a plumb bob as a guide (top). Mark the sole plate locations by drawing lines perpendicular to the wall, connecting each pair of points (bottom).

**Cut the outer 2 × 4 sole plates** and position them perpendicular to the wall, just inside the outlines. Shim plates to level if needed, then attach to the floor with a powder-actuated nailer or 3" screws. Attach a center sole plate midway between the outer sole plates.

**Prepare the shelf risers** by cutting ⅞"-wide, ¾"-deep dadoes with a router. Cut dadoes every 4" along the inside face of each 2 × 4 riser, with the top and bottom dadoes cut about 12" from the ends of the 2 × 4. *Tip: Gang cut the risers by laying them flat and clamping them together, then attaching an edge guide to align the dado cuts. For each cut, make several passes with the router, gradually extending the bit depth until dadoes are ¾" deep.*

**Trim the shelf risers** to uniform length before unclamping them. Use a circular saw and a straightedge guide.

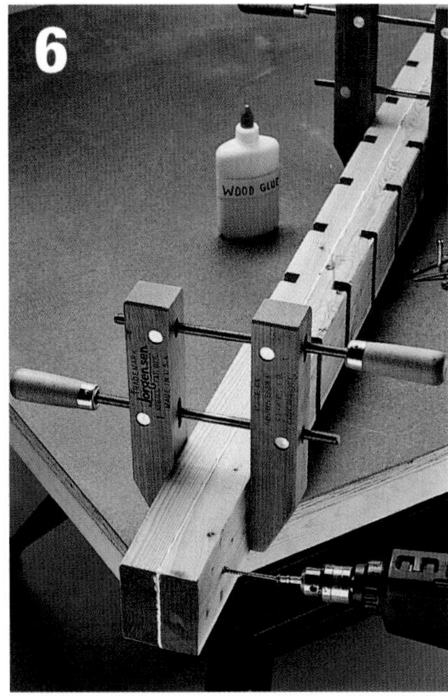


**Build two center shelf supports** by positioning pairs of shelf risers back-to-back and joining them with wood glue and 2½" screws.

**Build four end shelf supports** by positioning the back of a dadoed shelf riser against a 2 × 4 of the same length, then joining the 2 × 4 and the riser with glue and 2½" screws.

**Position an end shelf support** at each corner of the shelving unit between the top and the sole plates. Attach the supports by driving 3" screws toenail-style into the top plate and sole plates.

**Position a center shelf support** (both faces dadoed) at each end of the center sole plate, then anchor shelf supports to the sole plate using 3" screws driven toenail-style. Use a framing square to align the center shelf supports perpendicular to the top plates, then anchor to top plates.

**Measure the distance** between the facing dado grooves and subtract ¼". Cut the plywood shelves to fit and slide the shelves into the grooves.

# Installing Garage Cabinets

If you'd prefer to keep your garage storables behind closed doors, a set of cabinets might be just the solution you're looking for. Any interior kitchen cabinets can be used in a garage, including both base and upper cabinets. Base cabinets really offer several benefits: deep inner storage for large items; drawers for fasteners, hardware, or other small tools; and, of course, a convenient flat work surface. If you're upgrading your garage storage on a budget, utility-grade melamine or unfinished cabinets are actually quite affordable. You could also shop at a second-hand building materials outlet or put to use cabinets removed during a kitchen remodel. If you have limited floor space in your garage, look for utility cabinets with a shallower base. Some manufacturers offer a 15"-deep model that's 9" shallower than standard base cabinet. As you plan, make sure there's still room to park the car, bikes, and other yard and garden equipment.

The process for installing cabinets in a garage is the same as in a kitchen. Cabinets must be firmly attached to wall studs, and they should be level and plumb. Using a level as a guide, draw reference lines along the project wall to indicate the locations of base and wall cabinets. If your garage floor is uneven, find the highest point of the floor along the wall and use this as your initial reference for drawing the other layout lines.

The best way to ensure an even, level installation of upper cabinets is to install a temporary ledger board to the wall, and rest the cabinets on it when fastening them to the wall studs. Many pros install upper cabinets first to take advantage of the full wall access, but you might want to begin with the base cabinets and use them to help support the uppers during their installation. If your garage cabinet system will include a corner cabinet, install it first and work outward to make sure the corner cabinet will fit the space properly. If your garage floor tends to be damp, it's a good idea to install leveler feet on the base cabinets beforehand.

## Tools & Materials ▸

- Eye protection & work gloves
- Long level
- Grease pencil
- Tape measure
- Stud finder
- Combination square
- Drill
- Handscrew clamps
- Hammer
- Caulk gun
- 1 × 4 ledger boards
- 2½" drywall screws
- 1¼" panhead screws
- Base & wall cabinets
- Shims
- Toekick boards or side panel trim, as needed
- ¾" plywood
- Panel adhesive
- 1 × 2 lumber for edging strips
- Finish nails
- ¼" hardboard
- 1" brads
- L-brackets

**Garage utility cabinets** are inexpensive and because the base cabinets are not as deep as kitchen cabinets, they have a compact footprint that's well suited to a garage. A durable melamine surface is easy to clean, and a double plywood work top with a replaceable hardboard surface stands up well to hard use.

## How to Install Garage Cabinets

**Find the high point** of the floor in the installation area by leveling a long, straight board and identifying the principal contact point with the floor. Mark the point on the floor with a grease pencil or tape.

**Draw a level line** along the wall to create a base cabinet top reference

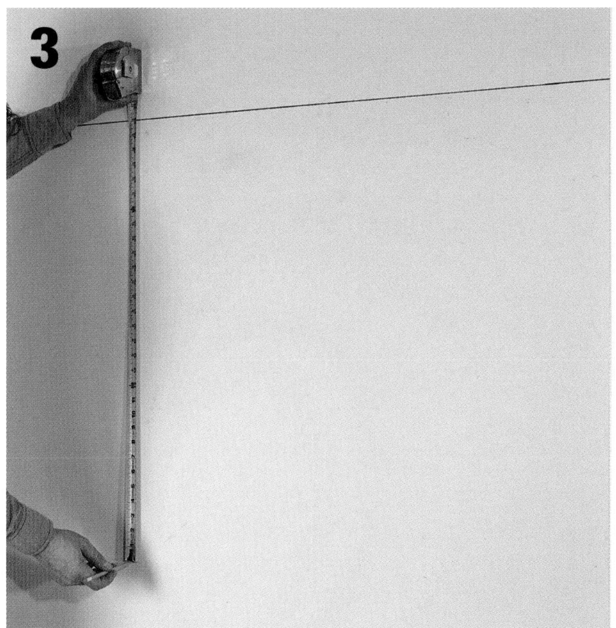

**Draw reference lines** for the upper cabinets based on the base cabinet line. If your base cabinets are 34½" tall (standard height not including countertop) then the line for the tops of the upper cabinets should be 49½" above the base cabinet line and parallel to it. Measure down from the upper cabinet top line 30" and mark reference lines for the bottom of the upper cabinets (make sure your cabinets are 30" high first—this is a standard but there is occasional variation).

**Mark wall stud locations** clearly on the wall just above the base cabinet line and just below the bottom upper cabinets line. Also mark stud locations slightly above the top upper cabinet line. Use a stud finder to identify the locations of the studs.

(continued)

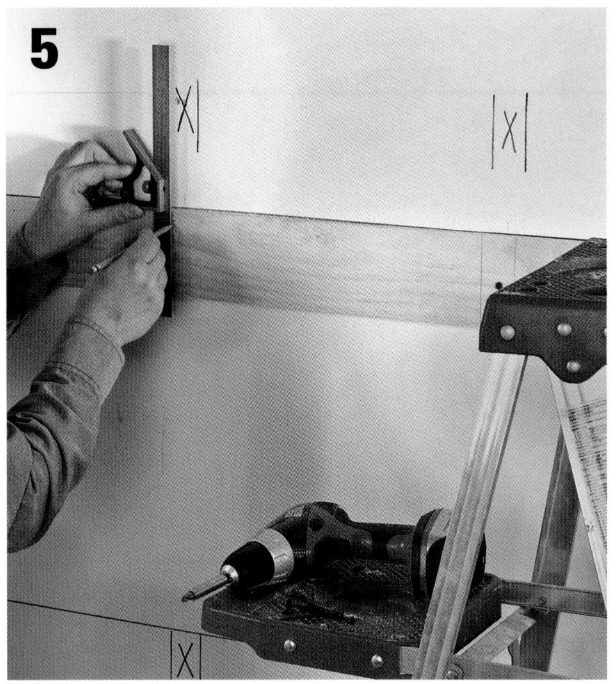


**Attach ledgers** to the wall or walls to provide temporary support for the upper cabinets while you install them. The ledgers (1 × 4 is being used here) should just touch the reference line for the bottom of the wall cabinet. Attach the ledger with a drywall screw driven at each stud location. Transfer stud location marks to the ledger.

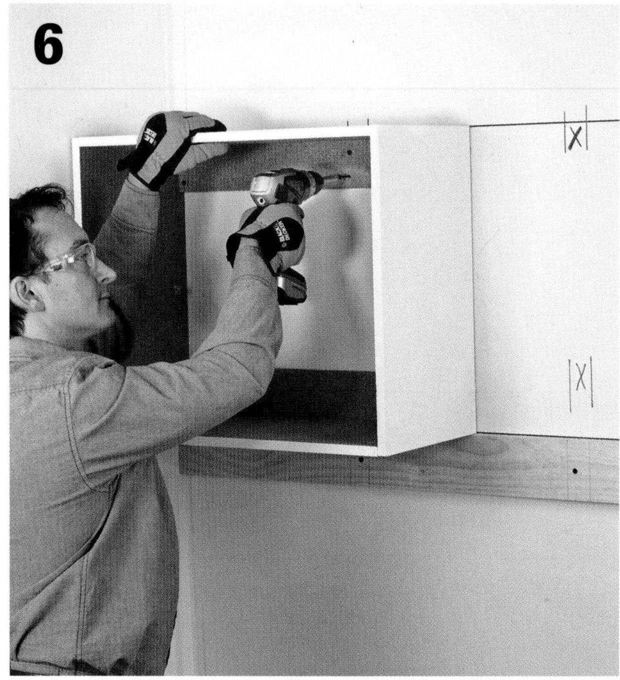


**Attach the first wall cabinet** with 2½" drywall screws. If the cabinet has a mounting strip at the top of the back panel (most do), drive a pair of screws through the strip at each stud location. Attach all wall cabinets to the wall.

**Join wall cabinets** by driving 1¼" panhead screws through one cabinet side and into the adjoining cabinet side. Clamp the cabinets together first to make sure the fronts and tops stay flush.

**Install the first base cabinet** directly under the first wall cabinet. Position the cabinet and shim it as needed until it is level, plumb, and touches the reference line (see step 2). Secure it to the wall with 2½" drywall screws.

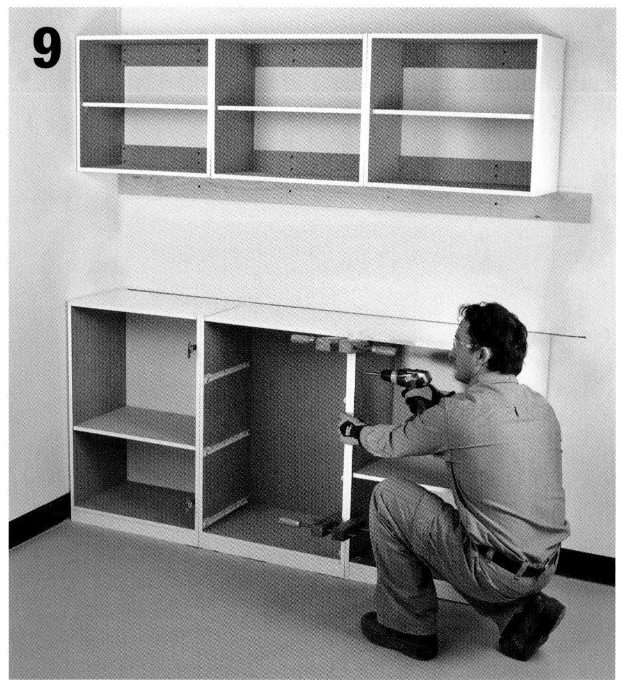


**Install the remaining base cabinets** by leveling the cabinet sides, screwing them to the wall studs, and then fastening them together. Attach toe-kick trim boards or side panel trim, if desired. Remove the upper cabinet wall ledger or ledgers.

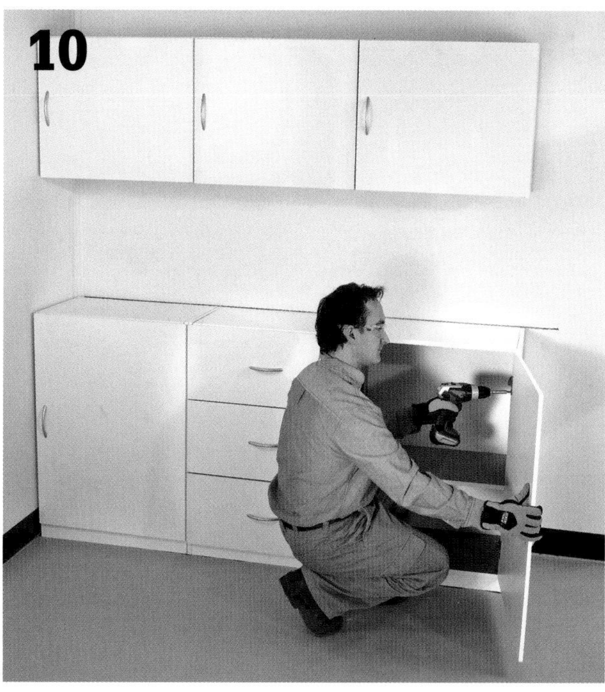


**Attach cabinet doors** and drawers if you removed them during installation or if they were not preattached. Adjust the hinges according to the manufacturer's instructions so the gaps between doors are even and they all open and close smoothly.

**Make the work top.** While a piece of postform countertop makes a suitable and easy-to-install work top, you can create a heavier, more durable top with plywood. Simply cut two pieces of ¾" plywood so they overhang each side and the front of the cabinet base by 1". Secure them with panel adhesive and countersunk 1¼" screws. Use plenty of screws. Then cover the front and side edges with strips of 1 × 2. The front strip should overhang the front ends of the side strips. Attach the strips with adhesive and finish nails. Finally, cut a piece of ¼"-thick hardboard so all edges are flush with the base. Attach it with 1" brads driven through slightly countersunk pilots holes (the heads need to be recessed). When the hardboard top becomes worn, you can easily remove it and replace it.

**Attach the work top.** If your base cabinets do not have preattached mounting strips for a countertop, fasten L-brackets around the inside perimeter of each cabinet, and then drive screws up through the L-brackets and into the underside of the work top. Apply a bead of panel adhesive to all cabinet top surfaces for a better bond and to reduce clattering. Add a bench vise, if desired.

# Installing a Ceiling Storage Unit

Some garage storables, such as empty coolers, luggage, and cartop carriers, tend to be bulky but lightweight. They take up an inordinate amount of shelf or floor space that could be better used for heavier items. One storage option for these items is right above your head—on your garage ceiling. Aside from a few lights and the track rails for your garage door, there isn't much on the ceiling of most garages. If your garage has roof trusses, you've got the perfect location for some lightweight shelf storage.

There are several ceiling-hung shelf kits available in a range of lengths and widths. The typical ceiling storage unit consists of four downrods that bolt to the bottom truss or joist members. A pair of crossbraces attaches to the downrods to form support frameworks for wire shelf grids. Other styles of ceiling storage are available for hoisting bicycles, truck toppers, or canoes up and out of the way.

Installing ceiling storage involves locating truss chords, joists, or rafter ties to support the four downrods, and then attaching the rods to the ceiling framing with lag bolts. The crossbraces and grids fit between the downrods and attach with nuts and bolts.

It's possible to install the system by yourself, but a helper makes the job much easier. Once the parts are assembled, carefully double-check all connections before loading up the shelf.

Be careful to position your ceiling storage unit clear of the path of your sectional garage door and the moving parts of your garage door opener. Use a stud finder to help determine the thickness of the trusses so you can locate the attachment bolts as close as possible to their centers. Refer to the instructions that come with your kit to be clear about the maximum weight load your unit can hold.

## Tools & Materials ▸

- Stepladder
- Stud finder
- Tape measure
- Drill
- Screwdriver
- Ratchet wrench & sockets
- Overhead shelving kit

**A ceiling shelf unit** takes advantage of underused space between the hood of your parked car and the ceiling. Most units are rated only for relatively light storage items.

## How to Install a Ceiling Storage Unit

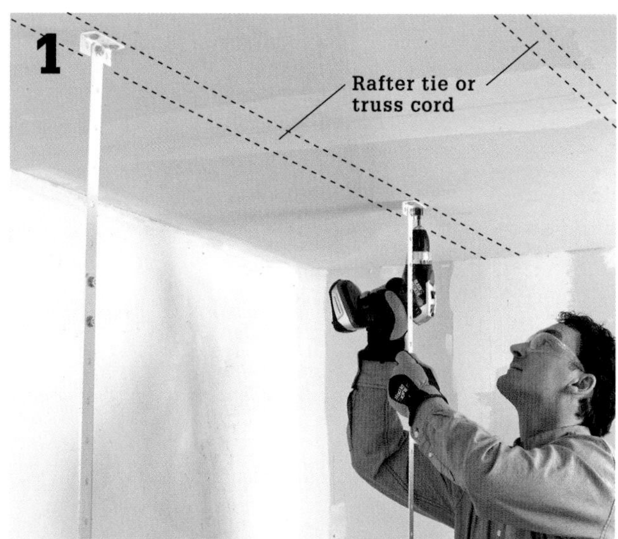


**Attach the downrods** for the first pair of horizontal support bars using the fasteners recommended by the manufacturer. The fasteners must be driven into structural members in the ceiling, be they truss chords, rafter ties, or ceiling joists. The outside edges of the two footplates should follow the spacing recommended in the instructions (69" apart for the model seen here). Install the second pair of downrod footplates on the next rafter or truss chord in 24" on-center framing. If the ceiling is 16" O.C., skip one member so the footplates are 32" apart.

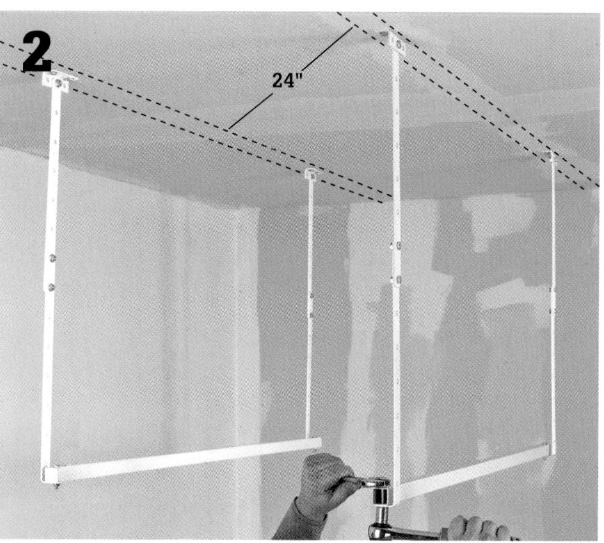


**Install the horizontal support bars.** The bottom ends of the downrods are secured to the horizontal bars that support the shelving. This is often done with the use of L-shaped corner rods with female ends that accept the male ends of the downrod and the horizontal bars. How deeply the corner rods are inserted into the downrod determines the height of the storage platform. Set the height you want and then insert bolts through the aligned bolt holes in the downrods and corner rods. Align all parts and secure with bolts and nuts.

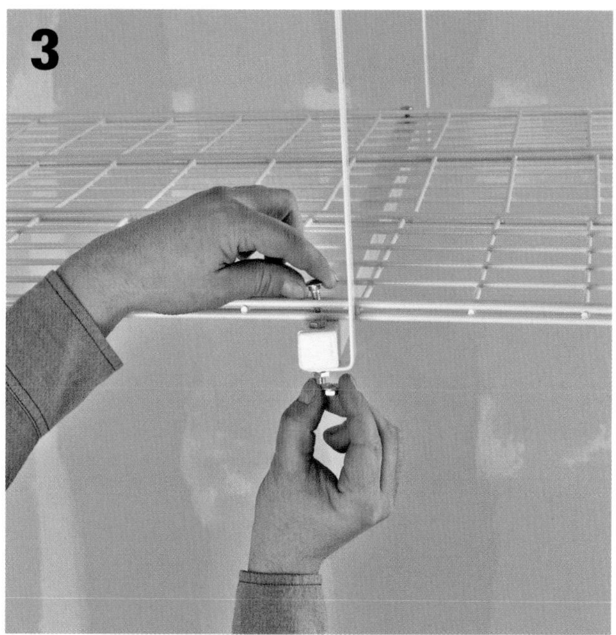


**Install the shelving grids.** Position the wire grid shelves so they span the support bars with even overhang (if possible). Thread bolts through the parallel wires and support framework as directed. Hand tighten nuts and washers onto bolts.

**Join the grids** together with the supplied fasteners. Load the storage items onto the shelves. Do not overload. Your instruction manual will inform you of the weight capacity. The model shown here is rated for up to 300 pounds provided the weight is distributed evenly.

# Electrical & Lighting Improvements

If your garage has too few outlets or just a single light bulb that hangs starkly from the ceiling, that may be part of the reason why you don't use your garage more often. It's frustrating to work in a poorly lit room and inconvenient to have to plug everything into extension cords. Truth be told, many garages are built with just one or two outlets and a single overhead light—just enough service to operate a garage door opener and get you in and out of your car.

Adding more outlets, lights, or even a skylight will dramatically improve the working conditions in your garage. Suddenly, you'll be able to plug in all those electric tools, add an air conditioner or heater, and actually see what you're working on. These sorts of projects could be the keys to jump-starting that garage workshop you've always dreamed about.

This section will show you how to install electrical boxes, run wire, connect receptacles and switches, and install circuit breakers. These are all the steps you need to bring juice where you want it. Pages 180 to 205 provide practical instructions for extending service into your garage. If your garage suffers from poor lighting, you'll learn how to install new fluorescent light fixtures or add a new garage window or fixed skylight. We'll also show you how to hardwire an electric heater to make your garage more habitable during the winter months.

If you are inexperienced with wiring or uncomfortable working with electricity, by all means hire a professional licensed electrican to complete this work. Professionals can do the job quickly and safely, and they secure the proper permit inspections. Even if you have the work performed by someone else, review the included wiring diagrams to familiarize yourself with your options. Draw up a plan to determine where you'd like to have outlets and switches installed so you can share it with the electrician.

**Upgrading** to a full 8-ft.-long fluorescent light fixture is an efficient way to improve the quality of the light in your garage (see pages 192 to 193).

# Wiring Safety

**Shut power OFF at the main service** panel or the main fuse box before beginning any work.

**Confirm power is OFF by testing** at the outlet, switch, or fixture with a current tester.

**Wear rubber-soled shoes** while working on electrical projects. On damp floors, stand on a rubber mat or dry wooden boards.

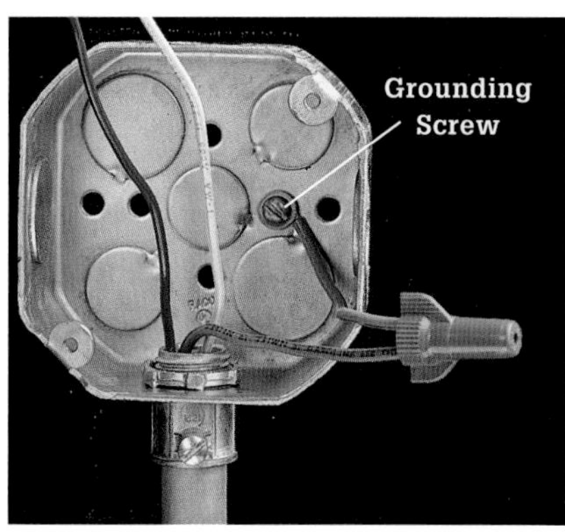


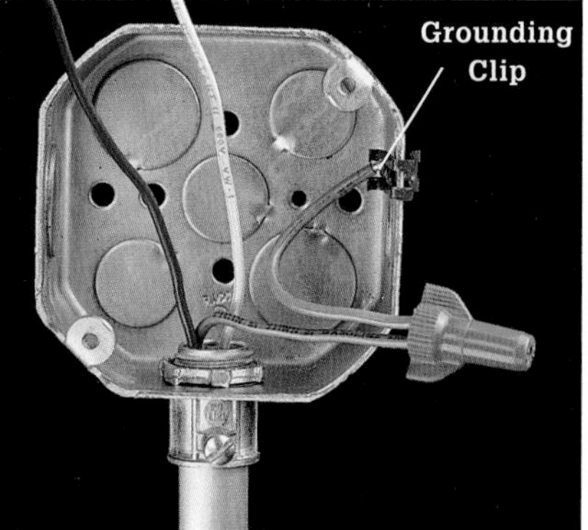


**Install a green insulated grounding** wire for any circuit that runs through metal conduit. Although code allows the metal conduit to serve as the grounding conductor, most electricians install a green insulated wire as a more dependable means of grounding the system. The grounding wires must be connected to metal boxes with a pigtail and grounding screw (left) or grounding clip (right).

**The ground-fault circuit-interrupter**, or GFCI receptacle, is a modern safety device. When it detects slight changes in current, it instantly shuts off power.

**Learn about codes.** The National Electrical Code (NEC), and local electrical and building codes, provide guidelines for determining how much power and how many circuits your home needs. Your local electrical inspector can tell you which regulations apply to your job.

# Bringing Electrical Service to a Garage

Nothing improves the convenience and usefulness of a garage more than electrifying it. Running a new underground circuit from your house to the garage lets you add receptacles and light fixtures both inside the outbuilding and on its exterior.

Adding an outdoor circuit is not complicated, but every aspect of the project is strictly governed by local building codes. Therefore, once you've mapped out the job and have a good idea of what's involved, **visit your local building department to discuss your plans and obtain a permit for the work**.

This project demonstrates standard techniques for running a circuit cable from the house exterior to the garage, plus the wiring and installation of devices inside the building. The building department may recommend or require using a GFCI breaker to protect the entire circuit. Alternatively, you may be allowed to provide GFCI protection to the circuit devices via the receptacle inside the shed. GFCI protection is required on all outdoor circuits.

For basic electrical needs, such as powering a standard light fixture and small appliances or power tools, a 15-amp circuit should be sufficient. However, if you plan to run power-hungry equipment like stationary woodworking or welding tools, you may need one or more dedicated 20-amp circuits. Also, if the shed is more than 50 feet away from the house, you may need heavier-gauge cable to account for voltage drop.

Most importantly, don't forget to call before you dig. Have all utility and service lines on your property marked even before you make serious project plans. This is critical for your safety, of course, and it may affect where you can run the circuit cable.

**Warning: All electrical work must be reviewed and passed by a building inspector. Unless you have experience, electrical installations should be done by a licensed electrician.**

**Adding electrical service to a garage** greatly expands the activities the building will support and is also beneficial for home security.

## Tools & Materials

Spray paint
Trenching shovel (4" wide blade)
4" metal junction box
Metal L-fittings (2) and conduit nipple for IMC conduit
Wood screws
IMC conduit with watertight threaded and compression fittings
Wrenches
Hacksaw
90° sweeps for IMC conduit
Plastic conduit bushings
Pipe straps
Silicone caulk and caulk gun
Double-gang boxes, metal
One exterior receptacle box (with cover)
Single-pole switches
Interior ceiling light fixture and metal fixture box
Exterior motion detector fixture and plastic fixture box
EMT metal conduit and fittings for inside the shed
Utility knife
Wire stripper
UF two-wire cable (12 gauge)
NM two-wire cable (12 gauge)
15-amp GFI-protected circuit breaker
Pliers
Screwdrivers
Wire connectors
Hand tamper
Masking tape
Grease pencil
Scraps of lumber

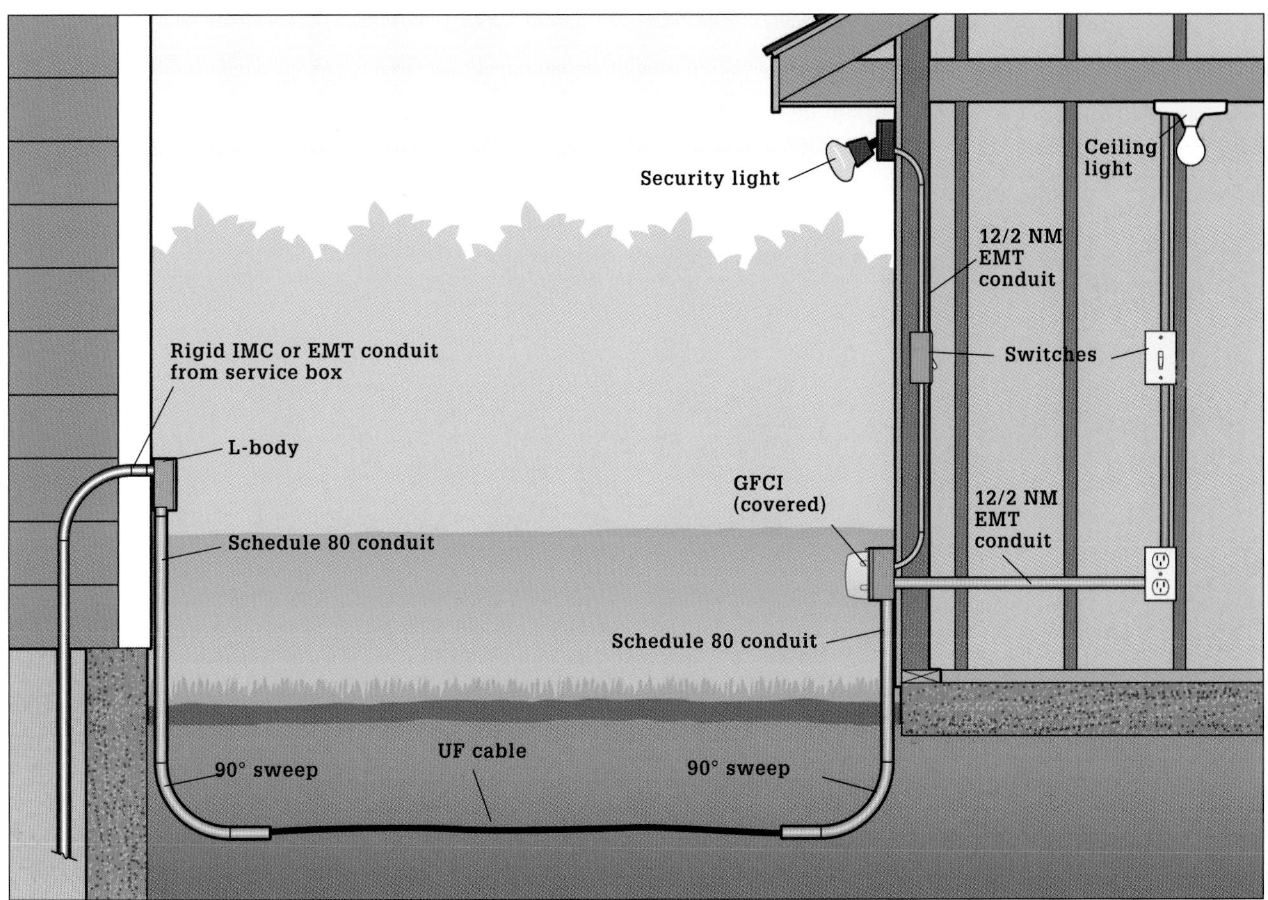


**A basic outdoor circuit** starts with a waterproof fitting at the house wall connected to a junction box inside. The underground circuit cable—rated UF (underground feeder)—runs in an 18"- to 24"- deep trench and is protected from exposure at both ends by metal or PVC conduit. Inside the garage, standard NM cable runs through metal conduit to protect it from damage (not necessary if you will be adding interior wall coverings). All receptacles and devices in the garage must be GFCI protected.

## How to Supply Electrical Service to a Garage

**Identify the circuit's exit point** at the house and entry point at the garage and mark them. Mark the path of the trench between the exit and entry points using spray paint. Make the route as direct as possible. Dig the trench to the depth required by local code using a narrow trenching shovel.

**From outside, drill a hole** through the exterior wall and the rim joist at the exit point for the cable (you'll probably need to install a bit extender or an extralong bit in your drill). Make the hole just large enough to accommodate the L-body conduit fitting and conduit nipple.

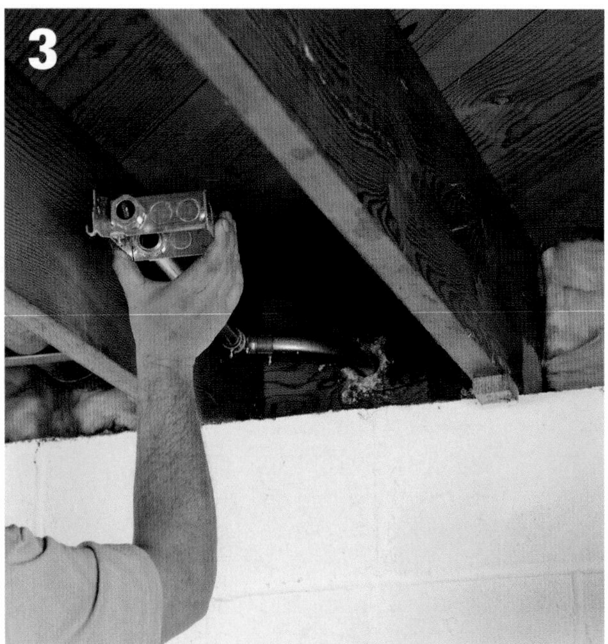

**Assemble the conduit and junction box fittings** that will penetrate the wall. Here, we attached a 12" piece of ¾" conduit and a sweep to a metal junction box with a compression fitting, and then inserted the conduit into the hole drilled in the rim joist. The junction box is attached to the floor joist.

**From outside, seal the hole** around the conduit with expandable spray foam or caulk, and then attach the free end of the conduit to the back of a waterproof L-body fitting. Mount the L-body fitting to the house exterior with the open end facing downward.

**Cut a length of IMC** to extend from the L-fitting down into the trench using a hacksaw. Deburr the cut edges of the conduit. Secure the conduit to the L-fitting, then attach a 90° sweep to the bottom end of the conduit using compression fittings. Add a bushing to the end of the sweep to protect the circuit cable. Anchor the conduit to the wall with a corrosion-resistant pipe strap.

**Inside the shed,** drill a ¾" dia. hole in the shed wall. On the interior of the garage, mount a junction box with an open back to allow the cable to enter through the hole. On the exterior side directly above the end of the UF trench, mount an exterior-rated receptacle box with cover. The plan is to bring power into the garage through the hole in the wall behind the exterior receptacle.

**Run conduit from the exterior box** down into the trench. Fasten the conduit to the building with a strap. Add a 90° sweep and bushing, as before. Secure the conduit to the box with an offset fitting. Anchor the conduit with pipe straps, and seal the entry hole with caulk.

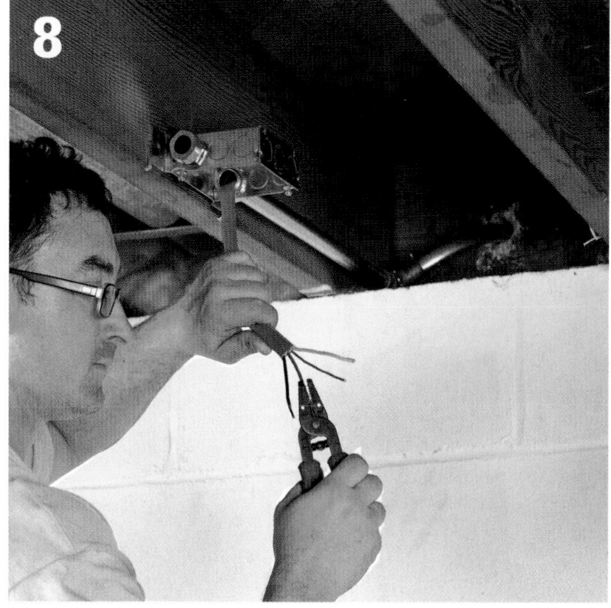


**Run underground feeder (UF) cable** from the house to the outbuilding. Feed one end of the UF circuit cable up through the sweep and conduit and into the L-fitting at the house (the back or side of the fitting is removable to facilitate cabling). Run the cable through the wall and into the junction box, leaving at least 12" of extra cable at the end.

(continued)

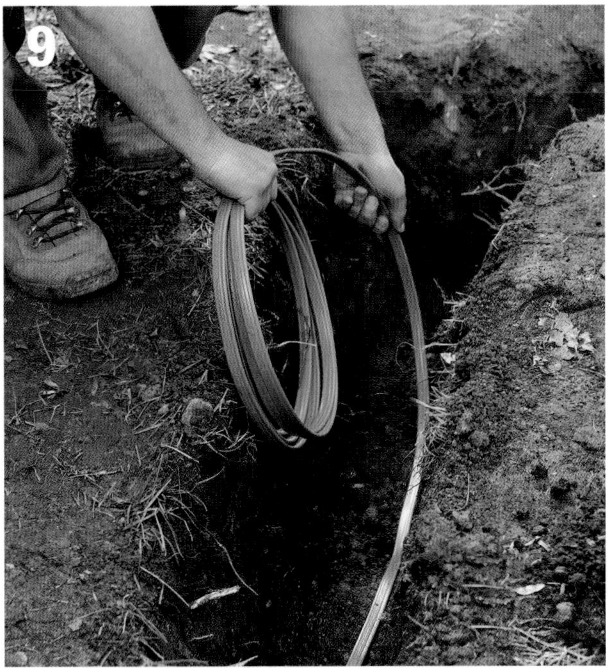

**Lay the UF cable into the trench,** making sure it is not twisted and will not contact any sharp objects. Roll out the cable and then feed the other end of the cable up through the conduit and into the receptacle box in the garage, leaving 12" of slack.

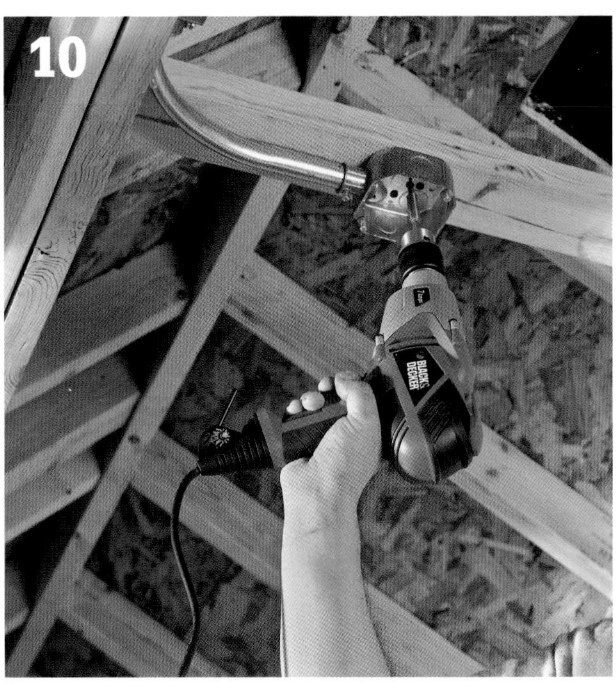

**Inside the garage,** install the remaining boxes for the other switches, receptacles, and lights. With the exception of plastic receptacle boxes for exterior exposure, use metal boxes if you will be connecting the boxes with metal conduit.

**Connect the electrical boxes** with conduit and fittings. Inside the garage, you may use inexpensive EMT to connect receptacle, switch, and fixture boxes. Once you've planned your circuit routes, start by attaching couplings to all of the boxes.

**Cut a length of conduit** to fit between the coupling and the next box or fitting in the run. If necessary, drill holes for the conduit through the centers of the wall studs. Attach the conduit to the fitting that you attached to the first box.

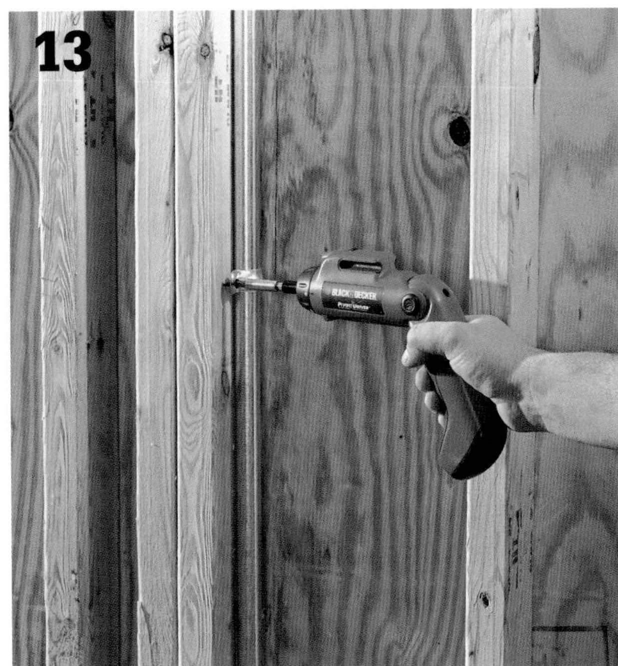


**If you are surface mounting the conduit** or running it up or down next to wall studs, secure it with straps no more than 3 ft. apart. Use elbow fittings for 90° turns and setscrew couplings for joining straight lengths as needed. Make holes through the wall studs only as large as necessary to feed the conduit through.

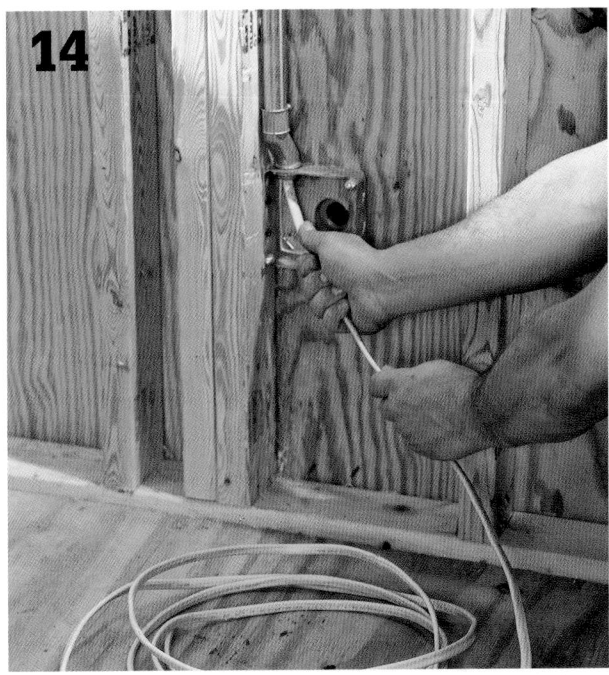


**Measure to find how much NM cable you'll need** for each run, and cut a piece that's a foot or two longer. Before making L-turns with the conduit, feed the cable through the first conduit run.

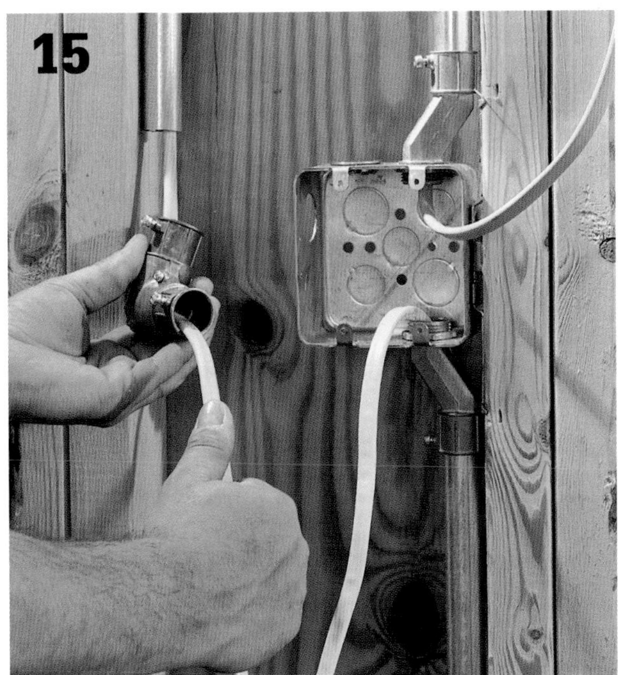


**Feed the other end of the cable** into the next box or fitting in line. It is much easier to feed cable into 45° and 90° elbows if they have not been attached to the conduit yet. Continue feeding cable into the conduit and fitting until you have reached the next box in line.

**Once you've reached the next box in line,** coil the end of the cable and repeat the process with new cable for the next run. Keep working until all of the cable is run and all of the conduit and fittings are installed and secured. If you are running multiple cables into a single box, write the origin or destination on a piece of masking tape and stick it to each cable end.

(continued)

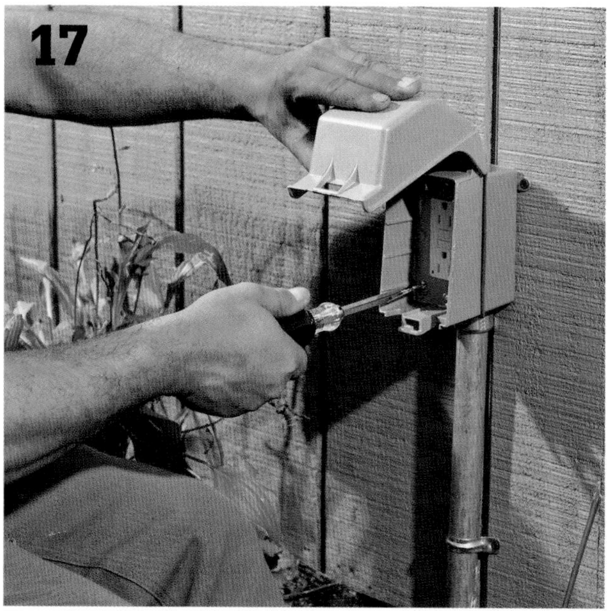


**Make the wiring connections at the receptacles.** Strip ¾" of insulation from the circuit wires using a wire stripper. Connect the white (neutral) wire and black (hot) wire of the UF cable to the LINE screw terminals on the receptacle. Connect the white (neutral) and black (hot) wires from the NM cable to the LOAD terminals. Pigtail the bare copper ground wires and connect them to the receptacle ground terminal and the metal box. Install the receptacle and cover plate.

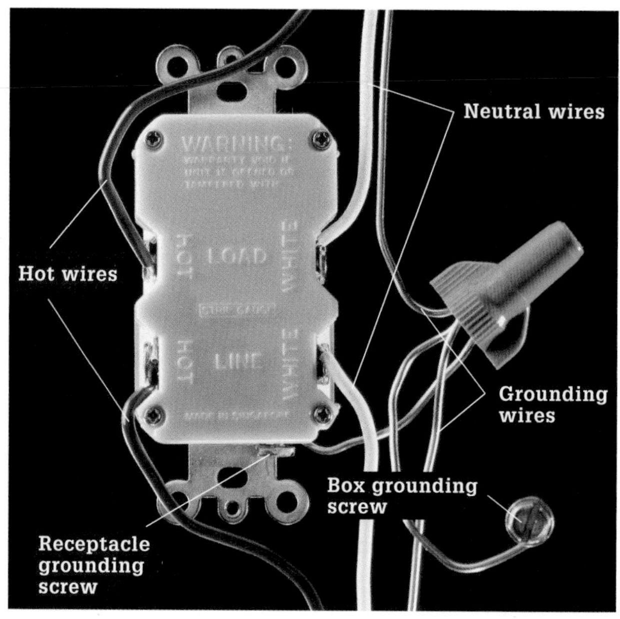


**Variation:** Installing a GFCI-protected breaker for the new circuit at the main service panel is the best way to protect the circuit and allows you to use regular receptacles in the building. An alternative that is allowed in many areas is to run the service into a GFCI-protected receptacle, and then wire the other devices on the circuit in series. If you use this approach, only the initial receptacle needs to be GFCI protected.

**Continue installing receptacles in the circuit run,** and then run service from the last receptacle to the switch box for the light fixture or fixtures. (If you anticipate a lot of load on the circuit, you should probably run a separate circuit for the lights.) Twist the white neutral leads and grounding leads together and cap them. Attach the black wires to the appropriate switches. Install the switches and cover plate.

**Install the light fixtures.** For this garage, we installed a caged ceiling light inside the garage and a motion-detector security light on the exterior side.

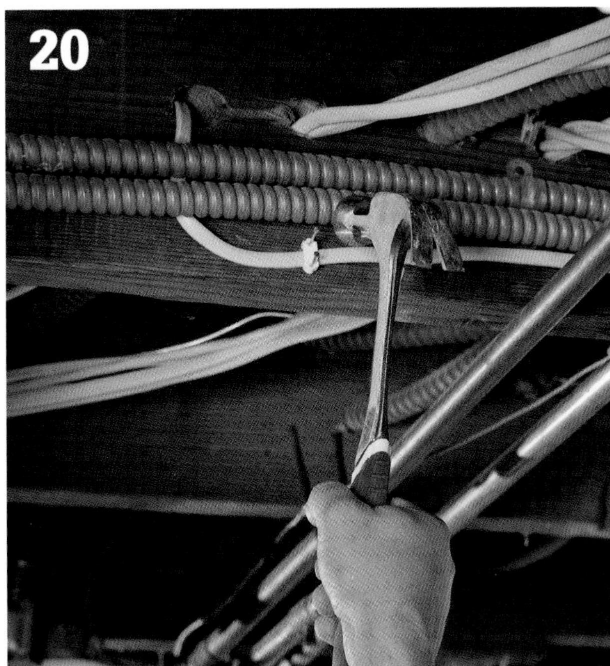


**Run NM cable** from the electrical box in the house at the start of the new circuit to the main service panel. Use cable staples if you are running the cable in floor joist cavities. If the cable is mounted to the bottom of the floor joists or will be exposed, run it through conduit.

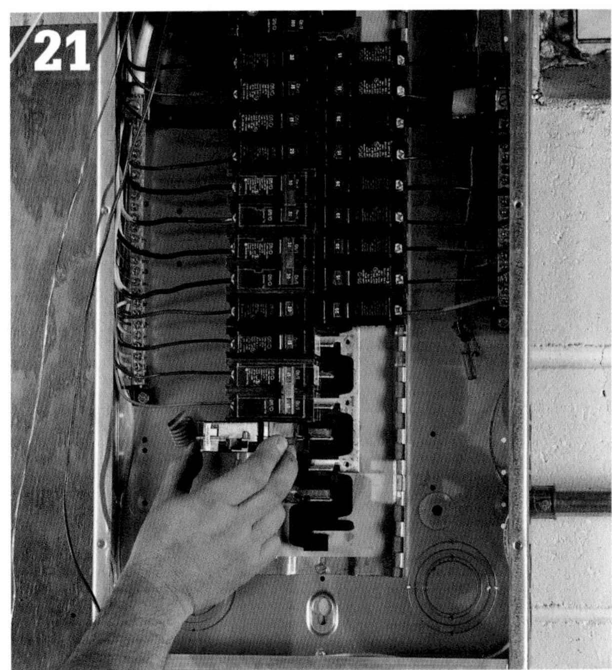


**At the service panel,** feed the NM cable in through a cable clamp. Arrange for your final electrical inspection before you install the breaker. Then attach the wires to a new circuit breaker and install the breaker in an empty slot. Label the new circuit on the circuit map.

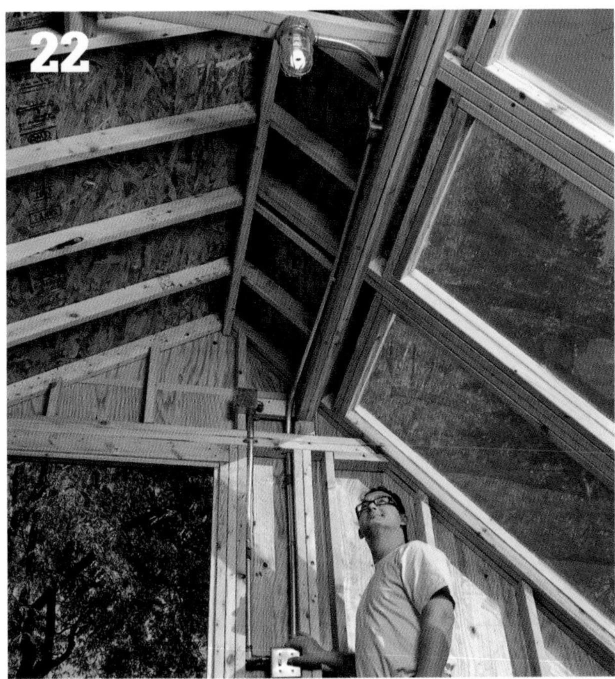


**Turn on the new circuit** and test all of the receptacles and fixtures. Depress the Test button and then the Reset button if you installed a GFCI receptacle. If any of the fixtures or receptacles is not getting power, check the connections first, and then test the receptacle or switch for continuity with a multimeter.

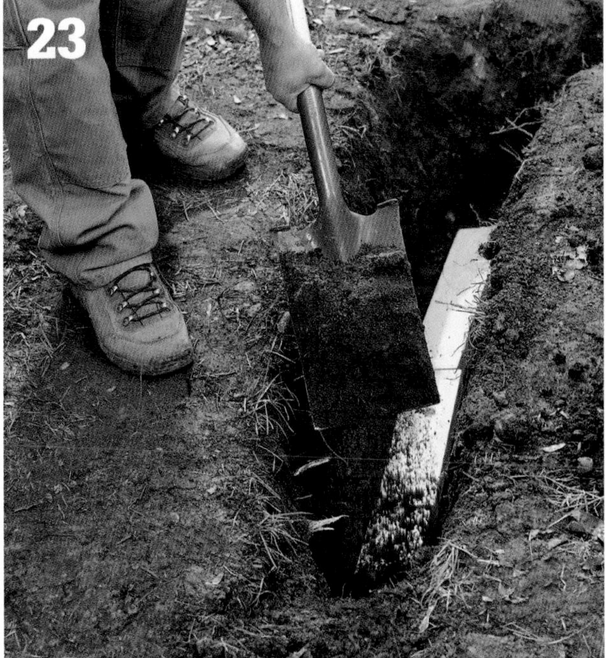


**Lay narrow scraps of lumber** over the cable in the trench as an extra layer of protection from digging, and then backfill with dirt to cover. Replace the sod in the trench if you saved it.

# Motion-Sensing Floodlights

Most garages have floodlights on their exteriors. You can easily upgrade these fixtures so that they provide additional security by replacing them with motion-sensing floodlights. Motion-sensing floods can be set up to detect motion in a specific area—like a walkway or driveway—and then cast light into that area. And there are few things intruders like less than the spotlight. These lights typically have timers that allow you to control how long the light stays on and photosensors that prevent the light from coming on during the day.

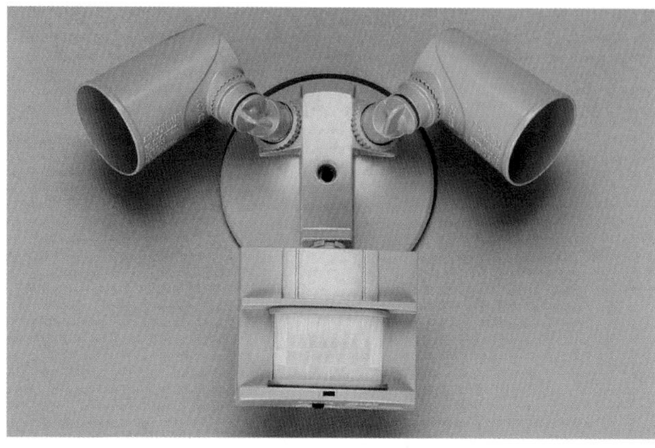

**A motion-sensing light fixture** provides inexpensive and effective protection against intruders. It has an infrared eye that triggers the light fixture when a moving object crosses its path. Choose a light fixture with: a photo cell to prevent the light from turning on in daylight; an adjustable timer to control how long the light stays on; and range control to adjust the reach of the motion-sensor eye.

## Tools & Materials ▸

- Marker
- Drill
- Jig saw
- Fish tape
- Cable ripper
- Combination tool
- Screwdriver
- Voltage sensor
- Light fixture box
- Motion sensor fixture
- Wire connectors

**An exterior floodlight with a motion sensor** is an effective security measure. Keep the motion sensor adjusted to cover only the area you wish to secure—if the coverage area is too large the light will turn on frequently.

## How to Install a New Exterior Fixture Box

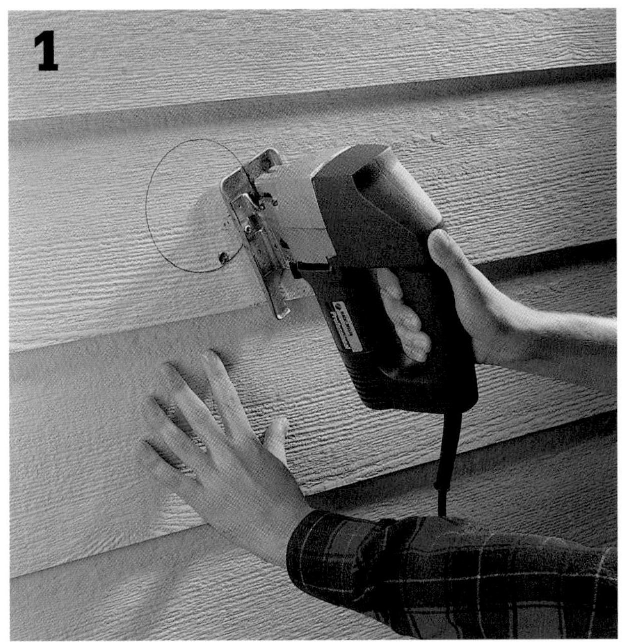


**On the outside of the house,** make the cutout for the motion-sensor light fixture in the same stud cavity with the GFCI cutout. Outline the light fixture box on the wall, then drill a pilot hole and complete the cutout with a wallboard saw or jigsaw.

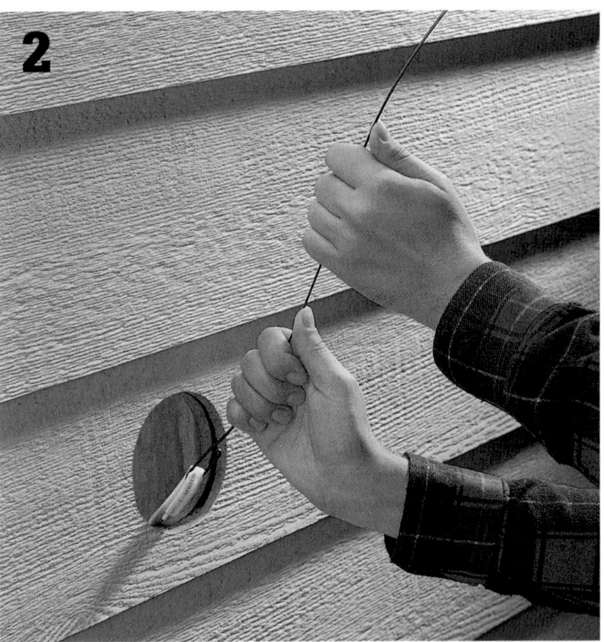


Estimate the distance between the indoor switch box and the outdoor motion-sensor box, and cut a length of NM cable about 2 ft. longer than this distance. Use a fish tape to pull the cable from the switch box to the motion-sensor box.

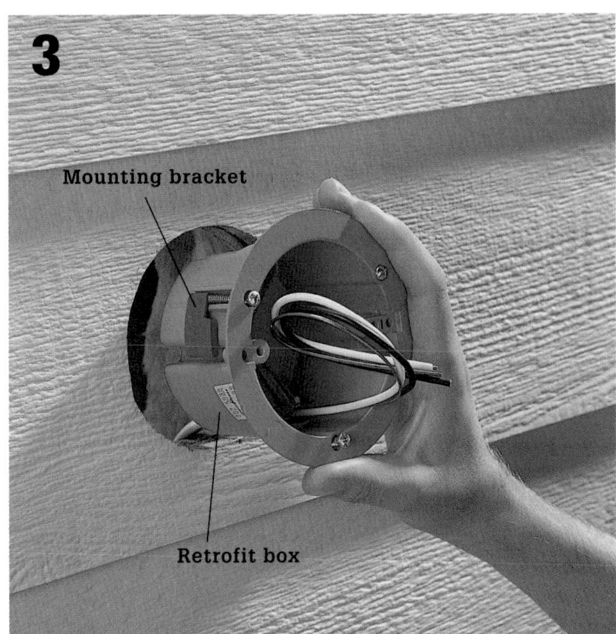


**Strip about 10" of outer insulation** from the end of the cable using a cable ripper. Open a knockout in the retrofit light fixture box with a screwdriver. Insert the cable into the box so that at least ¼" of outer sheathing reaches into the box.

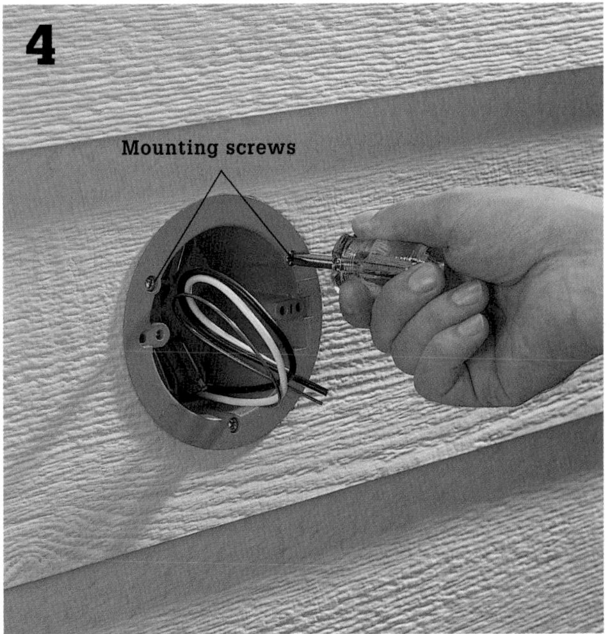


**Insert the box into the cutout opening,** and tighten the mounting screws until the brackets draw the outside flange firmly against the siding.

## How to Replace a Floodlight with a Motion-Sensor Light

**Turn off power to the old fixture.** To remove it, unscrew the mounting screws on the part of the fixture attached to the wall. There will probably be four of them. Carefully pull the fixture away from the wall, exposing the wires. Don't touch the wires yet.

**Before you touch any wires,** use a voltage sensor to verify that the circuit is dead. With the light switch turned on, insert the sensor's probe into the electrical box and hold the probe within ½" of the wires inside to confirm that there is no voltage flow. Disconnect the wire connectors and remove the old fixture.

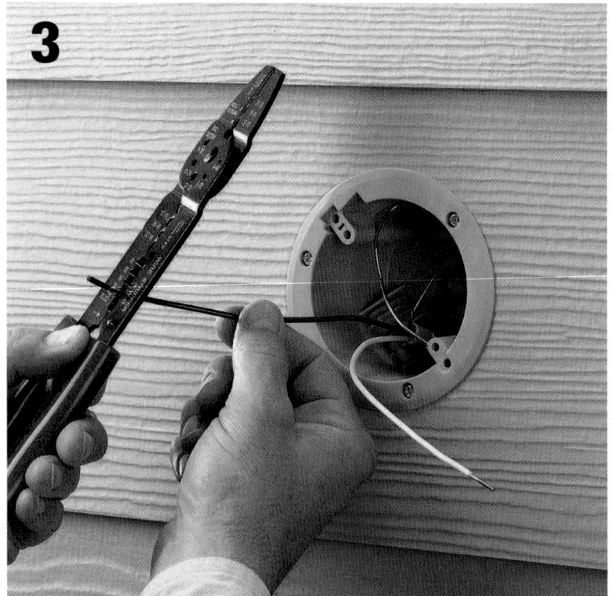

**Examine the ends of the three wires** coming from the box (one white, one black, and one bare copper). They should be clean and free of corrosion. If the ends are in poor condition, clip them off and then strip ¾" of wire insulation with a combination tool.

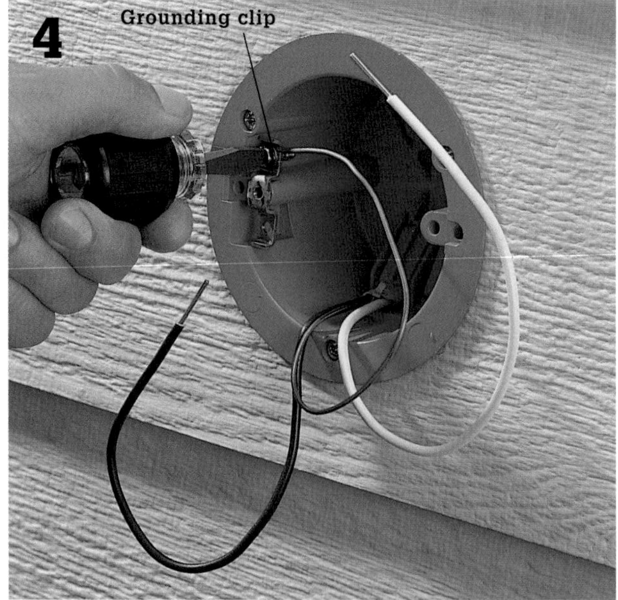


**If the electrical box is nonmetallic** and does not have a metal grounding clip install a grounding clip or replace the box with one that does have a clip, and make sure the ground wire is attached to it securely. Some light fixtures have a grounding terminal on the base. If yours has one, attach the grounding wire from the house directly to the terminal.

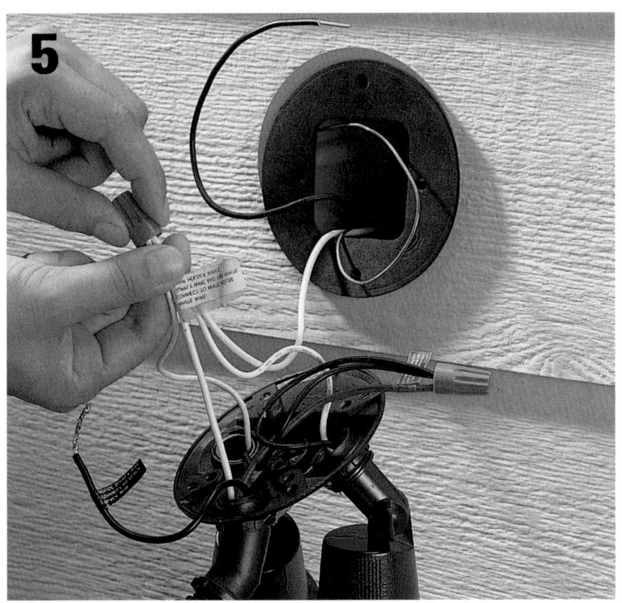


**Now you can attach the new fixture.** Begin by sliding a rubber or foam gasket (usually provided with the fixture) over the wires and onto the flange of the electrical box. Set the new fixture on top of a ladder or have a helper hold it while you make the wiring connections. There may be as many as three white wires coming from the fixture. Join all white wires, including the feed wire from the house using a wire connector.

Next, join the black wire from the box and the single black wire from the fixture with a wire connector. You may see a couple of black wires and a red wire already joined on the fixture. You can ignore these in your installation.

**Neatly tuck all the wires into the box** so they are behind the gasket. Align the holes in the gasket with the holes in the box, and then position the fixture over the gasket so its mounting holes are also aligned with the gasket. Press the fixture against the gasket and drive the four mounting screws into the box. Install floodlights (exterior rated) and restore power.

Test the fixture. You will still be able to turn it on and off with the light switch inside. Flip the switch on and pass your hand in front of the motion sensor. The light should come on. Adjust the motion sensor to cover the traffic areas and pivot the light head to illuminate the intended area.

# Installing Fluorescent Light Fixtures

Aside from natural lighting, fluorescent lights are the most economical way to brighten up your garage. The fixtures are relatively inexpensive, the bulbs burn for thousands of hours before they need replacement, and fluorescent lights use a fraction of the energy of incandescent bulbs. If you buy bulbs rated as daylight in the 3,000 kelvin range, you'll have bright, white light that will make excellent ambient or task lighting for a garage.

In this project, we show you how to install an 8-foot fluorescent ceiling fixture, but you can follow the same procedure for mounting shorter fixed 4-foot lamps. Either way, once you disassemble the fixture to hang it, you'll want to work with a helper. The fixtures are bulky and fairly delicate. If your only option is to work alone, consider renting a wallboard lift to hold the fixture against the ceiling while you fasten it in place.

You might wonder how to determine the number of fixtures you need for your garage. The rule of thumb is one overhead fixture will illuminate an area that extends about 4 feet out from the fixture in all directions. So, a single 4-foot light will illuminate approximately 96 square feet of floor space below it. You'll want to have at least two 4-foot fixtures for a single-car garage and four 4-foot or two 8-foot fixtures for a two-car garage. Of course, adding more fixtures only helps, particularly if you want to eliminate most or all of the shadows in your garage workspace. If you install the minimum number of ceiling fixtures, supplement the overhead lighting with windows and additional task lights where you need them.

Although it might be tempting to buy economy fixtures, you get better value and performance in the long run if you invest in industrial-grade fluorescents. These fixtures have cold-weather ballasts that start immediately in the winter, and they won't flicker or buzz as loudly as economy lights. The ballasts also last much longer than those in bargain-priced lights.

## Tools & Materials ▸

- Stepladder
- Tape measure
- Stud finder
- Drill
- Screwdriver
- Combination tool
- Fluorescent fixture
- Cable clamp
- Wire connectors

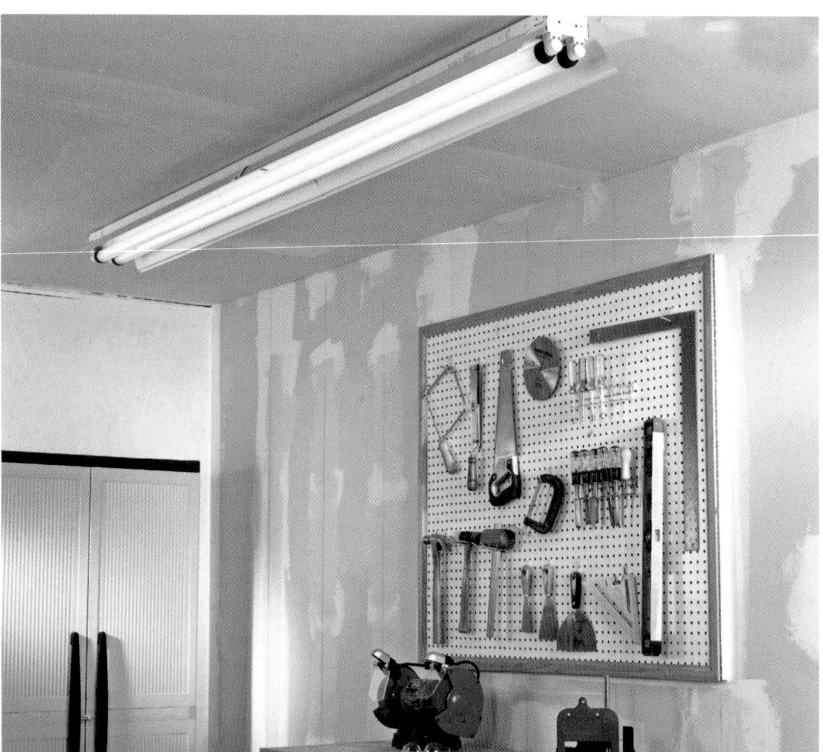

**An 8-ft.-long fluorescent light fixture** can illuminate your entire garage. This model has a heavy-duty ballast that withstands cold weather, making it a good choice for a garage setting.

## How to Install a Hard-wired Light Fixture

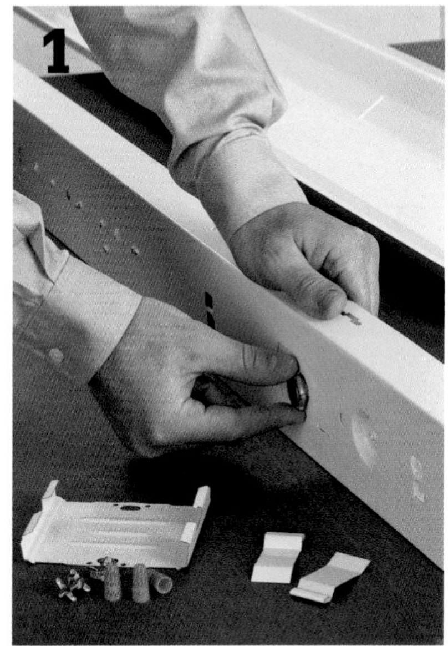

**Prepare the fixture box** for installation by removing the knockout in the box that will align with the electrical box in the ceiling. Raise the fixture to the ceiling. Although fluorescent fixtures are not especially heavy, once you've removed the diffuser there is a danger they will buckle. Have a helper support the other end of the fixture. Position it against the ceiling, threading the end of the cable through the cable clamp installed in the light fixture knockout. *Note: The light fixture must be supplied with 120-volt power from a ceiling box with 12- or 14-gauge NM cable. The cable should be routed through finished walls or through conduit, and it should originate from a switch next to the service door. If you do not have wiring experience, hire a professional to provide power to the fixture box. Shut power OFF at the service panel.*

**Attach the fixture box** to the ceiling by driving screws through mounting holes in the box and into ceiling framing members. If the mounting holes do not align with rafters or trusses, mark the holes, remove the fixture, and then install toggle bolts. Or drill new mounting holes in the metal box at the framing member locations.

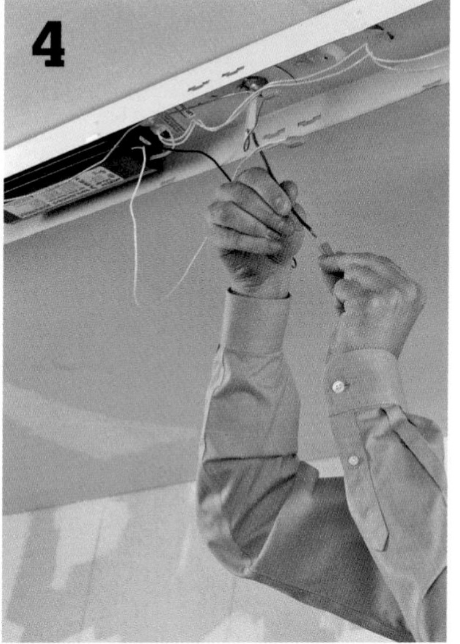

**Make wiring connections.** Connect the bare copper ground in the NM cable to the grounding terminal on the fixture box. (This may require a short pigtail wire.) Connect the black power wire from the switch to the black fixture wire with a wire connector. Connect the white neutral from the switch box to the white fixture wire.

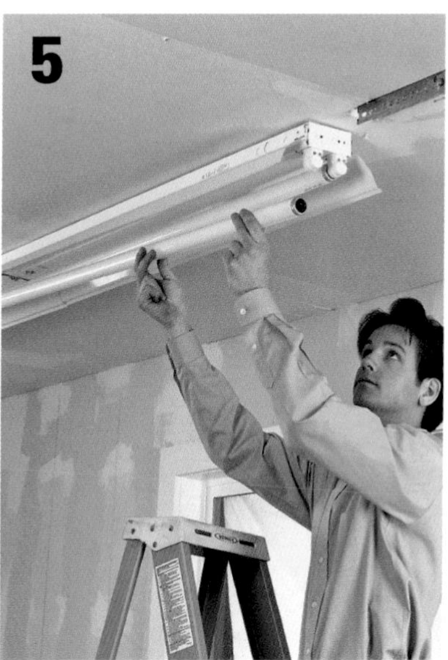

**Install the bulb and test the fixture.** If everything works, remove the bulb and install the deflector shield over the wiring connections. Reinstall the bulb, and then attach the diffuser.

# Installing an Electric Heater

A plug-in portable electric heater is one option for warming your garage, but most of these small room units won't deliver adequate heat. A better solution is to install a thermostatically controlled, hard-wired heater such as the one shown in this project. It has a built-in fan to circulate heat quickly and evenly, and you can mount it to the ceiling where it's out of your way. Louvers on the front of the heater enable you to direct the airflow where it's needed most. The unit has a thermal cutout that automatically shuts it off in the event of overheating.

A hard-wired heater generally requires 220-volt electric service, and it should be wired to a dedicated circuit breaker. If you are experienced with advanced wiring projects, you could wire this project yourself. However, in the interest of personal safety and in order to meet local building codes, it may make more sense to hire a professional electrician for this job.

The heater shown here hangs from a bracket that fastens to a ceiling joist or roof truss. Installing the bracket and mounting the heater isn't difficult. Be sure to follow the manufacturer's recommendations regarding important wall and ceiling clearances before proceeding with the installation. If your garage hobbies create a lot of dust, remember to inspect and clean the heater on a regular basis to keep it working safely and efficiently. If you do not have experience with home wiring, hire a professional to install a new circuit and run the cable to the device.

## Tools & Materials ▸

- Drill
- Studfinder
- Stepladder
- Screwdrivers
- 240-volt heater with mounting bracket
- Flexible metal conduit with 10/2 wire
- Lag screws (3⁄8" × 4")
- Cable clamp

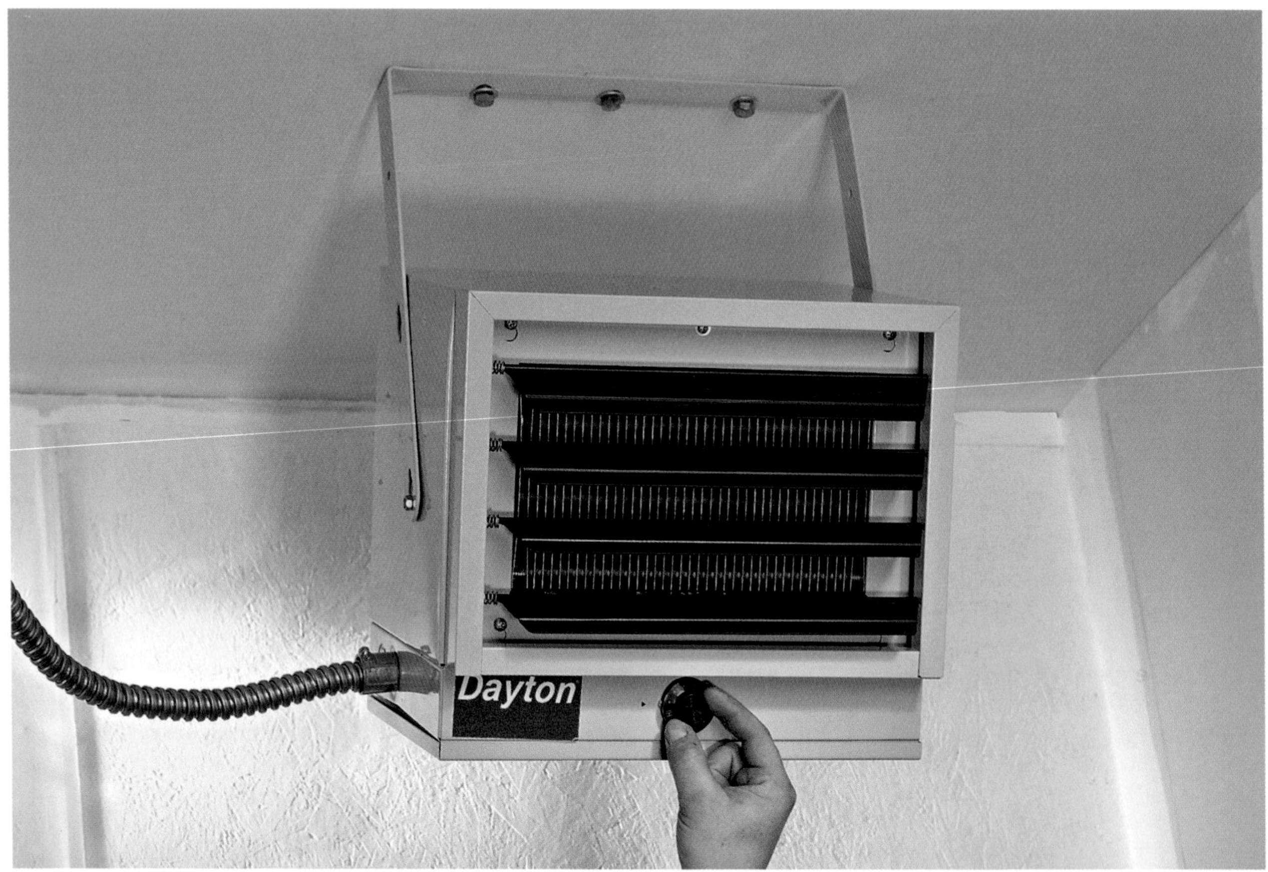


**A high-output electric heater** can improve the working conditions in your garage dramatically, extending your working-in-the-garage season by weeks or months.

## How to Install an Electric Heater

**Turn off power** to the circuit at the main service panel. Mount the heater hanger bracket to the ceiling at a joist location. So you can pivot the heater from side to side, use a single ⅜ x 4" lag screw with a washer on each side of the bracket strap to hang the unit. Don't overtighten the screws.

**Hang the heater unit** in the mounting bracket. Position it at the desired height and align the bracket screws with the screw slots in the hanger straps. Tighten screws to secure the unit. If you want to be able to point the heater downward, make sure to use the keyhole-shaped screw slots.

**Run electrical cable** to the heater. For finished garages, the easiest way to run cable is to encase it in metal conduit that's surface mounted to the walls and ceiling. The unit seen here requires 240-volt service delivered by 10/2 sheathed cable with a ground. Connections at the circuit breaker box should be made by an electrician. The cable is routed through an electrical box located within 2 ft. of the heater.

**Run flexible metal conduit** containing 10/2 cable from the electrical box to the heater unit. Use cable clamps to secure the conduit and leave 8 to 10" of free wire extending into the electrical box. Connect the other end of the conduit to the cable entry opening in the heater unit.

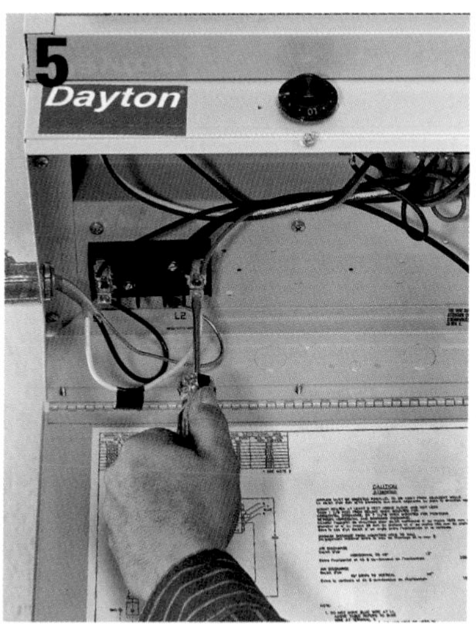


**Make wiring connections** inside the heater unit at the power block and inside the electrical box. A 240-volt heater will have two connection terminals. Connect the black wire from the box to one terminal and connect the white wire to the other terminal. The white wire should be tagged black with electrical tape. Connect the ground wire to the grounding screw terminal.

**Set the thermostat** once you have restored power and tested to make sure the heater is operating properly. On the model shown here, you set the thermostat to high and then dial it back once the garage reaches your desired temperature. Adjust the heater to the desired position.

# Adding a Garage Window

Artificial lighting is only one option for illuminating your garage. Another sensible approach is to add a window or two. No matter which direction your garage faces, a window increases the ambient lighting during daylight hours. Any window size and style can work in a garage, but smaller windows are less vulnerable to break-ins. If you want your garage window to serve as a source of ventilation as well as light, a double-hung style will allow breezes from all directions and it won't project out from the garage when it's open. Be sure to buy insect screens for your new window.

This project shows you how to install a flange-style window in a finished garage wall. The process involves locating the window on the inside wall, removing wallboard and existing framing, and then framing a new rough opening for the window. Once the exterior wall is opened up and the window is mounted, you patch the siding and interior wall surfaces to complete the job. Correct flashing and caulking techniques are critical to keep moisture out, so follow those steps carefully.

Be sure to defer to the installation manual that comes with your new window if the instructions differ from those you see here. Failing to do that and installing the window incorrectly could void the product warranty and lead to leaks or a shorter service life.

## Tools & Materials ▸

Work gloves & eye protection
Utility knife
Straightedge
Tape measure
Marker
Level
Combination square
Hammer
Stepladder
Circular saw
Reciprocating saw
Flat pry bar
Caulk gun
Chalkline
Aviation snips
Common nails (10d, 16d)
Panel adhesive
½" plywood
2× framing lumber
Self-adhesive flashing
Window
Shims
Silicone caulk
1½" roofing nails
Metal drip edge
Brickmold
Case moldings

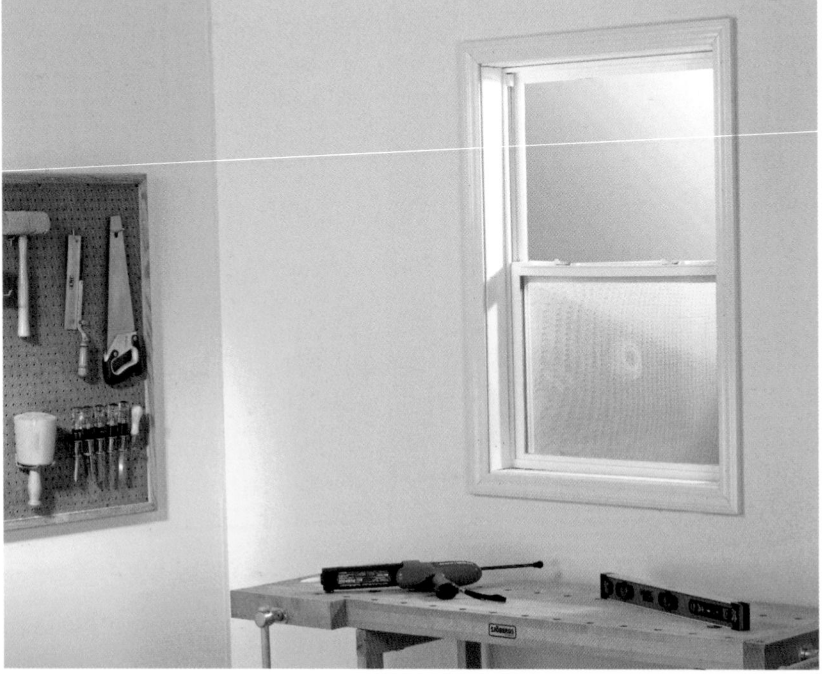

**Add a window** to a dark garage to increase natural light. Although hopper-style windows and fixed windows are common in garages, a double-hung such as this offers better ventilation.

## How to Add a Garage Window

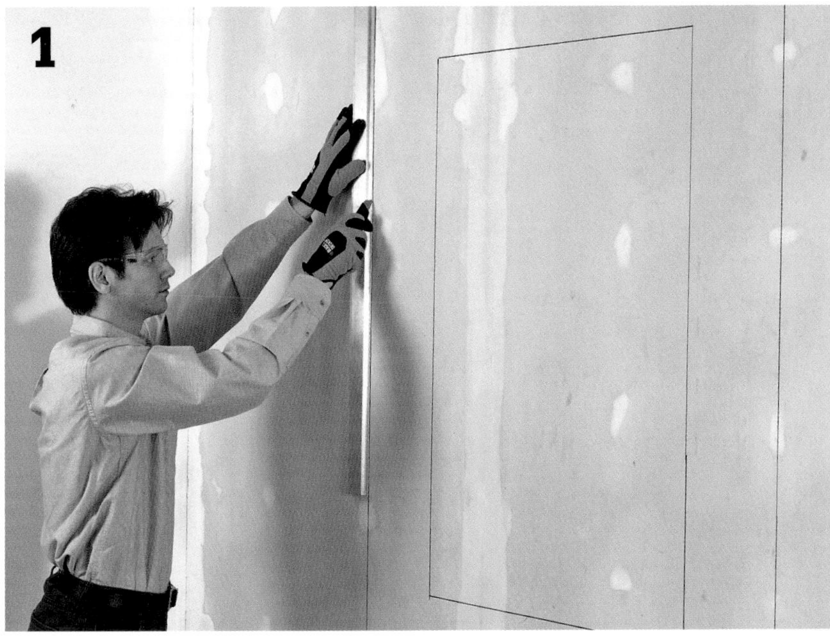

**Remove wall coverings** in the installation area. Lay out the location for the new window on the wall first, according to the rough opening requirements for the window unit you purchased. Extend the opening to the next wall stud on each side, and mark the centers of the studs to outline the removal area. Remove the wall covering material all the way from the ceiling to the floor in the removal area. This will create access for framing the window opening.

**Mark the rough opening width** on the sole plate of the garage wall. Mark locations for jack studs and king studs just outside the rough opening marks.

**Cut and attach the king studs** to the sole plate using 10d common nails driven toenail-style.

**Plumb the tops** of the king studs with a level, and then mark the edges onto the cap plate. Toenail the king studs to the cap plate.

**Mark the top of the rough opening** onto the king studs, measuring up from the floor. Cut the jack studs to this length.

(continued)

**Measure and mark the top** of the header and sill locations on the king studs, and then transfer the lines across the old studs in the rough opening area by positioning a straightedge between the header marks on the king studs. This creates a pair of cutting lines on each old stud.

**Cut the old studs** along the top and bottom cutting lines using a circular saw set to full cutting depth. Finish the cuts with a reciprocating saw or handsaw. Pry out the cut studs with a flat pry bar.

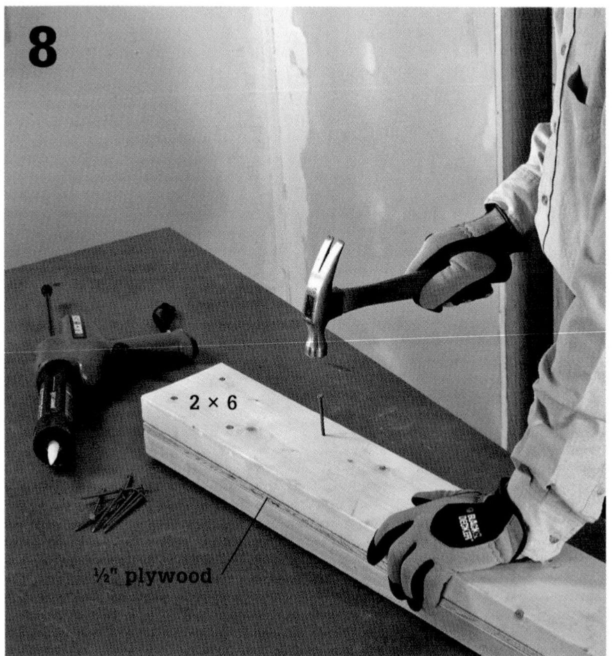


**Make the header.** For most garages, a window or door header made from a pair of 2 × 6s sandwiched around a strip of ½" plywood meets code requirements, but be sure to check with your local building department. Apply panel adhesive between all the parts, and drive 16d nails through both faces at regular intervals to secure the header parts.

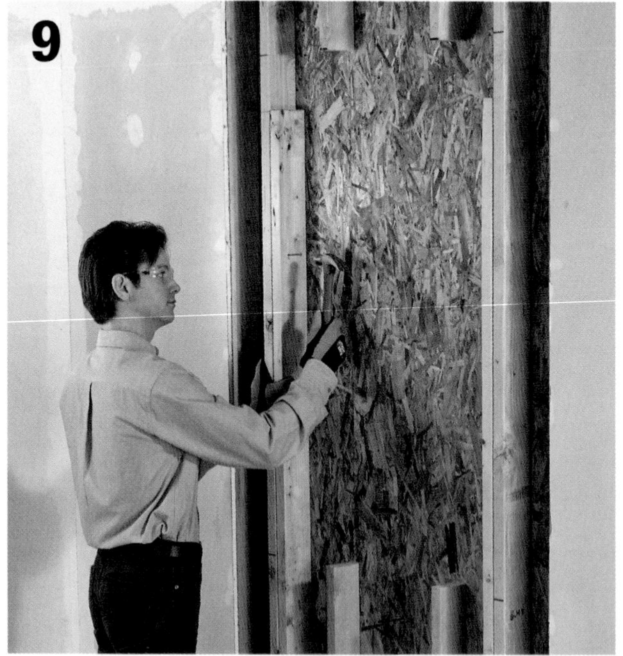


**Facenail the jack studs** to the king studs, making sure the tops align with the layout lines for the bottom of the header (the header will rest on the tops of the jack studs).

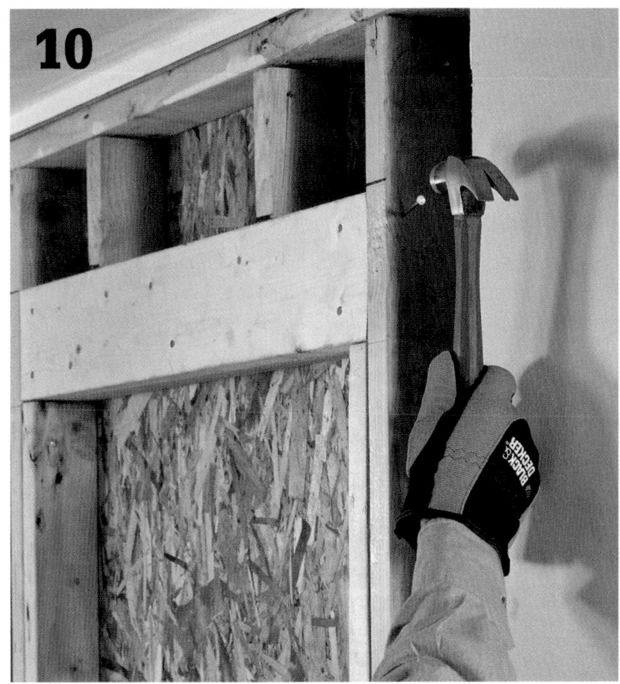

**Install the header.** Set the header (step 8) onto the tops of the jack studs. Attach it to the king studs by facenailing through the king studs and into the header with 10d common nails. Also toenail through the cut studs (called cripple studs) above the header.

**Install a doubled sill.** Attach one sill member by facenailing down and into the tops of the cripple studs. Then, facenail the second sill plate to the first. Also toenail the top sill to the jack studs. Finally, cut two cripple studs and install them beneath the ends of the sill.

**Mark the rough opening** on the exterior wall. First, drive a 10d casing nail through the siding at each corner of the opening, nailing from inside the garage. Then on the exterior side, snap a chalk line between the nails to outline the opening.

**Cut through the wall** with a reciprocating saw, following the cutting lines for the rough opening. Make your cutting lines as straight as you can.

(continued)

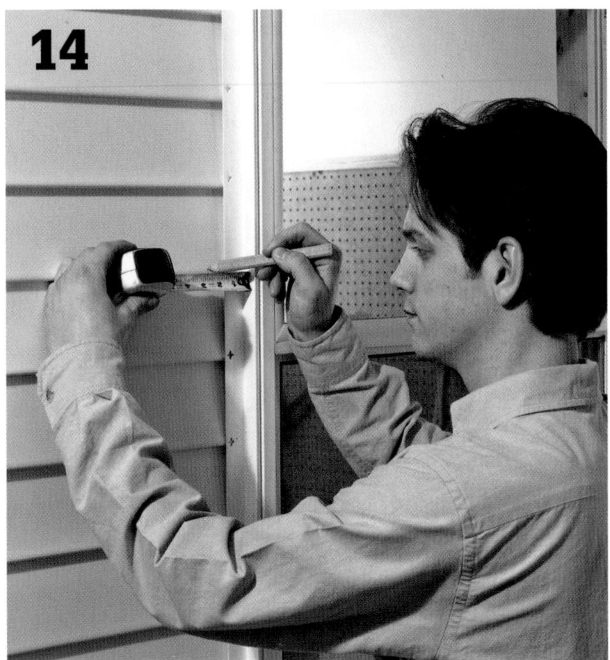


**Mark the siding** around the opening for trimming to create a recess for the window nailing flange and also the brickmold trim that will be installed (it is preinstalled on some windows). You need to temporarily set the window into the opening to trace the cutting lines.

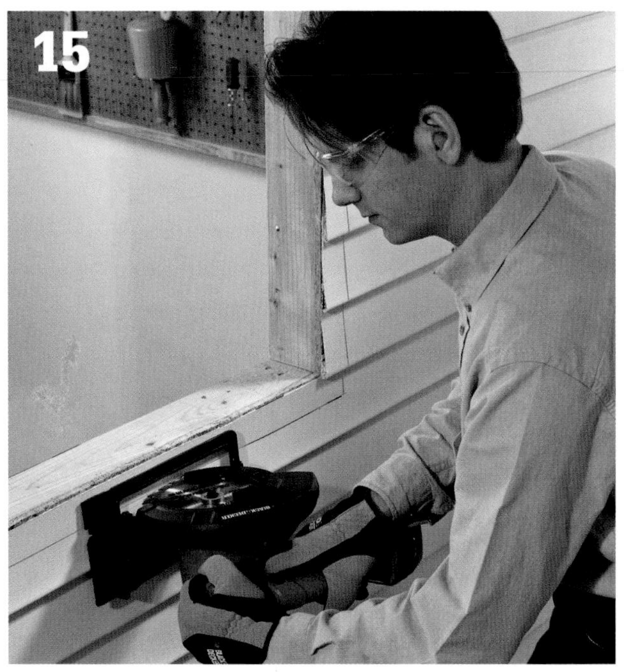


**Remove the siding** along the cutting lines. Vinyl, wood, or steel lap siding can be cut with a trim saw or circular saw. Other siding types, such as stucco or brick, require more complicated techniques. Check with a contractor or refer to other resources for more information. Remove all wall coverings down to the wall sheathing.

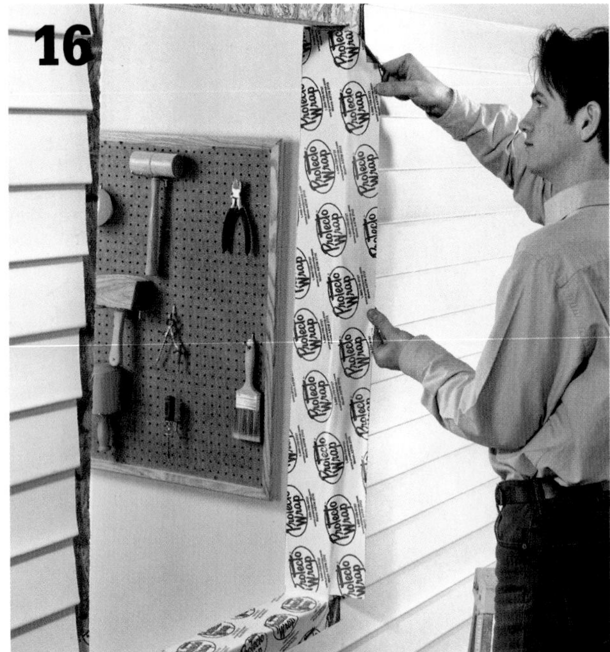


**Flash the rough opening** by installing self-adhesive flashing or strips of building paper around the opening. Tuck the flashing beneath the siding next to the window opening. Flash the sill first, then the side, and then the top so the strips overlap from above.

**Set the window in the opening.** Insert wood shims beneath the window and the sill and between the sides of the unit and rough opening. Adjust the shims until the unit is level in the opening and the side gaps are even. *Tip: For an extra seal, apply a bead of silicone caulk to the back of the nailing flange before installing the window.*

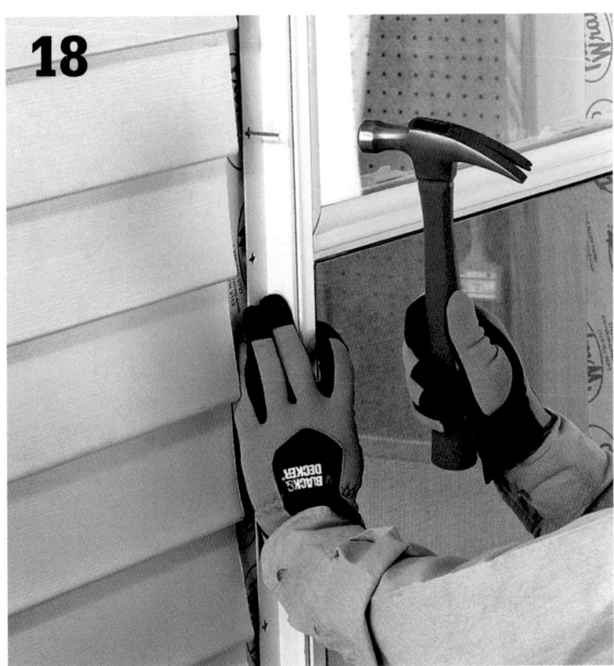


**Nail the window nailing flange** to the framing members with 1½" roofing nails. Unless the manufacturer's instructions direct otherwise, drive nails at corners and every 6" along the flanges. Most flanges are predrilled with guide holes for nails. For an extra seal, cut thin strips of self-adhesive flashing and cover the flanges once the nails are driven.

**Cut a piece of metal drip edge** molding (also called drip cap or window cap) and insert it behind the siding above the window. Use only caulk (no metal fasteners) to secure the drip edge.

**Install brickmold** if your window doesn't have preinstalled trim. Start with the top strip, miter cutting the ends at 45° to create miter joints with the side pieces. Then install the sides. Install the bottom last. Attach brickmold with 8 galvanized casing nails driven through pilot holes (brickmold is prone to splitting). Caulk between the brickmold and the siding.

**Finish the interior side.** Patch in with new drywall (see pages 154 to 157) or reuse the old drywall if possible. Then trim the window sill and jambs with mitered case molding.

# Installing a Skylight

A skylight will brighten any room in your house, including the garage. Skylights are reasonably priced, and today's new high-quality models have improved flashing that makes them as dependable and weather-tight as other windows. Any standard garage roof can accept a skylight, provided it has a reasonable pitch (at least 3-in-12) and good drainage. If your garage has an unfinished ceiling, you can simply mount the skylight and let it provide general ambient light. On finished ceilings, a skylight shaft is needed to direct the light down into the garage, which will create a more focused area of light.

A skylight frame has a header and sill, similar to a standard window frame. However, instead of king studs, it has king rafters as well as trimmers that define the sides of the rough opening. Follow the manufacturer's instructions for determining the proper rough opening size for your new skylight.

With standard rafter-frame roof construction, you can safely cut into one or two rafters as long as you permanently support the cut rafters. If your garage has a truss roof, the skylight needs to fit between two trusses. Never alter your roof trusses to accommodate a wider skylight by cutting or removing parts of their framework. If your garage has a heavy slate or clay tile roof, talk with an architect or building engineer regarding how to reinforce the new framing.

If you install your garage skylight facing west or south it will receive the greatest amount of direct sunlight, but the flip side is that the intensity of the light could overheat your space. For that reason, you may want to position it facing east or north for cooler general room lighting. Since installing a skylight requires working on the roof, carefully set up stepladders and wear fall-arresting gear. The job will go much more smoothly and safely with a helper.

## Tools & Materials ▸

- Work gloves & eye protection
- Tape measure
- Miter saw
- Hammer
- Drill
- Ladders
- Chalkline
- Circular saw
- Jigsaw
- Aviation snips
- 2× Framing lumber
- Utility screws
- 1 × 4 board
- Self-adhesive flashing
- Skylight with flashings

**A skylight** introduces natural light into a garage without posing the security risk that makes some homeowners reluctant to install an eye-level window in the garage (inset). A rafter-style garage roof provides clearspans that are impossible with trusses. Here's an attic space you can really use! If you're planning to build a new garage, give traditional rafters some serious thought.

# How to Install a Skylight

**Frame the rough opening** for the skylight according to the size specifications provided with the unit. Skylights are sized so they fit between 24 or 16" on-center roof members, so if you have chosen a model wisely, you only need to install a header and a sill to complete the rough framing. In most areas, single 2 × 4s may be used for the rough frame. For aesthetic purposes or if you will build a skylight shaft, however, you may prefer to use the same width dimensional lumber as the rafters.

**Mark the cutout area** for the roof sheathing by driving a long deck screw or a casing nail at each corner of the framed opening on the interior side.

**Outline the roof cutout** by snapping chalk lines between the points of the deck screws driven at the corners of the opening. Be sure to follow good safety practices for working on roofs: wear shoes, such as tennis shoes, with nonskid soles; and use roof jacks and fall-arresting gear on roofs with a pitch greater than 4-in-12. Also be aware of weather conditions.

**Cut out the roof opening.** Mount an old blade in a circular saw or cordless trim saw and plunge cut along the top and bottom cutting lines. Stop short of the corners so you don't overcut. Before making the side cuts, tack a long 1 × 4 across the opening, perpendicular to the top and bottom cuts, driving a couple of screws through the 1 × 4 and into the cutout area. The 1 × 4 will keep the waste from falling into the garage through the hole. Make the side cuts, and then finish the cuts at the corners with a jigsaw or reciprocating saw. Remove the waste.

(continued)

**Remove the shingles** surrounding the opening, but try and maintain the integrity of the building paper beneath. Try to salvage the shingles if you can so they can be reinstalled (they'll match better than new shingles). Start with the row of shingles above the opening. Once these are removed you'll have access to the roofing nails on lower courses.

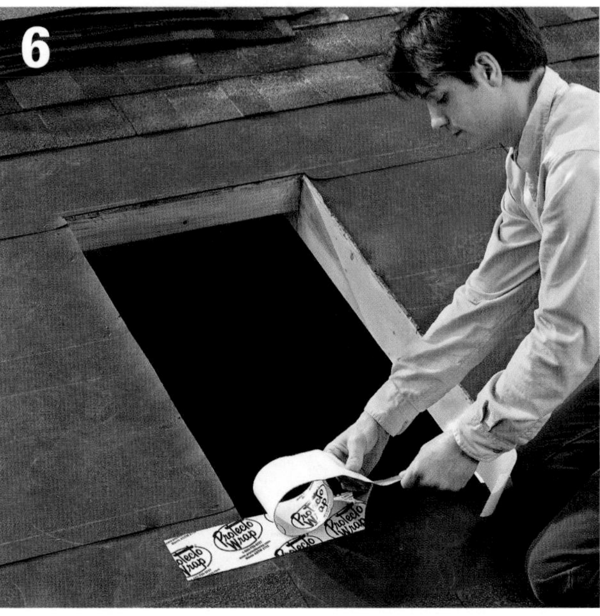

**Seal the bottom of the rough frame opening.** Apply a strip of self-adhesive flashing at the bottom of the roof opening to create a seal on the curb and to cover the seam between the underlayment and the roof deck. This is for extra protection.

**Position the skylight in the opening.** Different models use different fastening and centering devices. The one seen here is installed using pairs of adjustable brackets that are fastened to the roof deck and to the sides of the skylight frame.

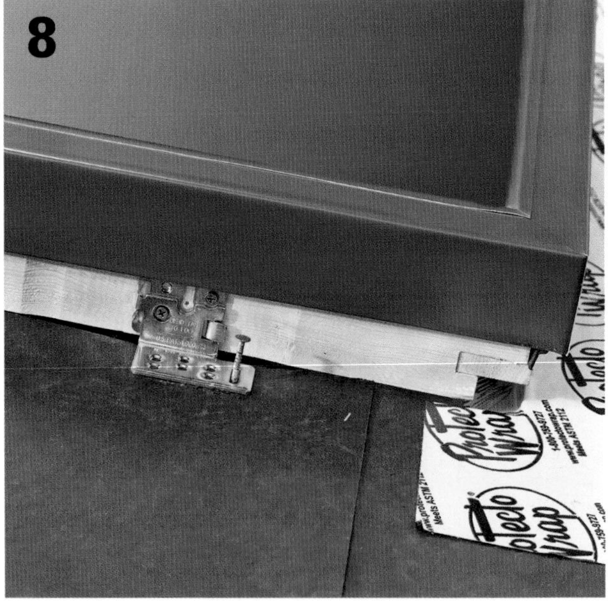

**Fasten the skylight unit.** Many models employ adjustable brackets like the ones seen here so the skylight can be raised or lowered and centered in the opening. The brackets seen here have a slot and several nail holes in the horizontal flange. Drive a ring shank nail in all four slots and then shift the unit side to side as necessary until it is centered in the opening. The brackets also allow the unit to be raised or lowered so the bottom edges of the cladding are the recommended distance above the finished roof surface (see manufacturer's recommendations).

**Install self-adhesive flashing strips** around the skylight curb. Start with the base strip, cutting slits in the corners so the flashing extends all the way up the curb (you'll need to remove metal cladding strips first). Install the head flashing last so all strips overlap from above.

**Install the metal flashing** beginning with the sill. Some skylights have a 4-piece flashing kit where the side flashing is simply shingled over. Others, like the one seen here, include solid base and head flashing components and step flashing that is woven in with the shingles as the roof coverings are installed.

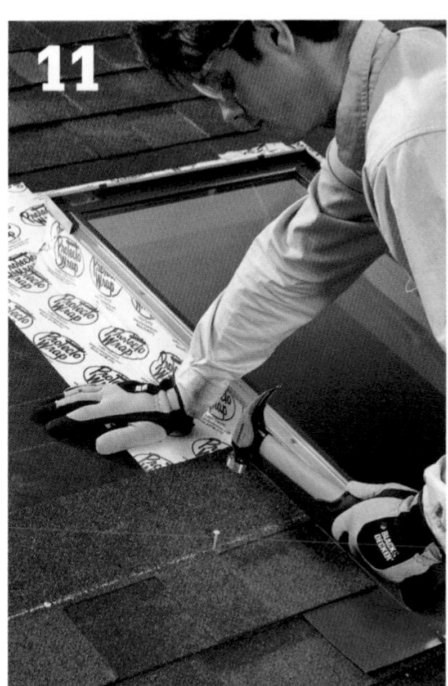


**Replace shingles** up to the skylight curb. Install shingles in complete rows, notching them to fit around the curb. Stop once the granular surfaces of the top row of shingles meet the curb.

**Install side flashing.** Here, metal step flashing is interwoven with the shingles during the shingling process. Whether it's the shingle layer or the step flashing layer, make sure that all components always overlap from above and the horizontal tabs on the step flashing are all covered with shingles. Do not nail through flashing.

**Install the head flashing** piece so it overlaps the last course of shingle and step flashing. Finish shingling in the installation area, again taking care not to nail through any metal flashing. Replace the metal cladding and caulk if recommended by the manufacturer.

# Floor Improvements

**Three flooring solutions** allow you to paint your floor or cover it up for a fresh, clean appearance, and all are manageable DIY projects. You won't have to put up with a dull, dirty, or damp garage floor.

If you plan to use your garage for anything more than parking or storage, you're going to spend a lot of time standing and walking on the floor, so it makes sense to improve its appearance, condition, and cleanliness. Garage slabs tend to be the most marginal floor areas of our homes. They can be damp, especially when the slab doesn't drain properly. If you've got an older garage, the slab may be cracked or show signs of deterioration from weathering and hard use. The good news is there are a number of ways to improve your garage floor economically as a do-it-yourselfer, without renting a jackhammer or sand blaster. This chapter will highlight several options.

For a garage floor that is dry and in sound condition the most cost-effective approach is to paint it. Garage floor paint is generally a two-part epoxy product that you can apply with a roller and brush. It comes in a range of colors, and you can add quartz crystals or sand to the paint to help improve traction. Paint will brighten dull concrete, and when applied correctly, it will stand up to both foot traffic and car tires. The first project of this section will show you how to apply garage floor paint properly.

The next two projects provide floor-covering options. If your garage floor has some minor cosmetic problems, such as tiny cracks or spalling, paint probably won't hide them adequately. One alternative is to install flexible rolled flooring. It's thick enough to hide surface imperfections in the slab, and it offers a bit of cushioning for your feet and legs. A third option—interlocking floor tiles—simply snap together to form a grid over the concrete. These tiles stand slightly off the floor to promote drainage underneath, so they're a good solution for damp concrete.

Because no flooring project should be conducted on a floor that is in disrepair, the following pages include a brief sequence showing how to patch your concrete garage floor.

## Patching Garage Floors ▸

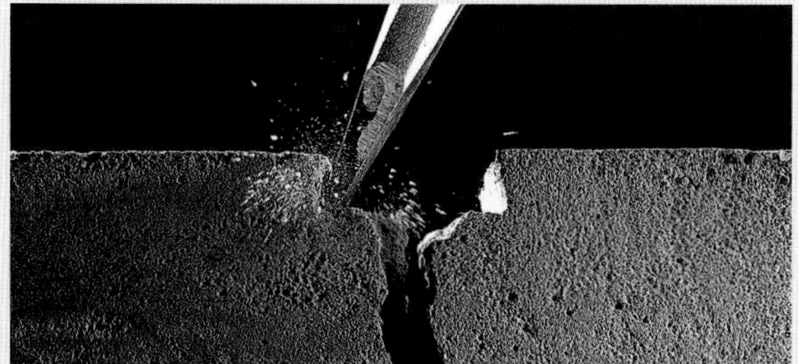

**Use a concrete chisel** (called a cold chisel) and a heavy hammer or mallet to deepen the edges of the damaged area until the outer edges are at least ⅛" thick. Most cracks and depressions in concrete floors are deeper in the center and are tapered at the edges; the feather-thin material around the perimeter of the hole is liable to peel or flake off.

**Clean out the area** to be patched using a wire brush or portable drill with a wire wheel attachment. Be sure to remove all dirt and loose material from the area to be patched. This step will also roughen the edges a bit, creating a better bond.

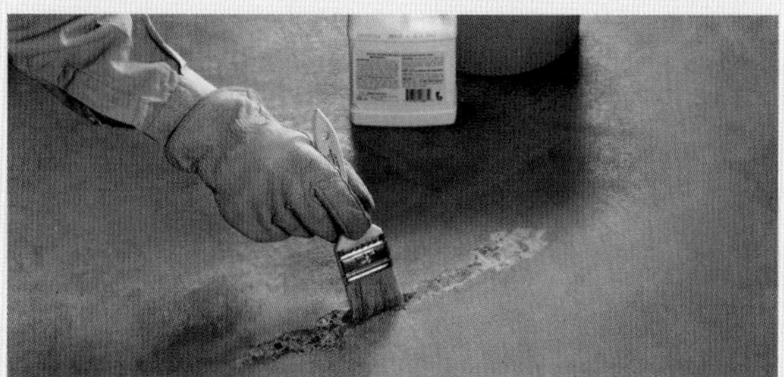

**A bonding agent** (also called a bonding adhesive) helps to chemically bond the patch material to the existing concrete, making the repair material less likely to loosen or dislodge. Apply a thin layer of bonding adhesive to the entire repair area with a paintbrush. Some bonding agents need to be applied to a wet surface, others should not. Follow the directions carefully.

**Mix your concrete** patching compound with clean water until all of the material is thoroughly wet and all of the lumps are worked out. Most mixing compounds start to set within 10 to 20 minutes. (Inset) Use a trowel to compact the material into the area being repaired until it is slightly raised above the surface of the surrounding concrete. If the hole is deeper than ¼", allow each layer to dry before applying the next layer.

**Use the edge of the trowel** to smooth the surface, removing any excess material. Slide the trowel back and forth on its edge, while also pulling the excess material toward you, until it is past the edge of the area you're working on. Scoop it up with the trowel and discard.

**Finishing work.** Slightly raise the flat face of the steel finishing trowel and smooth the patching material until it is even with the adjoining surfaces, creating a seamless repair. Keep the trowel clean and damp to prevent the mix from gumming up the trowel. Finishing is an art and takes practice, so keep trying.

## Garage Floor Treatments

If your garage floor is not perfectly dry, smooth, and in good repair, you have several options for improving it. A simple cleaning is the easiest and most obvious solution. For concrete floors, a process called etching is done in conjunction with basic cleaning with detergent. Etching uses mild acid to remove oil, grime, and other stains plain detergent won't take care of. Etching is recommended as a preparatory treatment for applying paint or acid-based stain. Prior to etching, any preexisting paint must be completely removed and any minor cracks or imperfections should be repaired (see following pages).

Once the garage floor is repaired, cleaned, and etched, you may choose simply to seal it. There is some debate about the advisability of sealing concrete because the sealing products remove the concrete's natural ability to breathe which can lead to problems related to moisture entrapment. But because garage floors receive so much traffic and filth, it is generally agreed that a seal coat is a definite aid in ongoing maintenance.

After etching, but before sealing, is the time to paint (or you can use an acid-based stain if you wish). To paint an etched concrete floor, use a two-part, epoxy-based product that you mix together before application. The paint can be applied with ordinary brushes and rollers. Each gallon provides approximately 250 square feet of floor coverage and dries in about 48 hours. When fully cured, the paint will resist oil and brake fluids and other automotive chemicals.

### Tools & Materials ▸

- Stiff-bristle push broom
- Leaf blower
- Pressure washer
- Power buffer
- Garden hose
- Long-handled paint roller or squeegee
- Paintbrush
- Baking soda
- Protective glasses
- Boots
- Painter's tape
- Plastic sheeting and tape
- Drill
- Mixing paddle attachment
- Cleaning and finishing products
- Shop vacuum
- Large plastic bucket
- Respirator

**Specially formulated epoxy-based paint** will give your concrete garage floor a low-cost facelift and comes in a variety of colors from which you can choose.

# Tools & Materials for Painting Garage Floors

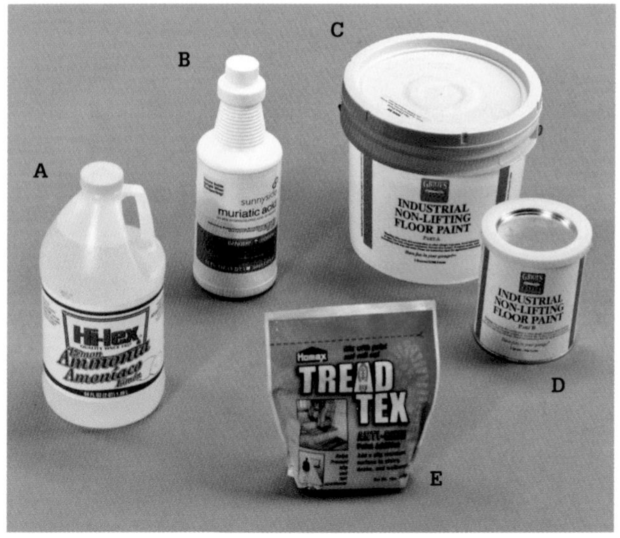


**Preparation and finishing materials include:** (A) ammonia-base detergent for general cleaning of concrete surface; (B) muriatic acid for final cleaning immediately before paint application; (C) two-part epoxy floor paint Part A; (D) two-part epoxy floor paint Part B; (E) antiskid granular additive (optional).

**A power washer** does a fast and thorough job of cleaning dirty garage floors prior to painting. Use these tools with caution. If handled carelessly, they are powerful enough to create more mess than they remove.

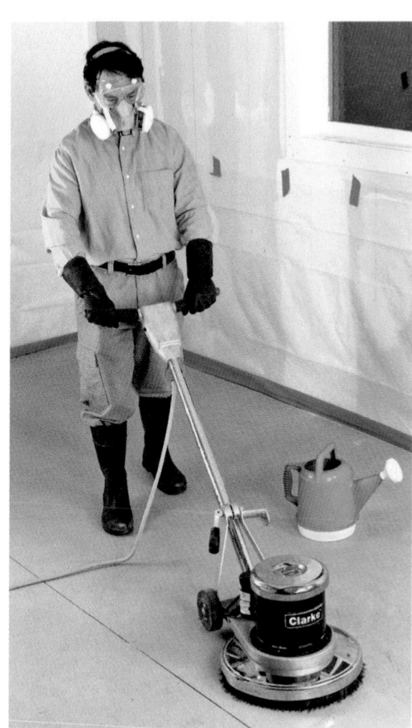


**A power scrubber/buffer** can be rented to clean dirty, oily floors and to help work floor treatment products into the concrete surface. These can be tricky to handle at first, so it's a good idea to practice with plain water before you use the scrubber with chemicals.

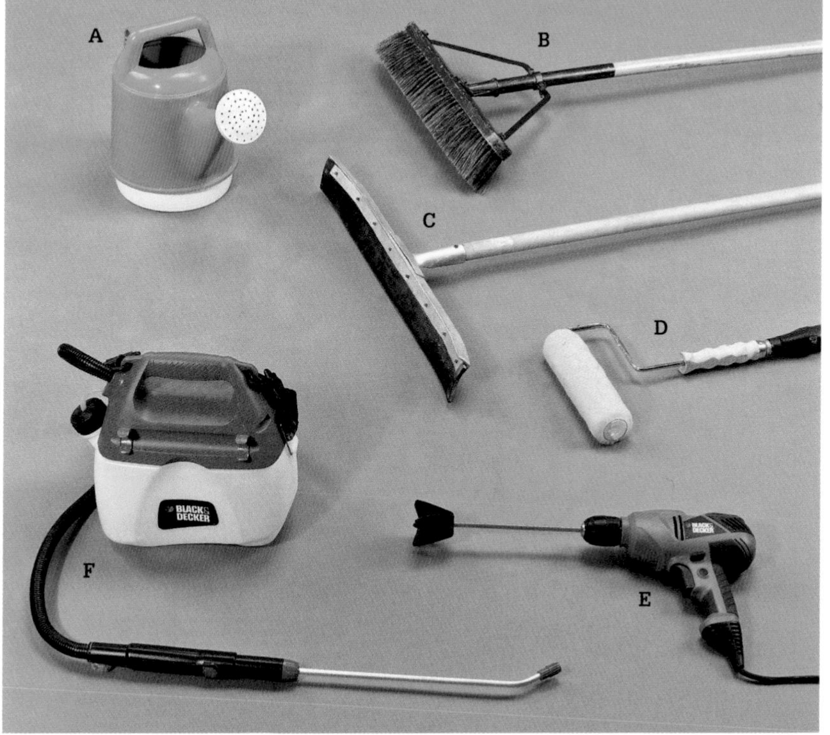


**General purpose tools** that are useful in a floor maintenance and painting project include: (A) a plastic watering can for broadcasting cleaning and finishing chemicals; (B) a push broom; (C) a long-handled squeegee; (D) a long-handled paint roller; (E) a drill outfitted with a paddle-type mixing attachment; (F) a plastic-body garden sprayer for applying chemical treatments.

# How to Clean & Etch a Garage Floor

## Testing Tip ▸

**Test the floor** to make sure moisture is not migrating up from below. Tape a large piece of plastic to the floor and let it rest overnight. If condensation forms on the underside of the plastic it means that transpiration is occurring and the paint will likely fail. Test the floor more than once and in multiple spots to be sure of its suitability for paint.

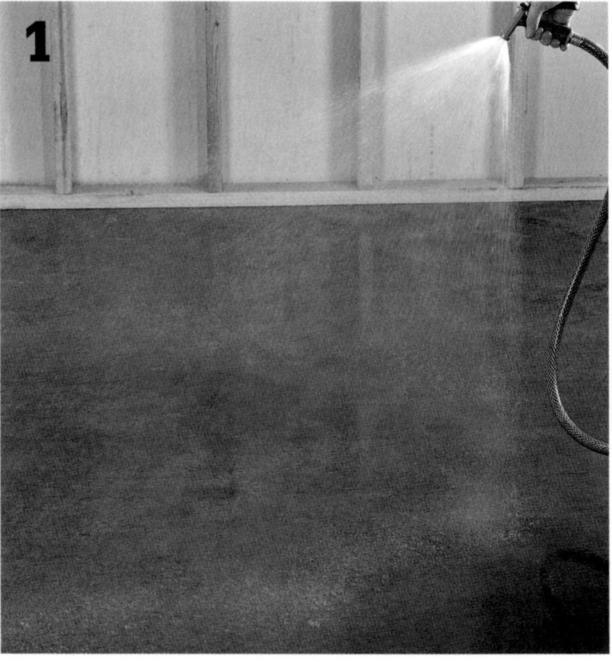

**Rinse the floor thoroughly** after sweeping or vacuuming. A simple garden hose can be used for this process, or you can employ a pressure washer for deep cleaning. Use grease-cutting detergent and also scrub with a stiff-bristle brush as necessary to remove oily stains.

**Prepare the acid-based etching solution** by pouring one cup of muriatic acid into a pump sprayer or a plastic watering can containing clean water for the recommended dilution ratio (see acid container label). **Always add acid to water: never add water to acid.** *Caution: Follow the safety precautions on the acid product container at all times.*

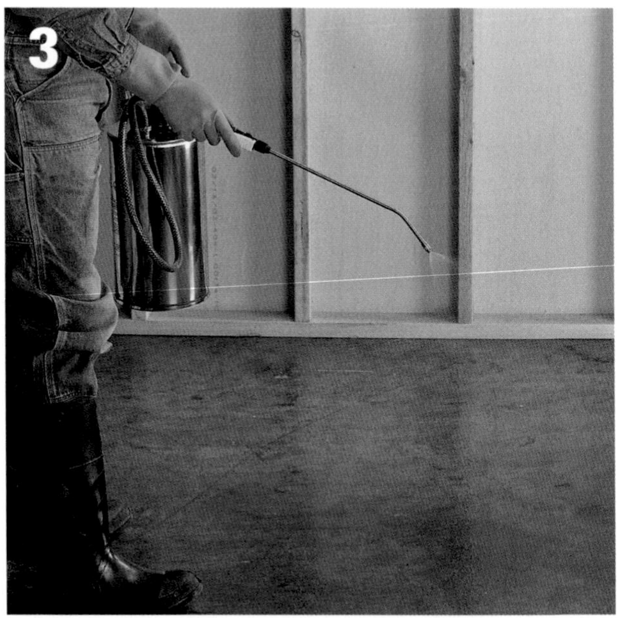

**Broadcast the acid** etching solution with a sprayer or a watering can. Apply it evenly in areas small enough that they will not dry before you can work the acid into the concrete surface (100 sq. ft. at a time is a good guideline).

**Work the acid solution** into the floor surface with a stiff-bristle push broom or a power scrubber/buffer. Let the acid solution rest for 5 to 10 minutes. A mild foaming action indicates that the product is working.

**Neutralize the acid** by brushing the floor with a solution of baking soda dissolved in water (1 cup per gallon of water) only after all of the floor surface has been etched. Rinse with a power washer and then vacuum with a wet/dry shop vacuum. Let the floor dry overnight before applying paint.

**Rinse the garage floor** thoroughly with a hose and clean water, or with a pressure washer. Multiple rinsing is advised.

**Vacuum the wet floor** thoroughly with a wet/dry shop vacuum after you have finished rinsing it. Vacuuming will help prevent any residue from forming on the floor when it dries.

# How to Seal a Garage Floor

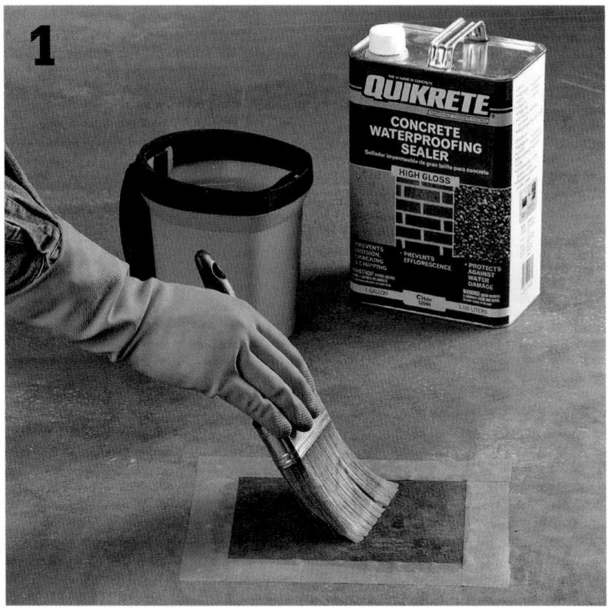


**Once etched,** clean, and dry, your concrete is ready for clear sealer or liquid repellent. Mix the sealer in a bucket with a stir stick. Lay painter's tape down for a testing patch. Apply sealer to this area and allow to dry to ensure desired appearance. Concrete sealers tend to make the surface slick when wet. Add an antiskid additive to aid with traction, especially on stairs.

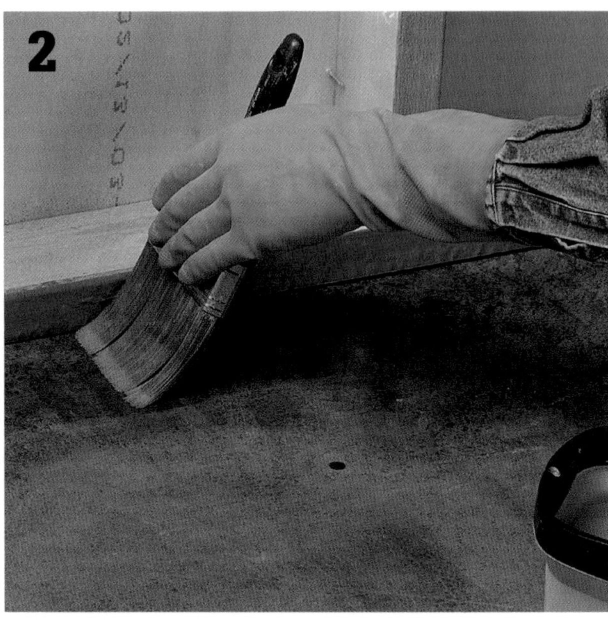


**Use wide painter's tape** to protect walls, and then use a good-quality 4"-wide synthetic-bristle paintbrush to coat the perimeter with sealer.

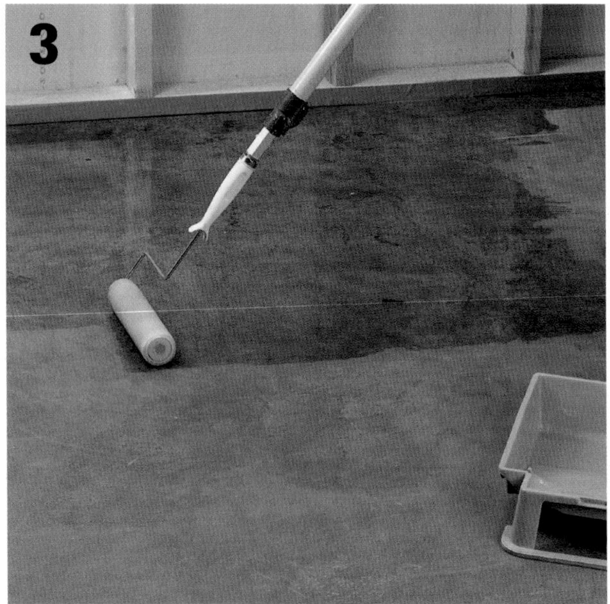


**Use a long-handled paint roller** with at least ½" nap to apply an even coat to the rest of the surface. Do small sections at a time (about 2 × 3 ft.). Work in one orientation (e.g., north to south). Avoid lap marks by always maintaining a wet edge. Do not work the area once the coating has partially dried; this could cause it to lift from the surface.

**Allow the surface to dry** according to the manufacturer's instructions, usually 8 to 12 hours minimum. Then apply a second coat in the opposite direction of the first coat. If the first coat was north to south, the second coat should be east to west.

# How to Paint a Garage Floor

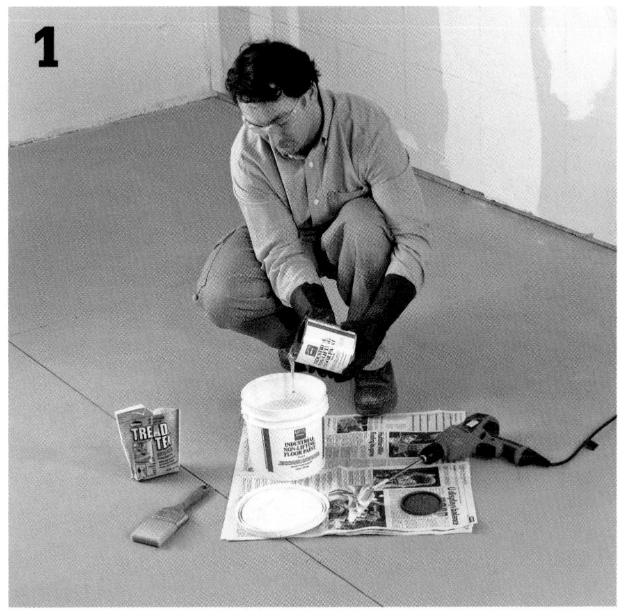


**Mix the first part** (Part A) of the two-part epoxy paint. Following the instructions on the can label precisely, add the Part B liquid to the Part A and blend with a mixing paddle attachment mounted in an electric drill. If you plan to add antiskid granules, add them at this point and mix them in well.

**Paint the perimeter** of the room with a large brush, making sure to get paint all the way into the corners and up against the bottom of the walls. Feather the paint out on the room side so you do not leave any ridges that will show.

**Paint the floor** with a long-handled roller extension and a short-nap sleeve. Work from one corner opposite the garage door and make your way to the overhead door. Don't make the coat too thick; a couple of thin coats is much better than one thick one. Once you have completed the first coat, close all doors and do not open them until the paint has dried. Sweep or vacuum the floor after the first coat (the primer coat) dries. Wear clean shoes and try and get up as much debris as you can.

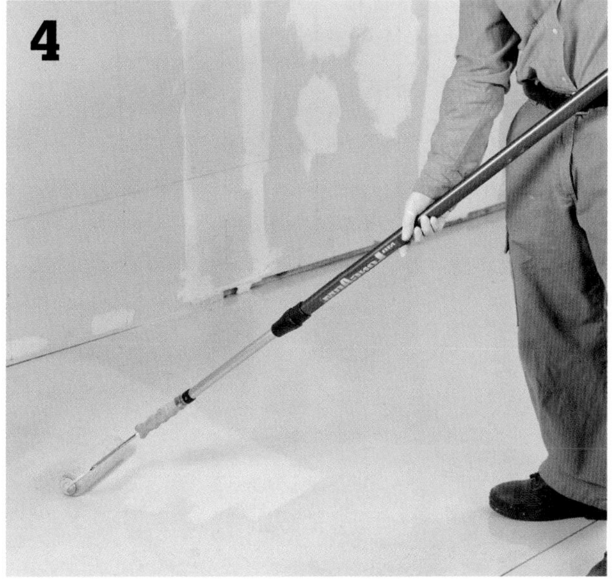


**Apply the second coat** of paint in the same manner as you applied the first. Instructions may vary, but in general it isn't a good idea to apply more than two coats. Reserve any leftover paint for occasional touch-ups in high-wear areas.

# Installing Roll-out Floor Covering

A quick, simple alternative to painting your garage floor is to cover it with rolled PVC flooring. Rolled flooring is manufactured in several colors and surface textures, including rib, coin, and tread patterns. This is the soft floor covering you often see in airports, shopping malls, gyms, and other high-traffic areas. The material is impervious to most automotive chemicals as well as road salt and water. Patterns help to hide minor concrete blemishes and improve traction. Rolled garage flooring is manufactured in 7½- to 10-foot-wide rolls and in various lengths up to 60 feet.

Installing roll-out covering requires much less preparation than garage floor paint, and the material is thick enough to lay flat and stay in place without bonding it to the concrete. To prepare for installation, sweep and clean your garage floor. Use cleaning chemicals, and then rinse thoroughly to remove stubborn oil and chemical stains. Plan to install the flooring on a warm, sunny day.

## Tools & Materials ▸

- Stiff-bristle push broom
- Tape measure
- Straightedge
- Utility knife
- Roll-out floor covering
- Double-sided carpet tape

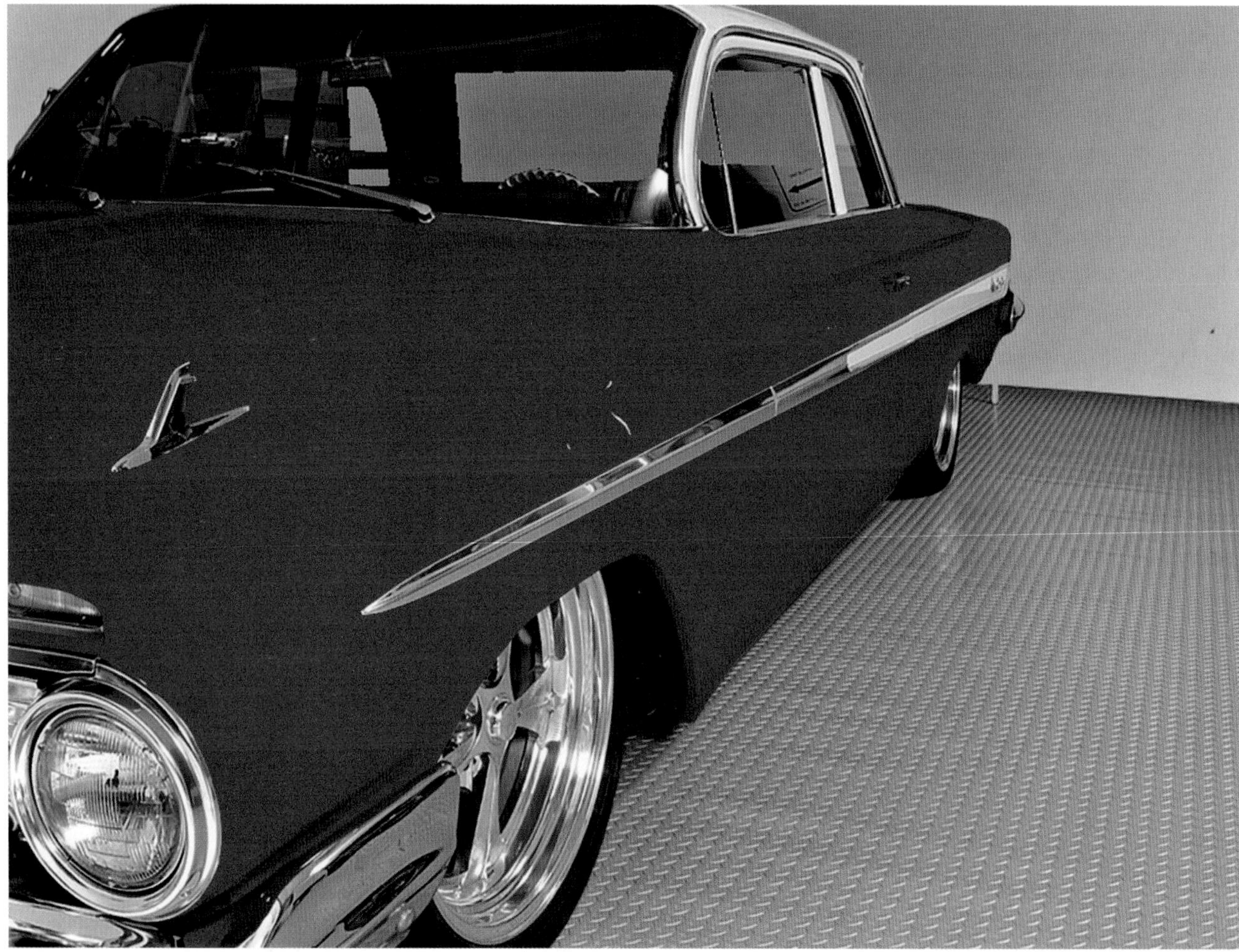

**Roll-out flooring** is a durable floating-floor solution that requires no special adhesives to install. In fact, you can lift up and pull the sheets outside for easy cleaning. It's an excellent option for concealing aged, stained, or damp concrete slabs.

## How to Install Roll-out Flooring

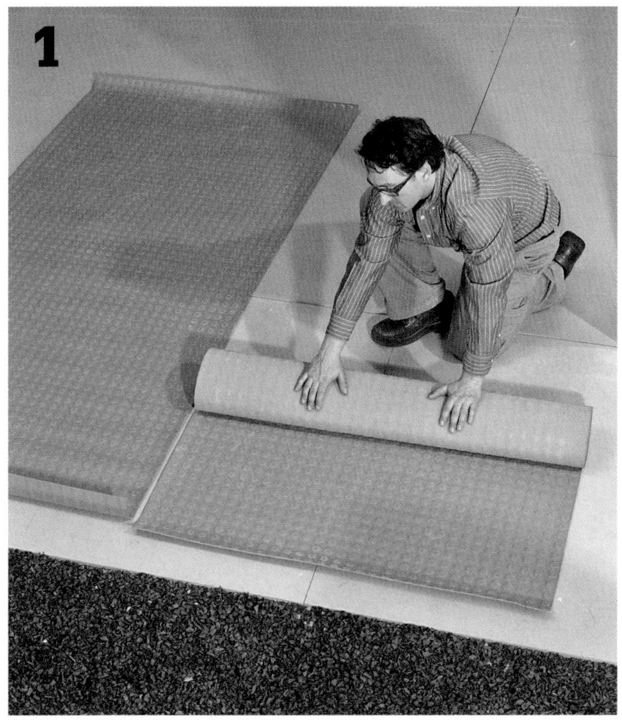


**Unroll the flooring material,** preferably in a clean driveway on a sunny day. Let the material rest for a few hours to flatten.

**Lay the material on the garage floor** in rough position and use a push broom to sweep out any air bubbles.

**Trim the material** to fit around door openings and any obstructions using a sharp utility knife. For larger garages, roll out additional rolls of floor covering as needed.

**Tape seams between rolls** by curling the edge over and applying double-sided carpet tape to one roll. Lay the edges back down so the edge of the other roll is pressed into the tape.

# Installing Interlocking Floor Tiles

Interlocking floor tiles are another quick, DIY-friendly solution that can give your garage floor a custom checkerboard look. These 1 × 1–ft. tiles are molded in a range of colors and are made of recycled PVC or other composites. You have several surface pattern styles to choose from, depending on the manufacturer. Some types are ventilated to promote drying, which makes them a good option for installing over damp concrete. The tiles will resist gasoline, oil, and most other solvents, so they're well suited for parking spaces or other garage workspace applications.

Interlocking tiles create a floating floor system similar to roll-out flooring (see pages 214 to 215). The four edges have locking tabs that clip together like a jigsaw puzzle. Once installed, the tile grid holds itself in place, so there's no need to fasten or glue the tiles permanently to the concrete. You can cut them with standard woodworking saws and tap them together with a mallet. Most tile brands offer beveled transition pieces to border the garage door edge.

The process for installing locking floor tiles is quite similar to laying permanent floor tile. Clean the floor thoroughly, then measure it and snap chalk lines to determine the exact center. Start by laying a row of tiles along the lengthwise chalk line from the garage door to the intersecting chalk line. Adjust the row as needed to allow for full tiles along the front edge of the garage. It's fine to have partial tiles along the back wall. Now, build out the tile grid left and right of the center row to fill in the rest of the floor. Measure and cut partial tiles as needed to fit against the side and back walls. Finish up by adding beveled transition pieces along the garage door, and cover the edges of the floor at the walls with sanitary base or other base moldings. With a helper, you should be able to complete your new tiled floor in an afternoon.

## Tools & Materials ▸

- Push broom or leaf blower
- Tape measure
- Chalk line
- Stiff-bristle brush
- Cleaning detergent
- Backer board
- Plastic bucket
- Straightedge guide
- Rubber mallet
- Jigsaw or circular saw
- Grease pencil
- Surface sealer
- Floor tiles

**Interlocking floor tiles** snap together for a virtually foolproof installation, and you'll have all the conveniences that a floating floor can offer.

# How to Install Interlocking Floor Tiles

**Clean the floor** by sweeping, vacuuming, or blowing off any debris with a leaf blower.

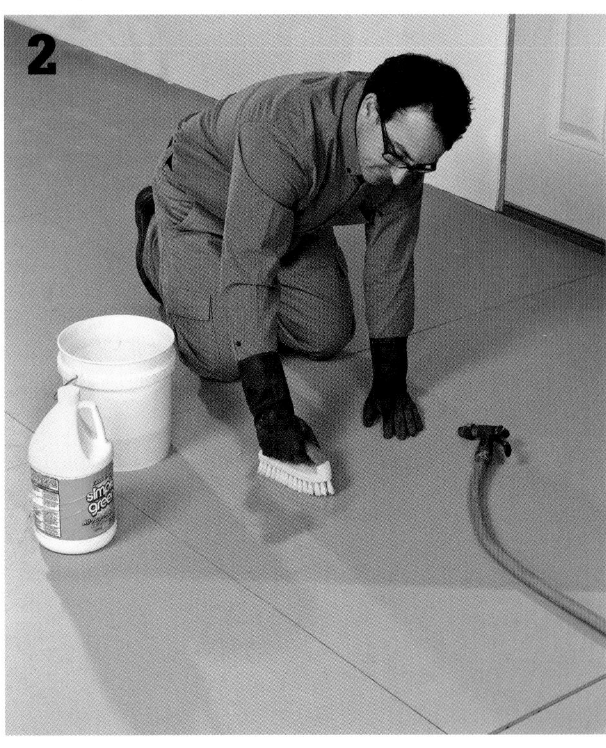

**Remove any oily stains** by scrubbing with detergent and a stiff-bristle brush.

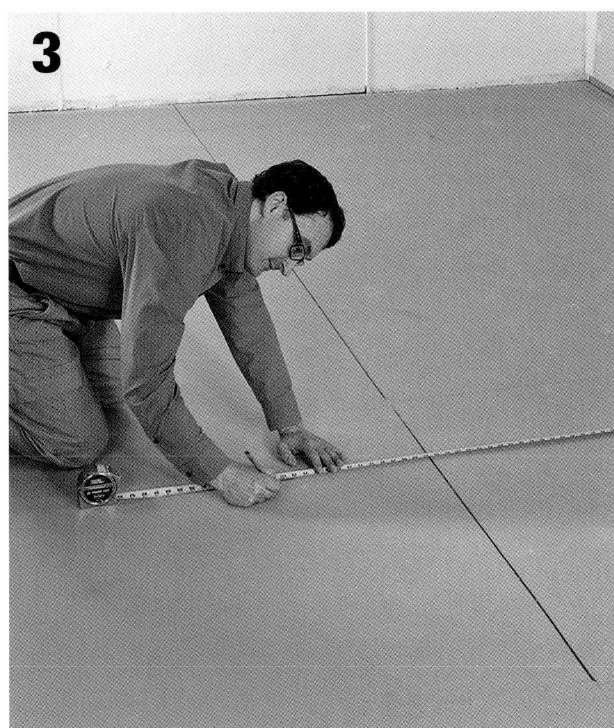

**Measure the floor** in both directions, and mark the locations of the centerlines.

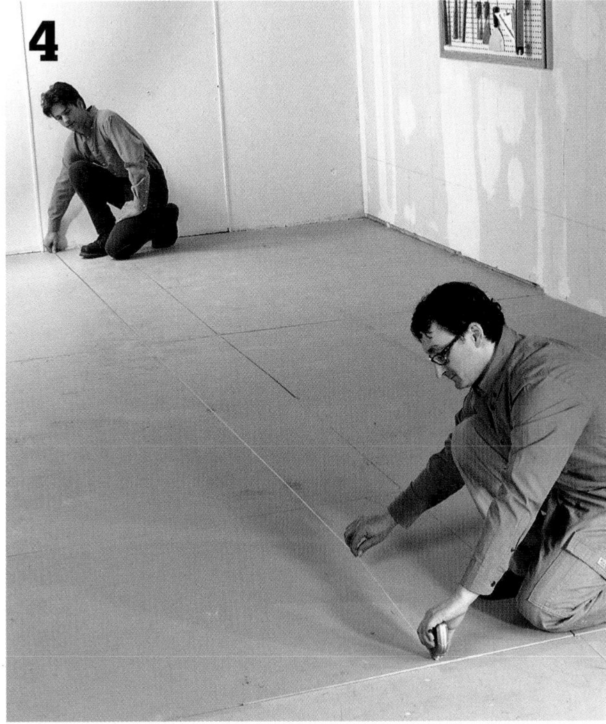

**Snap chalk lines** to connect the center points in both directions, forming a point of intersection in the middle of the garage and dividing the floor into four quadrants.

(continued)

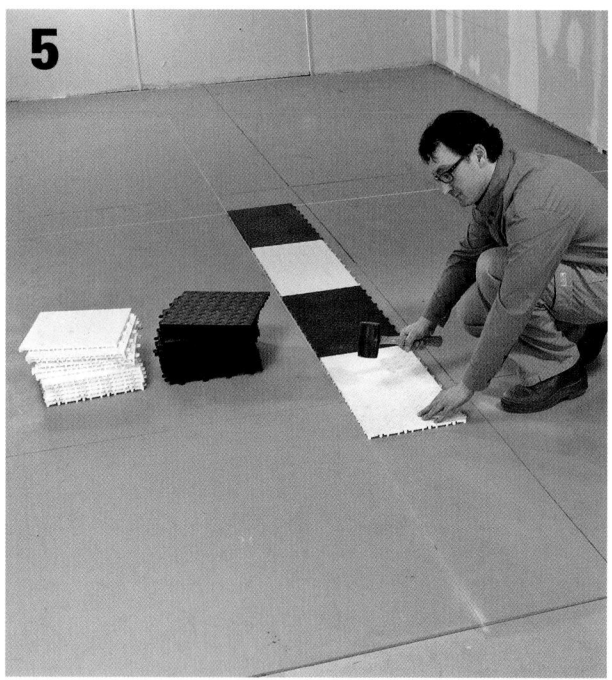

**Lay tiles** along one leg of the layout reference line, stopping just short of the wall. Snap the tiles together as you work. Use a rubber mallet to gently tap and set the tiles, if necessary.

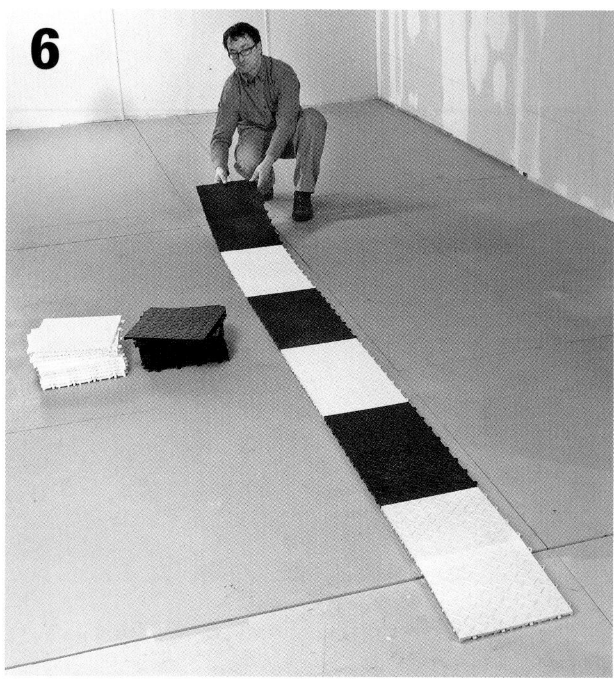

**Adjust the position** of the first row of tiles so the last tile will fit just short of the overhead door opening without cutting. It is best to have the cut tiles against the far wall. If you plan to install a beveled transition strip (some, but not all, manufacturers carry them), be sure to allow room for it when repositioning the row. Snap new chalk lines parallel to the originals.

**Add tiles** along the adjusted reference lines to establish the layout. If you find that one row of tiles will need to terminate with tiles that are cut to a couple of inches or less, adjust the layout side to side so the cut tiles will be evenly balanced at both ends of the line. Fill in the tiles in the field area of all quadrants.

**Measure the gaps** at the ends of the rows requiring cut tiles and subtract ¼" for expansion.

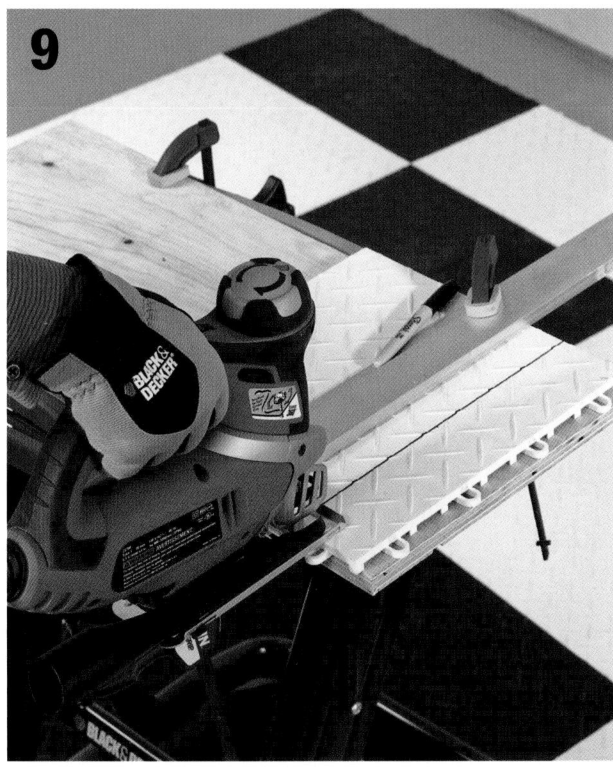


**Cut the tiles** that need cutting with a jigsaw. Be sure to place a backer board underneath the tile. Use a straightedge guide for a clean cut.

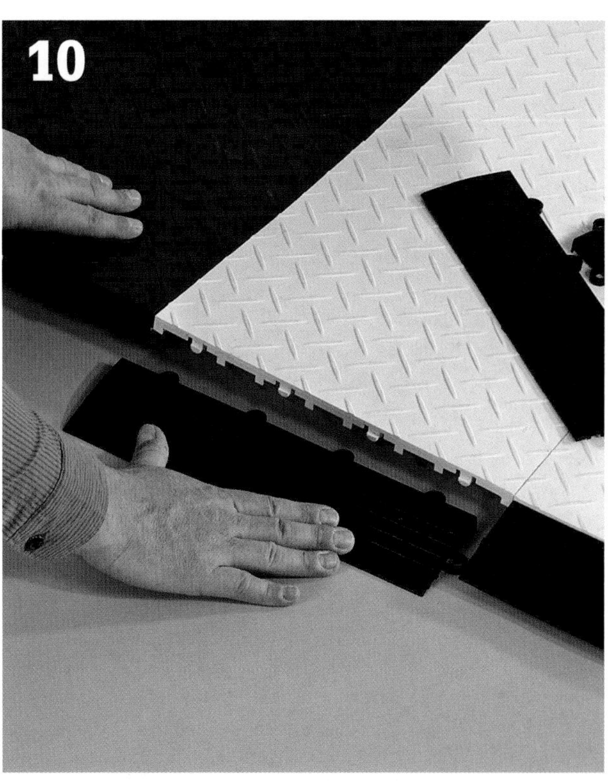


**Install transition strips** at doorways. Not all brands of interlocking tiles have transition strips available.

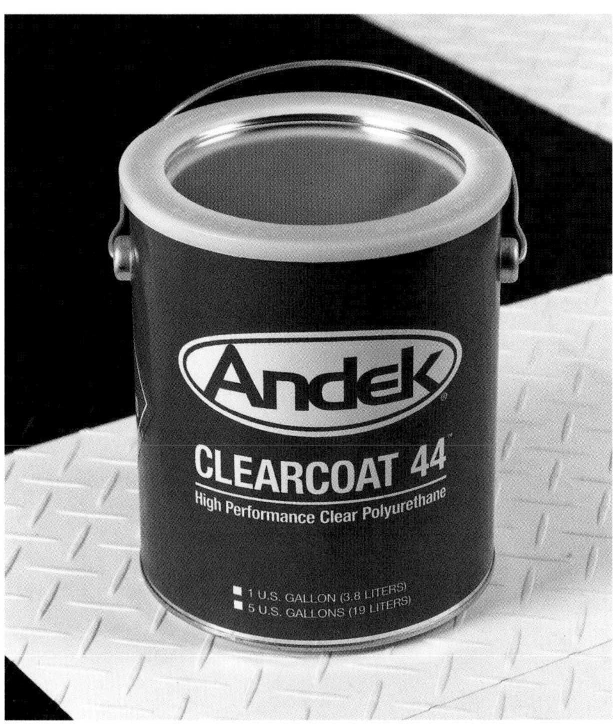


**Option:** Seal the tiles to protect against tire marks and other discoloration by applying a surface sealer. (Check with the tile manufacturer for its recommendations.)

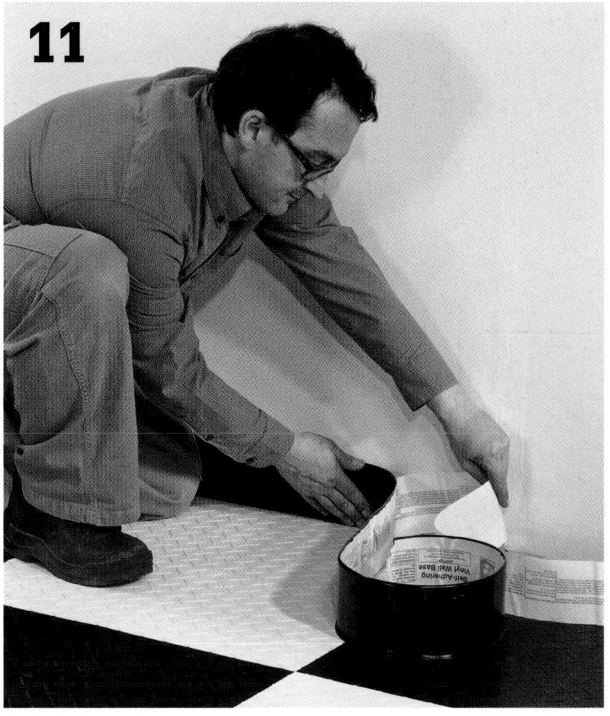


**Add base trim.** Conceal the expansion gaps around the perimeter of the installation with molding, such as vinyl-cove base molding.

CAUTION

# Garage Maintenance

Most of the chores required when taking care of your garage are not much different from those you'd perform on your house: some fresh paint, a little caulk around windows and doors, a new roof every 10 or 20 years, and some basic dusting up and washing. But there are some maintenance activities that are unique to the garage. Concrete garage floors get more abuse than most floor surfaces and need regular cleaning as well as the occasional touching up of cracks or pop-outs. If your garage is home to a car or other gas-powered vehicle equipment, you will almost certainly face an occasional stain from engine oil or other fluid. In colder climates, road salt tracked in by your vehicles can cause the floor to discolor and degrade.

The garage door is another hot spot for garage maintenance. Anything that's as big as a garage door and moves regularly will undoubtedly need occasional lubrication and adjusting. If you have a garage door opener, you can plan on some regular maintenance, as well as eventual replacement.

The trick to garage maintenance is really no trick at all: don't procrastinate. Fix problems as soon as you spot them so they don't get worse, and stick to a regular cleaning and maintenance schedule.

### In this chapter


- Renewing a Garage Floor
- Tuning Up Garage Doors
- Garage Door Openers

# Renewing a Garage Floor

Over time, exposed concrete surfaces can start to show a lot of wear. Weather, hard use, and problems with the initial pour and finishing are among the most common causes of surface blemishes. But despite a shabby appearance, old concrete is often structurally sound and can last for many more years. So instead of breaking up and replacing an old garage floor, you can easily renew its surface with concrete resurfacer. With this simple application, your concrete will have a freshly poured look and a protective surface layer that's typically stronger than the garage floor itself.

Concrete resurfacer is suitable for any size of garage floor, outdoors or indoors. You can also apply it to vertical surfaces to put a fresh face on steps, curbs, and exposed patio edges. Depending on the condition of the old surface, the new layer can range in thickness from $\frac{1}{16}$ to $\frac{1}{4}$". For a smooth finish, spread the resurfacer with a squeegee or trowel. For a textured or nonslip surface, you can broom the surface before it dries or use a masonry brush for smaller applications.

## Tools & Materials ▸

- Protective gloves & eyewear
- Scrub brush
- Pressure washer
- Trowel
- 5-gal. bucket
- Drill with mixing paddle
- Squeegee
- Concrete cleaner
- Concrete resurfacer
- Duct tape

**Concrete resurfacer** offers an easy, inexpensive solution for renewing garage floors that have become chipped and flaked with age.

## How to Resurface a Garage Floor

**Thoroughly clean** the entire project area. If necessary, remove all oil and greasy or waxy residue using a concrete cleaner and scrub brush. Water beading on the surface indicates residue that could prevent proper adhesion with the resurfacer; clean these areas again as needed.

**Wash the concrete** with a pressure washer. Set the washer at 3,500 psi and hold the fan-spray tip about 3" from the surface or as recommended by the washer manufacturer. Remove standing water.

**Fill sizeable pits** and spalled areas using a small batch of concrete resurfacer. Mix about 5 pt. of water per 40-lb. bag of resurfacer for a trowelable consistency. Repair cracks or broken slab edges as shown on page 207. Smooth the repairs level with the surrounding surface and let them harden.

**On a large project,** section off the slab into areas no larger than 100 sq. ft. It's easiest to delineate sections along existing control joints. On all projects, cover or seal off all control joints with duct tape, foam backer rod, or weather stripping to prevent resurfacer from spilling into the joints.

(continued)

**Mix the desired quantity** of concrete resurfacer with water following the mixing instructions. Work the mix with a ½" drill and a mixing paddle for 5 minutes to achieve a smooth, pourable consistency. If necessary, add water sparingly until the mix will pour easily and spread well with a squeegee.

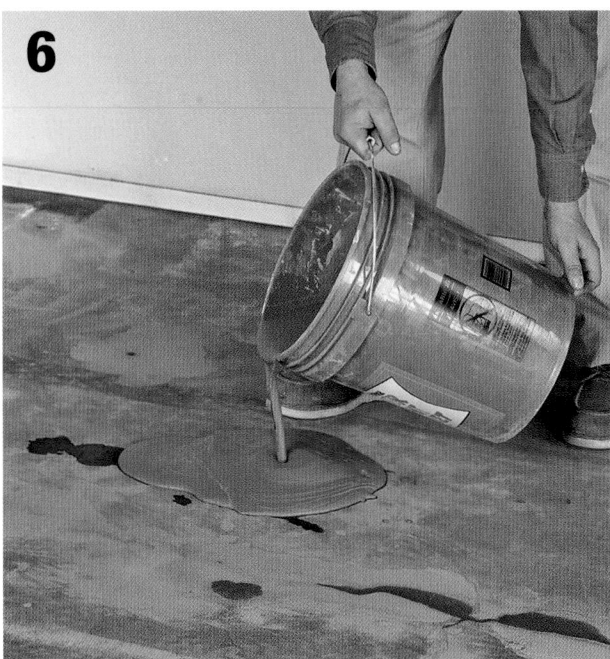


**Saturate the work area** with water, then use a squeegee to remove any standing water. Pour the mix of concrete resurfacer onto the center of the repair area or first repair section.

**Spread the resurfacer with the squeegee** using a scrubbing motion to make sure all depressions are filled. Then spread it into a smooth, consistent layer. If desired, broom the surface for a nonslip finish (opposite page). You can also tool the slab edges with a concrete edger within 20 minutes of application. Let the resurfacer cure.

## Options for Finishes

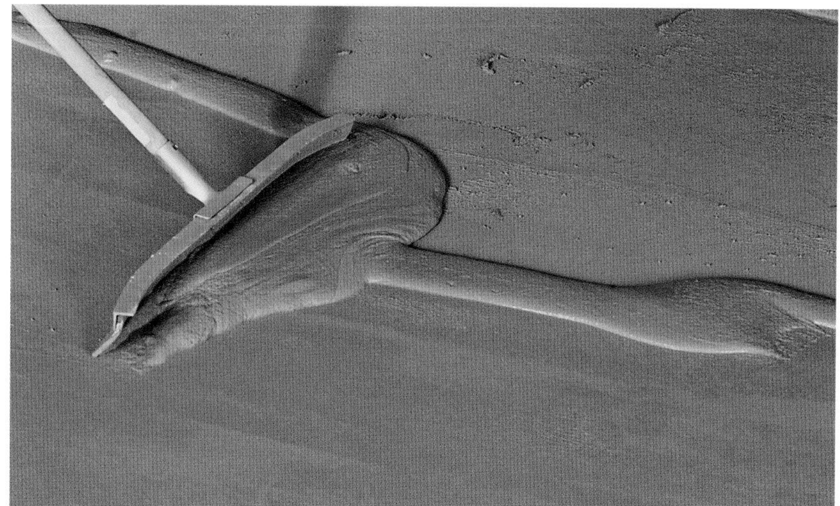

**For thicker resurfacing,** simply add more layers of resurfacer as needed. Wait until the surface can support foot traffic—typically 2 to 6 hours—before applying the next coat.

**Nonslip broomed finish:** Within 5 minutes of applying the resurfacer, drag a clean fine-bristle push broom across the surface. Pull the broom backward in a straight line, moving across the entire area without stopping. Repeat in parallel rows until the entire surface is textured.

**Trowel application:** A trowel is handy for resurfacing small areas. Use a stiffer mix for troweling—approximately 5 pt. of water per 40-lb. bag of dry mix. Spread and smooth the resurfacer with a steel concrete finishing trowel.

# Tuning Up Garage Doors

Imagine this: You're driving home late at night, it's pouring outside, and you're shivering because you've got the flu. Then you turn into your driveway, punch a little button, and your garage door opens, a light comes on, you pull in, and you're HOME. You didn't have to get drenched, or lift a door that felt like heavy metal, or scream at the heavens for making you so miserable. Thanks to a well-maintained garage door and opener, you escaped all of this, and that is a good thing.

Unfortunately, over time, many good things become bad things, especially if they aren't well maintained. An overhead garage door is no exception. To keep everything running smoothly requires effort on three fronts: the door, the opener, and the opener's electronic safety sensors. Here's what you need to know to keep all three in tiptop shape.

## Tools & Materials ▸

- Mineral spirits
- Graphite spray lubricant
- Garage door weather-stripping
- Level
- Soft-faced mallet
- Galvanized roofing nails
- Penetrating lubricant
- Toweling
- Socket wrenches
- Lightweight oil
- Pliers
- Open-end wrenches
- Old paintbrush or toothbrush
- Hammer

**A bit of routine maintenance** now and again will help keep your garage door working exactly as it should, rain or shine.

## How to Tune Up a Garage Door

**Begin the tune-up** by lubricating the door tracks, pulleys, and rollers. Use a lightweight oil, not grease, for this job. The grease catches too much dust and dirt.

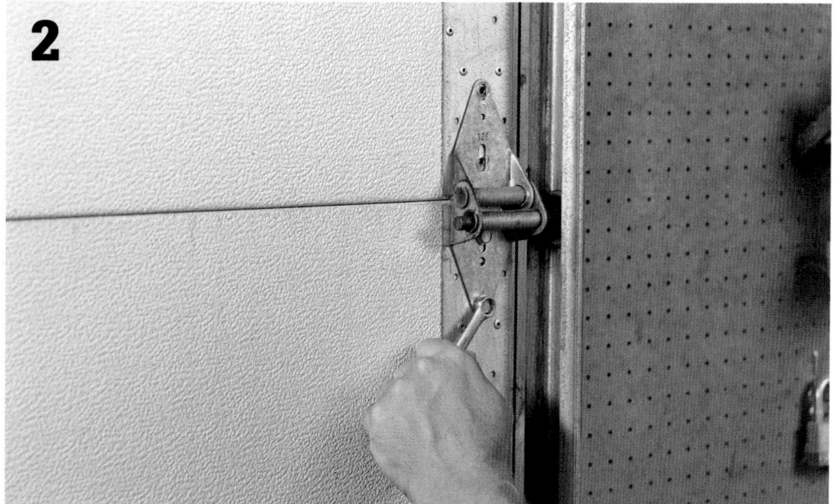


**Remove clogged or damaged rollers** from the door by loosening the nuts that hold the roller brackets. The roller will come with the bracket when the bracket is pulled free.

**Mineral spirits and kerosene** are good solvents for cleaning roller bearings. Let the bearing sit for a half-hour in the solvent. Then brush away the grime buildup with an old paintbrush or toothbrush.

(continued)

**If the rollers are making a lot of** noise as they move over the tracks, the tracks are probably out of alignment. To fix this, check the tracks for plumb. If they are out of plumb, the track mounting brackets must be adjusted.

**To adjust out-of-plumb tracks,** loosen all the track mounting brackets (usually 3 or 4 per track) and push the brackets into alignment.

**It's often easier** to adjust the brackets by partially loosening the bolts and tapping the track with a soft-faced mallet. Once the track is plumb, tighten all the bolts.

7

**Sometimes the door lock** bar opens sluggishly because the return spring has lost its tension. The only way to fix this is to replace the spring. One end is attached to the body of the lock; the other end hooks onto the lock bar.

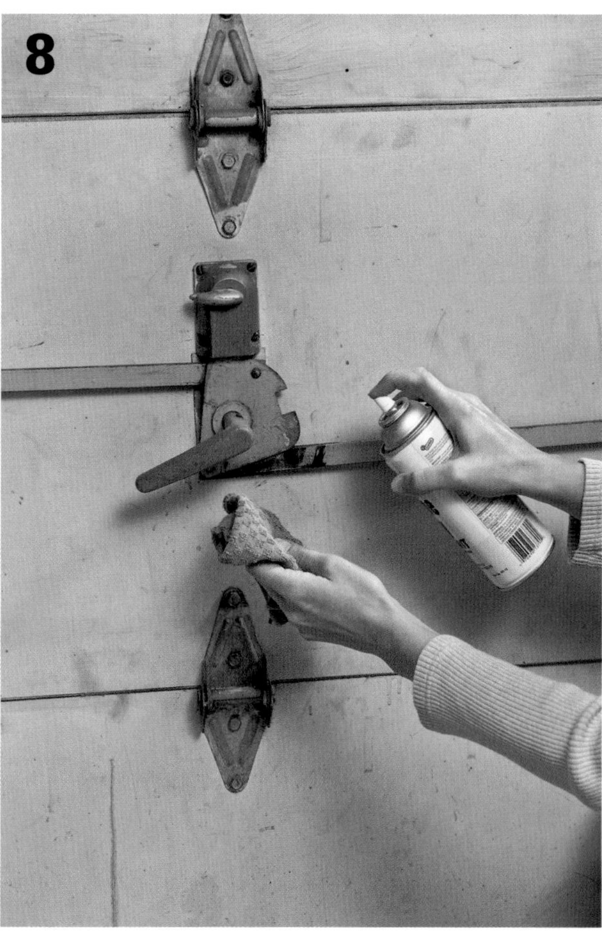

8

**If a latch needs lubrication,** use graphite in powder or liquid form. Don't use oil because it attracts dust that will clog the lock even more.

**Alternative:** Sometimes the lock bar won't lock the door because it won't slide into its opening on the door track. To fix this, loosen the guide bracket that holds the lock bar and move it up or down until the bar hits the opening.

(continued)

**Worn or broken weather stripping** on the bottom edge of the door can let in a lot of cold air and stiff breezes. Check to see if this strip is cracked, broken, or has holes along its edges. If so, remove the old strip and pull out any nails left behind.

**Measure the width** of your garage door, then buy a piece of weather stripping to match. These strips are standard lumber yard and home center items. Sometimes they are sold in kit form, with fasteners included. If not, just nail the stripping in place with galvanized roofing nails.

**If the chain** on your garage door opener is sagging more than ½" below the bottom rail, it can make a lot of noise and cause drive sprocket wear. Tighten the chain according to the directions in the owner's manual.

**On openers with a chain,** lubricate the entire length of the chain with lightweight oil. Do not use grease. Use the same lubricant if your opener has a drive screw instead.

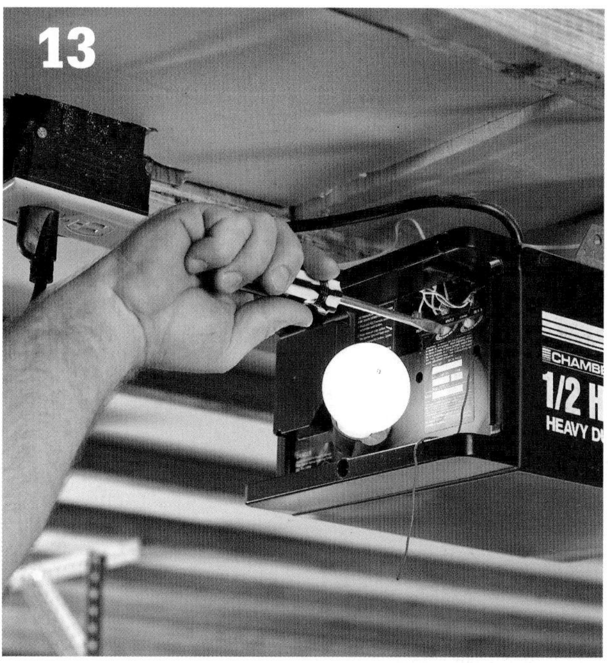


**Test the door's closing force** sensitivity and make adjustments at the opener's motor case if needed. Because both the sensitivity and the adjustment mechanism vary greatly between opener models, you'll have to rely on your owner's manual for guidance. If you don't have the owner's manual, you can usually download one from the manufacturer's website.

**Check for proper alignment** on the safety sensors near the floor. They should be pointing directly at one another and their lenses should be clean of any dirt and grease.

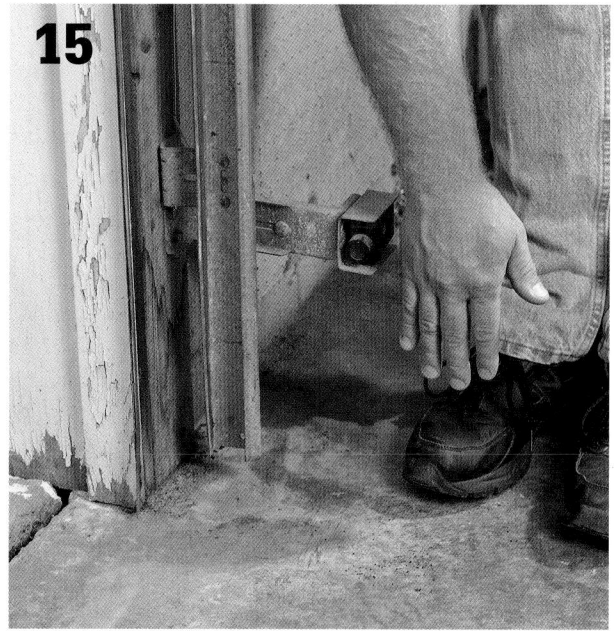


**Make sure that the sensors are "talking" to the opener** properly. Start to close the door, then put your hand down between the two sensors. If the door stops immediately and reverses direction, it's working properly. If it doesn't, make the adjustment recommended in the owner's manual. If that doesn't do the trick, call a professional door installer and don't use the door until it passes this test.

# Garage Door Openers

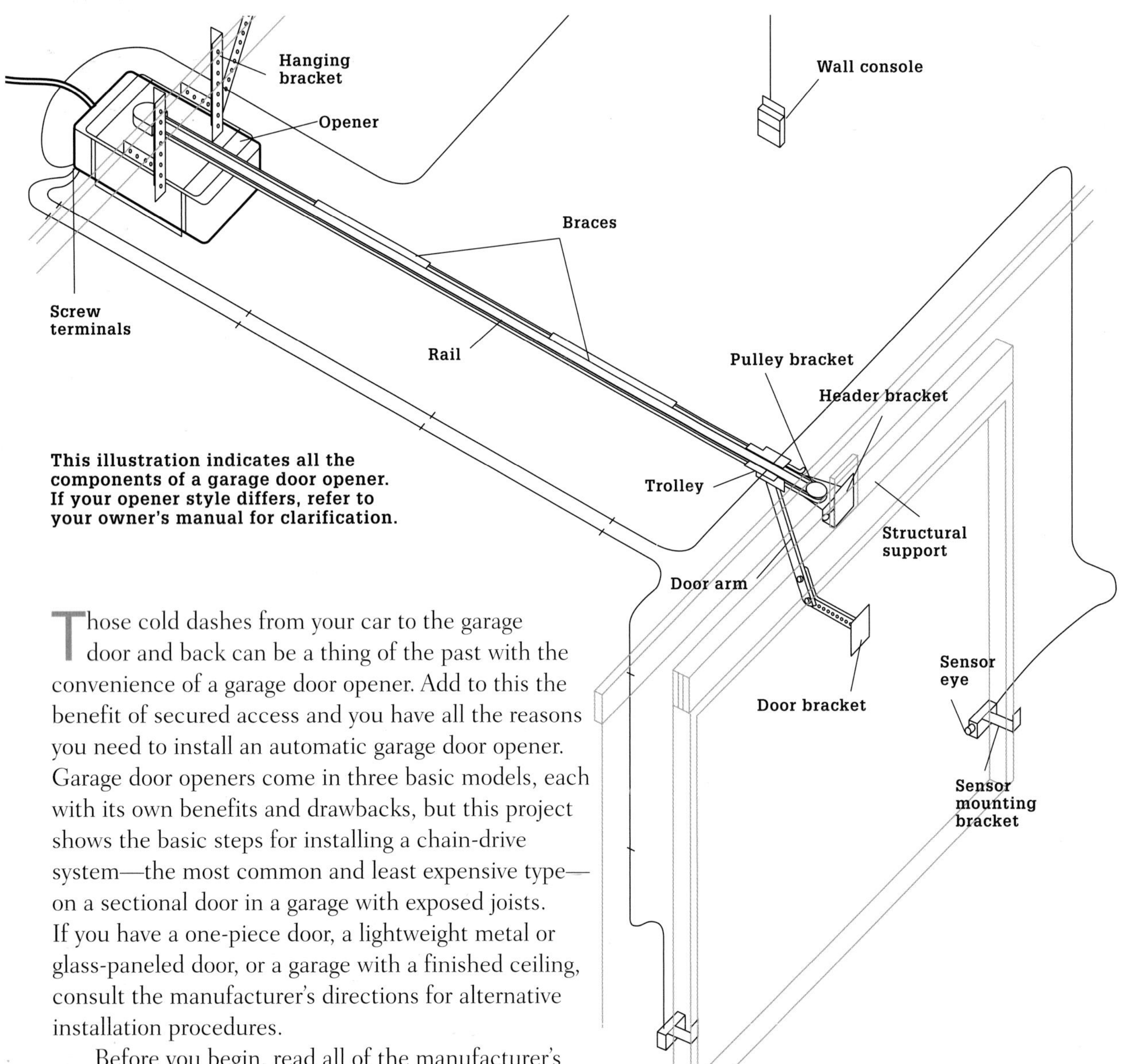


**This illustration indicates all the components of a garage door opener. If your opener style differs, refer to your owner's manual for clarification.**

Those cold dashes from your car to the garage door and back can be a thing of the past with the convenience of a garage door opener. Add to this the benefit of secured access and you have all the reasons you need to install an automatic garage door opener. Garage door openers come in three basic models, each with its own benefits and drawbacks, but this project shows the basic steps for installing a chain-drive system—the most common and least expensive type—on a sectional door in a garage with exposed joists. If you have a one-piece door, a lightweight metal or glass-paneled door, or a garage with a finished ceiling, consult the manufacturer's directions for alternative installation procedures.

Before you begin, read all of the manufacturer's instructions and the list of safety tips on the next page. Then make sure your garage door is properly balanced and moves smoothly. Open and close the door to see if it sticks or binds at any point. Release the door in the half-open position. It should stay in place supported by its own springs. If your door is not balanced or sticks at any point, call a garage door service professional before installing the opener.

Most garage door openers plug into a standard grounded receptacle located near the unit. Some local codes may require openers to be hard-wired into circuits. Consult the manufacturer's directions for hard-wiring procedures.

## Tools & Materials ▸

- Stepladder
- Tape measure
- Screwdriver
- Pliers
- Wire cutters
- Pencil
- Hammer
- Adjustable wrench
- ½ and 7/16" sockets and ratchet wrench
- Drill and bits
- Garage door opener kit
- 2× lumber
- Grease pencil
- Staple gun
- Insulated staples

## How to Install a Garage Door Opener

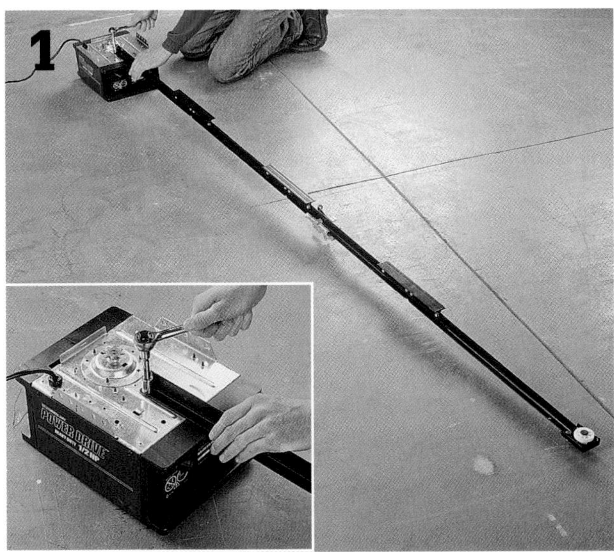


**Start by aligning the rail pieces** in proper order and securing them with the included braces and bolts. Screw the pulley bracket to the door end of the rail and slide the trolley onto the rail. Make sure the pulley and all rail pieces are properly aligned and that the trolley runs smoothly without hitting any hardware along the rail. Remove the two screws from the top of the opener, then attach the rail to the opener using these screws (inset).

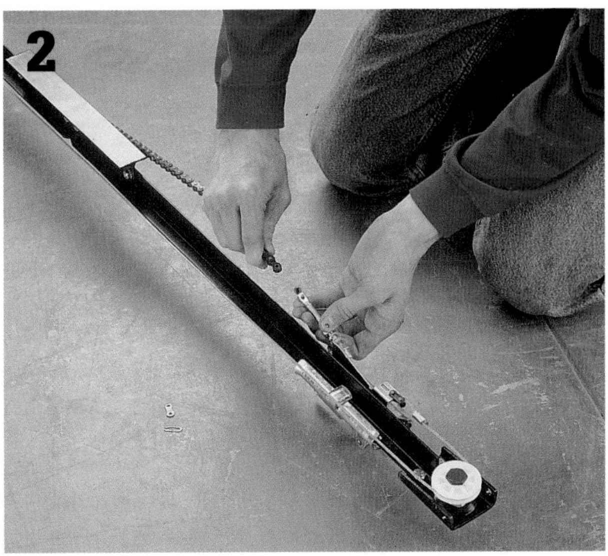

**The drive chain/cable** should be packaged in its own dispensing carton. Attach the cable loop to the front of the trolley using the included linking hardware. Wrap the cable around the pulley, then wrap the remaining chain around the drive sprocket on the opener. Finally, attach it to the other side of the trolley with linking hardware. Make sure the chain is not twisted, then attach the cover over the drive sprocket. Tighten the chain by adjusting the nuts on the trolley until the chain is ½" above the base of the rail.

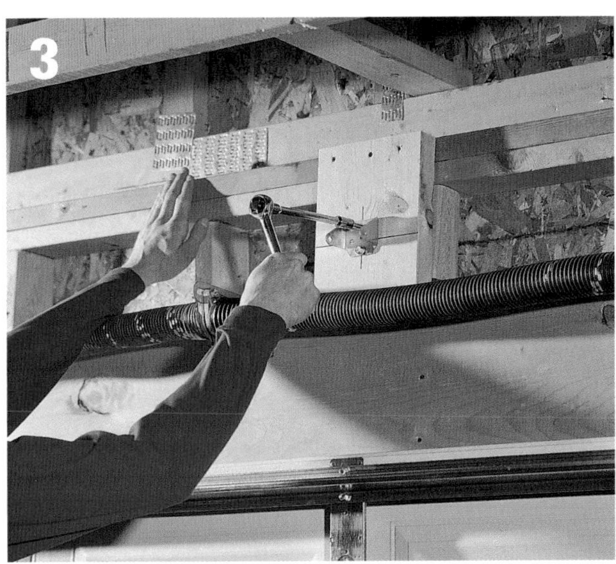

**To locate the header bracket,** first extend a vertical line from the center of the door onto the wall above. Raise the door and note the highest point the door reaches. Measure from the floor to this point. Add 2" to this distance and mark a horizontal line on the front wall where it intersects the centerline. If there is no structural support behind the cross point, fasten 2 × lumber across the framing. Then fasten the header bracket to the structural support with the included screws.

**Support the opener on the floor** with a board or box to prevent stress and twisting to the rail. Attach the rail pulley bracket to the header bracket above the door with the included clevis pin. Then place the opener on a stepladder so it is above the door tracks. Open the door and shim beneath the opener until the rail is 2" above the door.

(continued)

**Hang the opener** from the ceiling joists with the included hanging brackets and screws. Angle at least one of the hanging brackets to increase the stability of the unit while in operation. Attach the manual release cord and handle to the release arm of the trolley.

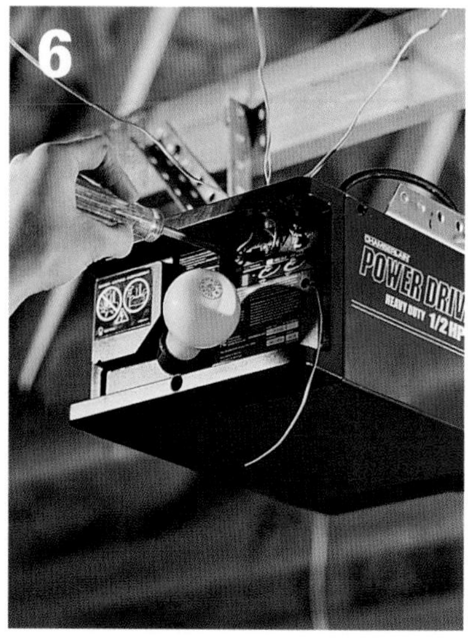


**Strip ¼" of sheathing** from the wall-console bell wire. Connect the wire to the screw terminals on the console, then attach it to the inside wall of the garage with the included screws. Run the wires up the wall and connect them to the proper terminals on the opener. Secure the wire to the wall with insulated staples, being careful not to pierce the wire. Install the light bulbs and lenses.

**Install the sensor-eye mounting** brackets at each side of the garage door, parallel to each other, about 4 to 6" from the floor. The sensor brackets can be attached to the door track, the wall, or the floor, depending upon your garage layout. See the manufacturer's directions for the best configuration for your garage.

**Attach the sensor eyes** to the brackets with the included wing nuts, but do not tighten the nuts completely. Make sure the path of the eyes is unobstructed by the door tracks. Run wires from both sensors to the opener unit and connect the wires to the proper terminals. Plug the opener into a grounded receptacle and adjust the sensors until the indicator light shows the correct eye alignment (inset), then tighten the wing nuts. Unplug the unit and attach the sensor wires to the walls with insulated staples.

**Center the door bracket** 2 to 4" below the top of the door. Drill holes and attach the bracket with the included carriage bolts. Connect the straight and curved arm sections with the included bolts. Attach the arm to the trolley and door bracket with the included latch pins. Plug the opener into a grounded receptacle and test the unit. See the manufacturer's directions for adjustment procedures.

# Contributors

American Garage Floor, LLC
800 401 4537
www.americangaragefloor.com

Andrea Rugg Photography
www.andrearugg.com

Armor Poxy
888 751 7361
email: info@armorpoxy.com
www.armorpoxy.com

Black & Decker
800 544 6986
www.blackanddecker.com

California Closets
All photos © 2008 California Closet Co. Inc. All Rights Reserved.
For a complimentary in-home design consultation, visit
www.californiaclosets.com or call 800.274.6754

ClosetMaid
800 874 0008
www.closetmaid.com

Cocinero Pty Ltd T/A Sydney Sheds and Garages
14 / 46-48 Jedda Rd
Prestons NSW 2170
+61 2 8783 8177
www.sydneysheds.com.au

CSNSheds.com (CSN Stores)
800 505 6893
www.csnsheds.com

diamondLife
888 983 4327
www.diamondlifegear.com

Robert Genat, photographer
www.robertgenat.com

IKEA Home Furnishings
800 434 4532
www.IKEA-usa.com

Lee Klancher, photographer
www.leeklancher.com

Mills Pride
www.millspride.net

Schulte, Strong Home Storage
800 669 3225
www.schultestorage.com

Beth Singer Photographer, Inc.
www.bethsingerphotographer.com

Swisstrax Corp.
866 748 7940
www.swissfloors.com

VAULT (Vault Brands, Inc.)
866 828 5810
www.vaultgarage.com

# Resources

American Garage Floor
Garage floorcoverings, pages 214 to 217
800-401-4537
www.americangaragefloor.com

Black & Decker Corp.
Power tools, utility cabinets
800-544-6986
www.blackanddecker.com

HDA Inc.
Garage plans, pages 92 to 101
800-373-2646/ plan sales
314-770-2228/ technical assistance
www.projectplans.com

Quikrete Cos.
Concrete sealer p. 33
800-282-5828
www.quikrete.com

# Photo Credits

p. 3 (second from bottom) Swiss Trax
p. 8 (top) IKEA, (lower left & right) Clopay
p. 9 (top left & right) Shutterstock, (lower) California Closets
p. 10 (top) Beth Singer, (lower left) Swiss Trax, (lower right) Andrea Rugg
p. 11 (top left) Shutterstock, (top right) iStockphoto, (lower) IKEA
p. 12 (top) California Closets, (lower left & right) Lee Klancher
p. 13 (top left & right) Photolibrary, (lower) Black & Decker
p. 14 (top left) IKEA, (top right) Closet Maid, (lower) Armor Poxy
p. 15 (top left) Shutterstock, (top right) Lee Klancher, (lower) Clopay
p. 16 (top left & right) Lee Klancher, (lower) Robert Genant
p. 17 (top) CSN, (lower) Schulte
p. 18 (top & lower right) Mill's Pride, (lower left) Clopay
p. 19 (top) Swiss Trax, (lower left) Closet Maid, (lower right) Armor Poxy
p. 20 (top left) elfa, (top right) Vault, (lower) Armor Poxy
p. 21 (top) Vault, (lower) Beth Singer
p. 50 (top) iStockphoto
p. 132 Cocinero Pty Ltd T/A Sydney Sheds and Garages
p. 151 Swiss Trax
p. 152 IKEA
p. 164 California Closets
p. 180 Robert Genant
p. 202 (inset) iStockphoto
p. 214 BLTC

# Conversion Charts

## Metric Equivalent

| Inches (in.) | 1/64 | 1/32 | 1/25 | 1/16 | 1/8 | 1/4 | 3/8 | 2/5 | 1/2 | 5/8 | 3/4 | 7/8 | 1 | 2 | 3 | 4 | 5 | 6 | 7 | 8 | 9 | 10 | 11 | 12 | 36 | 39.4 |
|---|---|---|---|---|---|---|---|---|---|---|---|---|---|---|---|---|---|---|---|---|---|---|---|---|---|---|
| Feet (ft.) | | | | | | | | | | | | | | | | | | | | | | | | 1 | 3 | 3 1/12 |
| Yards (yd.) | | | | | | | | | | | | | | | | | | | | | | | | | 1 | 1 1/12 |
| Millimeters (mm) | 0.40 | 0.79 | 1 | 1.59 | 3.18 | 6.35 | 9.53 | 10 | 12.7 | 15.9 | 19.1 | 22.2 | 25.4 | 50.8 | 76.2 | 101.6 | 127 | 152 | 178 | 203 | 229 | 254 | 279 | 305 | 914 | 1,000 |
| Centimeters (cm) | | | | | | | 0.95 | 1 | 1.27 | 1.59 | 1.91 | 2.22 | 2.54 | 5.08 | 7.62 | 10.16 | 12.7 | 15.2 | 17.8 | 20.3 | 22.9 | 25.4 | 27.9 | 30.5 | 91.4 | 100 |
| Meters (m) | | | | | | | | | | | | | | | | | | | | | | | | .30 | .91 | 1.00 |

## Converting Measurements

| To Convert: | To: | Multiply by: |
|---|---|---|
| Inches | Millimeters | 25.4 |
| Inches | Centimeters | 2.54 |
| Feet | Meters | 0.305 |
| Yards | Meters | 0.914 |
| Miles | Kilometers | 1.609 |
| Square inches | Square centimeters | 6.45 |
| Square feet | Square meters | 0.093 |
| Square yards | Square meters | 0.836 |
| Cubic inches | Cubic centimeters | 16.4 |
| Cubic feet | Cubic meters | 0.0283 |
| Cubic yards | Cubic meters | 0.765 |
| Pints (U.S.) | Liters | 0.473 (Imp. 0.568) |
| Quarts (U.S.) | Liters | 0.946 (Imp. 1.136) |
| Gallons (U.S.) | Liters | 3.785 (Imp. 4.546) |
| Ounces | Grams | 28.4 |
| Pounds | Kilograms | 0.454 |
| Tons | Metric tons | 0.907 |

| To Convert: | To: | Multiply by: |
|---|---|---|
| Millimeters | Inches | 0.039 |
| Centimeters | Inches | 0.394 |
| Meters | Feet | 3.28 |
| Meters | Yards | 1.09 |
| Kilometers | Miles | 0.621 |
| Square centimeters | Square inches | 0.155 |
| Square meters | Square feet | 10.8 |
| Square meters | Square yards | 1.2 |
| Cubic centimeters | Cubic inches | 0.061 |
| Cubic meters | Cubic feet | 35.3 |
| Cubic meters | Cubic yards | 1.31 |
| Liters | Pints (U.S.) | 2.114 (Imp. 1.76) |
| Liters | Quarts (U.S.) | 1.057 (Imp. 0.88) |
| Liters | Gallons (U.S.) | 0.264 (Imp. 0.22) |
| Grams | Ounces | 0.035 |
| Kilograms | Pounds | 2.2 |
| Metric tons | Tons | 1.1 |

## Converting Temperatures

Convert degrees Fahrenheit (F) to degrees Celsius (C) by following this simple formula: Subtract 32 from the Fahrenheit temperature reading. Then mulitply that number by 5/9. For example, 77°F - 32 = 45. 45 × 5/9 = 25°C.

To convert degrees Celsius to degrees Fahrenheit, multiply the Celsius temperature reading by 9/5, then add 32. For example, 25°C × 9/5 = 45. 45 + 32 = 77°F.

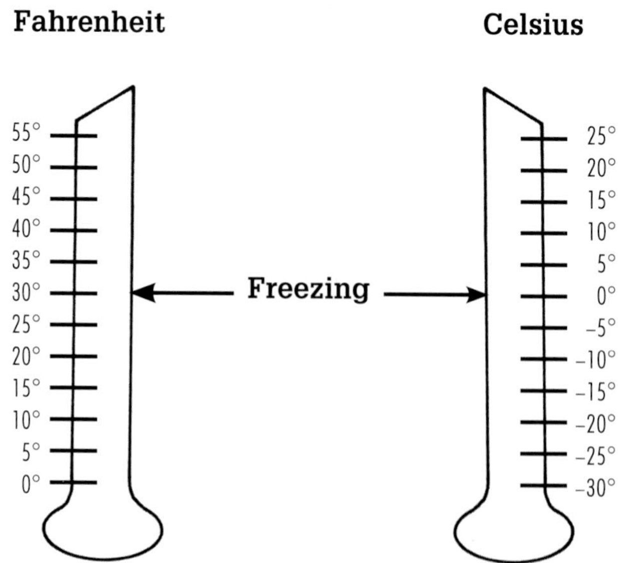

# Index


**A**

Air quality & ventilation for workshops, 146
Asphalt shingles
  choosing, 61
  installing, 63–66

**B**

Base trim, installing, 219
Bleed water, 33
Building section plans
  for carport, 135
  for compact garage, 105
  example, 24
  for gambrel garage, 119

**C**

Cabinets
  ideas, 12–13, 15, 16, 17, 18, 21
  installing, 172–175
  safety, 19
Carport
  about, 132
  building, 137–141
  materials & cutting list, 133
  plans, 134–136
Cast veneer stone siding
  about, 83–84
  idea, 83
  installing, 84–85
Ceiling storage units, installing, 176–177
Closets
  ideas, 12–13, 15, 16, 18, 21
  safety, 19
Color, use of, 17
Compact garage with storage
  about, 102–103
  building, 111–115
  materials & cutting list, 104
  plans, 105–110
    building section, 105
    door details, 109
    elevation, 106
    flooring, 108
    foundation, 105
    wall framing, 107–108
    windows, 108, 110
Concrete
  cleaning, 210–211
  etching, 208, 210–211
  painting, 208–209, 213
  patching, 207
  resurfacing, 222–225
  sealing, 212
Concrete slab foundation, building
  about, 28
  estimating amount of concrete, 31
  plans for, 29
  pouring concrete, 30–33
Condensation, checking for, 210

**D**

Doors. See Overhead doors; Service doors
Drawings of plans, 24–25
Drywall
  fire-rated (type X), 155
  hanging, 156

**E**

Electric heaters, installing, 194–195
Electricity
  bringing service to garage
    about, 180–181
    steps in, 182–187
  installing subpanels, 188–191
  planning for needs, 146
  wiring safety, 179, 180
Elevation plans
  for carport, 134
  for compact garage with storage, 106
  examples of, 25
  for gambrel garage, 122, 124–125
  for single detached garage, 94
Epoxy floor coating
  about, 19, 206, 208
  applying, 207, 209–213
  condensation testing, 210
  tools & materials for, 209
Etching concrete, 208, 210–211

**F**

Fascia, installing roof, 56–59
Faux stone siding
  about, 83–84
  idea, 83
  installing, 84–85
Fiber-cement lap siding
  about, 83
  installing, 86–89
  tools for, 86
Fire-rated drywall, 155
Flooring
  about, 206
  cleaning, 210–211
  condensation, checking for, 210
  etching, 208, 210–211
  ideas, 10, 16, 18, 206
  installing
    base trim, 219
    interlocking tiles, 216–219
    roll-out PVC, 214–215
  painting
    about, 19, 206, 208
    applying, 207, 209–213
    tools & materials for, 209
  patching, 207
  plans for compact garage with storage, 108
  resurfacing concrete, 222–225
  sealing, 212
  texturized, 20
Fluorescent lighting
  installing fixtures, 192–193
  types of, 145
Foundation
  building, 28–33
  building concrete slab
    about, 28
    estimating amount of concrete, 31
    plans for, 29
    pouring concrete, 30–33
  plans
    for compact garage, 105
    for single detached garage, 94, 96
Framing
  roofs
    using rafters, 44–49
    using trusses, 50–51
  service door openings, 40
  walls
    about, 34
    plans
      for compact garage with storage, 107–108
      for gambrel garage, 125
      for single detached garage, 95, 97
    steps in, 36–43
    tips for, 35
  window openings, 40
  window plans for
    box bay, 109, 110
    jamb detail, 124

**G**

Gambrel garage
  about, 116–117
  building, 126–131
  materials & cutting list, 118

plans, 119–125
building section, 119
doors, 124
elevations, 122, 125
floor, 120
overhangs, 123
roof, 121
window, 124
Garage door openers
installing, 232–234
safety tips, 81
tuning up, 230–231
Green insulated grounding wire, 179
Ground-fault circuit-interrupter (GFCI receptacle), 179

**H**

Heaters, installing electric, 194–195
Hobby areas, idea, 8
Housewrap, installing, 54–55

**I**

Interlocking floor tiles, installing, 216–219

**L**

Lap siding
fiber-cement
about, 83
installing, 86–89
tools for, 86
ideas, 82
types, 83
Lighting
fluorescent
installing fixtures, 192–193
types of, 145
natural
ideas, 8, 15
installing skylights, 202–205
recessed, 20
safety and, 179
skylights, installing, 202–205
for workshops, 144–145
Living space idea, 8
Locksets, installing, 75
Loft, idea and plan for garage with, 101

**M**

Multitab shingles, 61

**N**

National Electrical Code (NEC), 179
Nonservice rated panels, installing, 188–191

**O**

Overhead doors
about, 76, 81
idea, 14
installing, 77–80
openers
installing, 232–234
safety tips, 81
tuning up, 230–231
plans
for compact garage with storage, 109
for gambrel garage, 124
for single detached garage, 95
tuning up, 226–230

**P**

Painting floors
about, 19, 206, 208
applying, 207, 209–213
condensation testing, 210
ideas, 16, 18
tools & materials for, 209
Pegboard
about, 158
hanging, 160–161
styles, 159
Plans
for attached porch, 98
for compact garage with storage, 105–110
building section, 105
door details, 109
elevation, 106
flooring, 108
foundation, 105
wall framing, 107–108
windows, 108, 110
considerations when making, 25
drawings needed
making, 24–25
for roof, 45
for slab, 29
for gambrel garage, 119–125
building section, 119
doors, 124
elevations, 122, 125
floor, 120
overhangs, 123
roof, 121
window, 124
for single detached garages, 94–97
elevation, 94
foundation, 94, 96
wall framing, 95, 97
for workshops, 100
Porch, idea and plan for garage with, 98
PVC flooring, installing roll-out, 214–215

**R**

Racking and shelf systems
ideas, 9, 10, 11, 16, 18, 152
installing adjustable shelves, 162–163
installing slatted shelves, 164–167
installing utility shelves, 168–171
Reverse gable detached garage, idea and plan for, 100
Ridge caps
cutting, 65
installing, 141
Ridge vents, installing continuous, 66–67
Roll-out PVC flooring, installing, 214–215
Roofs
building
about, 60
continuous ridge vents, 66–67
preparing roof deck, 62–63
shingles, choosing, 61
shingles installing, 63–66
gable-style framing
about, 44–45
using rafters, 46–49
using trusses, 50–51
installing fascia & soffits, 56–59
installing metal panels, 140–141
plans
for carport, 135–136
for compact garage, 110
for gambrel garage, 121, 123
safety measures, 64

**S**

Safety
cabinets and closets, 19
door security, 75
lighting and, 20
roofs and, 64
wiring, 179, 180
Service doors
about, 68–69
choosing, 73
framing openings, 40
installing, 73–75
plans
for compact garage, 109
for single detached garage, 95
security, 75
Service panel, installing subpanels, 188–191
Shelf systems
ideas, 9, 11, 15, 18, 152
installing adjustable, 162–163
installing slatted, 164–167
installing utility shelves, 168–171
Shingles, asphalt for roof
choosing, 61
installing

preparing roof deck, 62–63
steps in, 63–66
Siding
about, 82
cast veneer stone
about, 83–84
idea, 83
installing, 84–85
fiber-cement lap
about, 83
installing, 86–89
tools for, 86
types of, 83–84
Single detached garage, building
about, 92
materials & cutting list, 93
plans
elevation, 94
foundation, 94, 96
wall framing, 95, 97
steps in, 26–27
Skylights
idea, 8
installing, 202–205
Slab-on-grade foundation, building
about, 28
estimating amount of concrete, 31
plans for, 29
pouring concrete, 30–33
Soffits, installing, 56–59
Speed squares, using, 45
Storage
building compact garage with
about, 102–103
materials & cutting list, 104
plans, 105–110
building section, 105
door details, 109
elevation, 106
flooring, 108
foundation, 105
wall framing, 107–108
windows, 108, 110
steps in, 111–115
ideas, 142
cabinets and closets, 12–13, 15, 16, 17, 18, 21
racking and shelf systems, 9, 10, 11, 15, 16, 18, 152
installing
cabinets, 172–175
ceiling units, 176–177
shelf systems
adjustable, 162–163
slatted, 164–167
utility shelves, 168–171
pegboard
about, 158
hanging, 160–161
styles, 159


**T**


Templates, 25
Texturized flooring idea, 20
Three-car detached garage, ideas and plans for, 98, 101
Three-car detached garage/workshop, idea and plan for, 100
Tiles, installing interlocking, 216–219
Two-car detached garage, idea and plan for, 99
Type X drywall, 155


**U**


Utility shelves, installing, 168–171


**V**


Victorian detached garage, idea and plan for, 99
Vinyl lap siding, about, 83


**W**


Walls
finishing interior
about, 154–155
hanging drywall, 156
with sheathing, 157
Framing
about, 34
plans
for compact garage with storage, 107–108
for gambrel garage, 125
for single detached garage, 95, 97
steps in, 36–43
tips for, 35
insulating, 153
raising, 39, 41–43
sheathing, 52–55, 157
siding
about, 82
cast veneer stone
about, 83–84
idea, 83
installing, 84–85
fiber-cement lap
about, 83
installing, 86–89
tools for, 86
types of, 83–84
trophy ideas, 14
Windows
about, 68–69
adding, 196–201
framing openings, 40
framing plans
box bay, 109, 110
jamb detail, 124
idea, 11
installing, 70–72
plans for compact garage with storage, 108, 110
Wiring safety, 179, 180
Wood lap siding, about, 83
Workbenches, 146–147
Workout area idea, 10
Workshops
about, 142–143
doors for, 73
floor plans, 148–149
ideas, 8, 11, 12–13, 21, 100
plan, 100
planning
air quality & ventilation, 146
electricity needs, 146
layout, 146–149
lighting, 144–145

# STUDENT'S GUIDE

As you begin each lab, take a few moments to read the **Case Study** and the Concept Preview. The case study introduces a real-life setting that is interwoven throughout the entire lab, providing the basis for understanding the use of the application. Also, notice the Additional Information, Having Trouble?, and Another Method boxes scattered throughout the book. These tips provide more information about related topics, help get you out of trouble if you are having problems, and offer suggestions on other ways to perform the same task. Finally, read the text between the steps. You will find the few minutes more it takes you is well worth the time when you are completing the practice exercises.

Many learning aids are built into the text to ensure your success with the material and to make the process of learning rewarding. The pages that follow call your attention to the key features in the text.

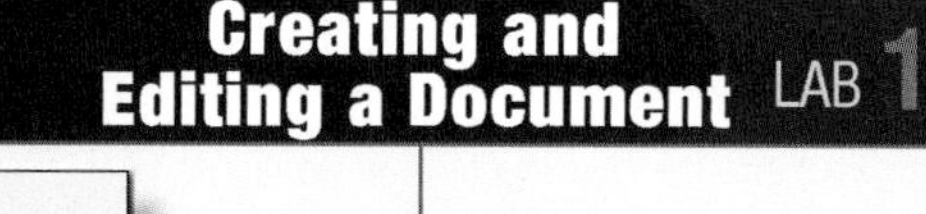


### Objectives

Appear at the beginning of the lab and identify the main features you will be learning.

**Objectives**

After you have read this chapter, you should be able to:

1. Develop a document as well as enter and edit text.
2. Insert and delete text and blank lines.
3. Reveal formatting marks.
4. Use AutoCorrect, AutoText, and AutoComplete.
5. Use automatic spelling and grammar checking.
6. Save, close, and open files.
7. Select text.
8. Undo and redo changes.
9. Change fonts and type sizes.
10. Bold and color text.
11. Change alignment.
12. Insert, size, and move pictures.
13. Preview and print a document.
14. Set file properties.

WD1.1

### Case Study

Introduces a real-life setting that is interwoven throughout the lab, providing the basis for understanding the use of the application.

Case Study

**Adventure Travel Tours**

As a recent college graduate, you have accepted a job as advertising coordinator for Adventure Travel Tours, a specialty travel company that organizes active adventure vacations. The company is headquartered in Los Angeles and has locations in other major cities throughout the country. You are responsible for coordination of the advertising program for all locations. This includes the creation of many kinds of promotional materials: brochures, flyers, form letters, news releases, advertisements, and a monthly newsletter. You are also responsible for creating Web pages for the company Web site.

Adventure Travel is very excited about four new tours planned for the upcoming year. They want to promote them through informative presentations held throughout the country. Your first job as advertising coordinator will be to create a flyer advertising the four new tours and the presentations about them. The flyer will be modified according to the location of the presentation.

The software tool you will use to create the flyer is the word processing application Microsoft Word Office 2003. It helps you create documents such as letters, reports, and research papers. In this lab, you will learn how to enter, edit, and print a document while you create the flyer (shown right) to be distributed in a mailing to Adventure Travel Tours clients.

© PhotoDisc

WD1.2

# • Objectives, Case Study
# • Concept Preview, Another Method, Having Trouble?

**Concept Preview**
Provides an overview to the concepts that will be presented throughout the lab.

**Another Method**
Offers additional ways to perform a procedure.

**Having Trouble?**
Helps resolve potential problems as you work through each lab.

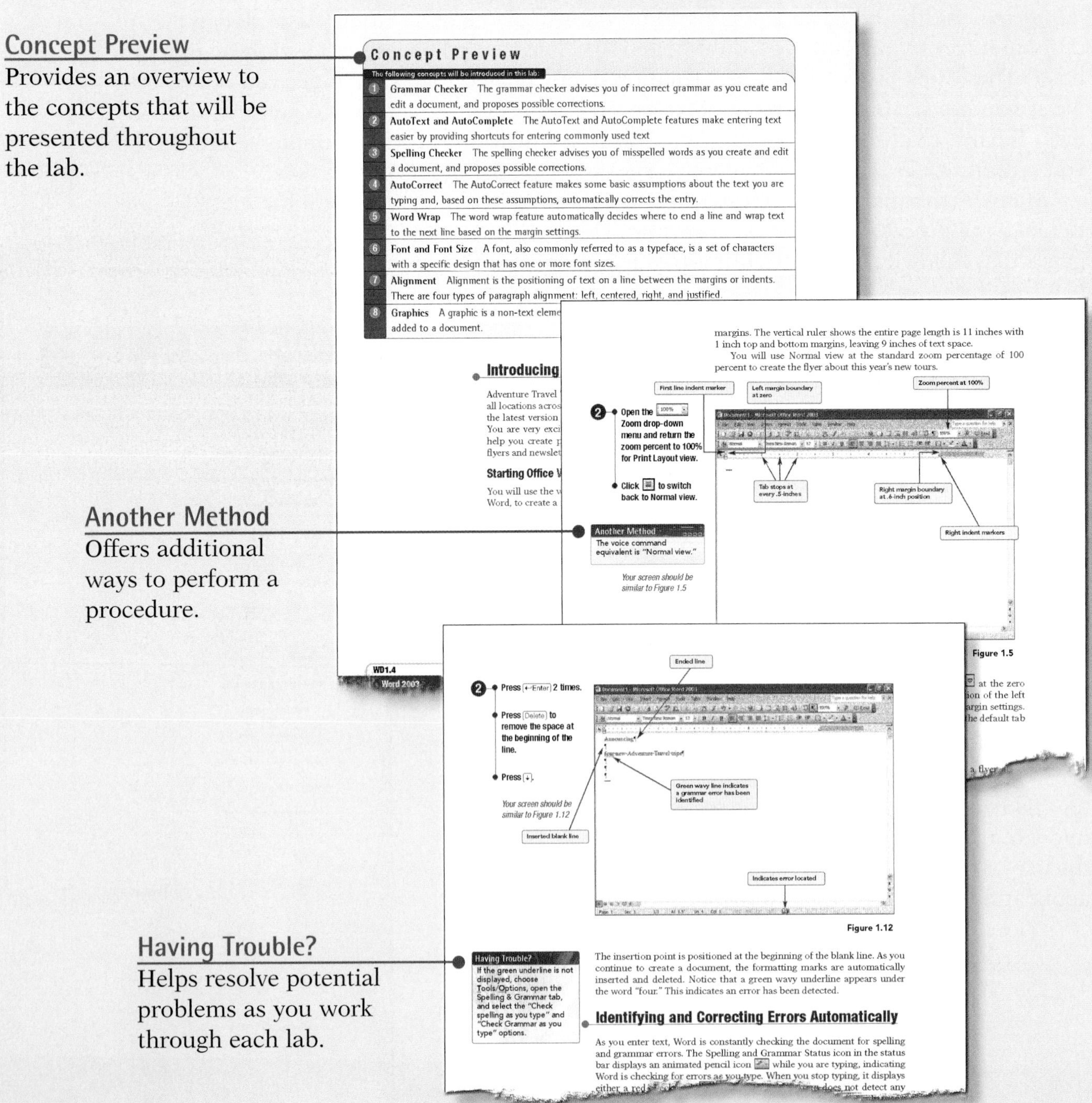

# Numbered and Bulleted Steps, Additional Information

## Numbered and Bulleted Steps

Provide clear Step-by-Step Instructions on how to complete a task, or series of tasks.

## Additional Information

Offers brief asides with expanded coverage of content.

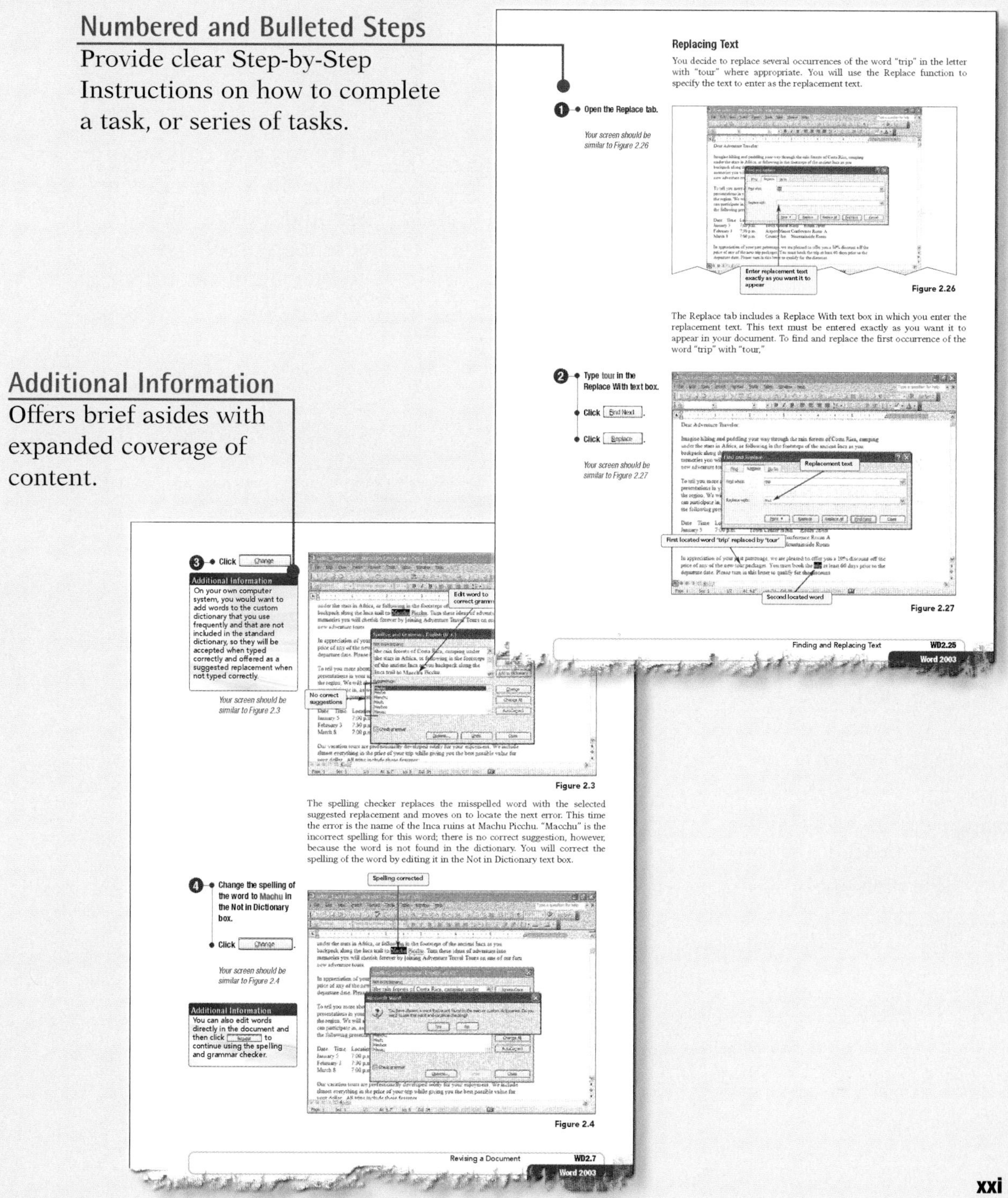

Replacing Text
You decide to replace several occurrences of the word "trip" in the letter with "tour" where appropriate. You will use the Replace function to specify the text to enter as the replacement text.
Open the Replace tab.
Your screen should be similar to Figure 2.26
Enter replacement text exactly as you want it to appear
Figure 2.26
The Replace tab includes a Replace With text box in which you enter the replacement text. This text must be entered exactly as you want it to appear in your document. To find and replace the first occurrence of the word "trip" with "tour,"
Type tour in the Replace With text box.
Click Find Next.
Click Replace.
Your screen should be similar to Figure 2.27
Replacement text
First located word 'trip' replaced by 'tour'
Second located word
Figure 2.27
Finding and Replacing Text
WD2.25
Word 2003
Click Change.
Additional Information
On your own computer system, you would want to add words to the custom dictionary that you use frequently and that are not included in the standard dictionary, so they will be accepted when typed correctly and offered as a suggested replacement when not typed correctly.
Your screen should be similar to Figure 2.3
Edit word to correct grammar
No correct suggestions
Figure 2.3
The spelling checker replaces the misspelled word with the selected suggested replacement and moves on to locate the next error. This time the error is the name of the Inca ruins at Machu Picchu. "Macchu" is the incorrect spelling for this word; there is no correct suggestion, however, because the word is not found in the dictionary. You will correct the spelling of the word by editing it in the Not in Dictionary text box.
Change the spelling of the word to Machu in the Not in Dictionary box.
Click Change.
Your screen should be similar to Figure 2.4
Spelling corrected
Additional Information
You can also edit words directly in the document and then click Resume to continue using the spelling and grammar checker.
Figure 2.4
Revising a Document
WD2.7
Word 2003

# • Figures and Callouts, Tables

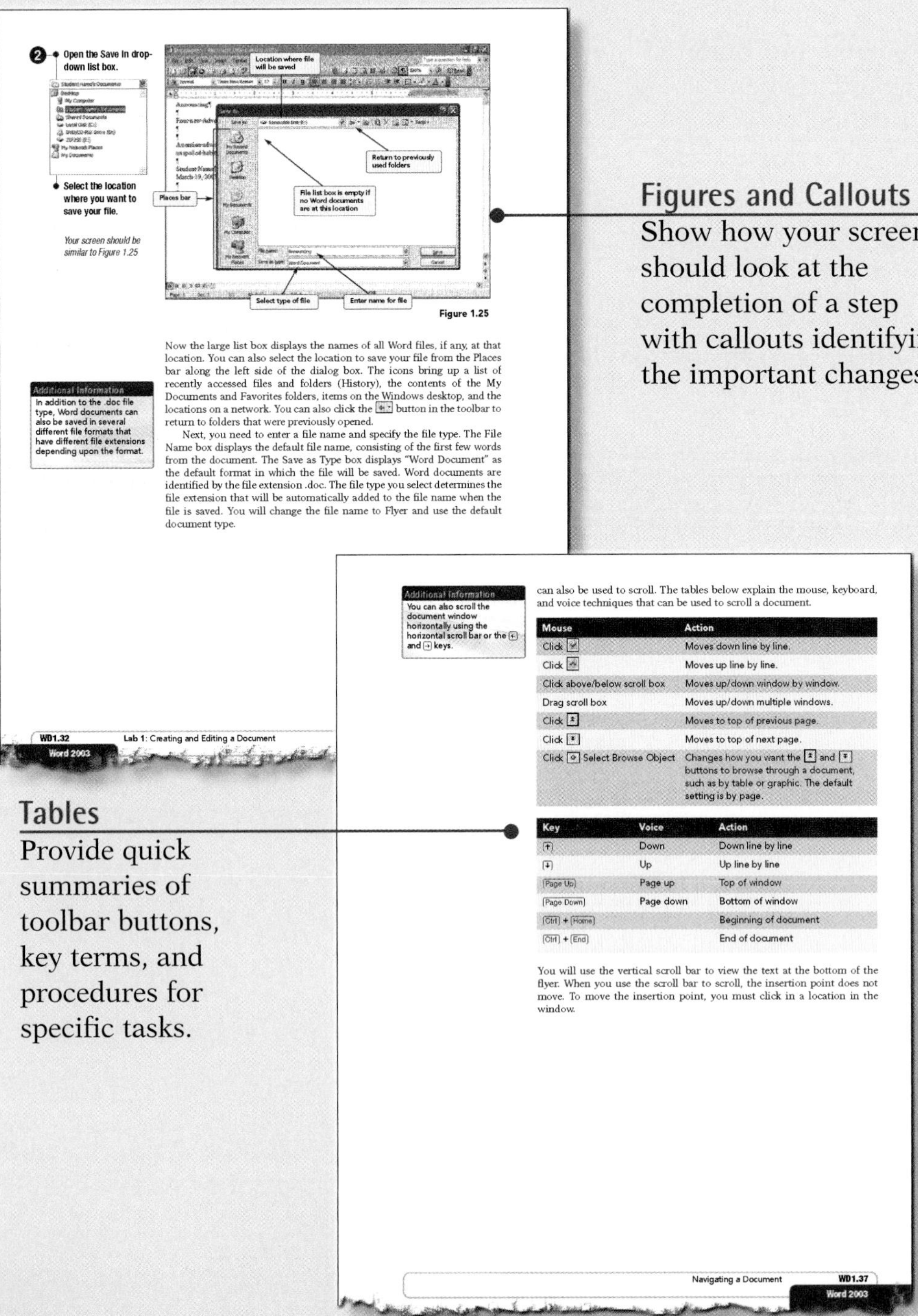

2 Open the Save In drop-down list box.

Select the location where you want to save your file.

*Your screen should be similar to Figure 1.25*



Figure 1.25

Now the large list box displays the names of all Word files, if any, at that location. You can also select the location to save your file from the Places bar along the left side of the dialog box. The icons bring up a list of recently accessed files and folders (History), the contents of the My Documents and Favorites folders, items on the Windows desktop, and the locations on a network. You can also click the button in the toolbar to return to folders that were previously opened.

Next, you need to enter a file name and specify the file type. The File Name box displays the default file name, consisting of the first few words from the document. The Save as Type box displays "Word Document" as the default format in which the file will be saved. Word documents are identified by the file extension .doc. The file type you select determines the file extension that will be automatically added to the file name when the file is saved. You will change the file name to Flyer and use the default document type.

**Additional Information**
In addition to the .doc file type, Word documents can also be saved in several different file formats that have different file extensions depending upon the format.

WD1.32 Lab 1: Creating and Editing a Document
Word 2003

**Additional Information**
You can also scroll the document window horizontally using the horizontal scroll bar or the ← and → keys.

can also be used to scroll. The tables below explain the mouse, keyboard, and voice techniques that can be used to scroll a document.

| Mouse | Action |
|---|---|
| Click [▼] | Moves down line by line. |
| Click [▲] | Moves up line by line. |
| Click above/below scroll box | Moves up/down window by window. |
| Drag scroll box | Moves up/down multiple windows. |
| Click [⇞] | Moves to top of previous page. |
| Click [⇟] | Moves to top of next page. |
| Click [○] Select Browse Object | Changes how you want the [⇞] and [⇟] buttons to browse through a document, such as by table or graphic. The default setting is by page. |

| Key | Voice | Action |
|---|---|---|
| ↑ | Down | Down line by line |
| ↓ | Up | Up line by line |
| Page Up | Page up | Top of window |
| Page Down | Page down | Bottom of window |
| Ctrl + Home | | Beginning of document |
| Ctrl + End | | End of document |

You will use the vertical scroll bar to view the text at the bottom of the flyer. When you use the scroll bar to scroll, the insertion point does not move. To move the insertion point, you must click in a location in the window.

Navigating a Document WD1.37
Word 2003

## Figures and Callouts

Show how your screen should look at the completion of a step with callouts identifying the important changes.

## Tables

Provide quick summaries of toolbar buttons, key terms, and procedures for specific tasks.

# • Focus on Careers, Concept Summary

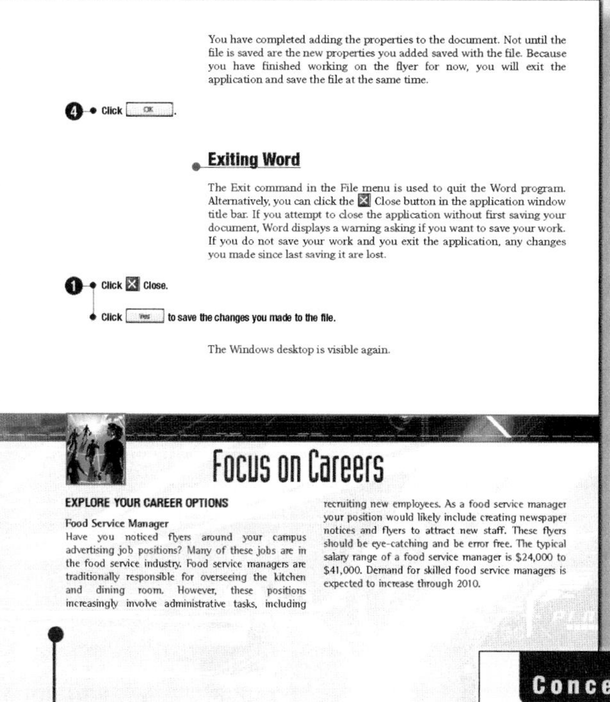

You have completed adding the properties to the document. Not until the file is saved are the new properties you added saved with the file. Because you have finished working on the flyer for now, you will exit the application and save the file at the same time.

4 • Click OK.

## Exiting Word

The Exit command in the File menu is used to quit the Word program. Alternatively, you can click the ☒ Close button in the application window title bar. If you attempt to close the application without first saving your document, Word displays a warning asking if you want to save your work. If you do not save your work and you exit the application, any changes you made since last saving it are lost.

1 • Click ☒ Close.

• Click Yes to save the changes you made to the file.

The Windows desktop is visible again.

## Focus on Careers

**EXPLORE YOUR CAREER OPTIONS**

**Food Service Manager**
Have you noticed flyers around your campus advertising job positions? Many of these jobs are in the food service industry. Food service managers are traditionally responsible for overseeing the kitchen and dining room. However, these positions increasingly involve administrative tasks, including recruiting new employees. As a food service manager your position would likely include creating newspaper notices and flyers to attract new staff. These flyers should be eye-catching and be error free. The typical salary range of a food service manager is $24,000 to $41,000. Demand for skilled food service managers is expected to increase through 2010.

Exiting Word

**Focus on Careers**
Provides an example of how the material covered may be applied in the "real world."

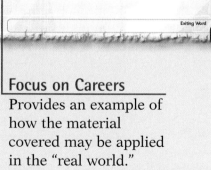

**Concept Summary**
Offers a visual summary of the concepts presented throughout the lab.

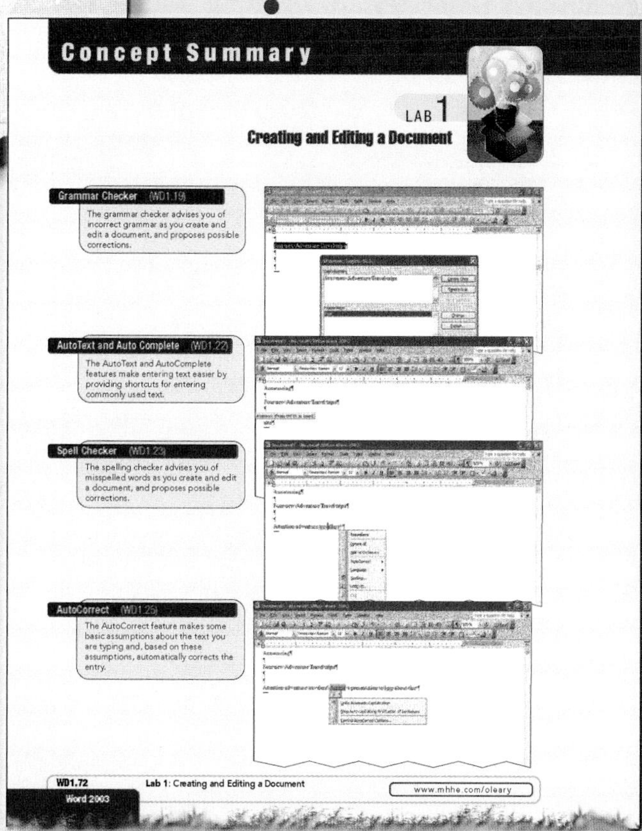

## Concept Summary

LAB 1
**Creating and Editing a Document**

**Grammar Checker** (WD1.19)
The grammar checker advises you of incorrect grammar as you create and edit a document, and proposes possible corrections.

**AutoText and Auto Complete** (WD1.22)
The AutoText and AutoComplete features make entering text easier by providing shortcuts for entering commonly used text.

**Spell Checker** (WD1.23)
The spelling checker advises you of misspelled words as you create and edit a document, and proposes possible corrections.

**AutoCorrect** (WD1.25)
The AutoCorrect feature makes some basic assumptions about the text you are typing and, based on these assumptions, automatically corrects the entry.

WD1.72 Word 2003 Lab 1: Creating and Editing a Document www.mhhe.com/oleary

# • Key Terms and Microsoft Office Specialist Skills, Command Summary

## Key Terms and Microsoft Office Specialist Skills

Includes a list of all bolded terms with page references and a table showing the Microsoft Office Specialist certification skills that were covered in the lab.

**lab review**

LAB 3

**Creating Reports and Tables**

**key terms**

alignment WD1.58
AutoComplete WD1.22
AutoCorrect WD1.25
AutoText WD1.22
character formatting WD1.50
cursor WD1.5
custom dictionary WD1.23
default WD1.68
document window WD1.5
drawing object WD1.60
edit WD1.11
embedded object WD1.60
end-of-file marker WD1.5
file property WD1.69
font WD1.51
font size WD1.51
format WD1.11
formatting mark WD1.14
Formatting toolbar WD1.5
grammar checker WD1.16
graphic WD1.60
Insert mode WD1.40
insertion point WD1.5
main dictionary WD1.23
object WD1.60
Overtype mode WD1.41
pane WD1.6
paragraph formatting WD1.50
picture WD1.60
ruler WD1.5
sans serif font WD1.51
select WD1.6
selection rectangle WD1.65
serif font WD1.51
sizing handles WD1.65
Smart Tag WD1.29
soft space WD1.58
source program WD1.60
spelling checker WD1.23
Standard toolbar WD1.5
thumbnail WD1.62
TrueType WD1.52
typeface WD1.51
word wrap WD1.28

**microsoft office specialist skills**

The Microsoft Office Specialist (MOS) certification program is designed to measure your proficiency in performing basic tasks using the Office 2003 applications. Getting certified demonstrates that you have the skills and provides a valuable industry credential for employment. After completing this lab, you have learned the following Microsoft Office Specialist skills:

| Skill | Description | Page |
|---|---|---|
| Creating Content | Insert and edit text, symbols, and special characters | WD1.XX |
| | Insert frequently used and predefined text | WD1.XX, |
| | Insert, position, and size graphics | WD1.XX |
| Formatting Content | Format text | WD1.XX |
| | Format paragraphs | WD1.XX |
| Formatting and Managing Documents | Preview and print documents | WD1.XX |
| | Review and modify document properties | WD1.XX |
| | Save documents in appropriate formats for different uses | WD1.XX |
| | Print documents, envelopes, and labels | WD1.XX |
| | Preview documents and Web pages | WD1.XX |
| | Change and organize document views and windows | WD1.XX |

WD1.74 Word 2003 Lab 1: Creating and Editing a Document www.mhhe.com/oleary

## Command Summary

Provides a table of commands and keyboard and toolbar shortcuts for all commands used in the lab.

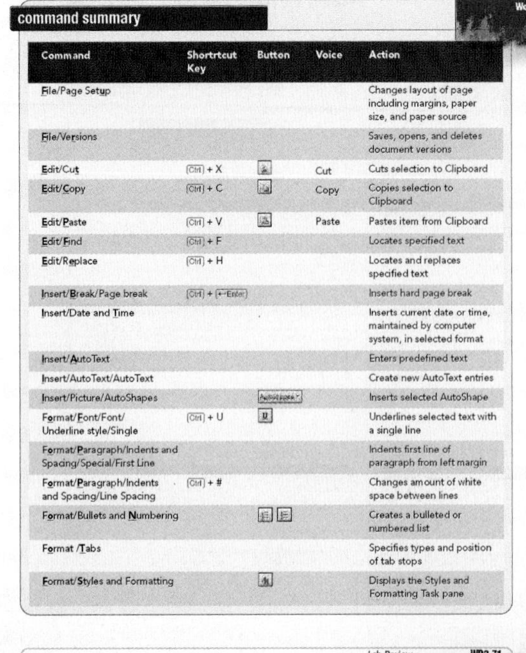

**command summary**

| Command | Shortrtcut Key | Button | Voice | Action |
|---|---|---|---|---|
| File/Page Setup | | | | Changes layout of page including margins, paper size, and paper source |
| File/Versions | | | | Saves, opens, and deletes document versions |
| Edit/Cut | Ctrl + X | | Cut | Cuts selection to Clipboard |
| Edit/Copy | Ctrl + C | | Copy | Copies selection to Clipboard |
| Edit/Paste | Ctrl + V | | Paste | Pastes item from Clipboard |
| Edit/Find | Ctrl + F | | | Locates specified text |
| Edit/Replace | Ctrl + H | | | Locates and replaces specified text |
| Insert/Break/Page break | Ctrl + ←Enter | | | Inserts hard page break |
| Insert/Date and Time | | | | Inserts current date or time, maintained by computer system, in selected format |
| Insert/AutoText | | | | Enters predefined text |
| Insert/AutoText/AutoText | | | | Create new AutoText entries |
| Insert/Picture/AutoShapes | | AutoShapes | | Inserts selected AutoShape |
| Format/Font/Font/Underline style/Single | Ctrl + U | U | | Underlines selected text with a single line |
| Format/Paragraph/Indents and Spacing/Special/First Line | | | | Indents first line of paragraph from left margin |
| Format/Paragraph/Indents and Spacing/Line Spacing | Ctrl + # | | | Changes amount of white space between lines |
| Format/Bullets and Numbering | | | | Creates a bulleted or numbered list |
| Format /Tabs | | | | Specifies types and position of tab stops |
| Format/Styles and Formatting | | | | Displays the Styles and Formatting Task pane |

Lab Review WD2.71 Word 2003

# • Lab Exercises: Screen Identification, Matching, Multiple Choice, True/False, Fill-in

## Lab Exercises

Reinforce the terminology and concepts presented in the lab through Screen Identification, Matching, Multiple Choice, True/False, and Fill-in questions.

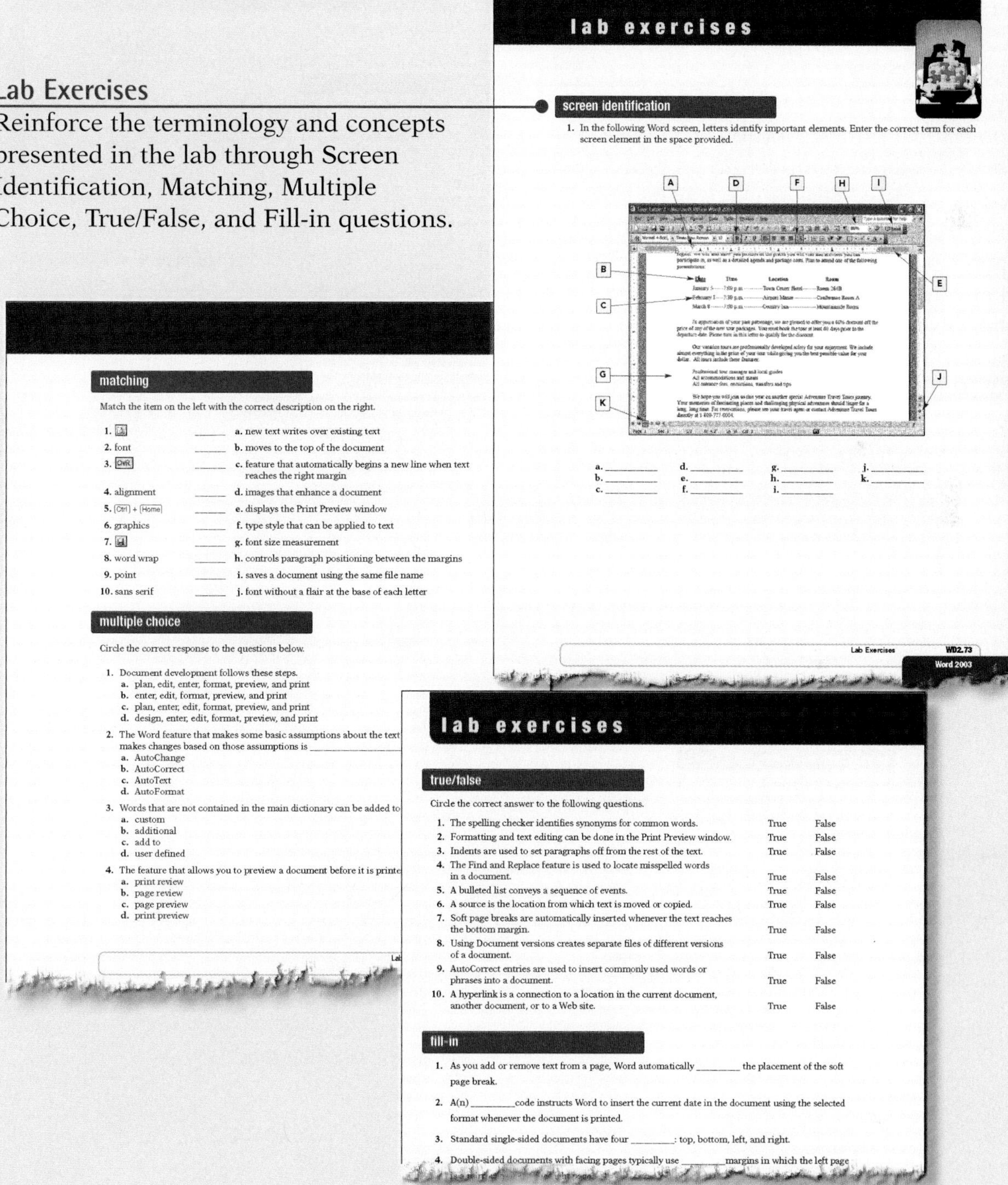

**lab exercises**

**screen identification**

1. In the following Word screen, letters identify important elements. Enter the correct term for each screen element in the space provided.

a. ________ b. ________ c. ________ d. ________ e. ________ f. ________ g. ________ h. ________ i. ________ j. ________ k. ________

Lab Exercises WD2.73 Word 2003

**matching**

Match the item on the left with the correct description on the right.

| | | |
|---|---|---|
| 1. [icon] | ______ | a. new text writes over existing text |
| 2. font | ______ | b. moves to the top of the document |
| 3. OVR | ______ | c. feature that automatically begins a new line when text reaches the right margin |
| 4. alignment | ______ | d. images that enhance a document |
| 5. Ctrl + Home | ______ | e. displays the Print Preview window |
| 6. graphics | ______ | f. type style that can be applied to text |
| 7. [icon] | ______ | g. font size measurement |
| 8. word wrap | ______ | h. controls paragraph positioning between the margins |
| 9. point | ______ | i. saves a document using the same file name |
| 10. sans serif | ______ | j. font without a flair at the base of each letter |

**multiple choice**

Circle the correct response to the questions below.

1. Document development follows these steps.
   a. plan, edit, enter, format, preview, and print
   b. enter, edit, format, preview, and print
   c. plan, enter, edit, format, preview, and print
   d. design, enter, edit, format, preview, and print
2. The Word feature that makes some basic assumptions about the text makes changes based on those assumptions is ____________
   a. AutoChange
   b. AutoCorrect
   c. AutoText
   d. AutoFormat
3. Words that are not contained in the main dictionary can be added to
   a. custom
   b. additional
   c. add to
   d. user defined
4. The feature that allows you to preview a document before it is printe
   a. print review
   b. page review
   c. page preview
   d. print preview

**lab exercises**

**true/false**

Circle the correct answer to the following questions.

| | | |
|---|---|---|
| 1. The spelling checker identifies synonyms for common words. | True | False |
| 2. Formatting and text editing can be done in the Print Preview window. | True | False |
| 3. Indents are used to set paragraphs off from the rest of the text. | True | False |
| 4. The Find and Replace feature is used to locate misspelled words in a document. | True | False |
| 5. A bulleted list conveys a sequence of events. | True | False |
| 6. A source is the location from which text is moved or copied. | True | False |
| 7. Soft page breaks are automatically inserted whenever the text reaches the bottom margin. | True | False |
| 8. Using Document versions creates separate files of different versions of a document. | True | False |
| 9. AutoCorrect entries are used to insert commonly used words or phrases into a document. | True | False |
| 10. A hyperlink is a connection to a location in the current document, another document, or to a Web site. | True | False |

**fill-in**

1. As you add or remove text from a page, Word automatically ________ the placement of the soft page break.
2. A(n) ________code instructs Word to insert the current date in the document using the selected format whenever the document is printed.
3. Standard single-sided documents have four ________: top, bottom, left, and right.
4. Double-sided documents with facing pages typically use ________margins in which the left page

# • Lab Exercises: Step-by-Step, On Your Own

## Lab Exercises

Provide hands-on practice and develop critical thinking skills through step-by-step and on-your-own practice exercises. These exercises have a rating system from easy to difficult and test your ability to apply the knowledge you gained in each lab. Exercises that build off of previous exercises are noted with a Continuing Exercise icon.

## On Your Own

**lab exercises**

rating system
★ Easy
★★ Moderate
★★★ Difficult

**step-by-step**

**Writing a Memo ★**

1. Adventure Travel Tours is planning to update its World Wide Web site in the near future. You have been asked to solicit suggestions from the travel agents about changes they would like to see made to the current Web site. You decide to send all the travel agents a memo asking them for their input. Your completed memo is shown here.

   a. Open a blank Word document and create the following memo in Normal view. Press Tab twice after you type colons (:) in the To, From, and Date lines. This will make the information following the colons line up evenly. Enter a blank line between paragraphs.

   To: Travel Agents
   From: Student Name
   Date: [Current date]
   RE: Web Site Revision

   Next month we plan to begin work on updating the Adventure Travel Tours Web site. In preparation for this project, I would like your input about the Web site.

   In the next few days as you use the Web site, pay attention to the layout, colors, ease of use, and content. Then send your comments back to me about both the positive and negative features of the current Web site and suggestions for changes you would like to see made in the new Web site.

   Thank you in advance for your input.

   **To: Travel Agents**
   **From: Student Name**
   **Date: [Current date]**
   **Next month we plan to begin work on updating the current Adventure Travel Tours Web site. In preparation for this project, I would like your input about the current Web site. In the next few days as you use the Web site, pay attention to such things as the layout, colors, and content. Then send your comments back to me about both the positive and negative features of the current Web site and suggestions for changes you would like to see made in the new Web site.**

   **Thank you in advance for your input.**

   b. Turn on the display of formatting marks.

   c. Correct any spelling and grammar errors that are identified.

   d. Delete the word "current" from the first and second sentences. Delete the phrase "such things ... hird sentence. Insert the text "ease of use," after the word "colors," in the third

   ...aragraph beginning with the third sentence. Include a blank line between

   ...t size for the entire memo to 14 pt and the alignment of the body of the memo to

   ...line insert the AutoText reference line "RE:".

...b 1: Creating and Editing a Document www.mhhe.com/oleary

p. Increase the font size of the line above "Roast Coffee" to 18 pt. Reset its line spacing to single. Insert a blank line below it.

q. Copy the remaining paragraph from the wd02_Coffee Flyer document, and insert it at the bottom of the new document. Include two blank lines between the table and the paragraph.

r. Bold and center the final paragraph. Remove the hyperlink format from the URL. Format the URL as italic, bold, and red.

s. Increase the top, left, and right margins to 1.5 inches.

t. Create the Explosion 1 AutoShape from Stars and Banners. Enter and center the word **Sale!** in red within it, and choose the gold fill color. Size the shape appropriately. Move the shape to the top left corner of the document. Delete the drawing canvas.

u. Add your name and a field with the current date several lines below the final paragraph.

v. Save the document as Coffee Flyer2. Preview and print it.

**on your own**

**Requesting a Reference ★**

1. Your first year as a biology major is going well and you are looking for a summer internship with a local research lab. You have an upcoming interview and want to come prepared with a letter of reference from your last position. Write a business letter directed to your old supervisor, Rachel McVey, at your former lab, AMT Research. Use the modified block letter style shown in the lab. Be sure to include the date, a salutation, two paragraphs, a closing, and your name as a signature. Spell-check the document, save the document as Reference Letter, and print it.

**Long Distance Rates Survey ★**

2. American Consumer Advocates conducted a survey in October, 2002 comparing the costs of long distance rates. Create a tabbed table using the information shown below. Bold and underline the column heads. Add style 2 tab leaders to the table entries. Above the table, write a paragraph explaining the table contents.

| Company | Per Minute | Monthly Fee | Customer Service Wait |
|---|---|---|---|
| Zone LD | 3.5¢ | $2.00 | Less than 1 minute |
| Pioneer Telephone | 3.9¢ | none | 1 minute |
| Capsule | 3.9¢ | none | 17 minutes |
| ECG | 4.5¢ | $1.99 | 5 minutes |
| IsTerra | 4.9¢ | none | 10 minutes |

Include your name and the date below the table. Save the document as Phone Rates and print the document.

Lab Exercises WD2.85
Word 2003

The O'Leary Series

# Microsoft® Office PowerPoint® 2003

Introductory Edition

# Introduction to Microsoft Office 2003

## Objectives

After completing the Introduction to Microsoft Office 2003, you should be able to:

1. Describe Office System 2003.
2. Describe the Office 2003 applications.
3. Start an Office 2003 application.
4. Recognize the basic application window features.
5. Use menus, shortcut menus, and shortcut keys.
6. Use toolbars and task panes.
7. Use Office Help.
8. Exit an Office 2003 application.

## What Is Microsoft Office System 2003?

Microsoft Office System 2003 is a comprehensive, integrated system of programs, servers and services designed to solve a wide array of business needs. Although the programs can be used individually, they are designed to work together seamlessly making it easy to connect people and organizations to information, business processes and each other. The applications include tools used to create, discuss, communicate, and manage projects. If you share a lot of documents with other people, these features facilitate access to common documents. This version has expanded and refined the communication and collaboration features and integration with the World Wide Web. In addition, several new interface features are designed to make it easier to perform tasks and help users take advantage of all the features in the applications.

The Microsoft Office System 2003 is packaged in different combinations of components. The major components and a brief description are provided in the following table.

| Component | Description |
|---|---|
| Microsoft Office 2003 | |
| Office Word 2003 | Word Processor |
| Office Excel 2003 | Spreadsheet |
| Office Access 2003 | Database manager |
| Office PowerPoint 2003 | Presentation graphics |
| Office Outlook 2003 | Desktop information manager |
| Office FrontPage 2003 | Web site creation and management |
| Office InfoPath 2003 | Creates XML forms and documents |
| Office OneNote 2003 | Note-taking |
| Office Publisher 2003 | Desktop publishing |
| Office Visio 2003 | Drawing and diagramming |
| Office SharePoint Portal Server v2.0 and Services | |

The five components of Microsoft Office 2003—Word, Excel, Access, PowerPoint, and Outlook—are the applications you will learn about in this series of labs. They are described in more detail in the following sections.

### Office Word 2003

Office Word 2003 is a word processing software application whose purpose is to help you create text-based documents. Word processors are one of the most flexible and widely used application software programs. A word processor can be used to manipulate text data to produce a letter, a report, a memo, an e-mail message, or any other type of correspondence.

Two documents you will produce in the first two Word labs, a letter and flyer, are shown here.

March 25, 2005

Dear Adventure Traveler:

Imagine hiking and paddling your way through the rain forests of Costa Rica, camping under the stars in Africa, or following in the footsteps of the ancient Inca as you backpack along the Inca trail to Machu Picchu. Turn these dreams of adventure into memories you will cherish forever by joining Adventure Travel Tours on one of our four new adventure tours.

To tell you more about these exciting new adventures, we are offering several presentations in your area. These presentations will focus on the features and cultures of the region. We will also show you pictures of the places you will visit and activities you can participate in, as well as a detailed agenda and package costs. Plan to attend one of the following presentations:

| Date | Time |
|---|---|
| January 5 ----- | 7:00 p.m. -------- |
| February 3 ---- | 7:30 p.m. -------- |
| March 8 ------- | 7:00 p.m. -------- |

In appreciation of your past patr
price of any of the new tour packages. Y
departure date. Please turn in this letter t

Our vacation tours are professior
almost everything in the price of your to
dollar. All tours include these features:

- **Professional tour manager and**
- **All accommodations and meals**
- **All entrance fees, excursions, t**

We hope you will join us this ye
Your memories of fascinating places an
long, long time. For reservations, please
directly at 1-800-777-0004.

A letter containing a tabbed table, indented paragraphs, and text enhancements is quickly created using basic Word features.

# Announcing

## New Adventure Travel Tours

Attention adventure travelers! Attend an Adventure Travel presentation to learn about some of the earth's greatest unspoiled habitats and find out how you can experience the adventure of a lifetime. This year we are introducing four new tours and offering you a unique opportunity to combine many different outdoor activities while exploring the world.

India Wildlife Adventure
Inca Trail to Machu Picchu
Safari in Tanzania
Costa Rica Rivers and Rain Forests

Presentation dates and times are January 5 at 7:00 p.m., February 3 at 7:30 p.m., and March 8 at 7:00 p.m. All presentations are held at convenient hotel locations. The hotels are located in downtown Los Angeles, in Santa Clara, and at the airport.

**Call 1-800-777-0004 for presentation locations, a full color brochure, and itinerary information, costs, and trip dates.**

**Visit our Web site at www.AdventureTravelTours.com**

A flyer incorporating many visual enhancements such as colored text, varied text styles, and graphic elements is both eye-catching and informative.

The beauty of a word processor is that you can make changes or corrections as you are typing. Want to change a report from single spacing to double spacing? Alter the width of the margins? Delete some paragraphs and add others from yet another document? A word processor allows you to do all these things with ease.

Word 2003 includes many group collaboration features to help streamline how documents are developed and changed by group members. You can also create and send e-mail messages directly from within Word using all its features to create and edit the message. In addition, you can send an entire document as your e-mail message, allowing the recipient to edit the document directly without having to open or save an attachment.

Word 2003 is closely integrated with the World Wide Web, detecting when you type a Web address and automatically converting it to a hyperlink. You can also create your own hyperlinks to locations within documents, or to other documents, including those at external locations such as a Web site or file server. Its many Web-editing features, including a Web Page Wizard that guides you step by step, help you quickly create a Web page.

## Office Excel 2003

Office Excel 2003 is an electronic worksheet that is used to organize, manipulate, and graph numeric data. Once used almost exclusively by accountants, worksheets are now widely used by nearly every profession. Marketing professionals record and evaluate sales trends. Teachers record grades and calculate final grades. Personal trainers record the progress of their clients.

Excel includes many features that not only help you create a well-designed worksheet, but one that produces accurate results. Formatting features include visual enhancements such as varied text styles, colors, and graphics. Other features help you enter complex formulas and identify and correct formula errors. You can also produce a visual display of data in the form of graphs or charts. As the values in the worksheet change, charts referencing those values automatically adjust to reflect the changes.

Excel also includes many advanced features and tools that help you perform what-if analysis and create different scenarios. And like all Office 2003 applications, it is easy to incorporate data created in one application into another. Two worksheets you will produce in Labs 2 and 3 of Excel are shown on the next page.

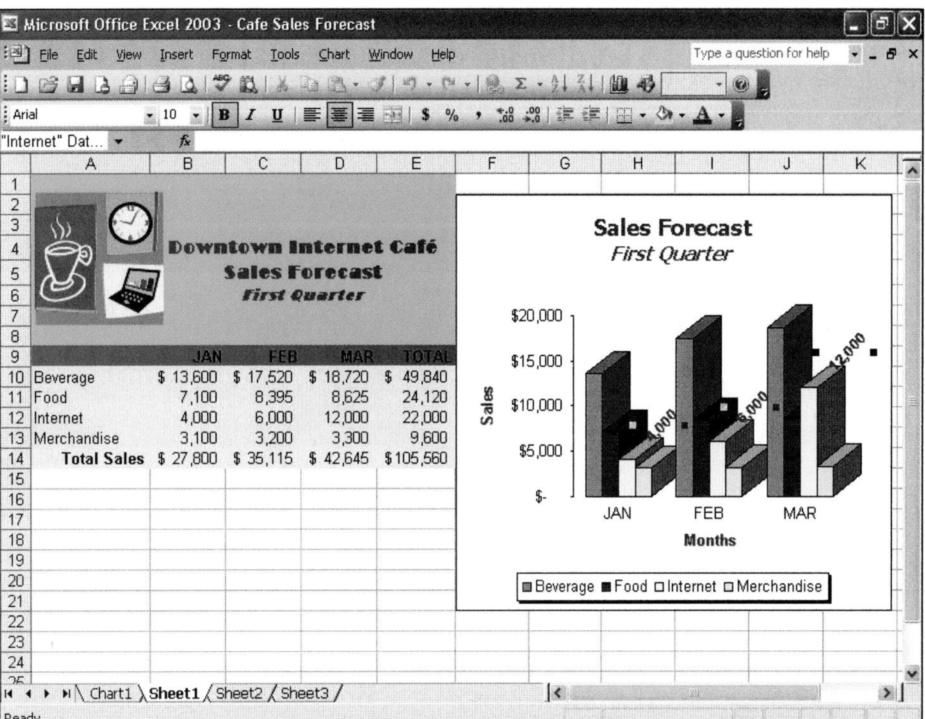


A worksheet showing the quarterly sales forecast containing a graphic, text enhancements, and a chart of the data is quickly created using basic Excel features.

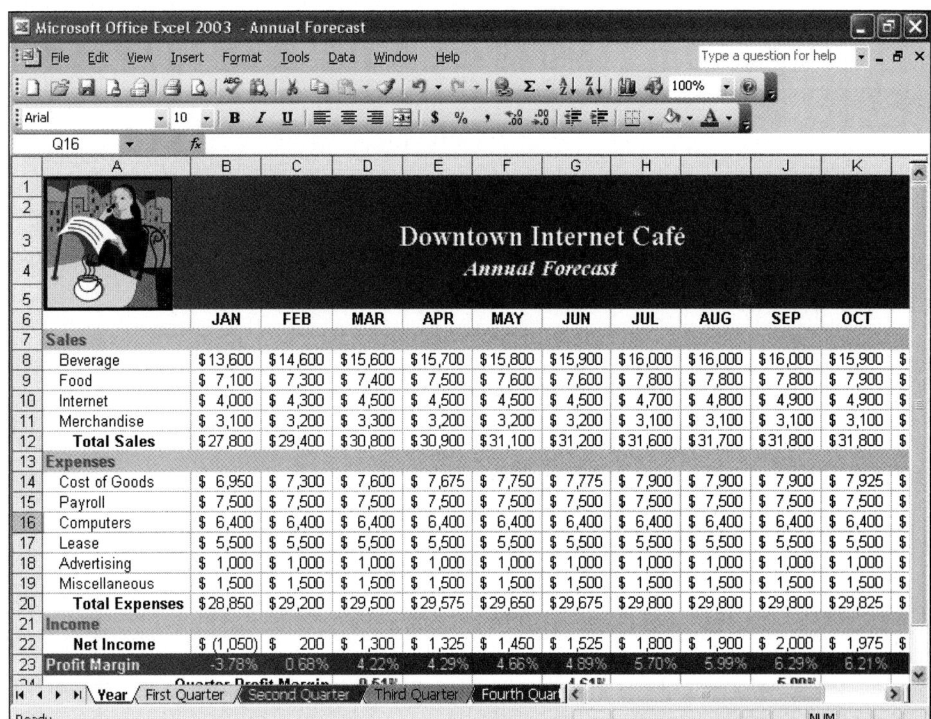


A large worksheet incorporating more complex formulas, visual enhancements such as colored text, varied text styles, and graphic elements is both informative and attractive.

You will see how easy it is to analyze data and make projections using what-if analysis and what-if graphing in Lab 3 and to incorporate Excel data in a Word document as shown in the following figures.

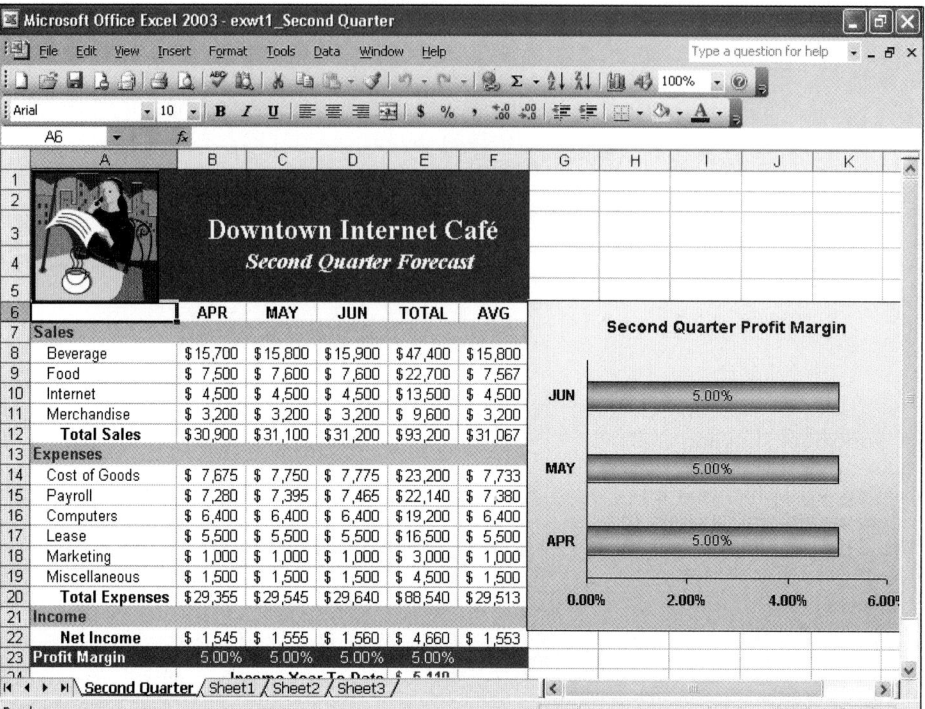


Changes you make in worksheet data while performing what-if analysis are automatically reflected in charts that reference that data.

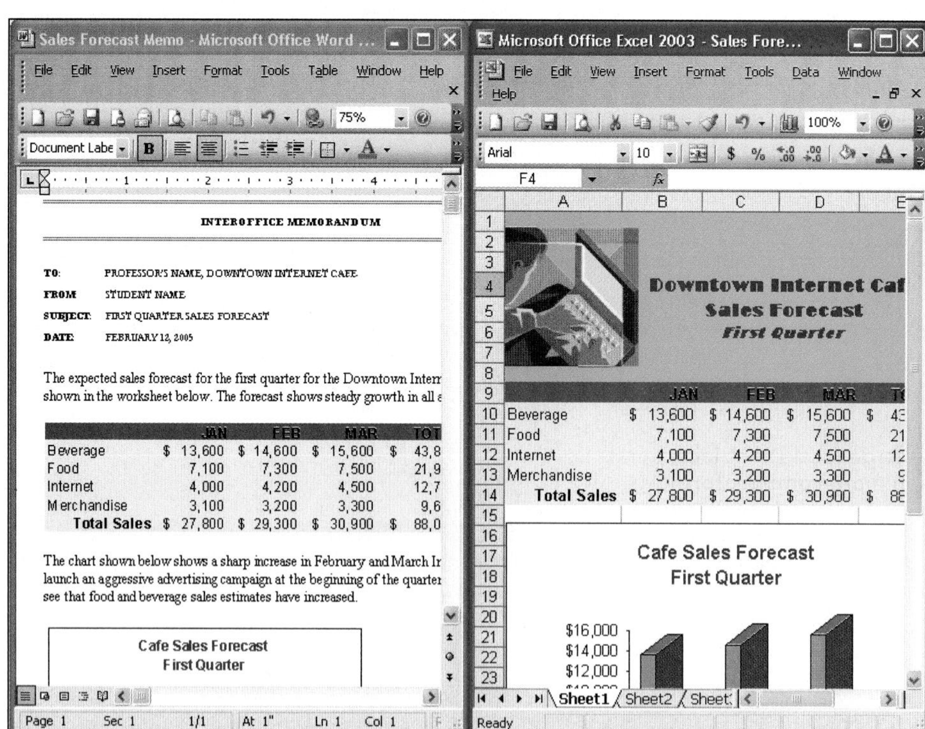


Worksheet data and charts can be copied and linked to other Office documents such as a Word document.

## Office Access 2003

Office Access 2003 is a relational database management application that is used to create and analyze a database. A database is a collection of related data. In a relational database, the most widely used database structure, data is organized in linked tables. Tables consist of columns (called fields) and rows (called records). The tables are related or linked to one another by a common field. Relational databases allow you to create smaller and more manageable database tables, since you can combine and extract data between tables.

The program provides tools to enter, edit, and retrieve data from the database as well as to analyze the database and produce reports of the output. One of the main advantages of a computerized database is the ability to quickly add, delete, and locate specific records. Records can also be easily rearranged or sorted according to different fields of data, resulting in multiple table arrangements that provide more meaningful information for different purposes. Creation of forms makes it easier to enter and edit data as well. In the Access labs you will create and organize the database table shown below.

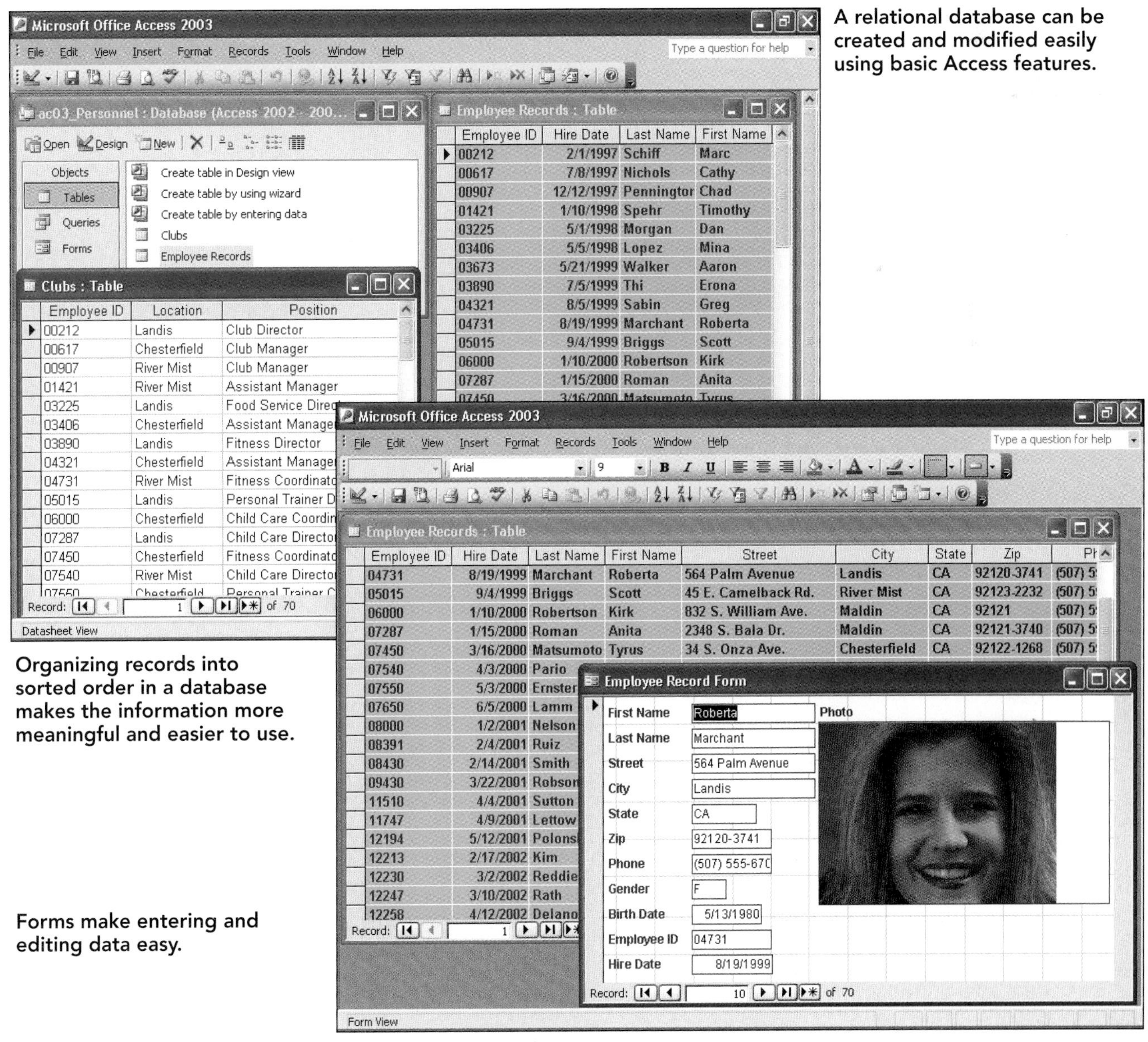


A relational database can be created and modified easily using basic Access features.

Organizing records into sorted order in a database makes the information more meaningful and easier to use.

Forms make entering and editing data easy.

Another feature is the ability to analyze the data in a table and perform calculations on different fields of data. Additionally, you can ask questions or query the table to find only certain records that meet specific conditions to be used in the analysis. Information that was once costly and time-consuming to get is now quickly and readily available. This information can then be quickly printed out in the form of reports ranging from simple listings to complex, professional-looking reports in different layout styles, or with titles, headings, subtotals, or totals.

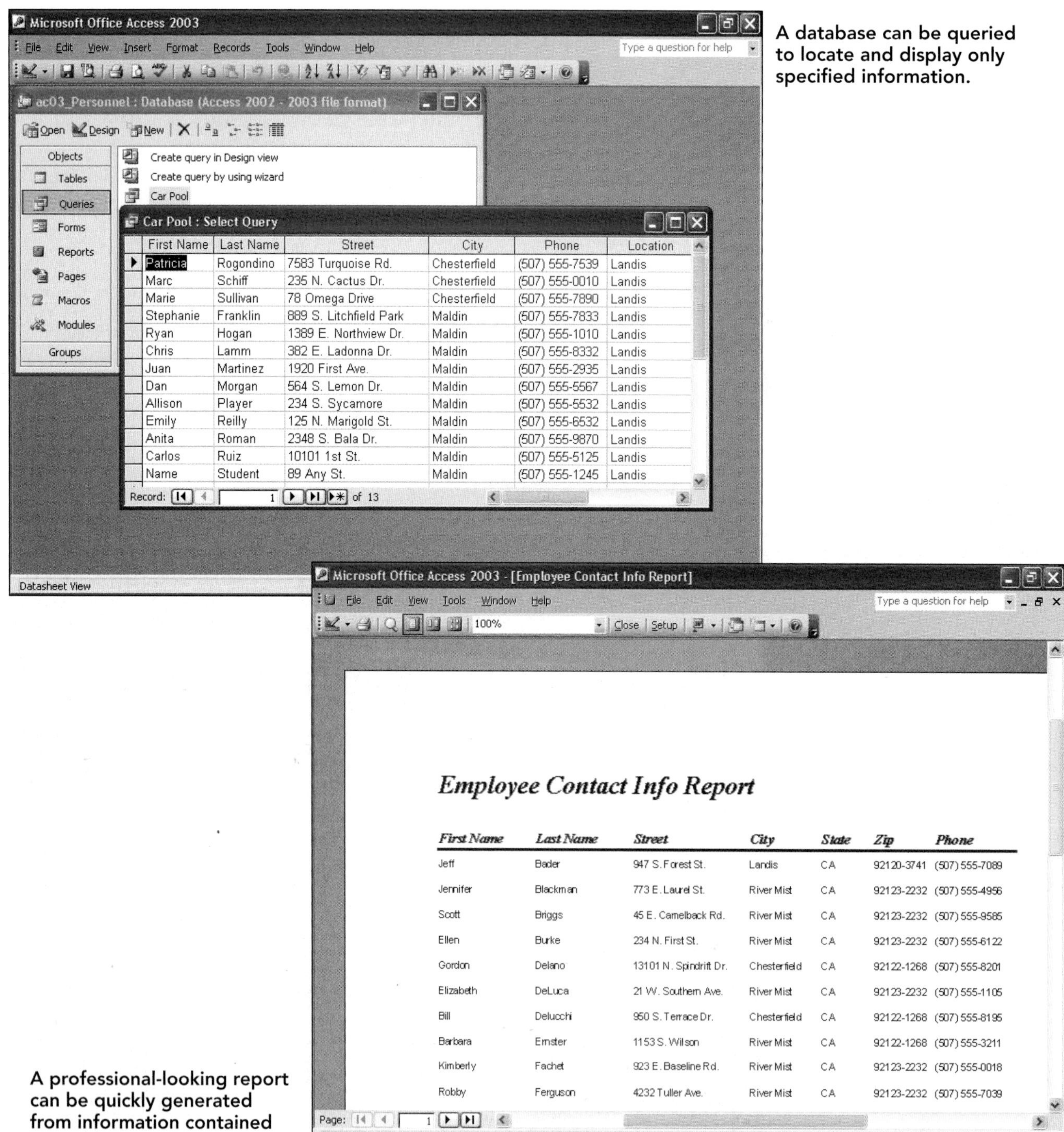


| First Name | Last Name | Street | City | Phone | Location |
|---|---|---|---|---|---|
| Patricia | Rogondino | 7583 Turquoise Rd. | Chesterfield | (507) 555-7539 | Landis |
| Marc | Schiff | 235 N. Cactus Dr. | Chesterfield | (507) 555-0010 | Landis |
| Marie | Sullivan | 78 Omega Drive | Chesterfield | (507) 555-7890 | Landis |
| Stephanie | Franklin | 889 S. Litchfield Park | Maldin | (507) 555-7833 | Landis |
| Ryan | Hogan | 1389 E. Northview Dr. | Maldin | (507) 555-1010 | Landis |
| Chris | Lamm | 382 E. Ladonna Dr. | Maldin | (507) 555-8332 | Landis |
| Juan | Martinez | 1920 First Ave. | Maldin | (507) 555-2935 | Landis |
| Dan | Morgan | 564 S. Lemon Dr. | Maldin | (507) 555-5567 | Landis |
| Allison | Player | 234 S. Sycamore | Maldin | (507) 555-5532 | Landis |
| Emily | Reilly | 125 N. Marigold St. | Maldin | (507) 555-6532 | Landis |
| Anita | Roman | 2348 S. Bala Dr. | Maldin | (507) 555-9870 | Landis |
| Carlos | Ruiz | 10101 1st St. | Maldin | (507) 555-5125 | Landis |
| Name | Student | 89 Any St. | Maldin | (507) 555-1245 | Landis |

A database can be queried to locate and display only specified information.



**Employee Contact Info Report**

| First Name | Last Name | Street | City | State | Zip | Phone |
|---|---|---|---|---|---|---|
| Jeff | Bader | 947 S. Forest St. | Landis | CA | 92120-3741 | (507) 555-7089 |
| Jennifer | Blackman | 773 E. Laurel St. | River Mist | CA | 92123-2232 | (507) 555-4956 |
| Scott | Briggs | 45 E. Camelback Rd. | River Mist | CA | 92123-2232 | (507) 555-9585 |
| Ellen | Burke | 234 N. First St. | River Mist | CA | 92123-2232 | (507) 555-6122 |
| Gordon | Delano | 13101 N. Spindrift Dr. | Chesterfield | CA | 92122-1268 | (507) 555-8201 |
| Elizabeth | DeLuca | 21 W. Southern Ave. | River Mist | CA | 92123-2232 | (507) 555-1105 |
| Bill | Delucchi | 950 S. Terrace Dr. | Chesterfield | CA | 92122-1268 | (507) 555-8195 |
| Barbara | Ernster | 1153 S. Wilson | River Mist | CA | 92122-1268 | (507) 555-3211 |
| Kimberly | Fachet | 923 E. Baseline Rd. | River Mist | CA | 92123-2232 | (507) 555-0018 |
| Robby | Ferguson | 4232 Tuller Ave. | River Mist | CA | 92123-2232 | (507) 555-7039 |

A professional-looking report can be quickly generated from information contained in a database.

## Office PowerPoint 2003

Office PowerPoint 2003 is a graphics presentation program designed to help you produce a high-quality presentation that is both interesting to the audience and effective in its ability to convey your message. A presentation can be as simple as overhead transparencies or as sophisticated as an on-screen electronic display. In the first two PowerPoint labs you will create and organize the presentation shown on the next page.

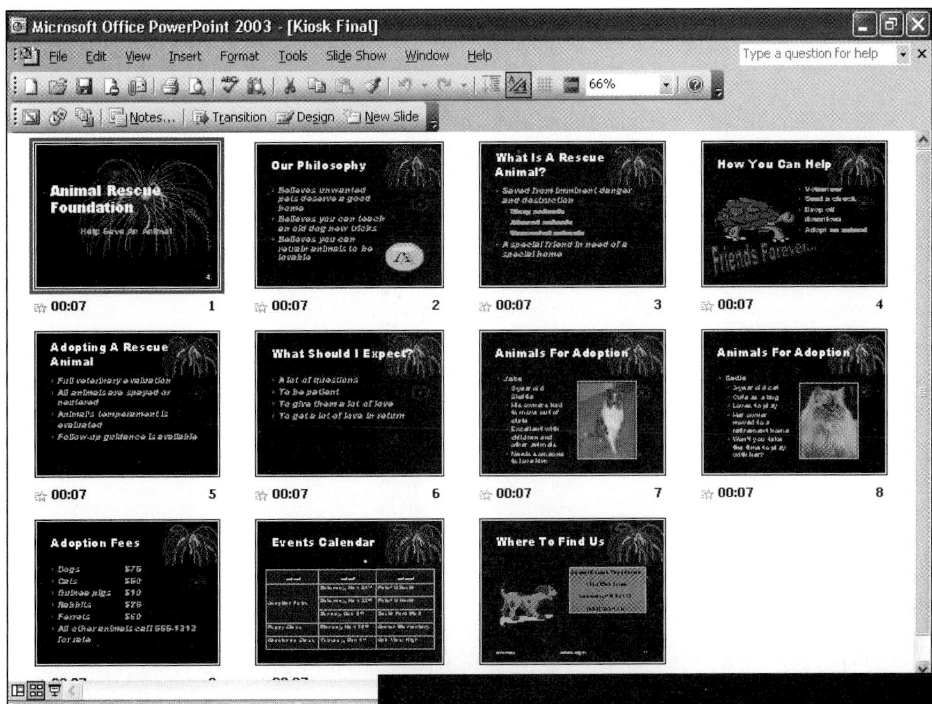


A presentation consists of a series of pages or "slides" presenting the information you want to convey in an organized and attractive manner.

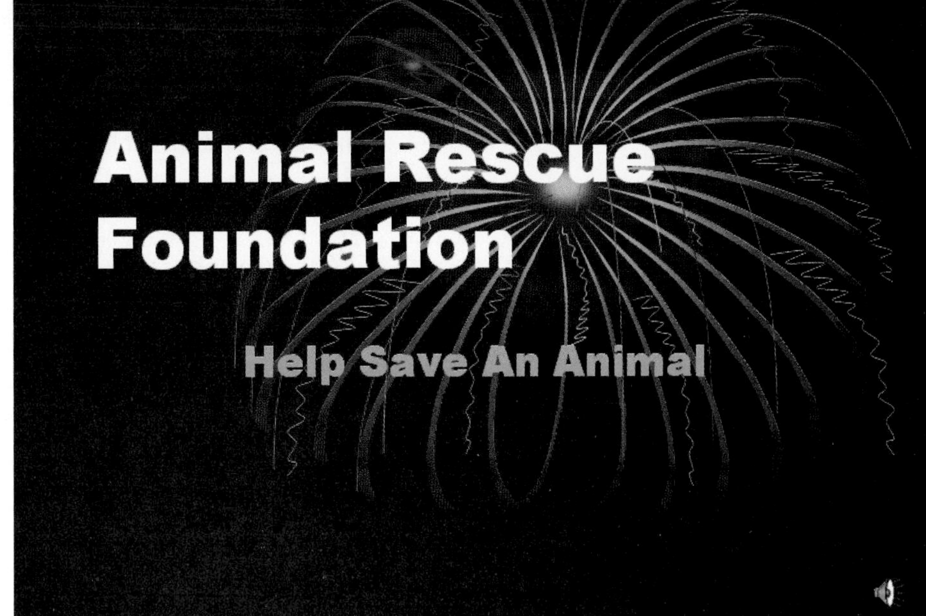


When running an onscreen presentation, each slide of the presentation is displayed full-screen on your computer monitor or projected onto a screen.

## Office Outlook 2003

Office Outlook 2003 is a personal information manager (PIM) program that is designed to get you organized and keep you organized. PIMs, also known as desktop managers, are designed to maximize your personal productivity by making it efficient and easy to perform everyday tasks such as scheduling meetings, recording contact information, and communicating with others, to name a few. Outlook 2003 includes an integrated e-mail program, a calendar, and contact and task management features.

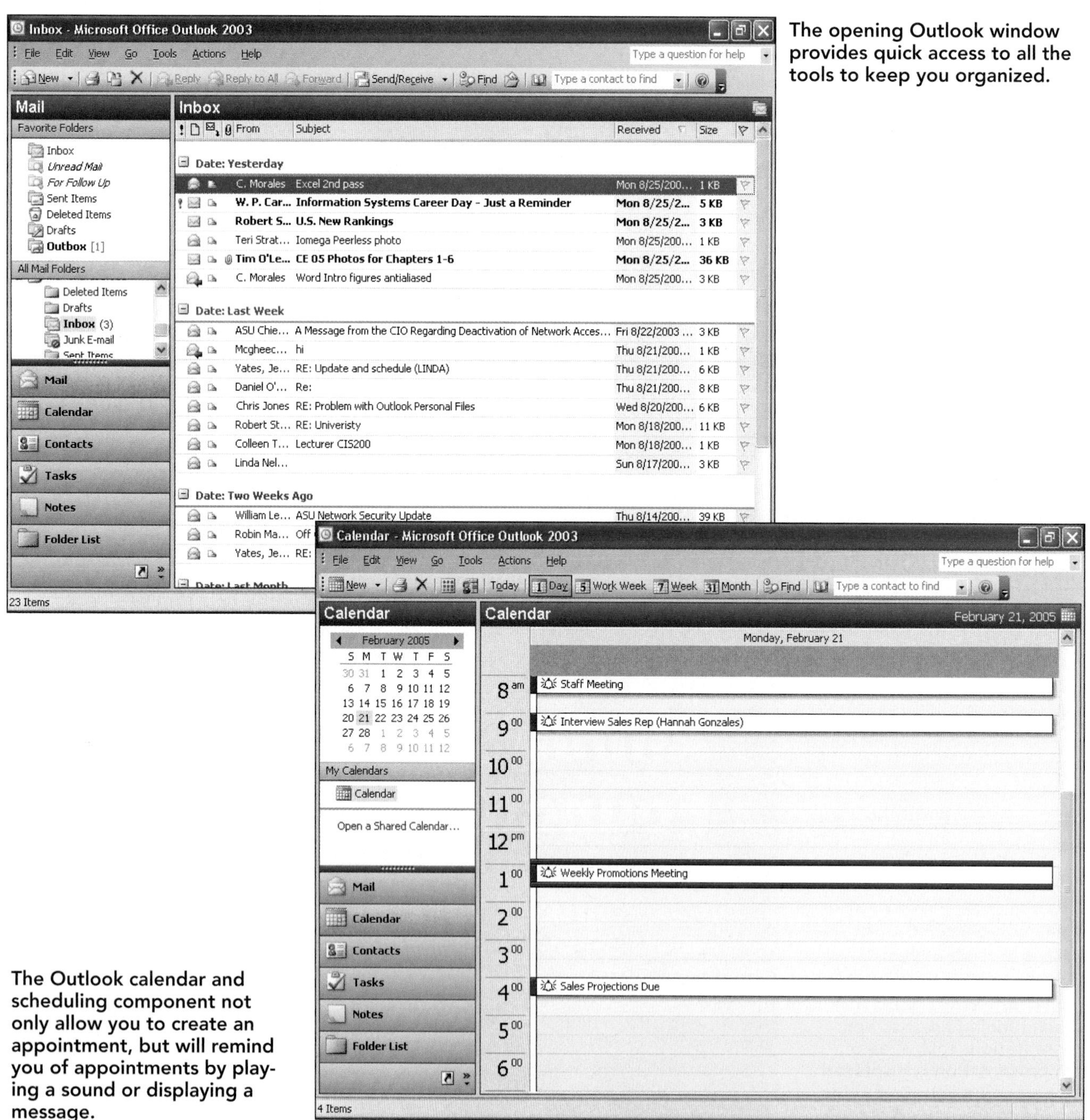

The opening Outlook window provides quick access to all the tools to keep you organized.

The Outlook calendar and scheduling component not only allow you to create an appointment, but will remind you of appointments by playing a sound or displaying a message.

# Common Office 2003 Features

**Additional Information**

Please read the Before You Begin and Instructional Conventions sections in the Overview to Office PowerPoint 2003 (PPO.3) before starting this section.

**Additional Information**

It is assumed that you are already familiar with basic Windows operating system features. To review these features, refer to your Windows text or if available, the O'Leary Series *Introduction to Windows* text.

Now that you know a little about each of the applications in Microsoft Office 2003, we will take a look at some of the features that are common to all Office 2003 applications. This is a hands-on section that will introduce you to the features and allow you to get a feel for how Office 2003 works. Although Word 2003 will be used to demonstrate how the features work, only common features will be addressed. These features include using menus, Office Help, task panes, toolbars, and starting and exiting an application. The features that are specific to each application will be introduced individually in each application text.

## Starting an Office 2003 Application

There are several ways to start an Office 2003 application. The two most common methods are by using the Start menu or by clicking a desktop shortcut for the program if it is available. If you use the Start menu, the steps will vary slightly depending on the version of Windows you are using.

**1** **Click start to display the Start menu.**

**Select All Programs.**

**Having Trouble?**

If you are using Windows 2002 or earlier, select Programs.

**Select Microsoft Office.**

**Choose Microsoft Office Word 2003.**

**OR**

**1** **Double-click the Microsoft Office Word 2003 shortcut on the desktop.**

**2** **If necessary, click Maximize in the title bar to maximize the window.**

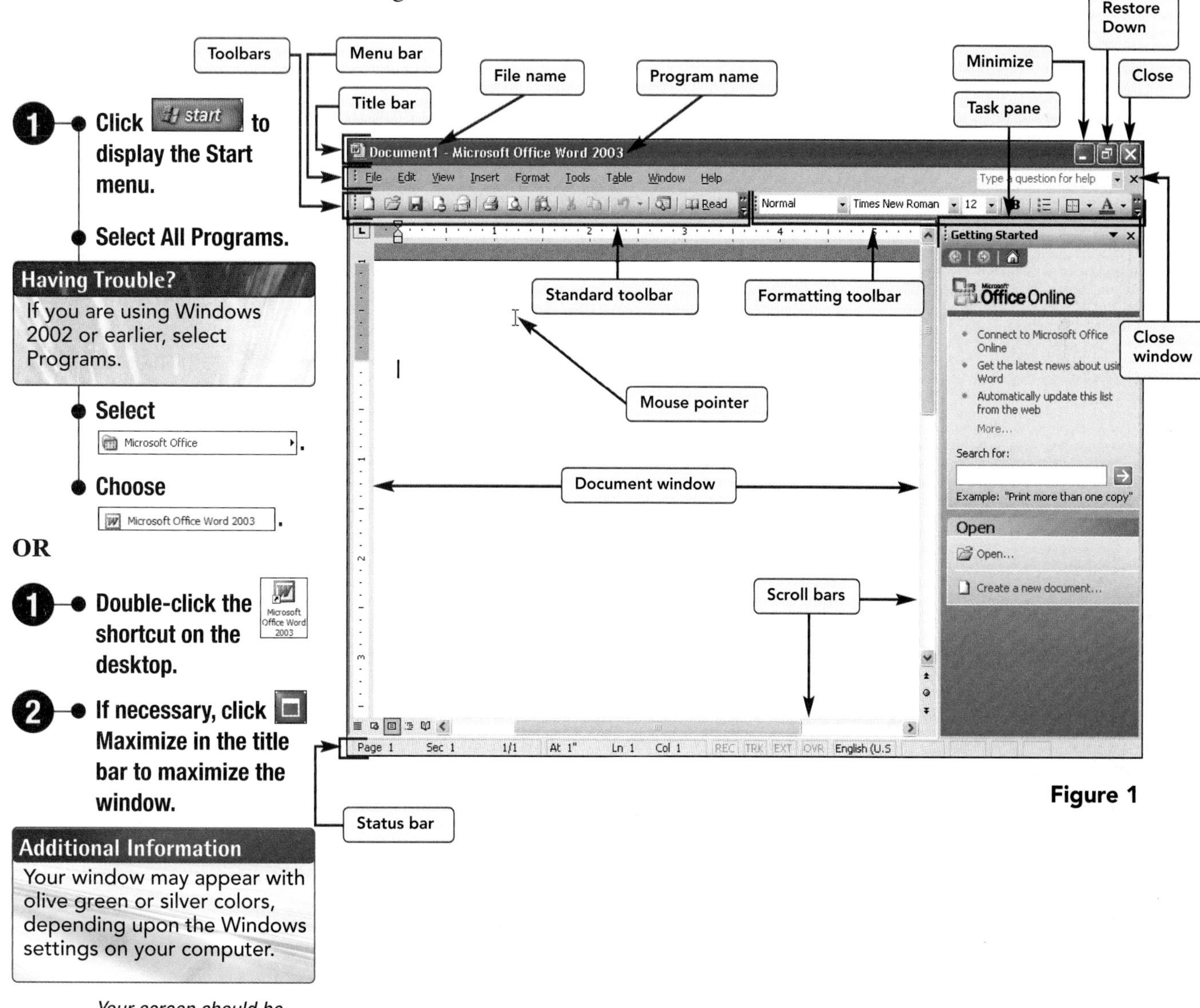


Figure 1

**Additional Information**

Your window may appear with olive green or silver colors, depending upon the Windows settings on your computer.

*Your screen should be similar to Figure 1*

**Additional Information**

Application windows can be sized, moved, and otherwise manipulated like any other windows on the desktop.

The Word program is started and displayed in a window on the desktop. The left end of the application window title bar displays the file name followed by the program name, Microsoft Office Word 2003. The right end of the title bar displays the Minimize, Restore Down, and Close buttons. They perform the same functions and operate in the same way as all Windows versions.

The **menu bar** below the title bar displays the application's program menu. The right end displays the document window's Close Window button. As you use the Office applications, you will see that the menu bar contains many of the same menus, such as File, Edit, and Help. You will also see several menus that are specific to each application.

The **toolbars** located below the menu bar contain buttons that are mouse shortcuts for many of the menu items. Commonly, the Office applications will display two toolbars when the application is first opened: Standard and Formatting. They may appear together on one row (as in Figure 1), or on separate rows.

**Additional Information**

Use Tools/Options and select Startup task pane to display the Getting Started task pane when starting the application.

The large center area of the program window is the **document window** where open application files are displayed. Currently, there is a blank Word document open. In Word, the mouse pointer appears as when positioned in the document window and as a when it can be used to select items. The **task pane** is displayed on the right side of the document window. Task panes provide quick access to features as you are using the application. As you perform certain actions, different task panes automatically open. In this case, since you just started an application, the Getting Started task pane is automatically displayed, providing different ways to create a new document or open an existing document.

The **status bar** at the bottom of the window displays location information and the status of different settings as they are used. Different information is displayed in the status bar for different applications.

On the right and bottom of the document window, are vertical and horizontal scroll bars. A **scroll bar** is used with a mouse to bring additional lines of information into view in a window. The vertical scroll bar is used to move up or down, and the horizontal scroll bar moves side to side in the window.

As you can see, many of the features in the Word window are the same as in other Windows applications. The common user interface makes learning and using new applications much easier.

## Using Menus

**Additional Information**

Use Tools/Customize/Options and check or clear the "Always show full menus" option to change how your menus operate.

A menu is one of many methods you can use to accomplish a task in a program. When opened, a menu displays a list of commands. When an Office program menu is first opened, it may display a short version of commands. The short menu is a personalized version of the menu that displays basic and frequently used commands and hides those used less often. An expanded version will display automatically after the menu is open for a few seconds.

**1** **Click File to open the File menu.**

**Point to each menu in the menu bar to see the full menu for each.**

**Additional Information**

Once one menu is expanded, others expand automatically until you choose a command or perform another action.

**Point to the View menu.**

*Your screen should be similar to Figure 2*

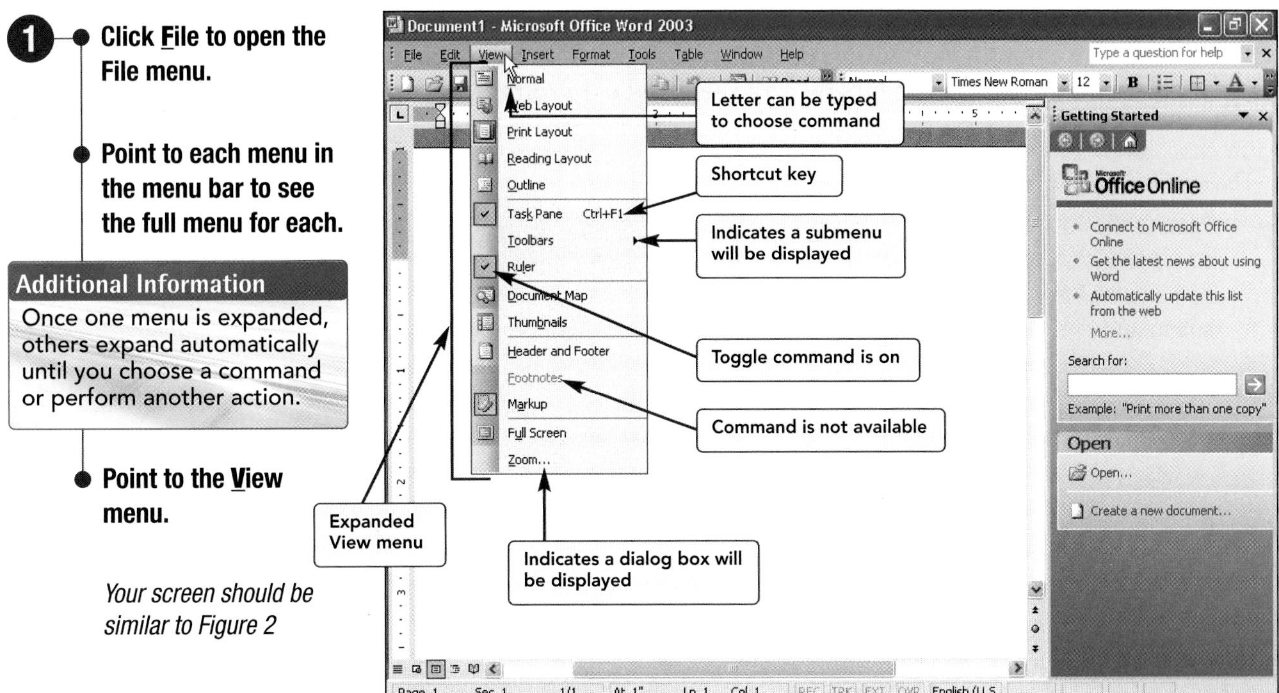


**Figure 2**

**Additional Information**

If you do not want to wait for the expanded menu to appear, you can click [⌄] at the bottom of the menu or double-click the menu name to display the full menu immediately.

Many commands have images next to them so you can quickly associate the command with the image. The same image appears on the toolbar button for that feature. Menus may include the following features (not all menus include all features):

| Feature | Meaning |
|---|---|
| Ellipsis (...) | Indicates a dialog box will be displayed. |
| ▸ | Indicates a submenu will be displayed. |
| Dimmed | Indicates the command is not available for selection until certain other conditions are met. |
| Shortcut key | A key or key combination that can be used to execute a command without using the menu. |
| Checkmark | Indicates a toggle type of command. Selecting it turns the feature on or off. A checkmark indicates the feature is on. |
| Underlined letter | Indicates the letter you can type to choose the command. |

**Additional Information**

If underlined command letters are not displayed, this feature is not active on your system.

On the View menu, two options, Task Pane and Ruler, are checked, indicating these features are on. The Task Pane option also displays the shortcut key combination, Ctrl + F1, after the option. This indicates the command can be chosen by pressing the keys instead of using the menu. The Footnotes option is dimmed because it is not currently available. The Toolbars option will display a submenu when selected, and the Zoom command a dialog box of additional options.

Once a menu is open, you can select a command from the menu by pointing to it. A colored highlight bar, called the **selection cursor**, appears over the selected command.

**2** **Point to the Toolbars command to select it and display the submenu.**

*Your screen should be similar to Figure 3*

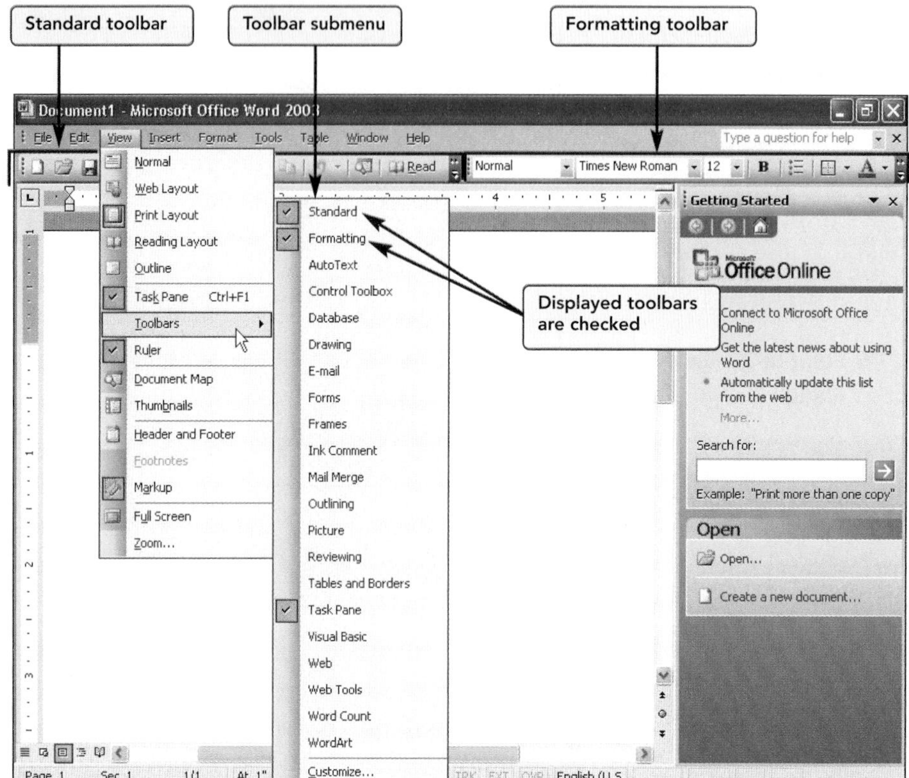


**Figure 3**

Currently there are three selected (checked) Toolbar options: Standard, Formatting, and although not technically a toolbar, the Task Pane. If other toolbars are selected in your menu, this is because once a toolbar has been turned on, it remains on until turned off.

To choose a command, you click on it. When the command is chosen, the associated action is performed. You will close the task pane and any other open toolbars and display the Drawing toolbar.

**3** **Click on Task Pane to turn off this feature.**

- **Open the View menu again, select Toolbars, and if it is not already selected, click on the Drawing toolbar option to turn it on.**

- **If necessary, choose View/Toolbars again and deselect any other toolbar options (there should be 3 selected toolbar options).**

*Your screen should be similar to Figure 4*

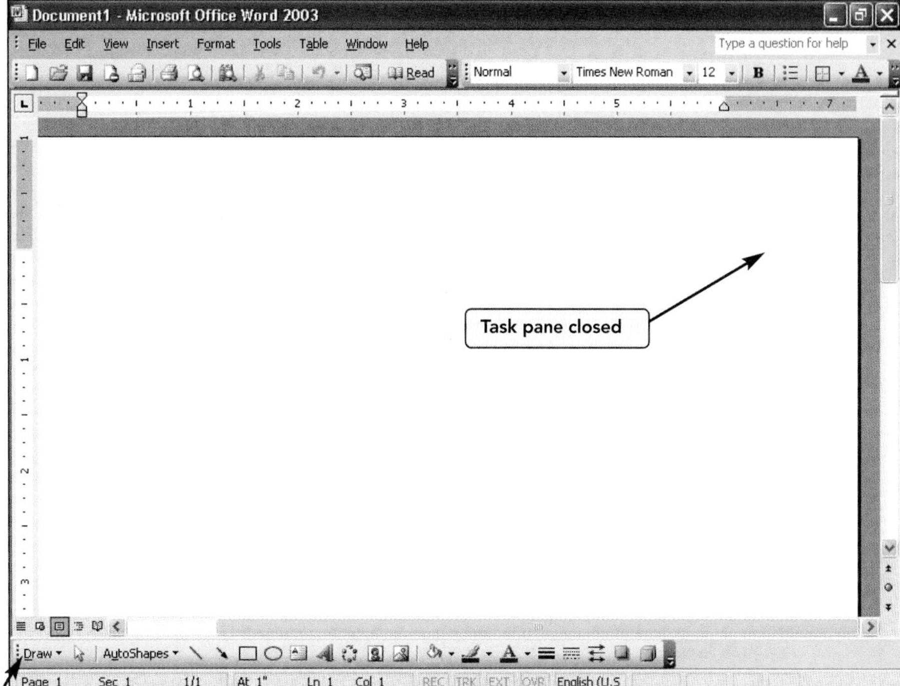


Figure 4

**Additional Information**

If you have a microphone and have installed and trained the Speech Recognition feature, you can speak the command sequences to open menus and choose commands. For example, to open a toolbar, you would say "View Toolbars."

**Additional Information**

Using voice commands, saying "Right click" will open the shortcut menu for the selected item.

The task pane is closed and the Drawing toolbar is displayed above the status bar. Any other toolbars that were open which you deselected are closed.

## Using Shortcut Menus

Another way to access menu options is to use the **shortcut menu**. The shortcut menu is opened by right-clicking on an item on the screen. This menu displays only those options associated with the item. For example, right-clicking on any toolbar will display the toolbar menu options only. You will use this method to hide the Drawing toolbar again.

**1** **Point to the Drawing toolbar and right-click.**

*Your screen should be similar to Figure 5*

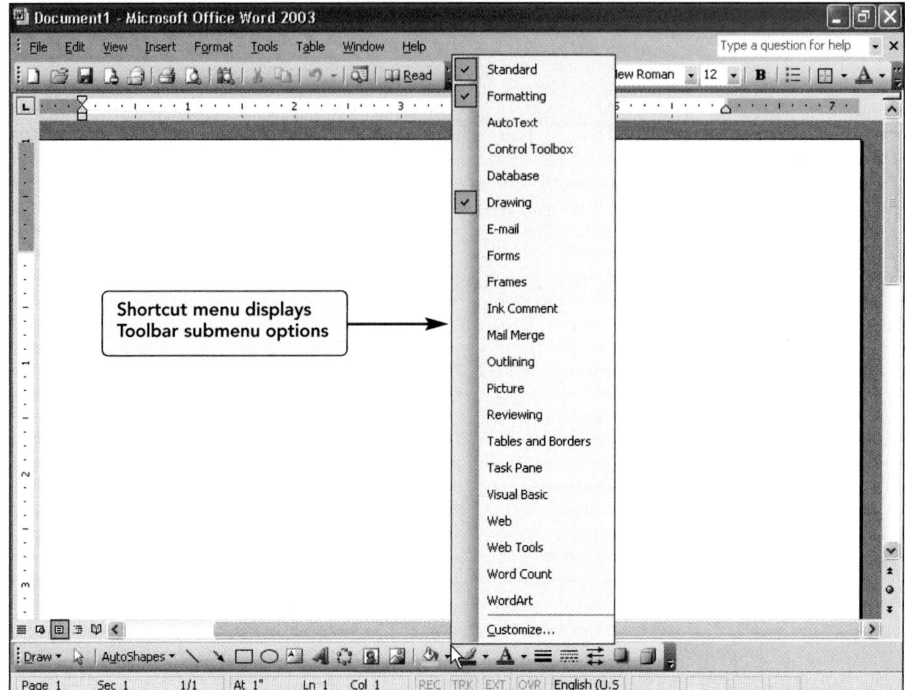


**Figure 5**

**Additional Information**

The Customize option can be used to change features of toolbars and menus.

The shortcut menu displays only the Toolbar submenu options on the View menu. Using a shortcut menu saves time over selecting the main menu command sequence.

**2** **Choose Drawing to turn off this feature.**

*Your screen should be similar to Figure 6*

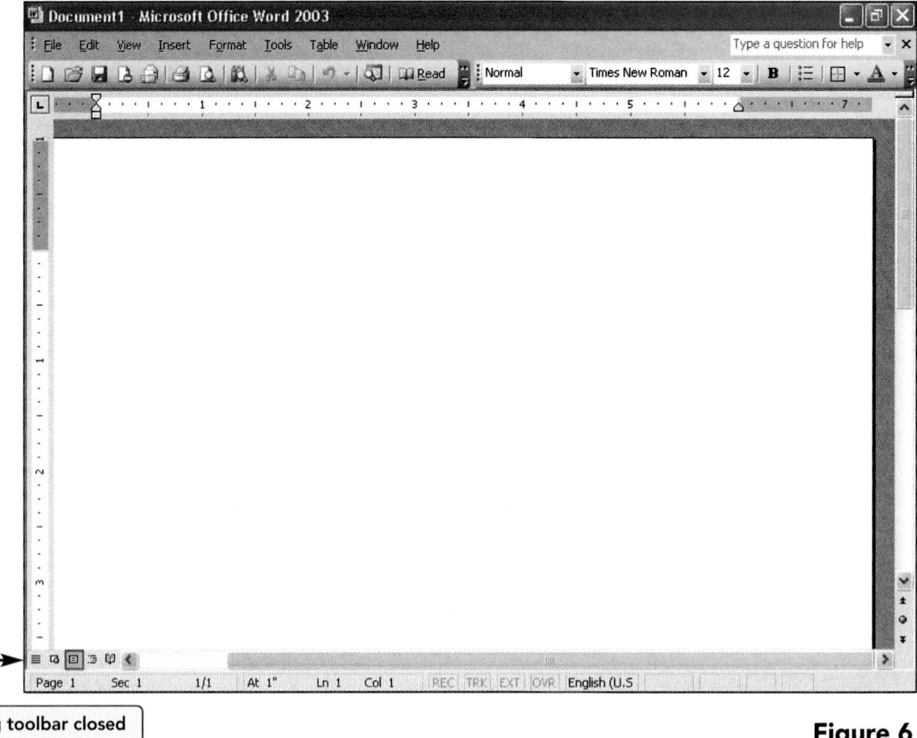


**Figure 6**

The Drawing toolbar is no longer displayed.

## Using Shortcut Keys

A third way to perform a command is to use the shortcut key or key combination associated with a particular command. If you will recall, the shortcut key associated with the **V**iew/Tas**k** Pane command is Ctrl + F1. To use the key combination, you hold down the first key while pressing the second.

**Additional Information**
Not all commands have shortcut keys.

**1 Hold down Ctrl and press the F1 function key.**

**Having Trouble?**
Function keys are located above the numeric keys on the keyboard.

*Your screen should be similar to Figure 7*

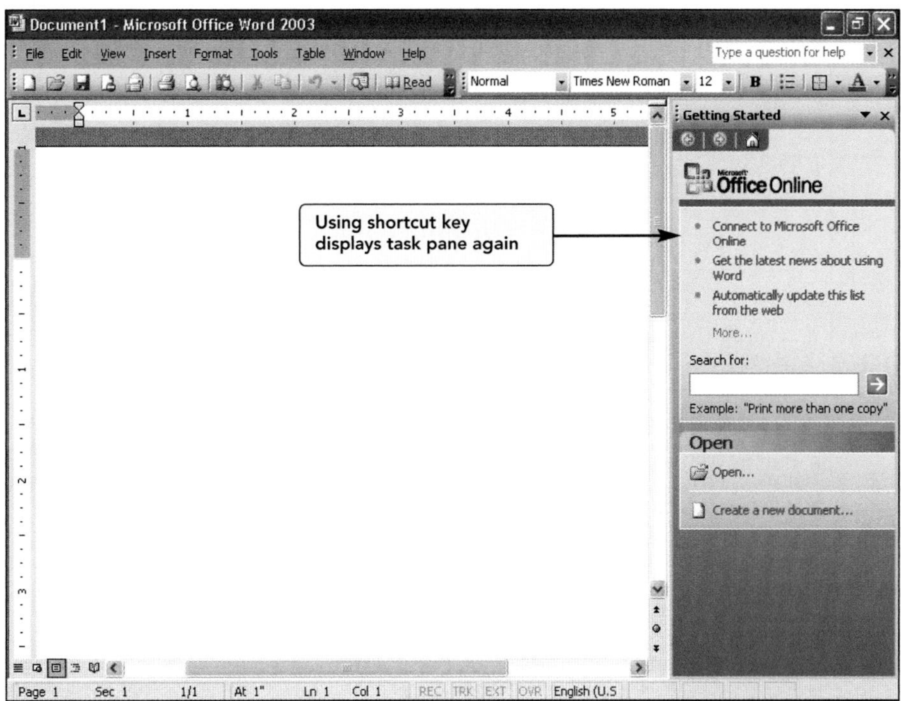


**Figure 7**

The task pane is displayed again. Using shortcut keys is the quickest way to perform many actions; however, you need to remember the key combination in order to use it.

**Additional Information**
Using the Speech Recognition feature, you can also use voice shortcuts for many commands. For example, to show the task pane, you would say "show task pane." Many voice commands also have several different words you can say to initiate the command. You could also say "task pane" or "view task pane."

## Using Toolbars

Initially, Word displays two toolbars, Standard and Formatting, below the menu bar (see Figure 3). The **Standard toolbar** contains buttons that are used to complete the most frequently used menu commands. The **Formatting toolbar** contains buttons that are used to change the appearance or format of the document. There are many features that can be used to make working with toolbars easier.

## Displaying Toolbars on Separate Rows

The default toolbar arrangement is to display both toolbars on one row. Because there is not enough space to display all the buttons on both toolbars on a single row, many buttons are hidden. The Toolbar Options button located at the end of a toolbar displays a drop-down button list of those buttons that are not displayed. Toolbars initially display the basic buttons. Like menus, they are personalized automatically, displaying those buttons you use frequently and hiding others. When you use a button from this list, it then is moved to the toolbar, and a button that has not been used recently is moved to the Toolbar Options list. It also contains an option to display the toolbars on separate rows. You will use this option to quickly see all the toolbar buttons.

**1** • **Click Toolbar Options.**

• **Choose Show Buttons on Two Rows.**

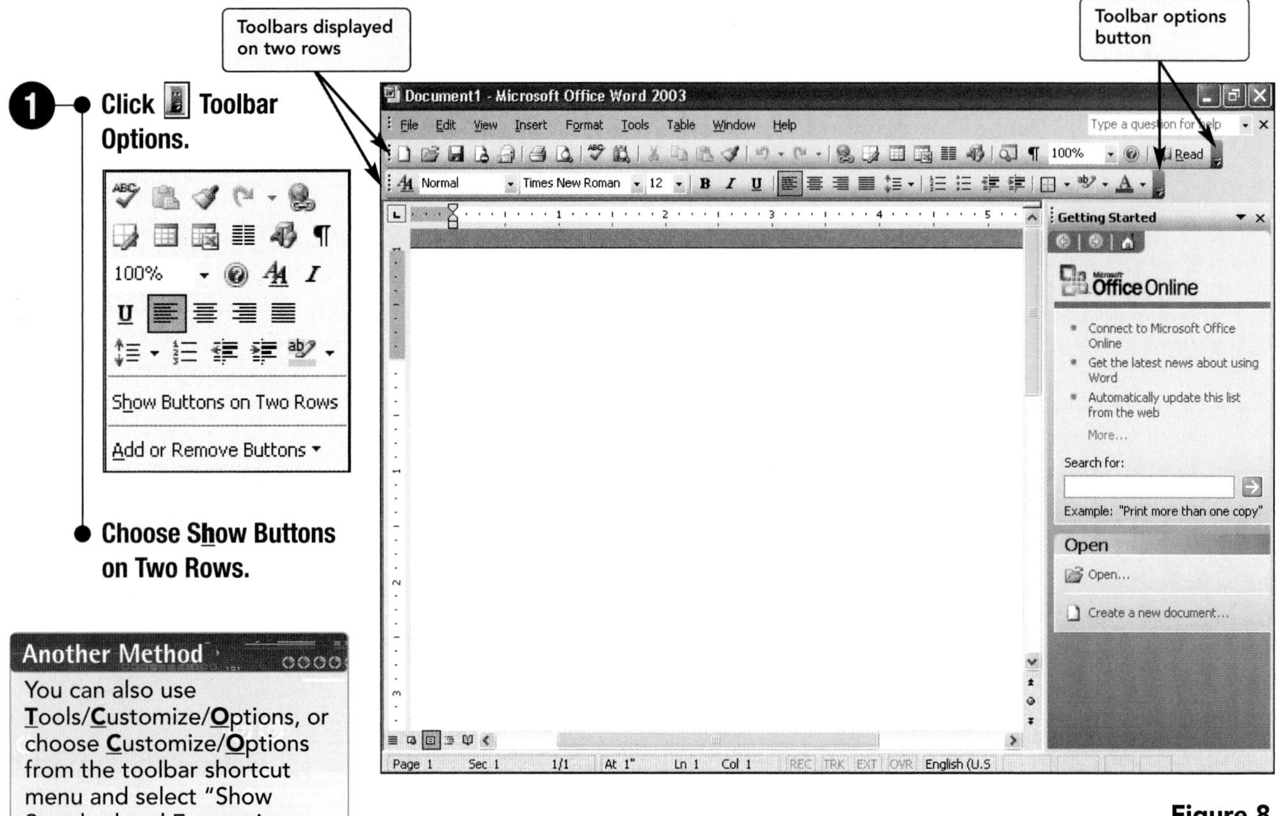


**Figure 8**

**Another Method**

You can also use Tools/Customize/Options, or choose Customize/Options from the toolbar shortcut menu and select "Show Standard and Formatting toolbars on two rows."

*Your screen should be similar to Figure 8*

**Additional Information**

The Add or Remove Buttons option allows you to customize existing toolbars by selecting those buttons you want to display and by creating your own customized toolbars.

The two toolbars now occupy separate rows, providing enough space for all the buttons to be displayed. Now using Toolbar Options is no longer necessary, and when selected only displays the options to return the toolbars display to one row and the Add or Remove Buttons option.

When a toolbar is open, it may appear docked or floating. A **docked toolbar** is fixed to an edge of the window and displays a vertical bar, called the move handle, on the left edge of the toolbar. Dragging this bar up or down allows you to move the toolbar. If multiple toolbars share the same row, dragging the bar left or right adjusts the size of the toolbar. If docked, a toolbar can occupy a row by itself, or several can be on a row together. A **floating toolbar** appears in a separate window and can be moved anywhere on the desktop.

**2** **Point to the move handle of the Standard toolbar and, when the mouse pointer appears as ✥, drag the toolbar into the document window.**

*Your screen should be similar to Figure 9*

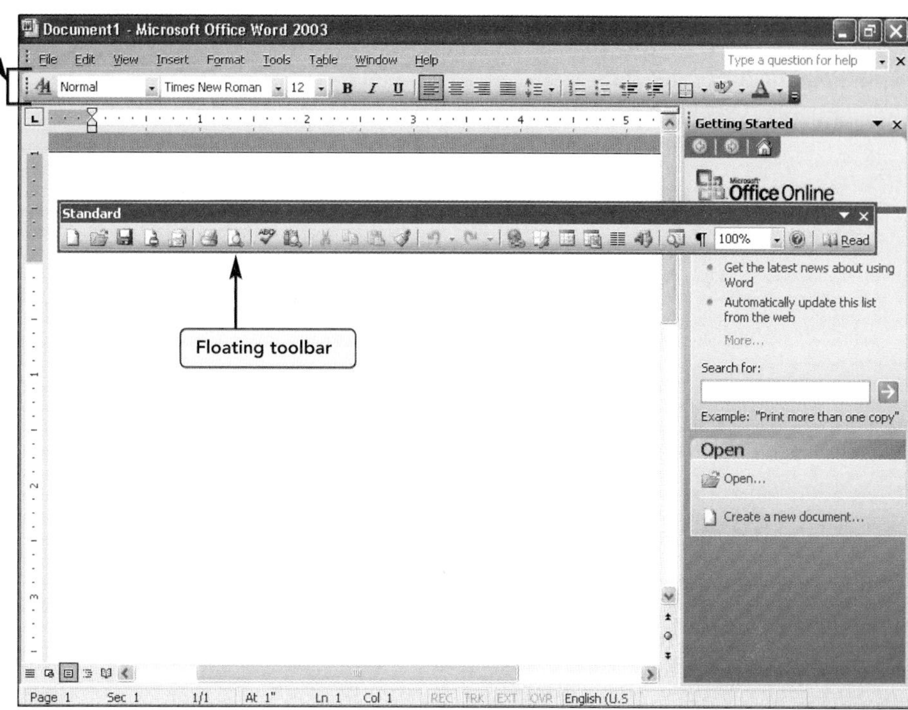


**Figure 9**

The Standard toolbar is now a floating toolbar and can be moved to any location in the window by dragging the title bar. If you move a floating toolbar to the edge of the window, it will attach to that location and become a docked toolbar. A floating toolbar can also be sized by dragging the edge of the toolbar.

**3** **Drag the title bar of the floating toolbar (the mouse pointer appears as ✥) to move the toolbar to the row below the Formatting toolbar.**

**Move the Formatting toolbar below the Standard toolbar.**

**Align both toolbars with the left edge of the window by dragging the move handle horizontally.**

*Your screen should be similar to Figure 10*

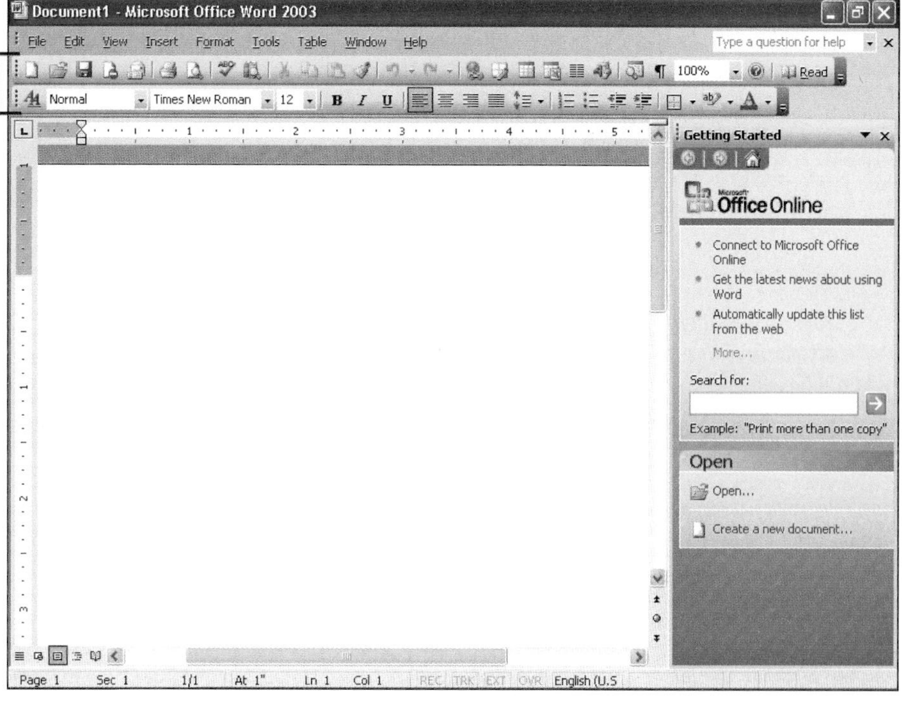


**Figure 10**

The two toolbars again occupy two rows. To quickly identify the toolbar buttons, you can display the button name by pointing to the button.

**4 Point to any button on the Standard toolbar.**

*Your screen should be similar to Figure 11*

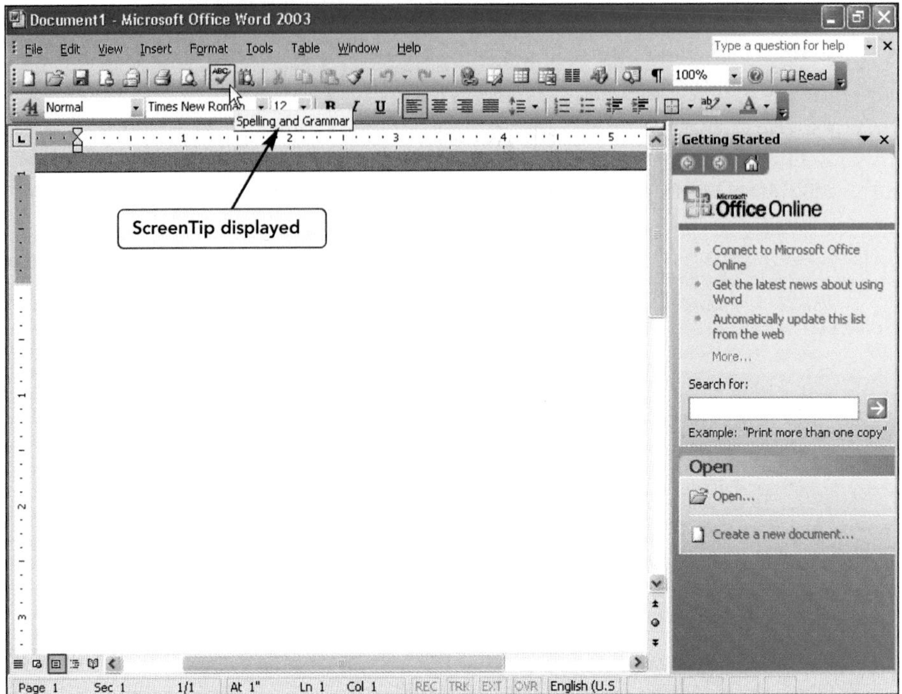


**Figure 11**

A ScreenTip containing the button name appears next to the mouse pointer. Clicking on a button will perform the associated action. You will use the Help button to access Microsoft Word Help.

**5 Click Microsoft Office Word Help.**

**Another Method**

You can also choose Help/Microsoft Office Word Help, or press F1 to access Help.

*Your screen should be similar to Figure 12*

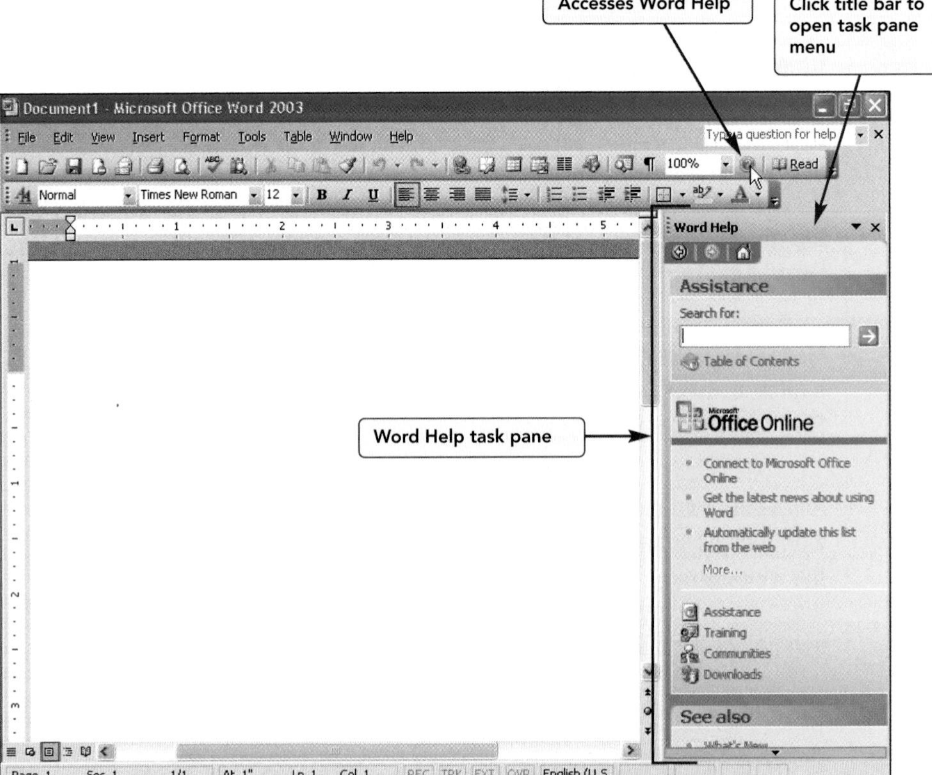


**Figure 12**

The Getting Started task pane is replaced by the Microsoft Word Help task pane. The name of the task pane appears in the task pane title bar.

## Using Task Panes

**Additional Information**

You can drag the pane divider line to adjust the width of the pane. When there is more information in the pane than can be displayed, [▲] and [▼] appear to scroll the information into view.

Task panes appear automatically when certain features are used. They can also be opened manually from the task pane menu. Clicking the task pane title bar displays a drop-down menu of other task panes you can select. In Word there are 14 different task panes. You will redisplay the Getting Started task pane. Then you will quickly return to the previously displayed task pane using the Back toolbar button in the task pane.

**1**

- **Click on the task pane title bar.**
- **Choose Getting Started.**

**Another Method**

You can also click the Home button to quickly display the Getting Started task pane.

- **Click Back.**

*Your screen should be similar to Figure 13*

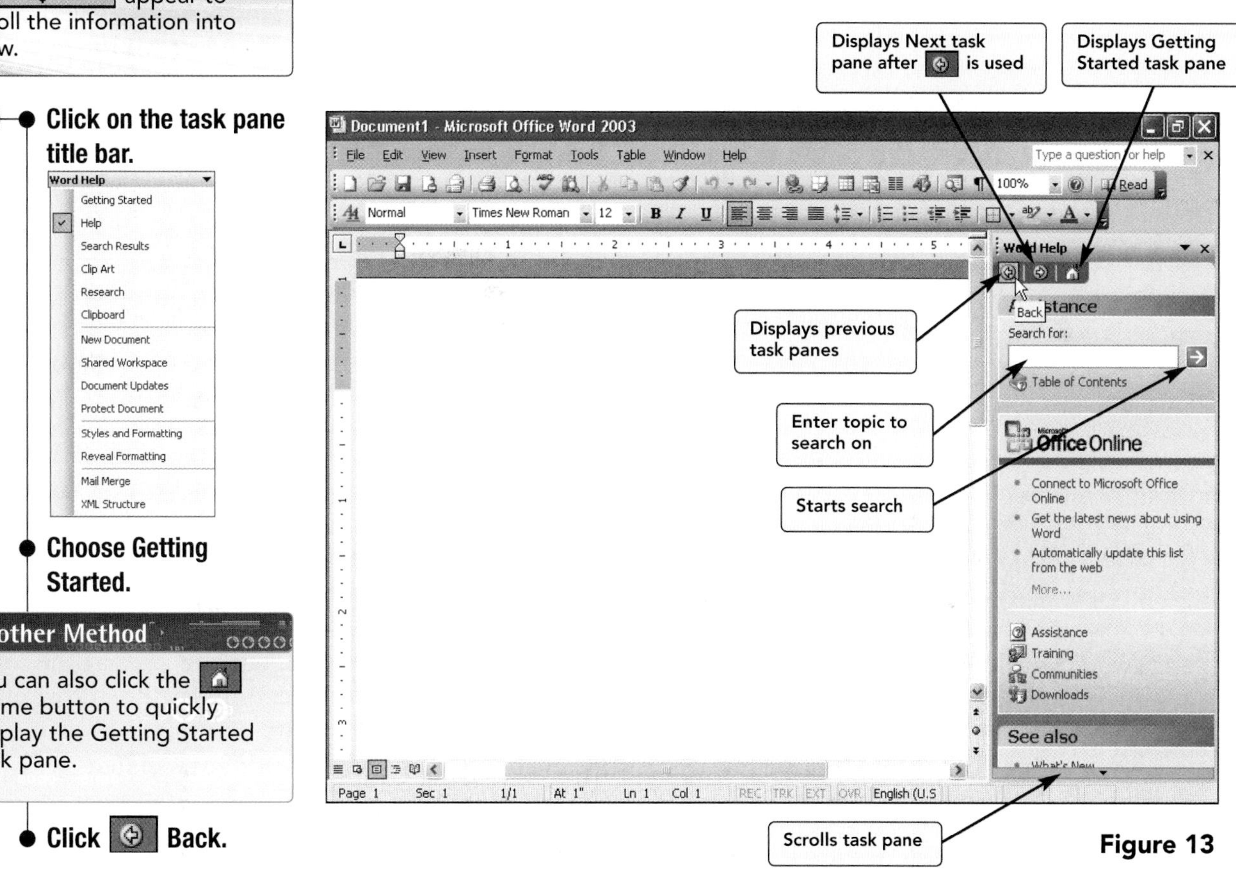


**Figure 13**

The Help task pane is displayed again. Likewise, clicking the Forward button will display the task pane that was viewed before using Back.

## Using Office Help

**Additional Information**

Although you can also simply enter a word or phrase in the Search box, the best results occur when you type a complete sentence or question.

There are several ways you can get help. One method is to conduct a search of the available help information by entering a sentence or question you want help on in the Search text box of the Help task pane. Notice the insertion point is positioned in the Search text box. This indicates it is ready for you to type an entry. You will use this method to learn about getting Help while you work.

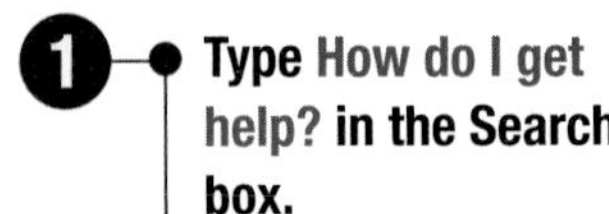

**1** **Type How do I get help? in the Search box.**

**Having Trouble?**

If the insertion point is not displayed in the Search box, simply click in the box to activate it.

**Click Start Searching.**

*Your screen should be similar to Figure 14*

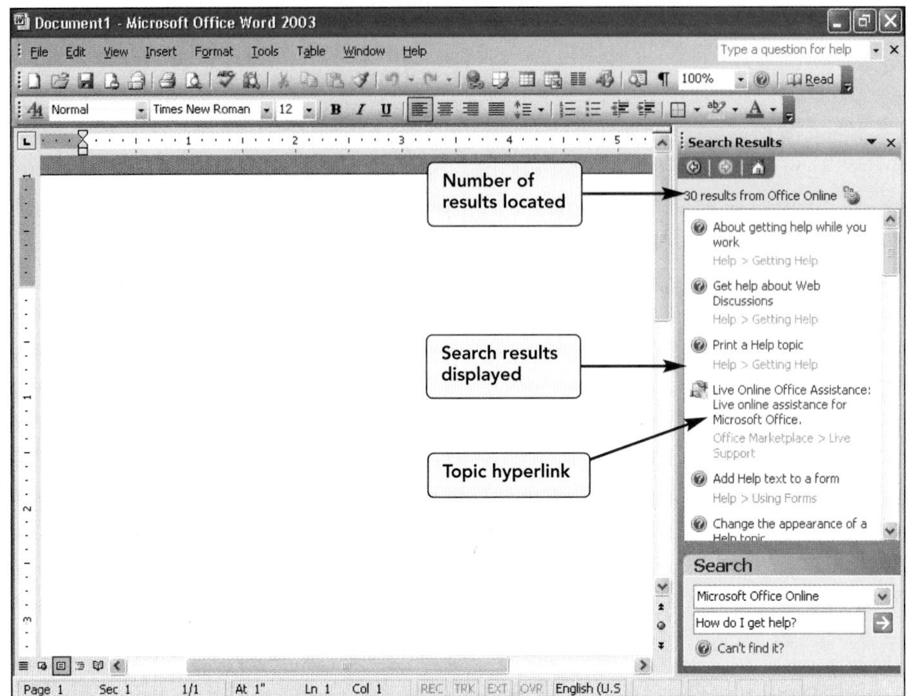


**Figure 14**

**Additional Information**

In addition to being connected to the Internet, the Online Content settings must be selected. Click Online Content Settings in the Help task pane and select all the options to turn on these features.

**Additional Information**

The number of results located and where they were found is displayed at the top of the list.

If you are connected to the Internet, the Microsoft Office Online Web site is searched and the results are displayed in the Search Results task pane. If you are not connected, the offline help information that is provided with the application and stored on your computer is searched. Generally the search results are similar, but fewer in number.

The Search Results pane displays a list of located results. The results are shown in order of relevance, with the most likely matches at the top of the list. Each result is a **hyperlink** or connection to the information located on the Online site or in Help on your computer. Clicking the hyperlink accesses and displays the information associated with the hyperlink.

You want to read the information in the topic "About getting help while you work."

**2** **From the Search Results list click the "About getting help while you work" hyperlink.**

**Additional Information**

When you point to the hyperlink, it appears underlined and the mouse pointer appears as 👆.

*Your screen should be similar to Figure 15*

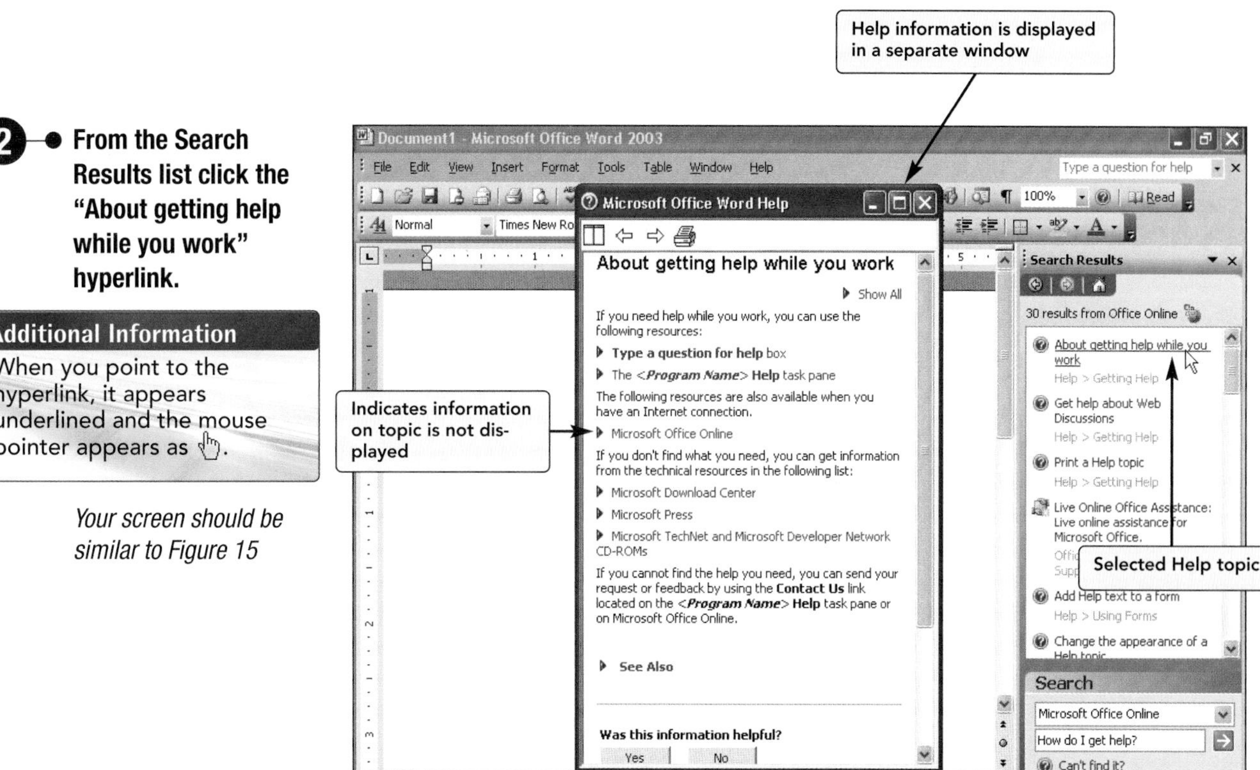


**Figure 15**

The information on the selected topic is displayed in a separate Help window. The Help window on your screen will probably be a different size and arrangement than in Figure 15. Depending on the size of your Help window, you may need to scroll the window to see all the Help information provided. As you are reading the help topic, you will see many subtopics preceded with ▶. This indicates the information in the subtopic is not displayed. Clicking on the subtopic heading displays the information about the topic.

**3**

- **If necessary, use the scroll bar to scroll the Help window to see the information on this topic.**
- **Scroll back up to the top of the window.**

> **Additional Information**
>
> Clicking the scroll arrows scrolls the text in the window line by line, and dragging the scroll bar up or down moves to a general location within the window area.

- **Click the "Type a question for help box" subtopic.**
- **Click the "The <Program name> Help task pane" subtopic.**
- **Read the information on both subtopics.**

*Your screen should be similar to Figure 16*

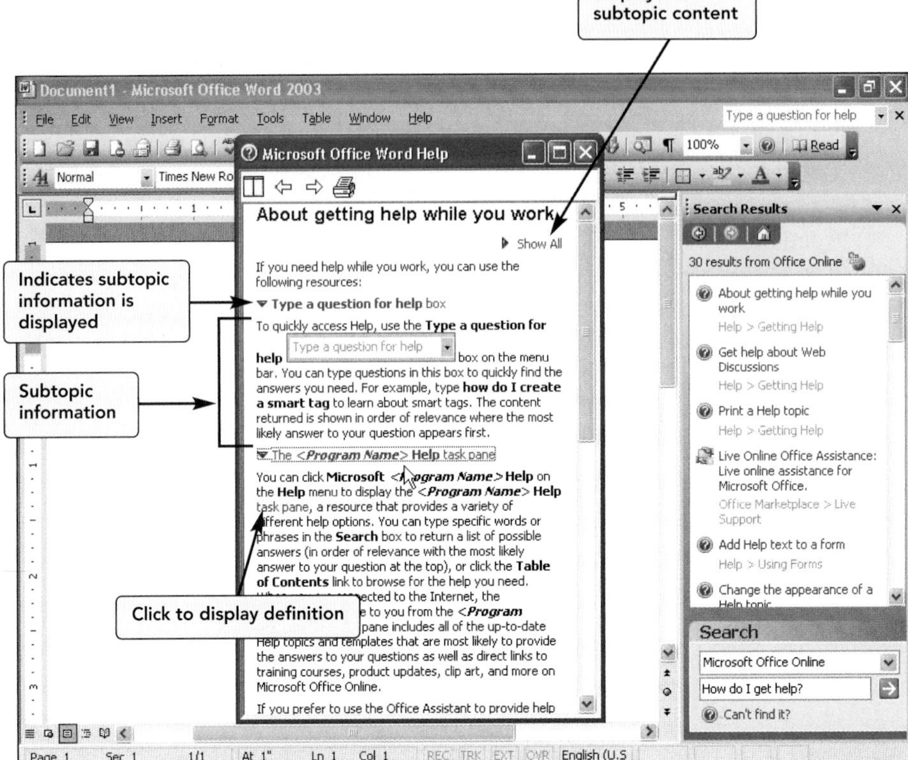


**Figure 16**

The ▸ preceding the subtopic has changed to ▾ indicating the subtopic content is displayed. The selected subtopics provide information about accessing Help using the "Type a question for help" box and the Help task pane. Notice the blue words "task pane" within the subtopic content. This indicates that clicking on the text will display a definition of the term. You can continue to click on the subtopic headings to display the information about each topic individually, or you can click Show All to display all the available topic information.

**4**

- **Click "task pane" to see the definition.**
- **Click Show All at the top of the Help window.**
- **Scroll the window to see the Microsoft Office Online subtopic.**
- **Read the information on this subtopic.**

*Your screen should be similar to Figure 17*

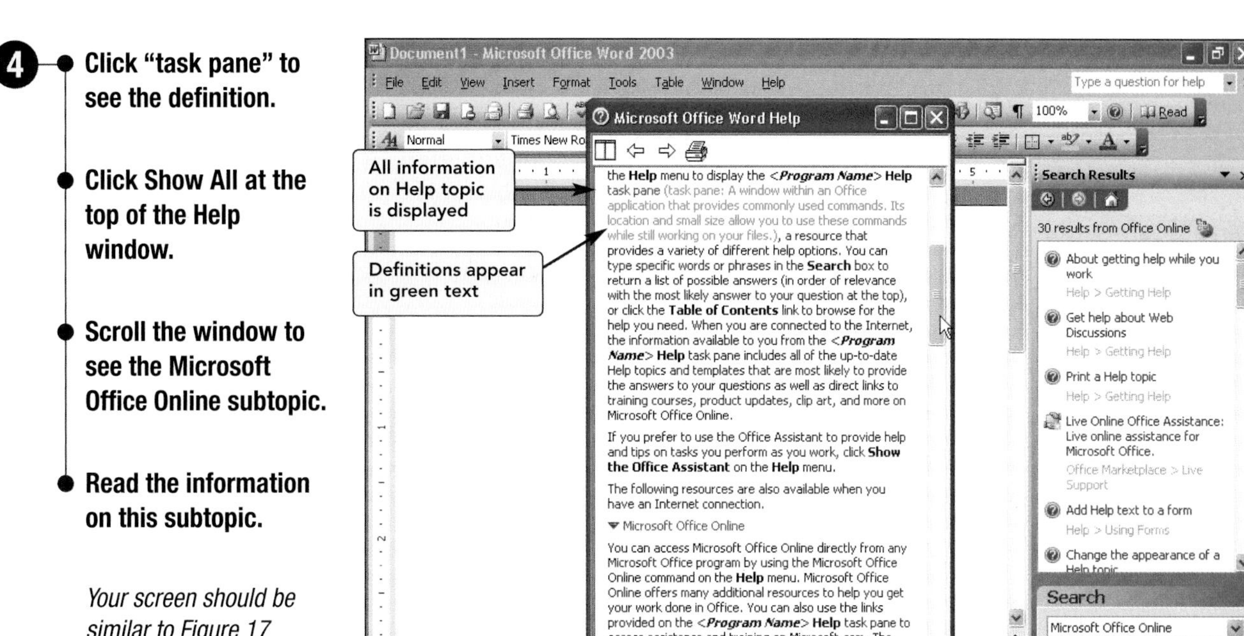


**Figure 17**

The information under all the subtopics is fully displayed, including definitions.

## Using the Help Table of Contents

Another source of help is to use the Help table of contents. Using this method allows you to browse the Help topics to locate topics of interest to you.

**1**

- **Click ☒ Close in the Help window title bar to close the Help window.**
- **Click ⊙ Back in the task pane.**
- **Click Table of Contents (below the Search box).**

*Your screen should be similar to Figure 18*

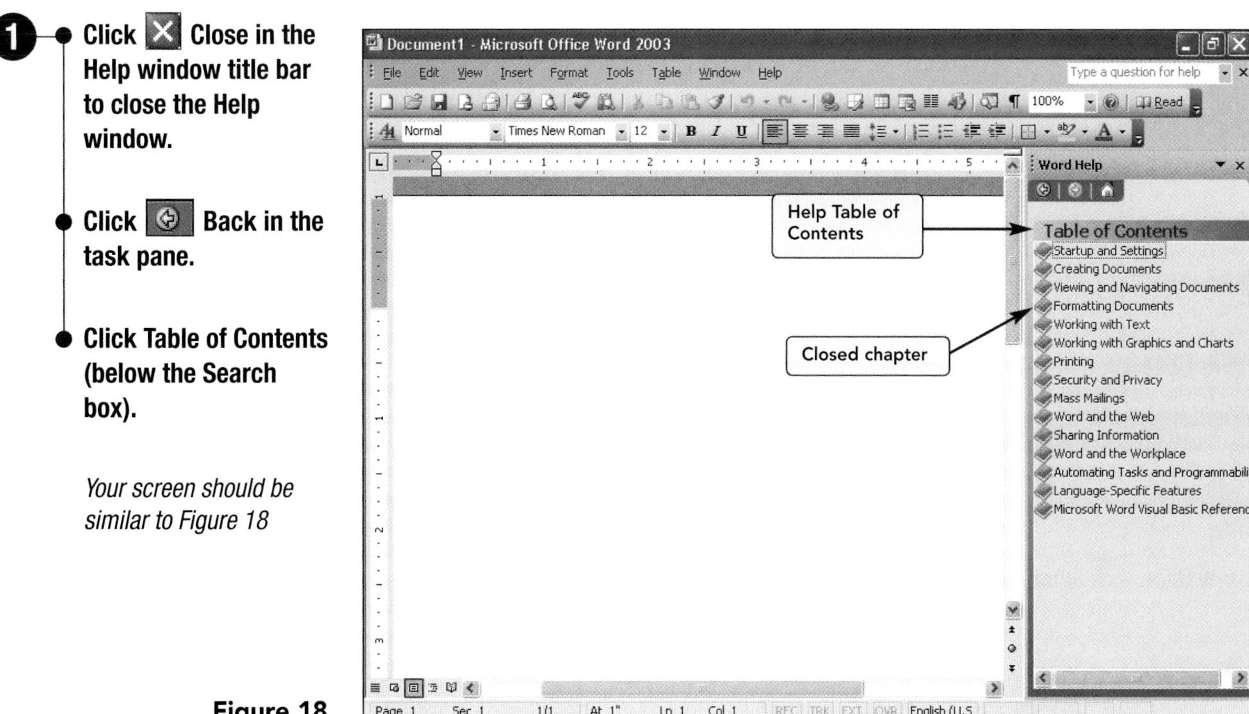


**Figure 18**

The entire Word Help Table of Contents is displayed in the Help task pane. Clicking on an item preceded with a Closed Book icon opens a chapter, which expands to display additional chapters or topics. The Open Book icon identifies those chapters that are open. Clicking on an item preceded with displays the specific Help information.

**2** **Click "Startup and Settings" to open this chapter.**

**Click "Getting Help."**

**Click "About getting help while you work."**

**Additional Information**

Pointing to an item in the Table of Contents that is not entirely visible in the pane displays a ScreenTip of the entire topic heading.

*Your screen should be similar to Figure 19*

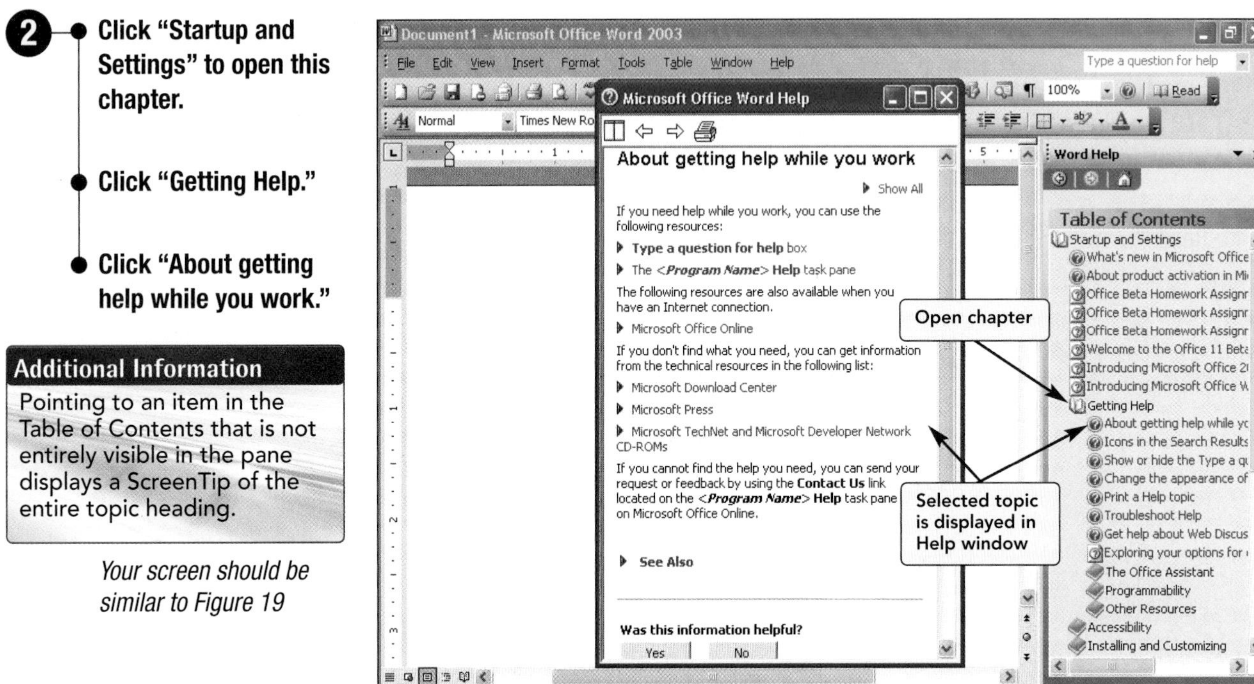


**Figure 19**

The Help window opens again and displays the information on the selected topic. To close a chapter, click the icon.

## Exiting an Office 2003 Application

Now you are ready to close the Help window and exit the Word program. The Exit command on the File menu can be used to quit most Windows programs. Alternatively, you can click the Close button in the program window title bar.

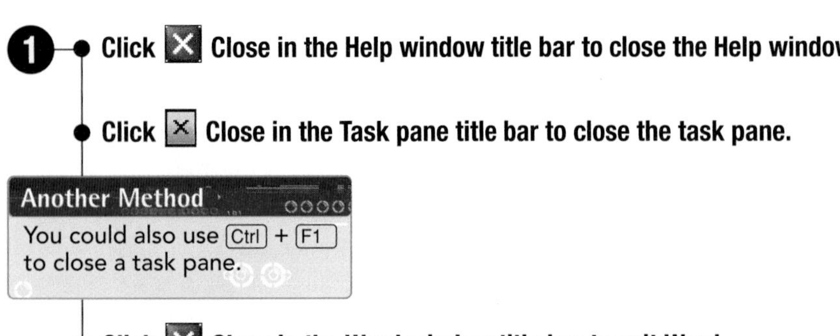

**1** **Click Close in the Help window title bar to close the Help window.**

**Click Close in the Task pane title bar to close the task pane.**

**Another Method**

You could also use Ctrl + F1 to close a task pane.

**Click Close in the Word window title bar to exit Word.**

The program window is closed and the desktop is visible again.

# Introduction to Microsoft Office 2003

## key terms

docked toolbar I.18
document window I.12
floating toolbar I.18
Formatting toolbar I.17
hyperlink I.22
menu bar I.12
scroll bar I.12
selection cursor I.14
shortcut menu I.15
Standard toolbar I.17
status bar I.12
task pane I.12
toolbar I.12

## command summary

| Command | Shortcut Key | Button | Voice | Action |
|---|---|---|---|---|
| start/All Programs | | | | Opens program menu |
| **F**ile/E**x**it | Alt + F4 | | | Exits Office program |
| **V**iew/**T**oolbars | | | View toolbars | Hides or displays toolbars |
| **V**iew/Tas**k** Pane | Ctrl + F1 | | Task pane<br>Show task pane<br>View task pane<br>Hide task pane | Hides or displays task pane |
| **T**ools/**C**ustomize/**O**ptions | | | | Changes settings associated with toolbars and menus |
| **H**elp/Microsoft Word **H**elp | F1 | | | Opens Help window |

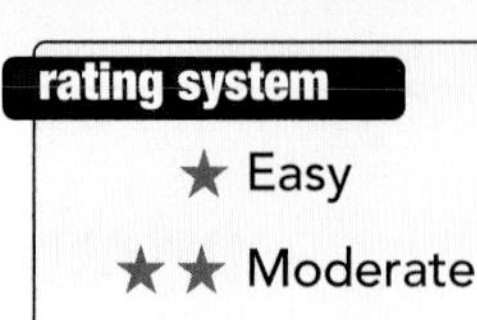

## step-by-step

### Using an Office Application ★

1. All Office 2003 applications have a common user interface. You will explore the Excel 2003 application and use many of the same features you learned about while using Word 2003 in this lab.

   a. Use the Start menu or a shortcut icon on your desktop to start Office Excel 2003. Close the Getting Started Task Pane.
   b. What shape is the mouse pointer when positioned in the document window area? ________
   c. Excel also has nine menus. Which menu is not the same as in Word? ________ Open the Tools Menu. How many commands in the Tools menu will display a submenu when selected? ______ How many commands are listed in the Formula Auditing submenu? __________
   d. Click on a blank space near the Formatting toolbar to open the toolbar shortcut menu. How many toolbars are available in Excel? ________
   e. Display the Chart toolbar. Dock the Chart toolbar above the Status bar. Change it to a floating toolbar. Close the Chart toolbar.
   f. Use the shortcut key combination to display the Task Pane. How many Task Panes are available? ___________
   g. Display the Help Task Pane and search for help information on "worksheet." How many search results were returned? ______ Read the "About viewing workbooks and worksheets" topic. What is the definition of a worksheet? ________________________________________________
   ________________________________________________________________________
   h. Close the Help window. Close the Excel window to exit the program.

## on your own

### Exploring Microsoft Help ★

1. In addition to the Help information you used in this lab, Office 2003 Online Help also includes many interactive tutorials. Selecting a Help topic that starts a tutorial will open the browser program on your computer. Both audio and written instructions are provided. You will use one of these tutorials to learn more about using Office 2003. Start Word 2003 and search for Help on "shortcut keys." Then select the "Work with the Keyboard in Office" topic. Follow the directions in the tutorial to learn about this feature. When you are done, close the browser window and the Word window.

# Overview of Microsoft Office PowerPoint 2003

## What Is a Presentation Program?

You are in a panic! Tomorrow you are to make a presentation to an audience and you want it to be good. To the rescue comes a powerful tool: graphics presentation programs. These programs are designed to help you create an effective presentation, whether to the board of directors of your company or to your fellow classmates. An effective presentation gets your point across clearly and in an interesting manner.

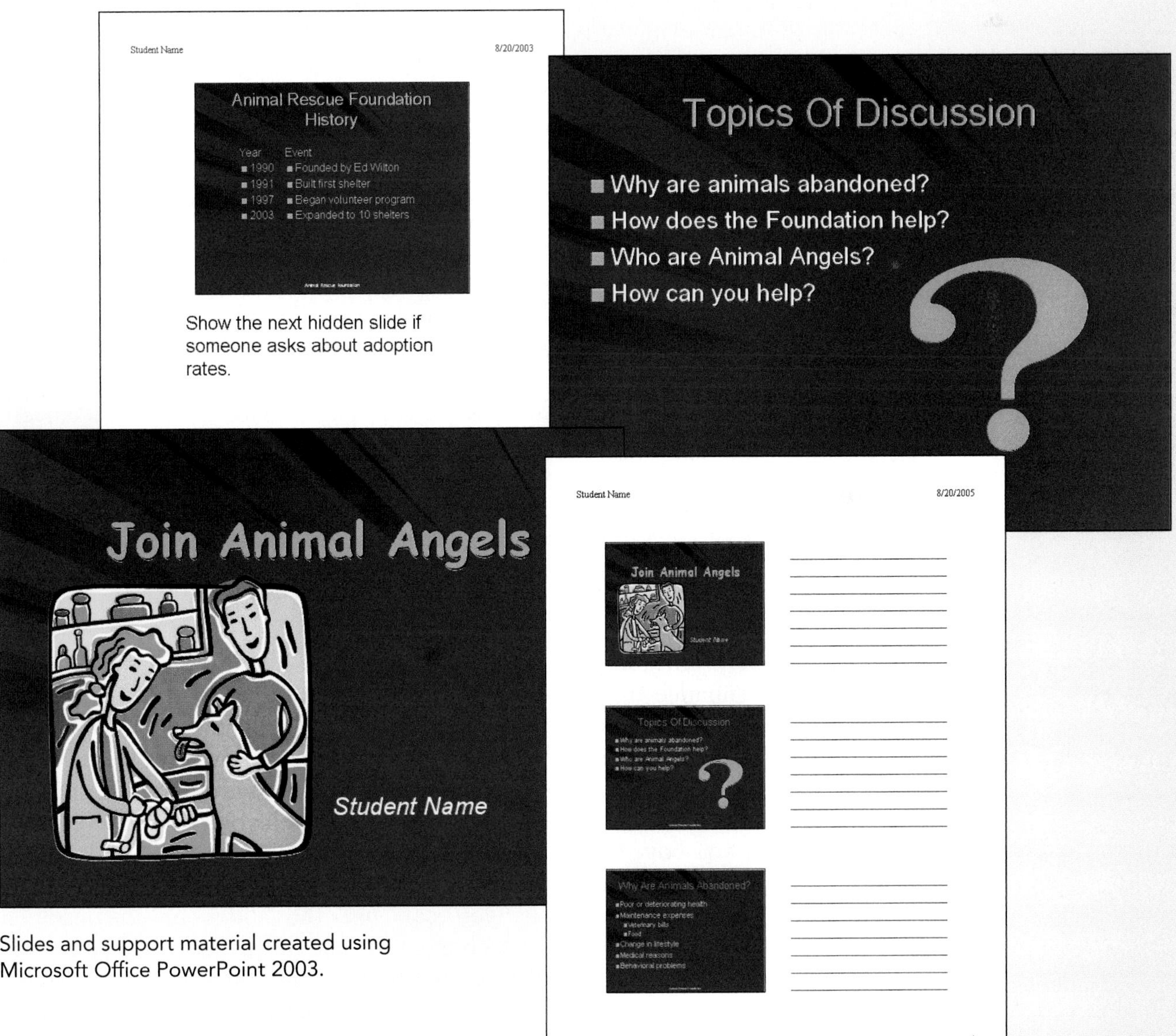


Slides and support material created using Microsoft Office PowerPoint 2003.

Graphics presentation programs are designed to help you produce a high-quality presentation that is both interesting to the audience and effective in its ability to convey your message. A presentation can be as simple as overhead transparencies or as sophisticated as an onscreen electronic display. Graphics presentation programs can produce black-and-white or color overhead transparencies, 35mm slides, onscreen electronic presentations called screen shows, Web pages for Web use, and support materials for both the speaker and the audience.

The graphics presentation program includes features such as text handling, outlining, graphing, drawing, animations, clip art, and multimedia support. With a few keystrokes, the user can quickly change, correct, and update the presentation. In addition, graphics presentation programs suggest layouts for different types of presentations and offer professionally designed templates to help you produce a presentation that is sure to keep your audience's attention.

## Office PowerPoint 2003 Features

Creating an effective presentation is a complicated process. Graphics presentation programs help simplify this process by providing assistance in the content development phase, as well as in the layout and design phase. In addition, these programs produce the support materials you can use when making a presentation to an audience.

The content development phase includes deciding on the topic of your presentation, the organization of the content, and the ultimate message you want to convey to the audience. As an aid in this phase, PowerPoint 2003 helps you organize your thoughts based on the type of presentation you are making. Several common types of presentations sell a product or idea, suggest a strategy, or report on the progress of a program. Based on the type of presentation, the program suggests ideas and organization tips. For example, if you are making a presentation on the progress of a sales campaign, the program would suggest that you enter text on the background of the sales campaign as the first page, called a slide; the current status of the campaign as the next slide; and accomplishments, schedule, issues and problems, and where you are heading on subsequent slides.

The layout for each slide is the next important decision. Again, PowerPoint 2003 helps you by suggesting text layout features such as title placement, bullets, and columns. You can also incorporate graphs of data, tables, organizational charts, clip art, and other special text effects in the slides.

PowerPoint 2003 also includes professionally designed templates to further enhance the appearance of your slides. These templates include features that standardize the appearance of all the slides in your presentation. Professionally selected combinations of text and background colors, common typefaces and sizes, borders, and other art designs take the worry out of much of the design layout.

After you have written and designed the slides, you can then have the slides made into black-and-white or color overhead transparencies or 35mm slides. Alternatively, you can use the slides in an onscreen electronic presentation or a Web page for use on the Web. An electronic presentation uses the computer to display the slides on an overhead projection screen. When you use this type of presentation, many programs also include a rehearsal feature, allowing you to practice and time your presentation. The length of time to display each slide can be set and your entire presentation can be completed within the allotted time. A presentation can be modified to display on a Web site and to run using a Web browser.

Finally, with PowerPoint 2003 you can also print out the materials you have created. You can print an outline of the text showing the titles of the slides and main text but not the art. The outline allows you to check the organizational logic of your presentation. You can also print speaker notes to which you can refer to while making your presentation. These notes generally consist of a small printout of each slide with any notes on topics you want to discuss while the slides are displayed. Finally, you can create printed handouts of the slides for the audience. The audience can refer to the slide and make notes on the handout page as you speak.

## Case Study for Office PowerPoint 2003 Labs

You have volunteered at the Animal Rescue Foundation, a nonprofit organization that rescues unwanted animals from local animal shelters and finds foster homes for them until a suitable adoptive family can be found. With your computer skills, you have been asked to create a powerful and persuasive presentation to entice the community to volunteer.

The organization has recently purchased the graphics presentation program Microsoft Office PowerPoint 2003. You will use this application to create the presentation.

**Lab 1:** You use PowerPoint to enter and edit the text for your presentation. You also learn how to reorganize the presentation and enhance it with different text attributes and by adding a picture. Finally, you learn how to run a slide show and print handouts.

**Lab 2:** You learn about many more features to enhance the appearance of your slides. These include changing the slide design and color scheme and adding clip art, animation, and sound. You also learn how to add transition effects to make the presentation more interesting. Finally, you create speaker notes to help you keep your cool during the presentation.

**Working Together:** Demonstrates the sharing of information between applications. First you learn how to copy and embed a table created in Word into a slide. Then you learn how to link a chart created in Excel to another slide.

## Before You Begin

*To the Student*

The following assumptions have been made:

- The Microsoft Office PowerPoint 2003 program has been installed on your computer system.

- You have the data files needed to complete the series of PowerPoint 2003 Labs and practice exercises. These may be supplied by your instructor and are also available at the online learning center Web site found at www.mhhe.com/oleary.
- You have completed the McGraw-Hill Windows Labs or you are already familiar with how to use Windows and a mouse.

*To the Instructor*

It is assumed that the complete version of the program has been installed prior to students using the labs. In addition, please be aware that the following settings are assumed to be in effect for the PowerPoint 2003 program. These assumptions are necessary so that the screens and directions in the text are accurate.

- The Getting Started task pane is displayed on startup (use Tools/Options/View).
- The status bar is displayed (use Tools/Options/View).
- The vertical ruler is displayed (use Tools/Options/View).
- The Paste Options buttons are displayed (use Tools/Options/Edit).
- The Standard, Formatting, Drawing, and Outlining toolbars are on (use Tools/Customize/Toolbars).
- The Standard and Formatting toolbars are displayed on separate rows (use Tools/Customize/Options).
- Full menus are always displayed (use Tools/Customize/Options).
- The Office Assistant feature is enabled but not on (right-click on the Assistant, choose Options, and clear the Use the Office Assistant option).
- Normal view is on (use View/Normal).
- The Clip Organizer is installed on the local disk or network.
- The automatic spelling check feature is on (use Tools/Options/Spelling and Style/Check spelling as you type).
- The style check feature is off (use Tools/Options/Spelling and Style and clear the Check Style option).
- All the options in the View tab are selected (use Tools/Options/View).
- All slide design templates have been installed.
- The feature to access Online Help is on (choose Online Content Settings from the Help task pane and select the Show content and links from Microsoft Office Online option).

In addition, all figures in the manual reflect the use of a standard VGA display monitor set at 800 by 600. If another monitor setting is used, it may display more or fewer lines of text displayed in the windows than in the figures. This setting can be changed using Windows setup.

## Microsoft Office Language Bar

The Microsoft Office Language bar may be displayed when you start the application. Commonly, it will appear in the title bar, however, it may appear in other locations depending upon your setup. The Language bar provides buttons to access and use the Speech Recognition and Handwriting recognition features of Office. To display the Language bar, choose Toolbars/Language bar from the Taskbar Shortcut menu.

## Instructional Conventions

Hands-on instructions that you are to perform appear as a sequence of numbered steps. Within each step, a series of bullets identifies the specific actions that must be performed. Step numbering begins over within each topic heading throughout the lab.

Command sequences that you are to issue appear following the word "Choose." Each menu command selection is separated by a /. If the menu command can be selected by typing a letter of the command, the letter will appear underlined and bold. Items that need to be selected will follow the word "Select" and will appear in black text. You can select items with the mouse or directional keys. (See Example A.)

**Example A**

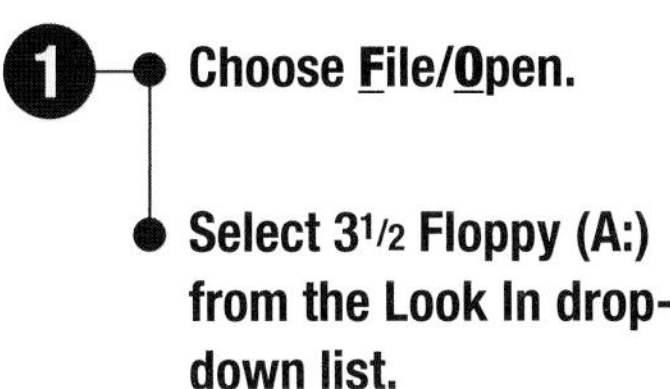


Commands that can be initiated using a button and the mouse appear following the word "Click." The icon (and the icon name if the icon does not include text) is displayed following "Click." The menu equivalent, keyboard shortcut and/or voice command appear in an Another Method margin note when the action is first introduced. (See Example B.)

**Example B**

**1 Click Open.**

Plain blue text identifies file names. Information you are asked to type appears in blue and bold. (See Example C.)

**Example C**

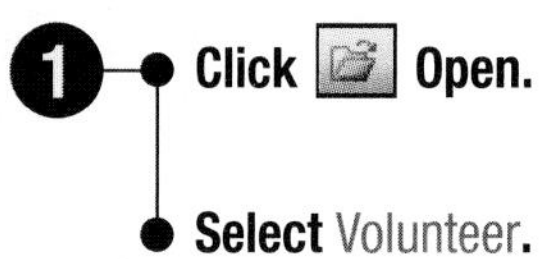


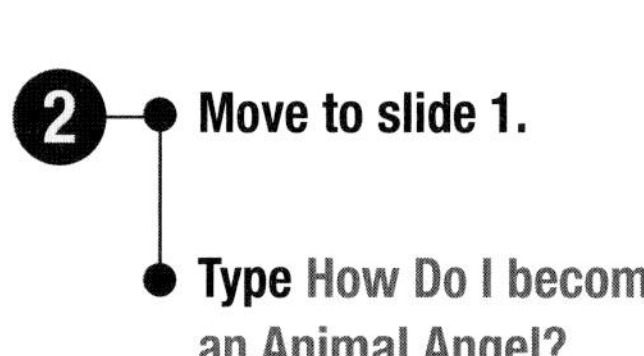

2
Move to slide 1.
Type How Do I become an Animal Angel?.

# Creating a Presentation

LAB 1

## Objectives

After completing this lab, you will know how to:

1. Use the AutoContent wizard to create a presentation.
2. View and edit a presentation.
3. Save, close, and open a presentation.
4. Check spelling.
5. Delete, move, and insert slides.
6. Size and move placeholders.
7. Run a slide show.
8. Change fonts and formatting.
9. Insert pictures and clip art.
10. Preview and print a presentation.

# Case Study

## Animal Rescue Foundation

You are the Volunteer Coordinator at the local Animal Rescue Foundation. This nonprofit organization rescues unwanted pets from local animal shelters and finds foster homes for them until a suitable adoptive family can be found. The agency has a large volunteer group called the Animal Angels that provides much-needed support for the foundation.

The agency director has decided to launch a campaign to increase community awareness about the Foundation. As part of the promotion, you have been asked to create a powerful and persuasive presentation to entice more members of the community to join Animal Angels.

The agency director has asked you to preview the presentation at the weekly staff meeting tomorrow and has asked you to present a draft of the presentation by noon today.

Although we would all like to think that our message is the core of the presentation, the presentation materials we use can determine whether the message reaches the audience. To help you create the presentation, you will use Microsoft Office PowerPoint 2003, a graphics presentation application that is designed to create presentation materials such as slides, overheads, and handouts. Using Office PowerPoint 2003, you can create a high-quality and interesting onscreen presentation with pizzazz that will dazzle your audience.

© Andy Sotiriou/Getty Images

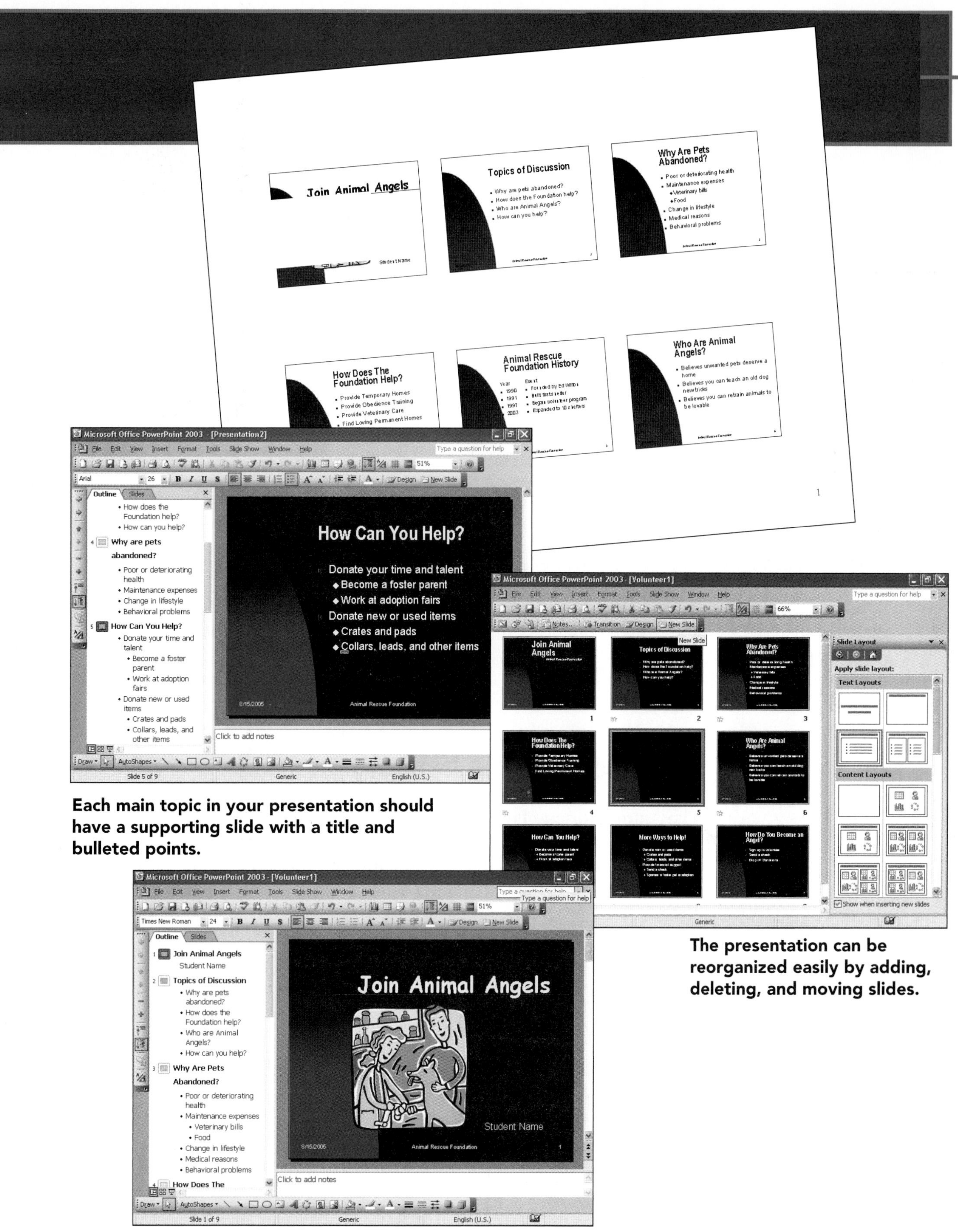


**Each main topic in your presentation should have a supporting slide with a title and bulleted points.**

**The presentation can be reorganized easily by adding, deleting, and moving slides.**

**Enhance the presentation with the addition of graphics and text colors.**

## Concept Preview

The following concepts will be introduced in this lab:

1. **Template** A template is a file containing predefined settings that can be used as a pattern to create many common types of presentations.
2. **Presentation Style** A PowerPoint presentation can be made using five different styles: onscreen presentations, Web presentations, black-and-white or color overheads, and 35mm slides.
3. **Slide** A slide is an individual "page" of your presentation.
4. **AutoCorrect** The AutoCorrect feature makes some basic assumptions about the text you are typing and, based on these assumptions, automatically corrects the entry.
5. **Spelling Checker** The spelling checker locates all misspelled words, duplicate words, and capitalization irregularities as you create and edit a presentation, and proposes possible corrections.
6. **Layout** The layout controls the way items are arranged on a slide.
7. **Font and Font Size** A font, also commonly referred to as a typeface, is a set of characters with a specific design. Each font has one or more sizes.
8. **Graphics** A graphic is a non-text element or object, such as a drawing or picture, that can be added to a slide.
9. **Stacking Order** Stacking order is the order in which objects are inserted into different layers of the slide.

## Introducing Office PowerPoint 2003

The Animal Rescue Foundation has just installed the latest version of the Microsoft Office Suite of applications, Office 2003, on their computers. You will use the graphics presentation program, Microsoft Office PowerPoint 2003, included in the office suite to create your presentation. Using this program, you should have no problem creating the presentation in time for tomorrow's staff meeting.

## Starting Office PowerPoint 2003

**1 Start the Office PowerPoint 2003 application.**

**Having Trouble?**

See "Introduction to Office System 2003" for information on starting the application and for a discussion of features that are common to all Office 2003 applications.

*Your screen should be similar to Figure 1.1*

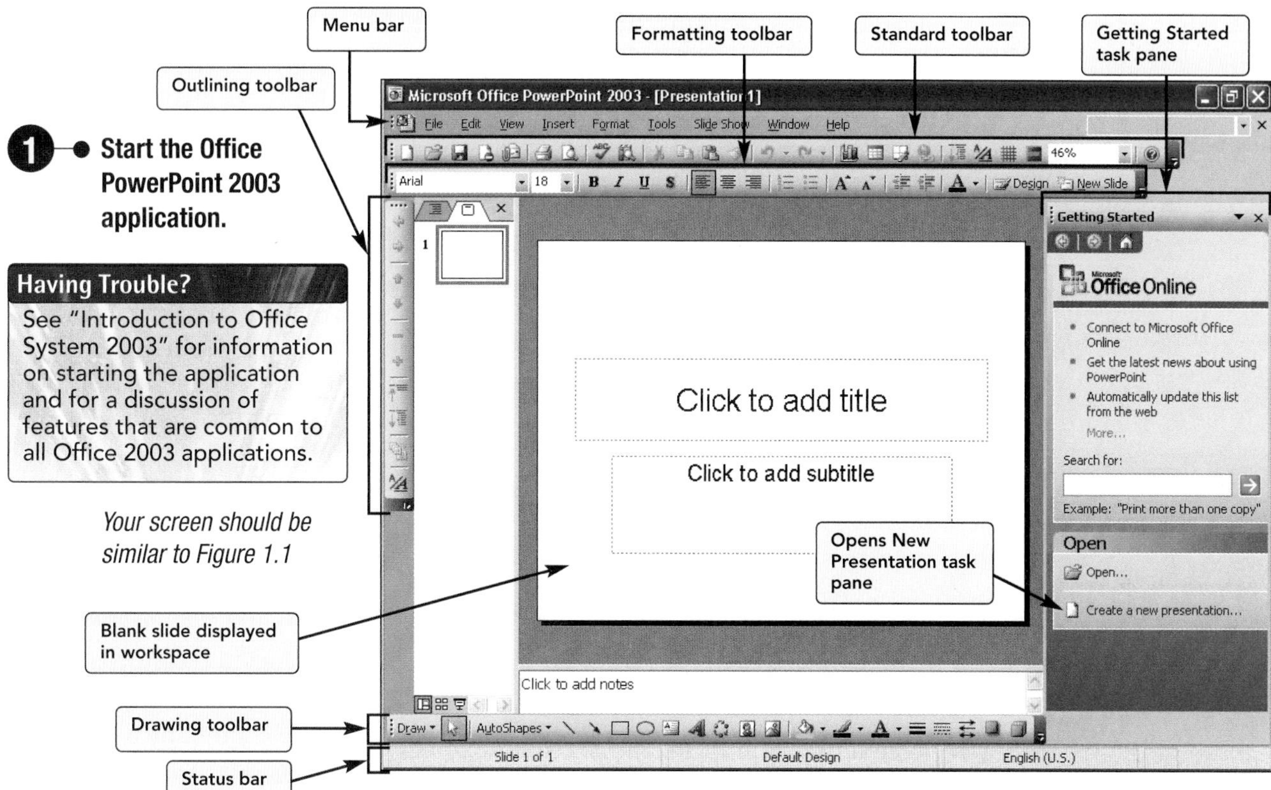


**Figure 1.1**

**Additional Information**

Because the Office 2003 applications remember settings that were on when the program was last exited, you screen may look slightly different.

The PowerPoint application window is displayed. The menu bar below the title bar displays the PowerPoint program menu. It consists of nine menus that provide access to the commands and features you will use to create and modify a presentation.

Located below the menu bar are the Standard and Formatting toolbars. The Standard toolbar contains buttons that are used to complete the most frequently used menu commands. The Formatting toolbar contains buttons that are used to change the appearance or format of the document. The **Drawing toolbar** is displayed along the bottom edge of the window. It contains buttons that are used to enhance text and create shapes. In addition, the **Outlining toolbar** may be displayed along the left edge of the window. It is used to enter and modify the content of the presentation. PowerPoint 2003 has 13 different toolbars. Many of the toolbars appear automatically as you use different features. Other toolbars may be displayed if they were on when the program was last exited.

**Additional Information**

If you have installed the Speech Recognition feature the voice command to display toolbars is "View Toolbars" and to display the task pane is "Task pane."

**2 If necessary, make the following changes to your screen to make it look like Figure 1.1:**

- **Use View/Toolbars and select or deselect the appropriate toolbar to display or hide it. There should be four toolbars displayed.**
- **The Standard, Formatting, Drawing and Outlining toolbars should be displayed.**
- **If your task pane is not displayed, choose View/Task Pane.**

**Additional Information**

Sixteen different task panes can be displayed depending on the task being performed.

The large area containing the blank slide is the **workspace** where your presentations are displayed as you create and edit them. Because you just started the program, the Getting Started task pane is automatically displayed on the right side of the window. It is used to open an existing presentation or create new presentations. The status bar at the bottom of the PowerPoint window displays messages and information about various PowerPoint settings.

## Developing New Presentations

During your presentation you will present information about the Animal Rescue Foundation and why someone should want to join the Animal Angels volunteer group. As you prepare to create a new presentation, you should follow several basic steps: plan, create, edit, enhance, and rehearse.

| Step | Description |
|---|---|
| Plan | The first step in planning a presentation is to understand its purpose. You also need to find out the length of time you have to speak, who the audience is, what type of room you will be in, and what kind of audiovisual equipment is available. These factors help to determine the type of presentation you will create. |
| Create | To begin creating your presentation, develop the content by typing your thoughts or notes into an outline. Each main idea in your presentation should have a supporting slide with a title and bulleted points. |
| Edit | While typing, you are will probably make typing and spelling errors that need to be corrected. This is one type of editing. Another type is to revise the content of what you have entered to make it clearer, or to add or delete information. To do this, you might insert a slide, add or delete bulleted items, or move text to another location. |
| Enhance | You want to develop a presentation that grabs and holds the audience's attention. Choose a design that gives your presentation some dazzle. Wherever possible add graphics to replace or enhance text. Add effects that control how a slide appears and disappears, and that reveal text in a bulleted list one bullet at a time. |
| Rehearse | Finally, you should rehearse the delivery of your presentation. For a professional presentation, your delivery should be as polished as your materials. Use the same equipment that you will use when you give the presentation. Practice advancing from slide to slide and then back in case someone asks a question. If you have a mouse available, practice pointing or drawing on the slide to call attention to key points. |

After rehearsing your presentation, you may find that you want to go back to the editing phase. You may change text, move bullets, or insert a new slide. Periodically, as you make changes, rehearse the presentation again to see how the changes affect your presentation. By the day of the presentation, you will be confident about your message and at ease with the materials.

During the planning phase, you have spoken with the Foundation director regarding the purpose of the presentation and the content in general. The purpose of your presentation is to educate members of the community about the organization and to persuade many to volunteer. In addition, you want to impress the director by creating a professional presentation.

## Creating a Presentation

When you first start PowerPoint, a new blank presentation is opened. It is like a blank piece of paper that already has many predefined settings. These settings, called **default** settings, are generally the most commonly used settings and are stored as a presentation template.

### Concept 1

#### Template

1 A **template** is a file containing predefined settings that can be used as a pattern to create many common types of presentations. Every PowerPoint presentation is based on a template. The default settings for a basic blank presentation are stored in the default design template file. Whenever you create a new presentation using this template, the same default settings are used.

Many other templates that are designed to help you create professional-looking presentations are also available within PowerPoint and in the Microsoft Office Template Gallery on the Microsoft Office Web site. They include design templates, which provide a design concept, fonts, and color scheme; and content templates, which suggest content for your presentation based on the type of presentation you are making. You can also design and save your own presentation templates.

The Getting Started task pane is used to specify how you want to start using the PowerPoint program. It provides a variety of ways to start a new presentation or to open an existing presentation. More options for starting a new presentation are available in the New Presentation task pane.

**1 Click Create a new presentation in the Getting Started task pane.**

**Another Method**

You could also select the task pane to open from the Other Task Panes drop-down menu.

*Your screen should be similar to Figure 1.2*

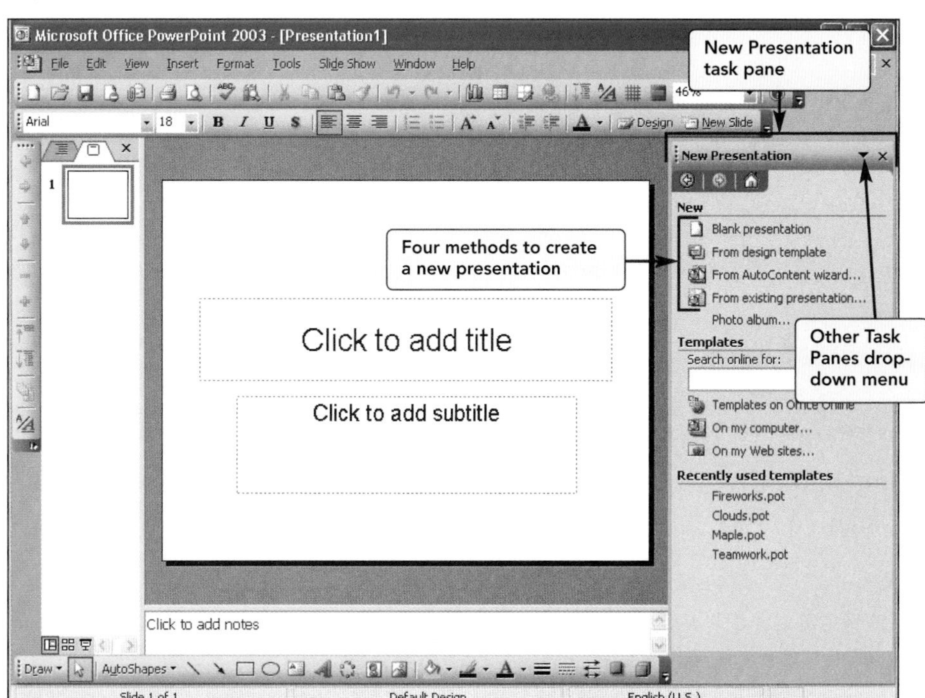


Figure 1.2

**Additional Information**

The Photo Album option allows you to create a specialized type of presentation consisting of pictures only.

Four methods can be used to create a presentation. The first method is to start with a blank presentation that has minimal design elements and add your own content and design changes. Another is to use one of the many design templates as the basis for your new presentation. The third method is to use the AutoContent wizard. A **wizard** is an interactive approach that guides you through the process of performing many complicated tasks. The AutoContent wizard creates a presentation that contains suggested content and design based on the answers you provide. Finally, you can use an existing presentation as the base for your new presentation by making the design or content changes you want for the new presentation.

## Using the AutoContent Wizard

Because this is your first presentation created using PowerPoint, you decide to use the AutoContent wizard.

**2** **From the New Presentation task pane, select From AutoContent wizard.**

*Your screen should be similar to Figure 1.3*

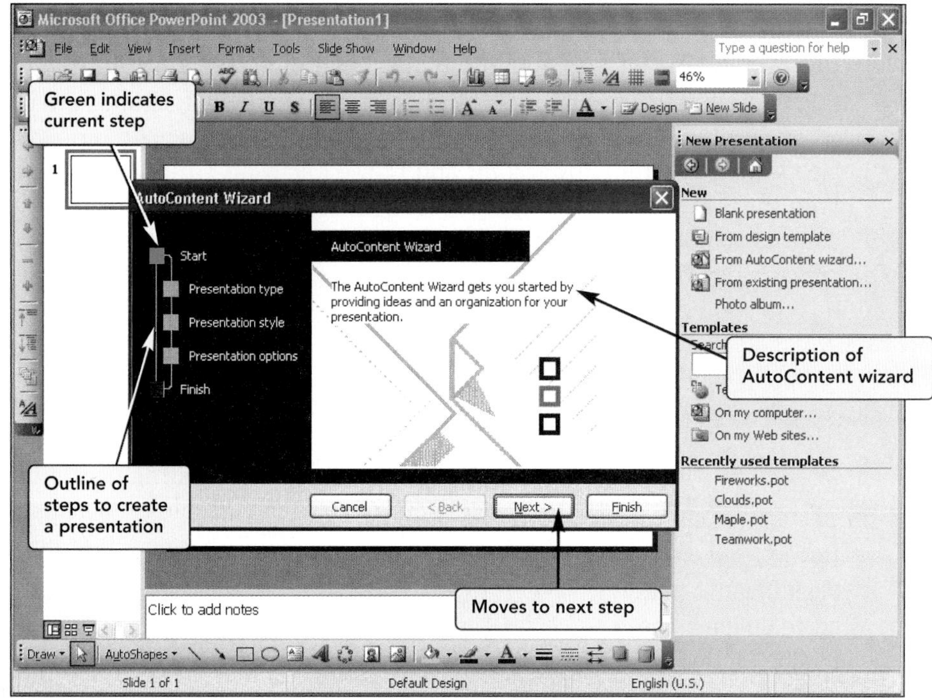


**Figure 1.3**

The opening dialog box of the AutoContent wizard briefly describes how the feature works. As the AutoContent wizard guides you through creating the presentation, it shows your progress through the steps in the outline on the left side of the dialog box. The green box identifies the current step.

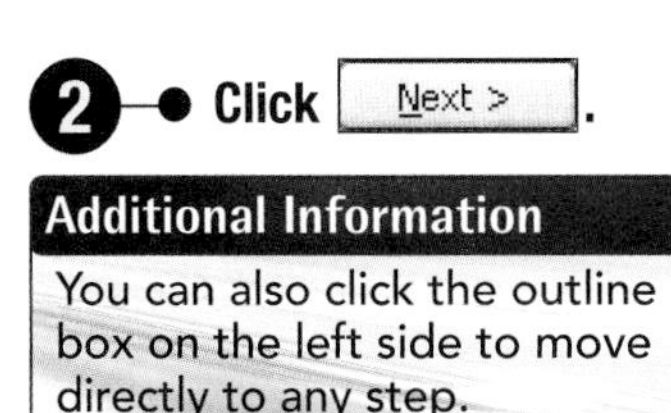

**2** Click Next >.

**Additional Information**

You can also click the outline box on the left side to move directly to any step.

*Your screen should be similar to Figure 1.4*

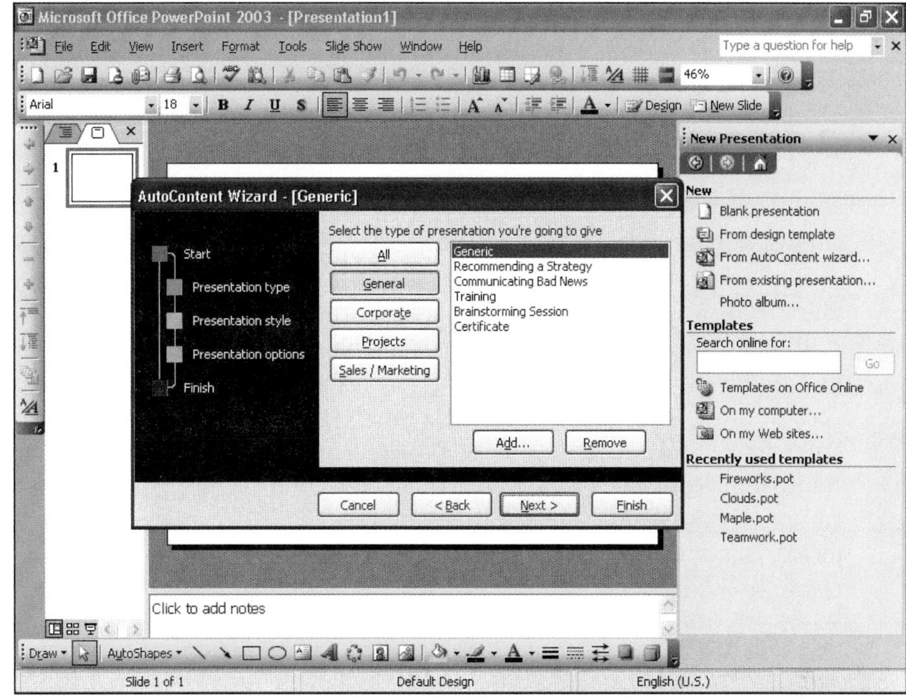


**Figure 1.4**

In the Presentation Type step, you are asked to select the type of presentation you are creating. PowerPoint offers 24 different types of presentations, each with a different recommended content and design. Each type is indexed under a category. Currently, only the names of the six presentation types in the General category appear in the list box. You will use the Generic presentation option.

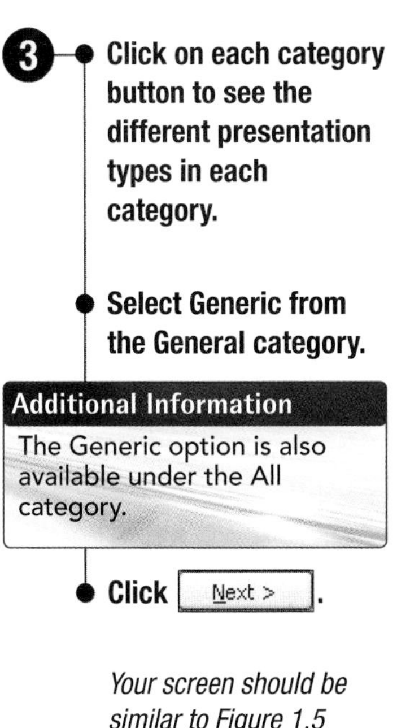

**3** Click on each category button to see the different presentation types in each category.

Select Generic from the General category.

**Additional Information**

The Generic option is also available under the All category.

Click Next >.

*Your screen should be similar to Figure 1.5*

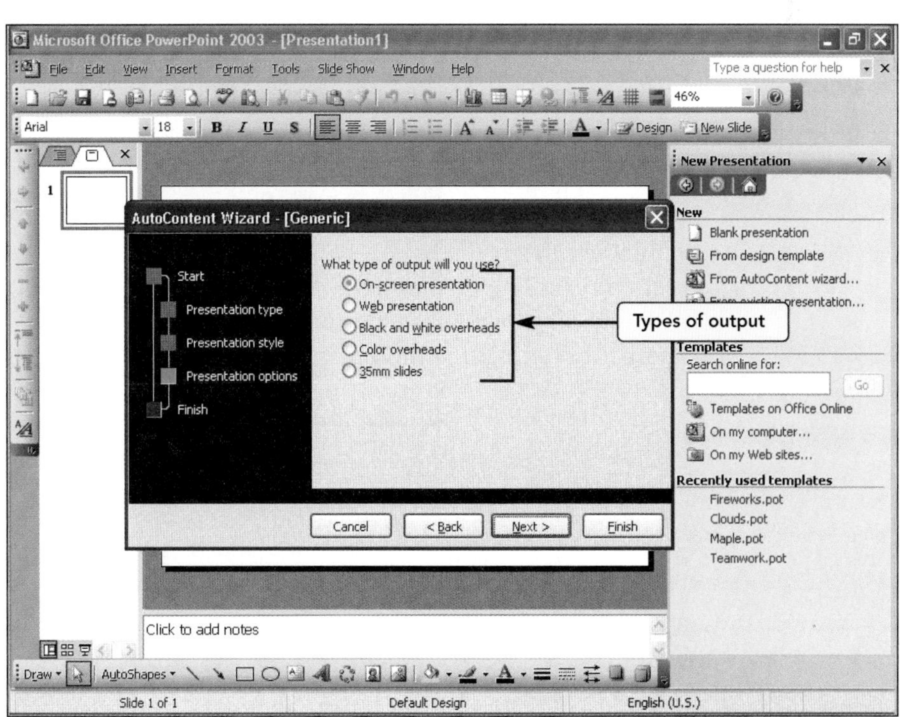


**Figure 1.5**

In the Presentation Style step, you select the type of output your presentation will use.

## Concept 2

### Presentation Style

2 A PowerPoint presentation can be made using five different styles: onscreen presentations, Web presentations, black-and-white or color overheads, and 35mm slides. The type of equipment that is available to you will affect the style of presentation that you create.

If you have computer projection equipment that displays the current monitor image on a screen, you should create a full-color onscreen presentation. You can also design your onscreen presentation specifically for the World Wide Web, where a browser serves as the presentation tool. Often you will have access only to an overhead projector, in which case you can create color or black-and-white transparencies. Most laser printers will print your overheads directly on plastic transparencies, or you can print your slides and have transparencies made at a copy center. If you have access to a slide projector, you may want to use 35mm slides. You can send your presentation to a service bureau that will create the slides for you.

The room in which you will be using to make your presentation is equipped with computer projection equipment, so you will create an onscreen presentation. The Wizard selects the color scheme best suited to the type of output you select. Because On-screen Presentation is the default selection, you will accept it and move to the next step.

*Your screen should be similar to Figure 1.6*

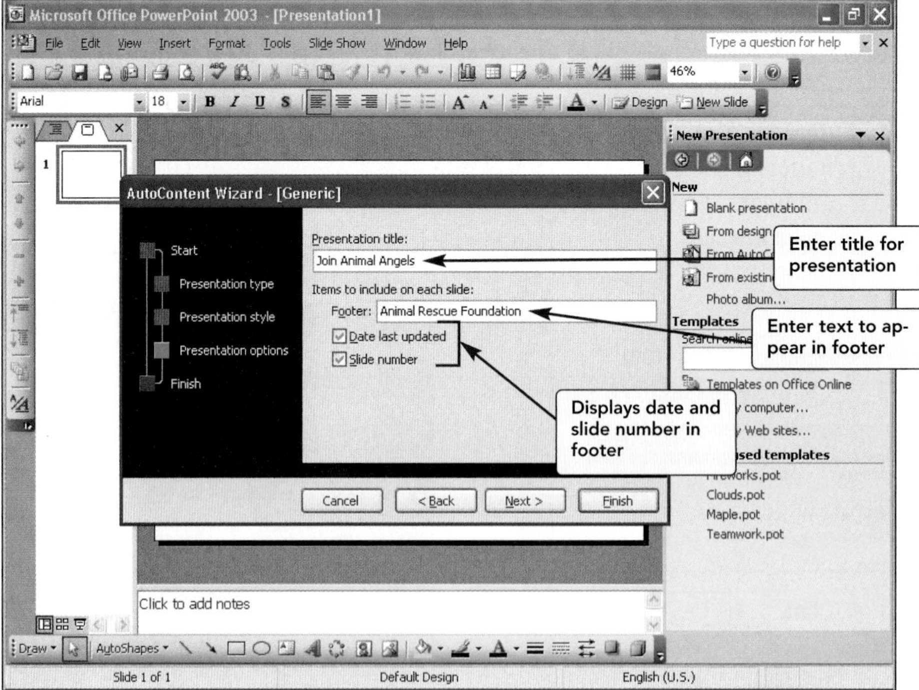


**Figure 1.6**

In the Presentation Options step, you are asked to enter some basic information that will appear on the title slide and in the footer of each slide in the presentation.

## Concept 3

### Slide

3 A **slide** is an individual "page" of your presentation. The first slide of a presentation is the title slide which is used to introduce your presentation. Additional slides are used to support each main point in your presentation. The slides give the audience a visual summary of the words you speak, which helps them understand the content and keeps them entertained. The slides also help you, the speaker, organize your thoughts, and prompt you during the presentation.

You would like to have the name of the presentation appear as the title on the first slide, and to have the name of the organization, date of the presentation, and the slide number appear on the footer of each slide. A **footer** consists of text or graphics that appear at the bottom of each slide. Because the options to display the date that the presentation was last updated and slide number are already selected, you only need to enter the title text and footer text.

**5** **Click in the Presentation title text box to display the insertion point.**

**Type Join Animal Angels.**

**Having Trouble?**

If you make a typing error, use the Backspace key to delete the characters to the left of the insertion point and then retype the current text.

**Press** **.**

**Type Animal Rescue Foundation in the Footer text box.**

*Your screen should be similar to Figure 1.7*

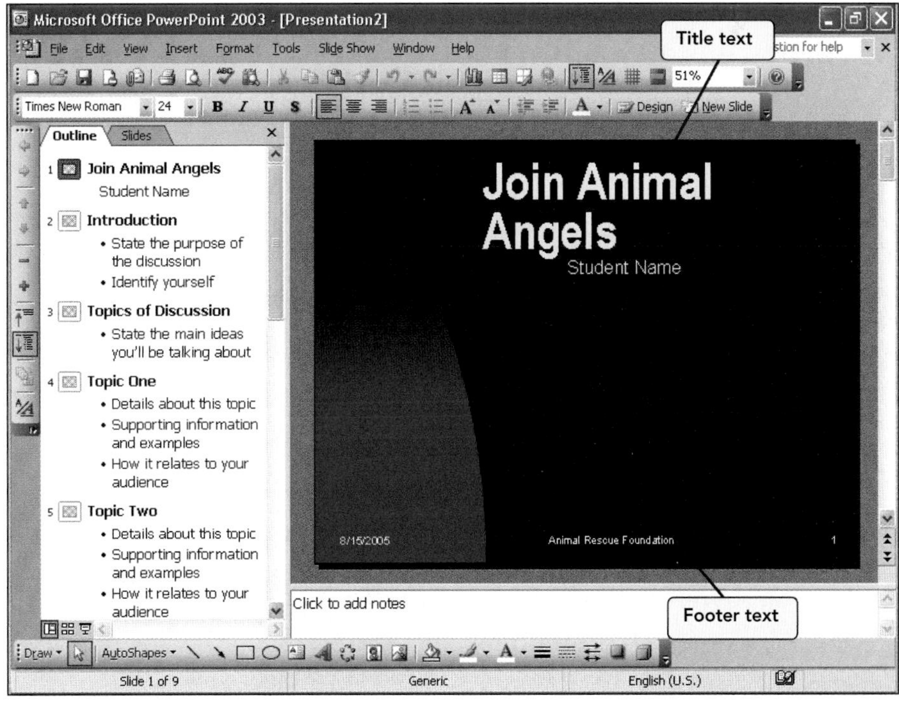


Figure 1.7

You have entered all the information PowerPoint needs to create your presentation.

**6** Click Next >.

Click Finish.

If necessary, maximize the document window.

*Your screen should be similar to Figure 1.8*

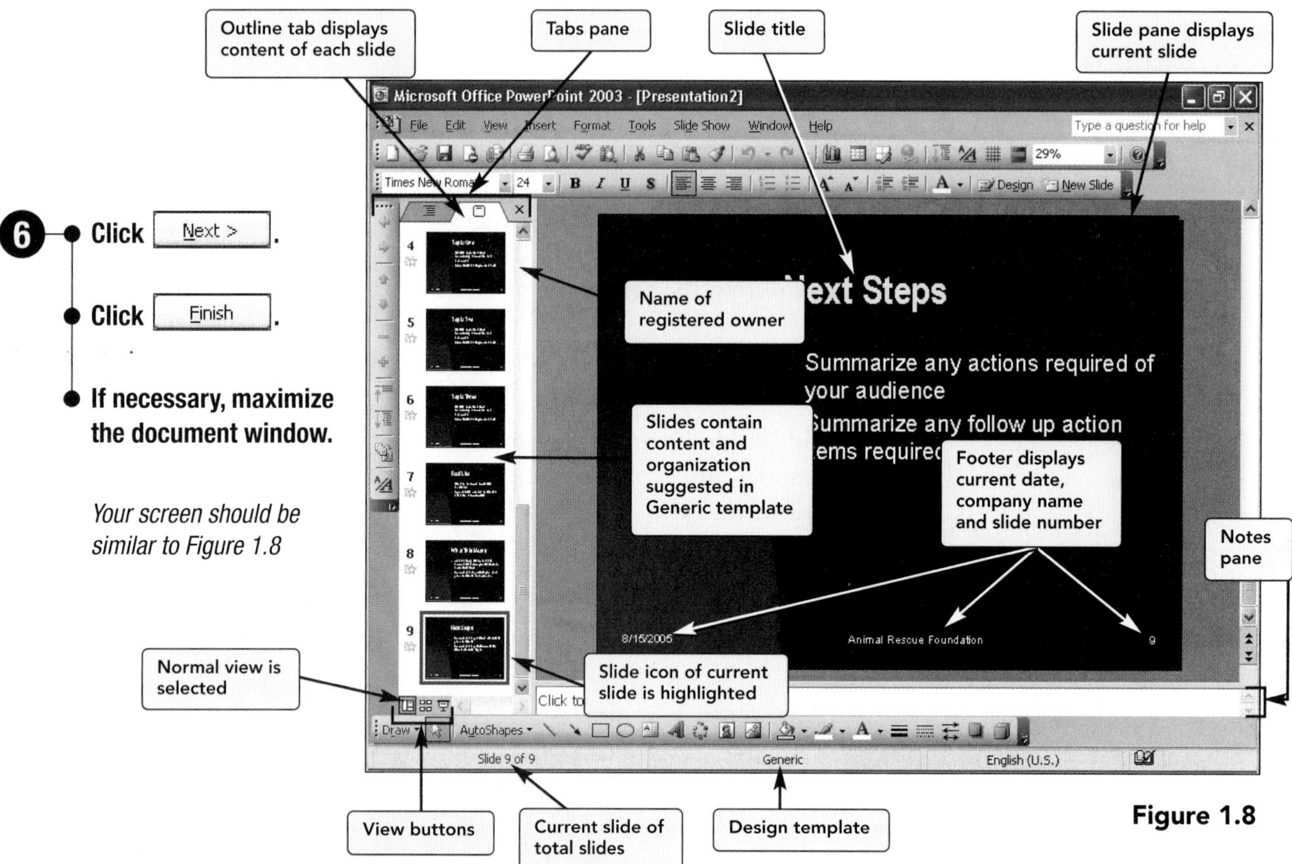

Outline tab displays content of each slide
Tabs pane
Slide title
Slide pane displays current slide
Name of registered owner
Slides contain content and organization suggested in Generic template
Footer displays current date, company name and slide number
Notes pane
Normal view is selected
Slide icon of current slide is highlighted
View buttons
Current slide of total slides
Design template
Next Steps
Summarize any actions required of your audience
8/15/2005
Animal Rescue Foundation
Slide 9 of 9
Generic
English (U.S.)

Figure 1.8

## Viewing the Presentation

**Additional Information**
You will learn how to change the color and design in Lab 2.

Based on your selections and entries, the AutoContent wizard creates a presentation and displays it in the workspace. The colors and design were selected by the wizard when you selected the Generic presentation type.

The presentation is initially displayed in Normal view showing the Outline tab. A **view** is a way of looking at a presentation. PowerPoint provides several views you can use to look at and modify your presentation. Depending on what you are doing, one view may be preferable to another. The commands to change views are located on the View menu. In addition, the three view buttons to the left of the horizontal scroll bar can be used to switch quickly from one view to another. The menu commands, buttons, and voice commands for the three main views are described in the table on the next page.

**Additional Information**
Many voice commands have several different words you can say to initiate the command.

| View | Command | Button | Voice | Description |
|---|---|---|---|---|
| Normal | View/Normal | | Normal or Normal view | Provides three working areas of the window that allow you to work on all aspects of your presentation in one place. |
| Slide Sorter | View/Slide Sorter | | Slide sorter | Displays a miniature of each slide to make it easy to reorder slides, add special effects such as transitions, and set timing between slides. |
| Slide Show | View/Slide Show | | View show, Begin slide show, Start slide show, or Slide show view | Displays each slide in final form using the full screen space so you can practice or present the presentation. |

## Using Normal View

**Additional Information**

Normal view is often referred to as a tri-pane view because it displays three panes simultaneously.

Normal view is displayed by default because it is the main view you use while creating a presentation. In Normal view, three working areas, called **panes**, are displayed. These panes allow you to work on all components of your presentation in one convenient location. The pane on the left side includes tabs that alternate between viewing the presentation in outline format and as slide miniatures. The pane on the right displays the selected slide. The notes pane below the slide pane includes space for you to enter speaker notes.

**Additional Information**

You will learn about speaker notes in Lab 2.

Currently, the Outline tab is open and displays the title and text for each slide in the presentation. It is used to organize and develop the content of your presentation. To the left of each slide title in the Outline tab is a slide icon and a number that identifies each slide (see Figure 1.8). The icon of the current slide is highlighted, and the current slide is displayed in the main working area, called the slide pane. The text for the first slide consists of the title and the footer text you specified when using the AutoContent wizard. Below the title, the name of the registered owner of the application program is displayed automatically. The other slides shown in the Outline tab contain sample text that is included by the Wizard based upon the type of presentation you selected. The sample text suggests the content for each slide to help you organize your presentation's content. Because the current view is Normal, the button is highlighted. The status bar displays the number of the current slide and total number of slides, and the name of the design template used.

**Additional Information**

You can adjust the size of each pane by dragging the splitter bar that borders each pane.

The Slides tab is used to display each slide in the presentation as a thumbnail. A **thumbnail** is a miniature representation of a picture, in this case of a slide. Clicking on the thumbnail selects the slide, making it the current slide, and displays it in the slide pane.

**1** **Click on the Slides tab to open it.**

**Another Method**

You can also press Ctrl + ⇧Shift + Tab to switch between the Slide and Outline tabs. The voice commands are "Slides" or "Outline."

- **Scroll the tabs pane to view the rest of the slides.**
- **Click on the last slide in the Slides tab.**

*Your screen should be similar to Figure 1.9*

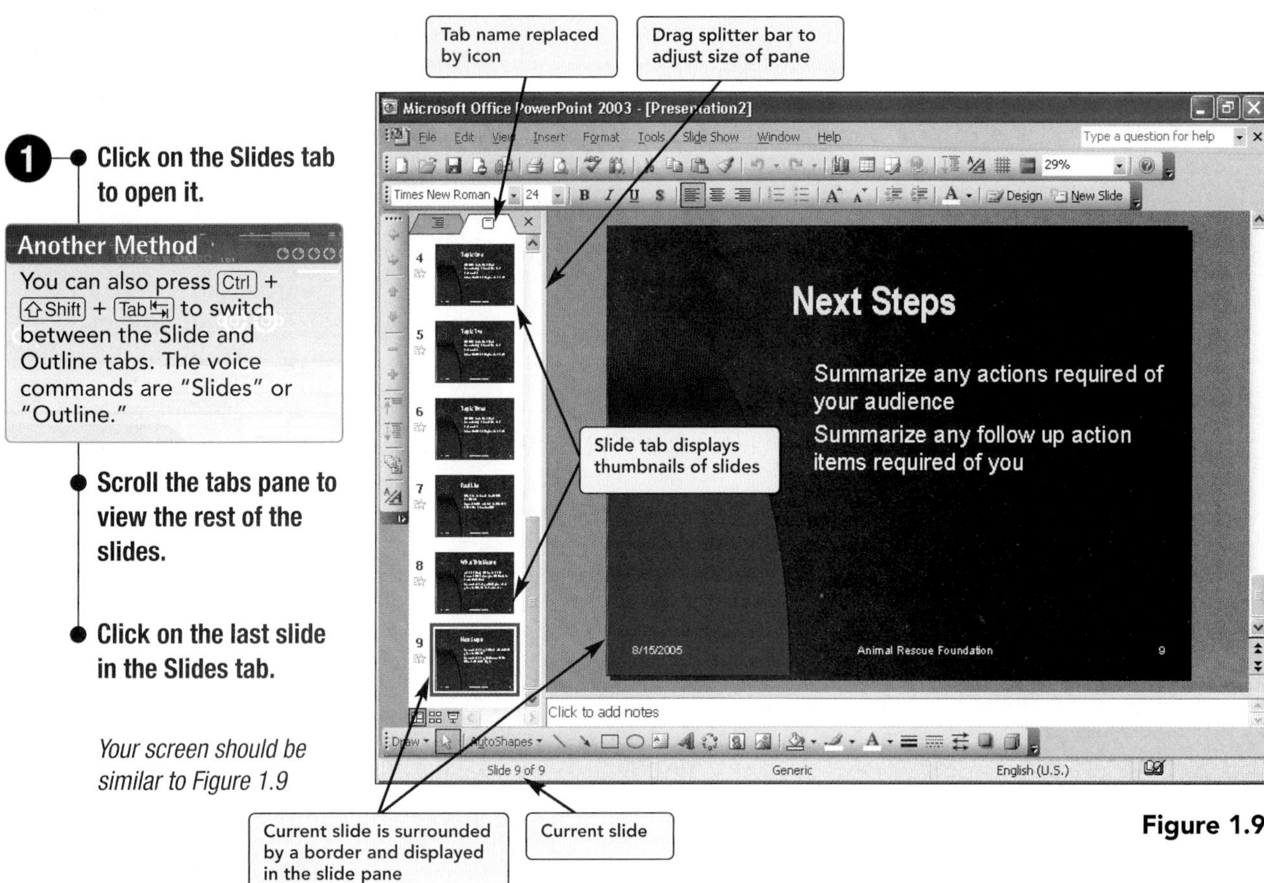


**Figure 1.9**

**Additional Information**

You can make the thumbnails larger by increasing the width of the tabs pane.

The size of the tabs pane adjusted to be just large enough to display the thumbnails. In addition, because the pane is narrower, the tab names are replaced by icons. The presentation has a total of nine slides. The status bar displays the number of the current slide.

## Using Slide Sorter View

The second main view that is used while creating a presentation is Slide Sorter view. This view also displays thumbnails of the slides.

**1** **Click Slide Sorter View.**

**Having Trouble?**

Pointing to a view button displays its name in a ScreenTip.

*Your screen should be similar to Figure 1.10*

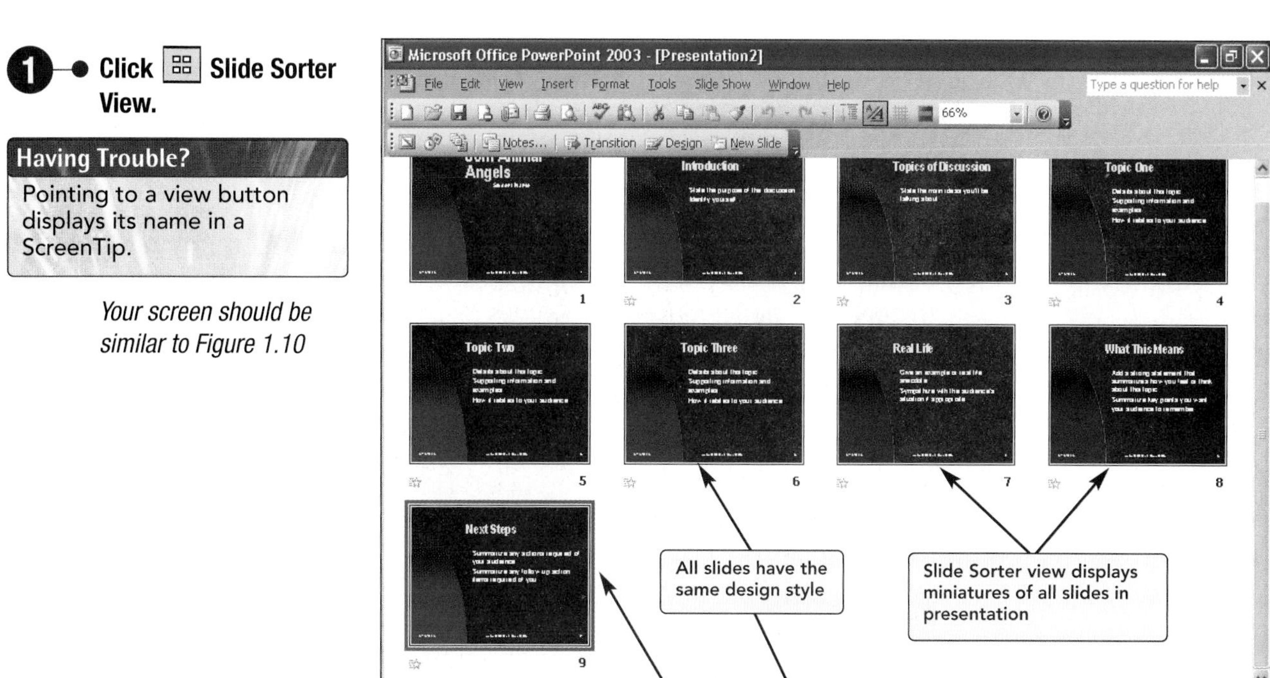

Microsoft Office PowerPoint 2003 - [Presentation2]
All slides have the same design style
Slide Sorter view displays miniatures of all slides in presentation
Border surrounds current slide
Slide Sorter view is selected

**Figure 1.10**

This view displays a miniature of each slide in the window. All the slides use the same design style, associated with a generic presentation. The design style sets the background design and color, as well as the text style, color, and layout. The currently selected slide, slide 9, appears with a blue border around it. Clicking on a thumbnail selects the slide and makes it the **current slide**, or the slide that will be affected by any changes you make.

**2** **Click on slide 1.**

*Your screen should be similar to Figure 1.11*

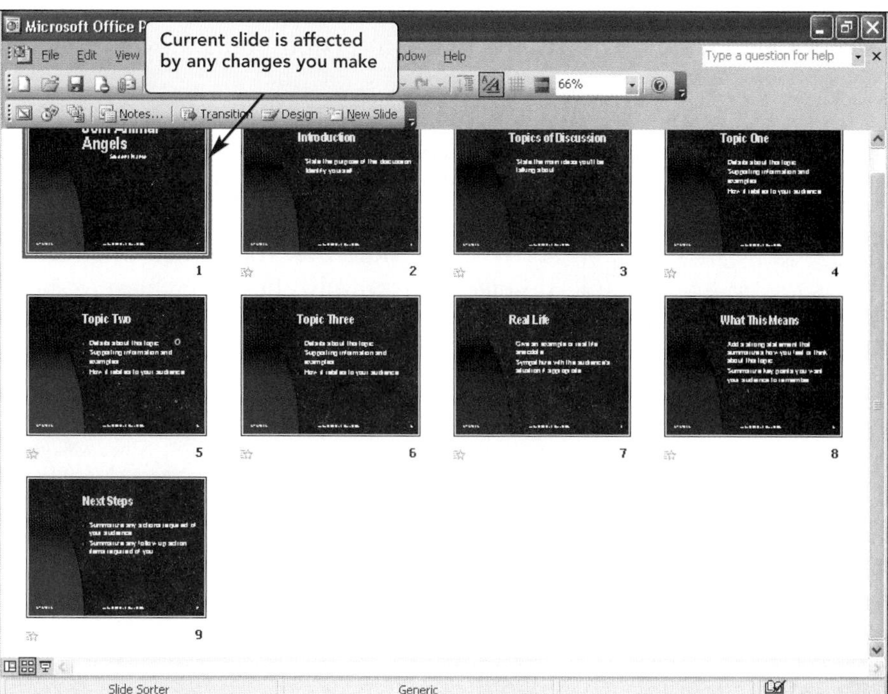

Current slide is affected by any changes you make

**Figure 1.11**

## Editing a Presentation

After creating a presentation using the AutoContent wizard, you need to replace the sample content with the appropriate information for your presentation. Editing involves making text changes and additions to the content of your presentation. It also includes making changes to the organization of content. This can be accomplished quickly by rearranging the order of bulleted items on slides as well as the order of slides.

While editing, you will need to move to specific locations in the text. You can use the mouse to move to selected locations simply by clicking on the location. An insertion point appears to show your location in the text. You can also use the arrow keys located on the numeric keypad or the directional keypad to move the insertion point. The keyboard directional keys and voice commands used to move within text are described in the following table.

| Key | Voice | Movement |
|---|---|---|
| → | Right | One character to right |
| ← | Left | One character to left |
| ↑ | Up | One line up |
| ↓ | Down | One line down |
| Ctrl + → | Next word | One word to right |
| Ctrl + ← | Back word | One word to left |
| Home | Home | Left end of line |
| End | Go end | Right end of line |

**Additional Information**

You can use the directional keys on the numeric keypad or the dedicated directional keypad area. If you use the numeric keypad, make sure the Num Lock feature is off, otherwise numbers will be entered in the document. The Num Lock indicator light above the keypad is lit when on. Press Num Lock to turn it off.

Holding down a directional key or key combination moves the insertion point quickly in the direction indicated, saving multiple presses of the key. Many of the insertion point movement keys can be held down to execute multiple moves.

While editing you will also need to select text. To select text using the mouse, first move the insertion point to the beginning or end of the text to be selected, and then drag when the mouse pointer is an I-beam to highlight the text you want selected. You can select as little as a single letter or as much as the entire document. To remove highlighting and deselect text, simply click anywhere in the document.

You can also quickly select a block of text, such as a word or line. The following table summarizes the mouse techniques used to select standard blocks.

| To Select | Procedure |
|---|---|
| Word | Double-click in the word. |
| Sentence | Press Ctrl and click within the sentence. |
| All text in a bullet | Triple-click in the bulleted text. |
| Multiple lines and bullets | Drag up or down across the lines |

You can also select text with the keyboard or using voice commands shown in the following table.

| Keyboard | Voice | Action |
|---|---|---|
| ⇧Shift + → | | Selects the next space or character. |
| ⇧Shift + ← | | Selects the previous space or character. |
| Ctrl + ⇧Shift + → | Select next word | Selects the next word. |
| Ctrl + ⇧Shift + ← | Select last word | Selects the last word. |
| Ctrl + ⇧Shift + ↑ | Select last line | Selects text going backward. |
| Ctrl + ⇧Shift + ↓ | Select next line | Selects text going forward. |
| Ctrl + A | Select all | Selects the entire document. |

## Using the Outline Tab

The easiest way to make text-editing changes is to use the Outline tab in Normal view. When working in the Outline tab, the Outlining toolbar is displayed. It is used to modify the presentation outline.

**1** **Click Normal View to switch to Normal view again.**

**Click the Outline tab.**

*Your screen should be similar to Figure 1.12*

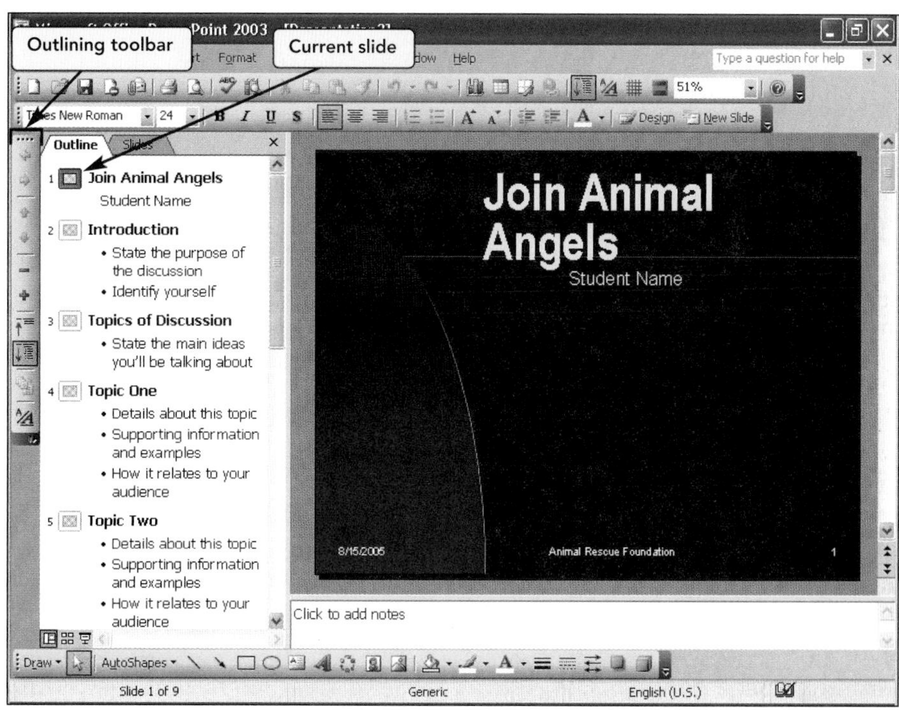


**Figure 1.12**

Slide 1 is still the current slide. The first change you want to make is to select the owner name on the first slide and delete it.

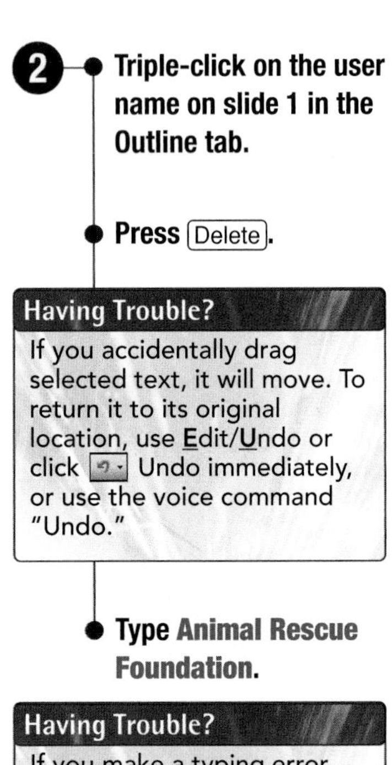

**2** • **Triple-click on the user name on slide 1 in the Outline tab.**

• **Press** Delete.

**Having Trouble?**

If you accidentally drag selected text, it will move. To return it to its original location, use Edit/Undo or click Undo immediately, or use the voice command "Undo."

• **Type Animal Rescue Foundation.**

**Having Trouble?**

If you make a typing error, press Backspace to delete the characters to the error and retype the entry.

*Your screen should be similar to Figure 1.13*

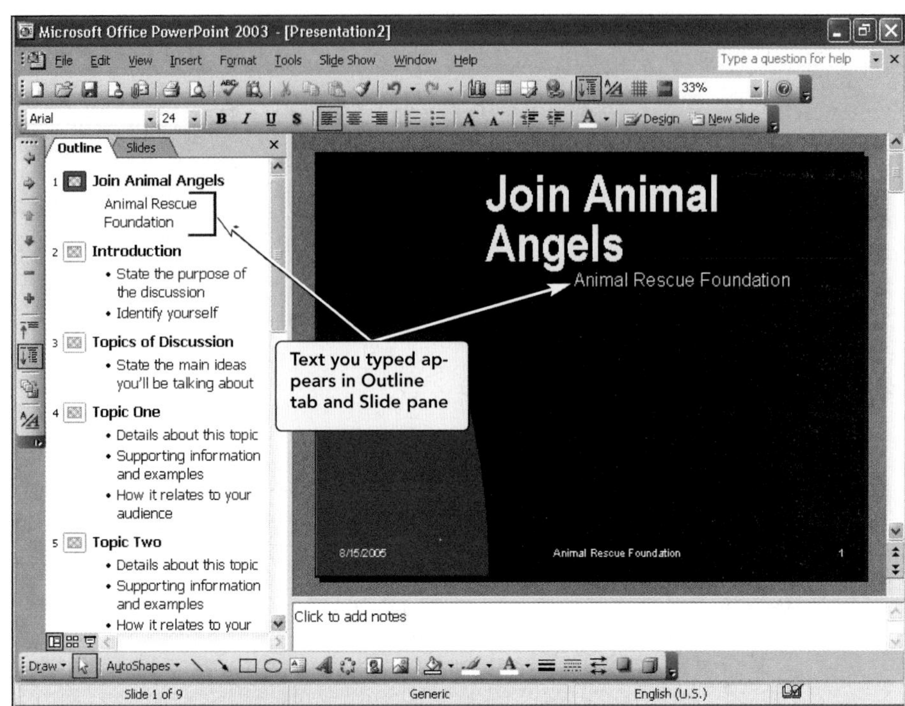


**Figure 1.13**

The selected text is removed and the new text is entered in the Outline tab as well as in the slide displayed in the slide pane. As you make changes in the Outline tab, the slide pane updates immediately.

**Additional Information**

If you click the slide icon to the right of the slide number, all text on the slide is selected.

The next change you want to make is in the Introduction slide. The sample text in this slide recommends that you enter an opening statement to explain the purpose of the discussion and to introduce yourself. You must replace the sample text next to the first bullet with the text for your slide. In the Outline tab, you can also select an entire paragraph and all subparagraphs by pointing to the left of the line and clicking when the mouse pointer is a ✥.

**3** Click on the slide 2 icon.

- Click to the left of the sample text "State the purpose of the discussion" in the Outline tab when the mouse pointer is a ✥.

- Type **volunter** (this word is intentionally misspelled).

- Press Spacebar.

*Your screen should be similar to Figure 1.14*

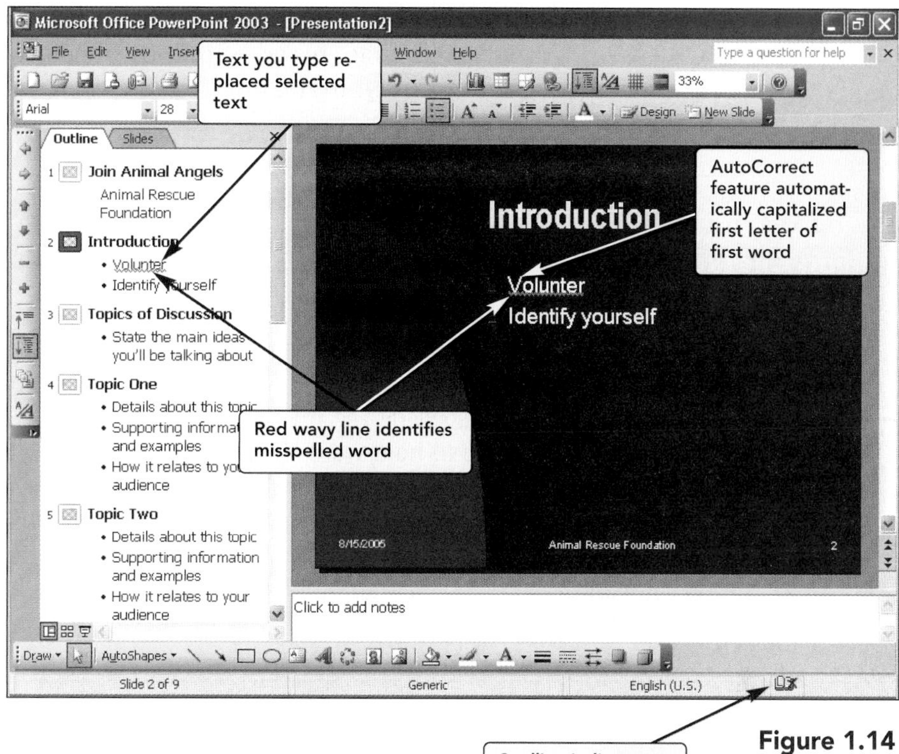


**Figure 1.14**

**Additional Information**

Bulleted items in a presentation are capitalized in sentence case format. Ending periods, however, are not included.

As soon as you pressed a key, the selected text was deleted and replaced by the new text you typed. Also, as you enter text, the program checks words for accuracy. First, PowerPoint capitalized the first letter of the word. This is part of the AutoCorrect feature of PowerPoint.

## Concept 4

### AutoCorrect

4 The AutoCorrect feature makes some basic assumptions about the text you are typing and, based on these assumptions, automatically corrects the entry. The AutoCorrect feature automatically inserts proper capitalization at the beginning of sentences and in the names of days of the week. It will also change to lowercase letters any words that were incorrectly capitalized due to the accidental use of the Caps Lock key. In addition, it also corrects many common typing and spelling errors automatically.

One way the program makes corrections automatically is by looking for certain types of errors. For example, if two capital letters appear at the beginning of a word, the second capital letter is changed to a lowercase letter. If a lowercase letter appears at the beginning of a sentence, the first letter of the first word is capitalized. If the name of a day begins with a lowercase letter, the first letter is capitalized.

Another way the program makes corrections is by checking all entries against a built-in list of words that are commonly spelled incorrectly or typed incorrectly. If it finds the entry on the list, the program automatically replaces the error with the correction. For example, the typing error "aboutthe" is automatically changed to "about the" because the error is on the AutoCorrect list. You can also add words to the AutoCorrect list that you want to be corrected automatically. Any such words are added to the list on the computer you are using and will be available to anyone who uses the machine after you.

Next, PowerPoint identified the word as misspelled by underlining it with a wavy red line. In addition, the spelling indicator in the status bar appears as [icon], indicating that the automatic spelling check feature has found a spelling error.

## Concept 5

### Spelling Checker

5 The **spelling checker** locates all misspelled words, duplicate words, and capitalization irregularities as you create and edit a presentation, and proposes possible corrections. This feature works by comparing each word to a dictionary of words. If the word does not appear in the main dictionary or in a custom dictionary, it is identified as misspelled. The **main dictionary** is supplied with the program; a **custom dictionary** is one you can create to hold words you commonly use, such as proper names and technical terms, but that are not included in the main dictionary.

If the word does not appear in either dictionary, the program identifies it as misspelled by displaying a red wavy line below the word. You can then correct the misspelled word by editing it. Alternatively, you can display a list of suggested spelling corrections for that word and select the correct spelling from the list to replace the misspelled word in the presentation.

**Additional Information**

The spelling checker works just as it does in the other Microsoft Office 2003 applications.

Because you have discovered this error very soon after typing it, and you know that the correct spelling of this word is "volunteer," you can quickly correct it by using the Backspace key. The Backspace key removes the character or space to the left of the insertion point; therefore, it is particularly useful when you are moving from right to left (backward) along a line of text. You will correct this word and continue entering the text for this slide.

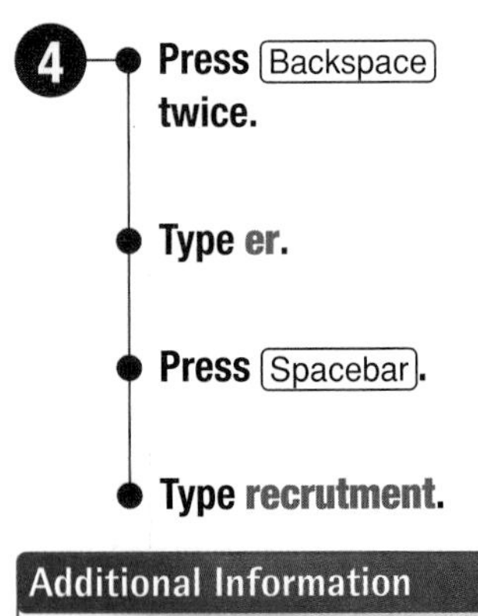

**4**
- **Press Backspace twice.**
- **Type er.**
- **Press Spacebar.**
- **Type recrutment.**

**Additional Information**

As you type, an animated pen appears over the spelling indicator while the spelling checker is in the process of checking for errors. When no spelling errors are located, the indicator appears as [icon].

*Your screen should be similar to Figure 1.15*

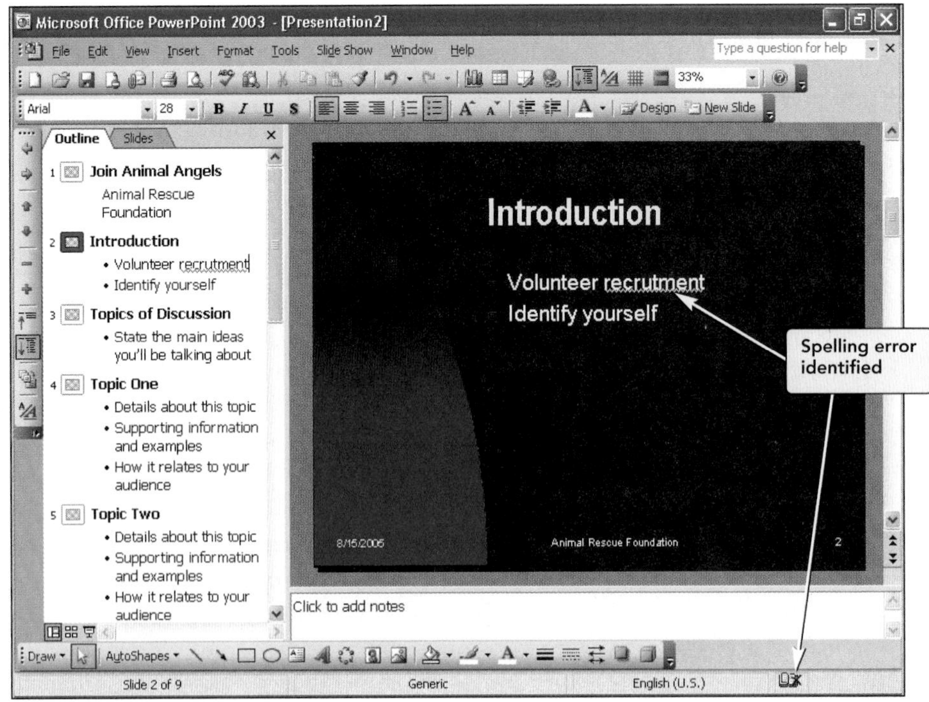


Figure 1.15

Again, the program has identified a word as misspelled. Another way to quickly correct a misspelled word is to select the correct spelling from a list of suggested spelling corrections displayed on the shortcut menu.

**5** **Right-click on the misspelled word in the Outline tab to display the shortcut menu.**

*Your screen should be similar to Figure 1.16*

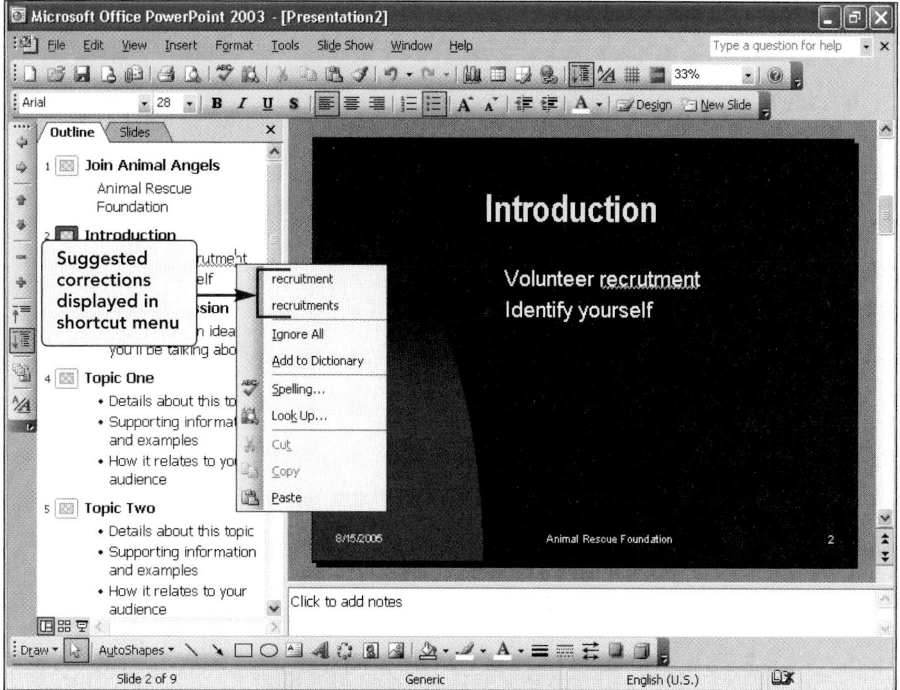


**Figure 1.16**

The shortcut menu displays two suggested correct spellings. The menu also includes several related menu options described below.

| Option | Effect |
|---|---|
| Ignore All | Instructs PowerPoint to ignore the misspelling of this word throughout the rest of this session. |
| Add to Dictionary | Adds the word to the custom dictionary list. When a word is added to the custom dictionary, PowerPoint will always accept that spelling as correct. |
| Spelling | Starts the spelling checker to check the entire presentation. |
| Look Up | Checks the spelling of text in another language. |

**Additional Information**

If only one suggested spelling correction is offered, the correction is automatically inserted.

Sometimes no suggested replacements are offered because PowerPoint cannot locate any words in its dictionary that are similar in spelling, or the suggestions offered are not correct. If either situation happens, you must edit the word manually. In this case, you will replace the word with the correct spelling and enter your name on this slide.

**6** Choose "recruitment."

Select "Identify yourself" in the Outline tab.

Type **your name.**

*Your screen should be similar to Figure 1.17*

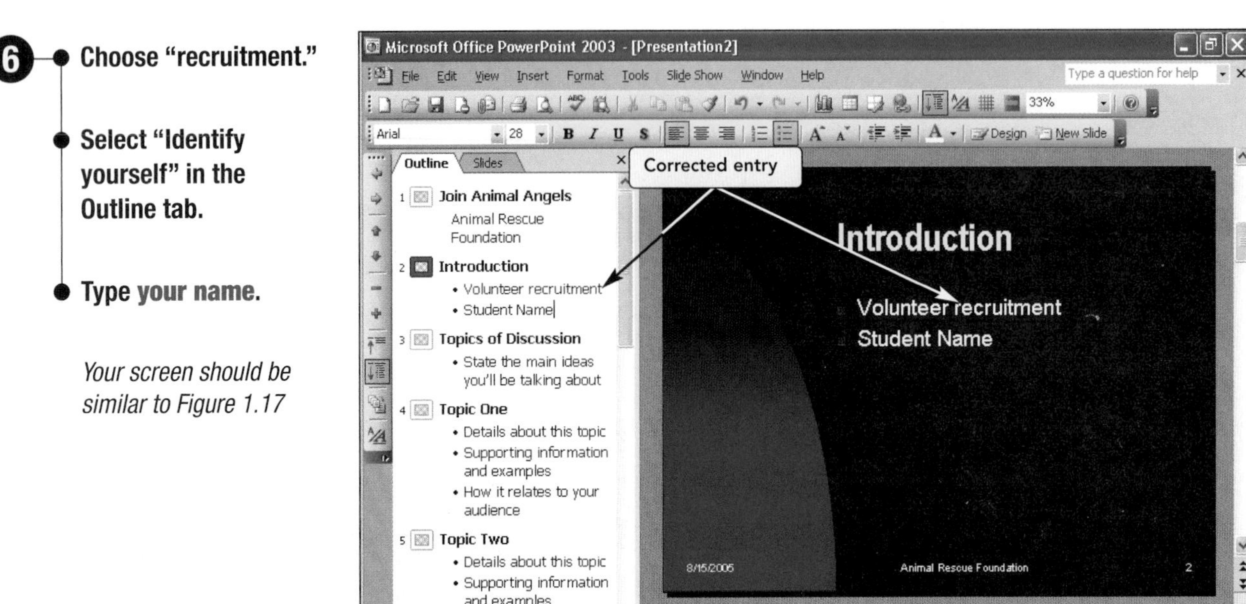


Figure 1.17

You are now ready to update the third slide in your presentation by entering the three main topics you will be discussing. You want to enter each topic on a separate bulleted line. The first bullet is already displayed and contains sample text that you will replace. To add additional lines and bullets, you simply press ↵Enter.

**7** In slide 3 of the Outline tab, select "State the main ideas you'll be talking about."

Type **Why are pets abandoned?.**

Press ↵Enter.

Type **How can you help?.**

Press ↵Enter.

Type **How does the Foundation help?** (do not press ↵Enter).

**Having Trouble?**

If you accidentally insert an extra bullet and blank line, press Backspace twice to remove them.

*Your screen should be similar to Figure 1.18*

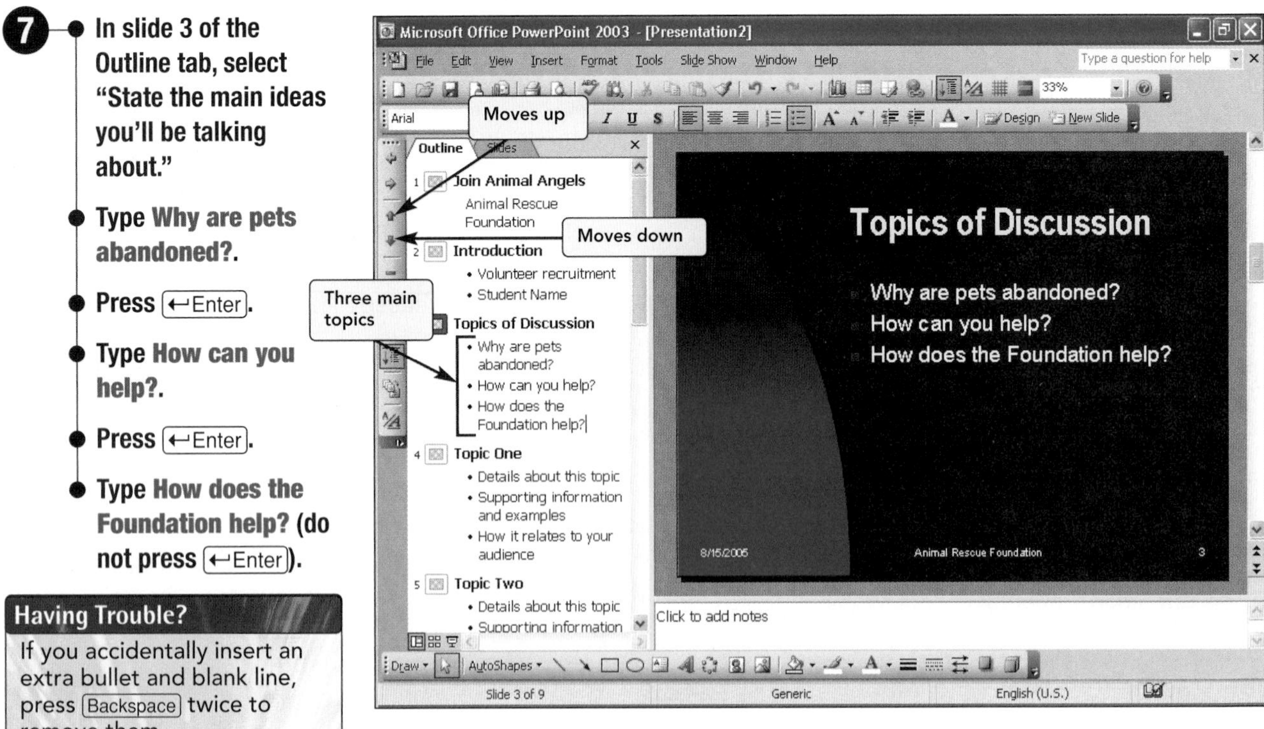


Figure 1.18

You realize that you entered the topics in the wrong order. You want the last item to be the second item in the list. A bulleted point can be moved easily by selecting it and dragging it to a new location, or by using the Move Up or Move Down buttons in the Outlining toolbar. When using the buttons, the insertion point must be on the bulleted item you want to move. You will move the bulleted item on the current line up one line.

**8** **Click Move Up.**

*Your screen should be similar to Figure 1.19*

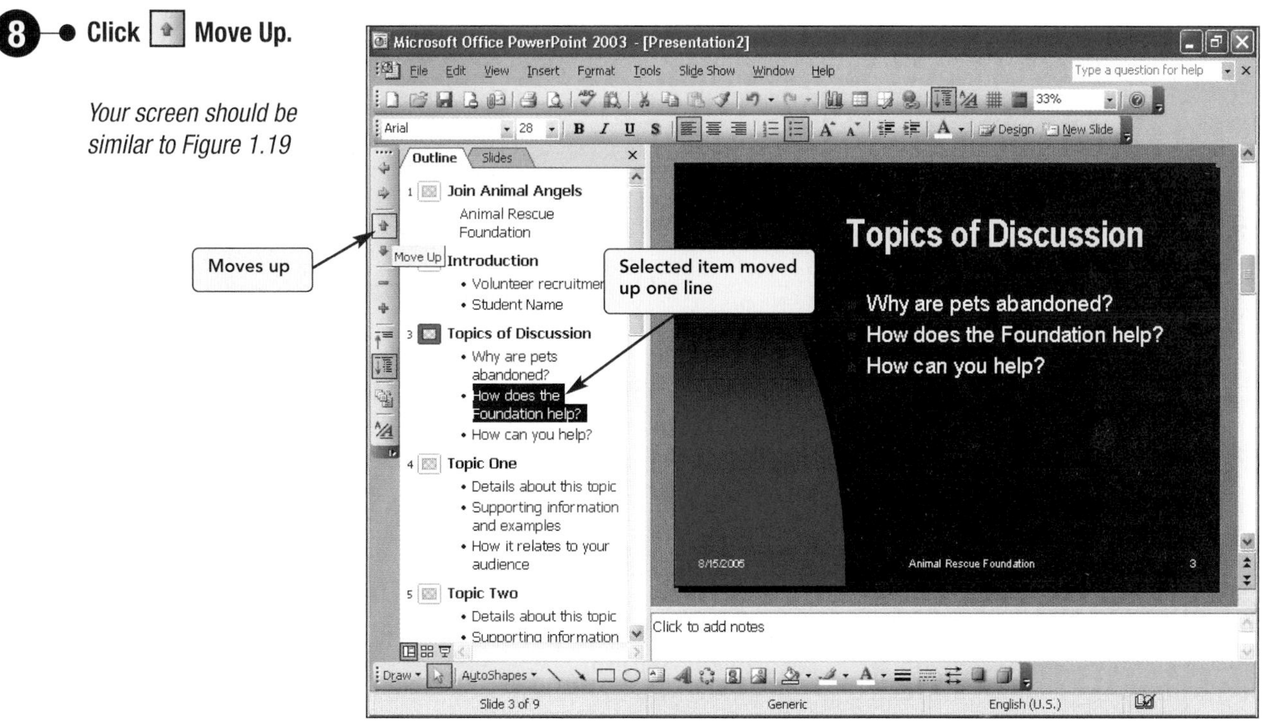


Figure 1.19

## Editing in the Slide Pane

Next, you want to update the content of the fourth slide. The fourth slide contains the title "Topic One" and a list of three bulleted items. The title and the bulleted list are two separate elements or placeholders on the slide. **Placeholders** are boxes that are designed to contain specific types of items or **objects** such as the slide title text, bulleted item text, charts, tables, and pictures. Each slide can have several different types of placeholders. To indicate which placeholder to work with, you must first select it. You will change the sample text in the title placeholder first in the slide pane.

**1** • **Click on slide 4 in the Outline tab to display it in the slide pane.**

• **Click anywhere on the slide title text in the slide pane.**

*Your screen should be similar to Figure 1.20*

Title placeholder

Insertion point

Selection rectangle with hatched border

Figure 1.20

**Additional Information**

You can also enter and edit text in Dictation mode using the Speech Recognition feature.

**Additional Information**

A dotted border around a selected object indicates that you can format the box itself. Clicking the hatch-marked border changes it to a dotted border.

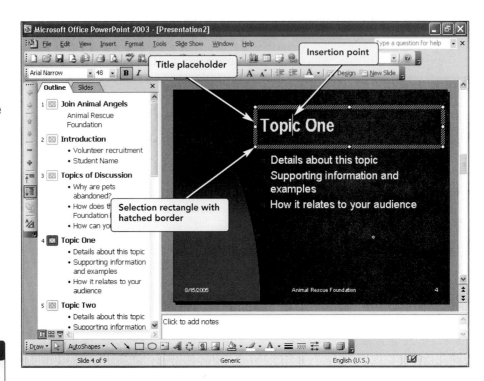

The title placeholder is now a selected object and is surrounded by a **selection rectangle**. The hatch-marked border of the selection rectangle indicates that you can enter, delete, select, and format the text inside the placeholder. An insertion point is displayed to show your location in the text and to allow you to select and edit the text. The mouse pointer appears as an I-beam to be used to position the insertion point. You will enter the new title for this slide.

**2** • **Select the title text.**

**Having Trouble?**

Drag to select a portion of the text, double-click to select a word, or triple-click to select a line.

• **Type Why Are Pets Abandoned?.**

*Your screen should be similar to Figure 1.21*

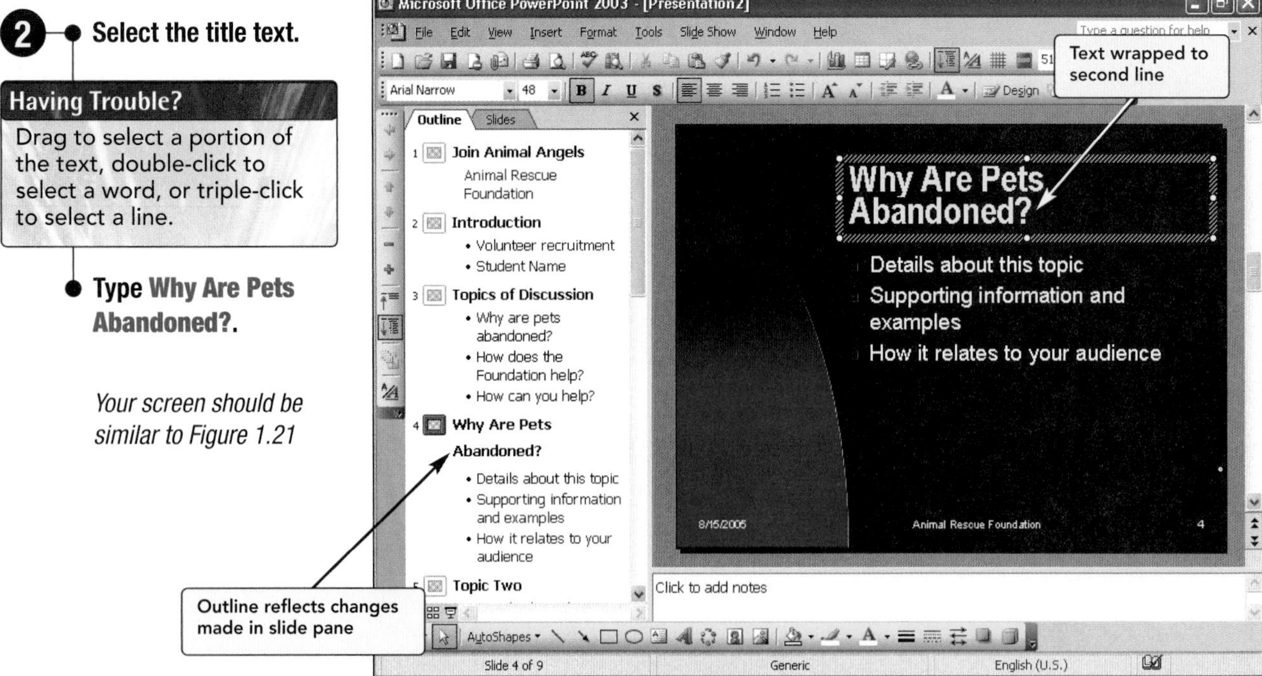


Figure 1.21

Notice that the text automatically wrapped to a second line when the length exceeded the width of the box. The Outline tab reflects the changes as they are made in the slide pane. Next, you need to replace the sample text in the bulleted list.

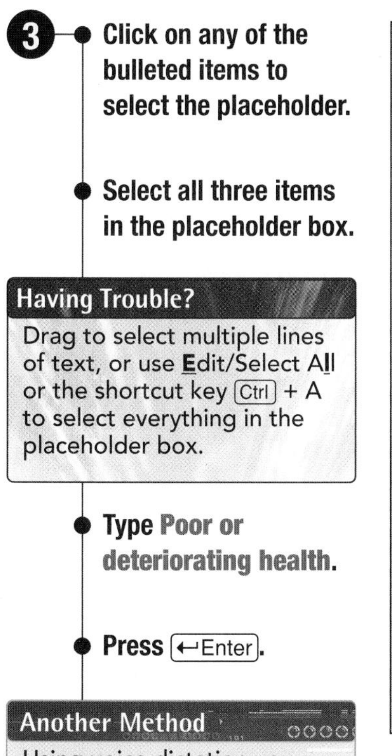

**3**

- **Click on any of the bulleted items to select the placeholder.**
- **Select all three items in the placeholder box.**

**Having Trouble?**

Drag to select multiple lines of text, or use Edit/Select All or the shortcut key Ctrl + A to select everything in the placeholder box.

- **Type Poor or deteriorating health.**
- **Press ←Enter.**

**Another Method**

Using voice dictation you would say "Enter" to start a new line.

- **Enter the following text for the next three bullets:**

  **Maintenance expenses**

  **Change in lifestyle**

  **Behavioral problems**

*Your screen should be similar to Figure 1.22*

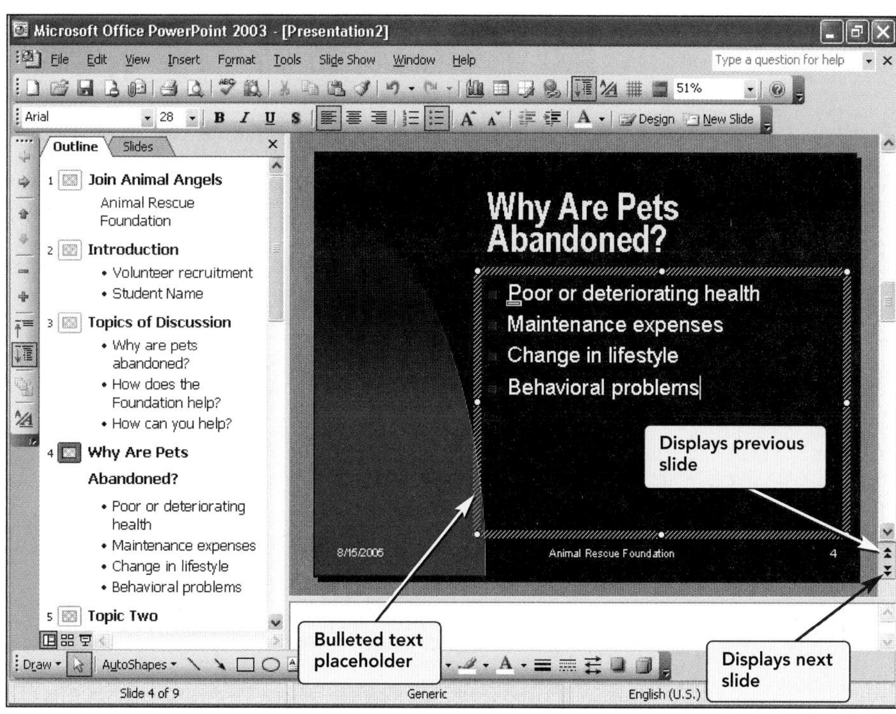


**Figure 1.22**

In the next slide you will enter information about how people can help the Animal Rescue Foundation. In addition to clicking on the slide in the Outline tab, the following features can be used to move to other slides in Normal view.

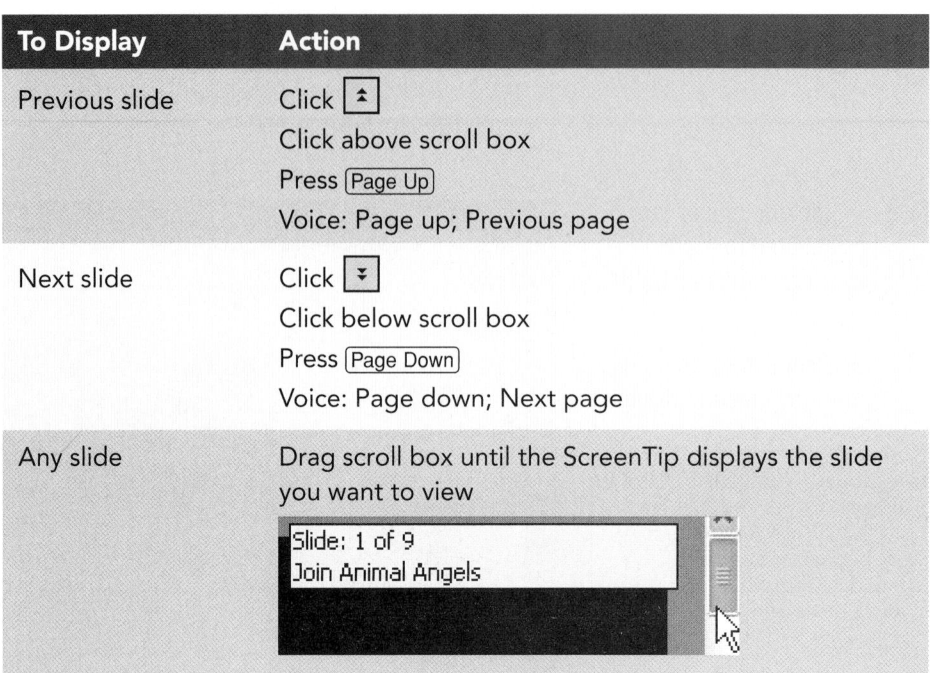

| To Display | Action |
|---|---|
| Previous slide | Click [▲]<br>Click above scroll box<br>Press Page Up<br>Voice: Page up; Previous page |
| Next slide | Click [▼]<br>Click below scroll box<br>Press Page Down<br>Voice: Page down; Next page |
| Any slide | Drag scroll box until the ScreenTip displays the slide you want to view |



You will enter a new slide title and text for the bulleted items.

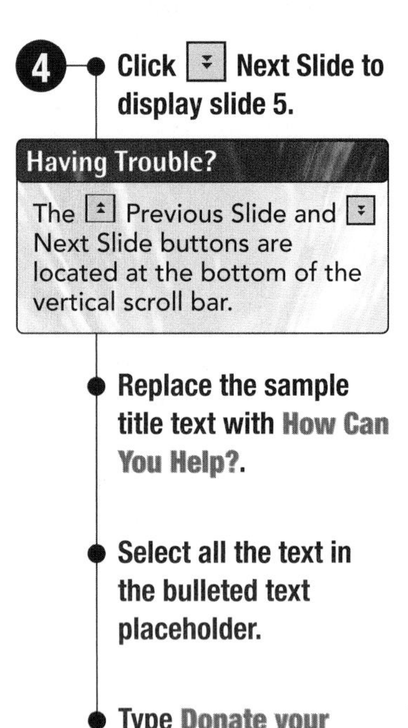

**4** • **Click [▼] Next Slide to display slide 5.**

**Having Trouble?**

The [▲] Previous Slide and [▼] Next Slide buttons are located at the bottom of the vertical scroll bar.

- **Replace the sample title text with How Can You Help?.**
- **Select all the text in the bulleted text placeholder.**
- **Type Donate your time and talent.**
- **Press ←Enter.**

*Your screen should be similar to Figure 1.23*

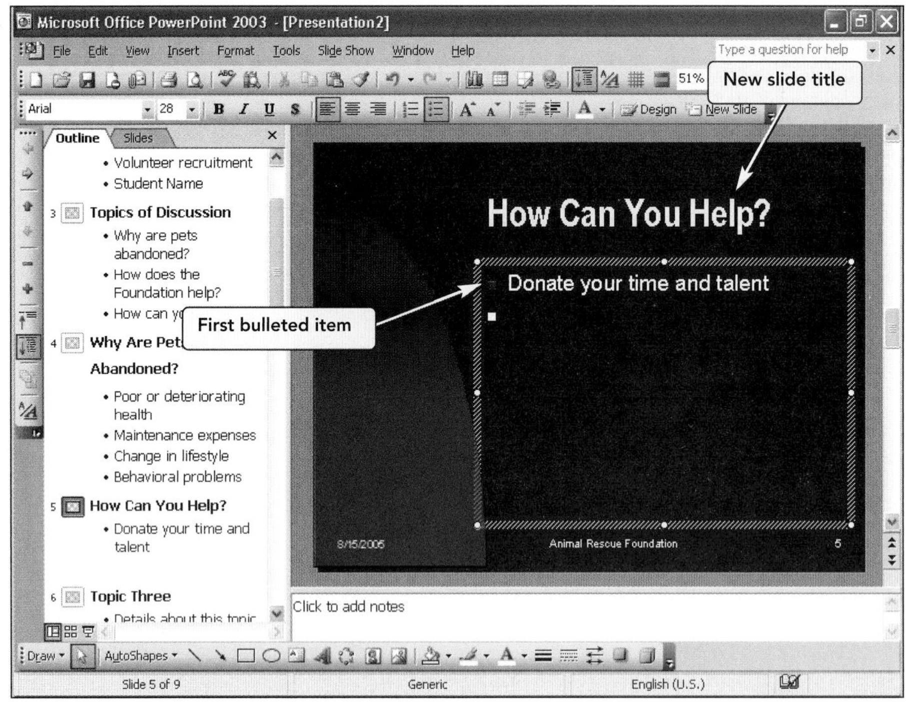



Figure 1.23

## Demoting and Promoting Bulleted Items

You want the next bulleted item to be indented below the first bulleted item. Indenting a bulleted point to the right **demotes** it, or makes it a lower or subordinate topic in the outline hierarchy.

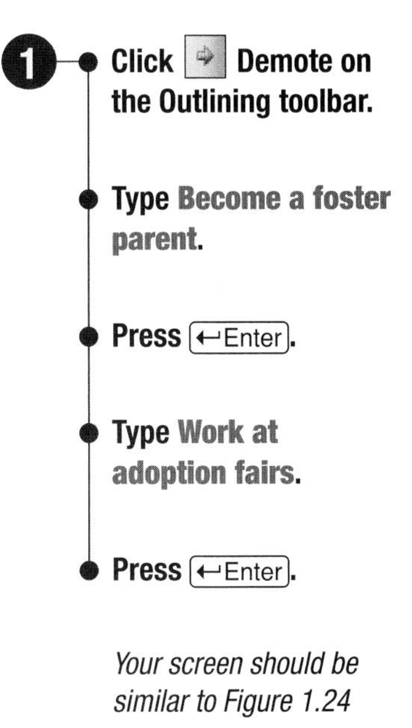

1
Click Demote on the Outlining toolbar.
Type Become a foster parent.
Press ←Enter.
Type Work at adoption fairs.
Press ←Enter.
Your screen should be similar to Figure 1.24


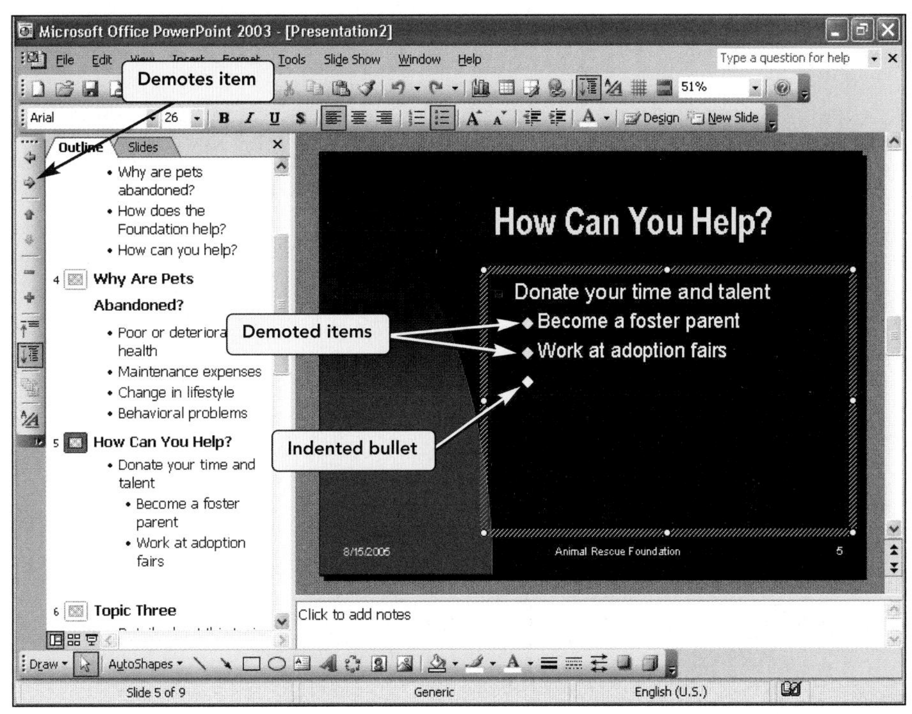


**Figure 1.24**

### Additional Information

You can also demote and promote bulleted items in the Outline tab using the same procedure. In addition, in the Outline tab you can drag a selected item to the left or right to promote or demote it.

The bullet style of the demoted lines is ◆. When you demote a bulleted point, PowerPoint continues to indent to the same level until you cancel the indent. Before entering the next item, you want to remove the indentation, or **promote** the line. Promoting a line moves it to the left, or up a level in the outline hierarchy.

**2** Click  Promote.

Type **Donate new or used items.**

Press ←Enter.

Enter the following two bulleted items:

**Crates and pads**

**Collars, leads, and other items**

*Your screen should be similar to Figure 1.25*

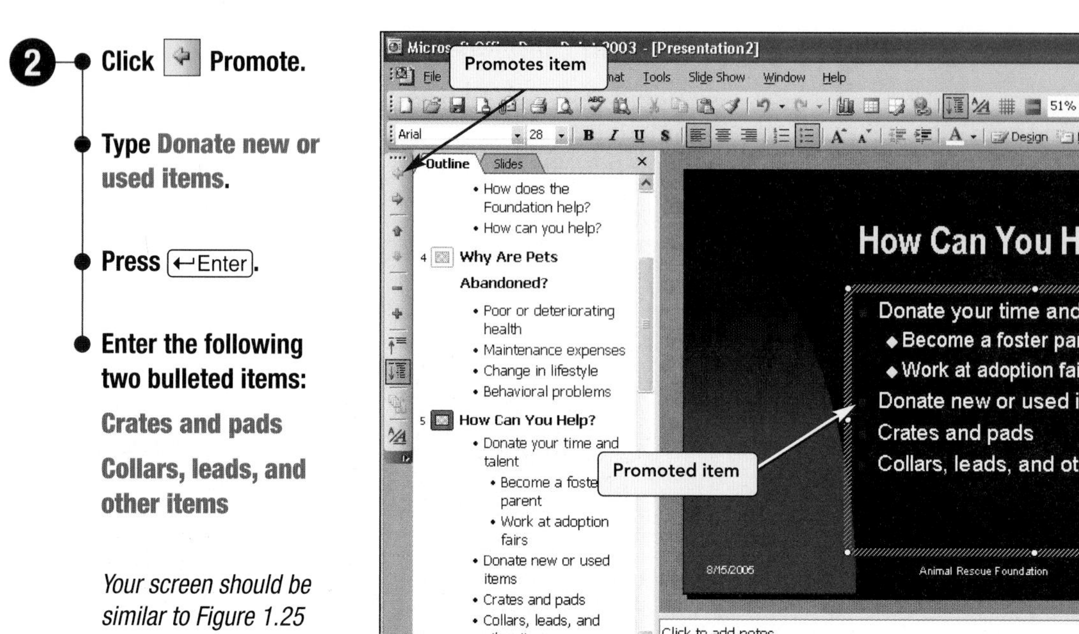


Figure 1.25

You can also promote or demote bulleted items after the text has been entered. The insertion point can be anywhere on the line to be promoted or demoted.

**3** Demote the items "Crates and pads" and "Collars, leads, and other items."

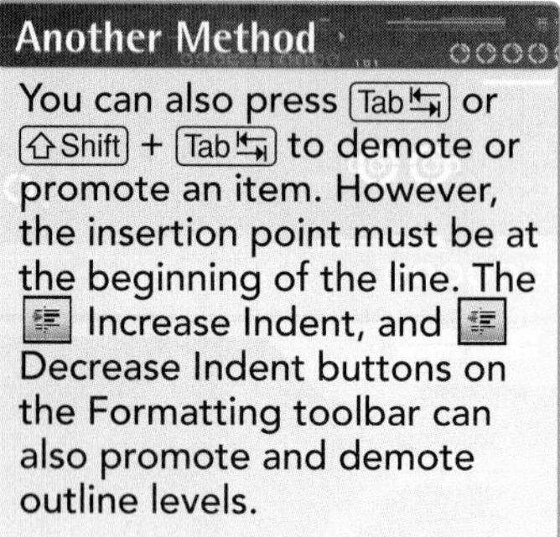

**Another Method**

You can also press Tab or ⇧Shift + Tab to demote or promote an item. However, the insertion point must be at the beginning of the line. The  Increase Indent, and  Decrease Indent buttons on the Formatting toolbar can also promote and demote outline levels.

*Your screen should be similar to Figure 1.26*

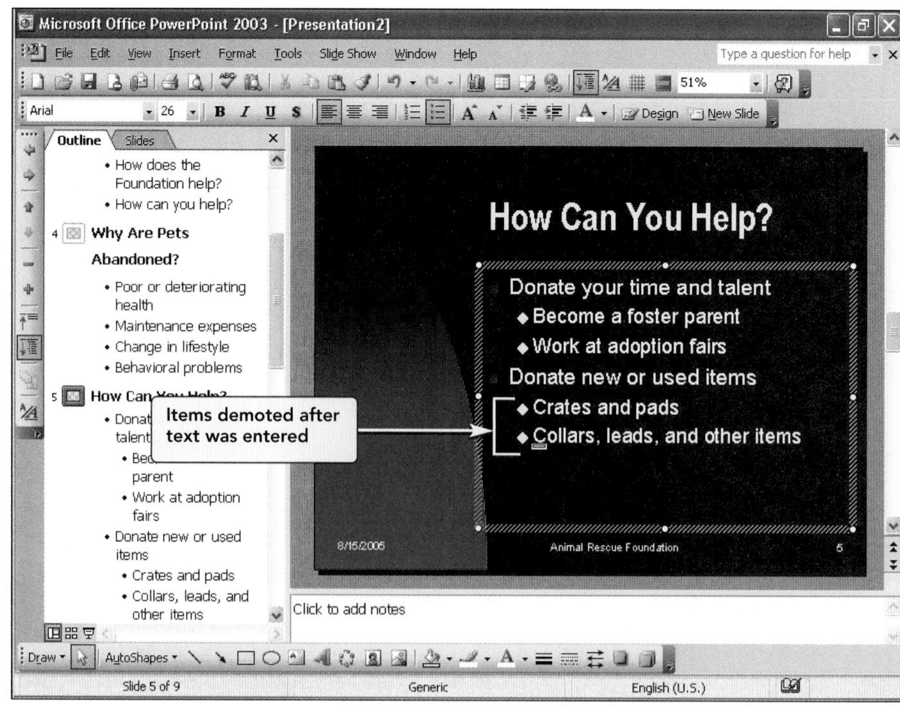


Figure 1.26

You still have three more bulleted items to add to this text placeholder. Notice, however, that the last item is near the bottom of the placeholder box. As you type the text the AutoFit feature will automatically reduce the line spacing and if needed the size of the text until the spillover text fits inside the placeholder.

4
- **Move to the end of "Collars, leads, and other items"**
- **Press ←Enter.**
- **Type Provide financial support**
- **Press ←Enter.**
- **Enter the following three bulleted items:**

  **Send a donation**

  **Sponsor a foster pet**

  **Sponsor an adoption**
- **Promote the "Provide Financial Support" bullet.**

*Your screen should be similar to Figure 1.27*

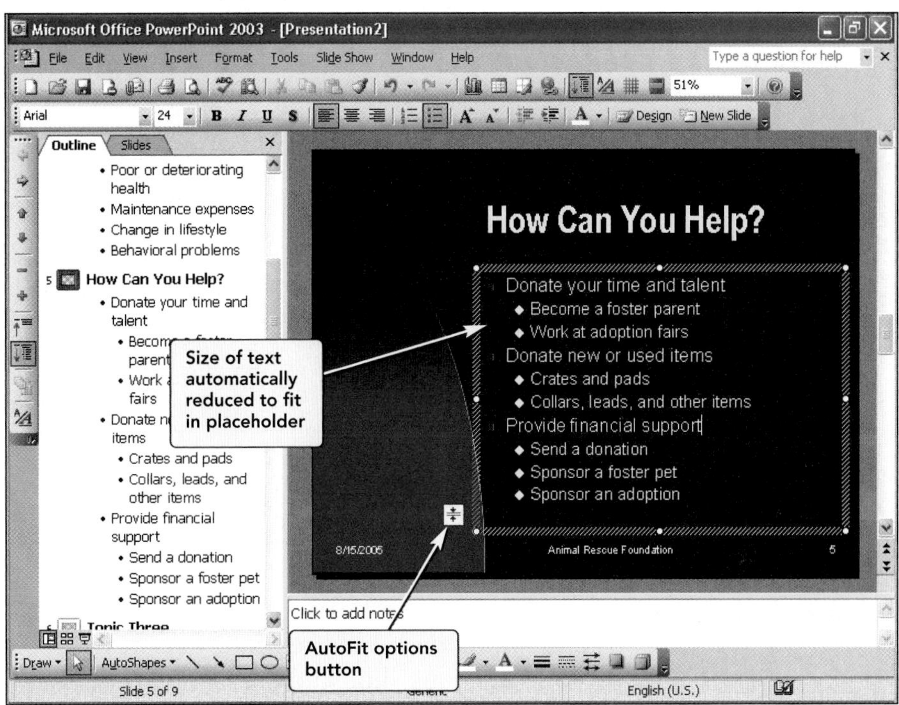


Figure 1.27

**Additional Information**

As you increase or decrease the size of the placeholder, the AutoFit feature will adjust the line spacing and text size appropriately.

As you continued entering more bulleted items, the text size reduced even more. Also notice that the AutoFit Options button appears next to the placeholder. It contains options that allow you to control the AutoFit feature and to handle the over-spilling text.

## Splitting Text Between Slides

Generally when creating slides, it is a good idea to limit the number of bulleted items on a slide to six. It is also recommended that the number of words on a line should not exceed five. In this case, because there are ten bulleted items on this slide, you want to split the slide content between two slides.

1. Click the AutoFit Options button.

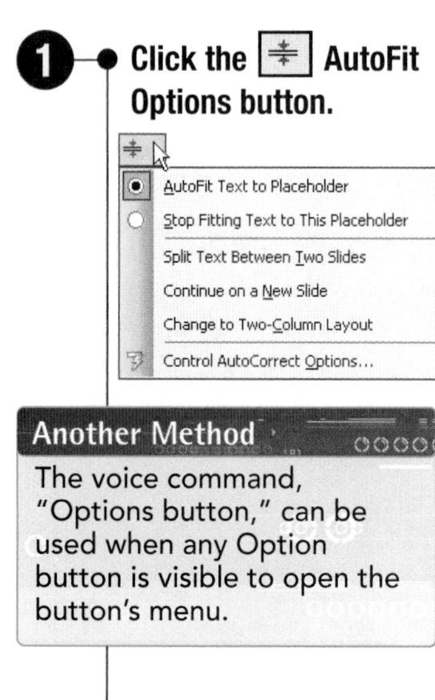


**Another Method**

The voice command, "Options button," can be used when any Option button is visible to open the button's menu.

- Choose Split Text Between Two Slides.

*Your screen should be similar to Figure 1.28*

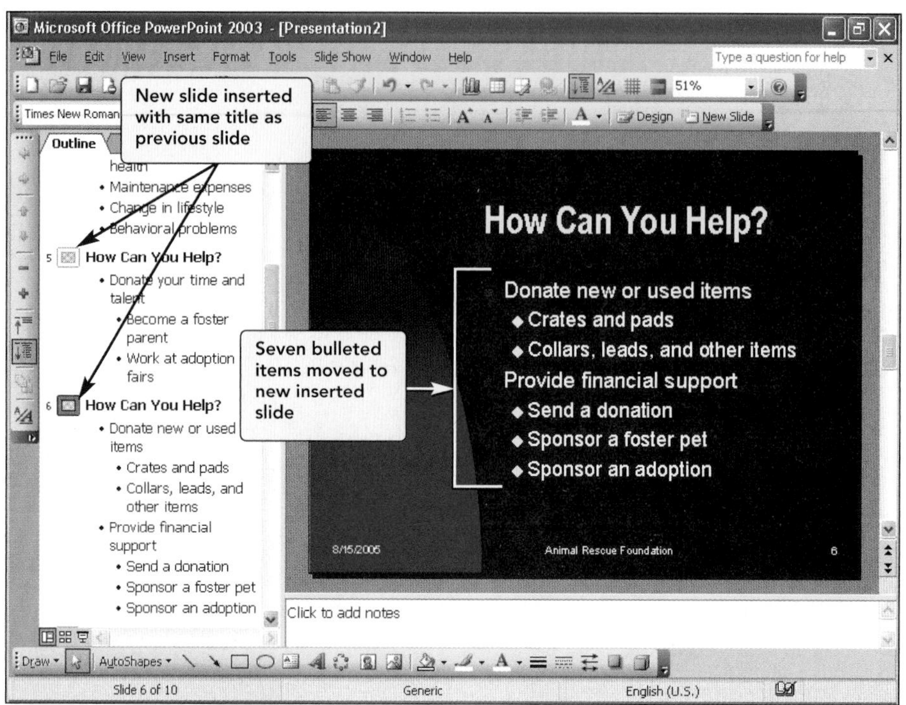


Figure 1.28

**Another Method**

You can split text into two slides in the Outline tab by positioning the insertion point at the end of a bulleted item and pressing ←Enter. Then promote it until a new slide icon and number appear. All text after the insertion point will become bulleted items on the new slide.

A new slide is inserted into the presentation containing the same title as the previous slide and the last two bulleted topic groups. Because the split occurs at a main topic, there are still seven bulleted items on the new slide. You will combine two items into one to reduce the number to six and change the title of the slide.

2. Click the title placeholder.

- Replace the title text with **More Ways to Help!**.
- Move to the end of the sixth bulleted item and press Delete.
- Edit the item to be "Sponsor a foster pet or adoption."

*Your screen should be similar to Figure 1.29*

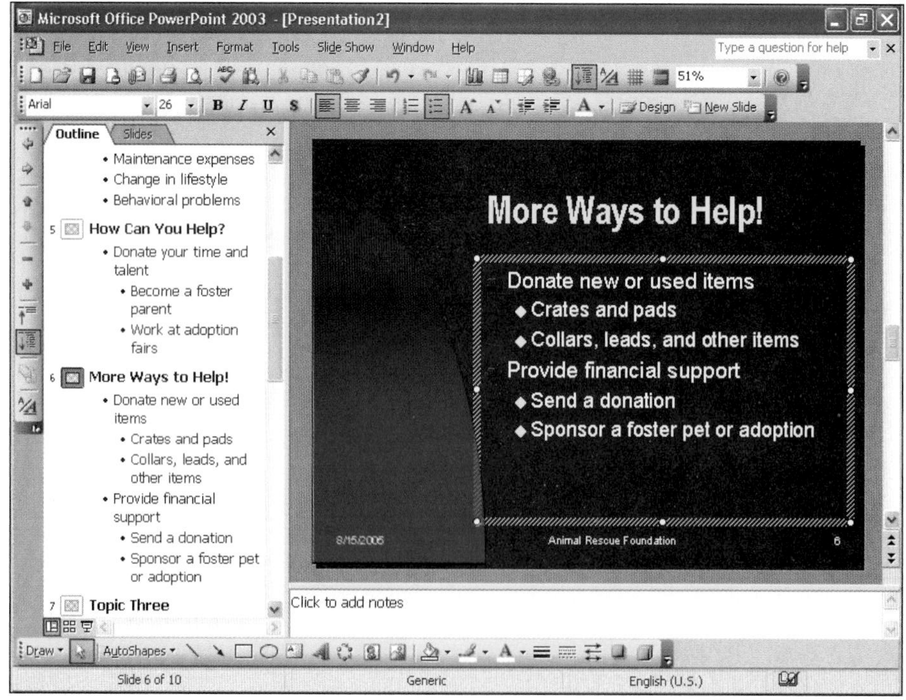


Figure 1.29

## Saving, Closing, and Opening a Presentation

You have just been notified about an important meeting that is to begin in a few minutes. Before leaving for the meeting, you want to save the presentation. As you enter and edit text to create a new presentation, the changes you make are immediately displayed onscreen and are stored in your computer's memory. However, they are not permanently stored until you save your work to a file on a disk. After a presentation is saved as a file, it can be closed and opened again at a later time to be edited further.

As a backup against the accidental loss of work caused by a power failure or other mishap, Office 2003 includes an AutoRecover feature. When this feature is on, as you work you may see a pulsing disk icon briefly appear in the status bar. This icon indicates that the program is saving your work to a temporary recovery file. The time interval between automatic saving can be set to any period you specify; the default is every 10 minutes. When you start up again, the recovery file containing all changes you made up to the last time it was saved by AutoRecover is opened automatically. You then need to save the recovery file. If you do not save it, it is deleted when closed. While AutoRecover is a great feature for recovering lost work, it should not be used in place of regularly saving your work.

### Saving the Presentation

You will save the work you have done so far on the presentation. The Save or Save As commands on the File menu are used to save files. The Save command or the Save button will save the active file using the same file name by replacing the contents of the existing file with the document as it appears on your screen. The Save As command allows you to save a file with a new file name and/or to a new location. This action leaves the original file unchanged. When a presentation is saved for the first time, either command can be used. It is especially important to save a new presentation very soon after you create it because the AutoRecover feature does not work until a file name has been specified.

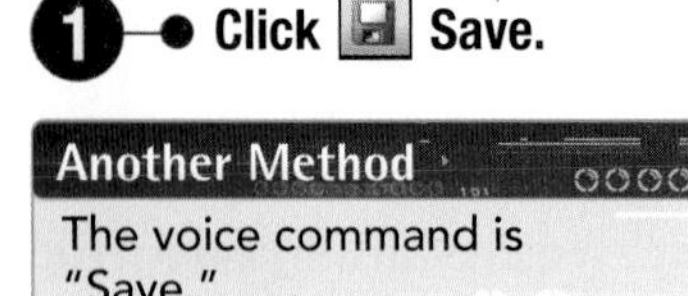

**1** Click Save.

**Another Method**

The voice command is "Save."

*Your screen should be similar to Figure 1.30*

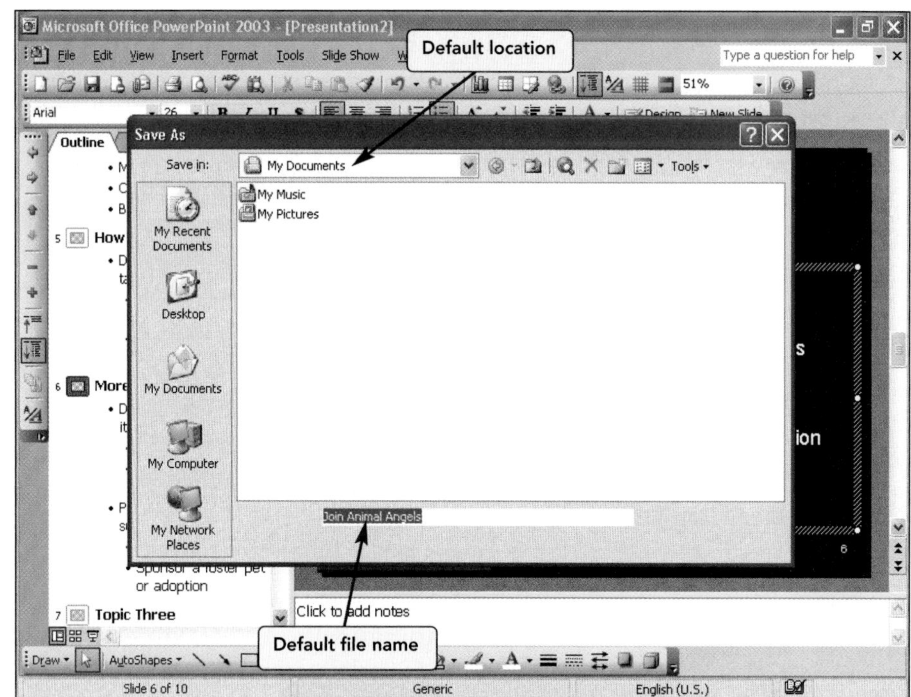


**Figure 1.30**

**Additional Information**

Windows documents can have up to 256 characters in the file name. Names can contain letters, numbers, and spaces; the symbols /,\,?,:,*,", <, > cannot be used.

The Save As dialog box is displayed in which you specify the location to save the file and the file name. The Save In list box displays the default location where files are stored. The File Name text box displays the title from the first slide as the default file name. You will change the location to the location where you save your files and the file name. Notice that the default name is highlighted, indicating that it is selected and will be replaced as you type the new name.

**Type Volunteer.**

**Additional Information**

The file name can be entered in either uppercase or lowercase letters and will appear exactly as you type it.

- **Open the Save In list box.**

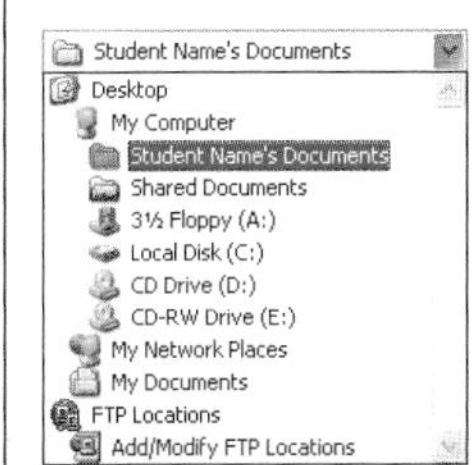


**Having Trouble?**

Click the text box arrow to open the drop-down list.

- **Select the location where you will save your files from the Save In drop-down list.**

**Having Trouble?**

If you are saving to a floppy disk and an error message is displayed, check that your disk is properly inserted in the drive and click .

*Your screen should be similar to Figure 1.31*

**Having Trouble?**

If your dialog box does not display file extensions, your Windows program has this option deactivated.

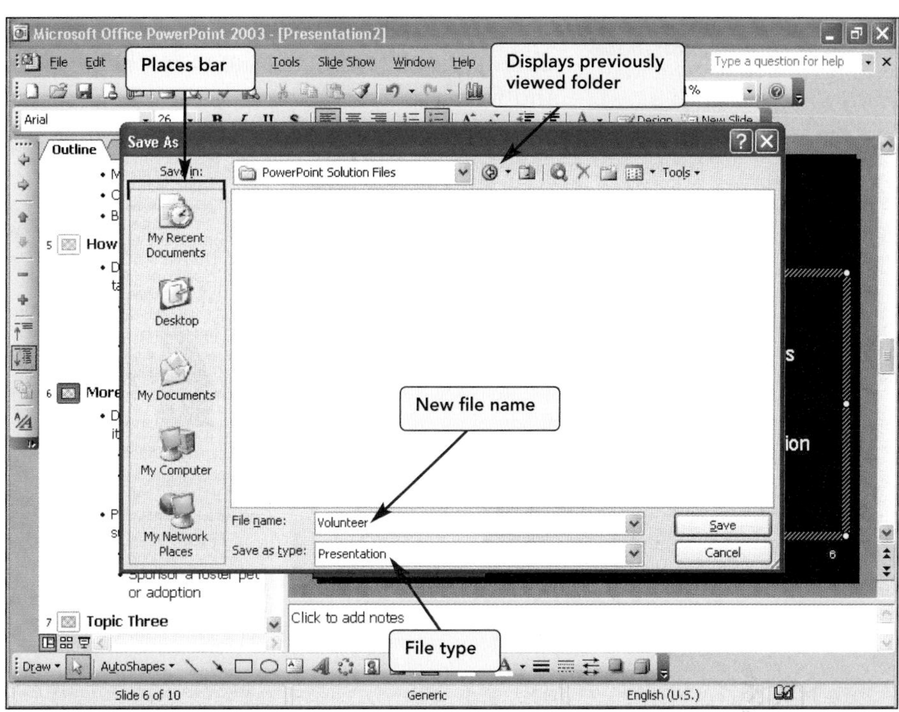


**Figure 1.31**

The large list box displays the names of any PowerPoint files (if any) stored in that location. Only PowerPoint presentation files are listed, because the selected file type in the Save As Type list box is Presentation. Presentation files have a default file extension of .ppt.

**Additional Information**

If your system uses Windows NT, My Network Places is Network Neighborhood.

You can also select the save location from the Places bar along the left side of the dialog box. The icons bring up a list of recently accessed files and folders, the contents of the My Documents and Favorites folders, the Windows desktop, and folders that reside on a network or Web through the My Network Places. Selecting a folder from one of these lists changes to that location. You can also click the button in the toolbar to return to folders that were previously opened during the current session.

**3** Click .

*Your screen should be similar to Figure 1.32*

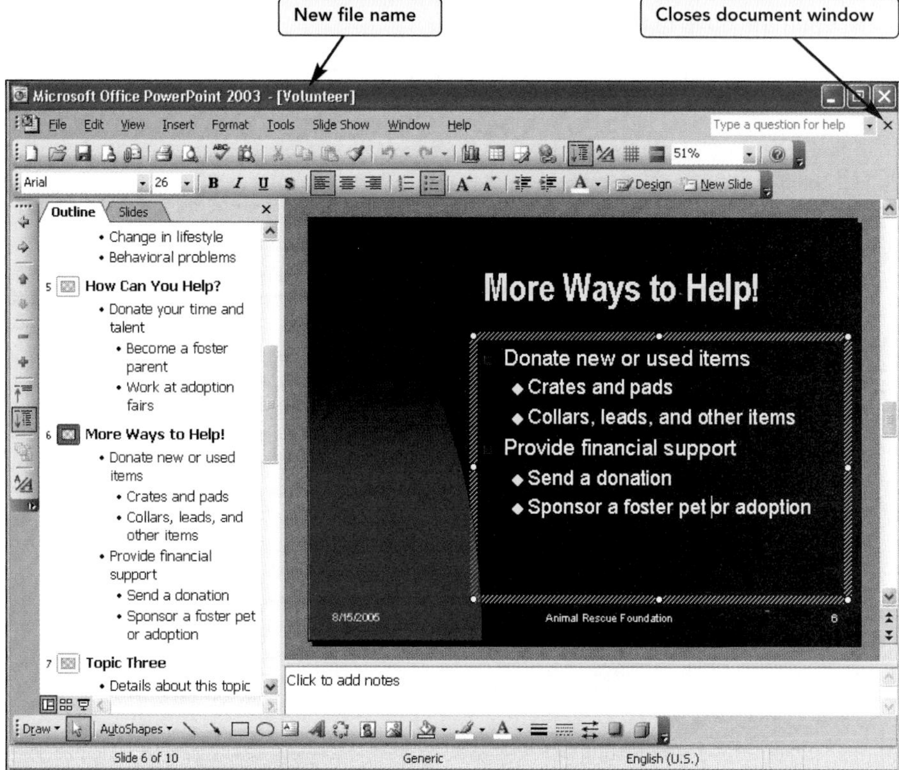


**Figure 1.32**

The new file name is displayed in the window title bar. The presentation is now saved in a new file named Volunteer. The view in use at the time the file is saved is also saved with the file.

## Closing a Presentation

You are now ready to close the file.

**1 Click Close Window (in the menu bar).**

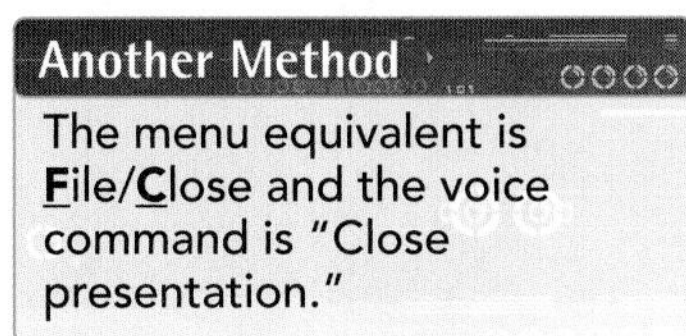



*Your screen should be similar to Figure 1.33*

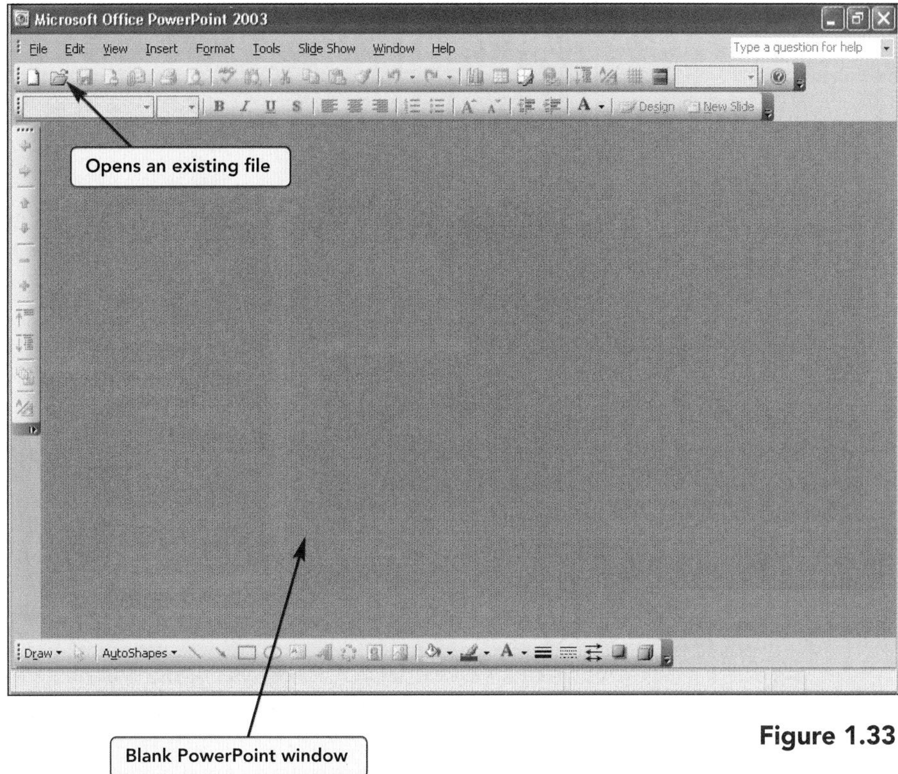



**Figure 1.33**

The presentation is closed, and a blank PowerPoint window is displayed. Always save your slide presentation before closing a file or leaving the PowerPoint program. As a safeguard against losing your work if you forget to save the presentation, PowerPoint will remind you to save any unsaved presentation before closing the file or exiting the program.

**Note:** If you are ending your lab session now, choose **F**ile/E**x**it to exit the program.

## Opening an Existing Presentation

After returning from your meeting, you hastily continued to enter the information for several more slides and saved the presentation using a new file name. You will open this file to see the information in the new slides and will continue working on the presentation.

**Click Open.**

**Another Method**

The menu equivalent is File/Open, the keyboard shortcut is Ctrl + O, and the voice command is "Open."

- **If necessary, select the location containing your data files from the Look In drop-down list box.**
- **Select** pp01_Volunteer1.

*Your screen should be similar to Figure 1.34*

**Having Trouble?**

The files in your file list and the previewed file may be different than shown in Figure 1.34. If a preview is not displayed, click Views and select Preview.

**Additional Information**

The File/New command or the button opens a blank new presentation. You can also quickly open a recently used file by selecting it from the list of file names displayed at the bottom of the File menu and at the bottom of the Getting Started task pane.

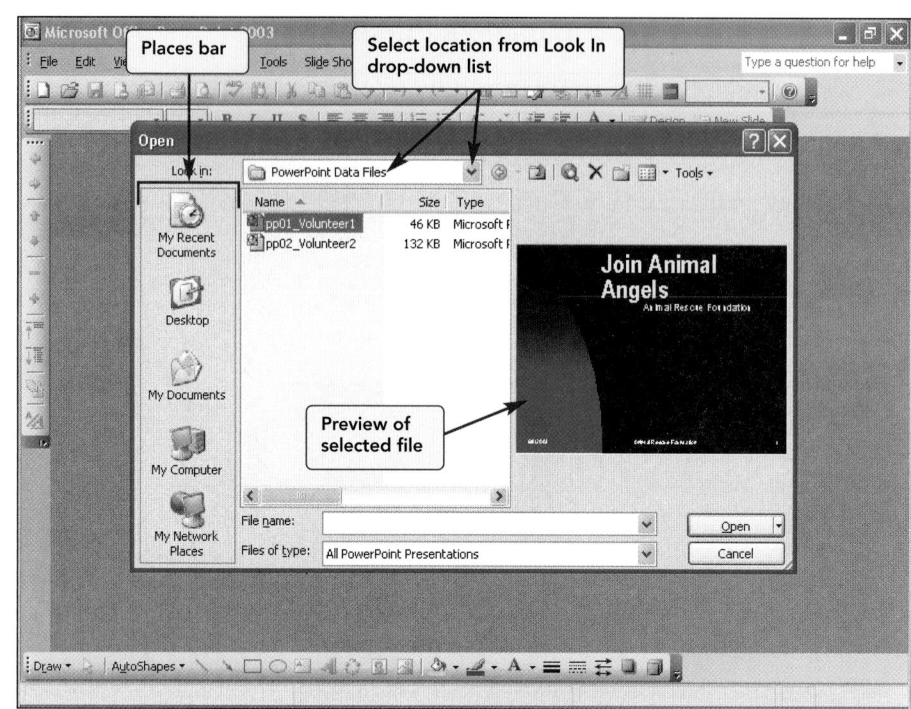


**Figure 1.34**

In the Open dialog box you specify the location and name of the file you want to open. The Look In drop-down list box displays the last specified location, in this case the location where you saved the Volunteer presentation. The large list box displays the names of PowerPoint presentation files only, as specified by the setting in the Files of Type box. As in the Save As dialog box, the Places bar can be used to quickly access recently used files. A preview of the selected file is displayed in the right side of the dialog box.

You will open the selected file next.

**2** Click [Open].

**Another Method**

You could also double-click the file name to both select it and choose [Open].

- If necessary, open the Outline tab.
- Edit slide 2 in the slide pane to display your name.
- Scroll the Outline pane to see the additional content that has been added to the presentation.

*Your screen should be similar to Figure 1.35*

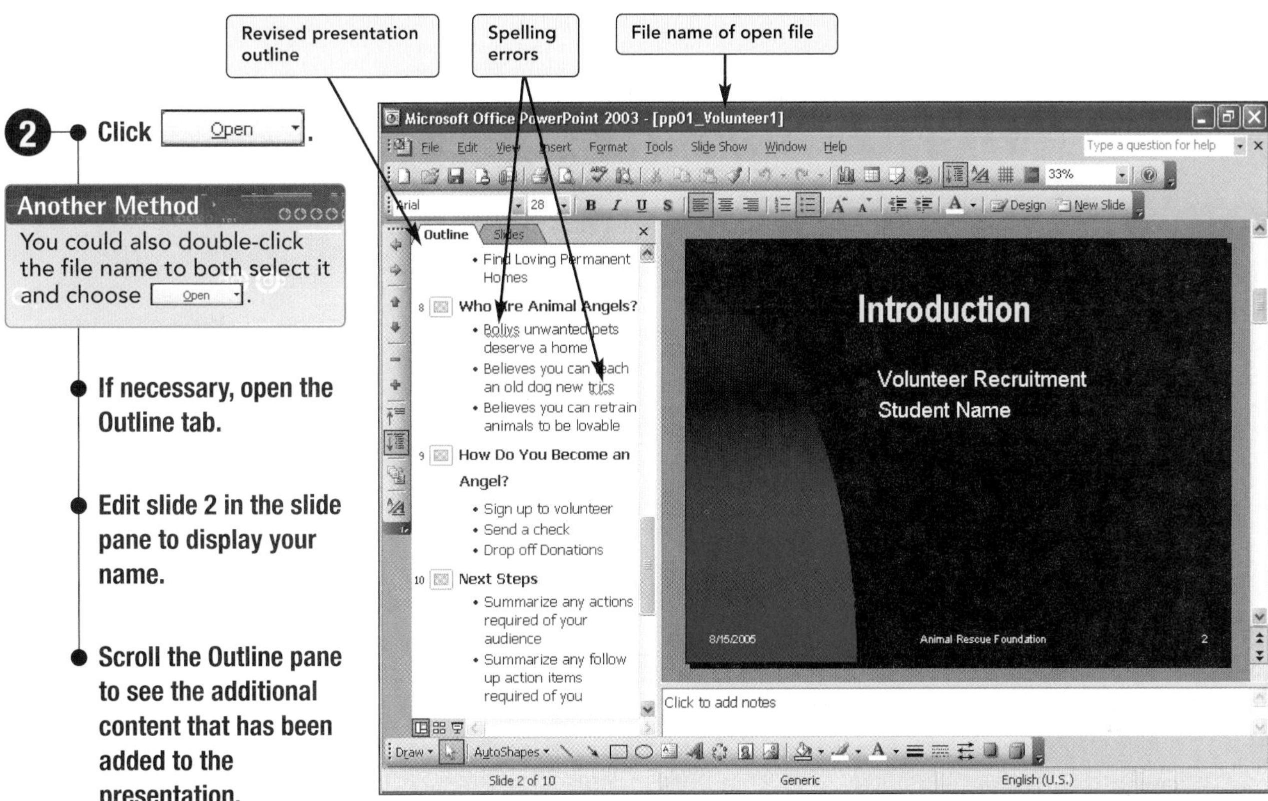


Figure 1.35

The presentation still contains ten slides, and all the sample text has been replaced with text for the volunteer recruitment presentation except for slide 10.

## Checking Spelling

As you entered the information on the additional slides, you left several typing errors uncorrected. To correct the misspelled words and grammatical errors, you can use the shortcut menu to correct each individual word or error, as you learned earlier. However, in many cases you may find it more efficient to wait until you are finished writing before you correct any spelling or grammatical errors. Rather than continually breaking your train of thought to correct errors as you type, you can check the spelling on all slides of the presentation at once.

**1 Click Speling.**

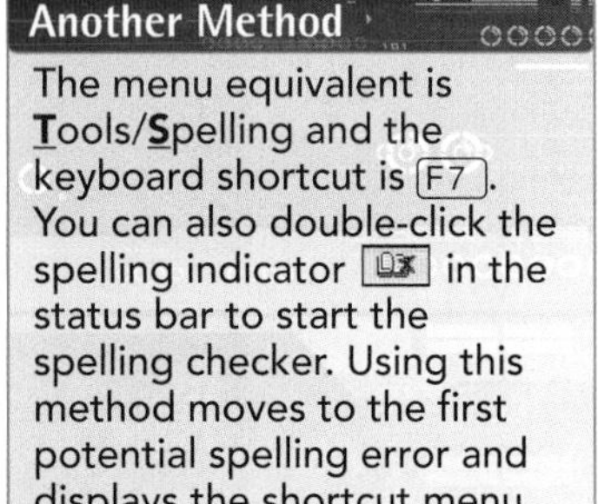

**Another Method**

The menu equivalent is Tools/Spelling and the keyboard shortcut is F7. You can also double-click the spelling indicator in the status bar to start the spelling checker. Using this method moves to the first potential spelling error and displays the shortcut menu.

*Your screen should be similar to Figure 1.36*

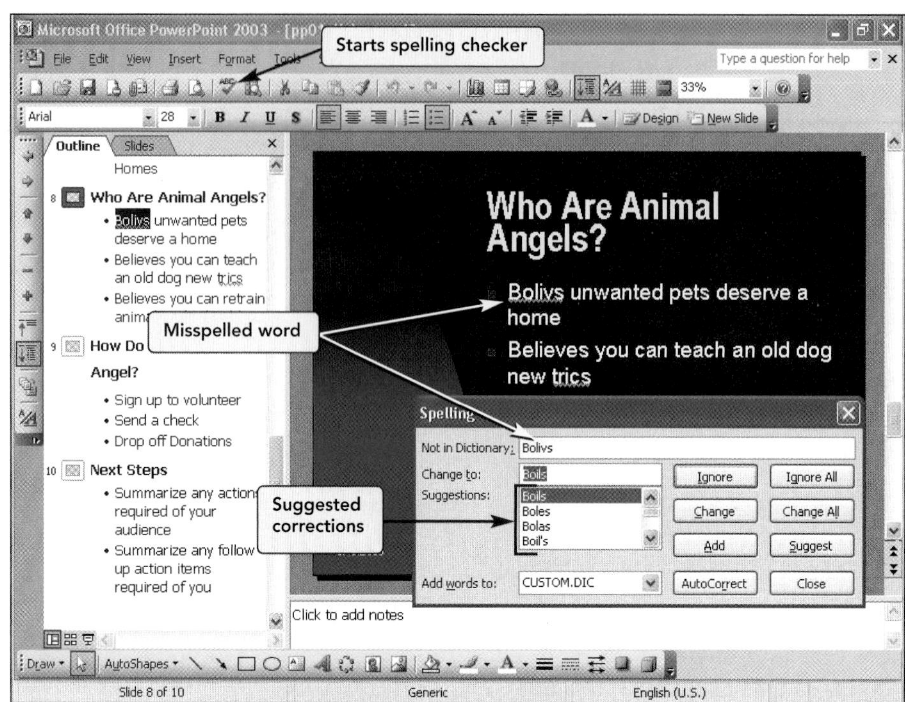


**Figure 1.36**

**Additional Information**

The spelling checker identifies many proper names and technical terms as misspelled. To stop this from occurring, use the Add Words To option to add those names to the custom dictionary.

The program jumps to slide 8, highlights the first located misspelled word, "Bolivs," in the Outline pane, and opens the Spelling dialog box. The Spelling dialog box displays the misspelled word in the Not in Dictionary text box. The Suggestions list box displays the words the spelling checker has located in the dictionary that most closely match the misspelled word. The first word is highlighted.

Although the list displays several additional suggestions, none of them is correct. Sometimes the spelling checker does not display any suggested replacements because it cannot locate any words in the dictionaries that are similar in spelling. If there are no suggestions, the Not in Dictionary text box simply displays the word that is highlighted in the text. When none of the suggestions is correct, you must edit the word yourself by typing the correction in the Change To text box.

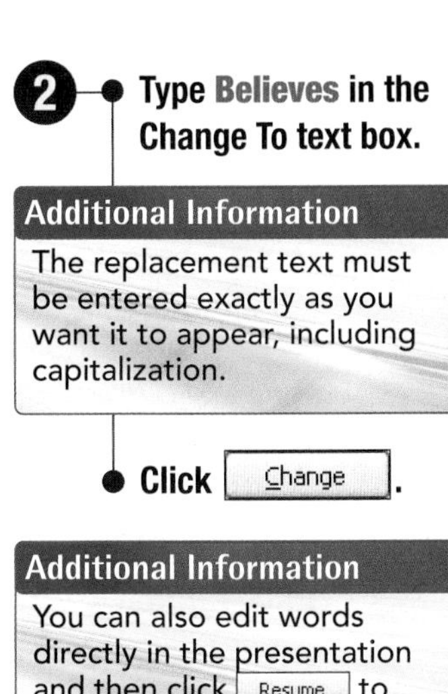

**2** **Type Believes in the Change To text box.**

**Additional Information**

The replacement text must be entered exactly as you want it to appear, including capitalization.

**Click** Change.

**Additional Information**

You can also edit words directly in the presentation and then click Resume to continue checking spelling.

*Your screen should be similar to Figure 1.37*

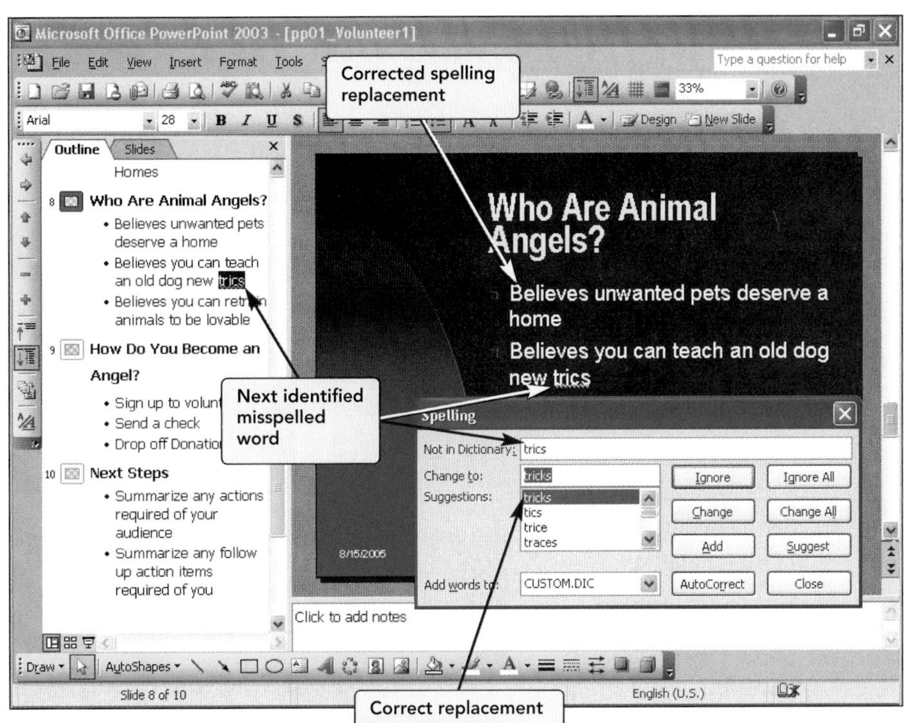


Figure 1.37

The corrected replacement is made in the slide. After the Spelling dialog box is open, the spelling checker continues to check the entire presentation for spelling errors. The next misspelled word, "trics," is identified. In this case, the suggested replacement is correct.

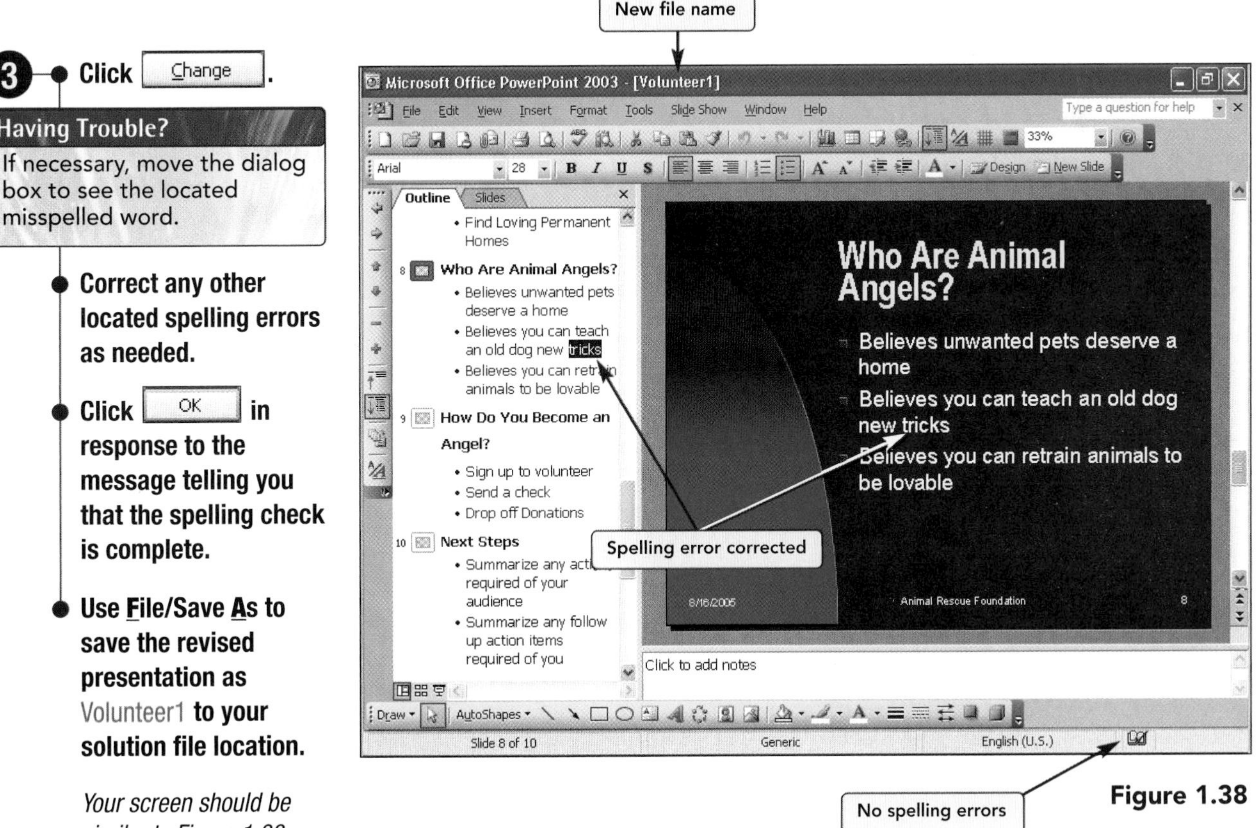

**3** **Click** Change.

**Having Trouble?**

If necessary, move the dialog box to see the located misspelled word.

- **Correct any other located spelling errors as needed.**
- **Click** OK **in response to the message telling you that the spelling check is complete.**
- **Use File/Save As to save the revised presentation as Volunteer1 to your solution file location.**

*Your screen should be similar to Figure 1.38*



Figure 1.38

## Working with Slides

To get a better overall picture of all slides in the presentation, you will switch to Slide Sorter view.

**1** **Click** [Slide Sorter icon] **Slide Sorter view.**

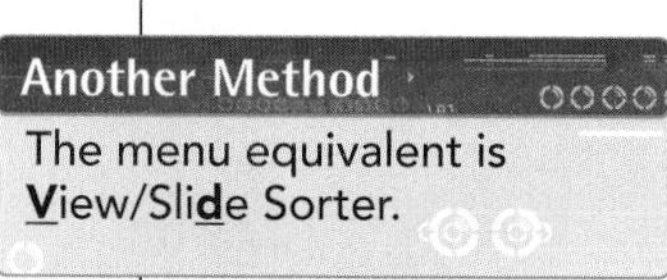

**Another Method**

The menu equivalent is View/Slide Sorter.

- **If necessary, move the Slide Sorter toolbar below the Standard toolbar.**

**Having Trouble?**

If the Slide Sorter toolbar is not displayed, select it from the toolbar shortcut menu and display it below the Standard toolbar.

*Your screen should be similar to Figure 1.39*

**Having Trouble?**

Do not be concerned if your screen displays a different number of slides per row. This is a function of your monitor settings.

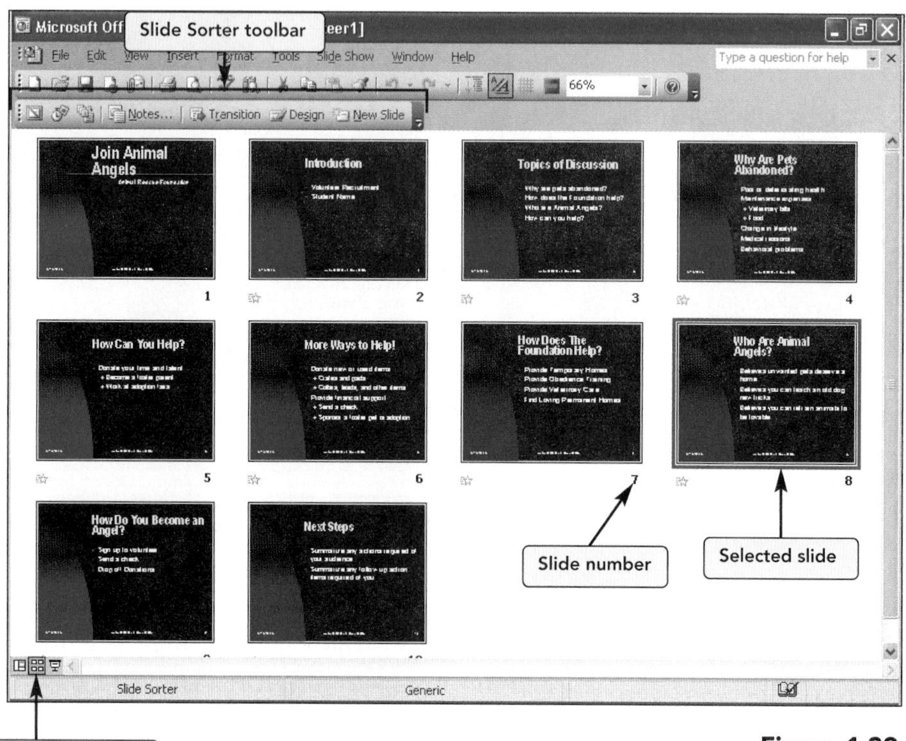


**Figure 1.39**

Viewing the slides side by side helps you see how your presentation flows. You can now see that slides 7 and 8 are out of order and do not follow the sequence of topics in the Topics for Discussion slide. You also see that you need to delete slide 10. As you continue to look at the slides, you also decide the second slide does not really add much to the presentation and you want to delete it.

This view also displays the Slide Sorter toolbar that is used to add enhancements to your presentation. The Formatting toolbar is not displayed because you cannot format slides in this view.

## Deleting Slides

First you will delete slide 10 and then slide 2.

**1** **Select slide 10.**

**Having Trouble?**

Clicking on a slide selects it.

- **Press** Delete**.**
- **In the same manner, select and delete slide 2.**

**Another Method**

The menu equivalent is Edit/Delete Slide.

*Your screen should be similar to Figure 1.40*

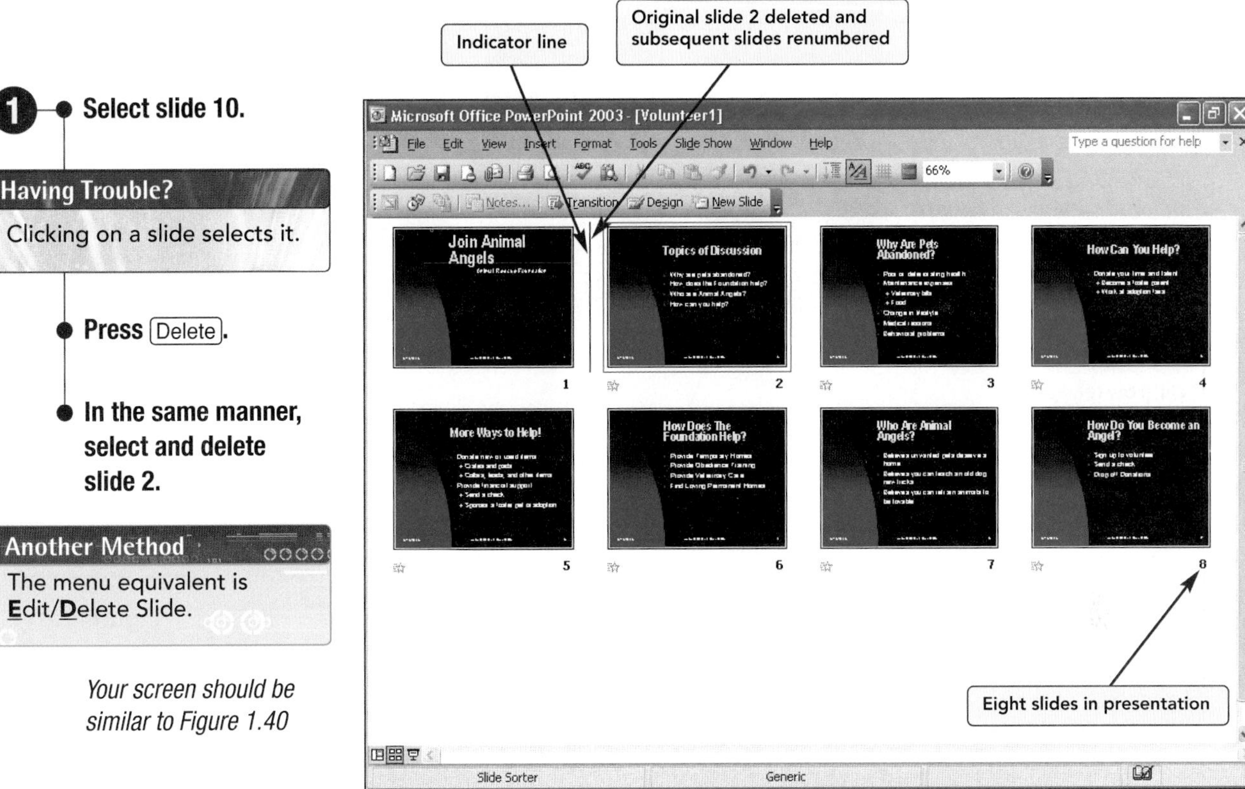


**Figure 1.40**

The slides have been deleted, and all remaining slides have been appropriately renumbered. An indicator line appears between slides 1 and 2 where the deleted slide once existed.

## Moving Slides

Now you want to correct the organization of the slides by moving slide 6, How Does the Foundation Help?, and slide 7, Who Are Animal Angels?, before slide 4, How Can You Help?. To reorder a slide in Slide Sorter view, you drag it to its new location using drag and drop. As you drag the mouse, an indicator line appears to show you where the slide will appear in the presentation. When the indicator line is located where you want the slide to be placed, release the mouse button. You will select both slides and move them at the same time.

1. Select slide 6.
   - Hold down Ctrl and click on slide 7.
   - Point to either selected slide and drag the mouse until the indicator line is displayed before slide 4.

**Additional Information**

The mouse pointer appears as [pointer] when you drag to move a slide.

   - Release the mouse button.

**Another Method**

You can also use the Edit/Cut and Edit/Paste commands to move slides in Slide Sorter view or the voice commands "Cut" and "Paste."

*Your screen should be similar to Figure 1.41*

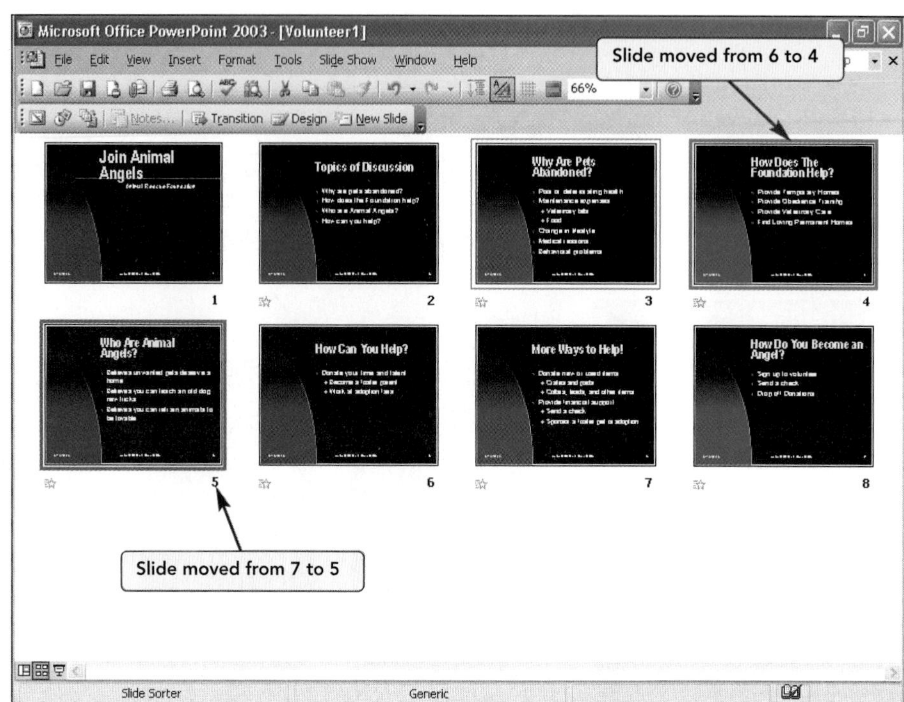


Figure 1.41

The slides now appear in the order you want them.

## Inserting Slides

During your discussion with the Foundation director, it was suggested that you add a slide showing the history of the organization. To include this information in the presentation, you will insert a new slide after slide 4.

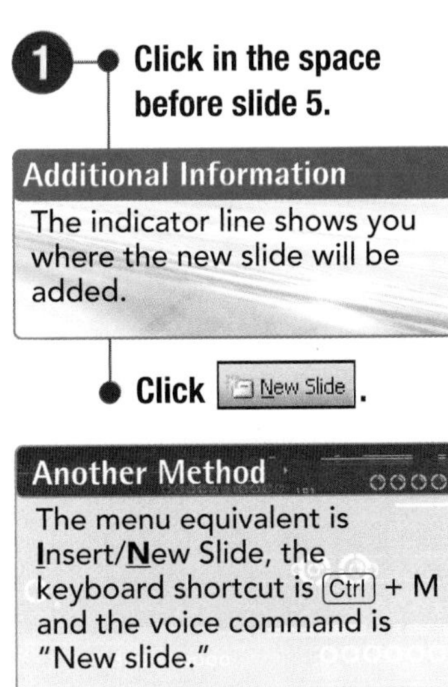

**1** **Click in the space before slide 5.**

**Additional Information**

The indicator line shows you where the new slide will be added.

**Click** New Slide.

**Another Method**

The menu equivalent is **I**nsert/**N**ew Slide, the keyboard shortcut is Ctrl + M and the voice command is "New slide."

*Your screen should be similar to Figure 1.42*

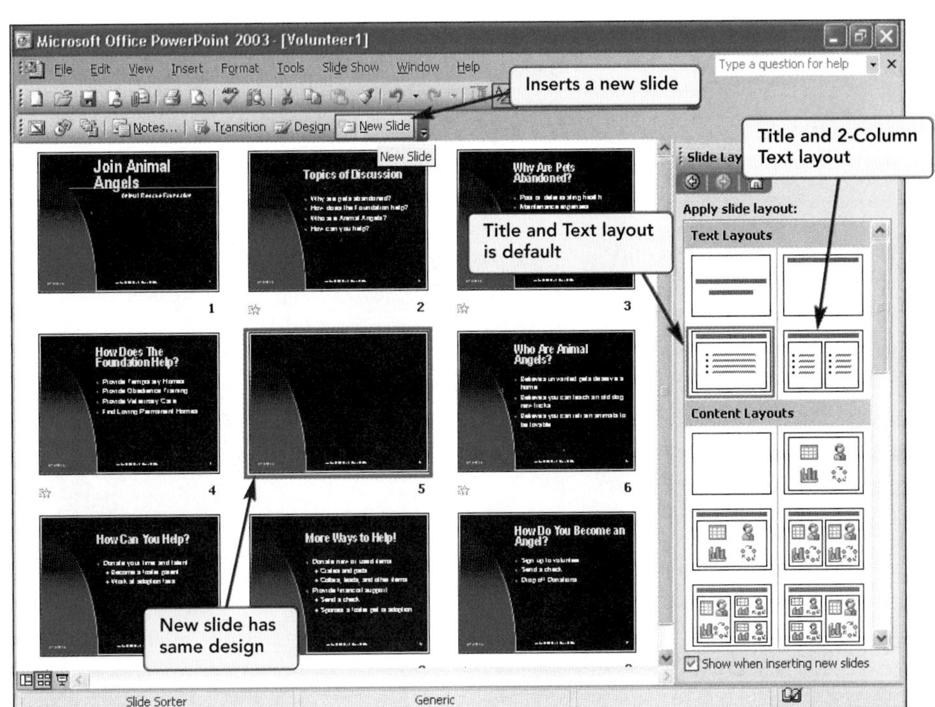


**Figure 1.42**

A blank new slide is inserted. It has the same design elements as the other slides in the presentation.

## Selecting the Slide Layout

The Slide Layout task pane is automatically displayed so that you can select a slide layout for the new slide.

## Concept 6

### Layout

6 The **layout** controls the way items are arranged on a slide. A layout contains placeholders for the different items such as bulleted text, titles, charts, and so on. PowerPoint includes 27 predefined layouts that can be selected and applied to slides. For example, there are text layouts that include placeholders for a title and bulleted text, and content layouts that include placeholders for a table, diagram, chart, or clip art.

You can change the layout of an existing slide by selecting a new layout. If the new layout does not include placeholders for objects that are already on your slide (for example, if you created a chart and the new layout does not include a chart placeholder), you do not lose the information. All objects remain on the slide and the selected layout is automatically adjusted by adding the appropriate type of placeholder for the object. Alternatively, as you add new objects to a slide, the layout automatically adjusts by adding the appropriate type of placeholder. You can also rearrange, size, and format placeholders on a slide any way you like to customize the slide's appearance.

To make creating slides easy, use the predefined layouts. The layouts help you keep your presentation format consistent and, therefore, more professional.

The Slide Layout task pane displays examples of the 27 layout designs organized into four categories. Pointing to a layout displays the layout name in a ScreenTip. The default layout, Title and Text, is selected.

Because this slide will contain two columns of text about the history of the organization, you will use the two-column text layout.

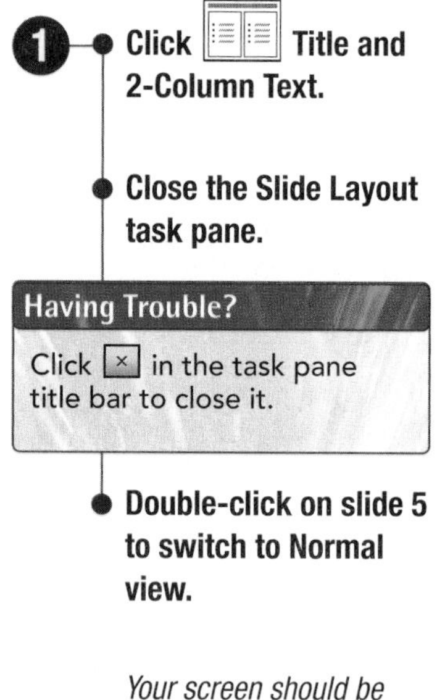

**1**

- **Click Title and 2-Column Text.**
- **Close the Slide Layout task pane.**

**Having Trouble?**

Click ☒ in the task pane title bar to close it.

- **Double-click on slide 5 to switch to Normal view.**

*Your screen should be similar to Figure 1.43*

**Additional Information**

The layout of an existing slide can be changed using Format/Slide Layout.

Three placeholders: title, and 2 columns

**Figure 1.43**

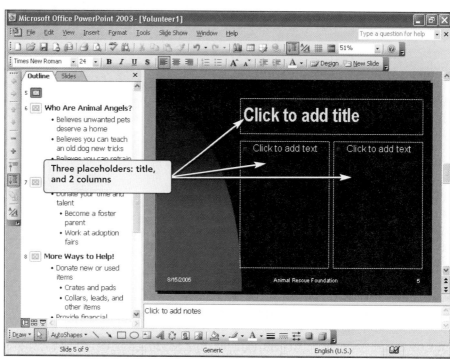

The slide displays the three placeholders created by the two-column text layout. Next, you will add text to the slide presenting a brief history of the Animal Rescue Foundation. First, you will enter the slide title and then the list of dates and events.

**2**

- Click in the title placeholder.
- Type **Animal Rescue Foundation History.**
- Click in the left text placeholder.
- Type **Year.**
- Press ←Enter.
- Continue entering the information shown below. Remember to press ←Enter to create a new line.

  **1990**

  **1991**

  **1997**

  **2003**
- In the same manner, enter the following text in the right text placeholder:

  **Event**

  **Founded by Ed Wilton**

  **Built first shelter**

  **Began volunteer program**

  **Expanded to 10 shelters**

*Your screen should be similar to Figure 1.44*

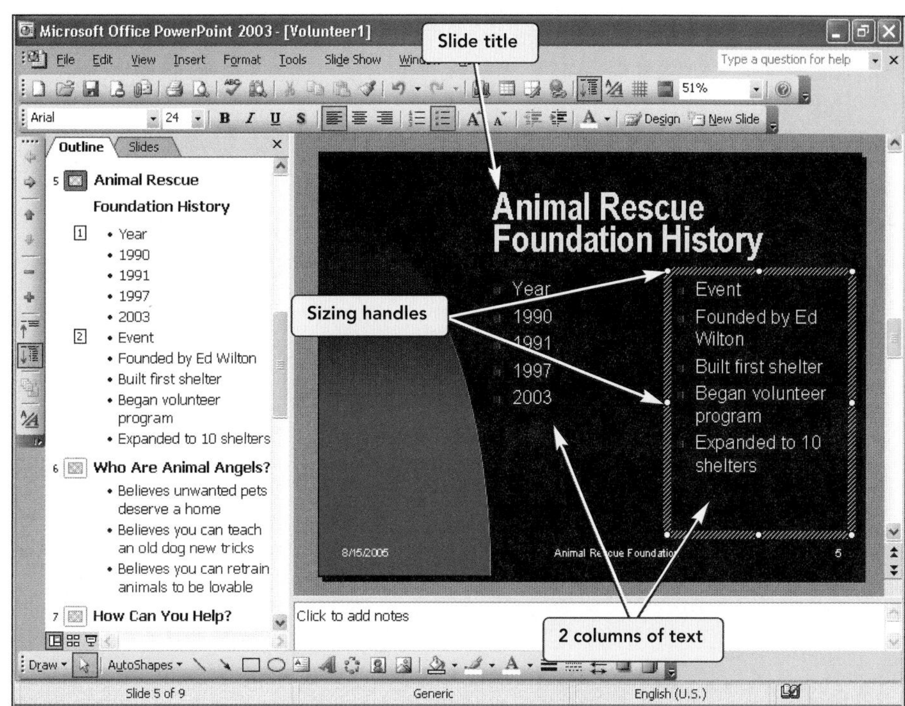


**Figure 1.44**

The left placeholder is too big for its contents, and the right placeholder is too small. To correct the size, you can adjust the size of the placeholders.

## Sizing a Placeholder

The eight boxes in the selection rectangle are **sizing handles** that can be used to adjust the size of the placeholder. Dragging the corner sizing handles will adjust both the height and width at the same time, whereas the center handles adjust the side borders to which they are associated. When you point to the sizing handle, the mouse pointer appears as ↔ indicating the direction in which you can drag the border to adjust the size.

1 **On the right text placeholder, drag the left-center sizing handle to the left until each item appears on a single line (see Figure 1.45).**

**Select the left text placeholder and drag the right-center sizing handle to the left (see Figure 1.45).**

*Your screen should be similar to Figure 1.45*

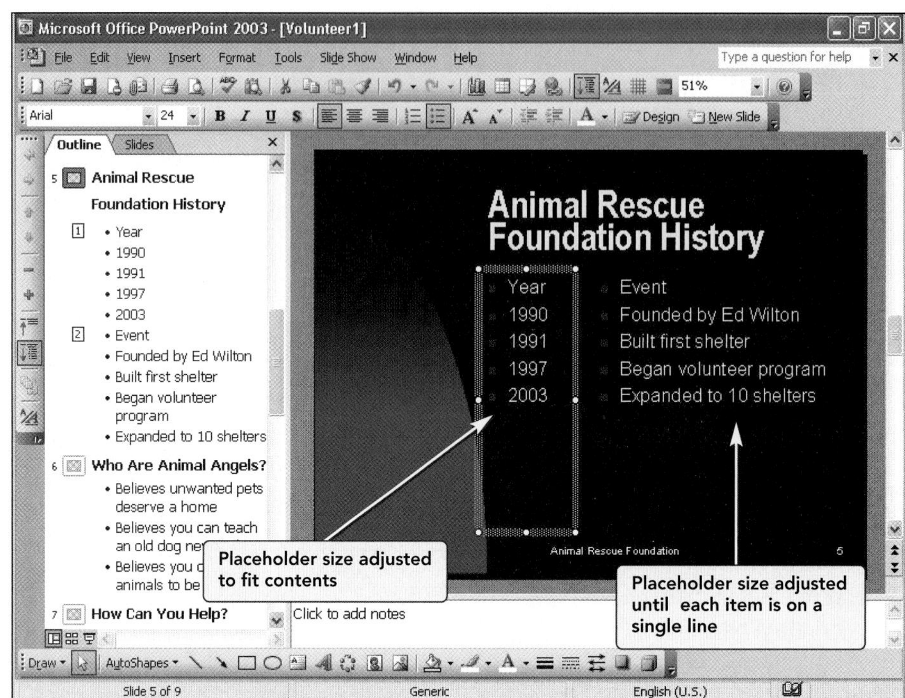


**Figure 1.45**

## Moving a Placeholder

Next, you want to move the Year column placeholder closer to the Event column. Then you want to move both placeholders so they appear more centered in the space. An object can be moved anywhere on a slide by dragging the selection rectangle. The mouse pointer appears as ✥ when you can move a placeholder. You will select both placeholders and move them at the same time. As you drag the placeholder a dotted outline is displayed to show your new location.

1 Point to the Year column selection rectangle (not a handle) and drag the selected placeholder to the right, closer to the Event column.

- With the left placeholder still selected, hold down Ctrl while clicking on the right placeholder to select both.
- Drag the selected placeholders to the left to their new location (see Figure 1.46).
- Save your changes to the presentation using the same file name.

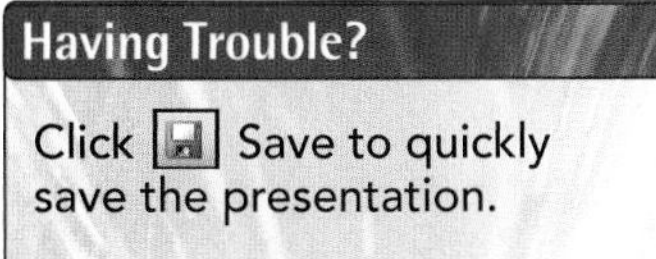

Having Trouble?
Click Save to quickly save the presentation.


*Your screen should be similar to Figure 1.46*

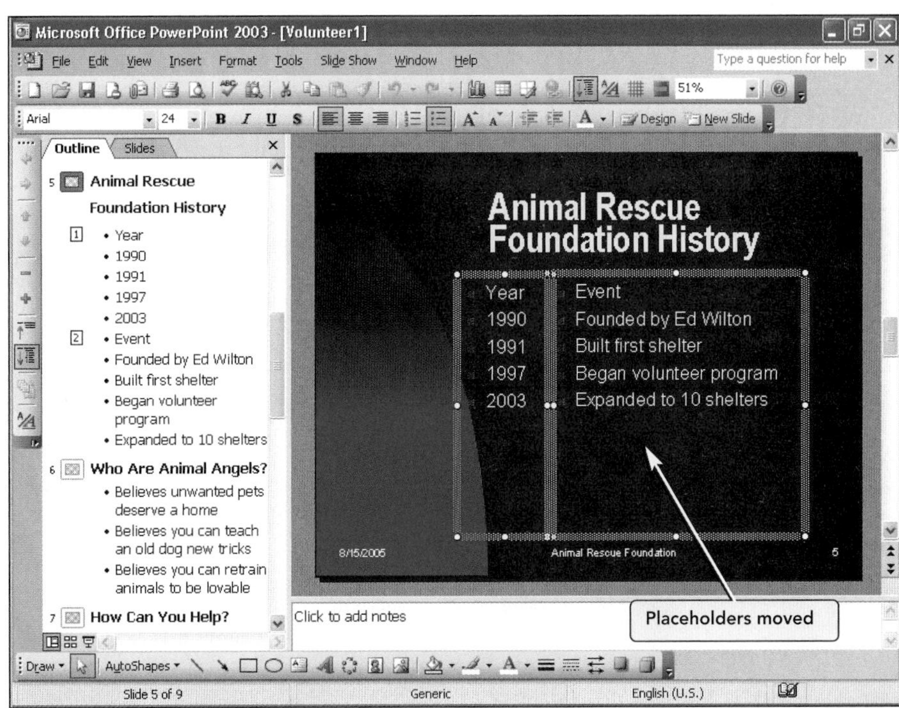


**Figure 1.46**

## Rehearsing a Presentation

Now that the slides are in the order you want, you would like to see how the presentation would look when viewed by an audience. Rather than set up the presentation as you would to present it for an audience, a simple way to rehearse a presentation is to view it electronically on your screen as a slide show. A **slide show** displays each slide full screen and in order. While the slide show is running, you can plan what you want to say to supplement the information provided on the slides.

## Using Slide Show View

When you view a slide show, each slide fills the screen, hiding the PowerPoint application window, so you can view the slides as your audience would. You will begin the slide show starting with the first slide.

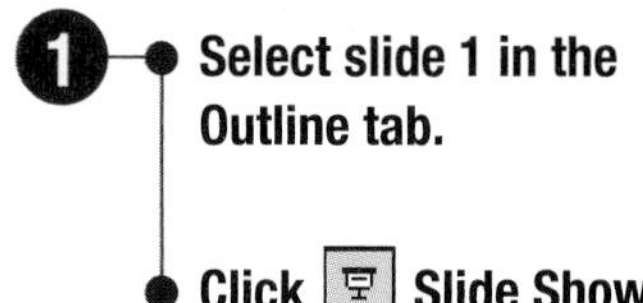

**1** **Select slide 1 in the Outline tab.**

**Click Slide Show.**

**Additional Information**

Using starts the slide show beginning with the currently selected slide.

**Another Method**

The menu equivalent is View/Slide Show and the voice command is "View show." Using these methods starts the slide show beginning with the first slide in the presentation.

*Your screen should be similar to Figure 1.47*

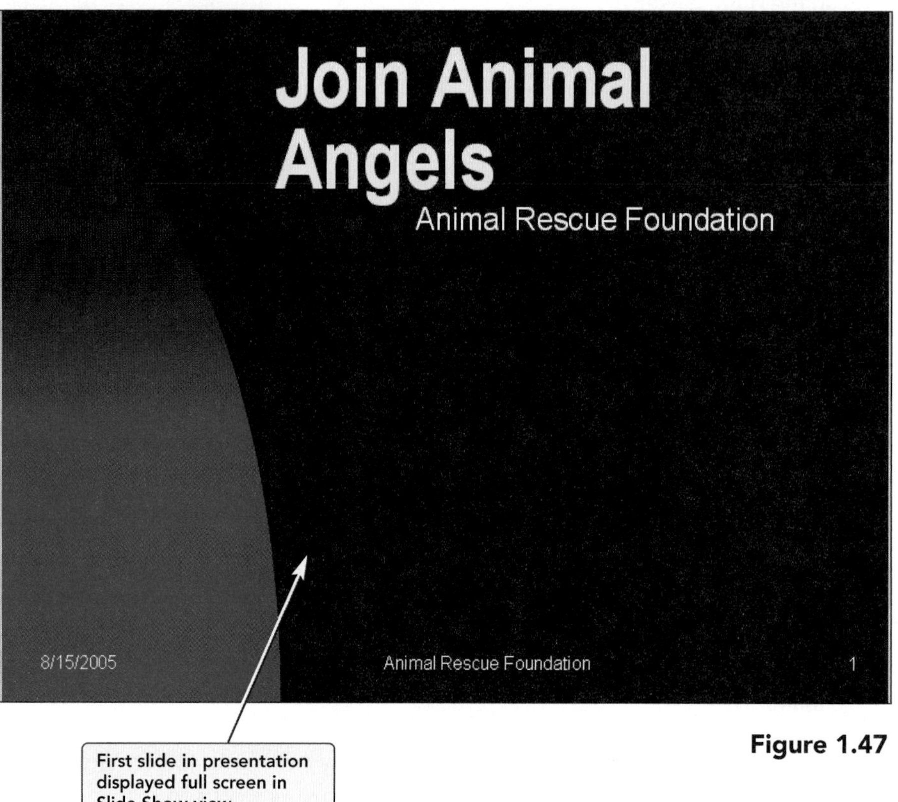


**Figure 1.47**

The presentation title slide is displayed full screen, as it will appear when projected on a screen using computer projection equipment. The easiest way to see the next slide is to click the mouse button. You can also use the keys shown below to move to the next or previous slide.

**Additional Information**

Pressing F1 while in Slide Show opens a Help window describing the actions you can use during the slide show.

| Next Slide | Previous Slide |
|---|---|
| Spacebar | Backspace |
| ←Enter | |
| → | ← |
| ↓ | ↑ |
| Page Down | Page Up |
| N (for next) | P (for previous) |

You can also select Next, Previous, or Last Viewed from the shortcut menu. Additionally, moving the mouse pointer in Slide Show displays the Slide Show toolbar in the lower left corner of the window. Clicking or moves to the previous or next slide and opens the shortcut menu.

Slide Show toolbar

**2**

- Click to display the next slide.
- Using each of the methods described, slowly display the entire presentation.
- When the last slide displays a black window, click again to end the slide show.

**Additional Information**

You can press Esc or use End Show on the shortcut menu at any time to end the slide show.

*Your screen should be similar to Figure 1.48*

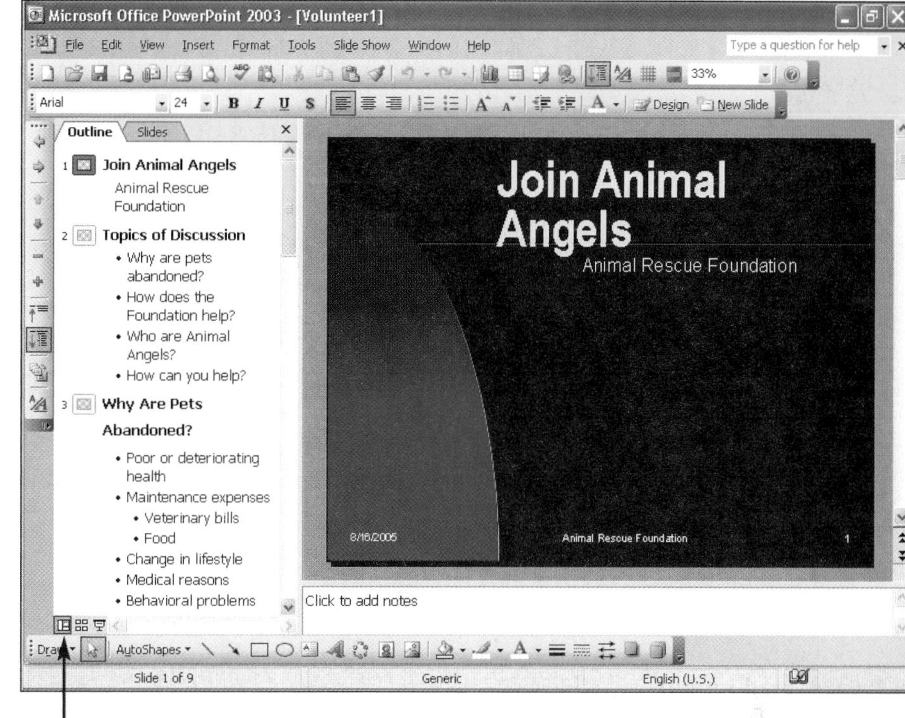


Figure 1.48

After the last slide is displayed, the program returns to the view you were last using, in this case Normal view.

## Formatting Slide Text

While looking at the slide show, you decide that the title slide needs to have more impact. You also want to remove the bullets from the items on the history slide. Enhancing the appearance of the slide to make it more readable or attractive is called **formatting**. The default design template already includes many basic formatting features.

Applying different formatting to characters and paragraphs can greatly enhance the appearance of the slide. **Character formatting** features affect the selected characters only. They include changing the character style and size, applying effects such as bold and italics, changing the character spacing, and adding animated text effects. **Paragraph formatting** features affect an entire paragraph. A paragraph is text that has a carriage return from pressing ←Enter at the end of it. Each item in a bulleted list, title, and subtitle is a paragraph. Paragraph formatting features include the position of the paragraph or its alignment between the margins, paragraph indentation, spacing above and below a paragraph, and line spacing within a paragraph.

## Changing Fonts

First, you will improve the appearance of the presentation title by changing the font of the title text.

### Concept 7

#### Font and Font Size

7 A **font,** also commonly referred to as a **typeface,** is a set of characters with a specific design. The designs have names such as Times New Roman and Courier. Using fonts as a design element can add interest to your presentation and give your audience visual cues to help them find information quickly.

There are two basic types of fonts: serif and sans serif. **Serif** fonts have a flair at the base of each letter that visually leads the reader to the next letter. Two common serif fonts are Roman and Times New Roman. Serif fonts generally are used for text in paragraphs. **Sans serif** fonts do not have a flair at the base of each letter. Arial and Helvetica are two common sans serif fonts. Because sans serif fonts have a clean look, they are often used for headings in documents. It is good practice to use only two or three different fonts in a presentation because too many can distract from your presentation content and can look unprofessional.

Each font has one or more sizes. Font size is the height and width of the character and is commonly measured in **points,** abbreviated pt. One point equals about 1/72 inch, and text in most documents is 10 pt or 12 pt.

Several common fonts in different sizes are shown in the following table.

| Font Name | Font Type | Font Size |
|---|---|---|
| Arial | Sans serif | This is 10 pt.<br>This is 16 pt. |
| Courier New | Serif | This is 10 pt.<br>This is 16 pt. |
| Times New Roman | Serif | This is 10 pt.<br>This is 16 pt. |

To change the font before typing the text, use the command and then type. All text will appear in the specified setting until another font setting is selected. To change a font setting for existing text, select the text you want to change and then use the command. If you want to apply font formatting to a word, simply move the insertion point to the word and the formatting is automatically applied to the entire word.

1 **Select the text "Join Animal Angels" in the slide pane.**

**Additional Information**

The font used in the title is Arial Narrow, as displayed in the Arial Narrow button.

**Open the Arial Narrow Font drop-down list.**

**Scroll the list and choose Comic Sans MS.**

**Another Method**

The menu equivalent is F**o**rmat/**F**ont/**F**ont.

*Your screen should be similar to Figure 1.49*

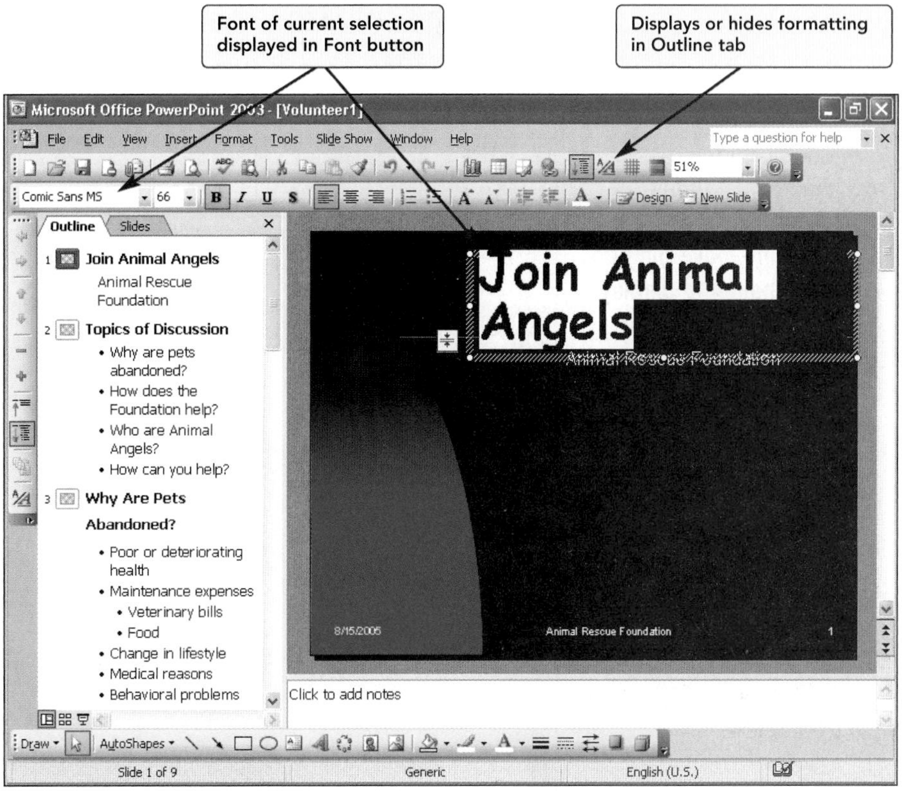


**Figure 1.49**

**Additional Information**

You can show or hide the text formatting in the Outline tab using Show Formatting.

The text has changed to the new font style, and the Font button displays the font name used in the current selection. The formatting effects appear in the slide pane but are not displayed in the Outline tab.

## Changing Font Size

The title text is also a little larger than you want it to be.

**1** **Click Decrease Font Size 2 times.**

- **Size and move the title placeholder to display the title on one line above the red graphic line.**

**Additional Information**

Use Increase Font Size to incrementally increase the point size of selected text.

**Another Method**

You could also specify the point size from the Font Size drop-down list or use Format/Font/Size.

*Your screen should be similar to Figure 1.50*

**Additional Information**

If a selection includes text in several different sizes, the smallest size appears in the Font Size button followed by a + sign.

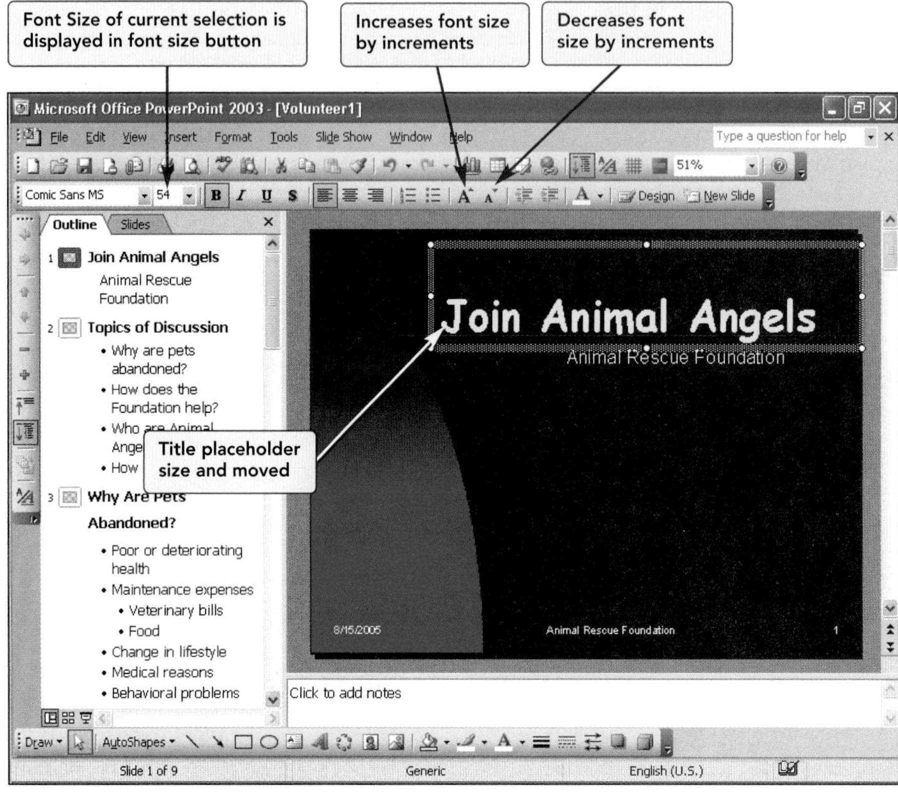


**Figure 1.50**

The Font Size button displays the point size of the current selection.

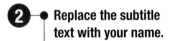

**2** **Replace the subtitle text with your name.**

- **Reduce the size of the subtitle placeholder to fit the contents.**

**Having Trouble?**

Drag the sizing handles to size the placeholder.

- **Move the placeholder to the location shown in Figure 1.51.**

*Your screen should be similar to Figure 1.51*

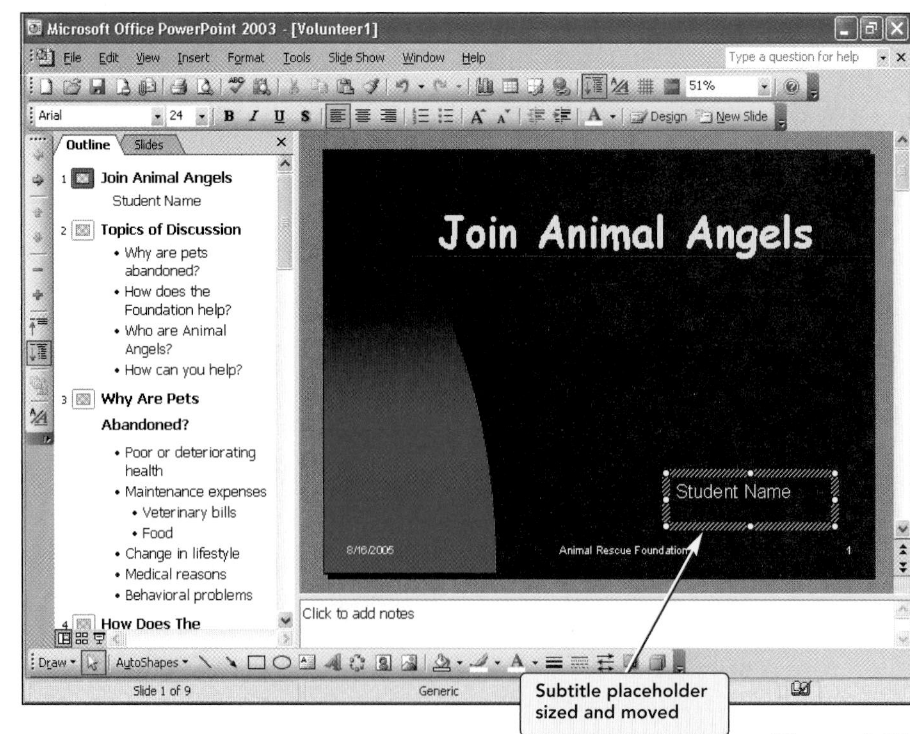


**Figure 1.51**

## Adding and Removing Bullets

Next, you want to remove the bullets from the items on the history slide. You can quickly apply and remove bullets using Bullets on the Formatting toolbar. This button applies the bullet style associated with the design template you are using. Because the placeholder items already include bullets, using this button will remove them.

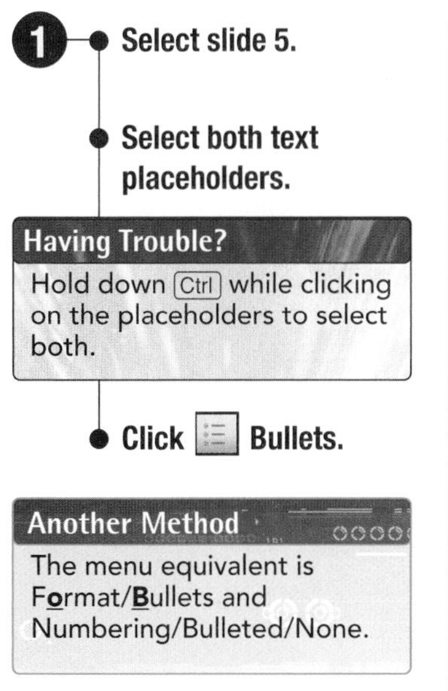

1. Select slide 5.
   - Select both text placeholders.

**Having Trouble?**

Hold down Ctrl while clicking on the placeholders to select both.

- Click Bullets.

**Another Method**

The menu equivalent is Format/Bullets and Numbering/Bulleted/None.

*Your screen should be similar to Figure 1.52*

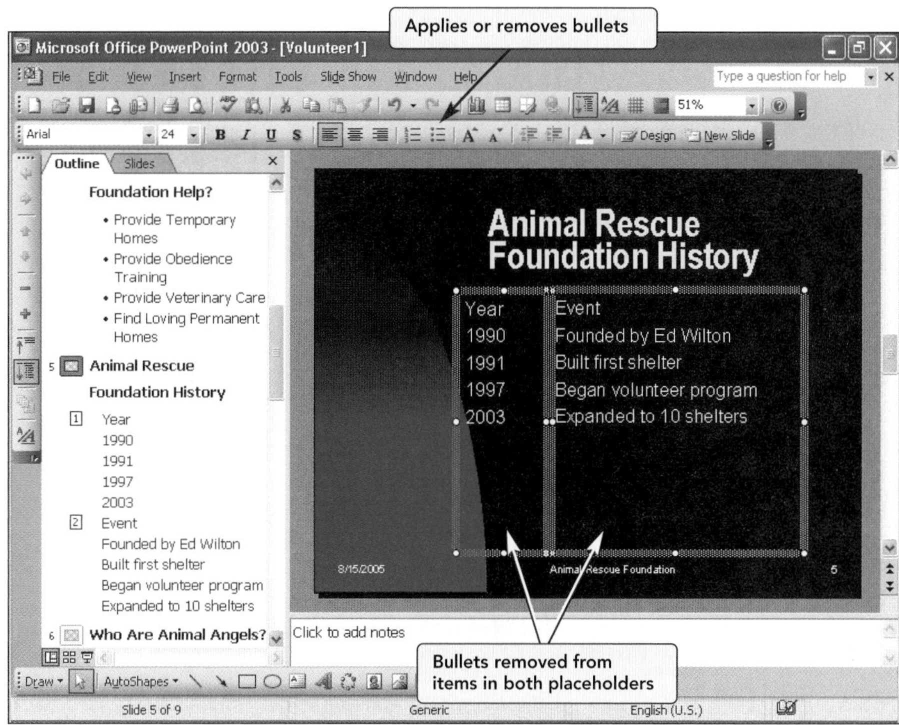


**Figure 1.52**

The bullets are removed from all the items in both placeholders. Now, however, you think it would look better to add bullets back to the four items under each column heading.

**2**

- Select the four years in the left column.
- Click Bullets.
- Apply bullets to the four events in the right column.
- Click outside the selected object to deselect it.
- Save the presentation again.

*Your screen should be similar to Figure 1.53*

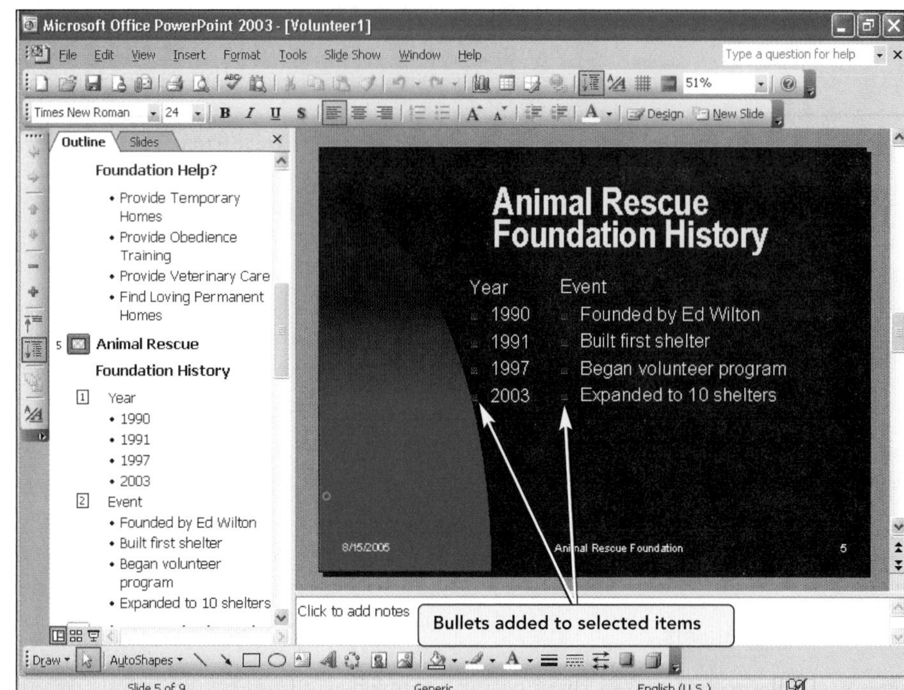


**Figure 1.53**

Bullets appear before the selected text items only.

## Working with Graphics

Finally, you want to add a picture to the title slide. A picture is one of several different graphic objects that can be added to a slide.

### Concept 8

#### Graphics

8 A **graphic** is a non-text element or object, such as a drawing or picture, that can be added to a slide. A graphic can be a simple **drawing object** consisting of shapes such as lines and boxes that can be created using features on the Drawing toolbar. A drawing object is part of your presentation document. A **picture** is an image such as a graphic illustration or a scanned photograph. Pictures are graphics that were created from another program and are inserted in a slide as embedded objects. An **embedded object** becomes part of the presentation file and can be opened and edited using the **source program**, the program in which it was created. Several examples of drawing objects and pictures are shown below.

Add graphics to your presentation to help the audience understand concepts, to add interest, and to make your presentation stand out from others.

Photograph

Clip Art

Drawing Object

## Inserting a Graphic from the Clip Organizer

You want to add a graphic to the slide below the title line. Graphic files can be obtained from a variety of sources. Many simple drawings called **clip art** are available in the Clip Organizer that comes with Office 2003. The Clip Organizer's files, or clips, include art, sound, animation, and movies you can add to a presentation.

**Additional Information**

You can also scan a picture and insert it directly into a slide without saving it as a file first.

You can also create graphic files using a scanner to convert any printed document, including photographs, to an electronic format. Most images that are scanned and inserted into documents are stored as Windows bitmap files (.bmp). All types of graphics, including clip art, photographs, and other types of images, can be found on the Internet. These files are commonly stored as .jpg or .pcx files. Keep in mind that any images you locate on the Internet may be protected by copyright and should only be used with permission. You can also purchase CDs containing graphics for your use.

You decide to check the Clip Organizer to find a suitable graphic.

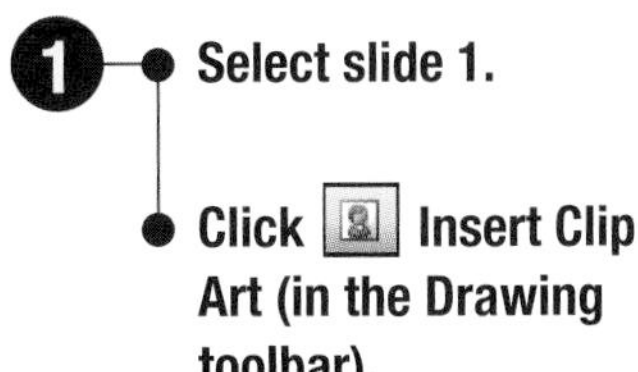

1. **Select slide 1.**

   **Click Insert Clip Art (in the Drawing toolbar).**

**Another Method**

The menu equivalent is Insert/Picture/Clip Art. You could also display the Getting Started task pane and select Clip Art from the task pane menu.

*Your screen should be similar to Figure 1.54*

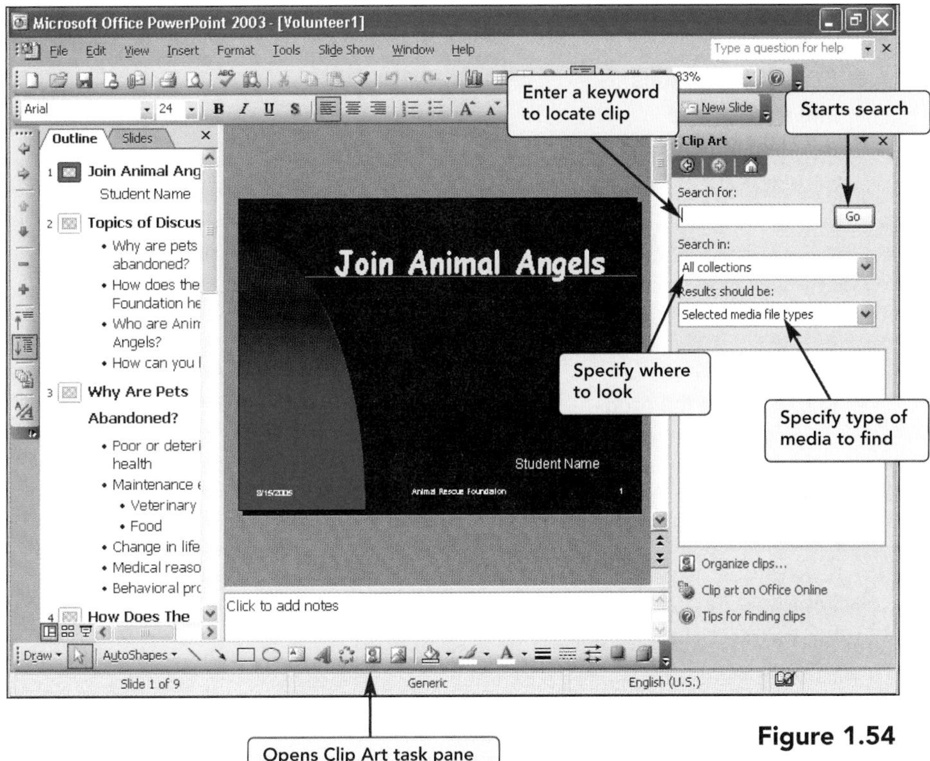


**Figure 1.54**

**Additional Information**

You can also insert graphics directly from files on your computer using Insert/Picture/From File.

The Clip Art task pane appears in which you can enter a keyword, a word or phrase that is descriptive of the type of graphic you want to locate. The graphics in the Clip Organizer are organized by topic and are identified with several keywords that describe the graphic. You can also specify the locations to search and the type of media files, such as clip art, movies, photographs or sound, to display in the search results. You want to find clip art and photographs of animals.

**2** **If necessary, select any existing text in the Search For text box.**

**In the Search for text box, type animal.**

**If All Collections is not displayed in the Search In text box, select Everywhere from the drop-down list.**

**Open the Results Should Be drop-down list.**

**Select Photographs and Clip Art and deselect Movies and Sounds.**

**Having Trouble?**

Click the box next to an option to select or deselect (clear the checkmark).

**Click outside the drop-down list to close it.**

**Click Go.**

**Point to a thumbnail in the Results area.**

*Your screen should be similar to Figure 1.55*

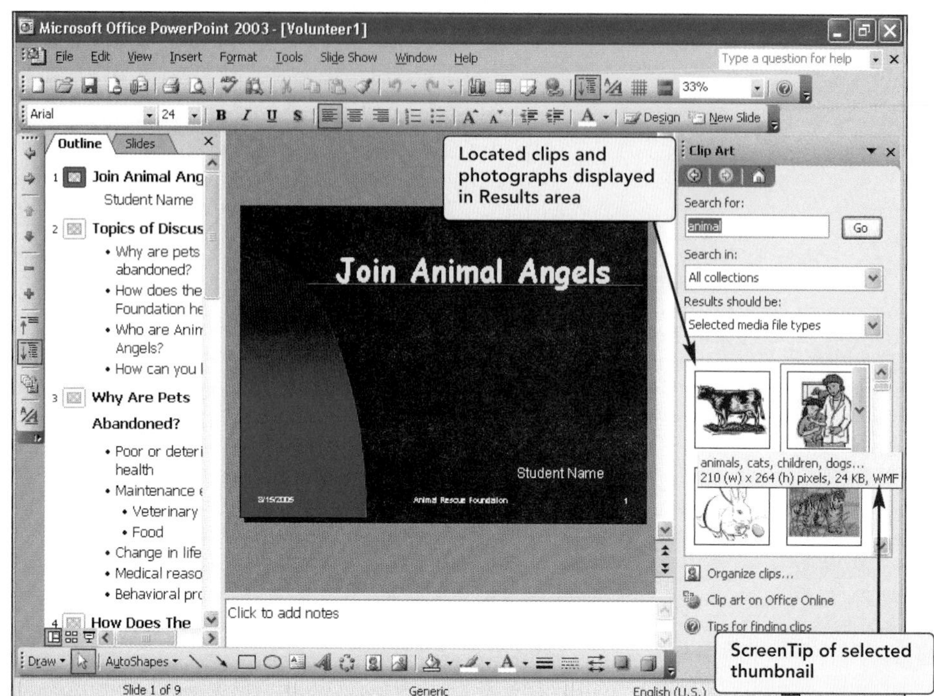


Figure 1.55

The program searches all locations on your computer and, if you have an Internet connection established, searches Microsoft's Clip Art and Media Web site for clip art and graphics that match your search term. The Results area displays thumbnails of all located graphics. Pointing to a thumbnail displays a ScreenTip containing the **keywords** associated with the picture and information about the picture properties. It also displays a drop-down list bar that accesses the item's shortcut menu.

**3** • **Scroll the results list to the bottom to view all of the located clips and photographs.**

*Your screen should be similar to Figure 1.56*

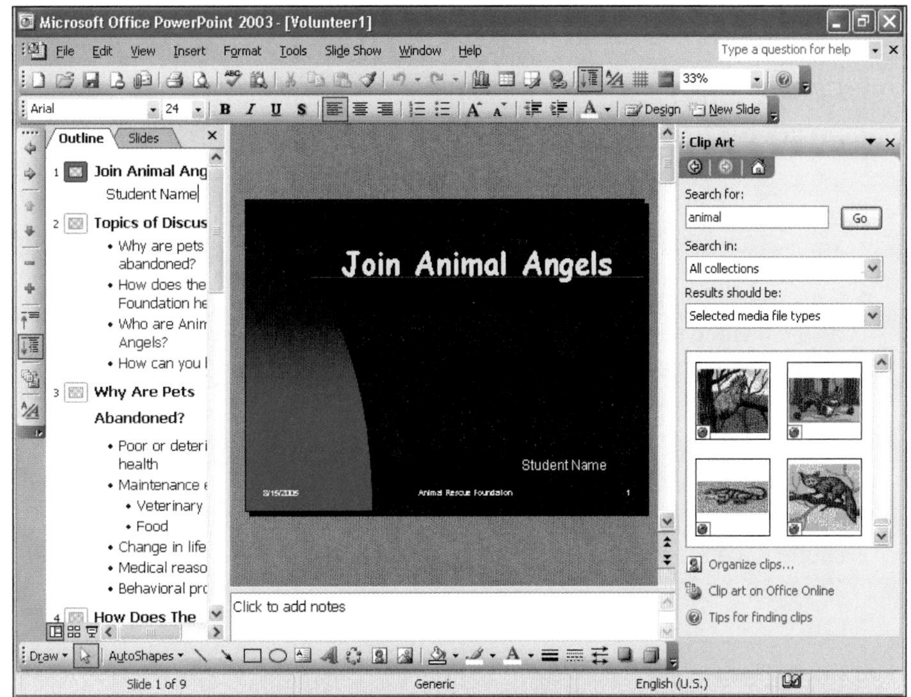


**Figure 1.56**

> **Additional Information**
>
> Entering keywords separated with a comma requires that either keyword be associated with the graphic and therefore expands the search.

Because so many pictures were located, you decide to narrow your search to display pictures of animals and healthcare only. Adding a second word to your search will narrow the number of graphics located. This is because it requires that both words must be associated with the graphic in order for it to appear in the results. Additionally, because the graphic is sometimes difficult to see, you can preview it in a larger size.

**4** **Add the word healthcare following the word "animal" in the Search For text box.**

- **Click Go.**
- **If necessary, scroll the results area to see the graphic of two people and a dog.**
- **Point to the graphic and click ▾ to open the shortcut menu.**

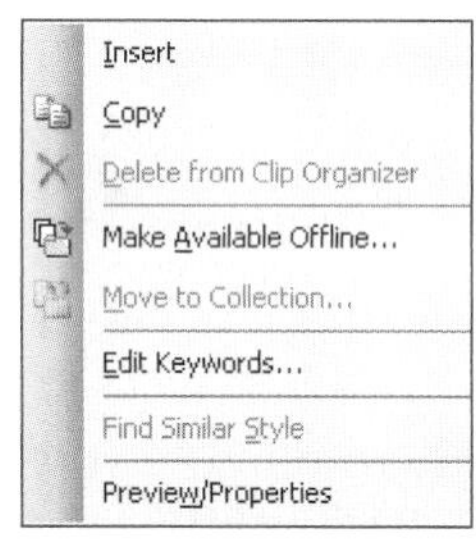


**Additional Information**

The shortcut menu commands are used to work with and manage the items in the Clip Organizer.

- **Choose Preview/Properties.**

*Your screen should be similar to Figure 1.57*

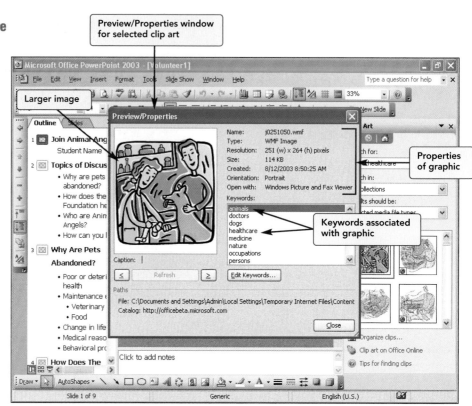

Preview/Properties window for selected clip art

Larger image

Properties of graphic

Keywords associated with graphic

**Figure 1.57**

**Having Trouble?**

If this graphic is not available in the Clip Organizer, close the Clip Art task pane and choose Insert/Picture/From File and insert pp01_Animalcare.bmp from your data file location. Skip to below Figure 1.58.

Because the search term is more specific, fewer results are displayed. The Preview/Properties dialog box displays the selected graphic larger so it is easier to see. It also displays more information about the properties associated with the graphic. You can now see that animals and healthcare are both keywords associated with this graphic. You think this looks like a good choice and will insert it into the document.

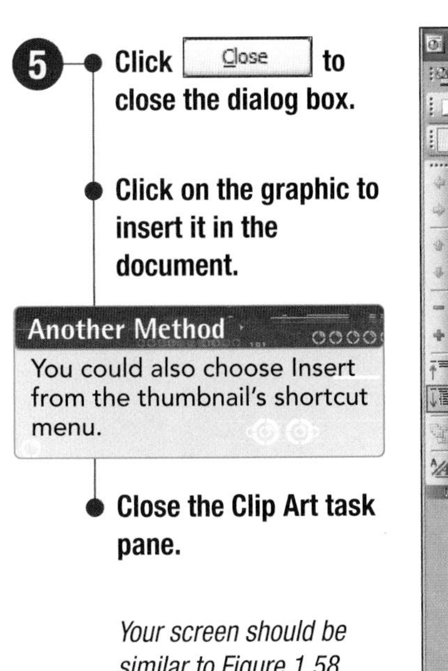

**5** • Click **Close** to close the dialog box.

• Click on the graphic to insert it in the document.

**Another Method**

You could also choose Insert from the thumbnail's shortcut menu.

• Close the Clip Art task pane.

*Your screen should be similar to Figure 1.58*

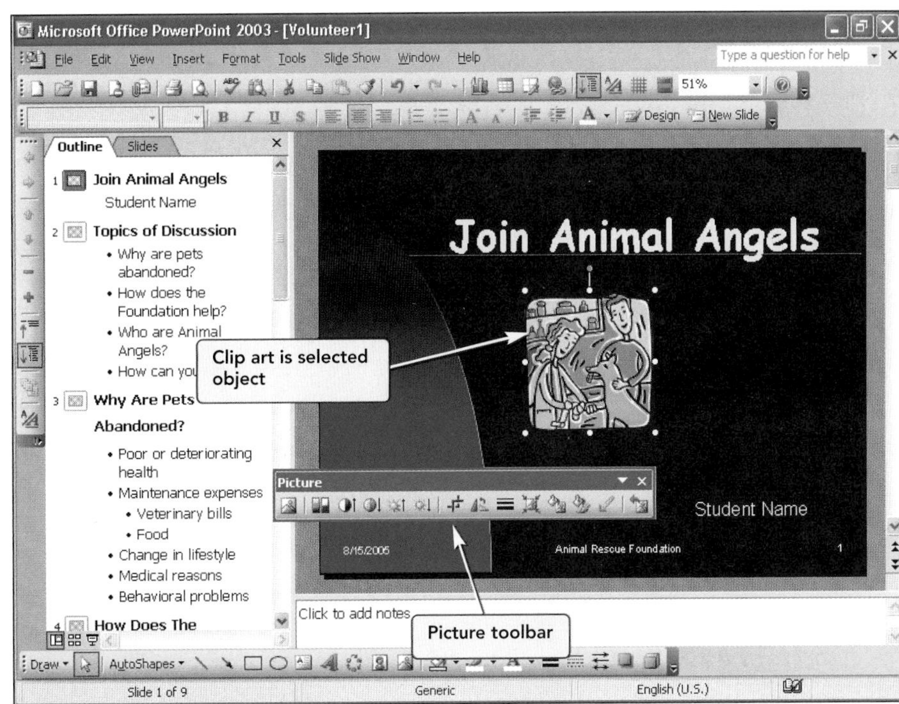


**Figure 1.58**

The clip art graphic is inserted in the center of the slide. It is a selected object and can be sized and moved like any other selected object. The **Picture toolbar** is also automatically displayed and is used to modify the graphic.

## Inserting a Graphic from a File

Although you think this graphic looks good, you want to see how a photograph you recently scanned of a puppy would look instead. The photograph has been saved as pp01_Puppy.jpg.

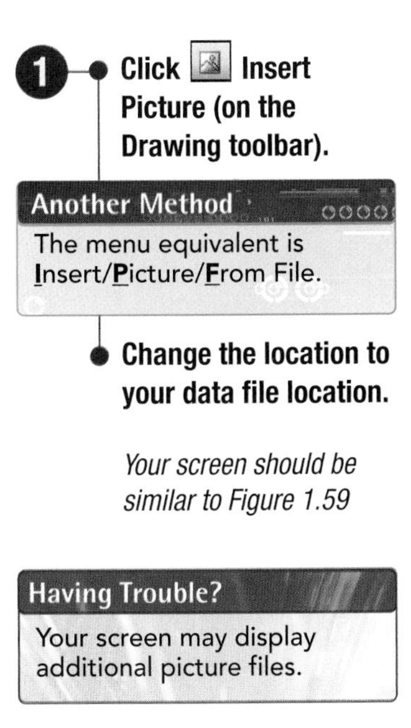

**1** • Click Insert Picture (on the Drawing toolbar).

**Another Method**

The menu equivalent is Insert/Picture/From File.

• Change the location to your data file location.

*Your screen should be similar to Figure 1.59*

**Having Trouble?**

Your screen may display additional picture files.

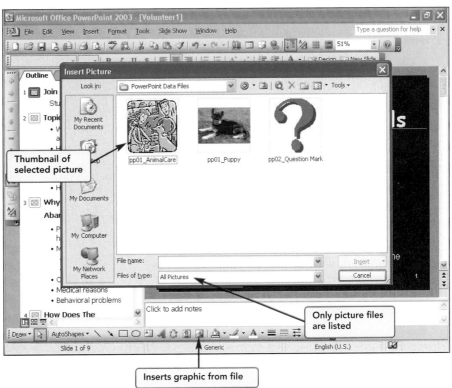

Thumbnail of selected picture

Only picture files are listed

Inserts graphic from file

**Figure 1.59**

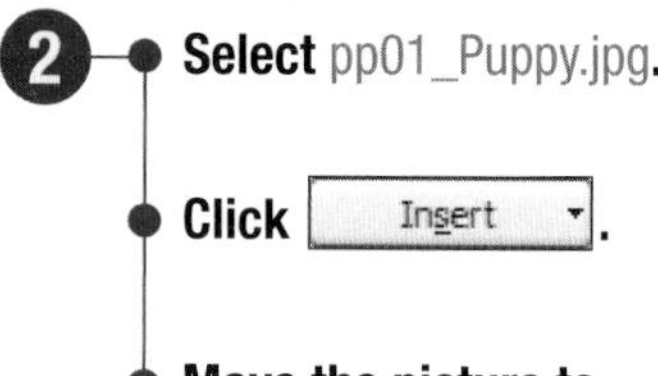

**Having Trouble?**

If the thumbnail preview is not displayed, click Views and choose Thumbnails.

The Insert Picture dialog box is similar to the Open and Save dialog boxes, except that the only types of files listed are files with picture file extensions. A thumbnail preview of each picture is displayed above the file name.

2 **Select** pp01_Puppy.jpg.

**Click** Insert.

**Move the picture to the right to see the underlying clip art.**

*Your screen should be similar to Figure 1.60*

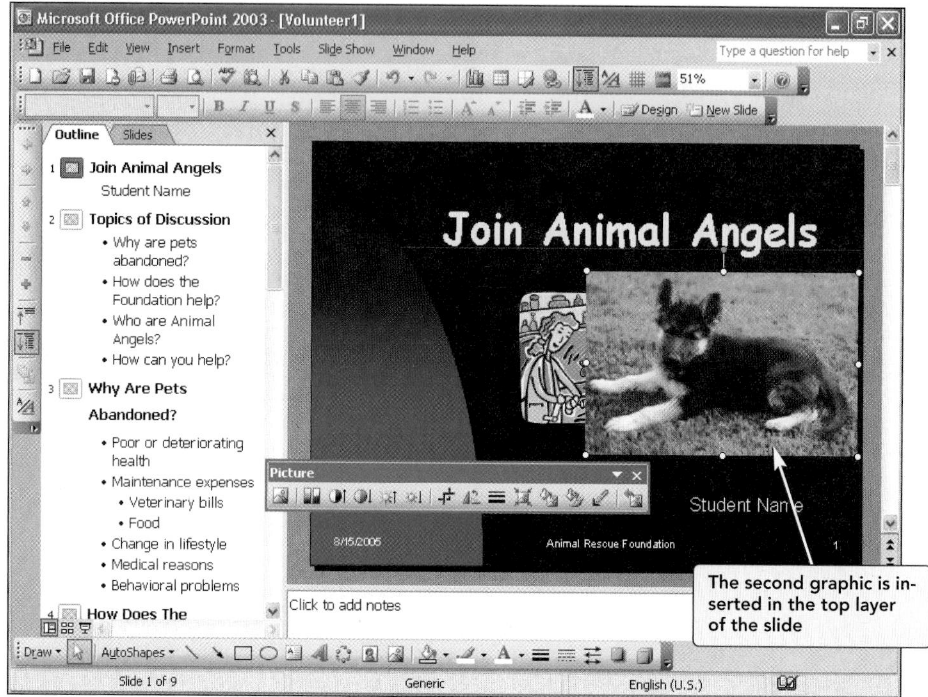


**Figure 1.60**

The second graphic is inserted on the slide on top of the clip art object. As objects are added to a slide, they automatically stack in individual layers.

## Concept 9
### Stacking Order

9 **Stacking order** is the order in which objects are inserted into different layers of the slide. As each object is added to the slide, it is added to the top layer. Adding objects to separate layers allows each object to be positioned precisely on the page, including in front of and behind other objects. As objects are stacked in layers, they may overlap. To change the stacking order, open the Draw menu on the Drawing toolbar and select Order.

**Additional Information**

Sometimes it is easy to lose an object behind another. If this happens, you can press Tab to cycle forward or Shift + Tab to cycle backward through the stacked objects until the one you want is selected.

Because the photograph was the last object added to the slide, it is on the top layer of the stack. Although the photograph looks good, you think the clip art introduces the topic of volunteering better.

**3 Click Undo (2 times).**

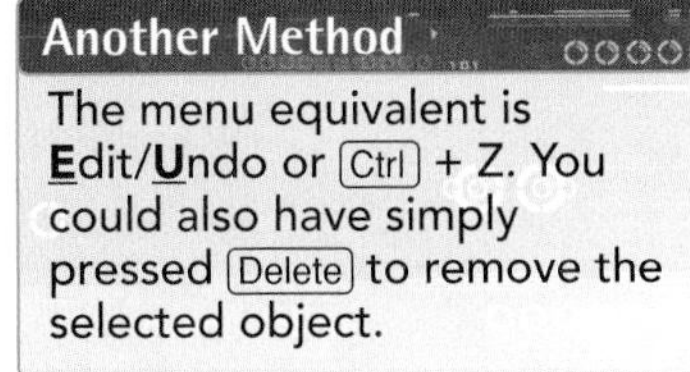

**Another Method**

The menu equivalent is **E**dit/**U**ndo or Ctrl + Z. You could also have simply pressed Delete to remove the selected object.

*Your screen should be similar to Figure 1.61*

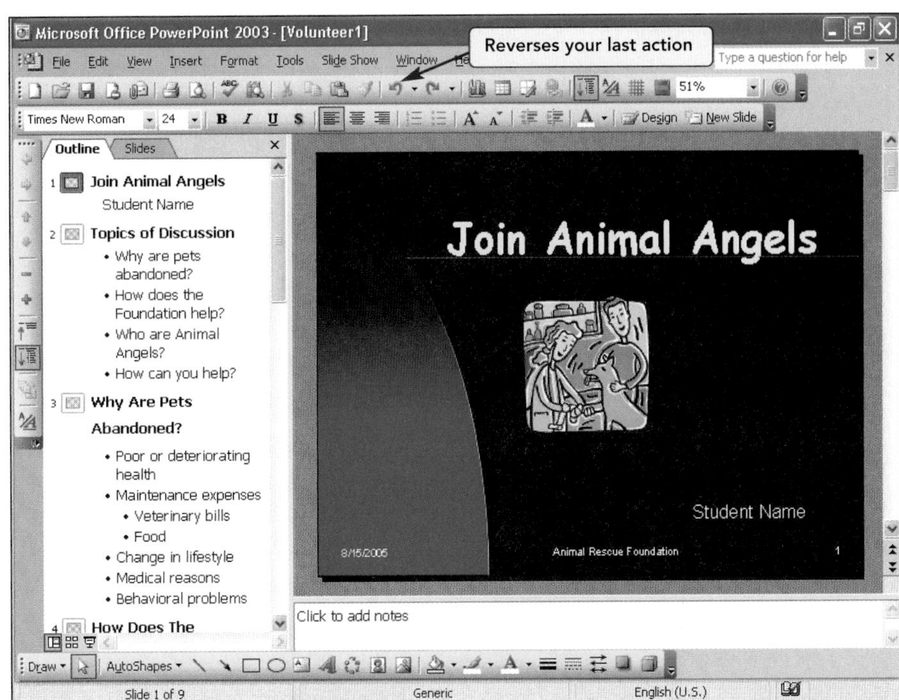


Figure 1.61

Using Undo reverses your last action. Notice that the Undo button includes a drop-down list button. Clicking this button displays a list of the most recent actions that can be reversed, with the most recent action at the top of the list. When you select an action from the drop-down list, you also undo all actions above it in the list.

## Sizing and Moving a Graphic

Frequently, when a graphic is inserted, its size or placement will need to be adjusted. A graphic object is sized and moved just like a placeholder. You want to increase the graphic size slightly and position it in the space below the title.

**1** • **Click on the graphic to select it.**

• **Drag the bottom left corner sizing handle to increase its size to that shown in Figure 1.62.**

• **Drag the graphic to position it as shown in Figure 1.62.**

• **Click outside the graphic to deselect it.**

*Your screen should be similar to Figure 1.62*

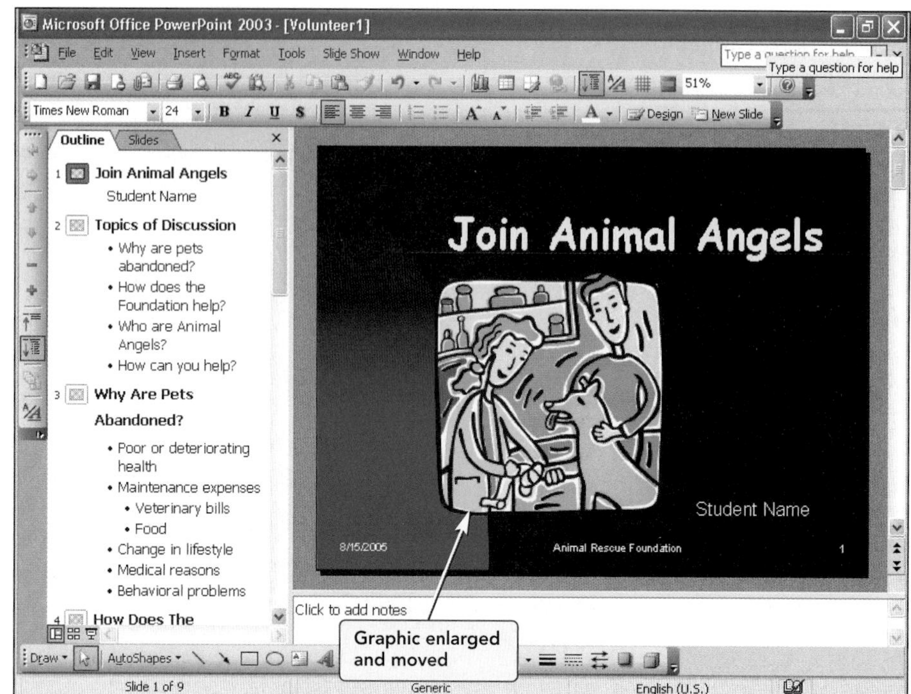


**Figure 1.62**

Now you think the title slide will make a much better impression. To see how the changes and enhancements you have made to the presentation will look full screen, you will run the slide show again.

**2** • **Save the presentation again.**

• **Run the slide show from the first slide.**

## Previewing and Printing the Presentation

Although you still plan to make many changes to the presentation, you want to give a copy of the slides to the Foundation director to get feedback regarding the content and layout. Although your presentation looks good on your screen it may not look good when printed. Previewing the presentation allows you to see how it will look before you waste time and paper printing it out. Many times, you will want to change the print and layout settings to improve the appearance of the output.

### Previewing the Presentation

Shading, patterns, and backgrounds that look good on the screen can make printed handouts unreadable, so you want to preview how the printout will look before making a copy for the director.

**1** **Click [Print Preview button] Print Preview.**

**Another Method**

The menu equivalent is **F**ile/Print Pre**v**iew and the voice command is "Print preview."

*Your screen should be similar to Figure 1.63*

**Having Trouble?**

Your Print Preview may appear in color if you have a color printer.

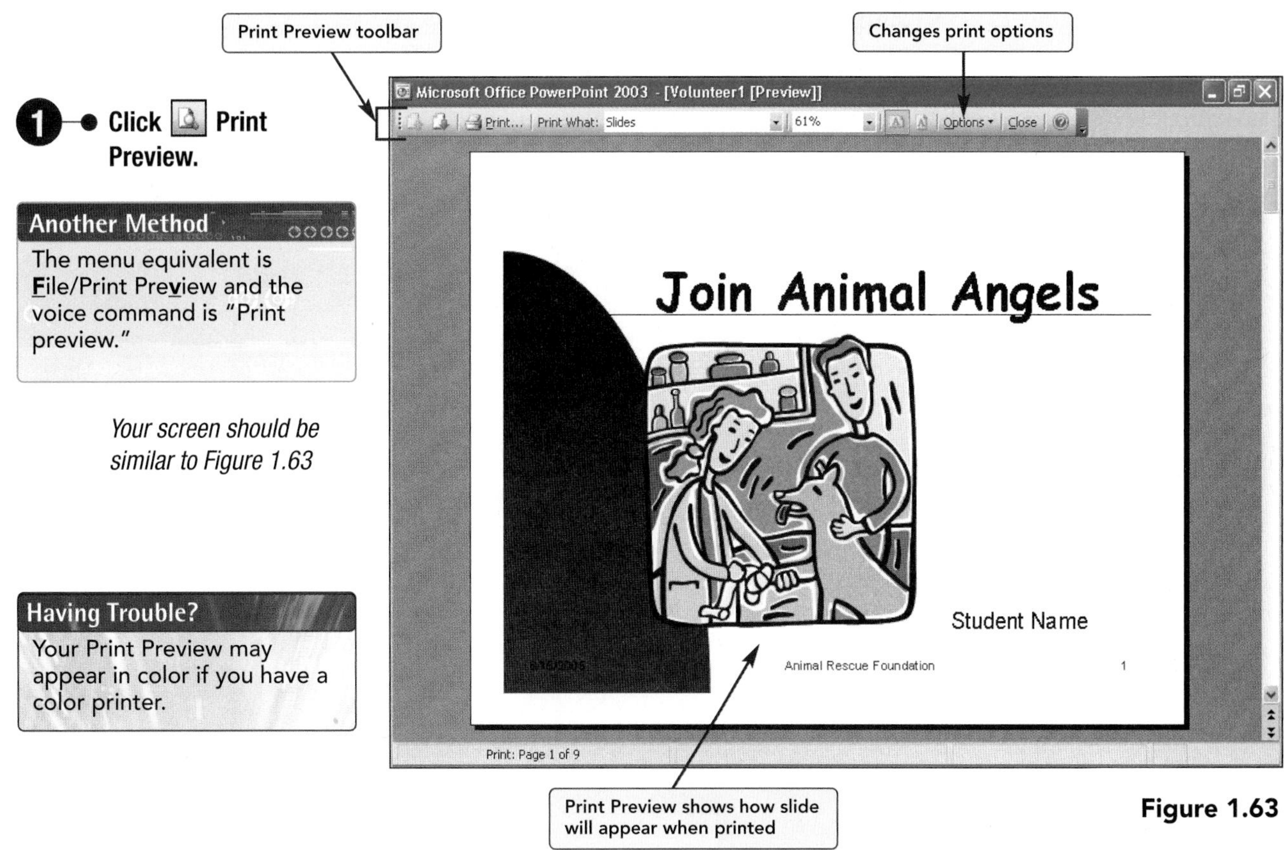


**Figure 1.63**

The Print Preview window displays the first slide in the presentation as it will appear when printed using the selected printer. It is displayed in color if your selected printer is a color printer; otherwise, it appears in grayscale (shades of gray) as in Figure 1.63. Even if you have a color printer, you want to print the slides in grayscale. The Print Preview window also includes its own toolbar that lets you modify the default print settings.

**2** **If you need to change to grayscale, click [Options ▾].**

**Choose Color/Grayscale/Grayscale.**

The default grayscale setting (shown in Figure 1.63) shows you how the slide would look with some of the background in white, with black text, and with patterns in grayscale.

## Specifying Printed Output

The Preview window displays a single slide on the page as it will appear when printed. This is the default print setting. You can change the type of printed output using the Print What option. The output types are described in the table below. Only one type of output can be printed at a time.

| Output Type | Description |
|---|---|
| Slides | Prints one slide per page. |
| Handouts | Prints multiple slides per page. |
| Outline View | Prints the slide content as it appears in Outline view. |
| Notes Pages | Prints the slide and the associated notes on a page. |

**Additional Information**

You will learn about notes in Lab 2.

You want to change the print setting to Handouts to print several slides on a page.

**1** **Open the Print What drop-down menu.**

**Choose Handouts (6 slides per page).**

*Your screen should be similar to Figure 1.64*

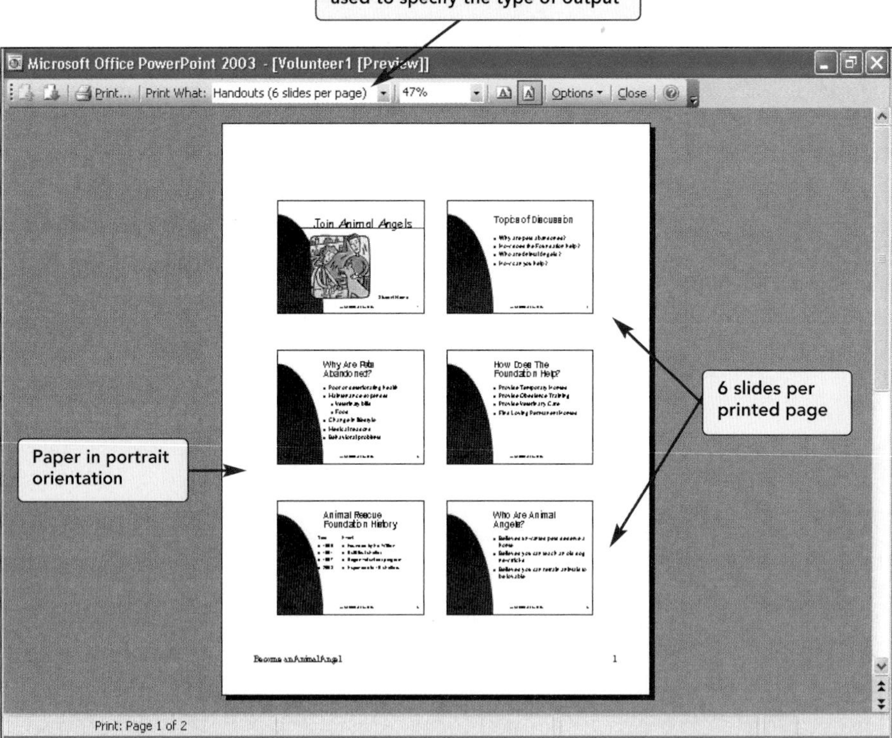


**Figure 1.64**

## Changing Page Orientation

You also want to change the orientation or the direction the output is printed on a page. The default orientation for handouts is **portrait**. This setting prints across the width of the page. You will change the orientation to **landscape** so that the slides print across the length of the paper. Then you will preview the other pages.

1. Click [Landscape icon] Landscape.
   - Click [Next Page icon] Next Page to view page 2 of the handout.

*Your screen should be similar to Figure 1.65*

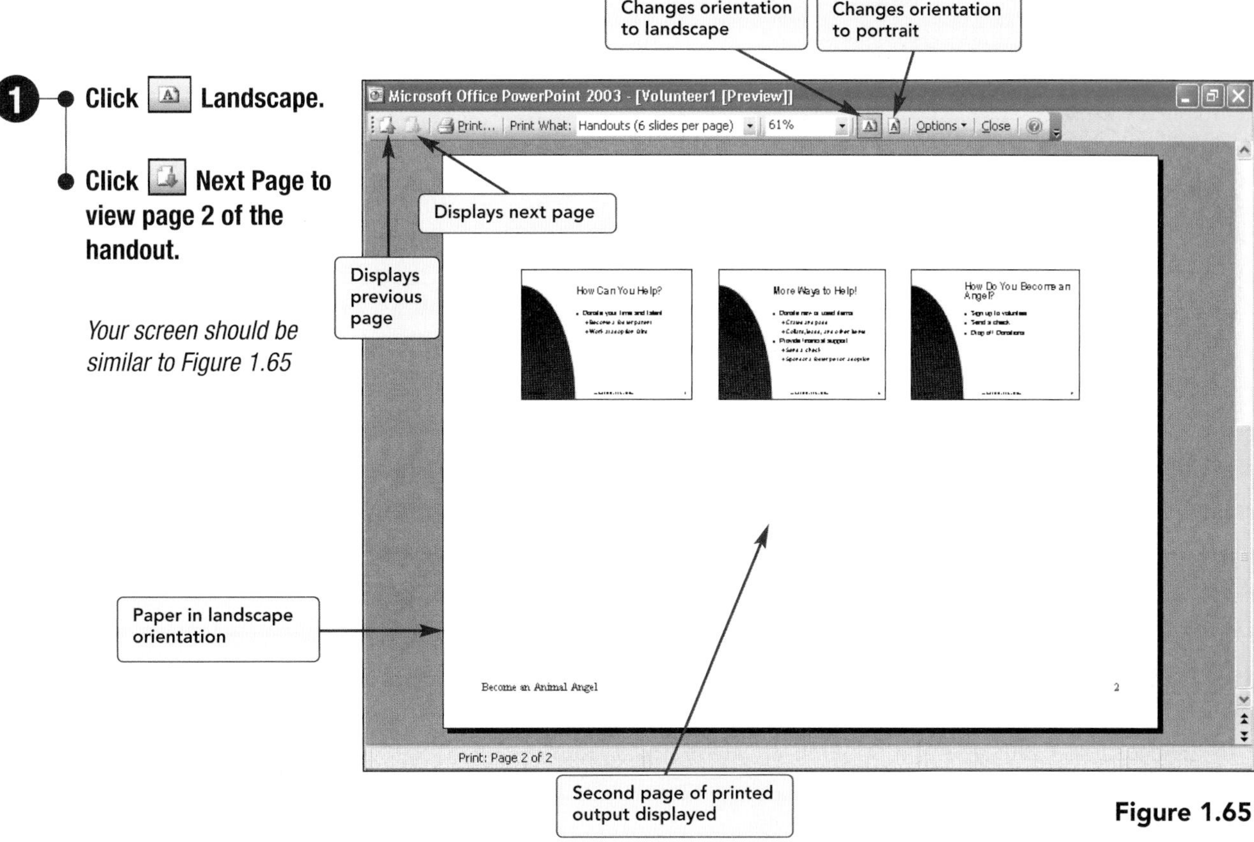


**Figure 1.65**

The last three slides in the presentation are displayed on the second page in landscape orientation.

## Printing the Presentation

Now, you are ready to print the handouts.

1. Click [Print...].

**Another Method**

The menu equivalent is File/Print and the keyboard shortcut is Ctrl + P. You can use [Print icon] Print on the Standard toolbar if you do not need to make any changes to the default print settings.

*Your screen should be similar to Figure 1.66*

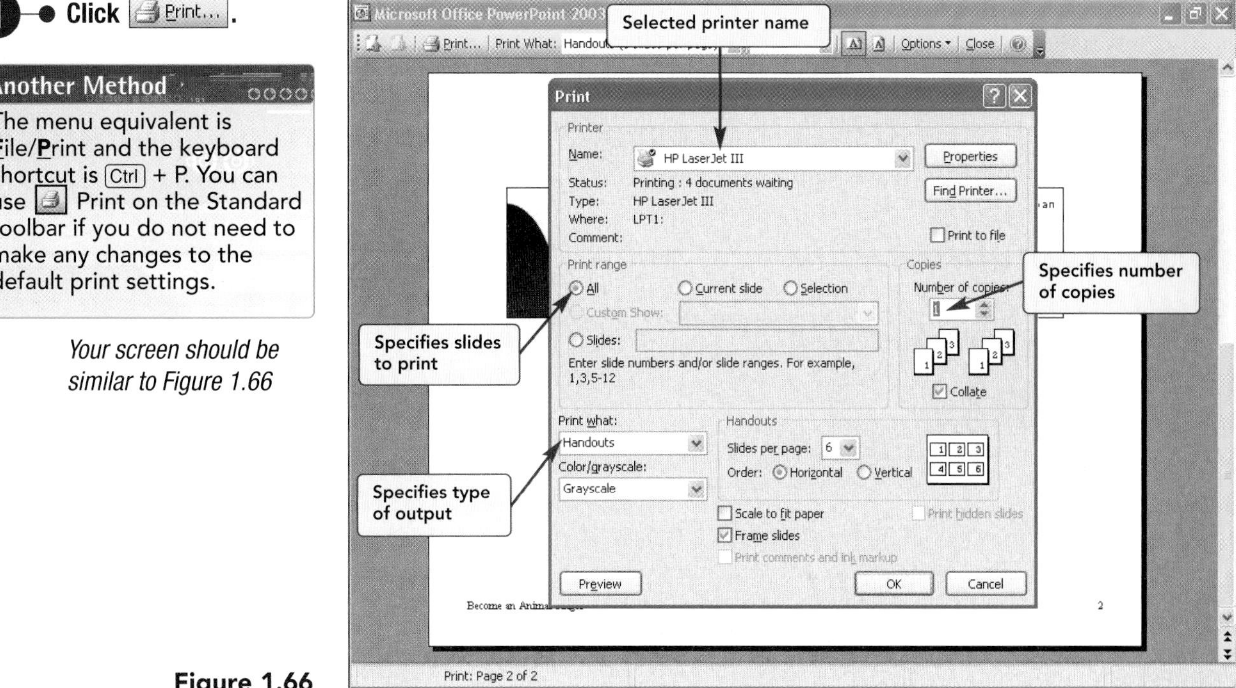


**Figure 1.66**

**Note:** Please consult your instructor for printing procedures that may differ from the following directions.

The Name text box in the Printer section displays the name of the selected printer. You may need to specify the printer you will be using. (Your instructor will provide the printer to select.) The Print Range settings specify the slides to print. The default setting, All, prints all the slides, while Current Slide prints only the slide you are viewing. The Slides option is used to specify individual slides or a range of slides to print by entering the slide numbers in the text box. The Copies section is used to specify the number of copies of the specified print range. The default is to print one copy.

At the bottom of the dialog box, PowerPoint displays options that allow you to print color slides as black-and-white slides, to make the slide images fill the paper, and to add a frame around the slide. The grayscale and handout options you specified in the Print Preview window are already selected. The Frame Slides option is selected by default and displays a border around each slide.

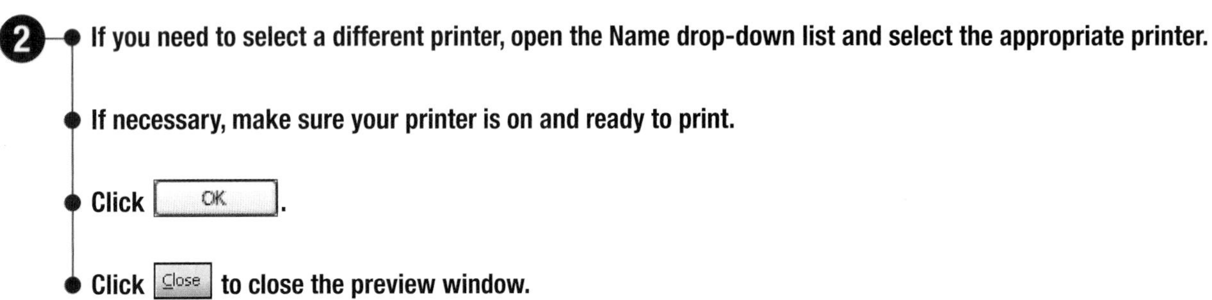

**2**

- **If you need to select a different printer, open the Name drop-down list and select the appropriate printer.**
- **If necessary, make sure your printer is on and ready to print.**
- **Click OK.**
- **Click Close to close the preview window.**

The Printer icon appears in the status bar, indicating that the program is sending data to the Print Manager, and your handouts should be printing. Your printed output should be similar to that shown in the Case Study at the beginning of the lab.

## Exiting PowerPoint

You have finished working on the presentation for now and will exit the PowerPoint program.

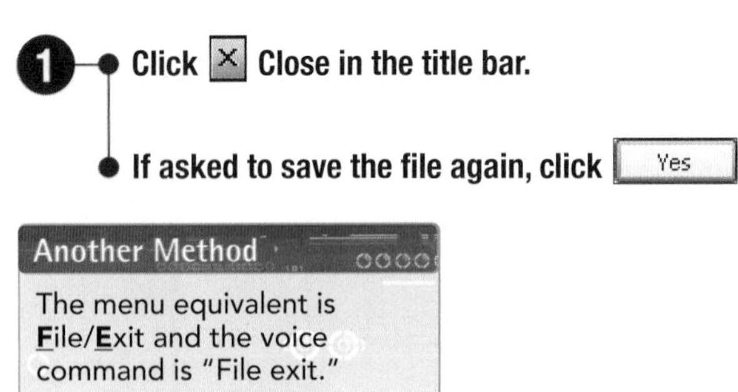

**1**

- **Click Close in the title bar.**
- **If asked to save the file again, click Yes.**

**Another Method**

The menu equivalent is File/Exit and the voice command is "File exit."

# Focus on Careers

## EXPLORE YOUR CAREER OPTIONS

Account Executive

Sales is an excellent entry point for a solid career in any company. Account Executive is just one of many titles that a sales professional may have; Field Sales and Sales Representative are two other titles. Account executives take care of customers by educating them on the company's latest products, designing solutions using the company's product line, and closing the deal to make the sale and earn their commission. These tasks require the use of effective PowerPoint presentations that educate and motivate potential customers. The salary range of account executives is limited only by his/her ambition; salaries range from $27,450 to more than $102,000. To learn more about this career visit http://www.bls.gov/oco/ocos119.htm, the Web site for the Bureau of Labor Statistics of the U.S. Department of Labor.

# LAB 1
# Creating a Presentation

**Template** (PP1.7)

A template is a file containing predefined settings that can be used as a pattern to create many common types of presentations.

**Presentation Style** (PP1.10)

A PowerPoint presentation can be made using five different styles: onscreen presentations, Web presentations, black-and-white or color overheads, and 35mm slides.

**Slide** (PP1.11)

A slide is an individual "page" of your presentation.

**AutoCorrect** (PP1.19)

The AutoCorrect feature makes some basic assumptions about the text you are typing and, based on these assumptions, automatically identifies and/or corrects the entry.

**Spelling Checker** (PP1.20)

The spelling checker locates all misspelled words, duplicate words, and capitalization irregularities as you create and edit a presentation, and proposes possible corrections.

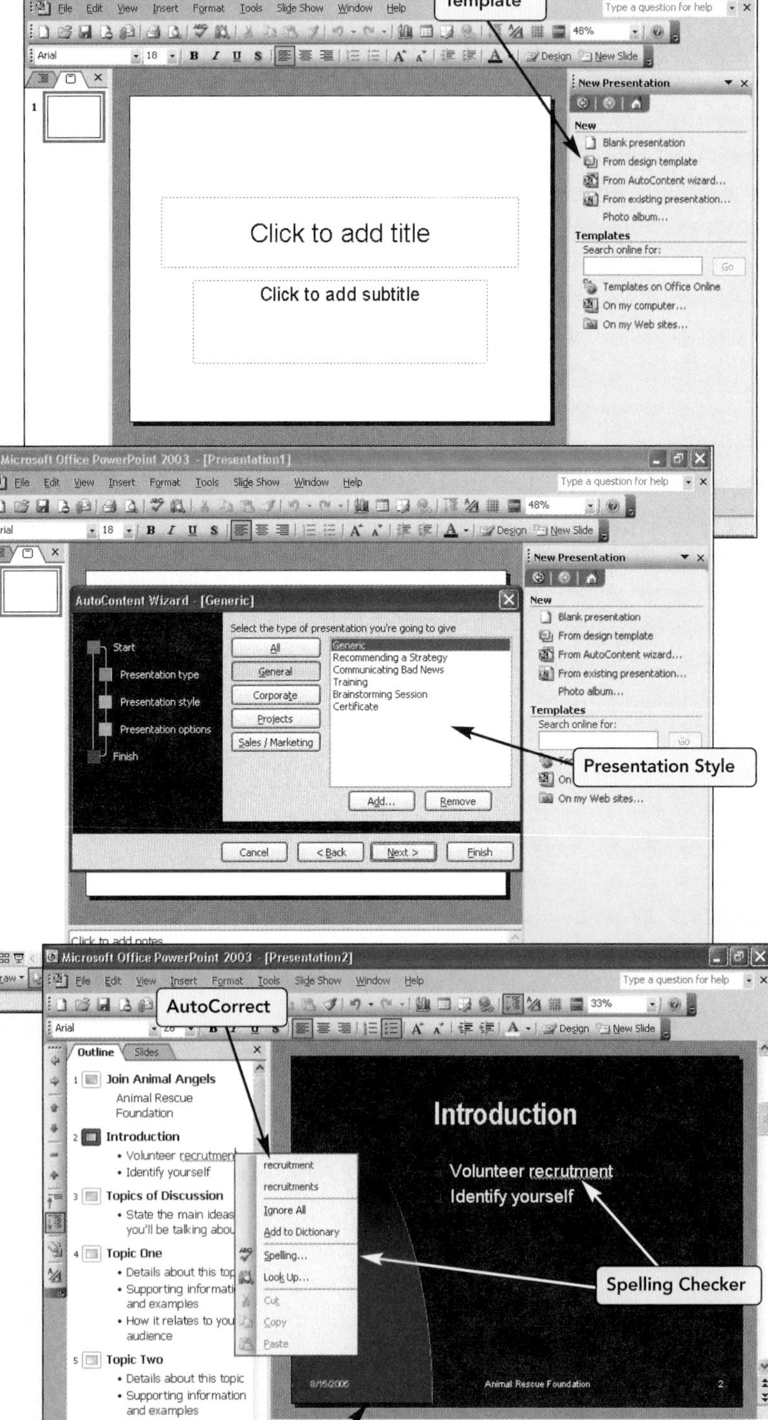

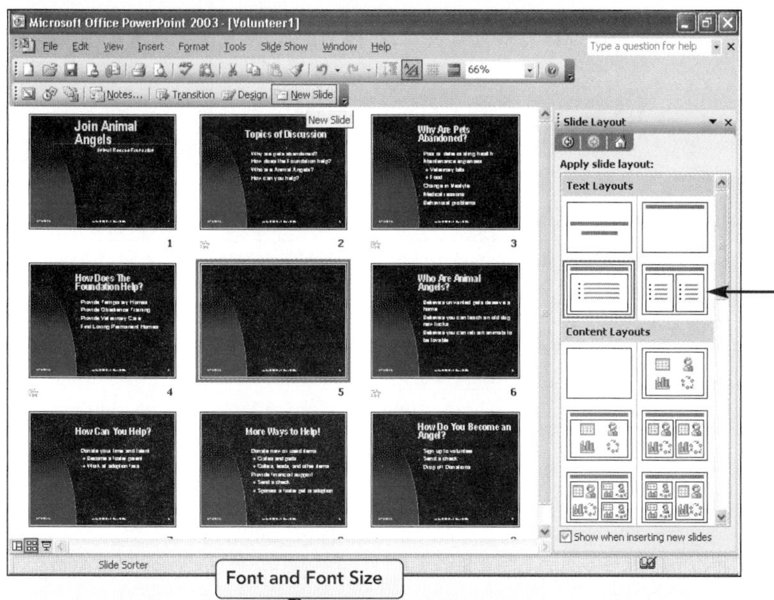


## Layout (PP1.43)

The layout controls the way items are arranged on a slide.

Font and Font Size

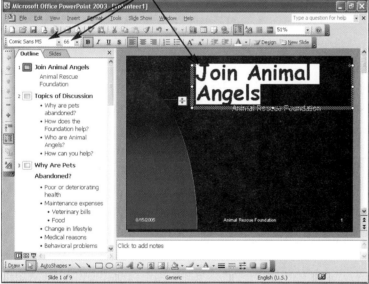

## Font and Font Size (PP1.50)

A font is a set of characters with a specific design. Each font has one or more sizes.

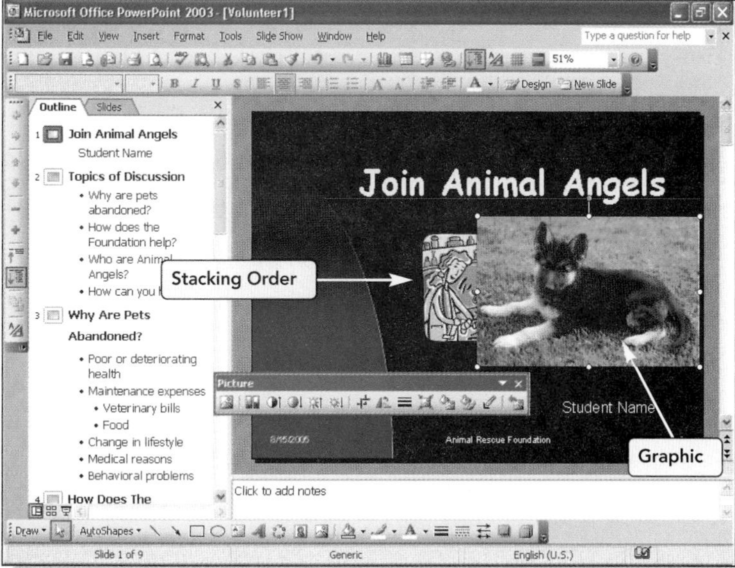


## Graphics (PP1.54)

A graphic is a non-text element or object, such as a drawing or picture, that can be added to a slide.

## Stacking Order (PP1.60)

Stacking order is the order in which objects are inserted in to different layers of the slide.

# LAB 1
## Creating a Presentation

## key terms

AutoCorrect PP1.19
character formatting PP1.49
clip art PP1.55
current slide PP1.15
custom dictionary PP1.20
default PP1.7
demote PP1.27
drawing object PP1.54
Drawing toolbar PP1.5
embedded object PP1.54
font PP1.50
font size PP1.50
footer PP1.11
format PP1.49
graphic PP1.54
keyword PP1.56
landscape PP1.64
layout PP1.43
main dictionary PP1.20
object PP1.23
Outlining toolbar PP1.5
pane PP1.13
paragraph formatting PP1.49
picture PP1.54
Picture toolbar PP1.59
placeholder PP1.23
point PP1.50
portrait PP1.64
promote PP1.27
sans serif PP1.50
selection rectangle PP1.24
serif PP1.50
sizing handles PP1.45
slide PP1.11
slide show PP1.47
source program PP1.54
spelling checker PP1.20
stacking order PP1.60
template PP1.7
thumbnail PP1.13
typeface PP1.50
view PP1.12
wizard PP1.8
workspace PP1.6

## microsoft office specialist skills

The Microsoft Office Specialist certification program is designed to measure your proficiency in performing basic tasks using the Office 2003 applications. Certification demonstrates that you have the skills and provides a valuable industry credential for employment. After completing this lab, you have learned the following Microsoft Office PowerPoint 2003 Specialist skills:

| Skill Sets | Skill Standards | Page |
|---|---|---|
| Creating Content | Create new presentations from templates | PP1.7 |
| | Insert and edit text-based content | PP1.16 |
| | Insert pictures, shapes, and graphics | PP1.54 |
| Formatting Content | Format text-based content | PP1.49 |
| | Format pictures, shapes, and graphics | PP1.61 |
| Managing and Delivering Presentations | Organize a presentation | PP1.12,1.40–1.45 |
| | Deliver presentations | PP1.47 |
| | Save and publish presentations | PP1.31 |
| | Print slides, outlines, handouts, and speaker notes | PP1.62 |

## command summary

| Command | Shortcut Key | Button | Voice | Action |
|---|---|---|---|---|
| File/New | Ctrl + N | | | Creates new presentation |
| File/Open | Ctrl + O | | Open<br>File open<br>Open file | Opens existing presentation |
| File/Close | | | Close presentation | Closes presentation |
| File/Save | Ctrl + S | | Save | Saves presentation |
| File/Save As | | | | Saves presentation using new file name and/or location |
| File/Print Preview | | | Print preview | Displays preview of file |
| File/Print | Ctrl + P | | | Prints presentation |
| Edit/Undo | Ctrl + Z | | Undo | Reverses last action |
| Edit/Cut | Ctrl + X | | Cut | Cuts selection to Clipboard |
| Edit/Paste | Ctrl + V | | Paste | Pastes item from Clipboard |
| Edit/Select All | Ctrl + A | | | Selects all objects on a slide or all text in an object, or (in Outline pane) an entire outline |
| Edit/Delete Slide | Delete | | | Deletes selected slide |
| View/Normal | | | Normal<br>Normal view | Switches to Normal view |
| View/Slide Sorter | | | Slide sorter | Switches to Slide Sorter view |
| View/Slide Show | | | View show<br>Begin slide show<br>Start slide show<br>Slide show view | Runs slide show |

## command summary (continued)

| Command | Shortcut Key | Button | Voice | Action |
|---|---|---|---|---|
| **I**nsert/**N**ew Slide | Ctrl + M | New Slide | New slide<br>Insert new slide | Inserts new slide |
| **I**nsert/**P**icture/**C**lip Art | | | | Opens Clip Organizer and inserts selected clip art |
| **I**nsert/**P**icture/**F**rom File | | | | Inserts a picture from file on disk |
| F**o**rmat/**F**ont/**F**ont | | Arial | | Changes font type |
| F**o**rmat/**F**ont/**S**ize | | 18 | | Changes font size |
| F**o**rmat/**B**ullets and Numbering/Bulleted | | | | Adds and removes selected bullets |
| F**o**rmat/Slide **L**ayout | | | | Changes the layout of an existing or new slide |
| **T**ools/**S**pelling | F7 | | | Spell-checks presentation |

## screen identification

1. In the following PowerPoint screen, several items are identified by letters. Enter the correct term for each item in the spaces that follow.

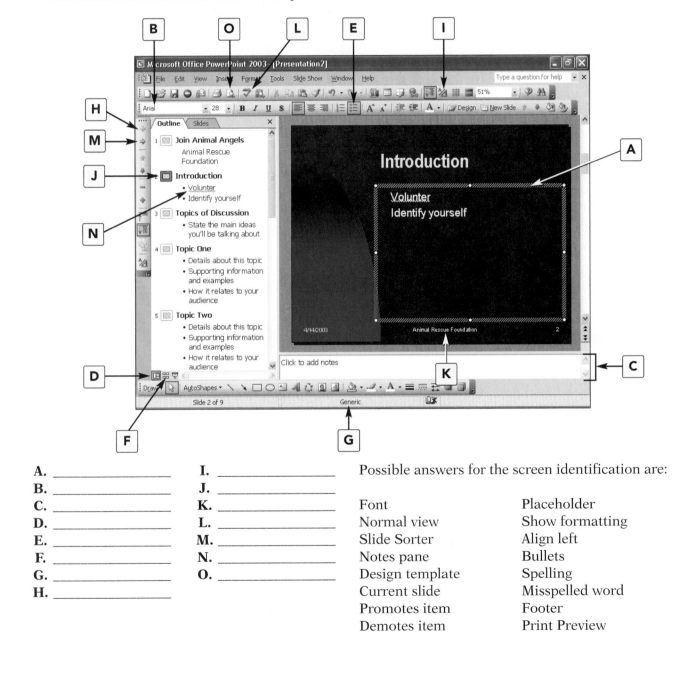

A. ______________

B. ______________

C. ______________

D. ______________

E. ______________

F. ______________

G. ______________

H. ______________

I. ______________

J. ______________

K. ______________

L. ______________

M. ______________

N. ______________

O. ______________

Possible answers for the screen identification are:

| | |
|---|---|
| Font | Placeholder |
| Normal view | Show formatting |
| Slide Sorter | Align left |
| Notes pane | Bullets |
| Design template | Spelling |
| Current slide | Misspelled word |
| Promotes item | Footer |
| Demotes item | Print Preview |

## matching

Match the numbered item with the correct lettered description.

| | | | |
|---|---|---|---|
| **1.** formatting | _____ | **a.** | allows text entry, deletion, selection, and formatting of an object when border appears hatched |
| **2.** title slide | _____ | **b.** | use to view and rearrange all slides |
| **3.** slide show | _____ | **c.** | demotes items in outline |
| **4.** [icon] | _____ | **d.** | controls the way items are arranged on a slide |
| **5.** .ppt | _____ | **e.** | file of predefined settings used as a pattern to create common types of presentations |
| **6.** Slide Sorter view | _____ | **f.** | displays each slide full screen and in order |
| **7.** workspace | _____ | **g.** | boxes that contain specific types of items or objects |
| **8.** template | _____ | **h.** | default file extension for PowerPoint documents |
| **9.** selection rectangle | _____ | **i.** | first slide in a presentation |
| **10.** layout | _____ | **j.** | large area of the screen where presentations are displayed |
| | _____ | **k.** | enhancing the appearance of the slide to make it more readable or attractive |

## multiple choice

Circle the letter of the correct response.

**1.** If you want to provide copies of your presentation to the audience showing multiple slides on a page, you would print _______________.
- **a.** slides
- **b.** handouts
- **c.** note pages
- **d.** outline area

**2.** If you only have access to an overhead projector, you should create _____________________.
- **a.** onscreen presentations
- **b.** Web presentations
- **c.** black-and-white or color transparencies
- **d.** all the above

**3.** The step in the development of a presentation that focuses on determining the length of your speech, the audience, the layout of the room, and the type of audiovisual equipment available is _____________________.
- **a.** planning
- **b.** creating
- **c.** editing
- **d.** enhancing

4. If you wanted to view the slides as your audience would, you would:
   a. print the notes pages
   b. run the slide show
   c. maximize the PowerPoint application window
   d. close the tabs pane

5. To make your presentation professional and easy to read, you would use a ________ font for the text and a __________ font for the headings.
   a. serif; sans serif
   b. large; small
   c. sans serif; serif
   d. red; black

6. If you want to work on all aspects of your presentation, switch to ____________________ view, which displays the slide pane, outline pane, and note pane.
   a. Slide Sorter
   b. Outline
   c. Slide
   d. Normal

7. When the spelling checker is used, you can create a ________________ dictionary to hold words that you commonly use but are not included in the main dictionary.
   a. custom
   b. official
   c. personal
   d. common

8. Dragging the _________________ sizing handles adjusts both the height and width of the placeholder at the same time.
   a. top
   b. bottom
   c. side
   d. corner

9. A(n)____________________is an onscreen display of your presentation.
   a. outline
   b. handout
   c. slide show
   d. slide

10. Onscreen presentations can be designed specifically for the World Wide Web, where a(n) ______________________ serves as the presentation tool.
    a. overhead projector
    b. browser
    c. white board
    d. computer screen

## true/false

Circle the correct answer to the following questions.

| | | | |
|---|---|---|---|
| 1. | A slide is a set of characters with a specific design. | True | False |
| 2. | The suggested maximum number of bullets on a slide is six. | True | False |
| 3. | All drawing objects are inserted into the same layer of the presentation. | True | False |
| 4. | Practicing the delivery of your presentation is the final step in presentation development | True | False |
| 5. | Sans serif fonts have a flair at the base of each letter that visually leads the reader to the next letter. | True | False |
| 6. | The page orientation can be landscape or portrait. | True | False |
| 7. | Graphics are objects, such as charts, drawings, pictures, and scanned photographs, that provide visual interest or clarify data. | True | False |
| 8. | Character formatting features affect selected characters only, while paragraph formatting features affect an entire paragraph. | True | False |
| 9. | A layout contains placeholders for the different items such as bulleted text, titles, charts, and so on. | True | False |
| 10. | Font size is the width of the character and is commonly measured in points. | True | False |

## fill-in

Complete the following statements by filling in the blanks with the correct terms.

1. ________________ order is the order objects are inserted in the different layers of the slide.
2. An embedded object is edited using the ______________ program.
3. The ____________________ Wizard is a guided approach that helps you determine the content and organization of your presentation through a series of questions.
4. The size of a ______________________ can be changed by dragging its sizing handles.
5. Boxes that are designed to contain specific types of objects such as the slide title, bulleted text, charts, tables, and pictures are called ______________________.
6. The ____________________ toolbar contains buttons that are used to change the appearance or format of the presentation.
7. A ________________ is text or graphics that appears at the bottom of each slide.
8. A ______________ is an individual "page" of your presentation.
9. ______________________________ is a PowerPoint feature that advises you of misspelled words as you add text to a slide and proposes possible corrections.
10. A ________________ is a miniature of a slide.

rating system

★ Easy

★★ Moderate

★★★ Difficult

## step-by-step

### Triple Crown Presentation ★

**1.** Logan Thomas works at Adventure Travel Tours. He is working on a presentation about lightweight hiking he will present to a group of interested clients. He has found some new information to add to the presentation. Logan also wants to rearrange several slides and make a few other changes to improve the appearance of the presentation. The handouts of the completed presentation are shown here.

- **a.** Open the file pp01_Triple Crown. Enter your name in the subtitle on slide 1.
- **b.** Run the slide show to see what Logan has done so far.
- **c.** Spell-check the presentation, making the appropriate corrections.
- **d.** Change the layout of slide 2 to Title, Text, and content. (Hint: Use Format/Slide Layout.) Increase the font size of the bulleted text on slide 2 from 28 to 32 points. Size and position the title, graphic, and text appropriately.
- **e.** Appropriately size and position the graphic on slide 3.
- **f.** Insert the picture pp01_Jump on slide 4. Size and position it appropriately.
- **g.** Move slide 6 before slide 5.
- **h.** Select slide 4. Open the Outline tab and click at the end of the last bullet under "Why go lightweight?" Press Enter and promote the new bullet twice. Enter the title **Less is More**.
- **i.** Change the layout of the new slide to Title, Text, and Content. Insert the picture pp01_Stream in the content placeholder.

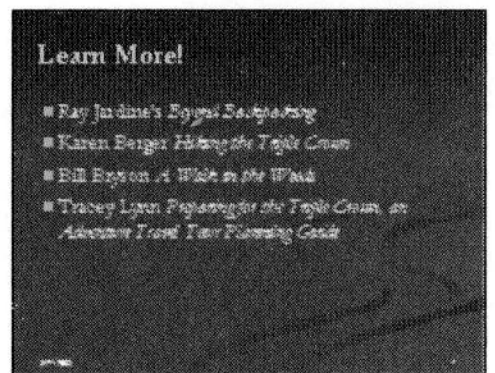

**j.** Change the layout of slide 7 to Title and Text layout. Add the following text in the text placeholder: **Contact Tracey Lynn at Adventure Travel Tours or visit us on the Web at www.AdventureTravelTours.com/hiking**.

**k.** Run the slide show.

**l.** Save the presentation as Triple Crown Presentation. Print the slides as handouts (four per page).

## Writing Effective Resumes ★ ★

**2.** You work for the career services center of a university and you are planning a presentation on how to write effective resumes and cover letters. A coworker has started such a presentation, but has not had time to edit or finalize it. You need to clean it up and enhance it a bit before presenting it. The handouts of the completed presentation are shown here.

**a.** Open the PowerPoint presentation pp01_Resume.

**b.** Run the Spelling Checker and correct any spelling errors.

**c.** In Normal view, change the font size of the title in the title slide to 44 pt. Increase the subtitle to 36 pt.

**d.** Replace "Student Name" in slide 2 with your name.

**e.** On slide 5, capitalize the first word of each bulleted item.

**f.** Since there is too much text on slide 6, split the slide content into two slides.

**g.** Reorganize the bulleted items on slide 10 so that "Types of cover letters" is the first item. To match the slide order with the way the topics are now introduced, move slide 13 before slide 11.

**h.** Break each bulleted item on slide 13 into two or three bullets

each as appropriate. Capitalize the first word of each bulleted item. Remove commas and periods at the end of the items. Split the slide content into three slides. Add an appropriate slide title to the slides.

i. On the title slide, insert the pp01_Success clip art. Resize and position it as shown in the example.

j. On slide 3, insert the pp01_Cover Letter clip art below the bulleted list. Position it in the lower right corner of the slide.

k. Save the presentation as Resume1.

l. Run the slide show.

m. Print the slides as handouts (nine per page in landscape orientation) and close the presentation.

## Massage Therapy ★ ★

3. Lifestyle Fitness Club is opening a new spa offering personal services that include therapeutic massage. Prior to opening, the club wants to promote the services to the community. The spa manager has asked you create a presentation that can be used as a sales tool with local groups and organizations. You have organized the topics to be presented and located several clip art graphics that will complement the talk. Now you are ready to begin creating the presentation. The handouts of the completed presentation are shown here.

a. Start PowerPoint 2003. Open the New Presentation task pane.

**b.** Using the AutoContent wizard, select Recommending a Strategy as the type of presentation, and select On-screen as the style of output for the presentation. Enter **Introducing Massage Therapy** in the Presentation Title text box. Enter your name in the footer text box. Keep the other footer options as they are.

**c.** Replace the owner name, your first name, on the title slide with **Lifestyle Fitness Club**.

**d.** Delete slide 2.

**e.** Replace the title and sample bullets on slide 2 with:

Title: **New Massage Facility**

Bullet 1: **Opens May 1**

Bullet 2: **Offers five certified massage therapists**

Bullet 3: **Provides service seven days a week**

Bullet 4: **Call now for an appointment**

**f.** Replace the title and sample bulleted text on slide 3 with:

Title: **Therapeutic Massage**

Bullet 1: **Manipulates soft body tissues**

Bullet 2: **Prevents injuries**

Bullet 3: **Alleviates pain**

Bullet 4: **Reduces stress**

Bullet 5: **Promotes health and wellness**

**g.** Change the title of slide 4 to **Reflexology** and replace the sample bullet text with the following bulleted items:

Bullet 1: **Massage points on hands and feet**

Bullet 2: **Points correspond to areas of the body**

Bullet 3: **Entire body affected**

**h.** Change the title of slide 5 to **Sports Massage Therapy** and include the following bulleted items:

Bullet 1: **Maintenance Massage**

Demoted Bullet 2: **Regular program of massage**

Demoted Bullet 3: **Helps athletes reach optimal performance**

Bullet 4: **Event Massage**

Demoted Bullet 5: **Readies athlete for top performance**

Demoted Bullet 6: **Stimulates circulation**

Bullet 7: **Rehabilitation Massage**

Demoted Bullet 8: **Speeds healing**

Demoted Bullet 9: **Reduces discomfort**

**i.** Change bullet 1 on slide 2 to **Opens June 1**. Delete bullet 4.

**j.** Insert a new slide after slide 2 using the Title and Text layout. Add the title **Benefits** and the following bulleted items:

Bullet 1: **Physical**

Demoted Bullet 2: **Relieves stress**

Demoted Bullet 3: **Reduces blood pressure**

Demoted Bullet 4: **Improves posture**

Demoted Bullet 5: **Strengthens immune system**

Bullet 6: **Mental**

Demoted Bullet 7: **Fosters peace of mind**

Demoted Bullet 8: **Helps relieve mental stress**

Demoted Bullet 9: **Fosters a feeling of well-being**

Change the order of bullets 3 and 4 on slide 4.

**k.** Insert a new slide after slide 5 using the Title and Text layout. Add the title **Shiatsu and Accupressure** and the following bulleted items:

Bullet 1: **Uses system of finger-pressure massage**

Bullet 2: **Based on Asian healing concepts**

Bullet 3: **Treats invisible channels of energy flow**

**l.** Change the title of slide 8 to **Swedish Massage** and include the following bulleted items:

Bullet 1: **Massages superficial muscle layer**

Bullet 2: **Promotes general relaxation**

Bullet 3: **Improves blood circulation**

Bullet 4: **Is most common type of massage**

**m.** Split the text on slide 3 between two slides. Title the first slide **Physical Benefits** and the second slide **Mental Benefits**. Delete the first bullet on both slides and promote the remaining bullets.

**n.** Change the font of the title on the title slide to 48 pt and the subtitle to 32 pt.

**o.** Insert the graphic pp01_Relaxation on slide 4. Size and position it appropriately.

**p.** Move slide 9 before slide 6.

**q.** Insert graphics of your choice to slides 3, 5, and 6. Size and position them appropriately.

**r.** Spell-check the presentation, making the appropriate changes.

**s.** Run the slide show.

**t.** Save the presentation as Massage Therapy.

**u.** Print the slides as handouts (six per page).

## Coffee Product Knowledge ★ ★ ★

4. As the manager of the Downtown Internet Café, you want to make a presentation to the other employees about the various blends of coffee that the cafe offers. The purpose of this presentation is to enable employees to answer the many questions that are asked by customers when looking at the Blend of the Day board or choosing the type of coffee beans they want to purchase. The handouts of the completed presentation are shown here.

   a. Start PowerPoint 2003. Open the new Presentation task pane.

   b. Using the AutoContent wizard, select Training as the type of presentation and select Color Overheads as the presentation style. Enter **Coffee Talk** in the Presentation Title text box. Enter your name in the footer text box and keep the other footer settings as they are.

   c. Replace your name in the title slide with **Downtown Internet Cafe**.

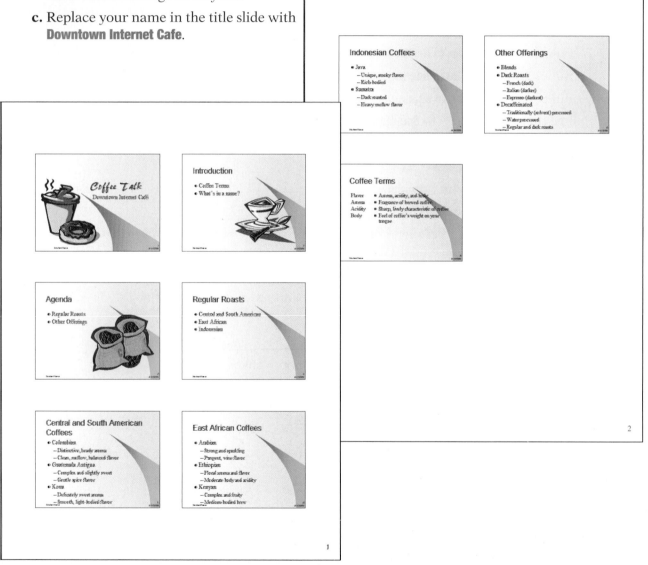

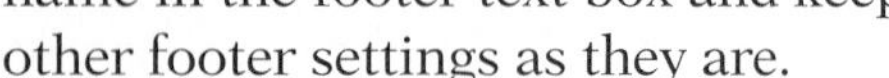

**d.** Replace the sample bulleted text on slide 2 with the following:

Bullet 1: **What's in a name?**

**e.** Replace the sample bulleted text on slide 3 with the following:

Bullet 1: **Regular Roasts**

Bullet 2: **Other Offerings**

**f.** Move slide 4 to the end of the presentation after slide 9.

**g.** In Normal view, change the title of slide 4 to **Regular Roasts** and replace the sample bulleted text with the following:

Bullet 1: **Central and South American**

Bullet 2: **East African**

Bullet 3: **Indonesian**

**h.** Change the title of slide 5 to **Central and South American Coffees** and replace the sample bulleted text with the following:

Bullet 1: **Colombian**

Demoted Bullet 2: **Distinctive, heady aroma**

Demoted Bullet 3: **Clean, mellow, balanced flavor**

Bullet 4: **Guatemala Antigua**

Demoted Bullet 5: **Complex and slightly sweet**

Demoted Bullet 6: **Gentle spice flavors**

Bullet 7: **Kona**

Demoted Bullet 8: **Delicately sweet aroma**

Demoted Bullet 9: **Smooth, light-bodied flavor**

**i.** Change the title of slide 6 to **East African Coffees** and replace the sample bulleted text with the following:

Bullet 1: **Arabian**

Demoted Bullet 2: **Strong and sparkling**

Demoted Bullet 3: **Pungent, wine flavor**

Bullet 4: **Ethiopian**

Demoted Bullet 5: **Floral aroma and flavor**

Demoted Bullet 6: **Moderate body and acidity**

Bullet 7: **Kenyan**

Demoted Bullet 8: **Medium-bodied brew**

Demoted Bullet 9: **Complex and fruity**

**j.** Change the title of slide 7 to **Indonesian Coffees** and replace the sample bulleted text with the following:

Bullet 1: **Java**

Demoted Bullet 2: **Unique, smoky flavor**

Demoted Bullet 3: **Rich-bodied**

Bullet 4: **Sumatra**

Demoted Bullet 5: **Dark roasted**

Demoted Bullet 6: **Heavy mellow flavor**

**k.** Change the title of slide 8 to **Other Offerings** and replace the sample bulleted text and graphic with the following:

Bullet 1: **Blends**

Bullet 2: **Dark Roasts**

Demoted Bullet 3: **French (dark)**

Demoted Bullet 4: **Italian (darker)**

Demoted Bullet 5: **Espresso (darkest)**

Bullet 6: **Decaffeinated**

Demoted Bullet 7: **Traditionally (solvent) processed**

Demoted Bullet 8: **Water processed**

Demoted Bullet 9: **Regular and dark roasts**

**l.** Change the order of the last two demoted bulleted items in slide 6.

**m.** Add a second bullet to slide 2 with the text **Coffee Terms**.

**n.** Change the title of slide 9 to **Coffee Terms**. Change the layout to Title and 2-Column Text. (Hint: Use Format/Slide Layout.) Select and delete the graphic. Replace the sample bulleted text with the following in the columns indicated:

| Left Column | Right Column |
|---|---|
| Bullet 1: **Flavor** | **Aroma, acidity, and body** |
| Bullet 2: **Aroma** | **Fragrance of brewed coffee** |
| Bullet 3: **Acidity** | **Sharp, lively characteristic of coffee** |
| Bullet 4: **Body** | **Feel of coffee's weight on your tongue** |

**o.** On slide 9, remove the bullets from the left column. Size and position the column placeholders to align the information in both columns as shown in the example.

**p.** On the title slide, position the subtitle directly under the title. Change the font and size of the title to improve its appearance.

**q.** On the title slide, insert the clip art pp01_Logo. Resize and position it in the lower left corner. Move the title and subtitle to the right of the logo.

**r.** Insert the clip art pp01_Cuppa on slide 2. Appropriately size and position the bulleted items and clip art on the slide.

**s.** Insert the clip art pp01_Beans on slide 3. Appropriately size and position the clip art on the slide.

**t.** Run the Spelling Checker and correct any spelling errors.

**u.** Save the presentation as Coffee.

**v.** Run the slide show.

**w.** Print the slides as handouts (six per page).

## Job Fair Presentation ★★

5. Jane is preparing for her talk on "Job Fairs" for her Career Club meeting. She has organized the topic to be presented and located several clip art graphics that will complement the talk. She is now ready to begin creating the presentation in PowerPoint. The handouts of the completed presentation are shown here.

   a. Start PowerPoint 2003 and open the new Presentation task pane. Using the AutoContent wizard, select Recommending a Strategy as the type of presentation, and select Color Overheads as the style of output for the presentation. Enter **Making a Job Fair Work for You** in the Presentation Title text box. Enter your name in the footer text box. Keep the other footer options as they are.

   b. Change the font of the title to 48 pts. Replace your name on the title slide with **University Career Club**.

   c. Delete slide 2.

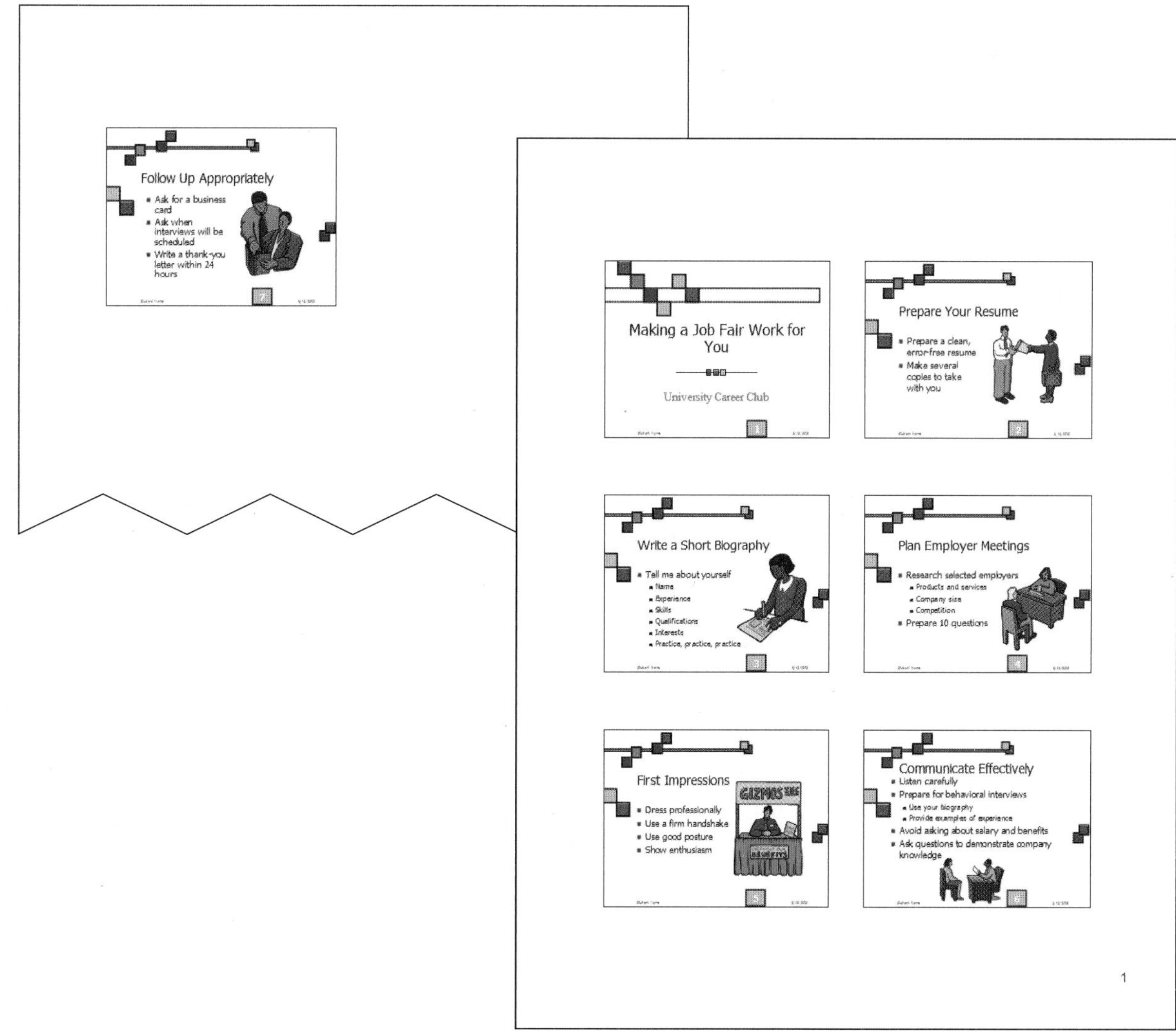

**d.** Replace the title and sample bulleted text on the new slide 2 with:

Title: **Prepare Your Resume**

Bullet 1: **Prepare a clean, error-free resume**

Bullet 2: **Make several copies to take with you**

**e.** Replace the title and sample bulleted text in slide 3 with:

Title: **Write a Short Biography**

Bullet 1: **Tell me about yourself**

Demoted Bullet 2: **Name**

Demoted Bullet 3: **Experience**

Demoted Bullet 4: **Skills**

Demoted Bullet 5: **Qualifications**

Demoted Bullet 6: **Interests**

Demoted Bullet 7: **Practice, practice, practice**

**f.** Replace the title and sample bulleted text in slide 4 with:

Title: **Plan Employer Meetings**

Bullet 1: **Research selected employers**

Demoted Bullet 2: **Products and services**

Demoted Bullet 3: **Company size**

Demoted Bullet 4: **Competition**

Bullet 5: **Prepare 10 questions**

**g.** Change the title of slide 5 to **Communicate Effectively** and include the following bulleted items:

Bullet 1: **Listen carefully**

Bullet 2: **Prepare for behavioral interviews**

Demoted Bullet 2: **Use your biography**

Demoted Bullet 3: **Provide examples of experience**

Bullet 3: **Avoid asking about salary and benefits**

Bullet 4: **Ask questions to demonstrate company knowledge**

**h.** Change the title of slide 6 to **First Impressions** and include the following bulleted items:

Bullet 1: **Dress professionally**

Bullet 2: **Use a firm handshake**

Bullet 3: **Use good posture**

Bullet 4: **Show enthusiasm**

**i.** Insert a new title and text slide after slide 6. Change the title to **Follow Up Appropriately** and include the following bulleted items:

Bullet 1: **Ask for a business card**

Bullet 2: **Ask when interviews will be scheduled**

Bullet 3: **Write a thank-you letter within 24 hours**

**j.** In Slide Sorter view, move slide 6 before slide 5.

**k.** Change the font of the subtitle on the title slide to Times New Roman and the size to 36 pt.

**l.** Insert the following graphics in the slides indicated. Adjust the slide layout as needed. Size and position the graphics appropriately.

Slide 2: pp01_Resume

Slide 3: pp01_Biography

Slide 4: pp01_Meeting

Slide 5: pp01_Booth

Slide 6: pp01_Interview

Slide 7: pp01_Follow Up

**m.** Run the slide show.

**n.** Save the presentation as Job Fairs.

**o.** Print the slides as handouts (six per page).

## on your own

### Internet Policy Presentation ★

**1.** You are working in the information technology department at Global Center Corporation. Your manager has asked you to give a presentation on the corporation's Internet policy to the new hire orientation class. Create your presentation in PowerPoint, using the information in the file pp01_InternetPolicy as a resource. Use the AutoContent wizard and the Generic template. Include your name in the footer. When you are done, run the spelling checker, then save your presentation as Internet Policy and print it.

### Telephone Training Course ★ ★

**2.** You are a trainer with Super Software, Inc. You received a memo from your manager alerting you that many of the support personnel are not using proper telephone protocol or obtaining the proper information from the customers who call in. Your manager has asked you to conduct a training class that covers these topics. Using the pp01_Memo data file as a resource, prepare the slides for your class. Use the AutoContent wizard and select an appropriate presentation type. Include your name in the footer. When you are done, save the presentation as Phone Etiquette and print the handouts.

### Pet Activities Presentation ★ ★

**3.** The director of Animal Rescue Foundation has asked you to prepare a presentation that introduces activities people can do with their new adopted pet. Using the pp01_Animals data file as a resource, create an onscreen presentation using the AutoContent wizard. Select an appropriate presentation type. Add clip art, where applicable. Include your name in the footer. When you are done, save the presentation as Pet Activities and print the handouts.

### Job Placement Services ★ ★ ★

**4.** You work at a job placement agency, and you have been asked to do a presentation for new clients that describes the services your company offers and the categories used to list available jobs. Visit a local placement agency or search the Web to gather information about job placement agency services and job listings. Using the AutoContent wizard, select an appropriate presentation type to create a short presentation. Include your name in the footer. When you are done, save the presentation as Placement Services and print the handouts.

### Careers with Animals ★ ★ ★

5. You have been volunteering at the Animal Rescue Foundation. The director has asked you to prepare a presentation on careers with animals to present to local schools in hopes that some students will be inspired to volunteer at the foundation. Using the pp01_AnimalCareers data file as a resource, create an onscreen presentation using the AutoContent wizard. Select an appropriate presentation type. Add some clip art where appropriate. Include your name in the footer. When you are done, save the presentation as Careers with Animals and print the handouts.

# Modifying and Refining a Presentation

LAB 2

## Objectives

After completing this lab, you will know how to:

1. Find and replace text.
2. Create and enhance a table.
3. Modify graphic objects and create a text box.
4. Create and enhance AutoShapes.
5. Change the presentation's design and color scheme.
6. Change slide and title masters.
7. Hide the title slide footer.
8. Duplicate and hide slides.
9. Add animation, sound, transition, and build effects.
10. Control and annotate a slide show.
11. Add speaker notes.
12. Check style consistency.
13. Document a file.
14. Customize print settings.

# Case Study

## Animal Rescue Foundation

The Animal Rescue Foundation director was very impressed with your first draft of the presentation to recruit volunteers, and asked to see the presentation onscreen. While viewing it together, you explained that you plan to make many more changes to improve the appearance of the presentation. For example, you plan to use a different design background and to include more art and other graphic features to enhance the appearance of the slides. You also explained that you will add more action to the slides using the special effects included with PowerPoint to keep the audience's attention.

The director suggested that you include more information on ways that volunteers can help. Additionally, because the organization has such an excellent adoption rate, the director wants you to include a table to illustrate the success of the adoption program.

Office PowerPoint 2003 gives you the design and production capabilities to create a first-class onscreen presentation. These features include artist-designed layouts and color schemes that give your presentation a professional appearance. In addition, you can add your own personal touches by modifying text attributes, incorporating art or graphics, and including animation to add impact, interest, and excitement to your presentation.

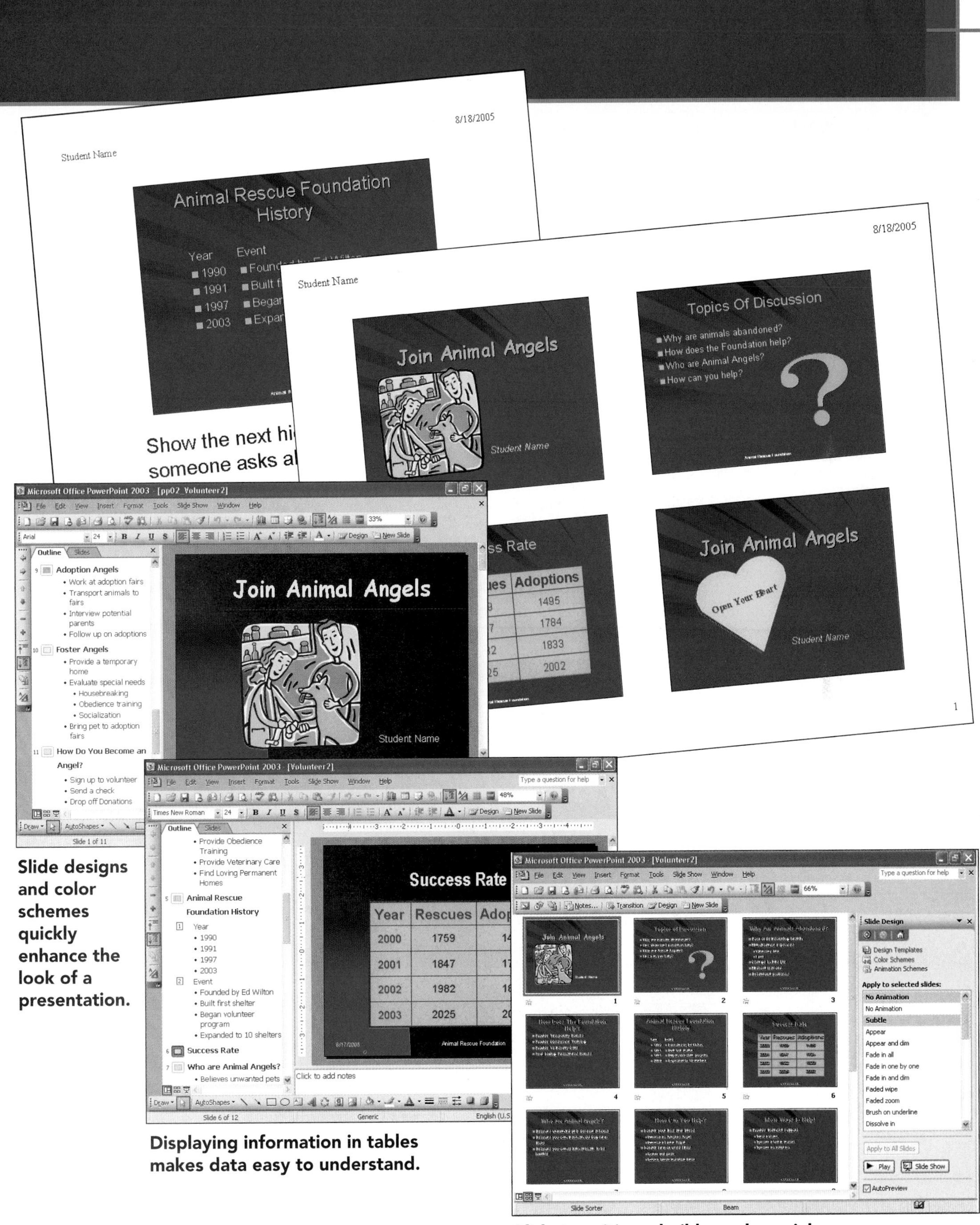


**Slide designs and color schemes quickly enhance the look of a presentation.**

**Displaying information in tables makes data easy to understand.**

**Slide transitions, builds, and special effects add action to a slide show.**

# Concept Preview

The following concepts will be introduced in this lab:

1. **Find and Replace** To make editing easier, you can use the Find and Replace feature to find text in a presentation and replace it with other text.
2. **Table** A table is used to organize information into an easy-to-read format of horizontal rows and vertical columns.
3. **Alignment** Alignment controls the position of text entries within a space.
4. **Design Template** A design template is a professionally created slide design that is stored as a file and can be applied to your presentation.
5. **Master** A master is a special slide or page that stores information about the formatting for all slides or pages in a presentation.
6. **Special Effects** Special effects such as animation, sound, slide transitions, and builds are used to enhance the onscreen presentation.

## Replacing Text

You have updated the content to include the additional information on ways that volunteers can help the Animal Rescue Foundation. You want to see the revised presentation.

**1**
- **Start Office PowerPoint 2003.**
- **Open the file** pp02_Volunteer2**.**
- **If necessary, switch to Normal view and close the task pane.**
- **Replace Student Name in slide 1 with your name.**
- **Scroll the Outline tab to view the content of the revised presentation.**

*Your screen should be similar to Figure 2.1*

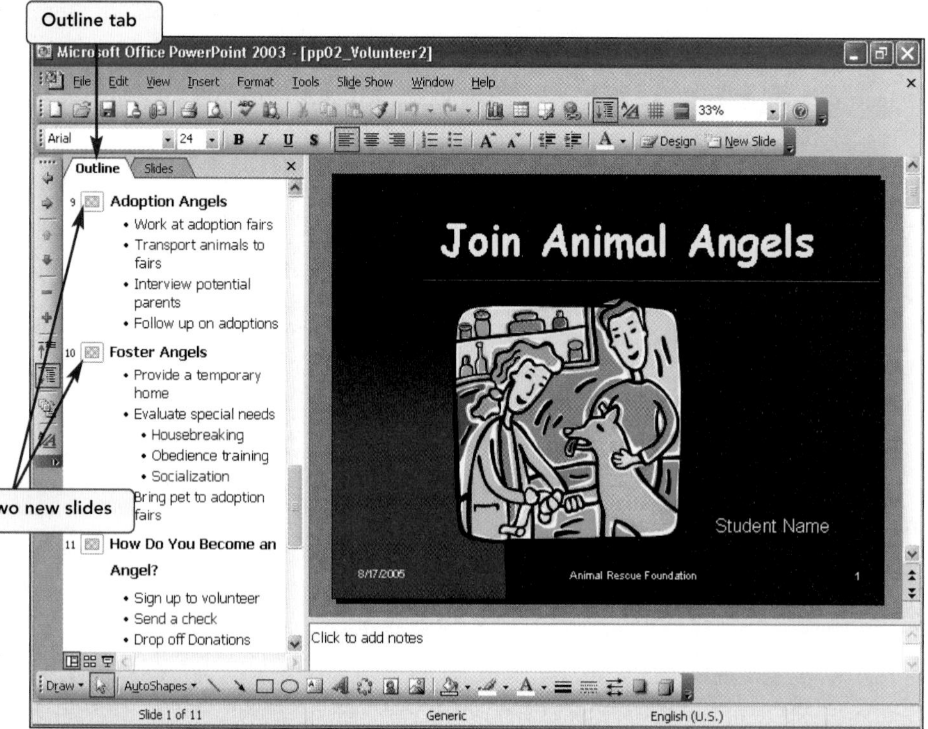


**Figure 2.1**

You added two new slides, 9 and 10, with more information about the Animal Angels volunteer organization, making the total number of slides in the presentation 11. As you reread the content of the presentation, you decide to edit the text by replacing the word "pet" in many locations with the word "animal."

## Concept 1
### Find and Replace

1 To make editing easier, you can use the **Find and Replace** feature to find text in a presentation and replace it with other text. For example, suppose you created a lengthy document describing the type of clothing and equipment needed to set up a world-class home gym, and then you decided to change "sneakers" to "athletic shoes." Instead of deleting every occurrence of "sneakers" and typing "athletic shoes," you can use the Find and Replace feature to perform the task automatically.

This feature is fast and accurate; however, use care when replacing so that you do not replace unintended matches.

## Using Find and Replace

You want to replace selected occurrences of the word "pet" with "animal" throughout the presentation.

**1** • **If necessary, display slide 1.**

• **Choose Edit/Replace.**

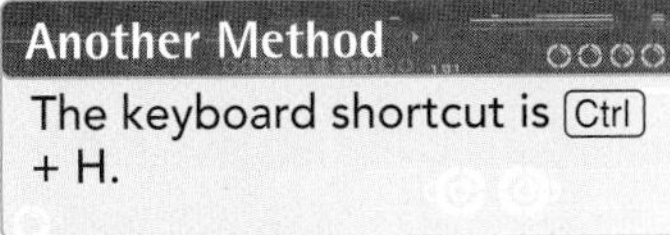


**Additional Information**

The Edit/Find command locates specified text only.

*Your screen should be similar to Figure 2.2*

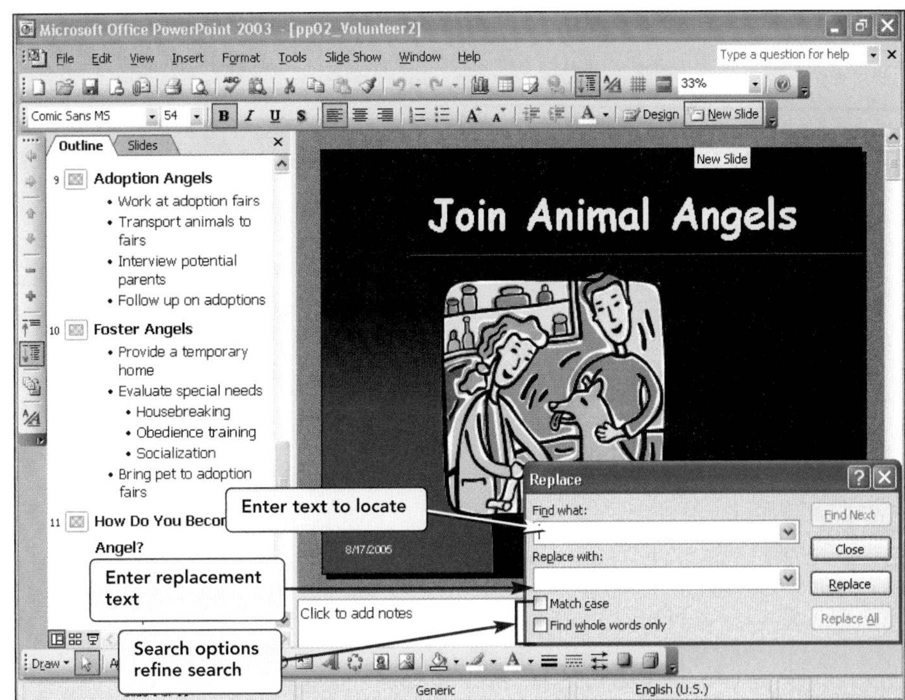


**Figure 2.2**

In the Find What text box, you enter the text you want to locate. The text you want to replace is entered in the Replace With text box. The replacement text must be entered exactly as you want it to appear in your presentation. The two options described in the following table allow you to refine the procedure that is used to conduct the search.

| Option | Effect on Text |
|---|---|
| Match Case | Distinguishes between uppercase and lowercase characters. When selected, finds only those instances in which the capitalization matches the text you typed in the Find What box. |
| Find Whole Words Only | Distinguishes between whole and partial words. When selected, locates matches that are whole words and not part of a larger word. For example, finds "cat" only and not "catastrophe" too. |

You want to find all occurrences of the complete word "pet" and replace them with the word "animal." You will not use either option because you want to locate all words regardless of case and because you want to find "pet" as well as "pets" in the presentation. You will enter the text to find and replace and begin the search.

**2**

- **Type pet in the Find What text box.**
- **Pres Tab or click in the Replace with text box.**

**Additional Information**

After entering the text to find, do not press ←Enter or this will choose Find Next and the search will begin.

- **Type animal in the Replace With text box.**
- **Click Find Next.**
- **If necessary, move the dialog box so you can see the located text.**

*Your screen should be similar to Figure 2.3*

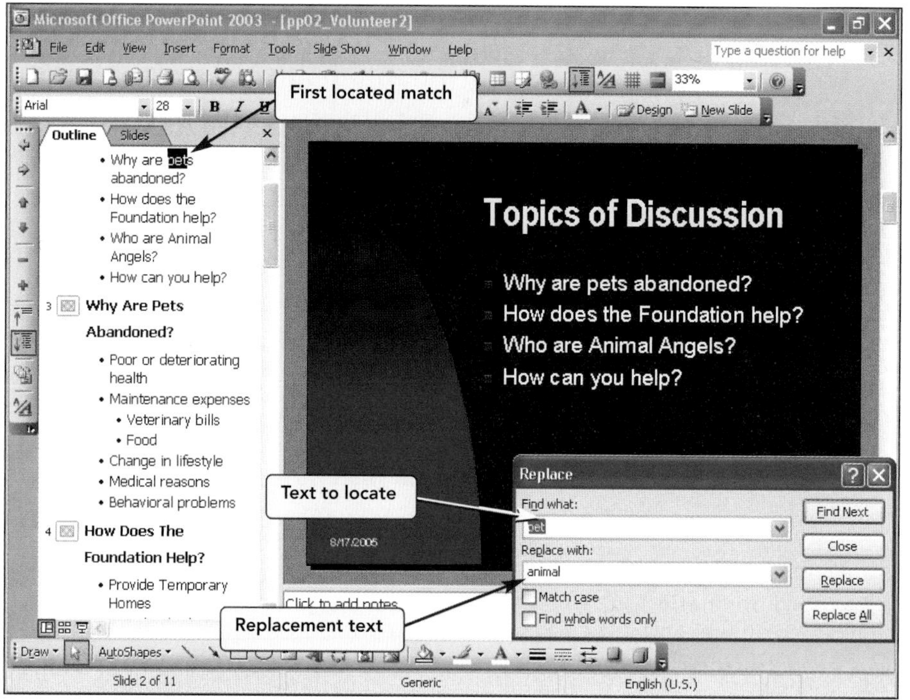


**Figure 2.3**

**Additional Information**

Find and Replace will highlight located text in whichever pane is current when the procedure started.

Immediately, the first occurrence of text in the presentation that matches the entry in the Find What text box is located and highlighted in the Outline tab. You will replace the located word in slide 2 with the replacement text.

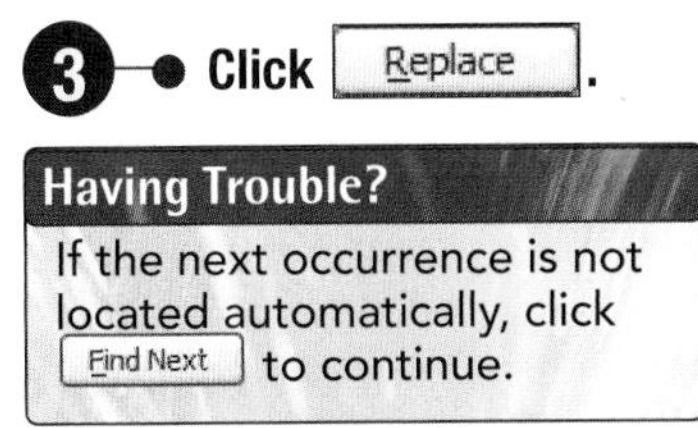


*Your screen should be similar to Figure 2.4*

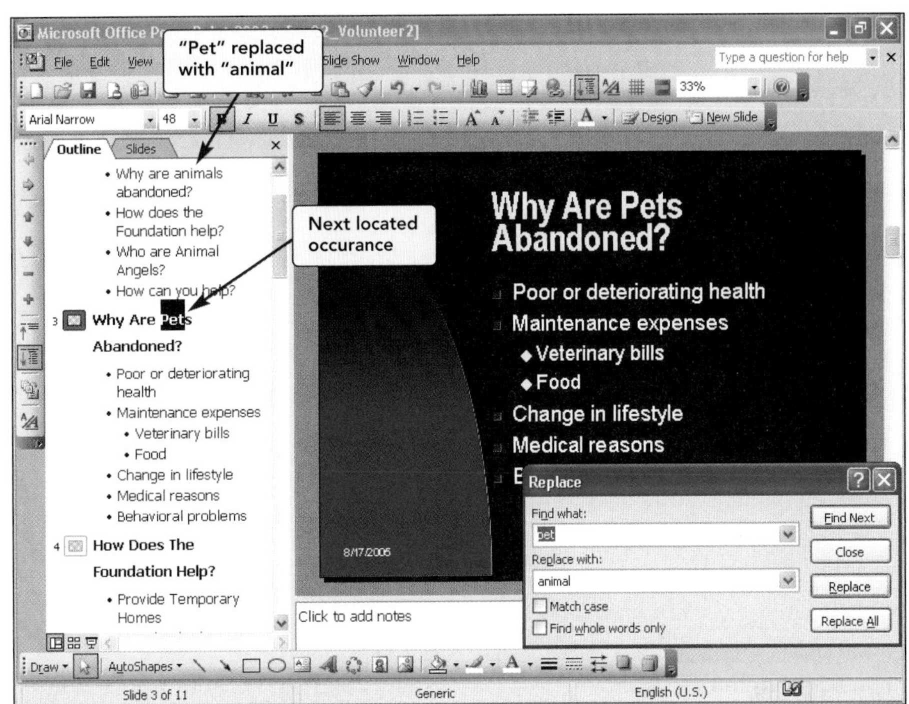


**Figure 2.4**

The highlighted text is replaced, and the next occurrence of the Find text is located in slide 3. Again, you want to replace this occurrence. As you do, notice the replacement is entered in lowercase even though it is replacing a word that begins with an uppercase character. You will correct this when you have finished using find and replace. If you do not want to replace a word, you can use Find Next to skip to the next occurrence without replacing it. You will continue to respond to the located occurrences.

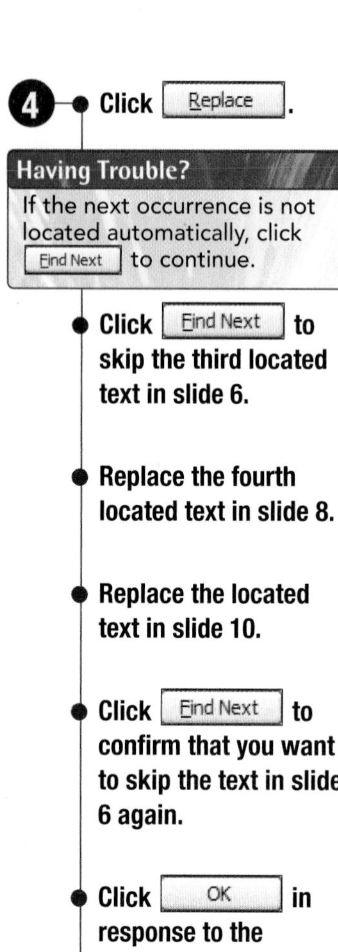

**4** **Click Replace.**

**Having Trouble?**

If the next occurrence is not located automatically, click Find Next to continue.

- **Click Find Next to skip the third located text in slide 6.**
- **Replace the fourth located text in slide 8.**
- **Replace the located text in slide 10.**
- **Click Find Next to confirm that you want to skip the text in slide 6 again.**
- **Click OK in response to the finished searching dialog box.**
- **Click Close to close the Replace dialog box.**
- **Edit the word "animals" to "Animals" in the title of slide 3.**
- **Save the presentation as Volunteer2.**

*Your screen should be similar to Figure 2.5*

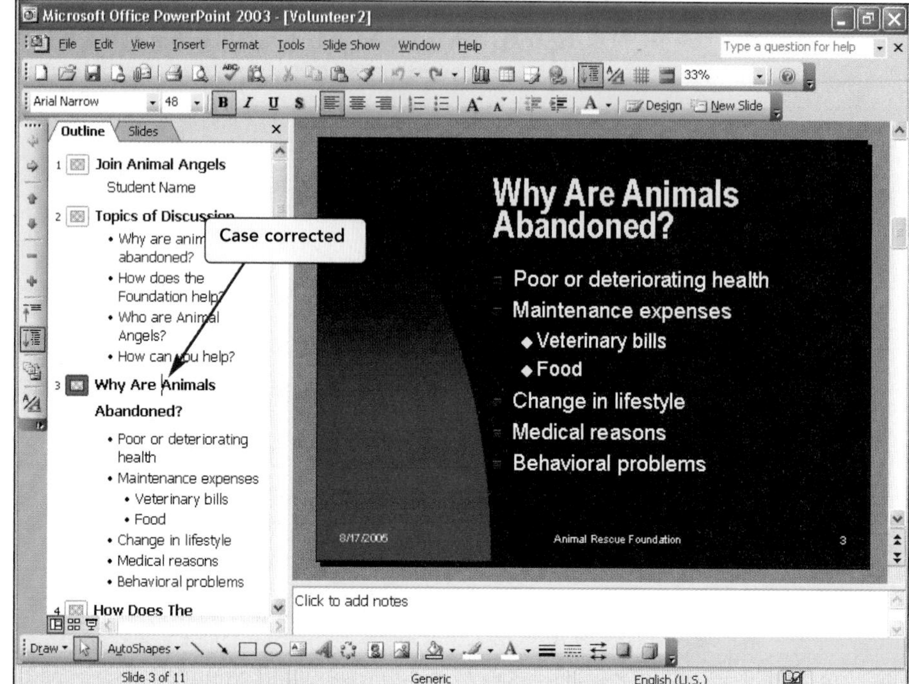


**Figure 2.5**

As you noticed, when you skip an occurrence, the program rechecks the presentation and asks you to reconfirm your choice before finishing. If you plan to change all occurrences, it is much faster to use the Replace All command button. Exercise care when using Replace All, however, because the search text you specify might be part of another word and you may accidentally replace text you want to keep.

In a similar manner you can find and replace fonts throughout a presentation using Format/Replace Fonts. When using this feature, however, all text throughout the presentation that is in the specified font to find is automatically changed to the selected replacement font.

## Creating a Simple Table

During your discussion with the director, he suggested that you add a slide containing data showing the success of the adoption program. The information in this slide will be presented using a table layout.

### Concept 2

**Table**

2 A **table** is used to organize information into an easy-to-read format of horizontal rows and vertical columns. The intersection of a row and column creates a **cell** in which you can enter data or other information. Cells in a table are identified by a letter and number, called a **table reference.** Columns are identified from left to right beginning with the letter A, and rows are numbered from top to bottom beginning with the number 1. The table reference of the top leftmost cell is A1 because it is in the first column (A) and first row (1) of the table. The third cell in column 2 is cell B3. The fourth cell in column 3 is C4.

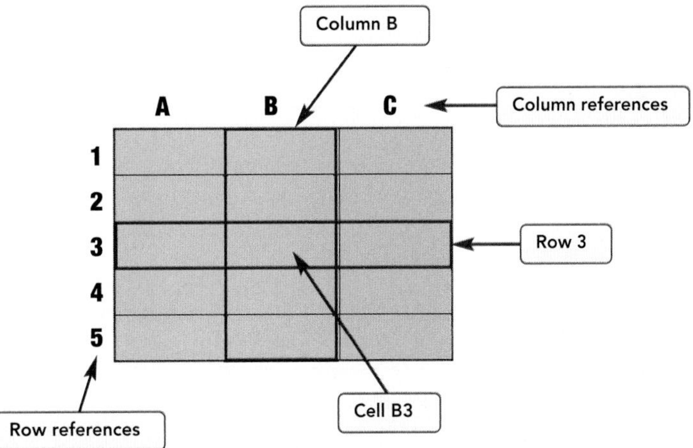


Tables are a very effective method for presenting information. The table layout organizes the information for readers and greatly reduces the number of words they have to read to interpret the data. Use tables whenever you can to make the information in your presentation easier to read.

The table you will create will display columns for the year, and for the number of rescues and adoptions. The rows will display the data for the past four years. Your completed table will be similar to the one shown here.

| Year | Rescues | Adoptions |
|---|---|---|
| 2000 | 1759 | 1495 |
| 2001 | 1847 | 1784 |
| 2002 | 1982 | 1833 |
| 2003 | 2025 | 2002 |

### Using the Table Layout

To include this information in the presentation, you will insert a new slide after slide 5. Because this slide will contain a table showing the adoption data, you want to use the table slide layout.

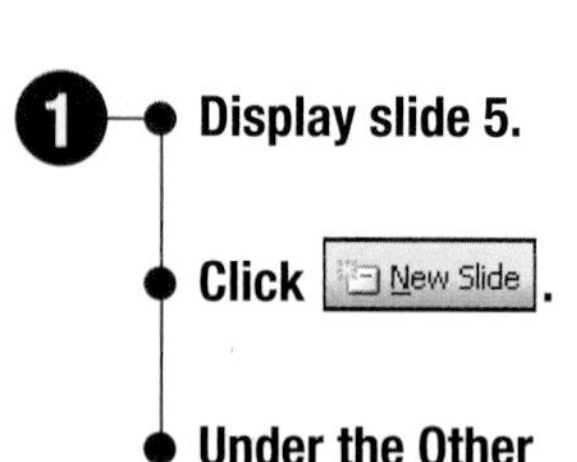

- **Display slide 5.**
- **Click New Slide.**
- **Under the Other Layouts group, click Title and Table.**
- **Close the Slide Layout task pane.**

*Your screen should be similar to Figure 2.6*

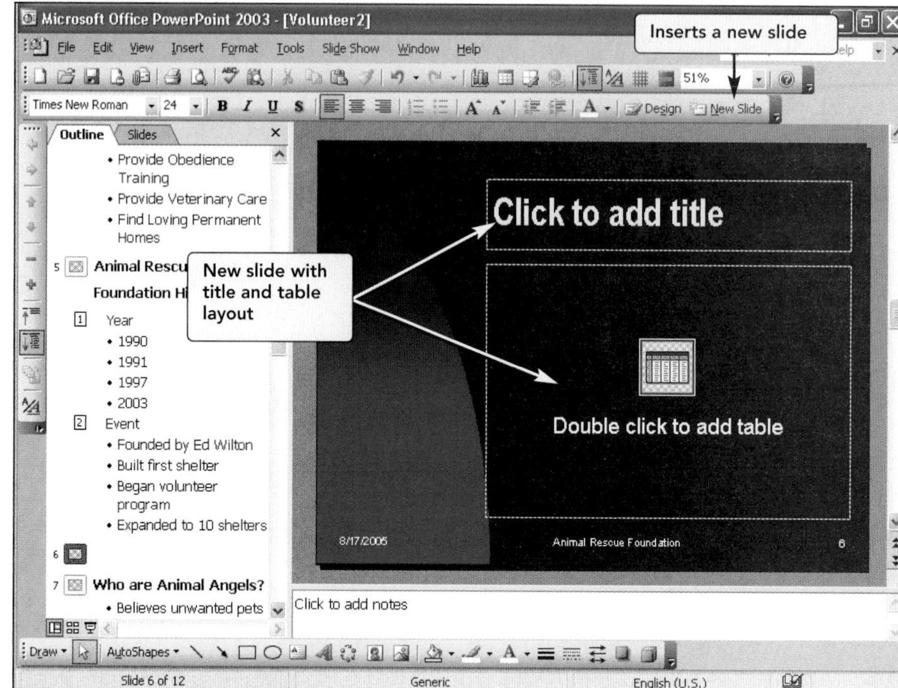


**Figure 2.6**

A new slide 6 with title and table placeholders is inserted.

## Inserting the Table

Next, you want to add a slide title and then create the table to display the number of adoptions and rescues.

- **Enter the title Success Rate in the title placeholder.**
- **Double-click the table placeholder.**

*Your screen should be similar to Figure 2.7*

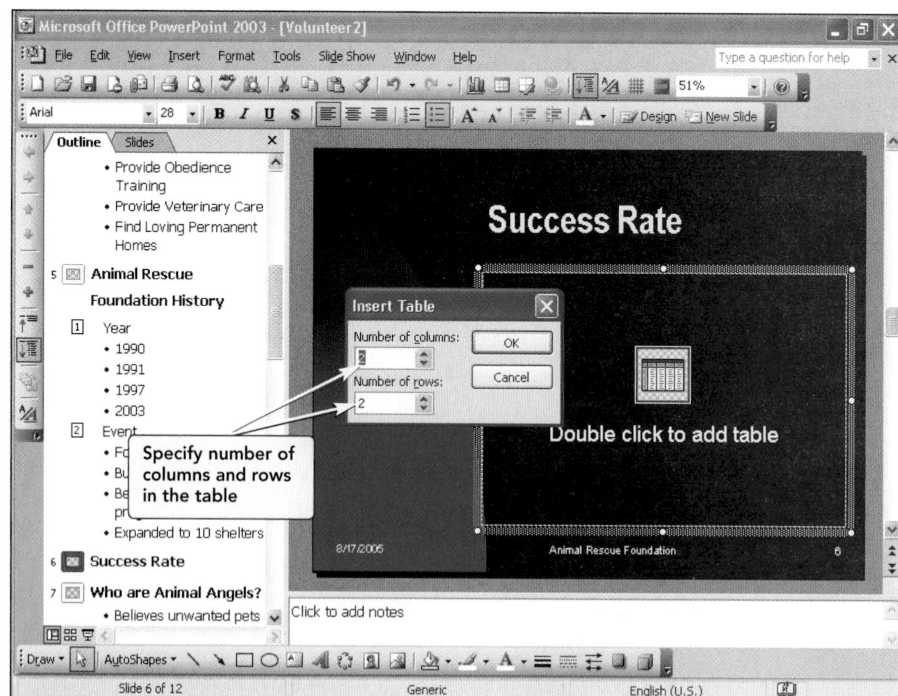


**Figure 2.7**

In the Insert Table dialog box, you specify the number of rows and columns for the table.

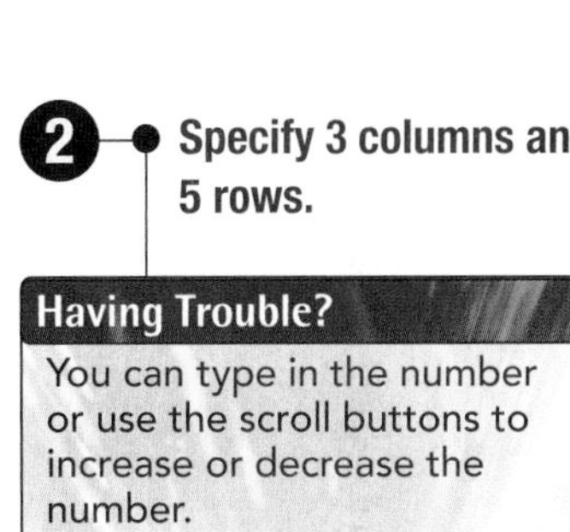

**2** **Specify 3 columns and 5 rows.**

**Having Trouble?**

You can type in the number or use the scroll buttons to increase or decrease the number.

- **Click** OK.
- **If necessary, move the Tables and Borders toolbar out of the way or dock it below the Formatting toolbar.**

*Your screen should be similar to Figure 2.8*

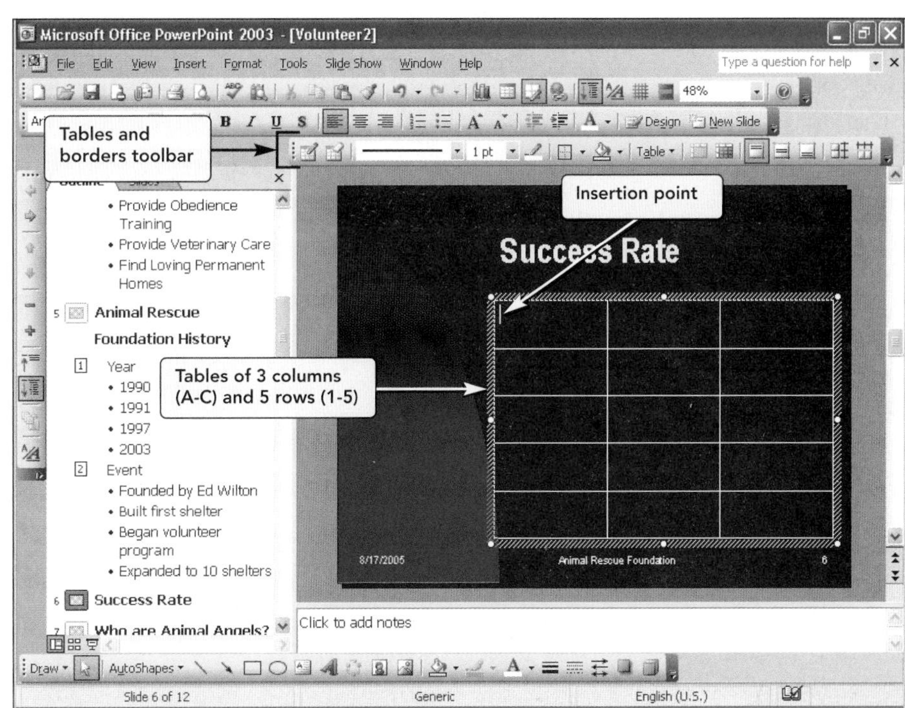


**Figure 2.8**

**Having Trouble?**

If the Tables and Borders toolbar is not displayed automatically, open it from the Toolbar shortcut menu.

A basic table consisting of three columns and five rows is displayed as a selected object. The Tables and Borders toolbar buttons (identified below) are used to modify features associated with tables.

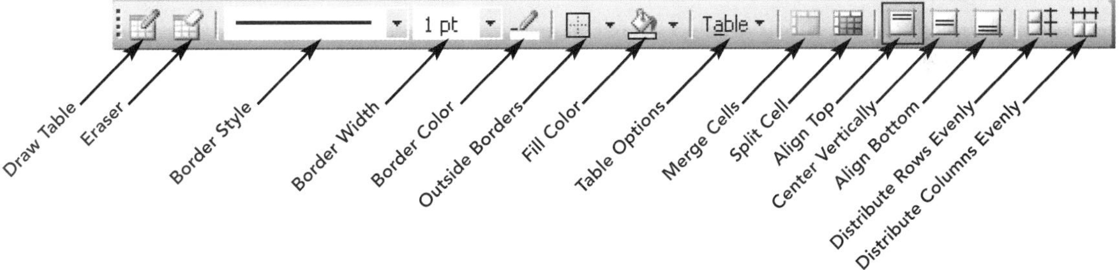


## Entering Data in a Table

Now, you can enter the information into the table. The insertion point appears in the top left corner cell, cell A1, ready for you to enter text. To move in a table, click on the cell or use Tab to move to the next cell to the right and ⇧Shift + Tab to move to the cell to the left. If you are in the last cell of a row, pressing Tab takes you to the first cell of the next row. You can also use the ↑ and ↓ directional keys to move up or down a row. When you enter a large amount of text in a table, using Tab to move rather than the mouse is easier because your hands are already on the keyboard.

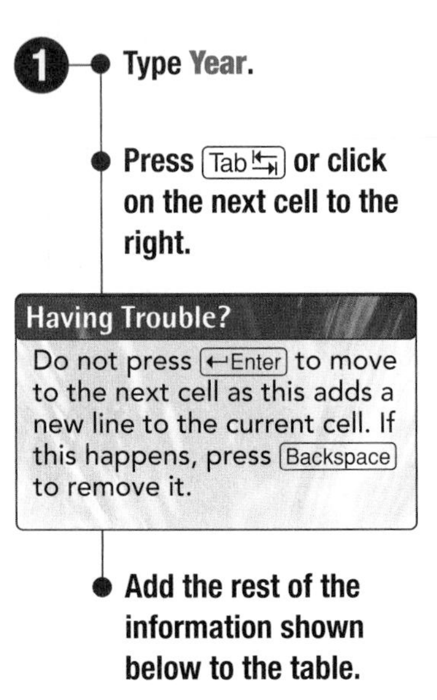

1. Type **Year.**

- Press Tab or click on the next cell to the right.

**Having Trouble?**

Do not press ←Enter to move to the next cell as this adds a new line to the current cell. If this happens, press Backspace to remove it.

- Add the rest of the information shown below to the table.

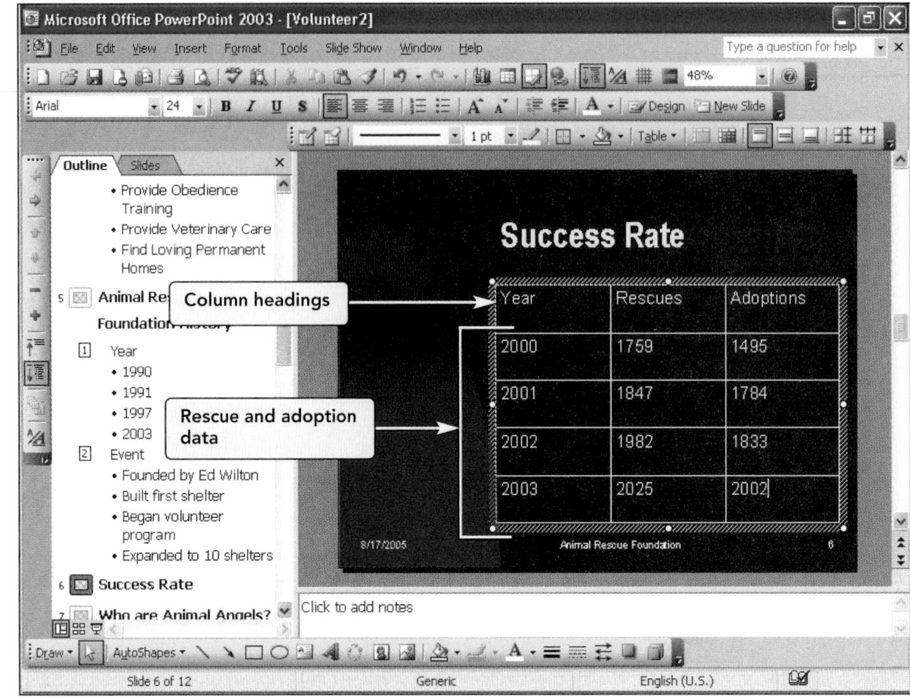


**Figure 2.9**

| | Col. A | Col. B | Col. C |
|---|---|---|---|
| Row 1 | Year | Rescues | Adoptions |
| Row 2 | 2000 | 1759 | 1495 |
| Row 3 | 2001 | 1847 | 1784 |
| Row 4 | 2002 | 1982 | 1833 |
| Row 5 | 2003 | 2025 | 2002 |

*Your screen should be similar to Figure 2.9*

Notice that text that is attached to an object, in this case a table, is not displayed in the outline pane.

## Applying Text Formats

**Additional Information**

Many of the Formatting toolbar buttons are toggle buttons, which means that you can click the button to turn on the feature for the selection, and then click it again to remove it from the selection.

Next, you want to improve the table's appearance by formatting the table text. Fonts and font size are two basic text attributes that you have used already. The table below describes some additional text formats and their uses. The Formatting toolbar contains buttons for many of the formatting effects.

| Format | Example | Use |
|---|---|---|
| Bold, italic | **Bold** *Italic* | Adds emphasis |
| Underline | Underline | Adds emphasis |
| Superscript | "To be or not to be."[1] | Used in footnotes and formulas |
| Subscript | $H_2O$ | Used in formulas |
| Shadow | Shadow | Adds distinction to titles and headings |
| Color | Color Color Color | Adds interest |

You will increase the font size of the table text and add bold and color.

**1**

- **Drag to select row 1 containing the column headings and increase the font size to 36 pt.**
- **Click B Bold to bold the selection.**

**Another Method**

The menu equivalent is Format/Font/Font Style/Bold and the voice command is "On bold" to apply it and "Off bold" to remove it.

- **Click A Font Color (in the Formatting or Drawing toolbar).**

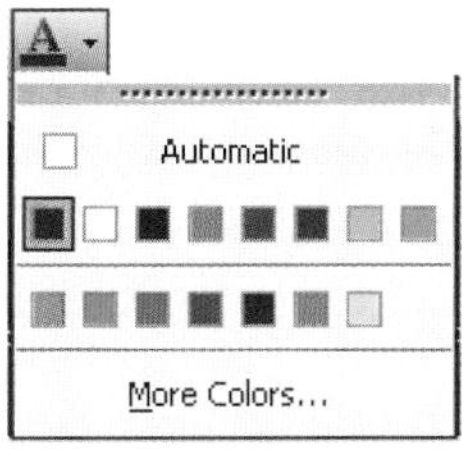


- **Click on the blue color.**

**Another Method**

The menu equivalent is Format/Font/Color.

- **Select rows 2 through 5 and increase the font size to 28.**

*Your screen should be similar to Figure 2.10*

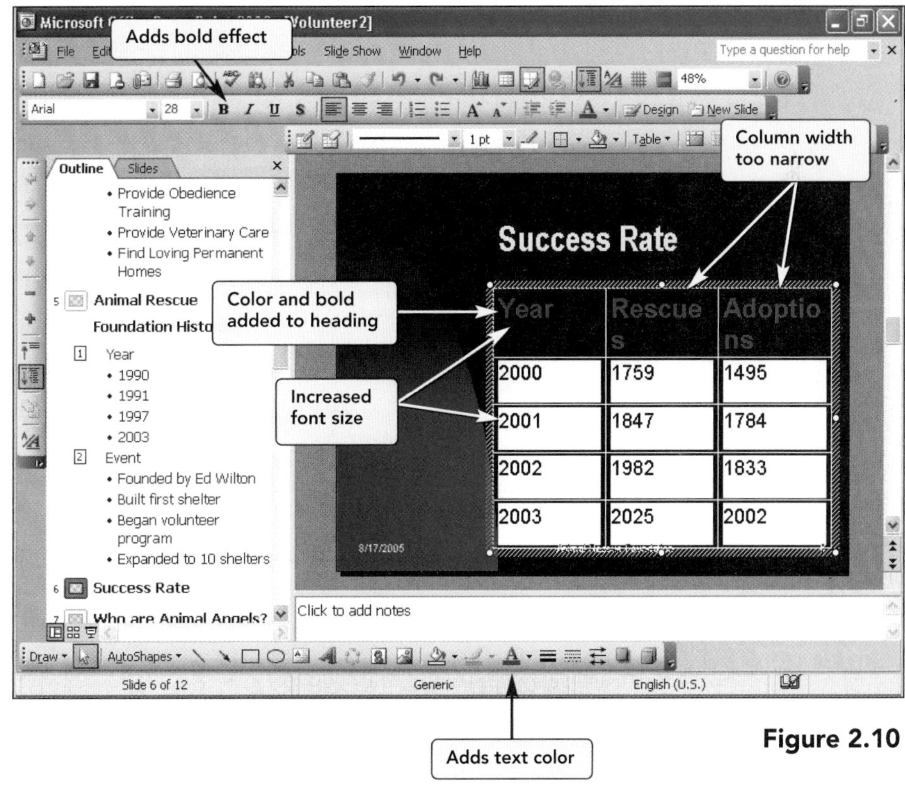


**Figure 2.10**

## Sizing the Table Columns

Because you increased the font size of the headings, two of the headings are too large to display on a single line in the cell space. To correct this problem, you will adjust the size of the columns to fit their contents. To adjust the column width or row height, drag the row and column boundaries. The mouse pointer appears as a ↔ when you can size the column and ↕ when you can size the row.

**1** **Decrease the width of the Year column and then adjust the width of the other two columns as in Figure 2.11.**

*Your screen should be similar to Figure 2.11*

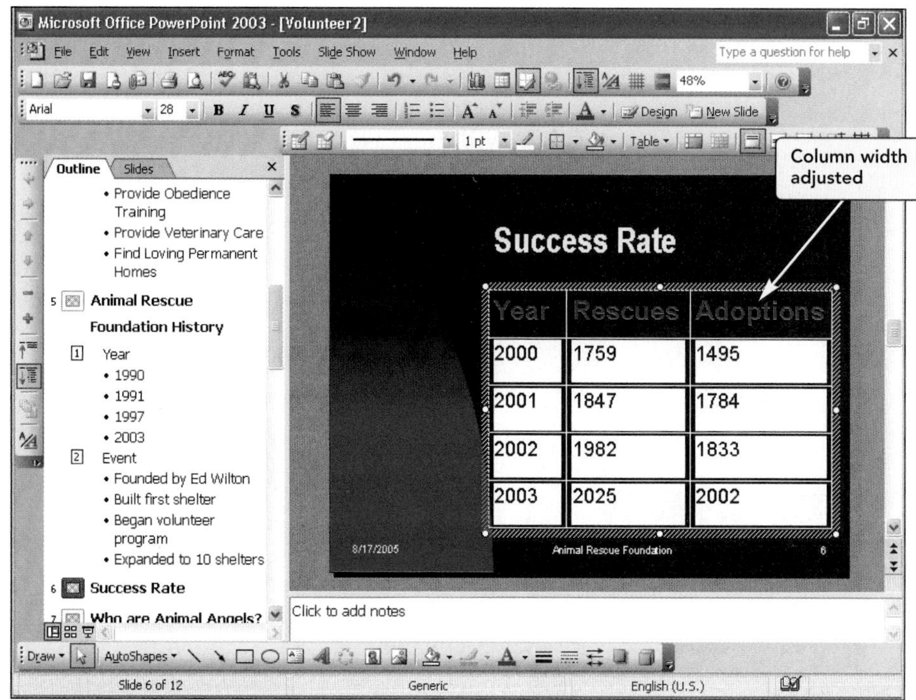


**Figure 2.11**

Now the column headings easily fit within the cell space.

## Aligning Text in Cells

Now that the columns are more appropriately sized, you want to center the text and data in the cells. To do this, you can change the alignment of the text entries.

## Concept 3

### Alignment

3 **Alignment** controls the position of text entries within a space. You can change the horizontal placement of an entry in a placeholder or a table cell by using one of the four horizontal alignment settings: left, center, right, and justified. You can also align text vertically in a table cell with the top, middle, or bottom of the cell space.

| Horizontal Alignment | Effect on Text | Vertical Alignment | Effect on Text |
|---|---|---|---|
| Left | Aligns text against the left edge of the placeholder or cell, leaving the right edge of text, which wraps to another line, ragged. | Top<br>Text | Aligns text at the top of the cell space. |
| Center | Centers each line of text between the left and right edges of the placeholder or cell. | Middle<br>Text | Aligns text in the middle of the cell space. |
| Right | Aligns text against the right edge of the placeholder or cell, leaving the left edge of multiple lines ragged. | Bottom<br>Text | Aligns text at the bottom of the cell space. |
| Justified | Aligns text evenly with both the right and left edges of the placeholder or cell. | | |

The commands to change horizontal alignment are options under the F<u>o</u>rmat/<u>A</u>lignment menu. However, using the shortcuts shown below is much quicker.

| Alignment | Keyboard Shortcut | Button | Voice |
|---|---|---|---|
| Left | Ctrl + L | | Left justify |
| Center | Ctrl + E | | Centered |
| Right | Ctrl + R | | Right justify |
| Justified | Ctrl + J | | |

You will center the cell entries both horizontally and vertically in their cell spaces.

**1**

- **Select the entire contents of the table.**
- **Click [Center icon] Center (on the Formatting toolbar).**
- **Click [Center Vertically icon] Center Vertically (on the Tables and Borders toolbar).**

*Your screen should be similar to Figure 2.12*

Centers text horizontally

Centers text vertically

Data centered horizontally and vertically within cell space

| Year | Rescues | Adoptions |
|---|---|---|
| 2000 | 1759 | 1495 |
| 2001 | 1847 | 1784 |
| 2002 | 1982 | 1833 |
| 2003 | 2025 | 2002 |

**Figure 2.12**

## Changing the Border Size and Color

Next, you will add a color to the outside border and increase the thickness or weight of the border line. The Tables and Borders toolbar is used to make these enhancements.

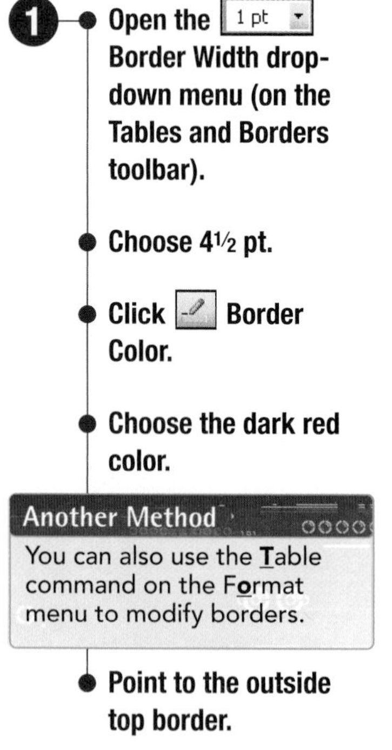

**1**

- **Open the [1 pt] Border Width drop-down menu (on the Tables and Borders toolbar).**
- **Choose 4½ pt.**
- **Click [Border Color icon] Border Color.**
- **Choose the dark red color.**

**Another Method**

You can also use the Table command on the Format menu to modify borders.

- **Point to the outside top border.**

*Your screen should be similar to Figure 2.13*

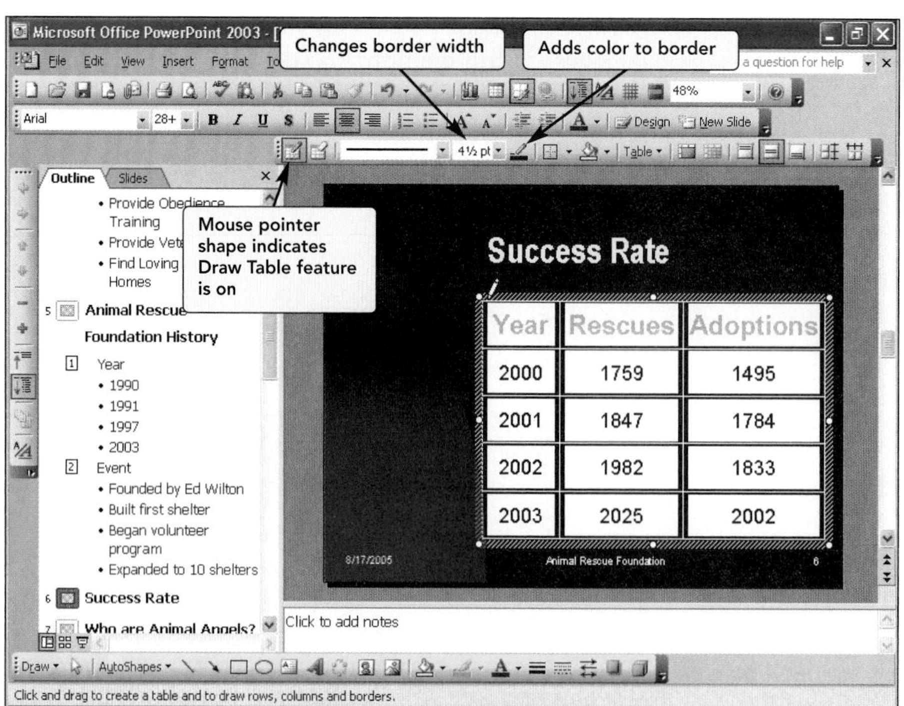


**Figure 2.13**

The mouse pointer is a ✎ indicating that the Draw Table feature has been turned on. When on, this feature allows you to add row and column lines to an existing table. It is also used to modify the settings associated with the existing lines. You will drag the mouse pointer over the existing outside border to modify it to the new settings you have selected. As you drag, a dotted line identifies the section of the border that will be modified.

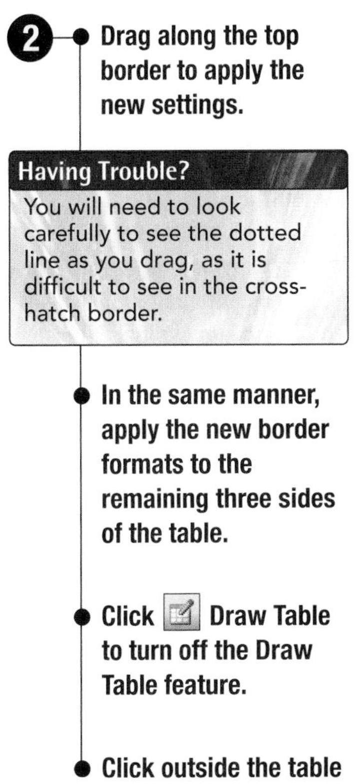

**2** **Drag along the top border to apply the new settings.**

**Having Trouble?**

You will need to look carefully to see the dotted line as you drag, as it is difficult to see in the cross-hatch border.

- **In the same manner, apply the new border formats to the remaining three sides of the table.**
- **Click Draw Table to turn off the Draw Table feature.**
- **Click outside the table to deselect it.**

*Your screen should be similar to Figure 2.14*

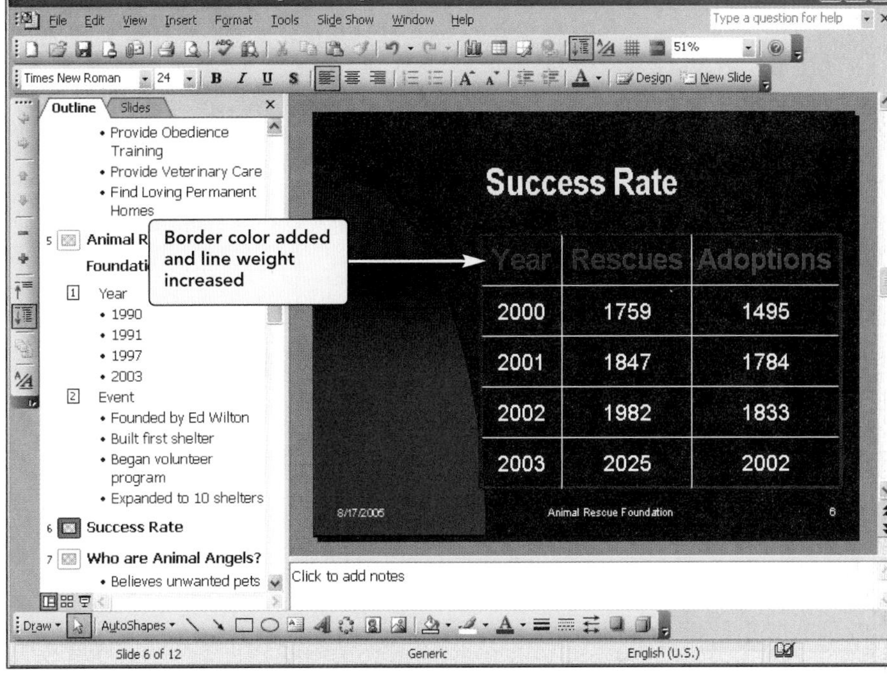


**Figure 2.14**

The increased weight and color have been applied to the outside border of the table.

## Adding Background Fill Color

Finally, you will add a background fill color to the table.

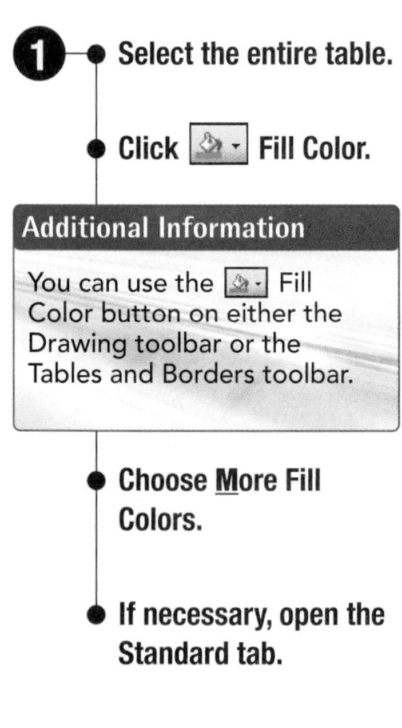

**1**

- **Select the entire table.**
- **Click Fill Color.**

**Additional Information**

You can use the Fill Color button on either the Drawing toolbar or the Tables and Borders toolbar.

- **Choose More Fill Colors.**
- **If necessary, open the Standard tab.**

*Your screen should be similar to Figure 2.15*

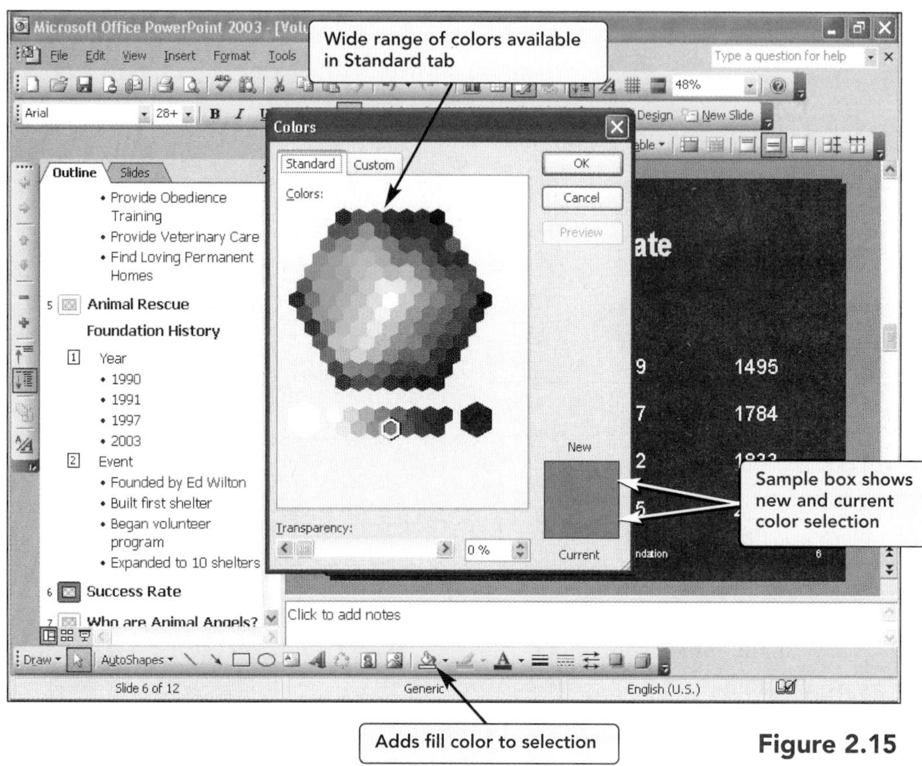


**Figure 2.15**

From the Standard tab of the Colors dialog box, you can select from a wider range of colors. The current fill color, gray, is selected. The sample box will show the new color you select in the upper half and the current color in the lower half. Because you have not yet selected a new color, only one color is displayed. You want to use a gold color for the table background.

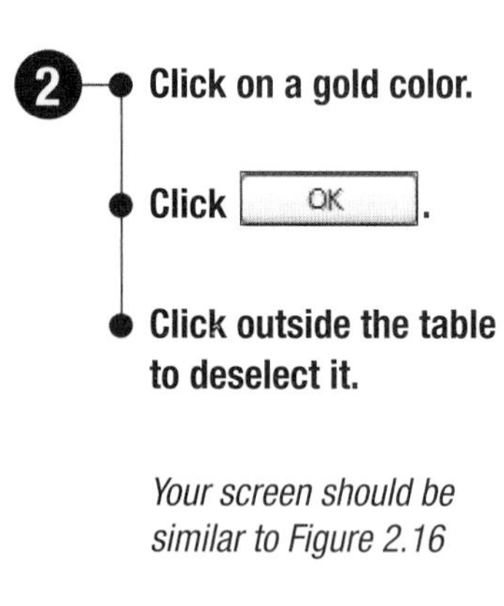

**2**

- **Click on a gold color.**
- **Click OK.**
- **Click outside the table to deselect it.**

*Your screen should be similar to Figure 2.16*

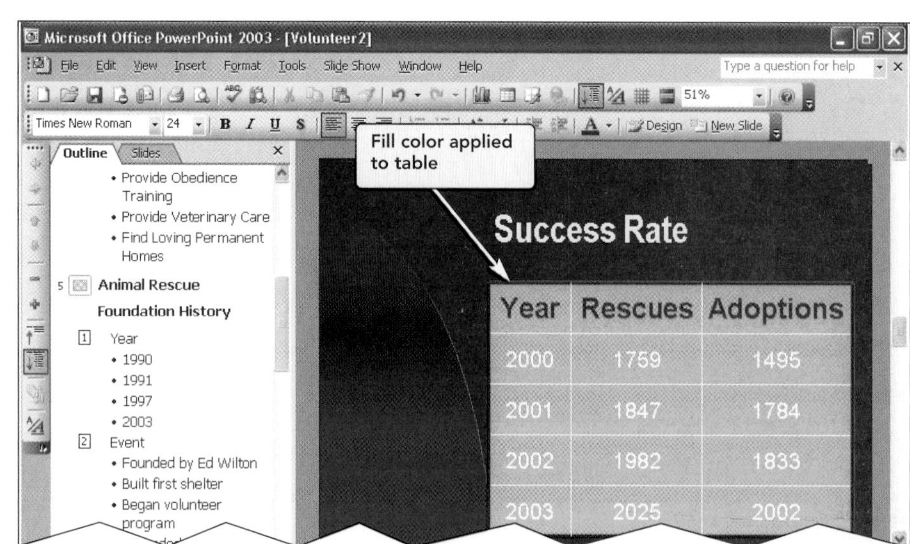


**Figure 2.16**

The new background color makes the data and row and column lines difficult to see. To correct this problem, you will change the color of the lines and data. You will change the interior line color to the same as the outside border color. Because there are many interior table lines, you will use the Format Table dialog box to make this change quickly.

**3** **Change the font color of the years to the same blue as the column headings.**

**Additional Information**

Because this was the last used font color, you can simply click Font Color to apply the color.

- **Change the font color of the numeric data to a dark color of your choice.**
- **Select the entire table.**
- **Choose Borders and Fill from the table shortcut menu.**

**Having Trouble?**

Right-click on the table to display the shortcut menu.

**Another Method**

You can also double-click on the table border to open the Format Table dialog box.

- **Select the red color from the Color drop-down palette.**
- **Click on the two interior table border lines in the diagram.**
- **Click Preview.**
- **If necessary, move the Format table dialog box to see the table.**

*Your screen should be similar to Figure 2.17*

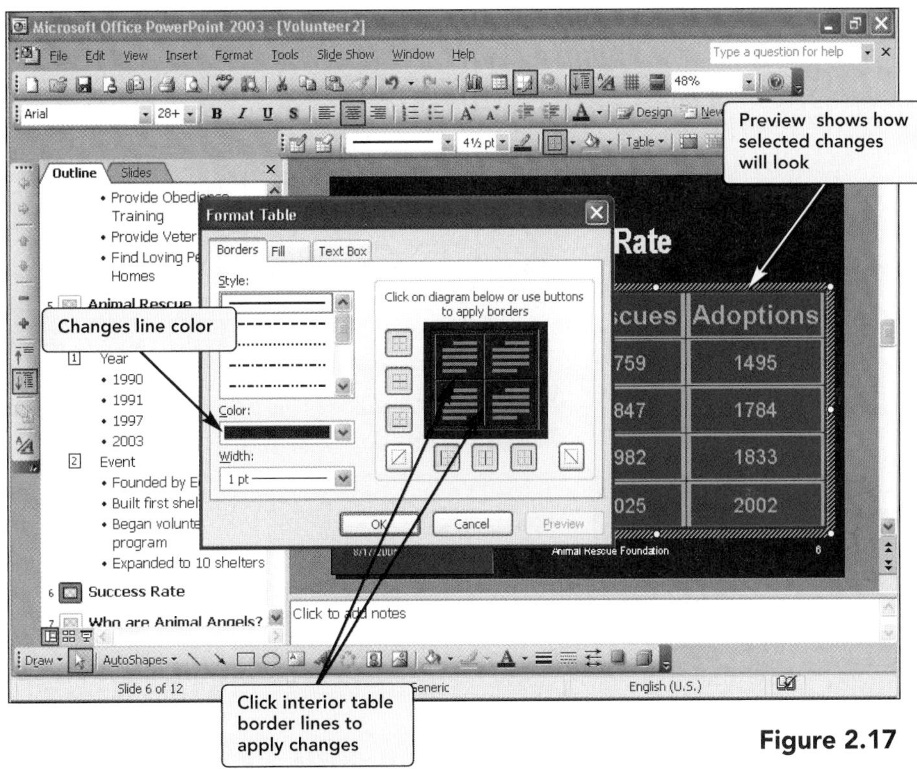


Figure 2.17

All interior table lines in the table in the slide have changed to the selected color. This was faster than changing each interior line color using the Draw Table feature.

4 Click  to apply the settings and close the dialog box.

- Choose **V**iew/**R**uler to display the ruler.

**Additional Information**

Use the ruler as a guide for placement of objects on the slide.

- Center the table horizontally on the slide as in Figure 2-18.

**Having Trouble?**

Drag the table placeholder border when the mouse pointer is ✥ to move the table.

**Having Trouble?**

Align the center sizing handle of the table placeholder with the 0 position on the horizontal ruler.

- Click outside the table to deselect it.
- Save the presentation.

*Your screen should be similar to Figure 2.18*

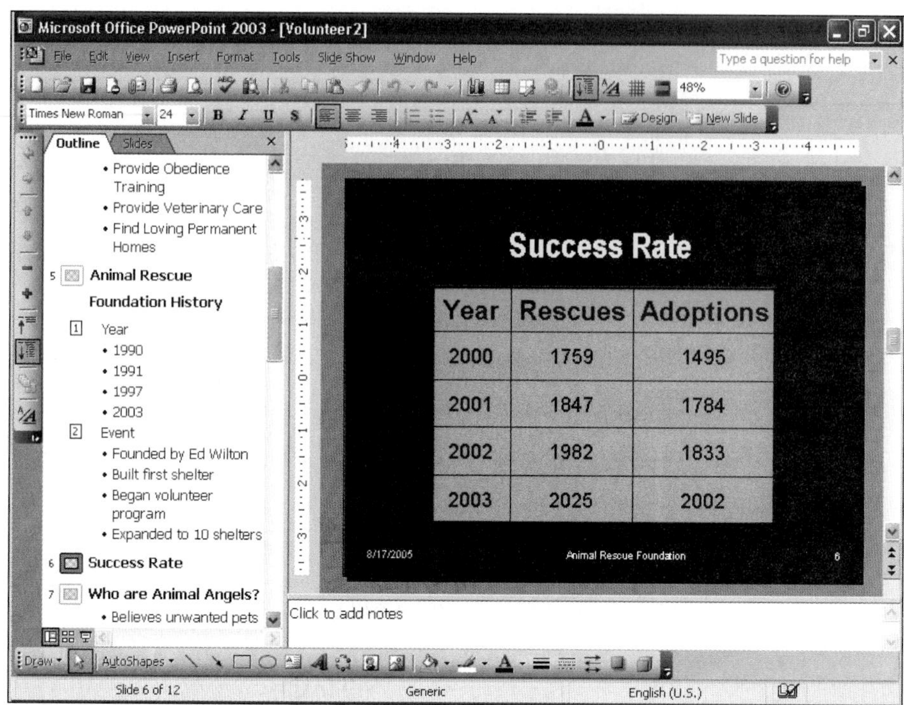


**Figure 2.18**

The enhancements you added to the table greatly improve its appearance.

## Modifying and Creating Graphic Objects

Now you are ready to enhance the presentation by adding several graphics. As you have seen, you can add many ready-made graphics to slides. Many of these can be customized to your needs by changing colors and adding and deleting elements. You can also create your own graphics using the AutoShapes feature.

### Changing the Slide Layout

First, you want to add a graphic to slide 2. Before adding the graphic, you will change the slide layout from the bulleted list style to a style that is designed to accommodate text as well as other types of content such as graphics.

- **Display slide 2.**
- **From the slide shortcut menu, choose Slide Layout.**

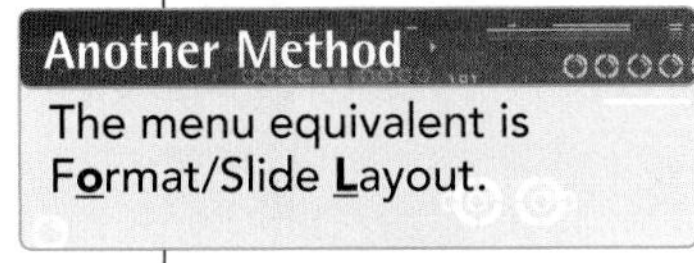

**Another Method**

The menu equivalent is Format/Slide Layout.

- **Click** **Title, Text, and Content (from the Text and Content Layouts category).**

*Your screen should be similar to Figure 2.19*

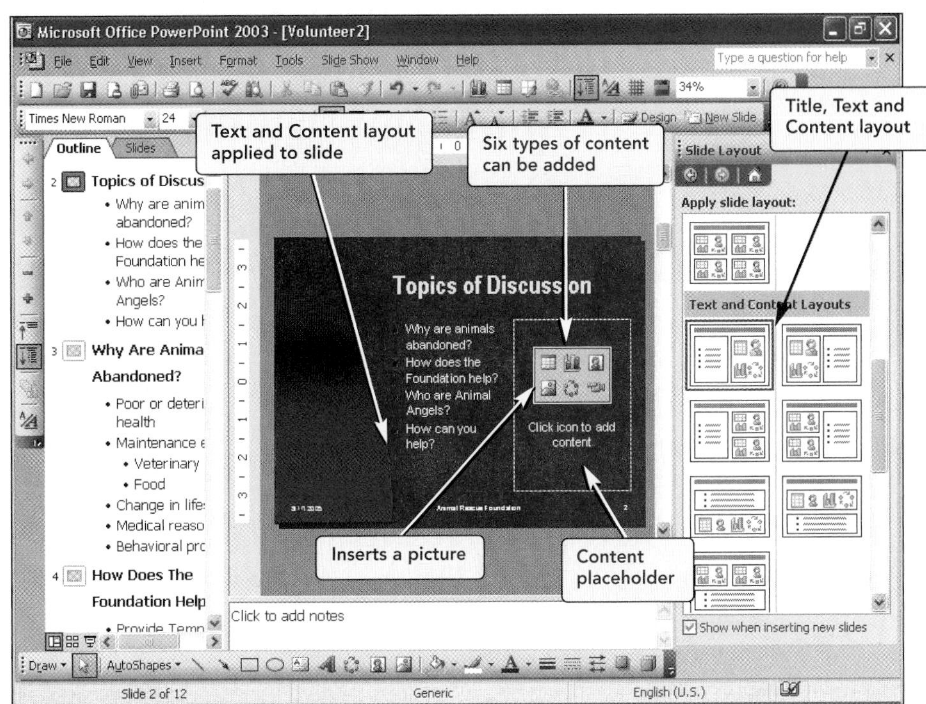


**Figure 2.19**

A content placeholder was added on the right side of the slide, and the bulleted text placeholder was resized and moved to the left side of the slide. Inside the content placeholder are six icons representing the different types of content that can be inserted. Clicking an icon opens the appropriate feature to add the specified type of content. You will add a clip art graphic of a question mark and then size the placeholder.

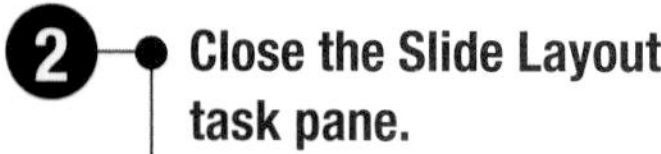

- **Close the Slide Layout task pane.**
- **Click Insert Picture in the content placeholder.**

**Additional Information**

A ScreenTip identifies the item as you point to it.

- **If necessary, change the Look In location to the location containing your data files.**
- **Locate and select the** pp02_Question Mark **clip art.**
- **Click Insert.**
- **Increase the size of the graphic and position it as in Figure 2.20.**

*Your screen should be similar to Figure 2.20*

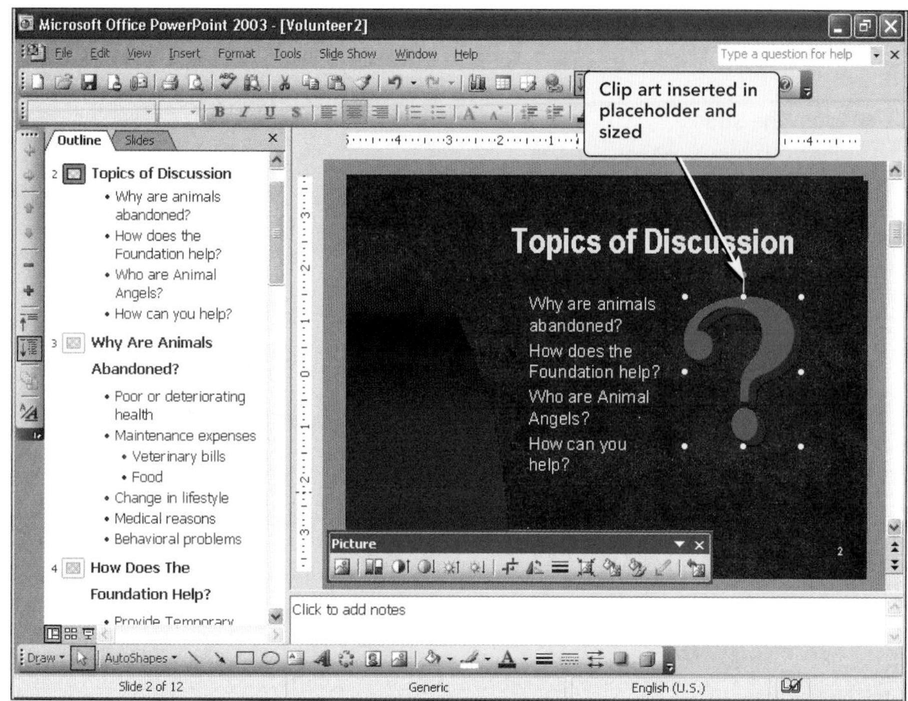


Figure 2.20

## Recoloring a Picture

Now you want to change the color of the graphic to a bright gold color.

- **If necessary, display the Picture toolbar.**
- **Click Recolor Picture.**

**Another Method**

The menu equivalent is Format/Picture/Recolor.

*Your screen should be similar to Figure 2.21*

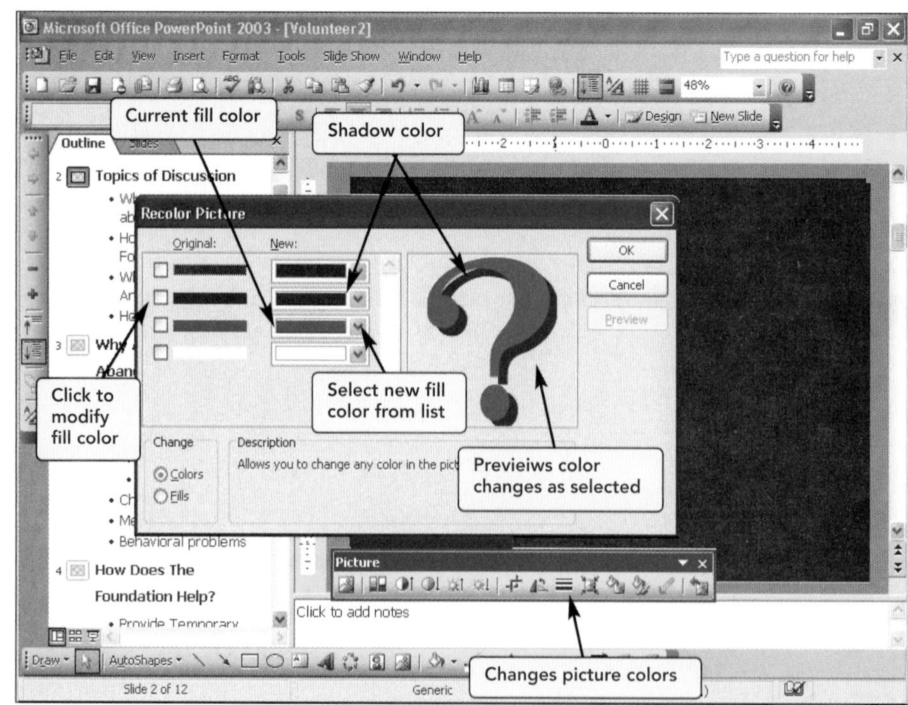


Figure 2.21

The original colors for each component of the picture are listed. Selecting the check box for a component allows you to change the color to a new color. You want to change the light blue color to gold. The preview area reflects your color changes as they are made.

**2**

- **Select the Original light blue color check box.**
- **Open the New color drop-down menu for the selected component and select gold.**

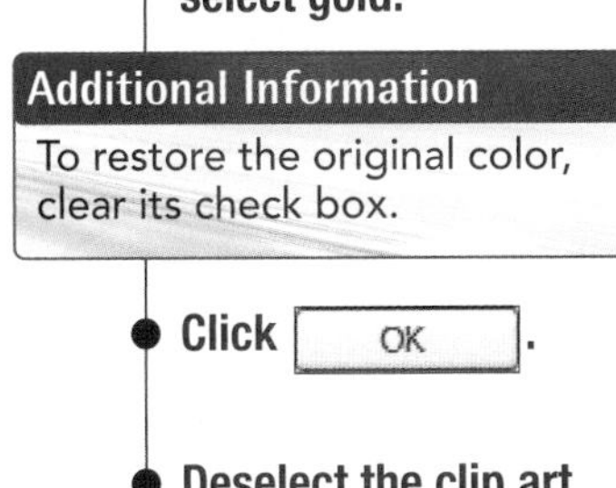

**Additional Information**

To restore the original color, clear its check box.

- **Click OK.**
- **Deselect the clip art and, if necessary, turn off the Picture toolbar.**

*Your screen should be similar to Figure 2.22*

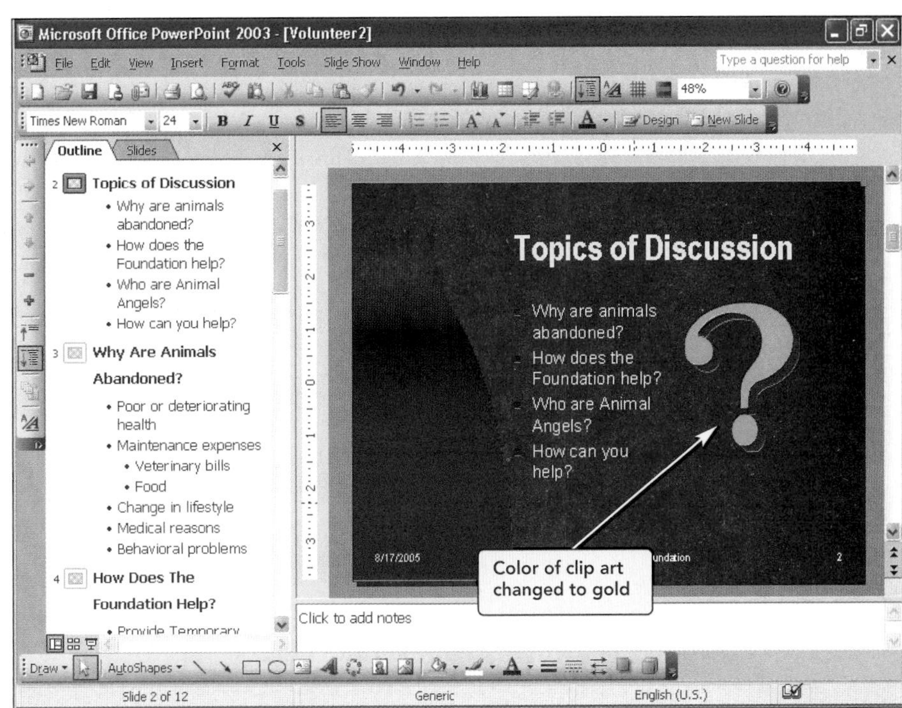


**Figure 2.22**

The graphic now adds much more color to the slide.

## Duplicating a Slide

At the end of the presentation, you want to add a concluding slide. This slide needs to be powerful, because it is your last chance to convince your audience to join Animal Angels. To create the concluding slide, you will duplicate slide 1 and then create a graphic to complement the slide.

Duplicating a slide creates a copy of the selected slide and places it directly after the selected slide. You can duplicate a slide in any view, but in this case you will use the Outline tab in Slide view to duplicate slide 1 and move it to the end of the presentation.

**1** • **Click slide 1 in the Outline tab.**

• **Choose Insert/Duplicate Slide.**

• **Drag slide 2 in the Outline tab to the end of the list of slides.**

**Another Method**

You can also duplicate a slide using the Copy and Paste commands on the Edit menu.

*Your screen should be similar to Figure 2.23*

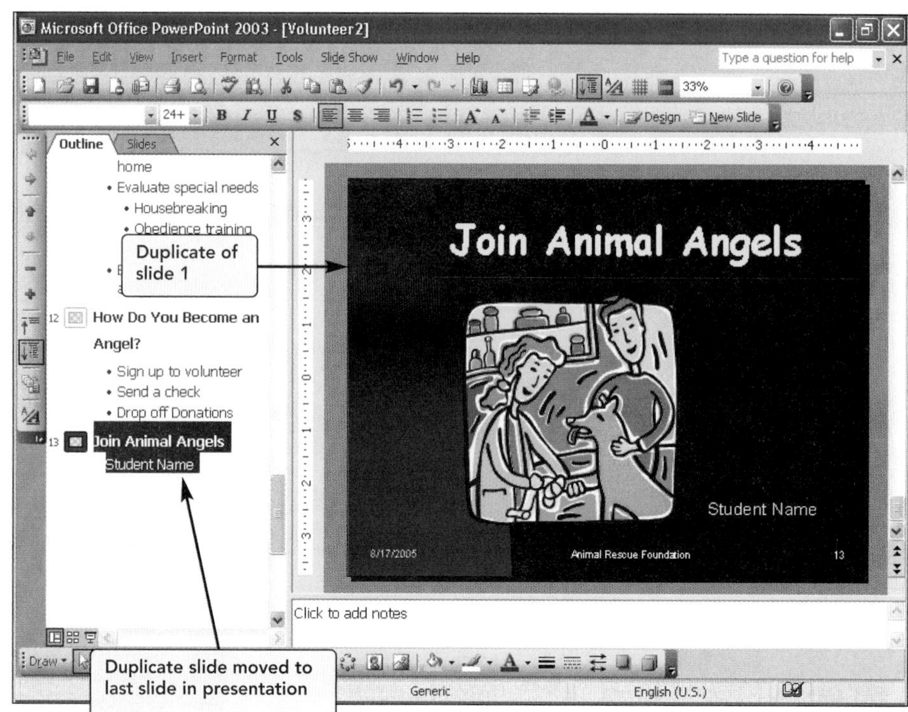


**Figure 2.23**

Duplicating the slide saved you time because you do not need to redo the changes to the title and subtitle.

## Inserting an AutoShape

**Additional Information**

Most shapes can also be inserted from the Clip Organizer as well.

You want to replace the graphic with another of a heart. To quickly add a shape, you will use one of the ready-made shapes supplied with PowerPoint called **AutoShapes**. These include such basic shapes as rectangles and circles, a variety of lines, block arrows, flowchart symbols, stars and banners, and callouts.

**1**

- **Select the graphic and press Delete.**
- **Click AutoShapes (in the Drawing toolbar).**
- **Select Basic Shapes.**

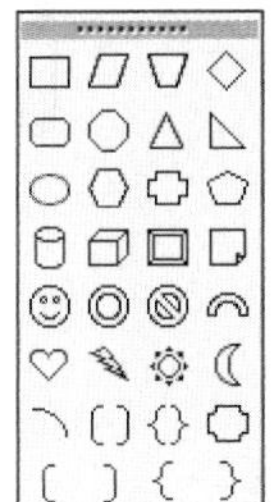

- **Click Heart.**
- **In the space on the left side of the slide, click and drag downward and to the right to create the heart.**

**Another Method**

The menu equivalent is Insert/Picture/AutoShapes.

- **If necessary, size and position the heart as in Figure 2.24.**

**Additional Information**

An AutoShape can be sized and moved just like any other object.

**Another Method**

To maintain the height and width proportions of the AutoShape, hold down Shift while you drag.

*Your screen should be similar to Figure 2.24*

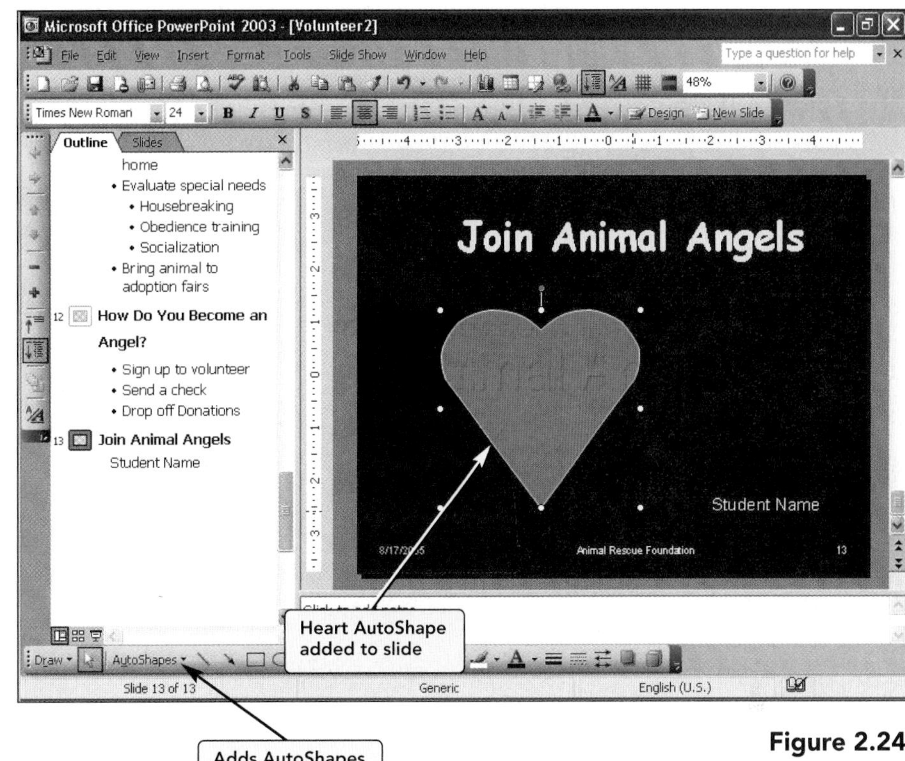


Figure 2.24

## Enhancing the AutoShape

Next, you will enhance its appearance by changing the fill color of the heart and adding a shadow behind the heart. Then you will change the color of the shadow. Generally, a darker shade of the object's color for a shadow is very effective.

**1** **Click Fill Color and select a bright yellow from the Standard Colors palette.**

- **Click Shadow Style (on the Drawing toolbar).**
- **Select any shadow style from the pop-up menu.**

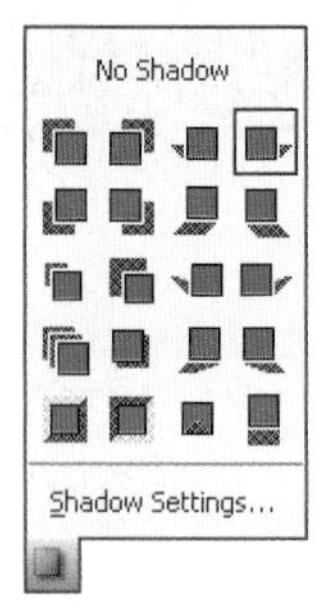


- **Click Shadow Style and choose Shadow Settings.**
- **Click Shadow Color from the Shadow Settings toolbar and select gold.**
- **Close the Shadow Settings toolbar.**

*Your screen should be similar to Figure 2.25*

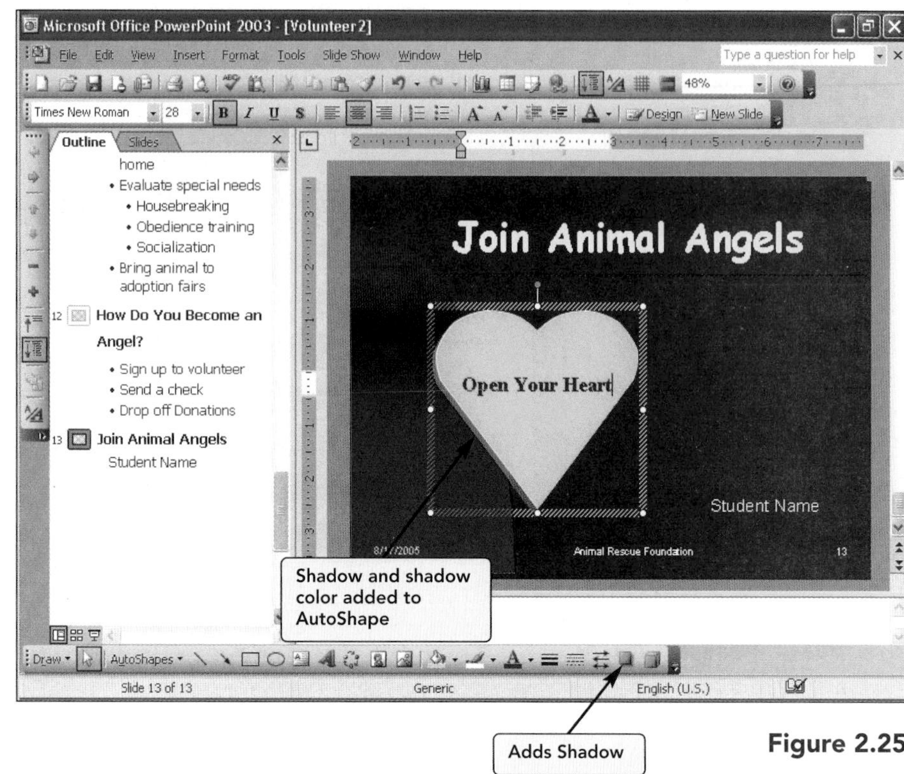


Figure 2.25

The addition of fill color and Shadow effect greatly improves the appearance of the heart.

## Adding Text to an AutoShape

Next, you will add text to the heart object. Text can be added to all shapes and becomes part of the shape; when the shape is moved, the text moves with it.

**1** • **Right-click on the AutoShape object to open the shortcut menu, and choose Add Text.**

• **Click [B] Bold.**

• **Increase the font size to 28 points.**

• **Change the font color to blue.**

• **Type Open Your Heart.**

• **If necessary, adjust the size of the heart to display the text on a single line.**

*Your screen should be similar to Figure 2.26*

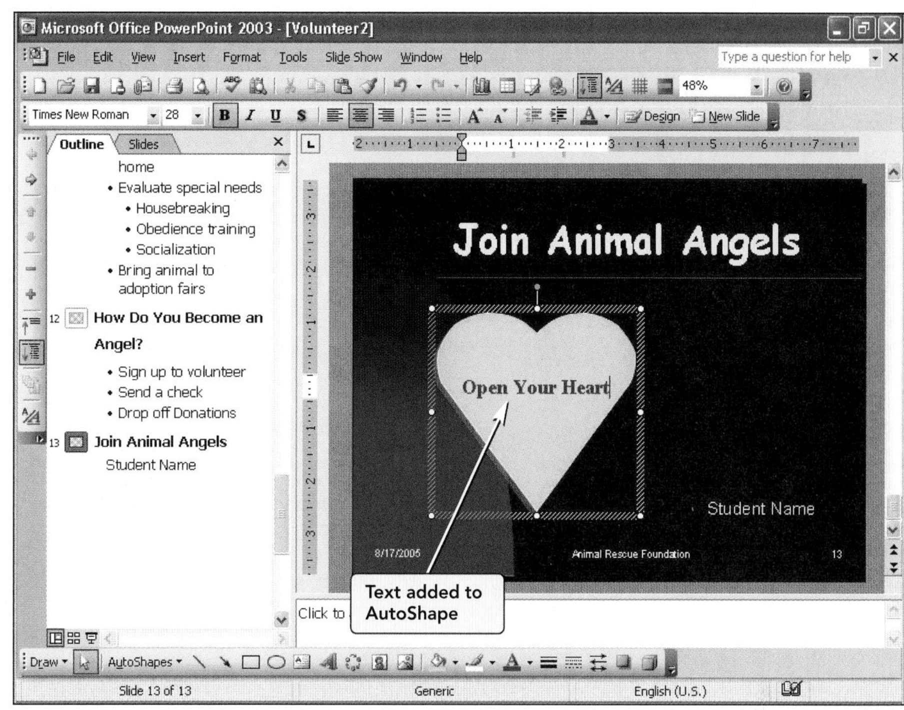


Figure 2.26

## Rotating the Object

**Additional Information**

Holding down ⇧Shift while using the rotate handle rotates the object in 15-degree increments.

Finally, you want to change the angle of the heart. You can rotate an object 90 degrees left or right, or to any other angle. You will change the angle of the heart to the right using the rotate handle for the selected object, which allows you to rotate the object to any degree in any direction.

**1** **Hold down Shift while you drag the rotate handle to the left one increment.**

**Additional Information**

The mouse pointer appears as ⟳ when positioned on the rotate handle.

*Your screen should be similar to Figure 2.27*

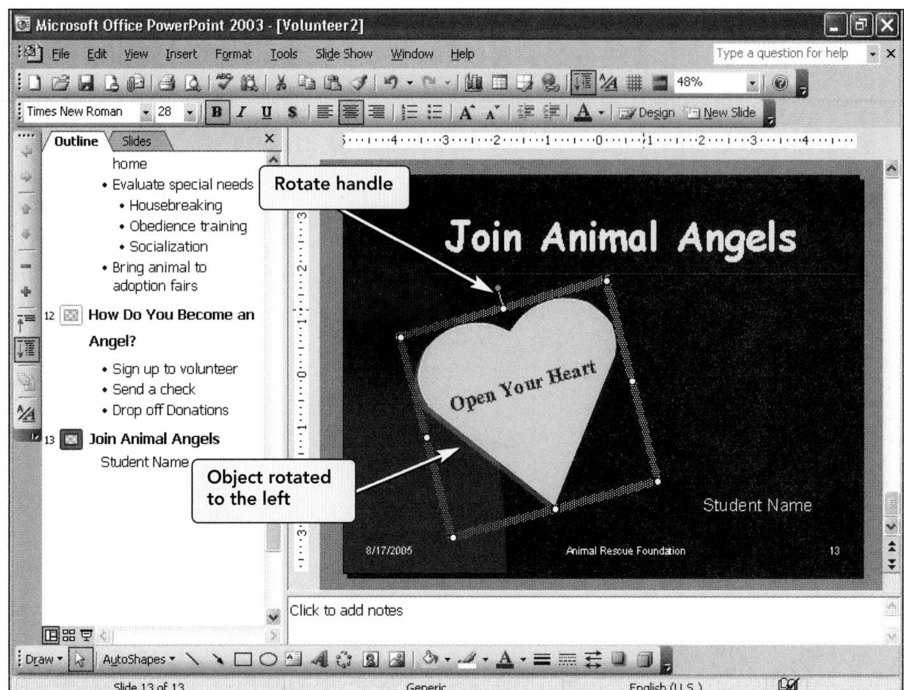


**Figure 2.27**

The graphic is a nice addition to the final slide of the presentation.

## Working with Text Boxes

On slide 12, you want to add the organization's name and address. To make it stand out on the slide, you will put it into a text box. A **text box** is a container for text or graphics. The text box can be moved, resized, and enhanced in other ways to make it stand out from the other text on the slide.

### Creating a Text Box

First you create the text box, and then you add the content.

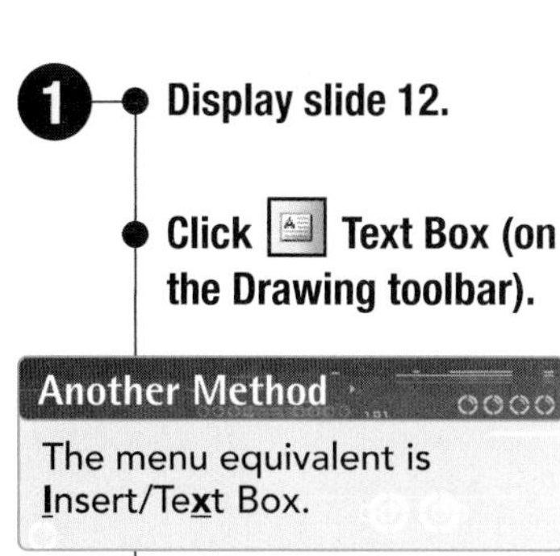

**1** • **Display slide 12.**

• **Click** **Text Box (on the Drawing toolbar).**

**Another Method**

The menu equivalent is Insert/Text Box.

• **Point to a blank area below the bullets and click to create a default size text box.**

**Additional Information**

Do not drag to create the text box. If you do, it will not resize appropriately when you enter text in the next step.

*Your screen should be similar to Figure 2.28*

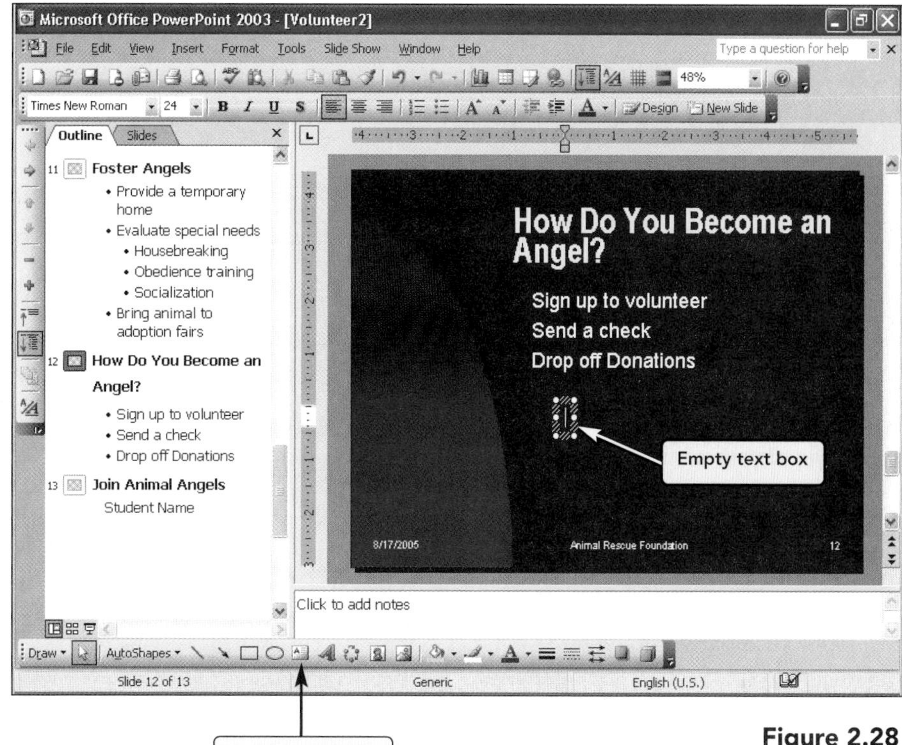


Figure 2.28

The text box is a selected object and is surrounded with a hatched border, indicating you can enter, delete, select, and format the text inside the box.

**Additional Information**

You could also copy text from another location and paste it into the text box.

## Adding Text to a Text Box

The text box displays an insertion point, indicating that it is waiting for you to enter the text. As you type the text in the text box, it will resize automatically as needed to display the entire entry.

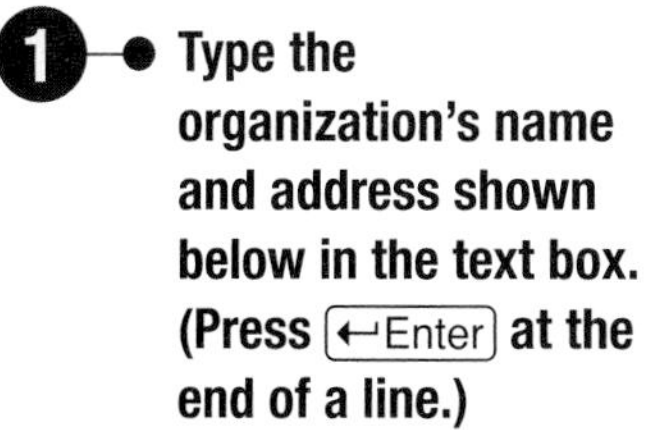

**1** • **Type the organization's name and address shown below in the text box. (Press ←Enter at the end of a line.)**

**Animal Rescue Foundation**

**1166 Oak Street**

**Lakeside, NH 03112**

**(603) 555-1313**

*Your screen should be similar to Figure 2.29*

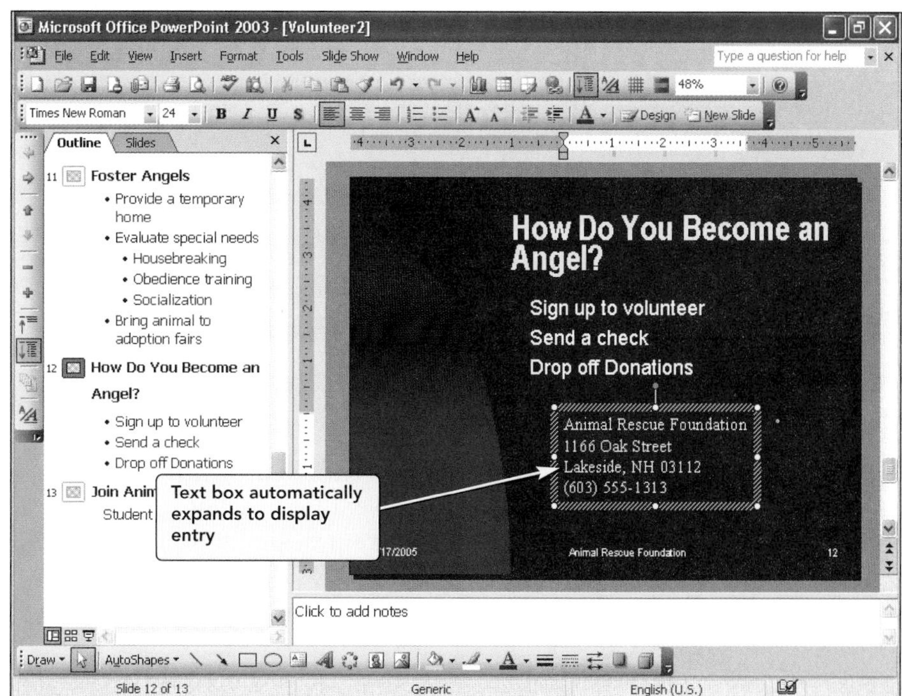


Figure 2.29

Again, because a text box is an object, the content is not displayed in the outline pane.

## Enhancing the Text Box

Like any other object, the text box can be sized and moved anywhere on the slide. It can also be enhanced by adding a border, fill color, shadow effect, or a three-dimensional effect to the box. You want to add a border around the box to define the space and add a fill color behind the text.

**1**

- **Click Line Style (on the Drawing toolbar) and select a style of your choice from the menu.**
- **Click Fill Color and select a color of your choice from the color palette.**
- **If the text does not look good with the fill color you selected, change the text color to a color of your choice.**
- **Position the text box as in Figure 2.30.**
- **Deselect the text box.**
- **Save the presentation.**

*Your screen should be similar to Figure 2.30*

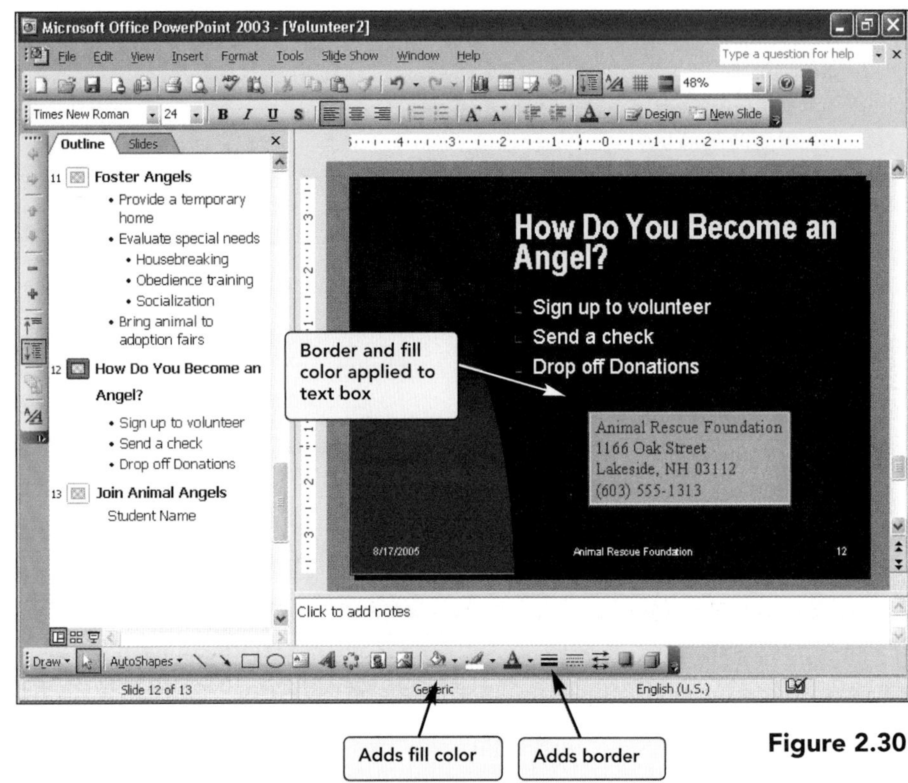


Figure 2.30

The information in the text box now stands out from the other information on the slide.

# Changing the Presentation Design

Now you are satisfied with the presentation's basic content and organization. Next you want to change its style and appearance by applying a different design template.

## Concept 4

### Design Template

4 A **design template** is a professionally created slide design that is stored as a file and can be applied to your presentation. Design templates include features that control the slide color scheme, the type and size of bullets and fonts, placeholder sizes and positions, background designs and fills, and other layout and design elements. PowerPoint provides more than 100 design templates that can be used to quickly give your presentations a professional appearance. Additional design templates are available at the Microsoft Office Template Gallery Web site, or you can create your own custom design templates.

A design template can be applied to all slides or selected slides in a presentation. You can also use more than one type of design template in a single presentation. Use a design template to ensure that your presentation has a professional, consistent look throughout.

## Applying a Design Template

A design template can be applied to the entire presentation or to selected slides. You want to change the design template for the entire presentation.

**1**

- **Display slide 1.**
- **Click Design on the Formatting toolbar.**

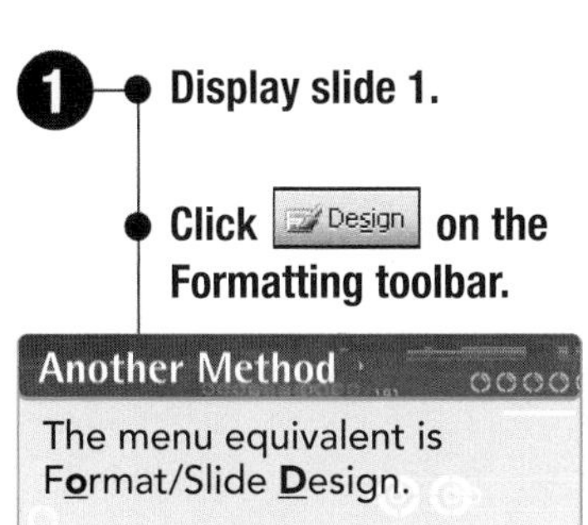

Another Method
The menu equivalent is Format/Slide Design.



- **Point to the first design preview in the task pane.**

**Having Trouble?**

If your task pane displays large preview images, open any preview's menu and clear the Show Large Previews option.

*Your screen should be similar to Figure 2.31*

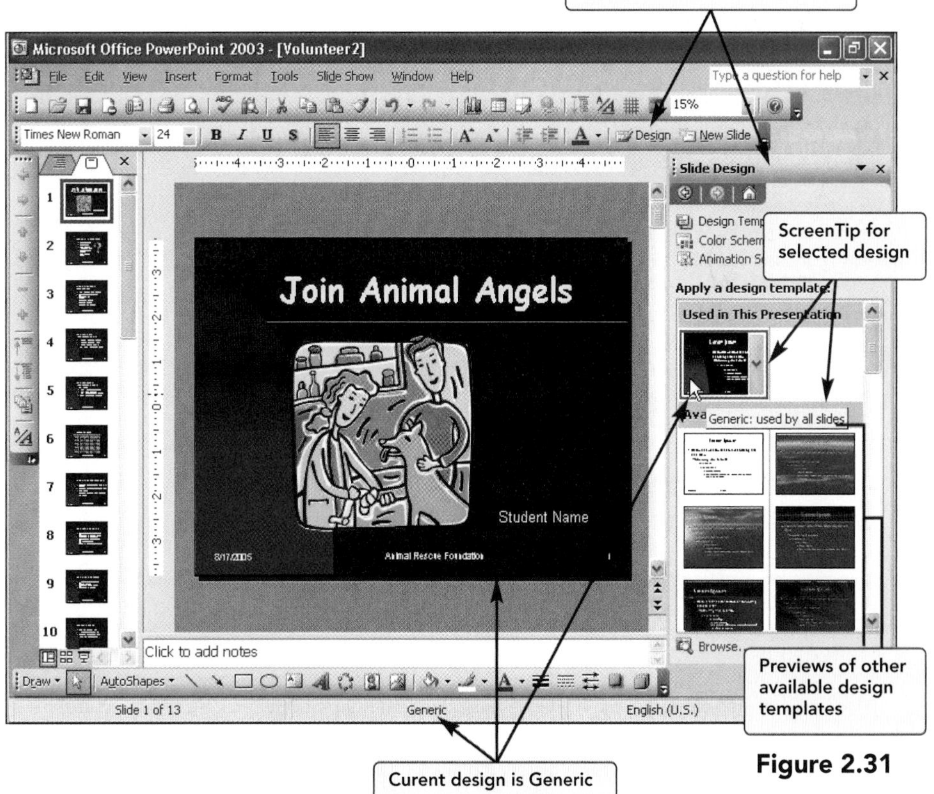



**Figure 2.31**

**Additional Information**

Design templates are stored in a file with a .pot file extension.

The Slide Design task pane displays previews of the design templates. The first design preview is the design that is currently used in the presentation. This is the Generic design as identified in the status bar and in the ScreenTip. If other designs were recently used, they appear in the Recently Used section. Previews of other available design templates are displayed in the Available For Use section of the pane.

**2** Click Balance in the Available For Use section to see how this design would look.

*Your screen should be similar to Figure 2.32*

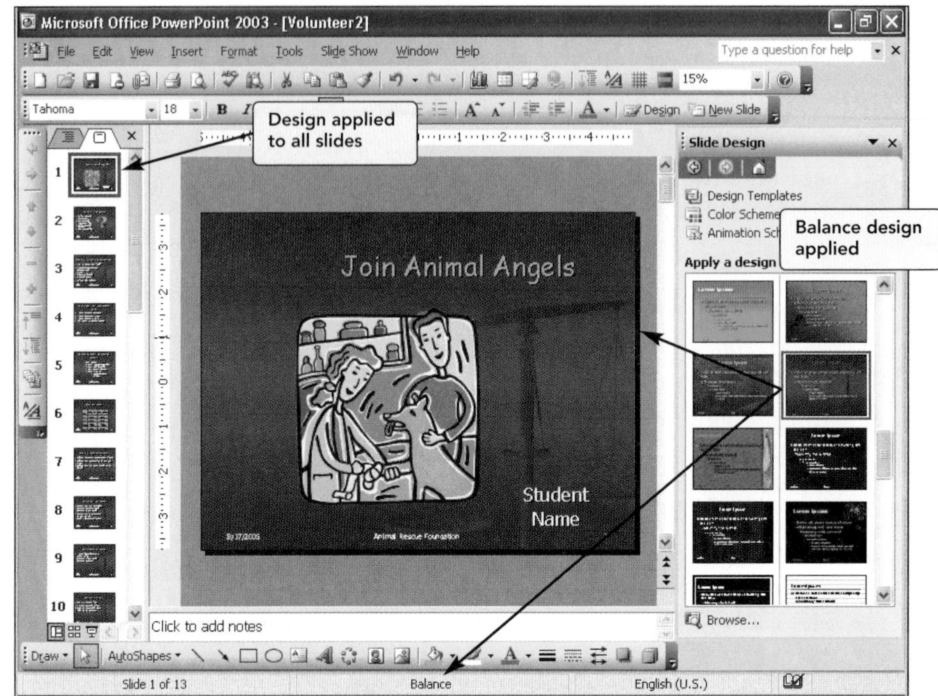


**Figure 2.32**

**Additional Information**

To apply a design to selected slides, preselect the slides to apply the design to in the Slide pane, and use the Apply to Selected Slides option from the design preview drop-down menu.

The Balance design template is applied to all slides in the presentation and the status bar displays the name of the current design. As different designs are selected, the previously used designs appear in the Recently Used section.

You will preview several other design templates, and then use the Beam template for the presentation.

**3** Preview several other design templates.

Choose the Beam template design.

**Having Trouble?**

If the Beam template design is not available, select a similar design of your choice.

*Your screen should be similar to Figure 2.33*

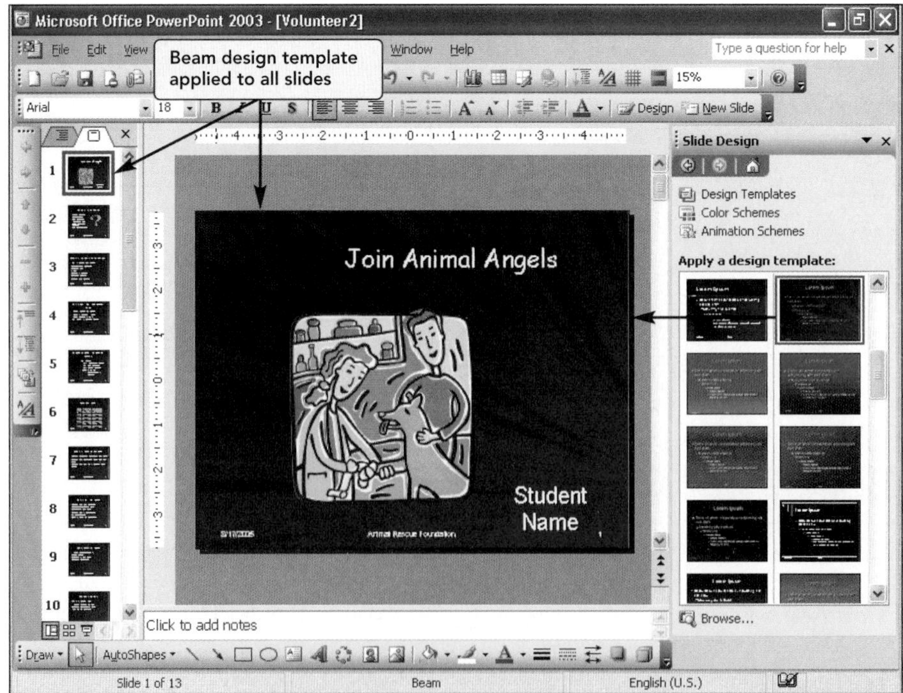


**Figure 2.33**

The Beam design template has been applied to all slides in the presentation. When a new template design is applied, the text styles, graphics, and colors that are included in the template replace the previous template settings. Consequently, the layout may need to be adjusted. For example, your name may appear on two lines because the font size of the subtitle using this design template is 36 points.

However, if you had made changes to a slide, such as changing the font of the title, these changes are not updated to the new design. In this case, the title is still the Comic Sans MS font you selected, however, its font size has been reduced and it is now too small. You will correct that shortly.

**4**

- **On the title slide, reduce the subtitle font size to 24 points and, if necessary, size the placeholder to display your name on a single line.**
- **Use the Slide tab to select each slide and check the layout.**
- **Make the adjustments shown in the table below to the indicated slide.**

*Your screen should be similar to Figure 2.34*

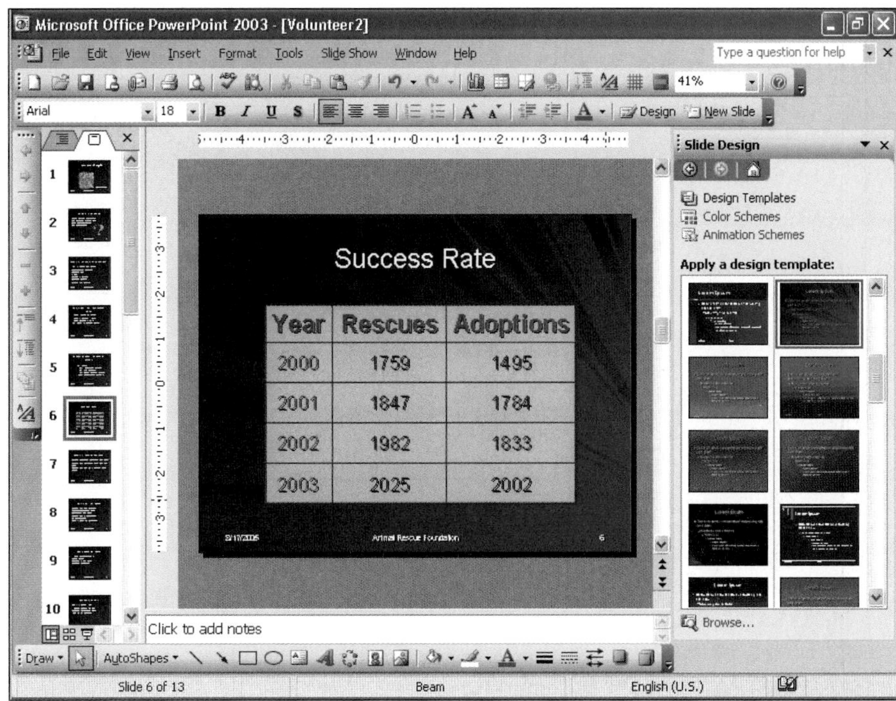


**Figure 2.34**

| Slide | Adjustment |
|---|---|
| 2 | Increase the text placeholder width to display each bulleted item on a single line. Move the question mark graphic to the lower right side of the slide. |
| 5 | Increase the width of the Event column to display each item on a single line. Center the Year and Event columns on the slide. |
| 6 | Adjust the size of the table columns and center the table below the title. If necessary, change the table text colors to coordinate with the new design. |

**Having Trouble?**

If you selected a different design template, you may need to make different adjustments than indicated in the table at left.

## Changing the Color Scheme

To make the presentation livelier, you decide to try a different color scheme. Each design template has several alternative color schemes from which you can choose.

**1** **Display slide 1.**

**Click Color Schemes in the Slide Design task pane.**

*Your screen should be similar to Figure 2.35*

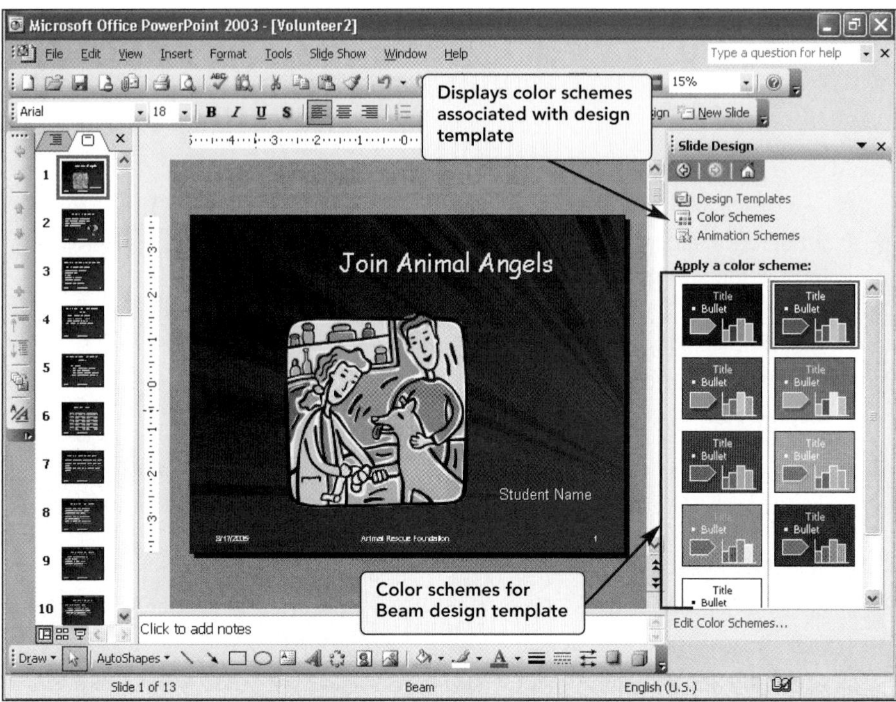


**Figure 2.35**

The nine color schemes for the Beam design template are displayed in the Slide Design pane. The color scheme with the medium blue background is selected. Each color scheme consists of eight coordinated colors that are applied to different slide elements. Using predefined color schemes gives your presentation a professional and consistent look. You want to see how the dark blue color scheme would look.

**2** • **Select the dark blue color scheme (first column, first row).**

*Your screen should be similar to Figure 2.36*

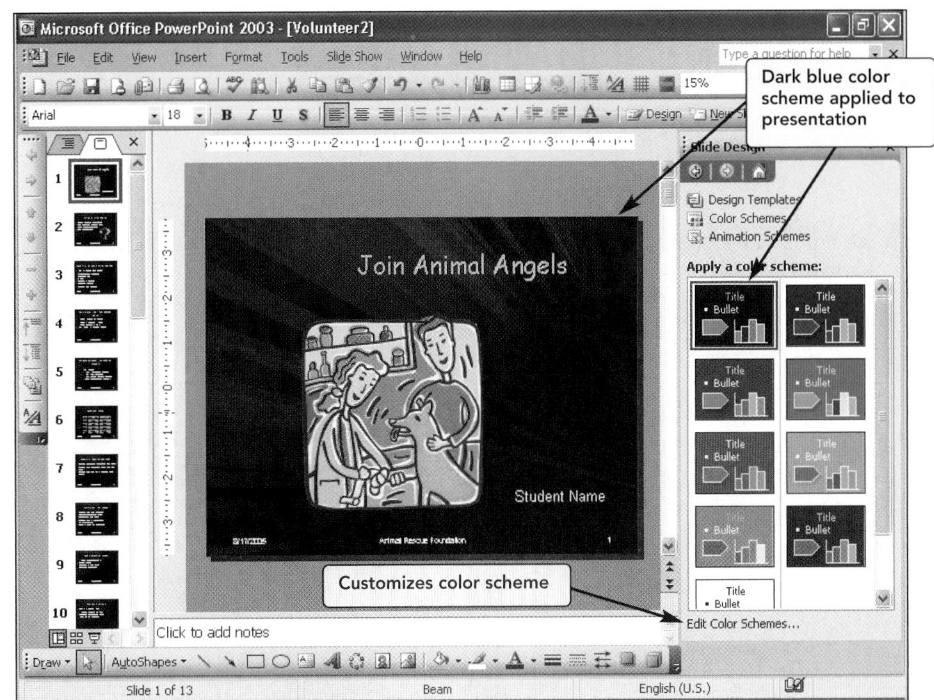


Figure 2.36

The slides display in the selected color scheme. Although you like this color scheme, you think it is a little dark. You can customize color schemes by changing colors associated with the different elements. You will change the background, shadow, and title text colors.

**3** • **Click Edit Color Schemes at the bottom of the Slide Design task pane.**

• **Open the Custom tab, if necessary.**

*Your screen should be similar to Figure 2.37*

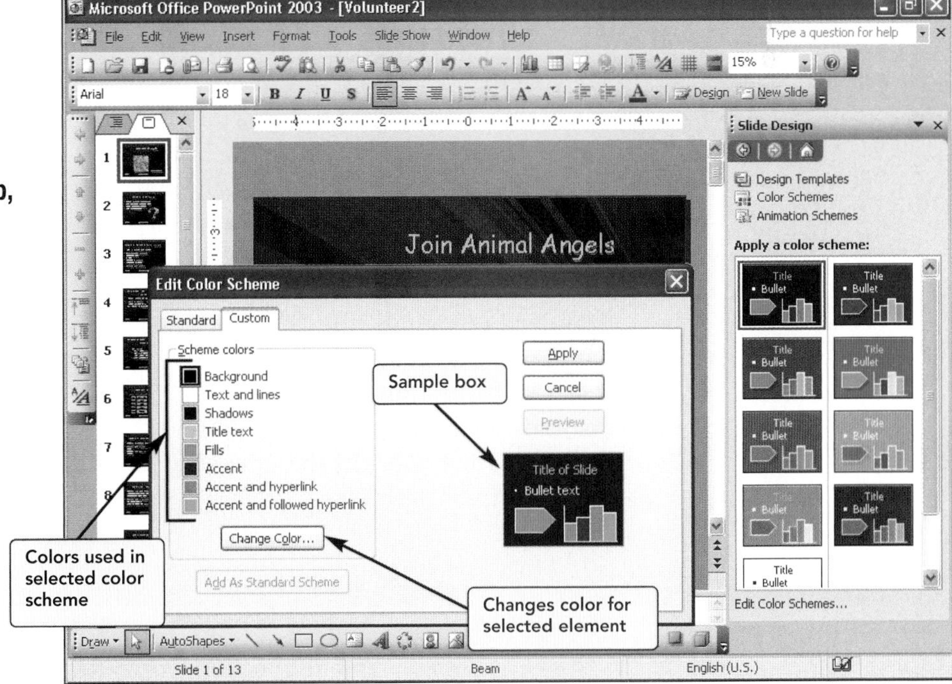


Figure 2.37

The Scheme Colors area of the dialog box shows you the eight colors that are applied to different elements of the template design. The sample box shows where the selected colors are used in a slide. The option to change the background color is selected by default. You will change the color of the background and title first.

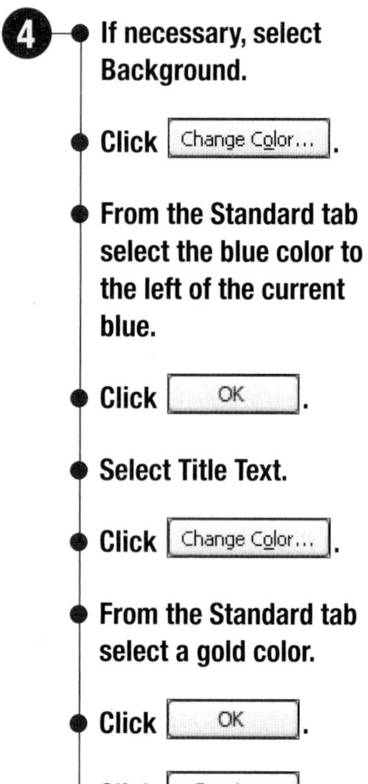

**4** **If necessary, select Background.**

- **Click** Change Color... .
- **From the Standard tab select the blue color to the left of the current blue.**
- **Click** OK .
- **Select Title Text.**
- **Click** Change Color... .
- **From the Standard tab select a gold color.**
- **Click** OK .
- **Click** Preview .
- **Move the Edit Color Scheme dialog box to see more of the slide.**

*Your screen should be similar to Figure 2.38*

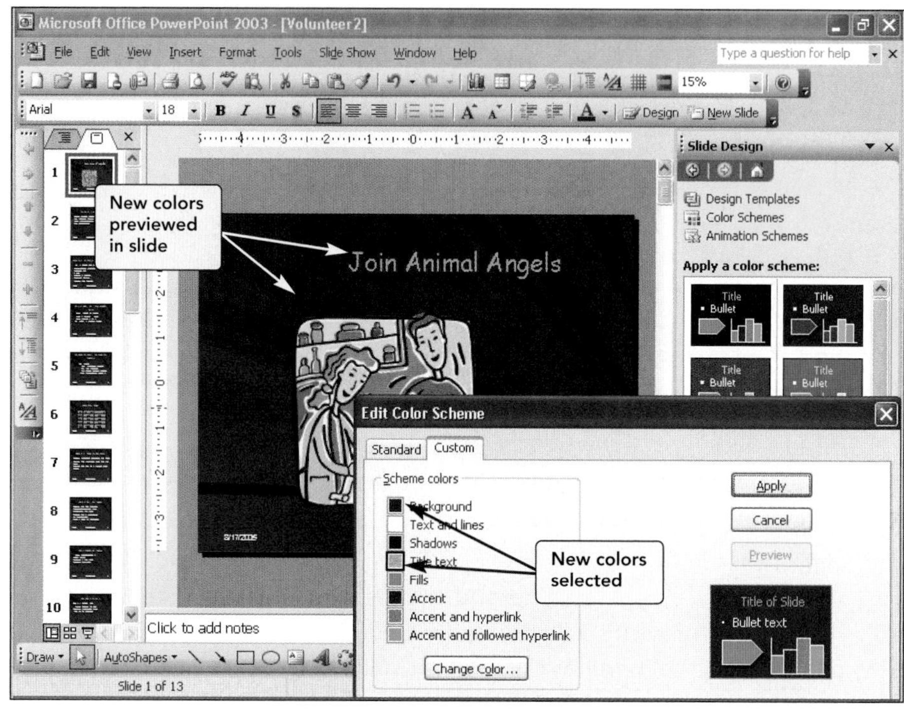


**Figure 2.38**

The background and title color has changed on all slides in the presentation. Changing the colors has made the slides much brighter. However, you do not like the dark blue used in the shadow color of the beams and will change it to a lighter blue. Because the shadow color is not a standard color found on the Standard color tab, the Custom tab will open automatically. Colors are selected from this tab by dragging the cross-hair to select a color and dragging the slider on the color bar to adjust the brightness.

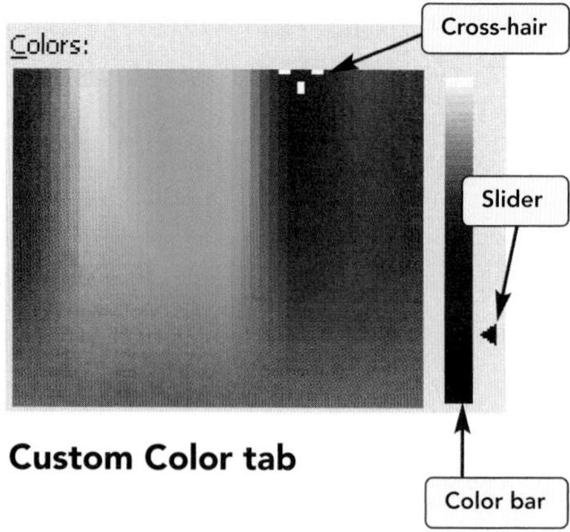


**Custom Color tab**

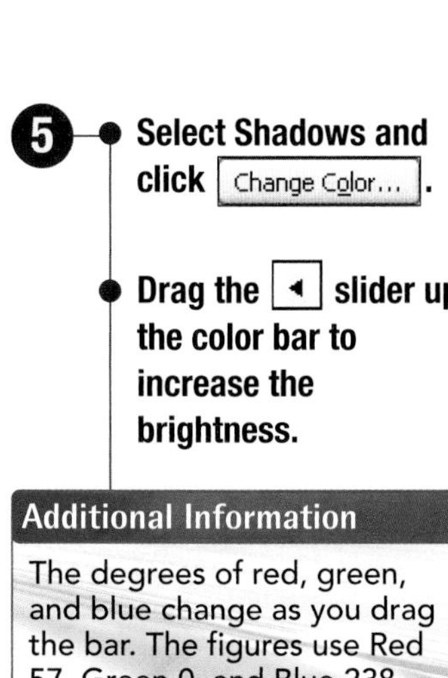

**5** **Select Shadows and click Change Color... .**

**Drag the ◂ slider up the color bar to increase the brightness.**

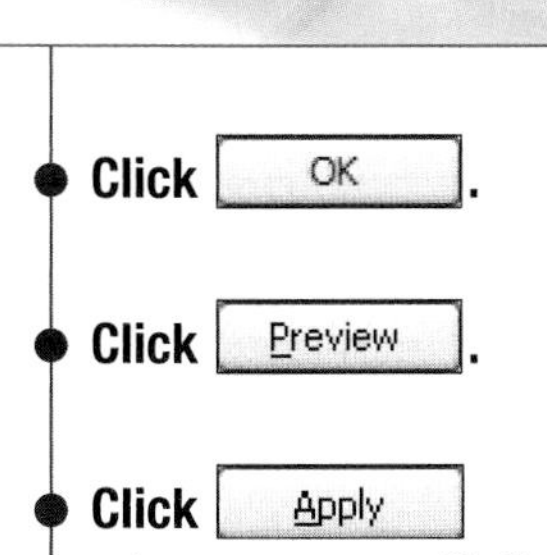

**Additional Information**

The degrees of red, green, and blue change as you drag the bar. The figures use Red 57, Green 0, and Blue 238.

**Click OK .**

**Click Preview .**

**Click Apply when you are satisfied with your shadow color selection.**

**Close the Slide Design pane.**

**Save the presentation.**

*Your screen should be similar to Figure 2.39*

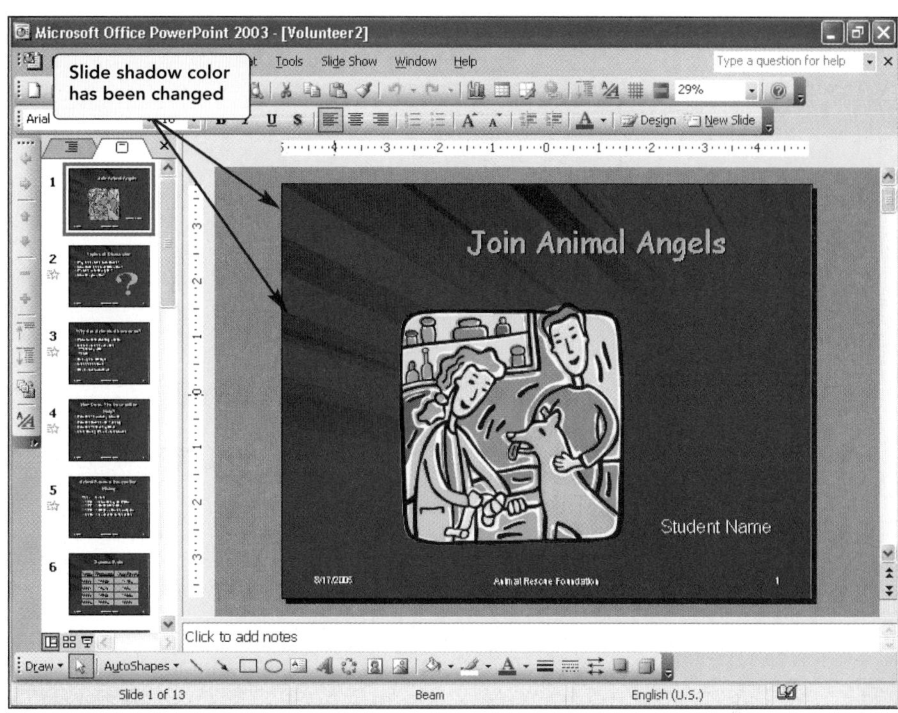


Figure 2.39

The new colors give the presentation much more impact. In addition, a new custom color scheme template is added to the available color schemes list in the task pane. This makes it easy to reapply your custom settings in the future.

## Working with Master Slides

While viewing the slides, you think the slide appearance could be further improved by changing the bullet design on all slides. Although you can change each slide individually as you did in Lab 1, you can make the change much faster to all the slides by changing the slide master.

## Concept 5

### Masters

5 A **master** is a special slide or page that stores information about the formatting for all slides or pages in a presentation. There are four key components of a presentation—slides, title slides, speaker notes, and handouts—and each has a master associated with it. The four masters are described below.

| Master | Function |
|---|---|
| Slide Master | Defines the format and placement of title, body, and footer text; bullet styles; background design; and color scheme of each slide in the presentation. |
| Title Master | Defines the format and placement of titles and text for slides that use the Title Slide layout. |
| Handout Master | Defines the format and placement of the slide image, text, headers, footers, and other elements that will appear on every handout. |
| Notes Master | Defines the format and placement of the slide image, note text, headers, footers, and other elements that will appear on all speaker notes. |

Any changes you make to a master affect all slides or pages associated with that master. Each design template comes with its own slide master and title master. When you apply a new design template to a presentation, all slides and masters are updated to those of the new design template. Using the master to modify or add elements to a presentation ensures consistency and saves time.

You can create slides that differ from the master by changing the format and placement of elements in the individual slide rather than on the master. For example, when you changed the font settings of the title on the title slide, the slide master was not affected. Only the individual slide changed, making it unique. If you have created a unique slide, the elements you changed on that slide retain their uniqueness even if you later make changes to the slide master. That is the reason that the title font did not change when you changed the design template.

## Modifying the Slide Master

You will change the bullet style in the slide master so that all slides in the presentation will be changed.

**1** Choose **View/Master/Slide Master.**

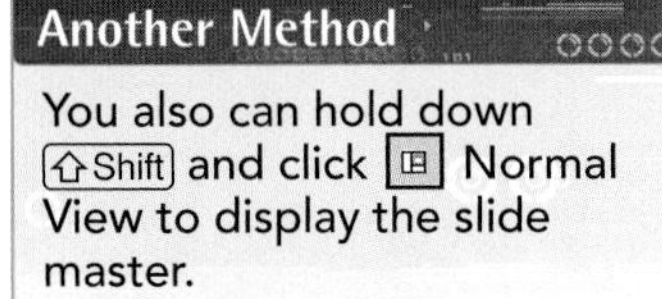

**Another Method**

You also can hold down Shift and click Normal View to display the slide master.

- **If necessary, dock the Slide Master View toolbar below the Formatting toolbar.**

*Your screen should be similar to Figure 2.40*

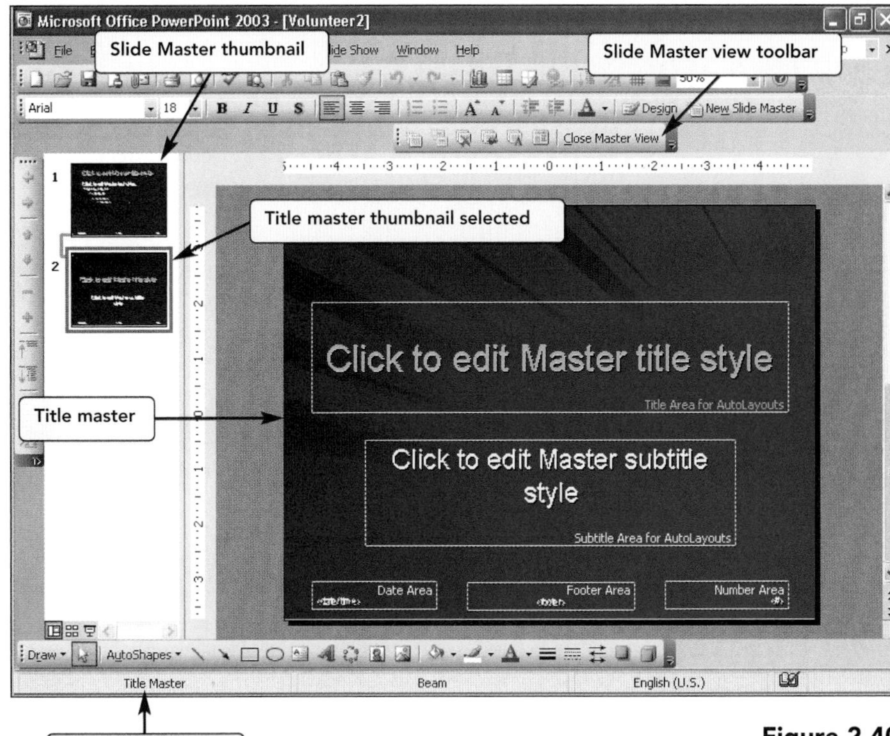


**Figure 2.40**

**Additional Information**

Pointing to the master thumbnail displays a ScreenTip that identifies the selected master and the slides where it is used in the presentation.

The view has changed to Master view, and the Slide Master View toolbar is displayed. Thumbnails for both the title master and slide master for the Beam design template appear in the left pane of this view. The second thumbnail for the title master is selected, and the slide pane displays the master for it. The status bar identifies the master you are viewing. You want to make changes to the slide master first.

**2** **Point to the slide master thumbnail to see the ScreenTip.**

- **Click on the first master thumbnail to select it.**

*Your screen should be similar to Figure 2.41*

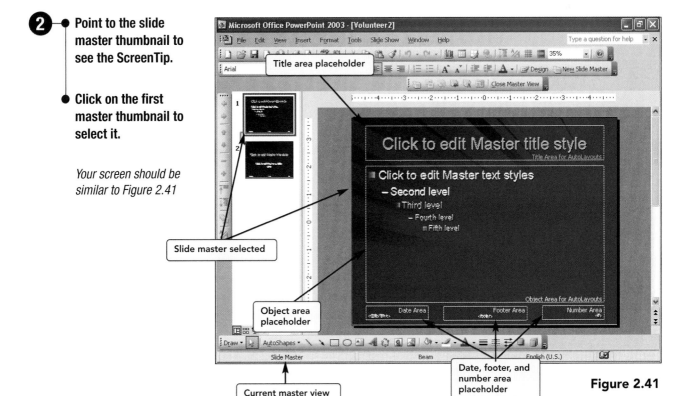

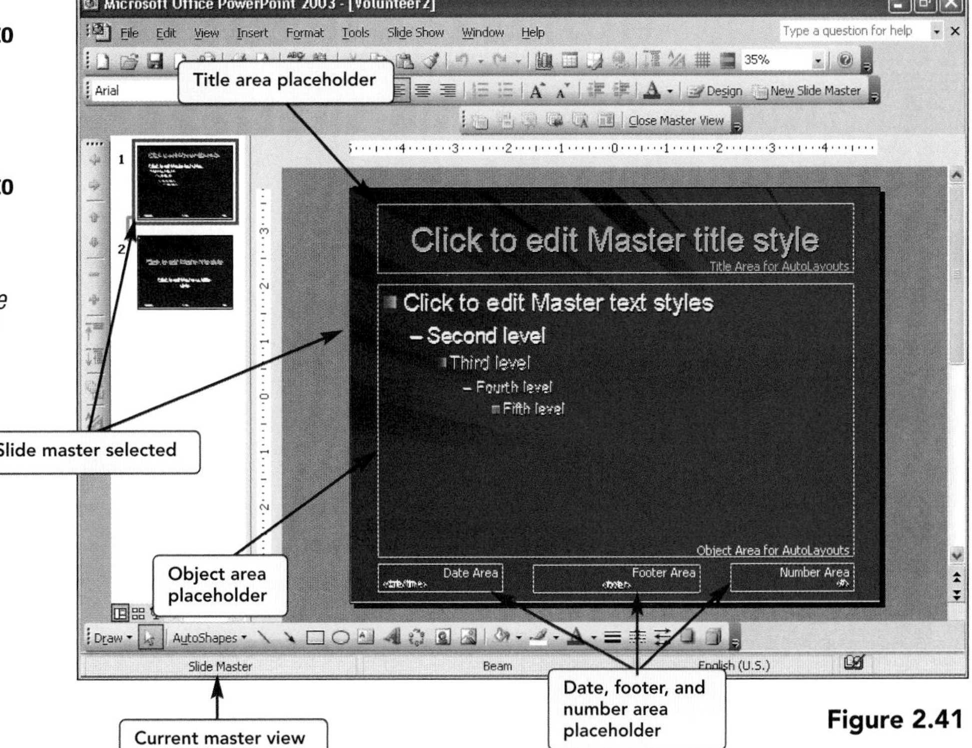


**Figure 2.41**

The slide master consists of five area placeholders that control the appearance of all slides except a title slide. Each placeholder displays sample text to show you how changes you make in these areas will appear. You make changes to the master slide in the same way that you change any other slide. You will modify the object area placeholder by changing the graphic that is used for the bullet style.

**3** • **Click the object area to select it.**

**Having Trouble?**

Do not select an individual item within the object area or the changes will be applied to the item only.

• **Choose Format/Bullets and Numbering.**

• **Click Picture... .**

*Your screen should be similar to Figure 2.42*

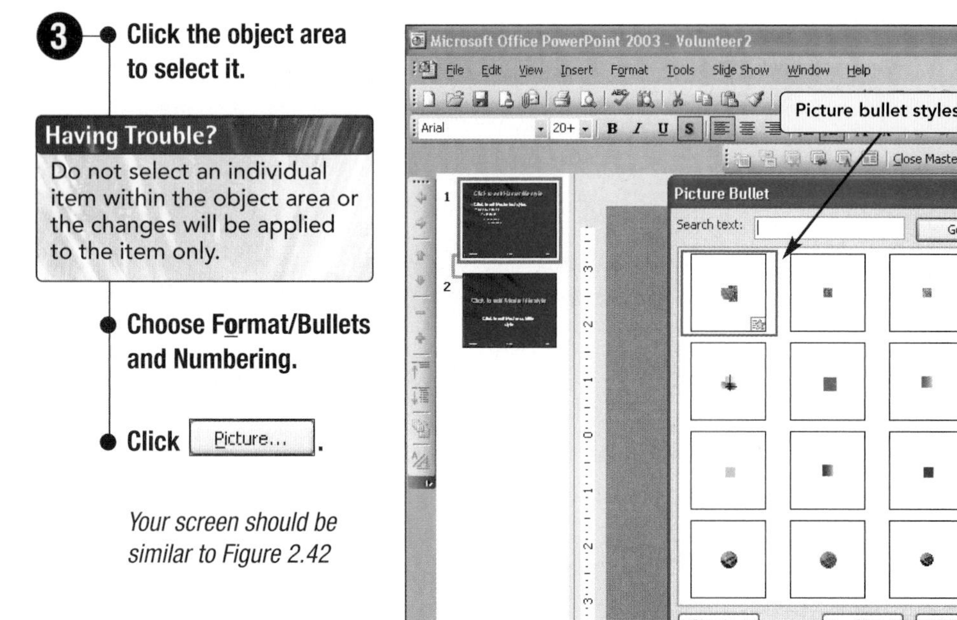

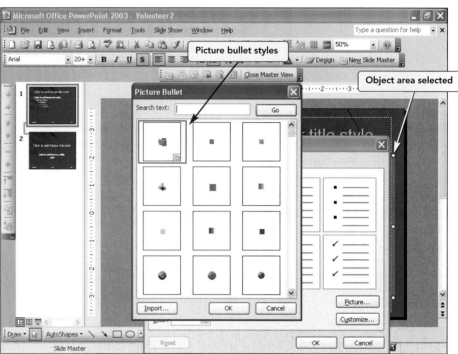

**Figure 2.42**

From the Picture Bullet dialog box, you select the bullet design you want to use from the bullet styles listed. You will use the square, yellow bullet design.

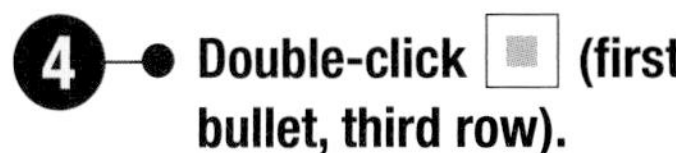

**Double-click ▪ (first bullet, third row).**

**Having Trouble?**

If this bullet style is not available, select another of your choice.

*Your screen should be similar to Figure 2.43*

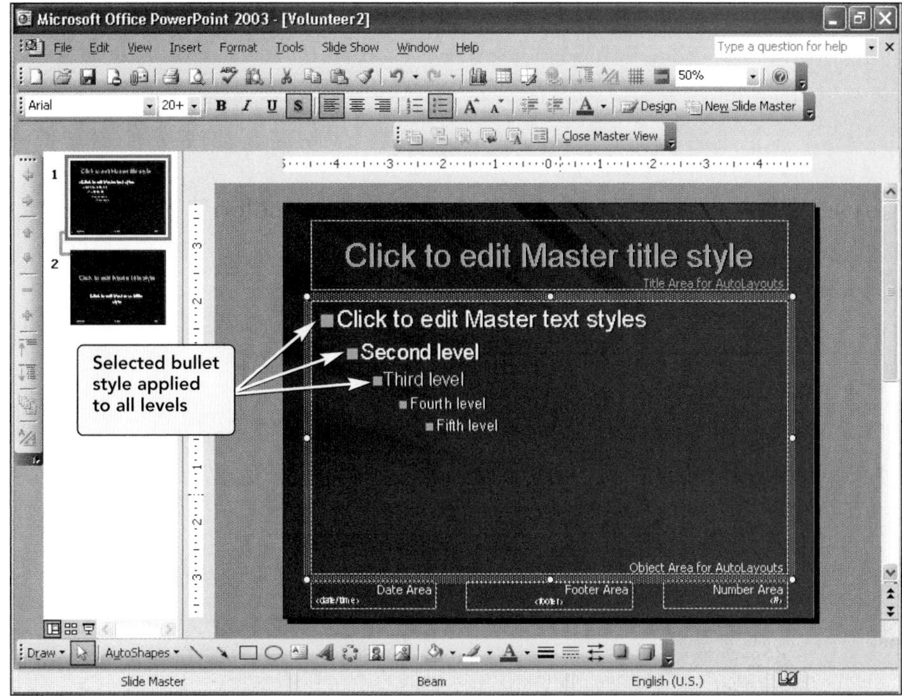


Figure 2.43

**Additional Information**

You can apply different bullet styles to each level by selecting each level individually.

The selected bullet style has been applied to all levels of items in the object area. Additionally, you decide to delete the date from the footer by deleting the Date Area placeholder.

**Select the Date Area placeholder.**

**Press Delete.**

**Additional Information**

You can restore deleted placeholders or add new placeholders to the slide master using F**o**rmat/**M**aster Layout and selecting the type of placeholder you want to add.

*Your screen should be similar to Figure 2.44*

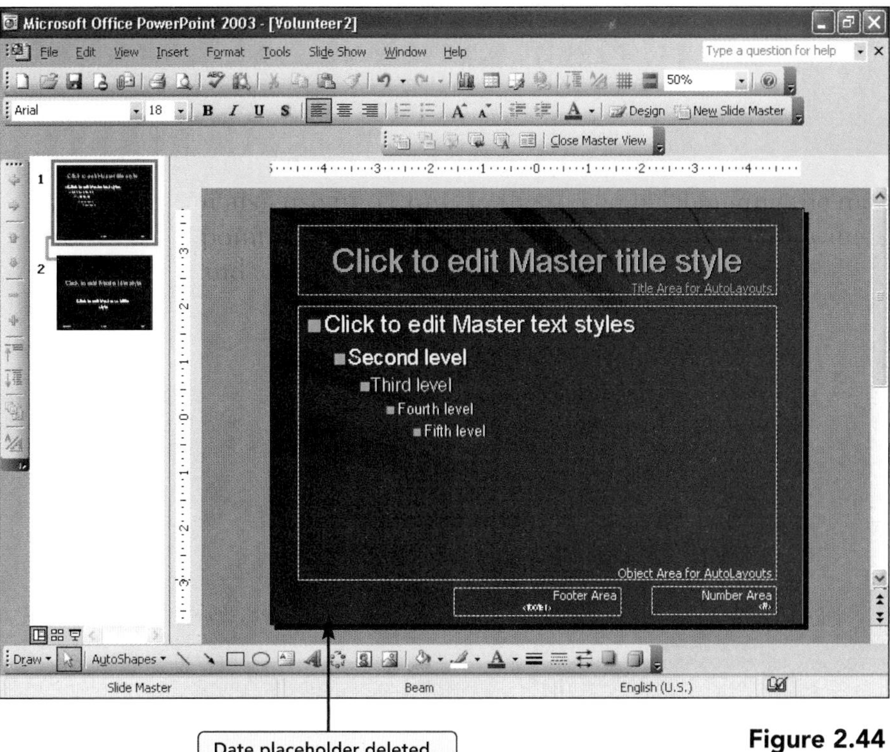


Figure 2.44

Now, you want to see how the changes you have made to the slide master have affected the slides.

**6** Click Slide Sorter view.

*Your screen should be similar to Figure 2.45*

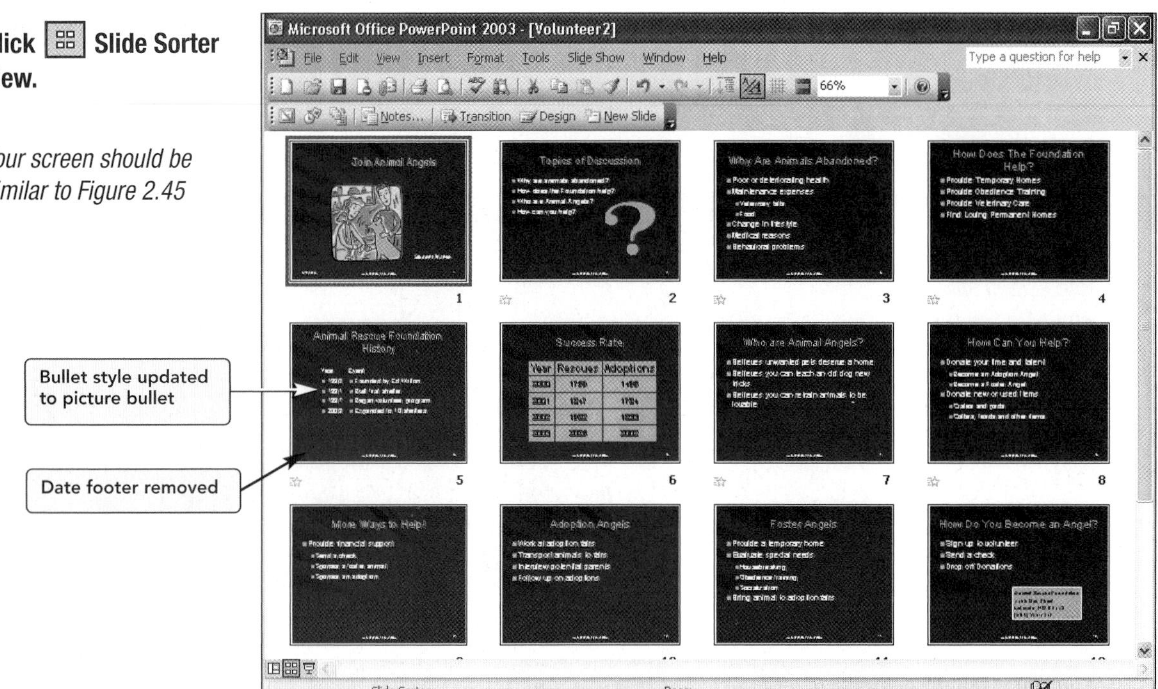


**Figure 2.45**

You can now see that the change you made to the bullet style in the slide master is reflected in all slides in the presentation. Additionally, none of the slides, except the title slides, displays the date in the footer. Using the slide master allows you to quickly make global changes to your presentation.

## Modifying the Title Master

Next you want to enhance the appearance of the two slides that use the title slide layout by changing the title and subtitle.

**1** Display slide 1 in Normal view.

*Your screen should be similar to Figure 2.46*

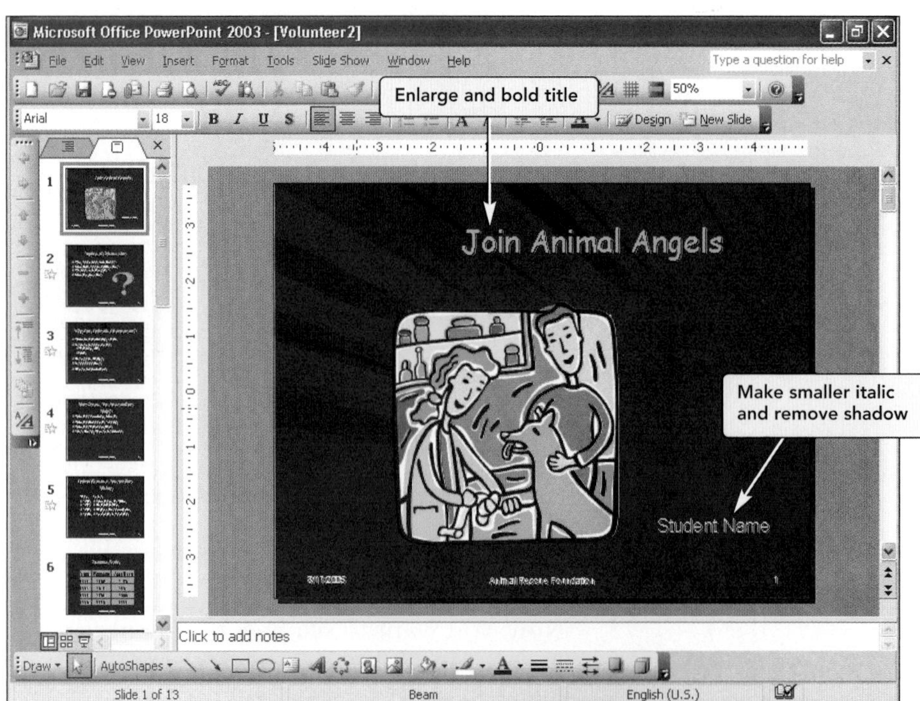


**Figure 2.46**

Earlier, you changed the font, size, and placement of the title and the placement and font size of the subtitle. Although you still like these changes, you want the title to be larger and the subtitle text smaller and italicized. You also want to remove the shadow from the subtitle.

**2**
- **Display the Slide Master view.**
- **Display the title master.**
- **Click the master title text placeholder.**

*Your screen should be similar to Figure 2.47*

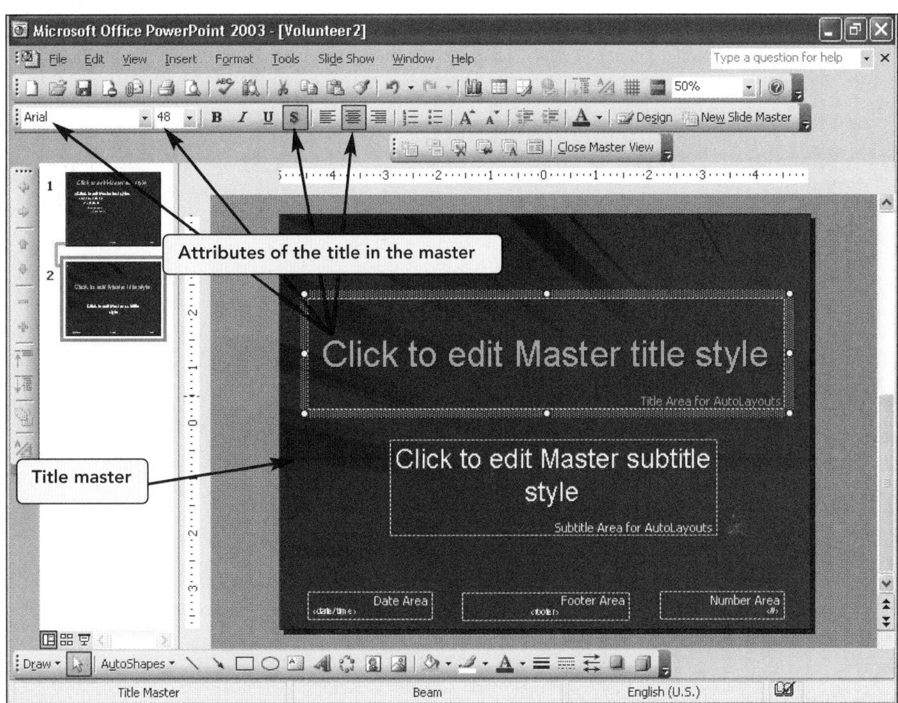


**Figure 2.47**

Notice that the title master has a slightly different appearance from the title slide in your presentation. This is because you modified the title slide by moving placeholders and changing the font, size, and color, making it a unique slide. The unique changes you made to that slide were not changed when the title master of the Beam design template was applied. The title master attributes reflect the attributes associated with the Beam template, such as the title font of Arial, 48 pt as shown in the toolbar buttons.

**3**

- **Change the font style to Comic Sans MS.**
- **Increase the font size to 54.**
- **Click B Bold.**
- **Move the title placeholder toward the top of the slide as in Figure 2.48.**
- **Select the subtitle area placeholder.**

**Another Method**

The menu equivalent is Format/Font/Font Style/Italic and the voice command is "Italic."

- **Click S Shadow to remove the shadow.**
- **Reduce the font size to 28.**
- **Click I Italic.**
- **Decrease the size of the placeholder and move it to the location shown in Figure 2.48.**

*Your screen should be similar to Figure 2.48*

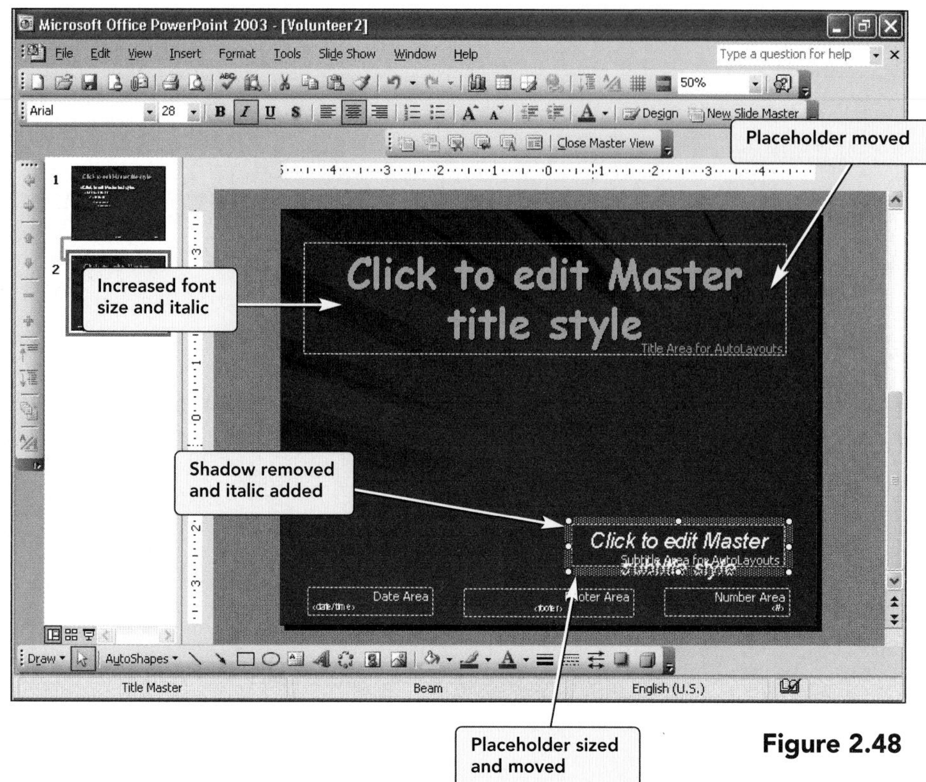


**Figure 2.48**

You want to see how the title slide looks with the changes you have made.

**4** **Switch to Normal view.**

**Click on the title placeholder.**

*Your screen should be similar to Figure 2.49*

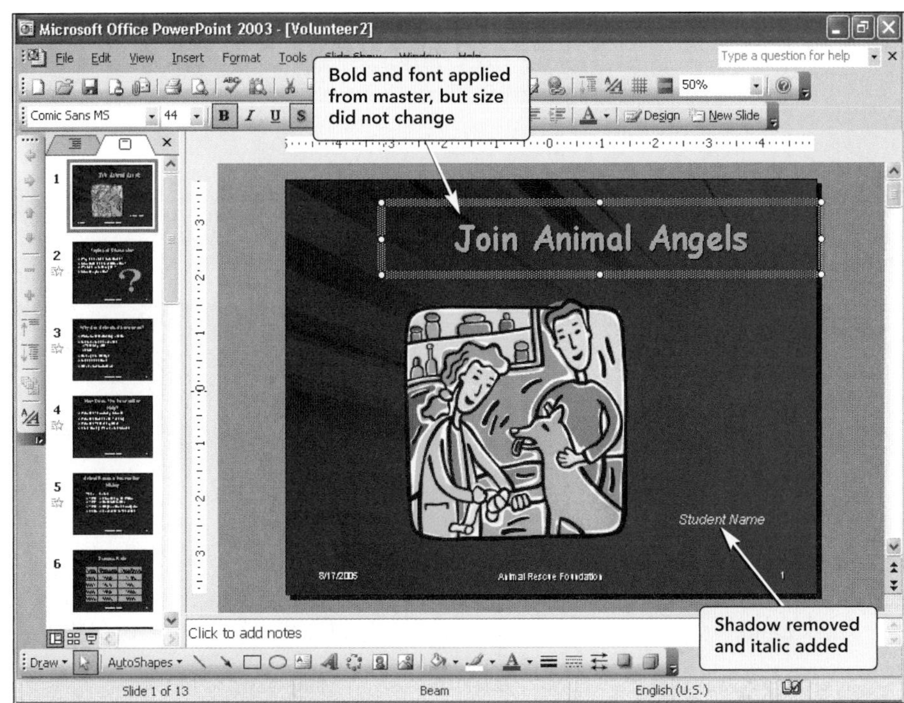


**Figure 2.49**

Some of the changes you made to the title master were applied to the title slide automatically; however, others were not. This is because the earlier changes you made, such as the font size, made the slide unique. Changes made to an individual slide override the master slide.

## Reapplying a Slide Layout

You decide to apply all the settings on the master title slide to the title slides in the presentation. To do this you reapply the slide layout.

**1** **Choose Format/Slide Layout.**

**Point to the Title Slide layout in the Slide Layout task pane.**

**Click ⌄ to open the drop-down menu for the Title Slide layout.**

| Apply to Selected Slides |
|---|
| Reapply Layout |
| Insert New Slide |

**Choose Reapply Layout.**

*Your screen should be similar to Figure 2.50*

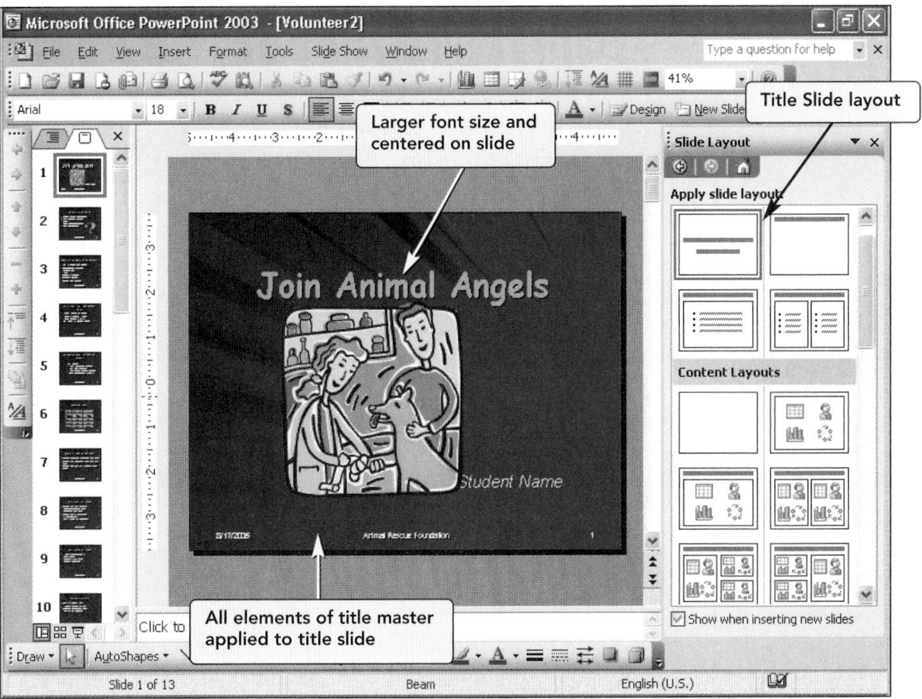


**Figure 2.50**

All elements of the title master slide have been applied to the title slide. The only adjustment you want to make to slide 1 is to reposition the graphic. Then you will reapply the slide layout to the concluding slide.

**2**

- **Move the graphic so it does not overlap the subtitle.**
- **Display slide 13 and reapply the Title Slide layout.**
- **Choose View/Ruler to hide the ruler.**
- **Close the Slide Layout task pane.**

*Your screen should be similar to Figure 2.51*

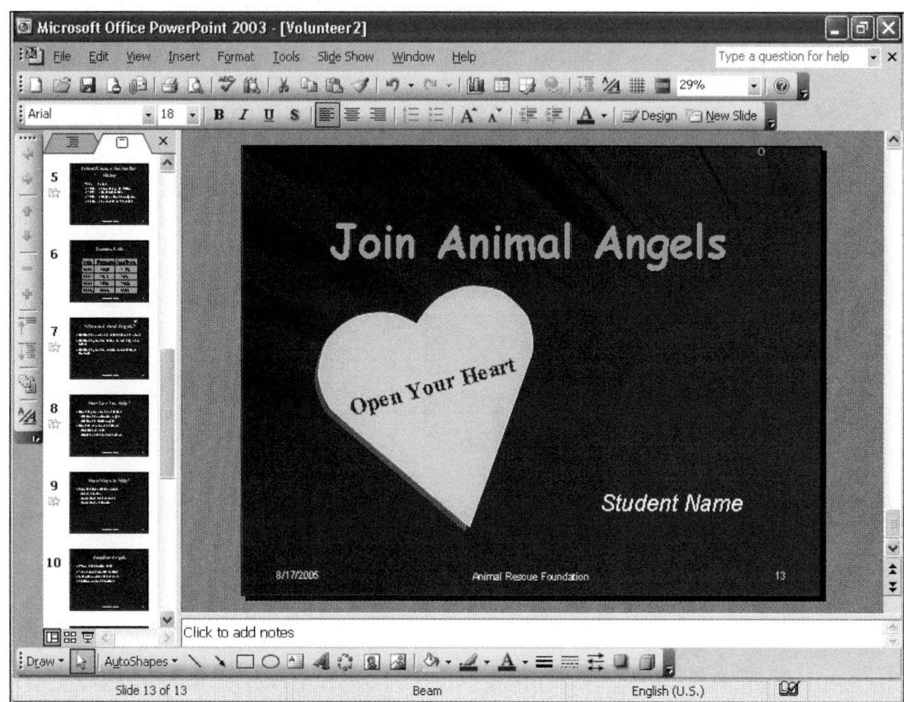


**Figure 2.51**

The layout settings have been applied and the concluding slide should not need any adjustments.

## Changing and Hiding Footer Text

You would also like to hide the display of the footer information on the title slides and change the information displayed in the other slides. When you created the presentation using the AutoContent Wizard, you specified the information to appear in the footer area for all slides in the presentation. The slide and title masters control the placement and display of the footer information, but they do not control the information that appears in those areas. As you have seen, one way to stop the footer information from appearing, is to delete the footer placeholder from the master. Alternatively, you can change or turn off the display of selected footer information or hide the footer in title slides only.

**1**

- **Choose View/Header and Footer.**
- **Open the Slide tab, if necessary.**

*Your screen should be similar to Figure 2.52*

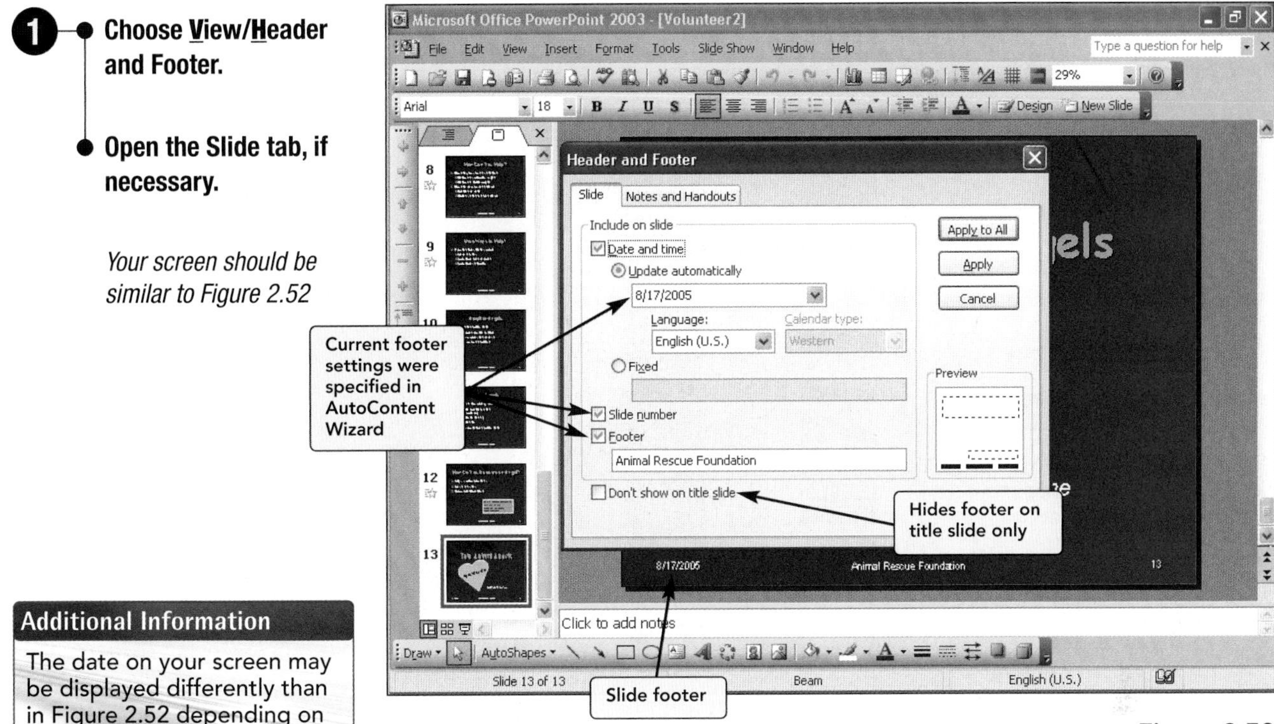


**Additional Information**

The date on your screen may be displayed differently than in Figure 2.52 depending on your Windows settings.

**Figure 2.52**

The Date and Time option is selected, and the date is set to update automatically using the current system date whenever the presentation is opened. However, because you deleted the Date area placeholder from the slide master, this information is not displayed on all (except title slides). You can also change this option to enter a fixed date that will not change.

Because the slide number option is selected, the slide number is displayed in the Number area placeholder on each slide. The text you entered, "Animal Rescue Foundation," appears in the footer text box and is displayed in the Footer area placeholder. You want to turn off the display of the slide number. Also, you do not want to display any footer information on the title slides, and will select the option to hide it.

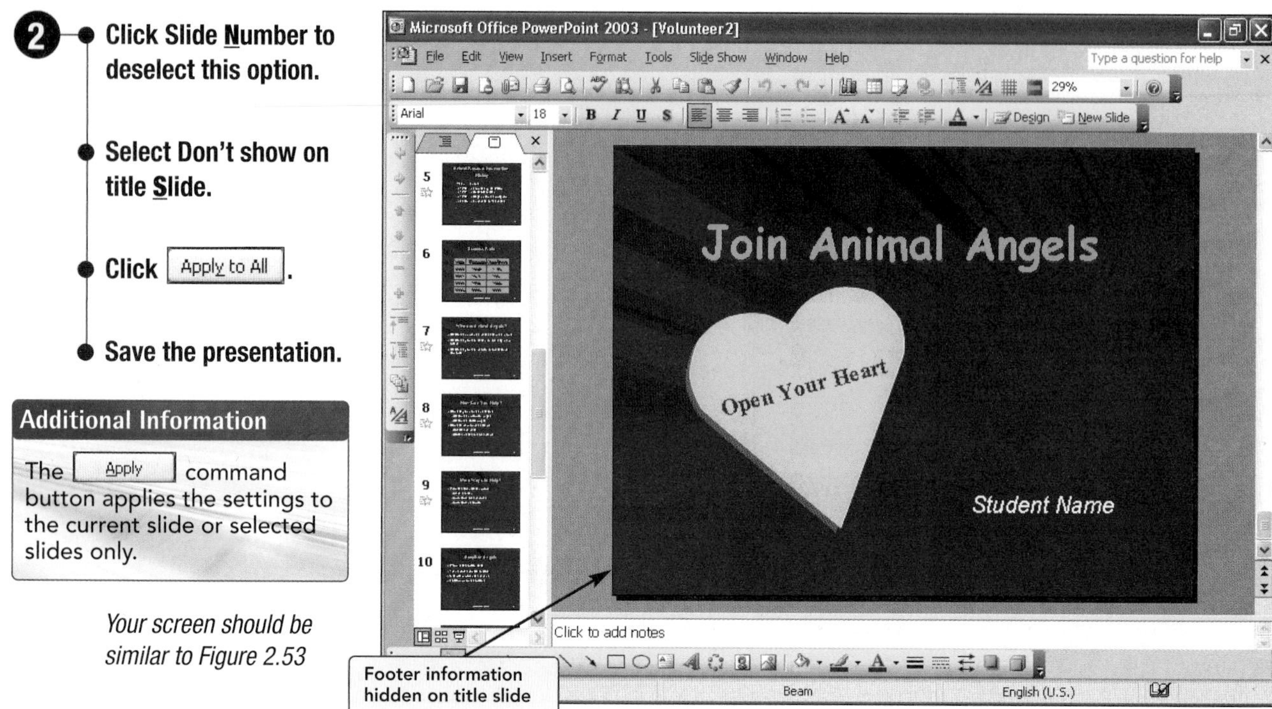


**2**
- **Click Slide Number to deselect this option.**
- **Select Don't show on title Slide.**
- **Click Apply to All.**
- **Save the presentation.**

**Additional Information**

The Apply command button applies the settings to the current slide or selected slides only.

*Your screen should be similar to Figure 2.53*

**Figure 2.53**

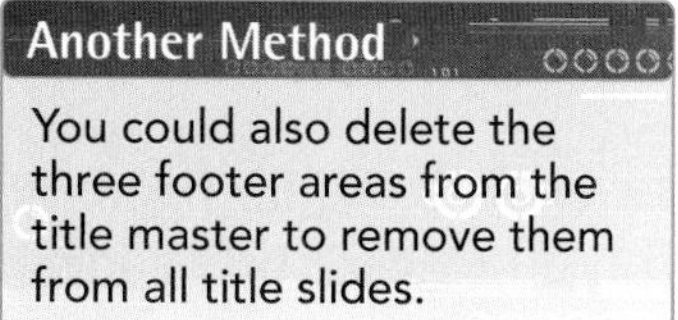

**Another Method**

You could also delete the three footer areas from the title master to remove them from all title slides.

No footer information is displayed on the concluding slide which uses the title slide layout. As you run the slide show next, you will also see that the footer does not display on the first slide. Additionally, the only footer information that appears on all other slides is the name of the organization because you deleted the Date area placeholder and deselected the slide number footer option.

**3**
- **Run the slide show beginning with slide 1.**
- **Click on each slide to advance through the presentation.**

You think the presentation looks quite good, but you have several changes in mind to make it more interesting.

**Note:** If you are ending your session now, save the presentation and exit PowerPoint. When you begin again, open this file.

## Using Special Effects

You decide to use some of PowerPoint's special effects to enhance the onscreen presentation.

## Concept 6

### Special Effects

6 **Special effects** such as animation, sound, slide transitions, and builds are used to enhance an onscreen presentation.

**Animation** adds action to text and graphics so they move around on the screen. You can assign sounds to further enhance the effect.

**Transitions** control the way that the display changes as you move from one slide to the next during a presentation. You can select from many different transition choices. You may choose Dissolve for your title slide to give it an added flair. After that you could use Wipe Right for all the slides until the next to the last, and then use Dissolve again to end the show. As with any special effect, use slide transitions carefully.

**Builds** are used to display each bullet point, text, paragraph, or graphic independently of the other text or objects on the slide. You set up the way you want each element to appear (to fly in from the left, for instance) and whether you want the other elements already on the slide to dim or shimmer when a new element is added. For example, because your audience is used to reading from left to right, you could design your build slides so the bullet points fly in from the left. Then, when you want to emphasize a point, bring a bullet point in from the right. That change grabs the audience's attention.

When you present a slide show, the content of your presentation should take center stage. You want the special effects you use, such as animation, builds, and transitions, to help emphasize the main points in your presentation—not draw the audience's attention to the special effects.

### Animating an Object and Adding Sound Effects

You will begin by adding animation and sound to the AutoShape object on the final slide.

**1** **Display slide 13.**

**From the heart AutoShape's shortcut menu select Custom Animation.**

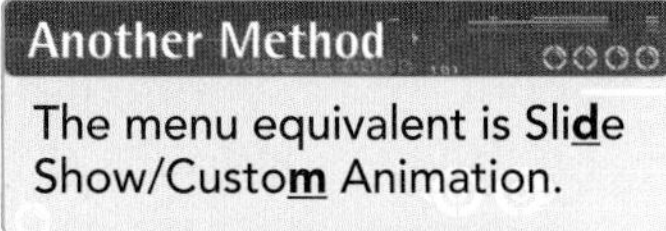

**Another Method**

The menu equivalent is Sli<u>d</u>e Show/Custo<u>m</u> Animation.

*Your screen should be similar to Figure 2.54*

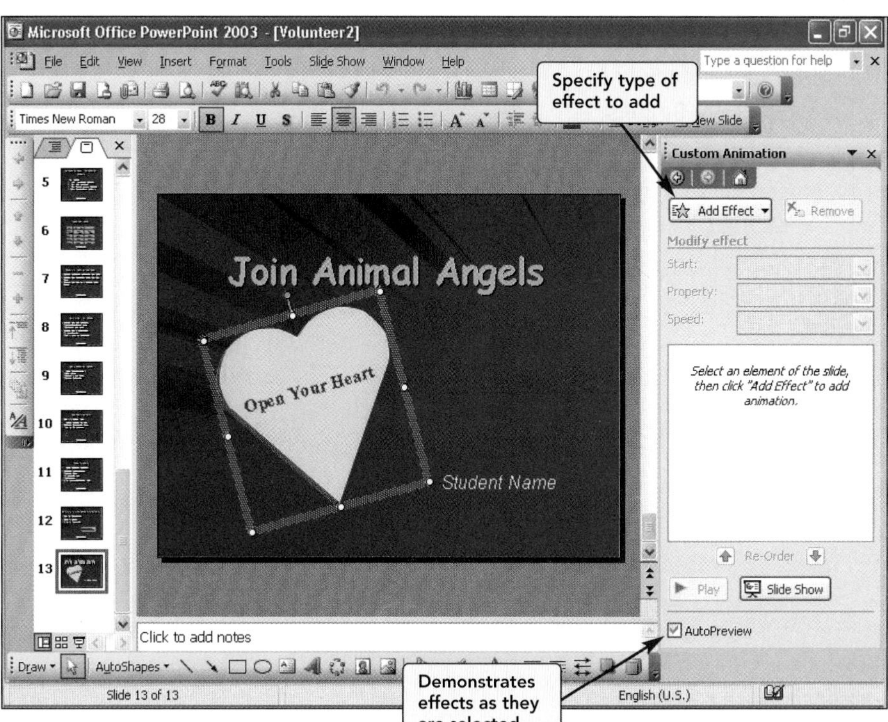


**Figure 2.54**

The Custom Animation task pane is used to assign animations and sound to objects on the slide. As you add animated items to a slide, each item is numbered. The number determines the order in which they display. A non-printing numbered tag appears on the slide near each animated item that correlates to the effects in the list.

You will animate the AutoShape object only. As you make selections, the Custom Animation list box will display the selected settings for the object and the effect will be demonstrated in the slide.

**2**

- **If necessary, select the AutoPreview option.**
- **Click Add Effect, select Entrance, and choose 5, Fly In.**

**Having Trouble?**

If Fly In is not available on the drop-down menu, select More Effects and select it from the dialog box.

- **From the Direction drop-down menu, select From Left.**
- **From the Speed drop-down menu, select Medium.**
- **Display the 1 Heart 3: Open Y... drop-down menu and select Effect Options.**

*Your screen should be similar to Figure 2.55*

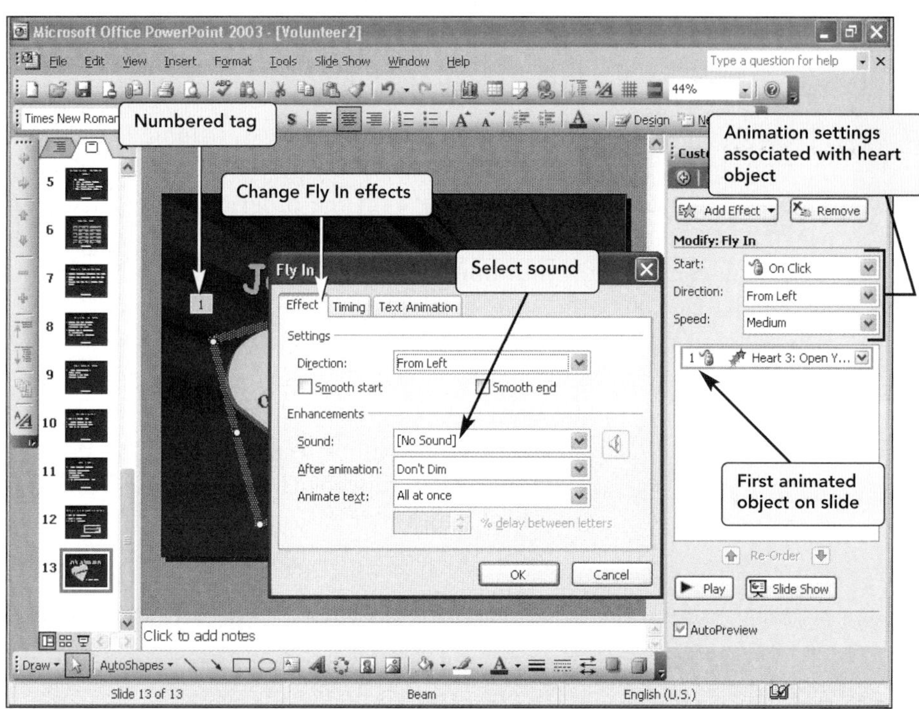


**Figure 2.55**

The list box in the task pane displays information about the first animated object on the slide. The numbered tag near the AutoShape identifies the animated object. The tag does not display when the slide show is run.

The Fly In dialog box includes the setting you already specified for the direction of the effect. You want to include a sound with the fly-in effect.

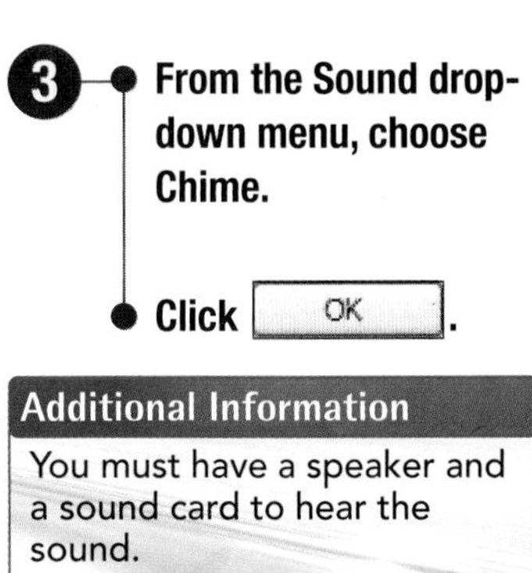

**3** **From the Sound drop-down menu, choose Chime.**

**Click OK.**

**Additional Information**

You must have a speaker and a sound card to hear the sound.

*Your screen should be similar to Figure 2.56*

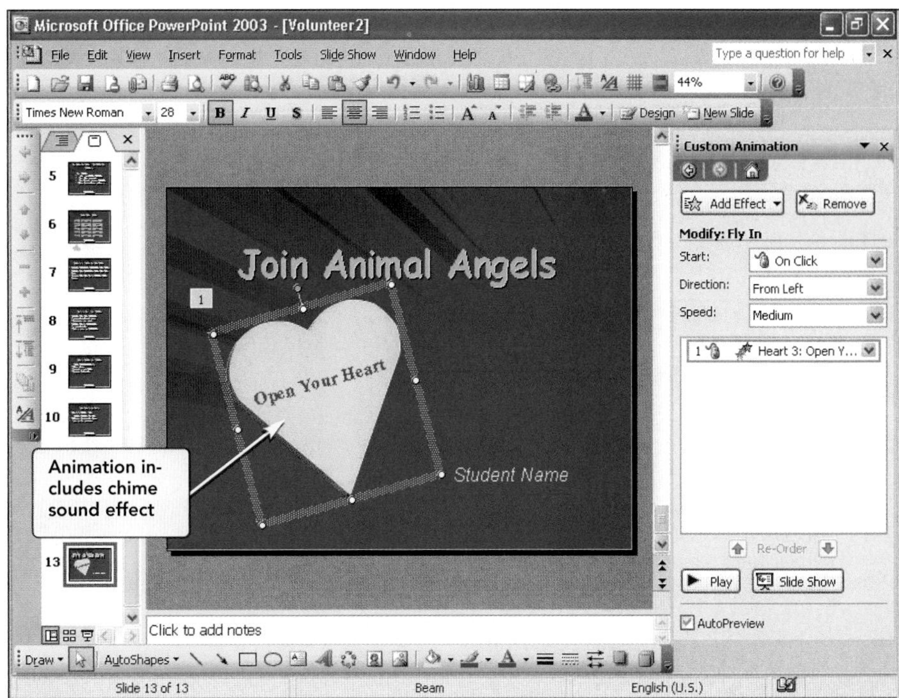


**Figure 2.56**

The heart appeared using the fly-in effect, and the chime sound played as it will when the slide show is run.

## Adding Transition Effects

Next, you want to add a transition effect to all the slides. Although you can add transitions in Normal view, you will use Slide Sorter view because it has its own toolbar that makes it easy to perform many different tasks in this view.

**1** **Switch to Slide Sorter view and select slide 1.**

**Having Trouble?**

If the Slide Sorter toolbar is not displayed, select it from the Toolbar shortcut menu.

**Click** Transition.

**Another Method**

The menu equivalent is Slide Show/Slide Transition.

*Your screen should be similar to Figure 2.57*

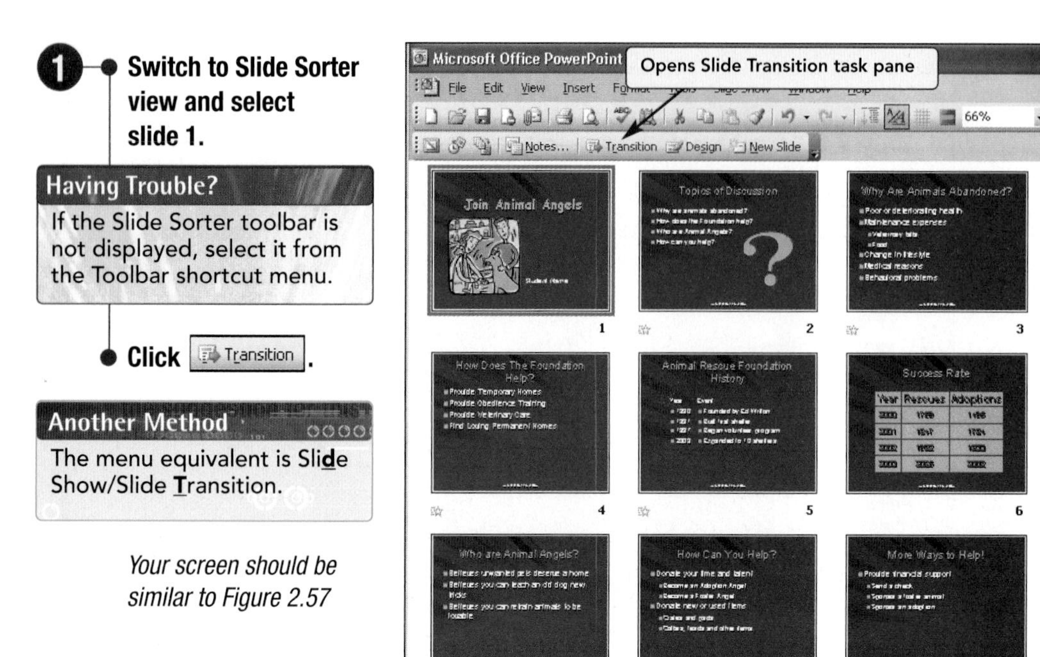

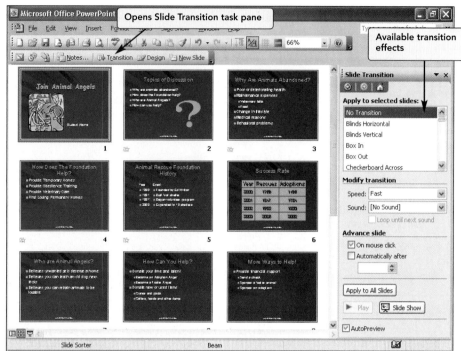

**Figure 2.57**

**Additional Information**

When AutoPreview is not on, you need to click Play to see the effect.

In the Slide Transition task pane, the list box displays the names of the transition effects that can be used on the slides. Currently, No Transition is selected, because the current slide does not include a transition effect. Because the AutoPreview option is selected, as you select a transition effect, the effect is displayed in the current slide. You can also replay the transition effect by clicking Play.

**2** **Scroll the list box and select Shape Diamond.**

**Click** Play **to replay the effect.**

*Your screen should be similar to Figure 2.58*

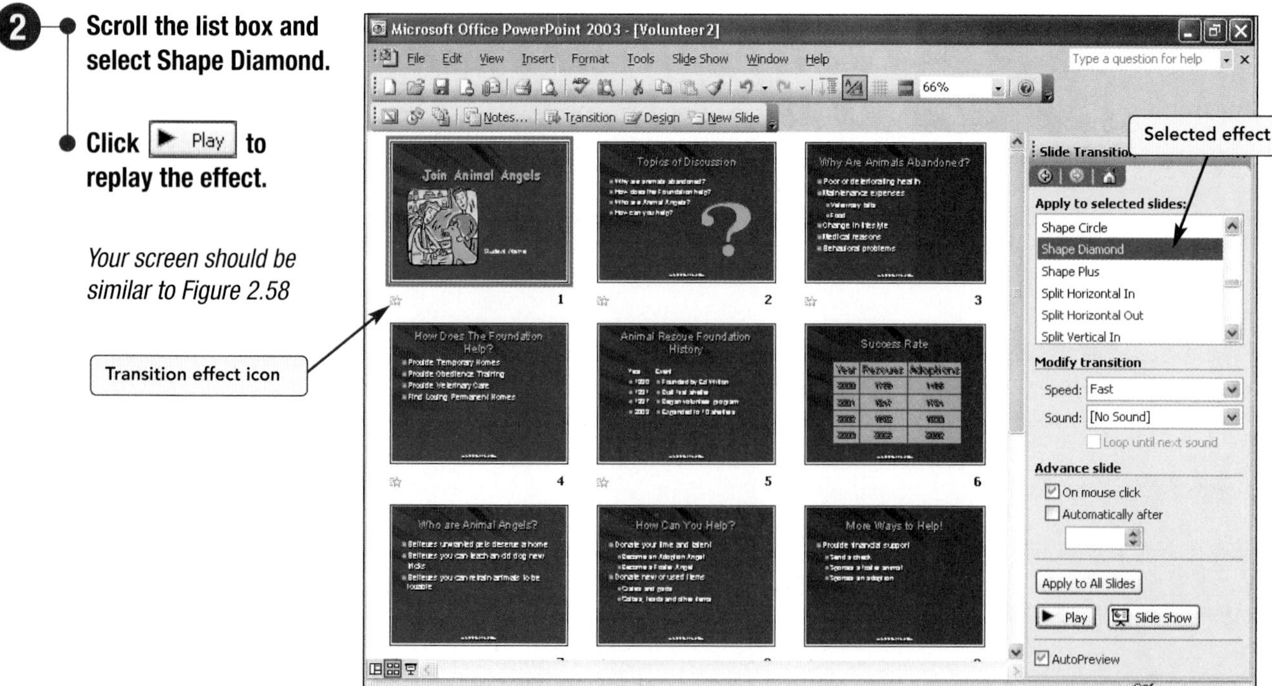


**Figure 2.58**

A preview of the selected transition effect is displayed on the current slide, and a [☆] transition icon is displayed below slide 1. This indicates that a transition effect has been applied to the slide. Several other slides in the presentation also display a transition effect icon. This is because the AutoContent Wizard automatically used the Cut transition effect on all slides, except the title slide, that were added when the presentation was created originally.

You like the way the transition effects work and decide to use the Random Transition effect, which will randomly select different transition effects, on all the slides. You will select and change all the slides at once.

**3**

- **Choose Random Transition (last option in list).**
- **Click** Apply to All Slides.
- **Close the Slide Transition pane.**

*Your screen should be similar to Figure 2.59*

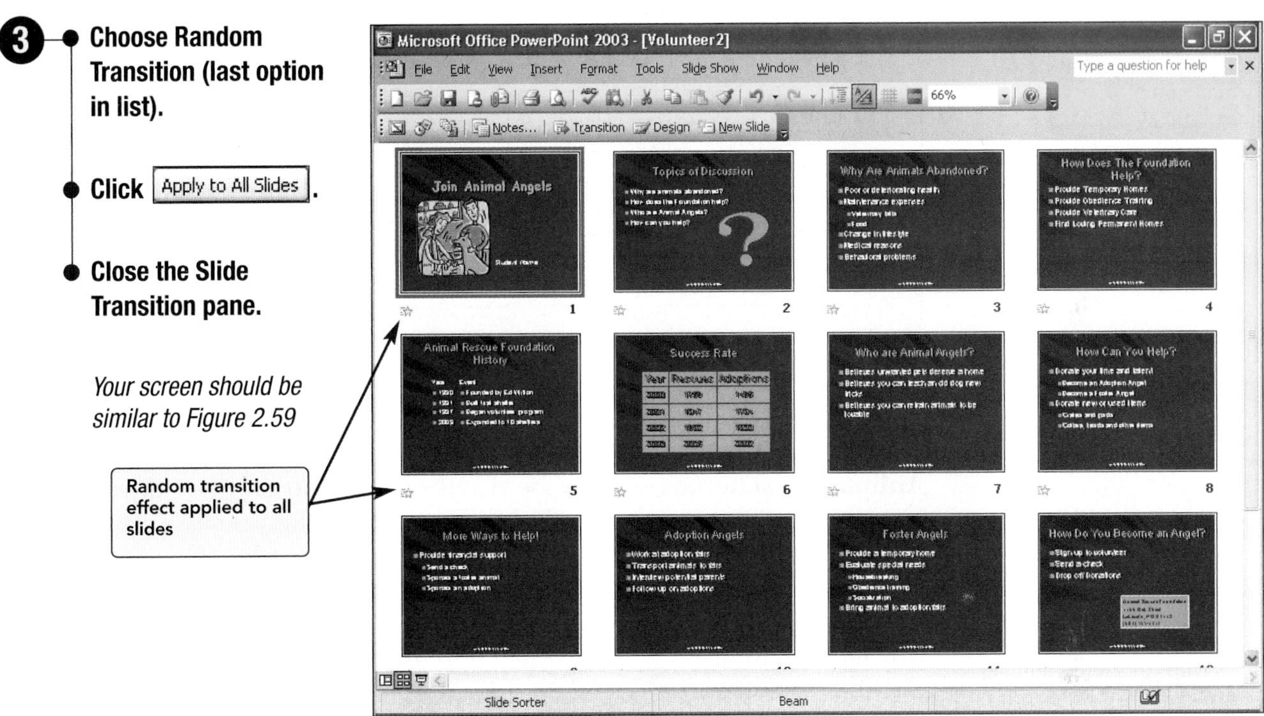


**Figure 2.59**

The transition icon appears below each slide, indicating that a transition effect has been applied to all slides.

**4**

- **Save the presentation.**
- **Run the slide show from the beginning to see the different transition effects.**

## Adding Build Effects

The next effect you want to add to the slides is a build effect that will display progressively each bullet on a slide. When a build is applied to a slide, the slide initially shows only the title. The bulleted text appears as the presentation proceeds. A build slide can also include different build transition effects, which are similar to slide transition effects. The effect is applied to the bulleted text as it is displayed on the slide.

1 • Click .

• Click Animation Schemes from the Slide Design task pane.

**Additional Information**

You can use the Animation Schemes and Custom Animation commands on the Slide Show menu to add sound build effects. To use this option, you must be in Normal view.

*Your screen should be similar to Figure 2.60*

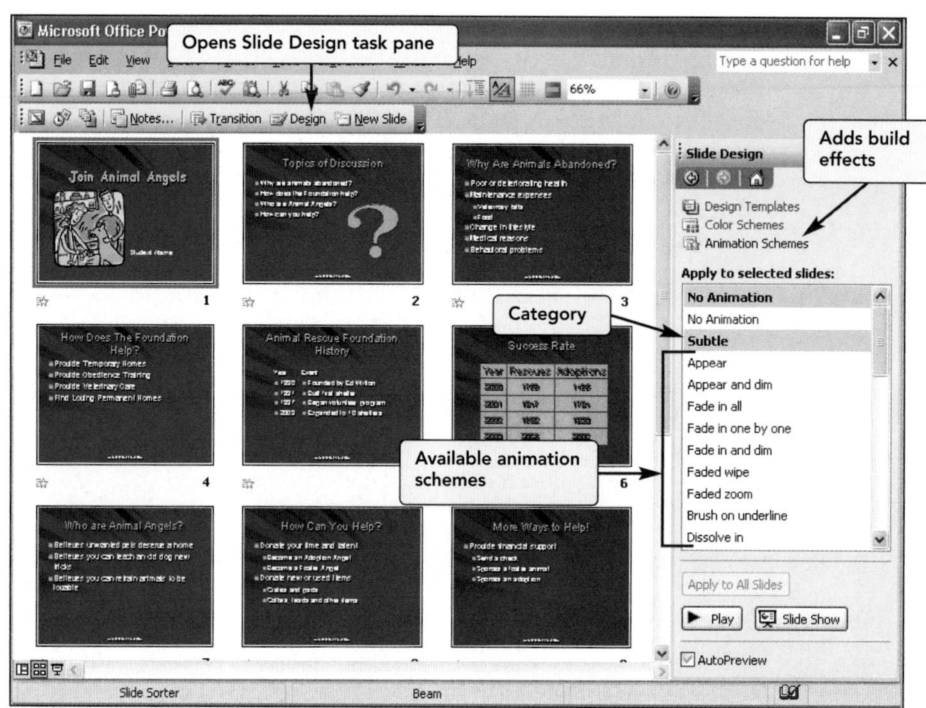


**Figure 2.60**

The Slide Design task pane displays a list of animation schemes. **Animation schemes** are preset visual effects that can be added to slide text. Each scheme usually includes an effect for the title as well as for the bulleted items. Some schemes include a slide transition effect as well. The schemes are divided into three categories: Subtle, Moderate, and Exciting.

**Additional Information**

Pointing to a scheme name displays a description of the effects in a ScreenTip.

You will use two different build effects in the presentation. The two title slides will use one build effect and all other slides except slides 5 and 6 will use another effect. You do not want slides 5 and 6 to have any build effects because they are tables and the content is not conducive to this type of animation.

**2**

- **If necessary, select AutoPreview to turn on this feature.**
- **Make slide 2 the current slide and select a few animation schemes to see how they look.**
- **Select Wipe from the Subtle category.**
- **Click Apply to All Slides.**
- **Select slides 5 and 6.**

**Having Trouble?**

You can select and deselect multiple slides by holding down Ctrl while making your selection.

- **Select No Animation from the No Animation category.**
- **Select slides 1 and 13.**
- **Select the Big Title effect from the Exciting category.**
- **Select slide 1 and click [Slide Show button] to start Slide Show.**
- **Click on the slide to display the subtitle.**

*Your screen should be similar to Figure 2.61*

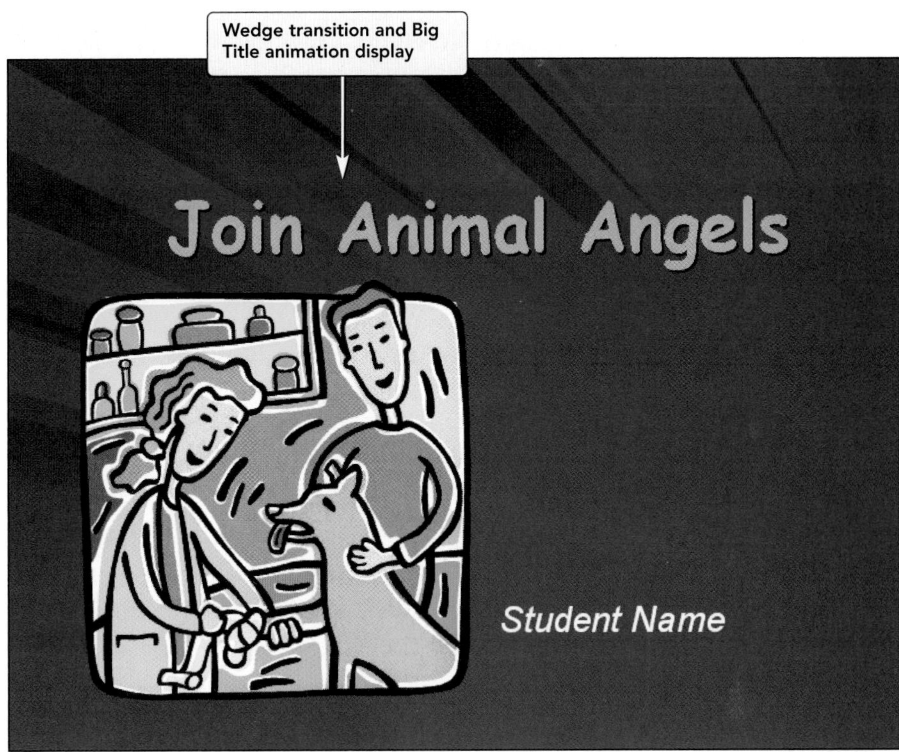

Wedge transition and Big Title animation display
Join Animal Angels
Student Name

Figure 2.61

The first slide is displayed using the Wedge transition effect and Big Title animation, but the subtitle did not display until you clicked on the slide. When a build is applied to a slide, the body items are displayed only when you click or use any of the procedures to advance to the next slide. This allows the presenter to focus the audience's attention and to control the pace of the presentation.

## Controlling the Slide Show

As much as you would like to control a presentation completely, the presence of an audience usually causes the presentation to change course. PowerPoint has several ways to control a slide show during the presentation. Before presenting a slide show, you should rehearse the presentation. To help with this aspect of the presentation, PowerPoint includes a Rehearse Timings option on the Slide Show menu that records the time you spend on each slide as you practice your narration. If your computer is set up with a microphone, you could even record your narration with the Record Narration option.

### Navigating in a Slide Show

Running the slide show and practicing how to control the slide show help you to have a smooth presentation. For example, if someone has a question about a previous slide, you can go backward and redisplay it. You will try out some of the features you can use while running the slide show.

**1 Continue to click or press Spacebar until slide 6, Success Rate, appears.**

**Press Backspace (2 times).**

> **Additional Information**
> You can return to the first slide in the presentation by holding down both mouse buttons for two seconds.

You returned the onscreen presentation to slide 4, but now, because the audience has already viewed slides 5 and 6, you want to advance to slide 7. To go to a specific slide number, you type the slide number and press ←Enter.

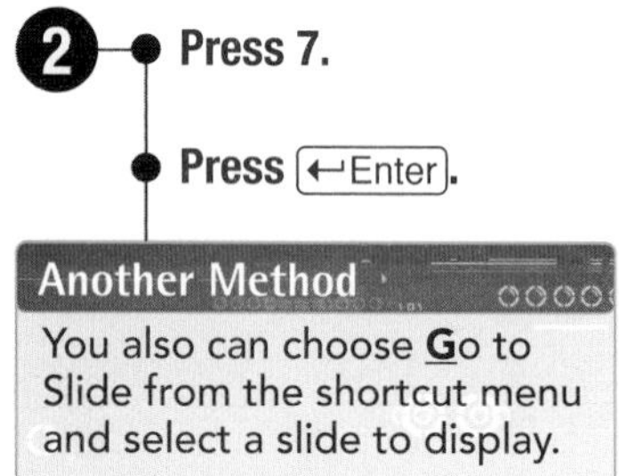

**2 Press 7.**

**Press ←Enter.**

> **Another Method**
> You also can choose Go to Slide from the shortcut menu and select a slide to display.

**Click 3 times to display the three bulleted items.**

> **Additional Information**
> You can also white out the screen by pressing W or using Screen/White Screen on the shortcut menu.

Slide 7, Who are Animal Angels?, is displayed. Sometimes a question from an audience member can interrupt the flow of the presentation. If this happens to you, you can black out the screen to focus attention onto your response.

**3 Press B.**

> **Another Method**
> The menu equivalent is Screen/Black Screen on the shortcut menu.

The screen goes to black while you address the topic. When you are ready to resume the presentation, you can bring the slide back.

**4 Click, or press B.**

## Adding Freehand Annotations

During your presentation, you may want to point to an important word, underline an important point, or draw checkmarks next to items that you have covered. To do this, you can use the mouse pointer during the presentation. When you move the mouse, the mouse pointer appears and the Slide Show toolbar is displayed in the lower left corner of the screen.

1 **Move the mouse on your desktop.**

*Your screen should be similar to Figure 2.62*

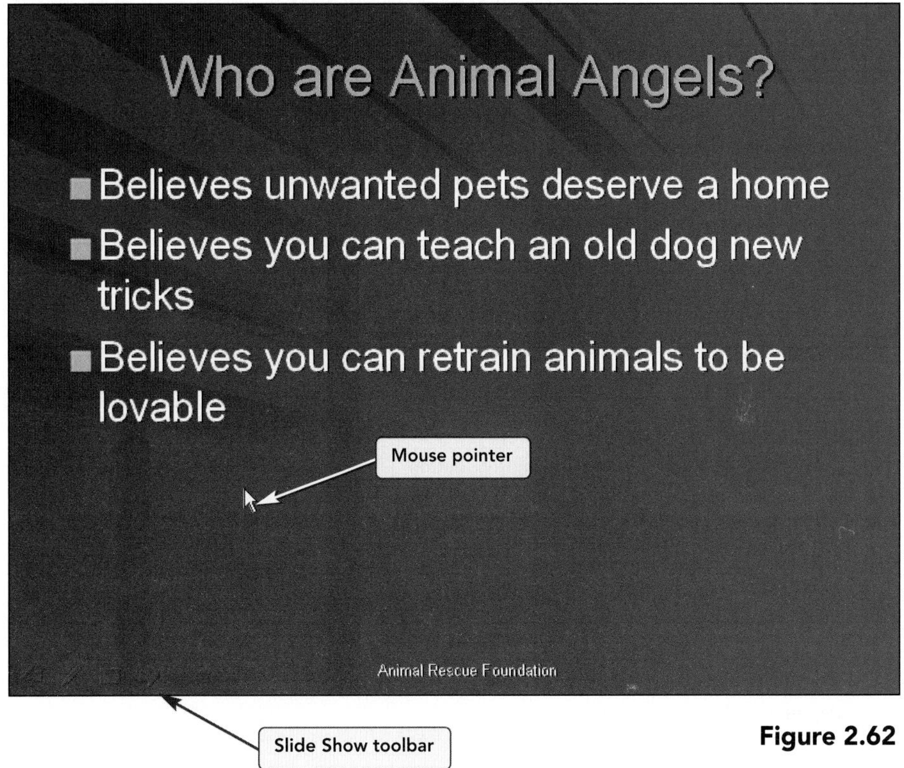

Who are Animal Angels?
Believes unwanted pets deserve a home
Believes you can teach an old dog new tricks
Believes you can retrain animals to be lovable
Mouse pointer
Animal Rescue Foundation
Slide Show toolbar


**Figure 2.62**

The mouse pointer in its current shape can be used to point to items on the slide. You can also use it to draw on the screen by changing the mouse pointer to a ballpoint pen, felt tip pen, or highlighter, which activates the associated freehand annotation feature.

**2** • **Click ![] to display the Pointer options menu.**

**Another Method**

You can also select Pointer Options from the shortcut menu.

*Your screen should be similar to Figure 2.63*

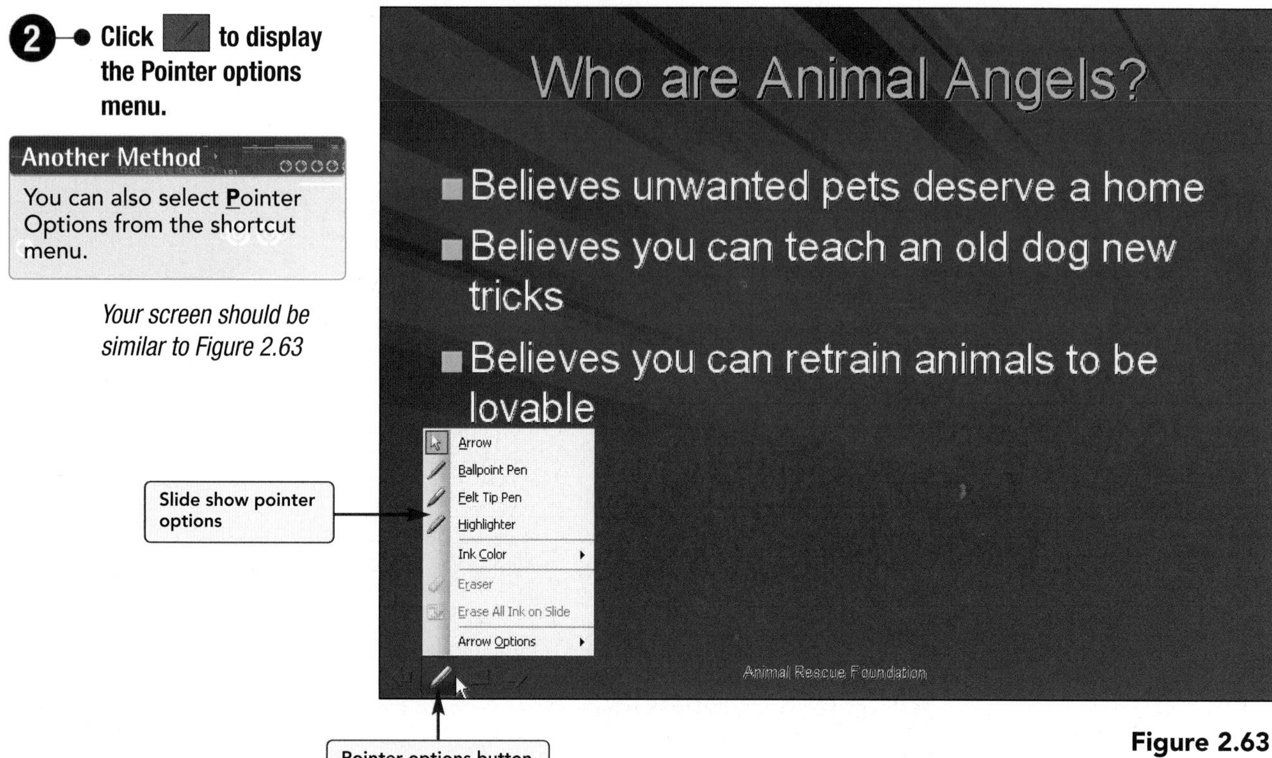


**Figure 2.63**

The mouse pointer and arrow options are described in the following table.

| Pointer Options | Effect |
|---|---|
| **A**rrow | Displays the mouse pointer as an arrow. |
| **B**allpoint Pen | Changes the mouse pointer to a diamond shape and turns on ballpoint pen annotation. |
| **F**elt Tip Pen | Changes the mouse pointer to a circle shape and turns on felt tip pen annotation. |
| **H**ighlighter | Changes the mouse pointer to a bar shape and turns on highlighter. |
| Ink **C**olor | Displays a color palette to select a color for the annotation tool. |
| E**r**aser | Erases selected annotations. |
| **E**rase All Ink on Slide | Removes all annotations from the slide. |
| **Arrow Options** | **(These options apply only if Arrow is selected.)** |
| A**u**tomatic | Hides the mouse pointer if it is not moved for 15 seconds. It reappears when you move the mouse. This is the default setting. |
| **V**isible | Displays the mouse pointer as an arrow and does not hide it. |
| **H**idden | Hides the mouse pointer until another pointer option is selected. |

You will try out several of the freehand annotation features to see how they work. To draw, you select the pen style and then drag the pen pointer in the direction you want to draw.

**3** • **Choose Felt Tip Pen.**

**Additional Information**

The mouse pointer changes shape depending upon the selected annotation tool.

• **Drag the dot pointer until a circle is drawn around the word "teach."**

• **Choose Highlighter from the Pointer options menu and highlight the word "retrain."**

• **Choose Ballpoint Pen from the Pointer options menu.**

**Another Method**

You can also use Ctrl + P to display the Ballpoint pen.

• **Choose Ink Color from the Pointer options menu and select gold.**

**Additional Information**

The Automatic ink color setting determines the default color to use for annotations based upon the slide design colors.

• **In the first bulleted item, draw a caret after the word "a" and write the word "good" above the line.**

*Your screen should be similar to Figure 2.64*

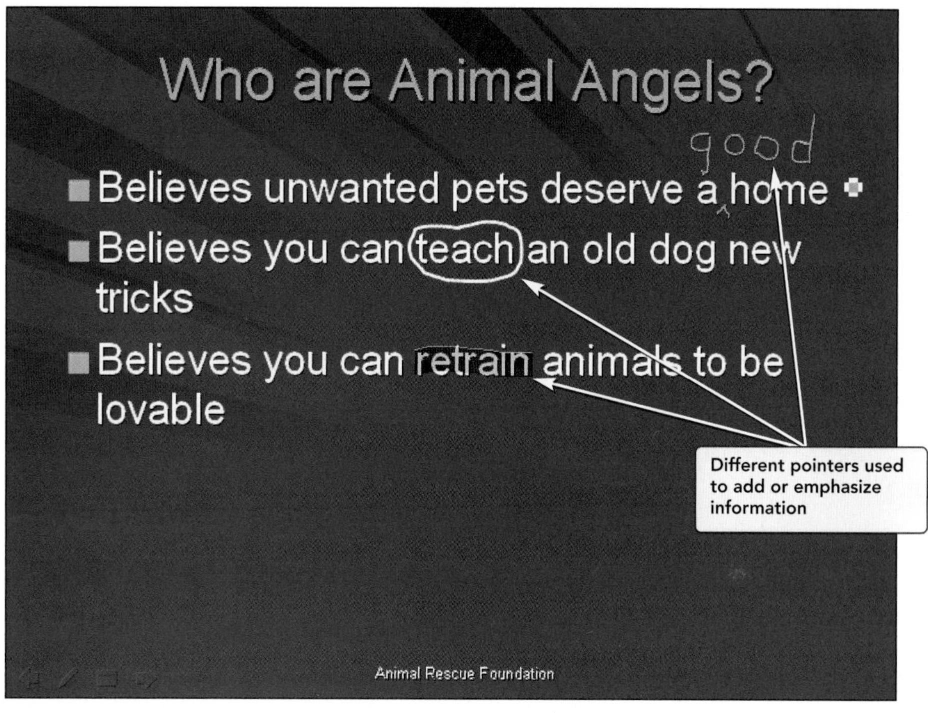


Figure 2.64

4 • **Practice using the freehand annotator to draw any shapes you want on the slide.**

• **To erase the annotations, select Erase All Ink on Slide from the Pointer options menu.**

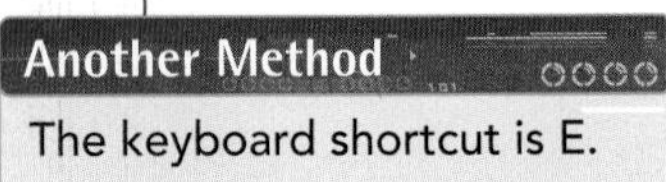


• **To turn off freehand annotation, select Arrow from the Pointer options menu.**

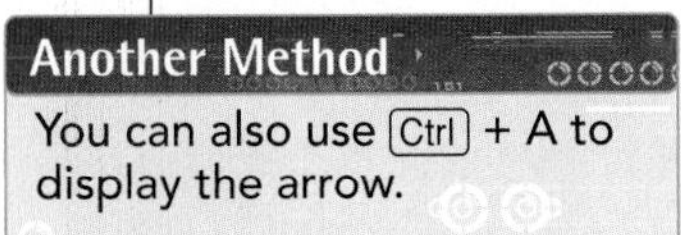

Another Method
You can also use Ctrl + A to display the arrow.


• **Press Esc to end the slide show.**

• **Close the task pane.**

If you do not erase annotations before ending the presentation, you are prompted to keep or discard the annotations when you end the slide show. If you keep the annotations they are saved to the slides and will appear as part of the slide during a presentation.

## Hiding Slides

As you reconsider the presentation, you decide to show the Success Rate slide only if someone asks about this information. To do this, you will hide the slide.

1 • **Select slide 6.**

• **Click Hide Slide.**

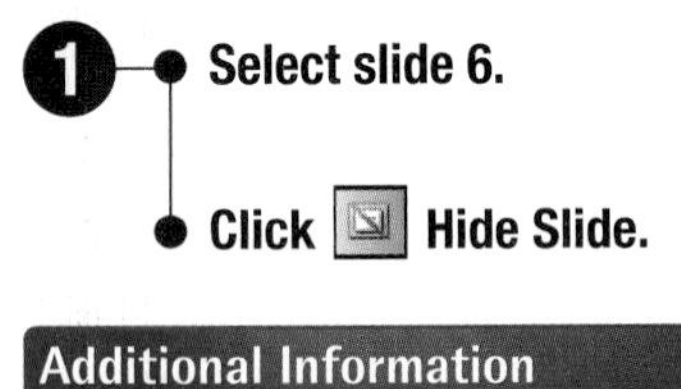

Additional Information
The menu equivalent is Slide Show/Hide Slide.


*Your screen should be similar to Figure 2.65*

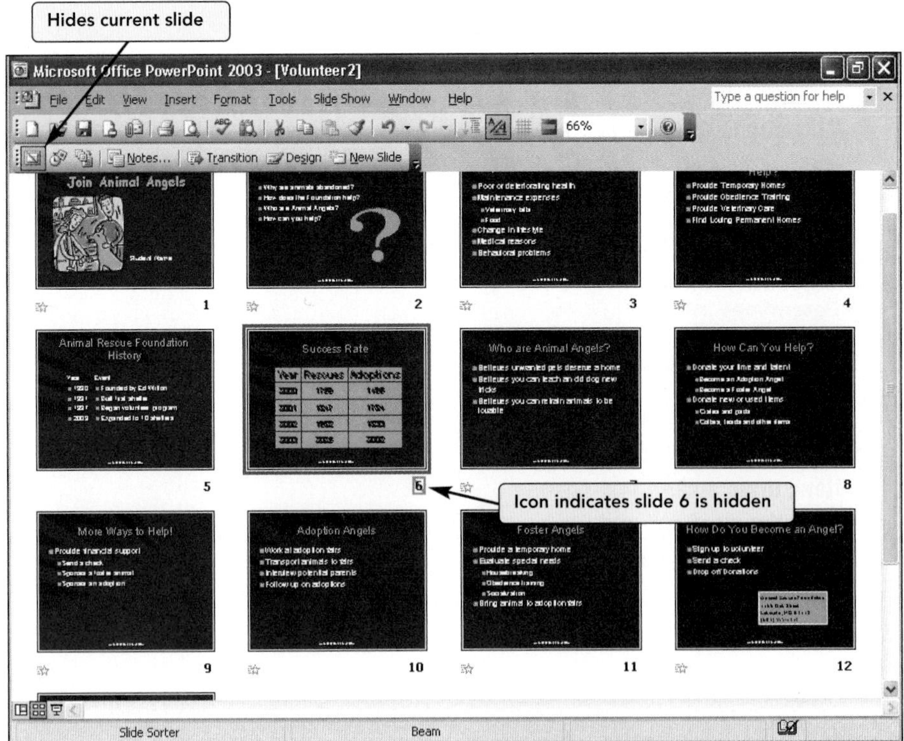


Figure 2.65

Notice that the slide number for slide 6 is surrounded by a box with a slash drawn through it which indicates that the slide is hidden. Next, you will run the slide show to see how hidden slides work. You will begin the show at the slide before the hidden slide.

**2**

- **Select slide 5.**
- **Click [icon] to run the slide show from the current slide.**
- **Click to display the next slide, which should be Who Are Animal Angels?**

*Your screen should be similar to Figure 2.66*

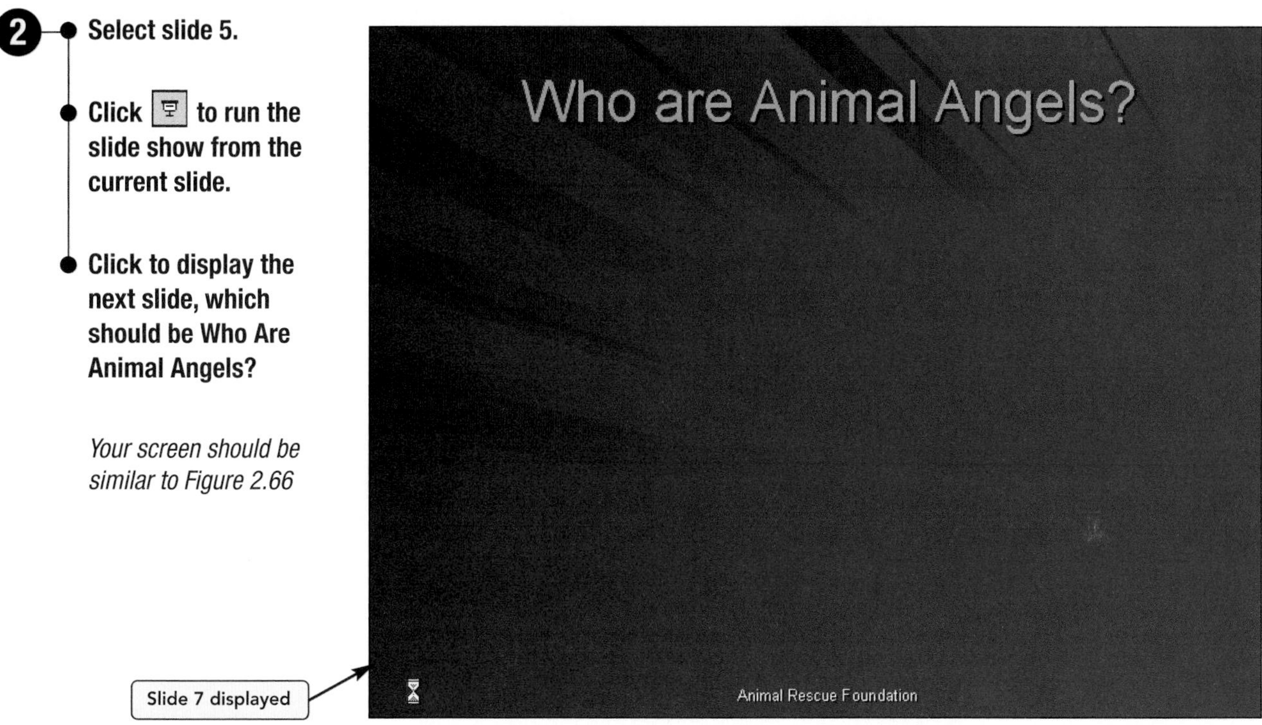


**Figure 2.66**

Slide 6 was not displayed because it is hidden. To show how to display a hidden slide, you will return to slide 5 and then display slide 6.

**3**

- **Press Page Up twice to display slide 5 again.**
- **Press H to see slide 6.**

*Your screen should be similar to Figure 2.67*

**Another Method**

You can also use **G**o to Slide on the shortcut menu to display a hidden slide.

| Year | Rescues | Adoptions |
|---|---|---|
| 2000 | 1759 | 1495 |
| 2001 | 1847 | 1784 |
| 2002 | 1982 | 1833 |
| 2003 | 2025 | 2002 |

**Figure 2.67**

## Adding Speaker Notes

When making your presentation, there are some critical points you want to be sure to discuss. To help you remember the important points, you can add notes to a slide and then print the **notes pages**. These pages display the notes below a small version of the slide they accompany. You can create notes pages for some or all of the slides in a presentation. You decide to add speaker notes on slide 5 to remind you about the hidden slide.

**1** • **Press Esc to end the slide show.**

• **Display slide 5 in Normal view.**

• **Click in the notes pane.**

• **Type Show the next hidden slide if someone asks about adoption rates..**

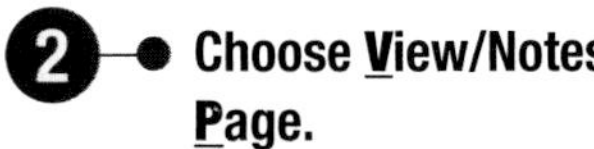

**Additional Information**

You can enlarge the notes area by dragging the pane divider line.

*Your screen should be similar to Figure 2.68*

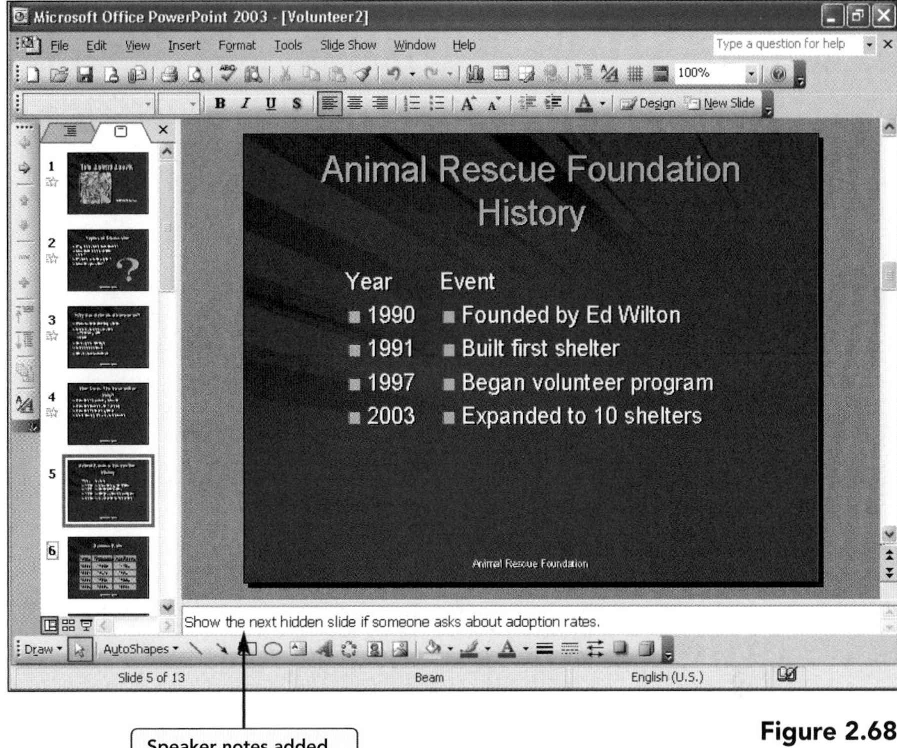


**Figure 2.68**

You want to preview the notes page to check its appearence before it is printed.

**2** • **Choose View/Notes Page.**

*Your screen should be similar to Figure 2.69*

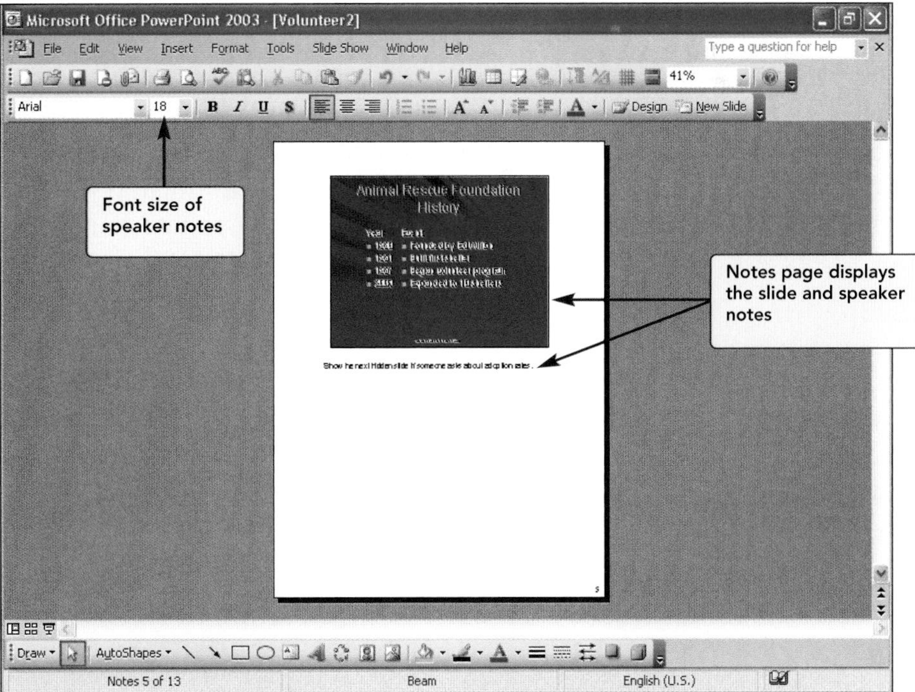


**Figure 2.69**

The notes pages display the notes you added below the slide that the note accompanies.

To make the speaker notes easy to read in a dimly lit room while you are making the presentation, you will increase the font size of the notes text.

**3**
- **Click on the note text to select the placeholder.**
- **Select the note text.**
- **Increase the font size to 24.**

*Your screen should be similar to Figure 2.70*

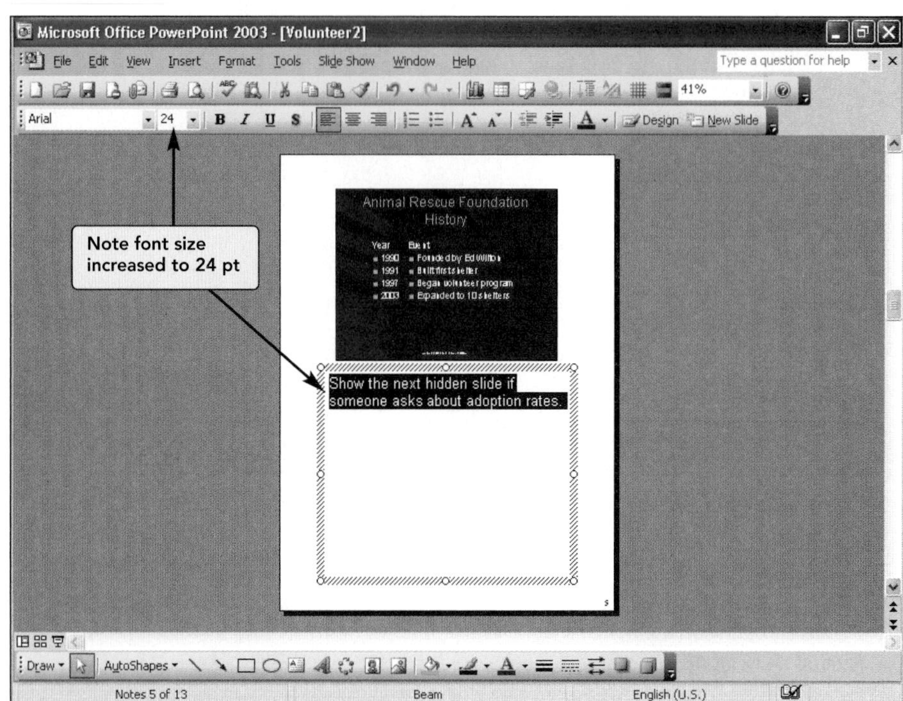


**Figure 2.70**

## Checking Style

**Having Trouble?**

If your school has disabled the Office Assistant, you will not be able to complete this section.

You want to make a final check of the presentation for consistency and style. To help with this, you can use the **style check** feature which checks for consistency in punctuation and capitalization as well as for visual elements such as the maximum number of bulleted items in a list. To use this feature, you need to turn it on and set the options to check. Additionally, the Office Assistant feature must be on, otherwise you will not be notified about located style inconsistencies.

**1** Display slide 1 in Normal view.

- Choose **T**ools/**O**ptions.
- Open the Spelling and Style tab and select **C**heck Style.
- If prompted, click  to turn on the Office Assistant.
- Click .

*Your screen should be similar to Figure 2.71*

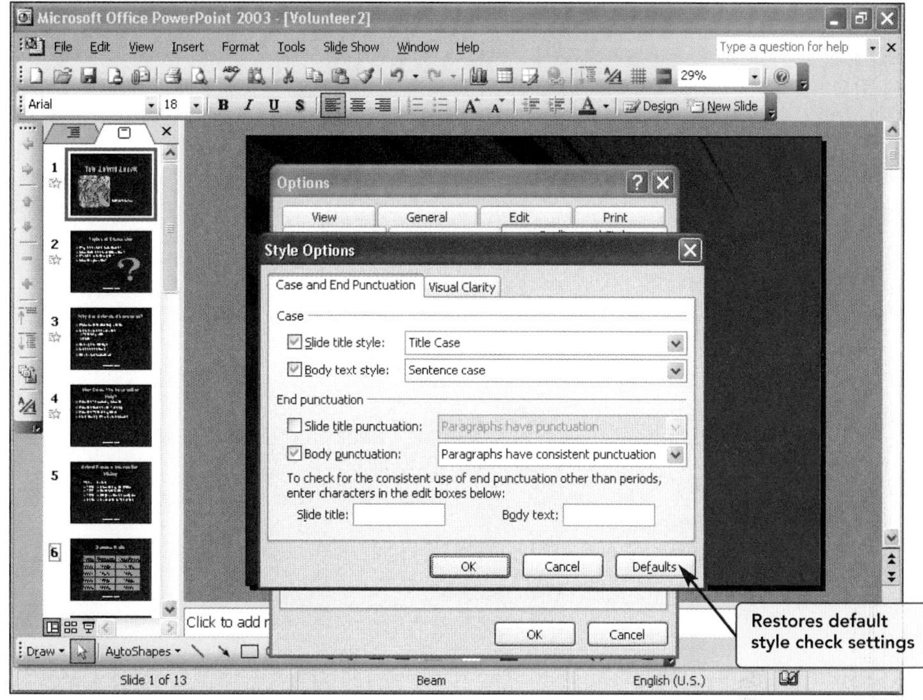


**Figure 2.71**

**Additional Information**

You can turn on/off options and change the default settings by selecting from the option's drop-down menu.

The Case and End Punctuation tab provides options that allow you to control the kind of style check used for capitalization and punctuation. The default style rule is to use title case (first letter of most words is capitalized) for slide titles and sentence case (only the first word is capitalized) for body text. Additionally, style checking looks for consistent use of end punctuation in body text.

You want to use the default settings for the style check.

**2** If necessary, click 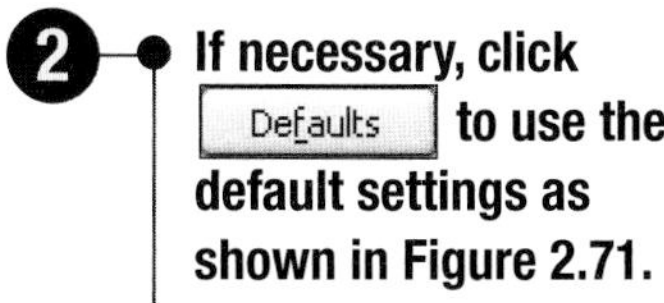 to use the default settings as shown in Figure 2.71.

- Open the Visual Clarity tab.
- If necessary, select all the options.

*Your screen should be similar to Figure 2.72*

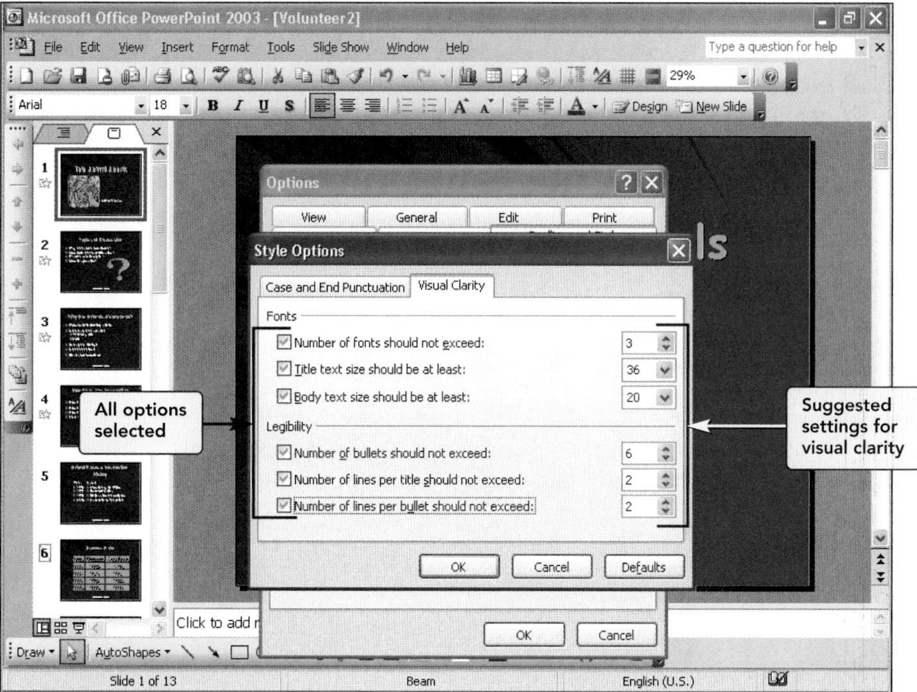


**Figure 2.72**

When a style check is made, each slide is examined for visual clarity. The default settings use guidelines for proper slide design: the font size is large, the number of fonts used is small, and the amount of text on a slide is limited. For example, the maximum number of bullets per slide is six and number of lines per bullet is two. All these settings help you adhere to good slide design.

The style check feature is active only when the Office Assistant is displayed. As you display each slide in Normal view, the style is evaluated. It displays a 💡 next to the placeholder area in any slides in which it detects a potential problem.

**3** **Click**  **2 times.**

- **Click on the slide pane of slide 1 to activate the pane.**
- **Because no problems were identified in slide 1, click in the scroll bar to display slide 2.**

**Having Trouble?**
If you advance to the next slide using the Slides tab, you must click on the slide pane each time to activate it and evaluate the style.

- **Click on the**  **.**
- **Move the Assistant character to the right side of the screen.**

*Your screen should be similar to Figure 2.73*

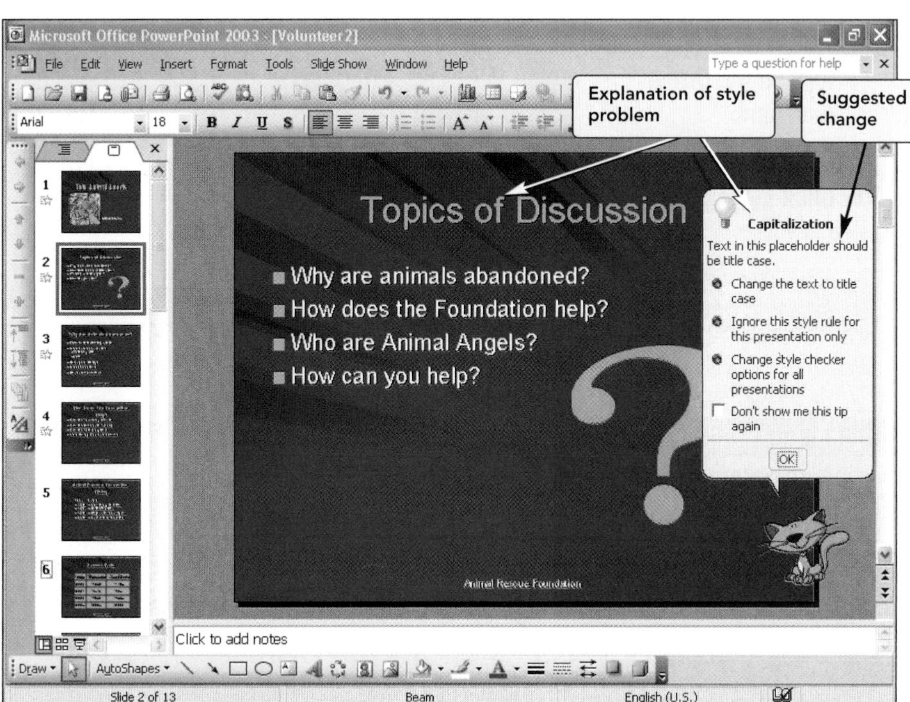


**Figure 2.73**

**Having Trouble?**
Your Assistant character may be different from the character shown here.

The Assistant displays an explanation of the problem it has located. In this case, because each word in the title is not capitalized, the title case rule has been violated. You will use the suggestion to correct the title case. As soon as you respond to the style checker, the correction is made and the next located potential problem is identified.

**4** Choose "Change the text to title case."

Click on the 💡 next to the object area placeholder.

*Your screen should be similar to Figure 2.74*

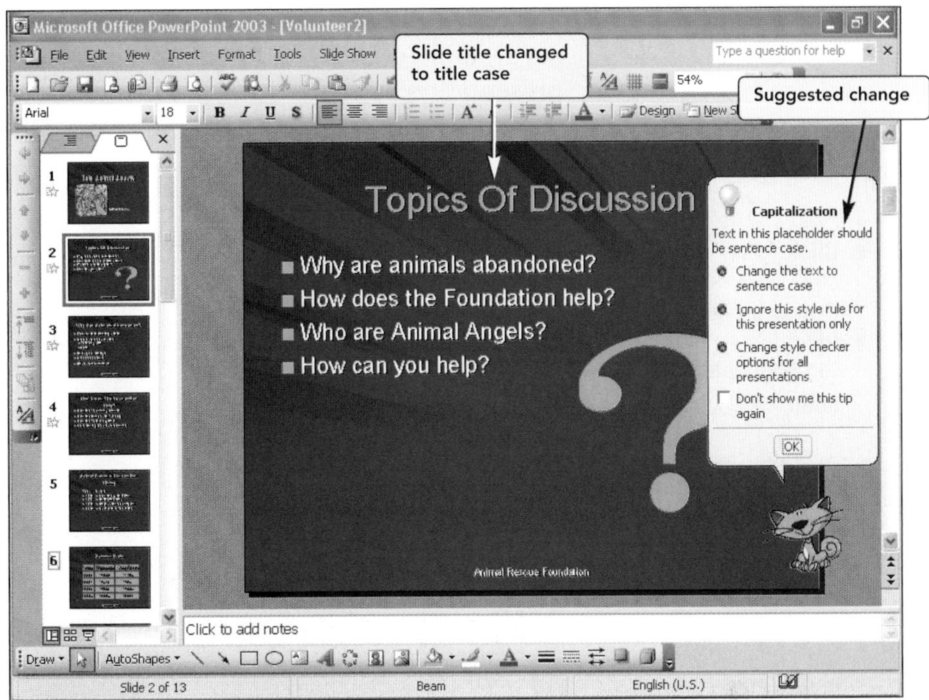


**Figure 2.74**

The title case is corrected and a second lightbulb appears indicating that another style problem has been identified. The suggested style change is to change the bulleted items to sentence case for body text.

**5** Choose "Change the text to sentence case."

*Your screen should be similar to Figure 2.75*

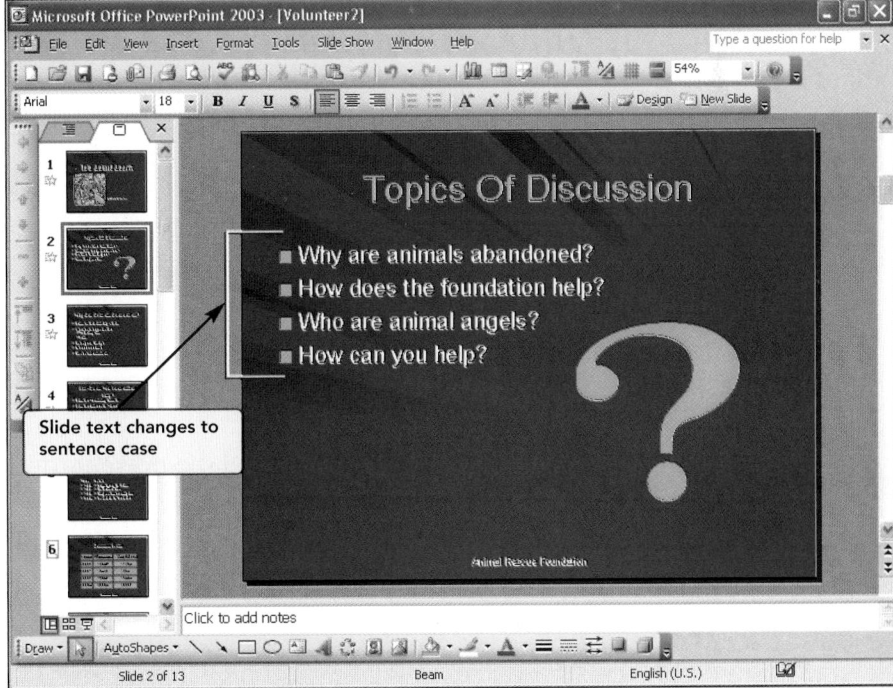


**Figure 2.75**

Making this change, however, changed proper names, such as the name of the volunteer organization, to lowercase. In this case, you do not want to keep this change. You will undo the change and skip the style check suggestion to clear it. Then you will continue checking the rest of the presentation.

**6** **Click Undo.**

- **Click** 💡.
- **Click OK to ignore the suggestion for this slide.**
- **Continue checking the style on the remaining slides in the presentation, making the changes shown in the table below Figure 2.76.**

*Your screen should be similar to Figure 2.76*

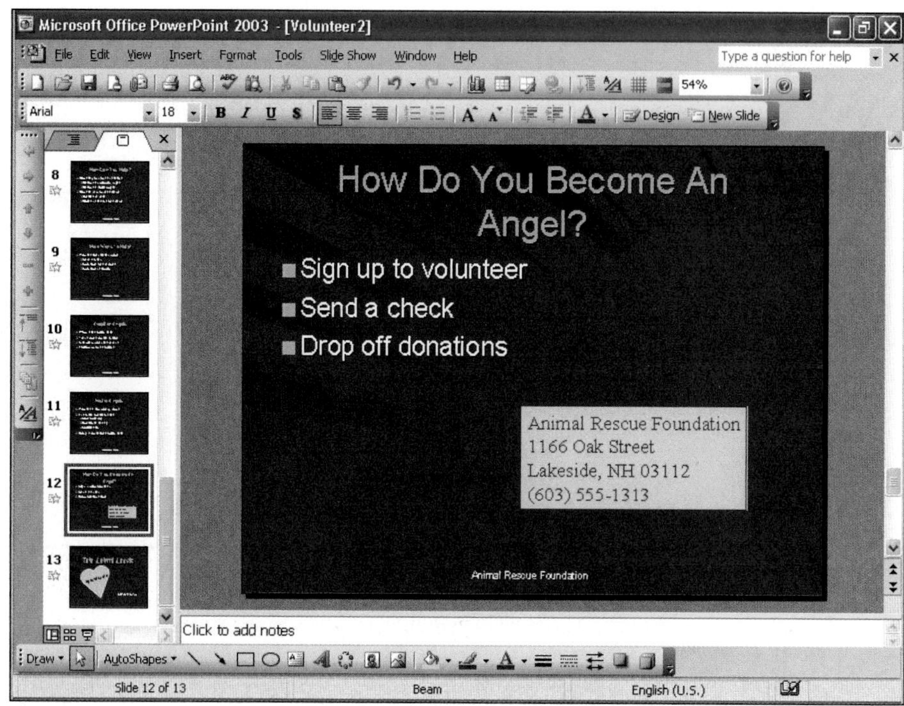


**Figure 2.76**

| Slide | Adjustment |
|---|---|
| 4 | Change the text to sentence case. |
| 5 | Click OK to ignore changes for this slide. |
| 7 | Change the text to title case. |
| 8 | Click OK to ignore change for this slide. |
| 9 | Change the text to title case. |
| 12 | Change the text to title case.<br>Change the text to sentence case. |

Now that you have checked the presentation, you will turn off this feature.

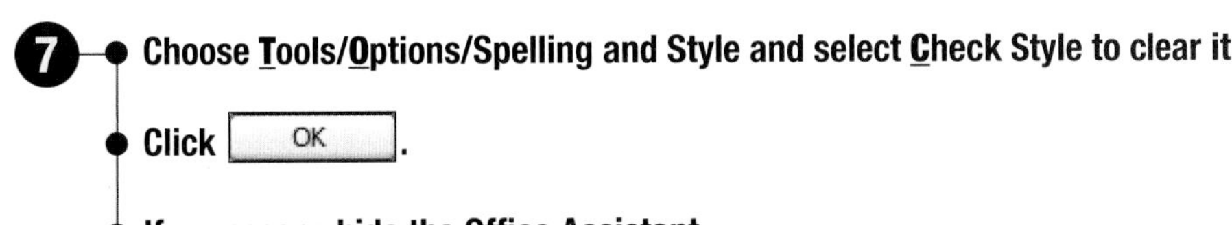

**7**
- **Choose Tools/Options/Spelling and Style and select Check Style to clear it.**
- **Click OK.**
- **If necessary, hide the Office Assistant.**

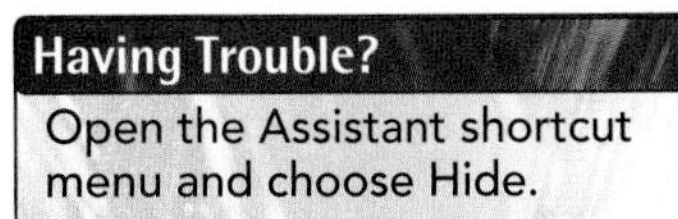

**Having Trouble?**

Open the Assistant shortcut menu and choose Hide.

## Documenting a File

Before saving the completed presentation, you want to include file documentation with the file when it is saved.

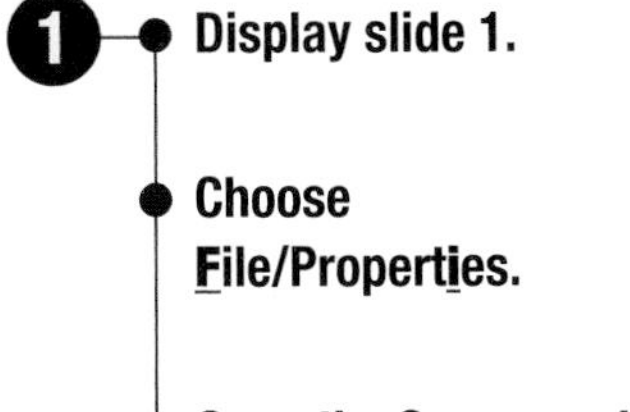

**1**
- **Display slide 1.**
- **Choose File/Properties.**
- **Open the Summary tab if necessary.**

*Your screen should be similar to Figure 2.77*

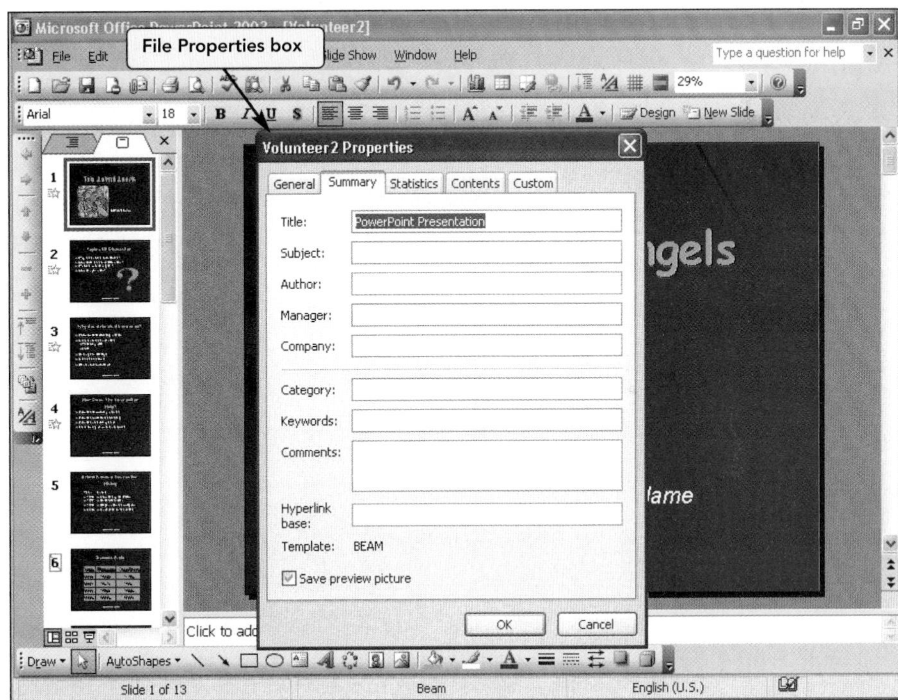


**Figure 2.77**

The Summary tab text boxes are used for the following:

| Option | Action |
|---|---|
| Title | Enter the presentation title. This title can be longer and more descriptive than the presentation file name. |
| Subject | Enter a description of the presentation's content. |
| Author | Enter the name of the presentation's author. By default this is the name entered when PowerPoint was installed. |
| Manager | Enter the name of your manager. |
| Company | Enter the name of your company. |
| Category | Enter the name of a higher-level category under which you can group similar types of presentations. |
| Keywords | Enter words that you associate with the presentation so the Find File command can be used. |
| Comments | Enter any comments you feel are appropriate for the presentation. |
| Hyperlink base | Enter the path or URL that you want to use for all hyperlinks in the document. |
| Template | Identifies the template that is attached to the file. |
| Save Preview Picture | Saves a picture of the first slide with the file to display in the Open dialog box. |

**2**

- **In the title text box, enter Animal Angels.**
- **In the subject text box, enter Volunteer recruitment.**
- **In the Author text box, enter your name.**
- **If necessary, select "Save preview picture."**

*Your screen should be similar to Figure 2.78*

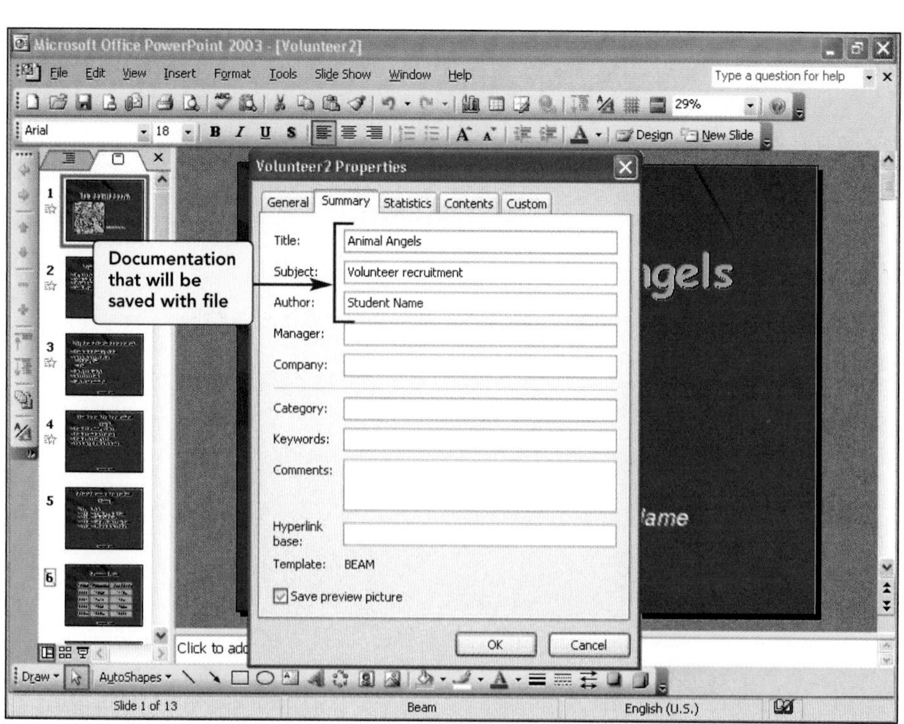


**Figure 2.78**

Save the presentation.

## Customizing Print Settings

You have created both slides and notes pages for the presentation. Now you want to print the notes page and some of the slides. Customizing the print settings by selecting specific slides to print and scaling the size of the slides to fill the page are a few of the ways to make your printed output look more professional.

### Printing Selected Slides

First you will print the notes page for the slide on which you entered note text.

**1**

- **Choose File/Print.**
- **If necessary, select the printer.**
- **From the Print Range section, select Slides.**
- **Type 5 in the Slides text box.**
- **From the Print What drop-down list box, select Notes Pages.**
- **If necessary, select Grayscale from the Color/Grayscale drop-down list box.**
- **Click Preview.**

*Your screen should be similar to Figure 2.79*

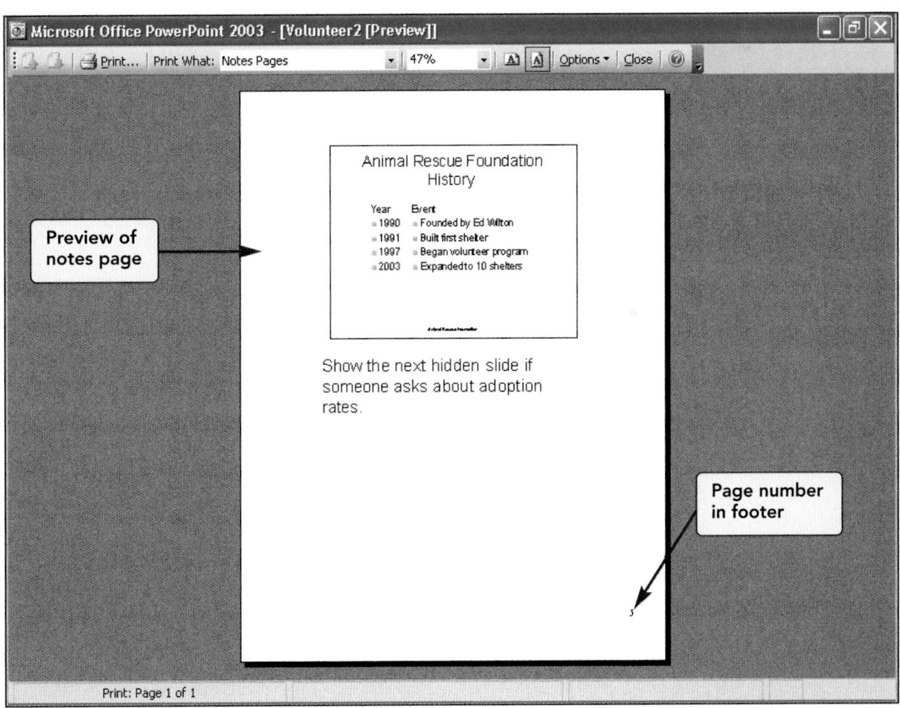


**Figure 2.79**

The notes page is displayed in portrait orientation as it will appear when printed.

## Adding Headers and Footers to Notes and Handouts

Currently, the only information that appears in the footer of the notes page is the page number. You want to include the date and your name in the header of the notes and handouts.

**1 Click Options and select Header and Footer.**

*Your screen should be similar to Figure 2.80*

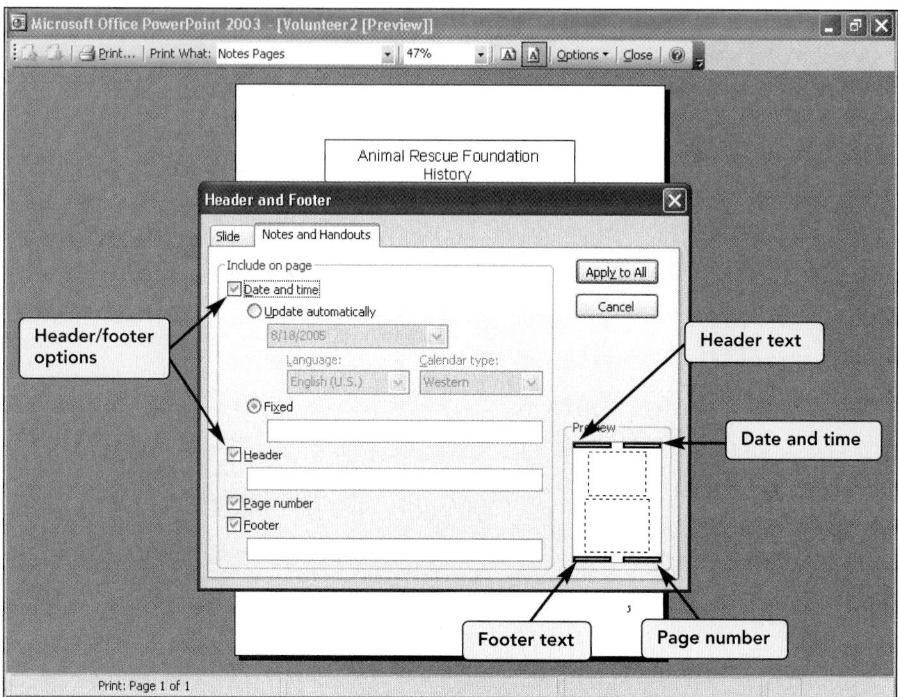


**Figure 2.80**

As in slides, you can display date and time information and footer text. In addition, on notes and handouts, you can include header text and a page number. The preview area identifies the four areas where this information will appear and identifies the currently selected areas in bold. The header option is selected, but because it does not include text, nothing is displayed.

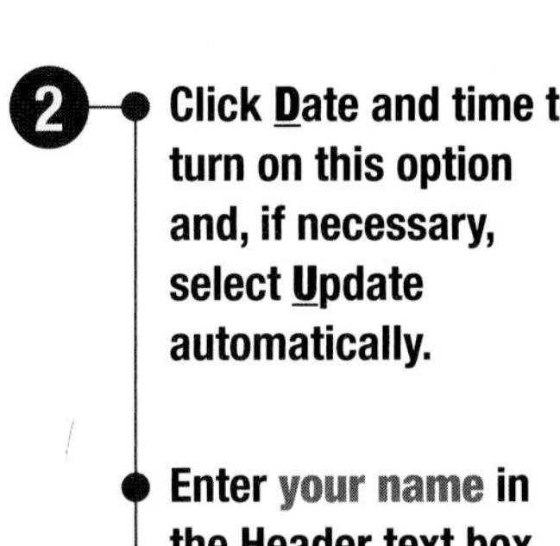

**2** • **Click Date and time to turn on this option and, if necessary, select Update automatically.**

• **Enter your name in the Header text box.**

• **Click Apply to All.**

*Your screen should be similar to Figure 2.81*

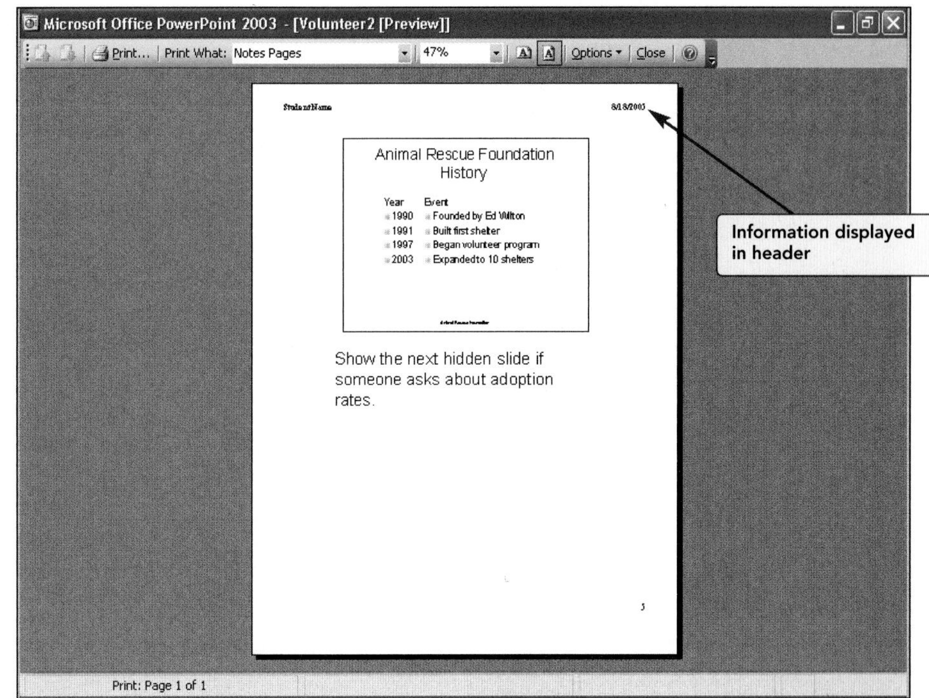


**Figure 2.81**

The information is displayed in the header as specified.

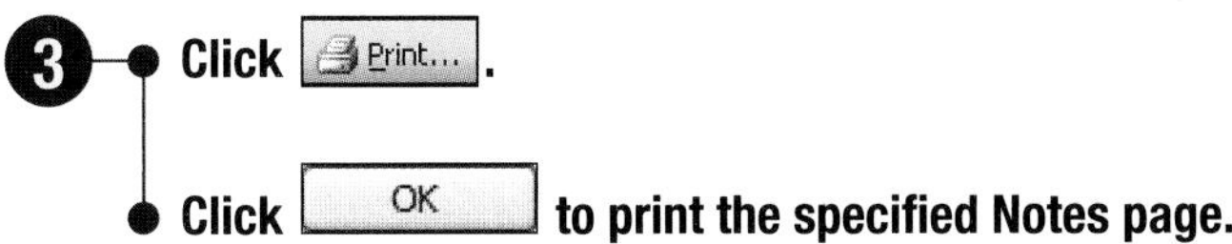

**3** • **Click Print... .**

• **Click OK to print the specified Notes page.**

## Scaling Slides

Next you will print a few selected slides to be used as handouts. You will change the orientation to landscape and scale the slides to fit the paper size.

**1** Click [Print...].

- In the Slides text box, type **1, 2, 6, 13.**
- Specify Handouts as the component to print and 4 slides per page.
- Click [Preview].
- Click [landscape button] to change to landscape orientation.
- Click [Options] and select Scale to Fit Paper.

*Your screen should be similar to Figure 2.82*

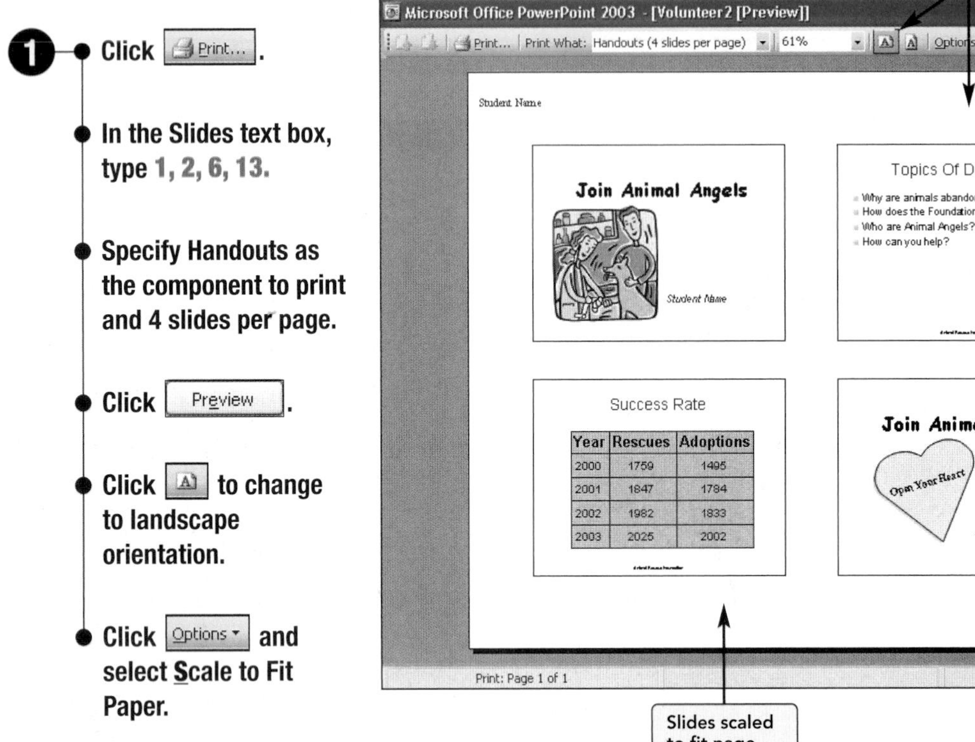


**Figure 2.82**

The four selected slides are displayed in landscape orientation and the slide images were sized as large as possible to fill the page.

**2** Print the handout.

- Close the Print Preview window.
- Save the completed presentation.
- Exit PowerPoint.

The view you are in when you save the file is the view that will be displayed when the file is opened. The print settings are also saved with the file.

# Focus on Careers

## EXPLORE YOUR CAREER OPTIONS

Marketing Communications Specialist

Are you interested in technology? Could you explain it in words and pictures? Marketing Communications Specialists assist sales and marketing management with communications media and advertising materials that represent the company's products and services to customers. In high-tech industries, you will take information from scientists and engineers and use PowerPoint to transform the data into eye-catching presentations that communicate effectively. You may also create brochures, develop Web sites, create videos, and write speeches. If you thrive in a fast-paced and high-energy environment and work well under the pressure of deadlines, then this job may be for you. Typically a bachelor's degree in journalism, advertising, or communications is desirable. The salary can range from $35,000 to $85,000, depending on the industry.

# LAB 2

# Modifying and Refining a Presentation

## Find and Replace (PP2.5)

To make editing easier, you can use the Find and Replace feature to find text in a presentation and replace it with other text as directed.

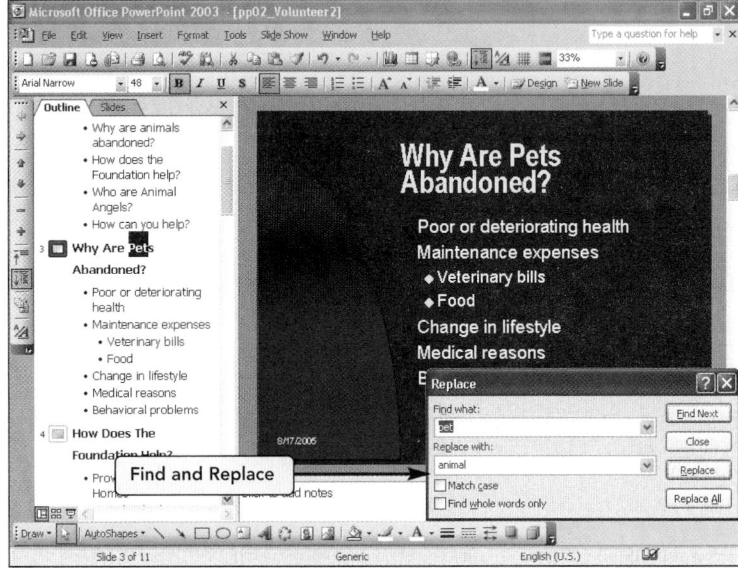


## Table (PP2.9)

A table is used to organize information into an easy-to-read format of horizontal rows and vertical columns.

## Alignment (PP2.15)

Alignment controls how text entries are positioned within a space.

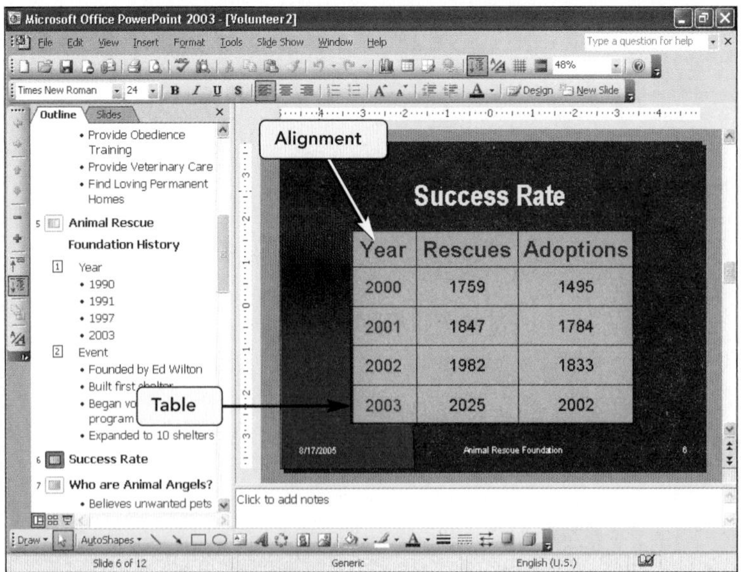

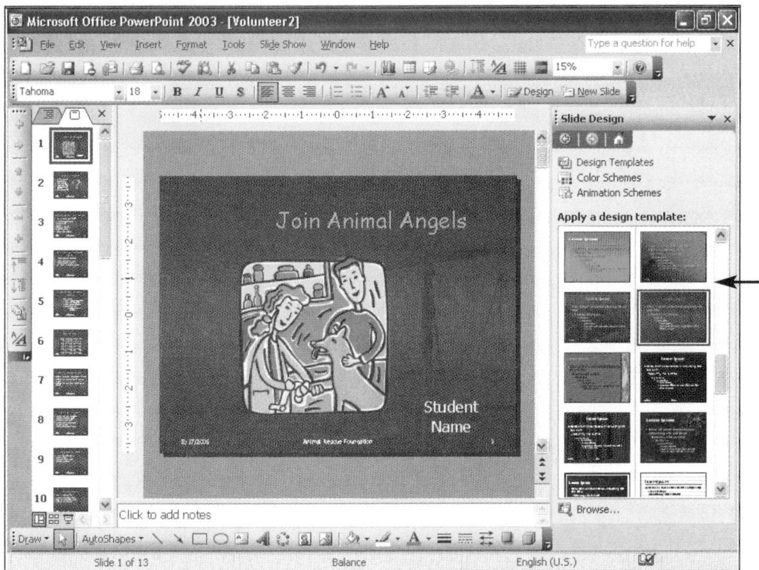


Design template

## Design Template (PP2.31)

A design template is a professionally created slide design that is stored as a file and can be applied to a presentation.

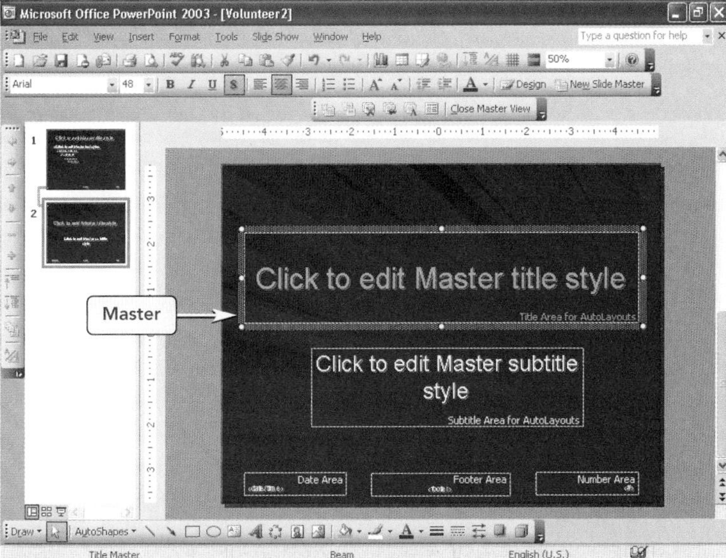


## Master (PP2.38)

A master is a special slide or page that stores information about the formatting for all slides in a presentation.

Special effects

## Special Effects (PP2.49)

Special effects such as animation, sound, slide transitions, and builds are used to enhance the onscreen presentation.

# LAB 2
# Modifying and Refining a Presentation

## key terms

alignment PP2.15
animation PP2.49
animation scheme PP2.54
AutoShape PP2.24
build PP2.49
cell PP2.9
design template PP2.31
Find and Replace PP2.5
master PP2.38
notes page PP2.62
rotate handle PP2.27
table PP2.9
table reference PP2.9
text box PP2.28
transition PP2.49

## microsoft office specialist skills

The Microsoft Office Specialist certification program is designed to measure your proficiency in performing basic tasks using the Office 2003 applications. Certification demonstrates that you have the skills and provides a valuable industry credential for employment. After completing this lab, you have learned the following Microsoft Office PowerPoint 2003 Specialist skills:

| Skill Sets | Skill Standards | Page |
|---|---|---|
| **Creating Content** | Insert and edit text-based content | PP2.5 |
| | Insert tables, charts, and diagrams | PP2.9 |
| | Insert pictures, shapes, and graphics | PP2.22, 2.24 |
| **Formatting Content** | Format text-based content | PP2.13, 2.15 |
| | Format pictures, shapes, and graphics | PP2.22, 2.25 |
| | Format slides | PP2.31, 2.33, 2.72 |
| | Apply animation schemes | PP2.54 |
| | Apply slide transitions | PP2.51 |
| | Work with masters | PP2.38 |
| **Managing and Delivering Presentations** | Organize a presentation | PP2.23, 2.63 |
| | Set up slide shows for delivery | PP2.60 |
| | Deliver presentations | PP2.56 |
| | Save and publish presentations | PP2.8 |
| | Print slides, outlines, handouts, and speaker notes | PP2.71 |

## command summary

| Command | Shortcut Key | Button | Voice | Action |
|---|---|---|---|---|
| File/Properties | | | | Displays statistics and stores information about presentation |
| Edit/Find | Ctrl + F | | | Finds specified text |
| Edit/Replace | Ctrl + H | | | Replaces located text with specified replacement text |
| View/Notes Page | | | | Displays notes page view |
| View/Master/Slide Master | ⇧Shift + | | | Displays slide master for presentation |
| View/Ruler | | | | Displays or hides ruler |
| View/Header and Footer | | | | Specifies information that appears as headers and footers on slides, notes, outlines, and handout pages |
| Insert/Duplicate Slide | | | | Inserts duplicate of current slide |
| Insert/Picture/AutoShapes | | | | Inserts selected AutoShape object |
| Insert/Text Box | | | | Adds a text box |
| Format/Font/Font Style/Bold | Ctrl + B | | On bold | Adds bold effect to selection |
| Format/Font/Font Style/Italic | Ctrl + I | | Italic | Adds italic effect to selection |
| Format/Font/Color | | | | Adds color to selection |
| Format/Alignment | Ctrl + L | | Left justify | Aligns text in a cell or placeholder to left, center, right, or justified |
| | Ctrl + E | | Centered | |
| | Ctrl + R | | Right justify | |
| | Ctrl + J | | | |

| Command | Shortcut Key | Button | Voice | Action |
|---|---|---|---|---|
| Format/Slide Design | | Design | | Changes appearance of slide by applying a different design template |
| Format/Replace Fonts | | | | Finds specified font and replaces it with another |
| Format/Picture/Recolor | | | | Changes color of a picture |
| Format/Master Layout | | | | Selects placeholder to be added |
| Format/Table | | | | Changes table border and fill color |
| Tools/Options/Spelling and Style | | | | Sets spelling and style options |
| Slide Show/Custom Animation | | | | Applies custom animation |
| Slide Show/Slide Transition | | Transition | | Adds transition effects |
| Slide Show/Hide Slide | | | | Hides selected slide |
| **Slide Show Pointer Options Menu** | | | | |
| Arrow | Ctrl + A | | | Changes pointer to arrow and turns off freehand annotation |
| Ballpoint Pen | Ctrl + P | | | Changes pointer to ballpoint pen and turns on freehand annotation |
| Felt Tip Pen | | | | Changes pointer to felt tip pen and turns on freehand annotation |
| Highlighter | | | | Changes pointer to a highlighter |
| Ink Color | | | | Shows color palette for annotation tool |
| Eraser | Ctrl + E | | | Changes pointer to eraser |
| Erase all Ink on Slide | E | | | Removes all annotations from slide |
| **Slide Show Screen Options Menu** | | | | |
| Go to Slide | | | | Displays specified slide |
| Screen/Black Screen | B | | | Blacks out screen |
| Screen/White Screen | W | | | Whites out screen |

## matching

Match the numbered item with the correct lettered description.

| | | |
|---|---|---|
| **1.** transition | ______ | **a.** indicates a transition effect has been applied to the slide |
| **2.** | ______ | **b.** ready-made shapes, such as block arrows, stars and banners, and callouts |
| **3.** design template | ______ | **c.** special slide that controls format for the title slide only |
| **4.** slide master | ______ | **d.** indicates the slide is hidden |
| **5.** build | ______ | **e.** printed output that displays a slide and its related notes |
| **6.** | ______ | **f.** controls the way one slide appears on the screen and the next appears |
| **7.** table | ______ | **g.** defines the background design, text format, and placeholder placement for each slide |
| **8.** Esc | ______ | **h.** professionally created slide design that can be applied to a presentation |
| **9.** AutoShapes | ______ | **i.** ends the slide show and displays the slide last viewed as the current slide |
| **10.** notes pages | ______ | **j.** special effect that controls how bulleted points appear during the slide show |
| | ______ | **k.** displays information in a row and column format |

## multiple choice

Circle the letter of the correct response.

**1.** If you wanted to display a black slide during a presentation, you would press ____________.

**a.** H
**b.** U
**c.** B
**d.** E

**2.** If you wanted to add a company logo on each slide in your presentation, you would place it on the ______________________________.

**a.** handout
**b.** notes page
**c.** outline slide
**d.** master

3. To substitute one word for another in a presentation, you would use the ______________ command on the Edit menu.
   a. Find
   b. Locate
   c. Replace
   d. Duplicate

4. To proportionally size an AutoShape, graphic, or picture, hold down ____________________ while you drag.
   a. Ctrl
   b. Alt
   c. ⇧Shift
   d. Ctrl + Alt

5. To display bullets on a slide one at a time, you would apply a(n) ________________________ .
   a. build
   b. transition
   c. animation
   d. motion

6. To ensure that your presentation has a professional, consistent look throughout, use a(n) __________________________.
   a. slide layout
   b. design template
   c. animation scheme
   d. transition

7. Using a ___________________ to modify or add elements to a presentation ensures consistency and saves time.
   a. design template
   b. slide layout
   c. table
   d. master

8. Slide transitions and build slides are ______________ that are used to enhance the onscreen presentation.
   a. animations
   b. slide masters
   c. graphics
   d. special effects

9. If you want to display information in columns and rows, you would create a(n) _________________.
   a. table
   b. text box
   c. slide layout
   d. AutoShape

10. To help you remember the important points during a presentation, you can add comments to slides and print ______________.
   a. notes pages
   b. slide handouts
   c. preview handouts
   d. handouts

## true/false

Circle the correct answer to the following questions.

| | | | |
|---|---|---|---|
| 1. | Builds control the way that the display changes as you move from one slide to another during a presentation. | True | False |
| 2. | Style checking looks for consistency in punctuation and capitalization. | True | False |
| 3. | Alignment controls the position of text entries in a placeholder. | True | False |
| 4. | Masters are professionally created slide designs that can be applied to your presentation. | True | False |
| 5. | An AutoShape is an object that can be enhanced using drawing tools and menu commands. | True | False |
| 6. | A handout master defines the format and placement of the slide image, text, headers, footers, and other elements that are to appear on every slide in the presentation. | True | False |
| 7. | A title master defines the format and placement of titles and text for slides that use the title layout. | True | False |
| 8. | Transitions are used to display each bullet point, text, paragraph, or graphic independently of the other text or objects on the slide. | True | False |
| 9. | An AutoShape is a container for text or graphics. | True | False |
| 10. | A master is a special slide or page on which the formatting for all slides or pages in your presentation is defined. | True | False |

## fill-in

Complete the following statements by filling in the blanks with the correct terms.

1. The ______________ master controls format, placement, and all elements that are to appear on every audience handout.
2. The ______________ feature checks the presentation for consistency in punctuation and capitalization.
3. ______________ add action to text and graphics so they move on the screen.
4. A ______________ is made up of rows and columns of cells that you can fill with text and graphics.
5. A ____________________ is a container for text or graphics.
6. Alignment controls the position of text entries within a ______________________ or ____________.
7. ______________ are used to define where text and graphics appear on a slide.
8. ______________ display each bullet point, text, paragraph, or graphic independently of the other text or objects on the slide.

9. ______________________ are professionally created slide designs that can be applied to your presentation.

10. The ______________ slide is a special slide on which the formatting for all slides in your presentation is defined.

**rating system**

★ Easy

★★ Moderate

★★★ Difficult

## step-by-step

### Enhancing a College Recruiting Presentation ★

1. Bonnie is the Assistant Director of New Admissions at Arizona State University. Part of her job is to make recruiting presentations at community colleges and local high schools about the University. She has already created the introductory portion of the presentation and needs to reorganize the topics and make the presentation more visually appealing. Several slides of the modified presentation are shown here:

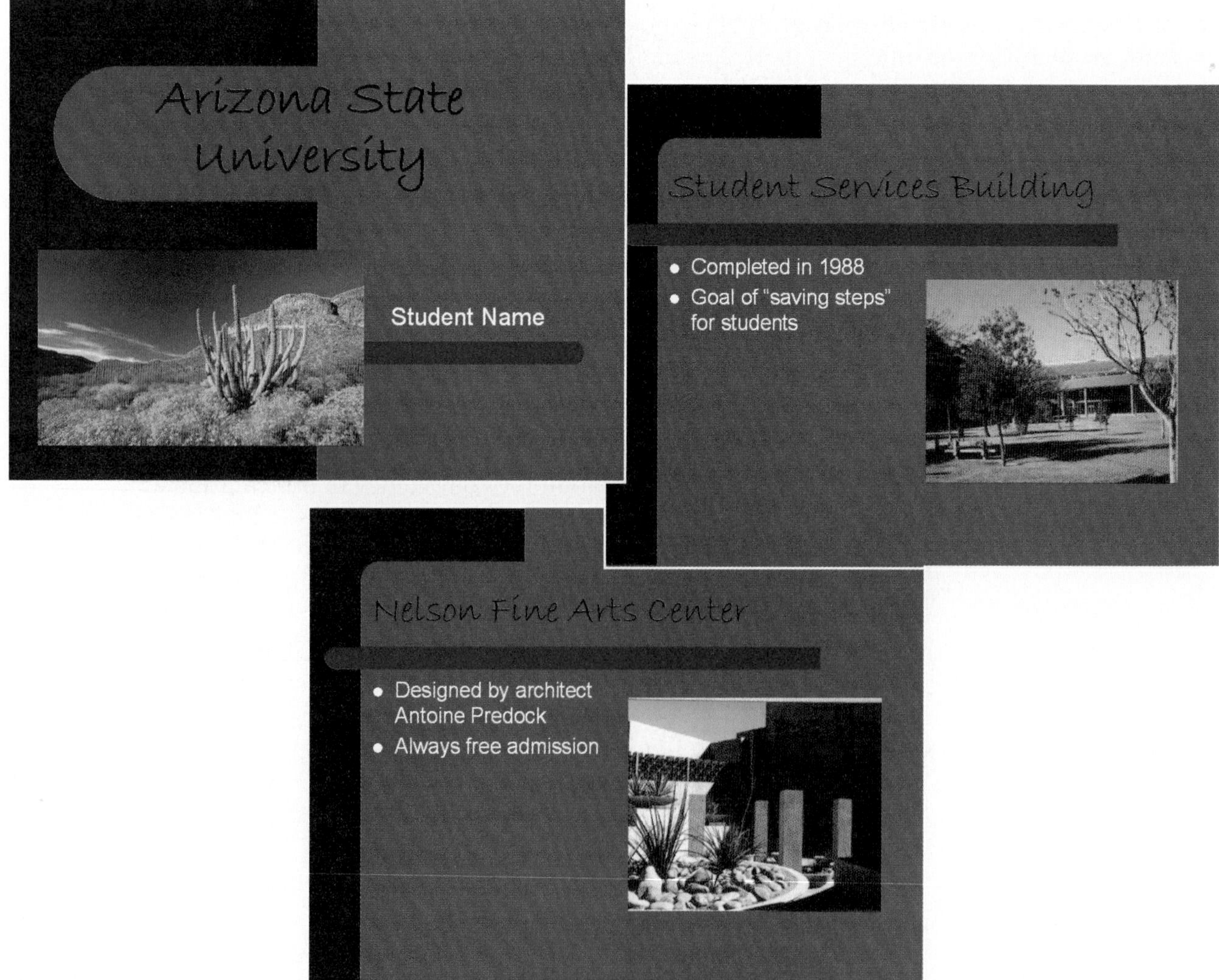

**a.** Open the file pp02_ASU Presentation.

**b.** Run the slide show to see what Bonnie has done so far.

**c.** Spell-check the presentation, making the appropriate corrections.

**d.** Move slide 5 before slide 3.

**e.** Move slide 5 before slide 4.

**f.** Use the Find and Replace command to locate all the occurrences of "Arizona State University" and replace them with **ASU** on all slides except the first and second slides.

**g.** Enter your name as the subtitle in slide 1. Insert the picture pp02_Arizona on the title slide. Size the picture and position the placeholders on the slide appropriately.

**h.** Demote all the bulleted items on slides 8 and 9 except the first item.

**i.** Apply a new presentation design of your choice to the presentation. Apply a new slide color scheme. Modify the font of the titles using the title and slide masters.

**j.** Duplicate slide 1 and move the duplicate to the end of the presentation. Delete the graphic. Replace your name with **Apply Now!**. Apply the Change Font Size custom animation Emphasis effect at a slow speed. Increase the font to a larger size.

**k.** Bonnie would like to add some pictures of the buildings at the end of the presentation. Switch to Slide Sorter view and select slides 12, 13, and 14. Apply the Title, Text and Content layout. Insert the picture pp02_Student Services in slide 12, the picture pp02_Library in slide 13, and the picture pp02_Fine Arts in slide 14.

**l.** Check the style of the presentation and make any changes you feel are appropriate. Turn the style check feature off when you are done.

**m.** Add a Wave custom animation at a medium speed and the Applause sound to the title text on the title slide.

**n.** Apply the Strips build effect at a medium speed in a Right Down direction to slides 3 through 7, 10, and 11.

**o.** Run the slide show.

**p.** Add file documentation and save the presentation as ASU Presentation1. Print slides 1, 2, and 12–15 as handouts (six per page).

## Completing the Massage Therapy Presentation ★ ★

2. To complete this problem, you must have completed Step-by-Step Exercise 3 in Lab 1. You have completed the first draft of the presentation on therapeutic massage, but still have some information to add. Additionally, you want to make the presentation look better using many of the PowerPoint design and slide show presentation features. Several slides of the modified presentation are shown here:

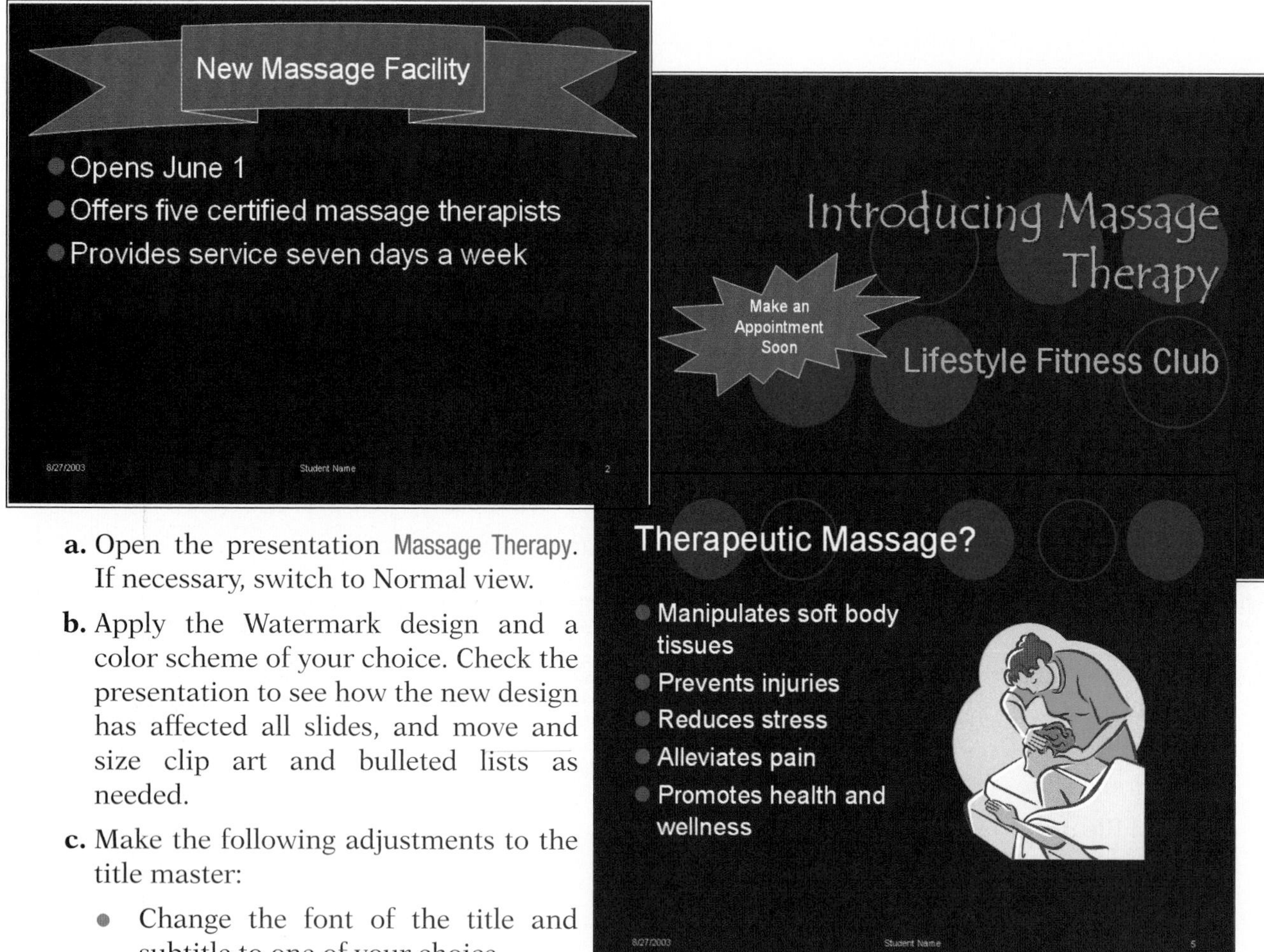


a. Open the presentation Massage Therapy. If necessary, switch to Normal view.

b. Apply the Watermark design and a color scheme of your choice. Check the presentation to see how the new design has affected all slides, and move and size clip art and bulleted lists as needed.

c. Make the following adjustments to the title master:

- Change the font of the title and subtitle to one of your choice.
- Change the font color of the title and subtitle to colors of your choice. Add a shadow.

d. On slide 2, replace the slide title with an AutoShape of your choice. Add the text **New Massage Facility** to the AutoShape. Add a medium speed Dissolve In or Out custom animation to the AutoShape. Add a medium speed Fly In custom animation to the bulleted list.

e. Duplicate the title slide and move it to the end of the presentation. Add an AutoShape to this slide that includes the text **Make an Appointment Soon**. Format the object and text appropriately. Move the title and subtitle to accommodate the drawing object.

f. Select an animation scheme of your choice to add transition and build effects to all the slides. Run the slide show.

g. Add the following note to slide 5 in a point size of 18:

**Basically, all massages are therapeutic.**

**h.** Add the following note to slide 10 in a point size of 18:

**Ask if there are any questions. Pass out brochures.**

**i.** Style-check the presentation and make any necessary changes. Turn off the style-check option when you are done.

**j.** Add file documentation and save the completed presentation as **Massage Therapy2**.

**k.** Print the notes page for slide 10. Print slides 1, 5, and 6 as handouts with three slides per page.

### Enhancing the Job Fairs Presentation ★★

**3.** To complete this problem, you must have completed Step-by-Step Exercise 5 in Lab 1. Tim has completed the first draft of the presentation for Job Fairs, but he still has some information he wants to add to the presentation. Additionally, he wants to make the presentation look better using many of the PowerPoint design and slide show presentation features. Several slides of the modified presentation are shown here:

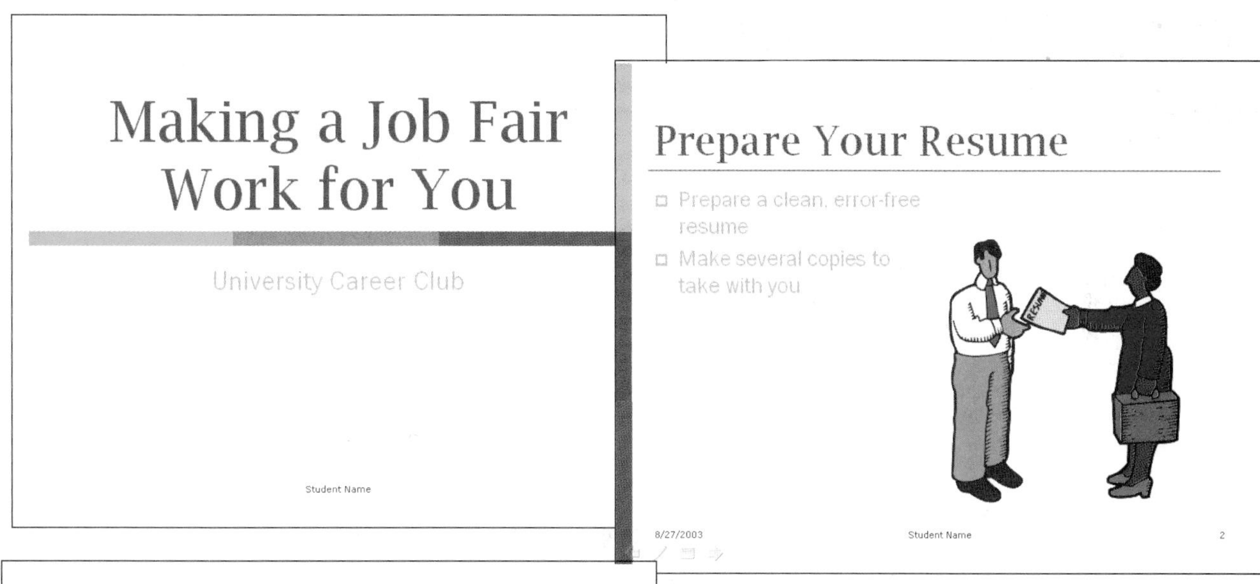


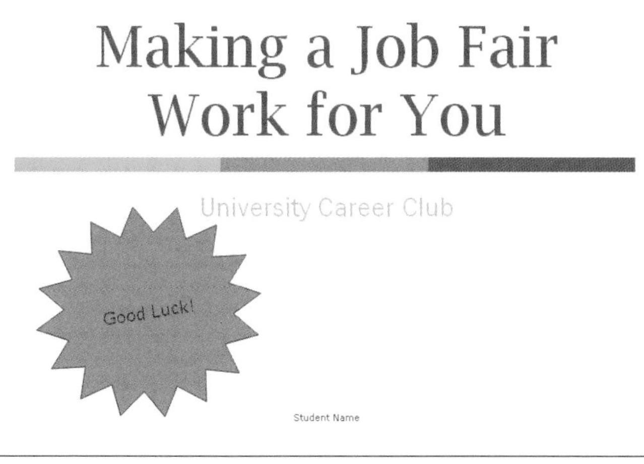

**a.** Open the presentation Job Fairs. If necessary, switch to Normal view.

**b.** Change the design template to Levels. Change the color scheme to a color of your choice.

**c.** Change to Slide Sorter view and check the slide layouts. Make the following adjustments:

- Slide master:
  - — Delete the Date area and Number area placeholders.
  - — Change the font of the title to one of your choice. Increase the font size. Change the font color to a color of your choice.
- Title master:
  - — Change the text color of the subtitle to a color of your choice, bold it, and change it to a font of your choice.

**d.** Check the slide layouts again in Slide Sorter view and fix the placement and size of the placeholders and pictures as needed.

**e.** Apply a custom animation to the clip art and bulleted list on slide 3 and add sound effects of your choice.

**f.** Duplicate the title slide and move it to the end of the presentation. Add a drawing object to this slide that includes the text **Good Luck!**. Format the object and text appropriately.

**g.** Select an animation scheme of your choice to add transition and build effects to all the slides. Run the slide show.

**h.** Add the following note to slide 3 in a point size of 18:

**You must be able to give a short biography when asked "Tell me about yourself." Practice until you can tell the story smoothly.**

**i.** Style-check the presentation and make any necessary changes. Turn off the style-check feature when you are done.

**j.** Add file documentation and save the completed presentation as Job Fairs2.

**k.** Print the notes page for slide 3. Print slides 1, 2, 6, and 8 as handouts with four slides per page.

## Enhancing the Triple Crown Presentation ★★★

4. To complete this problem, you must have completed Step-by-Step Exercise 1 in Lab 1. Logan's work on the Triple Crown Presentation was well received by his supervisor. She would like to see some additional information included in the presentation, including a table of upcoming qualifying hikes. Several of the slides from his updated presentation are shown here:

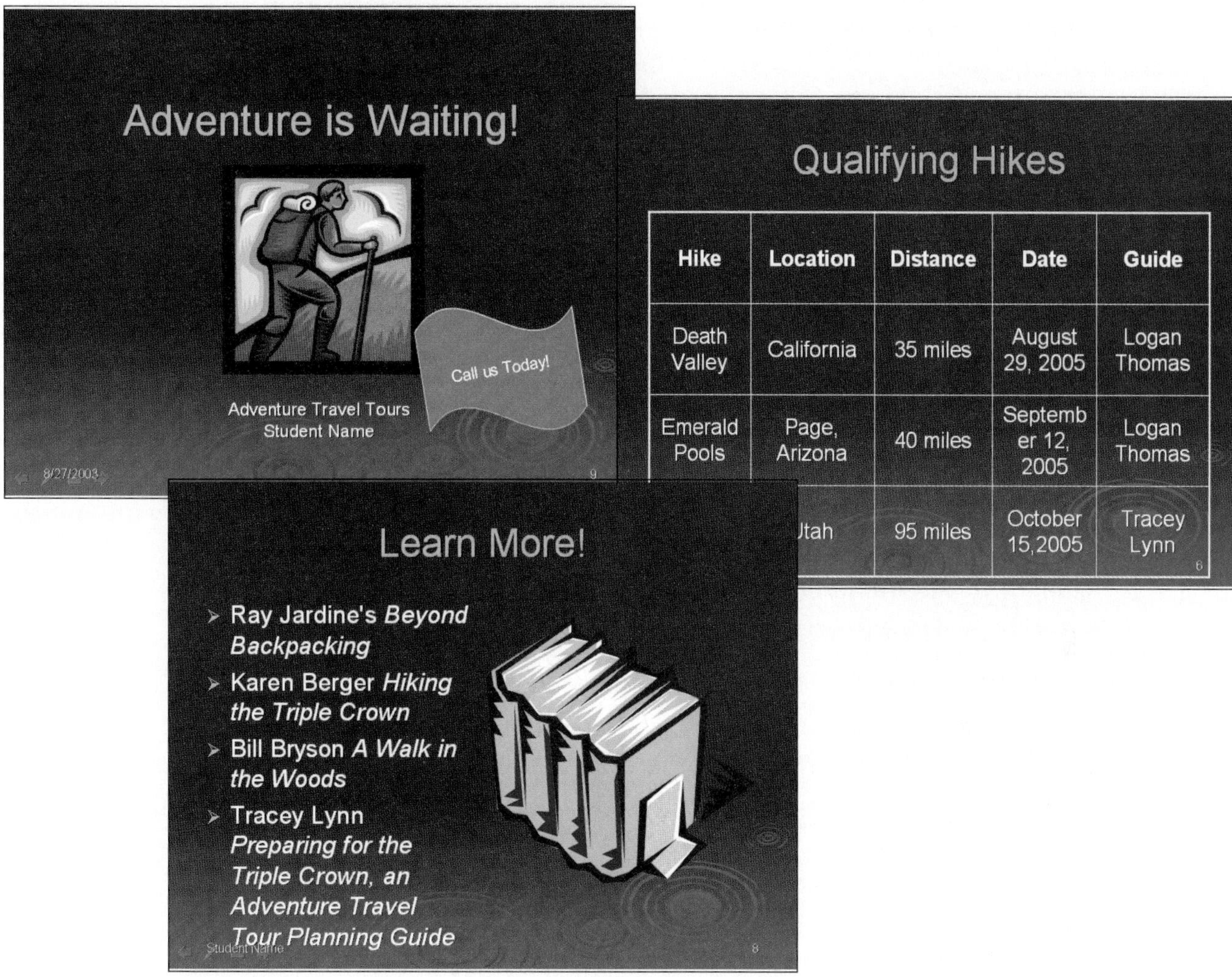


a. Open the file Triple Crown Presentation.

b. Apply a new presentation design and color scheme of your choice to the presentation. Check the presentation to see how the new design has affected all the slides, and move and size graphics and bulleted lists as needed.

c. Modify the text color of the titles using the title and slide masters.

d. Insert a Title and Table slide after slide 6, with 5 columns and 4 rows. Enter the title **Qualifying Hikes**. Enter the following information in the table:

| **Hike** | **Location** | **Distance** | **Date** | **Guide** |
|---|---|---|---|---|
| **Death Valley** | **California** | **35 miles** | **August 29, 2005** | **Logan Thomas** |
| **Paria Canyon** | **Page, Arizona** | **40 miles** | **September 12, 2005** | **Logan Thomas** |
| **Bryce to Zion** | **Utah** | **95 miles** | **October 15, 2005** | **Tracey Lynn** |

e. Size and position the table as shown in the example. Add bold to the table headings. Change the column and row size as needed. Center the table contents vertically and horizontally.

f. Change the border color to one of your choice.

g. Change the layout of slide 6 to Title, Text, and Content. Insert the clip art graphic pp02_Read. Change the coloring of the books from brown and tan to blue.

h. Duplicate slide 1 and place the copy at the end of the presentation. Change the title to **Adventure is Waiting!**.

i. Add a footer that contains your name left-aligned and the slide number right-aligned.

j. Add an AutoShape of your choice to the final slide with the text: **Call us Today!**.

k. Use the Find and Replace command to replace all occurrences of Paria Canyon with **Emerald Pools**.

l. Add the following information to the file properties:

   Title: **Triple Crown Presentation2**

   Subject: **Lightweight Backpacking Tours**

   Author: **Student Name**

   Company: **Adventure Travel Tours**

m. Save the file as Triple Crown Presentation2. Print slides 1, 6, 7, and 9 as a handout with all four slides on one page.

## Enhancing the Coffee Presentation ★ ★ ★

**5.** To complete this problem, you must have completed Step-by-Step Exercise 4 in Lab 1. Evan, the owner of the Downtown Internet Cafe, was so impressed with your presentation on coffee that he has decided to run it periodically throughout the day on a large screen in the cafe so customers can see it as well. To "spiff it up," he wants you to convert it to an onscreen presentation with more graphics as well as other design and animation effects. Several slides of the modified presentation are shown here:

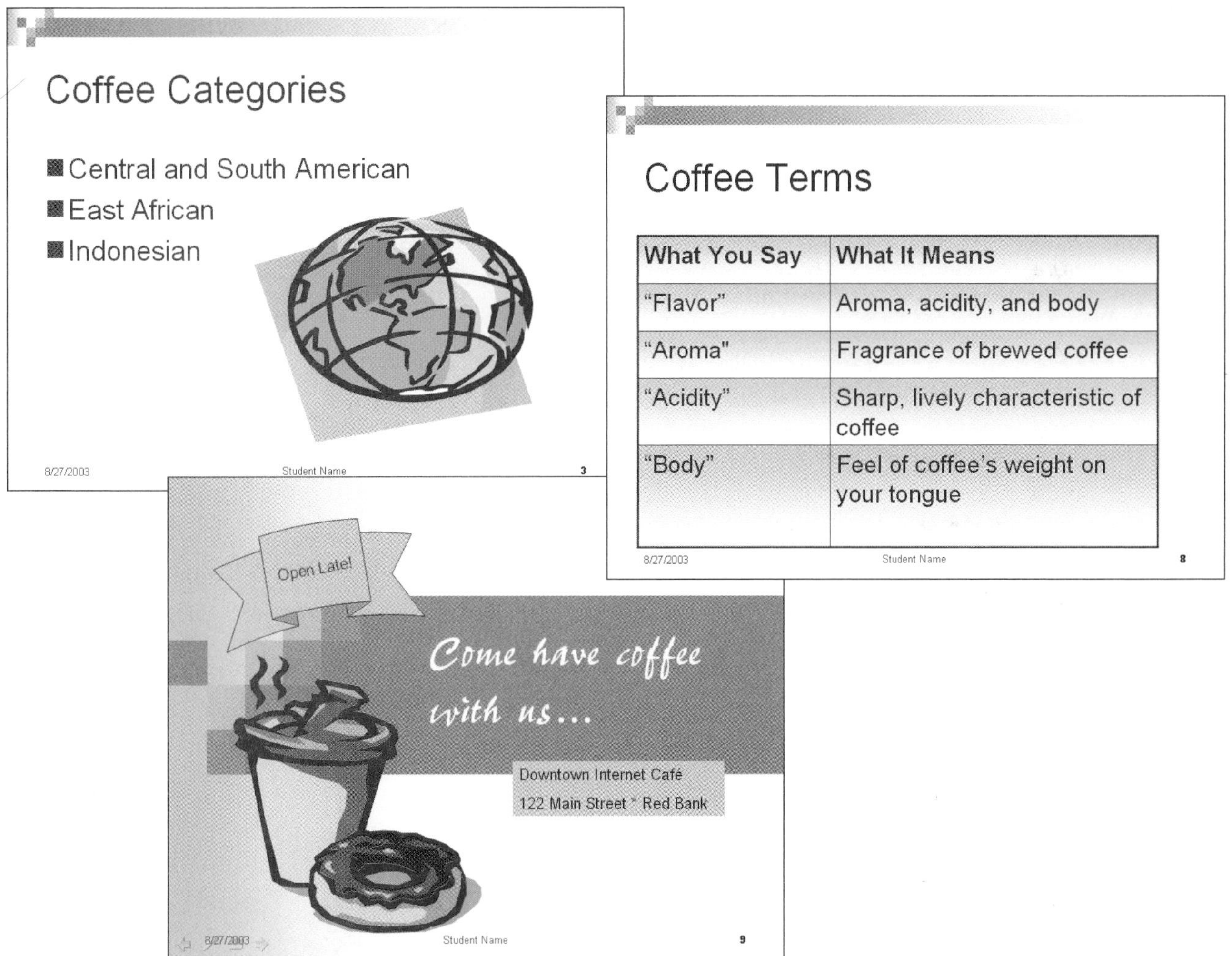


- **a.** Open the file Coffee.
- **b.** Use the Replace feature to replace both instances of the term "Regular Roasts" with **Coffee Categories**. Do the same to replace both instances of the term "Other Offerings" with **Coffee Types**.
- **c.** Change the design template to Pixel or a design of your choice. Select a color scheme of your choice. Check the presentation to see how the new design has affected all slides, and move and size clip art and bulleted lists as needed.
- **d.** Use the slide master to change the font color of all first-level bullet text to a different color.
- **e.** Apply a custom animation and sound of your choice to the coffee cup clip art on slide 2.
- **f.** Change the title of slide 3 to **What's Brewing?**. Delete the clip art.

**g.** Copy the clip art from slide 2 to slide 3 and size and position it appropriately. Add a third bullet to slide 3 with the text: **Coffee Terms**. Delete slide 2.

**h.** Insert the graphic pp02_Globe on slide 3. Recolor the background of the picture with colors that match the slide design.

**i.** Change the title "Central and South American Coffee" on slide 4 to **Coffees from the Americas**.

**j.** Insert a new slide with a table format after slide 7. Enter the title, **Coffee Terms**. Create the table with 2 columns and 5 rows. Enter **What You Say** as the first column heading and **What It Means** as the second column heading. Copy the terms and definitions from slide 9 into the table. Change the font size of the text as needed. Bold the column headings and put quotation marks around the terms. Center-align the What You Say column. Size the columns and table appropriately. Add a fill color to the table.

**k.** Delete slide 9.

**l.** Duplicate the title slide and move the duplicate to the end of the presentation. Change the title to **Come have coffee with us . . .** and delete the subtitle text. Delete the subtitle placeholder.

**m.** Add the following information in a text box on slide 9:

**Downtown Internet Cafe**

**122 Main Street * Red Bank**

**n.** Add a fill color and border to the text box.

**o.** Insert an AutoShape of your choice on the last slide with the text **Open Late!**.

**p.** Check the presentation style and make any necessary changes. Turn off the style-check feature when you are done.

**q.** Set the slide transition to automatically advance after 10 seconds. Run the slide show.

**r.** Add file documentation information and save the completed presentation as Coffee Show.

**s.** Print slides 1, 2, 8, and 9 as handouts, four per page.

## on your own

### Successful Interview Techniques ★

1. You work at an employment agency and your manager has asked you to create an onscreen presentation about interview techniques. This presentation will be loaded on all the computers that your company makes available to clients for online job searches, and instructions on how to run the presentation will be posted at each workstation. Select a presentation design that you like and create the presentation using the following notes for reference. Add clip art and build effects where applicable. Add your name to the footer on each slide except the title slide. Set the slide transition so that it automatically advances after an appropriate length of time (long enough for the person viewing the presentation to read each slide's contents). Save the presentation as Interview Techniques. Print all slides of your presentation, six per page.

   - Before a job interview, you should thoroughly research the company (use the library or the Web). For example, what is one event that occurred in the company within the last five years?
   - During the interview, demonstrate your expertise, using a consultant's style of communicating. Create open and clear communication, and effectively respond to open-ended questions. Examples of open-ended questions are: "Tell me about yourself." "What makes you stand out?" "What are your greatest weaknesses?" You should also be ready to answer questions about why you are interviewing with the company and how and where you fit within their organization. You must be prepared to handle both spoken and unspoken objections. And finally, you must justify your salary requirements; don't just negotiate them.

### Enhancing the Animal Careers Presentation ★

2. To finish creating the basic Careers with Animals presentation that you began in Lab 1, On Your Own Exercise 5, turn it into an onscreen presentation with a custom design, clip art, sound, transitions, and builds so it will hold your audience's interest. Add speaker notes and rehearse the presentation. When you are done, save the presentation as Animal Careers2, print the presentation as handouts, and print the notes pages for slides containing notes only.

### Explaining Fad Diets ★ ★

3. You have been asked to give a lunchbox presentation at the LifeStyle Fitness Club on fad diets. You plan to first describe all fad diets and then end with a summary of the benefits of eating according to the USDA's Food Pyramid and proper exercise. Do some research on the Web to obtain a list of fad diets, including a brief description, pros, and cons. Select an appropriate slide design and include some graphics to liven up the presentation. Add a table that includes some of your data. Include your name in the footer. When you are done, save the presentation as Fad Diets and print the handouts.

### Enhancing the Internet Policy Presentation ★ ★ ★

4. After completing the Internet Policy presentation in Lab 1, On Your Own Exercise 1, you decide it needs a bit more sprucing up. First of all, it would be more impressive as an onscreen presentation with a custom design. You also want to add some information about personal computing security. Do some research on the Web to find some helpful tips on protecting personal privacy and safeguarding your computer. Also, add some animated clip art pictures, non-standard bullets, builds, and

transitions to help liven up the content. Make these and any other changes that you think would enhance the presentation. Add a table and check the style consistency of the presentation. Add appropriate documentation to the file. When you are done, save it as Internet Policy2, print the presentation as handouts, and print the notes pages for slides containing notes only.

### Sharing Favorite Vacation Spots ★ ★ ★

**5.** You and your fellow Getaway Travel Club members have decided that each of you should do a presentation on your favorite vacation spot (one you have already been to or one you would like to go to). Pick a location and do some research on the Web and/or visit a local travel agency to get information about your chosen destination. Create a presentation using a custom design and include clip art, animation, sounds, transitions, and build effects to make the presentation more interesting. Include your name as a footer or subtitle on at least one slide. Create and enhance a table. Use speaker notes if necessary to remind yourself of additional information you want to relay that is not included in the slides. Add appropriate documentation to the file. Run the slide show and practice your presentation, then save as Travel Favorites and print your presentation and notes pages.

# Working Together 1: Copying, Embedding, and Linking Between Applications

# Case Study

## Animal Rescue Foundation

The director of the Animal Rescue Foundation has reviewed the PowerPoint presentation you created and has asked you to include a chart showing the adoption success rate that was created using Excel. Additionally, the director has provided a list of dates for the upcoming volunteer orientation meetings that he feels would be good content for another slide.

Frequently you will find that you want to include information that was created using a word processor, spreadsheet, or database application in your slide show. As you will see, you can easily share information between applications, saving you both time and effort by eliminating the need to recreate information that is available in another application. You will learn how to share information between applications while you create the new slides. The new slides containing information from Word and Excel are shown here.

**Note:** The Working Together section assumes that you already know how to use Office Word and Excel 2003 and that you have completed Lab 2 of PowerPoint. You will need the file Volunteer2, which you saved at the end of Lab 2 of PowerPoint. If this file is not available, use ppwt1_Volunteer2.

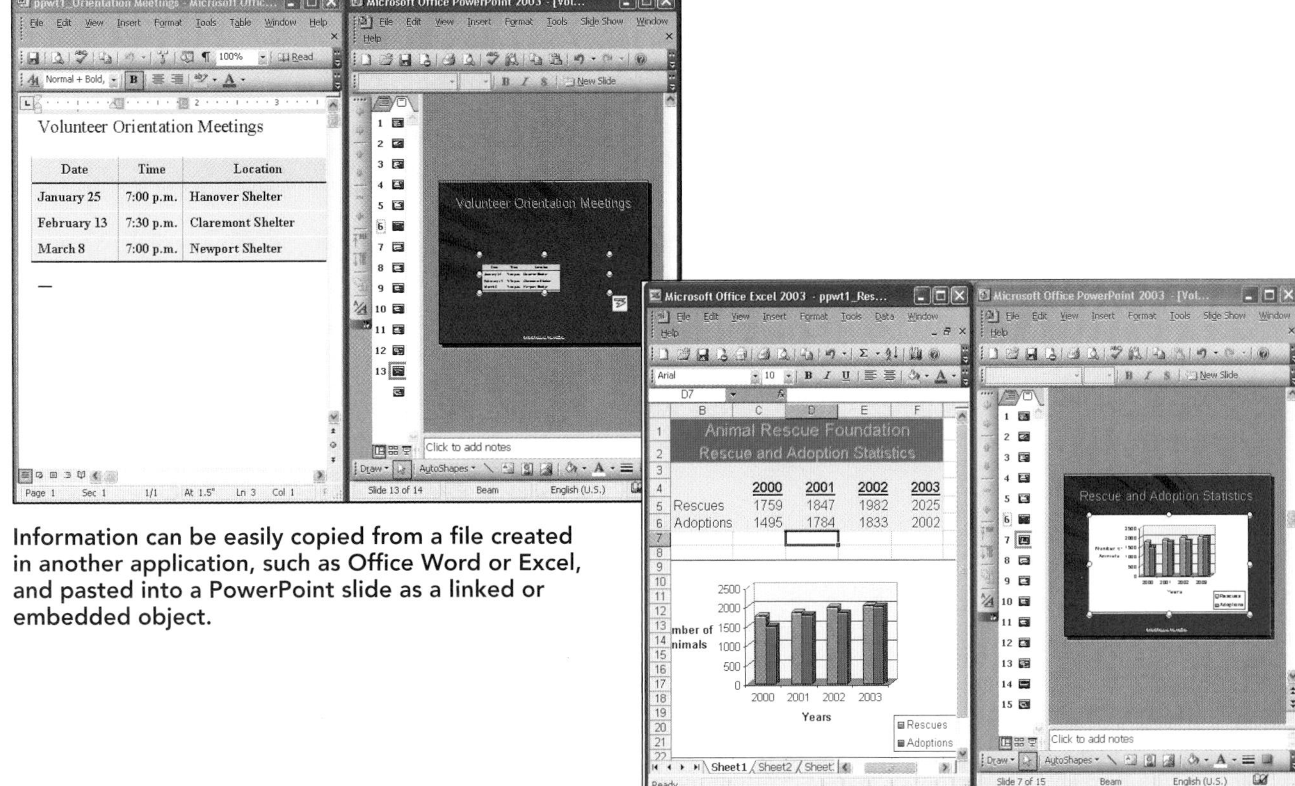


Information can be easily copied from a file created in another application, such as Office Word or Excel, and pasted into a PowerPoint slide as a linked or embedded object.

## Copying Between Applications

The orientation meeting information has already been entered in a document using Word. All the Microsoft Office System applications have a common user interface, such as similar commands and menu structures. In addition to these obvious features, they have been designed to work together, making it easy to share and exchange information between applications.

Rather than retype the list of orientation meeting dates provided by the director, you will copy it from the Word document into the presentation. You can also use the same commands and procedures to copy information from PowerPoint or other Office applications into Word.

### Copying from Word to a PowerPoint Slide

First, you need to modify the PowerPoint presentation to include a new slide for the orientation meeting dates.

**1**

- **Start Office PowerPoint 2003.**
- **Open the presentation** Volunteer2 **(saved at the end of Lab 2).**
- **Insert a new slide using the Title Only layout after slide 12.**
- **Close the Slide Layout task pane.**
- **Display the new slide in Normal view.**

*Your screen should be similar to Figure 1*

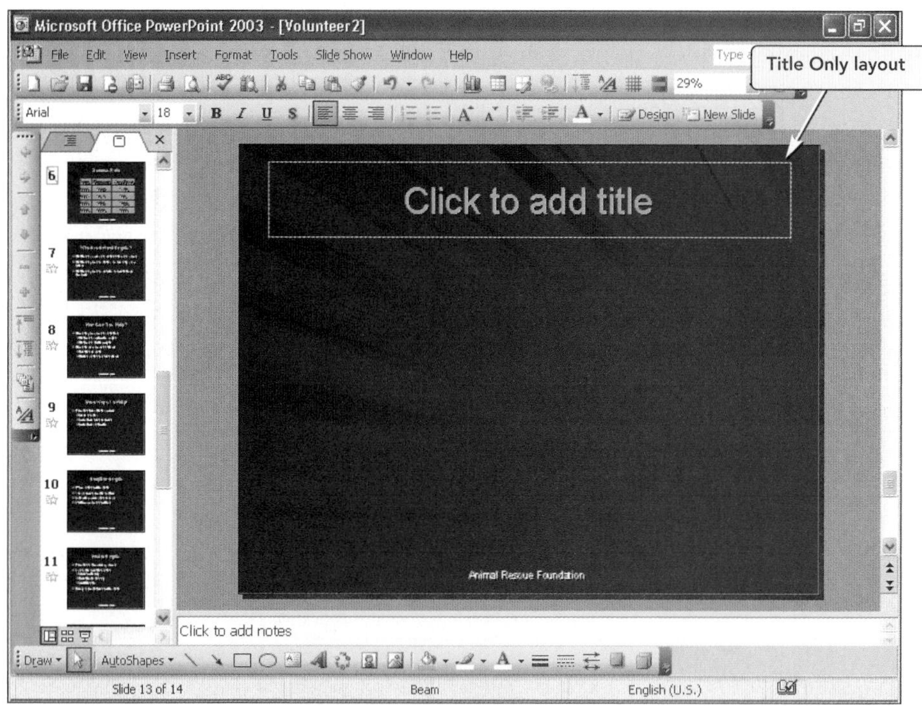


Figure 1

To copy the information from the Word document file into the PowerPoint presentation, you need to open the Word document.

**Start Office Word 2003.**

**Open the document** ppwt1_Orientation Meetings**.**

*Your screen should be similar to Figure 2*

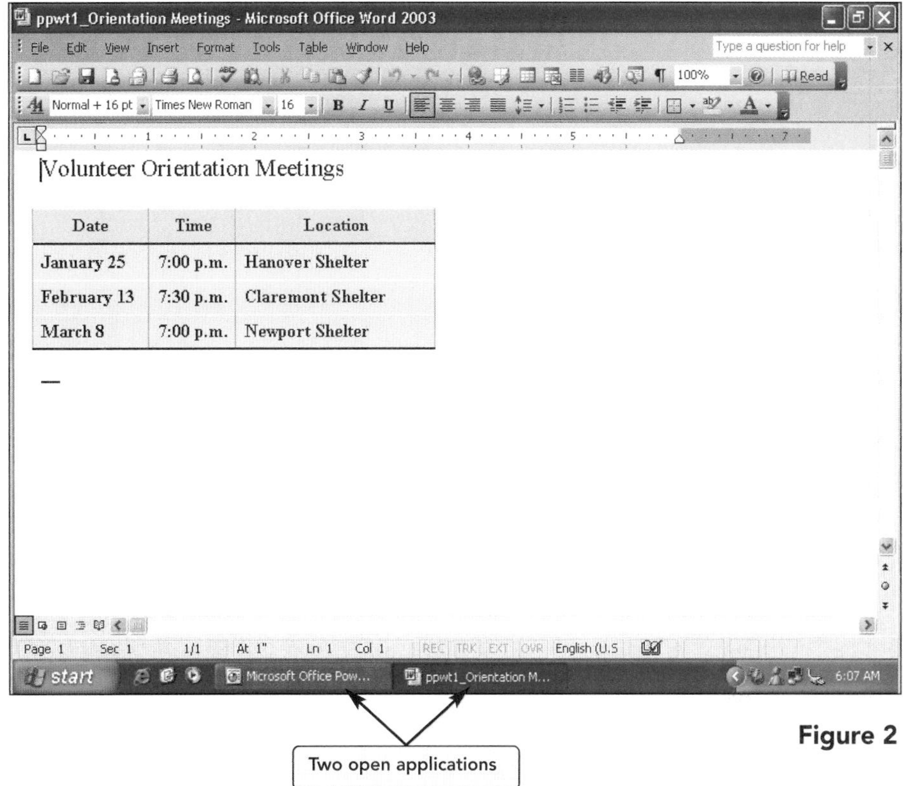


**Figure 2**

There are now two open applications, Word and PowerPoint. PowerPoint is open in a window behind the Word application window. Both application buttons are displayed in the taskbar. There are also two open files, Orientation Meetings in Word and Volunteer2 in PowerPoint. Word is the active application, and Orientation Meetings is the active file. To make it easier to work with two applications, you will tile the windows to view both on the screen at the same time.

**3**

**Right-click on a blank area of the taskbar to open the shortcut menu.**

**Select Tile Windows Vertically**

**Click on the Word document window to make it active.**

*Your screen should be similar to Figure 3*

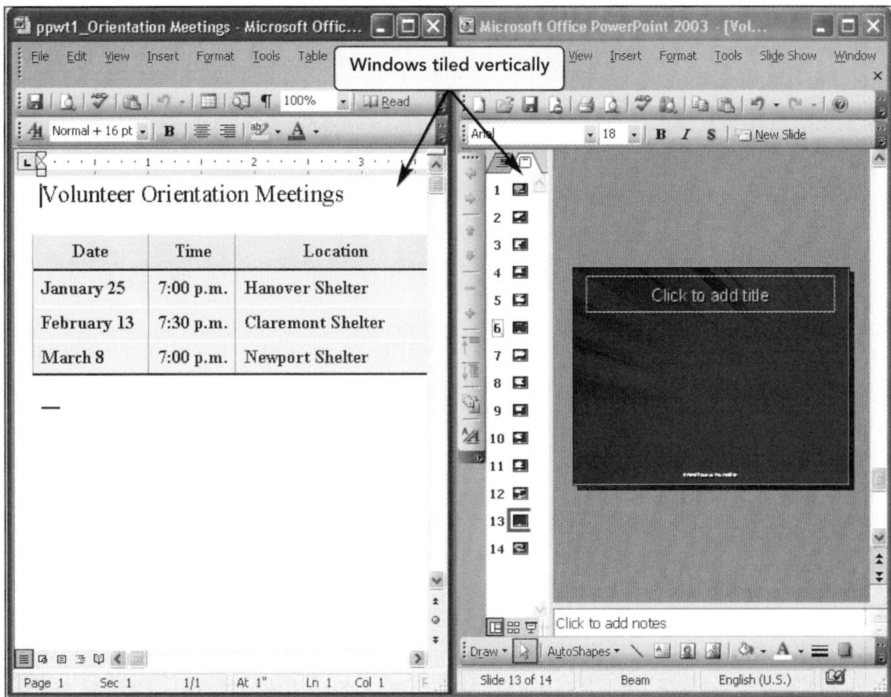


**Figure 3**

First, you will copy the title from the Word document into the title placeholder of the slide. While using the Office Word and PowerPoint applications, you have learned how to use cut, copy, and paste to move or copy information within the same document. You can also perform these same operations between documents in the same application and between documents in different applications. The information is pasted in a format that the application can edit, if possible.

**4** **Select the title "Volunteer Orientation Meetings."**

**Drag the selection using the right mouse button to the title placeholder in the slide.**

**Having Trouble?**

If you drag using the left mouse button, the selection is moved instead of copied.

**From the shortcut menu, select Copy.**

**Another Method**

You could also use Copy and Paste to copy the title to the slide.

**Click on the slide to deselect the placeholder.**

*Your screen should be similar to Figure 4*

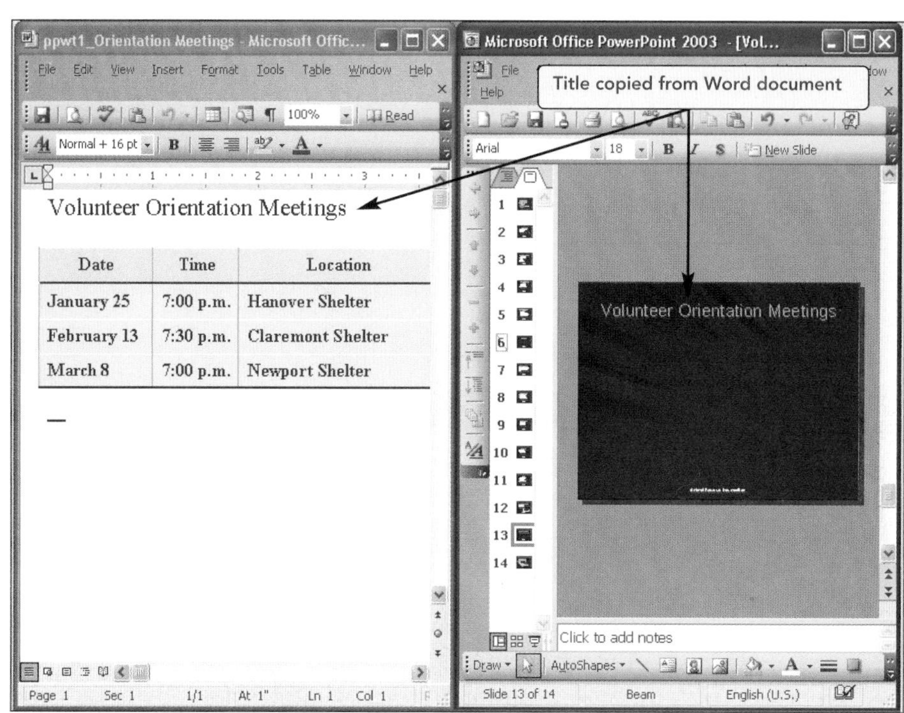


Figure 4

The title has been copied into the slide and can be edited and manipulated within PowerPoint. The formats associated with the slide master are applied to the copied text. If the copied text included formatting, such as color, it would override the slide master settings, just as if you formatted a slide individually to make it unique.

## Embedding a Word Table in a PowerPoint Slide

Next you want to display the table of orientation dates below the title in the slide. You will copy and embed the table in the slide. As you have seen, an object that is embedded is stored in the file that it is inserted into, called the **destination file**, and becomes part of that file. The embedded object can then be edited using features from the source program, the program in which it was created. Since the embedded object is part of the destination file, modifying it does not affect the original file called the **source file**.

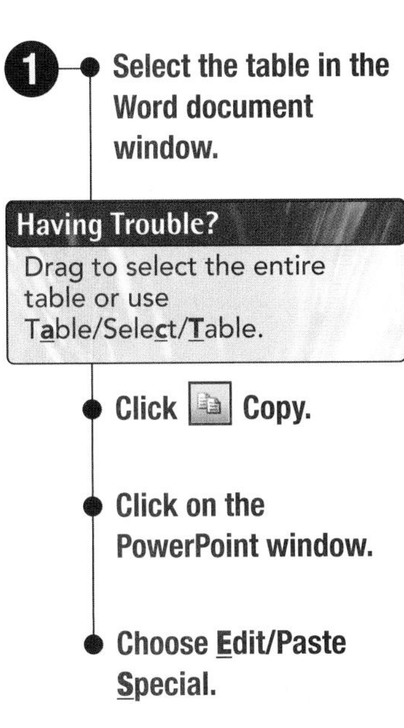

**1** Select the table in the Word document window.

**Having Trouble?**

Drag to select the entire table or use Table/Select/Table.

- Click Copy.
- Click on the PowerPoint window.
- Choose Edit/Paste Special.

*Your screen should be similar to Figure 5*

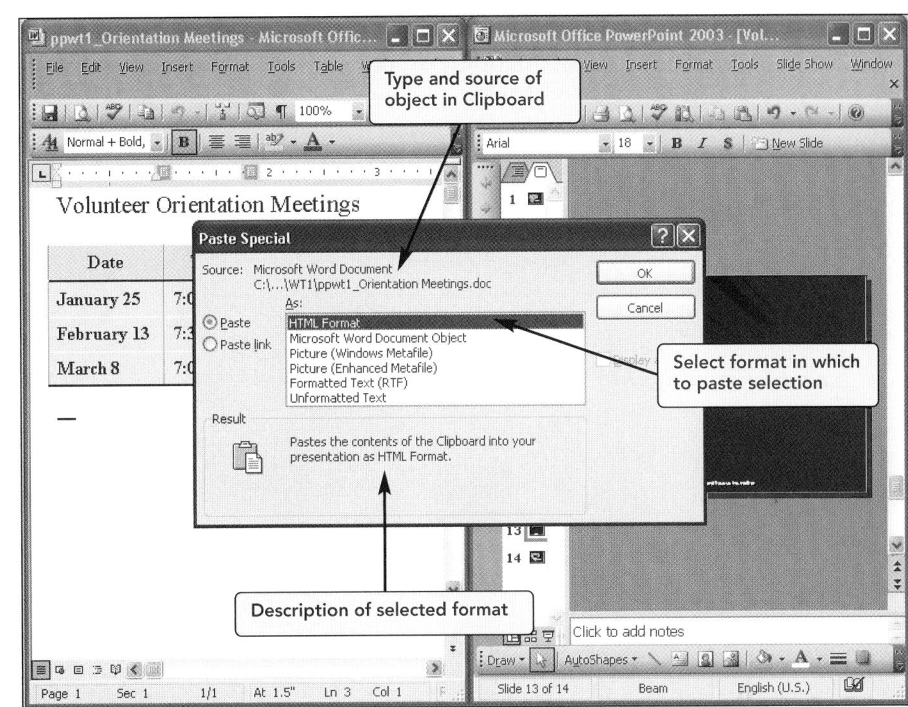


**Figure 5**

The Paste Special dialog box displays the type of object contained in the Clipboard and its location in the Source area. From the As list box, you select the type of format in which you want the object inserted into the destination file. The default option inserts the copy in HTML (HyperText Markup Language) format. The Result area describes the effect of your selections. In this case, you want the object inserted as a Word Document Object.

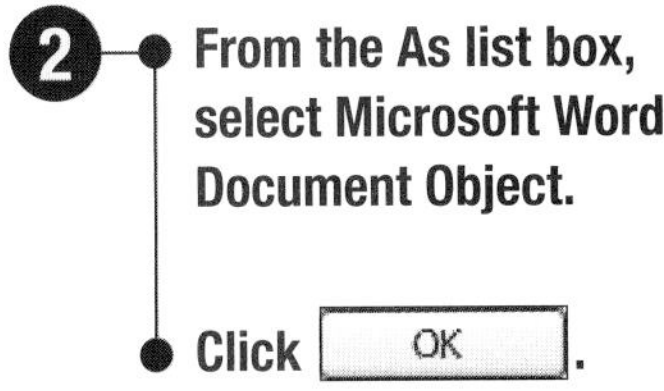

**2** From the As list box, select Microsoft Word Document Object.

- Click OK.

*Your screen should be similar to Figure 6*

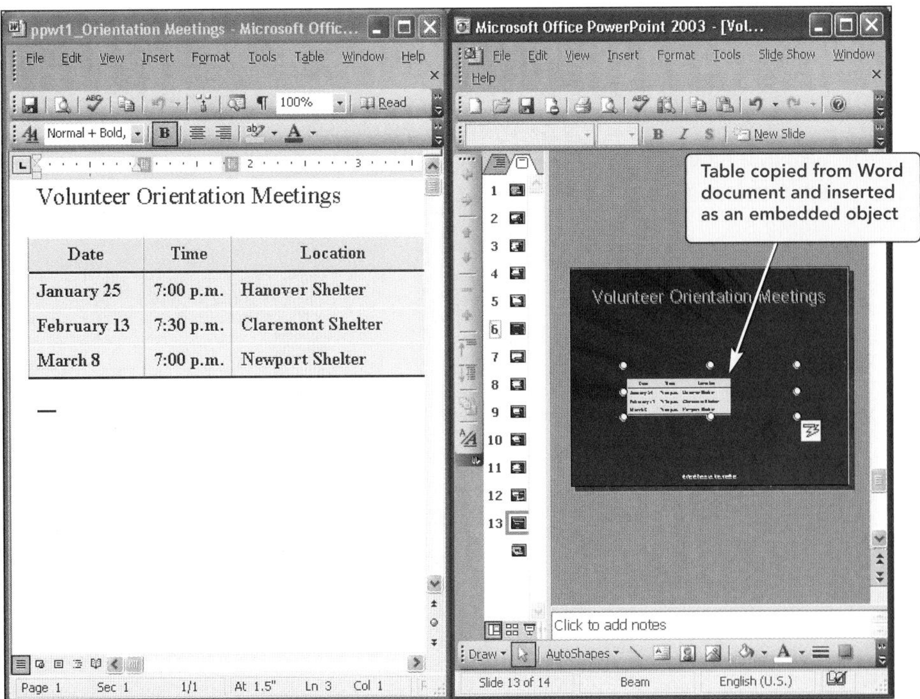


**Figure 6**

The table, including the table formatting, is copied into the slide as an embedded object that can be manipulated using the Picture toolbar. You will trim or crop the object so that the object size is the same size as the table. Then you will increase the size of the object and position it in the slide.

**3**

- **Choose Undo Tile from the taskbar shortcut menu.**
- **If necessary, maximize the PowerPoint window and select the table.**
- **Display the Picture toolbar.**
- **Click Crop.**
- **Position the cropping tool over a corner crop mark and drag inward to reduce the size of the object to the same size as the table.**

*Your screen should be similar to Figure 7*

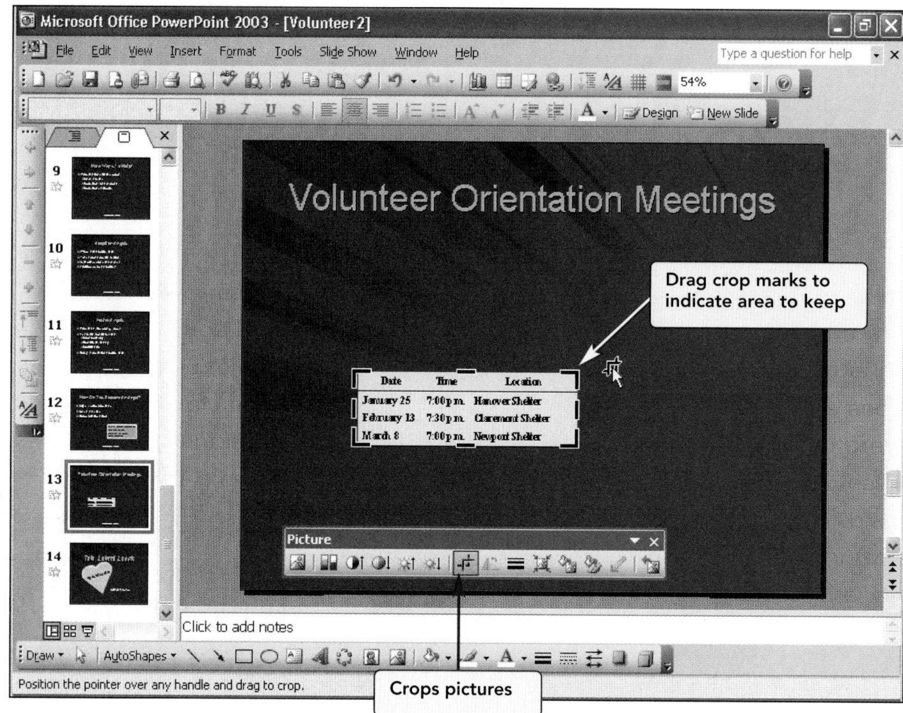


Figure 7

**4**

- **Click Crop to turn off the cropping tool.**
- **Size and move the table object as in Figure 8.**
- **Deselect the object.**
- **Close the Picture toolbar.**

*Your screen should be similar to Figure 8*

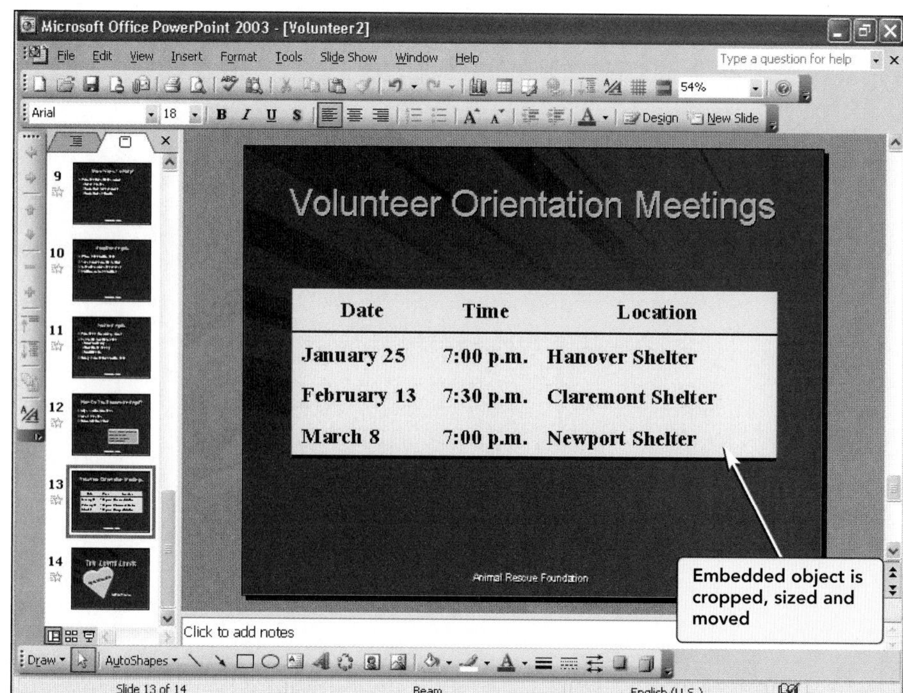


Figure 8

## Editing an Embedded Object

As you look at the table, you decide you want to change the appearance of the text in the headings. To do this, you will edit the embedded object using the source program.

❶ **Double-click the table.**

**Another Method**

The menu equivalent is Edit/Document Object/Edit.

*Your screen should be similar to Figure 9*

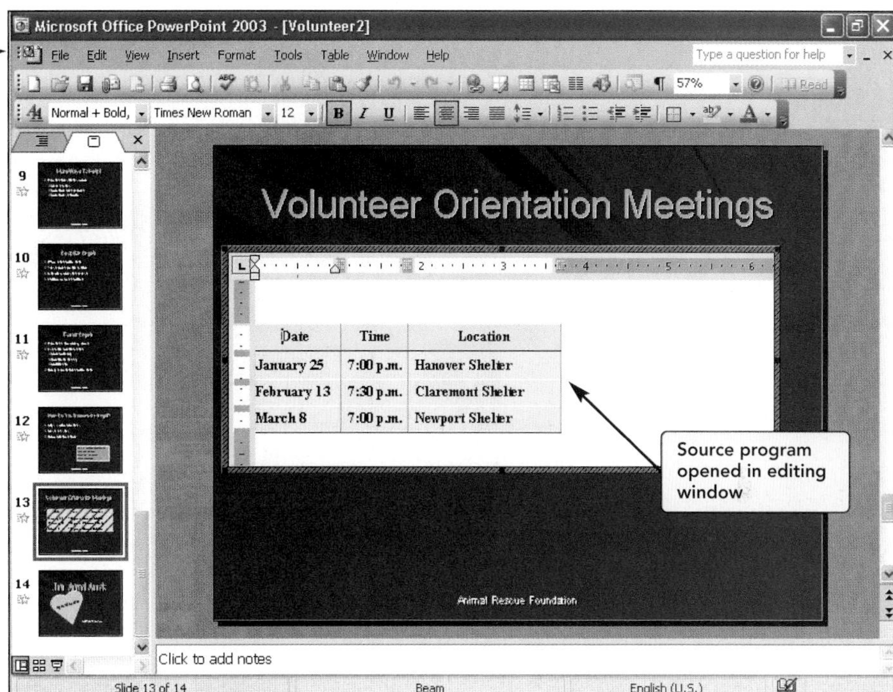


**Figure 9**

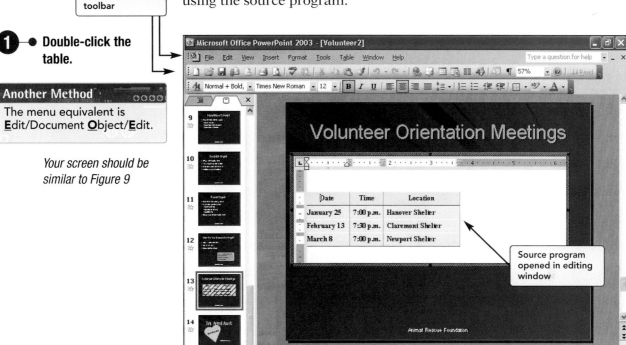

**Additional Information**

The user must have the source program on their system to be able to open and edit an embedded object.

The source program, in this case Word, is opened. The Word menus and toolbars replace some of the menus and toolbars in the PowerPoint application window. The embedded object is displayed in an editing window. Now, you can use the Word commands to edit the object.

**2** **Change the font color of the three headings to blue.**

**Left-align the three headings.**

**Close the source program by clicking anywhere outside the object.**

*Your screen should be similar to Figure 10*

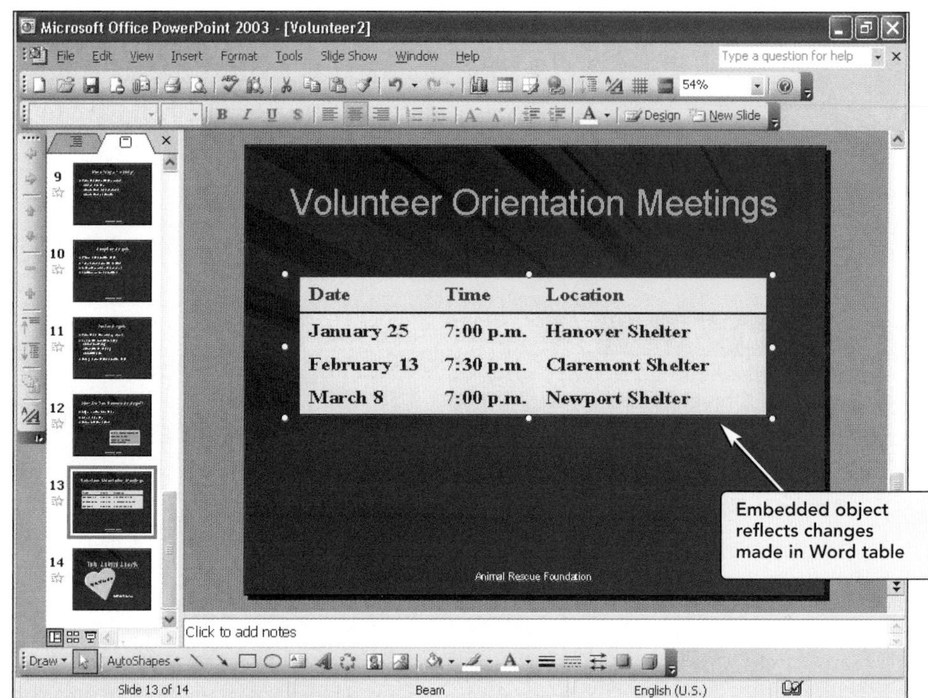


**Figure 10**

The embedded object in the PowerPoint slide is updated to reflect the changes you made in the Word table.

**3** **Click** [Orientation Meetings ...] **in the taskbar to switch to the Word application.**

**Deselect the table and notice that the source file has not been affected by the changes you made to the embedded object.**

**Exit Word.**

## Linking Between Applications

Next you want to copy the chart of the rescue and adoption data into the presentation. You will insert the chart object into the slide as a **linked object**, which is another way to insert information created in one application into a document created by another application. With a linked object, the actual data is stored in the source file (the document in which it was created). A graphic representation or picture of the data is displayed in the destination file (the document in which the object is inserted). A connection between the information in the destination file to the source file is established by creating a link. The link contains references to the location of the source file and the selection within the document that is linked to the destination file.

When changes are made in the source file that affect the linked object, the changes are automatically reflected in the destination file when it is opened. This connection is called a **live link**. When you create linked objects, the date and time on your machine should be accurate. This is because the program refers to the date of the source file to determine whether updates are needed when you open the destination file.

## Linking an Excel Chart to a PowerPoint Presentation

The chart of the rescue and adoption data will be inserted into another new slide following slide 6.

**1**

- **Insert a new slide following slide 6, using the Title Only layout.**
- **Close the Slide Layout task pane.**
- **Start Office Excel 2003 and open the workbook** ppwt1_RescueData **from your data files.**
- **Tile the application windows vertically.**

*Your screen should be similar to Figure 11*

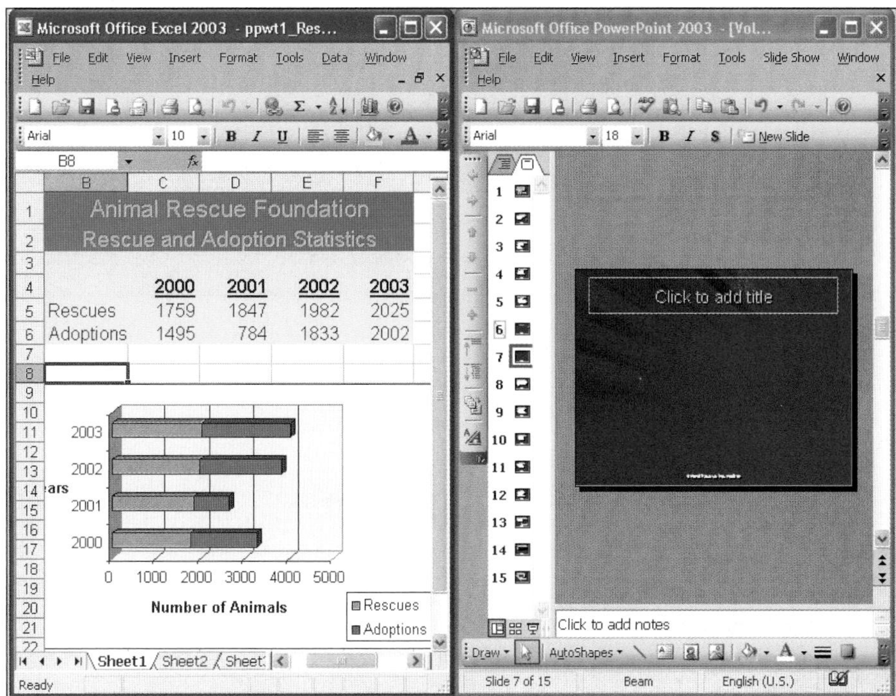


**Figure 11**

The worksheet contains the rescue and adoption data for the past four years as well as a column chart of the data. Again, you have two open applications, PowerPoint and Excel. Next you will copy the second title line from the worksheet into the slide title placeholder.

2 Select cell B2.

Click Copy.

Select the Title placeholder in the slide.

Choose **E**dit/Paste **S**pecial and select Formatted Text (RTF).

Click OK.

Remove the extra blank lines below the title and the extra space at the end of the title.

If necessary, size the placeholder and position the title appropriately on the slide.

Click on the slide to deselect the placeholder.

*Your screen should be similar to Figure 12*

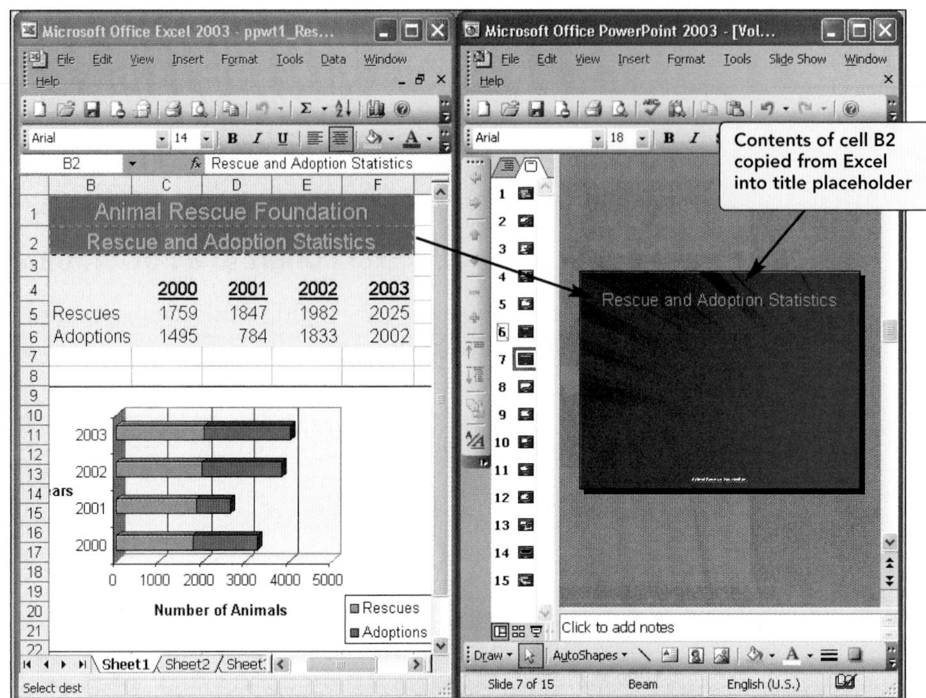


**Figure 12**

Now, you are ready to copy the chart. By making the chart a linked object, it will be updated automatically if the source file is edited.

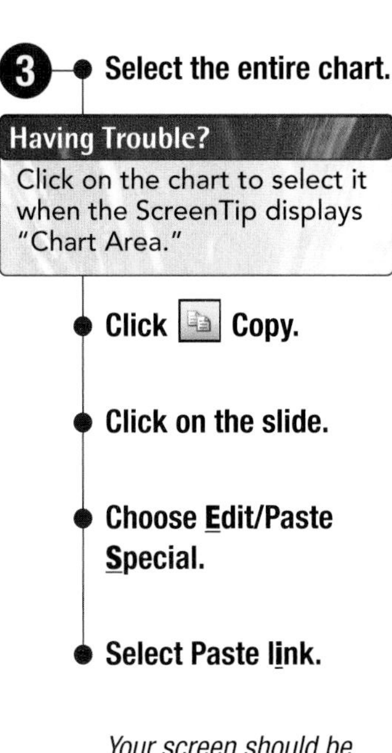

**3** Select the entire chart.

**Having Trouble?**

Click on the chart to select it when the ScreenTip displays "Chart Area."

- **Click Copy.**
- **Click on the slide.**
- **Choose Edit/Paste Special.**
- **Select Paste link.**

*Your screen should be similar to Figure 13*

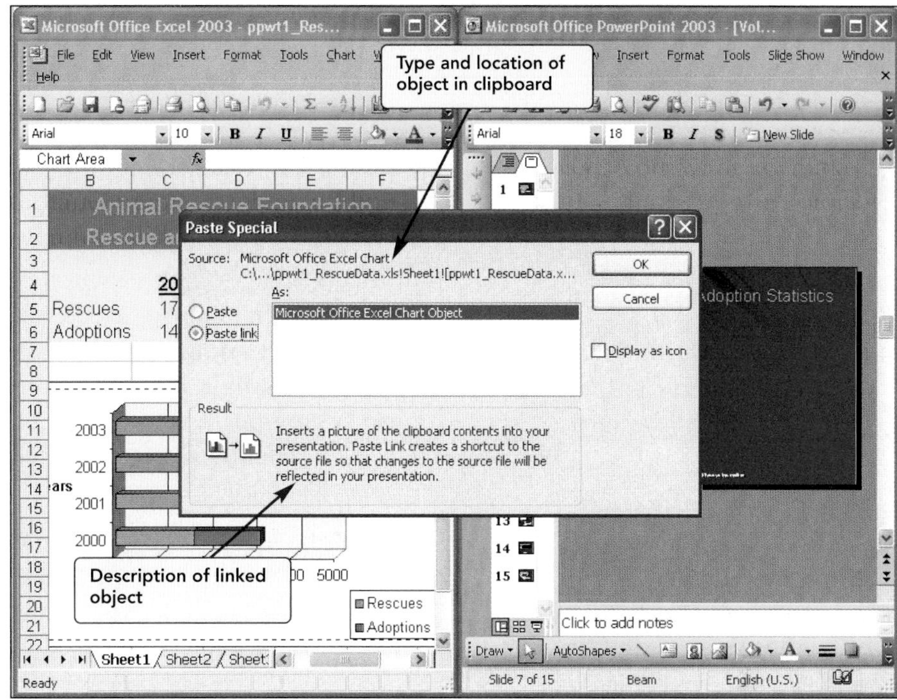


**Figure 13**

Again, from the As list box, you select the type of format in which you want the object inserted into the destination file. The only available option for this object is as a Microsoft Excel Chart Object. The Result area describes the effect of your selections. In this case, the object will be inserted as a picture, and a link will be created to the chart in the source file. Selecting the Display as Icon option changes the display of the object from a picture to an icon. Double-clicking the icon displays the object picture. The default selections are appropriate.

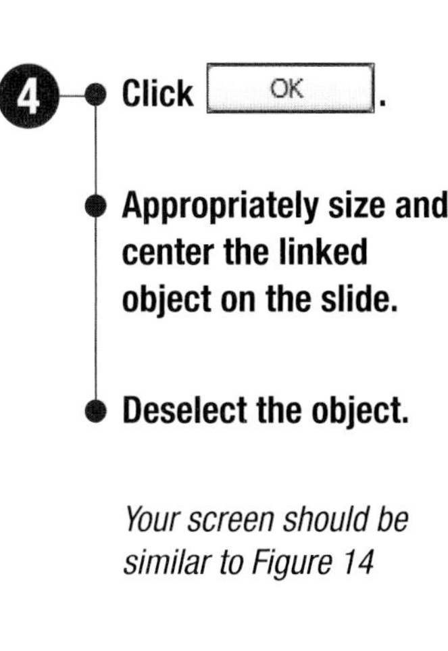

**4** Click OK.

- **Appropriately size and center the linked object on the slide.**
- **Deselect the object.**

*Your screen should be similar to Figure 14*

**Figure 14**

## Updating a Linked Object

While looking at the chart in the slide, you decide to change the chart type from a column chart to a bar chart. You believe that a bar chart will show the trends more clearly. You also notice the adoption data for 2001 looks very low. After checking the original information, you see that the wrong value was entered in the worksheet and that it should be 1784.

To make these changes, you need to switch back to Excel. Double-clicking on a linked object quickly switches to the open source file. If the source file is not open, it opens the file for you. If the application is not started, it both starts the application and opens the source file.

**1** **Double-click the chart object in the slide.**

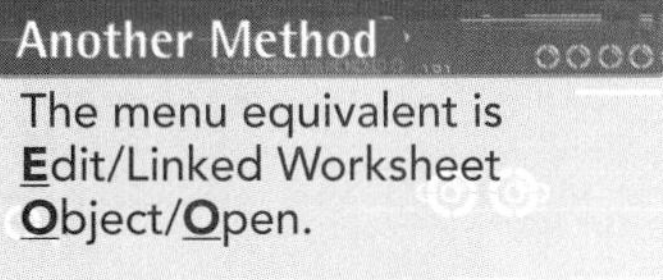

Another Method
The menu equivalent is Edit/Linked Worksheet Object/Open.


- **In Excel, right click on one of the columns in the chart and select Chart Type.**

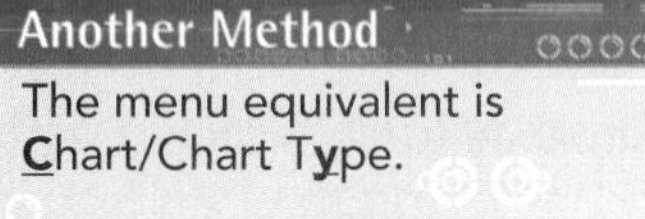

Another Method
The menu equivalent is Chart/Chart Type.


- **Select Column.**
- **Select Clustered column with a 3-D visual effect.**
- **Click** 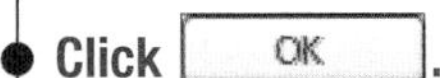 **.**
- **Edit the value in cell D6 to 1784.**

*Your screen should be similar to Figure 15*

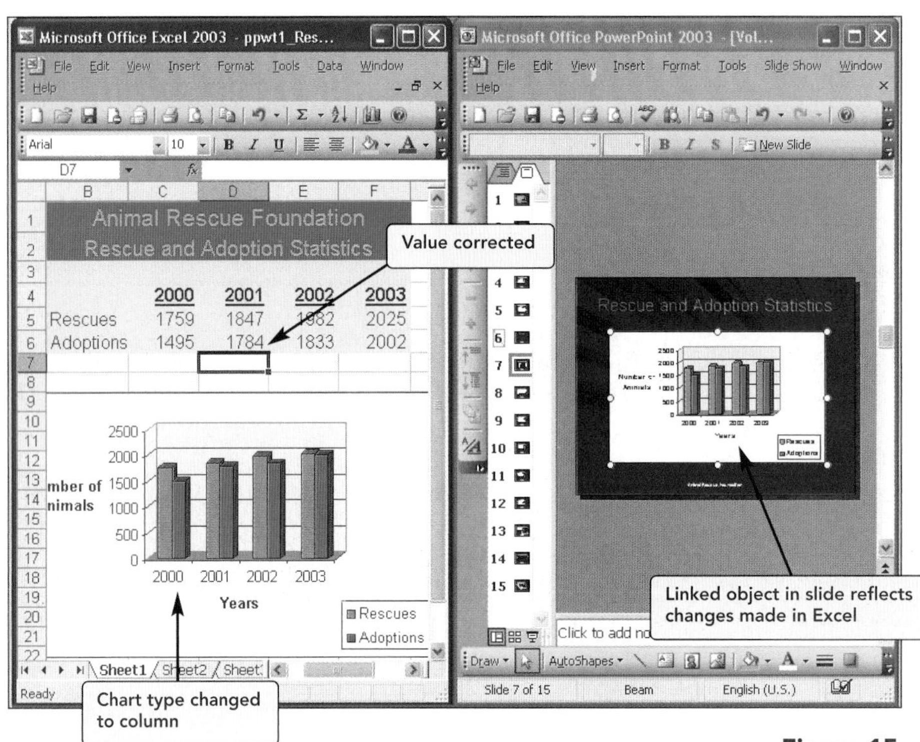


**Figure 15**

The chart in both applications has changed to a bar chart, and the chart data series has been updated to reflect the change in data. This is because any changes you make in the chart in Excel will be automatically reflected in the linked chart in the slide.

**2** • **Untile the application windows.**

• **Save the revised Excel workbook as RescueData Linked.**

• **Exit Excel.**

• **If necessary, maximize the PowerPoint window.**

## Editing Links

Whenever a document is opened that contains links, the application looks for the source file and automatically updates the linked objects. If there are many links, updating can take a lot of time. Additionally, if you move the source file to another location, or perform other operations that may interfere with the link, your link will not work. To help with situations like these, you can edit the settings associated with links. You will look at how to do this, though you will not actually edit the settings.

**1** • **If necessary, select the chart object.**

• **Choose Edit/Links.**

*Your screen should be similar to Figure 16*

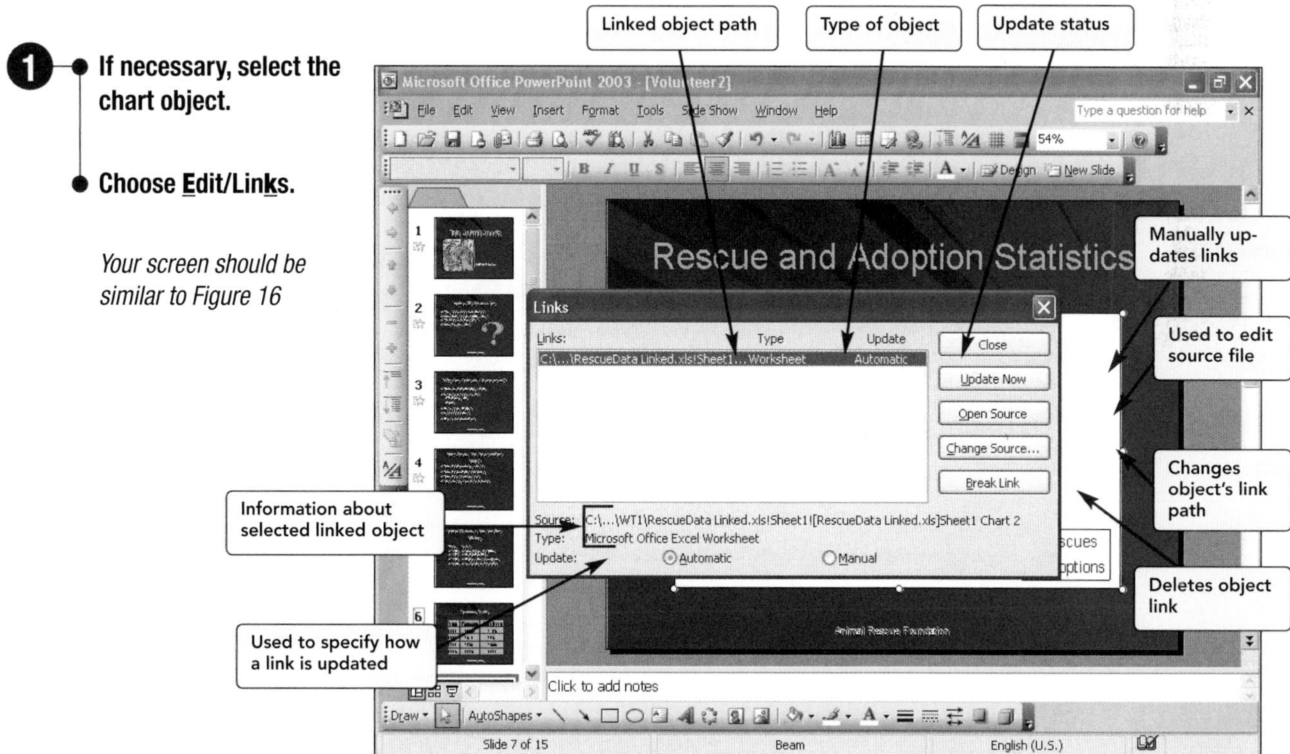


**Figure 16**

The Links dialog box list box displays information about all links in the document. This includes the path and name of the source file, the range of linked cells or object name, the type of file, and the update status. Below the list box the details for the selected link are displayed. The other options in this dialog box are described in the table on the next page.

| Option | Effect |
|---|---|
| Automatic | Updates the linked object whenever the destination document is opened or the source file changes. This is the default. |
| Manual | The destination document is not automatically updated, and you must use the Update Now command button to update the link. |
| Locked | Prevents a linked object from being updated. |
| Open Source | Opens the source document for the selected link. |
| Change Source | Used to modify the path to the source document. |
| Break Link | Breaks the connection between the source document and the active document. |

You do not want to make any changes to the link.

Linking documents is a very handy feature, particularly in documents whose information is updated frequently. If you include a linked object in a document that you are giving to another person, make sure the user has access to the source file and application. Otherwise the links will not operate correctly.

## Printing Selected Slides

Next, you will print the two new slides.

**1**

- **Switch to Slide Sorter view and select slides 7 and 14.**
- **Use View/Header and Footer to modify the slide footer to display your name on slides 7 and 14 only.**

> **Having Trouble?**
>
> Select the slides you want to modify, use the command, and click [Apply] to apply the new footer to the selected slides only.

- **Choose File/Print.**
- **If necessary, select the printer.**
- **Select Selection as the print range.**
- **Specify Slides as the type of output.**
- **Preview the output and change the print to grayscale if necessary.**
- **Print the slides.**
- **Save the PowerPoint presentation as** Volunteer2 Linked **and exit PowerPoint.**

*Your printed output should be similar to that shown here.*

Rescue and Adoption Statistics

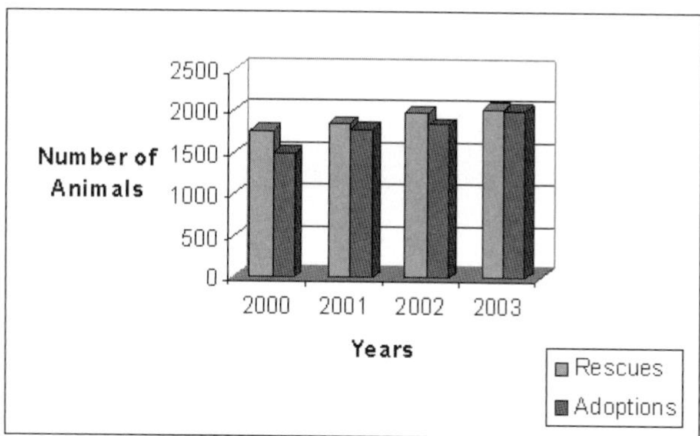


Student Name

Volunteer Orientation Meetings

| Date | Time | Location |
|---|---|---|
| January 25 | 7:00 p.m. | Hanover Shelter |
| February 13 | 7:30 p.m. | Claremont Shelter |
| March 8 | 7:00 p.m. | Newport Shelter |

Student Name

# WORKING TOGETHER 1
# Copying, Embedding, and Linking Between Applications

## key terms

destination file PPWT1.4
linked object PPWT1.8
live link PPWT1.9
source file PPWT1.4

## microsoft office specialist skills

The Microsoft Office Specialist certification program is designed to measure your proficiency in performing basic tasks using the Office 2003 applications. Certification demonstrates that you have the skills and provides a valuable industry credential for employment. After completing this lab, you have learned the following Microsoft Office PowerPoint 2003 Specialist skills:

| Skill Sets | Skill Standards | Page |
|---|---|---|
| Creating Content | Insert and edit text based content | PPWT1.2 |
| | Insert objects | PPWT1.11 |
| Managing and Delivering Presentations | Organize a presentation | PPWT1.2, 1.9 |
| | Print slides, outlines, handouts, and speaker notes | PPWT1.14 |

## command summary

| Command | Action |
|---|---|
| Edit/Paste Special/ <Object> | Inserts an item from Clipboard as an embedded object |
| Edit/Paste Special/Paste Link | Inserts an item from Clipboard as a linked object |
| Edit/Links | Changes settings associated with linked objects |
| Edit/Linked Worksheet Object/Open | Opens source application of linked object |
| Edit/Document Object/Edit | Opens source application of embedded object |

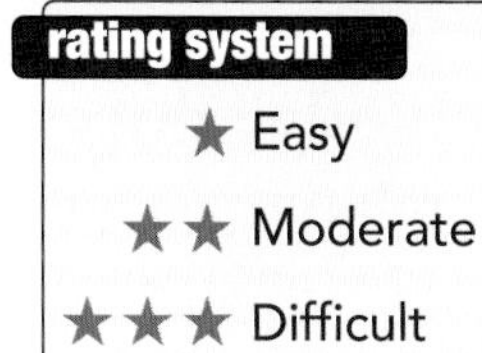

## step-by-step

### Embedding a Table of Massage Prices ★

1. To complete this problem, you must have completed Step-by-Step Exercise 2 in Lab 2. The Massage Therapy presentation is almost complete. You just need to add some information to the presentation about the prices. This information is already in a Word document as a table. You will copy and embed it into a new slide. The completed slide is shown here.
   - **a.** Start Word and open the document ppwt1_MassagePrices.
   - **b.** Start PowerPoint and open the Massage Therapy2 presentation.
   - **c.** Add a new slide after slide 9 using the Title Only layout.
   - **d.** Copy the title from the Word document into the slide title placeholder.
   - **e.** Copy the table into the slide as an embedded object. Exit Word.
   - **f.** Size and position the object on the slide appropriately.
   - **g.** Edit the table to increase the font size as needed.
   - **h.** Change the fill color of the table to match the slide design.
   - **i.** Save the presentation as Massage Therapy3.
   - **j.** Print the new slide.

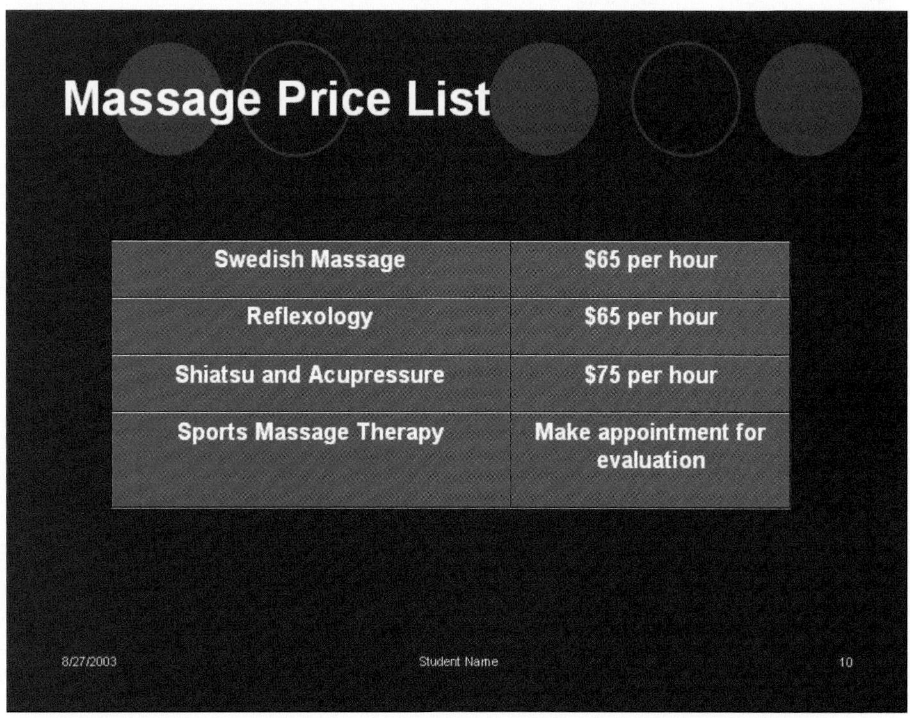

### Linking a Table of Coffee Prices ★★

2. To complete this problem, you must have completed Step-by-Step Exercise 4 in Lab 2. Evan, owner of the Downtown Internet Cafe, wants you to include information about special prices on coffee beans in the coffee slide show you created. You will link the coffee price information to the presentation, because the prices change frequently with market conditions and good buys. The completed slide is shown here.

   **a.** Start Word and open the document ppwt1_CoffeePrices.

   **b.** Start PowerPoint and open the presentation Coffee Show.

   **c.** Add a new slide at the end of the presentation using the Title Only layout.

   **d.** Enter the slide title **. . . Or Take Some Home**.

   **e.** Copy the table of prices into the slide as a linked object.

   **f.** Copy the text "Roast Coffee Specials" from the Word document into a text box on the slide. Apply a new font color and increase the font size.

   **g.** Size and position the objects appropriately.

   **h.** In the Word document, change the price of Kona to **$14.95**.

   **i.** Save the Word document as Coffee Prices Linked. Exit Word.

   **j.** Save the PowerPoint presentation as Coffee Show Linked.

   **k.** Print the new slide.

...Or Take Some Home

Roast Coffee Specials

| Coffee | Description | Cost/Pound |
|---|---|---|
| Columbian Blend | Classic body and aroma | $8.50 |
| Kona | Smooth, light bodied | $14.95 |
| Ethiopian | Floral aroma and flavor | $12.00 |
| Sumatra | Dark roasted | $7.95 |

8/27/2003 Student Name 10

## Linking a Worksheet on Forest Use ★★★

3. To complete this problem, you must have completed Step-by-Step Exercise 4 of Lab 2. Logan has found some interesting data on the increase in Americans hiking and wants to include this information in his lecture presentation. The completed slide is shown here.

   a. Start PowerPoint and open the Triple Crown Presentation2 presentation.

   b. Start Excel and open the ppwt1_Forest Use worksheet.

   c. Add a new slide after slide 6 using the Title Only layout.

   d. Enter the title **Most Popular Forest Activities**.

   e. Copy the worksheet range A2 through B6 as a linked object into slide 7. Size and position it appropriately.

   f. You notice that the percentage for hiking in the year 2002 seems low. After checking the original source, you see you entered the value incorrectly. In Excel, change the value in cell B5 to **36.4%**.

   g. Copy the text in cell A8 and paste it into the Notes for slide 7.

   h. Save the worksheet as Forest Use Linked. Exit Excel.

   i. Save the presentation as Triple Crown Presentation3.

   j. Print the new slide.

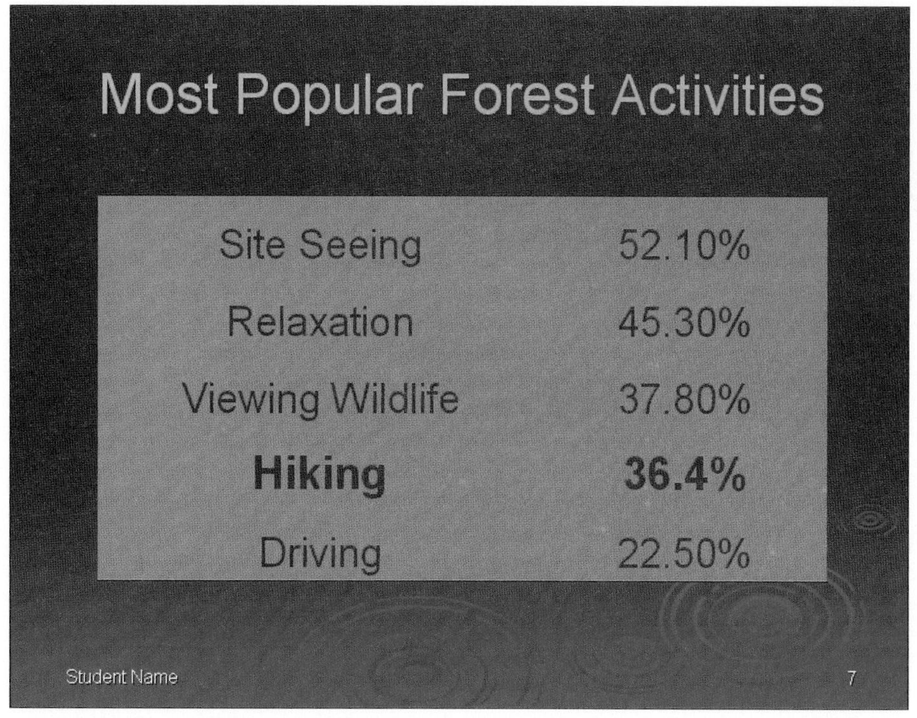

# Using Advanced Presentation Features

LAB 3

## Objectives

After completing this lab, you will know how to:

1. Create a new presentation from existing slides.
2. Create a numbered list.
3. Use Format Painter.
4. Create a custom background.
5. Change the design template.
6. Zoom slides.
7. Modify objects and change stacking order.
8. Wrap text in an object.
9. Group, ungroup, and align objects.
10. Create and modify a chart.
11. Create and modify an organization chart.
12. Export a presentation outline to Word.
13. E-mail a presentation.
14. Rehearse timings.
15. Package a presentation for a CD.
16. Prepare overheads or 35mm slides.

# Case Study

## Animal Rescue Foundation

The volunteer recruitment presentation you created for the Animal Rescue Foundation was a huge success. Now the agency director has asked you to create a presentation to use during new volunteer orientation programs. To create this presentation, you will modify and expand the recruitment presentation. This will include creating a new slide that presents an overview of the orientation, and another slide showing the organization of the agency. In addition, you plan to make the presentation more interesting by adding customized clip art and a custom background.

To help with these enhancements, PowerPoint 2003 includes several tools, such as graphs and organization charts that are designed to help present data. You will also use several Drawing tool features to customize a clip art graphic to enhance the presentation. Several slides from the completed presentation are shown here.

Ryan McVay/Corbis

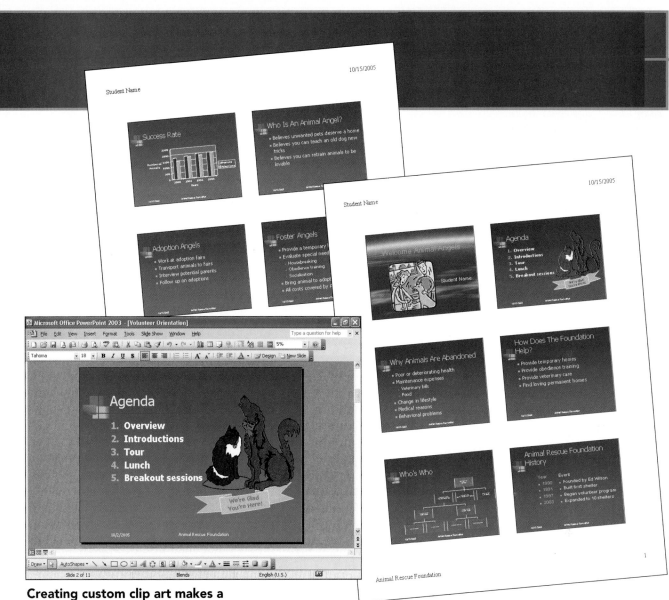

Creating custom clip art makes a presentation look more professional.

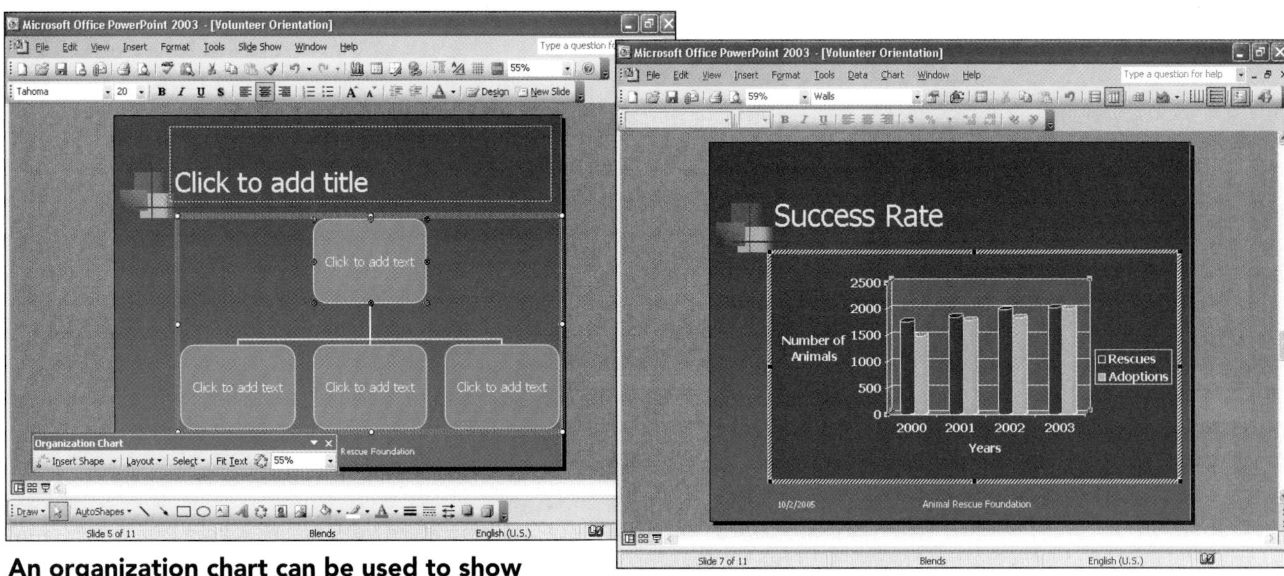


An organization chart can be used to show the hierarchy of an organization.

A graphic representation of table data as a chart makes data easier easier to understand.

## Concept Preview

The following concepts will be introduced in this lab:

1. **Group** A group is two or more objects that are treated as a single object.
2. **Object Alignment** Object alignment refers to the position of objects relative to each other by their left, right, top, or bottom edges; or horizontally by their centers or vertically by their middles; or in relation to the entire slide.
3. **Chart** A chart is a visual representation of numeric data that is used to help an audience grasp the impact of your data more quickly.
4. **Collect and Paste** The collect and paste feature is used to store multiple copied items in the Office Clipboard and then paste one or more of the items into another location or document.
5. **Organization Chart** An organization chart is a map of a group, which usually includes people, but can include any items that have a hierarchical relationship.

## Creating a New Presentation from Existing Slides

You worked very hard developing the content and layout for the volunteer recruitment presentation. Now you need to create a new presentation to be used during the volunteer orientation meeting. Much of the material in the volunteer recruitment presentation can also be used in the volunteer orientation presentation. To make the task of creating the new presentation easier, you will use the existing presentation, modify it to fit your needs, and save it as a new presentation. You have already made a few changes to the presentation. You changed the design and removed a few slides that you will not need in the orientation presentation.

**1**

- **Start Office PowerPoint 2003.**
- **Open the file** pp03_Recruitment**.**
- **If necessary, maximize the window and switch to Normal view.**
- **Change the title of slide 1 to Welcome Animal Angels.**
- **Replace Student Name on slide 1 with your name.**
- **Look at each of the slides to see the changes that have been made.**
- **Delete slide 10.**
- **Display slide 1 again.**

*Your screen should be similar to Figure 3.1*

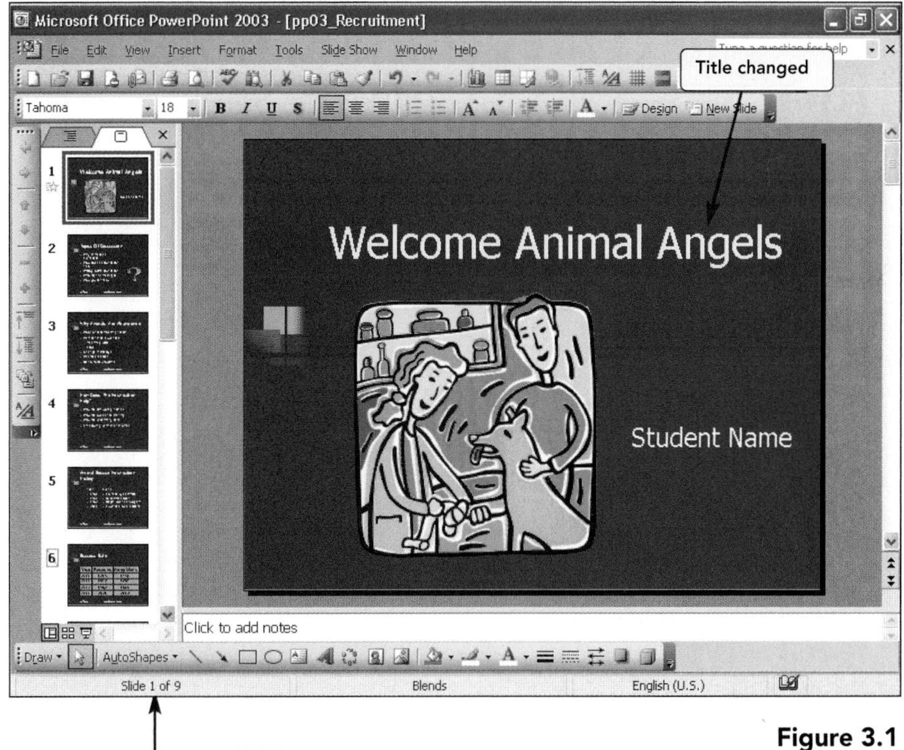


**Figure 3.1**

## Copying Slides from Another Presentation

Now you want to replace the ending slide you just deleted with a slide from another presentation you have been working on. To do this, you will copy the slide from the other presentation into the volunteer orientation presentation.

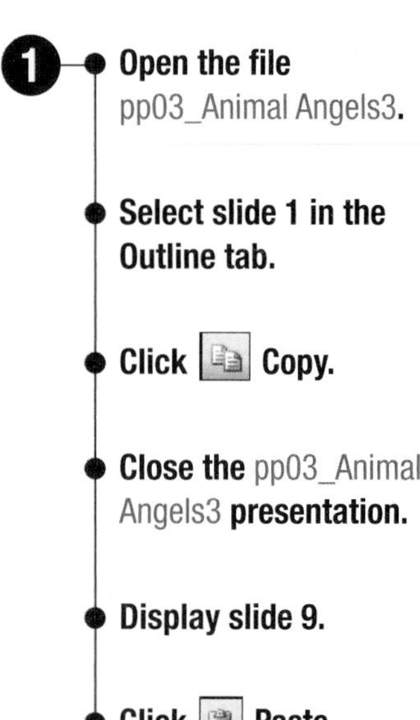

**1** **Open the file** pp03_Animal Angels3.

- **Select slide 1 in the Outline tab.**
- **Click Copy.**
- **Close the** pp03_Animal Angels3 **presentation.**
- **Display slide 9.**
- **Click Paste.**

*Your screen should be similar to Figure 3.2*

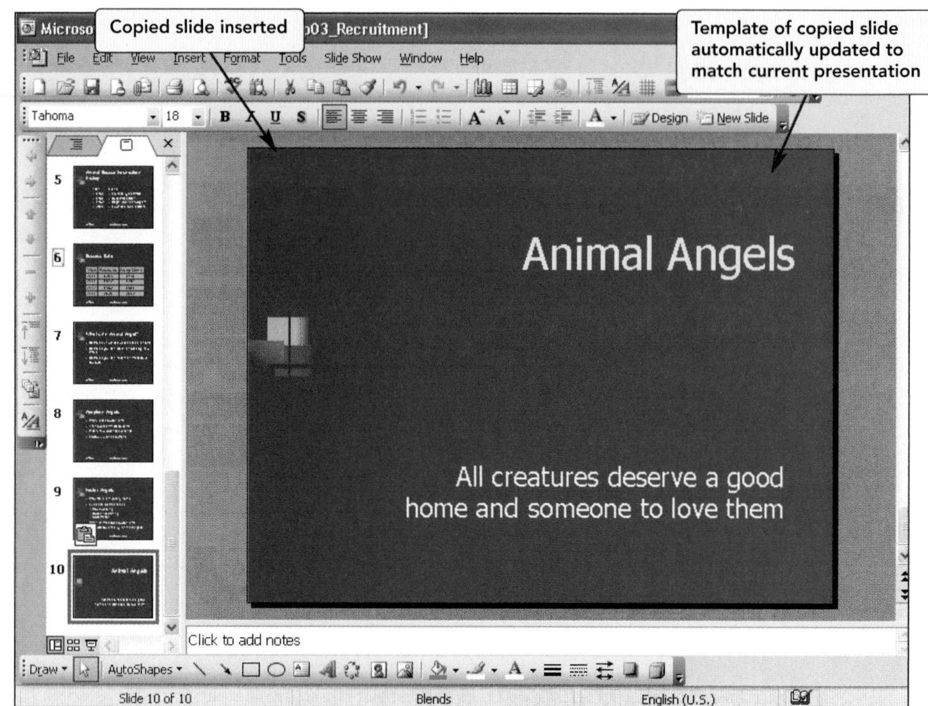


**Figure 3.2**

The copied slide is inserted into the presentation after the current slide. In addition, the slide template of the copied slide is updated automatically to match that of the current presentation.

## Saving the New Presentation

Before you make any additional changes, you will save the file as a new presentation.

**1** **Modify the title of slide 10 to Thank You for Joining Animal Angels.**

- **Save the revised presentation as** Volunteer Orientation.

*Your screen should be similar to Figure 3.3*

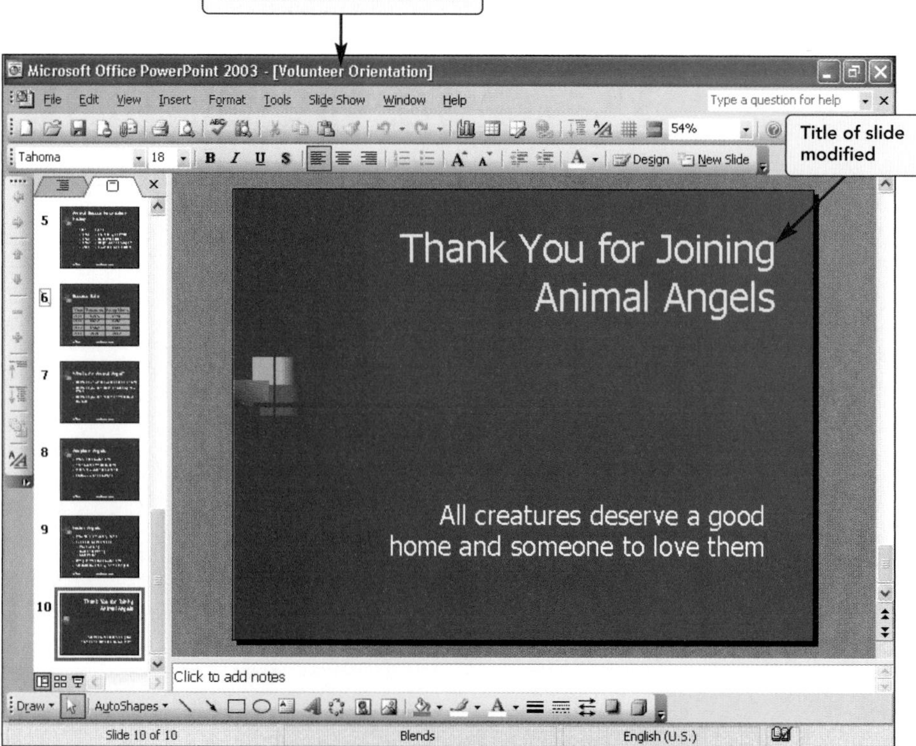


**Figure 3.3**

By modifying an existing presentation and saving it as a new presentation, you have saved a lot of time in the creation of your new presentation.

## Enhancing the New Presentation

Now that the basic presentation is assembled, you want to make some enhancements, such as adding an agenda slide, changing the color of text on a few slides, and adding some more content.

## Creating a Numbered List

First you want to change the second slide, which shows the topics of discussion, to a slide showing the agenda for the orientation. Since the agenda shows a sequential order of events, you want to use a numbered list rather than bullets.

**1**

- **Change the title of slide 2 to Agenda.**
- **Select the five bulleted items.**
- **Type the text for the following five bulleted items:**
  **Overview**
  **Introductions**
  **Tour**
  **Lunch**
  **Breakout sessions**
- **Select the five bulleted items on slide 2.**
- **Click Numbering.**

*Your screen should be similar to Figure 3.4.*

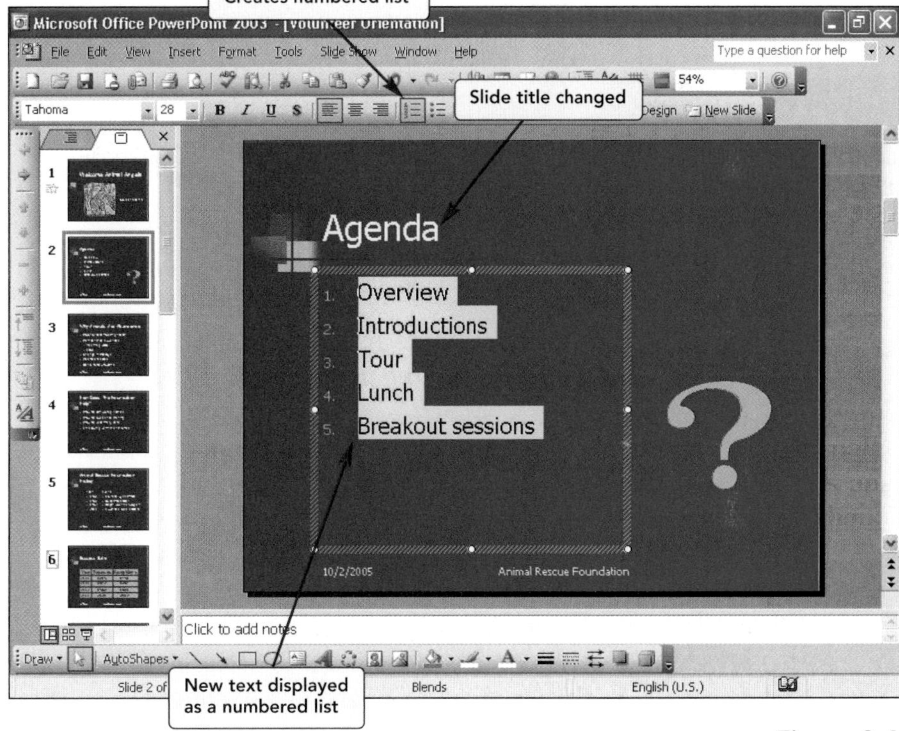


**Figure 3.4**

**Another Method**

You can also change a bulleted list to a numbered list by typing. To do this, press Backspace to remove the bullet at the beginning of the line, type 1, A, a, I, or i followed by a period or closing parenthesis, type the text, and then press ←Enter to start a new line. The next line is automatically numbered using the same style.

The bullets have been replaced with numbers, indicating a sequential order of events.

You would also like to change the size of the numbers so they will stand out more on the slide.

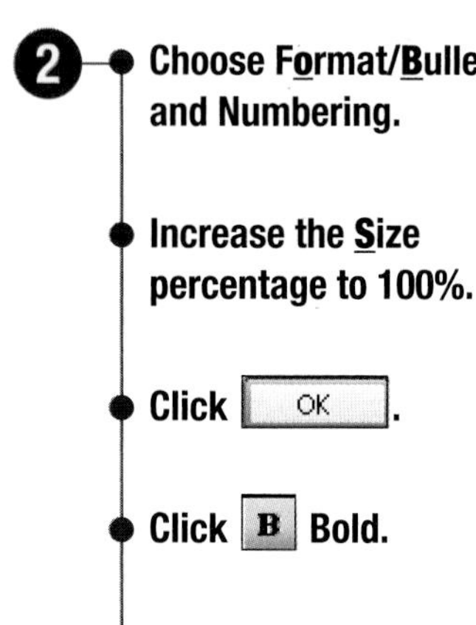

**2** **Choose Format/Bullets and Numbering.**

- **Increase the Size percentage to 100%.**
- **Click OK.**
- **Click B Bold.**
- **Deselect the text.**

*Your screen should be similar to Figure 3.5*

**Additional Information**

The Numbered tab of the Bullets and Numbering dialog box also allows you to select from several other numbering styles as well as specify a starting number.

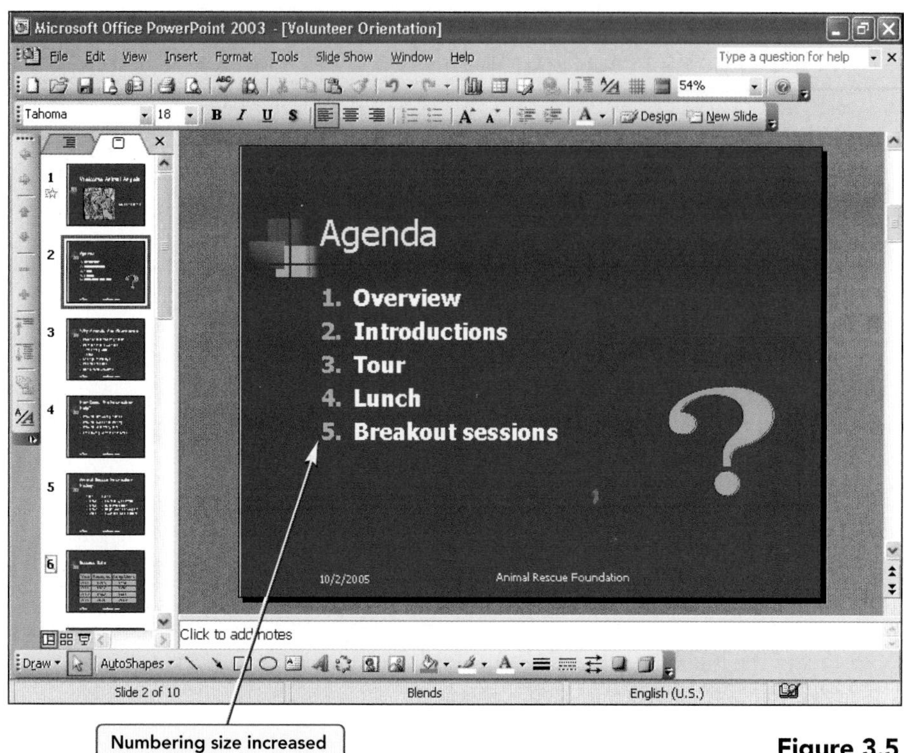


**Figure 3.5**

The numbers have changed to the size you selected and now stand out more from the text.

## Using Format Painter

You decide that slide 5, which shows the history of the Animal Rescue Foundation, could benefit from the addition of a little more color. To help you quickly apply the same formats to multiple selections, you will use the **Format Painter** tool. This feature applies the formats associated with the current selection to new selections. If the selection is a paragraph, the formatting is applied to entire paragraphs. If the selection is a character, it is applied to a word or selection you specify.

**1**

- **Display slide 5.**
- **Select the word "Year" in the slide.**
- **Change the font to Arial, bold, and the font color to gold.**
- **Double-click Format Painter.**
- **Click 1990.**

**Additional Information**

Single-clicking Format Painter applies the format to one selection, whereas double-clicking allows you to apply the format multiple times.

**Additional Information**

When the Format Painter feature is on, the mouse pointer appears as .

*Your screen should be similar to Figure 3.6*

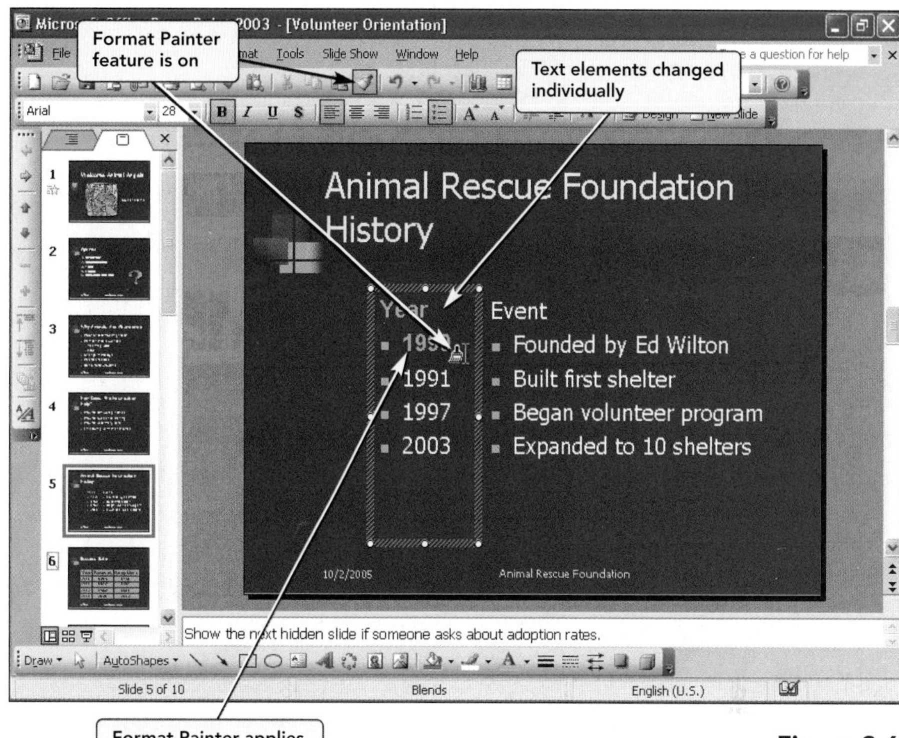


**Figure 3.6**

The text automatically changed to the same font settings associated with the selection when you turned on Format Painter. In one single click, you quickly applied three formats.

**2**

- **Use Format Painter to format the remaining three years.**
- **Click Format Painter to turn off the feature.**
- **Change "Event" to Arial and bold.**
- **Use Format Painter to change all the event text to match the heading.**
- **Turn off Format Painter.**

Another Method
You can also press Esc to turn off the Format Painter.


- **Deselect the text.**
- **Size the placeholder so each bullet is on one line.**

*Your screen should be similar to Figure 3.7*

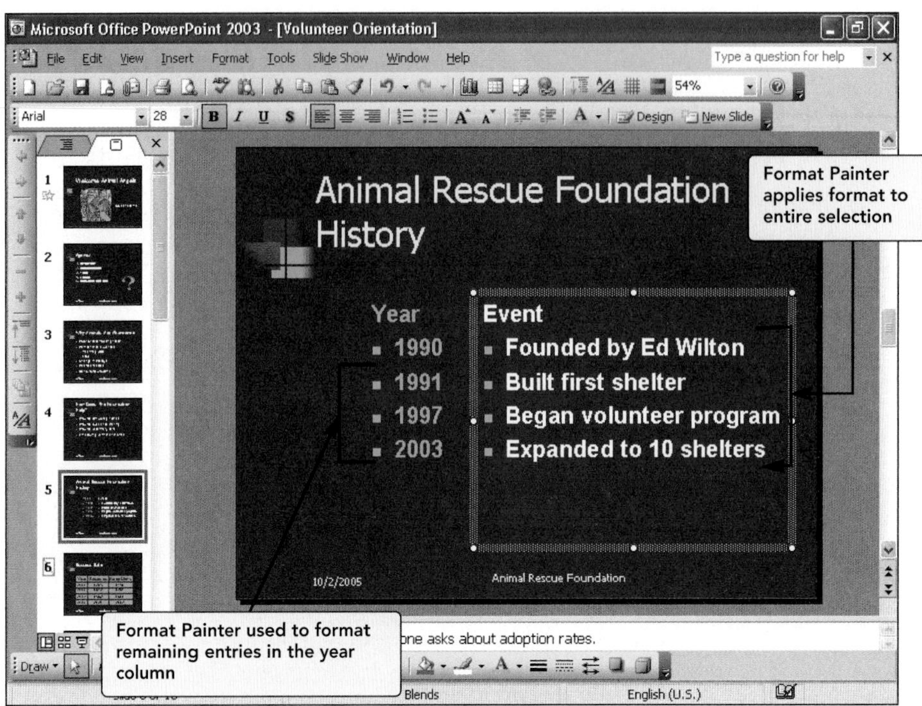


Figure 3.7

## Modifying the Design Template

Although you like the template design you selected for this presentation, you think the presentation design would benefit by adding a little variety. To do this, you decide to change the appearance of several of the slides by changing the slide background and using a different design template.

## Creating a Custom Background

As you look at the slides you decide you want to add a more interesting background. You will do this by adding a gradient color to the background.

**1**

- **Choose Format/ Background.**
- **Select Fill Effects from the Background Fill color drop-down list.**
- **Open the Gradient tab and select Two colors.**
- **From the Color 1 drop-down list, select the dark blue color from the top row.**
- **From the Color 2 drop-down menu, select More Colors.**
- **Select a lighter blue color from the Standard color palette and click OK.**
- **From the Shading styles area, select Horizontal and click OK.**

*Your screen should be similar to Figure 3.8*

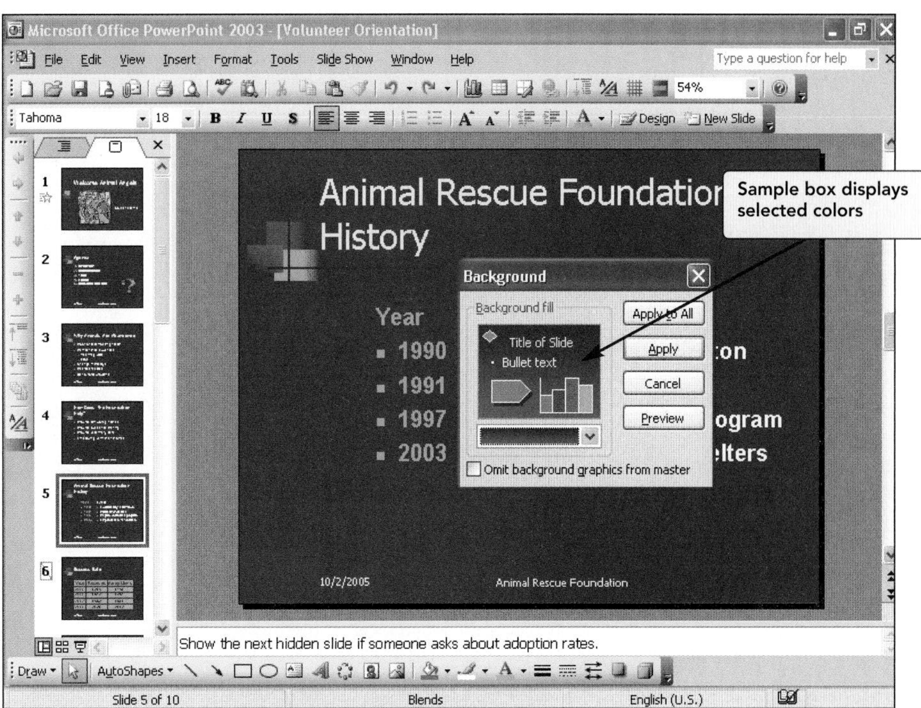


**Figure 3.8**

The selected colors in the gradient shading style you selected are displayed in the Sample box so you can see how it will look on the slide.

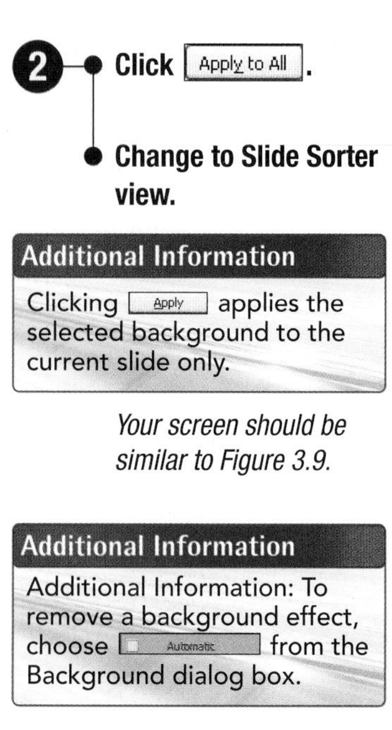

**2** Click Apply to All.

- Change to Slide Sorter view.

**Additional Information**

Clicking Apply applies the selected background to the current slide only.

*Your screen should be similar to Figure 3.9.*

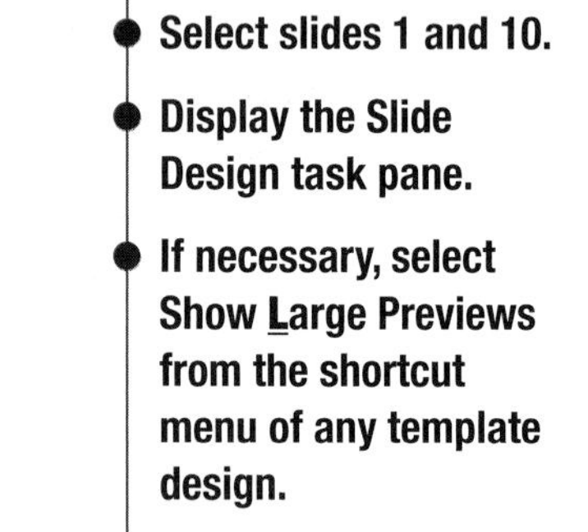

**Additional Information**

Additional Information: To remove a background effect, choose Automatic from the Background dialog box.

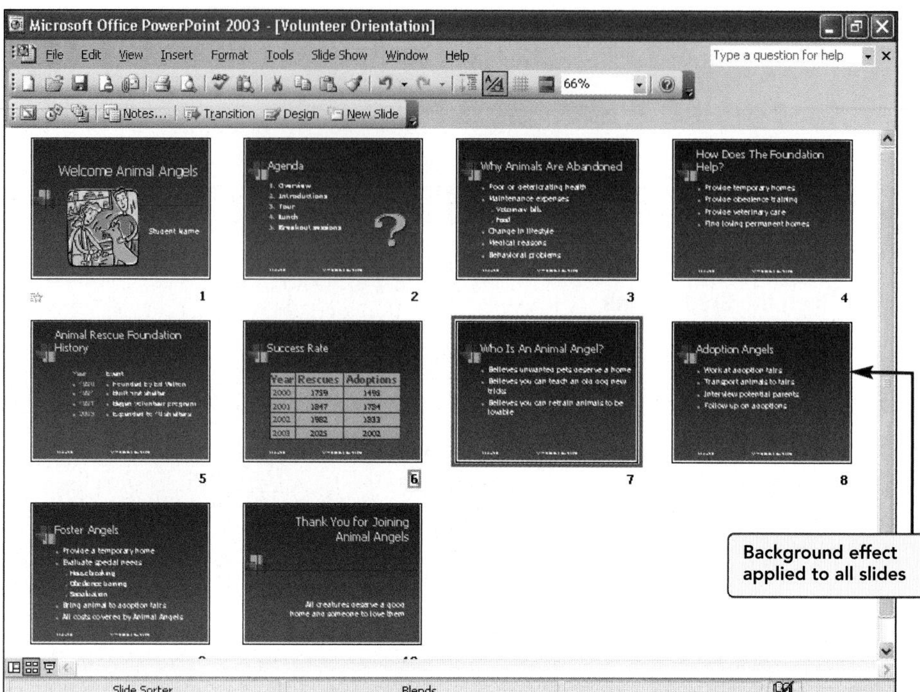


**Figure 3.9**

The gradient style background adds interest to the slides.

## Applying a Slide Master to Selected Slides

Next you want to change the design template for the first and last slides in the presentation to another template. Design templates can be applied to selected slides as well as to an entire presentation.

**1**

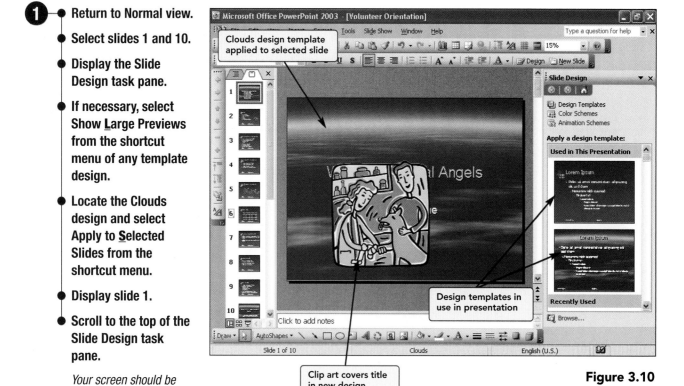

- Return to Normal view.
- Select slides 1 and 10.
- Display the Slide Design task pane.
- If necessary, select Show Large Previews from the shortcut menu of any template design.
- Locate the Clouds design and select Apply to Selected Slides from the shortcut menu.
- Display slide 1.
- Scroll to the top of the Slide Design task pane.

*Your screen should be similar to Figure 3.10*

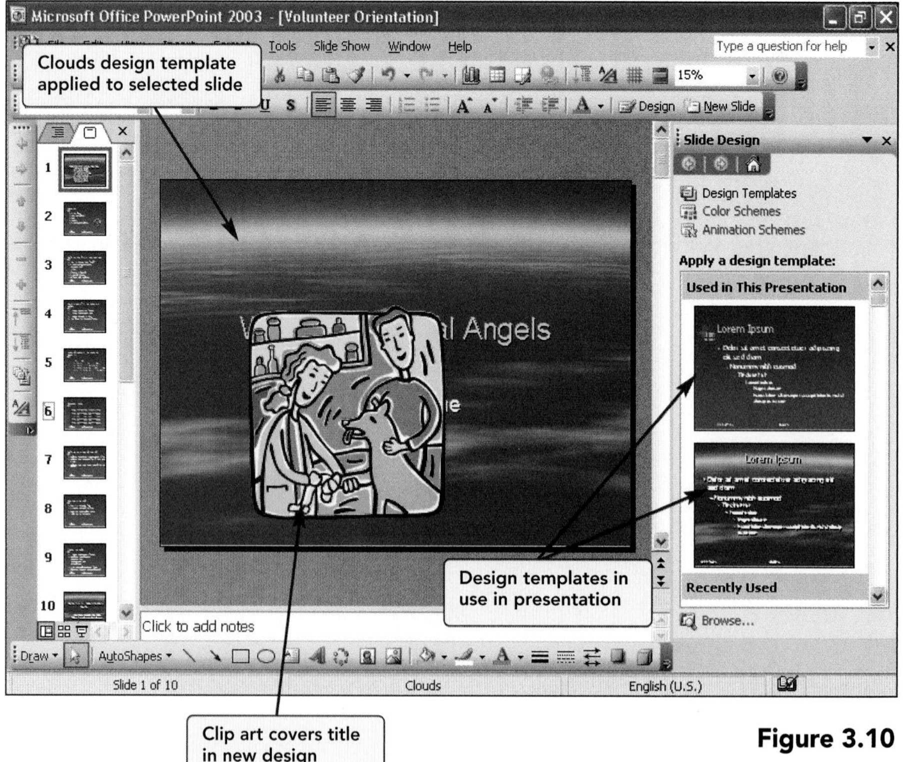


**Figure 3.10**

The Used in This Presentation section of the Slide Design task pane displays thumbnails for both design templates in use. As you can see by looking at slide 1, you need to make some changes to the title slide arrangement. You will make these changes to the slide title master.

**2**
- **Display Slide Master view.**
- **Point to the title slide master of the Clouds design (thumbnail 4).**

*Your screen should be similar to Figure 3.11*

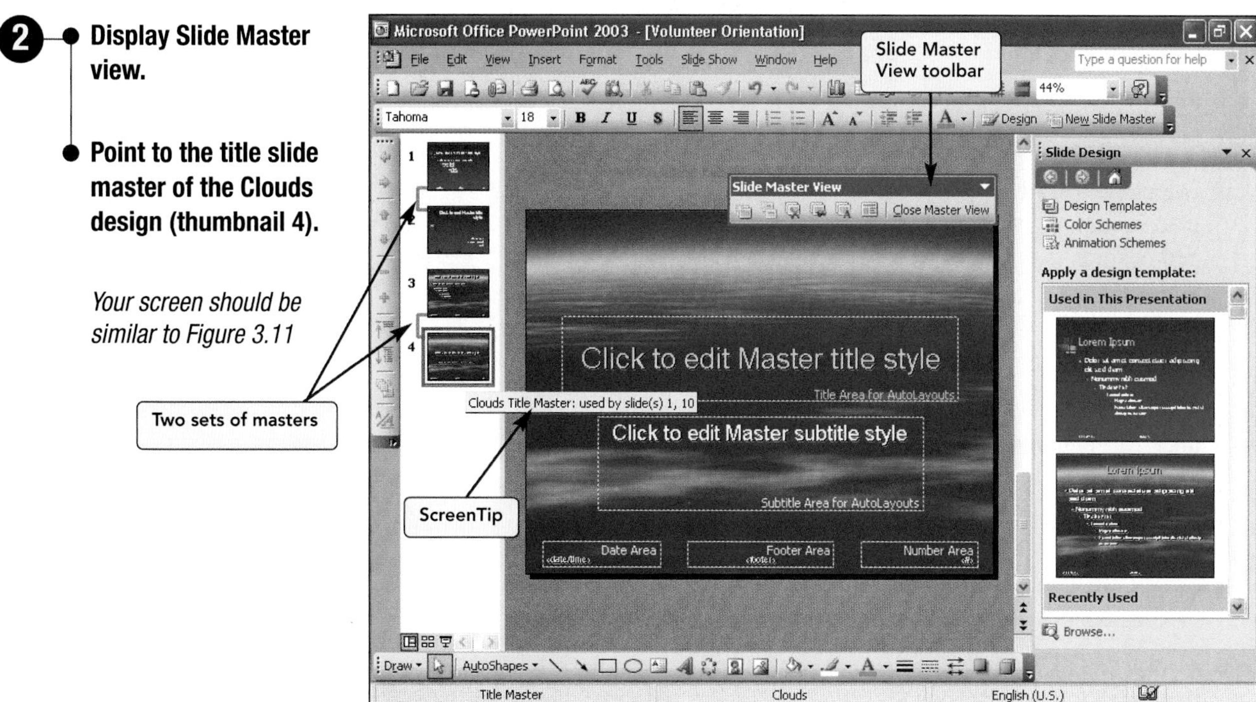


**Figure 3.11**

Because you are using two different slide designs in the presentation, there are two sets of masters, one for each design. Pointing to a slide master thumbnail displays a ScreenTip showing the design name and the slides in the presentation that use that template. Using menu commands and buttons on the Slide Master View toolbar, you can add, duplicate, rename, and delete masters. You can also preserve a master, which protects it from being deleted automatically in certain cases by PowerPoint.

You will modify the title master of the Clouds design and then you will rename it Sky.

**3**

- **Select the title placeholder and change the font color to dark gold and 48 pt.**
- **Move the title placeholder to the position shown in Figure 3.12.**
- **Select the subtitle placeholder and size and position it as in Figure 3.12.**
- **Right-align the subtitle text.**
- **Click Rename Master.**
- **Replace the existing name with Sky and click Rename.**
- **Point to the Sky thumbnail in the Slide Design task pane.**

*Your screen should be similar to Figure 3.12*

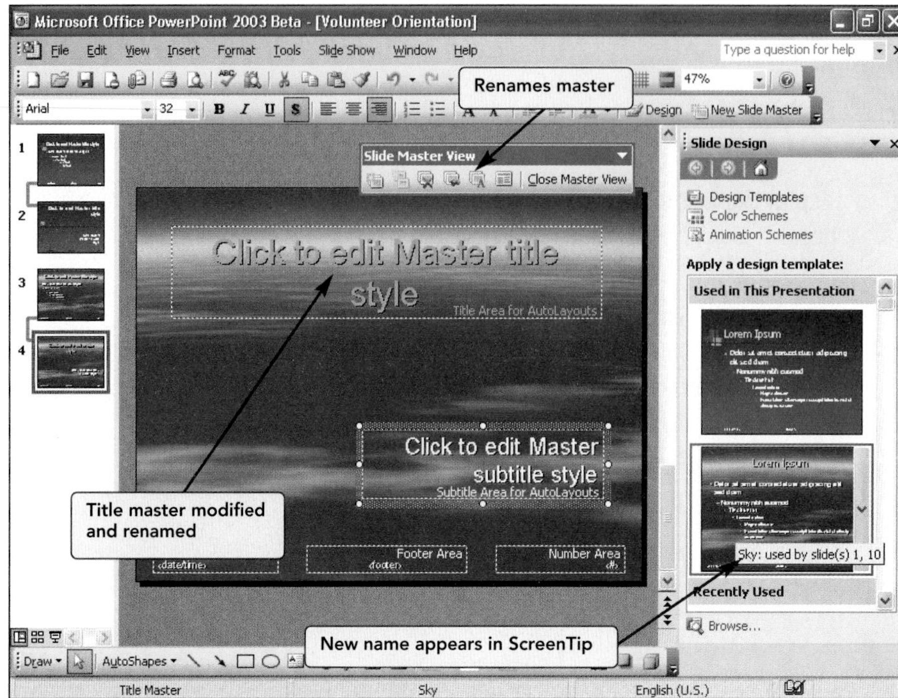


Figure 3.12

The new name appears in the ScreenTip.

**4**

- **Close Slide Master view.**
- **If necessary, reapply the slide layout.**

**Having Trouble?**

Use Format/Slide Layout and select Reapply Layout from the Title Slide layout shortcut menu.

- **Close the task pane and change to Slide Sorter view.**

*Your screen should be similar to Figure 3.13*

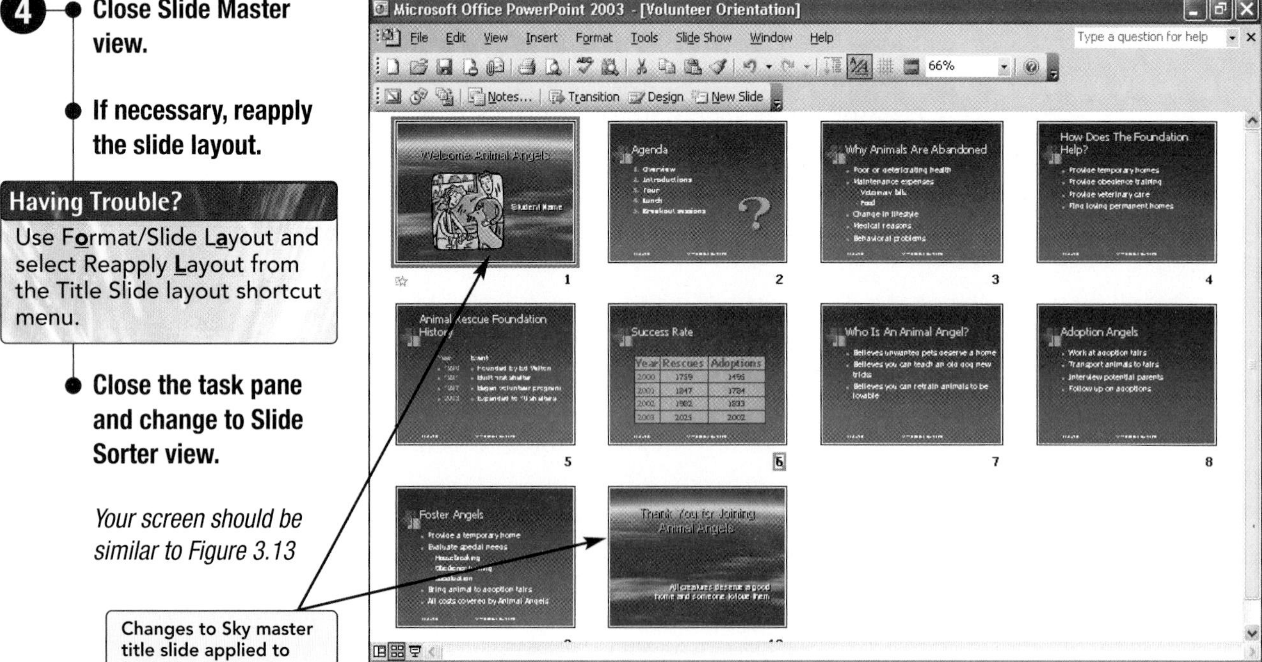


Figure 3.13

The changes you made to the master title slide are displayed in the two title slides in the presentation. In order to make changes throughout your presentation, you must make design changes to both pairs of masters.

## Adding a Picture Background

Finally, you decide to use a different slide background for the last slide in the presentation. You will use a picture of a sunrise in place of the clouds.

**1**

- **Display slide 10 in Normal view.**
- **Choose Format/Background**
- **Select Fill Effects from the Background Fill color drop-down list.**
- **Open the Picture tab.**
- **Click** Select Picture... **.**
- **Change the location to the location of your data files and select** pp03_Sunrise**.**
- **Click** Insert **.**
- **Click** OK **.**
- **Select Omit background graphics from master.**
- **Click** Apply **.**
- **Change to Slide Sorter view.**
- **Save the presentation.**

*Your screen should be similar to Figure 3.14*

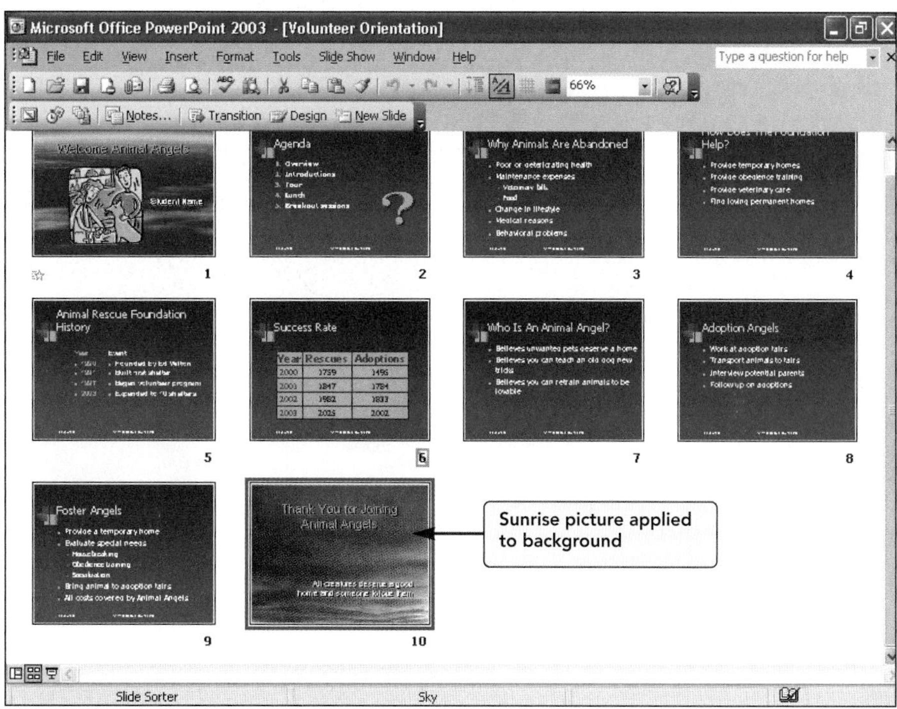


**Figure 3.14**

The sunrise background has been applied to the selected slide only.

## Customizing Graphics

You want to replace the question mark clip art on the Agenda slide with a graphic of a cat and a dog. You were unable to find a graphic of a cat and dog together that you liked, so you decide to create a custom graphic from two separate graphics. You will do this by opening and modifying the graphics individually, then grouping them into one object.

### Concept 1

#### Group

1 A **group** is two or more objects that are treated as a single object. Many clip art pictures are composed of several different elements that are grouped together. This allows you to easily move, resize, flip, or rotate all pieces of the group as a single unit. Features or **attributes**, such as line or fill color, associated with all objects in the group can also be changed at one time.

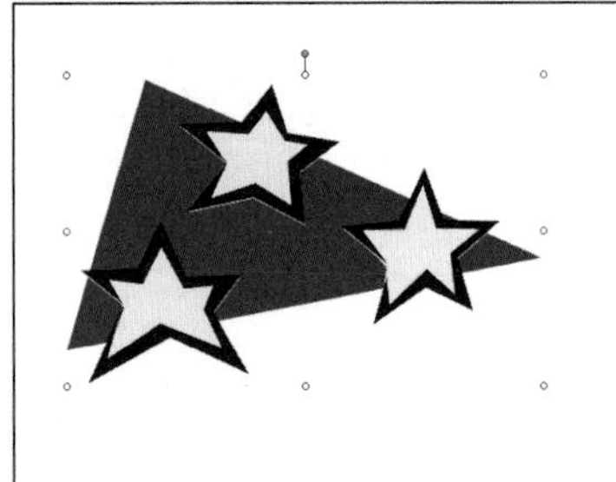

**Grouped**

**Ungrouped**

Sometimes you may want to ungroup the parts of an object so that the individual parts can be manipulated independently. Other times you may want to combine several objects to create your own graphic object that better suits your needs.

First you need to delete the existing clip art and placeholder. Then you will insert, position, and modify the new picture.

**1**

- **Display slide 2 in Normal view.**
- **Delete the question mark graphic and the clip art placeholder.**
- **Insert the graphic file** pp03_Cat **from your data file location.**
- **Move it to the right of the numbered list.**

*Your screen should be similar to Figure 3.15*

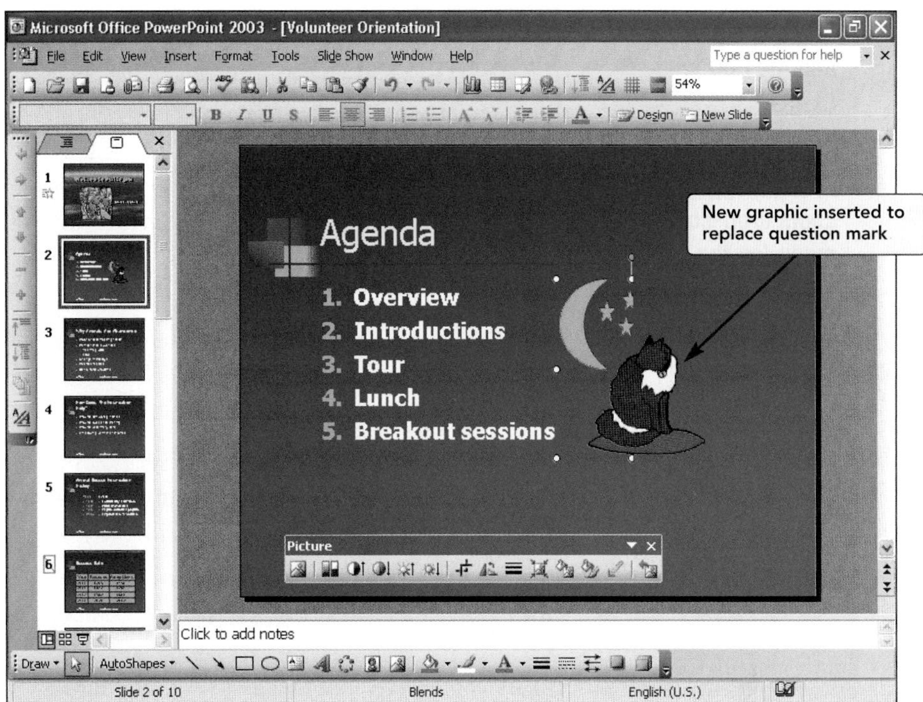


**Figure 3.15**

The cat graphic is made up of several elements grouped together.

## Zooming the Slide

To make complex graphics easier to work with, you can turn off the display of panes and increase the magnification of the slide. In Normal view the slide is sized by default to fit within the pane and is about 60 percent of full (100 percent) size. You can increase the onscreen display size up to four times normal display (400 percent) or reduce the size to 33 percent. Changing the Zoom percentage only affects the onscreen display of the slide; it does not change the actual font or object sizes.

**1** **Close the tabs pane and the Outlining toolbar.**

**Open the 55% Zoom drop-down menu (on the Standard toolbar) and choose 100%.**

**Another Method**

The menu equivalent is View/Zoom.

*Your screen should be similar to Figure 3.16*

**Figure 3.16**

The slide display is increased to 100 percent, and the entire slide is now too large to fully display in the window. The graphic is much larger, and as you make changes to the graphic, you will be able to more easily select different parts of the object.

You want to modify the graphic first by changing the color of the pillow below the cat. You can customize graphics by adding and deleting pieces of the graphic, changing the fill and line colors, and otherwise editing the graphic using features on the Drawing toolbar. However, to do this, the graphic must be a drawing object.

## Converting Graphics to Drawing Objects

Because this is an imported graphic (it was not originally created within PowerPoint using the Drawing features), it first needs to be converted to a drawing object that can be manipulated using features included within PowerPoint.

**1** **Right-click on the graphic and choose Edit Picture.**

**Click Yes to convert the graphic to a Microsoft Office drawing object.**

**Click on the red pillow to select it.**

*Your screen should be similar to Figure 3.17*

**Additional Information**

Not all types of graphics can be converted to drawing objects. Windows metafiles (.wmf) can be converted, but bitmap (.bmp), .jpg, .gif, and .png file types cannot.

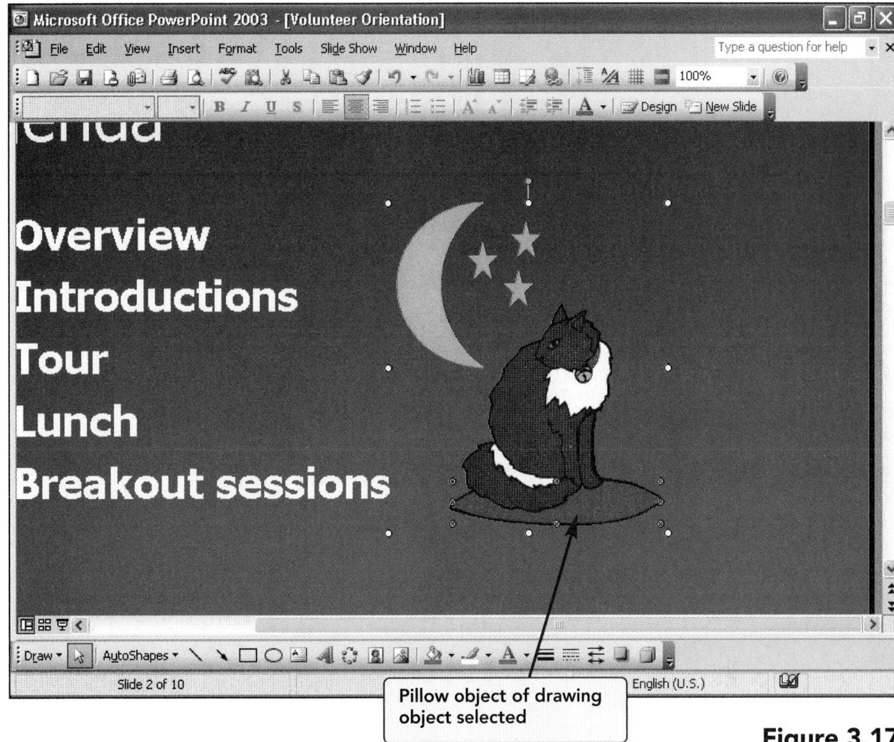


**Figure 3.17**

Once a graphic has been converted to a drawing object, the individual parts can be selected and edited just as you would an individual drawing object that you created using the Drawing features. You will change the fill color of the selected pillow and then the color of the collar to match.

**2** **Open the Fill Color drop-down list and select any color from the color scheme palette.**

**Select the collar and change the color to the same color as the pillow.**

*Your screen should be similar to Figure 3.18*

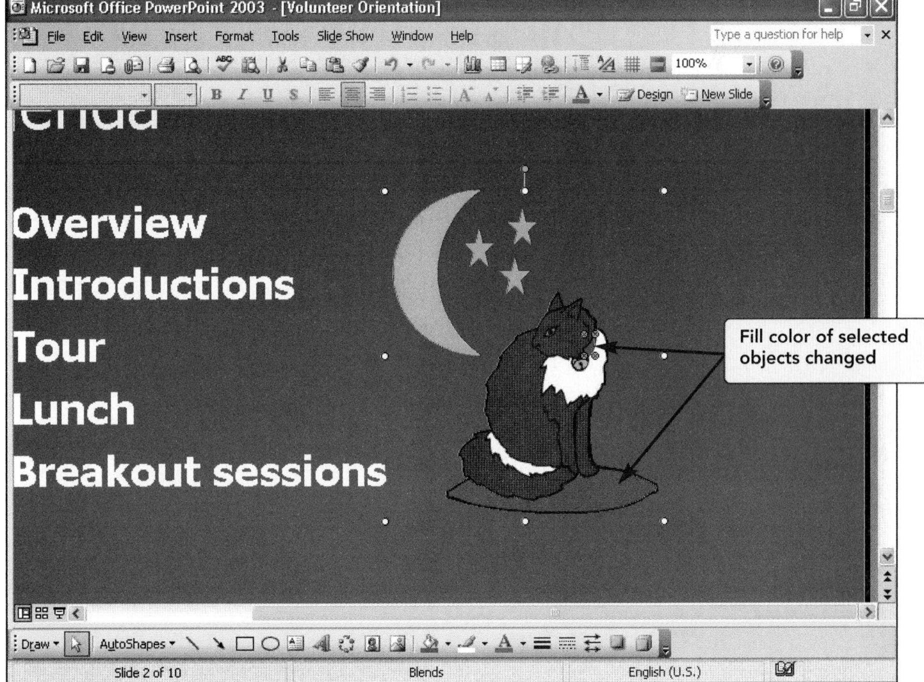


**Figure 3.18**

The color of the two selected objects within the graphic object has changed to the color you specified.

## Ungrouping an Object

You decide you do not like the moon and stars and you want to delete them. To delete individual objects from a graphic, you must first ungroup the object.

**1** **Right-click on the graphic and select Grouping/Ungroup from the shortcut menu.**

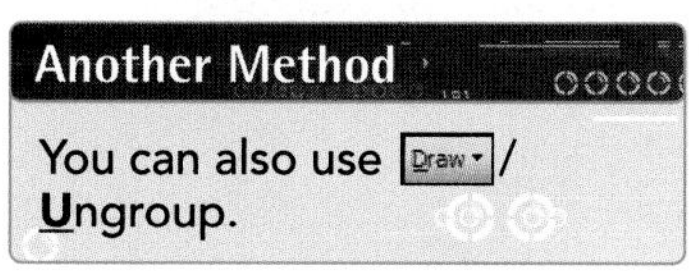


*Your screen should be similar to Figure 3.19*

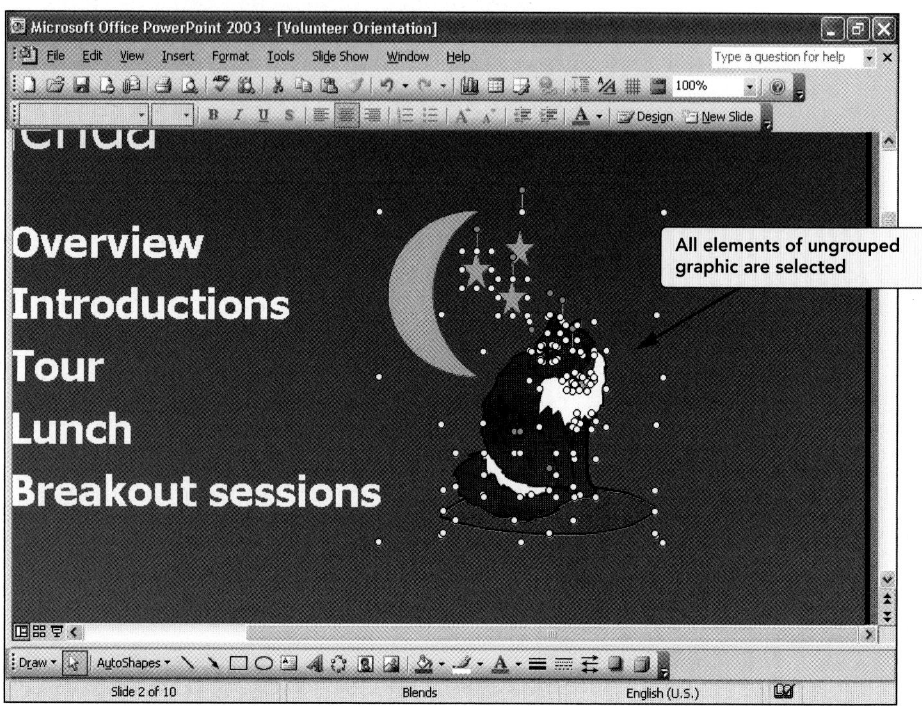


**Figure 3.19**

The graphic has been ungrouped and all the elements in the graphic are selected.

## Deleting a Graphic Element

You first need to deselect all the elements, and then select only the elements in the graphic object you want to delete. Clicking outside the selected object will deselect all elements. Then to select a specific object, you can click anywhere on a filled object or click on the border of an unfilled object.

1 • **Click anywhere outside the graphic to deselect all the elements.**

• **Click on the moon to select the object.**

• **Press Delete.**

• **In the same manner, delete the stars.**

**Additional Information**

Select multiple objects by holding down Ctrl while clicking on each object.

*Your screen should be similar to Figure 3.20*

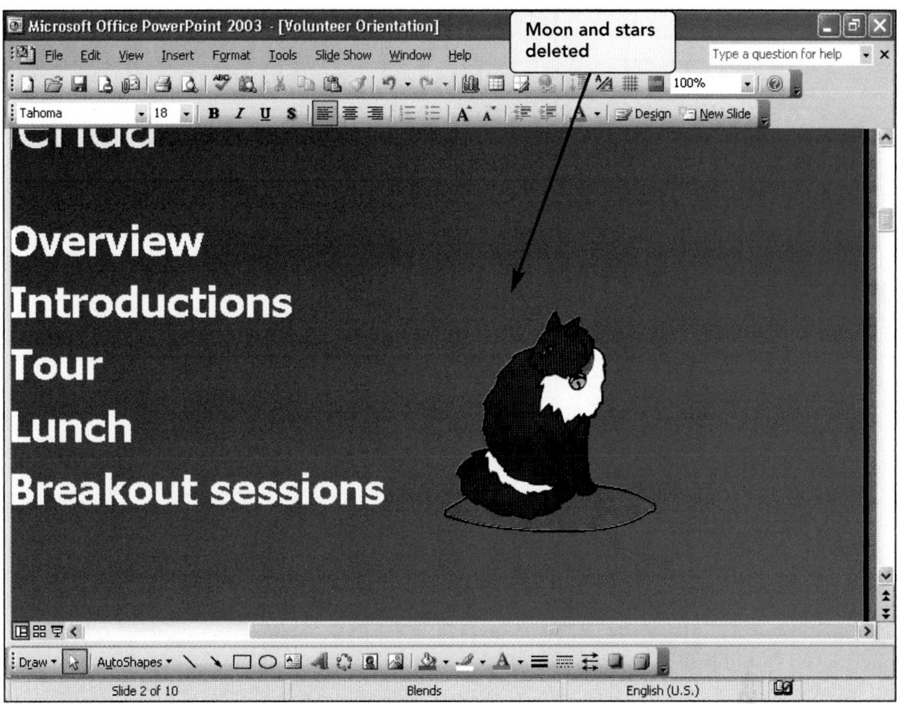


**Additional Information**

The graphic was made by starting with a black outline of the entire image filled with black, and then overlaying colored pieces to construct the cat. Because of this construction, certain areas of the graphic cannot be deleted.

**Additional Information**

The graphic does not need to be ungrouped to select and modify separate parts using features on the Drawing toolbar.

The moon and stars are deleted.

## Regrouping Objects

You think the graphic looks a lot better now. Next you will add a graphic of a dog to the slide and combine it with the cat graphic. You will regroup the parts of the cat graphic again and then insert the picture of the dog.

**1**

- **Click near the cat to select the entire cat graphic.**
- **Choose Grouping/ Regroup from the shortcut menu.**

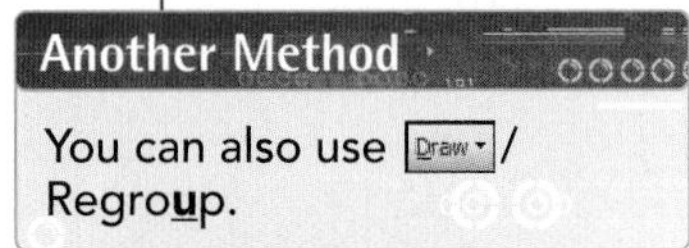

Another Method
You can also use Draw/ Regroup.


- **Open the Zoom drop-down menu and choose Fit.**
- **Insert the picture** pp03_Dog **from your data file location.**
- **Move and size the object as in Figure 3.21.**

*Your screen should be similar to Figure 3.21*

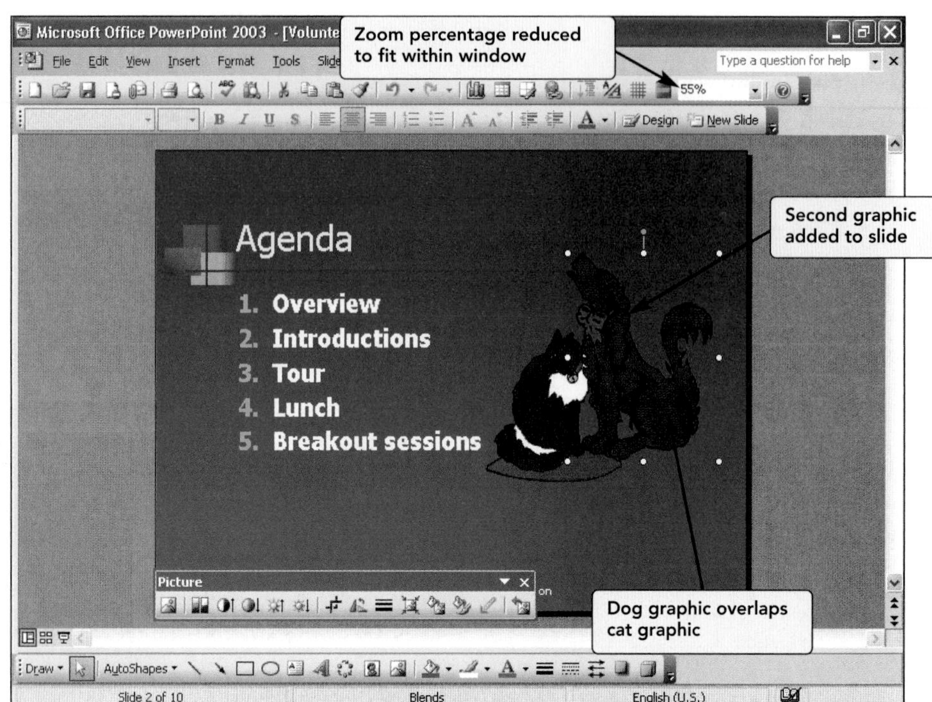


**Figure 3.21**

Did you notice when you moved the cat object, that all the objects in the group were identified and moved as a group? In contrast, when you moved and sized the dog object, because it has not been converted to a drawing object yet, separate parts were not identified as it was manipulated.

## Changing the Stacking Order

Notice the dog graphic overlaps the cat graphic. This is because as each new object is added to a slide, it is added to a separate drawing layer that stacks on top of the previous layer.

Now you want to see if the graphic would look better if the dog object were behind the cat. To change the order of these two objects, you will send the dog object to the back of the stack.

**1**

- **If necessary, select the dog graphic.**
- **Click Draw and choose Order/Send to Back.**
- **Size and position the graphics as in Figure 3.22.**

**Additional Information**

The Bring Forward and Send Backward options move the objects forward or backward in the stack one layer at a time.

*Your screen should be similar to Figure 3.22*

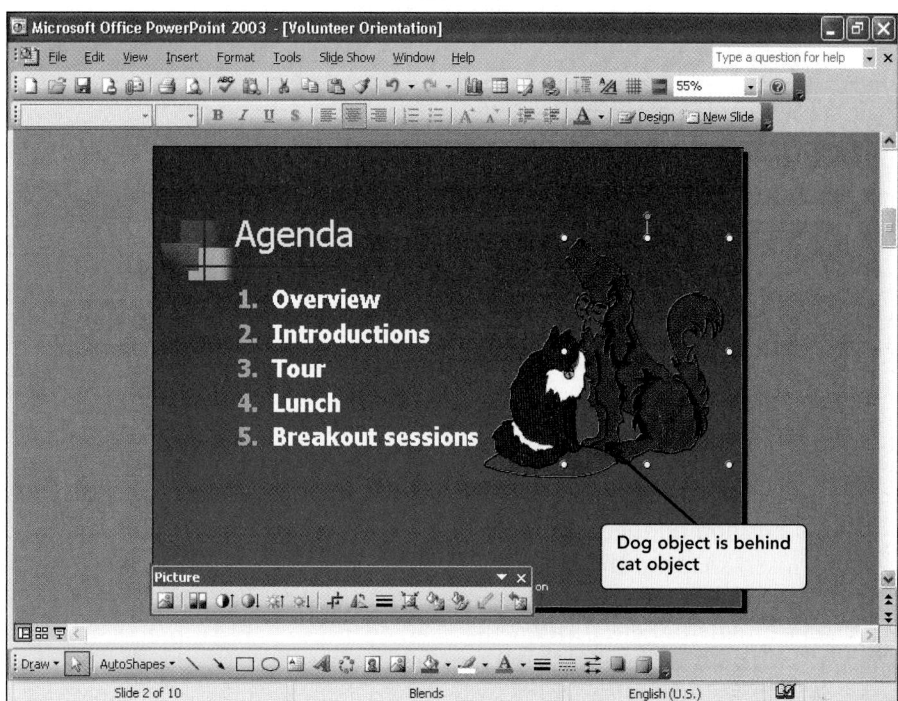


**Figure 3.22**

The dog is now behind the cat.

## Aligning Objects

Next you want to align the dog and cat so that the bottoms of the graphics are even. Although you can position objects on your slides visually by dragging to the approximate location, you can make your slides appear more professional by using tools in PowerPoint to precisely align and position objects.

## Concept 2

### Object Alignment

2 **Object alignment** refers to the position of objects relative to each other by their left, right, top, or bottom edges; or horizontally by their centers or vertically by their middles; or in relation to the entire slide.

There are several methods for aligning objects. You can align objects to a **grid**, a set of intersecting lines that form small squares on the slide. The grid is not displayed by default, but whenever you move, resize, or draw an object, the object's corners automatically "snap" to the nearest intersection of the grid. You can display the grid to help align objects more accurately. You can also snap an object to other shapes so that new objects align themselves with the pre-existing shapes. The grid lines run through the vertical and horizontal edges of other shapes, and the new shape aligns with the closest intersection of that grid.

Another way to align an object is to use a guide. A **guide** is a line, either vertical or horizontal, that you position on the slide. When an object is close to the guide, the object's center or corner (whichever is closer) snaps to the guide.

A third way to align objects is to other objects. For example, you can align the centers or the left edges of two objects. Using this method allows you to precisely align the edges or tops of selected shapes. At least two objects must be selected to align them.

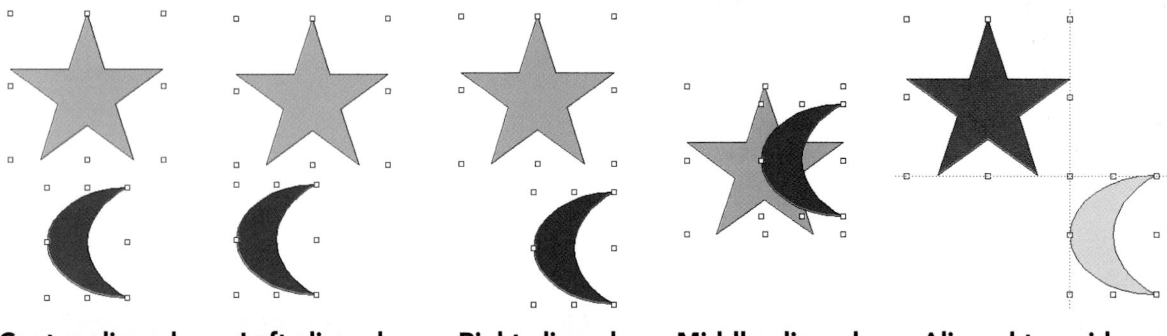

**Center aligned** **Left aligned** **Right aligned** **Middle aligned** **Aligned to guides**

Objects can also be aligned relative to the slide as a whole, such as to the top or side of a slide. Objects can further be arranged or distributed so that they are an equal distance from each other vertically, horizontally, or in relation to the entire slide. You must have at least three objects selected to distribute them.

You will display the slide gridlines and then evenly position the bottoms of the two graphics.

**1** • **Click Show/Hide Grid.**

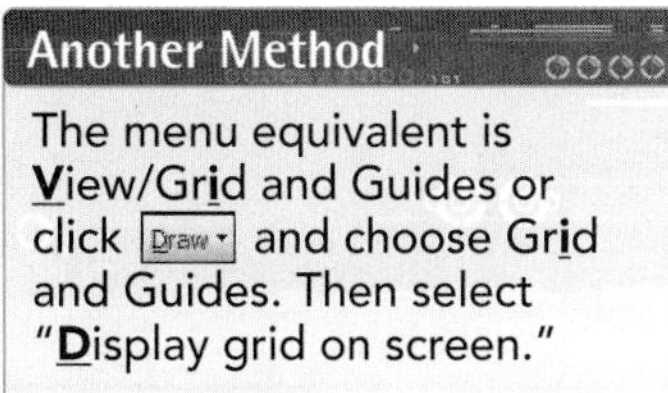

**Another Method**

The menu equivalent is View/Grid and Guides or click Draw and choose Grid and Guides. Then select "Display grid on screen."

*Your screen should be similar to Figure 3.23*

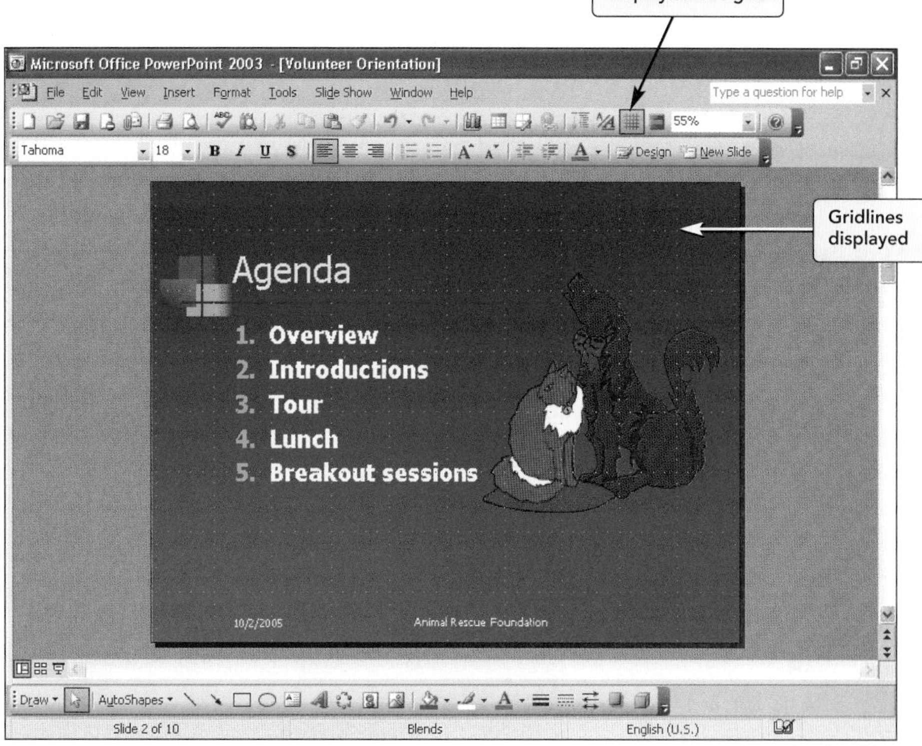


**Figure 3.23**

All slides in the presentation display a grid consisting of a crosshatch pattern of lines. Now you can easily align the bottom of the graphics.

**2** • **Align both graphics evenly with the horizontal gridline that runs below the fifth bulleted item.**

• **Position the dog graphic just to the right of the cat and bring it to the front of the cat.**

**Additional Information**

To override the snap-to settings, hold down Alt as you drag an object.

*Your screen should be similar to Figure 3.24*

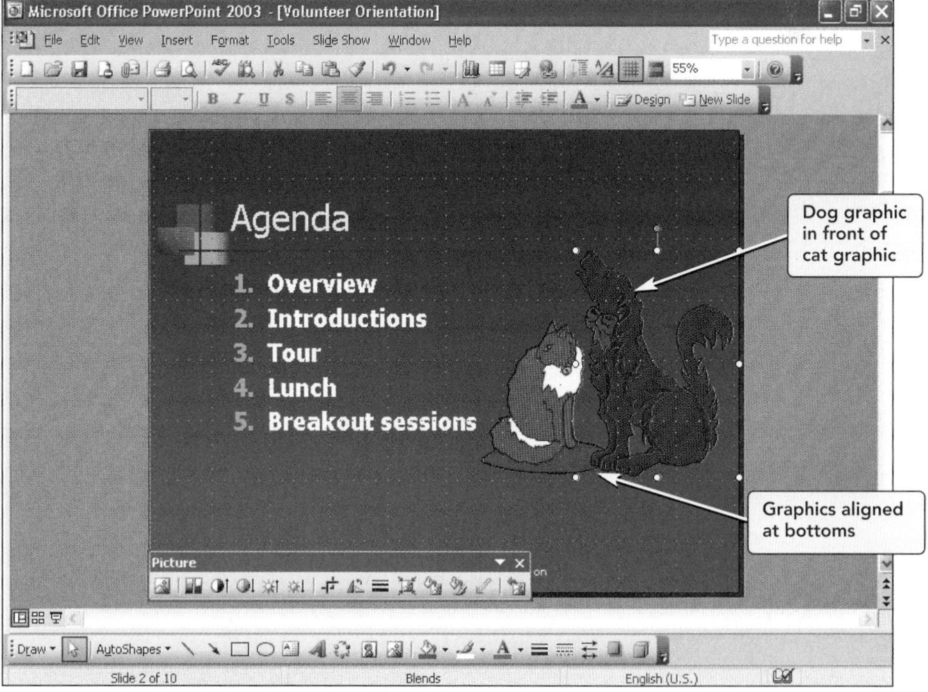


**Figure 3.24**

As you moved the objects, they automatically snapped to the nearest gridline when you released the mouse button.

## Grouping Objects

Now you want to combine the two graphics into one by grouping them, and then you will size them appropriately on the slide.

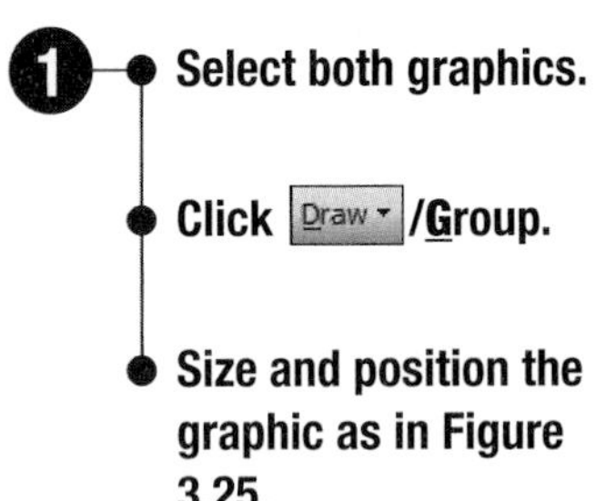

**1**

- **Select both graphics.**
- **Click Draw/Group.**
- **Size and position the graphic as in Figure 3.25.**

*Your screen should be similar to Figure 3.25*

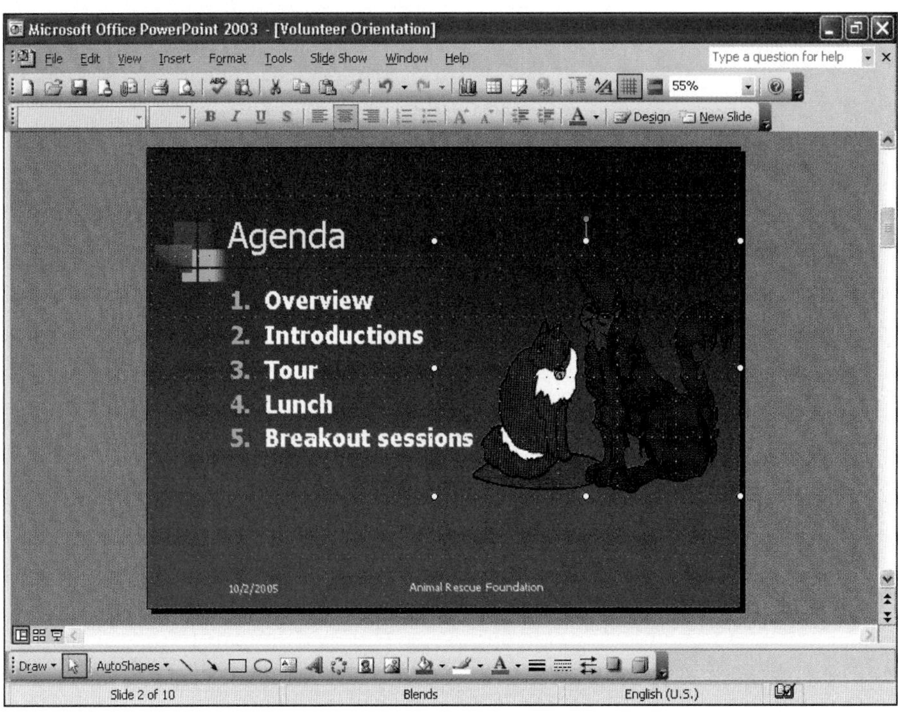


**Figure 3.25**

> **Additional Information**
>
> To select an object within a grouped object, select the group first, then click on the object you want to select.

Because the objects are grouped, they size and move as a single object. You could also change features associated with all objects in the group at once, such as changing the fill or line color of all objects. Even when objects are grouped, you can still select an object within a group and modify it individually without ungrouping the object.

## Wrapping Text in an Object

Below the graphic, you decide to add a banner that welcomes the volunteers.

**1**

- **Create a Curved Down Ribbon AutoShape banner below the graphic as shown in Figure 3.26.**
- **Change the fill color to gold.**
- **Right-click on the object and choose Add Text from the shortcut menu.**
- **Type We're Glad You're Here!.**
- **Change the font color to the same color as the pillow and apply bold.**
- **Click outside the AutoShape to turn off text editing.**

*Your screen should be similar to Figure 3.26*

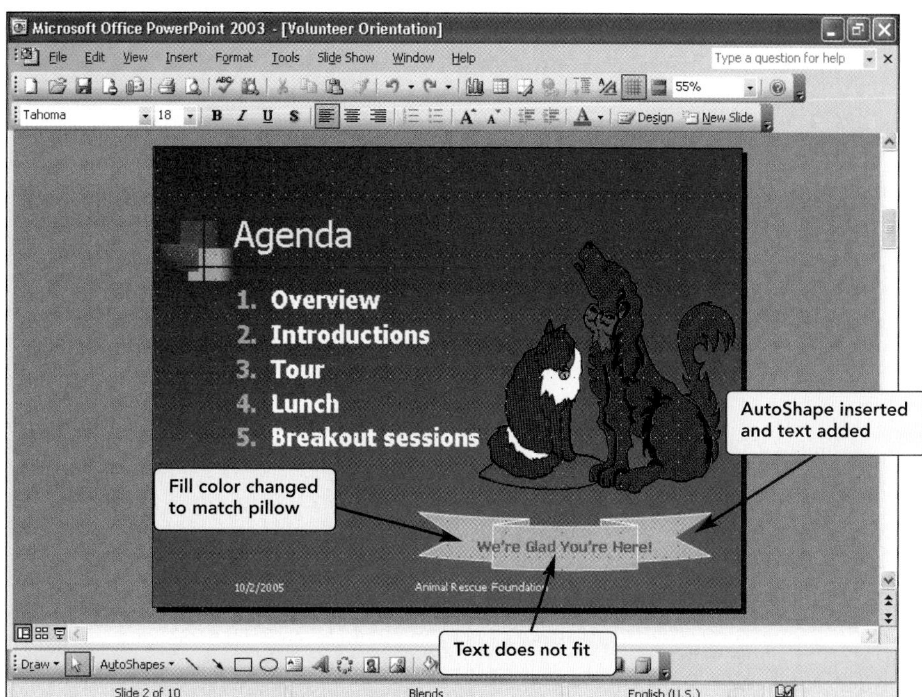


**Figure 3.26**

Notice that the text does not fit inside the center of the graphic. Although you could manually increase the size of the banner to fit the text, you would rather wrap the text in the AutoShape and then resize the banner to fit the text.

**2** — Choose Format AutoShape from the object's shortcut menu.

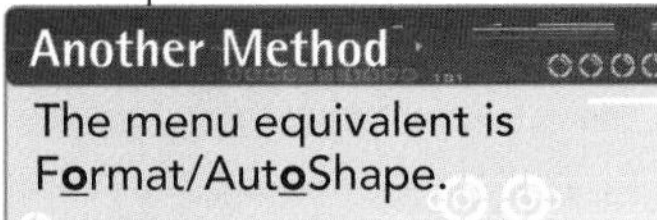

**Another Method**

The menu equivalent is Format/AutoShape.

- Open the Text Box tab.
- Select Word wrap text in AutoShape.
- Select Resize AutoShape to fit text.
- Click OK.
- Size, position, and rotate the AutoShape as shown in Figure 3.27.
- Move the AutoShape behind the animal graphic object.

*Your screen should be similar to Figure 3.27*

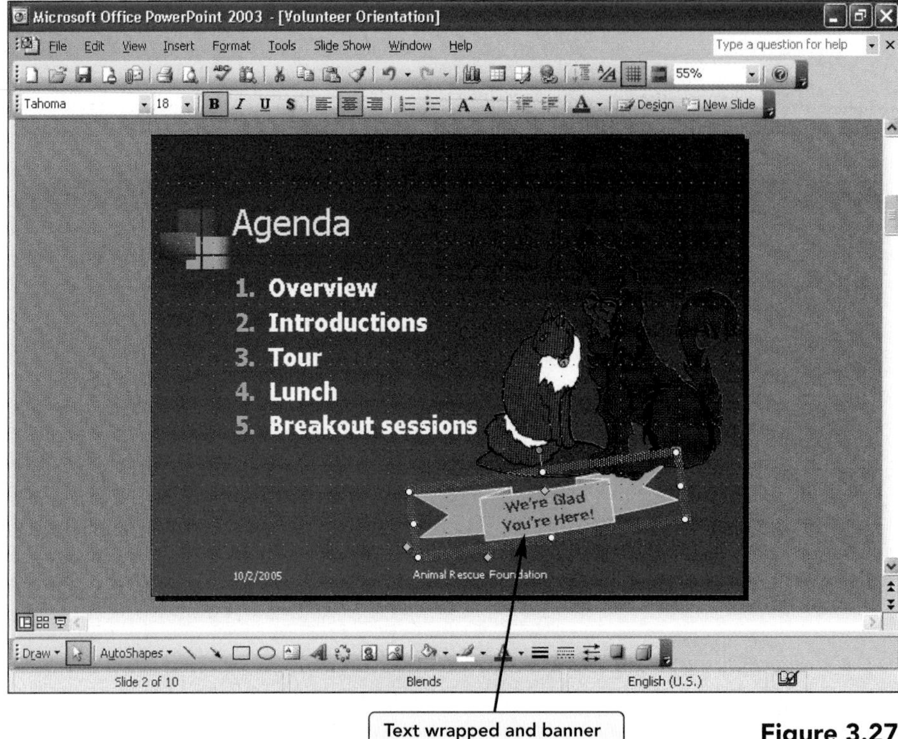


**Figure 3.27**

The text wraps to a second line and the size of the AutoShape has adjusted to fully display the two lines of text.

## Centering Objects

Next you want to center the banner below the graphic. You will align the centers of the two objects and then group them into one object.

**1**

- **Select both the banner and the animal graphic.**
- **Click Draw and choose Align or Distribute/Align Center.**

**Having Trouble?**

Make sure the Relative to Slide option is not selected. If it is, using Align Center will align the object with the center of the slide, not the other object.

- **Group the two objects together.**
- **Position the grouped object as in figure 3.28.**
- **Click on the slide to deselect the grouped object.**
- **Click [gridlines button] to turn off the display of gridlines.**
- **Save the presentation.**

*Your screen should be similar to Figure 3.28*

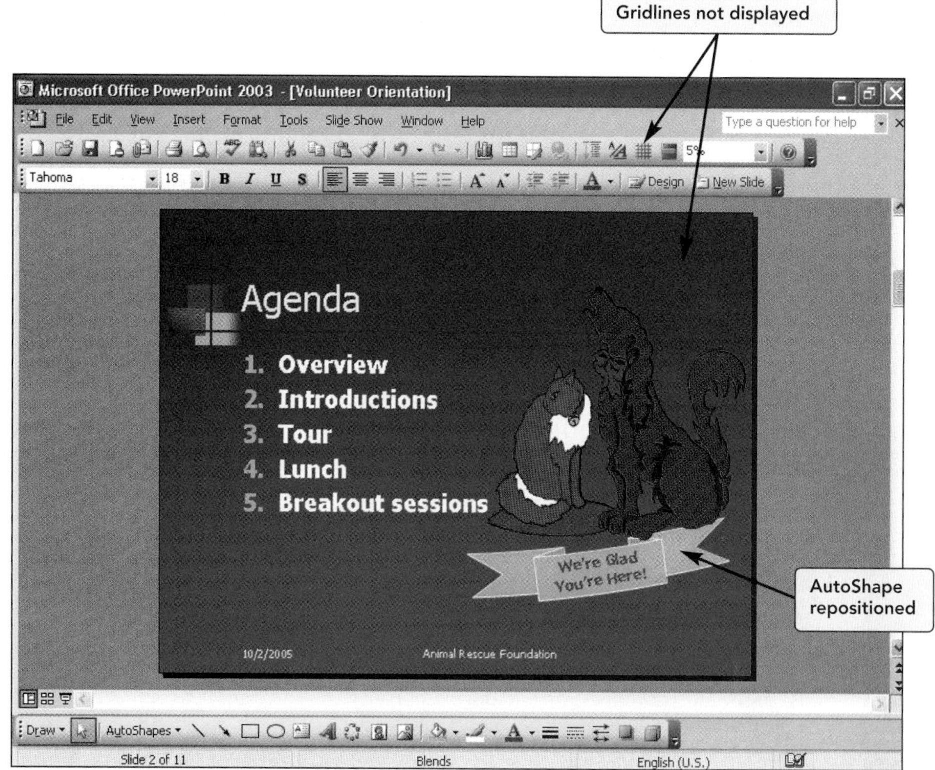


**Figure 3.28**

## Creating a Chart Slide

The next change you want to make is to show the adoption success rate data in slide 5 as a chart rather than a table.

### Concept 3

**Chart**

3 A **chart**, also called a **graph**, is a visual representation of numeric data. When you are presenting data to an audience, they will grasp the impact of your data more quickly if you present it as a chart. PowerPoint 2003 includes a separate program, Microsoft Graph, designed to help you create 14 types of charts with many different formats for each type.

Each type of chart represents the data differently and has a different purpose. It is important to select the type of chart that will provide the right emphasis to support your presentations. The basic chart types are described below.

| Type of Chart | Description |
|---|---|
| **Area** | Shows the relative importance of a value over time by emphasizing the area under the curve created by each data series. |
| **Bar** | Displays categories vertically and values horizontally, placing more emphasis on comparisons and less on time. Stacked-bar charts show the relationship of individual items to a whole by stacking bars on top of one another. |
| **Column** | Similar to a bar chart, except categories are organized horizontally and values vertically. Shows data changes over time or comparison among items. |
| **Line** | Shows changes in data over time, emphasizing time and rate of change rather than the amount of change. |
| **Pie** | Shows the relationship of each value in a data series to the series as a whole. Each slice of the pie represents a single value in a data series. |

Most charts are made up of several basic parts as identified and described below.

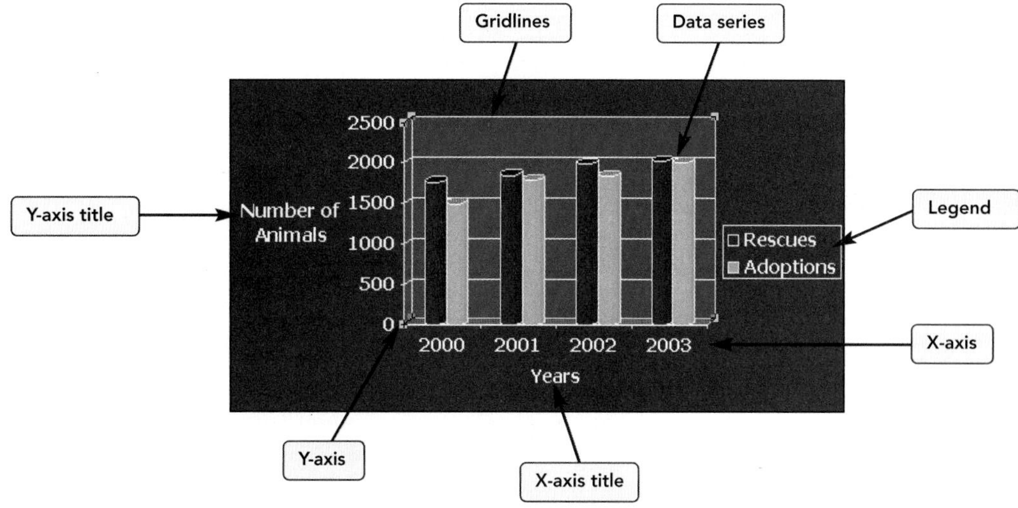


| Part | Description |
|---|---|
| **X axis** | The bottom boundary of the chart, also called the **category axis**, is used to label the data being charted; the label may be, for example, a point in time or a category. |
| **Y axis** | The left boundary of the chart, also called the **value axis**, is a numbered scale whose numbers are determined by the data used in the chart. Each line or bar in a chart represents a data value. In pie charts there are no axes. Instead, the data that is charted is displayed as slices in a circle or pie. |
| **Data Series** | Each group of related data that is plotted in a chart. |
| **Legend** | A box containing a brief description identifying the patterns or colors assigned to the data series in a chart. |
| **Titles** | Descriptive text used to explain the contents of the chart. |

You will create the chart in a new slide following the slide containing the table of data on success rates. PowerPoint includes a special slide layout for charts which contains a placeholder that opens the Graph application.

**1**

- **Switch to Slide Sorter view.**
- **Insert a new slide in Title and Chart slide layout after slide 6.**

> **Another Method**
> You can also use Insert/Chart or click [chart button] to add a chart object to a slide.

- **Double-click on slide 7.**
- **Choose View/Normal (Restore Panes).**
- **If necessary, display the Slides tab.**

*Your screen should be similar to Figure 3.29*

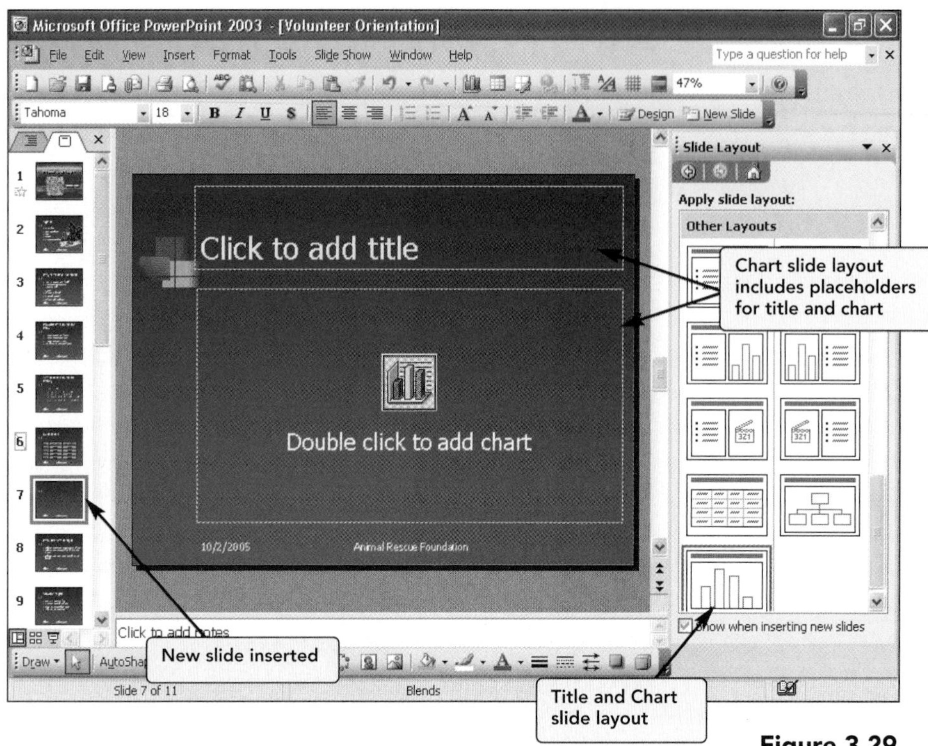


Figure 3.29

## Copying Data to the Office Clipboard

The chart slide layout includes a placeholder for the title and another placeholder for the chart. When you double-click on the chart placeholder, the Microsoft Graph application will open and you will be asked to enter the data you want to chart. Because this data is already contained in the table in slide 6, you will copy the data from the table into the chart. You will also copy the title text from slide 6 into the chart slide. You could copy and paste the selections one after the other, or you can use the Office Clipboard to collect multiple items and paste them as needed.

## Concept 4

### Collect and Paste

4 The **collect and paste** feature is used to store multiple copied items in the Office Clipboard and then paste one or more of the items into another location or document. For example, you could copy a chart from Excel and a paragraph from Word, then switch to PowerPoint and copy the two stored items into a slide in one easy step. This saves you from having to switch back and forth between documents and applications multiple times.

The Office Clipboard and the system Clipboard are similar, but separate, features. The major difference is that the Office Clipboard can hold up to 24 items, whereas the system Clipboard holds only a single item. The last item you copy to the Office Clipboard is always copied to the system Clipboard. When you use the Office Clipboard, you can select from the stored items to paste in any order.

The Office Clipboard is available in all Office 2003 applications, and is accessed through the Clipboard task pane. Once the Clipboard task pane is opened, it is available for use in any program, including non-Office programs. In some programs where the Cut, Copy, and Paste commands are not available, or in non-Office programs, the Clipboard task pane is not visible but it is still operational. You can copy from any program that provides copy and cut capabilities, but you can only paste into Word, Excel, Access, PowerPoint, and Outlook.

First you will copy the slide title text from slide 6 to the Office Clipboard.

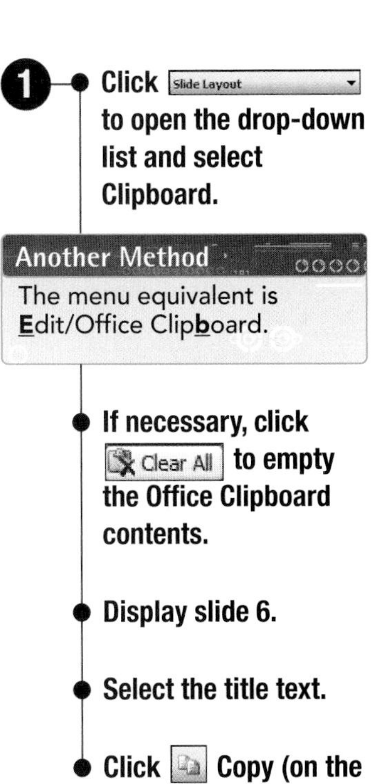

Click Slide Layout to open the drop-down list and select Clipboard.
Another Method
The menu equivalent is Edit/Office Clipboard.
If necessary, click Clear All to empty the Office Clipboard contents.
Display slide 6.
Select the title text.
Click


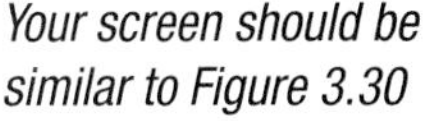


*Your screen should be similar to Figure 3.30*

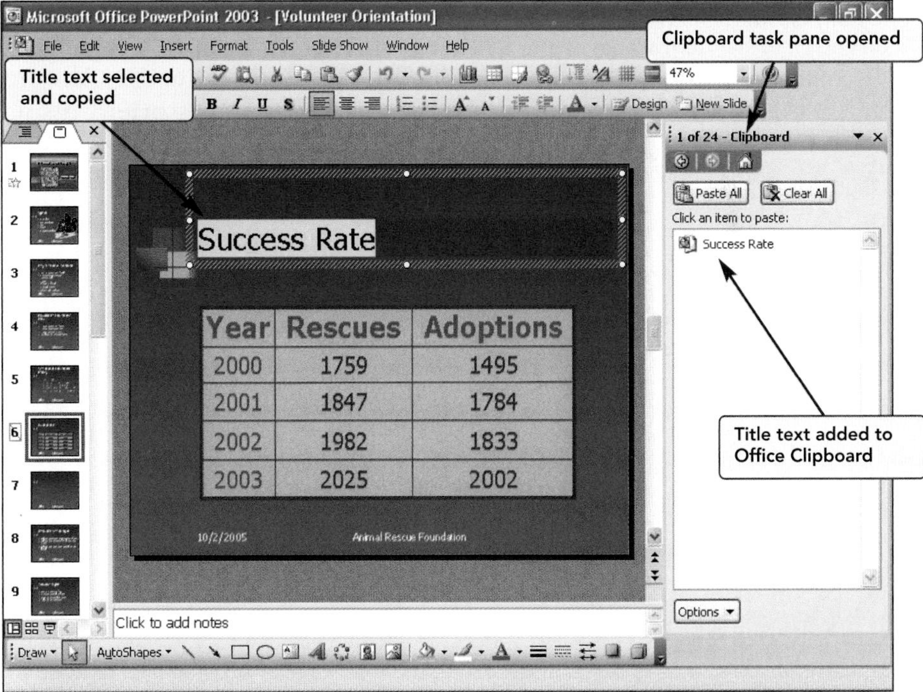


**Figure 3.30**

The Clipboard task pane displays a PowerPoint icon representing the copied item and the first few lines of the copied selection. Next you will copy the contents of the table into the Office Clipboard. As items are copied, they are added sequentially to the Office Clipboard with the last copied item at the top of the list.

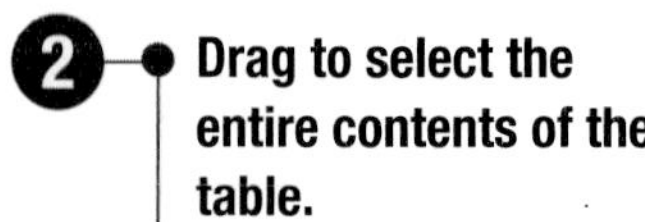

**2** **Drag to select the entire contents of the table.**

**Click Copy.**

*Your screen should be similar to Figure 3.31*

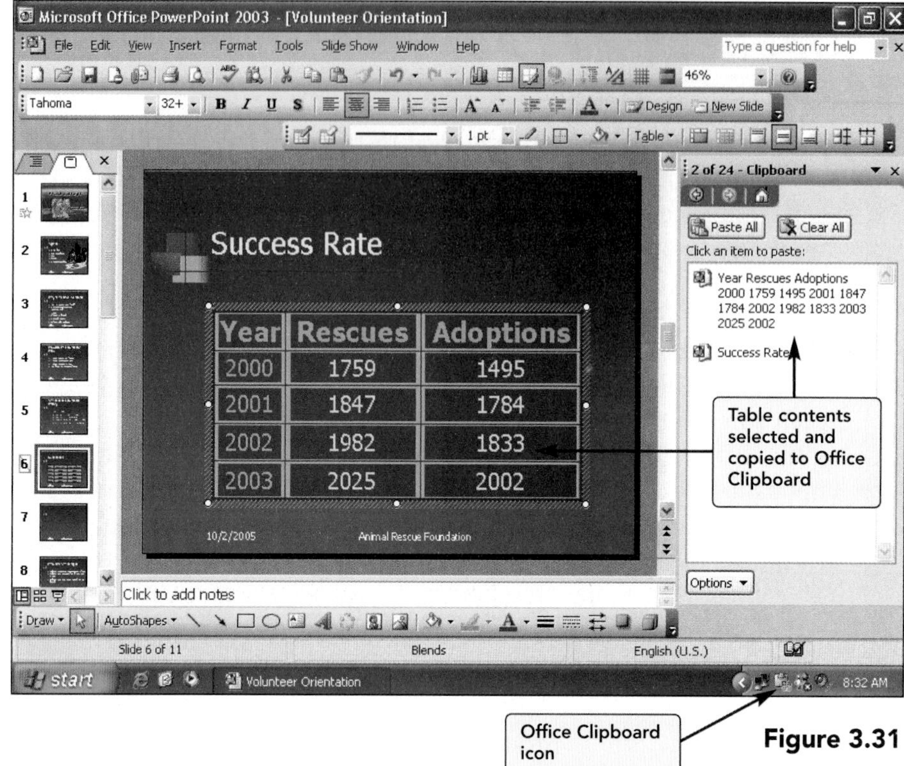


**Figure 3.31**

**Additional Information**

The Office Clipboard is automatically activated if you copy or cut two different items consecutively in the same program; if you copy one item, paste the item and then copy another item in the same program; or if you copy one item twice in succession.

The Office Clipboard now contains two PowerPoint document icons, one for each copied item. The Office Clipboard icon appears in the taskbar to show that the Clipboard is active. Also, as the selection is copied, the taskbar briefly displays a ScreenTip indicating that 1 out of a possible 24 items was collected.

**1 of 24 - Clipboard**
Item collected.

## Specifying the Chart Data

Now you are ready to start the Microsoft Graph application and use the table data to create the chart.

**1**

- **Display slide 7.**
- **Close the Tabs pane.**
- **Double-click [chart icon] in the placeholder.**
- **If necessary, display the toolbar on two rows.**

*Your screen should be similar to Figure 3.32*

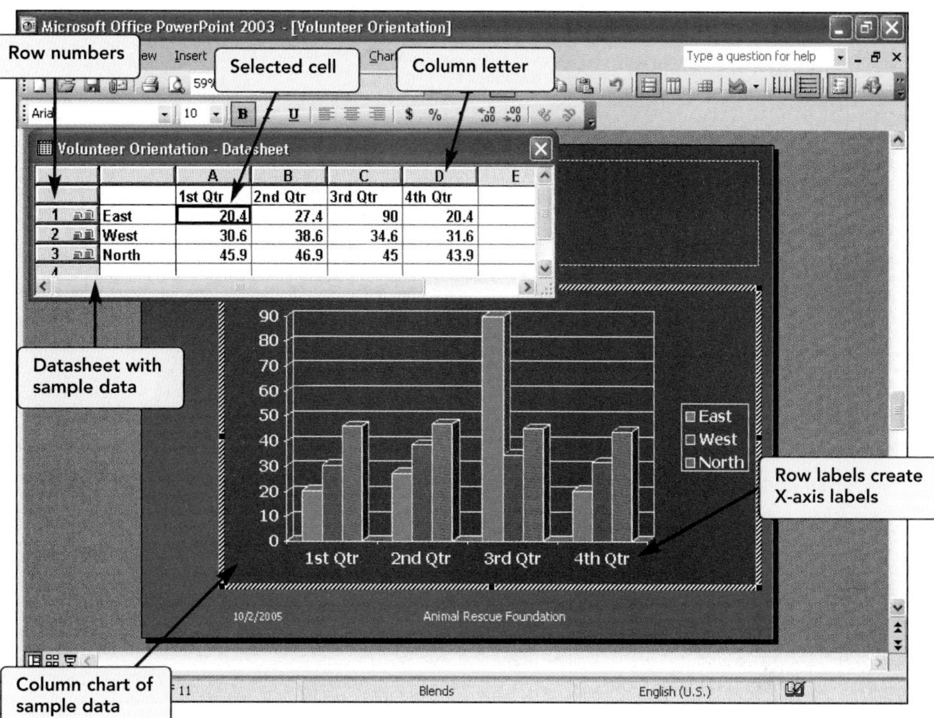


**Figure 3.32**

The Microsoft Graph program is activated and a column chart using the sample data from the datasheet is displayed in the slide. In addition, a datasheet containing sample data is displayed in the Datasheet window. A **datasheet** is a table consisting of rows and columns. As in a table, the intersection of a row and column creates a cell in which text or data is entered. Notice that the datasheet displays the column letters A through E and row numbers 1 through 4. Each cell has a unique name consisting of a column letter followed by a row number. For example, cell A1 is the intersection of column A and row 1. The cell that is surrounded by the border is the selected cell and is the cell you can work in.

In addition to displaying sample data, the datasheet also contains placeholders for the column labels, which are used as the legend in the chart, and for the row labels, which are used as X-axis labels.

You need to replace the sample data in the datasheet with the data you copied from slide 6. Unfortunately, because the Graph application is running, the Clipboard task pane is not displayed. However, because the table data was the last item copied to the Clipboard, you can simply click [Paste icon] Paste in the Standard toolbar to insert the last copied item from the system Clipboard into the datasheet.

**2** • **Click in the gray cell in the top left corner of the Datasheet window to select the entire datasheet.**

• **Click [Paste icon] Paste.**

• **Click [OK] in response to the advisory dialog box.**

*Your screen should be similar to Figure 3.33*

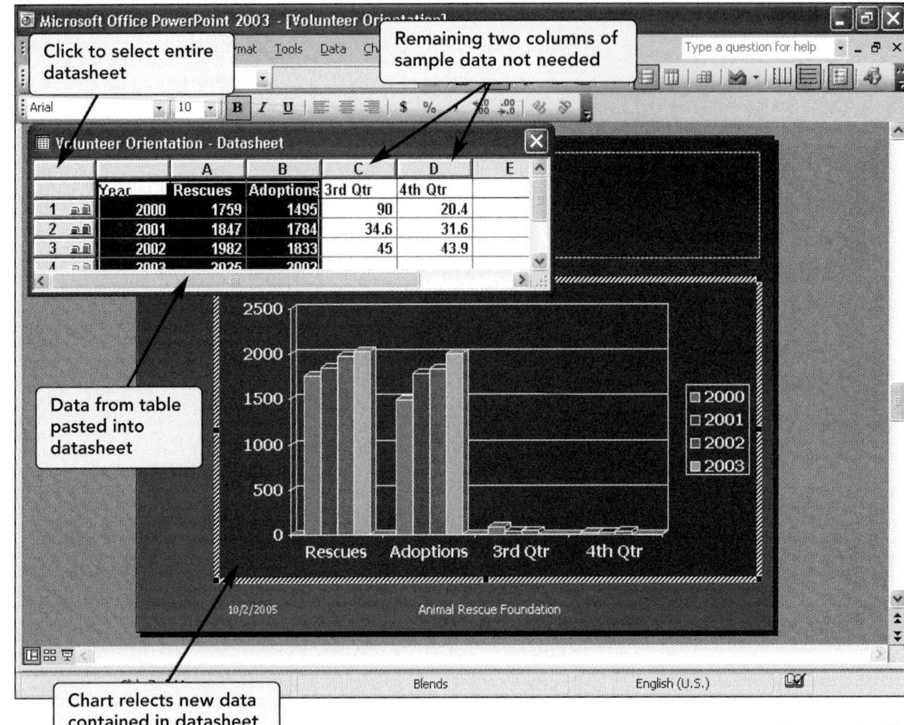


Figure 3.33

The datasheet is updated and displays the data from the table. The chart also reflects the change in data. Finally, you need to remove the remaining two columns of sample data.

**3** • **Drag over the column letters C and D to select both columns.**

• **Press Delete.**

*Your screen should be similar to Figure 3.34*

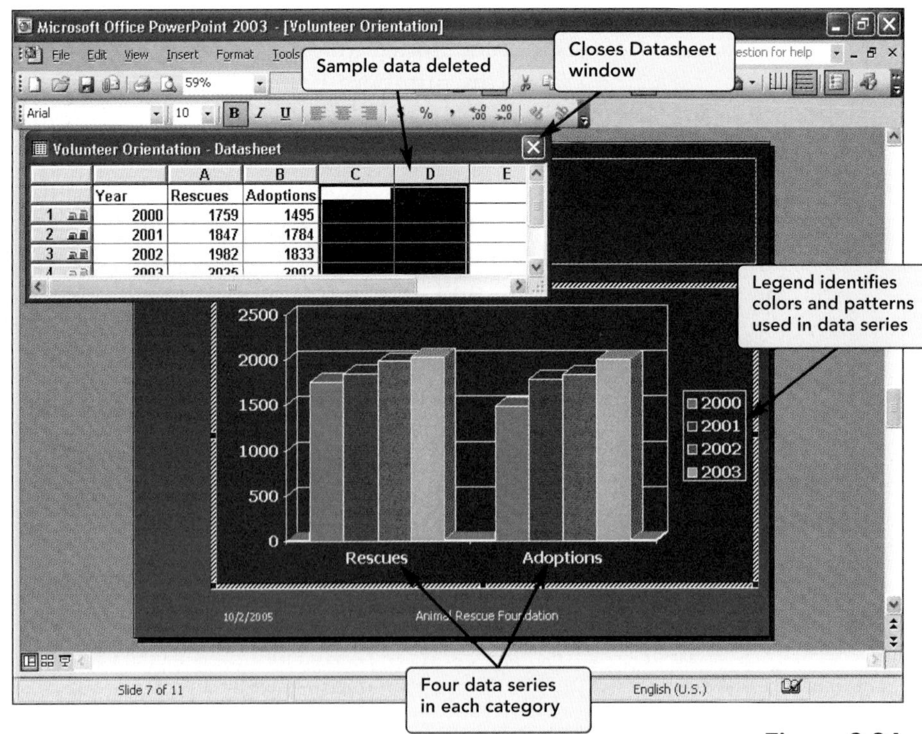


Figure 3.34

Each data series has a unique color or pattern assigned to it to identify the different series. The legend identifies the color or pattern associated with each data series. As you can see, the values and text in the chart are directly linked to the datasheet, and any changes you make in the datasheet are automatically reflected in the chart.

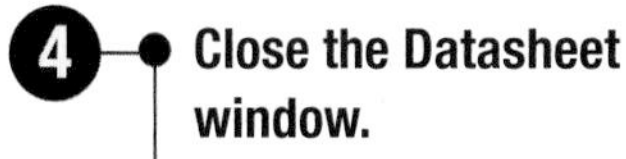

**4 Close the Datasheet window.**

Another Method
You can also click View Datasheet to hide and display the Datasheet window at any time.


**Click on the slide outside the chart.**

*Your screen should be similar to Figure 3.35*

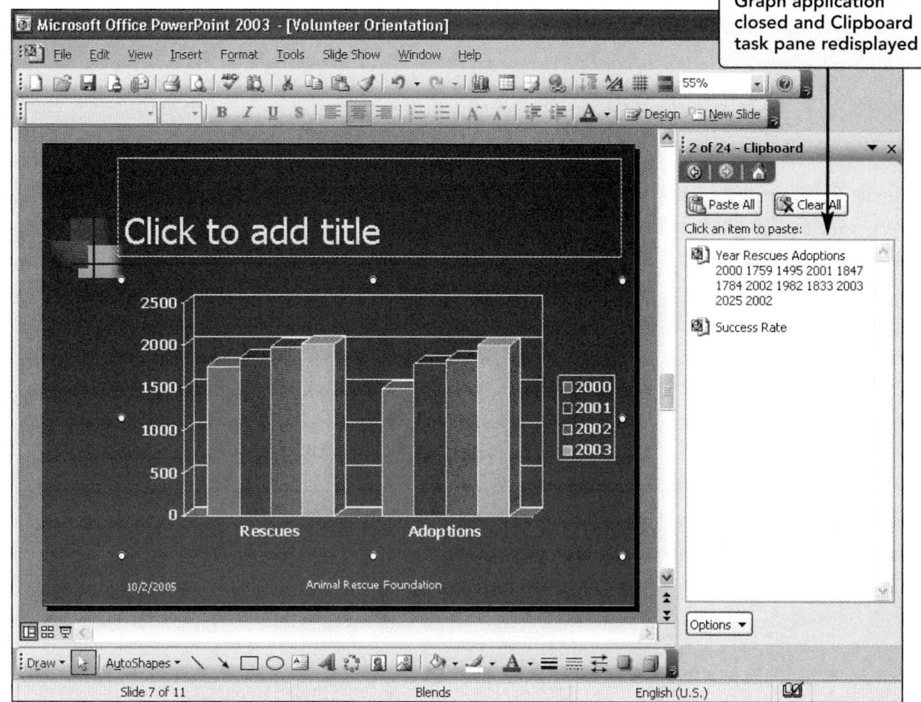


**Figure 3.35**

The Graph application is closed, and because the PowerPoint application is active again, the Office Clipboard task pane is displayed. Before modifying the chart, you will copy the title from the Office Clipboard into the slide.

**5 Click in the chart title placeholder.**

**Click on the Success Rate icon in the Clipboard task pane.**

**Click Clear All to clear the contents of the Office Clipboard.**

**Close the Clipboard task pane.**

*Your screen should be similar to Figure 3.36*

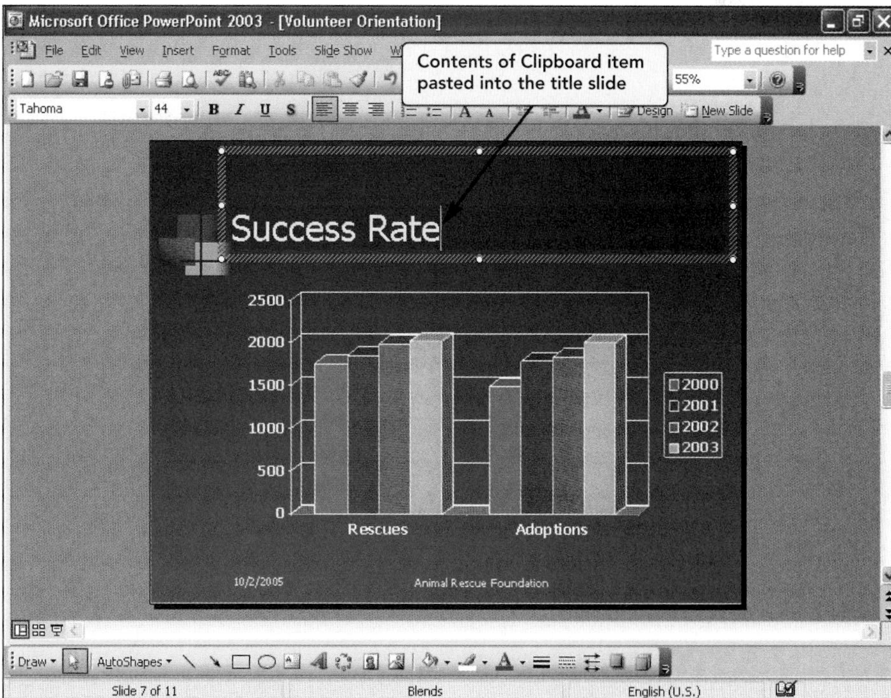


**Figure 3.36**

The contents of the first copied item are pasted from the Office Clipboard into the title of the slide.

## Modifying Chart Data

As you look at the chart, you decide you want to change it so that the data is displayed based on the columns of data (years), not the rows of data (Rescue and Adoption categories), which is the default. To modify the chart, you need to activate the Graph application again. Then you can use the features on the Graph menu and toolbar to edit the chart.

**1** **Double-click the chart object to open it for editing.**

**Another Method**

You can also use Chart Object/Edit from the chart objects shortcut menu.

**Click By Column.**

**Another Method**

The menu equivalent is Data/Series in Columns.

*Your screen should be similar to Figure 3.37*

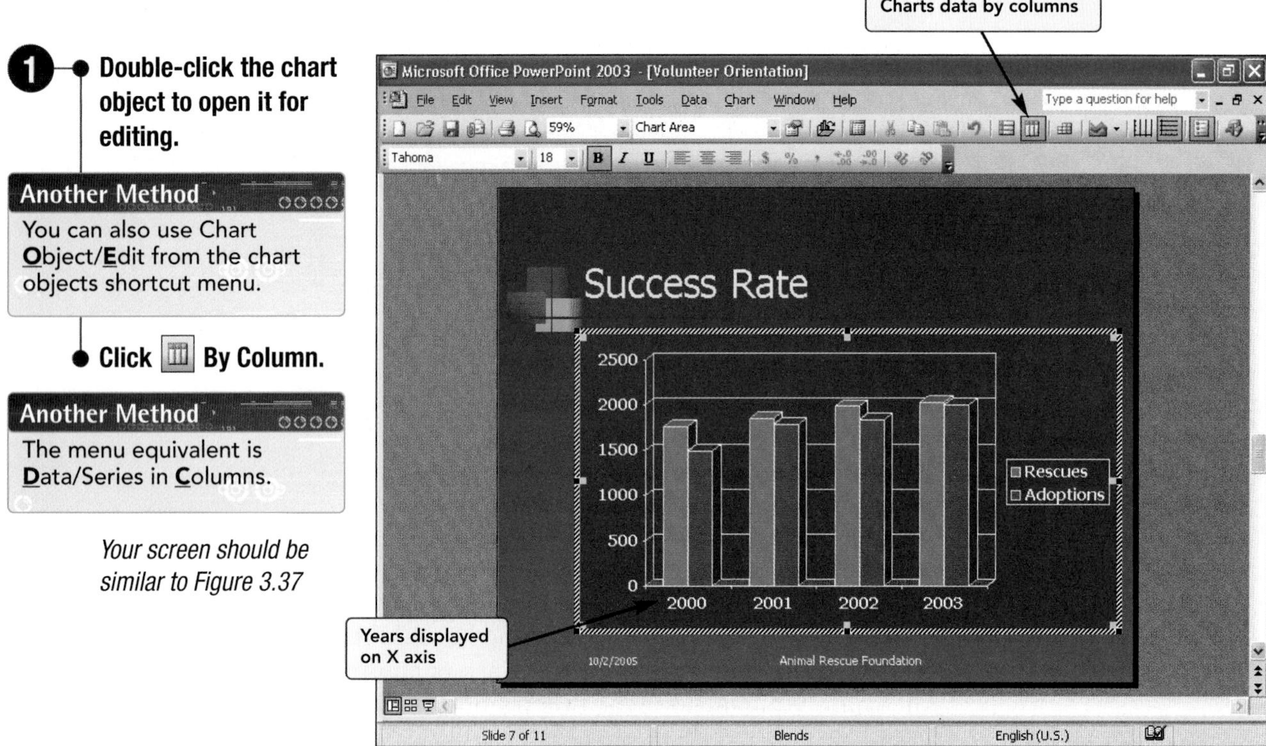


**Figure 3.37**

The years are now displayed along the X axis. The chart now shows the increasing success rate for adoptions and rescues over time more clearly.

## Adding Axis Titles

Next you want to add labels along the axes to clarify the information in the chart.

- **Choose Chart/Chart Options.**
- **If necessary, open the Titles tab.**

*Your screen should be similar to Figure 3.38*

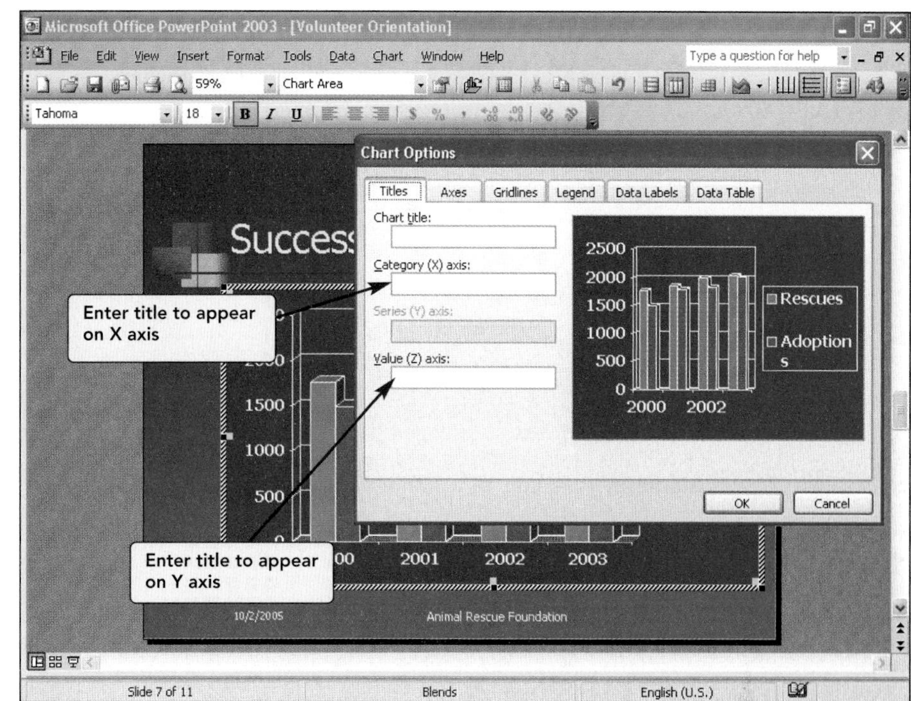


**Figure 3.38**

The Chart Options dialog box is used to add features to a chart, including titles, legends, and gridlines, that make it easier to understand the data in the chart. You will add titles along the two axis lines.

**2**

- **Type Years in the Category (X) Axis text box.**
- **Type Number of Animals in the Value (Z) Axis text box.**

**Additional Information**

Because this is a three-dimensional chart, a Z axis is used to display the values.

- **Click OK.**

*Your screen should be similar to Figure 3.39*

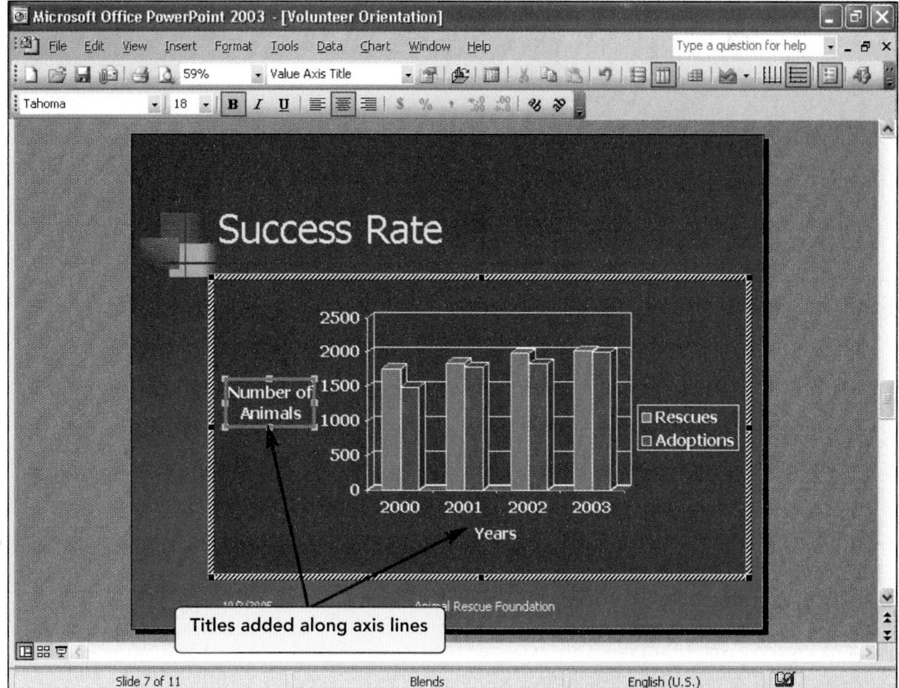


**Figure 3.39**

The labels you entered appear along the appropriate axes.

## Changing Chart Formats

Next you want to change the color and appearance of the data series to give them more visual interest.

1 **Click on any one of the Adoptions (purple) columns to select all the columns for that data series.**

**Click Format Data Series.**

**Another Method**

The menu equivalent is Format/Selected Data Series, and the keyboard equivalent is Ctrl + 1. You can also double-click the chart element or choose Format Data Series from the shortcut menu.

**If necessary, open the Patterns tab.**

*Your screen should be similar to Figure 3.40*

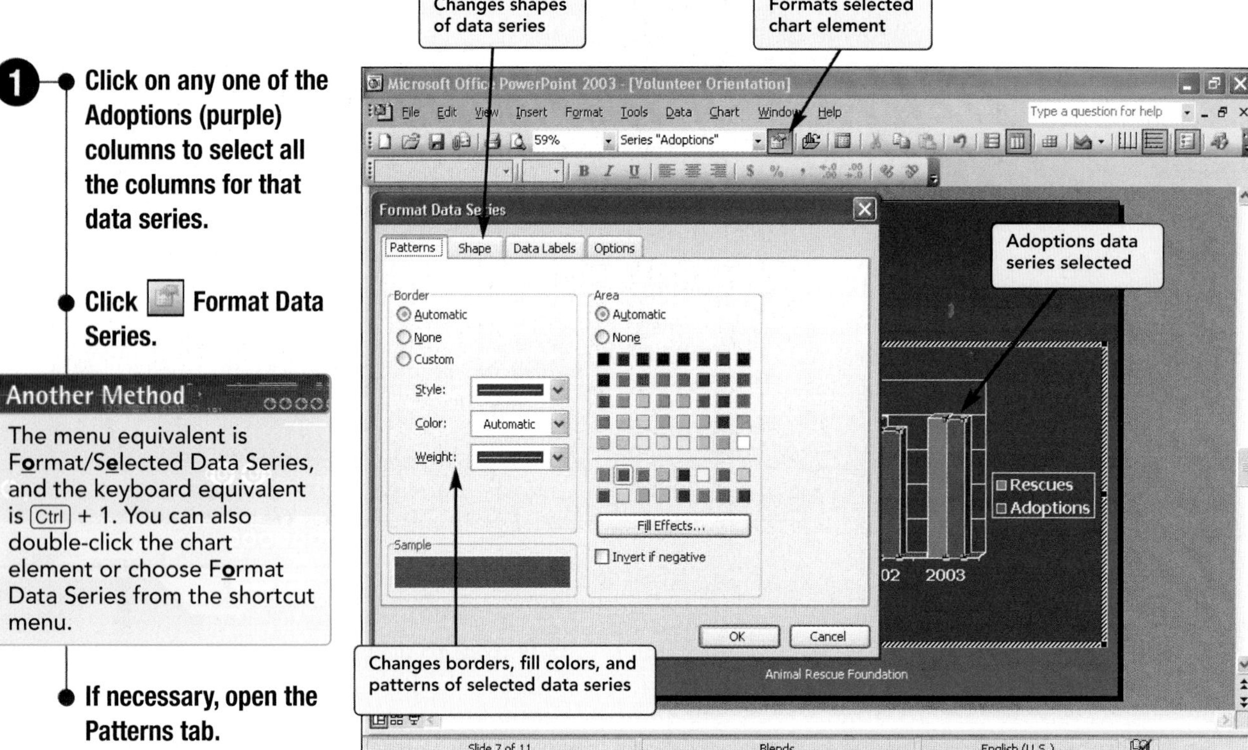


Figure 3.40

The Format Data Series dialog box is used to modify the appearance of the selected data series. The default chart colors are colors associated with the presentation design template. You want to change the color and shape of the bars. From the Patterns tab, you can select different borders and fill colors and patterns. The Shape tab is used to select different chart series shapes. You will change the color to gold and the shape to a cylinder.

**2** - **From the Area color palette, select a dark gold color.**
- **Open the Shape tab.**
- **Select the cylinder shape, 4.**
- **Click OK.**
- **Deselect the data series.**

*Your screen should be similar to Figure 3.41*

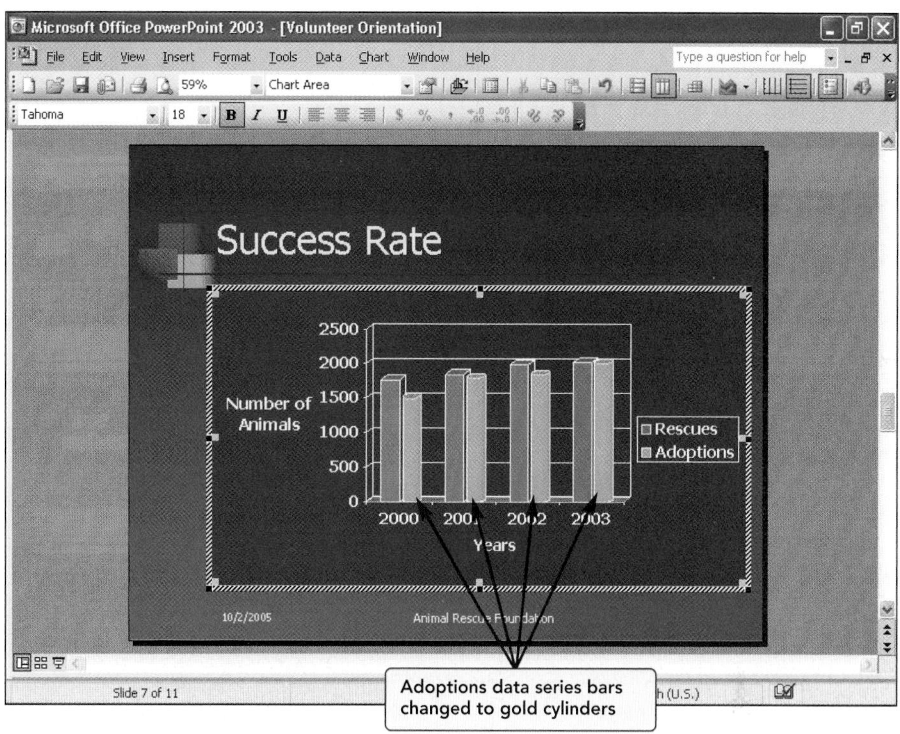


**Figure 3.41**

### Additional Information

You can also change other elements of the chart, such as the background and text color, gridlines, and scale.

The four Adoptions data series bars have changed to a dark gold cylinder shape.

**3** - **Change the Rescues data series in the same way, using a color of your choice and the same cylinder shape.**

*Your screen should be similar to Figure 3.42*

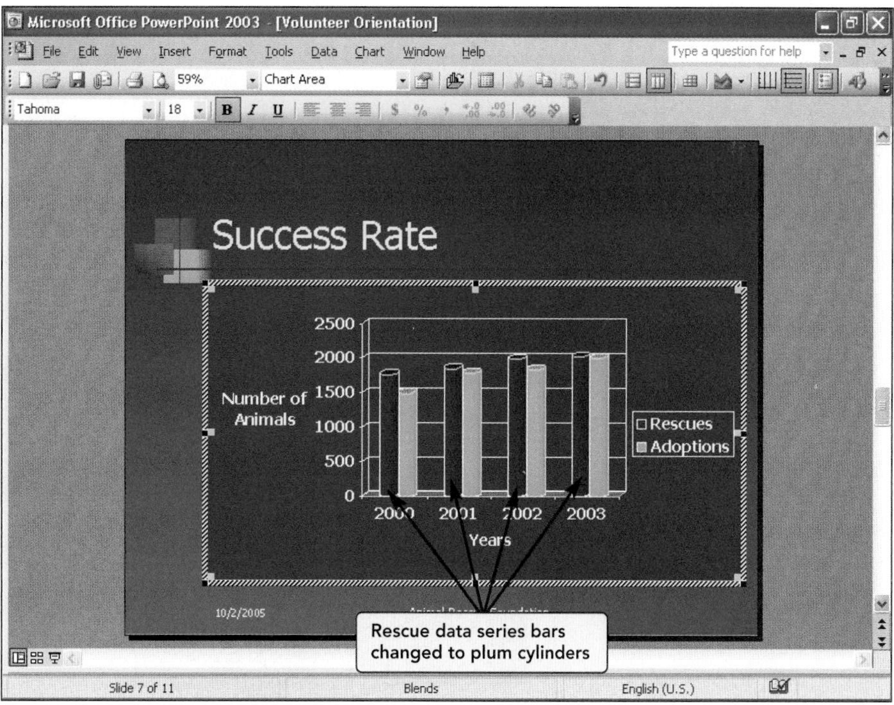


**Figure 3.42**

Next you want to add color to the chart walls.

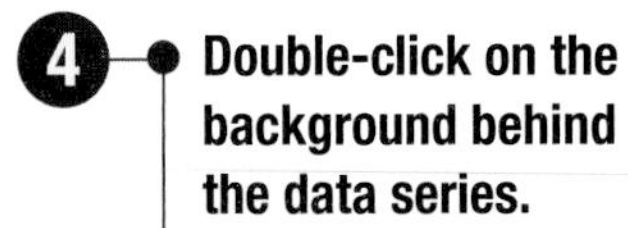

**4** • **Double-click on the background behind the data series.**

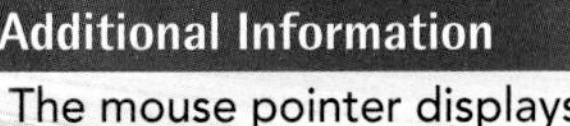

**Additional Information**

The mouse pointer displays "Walls" in a ScreenTip.

• **Select a lighter blue color from the Area color palette.**

• **Click OK.**

*Your screen should be similar to Figure 3.43*

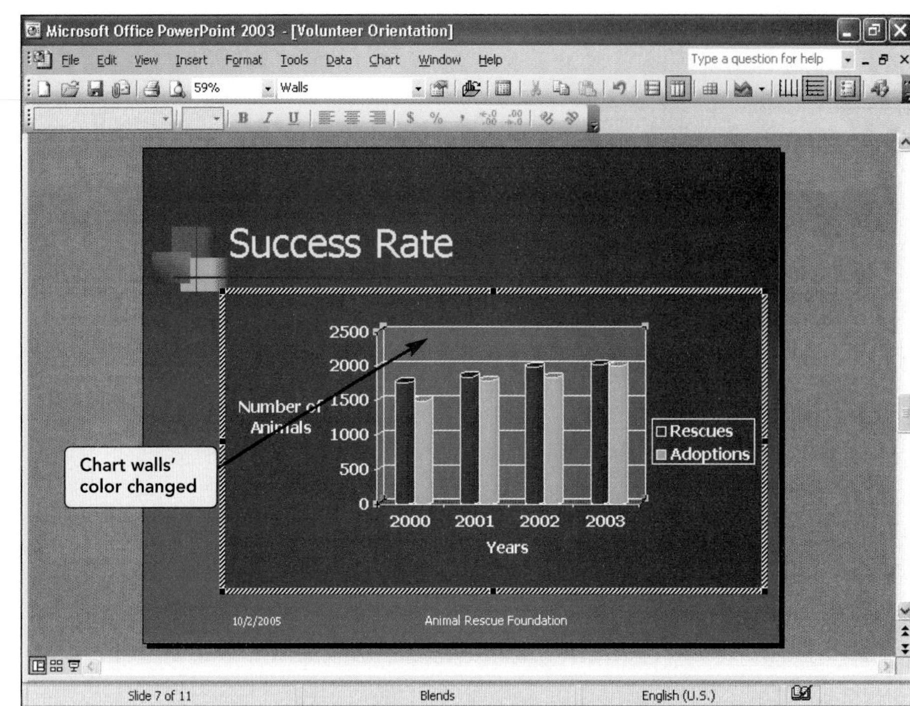


**Figure 3.43**

The chart is now much more attractive and more meaningful. Now that the success rate is represented in a chart, you decide to delete the slide containing the same information in table layout.

**5** • **Click outside the chart to close the Graph application.**

• **Switch to Slide Sorter view.**

• **Delete slide 6.**

• **Save the presentation.**

*Your screen should be similar to Figure 3.44*

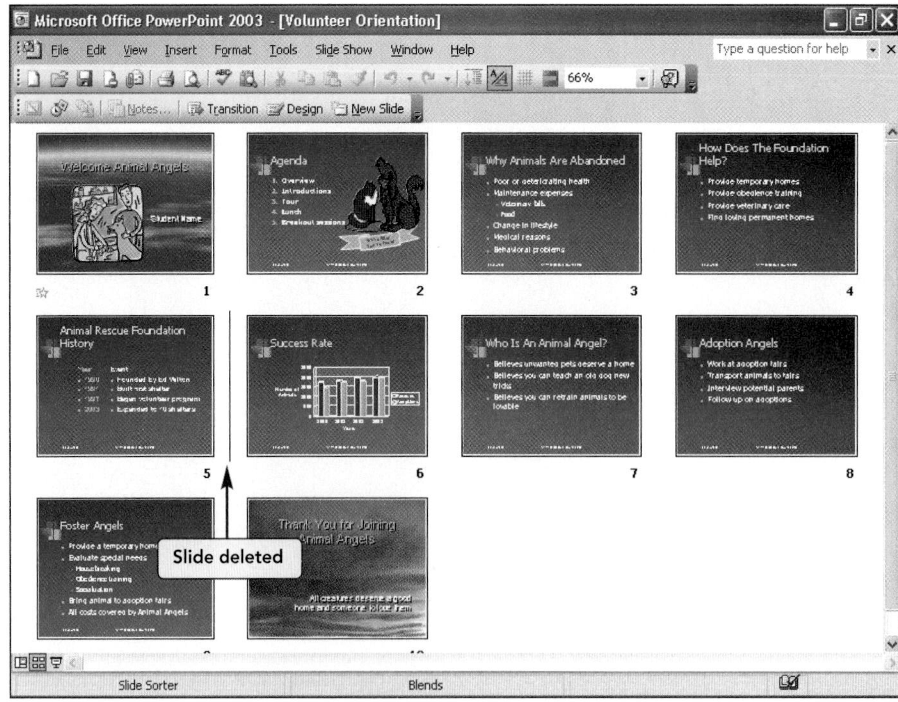


**Figure 3.44**

## Creating an Organization Chart

To provide the volunteers with an overview of the structure of the Animal Rescue Foundation organization, you want to include an organization chart in the presentation.

### Concept 5

#### Organization Chart

5 An **organization chart** is a map of a group, which usually includes people, but can include any items that have a hierarchical relationship. A **hierarchy** shows ranking, such as reporting structures within a department in a business. PowerPoint 2003 includes a separate application called Microsoft Organization Chart that is designed to help you quickly create organization charts.

There are several different styles of organization charts from which you can choose, depending on how you would like to display the hierarchy and how much room you have on your slide. A basic organization chart is shown below. All organization charts consist of different levels that represent the hierarchy. A **level** is all the boxes at the same hierarchical position regardless of the boxes each reports to. The topmost box in the organization chart is at level 1. All boxes that report directly to it are at level 2. Those boxes reporting to a level 2 box are at level 3, and so forth. An organization chart can have up to 50 levels.

The **manager box** is the top-level box of a group. **Subordinate boxes** report to the manager box. **Co-worker boxes** are boxes that have the same manager. Co-workers form a group. A **group** consists of all the boxes reporting to the same manager, excluding assistant boxes. **Assistant boxes** represent administrative or managerial assistants to a manager. A **branch** is a box and all the boxes that report to it.

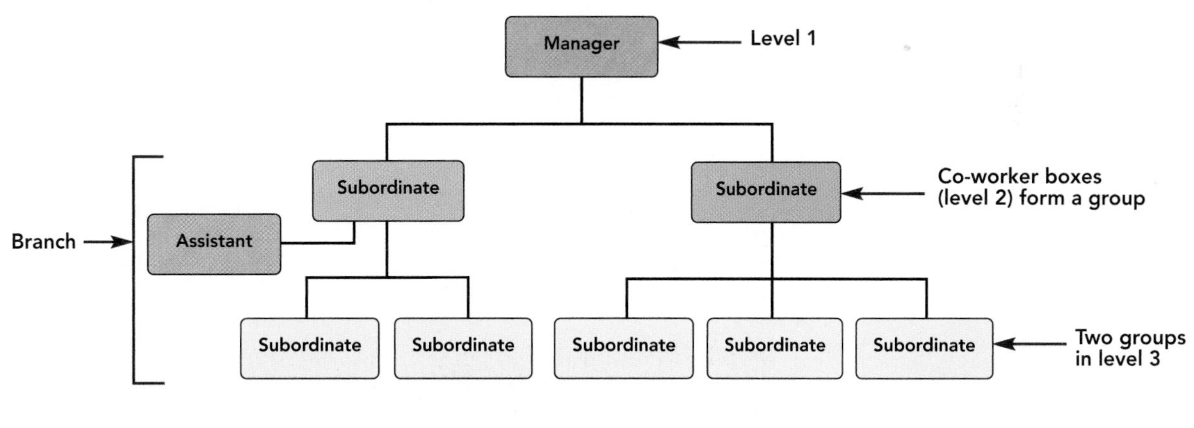


You will add a new slide following slide 4 to display the organization chart. Just as when creating a chart of data, there is a special slide layout for organization charts with a placeholder that opens the Organization Chart application.

**1**

- **Insert a new slide after slide 4 using the Title and Diagram or Organization Chart slide layout.**
- **Close the Slide Layout task pane.**
- **Double-click slide 5.**
- **Double-click [icon] in the organization chart placeholder.**

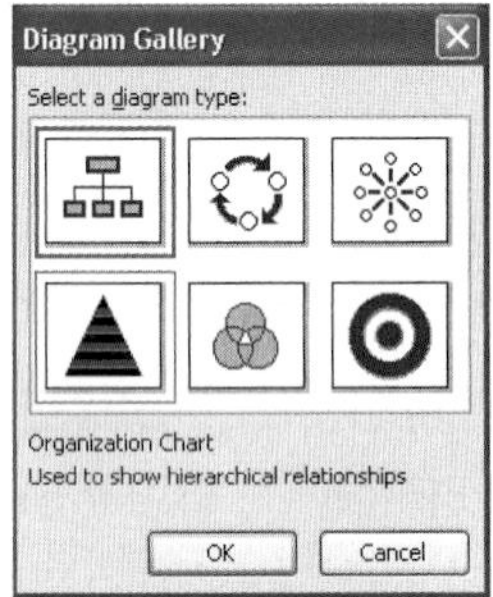


- **Double-click [icon] Organization Chart in the Diagram Gallery dialog box.**

*Your screen should be similar to Figure 3.45*

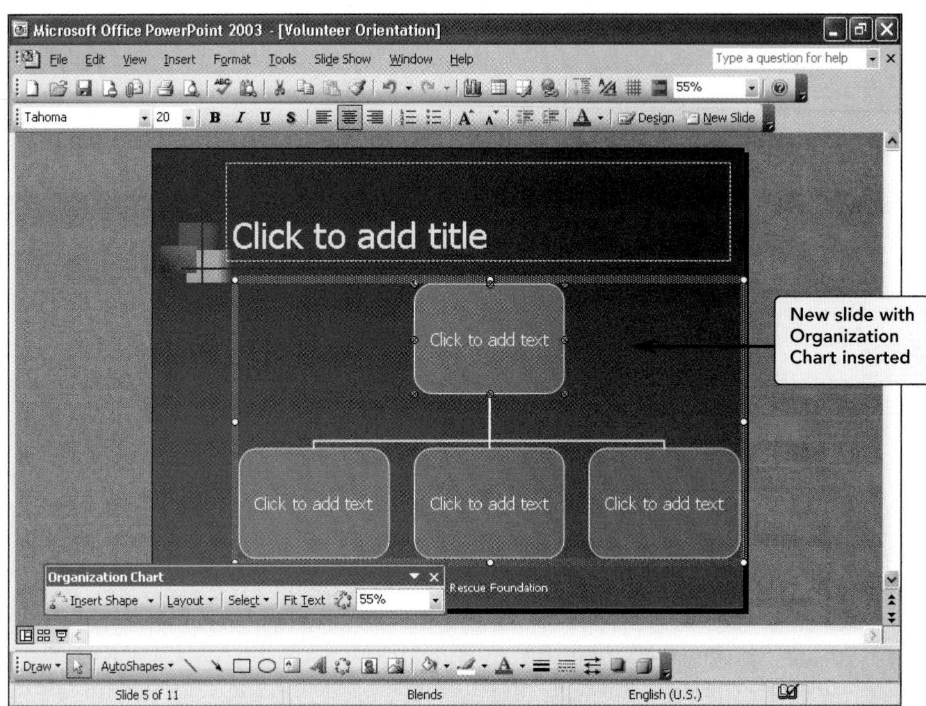


**Figure 3.45**

The Organization Chart toolbar contains the commands and tools to create and edit the organization chart.

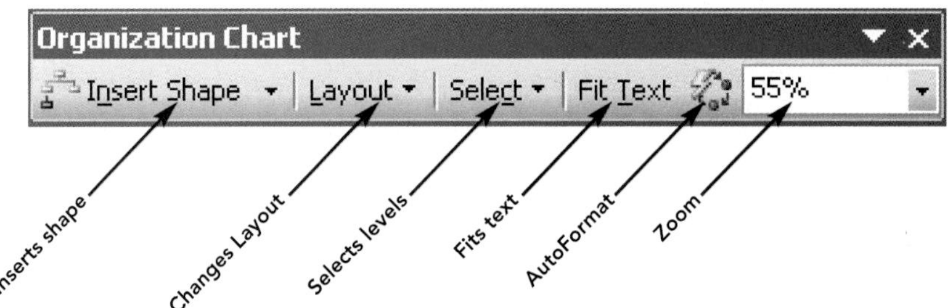


When you create a new organization chart, a chart containing four boxes (the default) is displayed. To enter information into a box, you type over the placeholder text. The top box in the organization chart is already selected. You will enter the name of the director of the Animal Rescue Foundation in the top-level box. You will also increase the zoom to make it easier to see the text in the boxes.

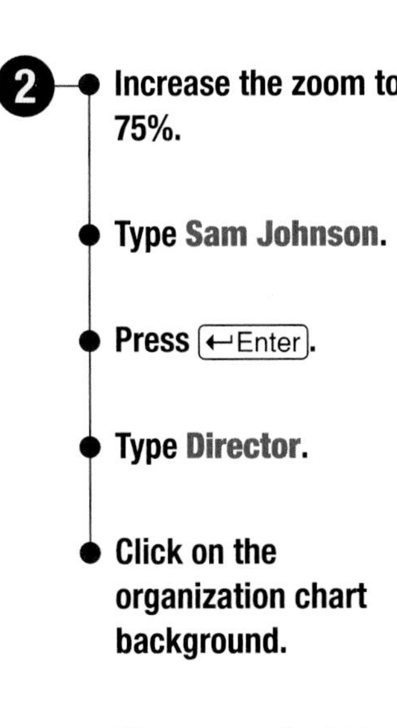

**2**

- **Increase the zoom to 75%.**
- **Type Sam Johnson.**
- **Press ←Enter.**
- **Type Director.**
- **Click on the organization chart background.**

*Your screen should be similar to Figure 3.46*

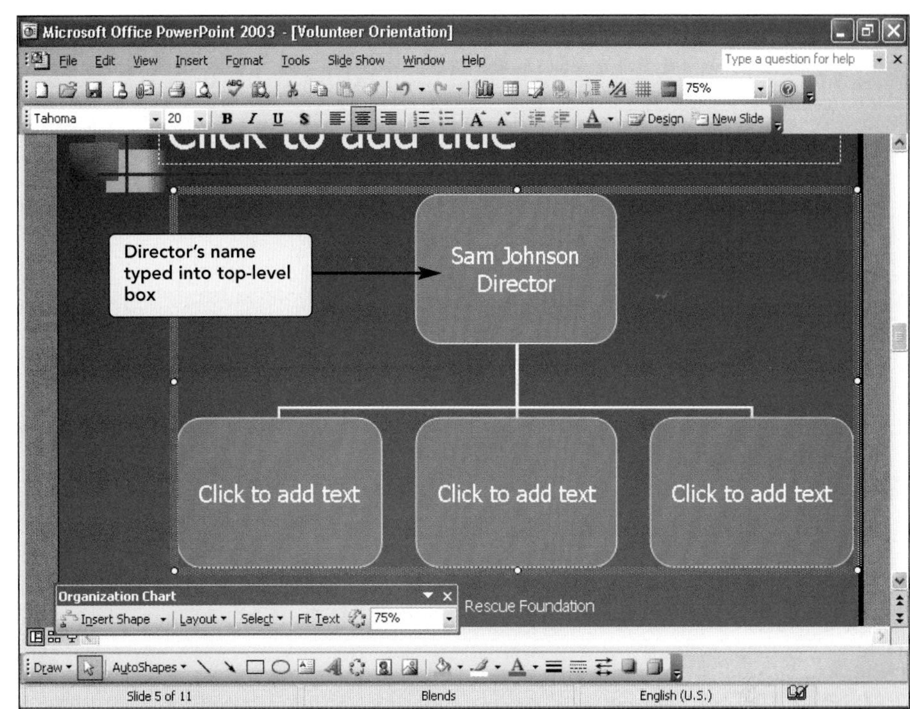


**Figure 3.46**

Next, you will add text to the other boxes. As you do, because some of the entries are too large to fit in the box, they will overlap. To fix this, you will size the text to fit within the box.

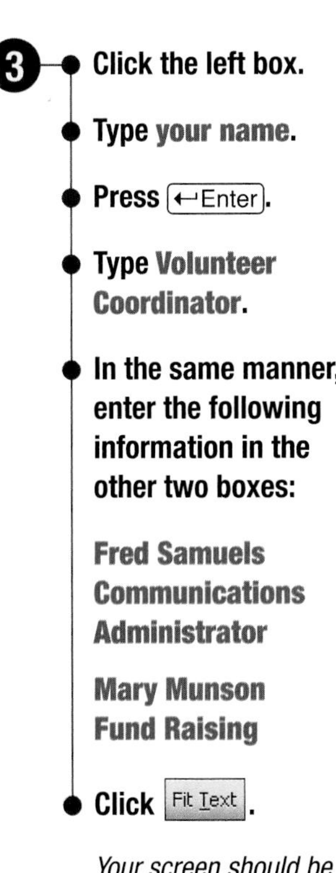

**3**

- **Click the left box.**
- **Type your name.**
- **Press ←Enter.**
- **Type Volunteer Coordinator.**
- **In the same manner, enter the following information in the other two boxes:**

  **Fred Samuels Communications Administrator**

  **Mary Munson Fund Raising**
- **Click Fit Text.**

*Your screen should be similar to Figure 3.47*

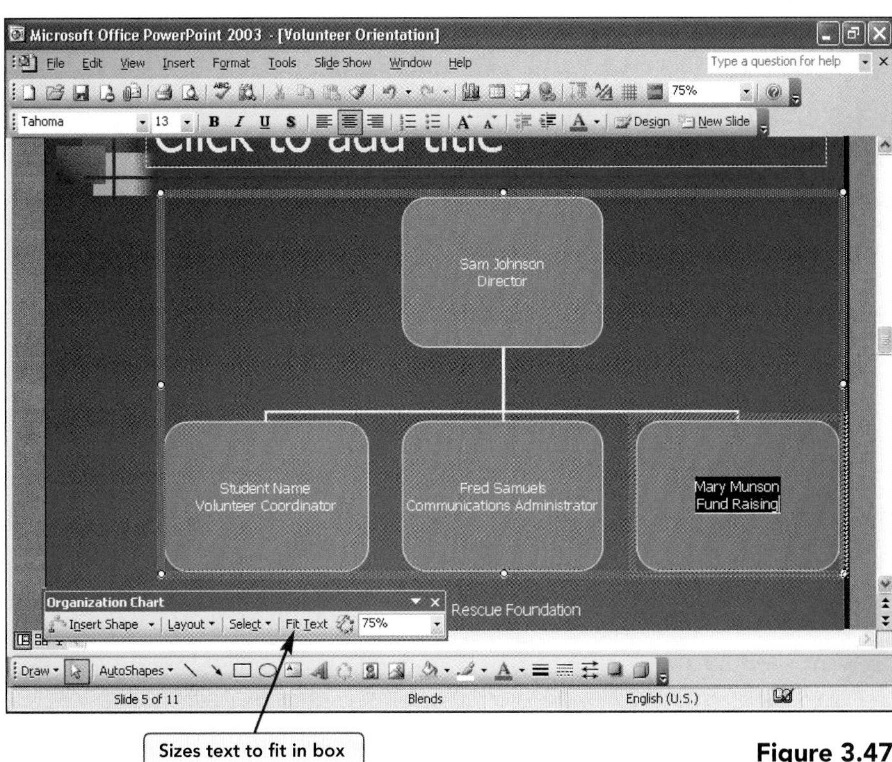


**Figure 3.47**

The font size of the text was reduced in all the boxes to the size needed to display the largest entry in the boxes.

## Adding Boxes

Since this orientation is for volunteers, you are going to expand only the Volunteer Coordinator section of the organization chart. To add a box, you first select the type of box to add and then select the box to link it to. You will add two subordinate boxes for the two people who report directly to you.

1
- **Click the Volunteer Coordinator box.**
- **Open the Insert Shape drop-down menu and select Subordinate.**
- **Click the new subordinate box.**
- **Type Martin Crane.**
- **Press ←Enter.**
- **Type Foster Angels.**
- **Click on the chart background.**

*Your screen should be similar to Figure 3.48*

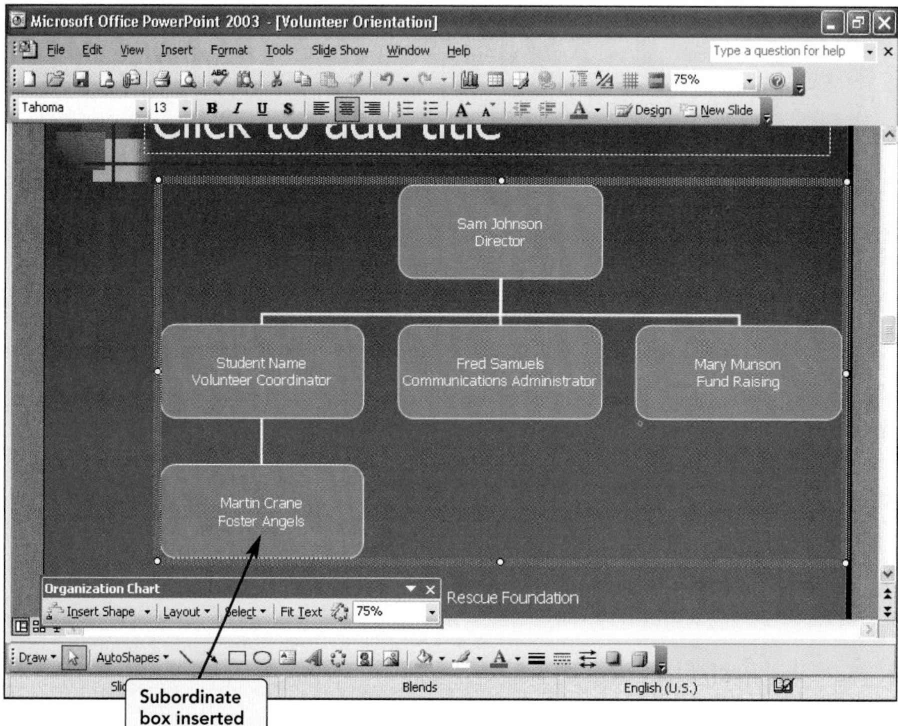


**Figure 3.48**

The new box appears in the same color background as the existing boxes. Next you will add a co-worker box next to Martin Crane.

**2** • Click on Martin Crane's box.

• Open the  drop-down menu and select Coworker.

• Click the new co-worker box.

• Type **Peg Ludwig**.

• Press ←Enter.

• Type **Adoption Angels**.

• Click on the chart background.

*Your screen should be similar to Figure 3.49*

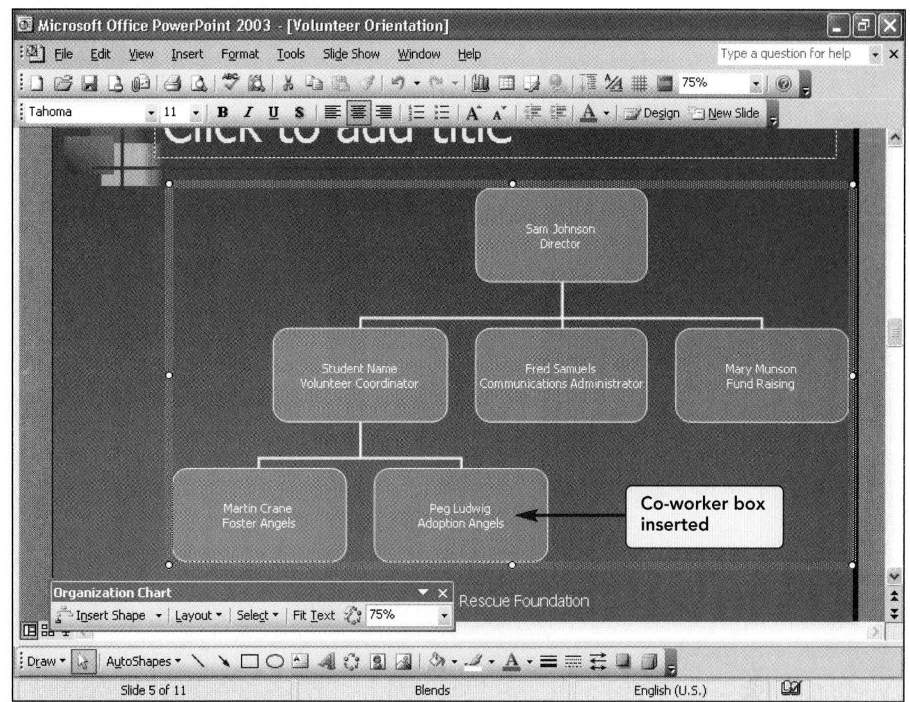


**Figure 3.49**

## Enhancing the Organization Chart

To make the organization chart more interesting, you decide to change the appearance of the boxes, text, and lines. You could select each element individually and make changes, but PowerPoint includes an AutoFormat option that provides prepackaged styles.

**1** • Click AutoFormat.

*Your screen should be similar to Figure 3.50*

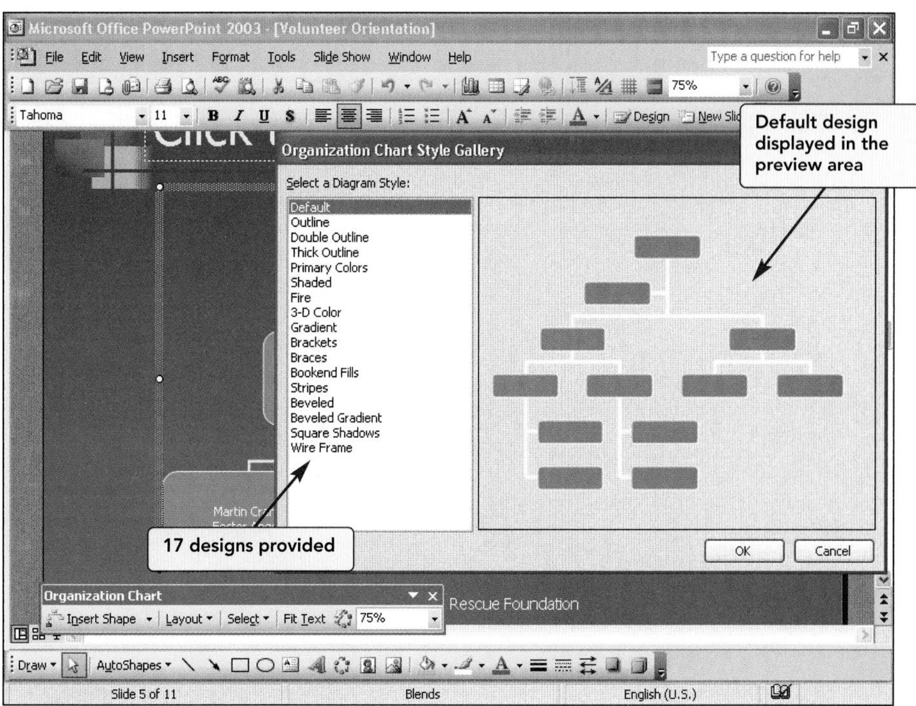


**Figure 3.50**

From the Organization Chart Style Gallery dialog box, you can select from 17 designs. The selected design, Default, is displayed in the preview area.

**2** Select several diagram styles and preview the samples.

- **Choose Bookend Fills.**
- **Click OK.**

*Your screen should be similar to Figure 3.51*

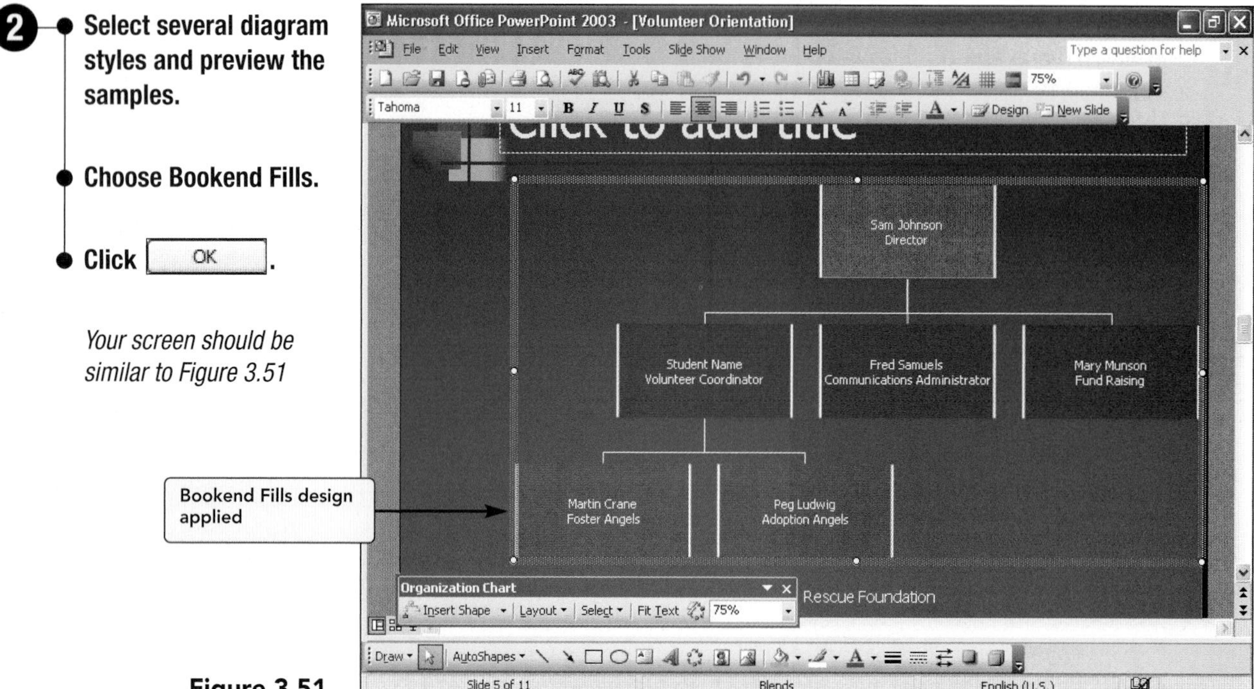


**Figure 3.51**

The final enhancement is to make the Volunteer branch of the organization chart stand out, so you decide to color and bold the names in the boxes.

**3** Click on the Volunteer Coordinator box to select it and drag to select your name.

- **Click B Bold.**
- **Click S Shadow.**
- **Click A Font Color and select gold.**
- **Use Format Painter to apply the same formats to the names in the two boxes below yours.**
- **Turn off Format Painter and click on the chart background.**

*Your screen should be similar to Figure 3.52*

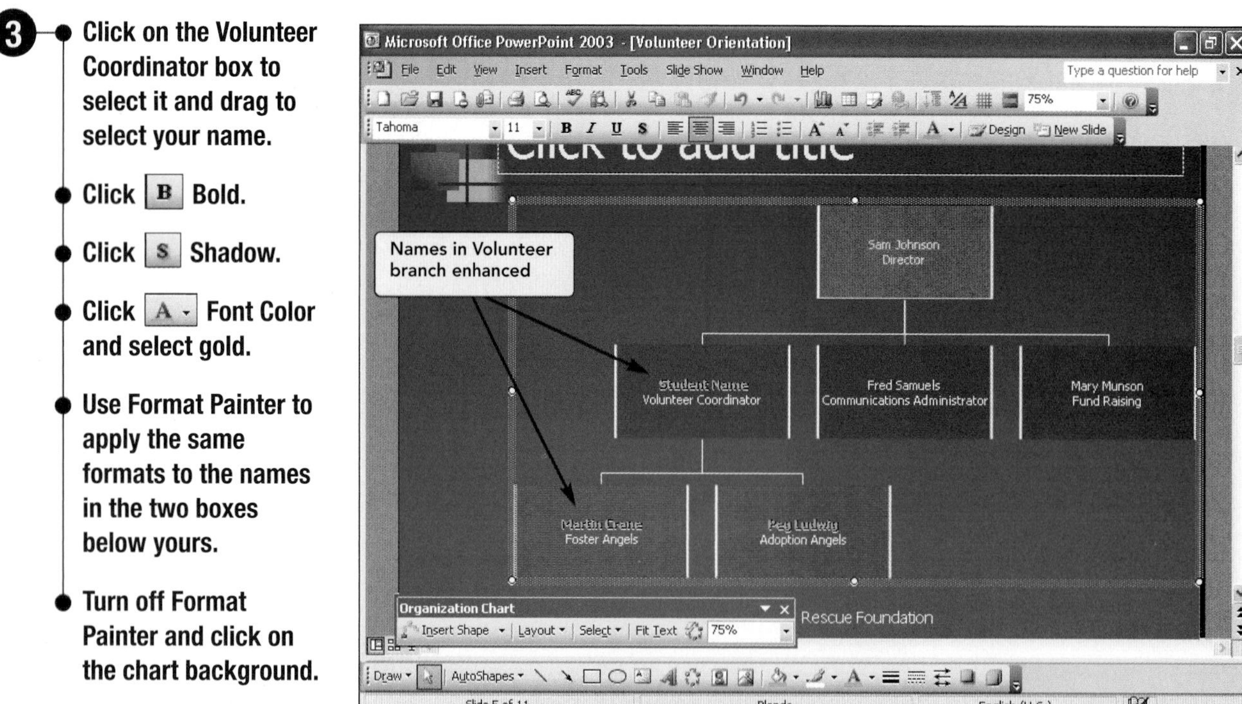


**Figure 3.52**

## Changing the Organization Chart Layout

You also decide to add to the chart the names of the volunteer assistants who work for the coordinators.

1. **Add two subordinate boxes under Martin Crane and enter the names Susan Allison and Maria Garcia.**

**Additional Information**

Clicking Insert Shape will insert the default shape of Subordinate.

- **In a similar manner, under Peg Ludwig add two subordinate boxes and enter the names Jamul Johnson and Kaye Benjamin.**

- **Change the font color to gold and bold in the new boxes.**

*Your screen should be similar to Figure 3.53*

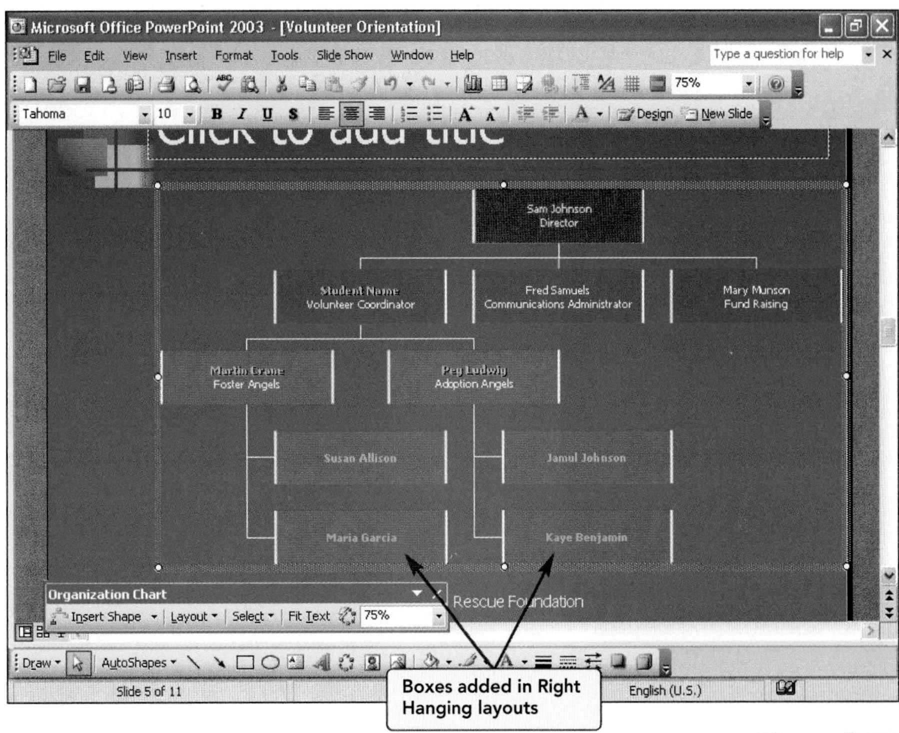


**Figure 3.53**

PowerPoint automatically adds the new subordinate boxes in a Right Hanging layout. You want to change the arrangement of the boxes. You can change the arrangement of the entire organization chart or only selected levels. You will rearrange the co-worker boxes to appear in the Standard layout to match the rest of the chart. To change a level, select the level above the level whose layout you want to change.

**2**

- **Click the box for Martin Crane.**
- **Open the Layout drop-down menu and choose Standard.**
- **In a similar manner, change the layout for the boxes beneath Peg Ludwig.**
- **Click on the slide background.**
- **Return the zoom to Fit.**

*Your screen should be similar to Figure 3.54*

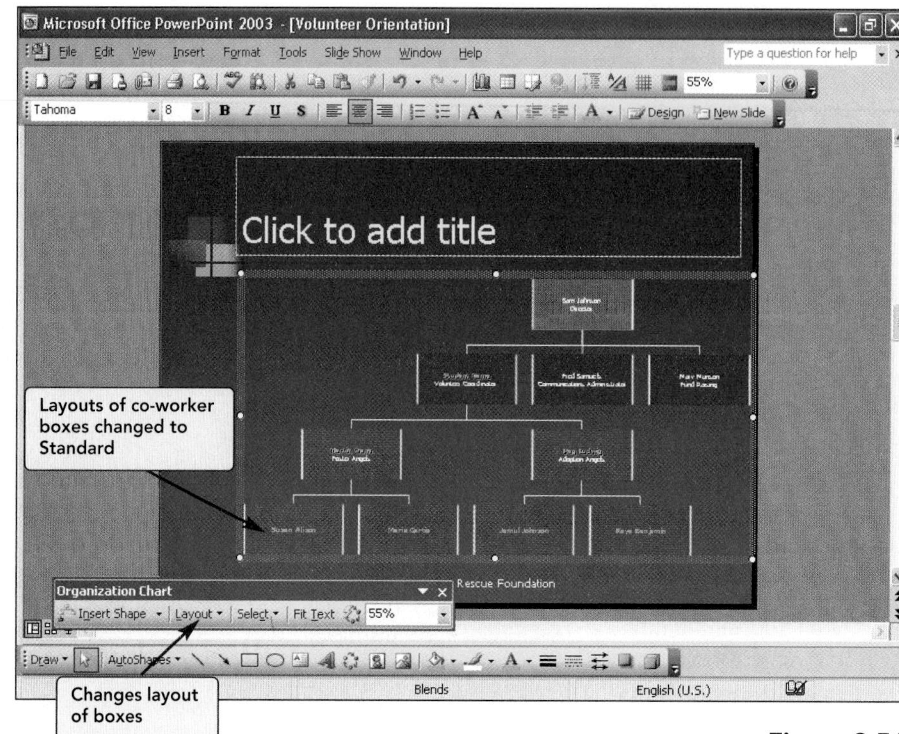


**Figure 3.54**

**Additional Information**

You can click on the chart to reopen the Organization Chart application to further modify the chart at any time.

The last step is to add the title.

**3** **Type Who's Who as the slide title.**

**Save the presentation.**

**Choose View/Normal (Restore Panes).**

*Your screen should be similar to Figure 3.55*

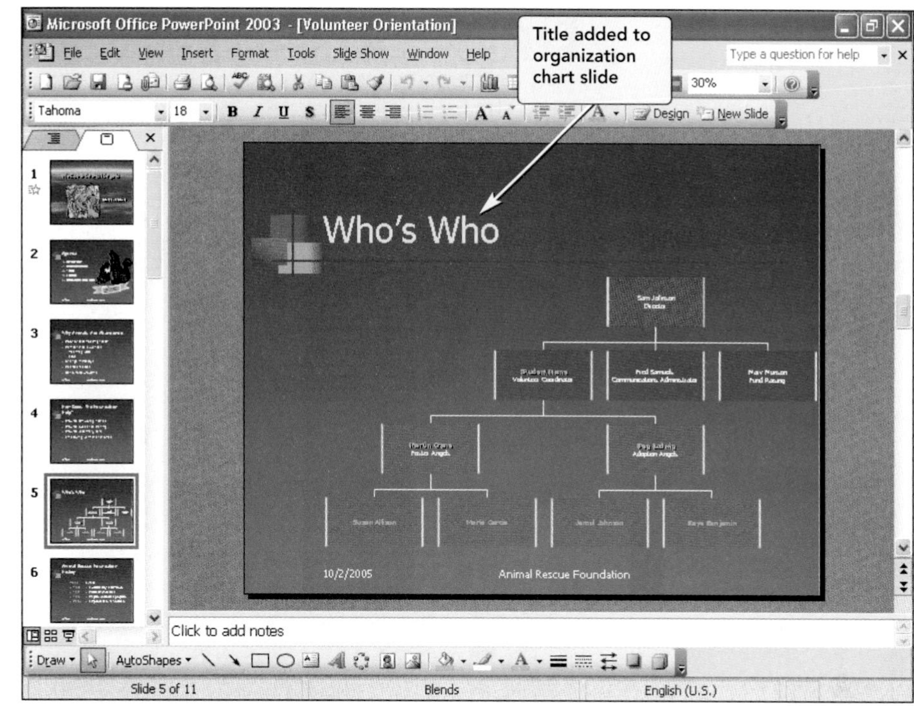


Figure 3.55

**4** **To see how all the changes you have made to the presentation look, run the presentation beginning with slide 1.**

**Print the presentation as handouts in portrait orientation, six per page.**

Your handouts will be similar to those shown here.

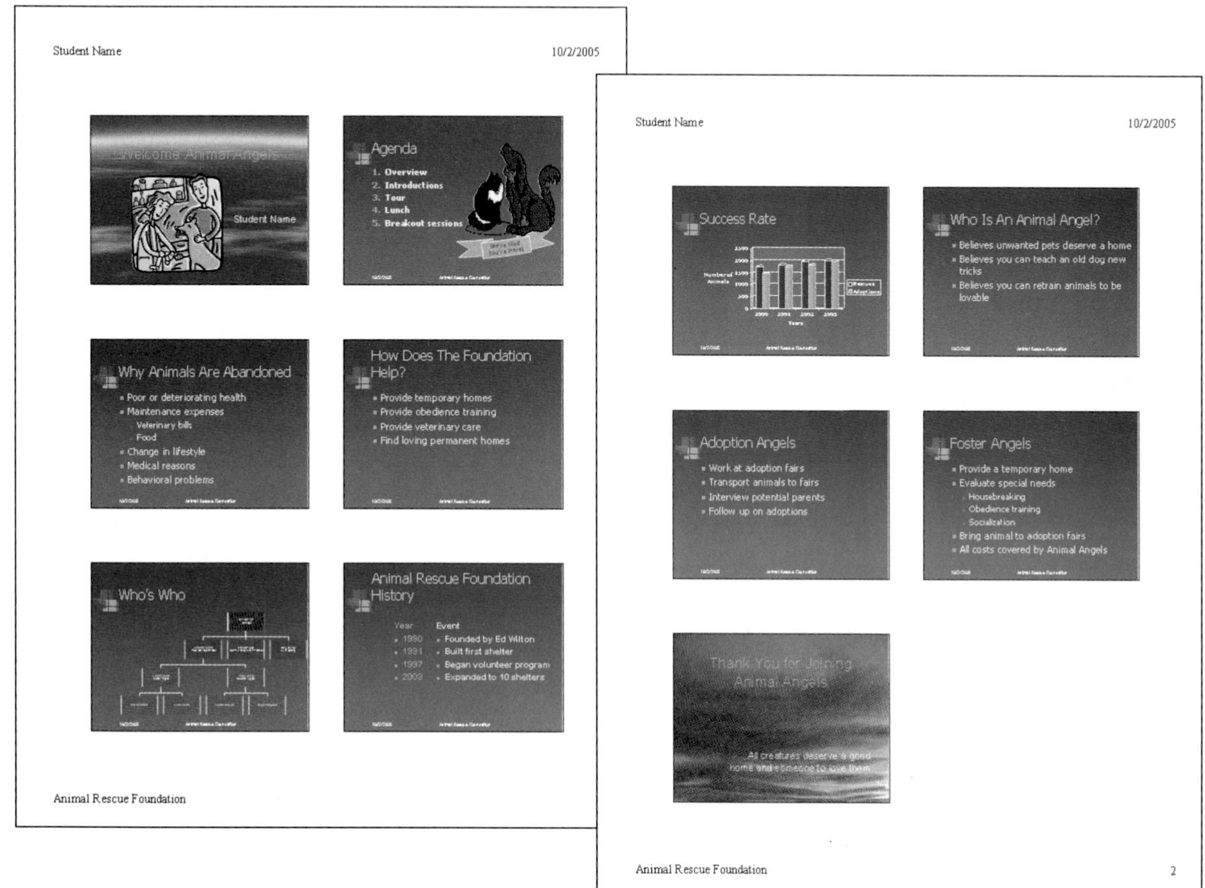

## Exporting a Presentation Outline to Word

Now that the presentation is nearly complete, you need to send a copy of the text portion of the presentation to the director for approval. To do this quickly, you can save the text of the presentation to a text file.

1 **Choose File/Send to/Microsoft Office Word.**

*Your screen should be similar to Figure 3.56*

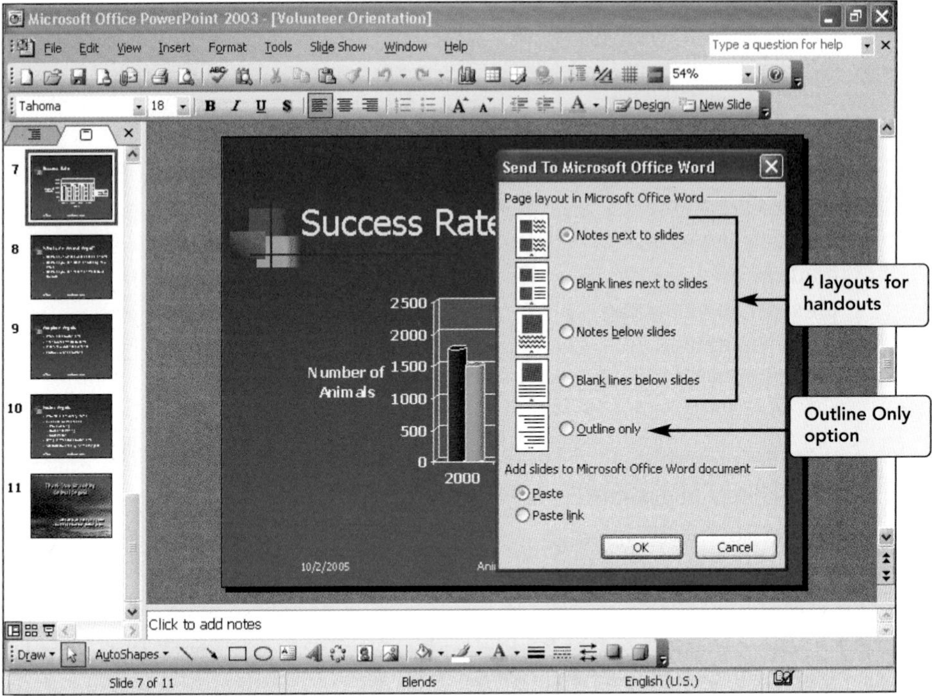


**Figure 3.56**

From the dialog box, you can select from four layouts for handouts, or you can create a document containing the outline only. If you choose a handout layout, you can also choose to include the slides in the handouts or just provide links to the slides. You want to create a Word document of just the outline of the presentation.

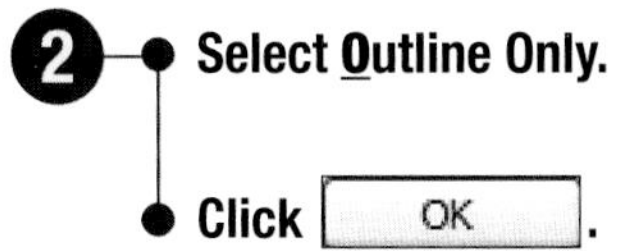

2 **Select Outline Only.**

**Click OK.**

*Your screen should be similar to Figure 3.57*

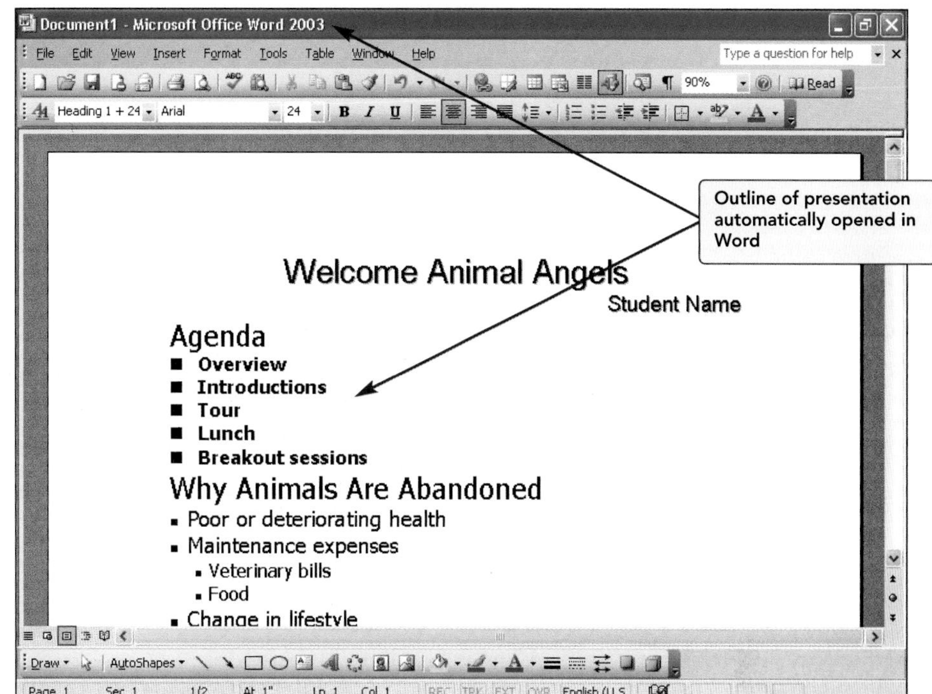


**Figure 3.57**

Word opens and displays the outline for the presentation.

3 **Scroll through the document to review the outline.**

**Save the document as** Orientation Outline **with a Word document (.doc) file type.**

**Print the outline and exit Word.**

## E-mailing a Presentation

The director has asked you to send a copy of the presentation for review by e-mail. To do this, you will send the presentation as an attachment to an e-mail message. An **attachment** is a copy of a file that is included with an e-mail message. The attached file can then be opened by the recipient using the application in which it was created.

**1** ● **Click [E-mail button] E-mail.**

**Having Trouble?**

If you do not have an e-mail program installed, the [E-mail button] button is not displayed and you will need to skip this section.

● **If necessary, click OK in the Choose Profile dialog box.**

**Another Method**

The menu equivalent is File/Send to/Mail Recipient (as Attachment).

*Your screen should look similar to Figure 3.58*

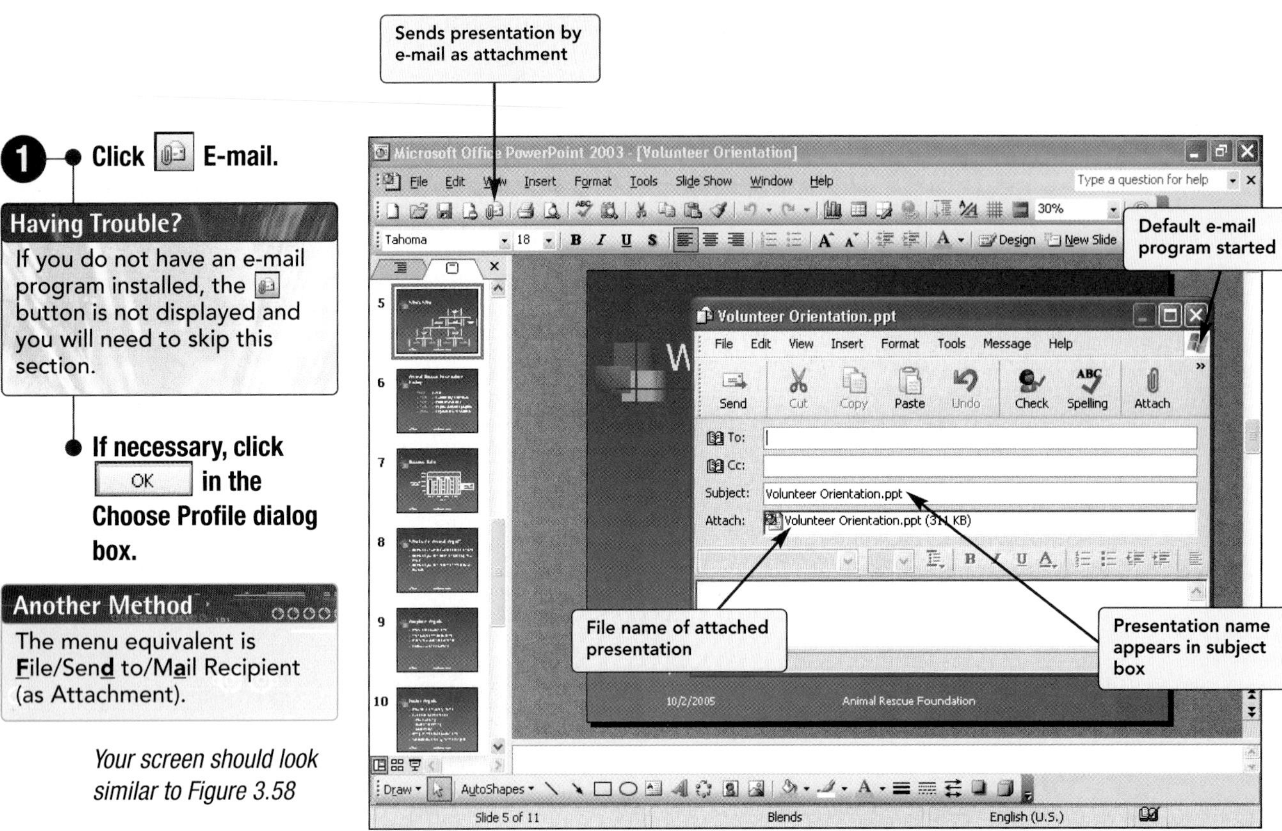


**Figure 3.58**

**Having Trouble?**

If your default e-mail program is other than Outlook Express, your e-mail window will look slightly different.

**Additional Information**

To send an e-mail message to multiple recipients, separate the e-mail addresses with semicolons.

The default e-mail program on your system is started, and a new message window is displayed.

You need to specify the recipient's e-mail address, the e-mail address of anyone you want to send a courtesy copy of this message to (CC:), and the subject and body of the message. You can use the toolbar buttons to select recipient names from your e-mail address book, attach a file to the message, set the message priority (high, normal, or low priority), include a follow-up message flag, and set other e-mail options. The file name of the presentation appears in the Subject box. The Attach box also displays the file name of the presentation file that will be sent with the e-mail message.

2 Enter the e-mail address of the person you want to send the message to in the To box.

**Additional Information**

Your instructor will provide the e-mail address to use. For example, if you have a personal e-mail address, your instructor may want you to use it for this exercise.

- **Enter the following in the message text area: Attached is the presentation I have been working on for the new volunteer orientation meeting. Please let me know if you have any suggestions..**
- **Press ←Enter twice and type your name.**

*Your screen should look similar to Figure 3.59*

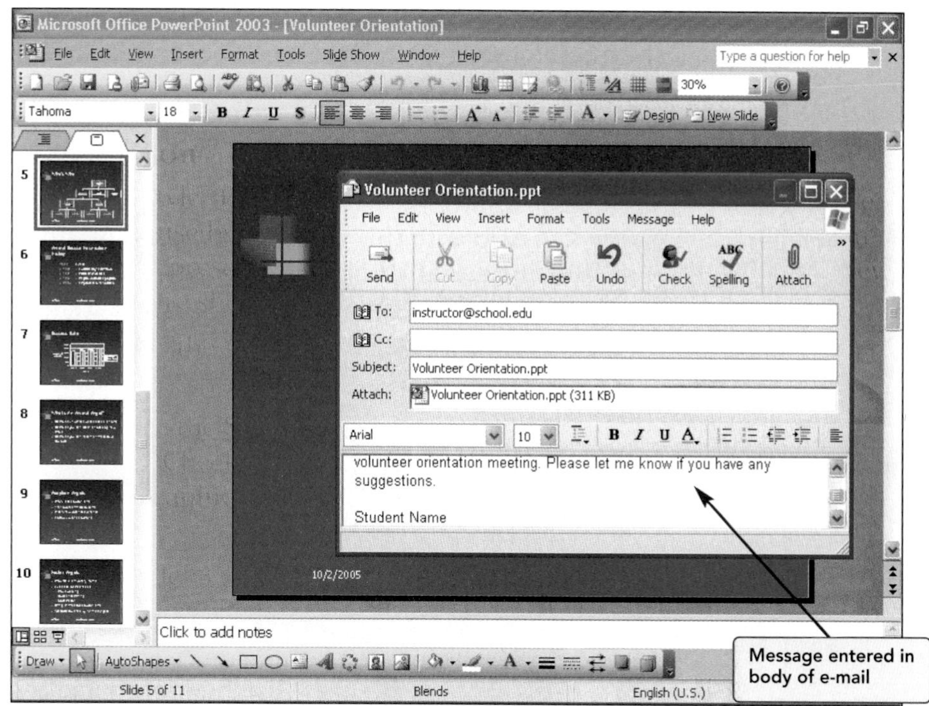


Figure 3.59

You are now ready to send the e-mail message. If you have an Internet connection, you could click Send to send the e-mail message. Instead, you will save it to be sent at a later time.

3 Choose **File/Save As and save the message as Volunteer Presentation to the location where you save your files.**

- **Close the e-mail window.**
- **If necessary, click No in response to the prompt to send the message.**

When the message is sent, the recipient can open the attachment and view the presentation using PowerPoint.

## Delivering Presentations

Typically presentations are delivered by connecting a computer to a projector to display the slides on a large screen. Before delivering a presentation, it is important to rehearse it so that you are well prepared and at ease with both the equipment and the materials. It is best to rehearse in a setting as close as possible to the real situation with a small audience who will give you honest feedback. Since most presentations are allotted a set amount of time, as part of the rehearsal you may also want to keep track of the time spent on each slide and the total time of the presentation.

## Rehearsing Timing

> **Additional Information**
> If your computer has a microphone, you could even record your narration using Sli**d**e Show/Record **N**arration.

To help with this aspect of the presentation, PowerPoint includes a timing feature that records the length of time spent on each slide and the total presentation time while you are rehearsing. If the presentation runs either too long or too short, you can quickly see which slides you are spending too much or too little time on and adjust the presentation accordingly.

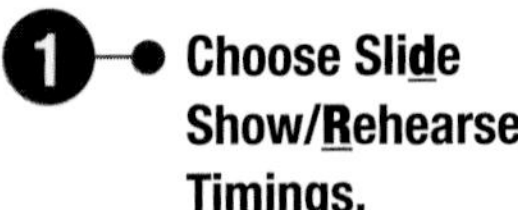

**1** **Choose Sli<u>d</u>e Show/<u>R</u>ehearse Timings.**

*Your screen should be similar to Figure 3.60*

**Figure 3.60**

The Rehearsal toolbar appears and starts a clock to time your delivery. The [Next] button advances to the next step in the show and the [Pause] will pause the timing. You can also return to the previous slide to repeat the rehearsal and apply new timings to the slide using the [Repeat] button on the toolbar.

Normally you would read your narration aloud while you rehearse the timing. For this exercise, think about what you would say for each slide. The toolbar will record the time for each slide. When you reach the end of the presentation, a message box displays the total time for the presentation.

**2** • **Advance through the slide show as you would during the actual presentation.**

• **Click Yes to keep the slide timings.**

• **Save the presentation.**

*Your screen should be similar to Figure 3.61*

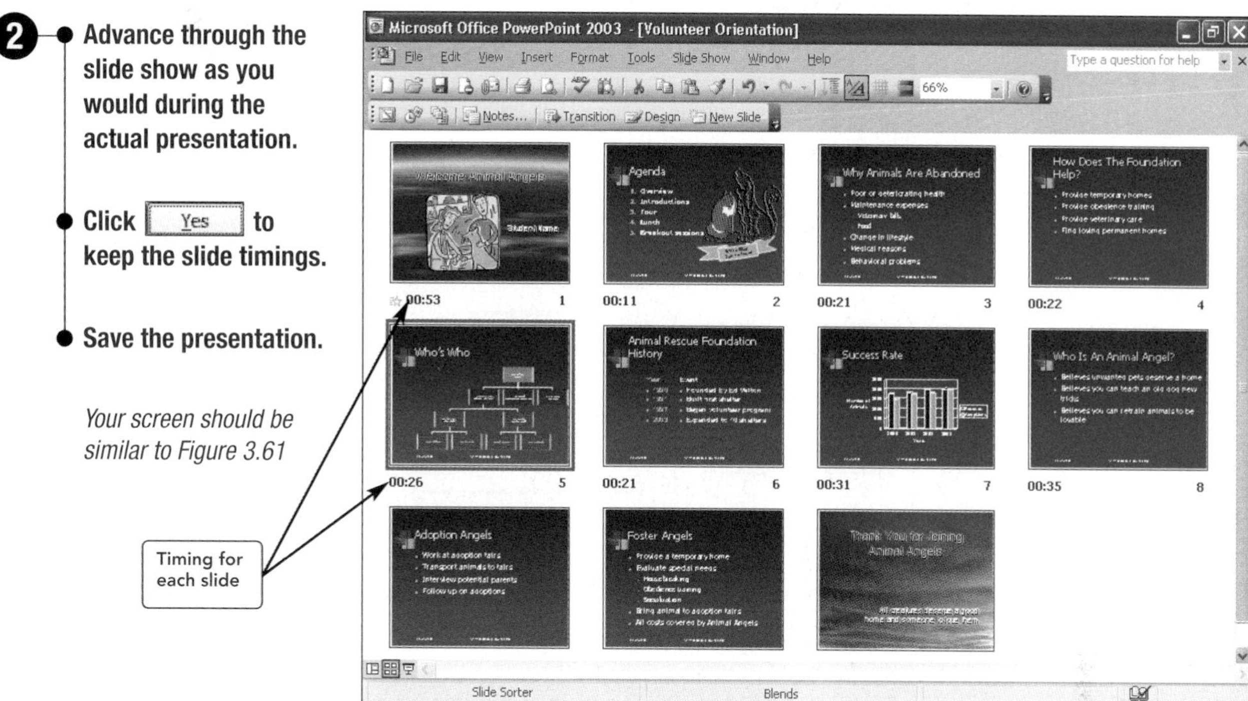


Figure 3.61

The presentation is displayed in Slide Sorter view, showing the timing for each slide. Now that you can see the individual timings, you can easily see where you are spending too little or too much time.

You can also preset timings for each slide, and the slides will be advanced automatically for you during the presentation. To turn on this feature use Slide Show/Set Up Show and select the Using Timings option to advance slides.

## Packaging Presentations for a CD

Finally, you are going to use the Package for CD feature to create an archive folder of your presentations. The Package for CD feature allows you to package your presentations and all of the supporting files to a folder, which can be copied to a CD. Viewers can then automatically run your presentations from the CD. The updated Microsoft Office PowerPoint Viewer is included on the CD so the viewer does not have to have PowerPoint installed on their PC to view your presentation.

**1** **Choose File/Package for CD.**

*Your screen should be similar to Figure 3.62*

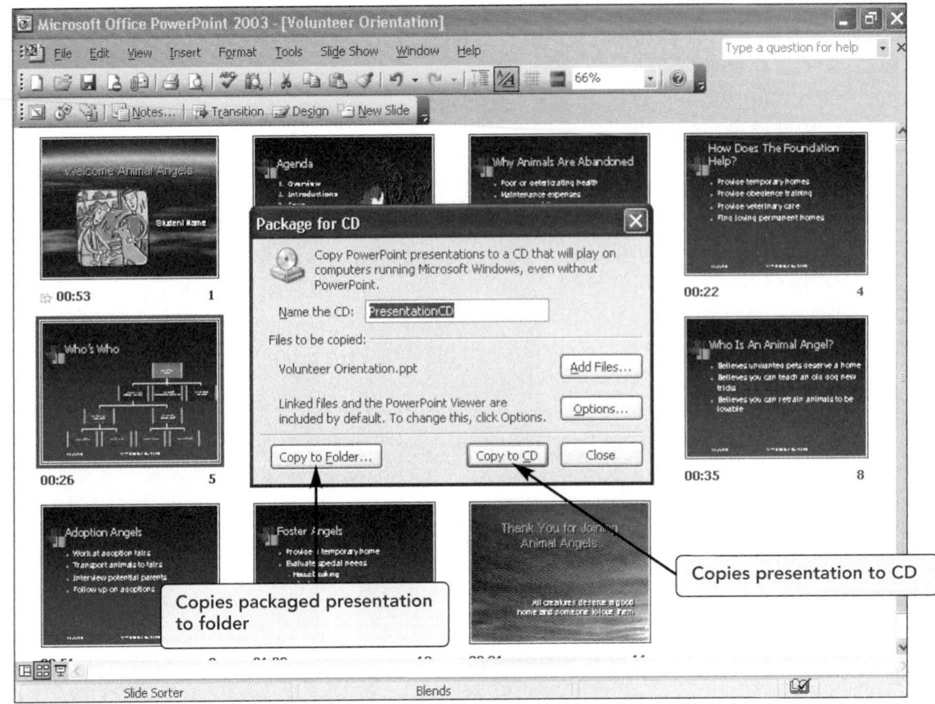


**Figure 3.62**

The Volunteer Orientation presentation is automatically added to the list for the CD. You also want to include the Animal Angels presentation on the CD.

**2** **Click** Add Files... **.**

**Select the file** pp03_Animal Angels3.ppt **from your data file location.**

**Click** Add **.**

*Your screen should be similar to Figure 3.63*

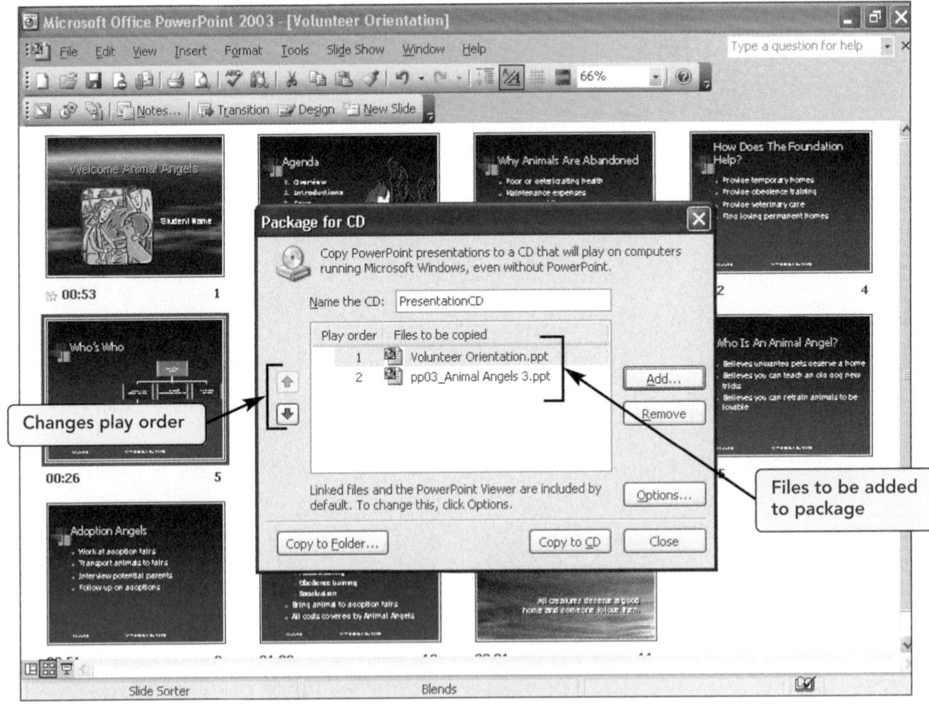


**Figure 3.63**

**Additional Information**

You could also copy the files directly to a CD at this point using Copy to CD.

Currently the Volunteer Orientation presentation will play before the Animal Angels presentation. You want to reverse the order, then copy the presentations to a folder.

3 • Click [⇩] to move the Volunteer Orientation presentation down the play list.

• Click [Copy to Folder...].

• Name the folder OrientationCD.

• Change the location to the location where you save your files.

• Click [OK].

• When the files are finished copying, click [Close].

• Exit PowerPoint.

When you are ready to create the CD, all you would need to do is copy the OrientationCD folder to the CD.

## Preparing Overheads and 35mm Slides

If you are unsure of the availability of a data projector, you may want to convert the presentation to overheads or 35mm slides. To create overheads, you print your presentation as black-and-white or color transparencies, using transparencies in the printer instead of paper. Be sure to order the type of transparency that is appropriate for your printer.

You can also transform your electronic slides to 35mm slides by contacting a local service bureau. Follow their instructions for sending the presentation.

# Focus on Careers

### EXPLORE YOUR CAREER OPTIONS

Training Specialist

In today's job market, learning new skills is the only way to keep current with ever-changing technology. A training specialist in a corporate environment is responsible for teaching employees how to do their jobs, which usually involves computer training. Training Specialists use PowerPoint to create materials for their lectures, and can automate the presentations and package to a CD to send to employees at remote locations. The position of training specialist usually requires a college degree and commands salaries from $35,000 to $75,000 depending on experience and skill.

# LAB 3
## Using Advanced Presentation Features

**Group** (PP3.16)

A group is two or more objects that are treated as a single object.

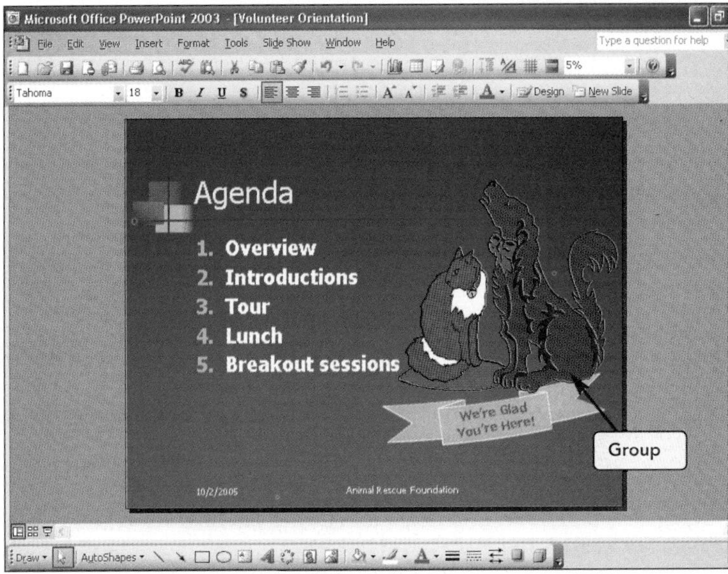


**Object Alignment** (PP3.24)

Object alignment refers to the position of objects relative to each other by their left, right, top, or bottom edges; or horizontally by their centers or vertically by their middles; or in relation to the entire slide.

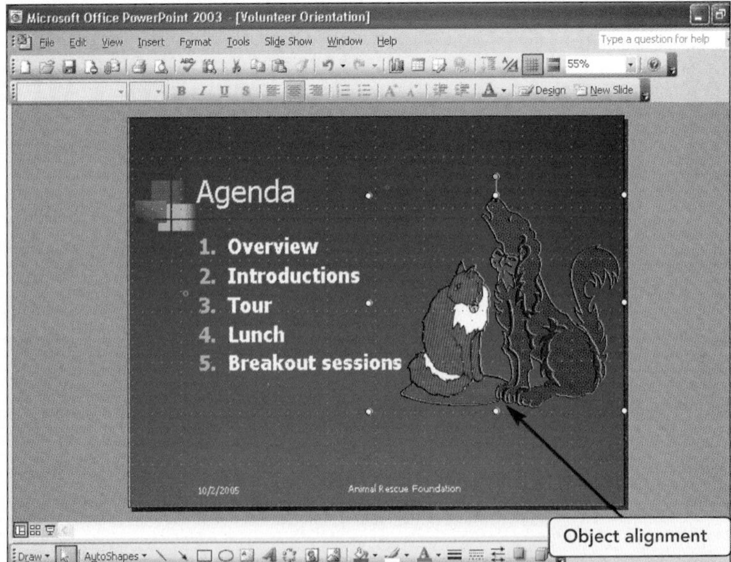

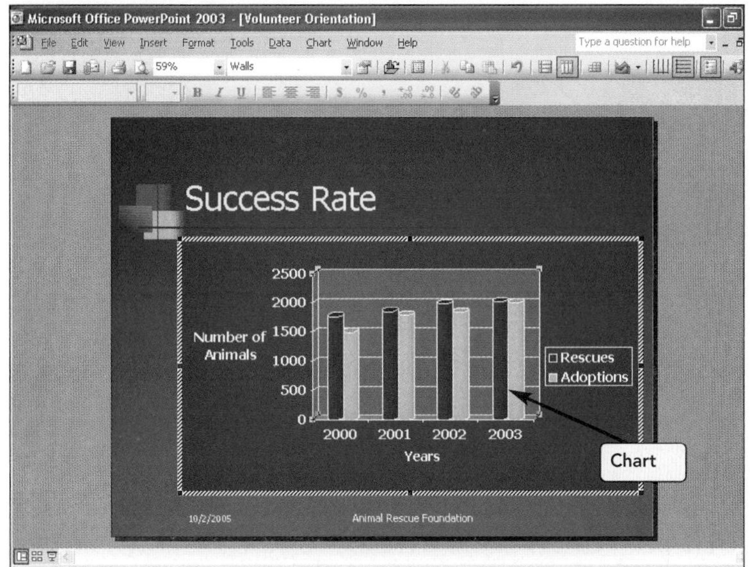


## Chart (PP3.30)

A chart is a visual representation of numeric data that is used to help an audience grasp the impact of your data more quickly.

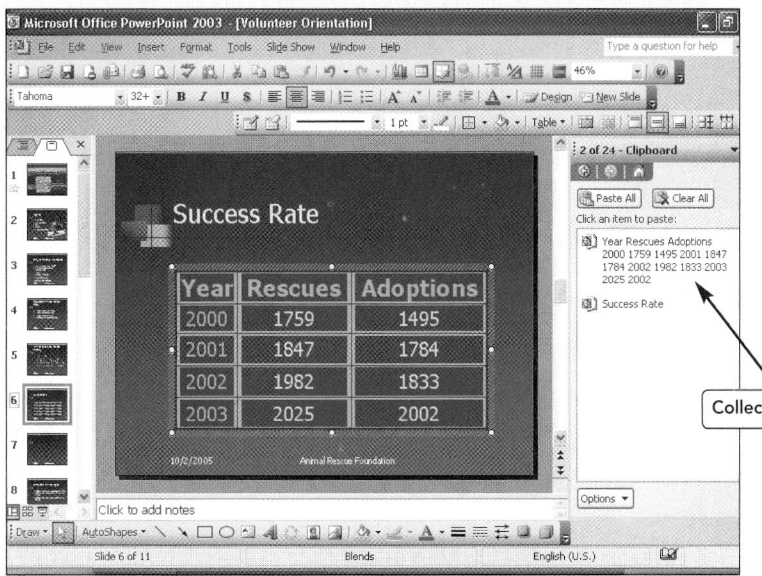


## Collect and Paste (PP3.33)

The Collect and paste feature is used to store multiple copied items in the Office Clipboard and then paste one or more of the items into another location or document.

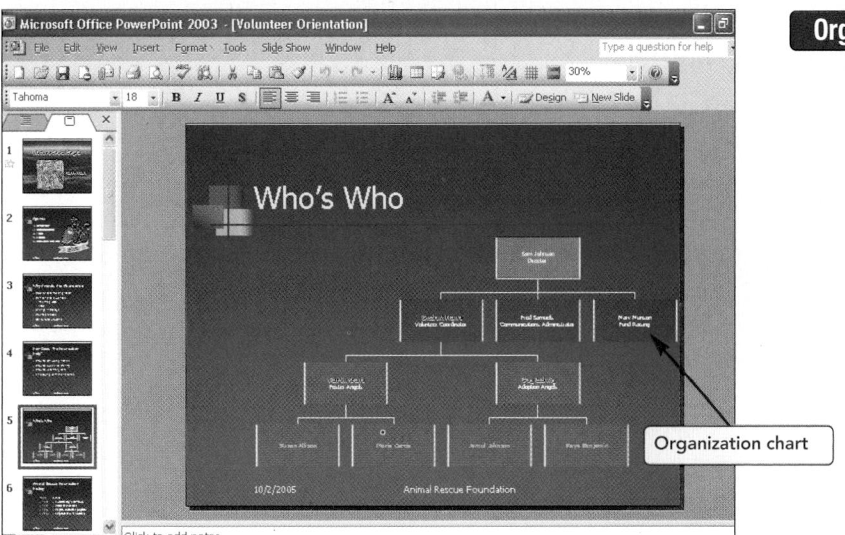


## Organization Chart (PP3.43)

An organization chart is a map of a group, which usually includes people, but can include any items that have a hierarchical relationship.

# LAB 3

## Using Advanced Presentation Features

## key terms

assistant box PP3.43
attachment PP3.53
attribute PP3.16
branch PP3.43
category axis PP3.31
chart PP3.30
collect and paste PP3.33
co-worker box PP3.43
data series PP3.31
datasheet PP3.35
Format Painter PP3.8
graph PP3.30
grid PP3.24
group PP3.16
guide PP3.24
hierarchy PP3.43
legend PP3.31
level PP3.43
manager box PP3.43
object alignment PP3.24
organization chart PP3.43
subordinate box PP3.43
titles PP3.31
value axis PP3.31
X axis PP3.31
Y axis PP3.31

## microsoft office specialist skills

The Microsoft Office Specialist certification program is designed to measure your proficiency in performing basic tasks using the Office System applications. Certification demonstrates that you have the skills and provides a valuable industry credential for employment. After completing this lab, you have learned the following Microsoft Office PowerPoint 2003 Specialist skills:

| Skill Sets | Skill Standard | Page |
|---|---|---|
| Creating Content | Insert and edit text-based content | PP3.5 |
| | Insert tables, charts, and diagrams | PP3.30,3.43 |
| | Insert pictures, shapes, and graphics | PP3.16,3.26 |
| Formatting Content | Format text-based content | PP3.8 |
| | Format pictures, shapes, and graphics | PP3.19,3.23,3.28 |
| | Format slides | PP3.10 |
| | Work with masters | PP3.13 |
| Managing and Delivering Presentations | Organize a presentation | PP3.5,3.24,3.44 |
| | Rehearse timing | PP3.56 |
| | Prepare presentations for remote delivery | PP3.57 |
| | Export a presentation to another Microsoft Office program | PP3.52 |

## command summary

| Command | Shortcut Key | Button | Voice | Action |
|---|---|---|---|---|
| File/Package for CD | | | | Saves presentation and all supporting files to a folder for use on a CD |
| File/Send To/Microsoft Office Word | | | | Exports text of presentation to Word |
| File/Send To/Mail Recipient (as Attachment) | | | | Sends presentation or selected slide as an e-mail attachment |
| Edit/Office Clipboard | | | | Opens Clipboard task pane |
| View/Grid and Guides | | | | Displays guidelines that help align objects |
| View/Zoom | | 45% | | Changes size of onscreen display of slide |
| Insert/Chart | | | | Adds a chart object to a slide |
| Format/Bullets and Numbering | | | | Creates bulleted or numbered lists |
| Format/Background | | | | Applies colors, patterns, or pictures to a slide background |
| Format/AutoShape | | | | Changes characteristics of an AutoShape |
| Slide Show/Set Up Show/Using Timings | | | | Sets up slide show to advance automatic calls by preset timings |
| Slide Show/Rehearse Timings | | | | Starts slide show and sets timings for slide |
| Slide Show/Record Narration | | | | Records Narration while rehearsing the presentation |
| Draw/Group | | | | Groups objects together |

## command summary

| Command | Shortcut Key | Button | Voice | Action |
|---|---|---|---|---|
| Draw/Ungroup | | | | Ungroups objects |
| Draw/Regroup | | | | Groups objects together again that were previously ungrouped |
| Draw/Order/Send to Back | | | | Sends object to bottom of stack |
| Draw/Grid and Guides/ Display grid on screen | | | | Displays or hides grid lines |
| Draw/Align or Distribute | | | | Aligns or distributes objects |
| ***Chart*** | | | | |
| Format/Selected Data Series | Ctrl + 1 | | | Applies patterns, shapes, and other formats to selected data series |
| Data/Series in Columns | | | | Arranges chart based on columns in Datasheet window |
| Chart/Chart Options | | | | Adds and modifies chart options such as titles, legends, and gridlines |
| ***Organization Chart*** | | | | |
| Insert Shape/Subordinate | | | | Adds a box below selected box |
| Insert Shape/Co-worker | | | | Adds a box at same level as selected box |
| Insert Shape/Standard | | | | Applies Standard layout to selected boxes |
| | | | | Applies selected design to boxes of organization chart |

## matching

Match the numbered item with the correct lettered description.

| | | |
|---|---|---|
| 1. [icon] | _____ | a. two or more objects treated as a single object |
| 2. legend | _____ | b. shows ranking within a department |
| 3. titles | _____ | c. descriptive text used to explain the content of a chart |
| 4. grid | _____ | d. used to convert text to a bulleted list |
| 5. data series | _____ | e. series of lines used to position objects on a slide |
| 6. attachment | _____ | f. intersection of a row and column in a table |
| 7. group | _____ | g. description of patterns or colors in a data series |
| 8. [icon] | _____ | h. visual representation of numeric data |
| 9. hierarchy | _____ | i. applies multiple formats to the selected text |
| 10. chart | _____ | j. group of related data plotted in the chart |
| | _____ | k. file copied along with an e-mail message |

## true/false

Circle the correct answer to the following statements.

| | | |
|---|---|---|
| 1. Many clip art pictures are composed of several different elements that are grouped together. | True | False |
| 2. You can move objects up or down within a stack using the Group button on the Drawing toolbar. | True | False |
| 3. You can align objects to a grid, a set of intersecting lines that form small squares on the slide. | True | False |
| 4. To make changes throughout a presentation you must make changes to all pairs of masters. | True | False |
| 5. You must have at least three objects selected to distribute them. | True | False |
| 6. Column charts show data changes over time or comparison among items. | True | False |
| 7. The system Clipboard holds up to 24 items. | True | False |
| 8. All organization charts consist of different levels that represent the hierarchy. | True | False |
| 9. A branch is all the boxes at the same level regardless of the boxes each reports to. | True | False |
| 10. The Package for CD feature allows the viewer to automatically run your presentations from the CD. | True | False |

## fill-in

Complete the following statements by filling in the blanks with the correct terms.

1. The intersection of a row and column creates a(n) ______________ in which text or data is entered.
2. A(n) ______________ is a box and all the boxes that report to it.
3. The table used to create a chart in PowerPoint is called a ________________.
4. ________________ means to position objects relative to each other by their left, right, top, or bottom edges.
5. A(n) ______________ presentation can be opened and viewed from an e-mail.
6. A(n) _________ chart emphasizes the area under the curve.
7. The ______ or category axis contains the labels of the data being charted.
8. The _________ identifies the patterns or colors assigned to data in a chart.
9. ______________ boxes have the same manager.
10. Changing the ____________ percentage only affects the onscreen display of the slide; it does not change the actual font or object size.

## multiple choice

Circle the letter of the correct response to the questions below.

1. To work with separate parts of a graphic, you must ______________ the elements.
   - **a.** regroup
   - **b.** bring it to front
   - **c.** select
   - **d.** ungroup
2. If you wanted to align objects to a vertical or horizontal line, you would turn on the ________________.
   - **a.** grid
   - **b.** align gauge
   - **c.** guide
   - **d.** form gauge

3. If you needed to create a chart that shows the relationship of each value in the data series to the series as a whole, you would select the ________ chart.
   a. line
   b. pie
   c. column
   d. bar

4. PowerPoint documents can be ______________ to Microsoft Word.
   a. imported
   b. extracted
   c. exported
   d. moved

5. __________________ is the capability of a program to store multiple copied items in the Office Clipboard and then paste one or more of the items into another location or document.
   a. Collecting and pasting
   b. Copying and pasting
   c. Collecting and storing
   d. Duplicating and inserting

6. A(n) ______________________ chart can include any items that have a hierarchical relationship.
   a. pie
   b. organization
   c. bar
   d. area

7. The ______________ ensures that as each object is added to the slide, it is added to the top layer.
   a. stacking order
   b. grouping order
   c. object alignment
   d. branching

8. When an object is close to the ____________, the center or corner snaps to the line.
   a. center
   b. align gauge
   c. guide
   d. form gauge

9. The ______________ is the top-level box of a group.
   a. co-worker box
   b. manager box
   c. subordinate box
   d. branch

10. Features or _________________, such as line or fill color, associated with objects in a group can be changed.
    a. properties
    b. qualities
    c. elements
    d. attributes

rating system

★ Easy

★★ Moderate

★★★ Difficult

## step-by-step

### Employee Morale Presentation ★

1. Chirag Shah works in the personnel department of a manufacturing company. Chirag has recently been studying the ways that employee morale can affect production levels and employee job satisfaction. Chirag has been asked to hold a meeting with department managers to suggest methods that can be used to improve employee morale. He has already started a PowerPoint presentation to accompany his talk, but still needs to make several changes and enhancements to the presentation. Several slides of the completed presentation are shown here.

   a. Start PowerPoint and open the presentation pp03_Employee Motivation. Replace the Student Name placeholder with your name.

   b. Change the design layout on slide 5 to Title, Text, and Content. Insert the graphic pp03_Motivation on slide 5. Size and place the clip art to the right of the text.

   c. Convert the five demoted bullets on slide 3 to a numbered list. Change the color of the numbers.

   d. Demote the last three bullets on slide 5. Add a callout AutoShape containing the words **You're doing a good job, Thanks!** Bold the text in the AutoShape. Position the AutoShape appropriately on the slide.

   e. Insert the clip art of pp03_Success on slide 1. Size and position the clip art appropriately. Ungroup the clip art and delete the tan color from the roof of the building. Regroup the clip art.

   f. Change the design template of the presentation to one of your choice. Change the slide zoom to 100%. Adjust the text and graphics on the slides as needed.

   g. Save the presentation as Employee Motivation2. Print the presentation as handouts, six slides per page.

   h. Export the presentation outline to Word. Save the Word document as Motivation Outline using the Word document file type (.doc). Print the outline.

**Employee Motivation**

Student Name

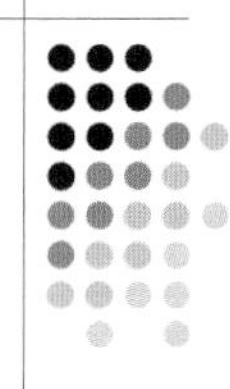

**Topics for Discussion**

- The following have been suggested:
  1. Flexibility
  2. Positive feedback
  3. Expert input
  4. Sharing the wealth
  5. Creating a team

**Positive Feedback**

- Talk with employees one-on-one weekly
- Acknowledge jobs well done publicly
  - in person
  - in monthly staff meeting
  - in company newsletter

You're doing a good job, Thanks!

## Traveling with Your Dog ★ ★

2. The Animal Rescue Foundation has asked you to help them create a presentation to inform the community about traveling with dogs. The presentation is partially completed, and you have been asked to enhance it so that it can be used at an upcoming meeting. Several slides of the completed presentation are shown here.

   a. Start PowerPoint and open the pp03_Doggie Travel presentation. Enter your name on the first slide in place of Student Name.

   b. Change the layout of slide 2 to Title and 2 Content. Insert the file pp03_Auto in the placeholder.

   c. Modify the clip art by changing the turquoise strip to the left of the car to green.

   d. On slide 2 enhance the column headings in the table by applying fill and text colors, increasing the row height, and vertically and horizontally centering the data. Bold all the text in the table.

   e. Increase the font size of the text in the first placeholder on slide 6 to 24.

   f. Insert a Title and Chart slide after slide 4. Delete the data in the datasheet. Copy the slide title and data (exclude the Total column and row) from slide 2. Paste the data into the chart datasheet on slide 5. Make the chart as large as possible and enhance it using the Microsoft Graph features. Paste the slide title you copied into the title for the chart slide.

   g. The travel tips have a duplicated slide. Delete slide 8. Apply a numbered list to the lists on slides 8 and 9. Set the numbering on slide 9 to begin at 5.

   h. Create an AutoShape of your choice on the last slide. Add the text **TRAVEL WITH YOUR DOG** in the AutoShape. Word wrap and resize the AutoShape to fit the text.

   i. Change the fill color to complement the slide. Increase the text size and bold the text. Resize the AutoShape if needed.

   j. Save the presentation as Doggie Travel Tips. E-mail the presentation to your instructor. Print the presentation as handouts with six slides per page.

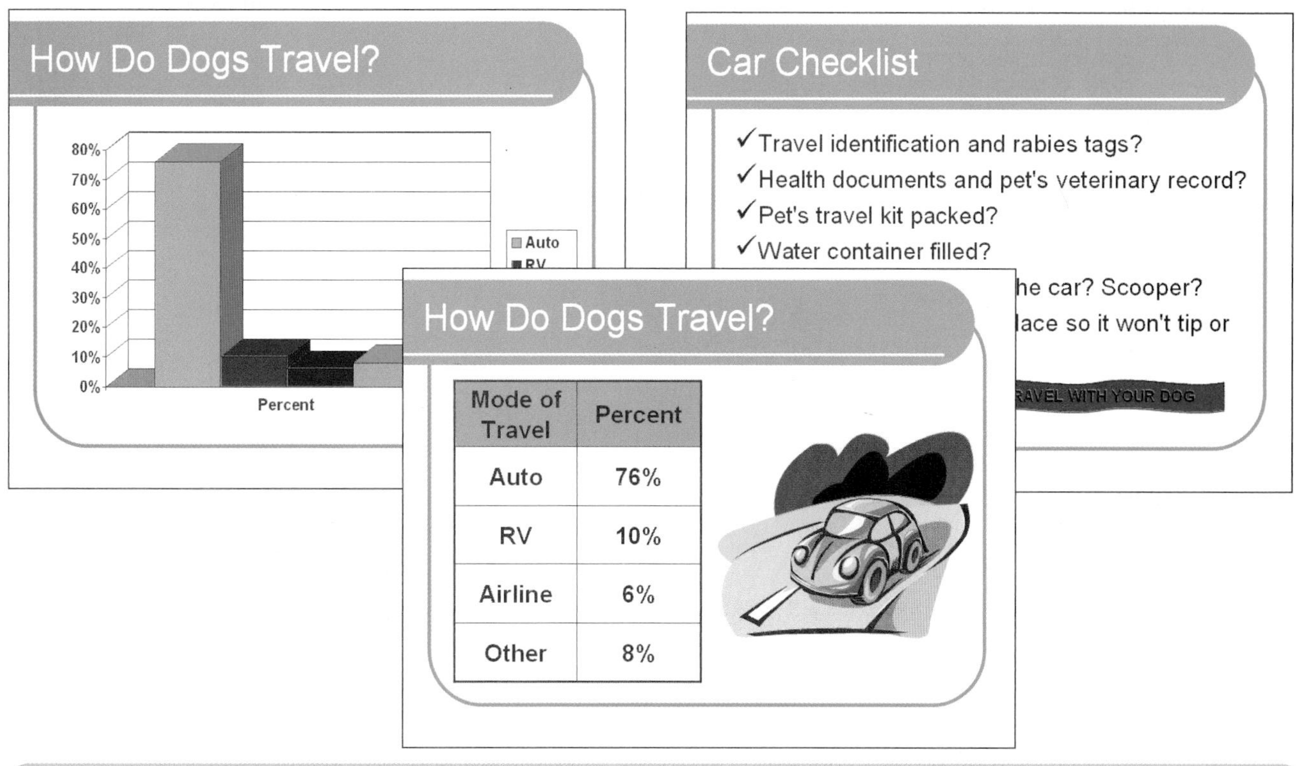

## Soccer Presentation ★ ★

3. You are the assistant coach for the girl's varsity soccer team at Valley High School. You are busy preparing for the upcoming team tryouts and need to finish a presentation you will make to the athletes before tryouts begin. You need to make several changes to the presentation, including a chart of the coaching staff. Several slides of the completed presentation are shown here.

   a. Start PowerPoint and open the file pp03_Valley Soccer.

   b. Change the slide zoom to 100%.

   c. Create a numbered list with the bulleted text on slide 2.

   d. Change the design template to Default Design. Insert the image pp03_Futbol on slide 1. Select slides 2 through 6. Insert the background image pp03_Varsity on these slides.

   e. Add red fill color to the title text box on slide 2. Use the Format Painter to add this color to all of the title text boxes on slides 3 through 6.

   f. Insert a new slide after slide 3 using the organization chart layout. Add an organization chart with the title **Coaching Staff**. Enter **Heather Mills, Head Coach** in the top-level box. Enter the following information into the other chart boxes:

      **Caroline Harrison, Assistant Coach** (second level)

      **Molly Hernandez, Assistant Coach** (second level)

      **Patricia Gardeta, Volunteer Assistant Coach** (second level)

   g. Add word wrap to the text in the Gardeta AutoShape. Add the Fire AutoFormat to the diagram.

   h. Add the date to the footer of the title slide. Adjust the formatting of the slides as needed.

   i. Save the presentation as Valley Soccer Presentation. Print the presentation with six slides per page. Rehearse the timing of the presentation.

   j. Export the presentation outline to Word. Save the outline in Word as Soccer Outline. E-mail the presentation to your instructor.

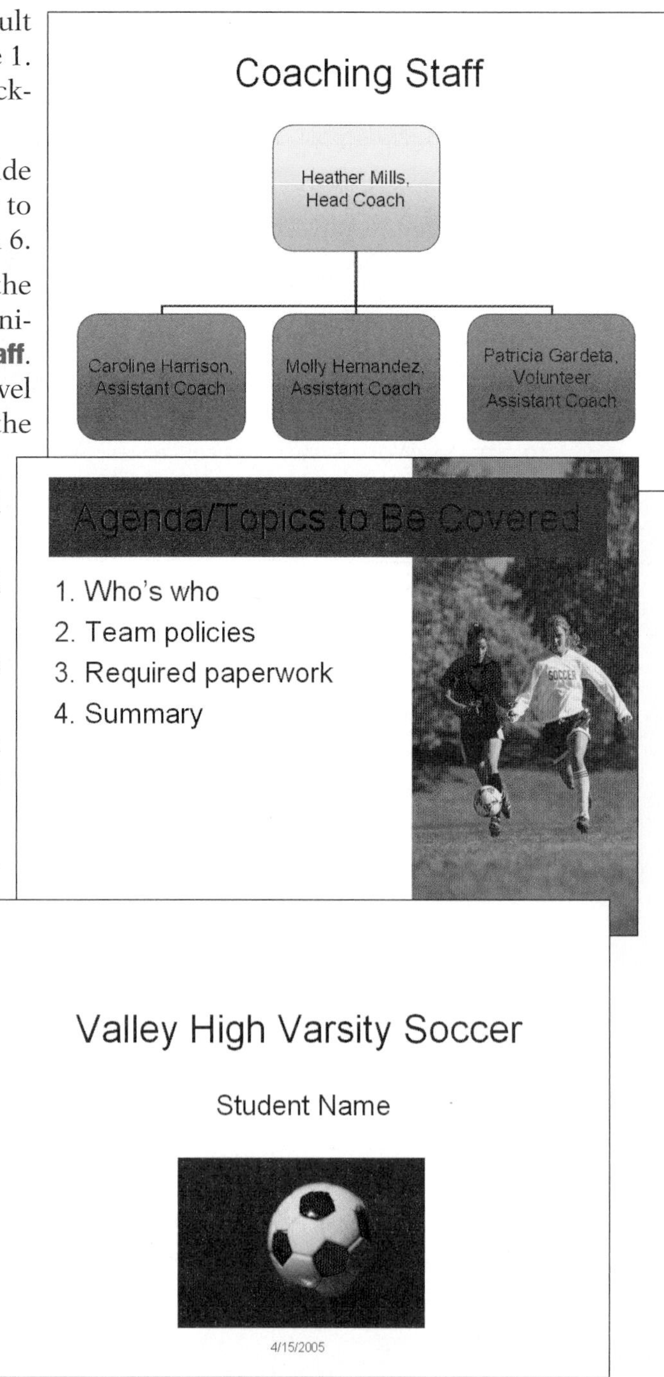

## Nutrition and Exercise Presentation ★★★

4. Annette Ramirez is the new Lifestyle Fitness Club nutritionist. She would like to use the presentation on exercise currently in use by the Club to discuss the benefits of a nutrition plan. She has asked you to modify the current presentation to include some nutrition information. Several slides of the completed presentation are shown here.

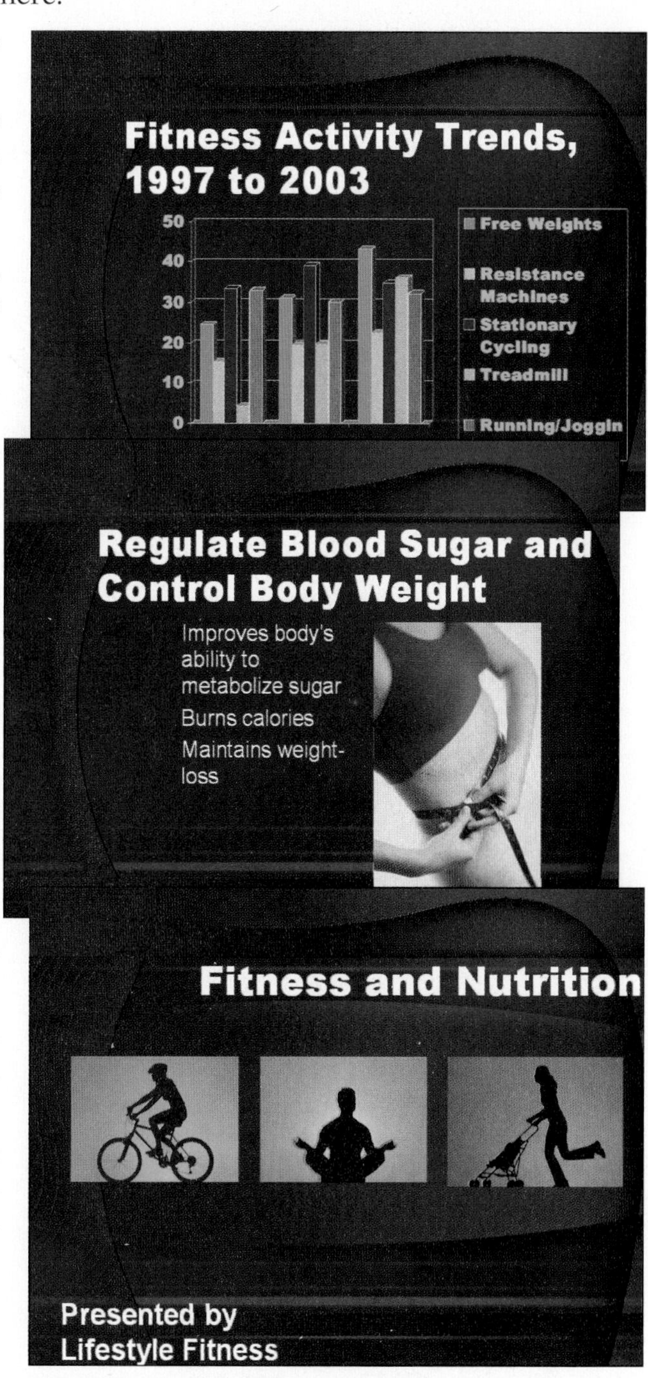


a. Start PowerPoint and open the file pp03_Exercise.

b. Change the zoom to 100%. Change the Slide Design to one of your choice. Check all slides and adjust the text and graphics as needed throughout.

c. Change the bulleted list on slide 3 to a numbered list. Change the color of the numbered list to blue.

d. Use Format Painter to change the bulleted list on slide 4 to a numbered list matching slide 3.

e. Change the title on slide 1 to **Fitness and Nutrition**.

f. Change the title on slide 2 to **What Exercise and Nutrition Can Do for You**.

g. Select and group the three images on slide 1.

h. Change the layout of slide 6 to Title, Text, and Content. Delete the clip art placeholder. Size and position the image to fit the slide.

i. Change the appearance of the table on slide 9 by using text colors, adjusting row heights, and vertically and horizontally centering the labels.

j. Circuit Training has been changed to Advanced Step. Adjust the entries accordingly.

k. Open the Excel file pp03_Fitness Trends. Using the Office Clipboard, copy the two title lines and then copy the worksheet data. Exit Excel.

l. Insert a new slide after slide 10 using the chart layout. Paste the worksheet data into the chart datasheet. Paste the title from Excel into the slide title placeholder. Size the title text appropriately.

m. Delete the border line around the legend. Modify the chart using the features you learned in the lab.

**n.** On the last slide, delete the text box and the subtitle placeholder. Create an AutoShape in a shape of your choice and add the text **Make it part of your life!**

**o.** Word wrap and size the AutoShape text. Change the fill color to match the colors on the slide. Adjust the text size and color as appropriate.

**p.** Insert the file pp03_LFC Logo. Ungroup the graphic. Remove the white border around each of the images (see the example). Size and position the graphic to the left of the title on slide 11.

**q.** Save the presentation as Fitness and Nutrition. Export the outline to Word. Save the Word file as Fitness and Nutrition Outline. Rehearse the timing of the presentation.

**r.** Print the outline. Print the presentation as handouts with six slides per page.

**s.** E-mail the presentation to your instructor.

### Future Job Statistics ★★★

**5.** Your presentation on Job Fairs has really turned out well (Exercise 5 of Lab 2). You did some additional research on the Department of Labor's Web site and found the projected number of college-level jobs in 2008. You think this new data will fit nicely into the presentation as a chart. Several slides of the completed presentation are shown here.

CONTINUING EXERCISES

**a.** Open the PowerPoint file JobFairs2.

**b.** Change the slide zoom to 100%.

**c.** On slide 7 change the bullets to numbers. Change the color of the numbers to red.

**d.** Use the Format Painter to change the text on slide 5 to a red numbered list.

**e.** Insert the image pp03_Hurry on slide 1 as the background.

**f.** Change the color of the woman's dress on slide 2 to gold. Regroup the image.

First Impressions

1. Dress professionally
2. Use a firm handshake
3. Use good posture
4. Show enthusiasm

6

College-Level Jobs

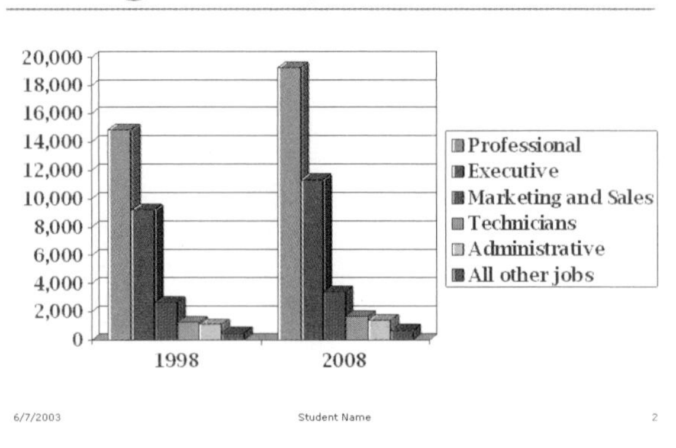


6/7/2003 Student Name 2

Making a Job Fair Work for You

University Career Club

Student Name

**g.** Insert a new Title and Chart slide after slide 1. Title the slide **College-Level Jobs**. Insert a 3-D bar chart and enter the following data into the datasheet:

| Occupational Group | 1998 | 2008 |
|---|---|---|
| Professional | 14,860 | 19,250 |
| Executive | 9,200 | 11,320 |
| Marketing and Sales | 2,640 | 3,400 |
| Technicians | 1,250 | 1,690 |
| Administrative | 1,090 | 1,390 |
| All other jobs | 510 | 690 |

**h.** Delete the clip art on slide 6 and insert the image pp03_Jobs. Adjust the image appropriately. Rehearse the timing of the presentation.

**i.** Save your completed presentation as JobFairs3. Print the presentation as handouts with six slides per page.

**j.** E-mail the presentation to your instructor. Export the presentation to Word as an Outline. Save the document as Jobs Outline.

**j.** Package the presentation for CD in a folder named Jobs.

## on your own

### Family Reunion Presentation ★

**1.** Your family is holding a reunion in your home town this year. They have heard all about your new computer skills, and one of your aunts has requested you put on a presentation following the welcome dinner. Using the skills you have learned so far, create a presentation that includes an organization chart for your family tree, photos you have scanned, family anecdotes, and graphics. Save your presentation as Family Reunion and print it with six slides per page. Consider e-mailing your completed work to a family member.

### Lifeguard Orientation ★

**2.** As part of your job as Head Lifeguard at the local pool, you have been asked to create a presentation for the new lifeguard training seminar. Use the data provided in pp03_Lifegaurd to create a presentation on pool safety. Use the skills you have learned in the lab to include a numbered list of steps on water safety. Create an organization chart to explain the chain of command. Format the slides as you like. Save your presentation as Lifeguard Presentation. Print the slides.

### Updating the Travel Presentation ★ ★

**3.** Your fellow Getaway Travel Club members are really excited about choosing the club's upcoming summer trip. Your presentation to the club went very well (Lab 2, On Your Own 5), and your locale was chosen to be among the finalists to present to the club officers. If chosen, your presentation will be placed on the club's Web site. You need to do more research on your locale to include the costs associated with the trip. You decide that the data would be easier to understand and more convincing if it were presented in chart form. Using your file Travel Favorites, modify the presentation. Create charts for the costs you researched. Update your information on the key tourist attractions with better graphics. Save your updated presentation as Travel Favorites2. Prepare the presentation for CD. Export the presentation to Word as an outline and print the slides.

### Storyland Fairytale Presentation ★ ★ ★

4. You work in a children's bookstore called Storyland. The owner has asked you to put together a presentation that highlights some of the more popular titles available at the store. The presentation will be used as part of new employee orientation. Your completed presentation should include a chart that tracks sales, a numbered list that includes sales tips, a custom background, modified graphics, and an organization chart. Save your presentation as Storyland Orientation. Prepare overheads of the presentation and e-mail your presentation to your instructor.

### Preventing Network Infection Presentation ★ ★ ★

5. Your computer survey class requires you to do a research project on computer viruses and worms. Do some research on the Web to learn more about viruses and worms and how companies and schools are protecting their networks from infection. Create a PowerPoint presentation that includes the features, products, and methodologies you have learned about. Search the Web for appropriate clip art images that you can group or ungroup as necessary to enhance your slides. If appropriate data is available, create a chart that displays the increase in viruses reported over the last five years. Include your name and the current date in a footer on the slides. Save your presentation as Preventing Network Infection. Export the slides to Word as an outline. Print the outline and six-slides-per-page handouts.

# Creating a Presentation for a Kiosk and the Web

# LAB 4

## Objectives

**After completing this lab, you will know how to:**

1. Create a presentation from a design template
2. Import text from other sources.
3. Insert slides from another presentation.
4. Create a complex table.
5. Add animated graphics.
6. Create and modify a WordArt object.
7. Add sound.
8. Set up a self-running presentation.
9. Create custom shows.
10. Create an agenda slide.
11. Add hyperlinks and action buttons.
12. Publish a presentation on the Web.
13. Create a design template.

# Case Study

## Animal Rescue Foundation

The director of the Animal Rescue Foundation has asked you to create a presentation promoting the organization that will run on a kiosk in the local shopping mall. This presentation needs to capture the attention of passers-by in a very busy area. Two ways to capture attention are to add animation and sound. You will add several different animation and sound features to your presentation, along with music that will play throughout the entire presentation. At the end, the presentation will loop back to the first slide and continue playing.

You also want to publish this presentation on the Animal Rescue Foundation's Web site. PowerPoint 2003 will automatically convert a presentation to a format that runs on the Web. Since you want to give the viewer a means to navigate through the presentation, you will add navigation buttons that go forward and back through the slides. You will also add a home page that contains links to key slides in the presentation. The completed self-running presentation and Web page are shown here.

© Getty Images

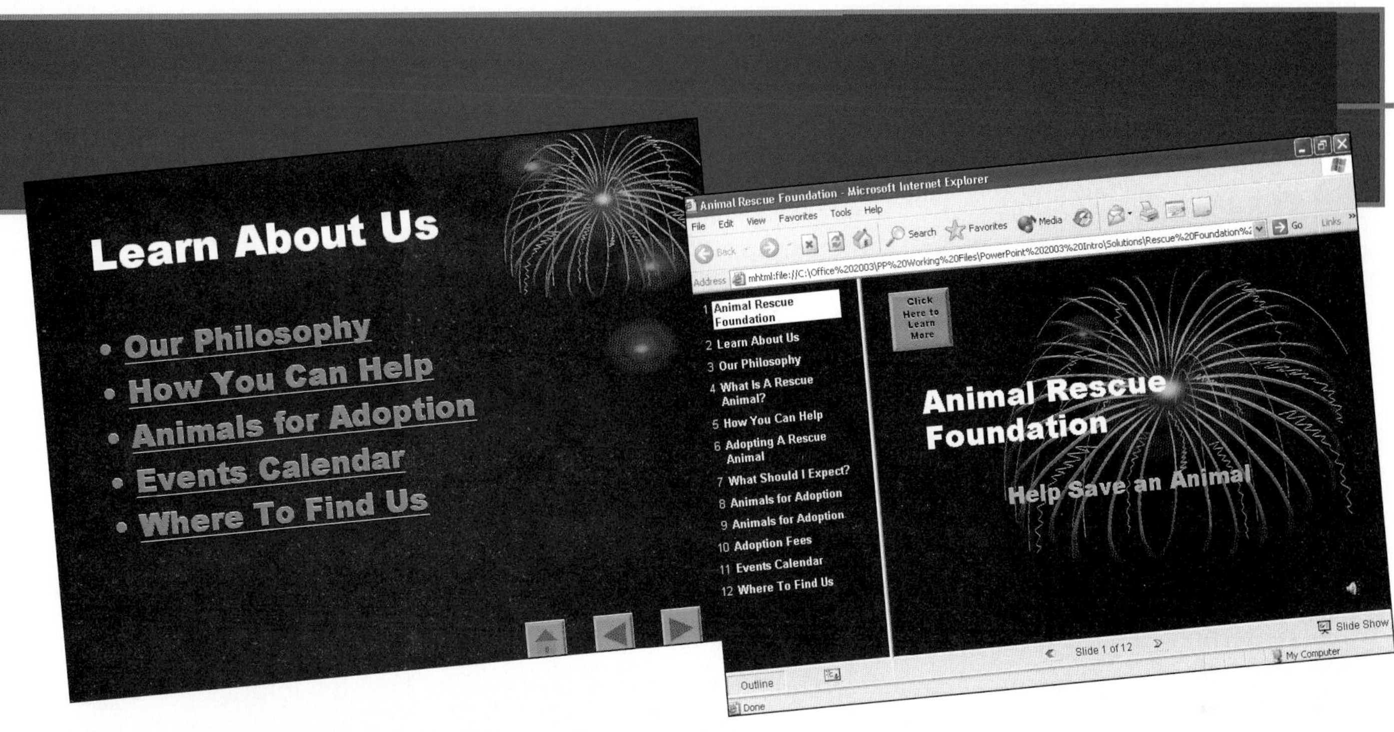


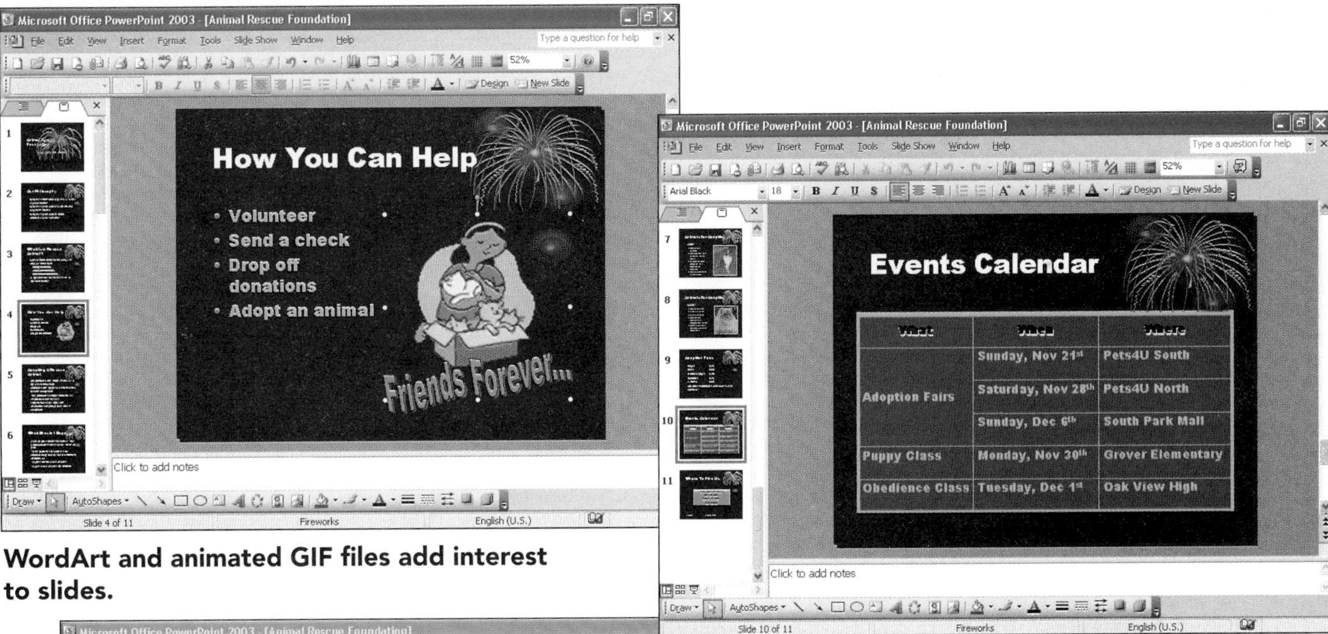


WordArt and animated GIF files add interest to slides.

Using tables makes information easier to read.

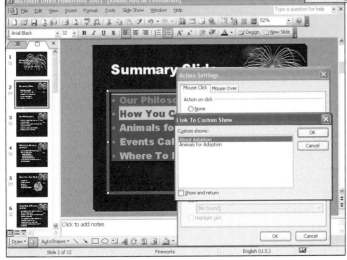

Creating a summary slide with hyperlinks adds custom navigation to a presentation.

## Concept Preview

The following concepts will be introduced in this lab:

1. **Animated GIF** An animated GIF file is a type of graphic file that has motion.
2. **WordArt** The WordArt feature is used to enhance slides by changing the shape of text, adding 3-D effects, and changing the alignment of text on a line.
3. **Sound and Movie Files** Almost all PCs today are equipped with multimedia capabilities, which means they can play the most commonly used sound and movie files.
4. **Custom Show** A custom show is a presentation that runs within a presentation.
5. **Hyperlinks** Hyperlinks provide a quick way to jump to other slides, custom shows, presentations, objects, e-mail addresses, or Web pages.
6. **Action Buttons** Action buttons consist of shapes, such as right- and left-facing arrows, that are used to navigate through a presentation.
7. **Hypertext Markup Language** All Web pages are written using a programming language called Hypertext Markup Language (HTML). HTML commands control how the information on a page, such as font colors and size, is displayed.

# Creating a Presentation from Multiple Sources

Often, as you are developing a presentation, you will have information from a variety of sources, such as text from a Word document or slides from other presentations. You can easily incorporate this information into a presentation without having to recreate it again.

## Creating a New Presentation from a Design Template

When you first start PowerPoint 2003, a blank new presentation in the default template design is open. Because you have already decided to use the Fireworks design template for the new presentation, you will create a new presentation using this design first.

**1** **Start PowerPoint 2003.**

- **Choose Create a New Presentation from the Getting Started task pane.**

**Additional Information**

Clicking New on the Standard toolbar opens a new blank presentation in the Default Design template and the Slide Layout task pane.

- **Choose From Design Template.**
- **If necessary, select Show Large Previews from the Slide Design task pane shortcut menu.**
- **Click on the Fireworks design template to apply it to the presentation.**

*Your screen should be similar to Figure 4.1*

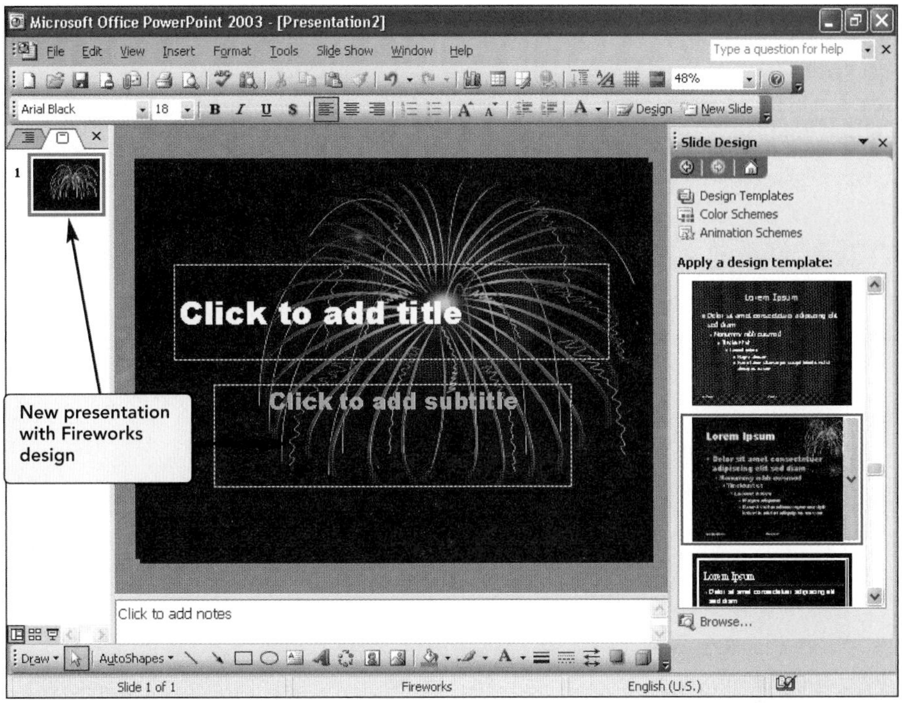

Figure 4.1

**Additional Information**

Each unnamed presentation you open during a session is assigned a number.

The default presentation is closed and a new presentation (Presentation2) consisting of one slide in the Fireworks design is displayed. Now you are ready to add content to the presentation.

**2**

- **Close the Slide Design task pane.**
- **Type Animal Rescue Foundation in the title text box.**
- **Type Help Save an Animal in the subtitle text box.**

*Your screen should be similar to Figure 4.2*

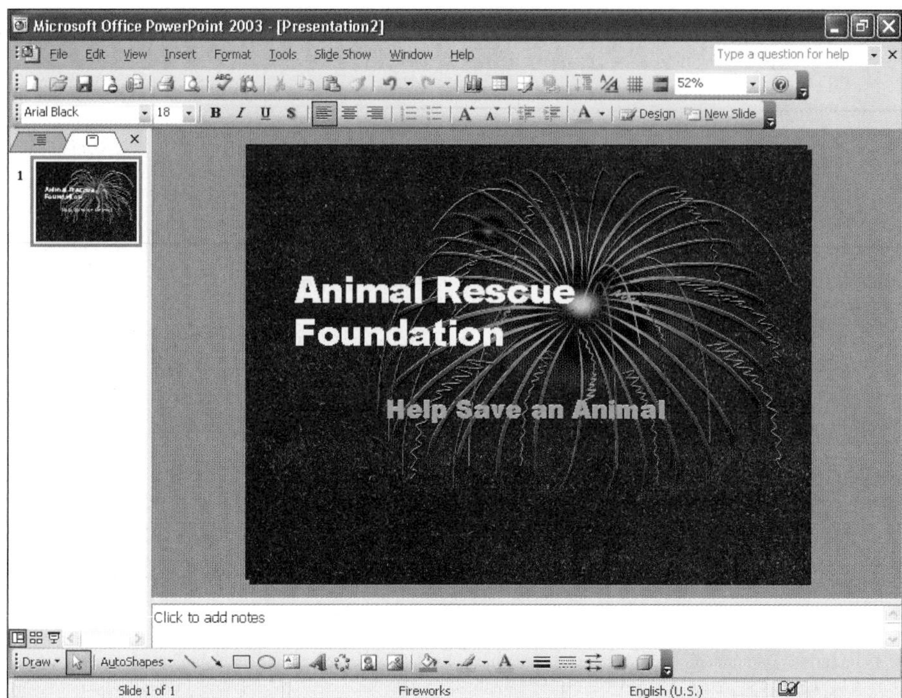


**Figure 4.2**

Before you can add additional text, you need to add slides to the presentation.

## Inserting Text from a Word Document

**Additional Information**

Text created in other word processing programs can also be used to create a new presentation. The text files that PowerPoint can import are Word (.doc), Rich Text Format (.rft), Plain Text Format (.txt), or HTML (.htm) files.

**Additional Information**

In Word, if you apply Outline Numbering styles to the outline text, save the file as a Rich Text Format (rtf) file before importing it to PowerPoint. This removes the Numbering style so that outline numbers do not appear on the slide, but maintains the heading style.

You have already started developing the content for the promotional presentation by creating an outline in Word. Instead of retyping this information, you will insert slides containing the text for the presentation by importing the outline. For best results, the document you want to import should be formatted using heading styles so PowerPoint can easily convert the file content to slides. PowerPoint uses the heading levels to determine the slide title and levels for the slide body text. If heading levels are not available, PowerPoint determines these features from the paragraph indentations.

Additionally, you have another document that contains information about specific animals that are available for adoption. You will use the information from both of these documents to quickly create the new presentation.

As you created the outline in Outline view in Word, heading styles were automatically applied. Now all you have to do is import the outline into PowerPoint.

**1**

- **Choose Insert/Slides from Outline.**
- **Change to your data file location.**
- **If necessary, change the file type to All Outlines.**
- **Select** pp04_Promotional Outline.
- **Click** Insert.

*Your screen should be similar to Figure 4.3*

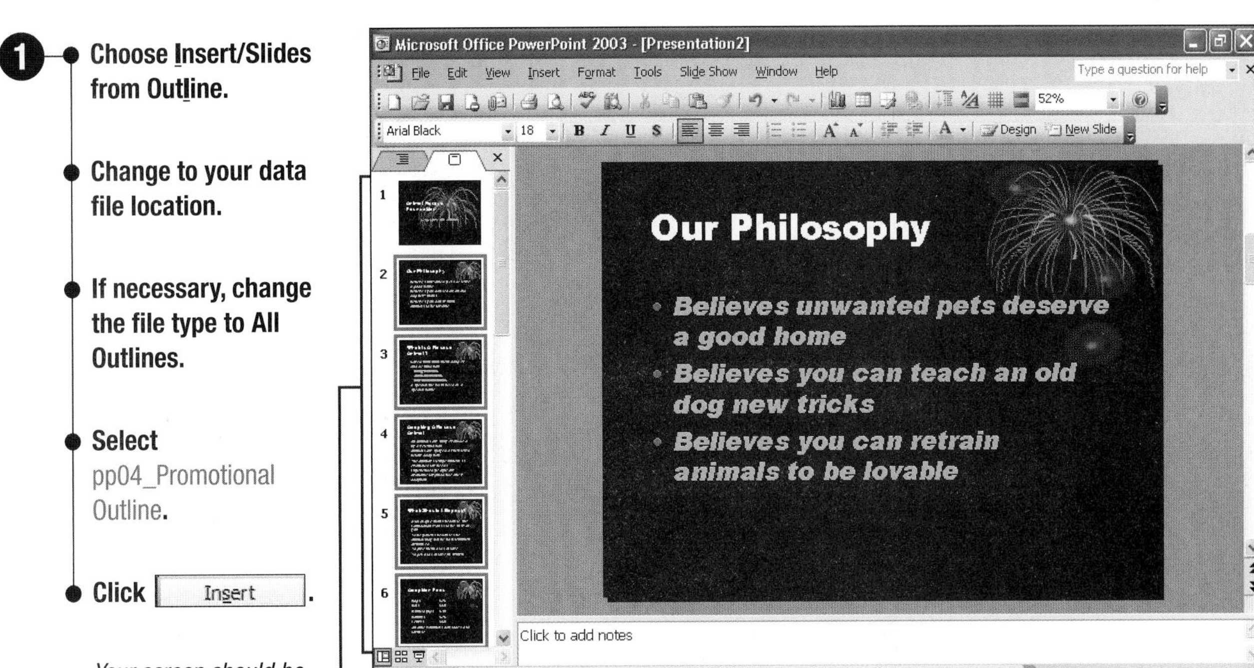


**Figure 4.3**

**Another Method**

You can create a presentation directly from within Word using File/Send to/Microsoft PowerPoint.

The outline text is imported into the blank presentation and inserted as separate slides. Each level 1 heading appears as an individual slide title. Text formatted as a level 2 heading is a main body text point, a level 3 heading is a second-level body text point, and so on.

Now you want to add the information about the animals available for adoption.

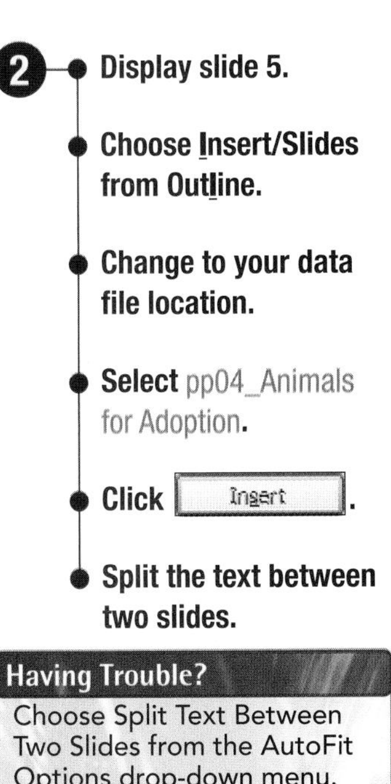

**2**

- **Display slide 5.**
- **Choose Insert/Slides from Outline.**
- **Change to your data file location.**
- **Select** pp04_Animals for Adoption.
- **Click** Insert.
- **Split the text between two slides.**

**Having Trouble?**

Choose Split Text Between Two Slides from the AutoFit Options drop-down menu.

*Your screen should be similar to Figure 4.4*

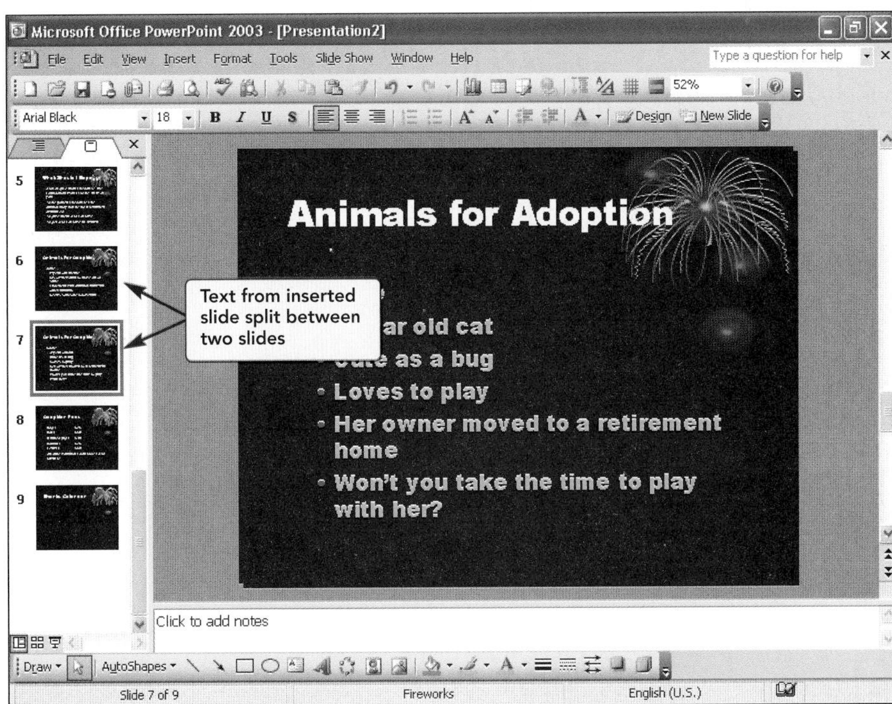


**Figure 4.4**

Slides 6 and 7 now contain the information about the animals currently available for adoption.

## Inserting Slides from Another Presentation

Next you want to add two more slides to the presentation. To save time, you will insert slides that have already been created in another presentation into your current presentation. First you will add a slide after slide 3.

**1**
- **Display slide 3.**
- **Choose Insert/Slides from Files.**
- **Open the Find Presentation tab, if necessary.**

*Your screen should be similar to Figure 4.5*

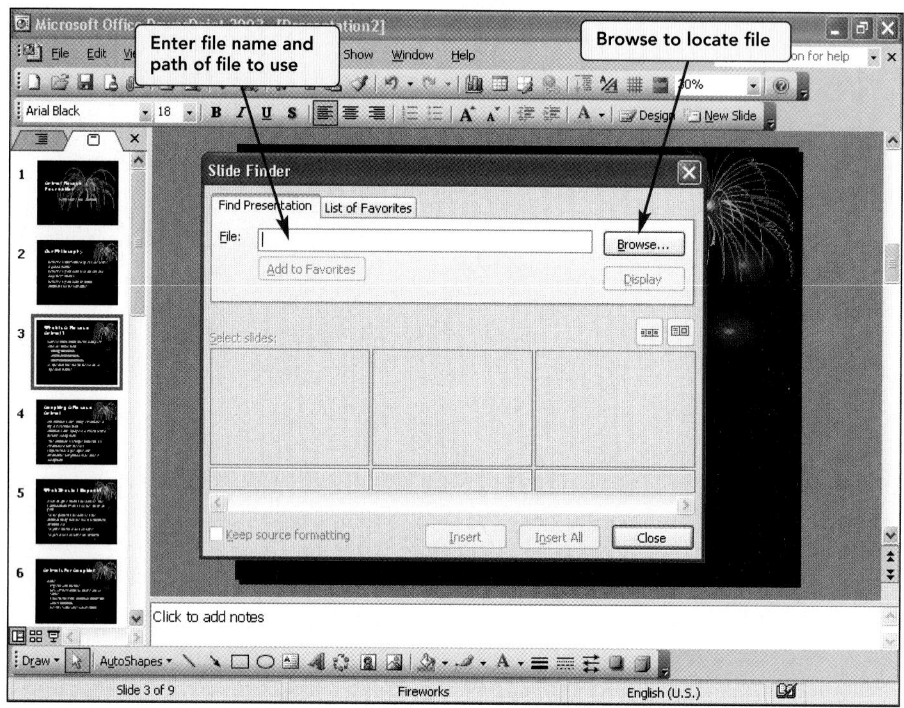


**Figure 4.5**

The Slide Finder dialog box is used to locate the presentation file containing the slides you want to copy into your current presentation. You can enter the file name and path directly in the File text box, or use the [Browse...] button to locate and select the file just as you would when opening an existing presentation.

**2** Click Browse... .

Change the Look In location to the location of your data files.

Select pp04_Foundation Introduction.

Click Open .

*Your screen should be similar to Figure 4.6*

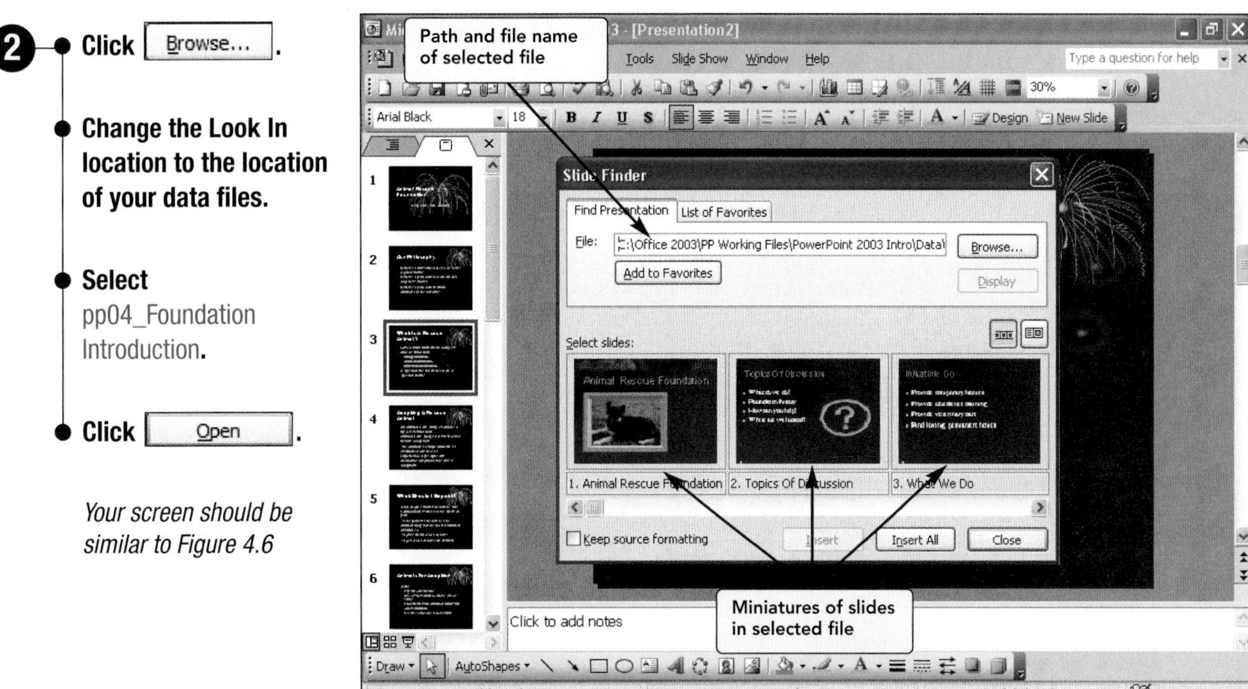


**Figure 4.6**

**Additional Information**

Click [horizontal icon] to switch to horizontal format and [list icon] to switch to list format.

The path and file name of the selected file are displayed in the File text box. In addition, miniatures of the slides in the presentation are displayed in the Select Slides area. You can view the slides in two different formats: horizontal or list. Horizontal format displays a miniature of each slide side by side with the slide title below each slide. This is the default view. List format displays the titles of all slides in the presentation in a list and a preview of the selected slide.

**3** Scroll the slides to the right and select slide 5, How You Can Help.

Click Insert .

*Your screen should be similar to Figure 4.7*

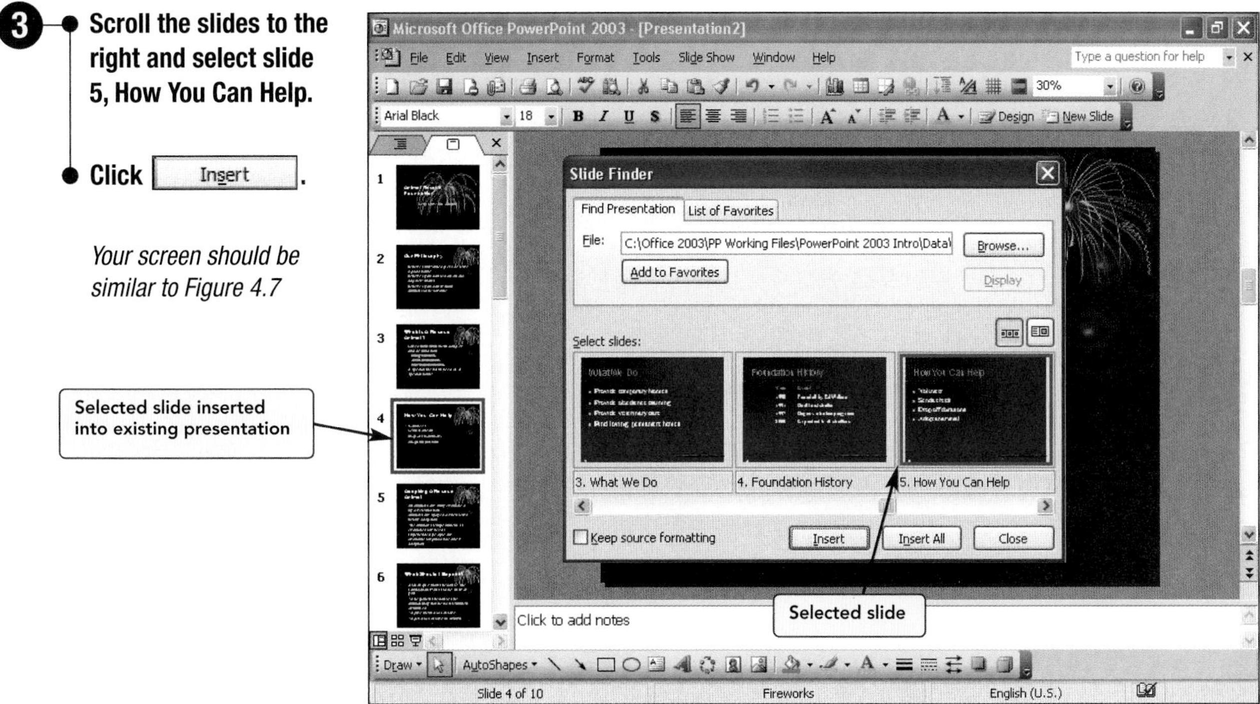


**Figure 4.7**

The selected slide from the Foundation Introduction presentation file is inserted into the new presentation and the template design is applied to the slide. Next you will insert the last slide from the Foundation Introduction presentation as the ending slide (11) of the new presentation.

**4**

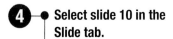

- **Select slide 10 in the Slide tab.**
- **Click on slide 5 from the Select Slides area of the dialog box to deselect it.**

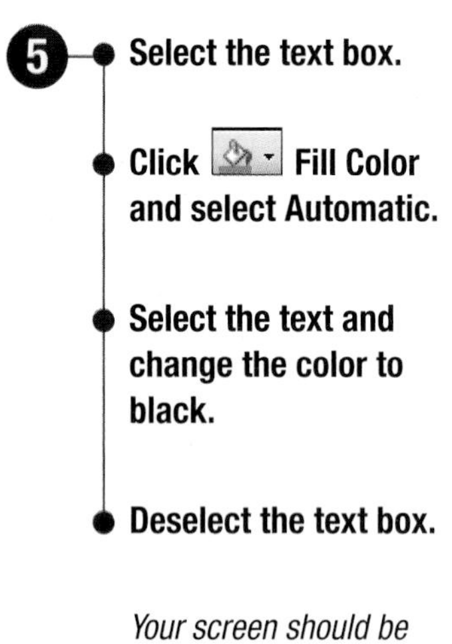

**Additional Information**

A dark border surrounds a selected slide.

- **Click on slide 6 from the Select Slides area of the dialog box to select it.**
- **Click Insert.**
- **Click Close.**

*Your screen should be similar to Figure 4.8*

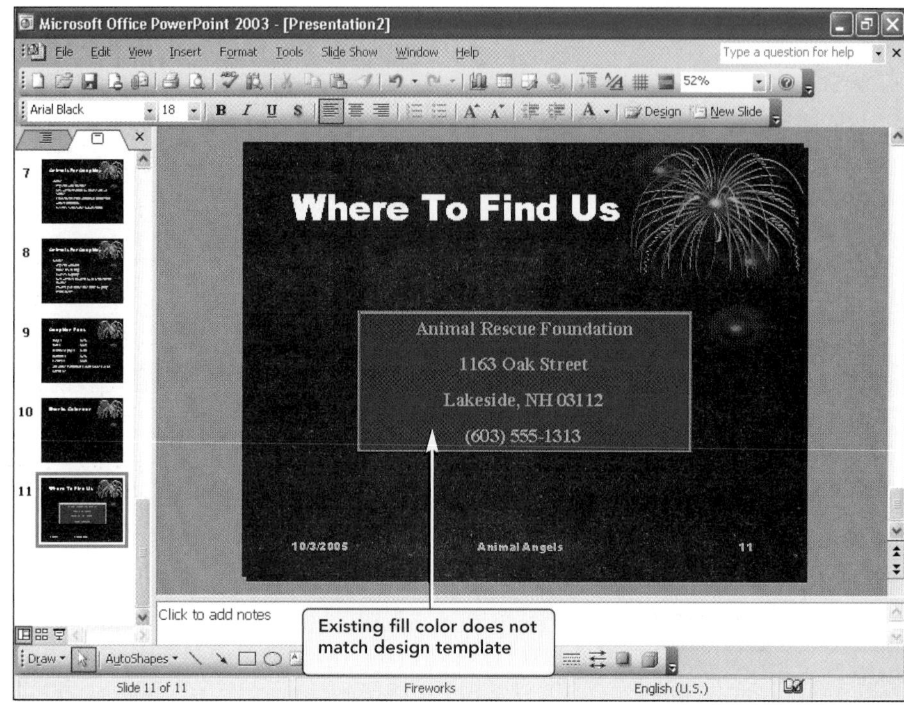


**Figure 4.8**

Now that all the slides you need have been added to the presentation, you need to make a few design adjustments. First you need to change the fill and font color of the text box to coordinate with the template colors.

**5**

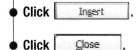

- **Select the text box.**
- **Click Fill Color and select Automatic.**
- **Select the text and change the color to black.**
- **Deselect the text box.**

*Your screen should be similar to Figure 4.9*

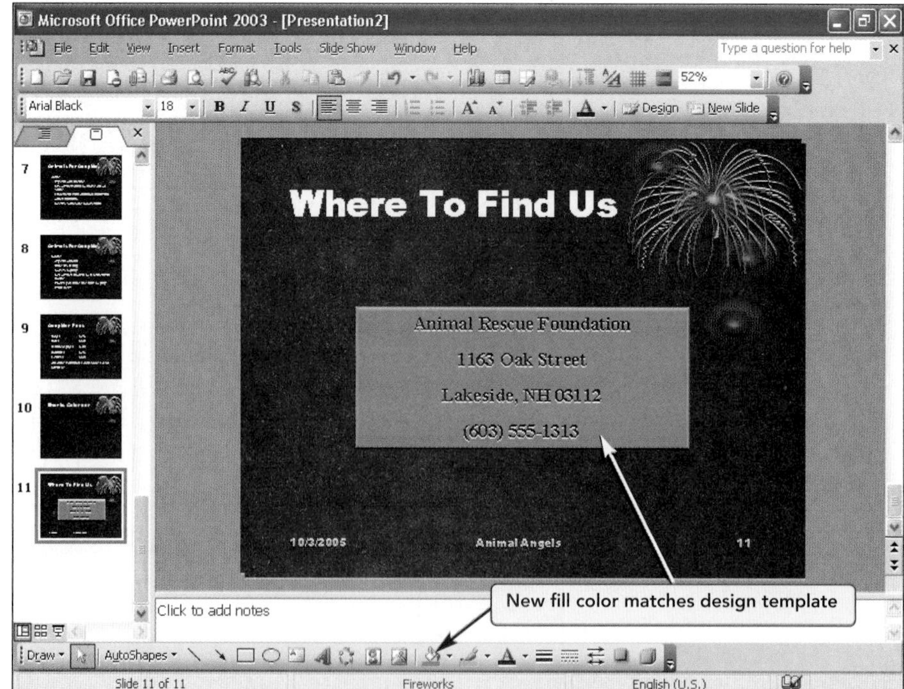


**Figure 4.9**

Next, make the following changes to the slides specified.

**6**

- **Change the slide layout of slide 7 to the Title, Text, and Content.**
- **Insert the picture file** pp04_Jake **from your data files on slide 7.**
- **Appropriately size and position the picture.**
- **Add a 6 pt dark gold border around the picture.**

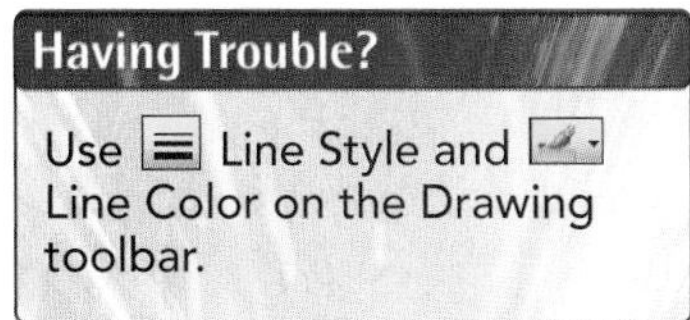

**Having Trouble?**

Use Line Style and Line Color on the Drawing toolbar.

*Your screen should be similar to Figure 4.10*

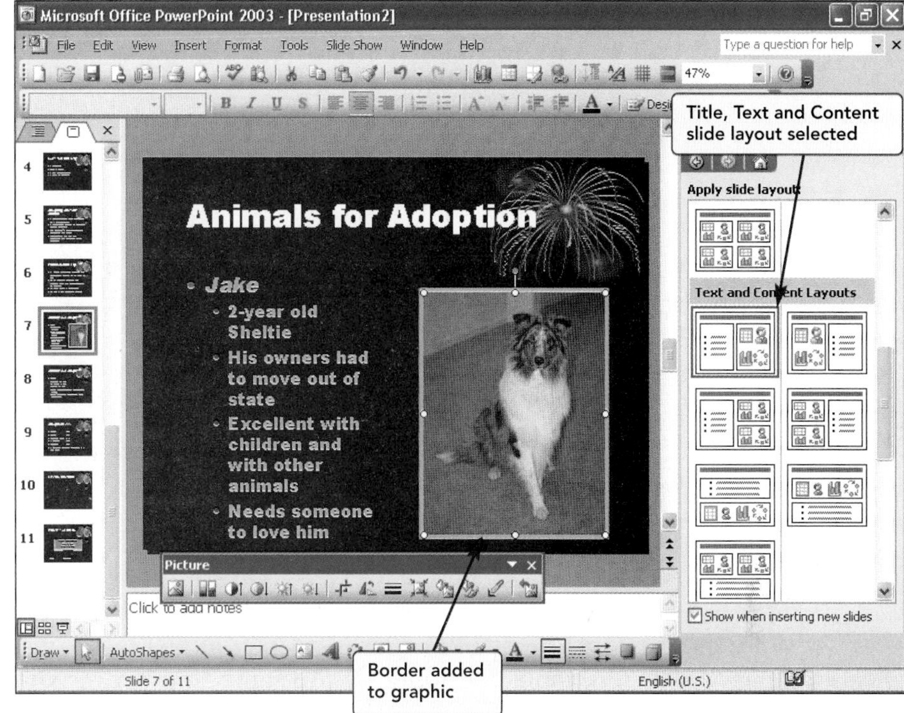


Figure 4.10

The addition of the graphic adds much more impact to the slide.

**7**

- **Repeat the same steps to add the picture file** pp04_Sadie **from your data files to slide 8.**
- **Change to Slide Sorter view.**
- **Run the slide show from the beginning to see how all the changes you have made so far look.**
- **Save the presentation as** Animal Rescue Foundation**.**

*Your screen should be similar to Figure 4.11*

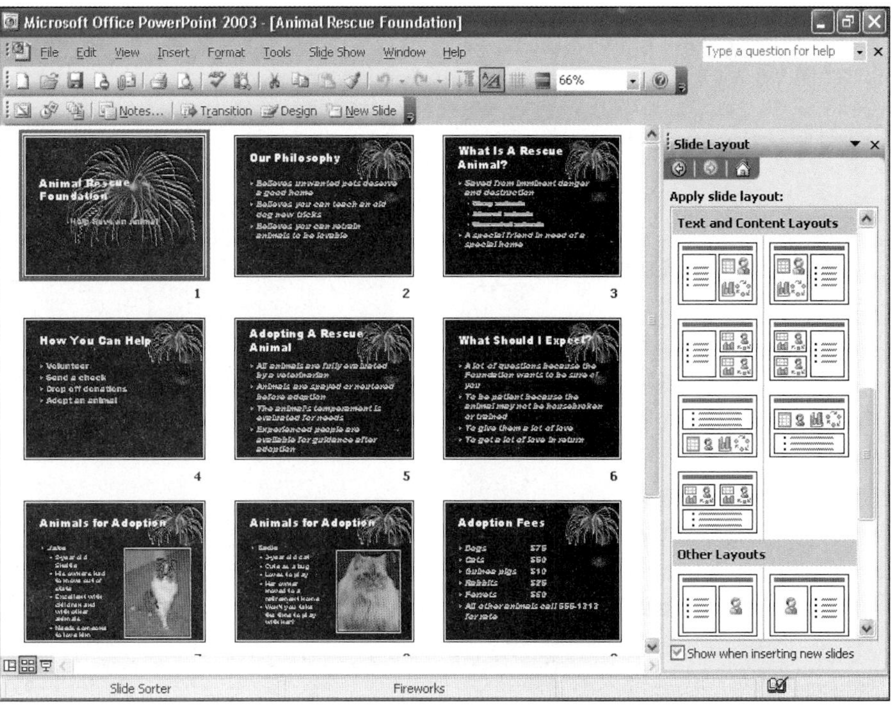


Figure 4.11

## Creating a Complex Table

Next you want to add a calendar of events in a table format. The table will display the type, date, and location of the event. Your completed table will be similar to the one shown below.

| [illegible] | [illegible] | [illegible] |
|---|---|---|
| Adoption Fairs | Sunday, Nov 21st | Pets4U South |
| | Saturday, Nov 28th | Pets4U North |
| | Sunday, Dec 6th | South Park Mall |
| Puppy Class | Monday, Nov 30th | Grover Elementary |
| Obedience Class | Tuesday, Dec 1st | Oak View High |

PowerPoint includes several different methods that you can use to create tables. One method is to apply the Table slide layout to a slide. You used this method to create a simple table in Lab 2. Another method uses the Insert/Table command or the Insert Table button to create a simple table consisting of the same number of rows and columns. Finally, Draw Table can be used to create any type of table, but is most useful for creating complex tables that contain cells of different heights or a varying number of columns per row. You will use the Draw Table feature to create this table.

**1**

- **Display slide 10, Events Calendar in Normal view.**
- **Apply the Title Only slide layout.**
- **Close the Slide Layout task pane.**
- **Click Tables and Borders.**
- **If necessary, dock the Tables and Borders toolbar below the Formatting toolbar.**

*Your screen should be similar to Figure 4.12*

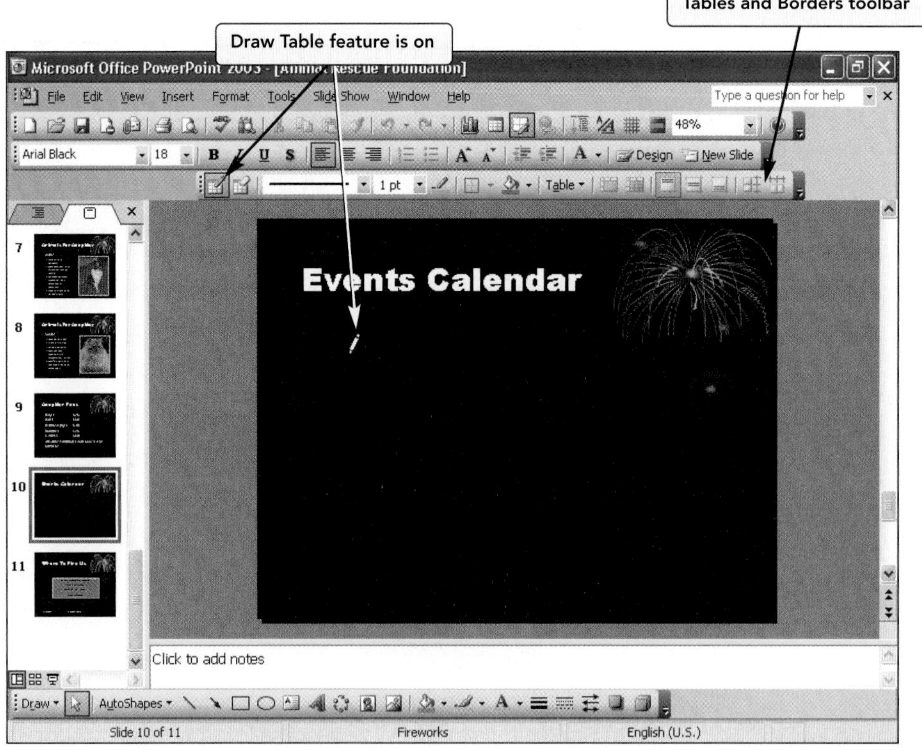


**Figure 4.12**

The Tables and Borders toolbar appears, and the mouse pointer changes to a pen when positioned on the slide. This indicates the Draw Table feature is on.

Using Draw Table to create a table is similar to the way you would use a pen to draw a table. First you define the outer table boundary by dragging diagonally to the size you want. Then you drag to create the column and row lines. A dotted line appears to show the boundary or lines you are creating as you drag. When creating row or column lines, drag from the beginning boundary to the end to extend the line the distance you want.

You will use Draw Table to create the table boundary and columns and rows. As you do, refer to Figure 4.13 for guidance. When creating a table using this feature, it is also helpful to display the ruler so you can more accurately draw the table lines.

**2**

- **Choose View/Ruler to display the ruler.**
- **Drag downward and to the right to create an outer table boundary of approximately 3.5 inches by 7.5 inches.**
- **Add two vertical column lines at positions 2.5 and 5.5 on the ruler.**
- **Draw five horizontal lines to create the rows as shown in Figure 4.13. (Lines 2 and 3 begin at the end of the first column.)**

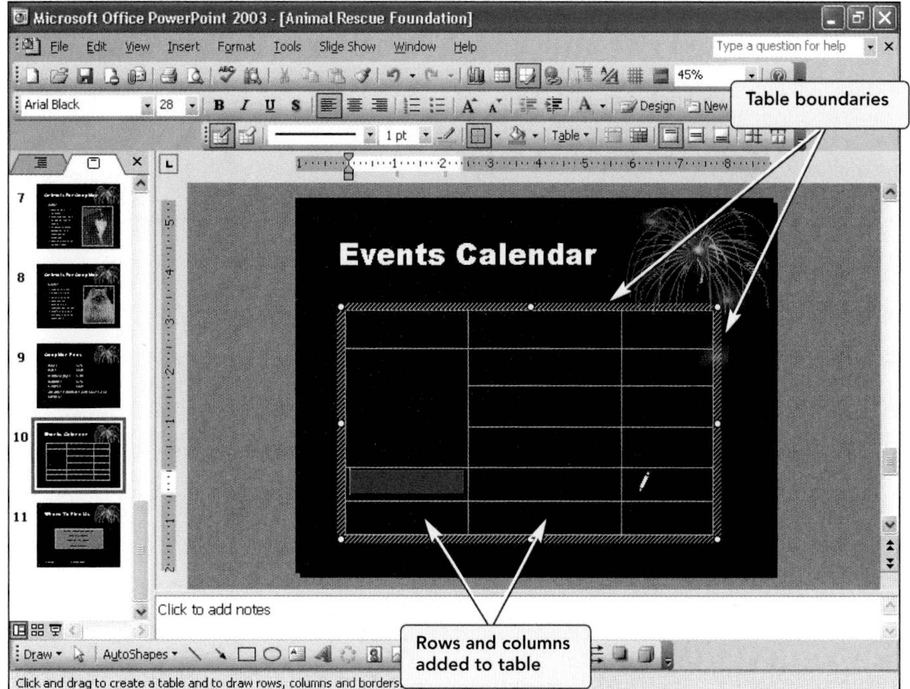


**Figure 4.13**

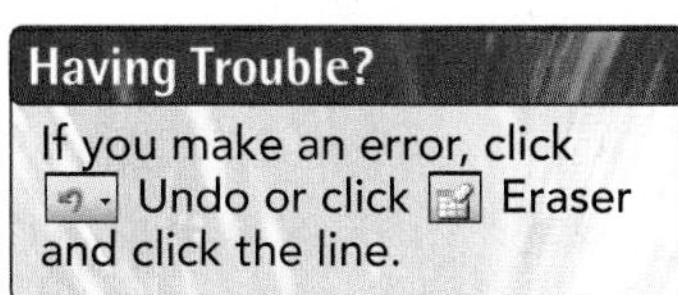
**Having Trouble?**

If you make an error, click Undo or click Eraser and click the line.

*Your screen should be similar to Figure 4.13*

Do not be concerned if your table is not exactly like that in Figure 4.13. You will adjust the table lines shortly.

Now you are ready to enter the information into the table. As you enter the text, the cells will automatically increase in size to accommodate the entries and the text will wrap in the cells.

**3** **Click Draw Table to turn off the Draw Table feature.**

**Another Method**

Typing in any cell will also turn off Draw Table.

**Enter the data shown at right.**

| | Col A | Col B | Col C |
|---|---|---|---|
| Row 1 | What | When | Where |
| Row 2 | Adoption Fairs | Saturday, Nov 21st | Pets4U South |
| Row 3 | | Saturday, Nov 28th | Pets4U North |
| Row 4 | | Sunday, Dec 6th | South Park Mall |
| Row 5 | Puppy Class | Monday, Nov 30th | Grover Elementary |
| Row 6 | Obedience Class | Tuesday, Dec 1st | Oak View High |

**Additional Information**

You can copy and edit similar table entries to save time.

**Additional Information**

The "st" and "th" following the date will automatically change to superscript as soon as you enter a space after the word.

*Your screen should be similar to Figure 4.14*

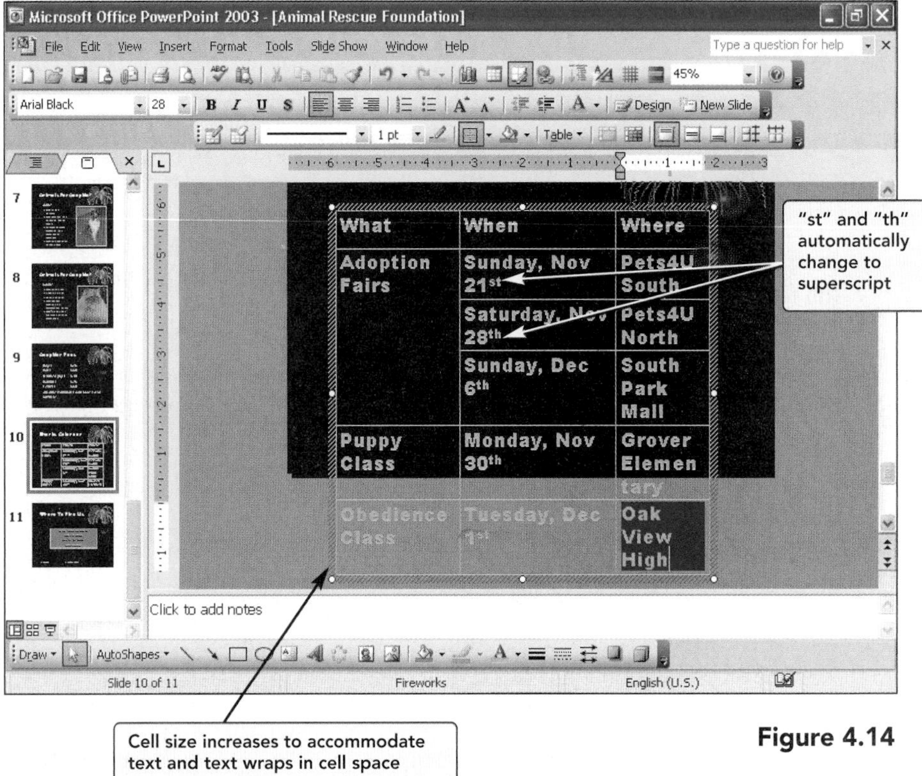


**Figure 4.14**

Because the table size has increased to accommodate the information in the table, it is too large to fit on the slide. You will fix this by making the font size of the text in the table smaller.

## Enhancing the Table

**Additional Information**

Many commands for working with tables are available by clicking Table on the Tables and Borders toolbar.

Next you need to adjust the size of the text, size the columns and rows appropriately, and add other enhancements to the table. As you continue to modify the table, the contents of many cells can be selected and changed at the same time. The following table describes how to select different areas of a table.

| Area to Select | Procedure |
|---|---|
| Cell | Drag across the contents of the cell. |
| Row | Drag across the row.<br>Use Table /Select Row. |
| Column | Drag down the column.<br>Use Table /Select Column. |
| Multiple cells, rows, or columns | Drag through the cells, rows, or columns.<br>Select the first cell, row, or column, and hold down ⇧Shift while clicking on another cell, row, or column. |
| Contents of next cell | Press Tab. |
| Contents of previous cell | Press ⇧Shift + Tab. |
| Entire table | Drag through all the cells.<br>Use Table /Select Table.<br>Click the crosshatched table border. |

**Additional Information**

A dotted table border indicates the entire table and all its contents are selected.

First you will reduce the size of the text. You could do this by selecting a point size from the drop-down list. Another way, however, is to decrease the size by units.

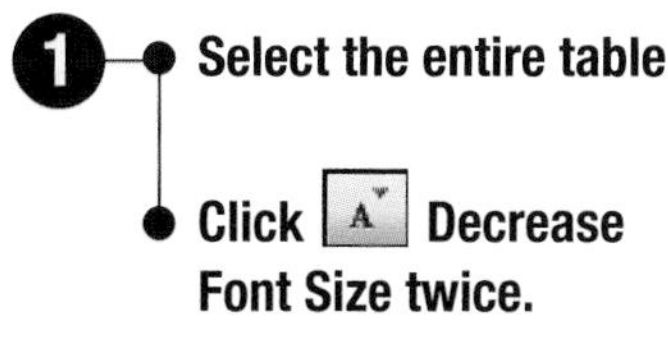

**1** **Select the entire table.**

**Click A Decrease Font Size twice.**

**Having Trouble?**

Clicking A increases the fonts size by units.

*Your screen should be similar to Figure 4.15*

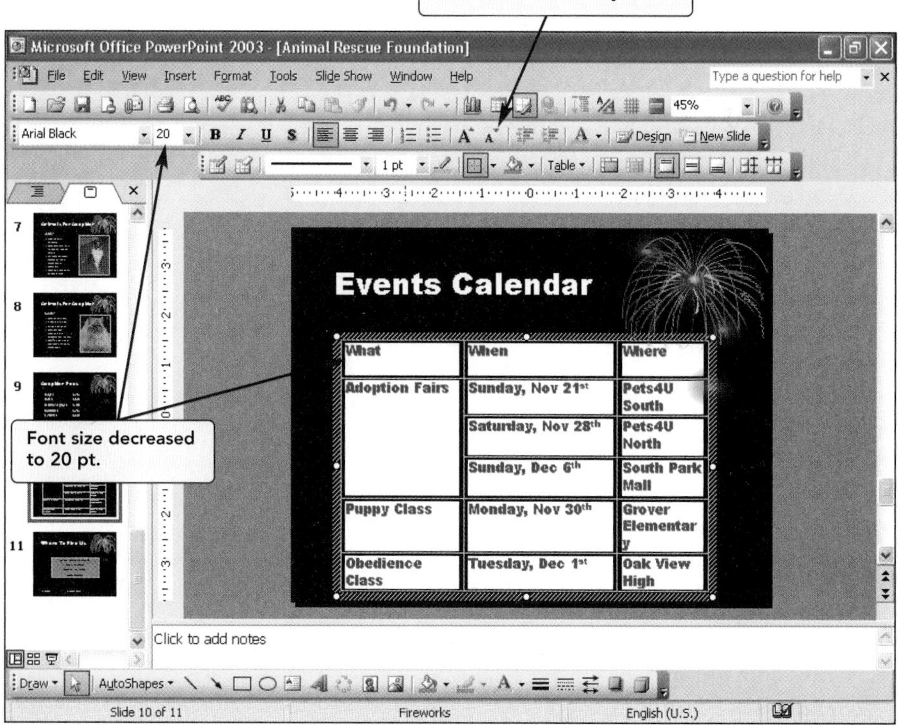


**Figure 4.15**

The font size has quickly been reduced by two units, and at 20 points the table now fits in the slide. Next, you will adjust the column widths so that the cell contents will display on a single line.

**2**

- Point to the right border of column A and drag to increase or decrease the column width until the information in the What column just fits on a single line.
- In the same manner, adjust the When and Where column widths as needed to display the cell contents on a single line.

**Having Trouble?**

You may need to increase the size of the entire table to display the cell contents on a single line.

- Position the table as in Figure 4.16.

*Your screen should be similar to Figure 4.16*

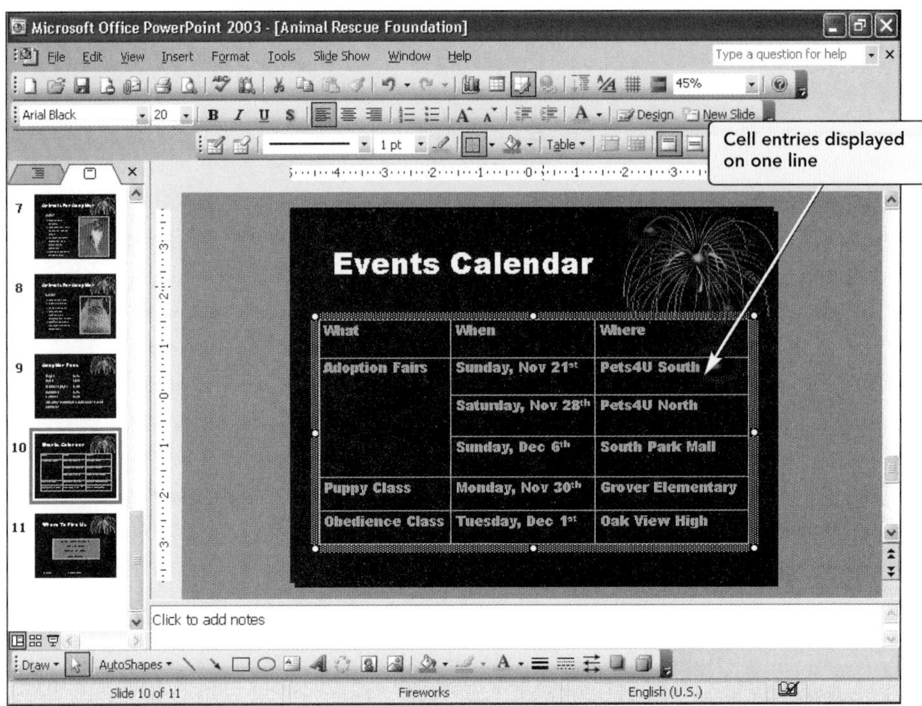


Figure 4.16

You also want to adjust the heights of the rows so they are all the same and center the text in several cells.

**3**

- Select the table.
- Click Distribute Rows Evenly (in the Tables and Borders toolbar).
- Select row 1 and click Center and Center Vertically to change the orientation of the text in the row to centered horizontally and vertically.
- Click to center vertically the text "Adoption Fairs" in row 2 of column A.

*Your screen should be similar to Figure 4.17*

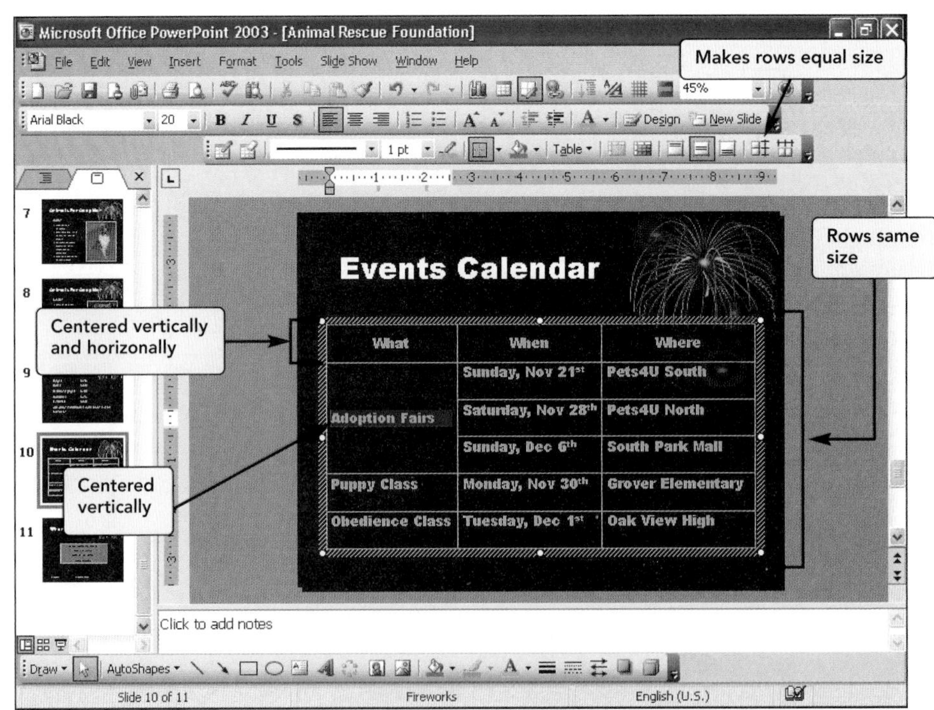


Figure 4.17

Next you will add some color to the table.

**4** **Select the entire table and apply a fill color of your choice to the selection.**

**Select row 1 and change the text to an appropriate color, bold, and shadowed.**

*Your screen should be similar to Figure 4.18*

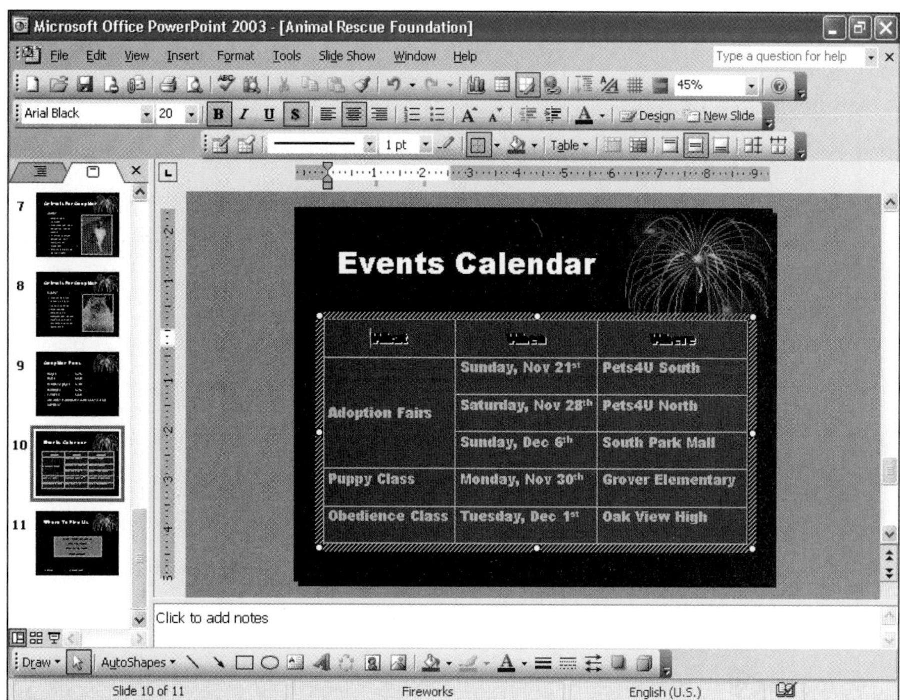


Figure 4.18

The final enhancement is to make the table border wider and a different color.

**5**

- **Select the entire table.**
- **Choose 6 pt from the [1 pt] Border Width drop-down list.**
- **Choose a color from the Border Color drop-down list.**
- **Click Outside Borders.**

**Having Trouble?**

You can also use the Format/Table command or /Borders and Fill to add, change, and remove borders and fills.

- **Turn off Draw Table and click outside the table to deselect it.**
- **Close the Tables and Borders toolbar.**
- **Turn off the display of the ruler.**
- **Save the presentation.**

*Your screen should be similar to Figure 4.19*

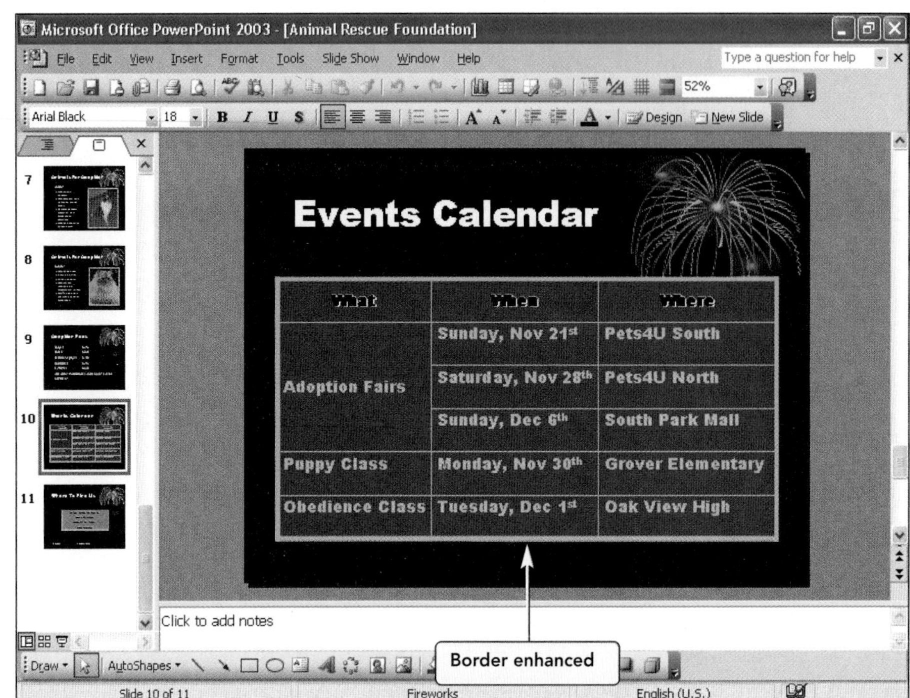


Figure 4.19

The table displays the information in an attractive and easy-to-read manner.

## Adding Interest to the Presentation

Although you like the look of the Fireworks template, you feel it is rather static for a kiosk presentation and want to add some action to the presentation. You will do this by adding an animated picture and graphic text to a slide.

### Adding Animated Graphics

First, you want to enhance the How You Can Help slide by adding a graphic from an animated GIF file.

## Concept 1

### Animated GIF

1 An **animated GIF** file is a type of graphic file that has motion. It consists of a series of GIF (Graphic Interchange Format) images that are displayed in rapid succession to produce an animated effect. They are commonly used on Web pages and can also be incorporated into PowerPoint presentations.

When an animated GIF file is inserted into a PowerPoint slide, it does not display action until you run the presentation. If you save the presentation as a Web page and view it in a browser, the animated GIF files run as soon as you view the page containing the graphic.

You cannot modify an animated graphic image using the features in the Picture toolbar. If you want to make changes to the graphic, such as changing the fill color or border, you need to use an animated GIF editing program.

You want to add an animated graphic that will really capture the attention of viewers.

1
- **Display slide 4 in Normal view.**
- **Apply the Title, Text, and Content slide layout to the slide.**
- **Click Insert Picture.**
- **Specify your data file location and select pp04_Adoptions.**
- **Click Insert.**

**Additional Information**

The Microsoft Clips Online Web site includes many animated graphics in the Motion category.

- **Size and position the graphic as shown in Figure 4.20.**

*Your screen should be similar to Figure 4.20*

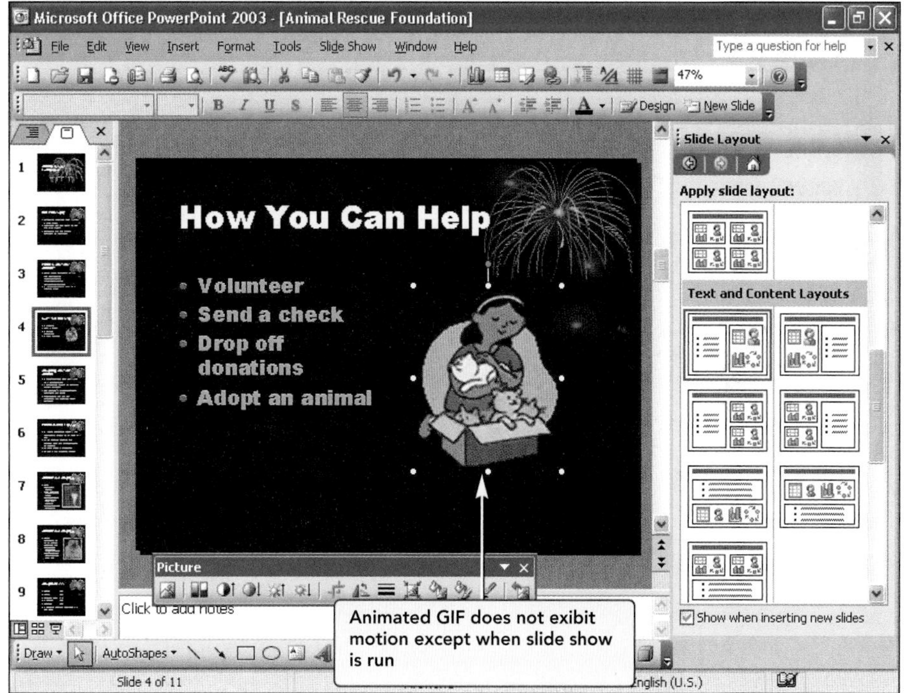


Figure 4.20

The graphic will not exhibit motion until you run the slide show.

2
- **Display the slide in Slide Show view to see the animation.**
- **Press Esc to stop the slide show.**

## Creating a WordArt Object

You also want to add graphic text to the slide to further enhance the slide. You will add the phrase "Friends Forever" below the picture. To make this phrase unique and more interesting, you will enter it using the WordArt feature.

### Concept 2

**WordArt**

2 The **WordArt** feature is used to enhance slides by changing the shape of text, adding 3-D effects, and changing the alignment of text on a line. You can also rotate, flip, and skew WordArt text. The text that is added to a slide using WordArt is a graphic object that can be edited, sized, or moved to any location on the slide.

Use WordArt to add a special touch to your presentations, but limit its use to a single element on a slide. You want the WordArt to capture the viewer's attention. Here are some examples of WordArt.

You will create a WordArt object for the text to appear below the animated graphic.

**1**

- **If necessary, deselect the graphic.**
- **Close the Slide Layout task pane.**
- **Click Insert WordArt.**

*Your screen should be similar to Figure 4.21*

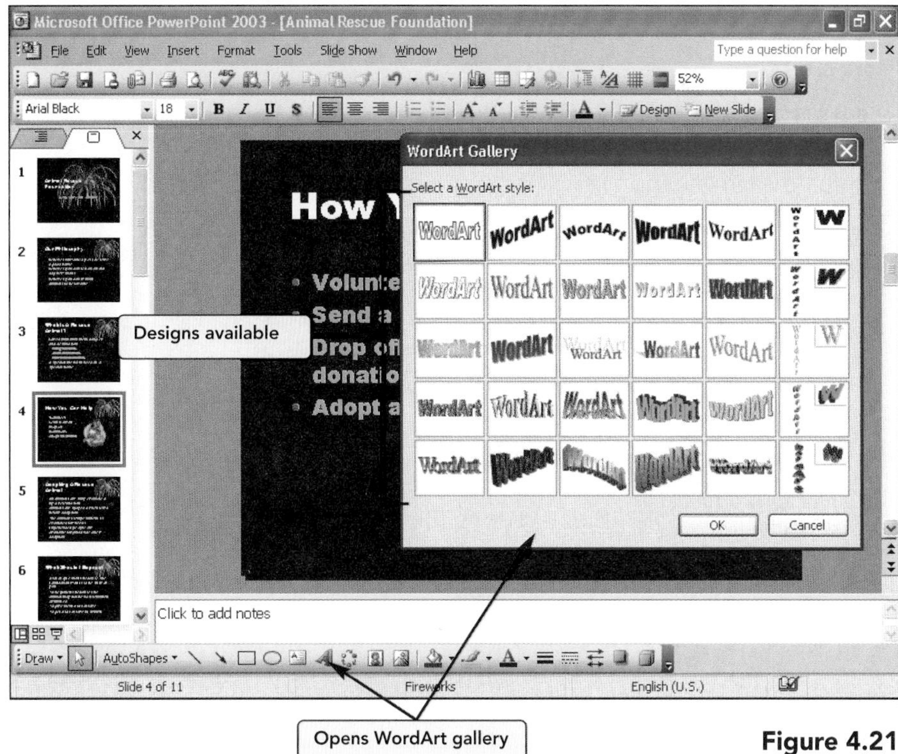


**Figure 4.21**

The first step is to select one of the 30 styles or designs of WordArt from the WordArt Gallery dialog box. These styles are just a starting point. As you will see, you can alter the appearance of the style by selecting a different color, shape, and special effect.

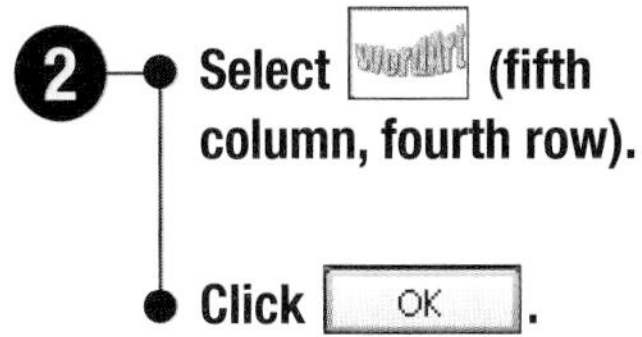

**2**

- **Select (fifth column, fourth row).**
- **Click OK.**

*Your screen should be similar to Figure 4.22*

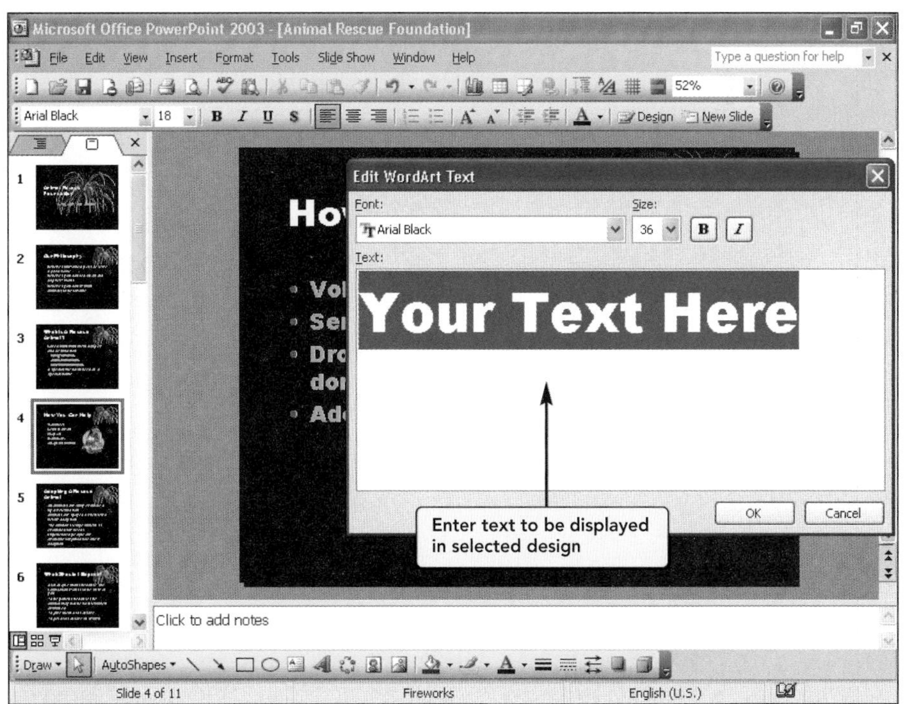


**Figure 4.22**

Next, in the Edit WordArt Text dialog box, you need to enter the text you want displayed using the selected WordArt design.

**3** **Type Friends Forever.**

- **From the 36 drop-down list, increase the font size to 44.**
- **Click OK.**
- **Move the WordArt object to the position shown in Figure 4.23.**

*Your screen should be similar to Figure 4.23*

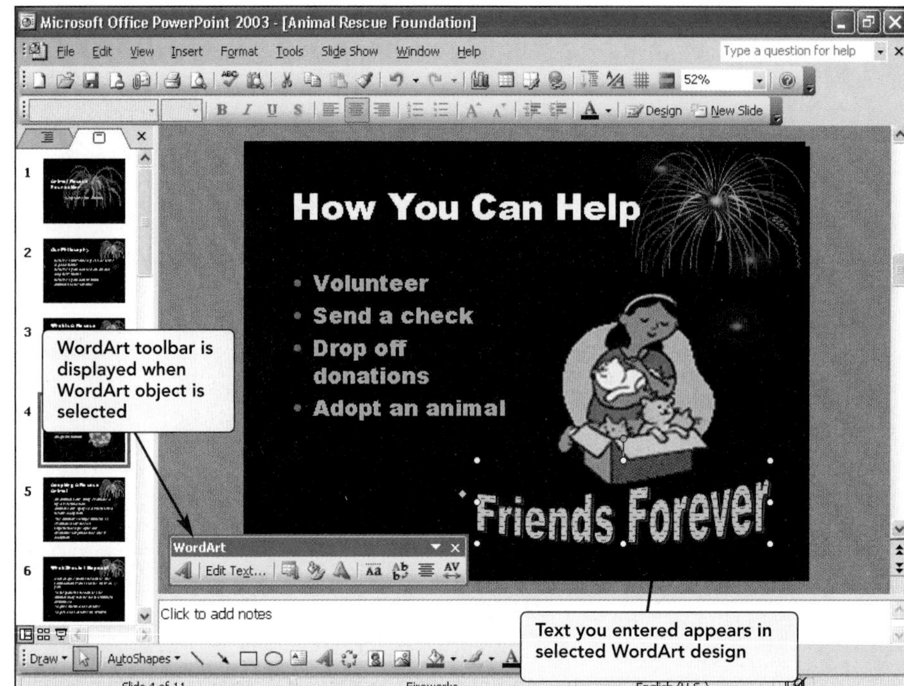


**Figure 4.23**

Now the text you entered is displayed in the selected WordArt style on the slide. The handles surrounding the WordArt object indicate that it is selected. Whenever a WordArt object is selected, the WordArt toolbar is displayed. The WordArt toolbar buttons (identified below) are used to modify the WordArt.

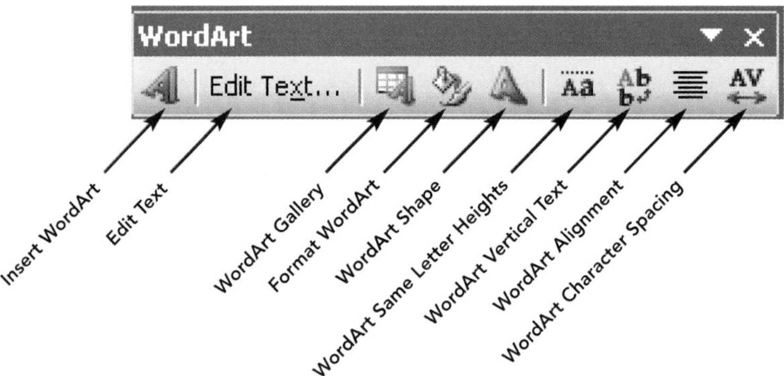

## Editing WordArt Text

As you look at the WordArt, you decide that you want to add an ellipsis following the text to lead the reader to the next slide. The text can be entirely changed or simply edited, as you will do.

1 Click Edit Text... on the WordArt toolbar.
Click at the end of the text to place the insertion point and type . . .
Click OK.


**Another Method**

You can also double-click the WordArt object to edit the text.

*Your screen should be similar to Figure 4.24*

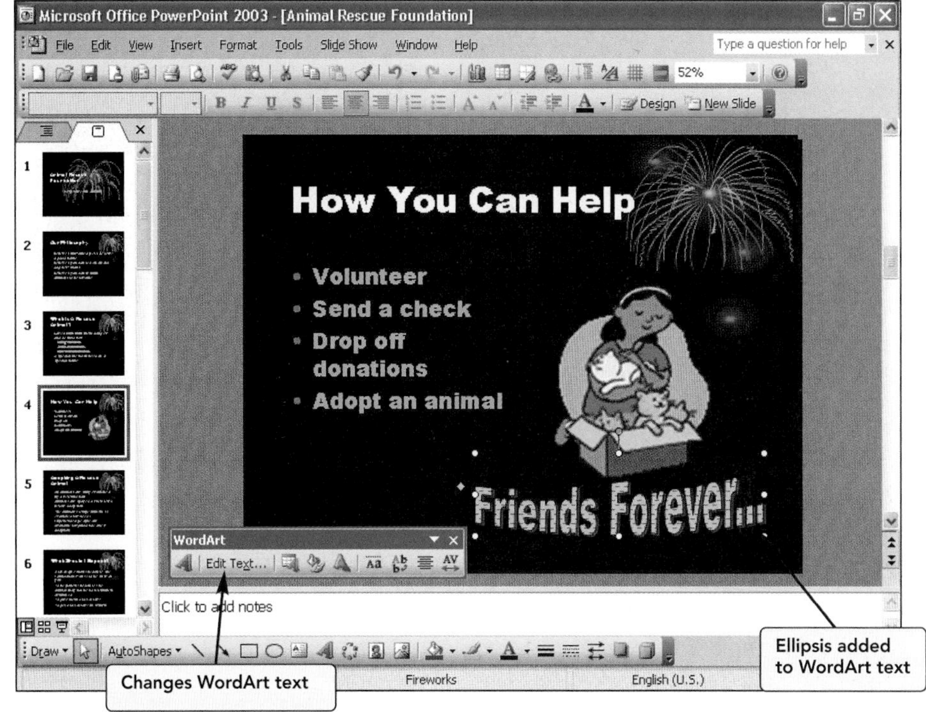


**Figure 4.24**

The change you made to the text in the Edit WordArt Text dialog box appears in the WordArt object.

## Enhancing a WordArt Object

Now you want to change the appearance of the WordArt object to make it more interesting. First you will change the shape of the object.

**Click WordArt Shape.**

**Choose Double Wave 2 (eighth column, third row).**

*Your screen should be similar to Figure 4.25*

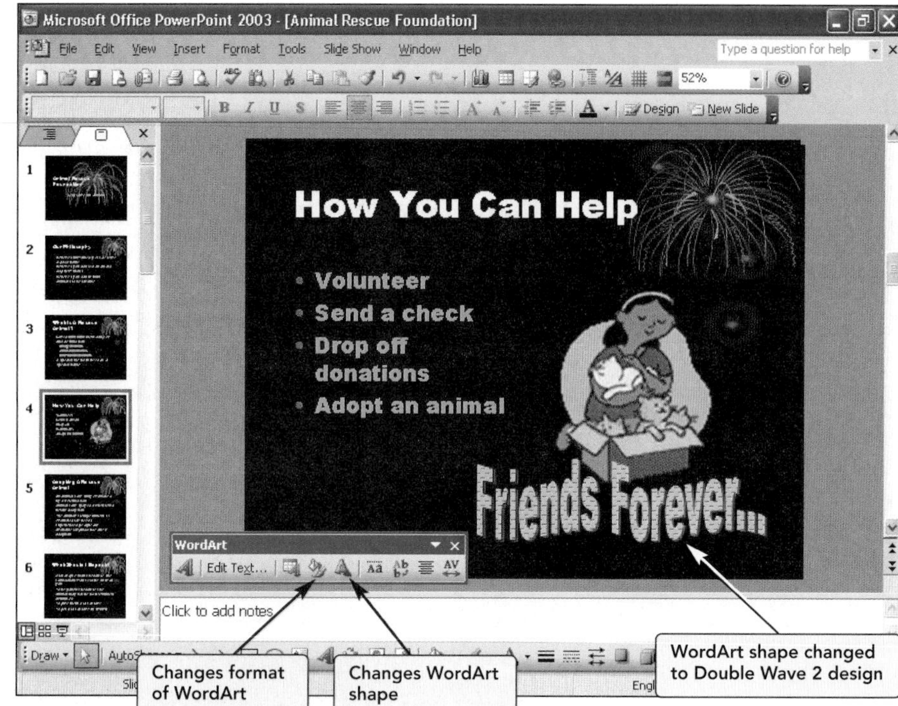


**Figure 4.25**

Next you want to change the color of the WordArt characters so they match the color scheme of the design template.

**Click Format WordArt.**

**Open the Colors and Lines tab.**

*Your screen should be similar to Figure 4.26*

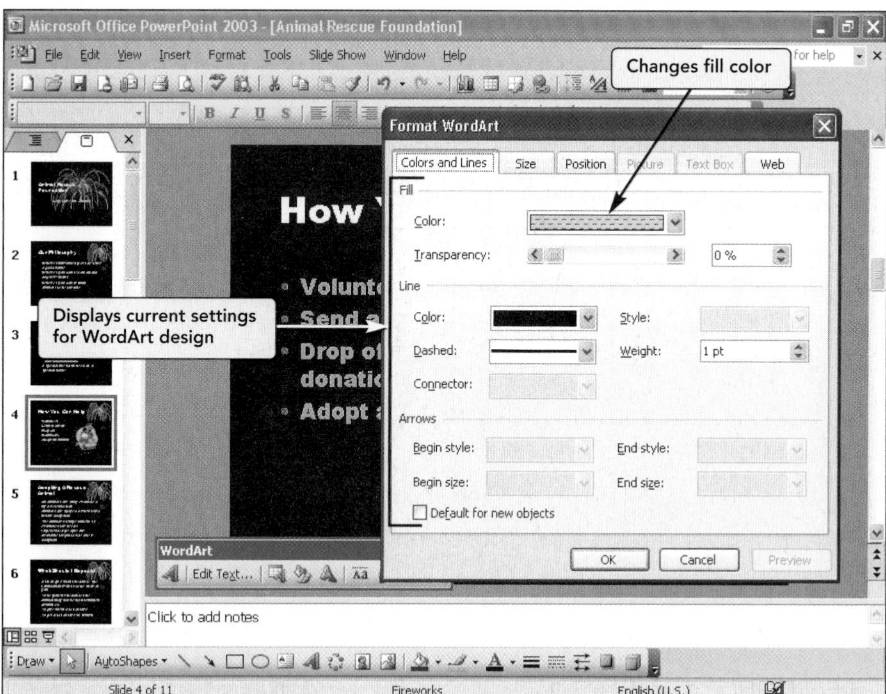


**Figure 4.26**

The Format WordArt dialog box shows the color and line settings for the selected WordArt design style. You want to change the colors to complement the color scheme of the design template.

**3**

- **Open the Fill Color drop-down list box.**
- **Select the orange color of the slide color scheme from the color palette.**
- **Click OK.**

*Your screen should be similar to Figure 4.27*

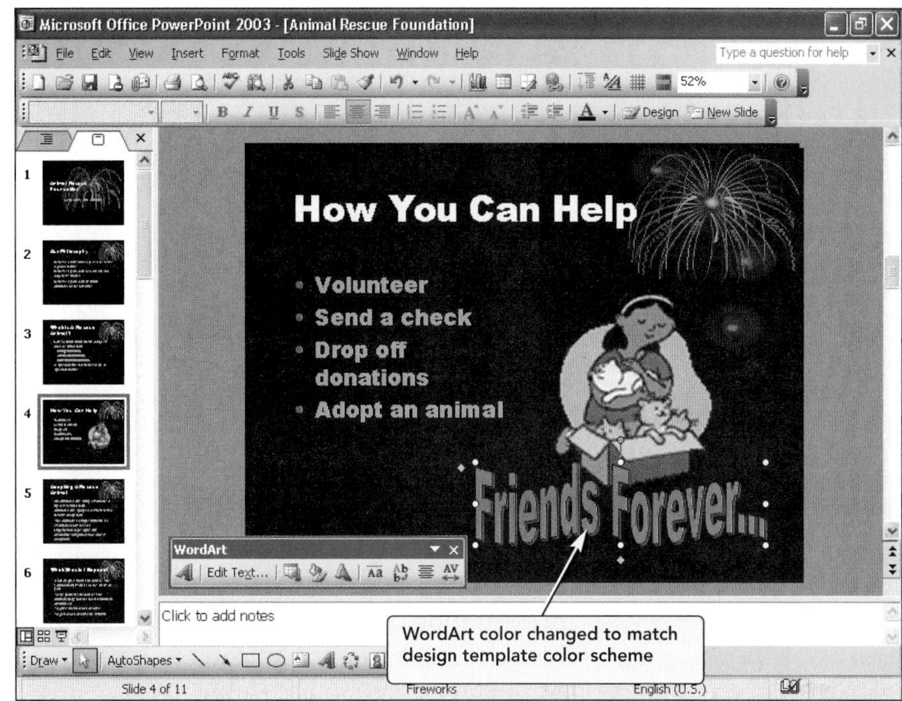


**Figure 4.27**

The selected fill color is used to fill the object. The last changes you want to make are to decrease the size of the WordArt object and to rotate the object to appear at an angle across the lower corner of the slide.

**4**

- **Drag the sizing handles to decrease the WordArt object size to that shown in Figure 4.28.**
- **Move the rotate handle slightly to the left to slant the text to the right.**

**Having Trouble?**

Drag the green rotate handle to rotate the object.

- **Position the object as in Figure 4.28.**
- **Group the two objects.**

*Your screen should be similar to Figure 4.28*

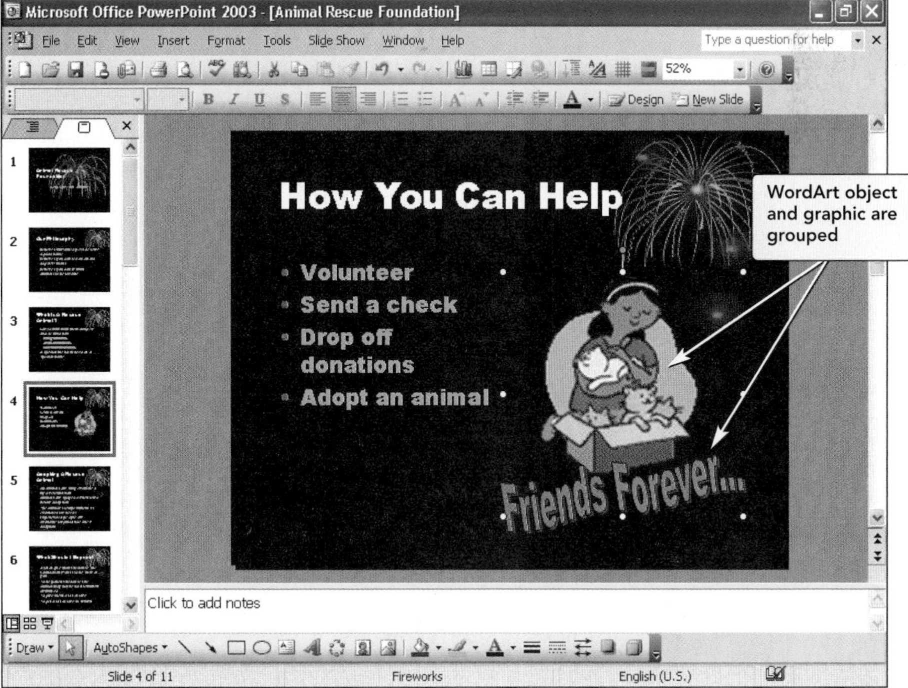


**Figure 4.28**

Now that you are finished enhancing the WordArt object, you want to see how it will look full screen.

**5**

- **Click [Slide Show icon] Slide Show.**
- **Press Esc and click outside the WordArt object to deselect it.**
- **If necessary, close the WordArt toolbar.**
- **Save the presentation.**

## Setting Up a Presentation for a Kiosk

**Additional Information**

When recording a voice narration, you need a sound card and a microphone. Use Slide Show/Record Narration. The slide show runs while you speak into the microphone. Once the slide show is complete, you can choose to save the timings along with the narration.

A presentation that is designed to run unattended on a kiosk has several special requirements. Because there is no one available while the slide show is running to clarify content and answer questions, you could record a narration to accompany the presentation. However, you feel the presentation content is both clear and complete and you decide to simply include background music to attract attention and to make the presentation more enjoyable as it runs. Next, you need to add slide transitions and to specify how long to display a slide before advancing to the next slide. Finally, you need to set up the presentation to be self-running.

### Adding Sound

Now that the content of the slides is complete, you want to add some background sound to the presentation as it is playing on the kiosk. There are several ways to add sound to a presentation. You can add discreet sounds that play when you click on an icon or automatically when the slide displays. You can play music from a file or a CD that runs continuously throughout the presentation. You can record a narration for your presentation; this, however, will override any other sounds you have programmed into it. You can also incorporate movie clips into a presentation.

## Concept 3

### Sound and Movie Files

3 Almost all PCs today are equipped with multimedia capabilities, which means they can play the most commonly used sound and movie files. A **sound file** is a type of file that plays sounds or music, and a **movie file** plays a motion picture with sound. This table lists the most common sound and movie file types.

| Format | File Extension |
|---|---|
| Waveform-audio | .wav |
| Musical Instrument Digital Interface | .mid |
| Video for Windows | .avi |
| Moving Picture | .mpeg |
| Quick Time for Windows | .mov |

WAV files are typically used for sounds, while MIDI files are typically used for music. Most sound cards are capable of playing MIDI files, but because these files were developed for synthesizers, you will not hear the true sound quality through a PC sound card.

AVI files do not require any special hardware or software to run, but they produce the lowest quality video. Both MPEG and MOV files produce better quality video, but both require special software, and MPEG requires special hardware.

When you choose to run a presentation on the Web, choose file types that are most commonly used. If you cannot control the computer on which your presentation will run, limit your audio to WAV files and your video to AVI files.

**Additional Information**

To play a CD, use Insert/Movies and Sounds/Play CD Audio Track.

For your kiosk, you want music to play continuously while the presentation runs. You could play tracks from a CD if the PC in the kiosk had a CD-ROM drive. You decide to use a short sound clip of music.

**1** • **Display slide 1.**

• **Choose Insert/Movies and Sounds/Sound from File.**

• **Select** pp04_Doggie **from your data file location.**

> **Additional Information**
>
> The Windows Media folder contains many short sound files.

• **Click OK.**

• **Click Automatically to confirm that you want the sound to play automatically.**

• **Move the sound icon to the lower right corner of the slide.**

*Your screen should be similar to Figure 4.29*

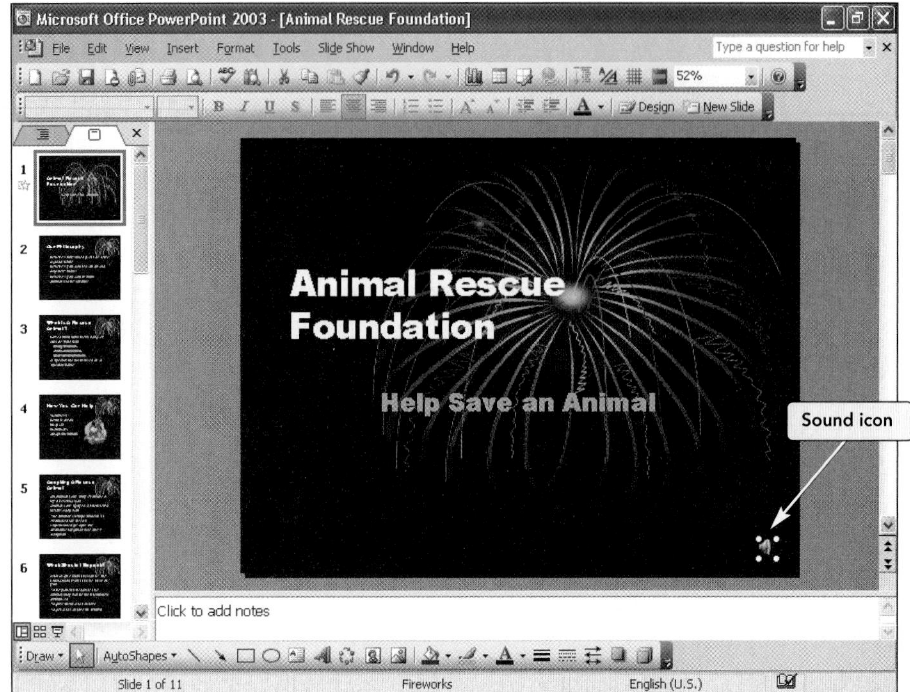


Figure 4.29

Now that you have added the music, you need to program how to play it during the slide show. You want the music to play continuously while the slide show runs.

**2** • **Choose Slide Show/Custom Animation.**

• **Open the** pp04_Doggie **drop-down list in the Custom Animation task pane.**

• **Choose Effect Options.**

• **If necessary, open the Effect tab.**

*Your screen should be similar to Figure 4.30*

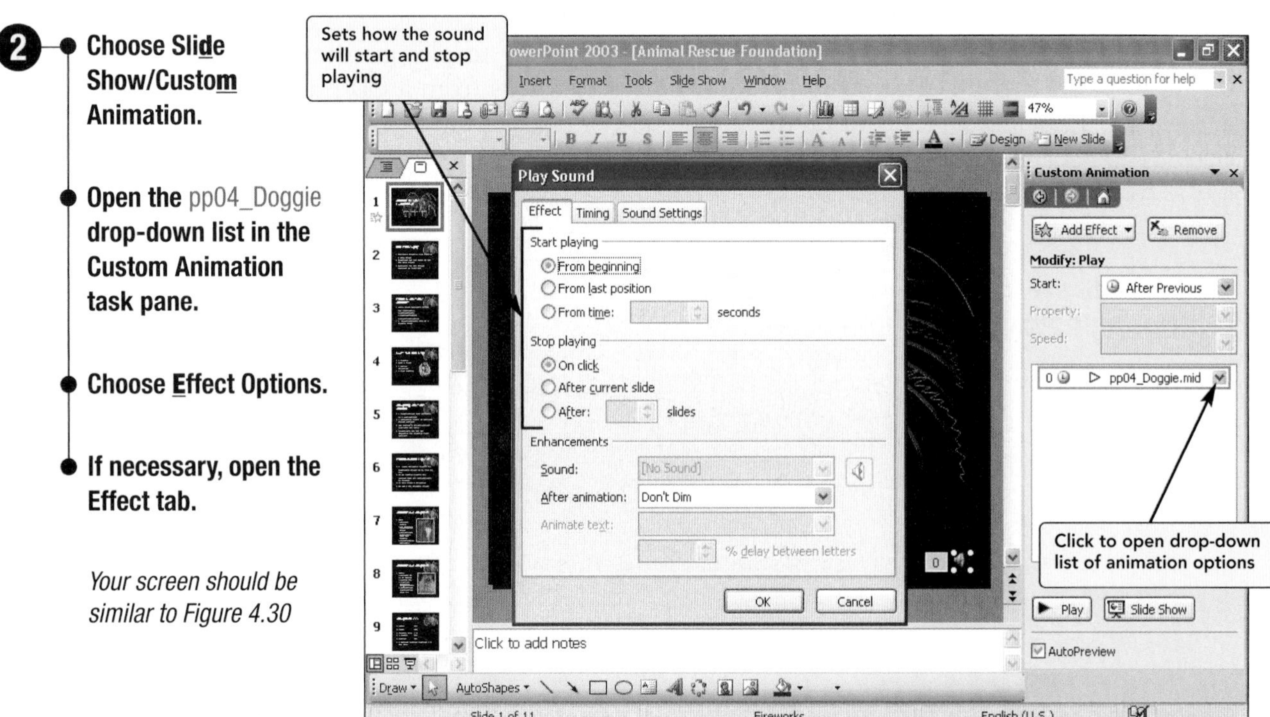


Figure 4.30

For each object on a slide, you can assign effects such as animation to the media element and control the order and timing. You want the music to start playing from the beginning of the presentation and to stop after the last slide (11). In addition, because the sound file is only 15 seconds long, you need to loop or repeat the sound so it will play the length of the presentation.

**3**
- **Under Stop Playing, select After, enter 11 in the text box, and click OK.**
- **Right click the sound icon and choose Edit Sound Object.**
- **Select Loop until stopped and and click OK.**
- **Run the slide show from the beginning.**

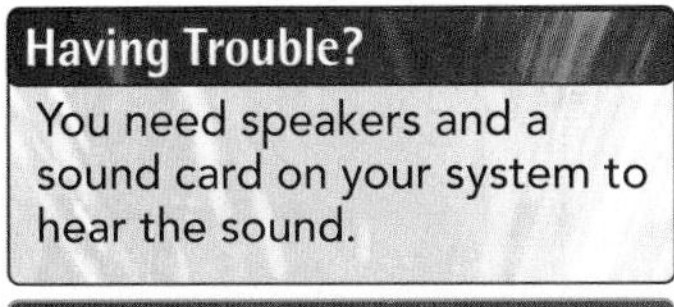

Having Trouble?
You need speakers and a sound card on your system to hear the sound.


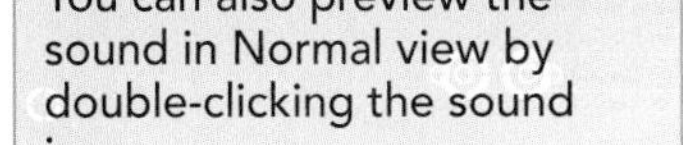


You can also preview the sound in Normal view by double-clicking the sound icon.

The music played continuously as you moved from slide to slide and stopped at the end of the presentation.

## Adding Slide Transitions

You also want the slide show to display different transition effects as it runs and to automatically advance to the next slide after a set time has elapsed.

**1**
- **Switch to Slide Sorter view.**
- **Select all the slides.**
- **Click Transition.**
- **Choose Random Transition at Medium speed as the effect.**
- **Select Automatically After.**
- **Change the timing to advance the slides automatically every 7 seconds.**
- **Click Apply to All Slides.**

*Your screen should be similar to Figure 4.31*

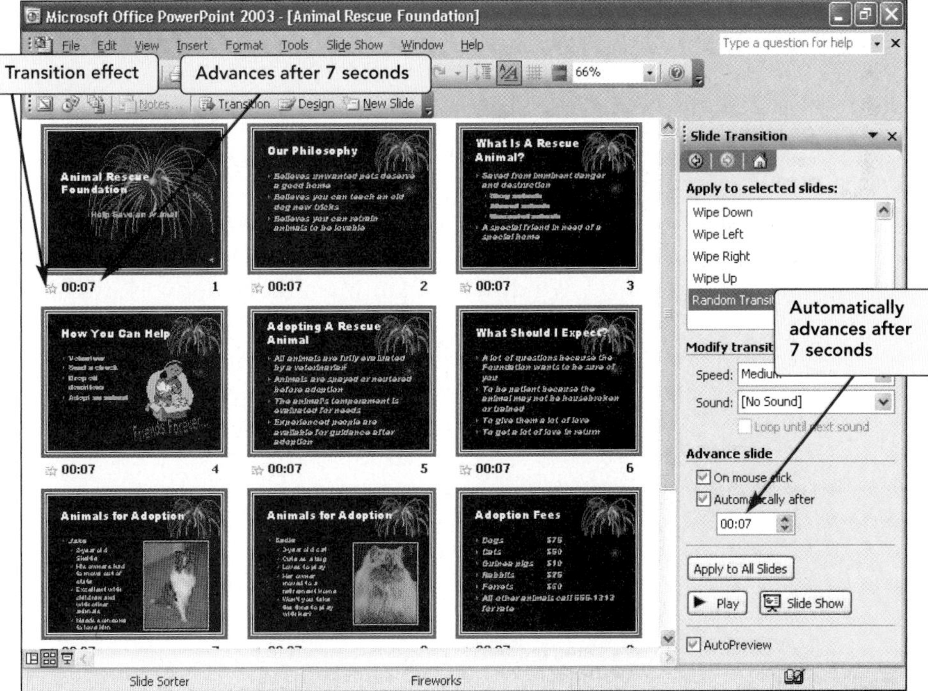


**Figure 4.31**

## Making the Presentation Self-Running

Now you will make the slide show self-running so that it will restart automatically when it has finished.

1. **Close the Slide Transition task pane.**

   **Choose Slide Show/Set Up Show.**

   *Your screen should be similar to Figure 4.32*

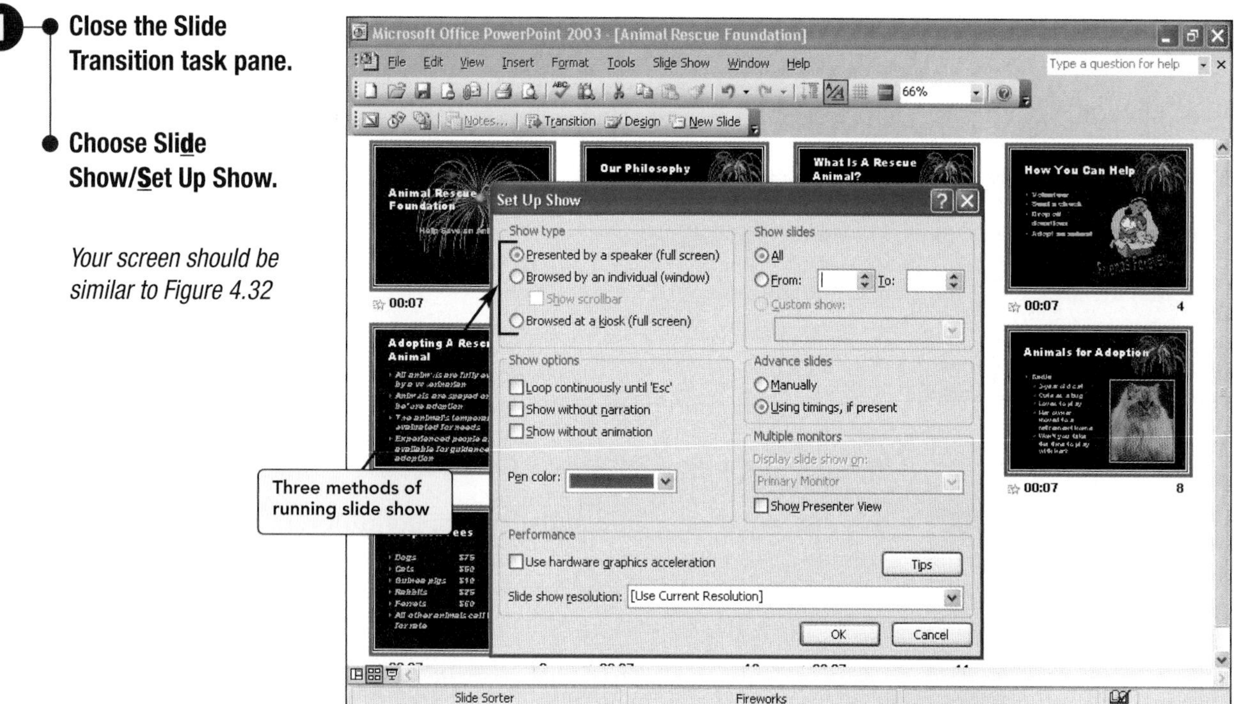


**Figure 4.32**

The Set Up Show dialog box allows you to choose from three ways of running a show. The first option, Presented by a Speaker, is the default and most frequently used style. As you have seen, this method requires that a speaker run the presentation. The second option, Browsed by an Individual, is used when one person views the presentation in a small window over an intranet (a network within an organization) or on a Web page. The third option, Browsed at a Kiosk, is the option you will use to create a self-running presentation that is displayed full screen. You can run the entire presentation or selected slides. The presentation will automatically play at full screen and restart automatically.

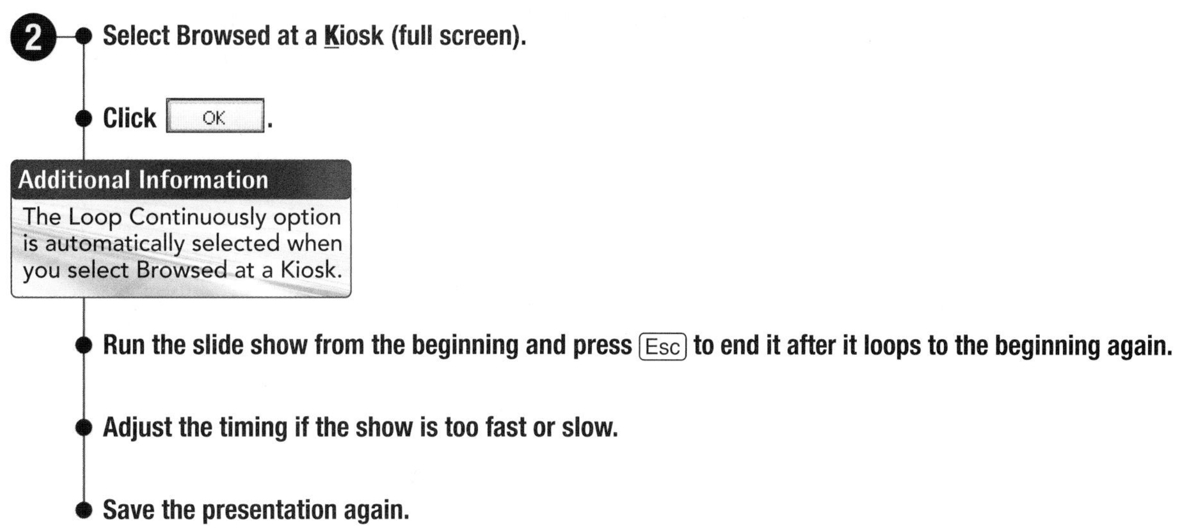

**2** Select Browsed at a Kiosk (full screen).

- Click OK.

**Additional Information**

The Loop Continuously option is automatically selected when you select Browsed at a Kiosk.

- Run the slide show from the beginning and press Esc to end it after it loops to the beginning again.
- Adjust the timing if the show is too fast or slow.
- Save the presentation again.

To deliver the presentation to the mall directors to run on the kiosks, you will package the presentation for CD.

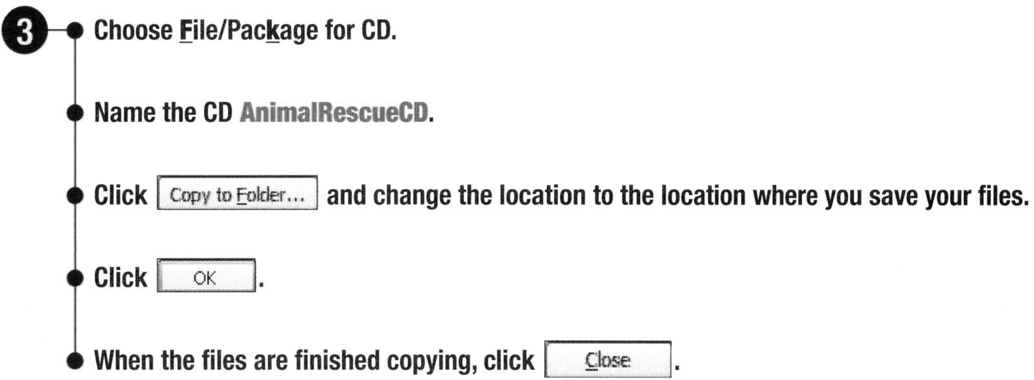

**3** Choose File/Package for CD.

- Name the CD **AnimalRescueCD**.
- Click Copy to Folder... and change the location to the location where you save your files.
- Click OK.
- When the files are finished copying, click Close.

## Setting Up the Presentation for Browsing

The Animal Rescue Foundation main shelter has a computer in the lobby that they want to use to show this same presentation. Rather than have the presentation loop continuously, you want to change it to a presentation that can be run by an individual using mouse control. This gives viewers the ability to control the slide show and go back to review a slide immediately or go forward more quickly to see other slides. To add this capability, you will create several custom shows and add hyperlinks and navigation controls to the presentation.

### Creating Custom Shows

First you will group some slides into custom shows.

# Concept 4

## Custom Show

4 A **custom show** is a presentation that runs within a presentation. For example, you may have one presentation that you need to give to two different groups. The overview slides are the same for both groups, but there are a few slides that are specific to each group. Rather than create two separate presentations, you can include all the slides in your main presentation and then group the specific slides into two custom shows that run after the overview slides. While you are running the slide show, you can jump to the specific custom show that you created for that audience.

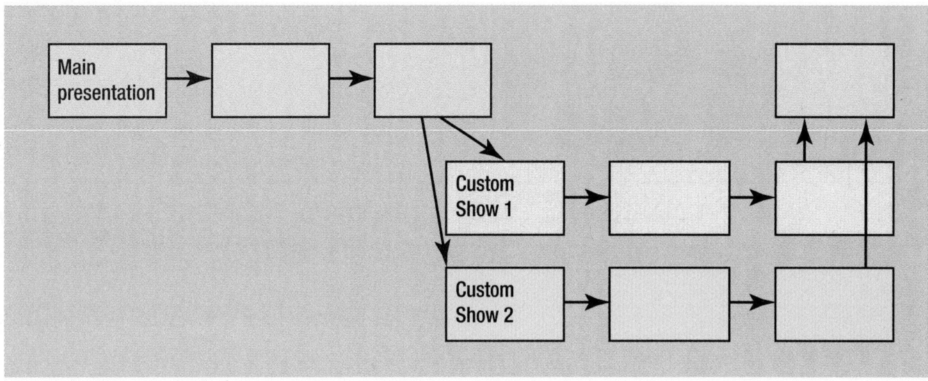


You are going to create two custom shows within your presentation. One custom show will run the slides that describe adopting rescue animals. The other custom show will run the slides that describe the animals that are available for adoption.

1. - Choose Slide Show/Custom Shows.
   - Click New... .

*Your screen should be similar to Figure 4.33*

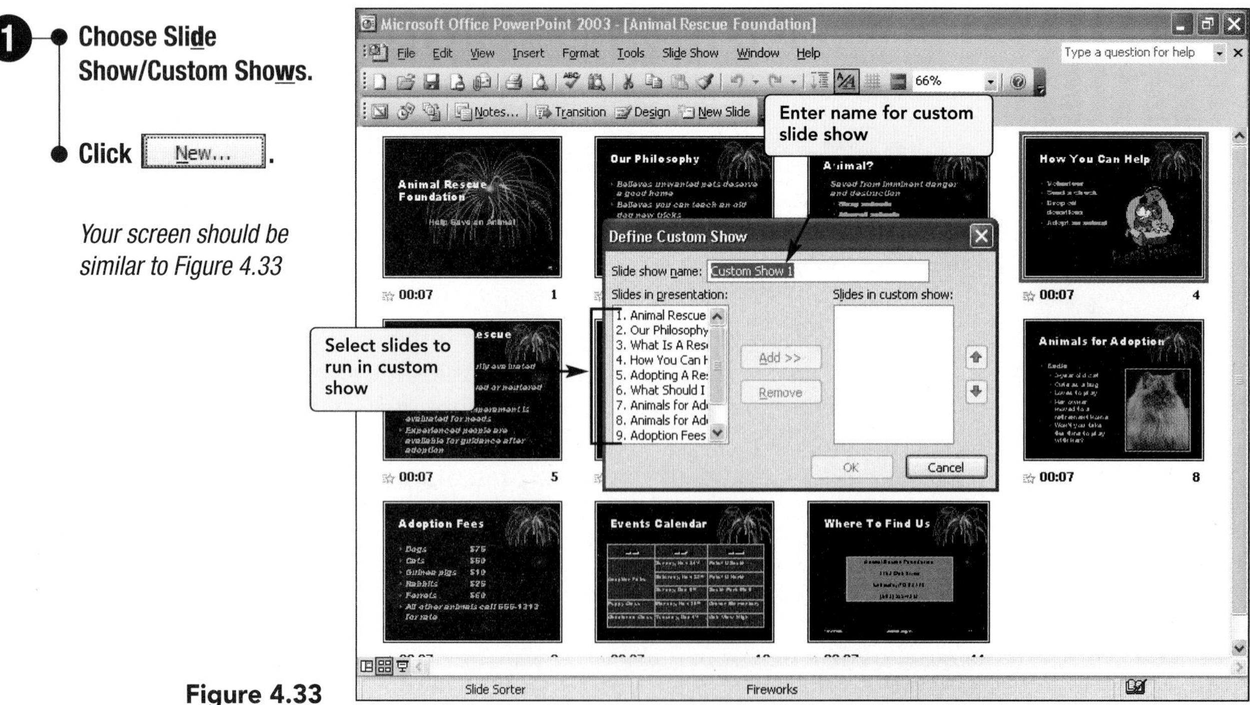


**Figure 4.33**

In the Define Custom Show dialog box, you name the custom show and select the slides that will run within the show. All the slides in a custom show must also be in the main presentation.

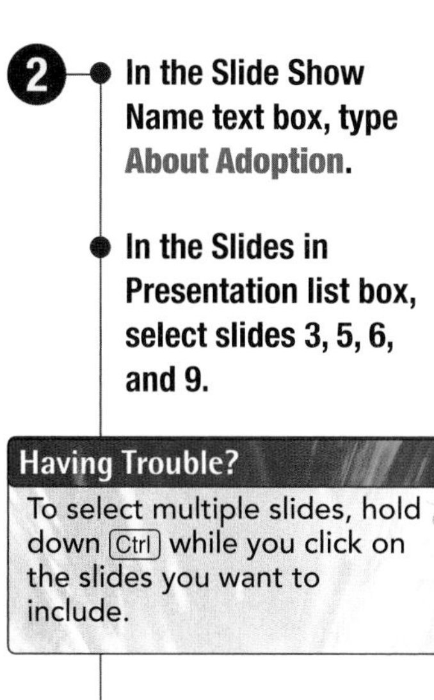

**2** • In the Slide Show Name text box, type **About Adoption**.

• In the Slides in Presentation list box, select slides 3, 5, 6, and 9.

**Having Trouble?**

To select multiple slides, hold down Ctrl while you click on the slides you want to include.

• Click Add >>.

*Your screen should be similar to Figure 4.34*

Figure 4.34

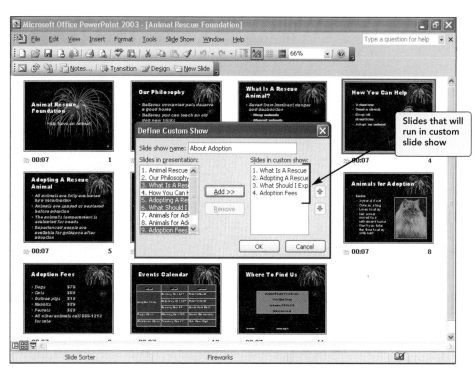

Next you want to make slide 2 in the custom show, slide 1. To change the order of the slides in the custom show, select a slide in the Slides in Custom Show list box, and then click one of the arrows to move the slide up or down the list. This will not change the order of the slides in the main presentation.

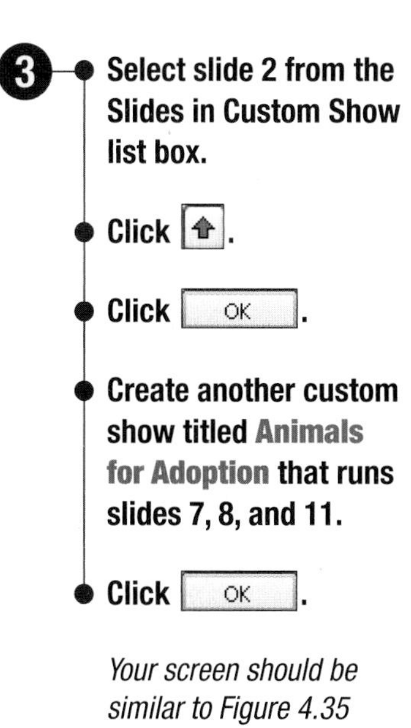

**3** • Select slide 2 from the Slides in Custom Show list box.

• Click ⬆.

• Click OK.

• Create another custom show titled **Animals for Adoption** that runs slides 7, 8, and 11.

• Click OK.

*Your screen should be similar to Figure 4.35*

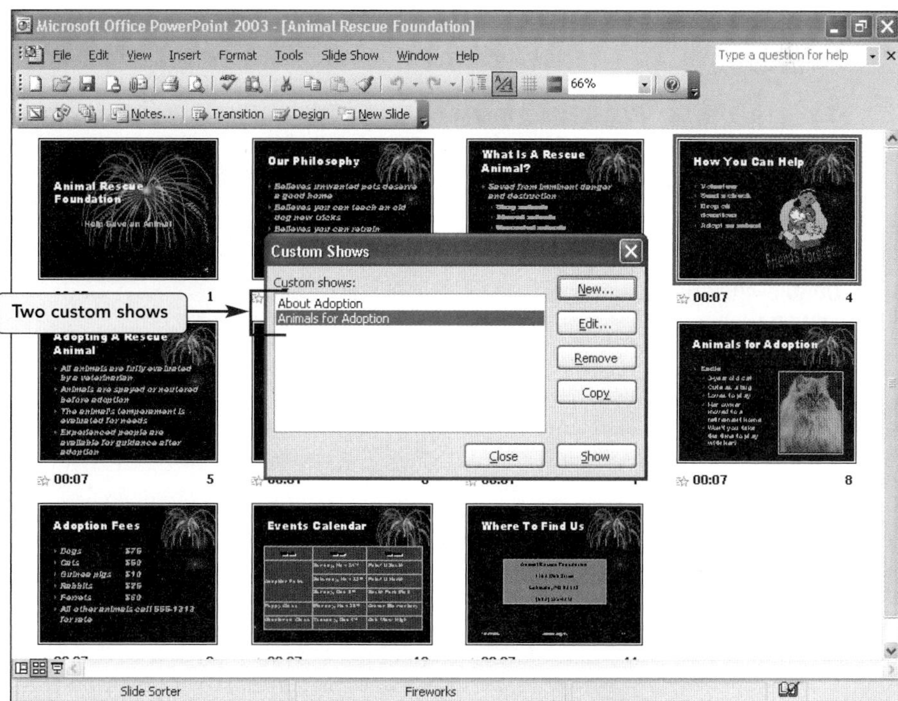


Figure 4.35

The name of the second custom show is added to the Custom Shows list. Now you will see how the About Adoption custom show runs.

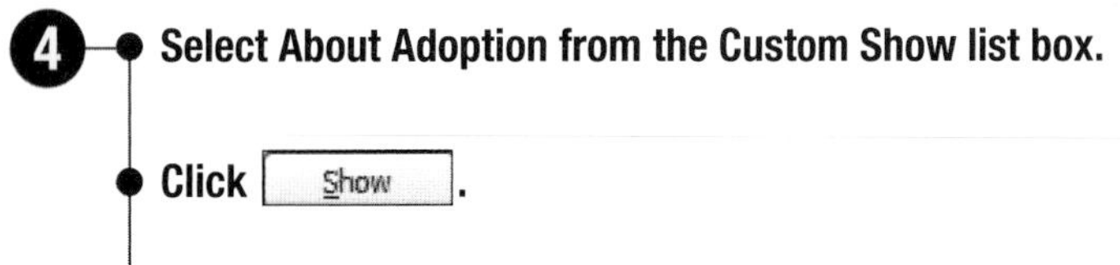

**4** 
- **Select About Adoption from the Custom Show list box.**
- **Click Show.**
- **View the four slides and press Esc to end the custom show.**

The custom show plays in a continual loop and does not play the sound. The sound only plays if you start the presentation from slide 1.

## Creating an Agenda Slide

Now that you have created the custom shows, you will create an agenda slide to use as a starting point for the entire presentation. An agenda slide contains a list of items or main topics from the presentation. Viewers can then make a selection from the list, and the presentation will jump directly to the slide containing the selected topic or a custom presentation will automatically run. When the custom show is finished, the presentation returns to the agenda slide.

An agenda slide is created from a summary slide consisting of a bulleted list of agenda items. A **summary slide** is created automatically from slides in the presentation whose titles you want to appear as agenda items.

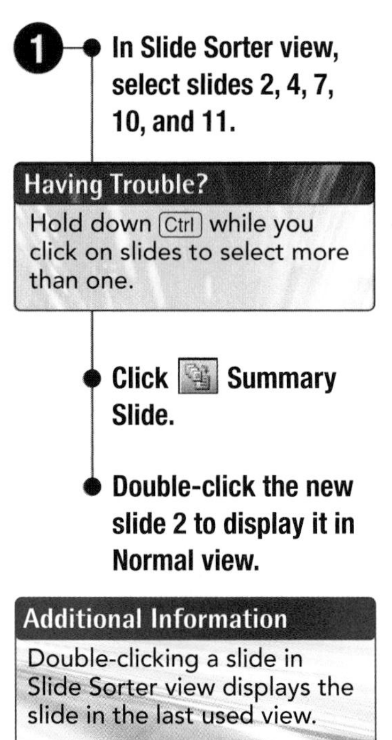

**1**
- **In Slide Sorter view, select slides 2, 4, 7, 10, and 11.**

**Having Trouble?**

Hold down Ctrl while you click on slides to select more than one.

- **Click Summary Slide.**
- **Double-click the new slide 2 to display it in Normal view.**

**Additional Information**

Double-clicking a slide in Slide Sorter view displays the slide in the last used view.

*Your screen should be similar to Figure 4.36*

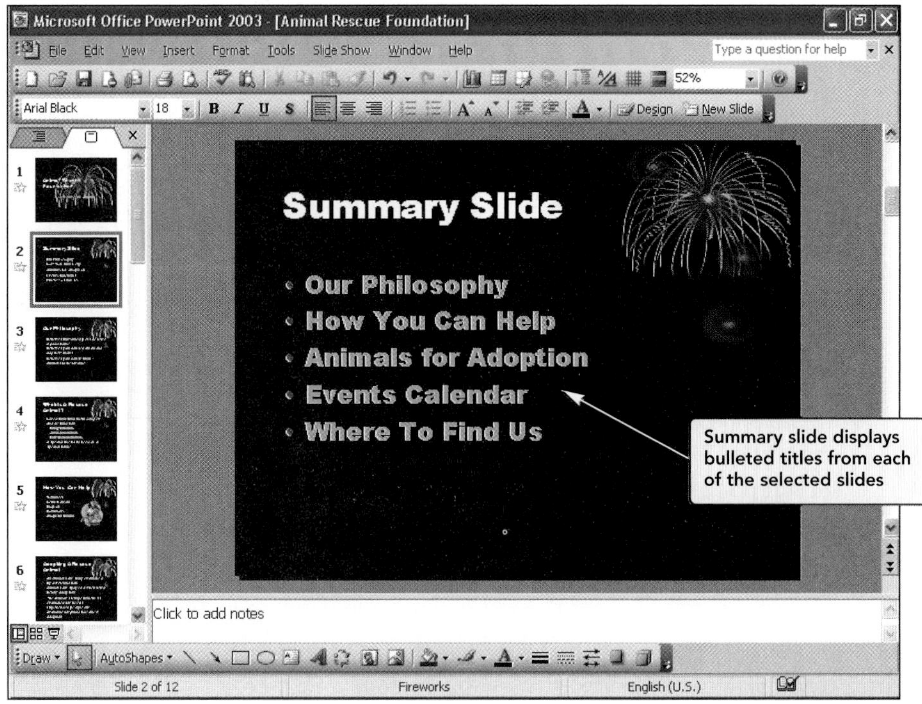


**Figure 4.36**

A new slide titled Summary Slide appears as slide 2. The summary slide is always inserted in front of the slide containing the first selected item. The slide contains bulleted titles from each of the selected slides.

## Adding Hyperlinks

The next step in creating an agenda slide is to create a hyperlink from each bulleted item to its corresponding slide or custom show.

### Concept 5

#### Hyperlinks

5 **Hyperlinks** provide a quick way to jump to other slides, custom shows, presentations, objects, e-mail addresses, or Web pages. You can assign the hyperlink to text or to any object, including pictures, tables, clip art, and graphs. You can jump to sites on your own system or network as well as to sites on the Internet and the Web. The user jumps to the referenced location by clicking on the hyperlink.

**1**

- **Select the first bulleted item.**
- **Choose Slide Show/Action Settings.**
- **If necessary, open the Mouse Click tab.**

*Your screen should be similar to Figure 4.37*

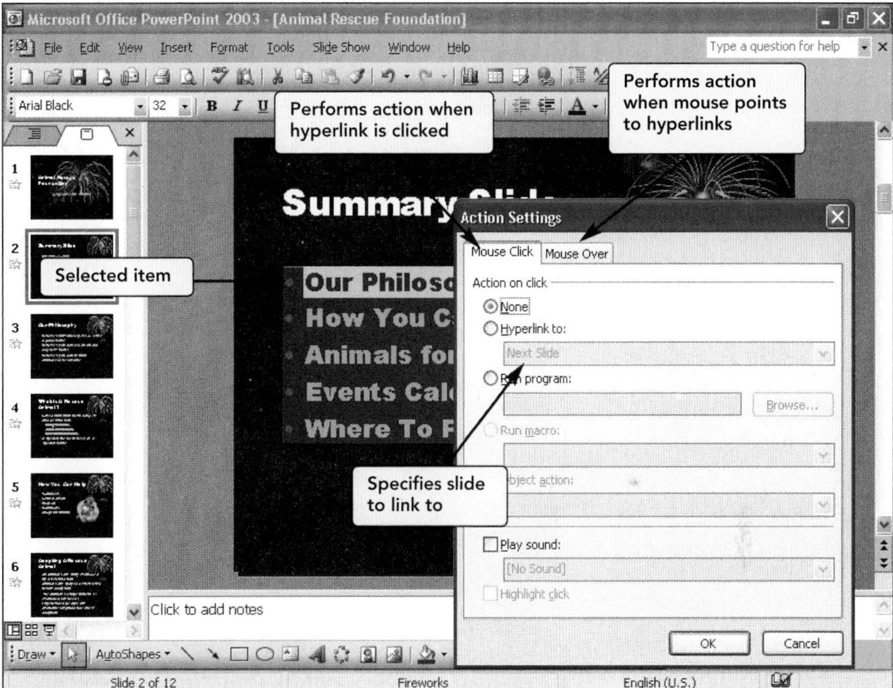


**Figure 4.37**

The two tabs in the Action Settings dialog box allow you to specify the action that is needed to activate the hyperlink. Mouse Click performs an action when the viewer clicks the hyperlink, and Mouse Over performs the action when the mouse pointer rests or passes over the hyperlink. Within each tab you specify the type of action you want to perform: jump to another location using a hyperlink, play a sound, or run a program or macro. Generally, it is best to use Mouse Click for hyperlinks so that you do not accidentally go to a location because you passed the mouse pointer over the hyperlink. Mouse Over is commonly used to play sounds or to highlight an object.

The first bulleted item will be a hyperlink to the next slide in the presentation. This is the default hyperlink selection.

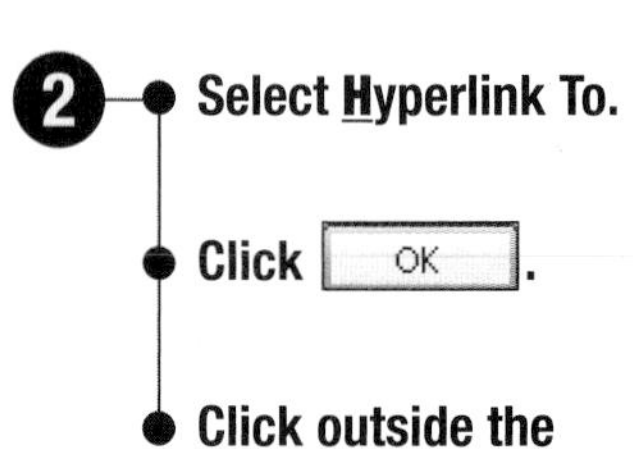

**2** Select **H**yperlink To.

Click OK.

Click outside the hyperlink to clear the selection.

*Your screen should be similar to Figure 4.38*

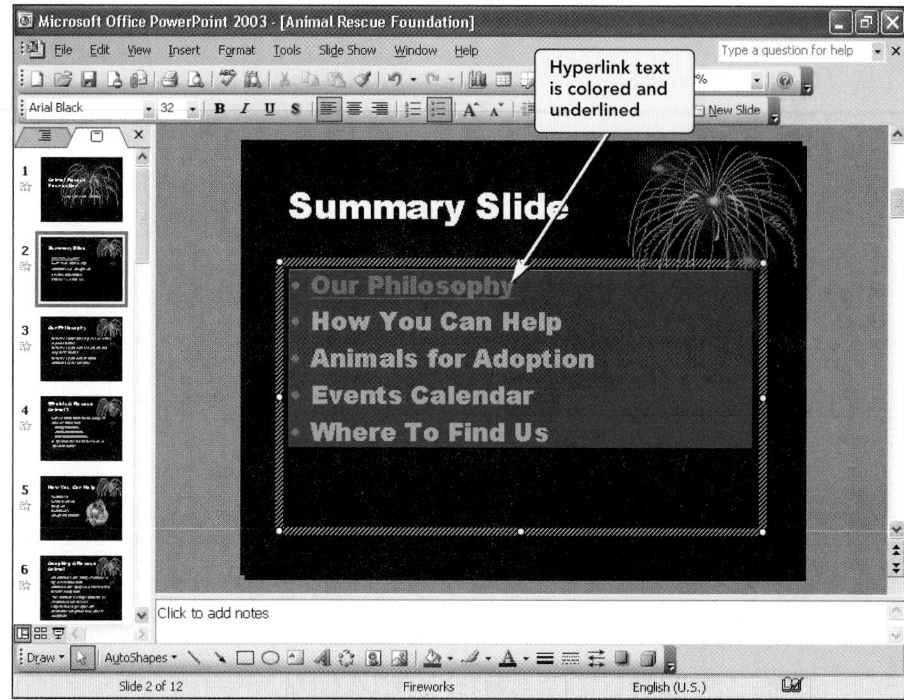


**Figure 4.38**

The hyperlink text appears underlined and in color. The color of the hyperlink text is determined by the presentation's color scheme.

The second bulleted item will be a hyperlink to the About Adoption custom show. You want the custom show to run and then return to the slide containing the hyperlink.

**3** Select the text in the second bulleted item.

Choose Sli**d**e Show/**A**ction Settings.

Select **H**yperlink To.

From the Hyperlink To drop-down list, select Custom Show.

**Having Trouble?**

Scroll the list box for the full list of options.

*Your screen should be similar to Figure 4.39*

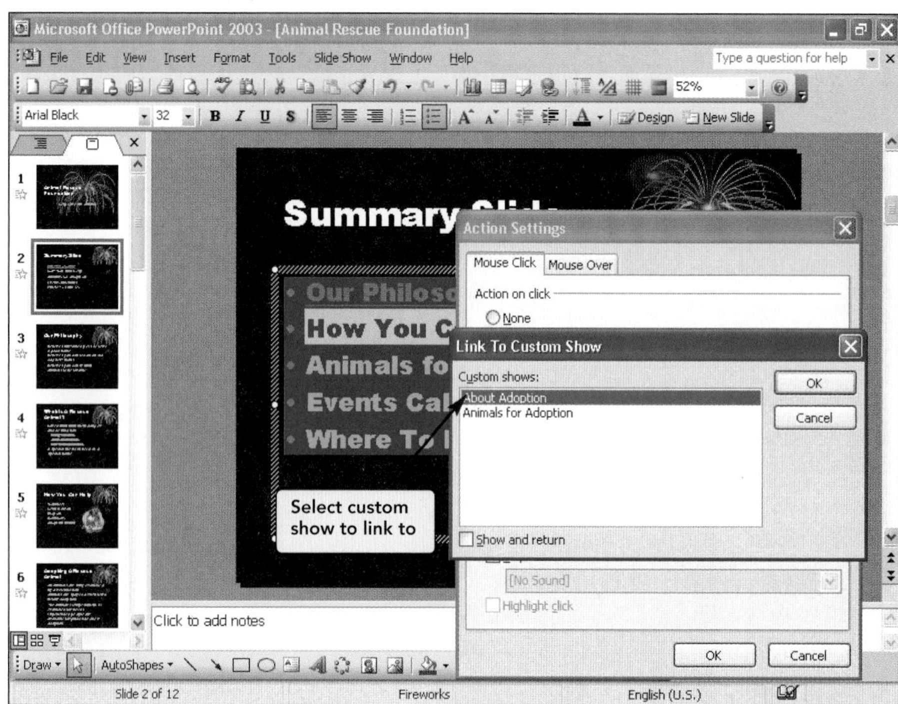


**Figure 4.39**

From the Link To Custom Show dialog box, you select the custom show to which you want to create a hyperlink.

**4**

- **Select About Adoption from the Custom Shows list.**
- **Select the Show and Return option.**
- **Click OK twice.**

*Your screen should be similar to Figure 4.40*

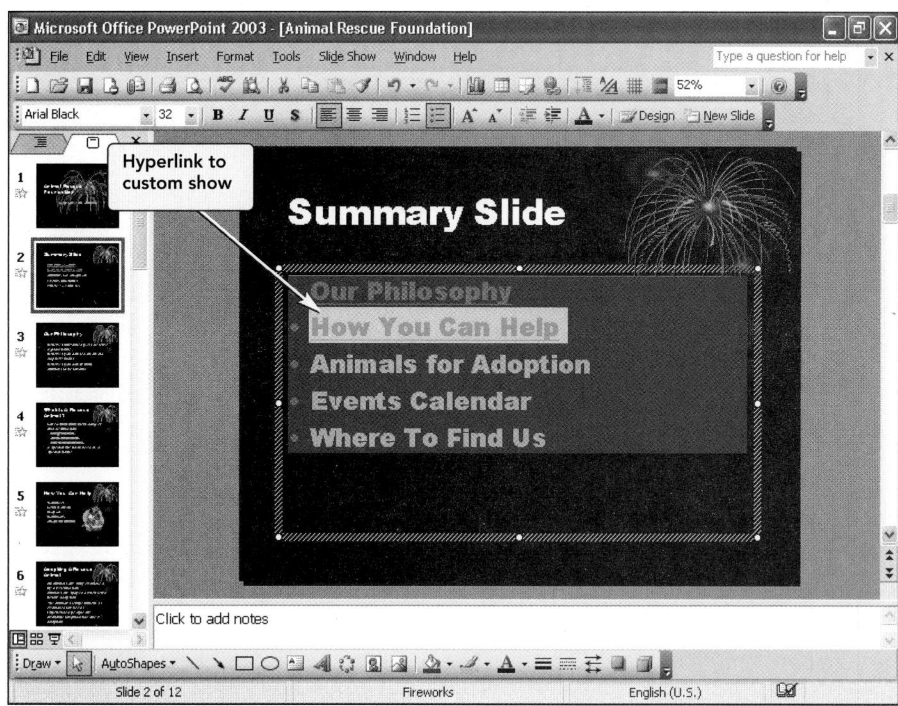


**Figure 4.40**

When the second bulleted item is selected, it will start the custom show. Now you need to add links for the remaining three items. The third bulleted item will be a hyperlink to the custom show named Animals for Adoption. The fourth and fifth will be to slides of the same name.

**5**

- **Link the third bulleted item to the Animals for Adoption custom show, selecting the Show and Return option.**
- **To link the fourth item, select Slide as the Hyperlink To option and select slide 11.**
- **To link the fifth item, select Slide as the Hyperlink To option and select slide 12.**
- **Change the title of the agenda slide to Learn About Us.**
- **Click outside the title to deselect it.**

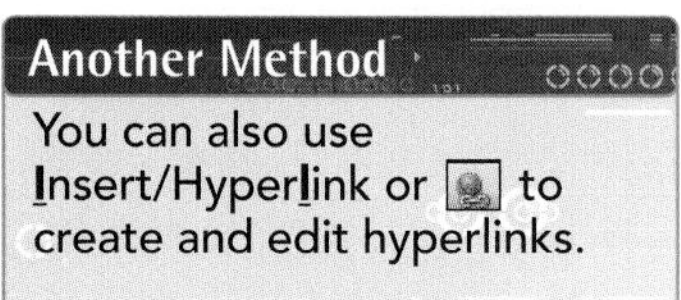


You can also use Insert/Hyperlink or [icon] to create and edit hyperlinks.

*Your screen should be similar to Figure 4.41*

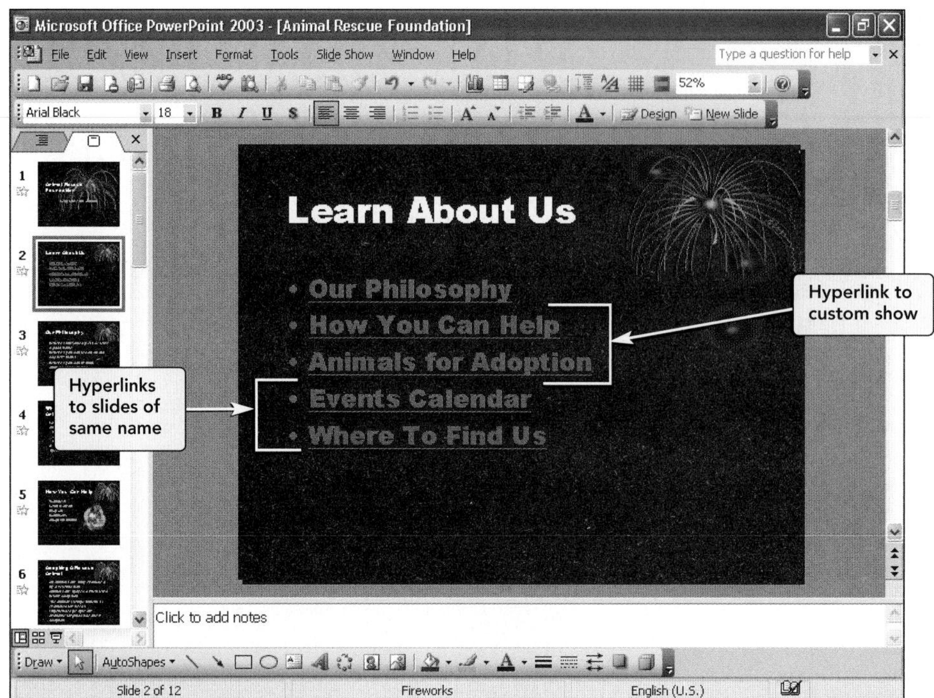


**Figure 4.41**

The addition of hyperlinks makes the summary slide an agenda slide, which can be used to jump to the selected topic.

## Using Hyperlinks

Next you want to try out one of the hyperlinks to see how they work. To activate the hyperlinks, you need to run the slide show.

**Run the slide show beginning with slide 2.**

**Having Trouble?**

To run the slide show starting from the current slide, click [icon]. Using Slide Show/View Show or F5 begins the presentation at slide 1.

**Additional Information**

The mouse pointer shape changes to a [hand] when pointing to a hyperlink.

**Click on the Animals for Adoption hyperlink.**

*Your screen should be similar to Figure 4.42*

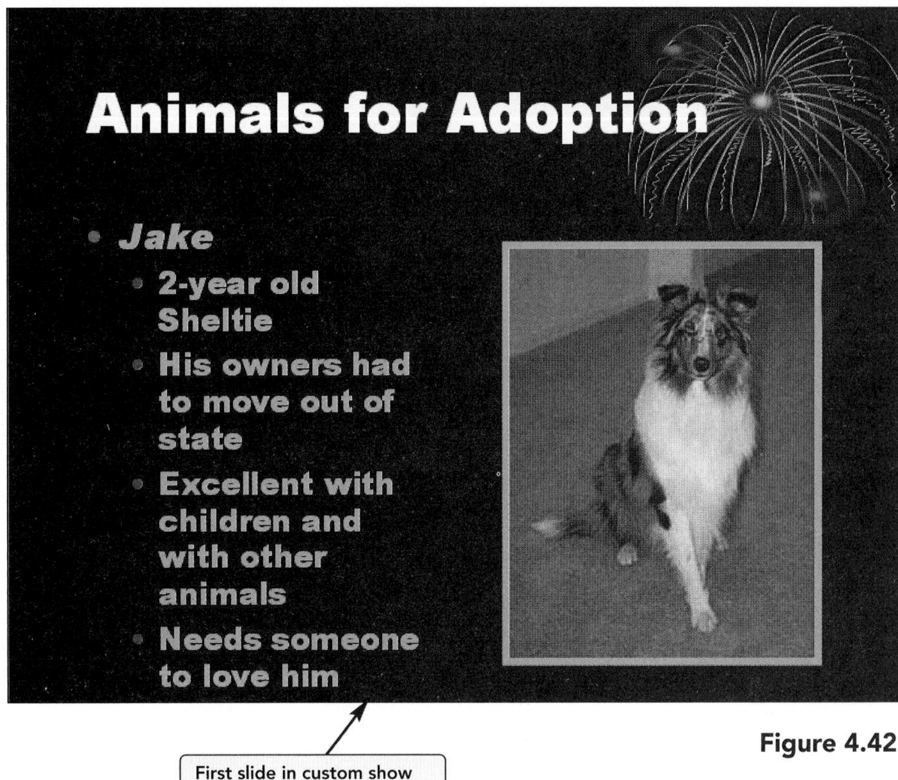


Figure 4.42

The slide show jumps to the first slide of the custom show and begins running the custom show.

2

- **When the custom show loops again to the first slide, press Esc to end the custom show and display the agenda slide.**
- **Press Esc to end the slide show presentation.**
- **Save the presentation as** Rescue Foundation Self Running**.**

**Additional Information**

The color of a selected hyperlink is different from those that have not been selected. This color change identifies those links that have already been viewed.

## Adding Action Buttons

To help the viewer navigate through the presentation, you decide to add action buttons to the slides.

## Concept 6

### Action Buttons

6 PowerPoint includes special objects called **action buttons** that can be inserted in a presentation and assigned a hyperlink. Action buttons consist of shapes, such as right- and left-facing arrows, that are used to navigate through a presentation. They are designed specifically for self-running presentations and presentations that run on a company network or the Web. Action buttons perform their associated action when you click on them or pass the mouse over them.

You have decided to have the first slide display continuously until the viewer clicks on a button to start the presentation. Once in the presentation, each slide will have a home button that will take the viewer back to the agenda slide, a forward button that will go to the next slide, and a backward button that will return to the previous slide.

**1**
- **Display slide 1 in Normal view.**
- **Choose Slide Show/Action Buttons.**

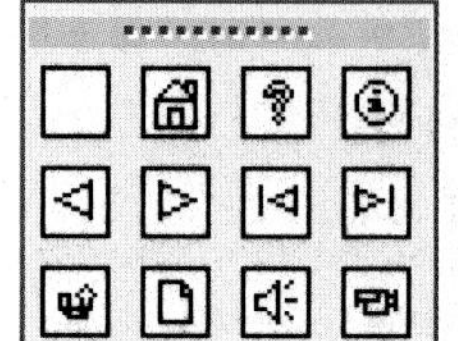

- **Click Custom (first column, first row).**
- **In the upper left corner of the slide, drag to create a button that is approximately 1 inch by 1 inch.**
- **In the Mouse Click tab of the Action Settings dialog box, make the button a hyperlink to the next slide.**
- **Click** 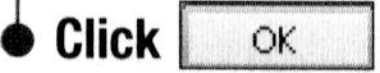 **.**

*Your screen should be similar to Figure 4.43*

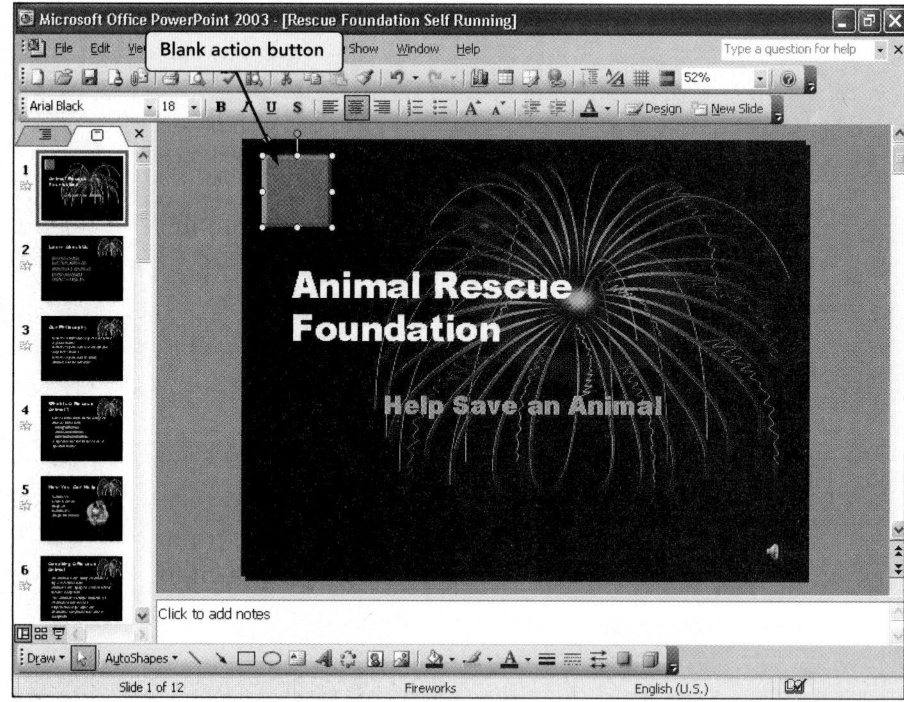


**Figure 4.43**

Next you need to add text to the button that contains the instructions for the viewer. You add button text just as you add text to a text box.

**2**

- **Right-click on the button and choose Add Text from the shortcut menu.**
- **Type Click Here to Learn More.**
- **Right-click on the button and choose Format AutoShape.**
- **Open the Text Box tab.**
- **Select Word wrap text in AutoShape.**
- **Select Resize AutoShape to fit text.**
- **Click OK.**
- **Change the text color to black and the font size to 14.**
- **Click outside the action button to deselect it.**

*Your screen should be similar to Figure 4.44*

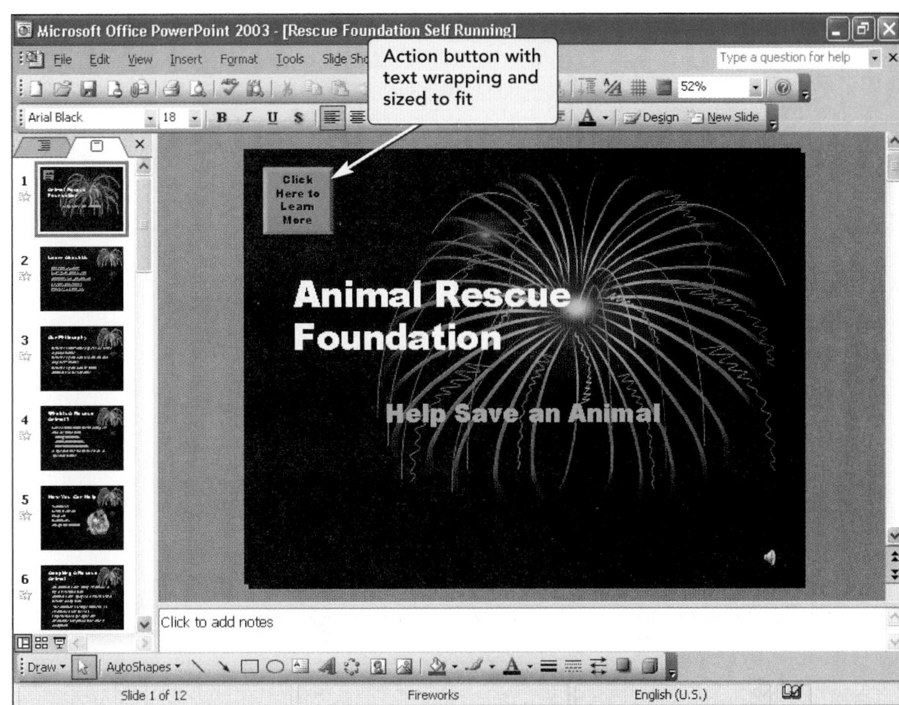


**Figure 4.44**

You will follow the same procedure to add three other buttons to the slides: home, forward, and backward. These buttons are predesigned, and contain icons that represent the action they perform. Therefore, you do not need to add text to the button. Since you want these buttons to appear on all slides other than title slides, you will add them to the Slide Master.

**3** • **Switch to Slide Master view and display the Slide Master.**

**Having Trouble?**

In Slide Master view, two slides appear in the Slide tab. Be sure to modify the Slide Master and not the Title Master.

- **Delete the three footer object boxes.**
- **Choose Slide Show/Action Buttons.**
- **Click Home (second column, first row).**
- **Click in the lower right of the footer area to create a default size button.**
- **Add a hyperlink to slide 2, the agenda slide.**
- **Click OK twice.**

*Your screen should be similar to Figure 4.45*

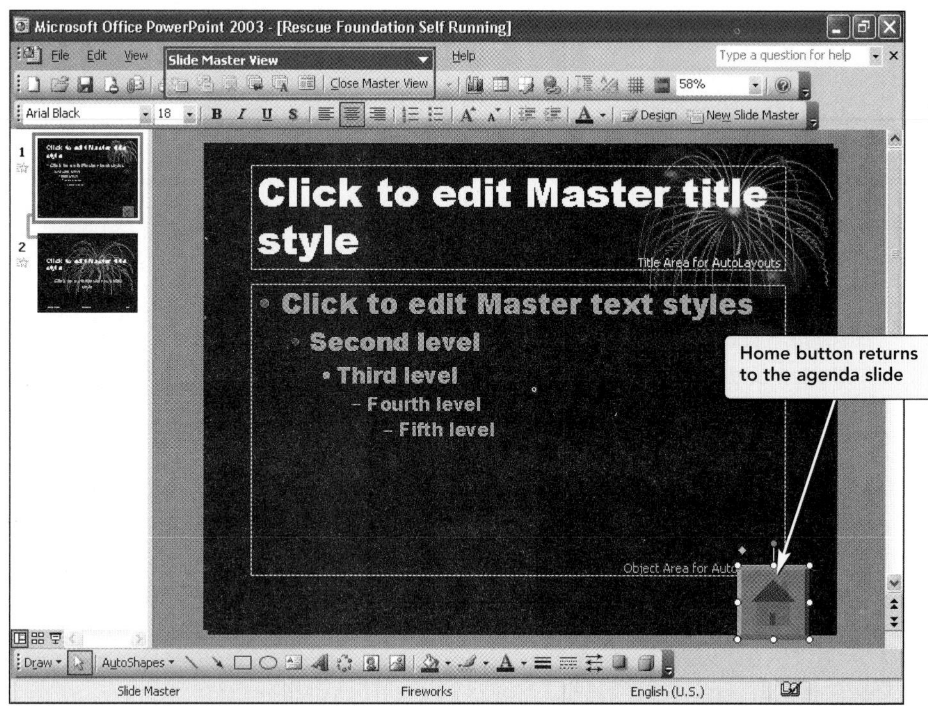


Figure 4.45

## Changing the Button Size

Now you want to reduce the size of the button by about half. In addition to changing the size of an object by dragging to an approximate size, you can change the size by entering an exact measurement for the object's height and width or by entering a percentage value to increase or decrease the object from its original size. Since you want to make the object about half its original size, you will reduce it by 50 percent.

1. 
   - Choose **Format/AutoShape**.
   - Open the Size tab.
   - Under Scale enter 50% in both the Height and Width boxes.
   - Click OK.
   - Move the button to the location shown in Figure 4.46.

**Additional Information**

If the slide miniature is displayed, you can see how the button looks on the current slide.

*Your screen should be similar to Figure 4.46*

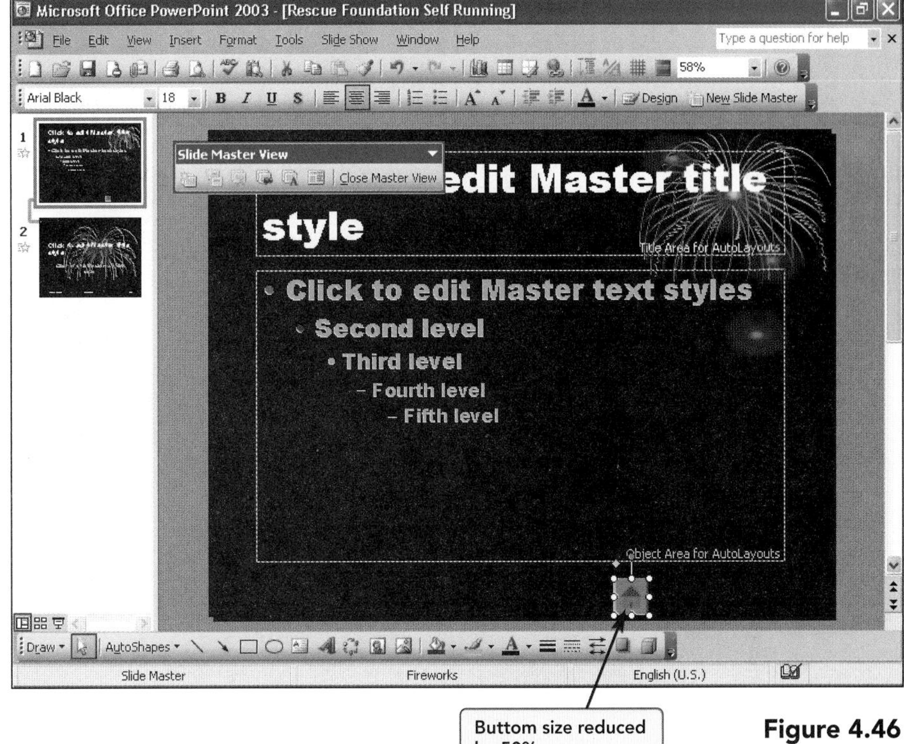


Figure 4.46

Now you will add the forward and back buttons.

2. 
   - To the right of the home button, add a default size Back or Previous button that hyperlinks to the previous slide.
   - To the right of the back button, add a default size Forward or Next button that hyperlinks to the next slide.
   - Select the two new buttons and reduce their size by 50 percent.

*Your screen should be similar to Figure 4.47*

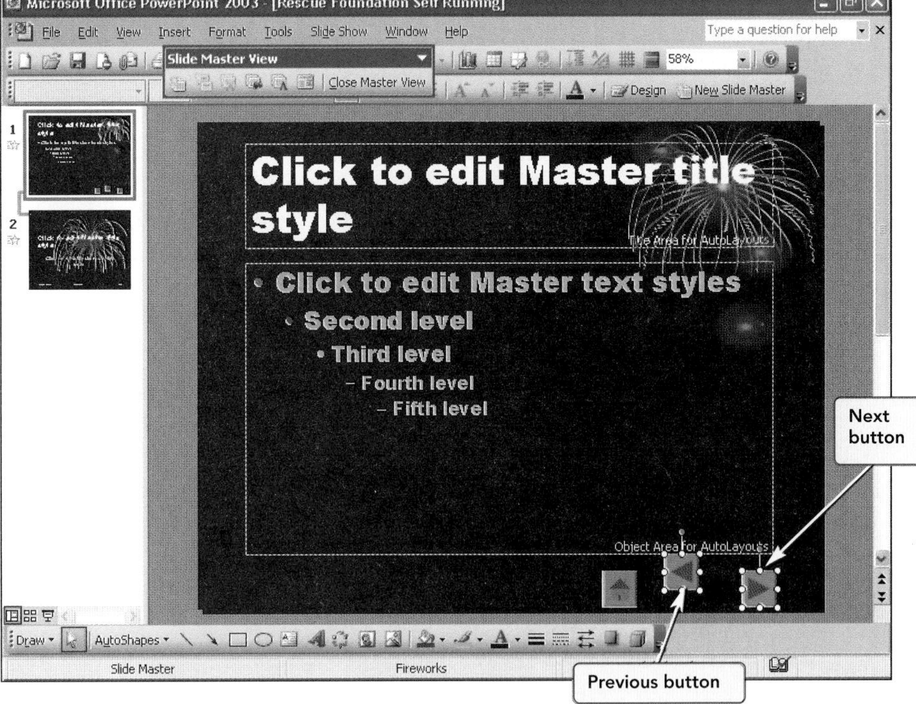


Figure 4.47

Finally, you want to position and align the three buttons.

**3** ● **Select the three buttons.**

● **Click Draw ▾ and choose Align or Distribute/Align Top.**

● **Click Draw ▾ and choose Align or Distribute/Distribute Horizontally.**

*Your screen should be similar to Figure 4.48*

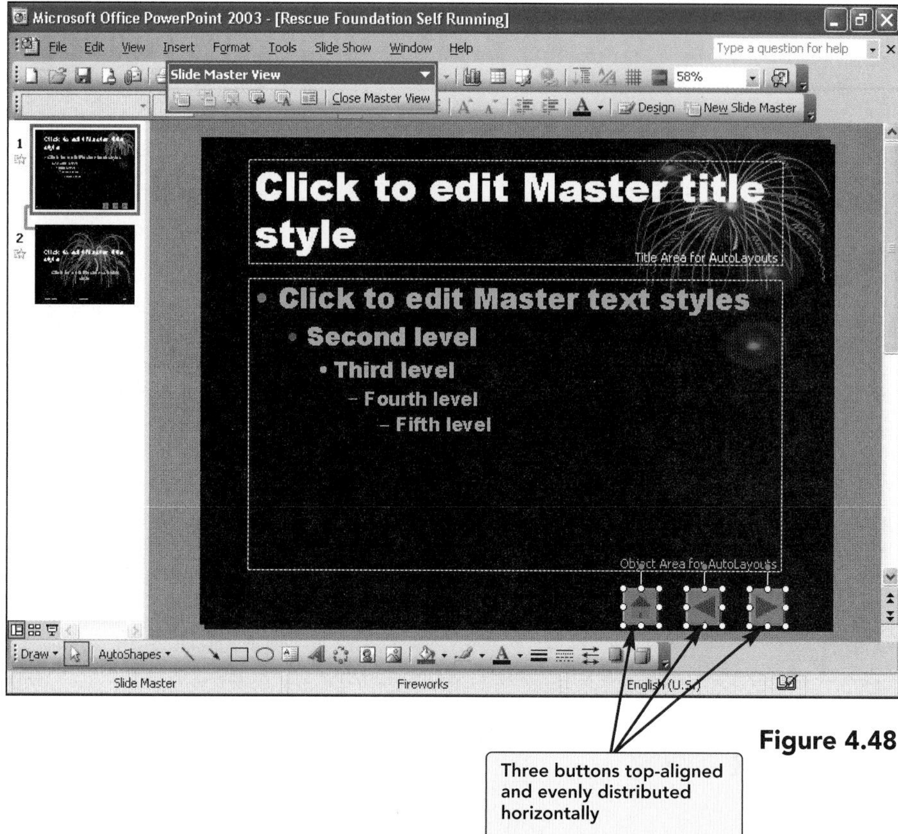


Figure 4.48

**Additional Information**

The outside buttons do not move; only the middle button moves to equalize the spacing.

The three buttons are evenly aligned with the top of the buttons and are an equal distance apart horizontally. Because the buttons were added to the slide master, they will appear in the same location on each slide in the presentation. You want to check the slides to make sure the buttons do not interfere with any of the text or graphics on the slides.

**4** ● **Switch to Slide Sorter view.**

● **Make any necessary adjustments to objects on the slides so they do not overlap the buttons.**

*Your screen should be similar to Figure 4.49*

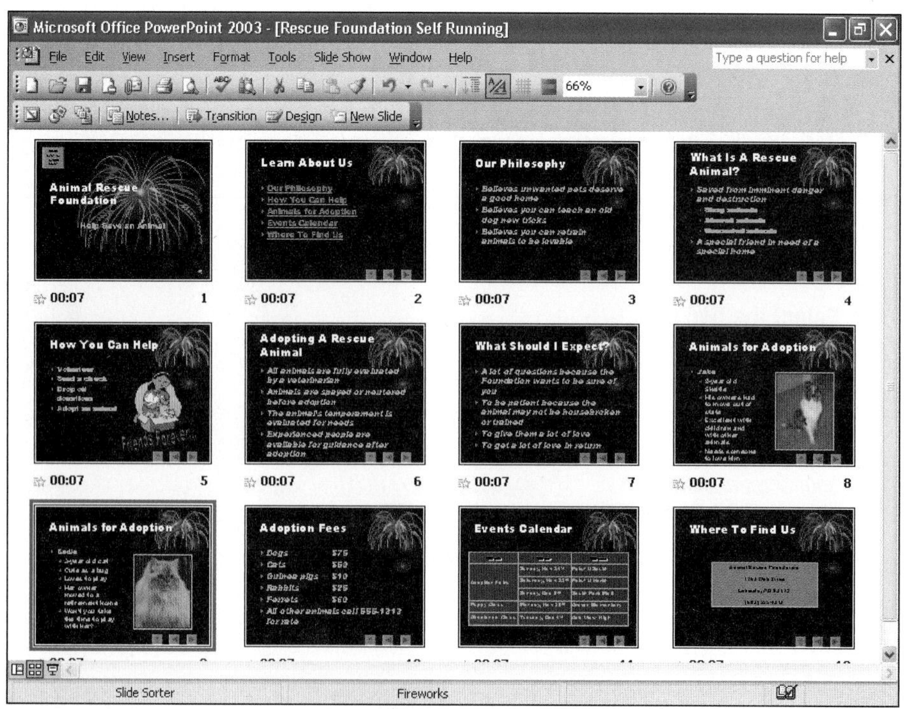


Figure 4.49

## Using Action Buttons

Now you are ready to run the revised presentation using the buttons. First you will turn off the features that make the presentation run continuously and change the music to play longer while the presentation is running.

1
- In Slide Sorter view, select all slides.
- Open the Slide Transition task pane.
- Clear the Automatically After option.
- Click Apply to All Slides.
- In Normal view, select the sound object on slide 1.
- Open the Custom Animation task pane.
- Open the pp04_Doggie drop-down list and select Effect Options.
- Increase the number of slides to stop playing after to 25.
- Click OK.
- Close the task pane and save the presentation.
- Run the slide show beginning at slide 1 and practice using the buttons.

*Your screen should be similar to Figure 4.50*

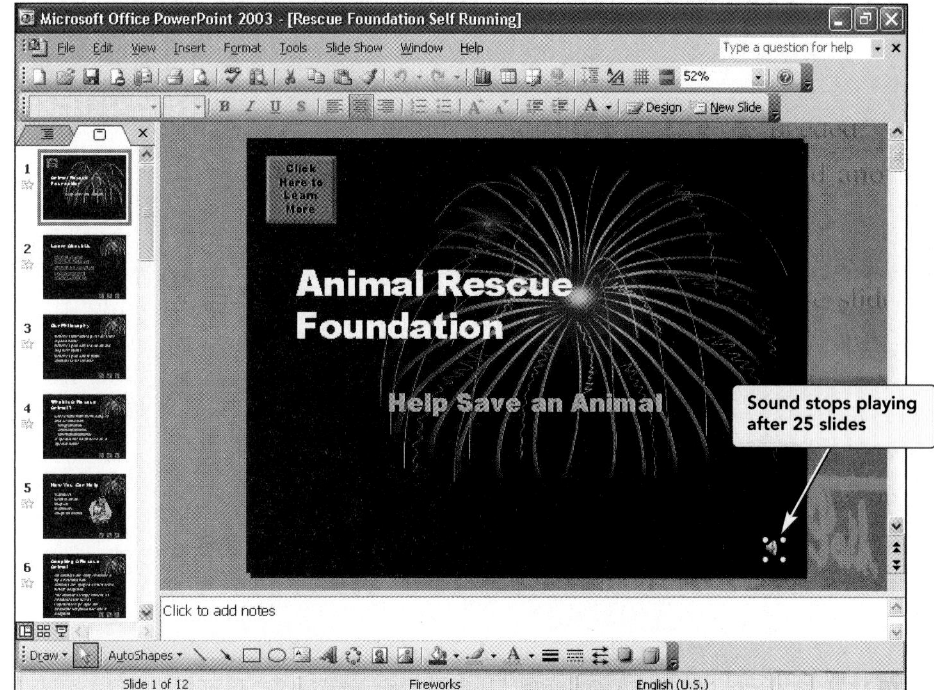


Figure 4.50

## Publishing a Presentation on the Web

You want to publish or save a copy of the presentation file for use on the World Wide Web (WWW). Publishing a file saves the file in Hypertext Markup Language (HTML) format.

## Concept 7

### Hypertext Markup Language

7 All Web pages are written using a programming language called **Hypertext Markup Language (HTML).** HTML commands control how the information on a page, such as font colors and size, is displayed. HTML also allows users to click on highlighted text or images and jump to other locations on the same page, to other pages in the same site, or to other sites and locations on the Web altogether.

HTML commands are interpreted by the browser software program you are using to access the WWW. A **browser** is a program that connects you to remote computers and displays the Web pages you request. The computer that stores the Web pages and sends them to a browser when requested is called the **server.**

**Additional Information**

If an older browser program is used, features that are not supported are unavailable.

Custom shows do not run in a Web browser, so before you publish the presentation, you first need to change the two hyperlinks to the custom shows to links to the first slide in the sequence. Most other features, including transitions and sound, will run in newer versions of browser programs.

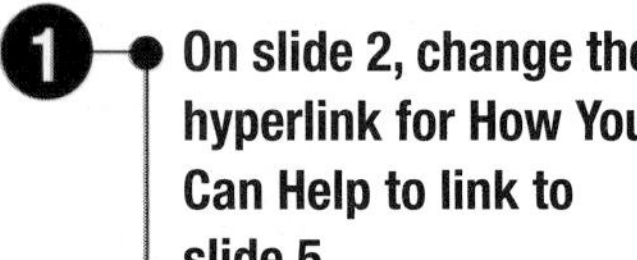

1. **On slide 2, change the hyperlink for How You Can Help to link to slide 5.**
   - **Change the Animals for Adoption hyperlink to link to slide 8.**

### Saving the presentation as a Single-File Web Page

Now that the presentation is ready for Web delivery, you can save it as a Web page. You can save a presentation in two ways:

- Web Page—Saves the presentation as a Web page and creates an associated folder that contains supporting files such as bullets, background textures, and graphics.
- Single-File Web Page—Saves the presentation as a Web page that integrates all supporting information, including graphics and other files, into a single file.

You will save the presentation to a single-file Web page, which is the default file type.

1. **Choose File/Save as Web Page.**
   - **Specify the location to save the file.**
   - **Enter the file name Rescue Foundation Web.**

*Your screen should be similar to Figure 4.51*

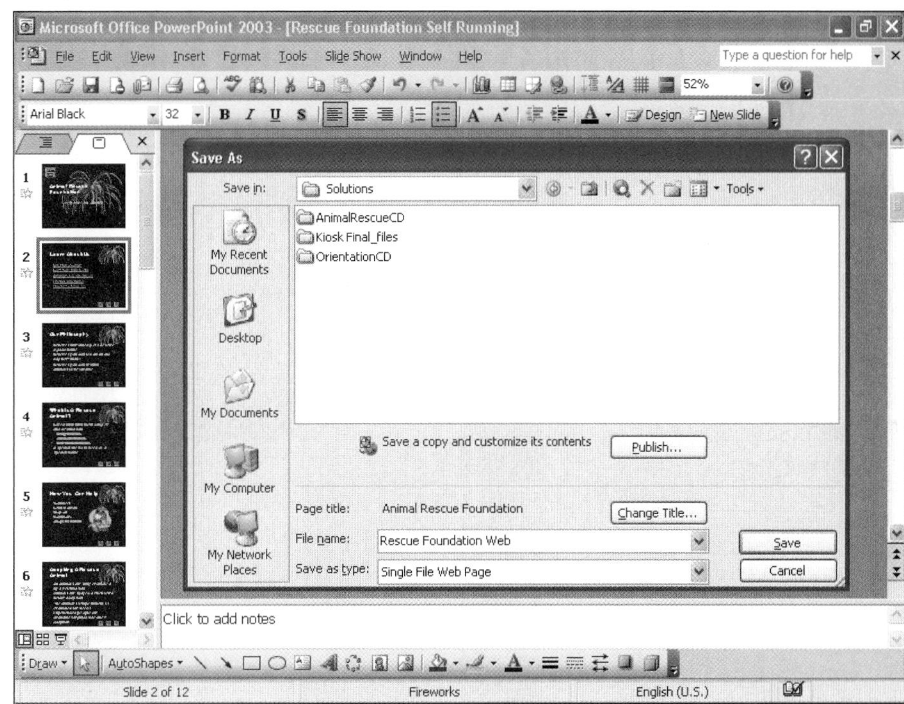


**Figure 4.51**

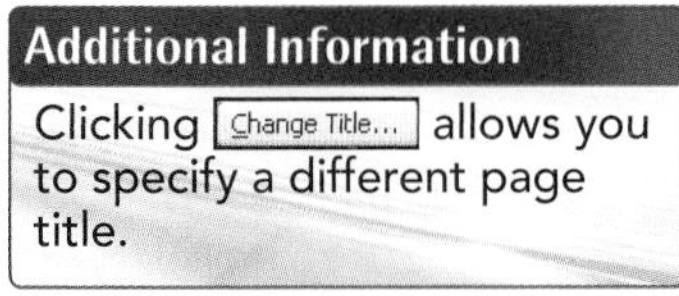

**Additional Information**

Clicking [Change Title...] allows you to specify a different page title.

Notice that the page title, the name that will appear in the title bar of the browser when the page is displayed, is the same as the title in the first slide. This is an appropriate page title and does not need to be changed. Next, you will set several additional Web page formatting and display options.

2. **Click [Publish].**

*Your screen should be similar to Figure 4.52*

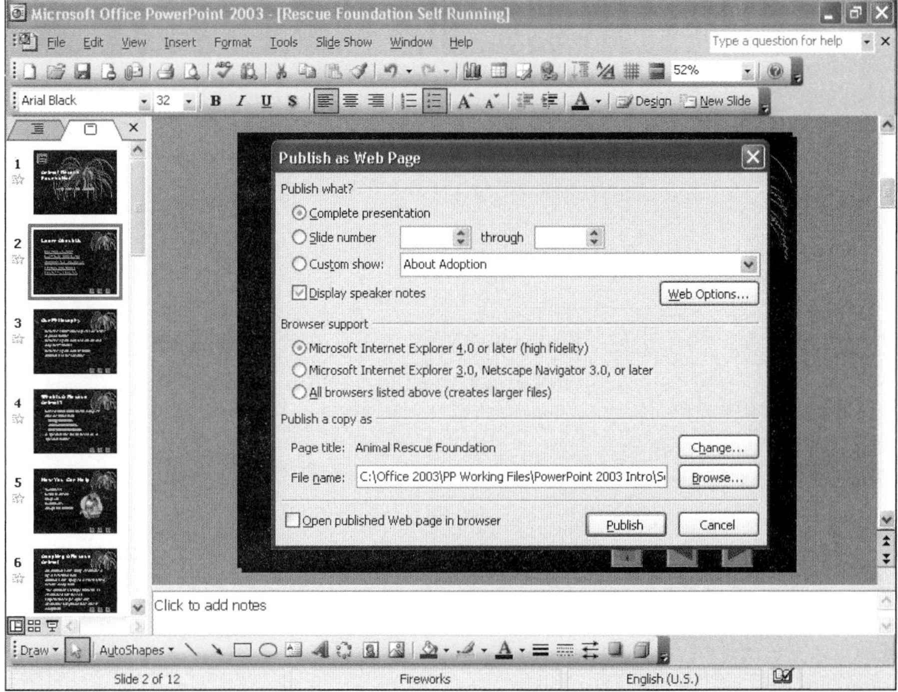


**Figure 4.52**

In the Publish as Web Page dialog box, you can specify the slides you want to publish under Publish What, and optimize the Web page for a particular browser or browser version under Browser support. The default settings, Complete Presentation and Microsoft Internet Explorer 4.0 or later, are appropriate for your needs. You do want to specify some additional Web options.

**3** **Click** 

- **In the General tab, select Show slide animation while browsing.**

*Your screen should be similar to Figure 4.53*

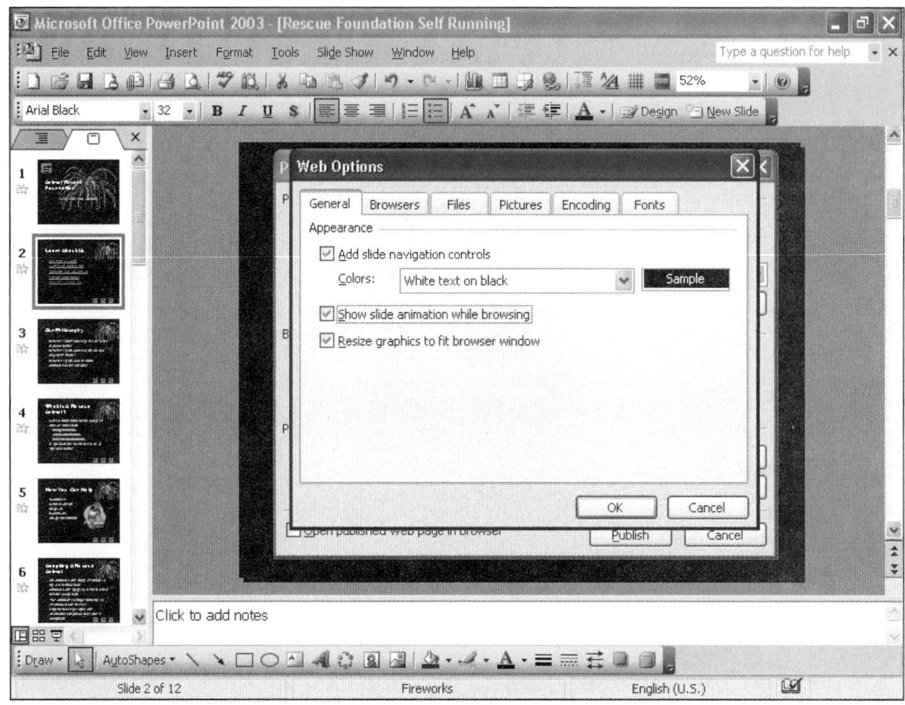


**Figure 4.53**

The three Appearance options on the General tab should be selected. The Add Slide Navigation Controls option will display a table of contents listing that can be used to navigate the presentation. The Resize Graphics to Fit Browser Window option automatically sizes the slides to fit the browser window.

**4** Click OK.

- To immediately see how your published Web presentation looks in your browser after you publish it, select **Open published Web page in browser.**
- Click Publish.
- If necessary, maximize the browser window.

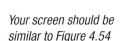

**Additional Information**

You can also use File/Web Page Preview to open your presentation in a Web browser.

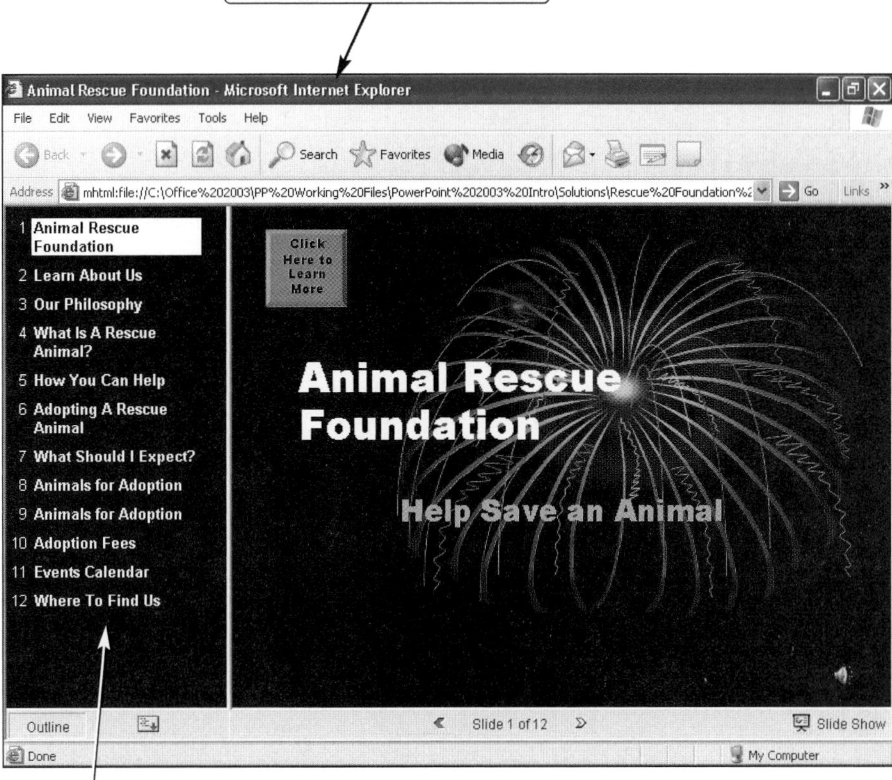


*Your screen should be similar to Figure 4.54*

**Figure 4.54**

**Additional Information**

A Single-File Web Page file type has a file extension of MHTML.

The file is converted to an HTML document and saved as a Single-File Web Page file type. This file contains all the elements on the page, such as images and hyperlinks, and all supporting files, such as those for bullets, graphics, and background. Any graphics that were added to the page that were not already JPEG or GIF files are converted to that format.

The browser on your system is loaded offline, and the page you created is displayed in the browser window. The left side of the window displays a table of contents listing consisting of the slide titles. Clicking on a title will display the associated slide on the right side.

## Navigating a Web Presentation

To navigate through the presentation, you can use the table of contents list, the action buttons, or the agenda slide hyperlinks.

**1**

- Try out the various methods of navigation in the presentation.
- When you are finished, click Close to exit the browser.
- Preview slides 2, 5, and 11 as handouts, three per page.
- Include a header on the handout that displays the current date and your name.

*Your screen should be similar to Figure 4.55*

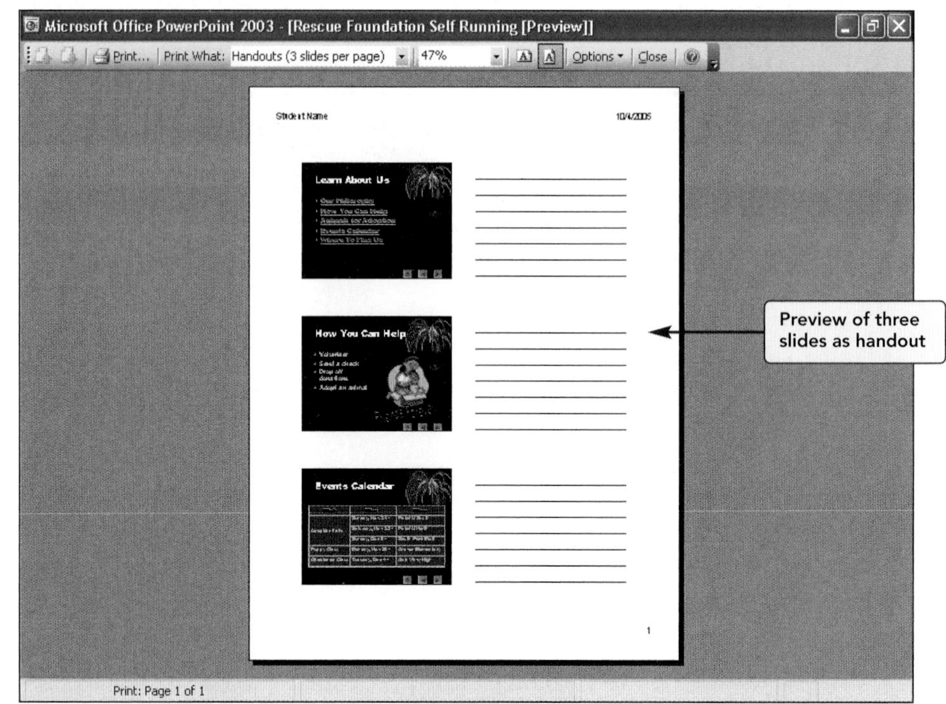


Figure 4.55

**2**

- Print the handout.
- Close the Print Preview window.
- Save the presentation.

## Saving a Presentation as a Design Template

Finally, you decide to save the first two slides of your presentation as a design template so you can quickly create another presentation that already contains the navigation items you added.

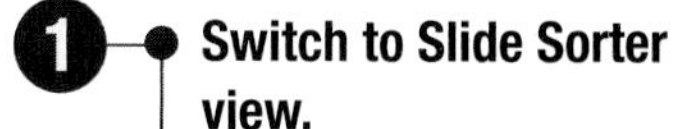

**Switch to Slide Sorter view.**

**Delete slides 3 through 12.**

**Choose File/Save As.**

**From the Save As Type box, select Design Template.**

**Change the file location to the location of your solution files.**

**Enter the file name Self Running.**

*Your screen should be similar to Figure 4.56*

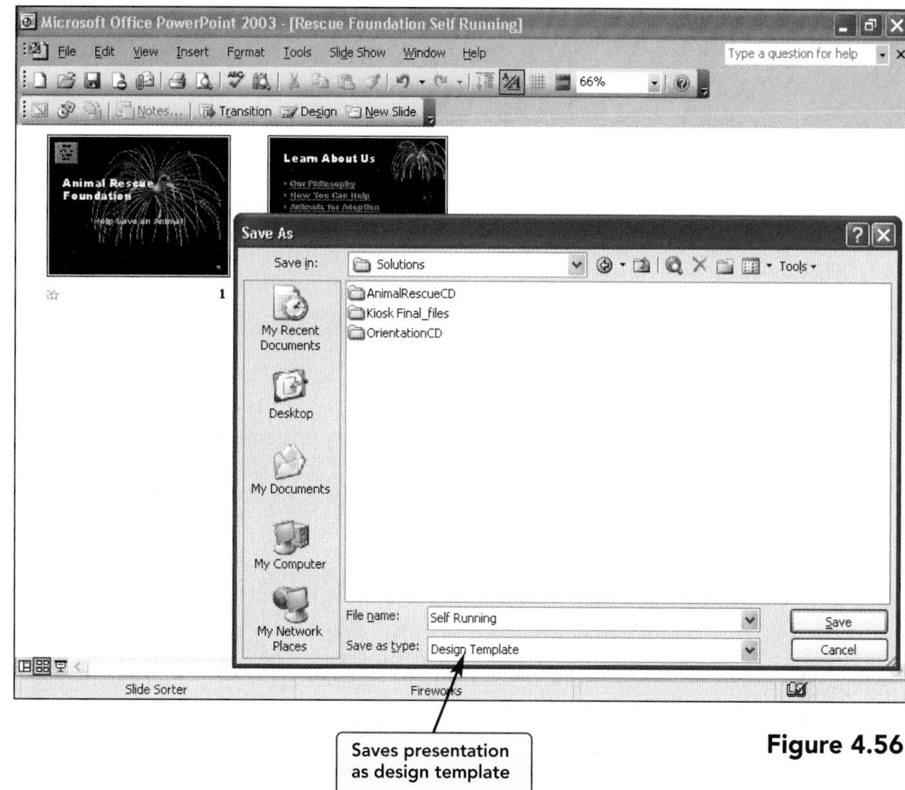


Figure 4.56

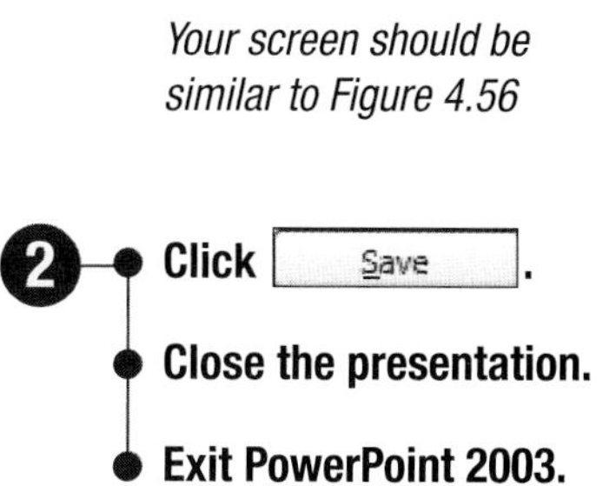

**Click Save.**

**Close the presentation.**

**Exit PowerPoint 2003.**

The default location to save a design template is the Template folder on your computer's hard drive. Saving it to this location will display the template name in the list of templates in the task pane. However, because you are saving it to your solution file location, it will not display in the template list.

The presentation is saved with a .pot file extension in your solution file folder and can be opened and modified to a new presentation. Because the extension is a template extension, when you save the modified presentation you will be prompted to give it a new file name, thereby preserving the template file for future use.

# Focus on Careers

## EXPLORE YOUR CAREER OPTIONS

### Public Relations Specialists

Informing the general public of an organization's policies, activities, and accomplishments is an important part of a public relations specialist's job. In addition to radio, print, and televised media, PowerPoint can be used to create presentations that can be viewed in public places, such as a kiosk or on the Web. The position of public relations specialist usually requires a college degree and commands salaries from $39,000 to over $75,000 depending on experience and skill.

# LAB 4
# Creating a Presentation for a Kiosk and the Web

## Animated GIF (PP4.19)

An animated GIF file is a type of graphic file that has motion.

Animated GIF

## WordArt (PP4.20)

The WordArt feature is used to enhance slides by changing the shape of text, adding 3-D effects, and changing the alignment of text on a line.

WordArt

## Sound and Movie Files (PP4.27)

Almost all PCs today are equipped with multimedia capabilities, which means they can play the most commonly used sound and movie files.

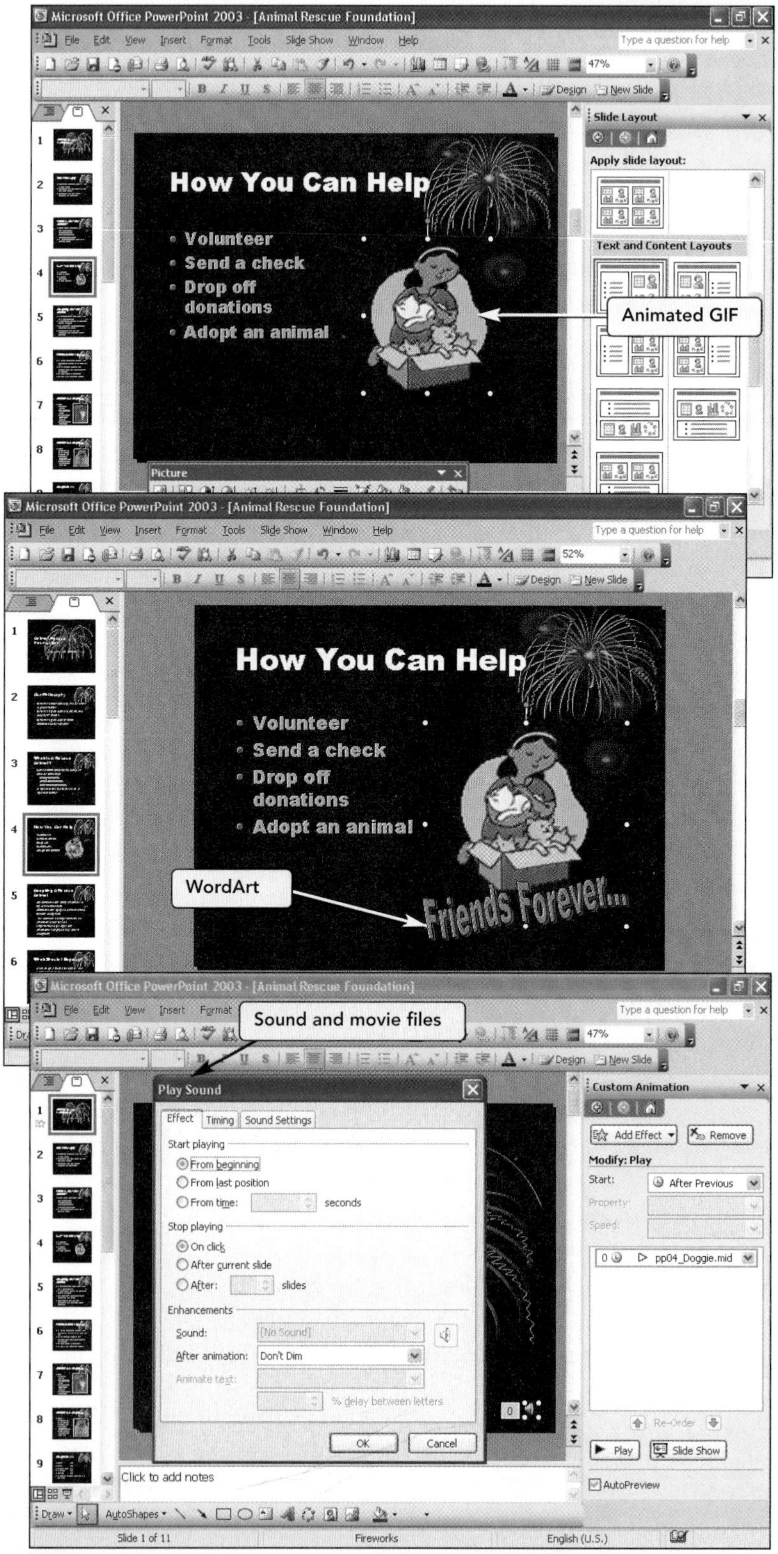

Sound and movie files

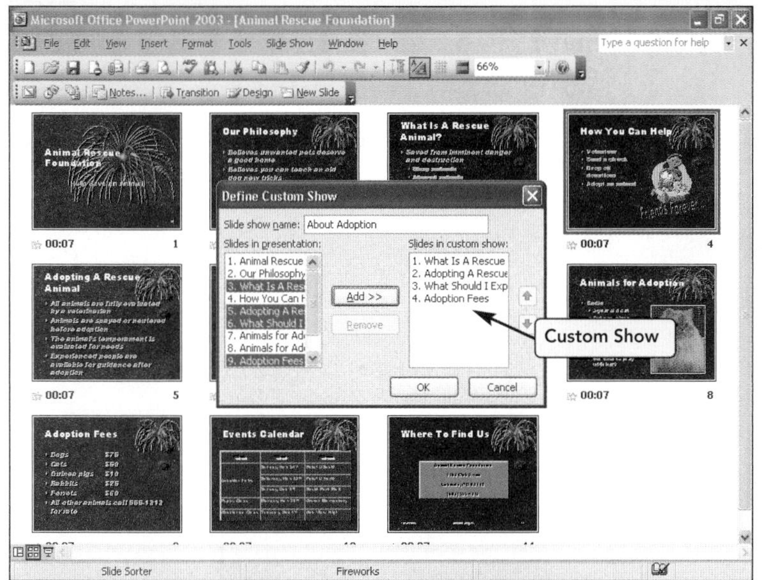


## Custom Show (PP4.32)

A custom show is a presentation that runs within a presentation.

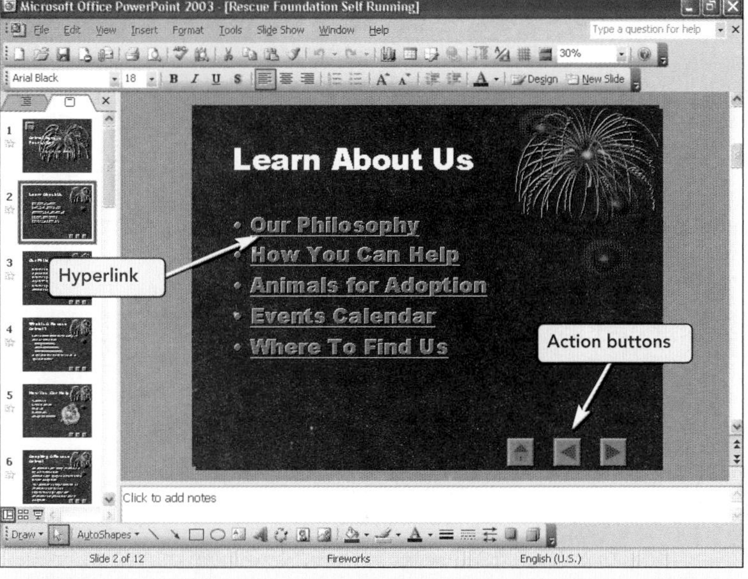


## Hyperlink (PP4.35)

Hyperlinks provide a quick way to jump to other slides, custom shows, presentations, objects, e-mail addresses, or Web pages.

## Action Buttons (PP4.40)

Action buttons consist of shapes, such as right- and left-facing arrows, that are used to navigate through a presentation.

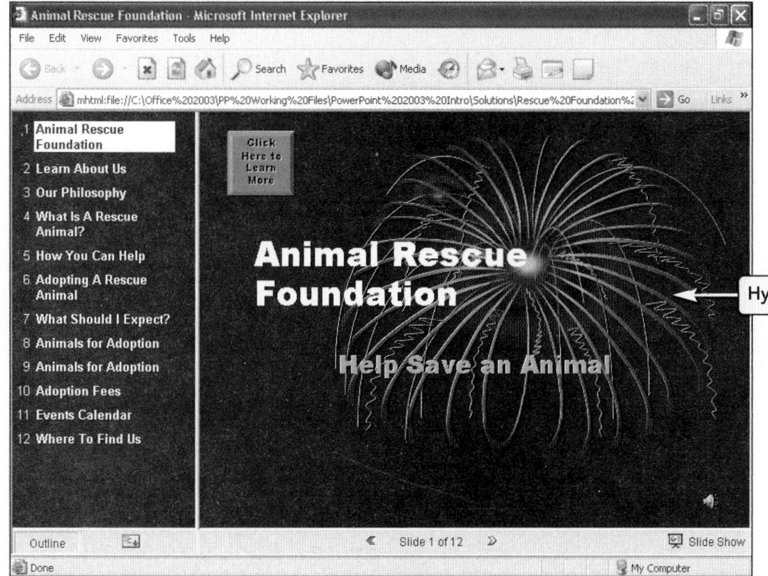

## Hypertext Markup Language (PP4.46)

All Web pages are written using a programming language called Hypertext Markup Language (HTML). HTML commands control how the information on a page, such as font colors and size, is displayed.

# LAB 4
# Creating a Presentation for a Kiosk and the Web

## key terms

action button PP4.40
animated GIF PP4.19
browser PP4.46
custom show PP4.32
hyperlink PP4.35
Hypertext Markup Language (HTML) PP4.46
publish PP4.45
server PP4.46
summary slide PP4.34
WordArt PP4.20

## microsoft office specialist skills

The Microsoft Office Specialist certification program is designed to measure your proficiency in performing basic tasks using the Office System applications. Certification demonstrates that you have the skills and provides a valuable industry credential for employment. After completing this lab, you have learned the following Microsoft Office PowerPoint 2003 Specialist skills:

| Skill Sets | Skill Standard | Page |
|---|---|---|
| Creating Content | Create new presentations from templates | PP4.4 |
| | Insert and edit text-based content | PP4.6 |
| | Insert tables, charts, and diagrams | PP4.12 |
| | Insert pictures, shapes, and graphics | PP4.20 |
| | Insert objects | PP4.26 |
| Formatting Content | Apply slide transitions | PP4.29 |
| | Customize slide templates | PP4.50 |
| Managing and Delivering Presentations | Organize a presentation | PP4.7 |
| | Set up slide shows for delivery | PP4.31,4.39 |
| | Prepare presentations for remote delivery | PP4.31 |
| | Save and publish presentations | PP4.45 |

## command summary

| Command | Button | Voice | Action |
|---|---|---|---|
| File/Save as Web Page | | | Publishes presentation on Web |
| Insert/Slides from Files | | | Inserts selected slides from another presentation |
| Insert/Slides from Outline | | | Creates slides from outline text |
| Insert/Movies and Sounds/ Sound from File | | | Inserts sound or movie files into selected slide |
| Insert/Movies and Sounds/ Play CD Audio Track | | | Plays a CD |
| Insert/Table | | | Inserts a table consisting of the specified number of rows and columns |
| Insert/Hyperlink | | | Creates a hyperlink |
| Format/AutoShape/Size | | | Changes size and scale of selected AutoShape |
| Format/Table | | | Formats borders and fill color of selected table |
| Slide Show/Set Up Show | | | Sets up presentation to run for specific situations |
| Slide Show/Custom Shows | | | Creates presentations within a presentation |
| Slide Show/Action Buttons | | | Adds navigation buttons to a slide |
| Slide Show/Action Settings | | | Specifies action that is needed to activate hyperlinks |
| Slide Show/Custom Animation | | | Adds motion and determines how sound is played |

## matching

Match the numbered item with the correct lettered description.

| | | | |
|---|---|---|---|
| **1.** agenda slide | _____ | **a.** | vertically centers cell contents |
| **2.** server | _____ | **b.** | combination of multiple images that appear to move |
| **3.** .mpeg | _____ | **c.** | creates a home action button |
| **4.** [icon] | _____ | **d.** | a single-file Web page file type |
| **5.** action buttons | _____ | **e.** | moving picture file extension |
| **6.** [icon] | _____ | **f.** | contains a list of items or main topics from the presentation |
| **7.** custom show | _____ | **g.** | computer that stores Web pages and sends them to a browser |
| **8.** hyperlink | _____ | **h.** | shapes that are used to navigate through a presentation |
| **9.** .WAV | _____ | **i.** | allows user to jump to a new location in the presentation |
| **10.** animated GIF | _____ | **j.** | presentation that runs within another presentation |
| **11.** .MHTML | | | |

## multiple choice

Circle the letter of the correct response to the questions below.

**1.** The feature that is used to enhance your presentation by changing the shape of text, adding 3-D effects, and changing the alignment of text is called ________________.
- **a.** TextArt
- **b.** WordArt
- **c.** DrawShape
- **d.** WordWrap

**2.** A(n) ________________ is a presentation that runs within a presentation.
- **a.** custom show
- **b.** moving picture
- **c.** hyperlink
- **d.** agenda slide

**3.** If you do not have control over what computer your presentation will run on, use _______ and _________ files for audio and video.
- **a.** WAV, MPEG
- **b.** MIDI, AVI
- **c.** WAV, AVI
- **d.** MIDI, MOV

4. The _______________ feature is most useful for creating complex tables that contain cells of different heights or varying number of columns per row.
   a. Insert Table
   b. Draw Table
   c. Table Slide Layout
   d. Create Table

5. ___________ control(s) how the information on a Web page is displayed.
   a. Formatting
   b. Browsers
   c. HTML commands
   d. Servers

6. A(n) __________________ file is a type of graphic file that has motion.
   a. animated GIF.
   b. moving graphic
   c. static GIF
   d. animated WAV

7. A(n) _____________________ loops back to the beginning slide and allows users to select what parts of the presentation they want to view.
   a. special show
   b. continuous show
   c. custom show
   d. agenda show

8. ____________________ provide a quick way to jump to other slides or Web pages.
   a. Action buttons
   b. Text links
   c. Hyperlinks
   d. Hypertext commands

9. Pages on the Web are written using the ________________ programming language.
   a. WWW
   b. HTML
   c. MPMC
   d. HMCL

10. A __________________ is a program that displays Web pages.
   a. viewer
   b. browser
   c. server
   d. control

## true/false

Check the correct answer to the following statements.

| | | | |
|---|---|---|---|
| **1.** | A presentation can be created from a Word outline document. | True | False |
| **2.** | WordArt is used to enhance predrawn images. | True | False |
| **3.** | Individual slides from one presentation can be inserted into another presentation. | True | False |
| **4.** | Animated images only move when the slide show is run. | True | False |
| **5.** | When a table is created in PowerPoint, it must have an equal number of columns and rows. | True | False |
| **6.** | Movies can be inserted into a PowerPoint presentation. | True | False |
| **7.** | When a presentation is run on a kiosk, it must have user interaction to repeat itself. | True | False |
| **8.** | A unique show runs a presentation within a presentation. | True | False |
| **9.** | An agenda slide can be linked to other slides in the presentation. | True | False |
| **10.** | Action buttons can be added to the slide master and appear on all slides in the presentation. | True | False |

## fill-in

Complete the following statements by filling in the blanks with the correct terms.

1. Text that is added to a slide using _________________ is a graphic object that can be edited, sized, or moved to any location on the slide.
2. When a(n) _____________ file is inserted into a PowerPoint slide, it does not display action until you run the presentation.
3. ______ files are typically used for sounds, and _________ files are typically used for music.
4. The programming language used on the Web is called ____________________.
5. ____________ files do not require any special hardware but they produce the lowest quality video.
6. When a custom show is finished, the presentation returns to the ________________.
7. A(n) _________________ is a presentation within a presentation.
8. A(n) __________________ slide is created from the titles of the selected slides.
9. _______________ buttons can be added to a presentation to move to other slides in the presentation.
10. _______________ provide a quick way to jump to other locations in a presentation.

rating system

★ Easy

★★ Moderate

★★★ Difficult

## step-by-step

### Betty's Birds Kiosk ★

1. You work at Betty's Birds, and are in charge of new customer orientation. Betty has requested that you create a kiosk presentation that will run in the store and help customers choose the right pet bird. Some of the completed slides are shown here.

   a. Open PowerPoint 2003. Create a new presentation using the Echo design template. Change the color scheme with the teal background choice.

   b. Add the title **Betty's Birds** and the subtitle **Your First Bird** to slide 1.

   c. Insert the graphic pp04_Birds to the right of the subtitle.

   d. Import text from the file pp04_Bird Outline. View the new slides and adjust the text as needed.

   e. Insert the graphic pp04_Dancing Parrot on slide 8.

   f. Insert a new Title Only slide at the end of the presentation. Insert the title **Betty's Birds**. Create a WordArt object with the text **Thank You** in a font of your choice. Position the WordArt object in the lower right corner of the slide.

   g. Search for the bird sound file pp04_Parrot Talk and insert it on slide 1 with the automatic play option selected.

   h. Add clip art of your choice to slides 3 and 9.

   i. Create an agenda slide as slide 2 with hyperlinks to the appropriate slides.

   j. Add home, next, and previous action buttons to the slide master that link to the agenda slide, next, and previous slides.

   k. Save the presentation as a Web page named Betty's Birds.

   l. Delete all slides except the first and last slides. Save the presentation as a template named Birds.

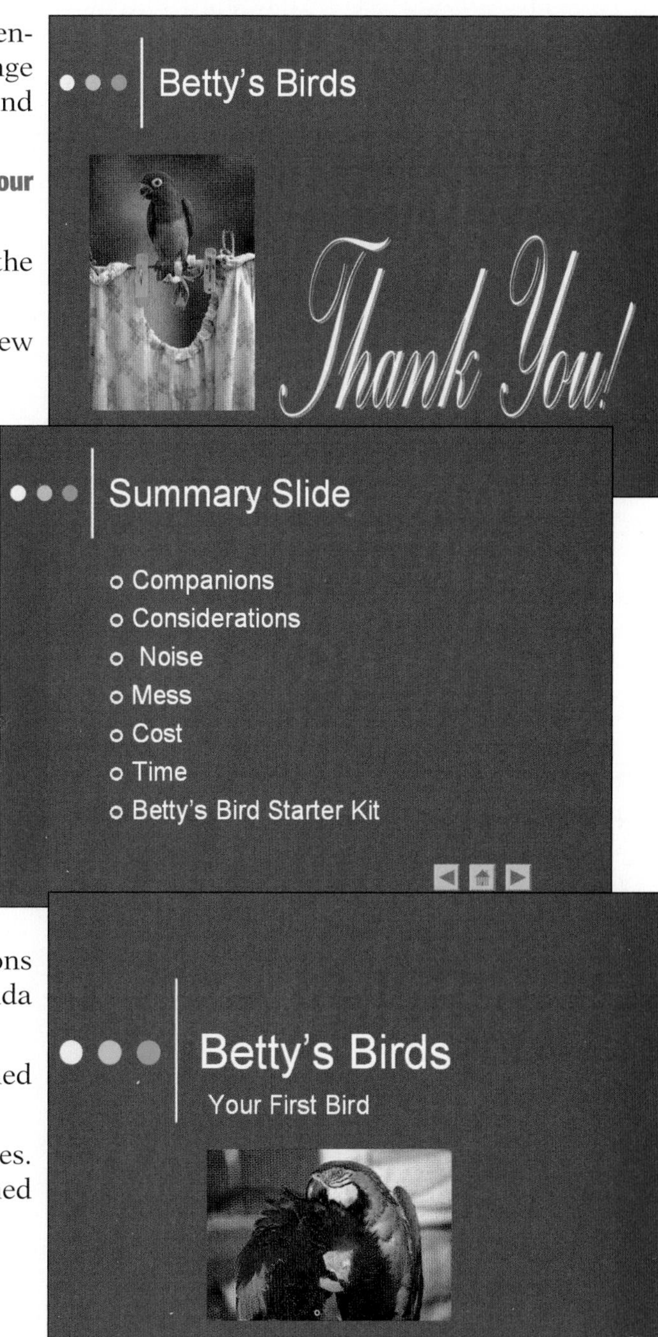

### Anthology Cinema Web Presentation ★ ★

**2.** You work at Anthology Cinema in the media and customer relations department. You have been asked to create a presentation about the summer movie matinees that will run on the company's Web site. Some of the completed slides from your presentation are shown here.

   **a.** Open PowerPoint 2003. Create a new presentation using the Glass Layers design template. Change the color scheme to the light orange background choice.

   **b.** Add the title **Saturday Matinee** and the subtitle **Thrill-a-Minute Movies** to slide 1.

   **c.** Insert the graphic pp04_Anthology Logo on slide 1. Center the logo on the slide and adjust the title and subtitle as shown in the example.

   **d.** Import text from the file pp04_Anthology Outline. View the new slides and adjust the text as needed.

   **e.** Change the layout of slide 5 to Title, Text, and Content. Insert the graphic pp04_Popcorn in the placeholder. Adjust the size of the image to fill the slide. View the slide show to see the animation.

   **f.** Insert a new slide at the end of the presentation with a Blank layout. Create a WordArt object with the text **Visit us soon!** in a font of your choice. Change the WordArt shape to Arch Up. Insert the graphic pp04_Ticket below the WordArt object.

   **g.** Create a WordArt object with the text **Anthology Cinema** in the same font as the first WordArt object. Change the WordArt shape to Arch Down.

   **h.** Add the sound file pp04_Film and select the automatic start option.

   **i.** Preview slides 1, 5, and 6 as handouts, three per page.

   **j.** Save the presentation as a Web page named Anthology Cinema Web Presentation.

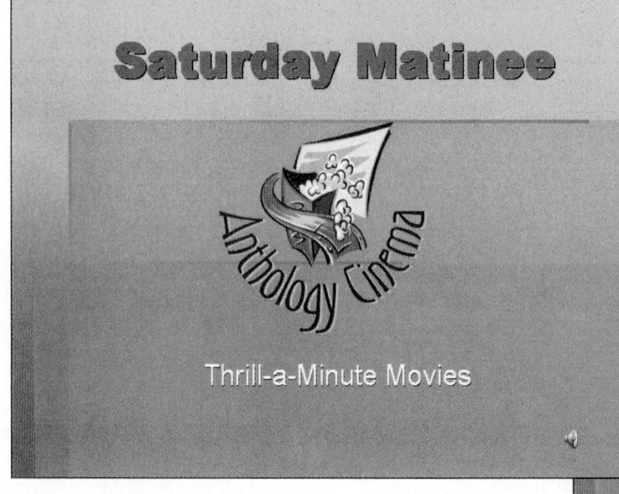

## Adventure Travel Tours ★ ★

3. Adventure Travel Tours would like to create more business in their student travel division. You have been asked to create a Web presentation that highlights the Student Abroad Tour and gives advice to potential clients on what to expect from the trip. Some of the completed slides are shown here.

   a. Start PowerPoint and open the file pp04_Europe. Include your name on the title slide. Insert the graphic pp04_Champs Elysees in the lower left corner of slide 1. Adjust slide layout as needed.

   b. Create two custom slide shows, one titled **Food** that displays slides 5 through 8, and another titled **Favorite Places** that displays slides 7 and 10.

   c. Create a summary slide that includes slides 3 through 11. Title the slide **Topics**.

   d. Add Mouse Click hyperlinks from each item on the agenda slide to the appropriate slide or custom slide show (Jambon & Fromage links to the Food custom show).

   e. Insert the graphic pp04_Dinner on slide 6 and adjust the layout as required.

   f. Add home, back, and forward action buttons to the slide master. The home button should return to the agenda slide. Size and position the buttons appropriately. Reposition any text or graphics in the presentation as needed.

   g. Set the slides to advance automatically after 10 seconds with slow transition. Set the presentation to run on a kiosk as a continuous loop.

   h. Insert an audio of your choice to run while the presentation runs.

   i. Insert the animated graphic pp04_Train on slide 11.

   j. Add a WordArt object with the text **Off the Beaten Path** in a font of your choice on slide 8. Apply the Wave 2 shape. Position the WordArt object over the upper left corner of the photo.

   k. Run the slide show and test all the hyperlinks. Edit any slides as necessary.

   l. Save the presentation as a Web page named Europe Web Presentation. Print the presentation with six slides per page.

   m. Turn off the automatic advance setting and remove the audio. Redo the two hyperlinks that linked to custom shows to link to the appropriate slides. Preview the Web page and run the presentation.

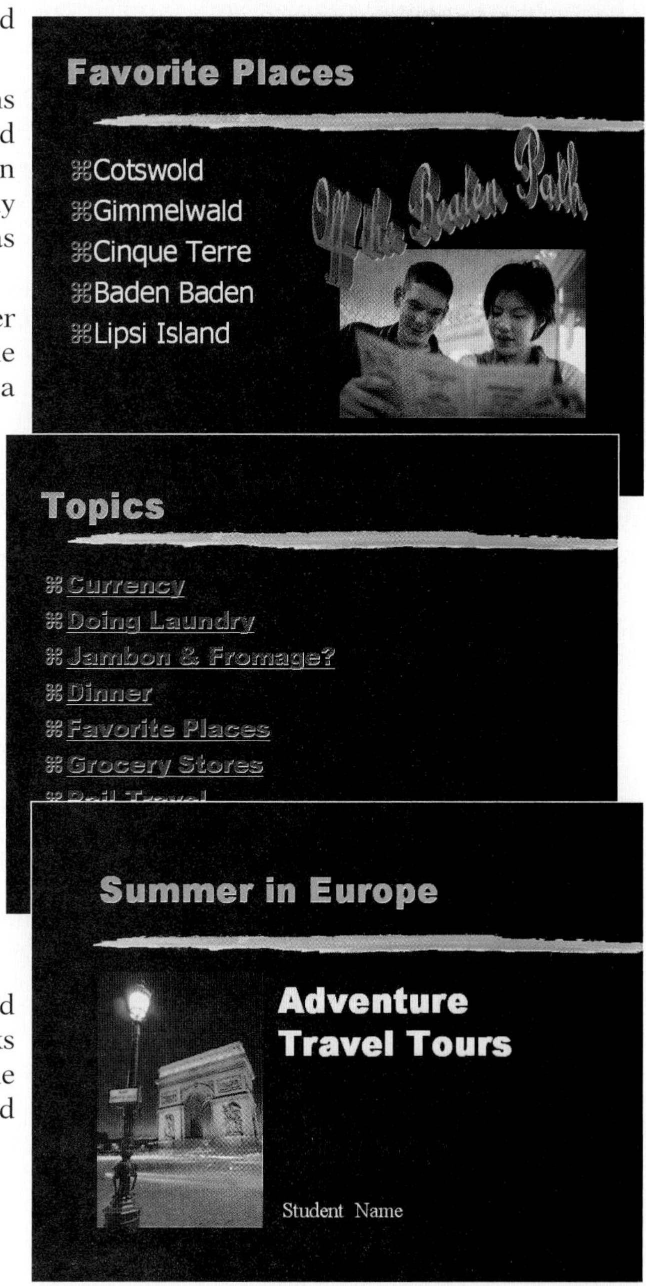

## Fitness Web Page ★★★

4. The Lifestyle Fitness Club would like you to create several new pages for their Web site. The outline containing the text for the pages has already been created. You will create a presentation using the information in this outline. Several slides of the completed presentation are shown here.

   a. Create a new presentation using the Shimmer design template. Add slides to the presentation using the Word outline pp04_Fitness Outline.

   b. Delete the blank first slide. Apply the Title slide layout to the first slide. Add your name as a subtitle on the title slide.

   c. Change the slide layout of slide 2 to Title, Text, and Content. Insert the graphic pp04_Exercise.

   d. Change the layout of slide 4 to Title, Text, and Content. Insert the file pp04_Stretching in the placeholder.

   e. Add a sound clip of your choice to the presentation.

   f. Use the numbered bullet style to consecutively number the tips on slides 5 and 6.

   g. Insert a new slide at the end of the presentation. Use the Title Only layout. Title the slide **Why People Go to Fitness Clubs**.

   h. Insert a table with 3 columns and 9 rows. Enter the following information. Include appropriate column headings and formatting.

| | | |
|---|---|---|
| **Tone my body** | **41%** | **159** |
| **Lose weight** | **31%** | **119** |
| **Meet people** | **0%** | **1** |
| **Reduce stress** | **3%** | **12** |
| **Bulk up** | **11%** | **41** |
| **Stay active** | **13%** | **49** |
| **Avoid feeling guilty** | **2%** | **7** |
| **Get out of house** | **1%** | **2** |

   i. Add home, back, and forward action buttons to the slide master. Appropriately size and position the buttons.

   j. Save the presentation as a Web page named Fitness Web Pages. Print the presentation with four slides per page.

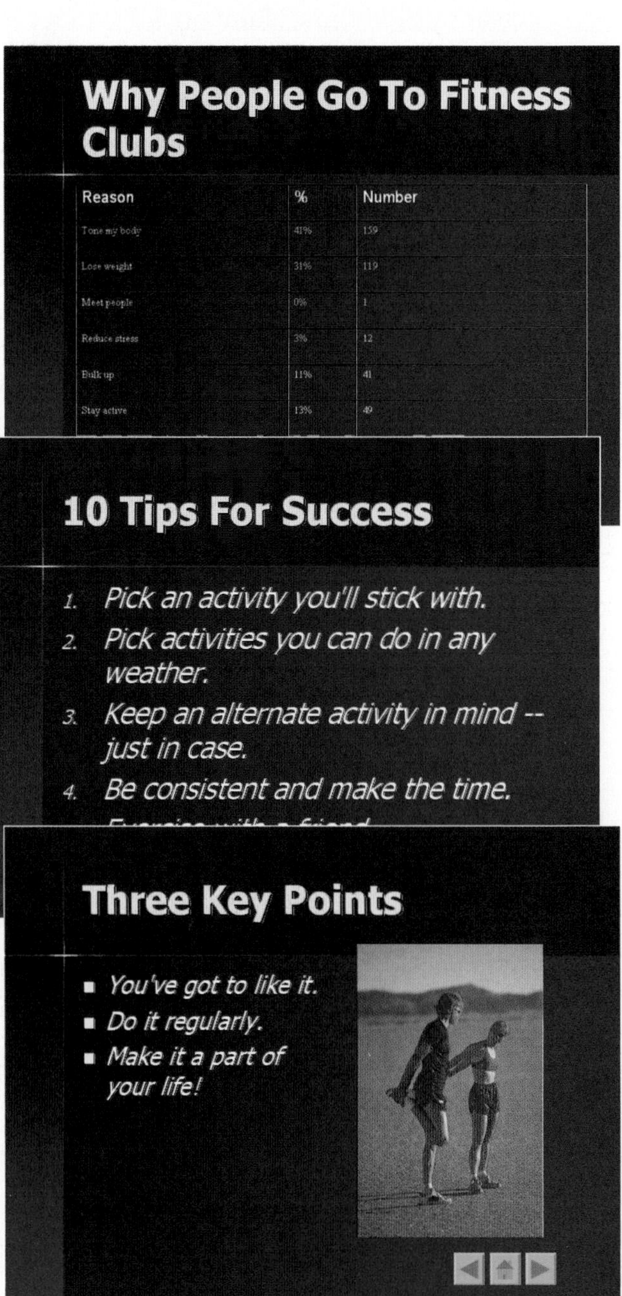

## Sports Company Kiosk and Web Page ★ ★ ★

5. The Sports Company is expanding its advertising. They would like to have a kiosk presentation to send to their stores that features some special products in the stores. They would also like the presentation available on the Web. Several slides of the completed presentation are shown here.

   a. Create a presentation using the Orbit design template. Add slides to the presentation by inserting the Word document file pp04_Sports Company Outline.

   b. Delete the blank slide 1. Apply the Title slide layout to slide 1. Enter your name as a subtitle on the title slide. Insert the graphic pp04_Weight Lifter. Adjust the slide layout as needed.

   c. Make two custom slide shows, one for **Products** and one for **Services**. The Products custom show should display slides 4, 5, and 6. The Services custom show should display slides 7 and 8.

   d. Hyperlink the titles of the Products and Services slides to the appropriate custom show.

   e. Insert the file pp04_Tennis Racquet in slide 6.

   f. Replace the main title on slide 1 with an appropriately sized and shaped WordArt that contains the same text. Change the color to match the presentation design.

   g. Insert the graphic pp04_Mountain Bike on slide 4. Size and position the graphic. Adjust the layout as needed.

   h. Insert the sound file pp04_Onestop on slide 1. Set the sound to play when the presentation starts and to play for all slides.

   i. Add an animation of your choice to slide 8.

   j. Add home, forward, and back action buttons to the slide master. Color, size, and position the buttons appropriately.

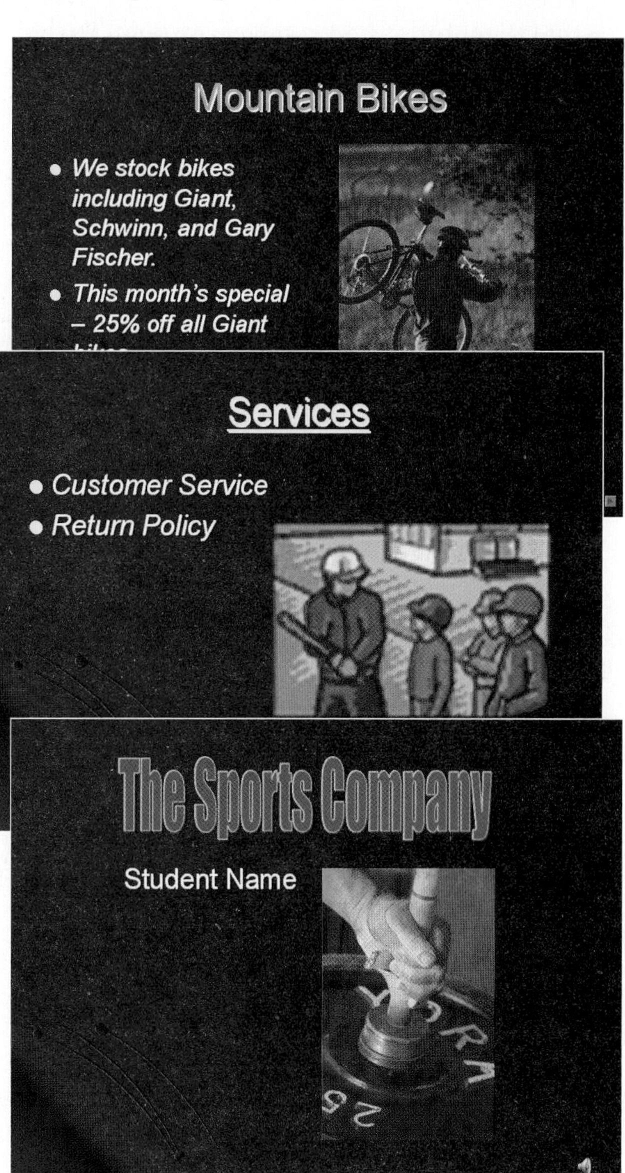


   k. Apply a random transition to all slides to advance automatically after 7 seconds. Set the slide show to run on a kiosk.

   l. Save the presentation as Sports Company Kiosk. Run the presentation to test the hyperlinks. Print the presentation with six slides per page.

   m. Remove the sound from the first slide. Remove the Products and Services hyperlinks. Add hyperlinks on the Products and Services slides for each bulleted item to the appropriate slide. Remove the transition settings and timings. Save the presentation as a Web presentation with the name Sports Company Web.

## on your own

### Pool Safety Kiosk ★

1. The response to your lifeguard safety presentation has been overwhelmingly positive. You decide that the information you have presented would make a good presentation to run on the kiosk in your public safety office. Modify the file Lifeguard Presentation for use on a kiosk. Add the name of your city in a WordArt design of your choice. Include appropriate animation and clip art, slide transitions, preset timing, and sound that runs continuously with the slide show. Set up the show to be browsed at a kiosk and to automatically play at full screen and loop continuously. Save the presentation as Pool Safety Kiosk and print the presentation with six slides per page.

### Carpooling Kiosk ★

2. As cities surrounding Seattle get larger, rush hour traffic to the business district increases. You have been hired by the Washington Department of Transportation to create a presentation for their office lobby on the benefits of mass transit and carpooling. Use the information in the file pp04_Mass Transit to create a presentation that will run on a kiosk giving people information on how mass transit use and carpooling will benefit their city. Use the features you learned in PowerPoint, including sound and animation. Include your name in a footer on all slides. Save the presentation as Mass Transit and print the presentation with six slides per page.

### Getaway Travel Club Web Page ★ ★

3. The Getaway Travel Club unanimously adopted your proposal to amend the itinerary for the Italy Trip this summer. They have asked you to post the information on the Web. Create a Web-based presentation. Open the presentation Favorites Travel (Lab 3, On Your Own 3) and create a custom show and an agenda slide with hyperlinks. Include action buttons, sound, animation, and WordArt. Include your name in the footer of all slides. Preview the presentation. Save the presentation as Travel Italy Web and print the presentation with six slides per page.

### Storyland Fairytale Web Page ★ ★ ★

4. Your presentation on popular children's book titles was very popular with parents. Many have contacted the store owner, Susan, for more information. Susan has decided that the information you have compiled in your previous presentations would be an excellent Web page. Modify the Storyland Orientation file for use on the Web. Create a custom show and an agenda slide with hyperlinks. Include action buttons, sound, animation, and WordArt with the company name (Storyland). Save the file as Storyland Web. Print the presentation.

### MusicFirst Web Presentation ★ ★ ★

5. MusicFirst, a large retail chain of stores that sells CDs, concert clothing, and jewelry would like you to create a presentation featuring a new artist monthly. This presentation will run on the company home page. Spotlight your favorite musician and his or her latest release. Create a presentation with the features you have learned in PowerPoint. Include music and custom slide shows within the presentation. Include your name and the date in a footer on the slides. Save your file as MusicFirst Web and print the presentation with six slides per page.

# Working Together 2: Reviewing, Embedding, and Broadcasting a Presentation

# Case Study

## Animal Rescue Foundation

**N**ow that the presentation to promote the Animal Rescue Foundation is nearly complete, you want to have several people review the presentation. To do this, you have sent copies of the presentation by e-mail to the agency director and several other administrators. You have asked them to add comments and make changes directly in the presentation and return it to you. When you receive the reviewed presentations back you will combine them with the original presentation and look at the comments and changes to determine which changes to make.

**O**nce the kiosk presentation is finalized, you want to send a copy to the local shopping malls that provide a kiosk for use by local volunteer organizations. You decide to create a letter that contains the presentation embedded in it. You will then e-mail the letter to the shopping mall directors.

**F**inally, you want to see how you can distribute the presentation over the Web to audiences at different locations. To do this, you will look into broadcasting the presentation.

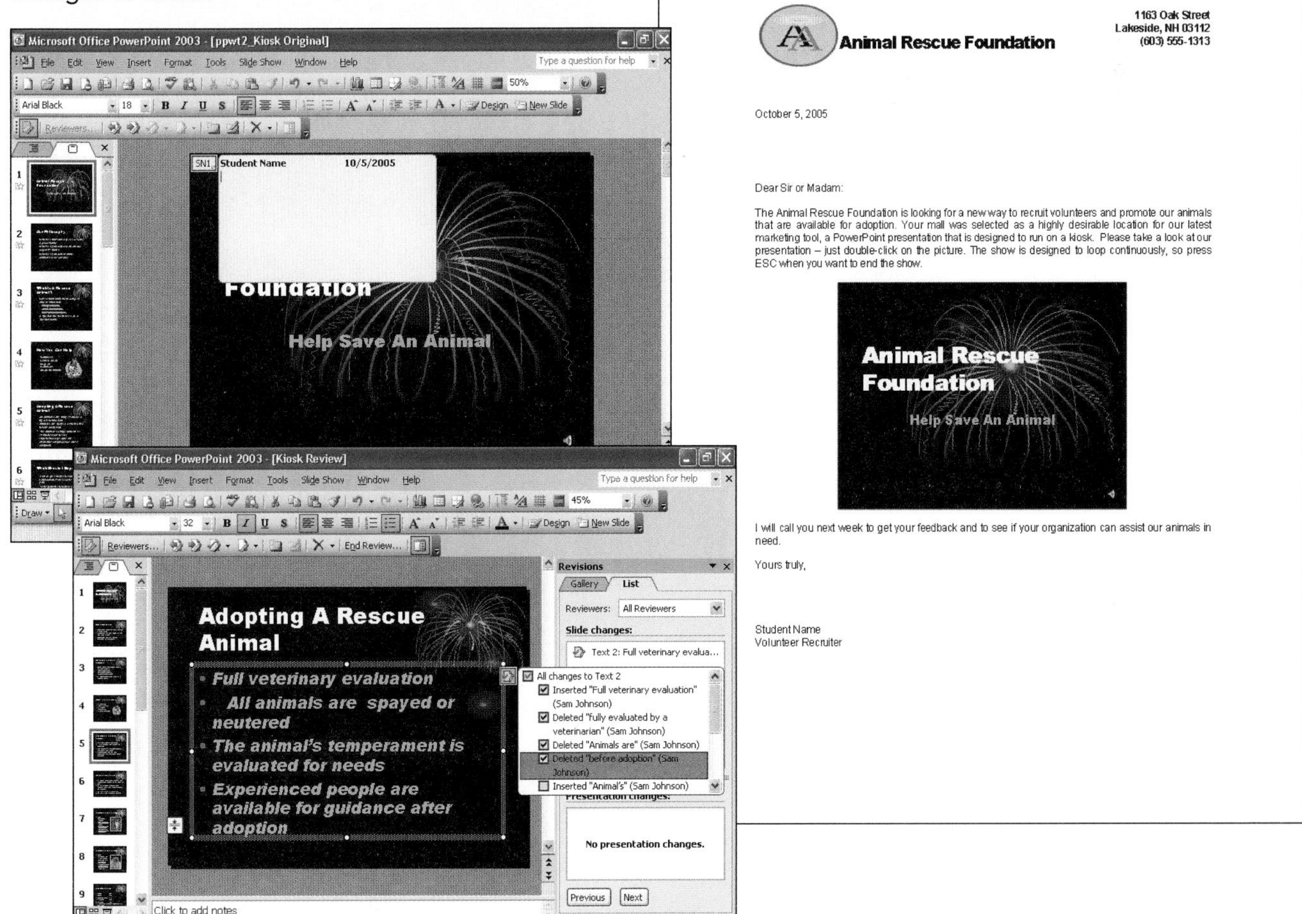

Animal Rescue Foundation

1163 Oak Street
Lakeside, NH 03112
(603) 555-1313

October 5, 2005

Dear Sir or Madam:

The Animal Rescue Foundation is looking for a new way to recruit volunteers and promote our animals that are available for adoption. Your mall was selected as a highly desirable location for our latest marketing tool, a PowerPoint presentation that is designed to run on a kiosk. Please take a look at our presentation – just double-click on the picture. The show is designed to loop continuously, so press ESC when you want to end the show.

Animal Rescue Foundation
Help Save An Animal

I will call you next week to get your feedback and to see if your organization can assist our animals in need.

Yours truly,

Student Name
Volunteer Recruiter

## Reviewing a Presentation

Before sending the presentation to the shopping malls for use in the kiosks, you want to get feedback from several people in the organization first. You will do this by sending a copy of the presentation by e-mail to each person for review. The review process consists of several steps: prepare the presentation to send to reviewers, send the presentation, receive the reviewed presentations back, merge the reviewed presentations and respond to changes, and end the review.

### Adding a Comment

Before you send the presentation for review, you want to add a comment to the reviewers. A **comment** is a remark that is displayed in a separate box and attached to a file.

**1**

- **Start Office PowerPoint 2003.**
- **Open the file** ppwt2_Kiosk Original**.**
- **Display slide 1 in Normal view.**
- **Choose Insert/Comment.**

*Your screen should be similar to Figure 1*

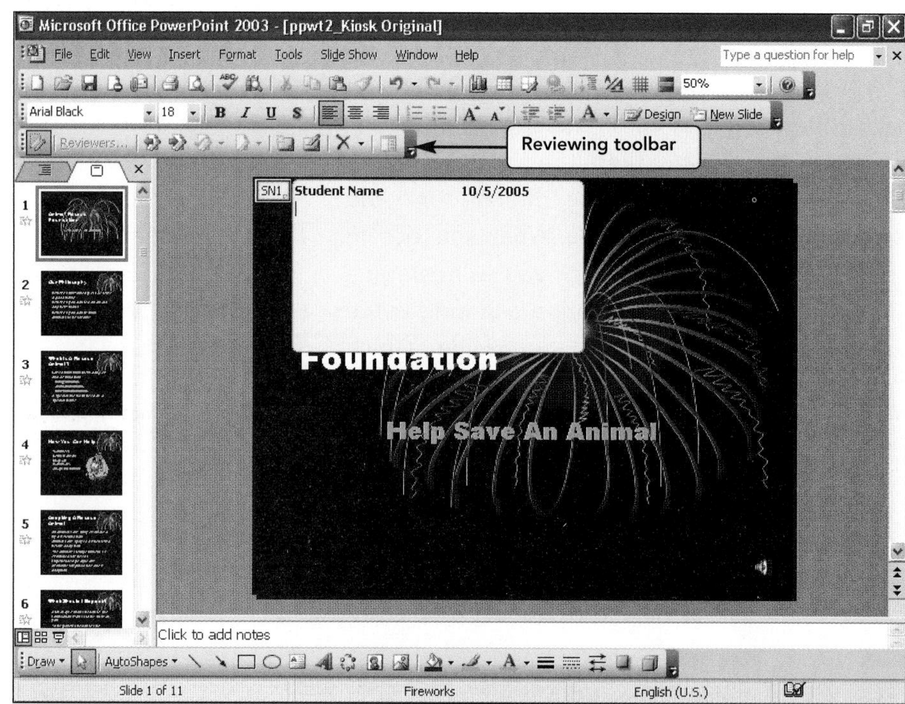


**Figure 1**

A comment box is displayed in which the text of the comment is entered. The name of the user inserting the comment appears on the first line followed by the system date. When you add a comment, the Reviewing toolbar automatically appears. You will use the Reviewing toolbar shortly, when you review the comments sent back to you by the reviewers.

**2** **Type the following comment text: Please add your comments and changes directly in the presentation and return it to me. Thank you for your help.**

*Your screen should be similar to Figure 2*

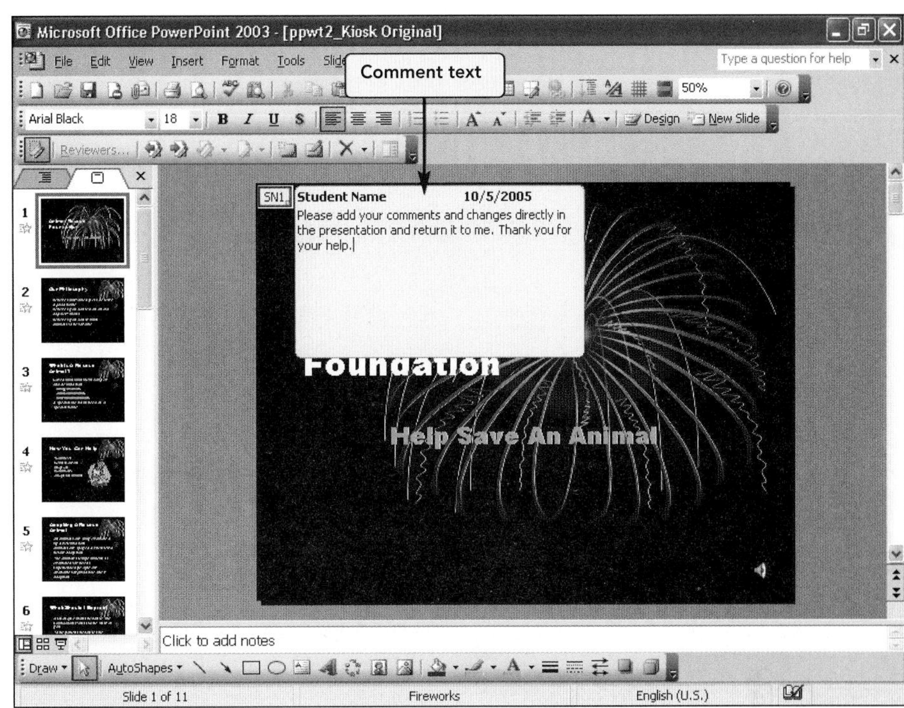


**Figure 2**

After entering comment text, clicking outside the comment closes it and displays an icon called a **comment marker** that indicates a comment has been added to the presentation. To see the comment text again, simply point to the marker.

**3** **Click outside the comment.**

**Point to the comment marker.**

*Your screen should be similar to Figure 3*

**Additional Information**

If you need to edit the comment, click Edit Comment on the Reviewing toolbar or double-click on the comment marker.

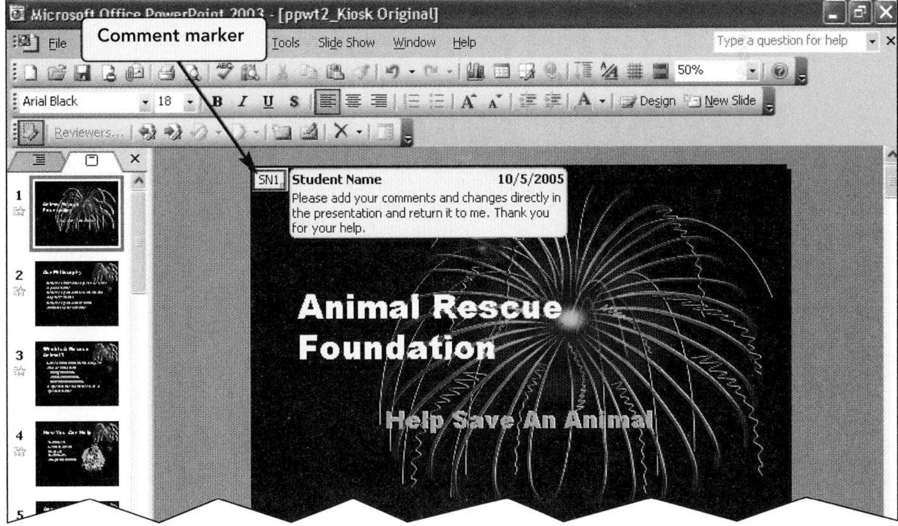


**Figure 3**

The comment is displayed in a balloon that is sized to fit the contents.

**4** **Save the presentation as Kiosk Review to your solution file location.**

## Sending the Presentation for Review

Now you will send the presentation to the director, Sam Johnson, and to the Fund Raising administrator, Mary Munson, via e-mail for them to review.

**1**

- **Choose File/Send to/Mail Recipient (for Review).**
- **In the To field, enter your e-mail address.**

*Your screen should be similar to Figure 4*

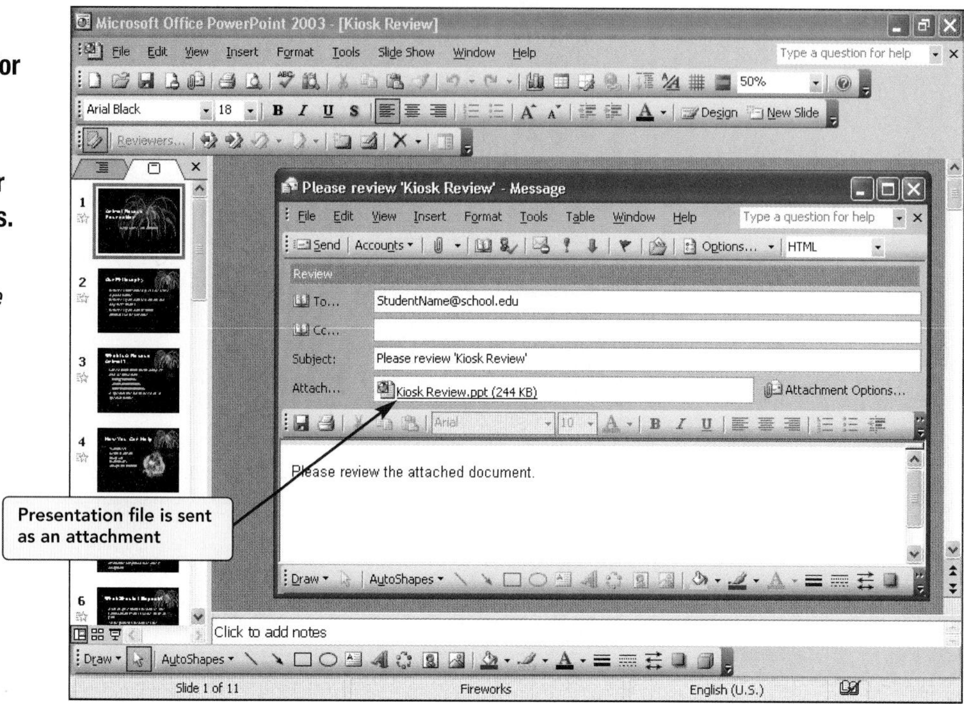


**Figure 4**

Because the command to send the presentation by e-mail was to send it for review, the subject and body of the message already include appropriate information. The presentation is included as an attachment to the e-mail message.

2 • In the body of the e-mail, type the following message below the default message: Please return your comments and changes to me by Friday. Thanks!

• Press ←Enter and type your name.

*Your screen should be similar to Figure 5*

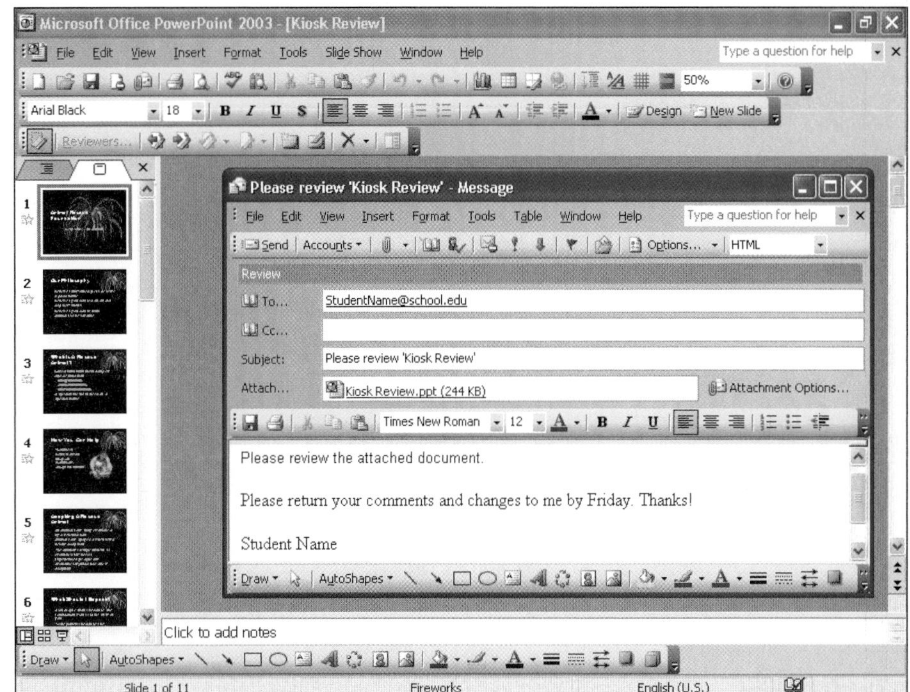


**Figure 5**

If you were connected to the Internet, you would send the message next. Instead, you will save the message as a text file.

3 • Choose File/Save As and save the message as a Word Document file type using the file name Kiosk Review E-mail to your solution file location.

• Close the e-mail window.

## Combining Reviewed Presentations

**Additional Information**

If all the reviewers are using Outlook, PowerPoint 2003 will prompt you to combine the reviewed presentations with the original when you double-click the attachment.

The next day while checking your e-mail for new messages, you see that both Sam and Mary have returned the presentation with their comments and changes. You have downloaded the attachments and saved them as files on your system. Now you want to review the suggested changes.

When you receive multiple reviewers' comments, the easiest way to review them is to merge the reviewed presentations with the original.

**1** • **Choose Tools/Compare and Merge Presentations.**

• **Change to your data file location and select** ppwt2_Kiosk Review (1) **and** ppwt2_Kiosk Review (2)**.**

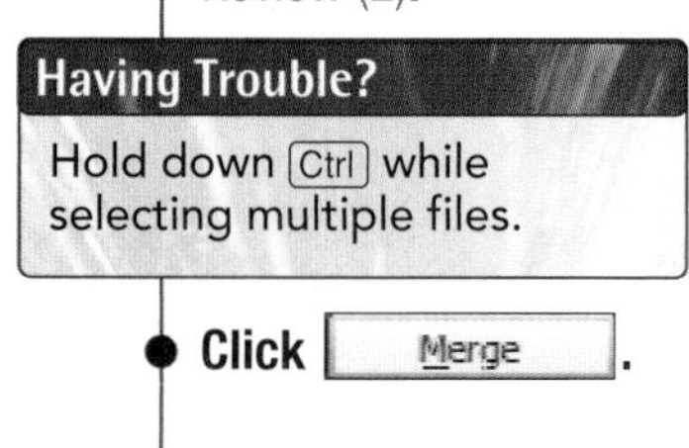

**Having Trouble?**

Hold down Ctrl while selecting multiple files.

• **Click** Merge**.**

• **If necessary, dock the Reviewing toolbar below the Formatting toolbar.**

**Additional Information**

When a presentation is sent for review, PowerPoint retains the name of the file but adds a number at the end in sequential order for each reviewer.

*Your screen should be similar to Figure 6*

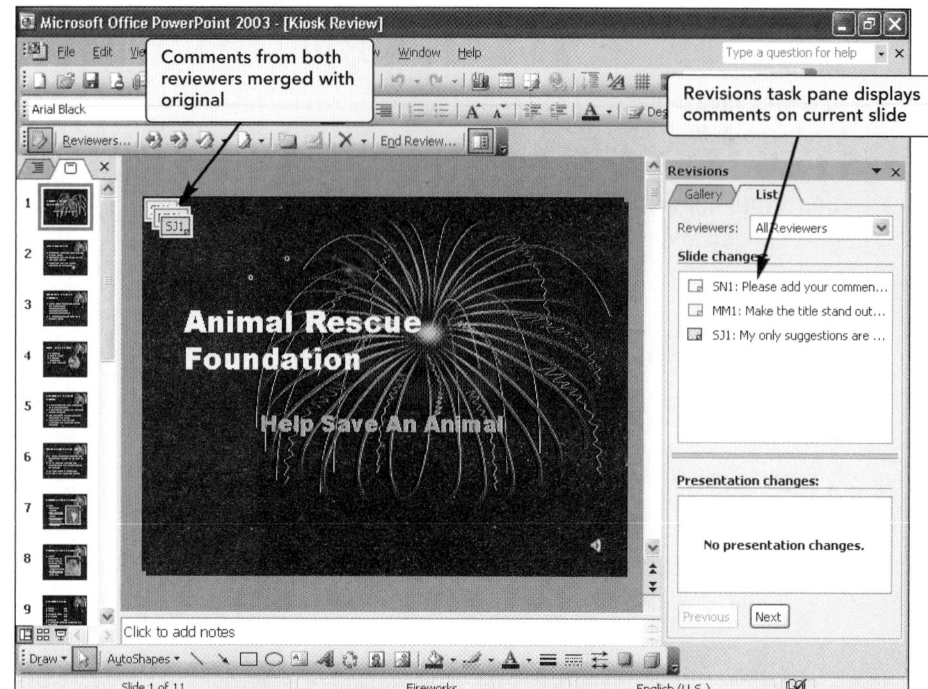


**Figure 6**

**Having Trouble?**

If the Revisions task pane is not displayed, click [button] in the Reviewing toolbar.

The changes and comments from both reviewed presentations are now included in the original presentation that was sent for review. The first slide has three comment markers in the upper left corner with the reviewer's initials and the number of the comment. Each reviewer's comments appear in a different color.

The Revisions task pane also opens to assist you in reviewing the comments and changes. The Revisions pane displays the comments on the current slide.

## Deleting a Comment

The comment you added when you sent the presentation for review is the first comment listed in the Revisions task pane. You want to delete this comment before you begin to review the comments from the reviewers.

**1** Click the first comment in the Slide changes list of the Revisions task pane.

*Your screen should be similar to Figure 7*

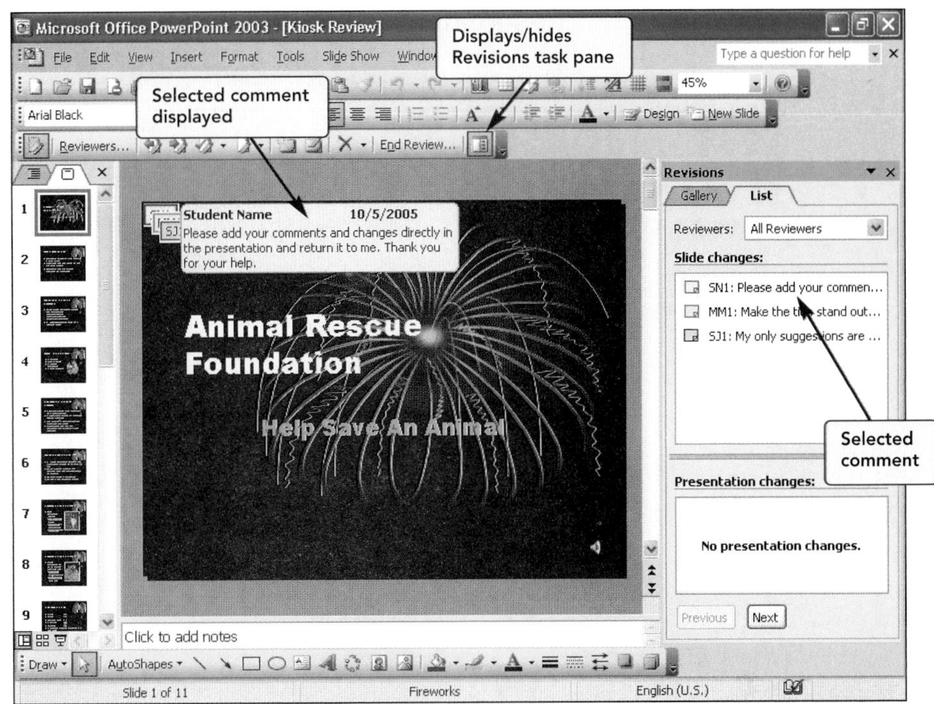


**Figure 7**

The comment box opens on the slide so you can delete the comment.

**2** Click Delete Comment on the Reviewing toolbar.

*Your screen should be similar to Figure 8*

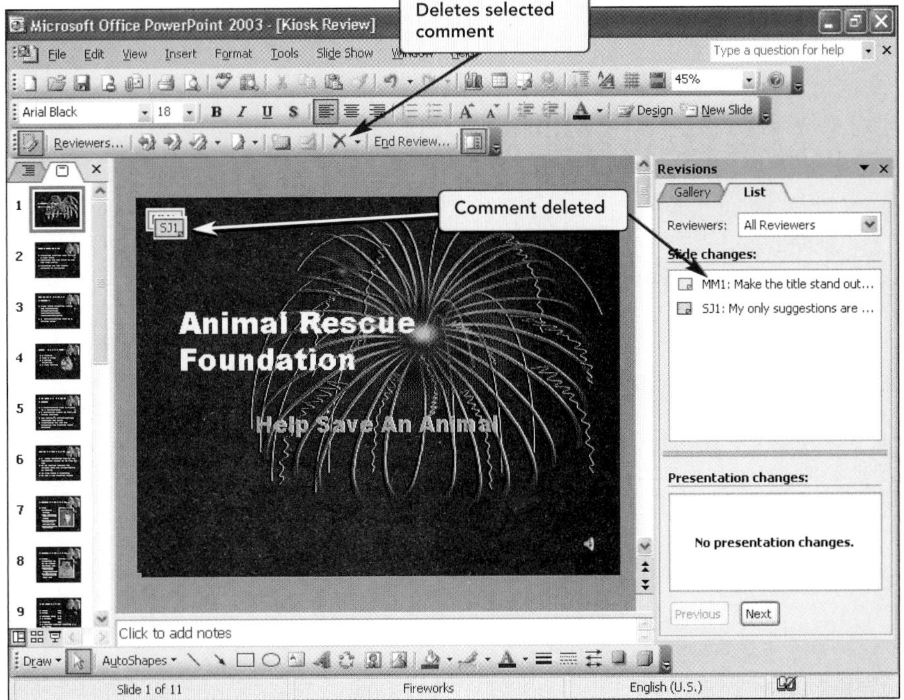


**Figure 8**

The comment is removed from the slide and the Revisions pane. You are now ready to start reviewing the comments and changes made by the reviewers.

## Responding to Comments and Changes

You will use the Reviewing toolbar to navigate through the comments and changes made to the presentation by the reviewers.

**1** **Click [Next Item icon] Next Item on the Reviewing toolbar.**

*Your screen should be similar to Figure 9*

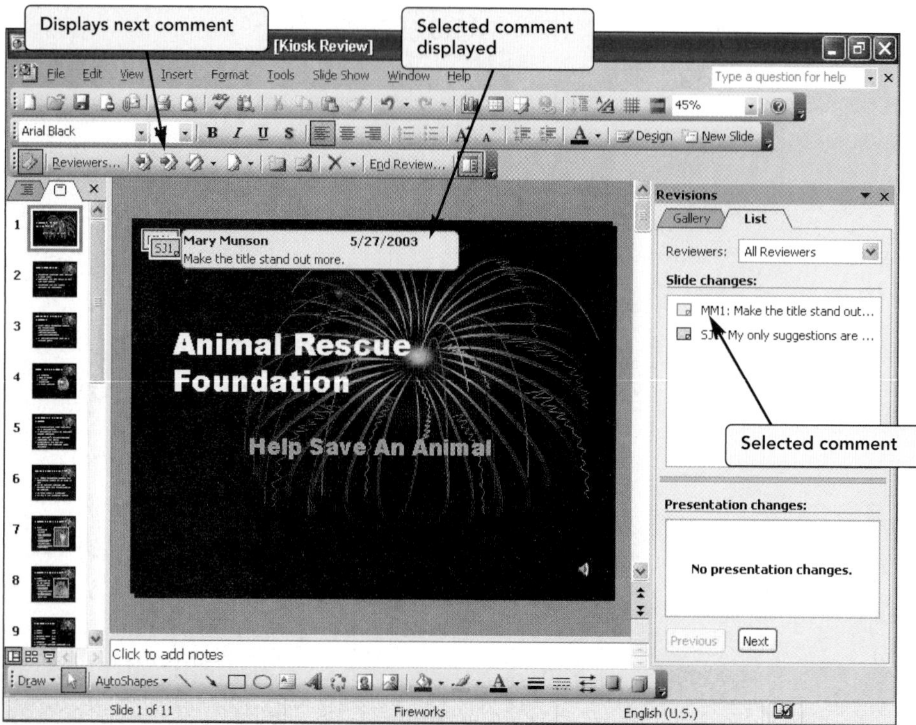


**Figure 9**

You think the suggestion in the first comment is a good idea. You decide to bold and make the title text larger.

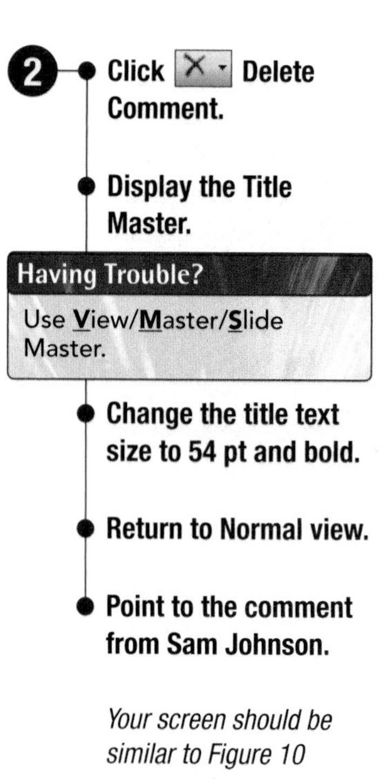

**2** **Click [Delete Comment icon] Delete Comment.**

- **Display the Title Master.**

**Having Trouble?**

Use <u>V</u>iew/<u>M</u>aster/<u>S</u>lide Master.

- **Change the title text size to 54 pt and bold.**
- **Return to Normal view.**
- **Point to the comment from Sam Johnson.**

*Your screen should be similar to Figure 10*

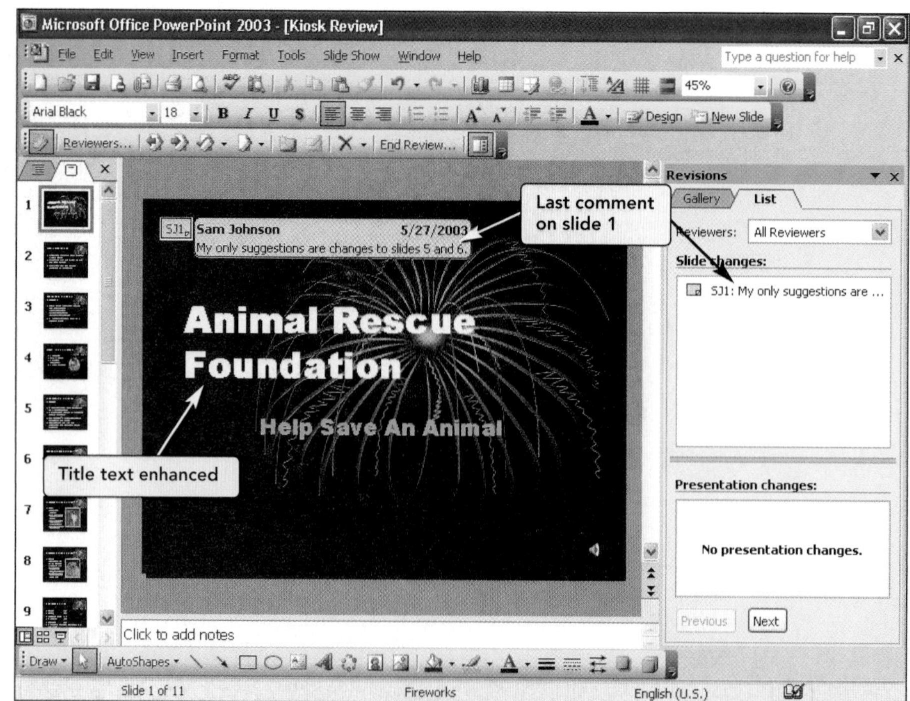


**Figure 10**

The title now stands out more. The last comment on this slide refers you to changes made to slide 5. You decide to go to slide 5 next and look at the changes.

**3**

- **Click on slide 5 in the slide tab.**
- **Select the comment.**

*Your screen should be similar to Figure 11*

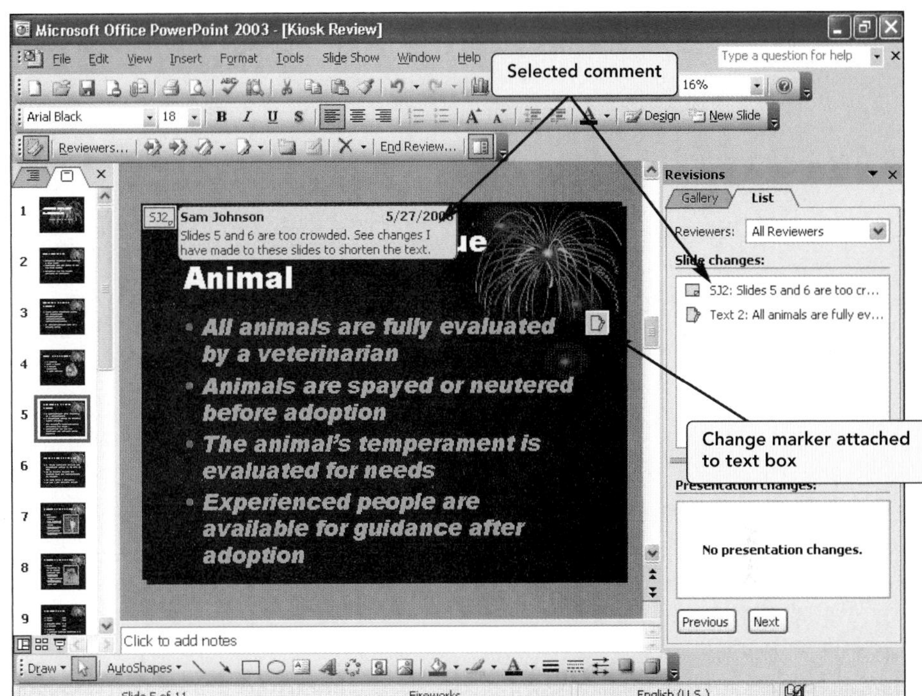


**Figure 11**

The comment on slide 5 notes that there is too much text on slides 5 and 6. The slide also displays a **change marker** attached to the text box indicating where a reviewer made changes to the presentation. You will delete the comment and look at the suggested changes.

**4** Delete the comment.

Click [icon].

*Your screen should be similar to Figure 12*

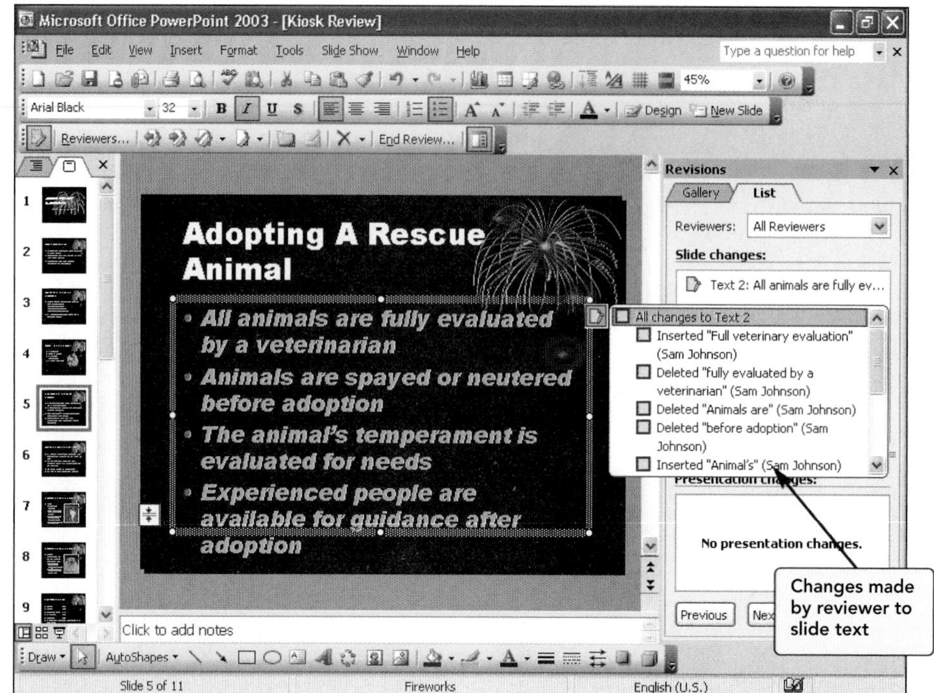


**Figure 12**

All the insertions and deletions that were made to the text are listed.

## Applying Reviewer Changes

Notice that each item in the All Changes to Text 2 box is preceded with a check box. Selecting the item will display the change in the slide.

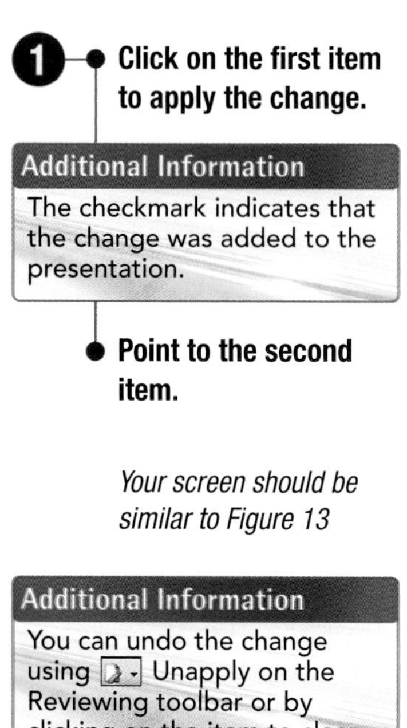

**1** Click on the first item to apply the change.

**Additional Information**

The checkmark indicates that the change was added to the presentation.

Point to the second item.

*Your screen should be similar to Figure 13*

**Additional Information**

You can undo the change using [icon] Unapply on the Reviewing toolbar or by clicking on the item to clear the checkmark.

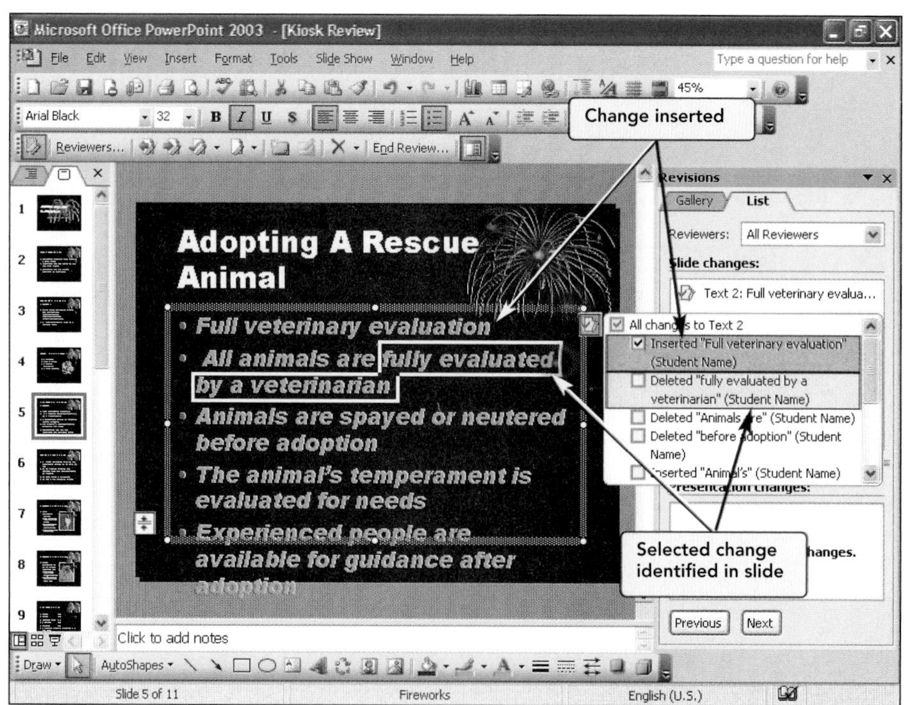


**Figure 13**

The first change is inserted, and the change you are pointing to is identified in the text box to show you the area that will be affected if you accept this change.

As you look at the next few changes, they all look good to you and you decide to incorporate them into the presentation.

**2 Click on the second, third, and fourth items.**

*Your screen should be similar to Figure 14*

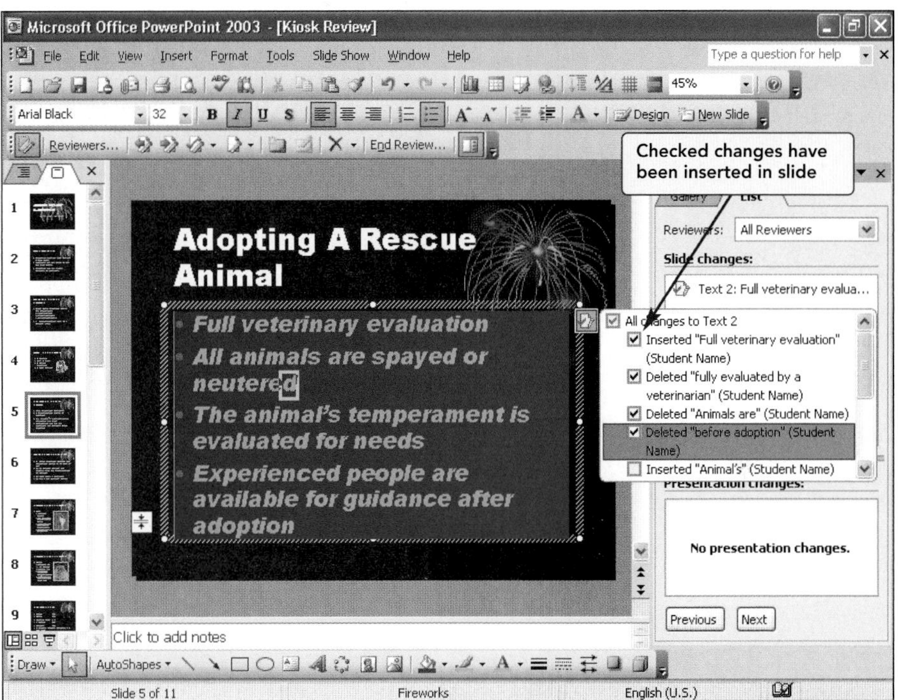


**Figure 14**

The three changes have been made in the slide. So far, you think all the changes look good and decide to just go ahead and apply all the changes to the slide.

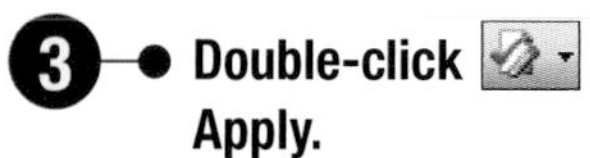

**3** **Double-click Apply.**

*Your screen should be similar to Figure 15*

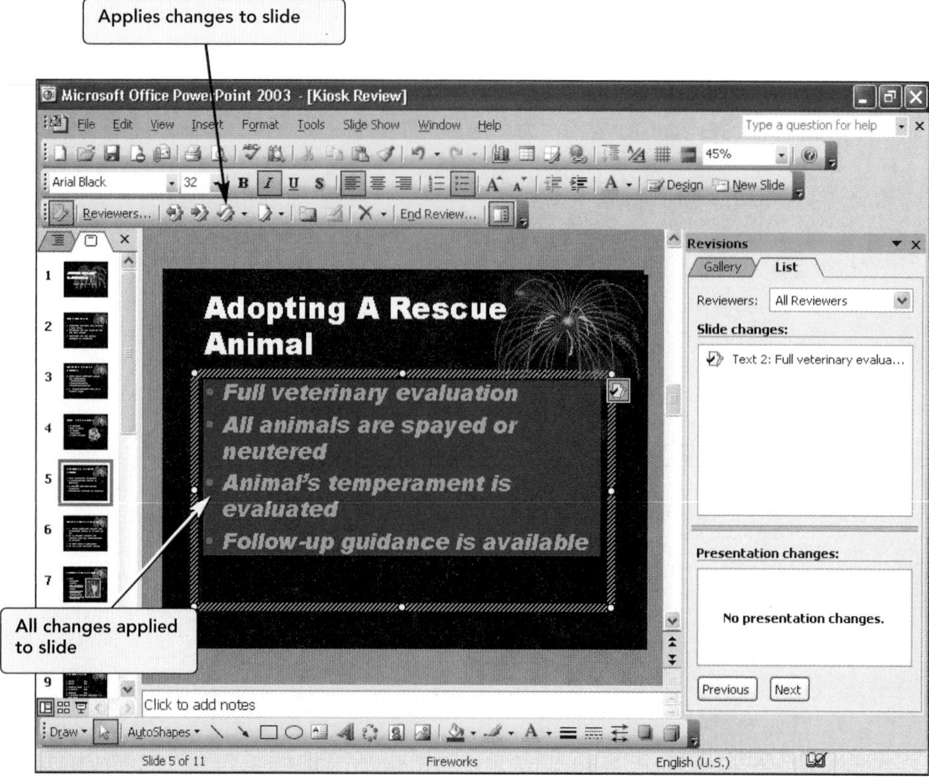


**Figure 15**

The changes look good and you just need to remove the change marker. Then you will look at the changes made to slide 6.

**4** **Click Delete to remove the change marker.**

**Display slide 6.**

**Click to display the changes.**

*Your screen should be similar to Figure 16*

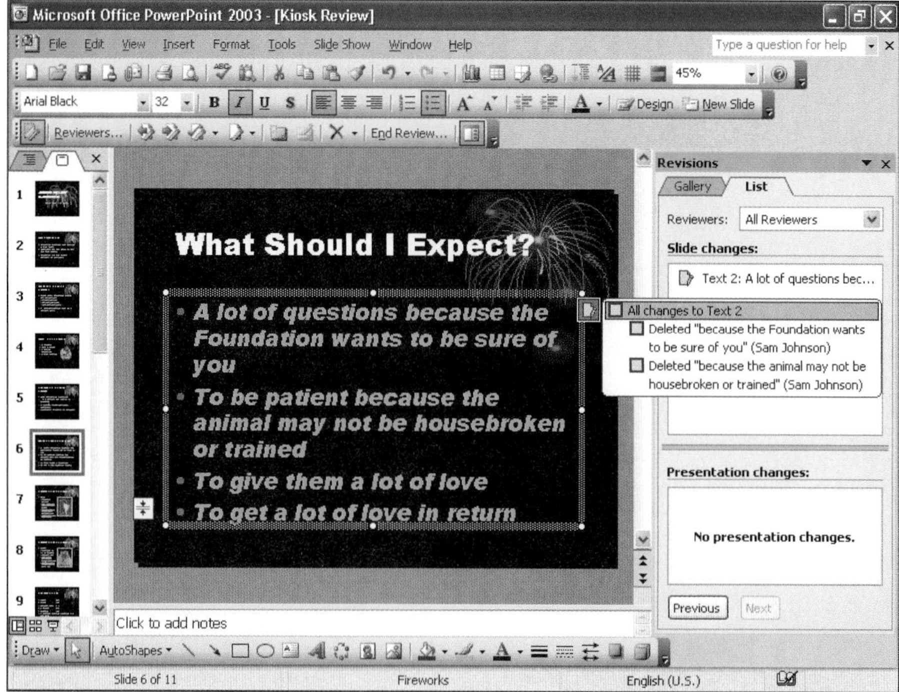


**Figure 16**

After reading the proposed changes, you again decide to accept them all. Then you will continue to look at and respond to any other comments as needed.

**5**

- **Click in the check box next to "All changes to Text 2" to insert all the changes.**
- **Delete the change marker.**
- **Click Next Item.**
- **Click Continue to look for more changes starting at the beginning of the presentation.**
- **Delete the comment on slide 1.**
- **Click Next Item.**

**Additional Information**

Notice the Slide Changes area of the Revisions pane indicates the location of the slide containing the next set of changes.

*Your screen should be similar to Figure 17*

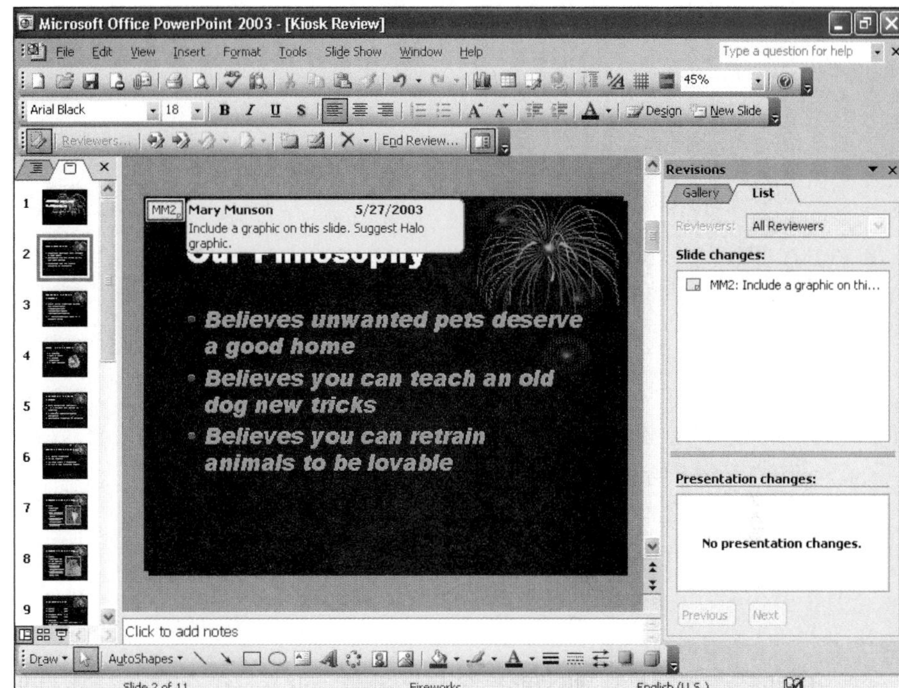


**Figure 17**

On this slide, Mary has suggested adding the Halo graphic to the slide. This graphic is one of the Animal Angels logo symbols that are frequently used in correspondence. Again, you like this idea.

**6** Delete the comment.

- **Insert the** ppwt2_Halo **graphic file from your data file location.**
- **Move the graphic to the lower right area of the slide as in Figure 18.**
- **Reduce the width of the text placeholder.**
- **Select the graphic.**
- **Increase the size of the graphic slightly.**

*Your screen should be similar to Figure 18*

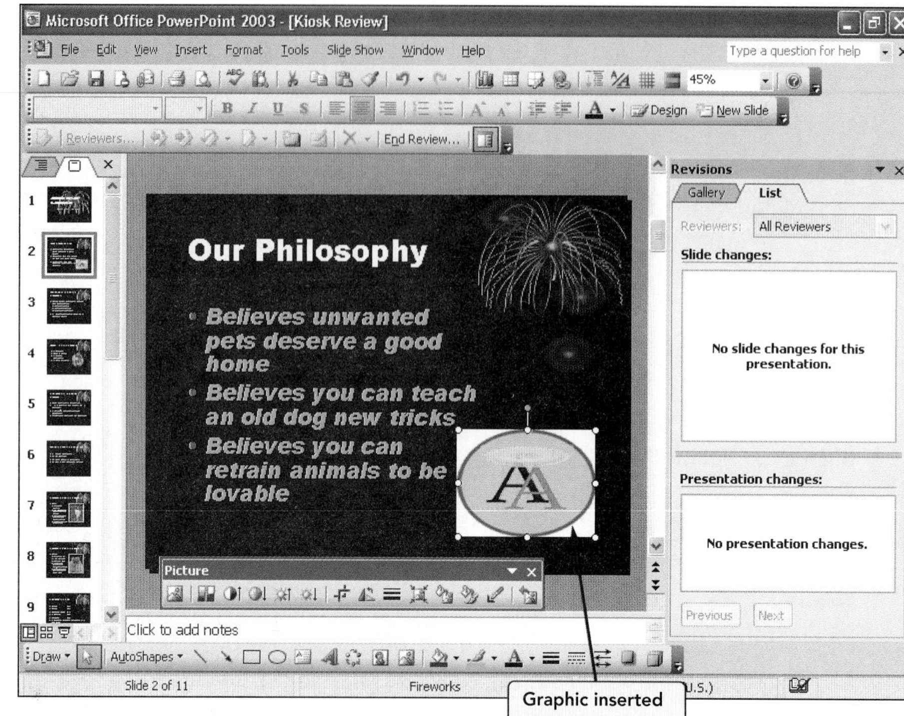


**Figure 18**

You think the graphic would look better without the white background. To quickly remove the background, you will make it transparent so that the slide background shows through instead.

**7** In the Picture toolbar, click 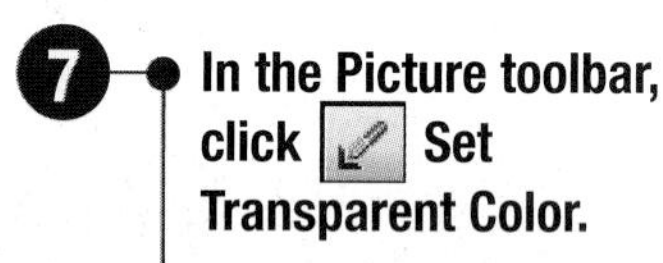 Set Transparent Color.

**Having Trouble?**

You may need to display and hide the Picture toolbar.

- **Click on the white background of the graphic to make it transparent.**

**Additional Information**

The mouse pointer appears as a pen when this feature is active.

- **Click outside the graphic to deselect it.**

*Your screen should be similar to Figure 19*

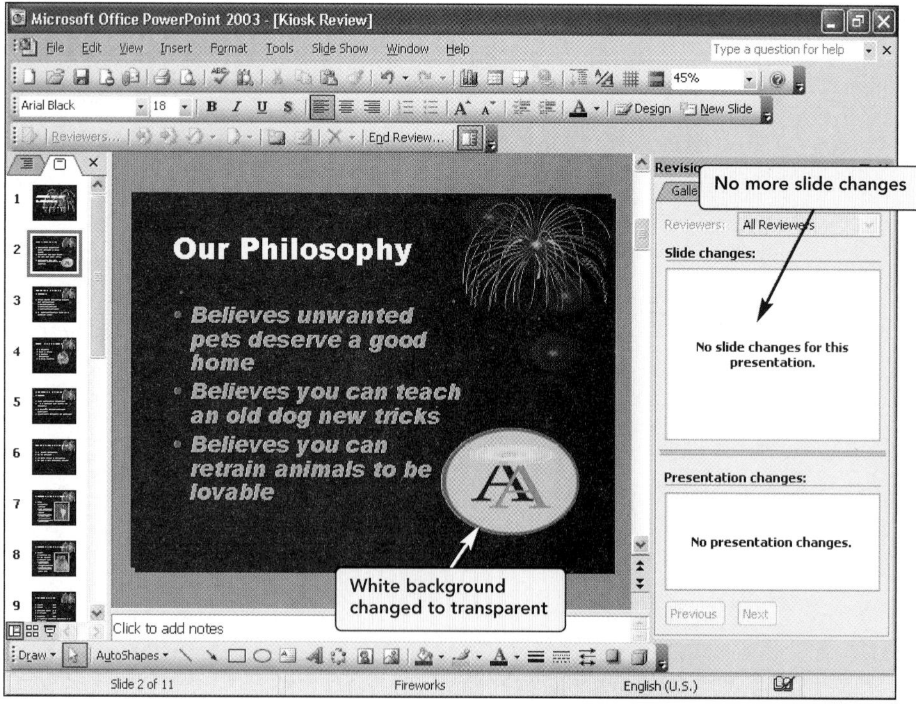


**Figure 19**

The graphic looks much better. Notice the Revisions pane indicates there are no more changes or comments in the presentation, and the buttons on the Reviewing toolbar are dimmed.

## Ending the Review

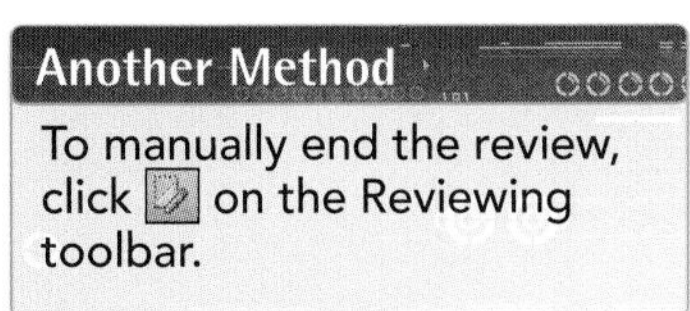

Another Method
To manually end the review, click on the Reviewing toolbar.


PowerPoint automatically ends the review process if you have applied the reviewer changes you want, deleted all change markers, and saved the presentation. When the review process is over, you cannot combine any more reviewed presentations with your original presentation. Since you do not plan to get any more reviews, you decide to save the file.

**1 Save the presentation as Kiosk Final to your solution file location.**

*Your screen should be similar to Figure 20*

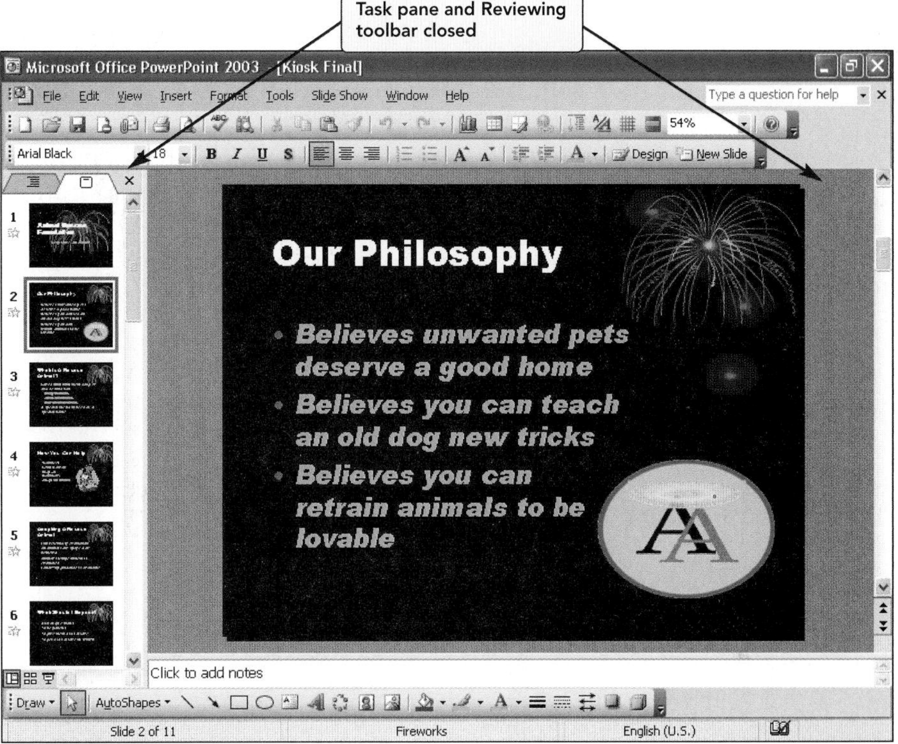


**Figure 20**

The review is ended, and the task pane and Reviewing toolbar are automatically closed.

## Collaborating Online

As suggested by the agency director, you looked into other methods you can use to have the presentation reviewed by other animal shelters and members of the Animal Protection Association.

There are two ways that you can collaborate with many reviewers at once. The first way is to hold an online meeting using the Microsoft Windows NetMeeting feature. Each person you invite to the online meeting must also be running NetMeeting to receive your invitation. In an online meeting, you are in control of the collaboration. Each person in the meeting can add comments to the presentation in real time, if you give them access. When you turn on collaboration, each person in the online meeting can take turns editing the presentation. The person who is controlling the presentation is the only one whose mouse will operate, and that person's initials appear next to the mouse pointer.

The second way to collaborate is by using the Web Discussion feature, which needs to be set up by a system administrator. It enables you and other people to insert comments into the same document at the same time. This makes your job as document author much easier. You can see all the comments made by the reviewers, and they can too, which means if there is a question about a comment, the reviewers can discuss it among themselves.

## Embedding a Presentation

The agency director is very pleased with the changes you made, and tells you to send out the presentation to the local malls. You have already created a letter to the mall directors and just need to insert the presentation file in the letter document file. Then you will send the letter as an e-mail attachment.

To insert the presentation in the letter, you will open the letter in Word and embed the PowerPoint presentation file in the document. An embedded object is inserted in a document and becomes part of that document, called the **destination document**. This means that you can modify it without affecting the **source document** where the original object resides.

**1**
- **Start Office Word 2003 and, if necessary, maximize the application window.**
- **Open the file** ppwt2_Mall Letter.

*Your screen should be similar to Figure 21*

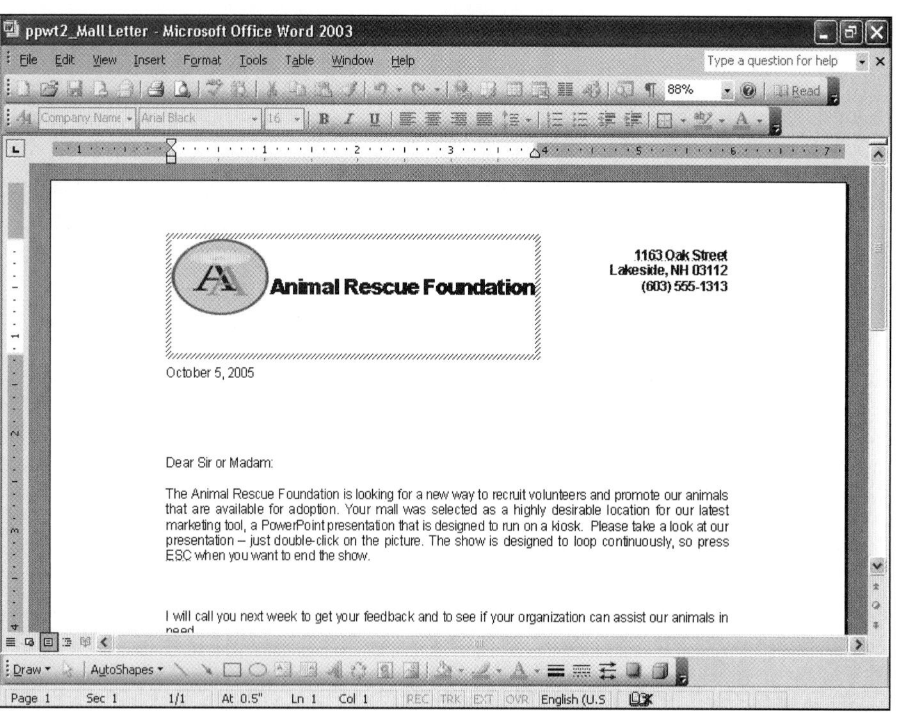


Figure 21

**Additional Information**

Always remove your personal information from the file's properties before distributing a presentation to avoid the distribution of this information to others.

Now you want to embed the presentation. When you embed a PowerPoint presentation, the first slide of the presentation is displayed in the document. You want the embedded presentation to appear below the first paragraph of the letter.

**2** **Move to the blank line below the first paragraph.**

- **Choose Insert/Object.**
- **Open the Create from File tab.**
- **Click Browse... .**
- **Change to your solution file location and select** Kiosk Final**.**
- **Click Insert .**
- **Click OK .**

*Your screen should be similar to Figure 22*

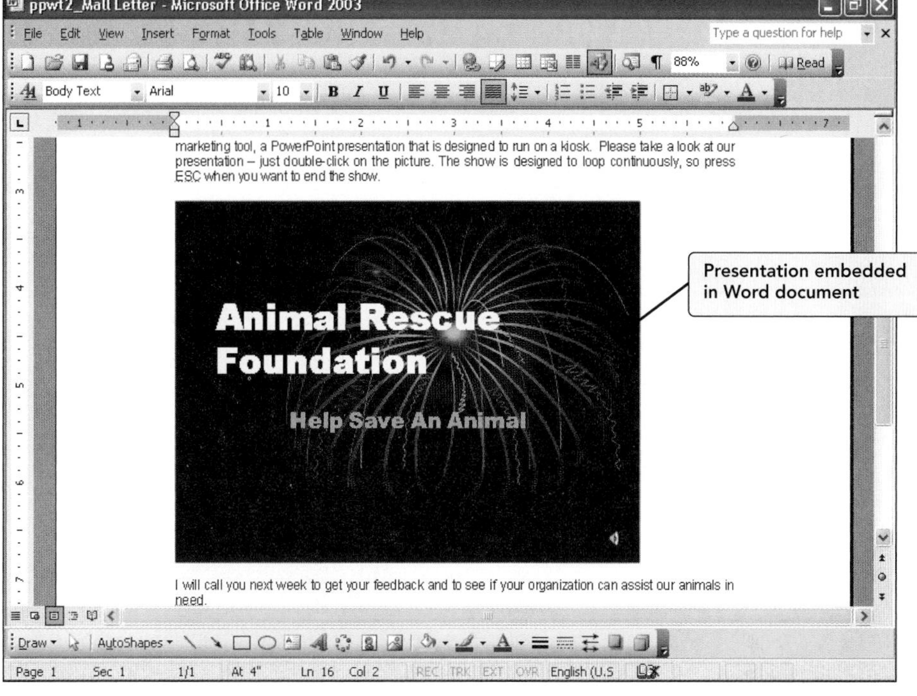


**Figure 22**

The opening slide of the presentation is inserted as an embedded object in the letter. Before you send the letter, you want to run the slide show to make sure that it looks good and runs correctly. The directions to run the presentation from within the Word document file are included in the first paragraph of the letter.

**3** **Double-click on the embedded object.**

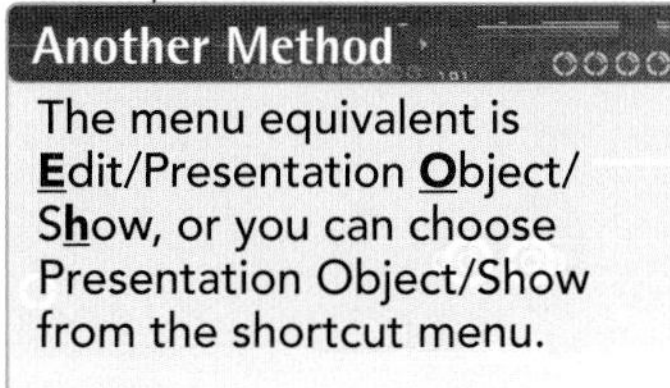

**Another Method**

The menu equivalent is Edit/Presentation Object/Show, or you can choose Presentation Object/Show from the shortcut menu.

- **View the entire presentation and press Esc to end the show when it begins over again.**

## Editing an Embedded Object

As you viewed the presentation, you think that the last slide would look better if it included a graphic. You decide to add an animated graphic of a dog wagging its tail to the slide. Rather than editing the PowerPoint presentation file and then reinserting it into the letter, you will make the changes directly to the object that is embedded in the letter. The source program, the program used to create the embedded object, is used to edit data in an embedded object.

**1** **Choose Presentation Object/Edit from the object's shortcut menu.**

**Another Method**

The menu equivalent is Edit/Presentation Object/Edit.

*Your screen should be similar to Figure 23*

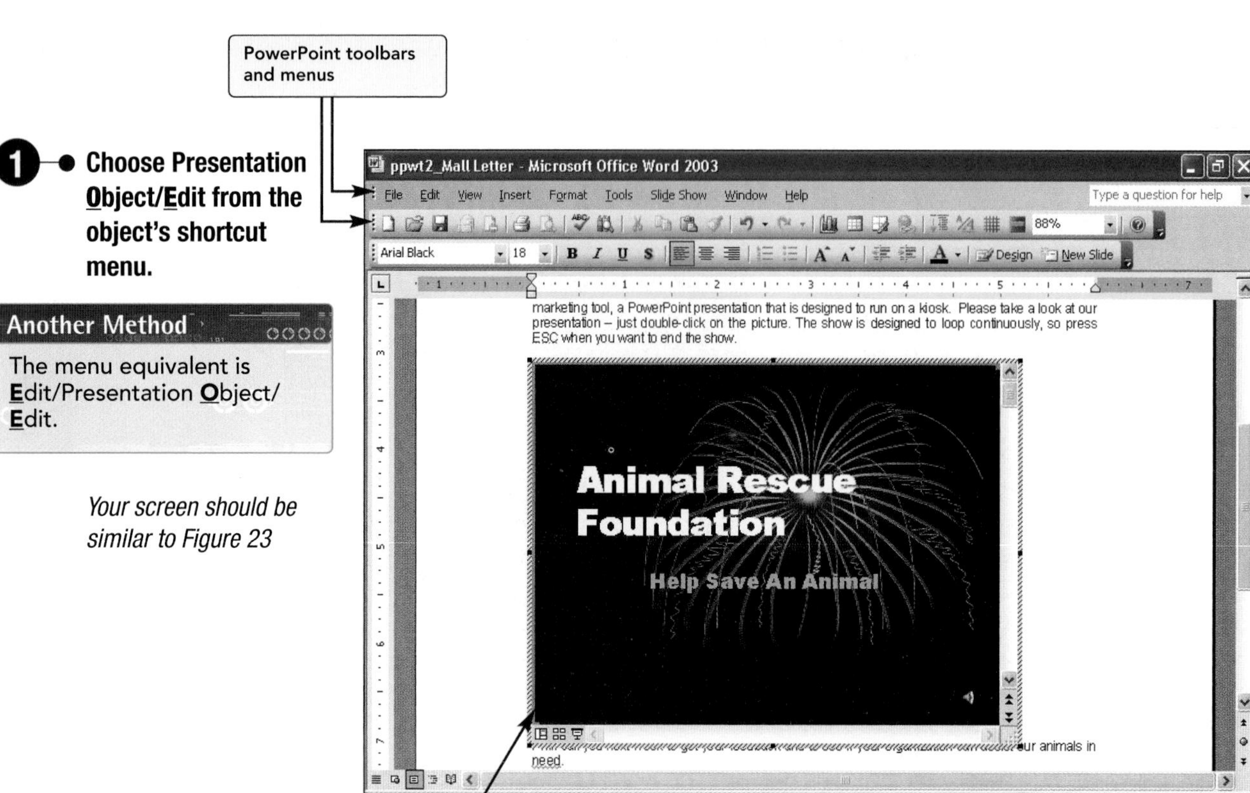


**Figure 23**

The presentation is open in an editing window, and the PowerPoint menus and toolbars replace some of the menus and toolbars in the Word application window. The first slide of the embedded object is displayed. Now you can use the PowerPoint commands to edit the object.

**2**

- **Use the editing window scroll bar to display the last slide.**
- **Insert the graphic** ppwt2_Dog Wagging **from your data file location.**
- **Position and size the graphic and text box as in Figure 24.**

**Having Trouble?**

Use the rotate handle to change the angle of the graphic.

- **Click Slide Show to run the slide show from the current slide.**
- **Press Esc to end the show after seeing the animated graphic.**

*Your screen should be similar to Figure 24*

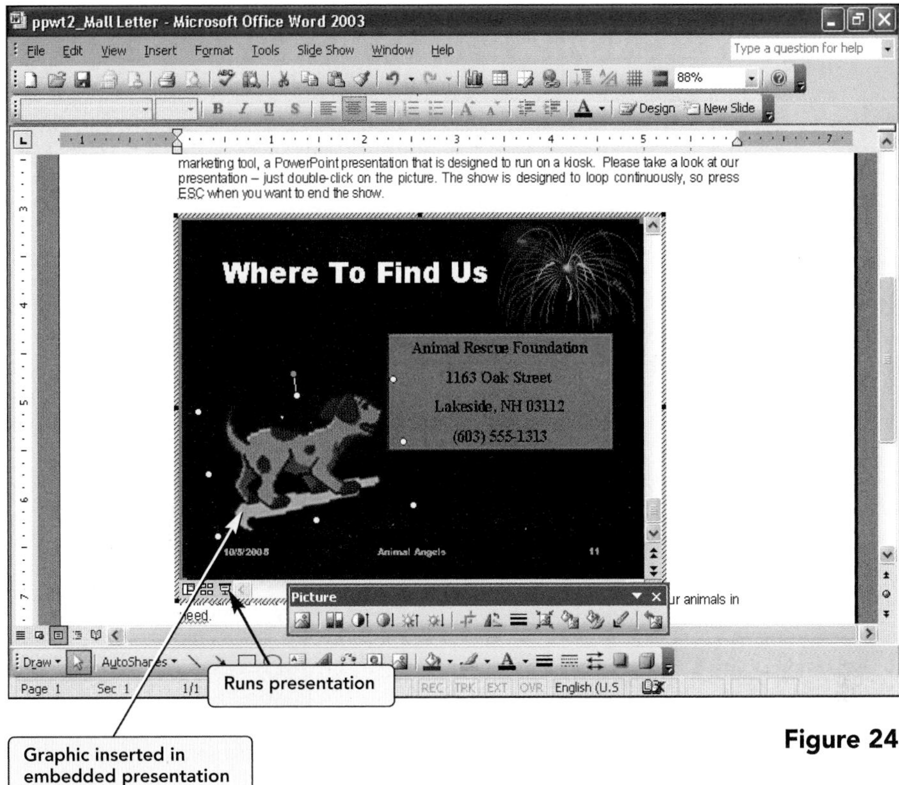


**Figure 24**

Now that the presentation is updated, you will close the source program.

**3**

- **Click outside the object to close the source application.**
- **Reduce the size of the embedded object and center it.**
- **Replace Student Name in the closing with your name.**
- **Save the letter as Kiosk Presentation Letter to your solution file location.**
- **Preview and print the letter.**
- **Exit Word.**

*Your printed letter should be similar to that shown here.*

1163 Oak Street
Lakeside, NH 03112
(603) 555-1313

October 5, 2005

Dear Sir or Madam:

The Animal Rescue Foundation is looking for a new way to recruit volunteers and promote our animals that are available for adoption. Your mall was selected as a highly desirable location for our latest marketing tool, a PowerPoint presentation that is designed to run on a kiosk. Please take a look at our presentation – just double-click on the picture. The show is designed to loop continuously, so press ESC when you want to end the show.

I will call you next week to get your feedback and to see if your organization can assist our animals in need.

Yours truly,

Student Name
Volunteer Recruiter

Next you will update the presentation in PowerPoint with the same change you made in the presentation in the Word document.

**4**

- **Display slide 11.**
- **Insert the** ppwt2_Dog Wagging **graphic in the slide.**
- **Position and size the graphic and text box as you did in the embedded presentation in the letter.**
- **Save the revised presentation.**

Additional Information

Most e-mail programs include the capability to create a distribution list that consists of the e-mail addresses of a group of people. The list is then assigned a name that is entered in the To box when you send the message. All addresses in the list receive the message.

Now that the letter is complete, you want to send the letter via e-mail to the list of local malls. This is only one way to distribute your presentation. You could also just send an e-mail with the presentation as an attachment or you could send a diskette in the mail containing the presentation along with a letter of introduction. By embedding the presentation in the letter, you create both an e-mail distribution method and also a printed letter that contains the first slide in your presentation as a graphic.

## Broadcasting a Presentation

**Note:** To complete this section, the Broadcast feature must be installed on your system.

Additional Information

Use Sli<u>d</u>e/Show/<u>O</u>nline Broadcast/<u>S</u>chedule a Live Broadcast to set up a live broadcast.

Another way to distribute a presentation is to broadcast a presentation over the Web. **Broadcasting** makes it possible to deliver a presentation to an audience at different locations. The viewers can view the presentation live or on demand. The presentation is saved in HTML format on a server that is accessible to the audience and is displayed in a Web browser. Your system administrator must set up a server location where you can store the files to be shared by all the viewers. Outlook can be set up to schedule and automatically start the presentation at a specified time. If you are using other e-mail applications, a hyperlink appears in the body of the e-mail and the audience double-clicks on the hyperlink to start the broadcast.

## Recording a Broadcast

You decide to try out this feature to see if you want to use it in the future, by recording and saving a broadcast.

1 **Choose Sli<u>d</u>e Show/<u>O</u>nline Broadcast/<u>R</u>ecord and Save a Broadcast.**

*Your screen should be similar to Figure 25*

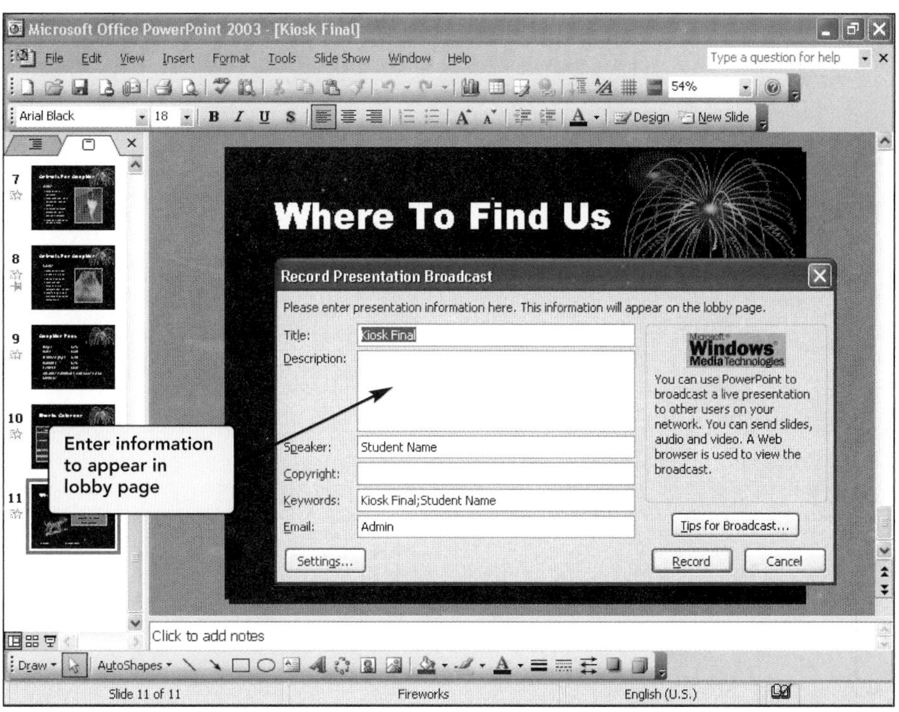


**Figure 25**

The first step is to enter information you want to appear on the lobby page. The **lobby page** is a page of information that is displayed in the viewer's browser before the broadcast starts. It includes information about the broadcast, including the title, subject, and host's name. It also displays a countdown to the starting time of the broadcast. The presentation file name is automatically displayed in the Title text box. You want to add a short description to appear on the lobby page when viewers receive the presentation.

2

- **In the Description text box type: This presentation is designed to encourage people to help the Foundation by adopting an animal or volunteering.**
- **Replace the name in the Speaker text box with your name.**
- **Click Settings... .**

*Your screen should be similar to Figure 26*

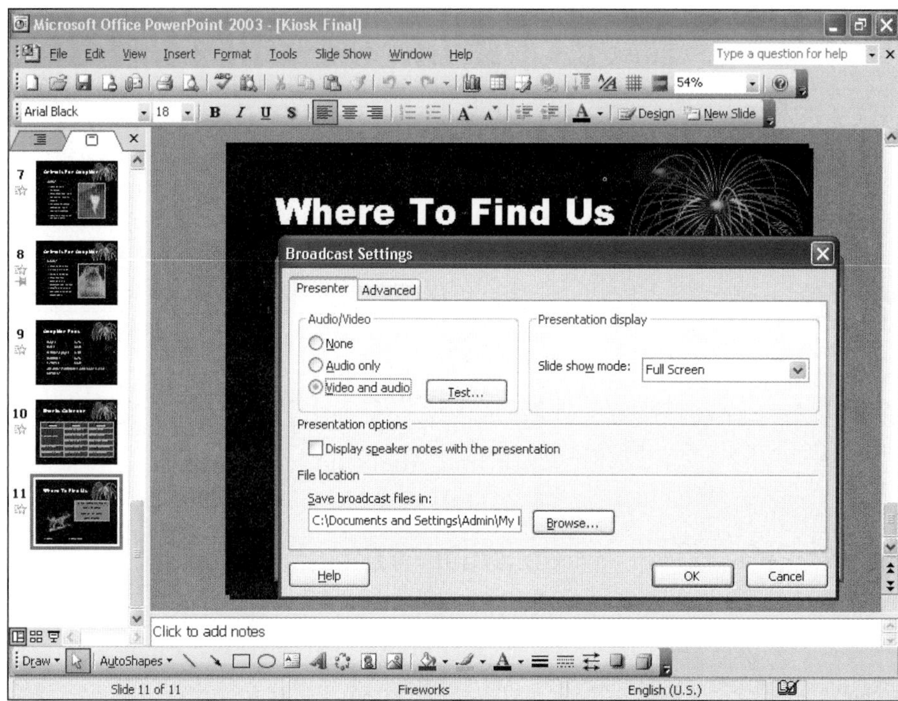


**Figure 26**

Next, in the Presenter tab, you define more features of the broadcast. You can send audio and video along with your presentation. Both of these types of files can slow down Web delivery, however, so you can turn them off if needed. You also need to specify the location where the broadcast files will be stored. If you are recording a broadcast, the location can be anywhere you want. However, when you actually schedule a broadcast, the location should be a server location that is accessible to the recipients. Once you have specified these items, you run the presentation to record it.

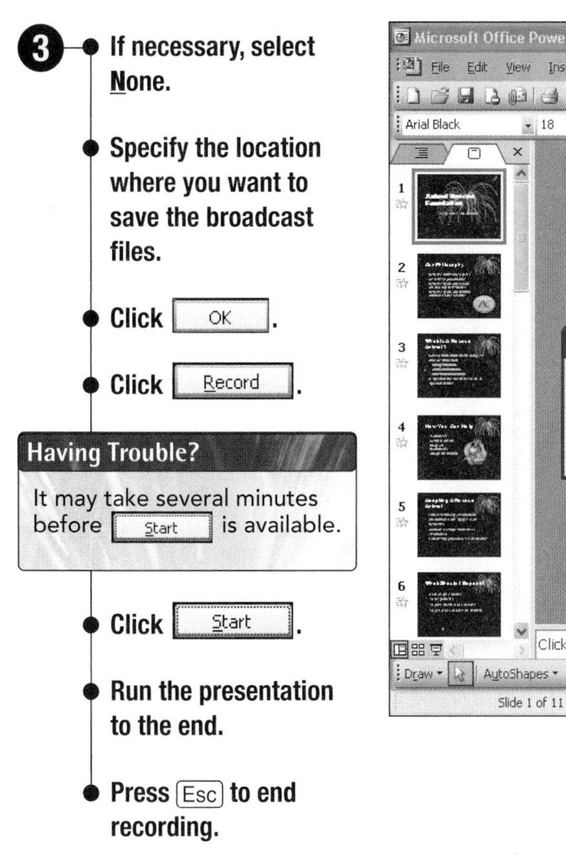

**3** • **If necessary, select None.**

• **Specify the location where you want to save the broadcast files.**

• **Click OK.**

• **Click Record.**

**Having Trouble?**

It may take several minutes before Start is available.

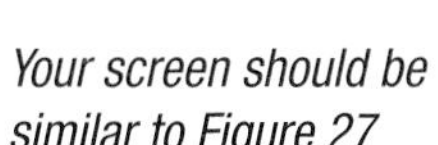

• **Click Start.**

• **Run the presentation to the end.**

• **Press Esc to end recording.**

*Your screen should be similar to Figure 27*

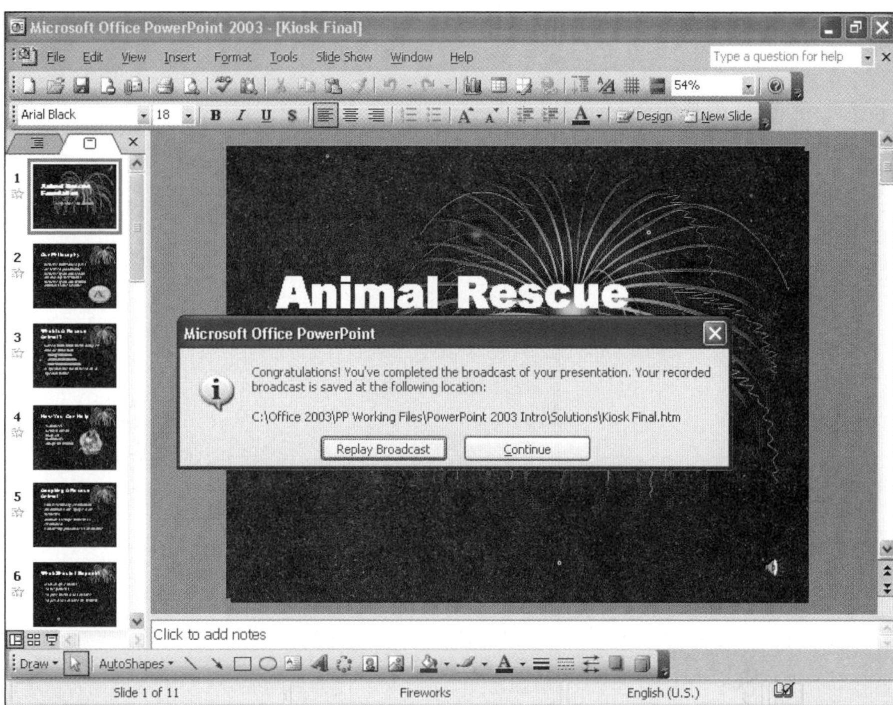


**Figure 27**

The slide show runs while it is being recorded. While it is running you could also record your narration to accompany the broadcast.

A congratulatory message appears indicating the slide show has successfully been recorded.

## Playing the Broadcast

Next you will replay the broadcast to make sure it recorded correctly.

1 Click .

If necessary, maximize the browser window.

*Your screen should be similar to Figure 28*

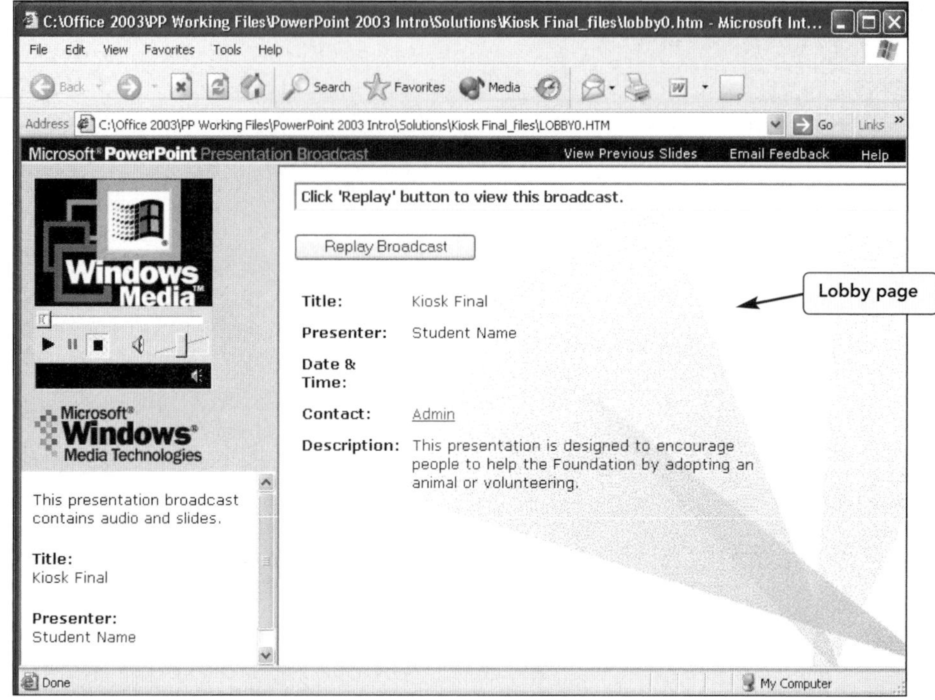


**Figure 28**

The lobby page with the information you entered is displayed in the browser window.

2 Click 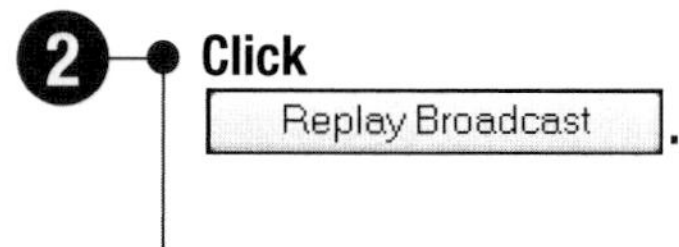.

When complete, close the browser window.

*Your screen should be similar to Figure 29*

**Figure 29**

The PowerPoint window is displayed again.

**Additional Information**

Use File/Save as Web Page/Publish and specify the location of the Web server where the presentation will be stored.

The presentation is saved in HTML format. To make the recorded presentation available to others, a copy of it needs to be published to a Web server. Then, you need to provide the link to the lobby page to users so they can access the presentation whenever they want. All the audience would need to view the presentation is a browser.

When you schedule a live broadcast, the recipients of the invitation receive an e-mail message with the broadcast date and time. If they are using Outlook and accept the invitation, they will receive a reminder 15 minutes before the broadcast begins. The reminder contains a View This Netshow button, which they click to open the lobby page in their browser. The lobby page starts a countdown to the broadcast, and when the timer reaches zero, the presentation broadcast begins. Depending on the options the presenter selected, audience members might be able to chat with one another and send e-mail messages to the presenter.

3

- **Close the presentation.**
- **Exit PowerPoint.**

# WORKING TOGETHER 2
## Reviewing, Embedding, and Broadcasting a Presentation

## key terms

broadcast PPWT2.21
change marker PPWT2.9
comment PPWT2.6
comment marker PPWT2.6
destination document PPWT2.16
lobby page PPWT2.24
source document PPWT2.16

## microsoft office specialist skills

The Microsoft Office Specialist certification program is designed to measure your proficiency in performing basic tasks using the Office System applications. Certification demonstrates that you have the skills and provides a valuable industry credential for employment. After completing this lab, you have learned the following Microsoft Office PowerPoint 2003 Specialist skills:

| Skill | Description | Page |
|---|---|---|
| Collaborating | Track, accept, and reject changes in a presentation | PPWT2.8 |
| | Add, edit, and delete comments in a presentation | PPWT2.2 |
| | Compare and merge presentations | PPWT2.6 |
| Managing and Delivering Presentations | Prepare presentations for remote delivery | PPWT2.21 |

## command summary

| Command | Action |
|---|---|
| File/Save as Web Page/Publish | Saves presentation in HTML format to a Web server |
| File/Send to/Mail Recipient (for Review) | Sends presentation as an e-mail attachment and activates recipient's Reviewing toolbar |
| Insert/Comment | Inserts a comment into presentation |
| Tools/Compare and Merge Presentations | Combines reviewed presentations with original |
| Slide Show/Online Broadcast/Record and Save a Broadcast | Records a presentation for online broadcast |
| Slide Show/Online Broadcast/Schedule a Live Broadcast | Sets up a live broadcast |
| Edit/Presentation Object/Edit | Edits an embedded object |
| Insert/Object/Create from File | Inserts contents of a file into document |

## step-by-step

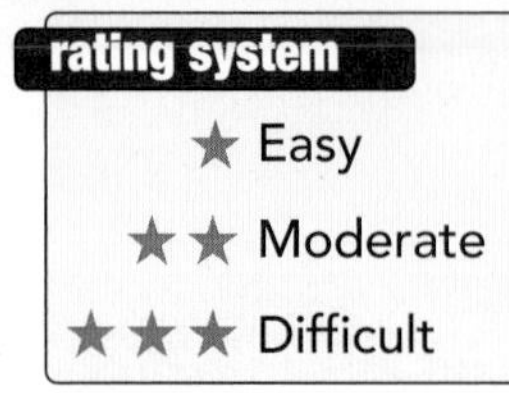

### Distributing the Europe Presentation ★

1. Because the presentation you created on European travel (Step-by-Step Exercise 3, Lab 4) for adventure Travel had such a positive response, you have been asked to distribute it to other branches of the company. You will do this by embedding it in a Word document and sending it via e-mail. The completed letter is displayed here.

   **a.** Start Word 2003 and open the ppwt2_Travel Letter file.

   **b.** Insert the Europe PowerPoint file you saved below the second paragraph. Reduce the size of the object and center it.

   **c.** Edit the embedded presentation by inserting a new slide before the last slide of the presentation listing the Travel agencies—**Flagstaff**, **Tucson**, and **Phoenix**—and the toll-free number of **1-800-555-5555**.

   **d.** Replace the name in the introduction with your name.

   **e.** Save the document as Europe Travel Memo.

   **f.** E-mail the document to your instructor for review.

   **g.** Print the letter.

   **h.** Make the same changes to the Water Presentation PowerPoint file and save it as Europe Web Presentation2.

**Memo**

**To:** Branch Managers
**From:** Student Name
**Date:** Wednesday, November 26, 2005
**Re:** European Tour Kiosk Presentation

We are currently looking to boost attendance of our European tours by 18% this summer, in order to attract potential clients, we have composed a PowerPoint presentation designed to run in the branch lobbies.

Please take a look at our presentation – just double-click on the picture. The show is designed to loop continuously, so press ESC when you want to end the show.

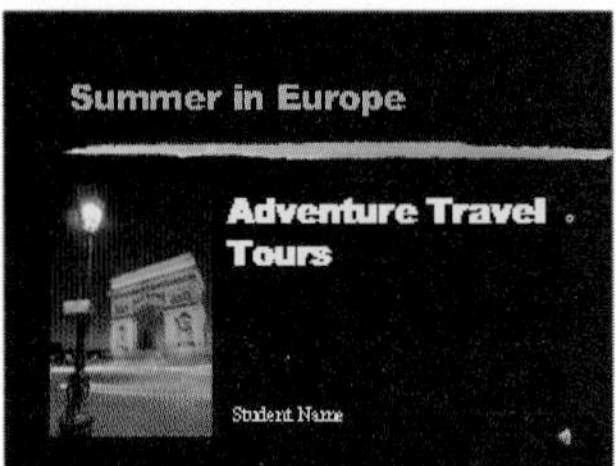


I will call you next week to get your feedback and to see if you can assist by running the presentation on the branch kiosk during the spring months.

1

## Promoting the Fitness Web Page ★ ★

2. The Lifestyle Fitness Club presentation you created for the Web (Step-by-Step Exercise 4, Lab 4) has received positive feedback from the members. You would like to provide the Web pages to affiliated clubs in other states to use on their Web sites. You decide to do this by embedding it in a Word document and sending it via e-mail. The completed letter is displayed here.

    **a.** Start Word 2003 and create a letter to let the recipients know how to view the presentation.

    **b.** Embed the Fitness and Nutrition PowerPoint file in the letter. Reduce the size of the object and center it.

    **c.** Edit the embedded presentation to include comments about how the recipients can customize the presentation for their own use.

    **d.** Insert your name in the closing of the letter.

    **e.** Save the document as Fitness Presentation Letter. E-mail the document as an attachment to your instructor for review.

    **f.** Print the letter.

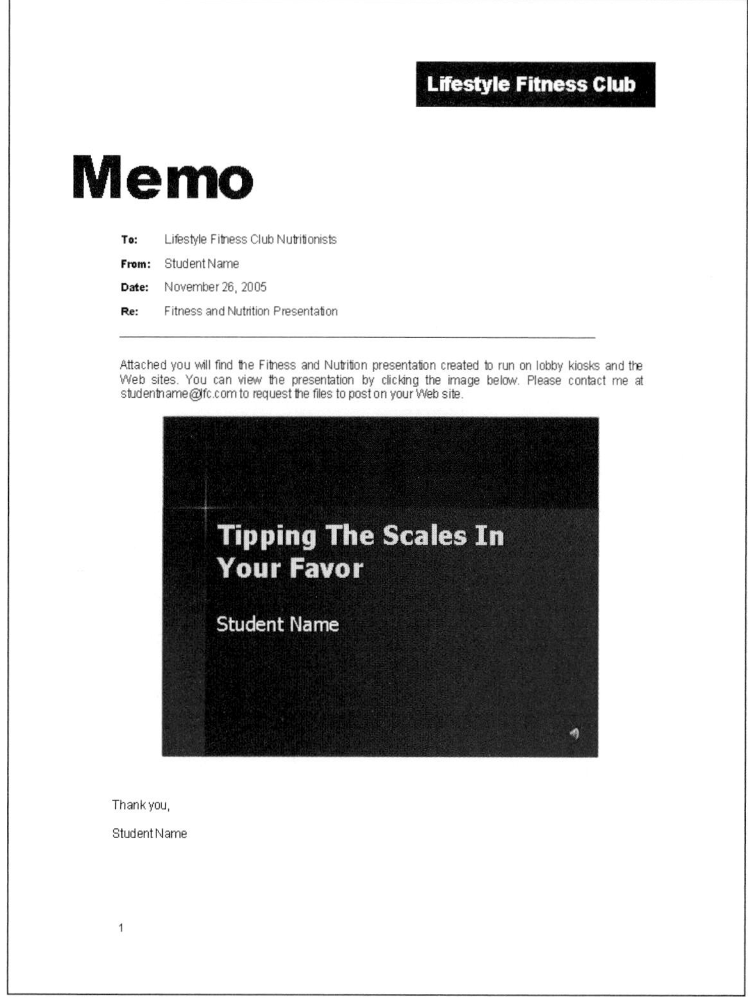

Lifestyle Fitness Club

**Memo**

**To:** Lifestyle Fitness Club Nutritionists

**From:** Student Name

**Date:** November 26, 2005

**Re:** Fitness and Nutrition Presentation

Attached you will find the Fitness and Nutrition presentation created to run on lobby kiosks and the Web sites. You can view the presentation by clicking the image below. Please contact me at studentname@lfc.com to request the files to post on your Web site.

Tipping The Scales In Your Favor

Student Name

Thank you,

Student Name

1

## Distributing the Sports Company Web Page ★★★

**3.** The Sports Company's kiosk presentation has worked out well. The store manager would like you to send the presentation you created (Step-by-Step Exercise 5, Lab 4) to the store managers of the other stores in the state. The completed letter is shown here.

**a.** Start Word 2003 and create a letter that describes the presentation and how to access it.

**b.** Embed the Sports Company Kiosk presentation in the letter. Reduce the size of the embedded object and center it.

**c.** Edit the embedded presentation to include comments suggesting changes they might make to customize the presentation for their own use.

**d.** Insert your name in the closing of the letter.

**e.** Save the document as Sports Company Letter.

**f.** E-mail the document to your instructor for review.

**g.** Print the letter.

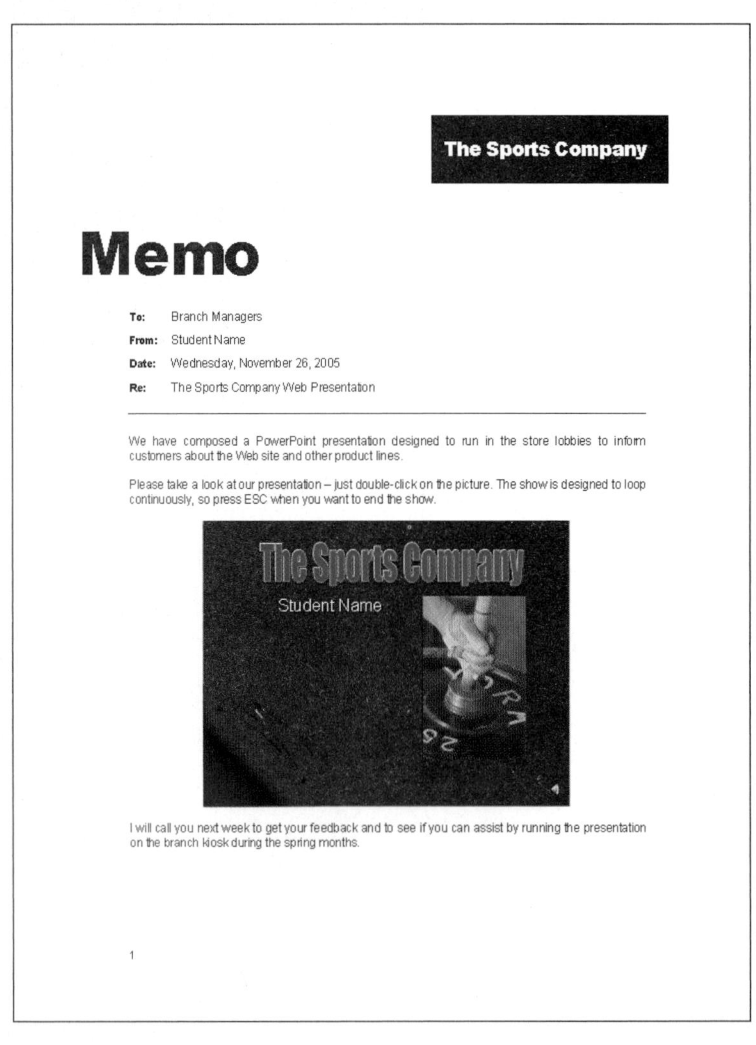

The Sports Company

# Memo

**To:** Branch Managers
**From:** Student Name
**Date:** Wednesday, November 26, 2005
**Re:** The Sports Company Web Presentation

We have composed a PowerPoint presentation designed to run in the store lobbies to inform customers about the Web site and other product lines.

Please take a look at our presentation – just double-click on the picture. The show is designed to loop continuously, so press ESC when you want to end the show.



I will call you next week to get your feedback and to see if you can assist by running the presentation on the branch kiosk during the spring months.

1

# Command Summary

| Command | Shortcut Key | Button | Voice | Action |
|---|---|---|---|---|
| start/All Programs | | | | Opens program menu |
| **F**ile/**N**ew | Ctrl + N | | | Creates new presentation |
| **F**ile/**O**pen | Ctrl + O | | Open<br>File open<br>Open file | Opens existing presentation |
| **F**ile/**C**lose | | | Close presentation | Closes presentation |
| **F**ile/**S**ave | Ctrl + S | | Save | Saves presentation |
| **F**ile/Save **A**s | | | | Saves presentation using new file name and/or location |
| **F**ile/Package for CD | | | | Saves presentation and all supporting files to a folder for use on a CD |
| **F**ile/Print Pre**v**iew | Ctrl + P | | Print preview | Displays preview of slide |
| **F**ile/**P**rint | | | | Prints presentation |
| **F**ile/Propert**i**es | | | | Displays statistics and stores information about presentation |
| **F**ile/Sen**d** To/Microsoft Office **W**ord | | | | Exports text of presentation to Word |
| **F**ile/Sen**d** To/M**a**il Recipient (as Attachment) | | | | Sends presentation or selected slide as an e-mail attachment |
| **F**ile/E**x**it | | | File exit | Exits PowerPoint program |
| **E**dit/**U**ndo | Ctrl + Z | | Undo | Reverses last action |
| **E**dit/Cu**t** | Ctrl + X | | Cut | Cuts selection to Clipboard |
| **E**dit/**P**aste | Ctrl + V | | Paste | Pastes item from Clipboard |
| **E**dit/Paste **S**pecial/<Object> | | | | Inserts an item from Clipboard as an embedded object |
| **E**dit/Paste Special/Paste **L**ink | | | | Inserts an item from Clipboard as a linked object |
| **E**dit/Select A**l**l | Ctrl + A | | | Selects all objects on a slide or all text in an object, or (in Outline pane) an entire outline |

| Command | Shortcut Key | Button | Voice | Action |
|---|---|---|---|---|
| **E**dit/**D**elete Slide | | | | Deletes selected slide |
| **E**dit/**F**ind | Ctrl + F | | | Finds specified text |
| **E**dit/Replace | Ctrl + H | | | Replaces located text with specified replacement text |
| **E**dit/Lin**k**s | | | | Changes settings associated with linked objects |
| **E**dit/Linked Worksheet **O**bject/**O**pen | | | | Opens source application of linked object |
| **E**dit/**D**ocument **O**bject/**E**dit | | | | Opens embedded object for editing by source program |
| **V**iew/Gr**i**d and Guides | | | | Displays guidelines that help align objects |
| **V**iew/**N**ormal | | | Normal<br>Normal view | Switches to Normal view |
| **V**iew/**Z**oom | | 45% | | Changes size of onscreen display of slide |
| **V**iew/Sli**d**e Sorter | | | Slide sorter | Switches to Slide Sorter view |
| **V**iew/Slide Sho**w** | | | View show<br>Begin slide show<br>Start slide show<br>Slide show view | Runs slide show |
| **V**iew/Notes **P**age | | | | Displays notes pages |
| **V**iew/**M**aster/**S**lide Master | Shift + [Normal View button] | | | Displays slide master for current presentation |
| **V**iew/Tas**k** pane | Ctrl + F1 | | Task pane<br>Show task pane<br>View task pane<br>Hide task pane | Hides or displays task pane |
| **V**iew/**T**oolbars | | | | Displays or hides selected toolbars |
| **V**iew/**R**uler | | | | Displays or hides ruler |
| **V**iew/**H**eader and Footer | | | | Specifies information that appears as headers and footers on slides, notes, outlines, and handout pages |

| Command | Shortcut Key | Button | Voice | Action |
|---|---|---|---|---|
| Insert/New Slide | Ctrl + M | New Slide | New slide<br>Insert new slide | Inserts new slide |
| Insert/Duplicate Slide | | | | Inserts duplicate of selected slide |
| Insert/Chart | | | | Adds a chart object to a slide |
| Insert/Picture/Clip Art | | | | Opens Clip Organizer and inserts selected clip art |
| Insert/Picture/From File | | | | Inserts a picture from file on disk |
| Insert/Picture/AutoShapes | | | | Inserts selected AutoShape object |
| Insert/Text Box | | | | Adds a text box |
| Format/Font/Font | | Arial | | Changes font type |
| Format/Font/Size | | 18 | | Changes font size |
| Format/Font/Font Style/Bold | Ctrl + B | B | on bold | Adds bold effect to selection |
| Format/Font/Font Style/Italic | Ctrl + I | I | italic | Adds italic effect to selection |
| Format/Font/Color | | A | | Adds color to selection |
| Format/Bullets and Numbering | | | | Creates bulleted or numbered lists |
| Format/Background | | | | Applies colors, patterns, or pictures to a slide background |
| Format/AutoShape | | | | Changes characteristics of an AutoShape |
| Format/Alignment | Ctrl + L | | Left justify | Aligns text in a cell or placeholder to left, center, right, or justified |
| | Ctrl + E | | Centered | |
| | Ctrl + R | | Right justify | |
| | Ctrl + J | | | |
| Format/Slide Design | | Design | | Changes appearance of slide by applying a different design template |
| Format/Replace Fonts | | | | Finds specified font and replace it with another |
| Format/Slide Layout | | | | Changes layout of an existing or new slide |
| Format/Picture/Recolor | | | | Changes color of a picture |

| Command | Shortcut Key | Button | Voice | Action |
|---|---|---|---|---|
| F**o**rmat/**M**aster Layout | | | | Selects the placeholder to be added |
| F**o**rmat/**T**able | | | | Changes table border and fill color |
| **T**ools/**S**pelling | | | | Spell-checks presentation |
| **T**ools/**C**ustomize/**O**ptions/ | | | | Shows Standard and Formatting toolbars in two rows |
| **T**ools/**O**ptions/Spelling and Style | | | | Sets spelling and style options |
| Sli**d**e Show/Custo**m** Animation | | A | | Applies custom animation |
| Sli**d**e Show/Slide **T**ransition | | Transition | | Adds transition effects |
| Sli**d**e Show/**H**ide Slide | | | | Hides selected slide |
| ***Slide Show Pointer Shortcut Menu*** | | | | |
| **A**rrow | Ctrl + A | | | Changes pointer to arrow and turns off freehand annotation |
| **B**allpoint Pen | Ctrl + P | | | Changes pointer to ballpoint pen and turns on freehand annotation |
| **F**elt Tip Pen | | | | Changes pointer to felt tip pen and turns on freehand annotation |
| **H**ighlighter | | | | Changes pointer to a highlighter |
| Ink **C**olor | | | | Shows color palette for annotation tool |
| E**r**aser | | | | Erases selected annotations |
| **E**rase all Ink on Slide | E | | | Removes all annotations from slide |
| ***Slide Show Screen Shortcut Menu*** | | | | |
| **G**o to Slide | | | | Displays hidden slide |
| S**c**reen/**B**lack Screen | B | | | Blacks out screen |
| S**c**reen/**W**hite Screen | W | | | Whites out screen |
| **H**elp/Microsoft Word **H**elp | F1 | | | Opens Help window |
| **E**dit/Office Clip**b**oard | | | | Opens Clipboard task pane |
| Sli**d**e Show/**S**et Up Show/ **U**sing Timings | | | | Sets up slide show to advance auto-math calls by preset timings |
| Sli**d**e Show/**R**ehearse Timings | | | | Starts slide show and sets timings for slide |

| Command | Shortcut Key | Button | Voice | Action |
|---|---|---|---|---|
| Slide Show/Record Narration | | | | Records narration while rehearsing the presentation |
| Draw/Group | | | | Groups objects together |
| Draw/Ungroup | | | | Ungroups objects |
| Draw/Regroup | | | | Groups objects together again that were previously ungrouped |
| Draw/Order/Send to Back | | | | Sends object to bottom of stack |
| Draw/Grid and Guides/ Display grid on screen | | | | Displays or hides grid lines |
| Draw/Align or Distribute | | | | Aligns or distributes objects |
| ***Chart*** | | | | |
| Format/Selected Data Series | Ctrl + 1 | | | Applies patterns, shapes, and other formats to selected data series |
| Data/Series in Columns | | | | Arranges chart based on columns in Datasheet window |
| Chart/Chart Options | | | | Adds and modifies chart options such as titles, legends, and gridlines |
| ***Organization Chart*** | | | | |
| Insert Shape/Subordinate | | | | Adds a box below selected box |
| Insert Shape/Coworker | | | | Adds a box at same level as selected box |
| Insert Shape/Standard | | | | Applies Standard layout to selected boxes |
| | | | | Applies selected design to boxes of organization chart |
| File/Save as Web Page | | | | Publishes presentation on Web |
| Insert/Slides from Files | | | | Inserts selected slides from another presentation |
| Insert/Slides from Outline | | | | Creates slides from outline text |
| Insert/Movies and Sounds/ Sound from File | | | | Inserts sound or movie files into selected slide |
| Insert/Movies and Sounds/ Play CD Audio Track | | | | Plays a CD |
| Insert/Table | | | | Inserts a table consisting of the specified number of rows and columns |

| Command | Shortcut Key | Button | Voice | Action |
|---|---|---|---|---|
| Insert/Hyperlink | | | | Creates a hyperlink |
| Format/AutoShape/Size | | | | Changes size and scale of selected AutoShape |
| Format/Table | | | | Formats borders and fill color of selected table |
| Slide Show/Set Up Show | | | | Sets up presentation to run for specific situations |
| Slide Show/Custom Shows | | | | Creates presentations within a presentation |
| Slide Show/Action Buttons | | | | Adds navigation buttons to a slide |
| Slide Show/Action Settings | | | | Specifies action that is needed to activate hyperlinks |
| Slide Show/Custom Animation | | | | Adds motion and determines how sound is played |
| File/Save as Web Page/Publish | | | | Saves presentation in HTML format to a Web server |
| File/Send to/Mail Recipient (for Review) | | | | Sends presentation as an e-mail attachment and activates recipient's Reviewing toolbar |
| Insert/Comment | | | | Inserts a comment into presentation |
| Tools/Compare and Merge Presentations | | | | Combines reviewed presentations with original |
| Slide Show/Online Broadcast/Record and Save a Broadcast | | | | Records a presentation for online broadcast |
| Slide Show/Online Broadcast/Schedule a Live Broadcast | | | | Sets up a live broadcast |
| Edit/Presentation Object/Edit | | | | Edits an embedded object |
| Insert/Object/Create from File | | | | Inserts contents of a file into document |

# Glossary of Key Terms

**action button** A special object that can be inserted into a presentation and assigned a hyperlink. Used in self-running presentations and presentations that work on a company network or Web site.

**agenda slide** A slide that lists the agenda items or main topics of a presentation from which viewers can select.

**alignment** Controls the position of text entries within a space.

**animated GIF** A type of graphic file that has motion.

**animation** Effect that adds action to text and graphics so they move around on the screen.

**animation scheme** A preset visual effect that can be added to slide text.

**assistant box** In an organization chart, a box representing administrative or managerial assistants to a manager.

**attachment** A file that is sent along with an e-mail message but is not part of the message.

**attribute** A features associated with an object that can be isolated and changed.

**AutoContent Wizard** A guided approach that helps you determine the content and organization of your presentation through a series of questions.

**AutoCorrect** Feature that makes certain types of corrections automatically as you enter text.

**AutoShape** A ready-made drawing shape supplied with PowerPoint.

**branch** In an organization chart, a box and all the boxes that report to it.

**broadcast** To deliver a presentation to an audience at different locations.

**browser** A program that connects you to remote computers and displays the Web pages you request.

**build** An effect that progressively displays bulleted items as the presentation proceeds.

**category axis** The bottom boundary of a chart, which is used to label the data being charted. Also called the X axis.

**cell** The intersection of a row and column in a table.

**change marker** An icon that indicates a reviewer made a change to a slide.

**chart** A visual representation of numeric data. Also called a graph.

**character formatting** Formatting features that affect the selected characters only.

**clip art** Professionally drawn images.

**collect and paste** The capability of the program to store multiple copied items in the Office Clipboard and then paste one or many of the items.

**comment** A remark that is displayed in a separate box and attached to a slide.

**comment marker** An icon that indicates a comment is attached to a slide.

**co-worker box** In an organization chart, a box having the same manager as another box. Co-workers from a group.

**custom dictionary** A dictionary you can create to hold words you commonly use but that are not included in the dictionary that is supplied with the program.

**custom show** A presentation that runs within a presentation.

**data series** Each group of related data that is plotted in a chart. Each data series has a unique color or pattern assigned to it so that you can identify the different series.

**datasheet** A table consisting of rows and columns that is used to enter the data that you want represented in a chart.

**default** Initial program settings.

**demote** To move a topic down one level in the outline hierarchy.

**design template** Professionally created slide design that can be applied to your presentation.

**destination document** The document where an embedded object is inserted.

**destination file** The document receiving the linked or embedded object.

**docked toolbar** A toolbar fixed to an edge of the window and displays a vertical bar called the move handle, on the left edge of the toolbar.

**document window** The area of the application window that displays the contents of the open document.

**drawing object** An object consisting of shapes such as lines and boxes that can be created using the Drawing toolbar.

**Drawing toolbar** A toolbar that is used to add objects such as lines, circles, and boxes.

**embedded object** An object that is inserted into another application and becomes part of the document. It can be edited from within the document using the source program.

**floating object** A graphic object that is inserted into the drawing layer and which can be positioned anywhere on the page.

**font** A set of characters with a specific design. Also called a typeface.

**font size** The height and width of a character, commonly measured in points.

**footer** Text or graphics that appear on the bottom of each slide.

**format** To enhance the appearance of a slide to make it more readable or attractive.

**Format Painter** A feature that applies the format associated with the current selection to new selections.

**Formatting toolbar** A toolbar that contains buttons used to modify text.

**graphic** A non-text element, such as a chart, drawing, picture, or scanned photograph, in a slide.

**grid** An invisible series of lines that form small squares on the slide and that are used to position objects.

**group** Two or more objects that are treated as a single object. In an organization chart, all the boxes reporting to the same manager, excluding assistant boxes.

**guide** A line, either vertical or horizontal, that you position on the slide. When an object is close to the guide, the center or corner (whichever is closer) snaps to the grid.

**hierarchy** A visual representation that shows ranking, such as reporting structures within a department in a business.

**hyperlink** A connection to locations in the current document, other documents, or Web pages. Clicking a hyperlink jumps to the specified location.

**Hypertext Markup Language (HTML)** The programming language used to write Web pages. It controls how information on the page, such as font colors and size, is displayed.

**keyword** A word or phrase that is descriptive of the type of graphic you want to locate.

**landscape** Orientation of the printed output across the length of the paper.

**layout** A predefined slide organization that is used to control the placement of elements on a slide.

**legend** A box containing a brief description that identifies the patterns or colors assigned to the data series in a chart.

**level** All the boxes in an organization chart at the same position in the hierarchy, regardless of the boxes each reports to.

**linked object** An object that is created in a source file and linked to a destination file. Edits made to the source file are automatically reflected in the destination file.

**live link** A link that automatically updates the linked object whenever changes are made to it in the source file.

**lobby page** In a broadcast, the page that displays information about the broadcast including the title, subject, and host's name.

**main dictionary** Dictionary that comes with the Office 2003 programs.

**manager box** In an organization chart, the top-level box of a group.

**master** A special slide on which the formatting of all slides in a presentation is defined.

**menu bar** Located below the title bar, this bar displays the application's program menu.

**notes page** Printed output that shows a miniature of the slide and provides an area for speaker notes.

**object** An item on a slide that can be selected and modified.

**object alignment** To position objects relative to each other by their left, right, top or bottom edges; or horizontally by their centers or vertically by their middles; or in relation to the entire slide.

**organization chart** A map of a group, which usually includes people, but can include any items that have a hierarchical relationship.

**Outlining toolbar** A toolbar that is used to modify the organization of the presentation text and slides.

**pane** In Normal view, the separate divisions of the window that allow you to work on all aspects of your presentation in one place.

**paragraph formatting** Formatting features that affect entire paragraphs.

**picture** An image such as a graphic illustration or a scanned photograph.

**placeholder** Box that is designed to contain objects such as the slide title, bulleted text, charts, tables, and pictures.

**point** A unit of type measurement. One point equals about 1/72 inch.

**portrait** Orientation of the printed output across the width of the paper.

**promote** To move a topic up one level in the outline hierarchy.

**publish** To save a presentation in HTML format to a Web server.

**rotate handle** The [icon] on the selection rectangle of a selected object that allows you to rotate the object in any direction.

**sans serif** A font that does not have a flair at the base of each letter, such as Arial or Helvetica.

**scroll bar** Used with a mouse to bring additional lines of information into view in a window.

**selection cursor** A colored highlight bar that appears over the selected command.

**selection rectangle** Hashed border that surrounds a selected placeholder.

**serif** A font that has a flair at the base of each letter, such as Roman or Times New Roman.

**server** The computer that stores Web pages and sends them to a browser when requested.

**Shortcut menu** By right clicking on an item, this menu displays only the options pertaining to that item.

**sizing handles** Small boxes surrounding selected objects that are used to change the size of the object.

**slide** An individual page of the presentation.

**slide show** Used to practice or to present the presentation. It displays each slide in final form.

**source document** The document from which an embedded object was obtained.

**source file** The file from which a linked or embedded object is obtained.

**source program** The program used to create the linked or embedded object.

**spelling checker** Locates all misspelled words, duplicate words, and capitalization irregularities as you create and edit a presentation, and proposes possible corrections.

**stacking order** The order in which objects are inserted into layers in the slide.

**Standard toolbar** A toolbar that contains buttons that give quick access to the most frequently used program features.

**status bar** A bar displayed at the bottom of the document window that advises you of the status of different program conditions and features as you use the program.

**subordinate box** In an organization chart, a box reporting to a manager box.

**summary slide** A slide that contains the title of selected slides in the presentation.

**table** An arrangement of horizontal rows and vertical columns.

**table reference** The letter and number that identifies a table cell.

**Task Pane** Displayed on the right side of the document window, it provides quick access to features as you are using the application.

**template** A file that includes predefined settings that can be used as a pattern to create many common types of presentations.

**text box** A container for text or graphics.

**thumbnail** A miniature view of a slide.

**titles** Descriptive text used to explain the content of a chart.

**transition** An effect that controls how a slide moves off the screen and the next one appears.

**typeface** A set of characters with a specific design. Also called a font.

**value axis** The left boundary of a chart, consisting of a numbered scale whose numbers are determined by the data used in the chart. Also called the Y axis.

**view** A way of looking at the presentation.

**WordArt** Used to enhance slide text by changing the shape of text, adding 3-D effects, and changing the alignment of text on a line.

**workspace** The large area containing the slide where your presentations are displayed as you create and edit them.

**X axis** The bottom boundary of the chart, which is used to label the data being charted. Also called the category axis.

**Y axis** The left boundary of the chart, consisting of a numbered scale whose numbers are determined by the data used in the chart. Also called the value axis.

# Reference 1

## Data File List

| Supplied/Used | Created/Saved As |
|---|---|
| **Lab 1** | |
| | Volunteer |
| pp01_Volunteer1 | Volunteer1 |
| pp01_Puppy (graphic) | |
| pp01_AnimalCare (graphic) | |
| **Step-by-Step** | |
| 1. pp01_Triple Crown<br>pp01_Jump (graphic)<br>pp01_Stream (graphic) | Triple Crown Presentation |
| 2. pp01_Resume (graphic)<br>pp01_Success (graphic)<br>pp01_Cover Letter (graphic) | Resume1 |
| 3. pp01_Relaxation | Massage Therapy |
| 4. pp01_Logo<br>pp01_Cuppa (graphic)<br>pp01_Beans (graphic) | Coffee |
| 5. pp01_Resume<br>pp01_Biography (graphic)<br>pp01_Meeting (graphic)<br>pp01_Booth (graphic)<br>pp01_Interview (graphic)<br>pp01_Follow Up (graphic) | Job Fairs |
| **On Your Own** | |
| 1. pp01_Internet Policy | Internet Policy |
| 2. pp01_Memo | Phone Etiquette |
| 3. pp01_Animals | Pet Activities |
| 4. | Placement Services |
| 5. pp01_Animal Careers | Careers with Animals |
| **Lab 2** | |
| pp02_Volunteer2 | Volunteer2 |
| pp02_QuestionMark (graphic) | |
| **Step-by-Step** | |
| 1. pp02_ASU Presentation<br>pp02_Arizona (graphic)<br>pp02_Student Services (graphic)<br>pp02_Library (graphic)<br>pp02_Fine Arts (graphic) | ASU Presentation1 |
| 2. Massage Therapy (from Lab 1) | Massage Therapy2 |
| 3. Job Fairs (from Lab 1) | Job Fairs2 |

| Supplied/Used | Created/Saved As |
|---|---|
| 4. Triple Crown Presentation (from Lab 1)<br>pp02_Read (graphic) | Triple Crown Presentation2 |
| 5. Coffee (from Lab 1)<br>pp02_Globe (graphic) | Coffee Show |
| **On Your Own** | |
| 1. | Interview Techniques |
| 2. Careers with Animals (from Lab 1) | Animal Careers2 |
| 3. | Fad Diets |
| 4. Internet Policy (from Lab 1) | Internet Policy2 |
| 5. | Travel Favorites |
| **Working Together 1** | |
| Volunteer2 (from Lab 2) | Volunteer2 Linked |
| ppwt1_OrientationMeetings (Word doc) | |
| ppwt1_RescueData (Excel chart) | Rescue Data Linked |
| **Step-by-Step** | |
| 1. ppwt1_MassagePrices (Word doc)<br>Massage Therapy2 (from Lab 2) | Massage Therapy3 |
| 2. ppwt1_Coffee Prices (Word doc)<br>Coffee Show (from Lab 2) | Coffee Prices Linked (Word doc)<br>Coffee Show Linked |
| 3. Triple Crown Presentation2 (from Lab 2)<br>ppwt1_Forest Use (Excel worksheet) | Triple Crown Presentation3<br>Forest Use Linked (Excel worksheet) |
| **Lab 3** | |
| pp03_Recruitment | Volunteer Orientation |
| pp03_Animal Angels3 | Volunteer Presentation (e-mail) |
| pp03_Sunrise (graphic) | OrientationCD (folder) |
| pp03_Cat (graphic) | |
| pp03_Dog (graphic) | |
| **Step-by-Step** | |
| 1. pp03_Employee Motivation<br>pp03_Motivation (graphic)<br>pp03_Success (graphic) | Employee Motivation2<br>Motivation Outline |
| 2. pp03_Doggie Travel<br>pp03_Auto | Doggie Travel Tips |
| 3. pp03_Valley Soccer<br>pp03_Futbol<br>pp03_Varsity | Valley Soccer Presentation<br>Soccer Outline |
| 4. pp03_Exercise<br>pp03_Fitness Trends<br>pp03_LFC Logo | Fitness and Nutrition<br>Fitness and Nutrition Outline |
| 5. Job Fairs2 (From Lab 2)<br>pp03_Hurry<br>pp03_Jobs | Job Fairs3<br>Jobs (CD folder) |
| **On Your Own** | |
| 1. | Family Reunion |
| 2. pp03_Lifeguard | Lifeguard Presentation |
| 3. Travel Favorites (from Lab 2) | Travel Favorites2 |
| 4. | Storyland Orientation |
| 5. | Preventing Network Infection |

| Supplied/Used | Created/Saved As |
|---|---|
| **Lab 4** | |
| pp04_Promotional Outline | Animal Rescue Foundation |
| pp04_Animals for Adoption (Word document) | AnimalRescueCD (folder) |
| pp04_Foundation Introduction | Rescue Foundation Self Running |
| pp04_Jake (picture) | Rescue Foundation Web |
| pp04_Sadie (picture) | |
| pp04_Adoptions (graphic) | |
| pp04_Doggie (sound) | Self Running (template) |
| **Step-by-Step** | |
| 1. pp04_Birds (graphic) | |
| pp04_Bird Outline | Betty's Birds |
| pp04_Dancing Parrot | Birds (template) |
| pp04_Parrot Talk (sound) | |
| 2. pp04_Anthology Logo | |
| pp04_Anthology Outline | Anthology Cinema Web Presentation |
| pp04_Popcorn (graphic) | |
| pp04_Ticket (graphic) | |
| pp04_Film (sound) | |
| 3. pp04_Europe | Europe Web Presentation |
| pp04_Champs Elysees (graphic) | |
| pp04_Dinner (graphic) | |
| pp04_Train (graphic) | |
| 4. pp04_Fitness Outline | Fitness Web Pages |
| pp04_Exercise (graphic) | |
| pp04_Stretching (graphic) | |
| 5. pp04_Sports Company Outline | Sports Company Kiosk |
| pp04_Weight Lifter (graphic) | Sports Company Web |
| pp04_Tennis Racquet (graphic) | |
| pp04_Mountain Bike (graphic) | |
| pp04_Onestop (sound) | |
| **On Your Own** | |
| 1. Lifeguard presenation | Pool Safety Kiosk |
| 2. pp04_Mass Transit | Mass Transit |
| 3. Italy Favorites2 | Travel Italy Web |
| 4. Storyland Orientation | Storyland Web |
| 5. | MusicFirst Web |

| Supplied/Used | Created/Saved As |
|---|---|
| **Working Together 2** | |
| ppwt2_Kiosk Original | Kiosk Review |
| | Kiosk Review E-mail |
| ppwt2_Kiosk Review (1) | Kiosk Final |
| ppwt2_ Kiosk Review (2) | |
| ppwt2_Halo (graphic) | |
| ppwt2_Mall Letter (Word document) | |
| ppwt2_Dog Wagging (graphic) | Kiosk Presentation Letter |
| **Step-by-Step** | |
| 1. ppwt2_Travel Letter | Europe Web Presentation2 |
| 2. Fitness Web Pages (from Lab 4) | Fitness Presentation Letter |
| 3. Sports Company Kiosk (from Lab 4) | Sports Company Letter |

# Reference 2

## Microsoft Office Specialist Skills

### Office PowerPoint 2003 Specialist Certification

| Standardized Coding Number | Skill Sets and Skill Standards | Lab Exercises | | | |
|---|---|---|---|---|---|
| | | Lab | Page | Step-By-Step | On Your Own |
| **PPO3S-1** | **Creating Content** | | | | |
| PPO3S-1-1 | Create new presentations from templates | 1 | PP1.7 | 3,4,5 | 1,2,3,4,5 |
| | | 4 | PP4.4 | 1,2,3,4,5 | 1,2,3,4,5 |
| PPO3S-1-2 | Insert and edit text-based content | 1 | PP1.16 | 1,2,3,4,5 | 1,2,3,4,5 |
| | | 2 | PP2.5 | 1,2,3,4,5 | 1,2,3,4,5 |
| | | 3 | PP3.5 | 1,2,3,4,5 | 1,2,3,4,5 |
| | | 4 | 4.6 | 1,2,3,4,5 | 1,2,3,4,5 |
| | | WT1 | PPWT1.2 | 1,2,3 | |
| PPO3S-1-3 | Insert tables, charts, and diagrams | 2 | PP2.9 | 4,5 | 3 |
| | | 3 | PP3.30,3.43 | 1,2,3,4,5 | 1,2,3,4,5 |
| | | 4 | PP4.12 | 1,2,3,4,5 | 1,2,3,4,5 |
| PPO3S-1-4 | Insert pictures, shapes and graphics | 1 | PP1.54 | 1,2,3,4,5 | 1,2,3,4,5 |
| | | 2 | PP2.23,2.24 | 1,2,3,4,5 | 1,2,3,4,5 |
| | | 3 | PP3.16,3.26 | 1,2,3,4,5 | 1,2,3,4,5 |
| | | 4 | PP4.20 | 1,2,3,4,5 | 1,2,3,4,5 |
| PPO3S-1-5 | Insert objects | WT1 | PPWT1.11 | | |
| | | 4 | PP4.26 | 1,2,3,4,5 | 1,2,3,4,5 |
| **PPO3S-2** | **Formatting Content** | | | | |
| PPO3S-2-1 | Format text-based content | 1 | PP1.49 | 1,2,3,4,5 | 1,2,3,4,5 |
| | | 2 | PP2.13,2.15 | 1,2,3,4,5 | 1,2,3,4,5 |
| | | 3 | PP3.8 | 1,2,3,4,5 | 1,2,3,4,5 |
| PPO3S-2-2 | Format pictures, shapes, and graphics | 1 | PP1.61 | 1,2,3,4,5 | 1,2,3,4,5 |
| | | 2 | PP2.22,2.25 | 1,2,3,4,5 | 1,2,3,4,5 |
| | | 3 | PP3.19,3.23,3.28 | 1,2,3,4,5 | 1,2,3,4,5 |
| PPO3S-2-3 | Format slides | 2 | PP2.31,2.33,2.72 | 1,2,3,4,5 | 1,2,3,4,5 |
| | | 3 | PP3.10 | 1,2,3,4,5 | 1,2,3,4,5 |
| PPO3S-2-4 | Apply animation schemes | 2 | PP2.54 | 1,4,5 | 1,2,3,4 |
| PPO3S-2-5 | Apply slide transitions | 2 | PP2.51 | 2,3,5 | 1,2,4,5 |
| | | 4 | PP4.29 | 1,2,3,4,5 | 1,2,3,4,5 |
| PPO3S-2-6 | Customizing slide templates | 4 | PP4.50 | 1 | |
| PPO3S-2-7 | Work with masters | 2 | PP2.38 | 1,2,3,4,5 | 1,2,3,4,5 |
| | | 3 | PP3.13 | 1,2,3,4,5 | 1,2,3,4,5 |
| **PPO3S-3** | **Collaborating** | | | | |
| PP03S-3-1 | Track, accept, and reject changes in a presentation | WT2 | PPWT2.8 | 1,2,3 | 1,2,3 |
| PP03S-3-2 | Add, edit, and delete comments in a presentation | WT2 | PPWT2.2 | 1,2,3 | 1,2,3 |
| PP03S-3-3 | Compare and merge presentations | WT2 | PPWT2.6 | 1,2,3 | 1,2,3 |

| Standardized Coding Number | Skill Sets and Skill Standards | Lab Exercises | | | |
|---|---|---|---|---|---|
| | | Lab | Page | Step-By-Step | On Your Own |
| **PPO3S-4** | **Managing and Delivering Presentations** | | | **3,4,5** | **2,3,4,5** |
| PPO3S-4-1 | Organize a presentation | 1 | PP1.12,1.40–1.45 | 1,2,3,4,5 | 1,2,3,4,5 |
| | | 2 | PP2.23,2.63 | 1,2,3,4,5 | 1,2,3,4,5 |
| | | WT1 | PPWT1.2,WT1.9 | 1,2,3 | |
| | | 3 | PP3.5,3.24,3.44 | 1,2,3,4,5 | 1,2,3,4,5 |
| | | 4 | PP4.7 | 1,2,3,4,5 | 1,2,3,4,5 |
| PPO3S-4-2 | Set up slide shows for delivery | 2 | PP2.60 | | |
| | | 4 | 4.31,4.39 | 3,5 | 1 |
| PPO3S-4-3 | Rehearse timing | 3 | 3.56 | 3,4,5 | 1,2,3,4,5 |
| PPO3S-4-4 | Deliver presentations | 1 | PP1.47 | 1,2,3,4,5 | 1,2,3,4,5 |
| | | 2 | PP2.56 | 1,2,3,4,5 | 1,2,3,4,5 |
| PPO3S-4-5 | Prepare presentations for remote delivery | 3 | 3.57 | 5 | 3 |
| | | 4 | 4.31 | 1,2,3,4,5 | 1,2,3,4,5 |
| | | WT2 | WT2.21 | | |
| PPO3S-4-6 | Save and publish presentations | 1 | PP1.31 | 1,2,3,4,5 | 1,2,3,4,5 |
| | | 2 | PP2.8 | 1,2,3,4,5 | 1,2,3,4,5 |
| | | 4 | 4.45 | 1,2,3,4,5 | 1,2,3,4,5 |
| PPO3S-4-7 | Print slides, outlines, handouts, and speaker notes | 1 | PP1.62 | 1,2,3,4,5 | 1,2,3,4,5 |
| | | 2 | PP2.71 | 1,2,3,4,5 | 1,2,3,4,5 |
| | | WT1 | PPWT1.14 | 1,2,3 | |
| PPO3S-4-8 | Export a presentation to another Microsoft office program | 3 | PP3.52 | 1,3,4 | 5 |

# Index


Action buttons, PP4.39–PP4.41, PP4.45
Action Settings dialog box, PP4.35
Adding interest to presentation
  animated graphics, PP4.18–PP4.19
  WordArt, PP4.20–PP4.26
Agenda slide, PP4.34
Alignment, PP2.15. *See also* Object alignment
Animated GIF, PP4.19
Animated graphics, PP4.18–PP4.19
Animation, PP2.49–PP2.51
Animation number tag, PP2.51
Animation schemes, PP2.54
Annotations, PP2.57–PP2.60
Any slide, PP1.26
Area chart, PP3.30
Assistant box, PP3.43
Attachment, PP3.53
Attributes, PP3.16
AutoContent Wizard, PP1.8, PP1.12
AutoCorrect, PP1.19
AutoFit, PP1.29
AutoFit Options button, PP1.29
AutoPreview, PP2.52
AutoRecover, PP1.31
AutoShape, PP2.24–PP2.27
Available For Use, PP2.31, PP2.32
AVI file (.avi), PP4.27
Axis titles, PP3.38–PP3.39

Background
  add gradient color, PP3.10–PP3.12
  fill color, PP2.18–PP2.19
  picture, PP3.15
  sunrise, PP3.15
Backspace key, PP1.20
Balance design template, PP2.32
Bar chart, PP3.30
Beam design template, PP2.32–PP2.33
Big Title animation, PP2.55
Bitmap files (.bmp), PP1.55, PP3.19
Black out the screen, PP2.56
.bmp, PP1.55, PP3.19
Bold, PP2.13
Border size/color, PP2.16–PP2.17
Bottom, PP2.15
Branch, PP3.43
Browser, PP4.46. *See* Set up presentation for browsing
Build, PP2.49
Build effects, PP2.53–PP2.55
Build slide, PP2.53–PP2.54
Bullet
  add/remove, PP1.22, PP1.53
  convert bulleted list to numbered list, PP3.7–PP3.8
  move, PP1.23
  picture, PP2.40–PP2.42
  promote/demote, PP1.27–PP1.28
Bulleted text placeholder, PP2.21
Buttons. *See* Command summary

Case and End Punctuation tab, PP2.65
Category axis, PP3.31
Cell, PP2.9
Center, PP2.15
Center alignment, PP3.24
Centering objects, PP3.28–PP3.29
Character formatting, PP1.49

Chart
axis titles, PP3.38–PP3.39
basic types, PP3.30
copy data to Office Clipboard, PP3.32–PP3.34
defined, PP3.30
formatting, PP3.40–PP3.42
modify data, PP3.38
organization, PP3.43–PP3.51. *See also* Organization chart
parts, PP3.31
specify chart data, PP3.34–PP3.38
Chart Options dialog box, PP3.39
Checking style, PP2.64–PP2.69
Chime sound effect, PP2.51
Clip art, PP1.55
Clip Art task pane, PP1.55
Clip Organizer, PP1.55
Clipboard
Office, PP3.32–PP3.34
system, PP3.33
Closing a presentation, PP1.35
Co-worker box, PP3.43
Collect and paste, PP3.33
Color, PP2.13
Background. *See* Background
border, PP2.17
fill, PP2.18–PP2.19
recolor a picture, PP2.22–PP2.23
Color scheme, PP2.34–PP2.37
Column chart, PP3.30
Command summary, PPCS.1–PPCS.6
Lab 1, PP1.71–PP1.72
Lab 2, PP2.79–PP2.80
Lab 3, PP3.63–PP3.64
Lab 4, PP4.55
Complex table, PP4.12–PP4.18
Content placeholder, PP2.21
Content templates, PP1.7
Controlling the slide show, PP2.56–PP2.62
black out the screen, PP2.56
checking style, PP2.64–PP2.69
freehand annotations, PP2.57–PP2.60
hiding slides, PP2.60–PP2.62
mouse pointer, PP2.57–PP2.58
navigating, PP2.56
speaker notes, PP2.62–PP2.64
Convert
bulleted list to numbered list, PP3.7–PP3.8
graphics to drawing objects, PP3.18–PP3.19
Copy
data to Office Clipboard, PP3.32–PP3.34
slides from another presentation, PP3.5–PP3.6
Corrections, PP1.19–PP1.20
Create
presentation, PP1.7–PP1.8
table, PP2.9–PP2.20
text box, PP2.28–PP2.29
Create presentation from existing slides, PP3.4–PP3.15
applying slide master to selected slides, PP3.12–PP3.15
background color, PP3.10–PP3.12
copying slides from another presentation, PP3.5–PP3.6
Format Painter, PP3.8–PP3.10
modifying design template, PP3.10–PP3.15
numbered list, PP3.7–PP3.8
picture background, PP3.15
saving new presentation, PP3.6
Create presentation from multiple sources, PP4.4–PP4.11
create new presentation from design template, PP4.4–PP4.6
insert slides from another presentation, PP4.8–PP4.11
insert text from Word document, PP4.6–PP4.8
Current slide, PP1.15
Custom Animation task pane, PP2.50
Custom dictionary, PP1.20
Custom shows, PP4.31–PP4.34
Customizing graphics, PP3.16–PP3.29
align objects, PP3.23–PP3.26
center objects, PP3.28–PP3.29
convert graphics to drawing objects, PP3.18–PP3.19
delete graphic element, PP3.20–PP3.21
group objects, PP3.26
regroup objects, PP3.21–PP3.22
stacking order, PP3.22–PP3.23
ungroup objects, PP3.20
wrap text in object, PP3.26–PP3.28
zoom the slide, PP3.17–PP3.18
Customizing print settings, PP2.71–PP2.74
Cut transition effect, PP2.53

Data series, PP3.31
Datasheet, PP3.35
Delivering presentations, PP3.55–PP3.59
Define Custom Show dialog box, PP4.32
Definitions (glossary), PPG.1–PPG.10
Default, PP1.7
Default design template, PP1.7
Delete
  graphic element, PP3.20–PP3.21
  slide, PP1.41
Demote, PP1.27–PP1.28
Design templates, PP1.7, PP2.31–PP2.33
Dictionary, PP1.20
Directional keys, PP1.16
Display slides, PP1.26
Documenting a file, PP2.69–PP2.71
Dotted border, PP1.24, PP4.15
Draw menu, PP1.60
Draw Table, PP2.17, PP4.12–PP4.13
Drawing object, PP1.54
Drawing toolbar, PP1.5, PP1.54
Duplicating a slide, PP2.23–PP2.24

E-mail attachment, PP3.53
E-mailing a presentation, PP3.53–PP3.55
Edit
  presentation, PP1.16–PP1.30
  slide pane, PP1.23–PP1.26
Edit Color Scheme dialog box, PP2.35, PP2.36
Edit WordArt Text dialog box, PP4.21
Embedded object, PP1.54
Exciting, PP2.54
Exiting PowerPoint, PP1.66
Expand Results, PP1.56, PP1.57
Exporting a presentation outline to Word,
  PP3.52–PP3.53

File documentation, PP2.69–PP2.71
File extensions
  .avi, PP4.27
  .bmp, PP1.55
  .jpg, PP1.55
  .mid, PP4.27
  .mov, PP4.27
  .mpeg, PP4.27
  .pcx, PP1.55
  .pot, PP2.31, PP4.51
  .ppt, PP1.33
  .wav, PP4.27
File name, PP1.32
File Properties box, PP2.69
Fill color, PP2.18–PP2.19
Find and Replace, PP2.5–PP2.8
Fly In dialog box, PP2.50
Fly-in effect, P2.51, PP2.50
Font, PP1.50–PP1.52
Font size, PP1.50, PP1.52
Footer, PP1.11, PP2.72–PP2.73
Footer placeholder, PP2.46
Footer text, PP2.46–PP2.48
Format
  character formatting, PP1.49
  chart, PP3.40–PP3.42
  paragraph formatting, PP1.49
  slide text, PP1.49–PP1.54
Format Data Series dialog box, PP3.40
Format Painter, PP3.8–PP3.10
Format Table dialog, PP2.19
Format WordArt dialog box, PP4.24
Formatting, PP1.49
Formatting toolbar, PP1.5, PP1.40, PP2.12
Freehand annotations, PP2.57–PP2.60

Generic design, PP2.31
Generic presentation, PP1.9
Getting Started task pane, PP1.6, PP1.7
.gif, PP3.19
Glossary of key terms, PPG.1–PPG.10
Gradient style background, PP3.10–PP3.12
Graph. *See* Chart
Graphics, PP1.54–PP1.62
  AutoShape, PP2.24–PP2.27
  customizing. *See* Customizing graphics
  defined, PP1.54
  duplicating a slide, PP2.23–PP2.24
  inserting, from Clip Organizer,
  PP1.55–PP1.59
  inserting, from file, PP1.59–PP1.60
  recoloring a picture, PP2.22–PP2.23
  rotating the object, PP2.27–PP2.28
  sizing/moving, PP1.61
  slide layout, PP2.20–PP2.22
Grayscale, PP1.63
Grid, PP3.24
Group
  objects, PP3.16, PP3.26
  organization chart, PP3.43
Guide, PP3.24

Handout, PP1.64
  headers/footers, PP2.72–PP2.73
  slides, PP2.73–PP2.74

Handout Master, PP2.38
Hatch-marked border, PP1.24
Headers, PP2.72–PP2.73
Hide
footer text, PP2.46–PP2.48
slide, PP2.60–PP2.62
Hierarchy, PP3.43
Horizontal alignment, PP2.15
Horizontal format, PP4.9
HTML, PP4.46
Hyperlinks, PP4.35–PP4.39
Hypertext Markup Language (HTML), PP4.46

Insert
AutoShape, PP2.24
graphic (Clip Organizer), PP1.55–PP1.59
graphic (file), PP1.59–PP1.60
slide, PP1.42–PP1.43
slide from another presentation, PP4.8–PP4.11
table, PP2.10–PP2.11
text from Word document, PP4.6–PP4.8
Insert Picture dialog box, PP1.60
Insert/Table command, PP4.12
Insert Table dialog box, PP2.10
Insertion point movement keys, PP1.16
Italic, PP2.13

.jpg, PP1.55, PP3.19
Justified, PP2.15

Keyboard directional, PP1.16
Keyboard shortcuts. *See* Command Summary; Voice Commands
Keyword, PP1.56
Kiosk presentation, PP4.26–PP4.31
self-running, make presentation, PP4.30–PP4.31
slide transitions, PP4.29
sound, PP4.26–PP4.29

Landscape, PP1.64
Layout, PP1.43
Left, PP2.15
Left alignment, PP3.24
Legend, PP3.31
Level, PP3.43
Line chart, PP3.30
Link To Custom Show dialog box, PP4.37
List format, PP4.9

Main dictionary, PP1.20
Manager box, PP3.43
Master view, PP2.39
Menu bar, PP1.5
Metafile (.wmf), PP3.19
Microsoft Graph, PP3.30, PP3.35
Microsoft Office Template Gallery, PP1.7
Microsoft Office Template Gallery Web site, PP2.31
Microsoft Organization Chart, PP3.43
MIDI file (.mid), PP4.27
Middle, PP2.15
Middle alignment, PP3.24
Moderate, PP2.54
Mouse Click, PP4.35
Mouse Over, PP4.35
Mouse pointer
crayon/pencil, PP2.17
cross, PP1.18, PP1.46
Draw Table feature, PP4.13
I-beam, PP1.16
sizing a column, PP2.14
sizing a row, PP2.14
slide show, PP2.57–PP2.58
MOV file (.mov), PP4.27
Move
bullets, PP1.23
graphic, PP1.61
placeholder, PP1.46
slides, PP1.41–PP1.42
Move Up/Move Down buttons, PP1.23
Movie file, PP4.27
MPEG file (.mpeg), PP4.27

Navigating
slide show, PP2.56
Web presentation, PP4.49
New presentation, PP1.6–PP1.12, PP1.36. *See also* Create presentation from existing slides
New Presentation task pane, PP1.7
Next slide, PP1.26, PP1.48
Normal view, PP1.12, PP1.13
Notes Master, PP2.38
Notes pages, PP1.64, PP2.62–PP2.64
Numbered list, PP3.7–PP3.8

Object, PP1.23
Object alignment, PP3.23–PP3.26
Office Assistant, PP2.66

Office Clipboard, PP3.32–PP3.34
Office Clipboard icon, PP3.34
Office Shortcut Bar, PP1.8
On-screen Presentation, PP1.10
Open
existing presentation, PP1.35–PP1.37
new presentation, PP1.36
Open dialog box, PP1.36
Organization chart, PP3.43–PP3.51
adding boxes, PP3.46
defined, PP3.43
enhancing, PP3.47–PP3.51
layout, PP3.49
levels, PP3.43
types of boxes, PP3.43
Organization Chart Style Gallery dialog box, PP3.48
Organization Chart toolbar, PP3.44
Outline tab, PP1.13, PP1.14, PP1.17–PP1.18
Outlining toolbar, PP1.5, PP1.17
Overheads, PP3.59

Package for CD feature, PP3.57–PP3.59
Page orientation, PP1.64–PP1.65
Pane, PP1.13
Paragraph formatting, PP1.49
.pcx, PP1.55
Pen style, PP2.58
Photo Album option, PP1.8
Picture, PP1.54
Picture Bullet dialog box, PP2.40
Picture toolbar, PP1.59
Pie chart, PP3.30
Placeholder
bulleted text, PP2.21
content, PP2.21
defined, PP1.23
footer, PP2.46
move, PP1.46
sizing, PP1.45
slide master, PP2.40
Places bar, PP1.36
.png, PP3.19
Point (pt.), PP1.50
Portrait, PP1.64
.pot, PP2.31, PP4.51
.ppt, PP1.33
Predefined color schemes, PP2.34
Predefined layouts, PP1.43
Presentation
close, PP1.35
create, PP1.7–PP1.8
edit, PP1.16–PP1.30
new, PP1.6–PP1.12, PP1.36
open, PP1.35–PP1.37
preview, PP1.62–PP1.63
print, PP1.65–PP1.66
rehearse, PP1.47–PP1.49
save, PP1.31–PP1.34
view, PP1.12–PP1.15
Presentation design
color scheme, PP2.34–PP2.37
design template, PP2.31–PP2.33
Presentation files, PP1.33
Presentation Options, PP1.10
Presentation style, PP1.10
Presentation types, PP1.9
Preview/Properties dialog box, PP1.58
Preview window, PP1.64
Previewing a presentation, PP1.62–PP1.63
Previous slide, PP1.26, PP1.48
Print
add headers/footers to handouts, PP2.72–PP2.73
customize print settings, PP2.71–PP2.74
handouts, PP1.64
notes pages, PP1.64
outline view, PP1.64
page orientation, PP1.64–PP1.65
presentation, PP1.65–PP1.66
scaling slides, PP2.73–PP2.74
selected slides, PP2.71
slides, PP1.64
Print Preview window, PP1.63
Print Range, PP1.66
Print What option, PP1.64
Printer icon, PP1.66
Promote, PP1.27–PP1.28
Publish as Web Page dialog box, PP4.48
Publishing presentation on Web, PP4.45–PP4.50
navigating Web presentation, PP4.49
saving presentation as single-file Web page, PP4.46–PP4.49

Random Transition effect, PP2.53
Recently Used, PP2.31, PP2.32
Recolor Picture, PP2.22
Record Narration, PP2.56

Regroup objects, PP3.21–PP3.22
Rehearse Timings, PP2.56
Rehearsal toolbar, PP3.56
Rehearsing, PP1.47–PP1.49, PP3.55–PP3.56
Resize. *See* Sizing
Results area, PP1.56
Right, PP2.15
Right alignment, PP3.24
Rotate handle, PP2.27
Rotating the object, PP2.27–PP2.28
.rtf, PP3.53

Sans serif, PP1.50
Save
  design template, as, PP4.50–PP4.51
  new presentation, PP3.16
  presentation, PP1.31–PP1.34
  single-file Web page, as, PP4.46–PP4.49
  Web page, as, PP4.46
Save As command, PP1.31
Save As dialog box, PP1.32
Save As Type list box, PP1.33
Scaling slides, PP2.73–PP2.74
ScreenTip
  Clipboard item collected, PP3.34
  design template, PP2.31
  layout, PP1.44
  master thumbnail, PP2.39
  renaming, PP3.14
  slide master thumbnail, PP3.13
  special effects, PP2.54
  thumbnail, PP1.56
Select
  sentence, PP1.16
  standard blocks, PP1.16
  table, areas of, PP4.15
  text, PP1.17
  word, PP1.16
Selection rectangle, PP1.24
Self-running, make presentation, PP4.30–PP4.31
Serif, PP1.50
Server, PP4.46
Set up presentation for browsing
  action buttons, PP4.39–PP4.41, PP4.45
  agenda slide, PP4.34
  change button size, PP4.42–PP4.44
  custom shows, PP4.31–PP4.34
  hyperlinks, PP4.35–PP4.39
Set Up Show dialog box, PP4.30
Shadow Settings toolbar, PP2.26
Shadow style, PP2.26
Shape Diamond, PP2.52
Shortcut keys. *See* Command summary; Voice commands
Single-file Web page, PP4.46–PP4.49
Sizing
  action buttons, PP4.42–PP4.44
  graphic, PP1.61
  placeholder, PP1.45
  table columns/rows, PP2.14
Sizing handles, PP1.45
Slide
  current, PP1.15
  defined, PP1.11
  delete, PP1.41
  display, PP1.26
  duplicate, PP2.23–PP2.24
  hide, PP2.60–PP2.62
  insert, PP1.42–PP1.43
  master, PP2.37–PP2.38
  move, PP1.41–PP1.42
  next/previous, PP1.26, PP1.48
  scale, PP2.73–PP2.74
Slide Design pane, PP2.34
Slide Design task pane, PP2.31, PP2.54
Slide Finder dialog box, PP4.8
Slide icon, PP1.13
Slide layout
  graphics, PP2.20–PP2.22
  Slide Master, PP2.45–PP2.46
  table, PP2.9–PP2.10
Slide Layout task pane, PP1.43–PP1.45
Slide Master, PP2.38–PP2.48
  apply to selected slides, PP3.12–PP3.15
  bullet style, PP2.40–PP2.42
  footer text, PP2.46–PP2.48
  function, PP2.38
  modifying, PP2.38–PP2.48
  modifying Title Master, PP2.42–PP2.45
  placeholders, PP2.40
  reapplying slide layout, PP2.45–PP2.46
Slide Master View toolbar, PP2.39, PP3.13
Slide pane, PP1.13, PP1.23–PP1.26
Slide show, PP1.47. *See also* Controlling the slide show
Slide show pointer options, PP2.58
Slide Show toolbar, PP1.48, PP2.57
Slide Show view, PP1.13, PP1.48
Slide Sorter toolbar, PP1.40
Slide Sorter view, PP1.13, PP1.14–PP1.15, PP1.40
Slide tab, PP1.13, PP1.14
Slide transition, PP4.29

Slide Transition task pane, PP2.52
Sound, kiosk presentation, PP4.26–PP4.29
Sound effects, PP2.50–PP2.51
Sound file, PP4.27
Source program, PP1.54
Speaker notes, PP2.62–PP2.64
Special effects, PP2.48–PP2.55
    animation, PP2.49–PP2.51
    build effects, PP2.53–PP2.55
    sound effects, PP2.50–PP2.51
    transition effects, PP2.51–PP2.53
Spelling checker, PP1.20–PP1.21, PP1.37–PP1.39
Splitting text between slides, PP1.29–PP1.30
Stacked-bar charts, PP3.30
Stacking order, PP1.60, PP3.22–PP3.23
Standard toolbar, PP1.5
Starting PowerPoint, PP1.5–PP1.6
Status bar, PP1.6
Style check, PP2.64–PP2.69
Subordinate box, PP3.43
Subscript, PP2.13
Subtle, PP2.54
Summary tab, PP2.69–PP2.70
Summary tab text boxes, PP2.70
Summary slide, PP4.34
Sunrise background, PP3.15
Superscript, PP2.13

Table, PP2.9–PP2.20
    aligning text, PP2.15–PP2.16
    background fill color, PP2.18–PP2.19
    border size/color, etc., PP2.16–PP2.17, PP4.15
    complex, PP4.12–PP4.18
    creating, PP4.12
    defined, PP2.9
    dotted table border, PP4.15
    enhancement, PP4.14–PP4.18
    entering data, PP2.11–PP2.12
    format changes, PP4.14–PP4.18
    inserting, PP2.10–PP2.11
    selecting segments of, PP4.15
    sizing columns/rows, PP2.14
    slide layout, PP2.9–PP2.10
    text formats, PP2.12–PP2.13
Table reference, PP2.9
Table slide layout, PP2.9–PP2.10
Tables and Borders toolbar, PP2.11, PP2.16, PP4.13
Tabs pane, PP1.14
Task panes, PP1.6
Template, PP1.7
Text
    add, to AutoShape, PP2.26–PP2.27
    add, to text box, PP2.29–PP2.30
    alignment, PP2.15
    footer, PP2.46–PP2.48
    insert, from Word document, PP4.6–PP4.8
    split, between slides, PP1.29–PP1.30
    WordArt, PP4.23
    wrap, in object, PP3.26–PP3.28
Text and Content Layouts, PP2.21
Text box, PP2.28–PP2.30
35mm slides, PP3.59
Title Master, PP2.38, PP2.42–PP2.45
Title slide, PP1.11
Titles, PP3.31
Toolbar, PP1.5
    Drawing, PP1.5, PP1.54
    Formatting, PP1.5, PP1.40, PP2.12
    Organization Chart, PP3.44
    Outlining, PP1.5, PP1.17
    Picture, PP1.59
    Rehearsal, PP3.56
    Shadow Settings, PP2.26
    Slide Master View, PP2.39
    Slide Show, PP1.48, PP2.57
    Slide Sorter, PP1.40
    Standard, PP1.5
    Tables and Borders, PP2.11, PP2.16
    WordArt, PP4.22
Top, PP2.15
Transition, PP2.49
Transition effect icon, PP2.53
Transition effects, PP2.51–PP2.53
Transparencies, PP3.59
Tri-pane view, PP1.13
Typeface, PP1.50

Underline, PP2.13
Undo, PP1.61
Ungroup, PP3.16, PP3.20
Unhide. *See* Hide

Value axis, PP3.31
Vertical alignment, PP2.15
View, PP1.12
View buttons, PP1.12, PP1.13
View menu, PP1.12, PP1.13

Voice commands
alignment, PP2.15
commands. *See* Command summary
directional keys, PP1.16
display slides, PP1.26
select text, PP1.17
views, PP1.13

WAV file (.wav), PP4.27
Web. *See* Publishing presentation on Web
Wedge transition effect, PP2.55
.wmf, PP3.19
WordArt, PP4.20
creating an object, PP4.20
enhancing an object, PP4.23–PP4.26
text, PP4.23
toolbar, PP4.22
WordArt Gallery dialog box, PP4.21
WordArt toolbar, PP4.22
Workspace, PP1.6

X axis, PP3.31

Y axis, PP3.31

Zooming the slide, PP3.17–PP3.18